Contemporary
Literary Criticism

Guide to Gale Literary Criticism Series

When you need to review criticism of literary works, these are the Gale series to use:

If the author's death date is: **You should turn to:**

After Dec. 31, 1959
(or author is still living)

CONTEMPORARY LITERARY CRITICISM

for example: Jorge Luis Borges, Anthony Burgess,
William Faulkner, Mary Gordon,
Ernest Hemingway, Iris Murdoch

1900 through 1959

TWENTIETH-CENTURY LITERARY CRITICISM

for example: Willa Cather, F. Scott Fitzgerald,
Henry James, Mark Twain, Virginia Woolf

1800 through 1899

NINETEENTH-CENTURY LITERATURE CRITICISM

for example: Fedor Dostoevski, Nathaniel Hawthorne,
George Sand, William Wordsworth

1400 through 1799

LITERATURE CRITICISM FROM 1400 TO 1800
(excluding Shakespeare)

for example: Anne Bradstreet, Daniel Defoe,
Alexander Pope, François Rabelais,
Jonathan Swift, Phillis Wheatley

SHAKESPEAREAN CRITICISM

Shakespeare's plays and poetry

Antiquity through 1399

CLASSICAL AND MEDIEVAL LITERATURE CRITICISM

for example: Dante, Homer, Plato, Sophocles, Vergil,
the Beowulf Poet

Gale also publishes related criticism series:

CHILDREN'S LITERATURE REVIEW

This series covers authors of all eras who have written for the preschool through high school audience.

SHORT STORY CRITICISM

This series covers the major short fiction writers of all nationalities and periods of literary history.

ISSN 0091-3421

Volume 54

Contemporary Literary Criticism

Excerpts from Criticism of the
Works of Today's Novelists, Poets,
Playwrights, Short Story Writers, Scriptwriters,
and Other Creative Writers

Daniel G. Marowski
Roger Matuz
EDITORS

Sean R. Pollock
David Segal
Thomas J. Votteler
Robyn V. Young
ASSOCIATE EDITORS

Detroit, New York, Fort Lauderdale, London

STAFF

Daniel G. Marowski, Roger Matuz, *Editors*

Sean R. Pollock, David Segal, Thomas J. Votteler, Robyn V. Young, *Associate Editors*

Cathy Beranek, Mary K. Gillis, Susan Miller Harig, Anne Sharp, Bridget Travers,
Assistant Editors

Jeanne A. Gough, *Production & Permissions Manager*
Linda M. Pugliese, *Production Supervisor*
Jennifer Gale, Suzanne Powers, Maureen A. Puhl, Lee Ann Welsh, *Editorial Associates*
Donna Craft, Christine A. Galbraith, David G. Oblender, Linda M. Ross,
Editorial Assistants

Victoria B. Cariappa, *Research Supervisor*
Karen D. Kaus, Eric Priehs, Maureen R. Richards, Mary D. Wise, *Editorial Associates*
Rogene M. Fisher, Filomena Sgambati, *Editorial Assistants*

Sandra C. Davis, *Permissions Supervisor (Text)*
H. Diane Cooper, Kathy Grell, Josephine M. Keene, Kimberly F. Smilay,
Permissions Associates
Lisa M. Lantz, Camille P. Robinson, Shalice Shah, Denise M. Singleton,
Permissions Assistants

Patricia A. Seefelt, *Permissions Supervisor (Pictures)*
Margaret A. Chamberlain, *Permissions Associate*
Pamela A. Hayes, Lillian Quickley, *Permissions Assistants*

Mary Beth Trimper, *Production Manager*
Anthony J. Scolaro, *Production Assistant*

Arthur Chartow, *Art Director*
C. J. Jonik, *Production Assistant*

Laura Bryant, *Production Supervisor*
Louise Gagné, *Internal Production Associate*
Shelly Andrews, Sharana Wier, *Internal Production Assistants*

Contents

Preface   vii

Acknowledgments   xi

Authors Forthcoming in *CLC*   xvii

Preface

Literary criticism is, by definition, "the art of evaluating or analyzing with knowledge and propriety works of literature." The complexity and variety of the themes and forms of contemporary literature make the function of the critic especially important to today's reader. It is the critic who assists the reader in identifying significant new writers, recognizing trends in critical methods, mastering new terminology, and monitoring scholarly and popular sources of critical opinion.

Until the publication of the first volume of *Contemporary Literary Criticism (CLC)* in 1973, there existed no ongoing digest of current literary opinion. *CLC,* therefore, has fulfilled an essential need.

Scope of the Work

CLC presents significant passages from published criticism of works by today's creative writers. Each volume of *CLC* includes excerpted criticism on about thirty-five authors who are now living or who died after December 31, 1959. Nearly 2,000 authors have been included since the series began publication. Since many of the writers covered by *CLC* inspire continual critical commentary, authors frequently appear in more than one volume. There is, of course, no duplication of reprinted criticism.

Authors are selected for inclusion for a variety of reasons, among them the publication or dramatic production of a critically acclaimed new work, the reception of a major literary award, revival of interest in past writings, or the dramatization of a literary work as a film or television screenplay. For example, the present volume includes Jessie Redmon Fauset, an important writer associated with the Harlem Renaissance, and André Breton, a seminal figure in the rise of surrealism; A. R. Gurney, past recipient of the Award of Merit from the American Academy and Institute of Arts and Letters; and Don DeLillo, whose latest novel, *Libra,* received much attention from critics and reviewers. Perhaps most importantly, authors who appear frequently on the syllabuses of high school and college literature classes are heavily represented in *CLC;* Ralph Ellison, whose widely studied novel *Invisible Man* is the focus of the current entry, and Robinson Jeffers are examples of writers of this stature in the present volume. Attention is also given to several other groups of writers—authors of considerable public interest—about whose work criticism is often difficult to locate. These include mystery and science fiction writers, literary and social critics, foreign writers, and authors who represent particular ethnic groups in the United States.

Format of the Book

Altogether there are about 600 individual excerpts in each volume—with approximately seventeen excerpts per author—taken from hundreds of literary reviews, general magazines, scholarly journals, and monographs. Contemporary criticism is loosely defined as that which is relevant to the evaluation of the author under discussion; this includes criticism written at the beginning of an author's career as well as current commentary. Emphasis has been placed on expanding the sources for criticism by including an increasing number of scholarly and specialized periodicals. Students, teachers, librarians, and researchers frequently find that the generous excerpts and supplementary material provided by *CLC* supply them with vital information needed to write a term paper, analyze a poem, or lead a book discussion group. In addition, complete bibliographical citations facilitate the location of the original source and provide all of the information necessary for a term paper footnote or bibliography.

A *CLC* author entry consists of the following elements:

- The **author heading** cites the author's full name, followed by birth date, and death date when applicable. The portion of the name outside parentheses denotes the form under which the author has most commonly published. If an author has written consistently under a pseudonym, the pseudonym will be listed in the author heading and the real name given on the first line of the biographical and critical introduction. Also located at the beginning of the introduction to the author entry are any important name variations under which an author has written. Uncertainty as to a birth or death date is indicated by question marks.

- A **portrait** of the author is included when available.

• A brief **biographical and critical introduction** to the author and his or her work precedes the excerpted criticism. However, *CLC* is not intended to be a definitive biographical source. Therefore, *cross-references* have been included to direct the reader to these useful sources published by Gale Research: *Contemporary Authors*, which includes detailed biographical and bibliographical sketches of more than 92,000 authors; *Children's Literature Review*, which presents excerpted criticism on the works of authors of children's books; *Something about the Author*, which contains heavily illustrated biographical sketches of writers and illustrators who create books for children and young adults; *Dictionary of Literary Biography*, which provides original evaluations and detailed biographies of authors important to literary history; *Contemporary Authors Autobiography Series*, which offers autobiographical essays by prominent writers; and *Something about the Author Autobiography Series*, which presents autobiographical essays by authors of interest to young readers. Previous volumes of *CLC* in which the author has been featured are also listed in the introduction.

• The **excerpted criticism** represents various kinds of critical writing—a particular essay may be descriptive, interpretive, textual, appreciative, comparative, or generic. It may range in form from the brief review to the scholarly exegesis. Essays are selected by the editors to reflect the spectrum of opinion about a specific work or about an author's literary career in general. The excerpts are presented chronologically, adding a useful perspective to the entry. All titles by the author featured in the entry are printed in boldface type, which enables the reader to easily identify the works being discussed. Publication information (such as publisher names and book prices) and parenthetical numerical references (such as footnotes or page and line references to specific editions of a work) have been deleted at the editors' discretion to provide smoother reading of the text.

• A complete **bibliographical citation** designed to help the user find the original essay or book follows each excerpt.

Other Features

• A list of **Authors Forthcoming in *CLC*** previews the authors to be researched for future volumes.

• An **Acknowledgments** section lists the copyright holders who have granted permission to reprint material in this volume of *CLC*. It does not, however, list every book or periodical reprinted or consulted during the preparation of the volume.

• A **Cumulative Author Index** lists all the authors who have appeared in *CLC, Twentieth-Century Literary Criticism, Nineteenth-Century Literature Criticism, Literature Criticism from 1400 to 1800*, and *Classical and Medieval Literature Criticism*, with cross-references to these Gale series: *Short Story Criticism, Children's Literature Review, Authors in the News, Contemporary Authors, Contemporary Authors Autobiography Series, Contemporary Authors Bibliographical Series, Dictionary of Literary Biography, Something about the Author, Something about the Author Autobiography Series*, and *Yesterday's Authors of Books for Children*. Readers will welcome this cumulated author index as a useful tool for locating an author within the various series. The index, which lists birth and death dates when available, will be particularly valuable for those authors who are identified with a certain period but whose death date causes them to be placed in another, or for those authors whose careers span two periods. For example, Ernest Hemingway is found in *CLC*, yet a writer often associated with him, F. Scott Fitzgerald, is found in *Twentieth-Century Literary Criticism*.

• A **Cumulative Nationality Index** alphabetically lists all authors featured in *CLC* by nationality, followed by numbers corresponding to the volumes in which they appear.

• A **Title Index** alphabetically lists all titles reviewed in the current volume of *CLC*. Titles are followed by the corresponding page numbers where they are discussed in the series. In cases where the same title is used by different authors, the authors' surnames are given in parentheses after the title, e.g., *Collected Poems* (Berryman), *Collected Poems* (Eliot). For foreign titles, a cross-reference is given to the translated English title. Titles of novels, novellas, dramas, films, record albums, and poetry, short story, and essay collections are printed in italics, while all individual poems, short stories, essays, and songs are printed in roman type within quotation marks; when published separately (e.g., T.S. Eliot's poem *The Waste Land*), the title will also be printed in italics.

• In response to numerous suggestions from librarians, Gale has also produced a **special paperbound edition** of the *CLC* title index. This annual cumulation, which alphabetically lists all titles reviewed in the series, is available to all customers and will be published with the first volume of *CLC* issued in each calendar year. Additional copies of the index are available upon request. Librarians and patrons will welcome this separate index: it saves shelf space, is easily disposable upon receipt of the following year's cumulation, and is more portable and thus easier to use than was previously possible.

Suggestions Are Welcome

The editors welcome the comments and suggestions of readers to expand the coverage and enhance the usefulness of the series. Please feel free to contact us by letter or by calling our toll-free number: 1-800-347-GALE.

Acknowledgments

The editors wish to thank the copyright holders of the excerpted criticism included in this volume, the permissions managers of many book and magazine publishing companies for assisting us in securing reprint rights, and Anthony Bogucki for assistance with copyright research. We are also grateful to the staffs of the Detroit Public Library, the Library of Congress, the University of Detroit Library, the University of Michigan Library, and the Wayne State University Library for making their resources available to us. Following is a list of copyright holders who have granted us permission to reprint material in this volume of *CLC*. Every effort has been made to trace copyright, but if omissions have been made, please let us know.

COPYRIGHTED EXCERPTS IN *CLC*, VOLUME 54, WERE REPRINTED FROM THE FOLLOWING PERIODICALS:

Authors Forthcoming in *CLC*

Contemporary Literary Criticism, Volume 55, will be a yearbook devoted to an examination of the outstanding achievements and trends in literature during 1988. Volumes 56 and 57 will feature critical excerpts on a number of authors not previously listed as well as criticism on newer works by authors included in earlier volumes.

To Be Included in Volume 56

Steven Berkoff (English dramatist)—Berkoff has gained notoriety for his satirical portrayals of British society and his innovative modernizations of classical dramas. Among his most recent productions is a controversial adaptation of Shakespeare's *Coriolanus.*

Edmund Blunden (English poet, critic, and biographer)—Greatly influenced by the English Romantic movement of the nineteenth century, Blunden evokes the beauty of nature in his predominantly pastoral poetry. Reflections on his experiences as a military officer during World War I temper the idyllic qualities of such collections as *The Shepherd* and *The Waggoner.*

Bruce Jay Friedman (American novelist, short story writer, dramatist, and scriptwriter)—Friedman's fiction focuses on the serious and comic aspects of Jewish assimilation into American society. In such novels as *Stern* and *A Mother's Kisses,* he examines the guilt and repression felt by his luckless protagonists and their families.

John Clellon Holmes (American novelist, essayist, poet, and short story writer)—Holmes is best remembered for his objective portrayals of the rebellious lifestyles of writers who were involved in the Beat movement of the 1950s. His novel *Go* is generally credited as the first authentic chronicle of the Beat phenomenon.

Ivan Klima (Czechoslovakian short story writer, novelist, dramatist, and essayist)—A dissident writer whose fiction has been banned in his native country since 1970, Klima portrays the lives of ordinary individuals living under communist rule. Among his works to be translated into English are *A Summer Affair* and *My Merry Mornings: Stories from Prague.*

Rhoda Lerman (American novelist)—Best known for such metaphorical novels as *Call Me Ishtar* and *The Book of the Night,* Lerman uses elements of fantasy to comment on contemporary sexual relationships and the role of women in society.

François Mauriac (French novelist, non-fiction writer, critic, dramatist, and poet)—Winner of the 1952 Nobel Prize in Literature, Mauriac is considered one of the most important Roman Catholic authors of the twentieth century. Both his fiction and nonfiction writings reflect his concern with sin, redemption, and other religious issues. Such novels as *Thérèse* and *Vipers' Tangle* also offer vivid depictions of life in the Bordeaux region of southwestern France.

J. D. Salinger (American novelist and short story writer) An influential and often imitated writer whose reclusiveness has contributed to his legendary stature, Salinger is best known for his controversial novel *The Catcher in the Rye.* This work, which concerns a young man's confrontations with hypocrisy and the difficult transition from adolescence to adulthood, will serve as the focus of Salinger's entry.

William Saroyan (American dramatist, short story writer, and novelist)—A prolific author of works in several genres, Saroyan was praised for his romantic and nostalgic celebrations of American innocence and idealism. Critical commentary in Saroyan's entry will focus on his Pulitzer Prize-winning drama, *The Time of Your Life.*

Arno Schmidt (German novelist, short story writer, translator, critic, biographer, and essayist)—An important figure in German literature, Schmidt is renowned for bold innovations with prose structure and typography and for satirical novels that present a dystopian vision.

Isabel Allende (Chilean novelist)—In her novels *The House of Spirits, Of Love and Shadows,* and the recent *Eva Luna,* Allende combines elements of realism and fantasy to examine the tumultuous social and political history of South America.

Samuel Beckett (Irish-born dramatist and novelist)—A recipient of the Nobel Prize in Literature, Beckett often combines humor and tragedy in his works to create an existential view of the human condition in which life is regarded as meaningless. Beckett's entry will focus on his seminal absurdist drama, *Waiting for Godot.*

T. S. Eliot (English poet, critic, and dramatist)—A principal founder of modernism, Eliot greatly influenced modern letters with his innovative and distinctively erudite verse and criticism. Eliot's entry will focus on *The Waste Land,* an epic widely considered among the major works of twentieth-century poetry.

Percival Everett (American novelist and short story writer)—An author of tragicomic fiction, Everett often focuses upon characters who transcend destructive personal relationships to achieve a sense of self-worth. His novels include *Suder* and *Walk Me to the Distance.*

Richard Greenberg (American dramatist and scriptwriter)—In his plays *The Moderati,* a satire of self-absorbed literary society, and *Eastern Standard,* a critique of young middle-class professionals, Greenberg uses sympathy and humor to explore the American obsession with wealth and materialism.

Danilo Kis (Yugoslavian novelist and short story writer)—Kis first attracted critical acclaim in Western countries for his novels *Garden, Ashes* and *A Tomb for Boris Davidovich,* both of which focus upon the persecution of European Jews during World War II. Kis's recently translated short story collection, *The Encyclopedia of the Dead,* has further enhanced his international reputation.

Peter Klappert (American poet)—Klappert garnered praise for the wit and technical innovations of his first poetry collection, *Lugging Vegetables to Nantucket,* for which he received the Yale Series of Younger Poets Award. His sequence *The Idiot Princess of the Last Dynasty* has been compared to such celebrated works as Ezra Pound's *Cantos* and John Berryman's *The Dream Songs.*

Cormac McCarthy (American novelist) —McCarthy is regarded as an important contributor to the Southern Gothic tradition as exemplified by such authors as William Faulkner, Carson McCullers, and Flannery O'Connor. McCarthy's novels, which are often set in his native Tennessee, are praised for their inventive dialect and powerful examinations of evil.

Mbongeni Ngema (South African dramatist)—Ngema's plays illustrate the consequences of apartheid and humanity's capacity for injustice. His recent musical drama *Sarafina!,* inspired by the Soweto uprising of 1976, chronicles the efforts of South African high school students to fashion a play from their country's tragic history.

Andrei Voznesensky (Russian poet)—A protégé of Boris Pasternak, Voznesensky is one of the Soviet Union's most prestigious contemporary poets. His complex experimental verse reveals a profound love for his country and often explores the alienation of youth in industrial society.

Gina Berriault

1926-

American novelist, short story writer, and scriptwriter.

In her fiction, Berriault utilizes detached, economical prose to explore psychological conflicts between perception and reality. Her socially varied yet uniformly isolated characters often find hope or action futile after confronting unrealized expectations concerning familial and sexual relationships, mortality, and success. Marjorie Spencer commented: "Berriault writes about what can (and must) happen without warning to each of us . . . ; about events that reduce our stake in the future to our stake in surviving the present, which in itself has come unhinged."

In Berriault's first novel, *The Descent* (1960), an idealistic member of a near-future President's Cabinet discovers the insanity of the politicians who control America's nuclear arsenal. Although faulted as unsophisticated, this novel garnered praise for effective characterizations and perceptive satire. Berriault's next two novels, *Conference of Victims* (1962) and *The Son* (1966), also received mixed reviews. *Conference of Victims* examines the reactions of relatives and friends following a man's suicide, while *The Son* chronicles an incestuous relationship between a mother and her adolescent child. Although several commentators viewed Berriault's psychological analyses as excessive, others lauded her incisive portraits of the emotional lives of her characters. In *The Lights of Earth* (1984), an obscure writer who has lost her married lover after his sudden literary fame is able to overcome personal and professional disillusionment and reach out for help to those closest to her. Critics generally praised Berriault's portrait of both the tension between success and failure and the possibilities of transcendence through human communication. Gary Davenport commented: "Gina Berriault's prose is an instrument of great subtlety and perfection, and her powers of observation, psychological and otherwise, are unrivaled in recent fiction."

Berriault has won two O. Henry awards for her short fiction. Her first collection, *The Mistress and Other Stories* (1965), examines a variety of characters whose rationalizations of indefensible actions ultimately fail them. While some critics considered Berriault's style overly pessimistic, most maintained that her talents suited the short story genre and commended her convincing depiction of diverse personalities. *The Infinite Passion of Expectation: Twenty-Five Stories* (1983) gathers pieces written throughout her career, including "The Stone Boy," from *The Mistress and Other Stories,* which Berriault adapted for film. Critics praised Berriault's precise dissection of the self-delusions and dormant hopes of her characters. Edith Milton observed: "In story after story, Mrs. Berriault focuses on lives that touch each other without intimacy. She magnifies the banal instances that are her fiction's raw material until we see a series of worlds in close-up, anatomies . . . simultaneously repellent and magnetic, exotic and familiar."

(See also *Contemporary Authors,* Vol. 116.)

THE NEW YORKER

[In *The Descent*], Mrs. Berriault, a writer of undoubted talent, chooses to write about the year 1964 and about the fate of a trusting Iowa man—an associate professor of history—who is selected by the President of the United States to fill the newly created Cabinet post of Secretary for Humanity. The personality of the professor, Arnold Elkins, is well drawn, and his predicament—a predicament that can most simply be described as that of an honest man in a dishonest world—is thoroughly examined, but his story, like all realistic stories that are set in the future, has a superfluous, undisciplined air, as though the novelist were assuming prerogatives that did not properly belong to her. The atmosphere throughout is ominous—braced, and at the same time disordered, by the threat of immediate atomic war. (pp. 181-82)

A review of "The Descent," in The New Yorker, Vol. XXXVI, No. 33, October 1, 1960, pp. 181-82.

MARCUS KLEIN

The Descent is a novel ineptly devised, patronizing and stone deaf to the rhythms of ordinary speech, but Gina Berriault is ablaze with constructive suggestions. And she can fix responsibility: foggy thinking in Washington, demagoguery, big business, selfish labor interests, Luce Publications, Inc., Public Relations, Motivational Research, optimism, beauty contests, intellectual pettiness in the academy and Billy Graham. For a wonder she does not include the violence on television, there isn't much that escapes her knowingness, but then hers is a very short novel forced to accommodate, too, the legions of light. Which are: irresistible demonstrations, principally at Hiroshima, stupendous petitions, non-violent sabotage, militant pacifism and Albert Schweitzer. Her Arnold Elkins becomes possessed of a plan—one evolved, and that is important, by qualified technicians—for compulsory total disarmament and conversion to peaceful pursuits. It is a sanguine plan, a serious plan, and one that sets Arnold back on his heels, but that is all of the plan there is. Details aren't Arnold's business, he is enthusiastic, and Miss Berriault is impatient of them. At her novel's climax Arnold's thirteen-year-old daughter demands unilateral disarmament. (pp. 401-02)

Marcus Klein, "A Slouch toward Bethlehem," in The Nation, *New York, Vol. 191, No. 17, November 19, 1960, pp. 398-402.*

BOOKS, NEW YORK

When Hal Costigan, popular candidate for Congress, was surprised in his car with a seventeen-year-old high school girl, he committed suicide. What his death does to his close survivors, his blind mother, his sister, brother, his wife and twelve-year-old son, and to the girl he physically awakened, is the story Gina Berriault unfolds in [*Conference of Victims*]. With the exception of the girl who embarks on a career of sordid affairs, confusedly seeking some stability in her relationships, the lives of the others touch each other closely.

All of them are people of meager fulfillments and meager hopes but each is an individual and to each the death of the man, whose future had held promise for all of them, carries its own questions and burden. With a touch that is at the same time compassionate and relentless, Miss Berriault probes the half truths, the lies, the evasions which make life supportable for them. Particularly effective are her portraits of Naomi, the spinster sister and of the alcoholic drifter, Dan O'Leary, who recognizes her hunger for love and experience, and of the weakling younger brother who stubbornly hangs on to the hero image of the dead man. The writing, strong, clean, rhythmic, captures the mood of the story.

R. F., in a review of "Conference of Victims," in Books, *New York, July 1, 1962, p. 6.*

WIRT WILLIAMS

[In *Conference of Victims*], the precipitating act is a man's suicide. The book is about the effect of his act upon those whose lives were joined to his: his mother, sister, brother, wife, mistress. Its work is done with little overt plot in the traditional sense, but with a massive, yet intricate rendering of the awareness and subconscious of the characters.

The man is Hal Costigan. . . . Just before the book begins, he has asphyxiated himself with the fumes from his auto exhaust. The inevitable investigation into his death reveals that he has been having a long affair with a high-school girl. His mother, sister and brother find this scandal curiously com-

forting; indeed, they cling with a kind of gratitude to the semi-official explanation of the suicide thus established, that Costigan destroyed himself because of a hopeless love. Yet, beneath their insistent acceptance of his explanation, they all have a sense of guilt, a feeling of having been, mysteriously, accessories to his action. For the next six years, the fact of his self-destruction pursues them like a hound of earth. When *Conference of Victims* ends, each character is either destroyed by it or reconciled to it.

The novel has considerable virtues: richness of language, complexity of insight, lifelike speech. Unfortunately, its supreme virtue—the author's marvelous exploration of the seacaves of the mind—is what ultimately limits it. Deep in these tunnels, it never generates a real narrative or true dramatic tension. In the end, it offers almost everything but excitement. Reservations are always relative, however, and *Conference of Victims,* whatever its deficiencies, is an important first novel by a remarkable talent. (pp. 24-5)

Wirt Williams, "The Repercussions of a Suicide," in The New York Times Book Review, *July 15, 1962, pp. 24-5.*

HASKEL FRANKEL

The central character of Gina Berriault's novel *Conference of Victims* is a suicide, already dead before the book opens. Hal Costigan, candidate for Congress, husband and father, took his own life shortly after being caught with a seventeen-year-old girl in a compromising situation. He left no note. Was the possibility of scandal his motive, or was there another reason? No one will ever know. It is from this situation that the novel grows, as each person involved with the dead man—wife, mother, sister, brother, and paramour—lives with his unexplained death.

Certainly this is a promising situation for a novel, given a writer of talent, and Gina Berriault is one. She can take little lives and the little incidents that make up those lives and create people well worth a reader's time and interest. If the ability to develop character and to write beneath the surface of people were all, *Conference of Victims* could be recommended without hesitation.

Unfortunately, it isn't all. There is the matter of plot, and this is where the book fails. Miss Berriault's victims are never in conference. The wife and the paramour leave town, each going her separate way, shortly after Hal Costigan's death. As for the Costigan family . . . they were strangers to each other even before Hal's death. Each person is already committed to his personal hell; the suicide is merely one more burden to be carried down that long, lonely road. Without vital interactions and conflicts, *Conference of Victims* becomes a series of short stories or character sketches.

If such probing is enough for the reader, these slices of life will make rewarding reading. For the fan of the novel, it is enough carefully to mark down Miss Berriault's name as one to watch for in the book columns. (pp. 26-7)

Haskel Frankel, "Suicide and Survivors," in Saturday Review, *Vol. XLV, No. 28, July 21, 1962, pp. 26-7.*

CHARLES POORE

The trouble with many short stories is that they are too long. Their advertised brevity is inauthentic. A point a reader grasps in two minutes gains nothing by being nested in words for half an hour.

That, I think, is why short story collections, by and large, are said not to sell. There are exceptions, of course, as we all know well. One, in fact, should be Gina Berriault's *The Mistress and Other Stories*. . . .

[With Berriault's stories you] usually know from the start whether you want to go on. The one called **"The Diary of KW,"** for example, gets nowhere in particular, and gets there rapidly, in a bitter crone's progress.

The title story, **"The Mistress,"** has just one lamentable point to make. A discarded high-spirited doxy is revengefully eager to let a boy know she once held his father's wayward affection. She does so, in the cruelest way.

Murder, Miss Berriault shows us, has many forms and devices. It is seemingly explicit in **"The Stone Boy,"** where a life ends in a shooting accident. How much of an accident was it? we are left to ask. At that point, the explicit and the implicit merge in shadows.

She does not stay for our answer. She is on to another event in another place. Always Miss Berriault displays a splendid gift for cutting her characters' gains—or losses—according to the point of view, with quick endings.

Not O. Henryesque Surprise! Surprise! endings, either. Her music, as T. S. Eliot liked to say, is successful with a dying fall.

The scene is often California. . . . Uppergrade beatniks, middlegrade beatniks, and the true beatniks of desperation are all over the place.

Miss Berriault swiftly fields their antics, their poses, their despairs. She shows us people who fight for what they want. Whether they deserve it or not becomes an irrelevancy in justice's scales. It is burningly germane to her stories.

The man or woman is always self-revealed. Assists are generously supplied by other characters. Offhand, it is hard to believe that any writer, in our passing day and age, could do much with the bit about the melancholy housewife romantically moping over her Bohemian fling in Paris. It's threadbare. It's passé. But read Miss Berriault's **"Death of a Lesser Man,"** and you'll see that life can be pumped into that antique vein. . . .

The moony yearning to meet someone who has been in a Fellini movie or knows Beckett is crisply anatomized [in **"Felis Catus"**] under Miss Berriault's razory words.

Her effects pour out in amazing combinations. Here, for example, she is about to describe a man literally throwing a fit. While she's at it, she satirizes a way of life. Look:

> In the midst of seven friends eating pickled mushrooms, cheeses, smoked oysters . . . and drinking Danish beer from tall green Mexican glasses in an apartment of red Naugahyde furniture and black shag rugs . . . his eyes rolled up . . .

So do ours, so do ours. Our eyes roll down again, though, when we come to another setting, in another story, where people live in hunger and want. And there is a synthesis, of sorts, when a girl from a slum is given patronizing work in the world of black shag rugs and Danish beer in tall Mexican glasses.

Charles Poore, "The Moment of Truth Doesn't Need Stretching," in The New York Times, *September 11, 1965, p. 25.*

THE CHRISTIAN SCIENCE MONITOR

Gina Berriault's preferred form of fiction seems to reach simultaneously toward the general and the particular. Providing a detailed sketch of individual characters who also represent social, if not literary, stereotypes, she obeys the categorizing impulse of the neorealist—but not unduly. Elements of her own special talent are present and lively in each of the stories [contained in *The Mistress and Other Stories*] while the collection as a whole is impressively varied and uniformly high in quality.

No bad or mediocre efforts have been included. Naturally some of the stories, particularly **"The Birthday Party"** and **"Around the Dear Ruin,"** are less memorable than the others, while two strike a different note by focusing on somewhat comical human categories. Of the latter, **"Anna Lisa's Nose"** is a study of a woman's excessive preoccupation with her appearance and **"Felis Catus"** is a laugh-sob portrait of a married couple who like cats to the exclusion of other people.

Such human types exist, but they do not have the same tragic impact as the aging, irresponsible flirt in [**"The Mistress"**], the Negro heroine of **"Myra"** or the ultrasensitive **"Stone Boy"** who reacts to his brother's fatal accident with temporarily frozen emotions and an icy façade that chills his parents into permanent hostility.

Gina Berriault's views are fundamentally pessimistic. Something awful happens to most of her characters and the collection itself is prefaced by a quotation from (of all people) Ortega y Gasset: "Every life is more or less a ruin among whose debris we have to discover what the person ought to have been."

Granted: passing days and simple experience mean that possibilities have been lost. But some lives are still less ruined and debris-strewn, without necessarily being more insipid, than others.

Pessimism appears to encourage people, including writers, to think in terms of categories and types. One wonders whether the flattened perspective and use of literary types that the neorealists, including Gina Berriault, seem to prefer are technical innovations or symptoms of a seek-nothing outlook.

F. C., "She Pokes among the Debris," in The Christian Science Monitor, *November 11, 1965, p. 11.*

DORRIE PAGONES

Gina Berriault's *The Mistress and Other Stories* is so good a book that it ought to be better. Reading several of the stories at a time is to be avoided, like looking too long at splendid scenery; one marvels while stifling a yawn. Gina Berriault is a formidably intelligent, observant, and analytical person, but indispensable though these qualities are, they are not enough to give her prose what the landscape lacks—the ordinary breath of life.

For all that, these fifteen stories are worth anyone's while. Miss Berriault takes a thoroughly pessimistic view of human nature. . . . No one behaves as he should, and even supposing anyone did, it is quite clear, as the title of one story puts it, that **"All Attempts Will End in Failure."** (p. 104)

In **"The Diary of KW"** an old woman loses her job as a school cafeteria helper because "it occurred to me that food was abominable and that . . . if they went on eating their hot lunches every day they would only be preparing themselves to suffer, they would only grow up to suffer." The parents obtusely fail the child in **"The Stone Boy,"** and the child inevitably fails the parent in **"The Bystander."** Most frequently of all, men and women fail each other, like the white woman and Negro man, former lovers, of **"Lonesome Road."** When he accidentally meets her in the park with her children he is unable to wave casually at them in parting "because his pity for her, the pity that he had failed to experience in the time of his love, forbade him small and amiable signals."

There are plenty of other kinds of failure here, as many as there are stories. Since no one particularly cares to think of his life and all other lives as foredoomed fiascoes, the temptation is to say that Miss Berriault has overdone it, that she is being academic about life. But if her book is, in any sense, a failure, it is better than many successes. (pp. 104-05)

> *Dorrie Pagones, in a review of "The Mistress and Other Stories," in* Saturday Review, *Vol. XLVIII, No. 46, November 13, 1965, pp. 104-05.*

PETER BUITENHUIS

It is difficult to know exactly what Gina Berriault set out to achieve in [**The Son**]. In fact, it's even difficult to know what motivates the characters. The style has all the bland, impersonal intimacy of peanut butter. It reduces all experience to the level of a Dead Sea.

Vivian Carpentier, the heroine and narrative center of the book, goes through several marriages and emerges from them with one son. The story is largely the account of her miserable experiences with the Men in her Life and how she succeeds in getting rid of them. . . .

As the title reveals, the son is the real Man in her Life. This becomes embarrassingly obvious when she leaves her last husband and goes moteling with the boy. The following extract gives the moment of revelation and reveals, incidentally, how a writer who is really practised at it can somehow knock all the resonance and rhythm out of words:

> She had wanted him to know her body again as he had known it as an infant or to know her body as he had not known it, like a lover who had been unconscious of who it was he had loved, who had loved a woman for a time and yet not known the person she was; and she wanted to know his body as she had known it and claimed it would be in the years to come when he was apart from her, and . . . .

This toneless drivel continues until the moment, near the end of the novel, when she sleeps with her son. After this adventure, "it seemed to her that all she had done in her life up to the time of their climbing the stairs, clinging together, had

been without her consciousness." This is precisely the case. But what earthly use to a novelist is an unconscious character? Novels can certainly have unconscious character in them. But their function should surely be never anything but auxiliary to the main task of the novelist—which is, in essence, the drama of consciousness.

Miss Berriault (who has been highly praised for her short stories) has chosen one of the oldest, most exciting and potentially dangerous themes that literature provides: incest. Yet she has managed to reduce it to the level of a woman's magazine serial. The very syntax of her style reveals the monotony and meaninglessness of the lives lived in the novel. Events are just one damned thing after another—even seductions, fights and death. The last sentence fits the case exactly and allows the reader to close the book feeling that the mediocre heroine has met her appropriately mediocre fate: "There was no illumination of anybody other than herself, lying alone waiting for one of the remote ones to return and lie down beside her."

> *Peter Buitenhuis, "Vivian's True Love," in* The New York Times Book Review, *November 13, 1966, p. 71.*

CHARLES POORE

The ink-stained heralds are trumpeting a pornographic revolution. Indeed they've been trumpeting it so lengthily that the idea has become a cliché. . . .

It is significant, I think, that . . . [**The Son** does not bother] much with that passé short cut to notoriety. Instead, [it concentrates] on less psychedelic manifestations of morality.

Miss Berriault, it is true, has a fearful unraveling in view for her novella. She is dealing with a case of incest in California. But she twirls her silver-cord lariat so artlessly that we know how the story is going to come out a long time before she is ready to call it a day.

She always writes well. Those who remember one of her earlier books, **The Mistress,** or her stories in *New World Writing, Esquire, Contact,* and other magazines, know that. . . .

To me, the best part of Miss Berriault's **The Son** lies in the deft way she sketches Bohemian manners and customs in San Francisco and the general Bay Area. Her heroine, a girl called Vivian, is launched on a strenuous career of promiscuousness before World War II.

Then we have the feverish glitter of wartime, while her doomed son is growing up. Toward the end there's almost everything short of a Free Speech Movement riot at Berkeley.

It is well that she approaches her incest theme with solemnity. The thematic history of that crime goes back very far in literature—and up to such more recent manifestations as F. Scott Fitzgerald's *Tender Is the Night* and Iris Murdoch's . . . *The Time of the Angels.*

> *Charles Poore, "Fiction Can Be Stranger than Truth," in* The New York Times, *November 24, 1966, p. 33.*

EDITH MILTON

Gina Berriault has been writing novels and short stories for some 25 years. And the 25 stories collected in **The Infinite**

Passion of Expectation are without exception nearly flawless miniatures in her particular mode. They always descend below the surface of the events and phenomena out of which they are woven, but they descend only minimally, so that their observations stay easily within the perceptions of the characters and the reader is given the illusion not merely of looking at alien lives but of moving through alien sensibilities. In story after story, Mrs. Berriault focuses on lives that touch each other without intimacy. She magnifies the banal instances that are her fiction's raw material until we see a series of worlds in close-up, anatomies as simultaneously repellent and magnetic, exotic and familiar, as a Chuck Close portrait.

In particular she is a virtuoso in the sort of claustrophobia from which Jean-Paul Sartre built his play *No Exit;* the emotional climate, I mean, that develops when two or three characters with conflicting fears and expectations jostle against each other in a rather small space. . . .

The characters of these stories, almost without exception, are humble people caught in emotional ambiguities and contradictions that have paralyzed them and made it easier to live in dreams or the past than to confront the present world. Often, in fact, their longing for the past and their illusions about the future reduce them to shadows. (p. 8)

The rewards for most of Mrs. Berriault's people are . . . usually brief and borrowed and often illusory. A large part of her characters' existence is spent rearranging their expectations, adjusting what they see and feel to what they had hoped to see and feel, which was quite different. . . . The most poignant story of the collection and my favorite is **"The Diary of K. W. ,"** in which an old woman dying of starvation listens to the sounds of the happy life in the apartment above hers, too shy and too conditioned by isolation and self-denigration to ask for help.

Although most of these stories take place in or around San Francisco, the experiences they represent are amazing in their variety: from bar nights to discussions of Camus, from the routines of farm chores to the hand-to-mouth improvisation of the urban ghetto. These are particular worlds drawn from the specific witness of the characters themselves.

And yet in some way difficult to describe, Mrs. Berriault's fiction remains oddly cerebral. Her characters' inner voices seem always to move toward generalization. "He was the parent who breaks down under the eyes of his child," the narrator of **"The Bystander"** says of his father, ". . . while the child stands and watches the end of the struggle and then walks away to catch a streetcar." That exquisite, aphoristic ending also seems disturbingly at odds with the gritty, down-at-heels realism of the story's characters and setting. The heroine of **"Death of a Lesser Man"** thinks about the man who has been following her and who she is afraid may attack her:

> The obscene dolt must have stolen away her dream
> of herself in the future, the dream that was only a
> memory of herself in the past. . . . The intruder
> must have stolen away the past and the future.

Surely an incredibly subtle insight for a woman who is both choked with fear and distressed by incongruous stirrings of sexual excitement.

In one of the longer stories in the collection, **"The Search for J. Kruper,"** a lionized writer of autobiographical schlock heads into the Mexican wilderness to find his antithesis and

idol, the great J. Kruper, who "forgot the self that bore a name and became all others." J. Kruper is, one assumes, Mrs. Berriault's own ideal of authorship, and the aim of her fiction, like his, is forgetting the self and becoming all others. But as the story wryly notes, the self is not easily forgotten and, far from obligingly becoming all others, often subverts all others to become the self instead.

In fact, it is hard to escape the author's voice in these stories: Their diction is sophisticated, their prose bristles with astute observation. An occasional witty quirk of syntax seems to grant control to the inanimate and the abstract . . . I suppose I may be quibbling over what is merely a shrewd exploitation of grammar to define human helplessness, but the mannerism adds to the sense that these pieces are more about the pattern of people's lives than about the people, that they develop less from the integral needs of their characters than from the ideas they have been created to contain.

The 25 stories of *The Infinite Passion of Expectation* are limited, then, by the control of their author's intellect. But within those limits they work brilliantly. None really moved me, none jarred my complacent prejudices or stirred my compassion; but there is not a story among them that is less than elegant, less than perfectly observed, perfectly resolved fiction. (pp. 8, 28-9)

> *Edith Milton, "Lives That Touch without Intimacy," in* The New York Times Book Review, *January 9, 1983, pp. 8, 28-9.*

RITA FINK

"Simplicity has always been held to be a mark of truth; it is also a mark of genius," wrote Schopenhauer in *The Art of Literature.* Gina Berriault's new novel is a study of simplicity in literature which leads to the mark of truth. As to the mark of genius, that is for the reader to award. For me, *The Lights of Earth* is a finely wrought novel which places Berriault in the excellent company of such top-flight contemporary writers as M.F.K. Fisher, Aharon Appelfeld and John Berger.

The story opens:

> Years after the night of that strange little party her
> memory played a trick on her. Her memory set him
> among the others, the guest of honor who heard
> every word, who saw every gesture and every expression
> on every face. But he wasn't there. He
> wasn't even expected that night.

Immediately, the sense of intrigue, wonderment and involvement in the story becomes irresistible.

Ilona, the lover of the absent, neo-celebrated writer Martin, has been invited to this arty-chic party since: "Any creature, she thought, no matter how microscropically small, that's on or near a person who's become famous, becomes famous also." Now that Martin's picture is on the cover of *Time,* those close to him are captured for the nuggets they recount of pre-celebrity days. . . .

The story emerges from the pains, experiences and (meager) joy of Ilona. Throughout, certain characters weave in and out of her daily life: the lover whom she is losing, her friend Claud, and her daughter who writes from Nepal. As they enter and reenter her life, their personalities grow more precisely defined.

Other characters play their strong roles in vignettes, yet their imprint is undeniable: the voyeuristic party host Jerome . . . ; Martin's ex-wife who tested suicide; and Ilona's mother restrained in poverty and illness, then death.

Ilona's musings are rich yet spare, sensuous yet stark. "Nobody was blessed and nobody abandoned. The world wasn't like that," she wants to believe. Still she knew that some, like Jerome's beautiful wife, appear blessed by being granted every desire of life. Others like friend Claud with his writer's block (and this is a faithful rendition of the disease) appear abandoned.

The dynamic, searing relationship is that of Ilona and her man-child, retarded older brother. . . . For a long time I will recall the moving passages and exquisite phrasing with which the author embraces the brother and seeks redemption for Ilona.

Very quickly I recognized that this book is to be read and reread. I was enthralled by this novel that neither depends on location nor description for the sake of using lush words, nor reaffirmation of the latest literary fashion, nor a rewriting of the '60s. *The Lights of Earth* is a miraculous restorative, a story exquisitely honed and a style richly imaginative.

> *Rita Fink, in a review of "The Lights of Earth," in* San Francisco Review of Books, *Spring, 1984, p. 19.*

ELIZABETH SPENCER

The locale of Gina Berriault's *Lights of Earth* is San Francisco, and this short, absorbing novel is permeated by a sense of the hills, mists and nearby beaches of that city. In a strong first chapter that could be read as a fine short story, Ilona, an unsuccessful writer who is the narrator, goes to a party honoring her married lover, Martin, who is absent. Her friend Claud, also a failed writer, is her escort. Martin has just scored a worldwide success—and this seems exaggerated—with the publication of a single novel, and the party is a shocked response to his sudden fame. While Ilona seems to be waiting for Martin's return from his journeys abroad, the truth is that he has already left her emotionally; and the remainder of the book is an evocation of her time of despair following the affair's end. The quality is that of a personal memoir.

Feelings of abandonment, remembered moments of passion, efforts to stem the tide of loss move repetitively through Ilona's mind, constantly shifting the scene between past and present. She is especially obsessed with the idea of saving, of salvage. Things—objects—assume magnified importance. . . .

Suddenly, in Chicago, Ilona's brother dies, a sweet, retarded man 10 years her senior. She feels she had abandoned him—as Martin has abandoned her—to live alone when he had wanted to live with her. In his room she finds the things their father had left when he died. "They were small enough, these possessions, to fit into her purse and small enough to be hidden away when she got home, where she would promise them to take them out later . . . . Claud reflects another time that a shoe dropped in the sea might circle the world, turn up on a distant shore. Ilona is constantly hoping to dispel "the vast

abandonment the world casts on everyone's face." Mementos . . . Claud saves them in boxes. He too has been abandoned—by a wife who lived alone for a time in his beach house.

There is a poetic association in all this, it would seem, with writing, though in a lyrical context the association is often elusive. Martin is a writer whom global recognition has saved from oblivion, Claud a writer who gave up writing after one book. The host at that opening party, Jerome, in a kind of suicidal acceptance of anonymity, deliberately burns a huge novel manuscript after his wife abandons him for Martin. There is talk of burning up love letters. Burning is instant destruction—the opposite of saving. The brother is cremated, his ashes to be scattered.

Martin cannot now be abandoned or lost because he has joined "the lights of earth"—that is to say, become permanently luminous through fame. . . .

Toward the end of the book, after Claud becomes her lover, there is a slow shift in the meaning of the novel's chief metaphor. At the beach house, she goes out as he is sleeping to risk swimming in a heavy sea. Martin's wife had done this very thing, as though to drown herself, but, drawn by the thought of Martin, had come to shore. Ilona too comes back, to Claud. "The lights of earth" are no longer related to fame or success but to love and human communication.

There is little in this book of the practical daily life that the novel usually assumes as its province. The few characters seem entirely patterned and controlled by their lovers, past, present and future. Only in the chapters concerning the brother do we have a welcome relief from this strict frame of reference. Perhaps because of the narrator's emotional strain, we never get a really clear view of Martin as a person. This is a central need of the narrative. The writing is sensuous and the texture closely woven, in colors that, though muted, form a memorable design.

> *Elizabeth Spencer, "Flotsam of the Heart," in* The New York Times Book Review, *April 8, 1984, p. 9.*

GARY DAVENPORT

[In *The Lights of Earth,* Berriault is] preoccupied with celebrity and obscurity—with three writers, one of whom has become, to all appearances, a light of earth, much courted and envied by the California cognoscenti and by the world. The deteriorating love relationship between this man and the central character, Ilona Lewis, is the main matter of the novel. She has nothing like his renown or his confidence (although he is himself a perplexed and ambiguous character): her simple vow as a writer has been "to see that certain persons would not pass by unknown, even if all she could do was imagine with a few faltering words their inaccessible selves." But she has let her brother die in obscurity and neglect, and her agony of guilt adds urgency to the crisis of her love.

Ilona is tortured by what she thinks of as "her archaic view of the world that saw it divided between those who appeared to be blessed and those who appeared to be forsaken." The blessed have always been someone else—artists, scientists, saints, lovers—and she has consistently regarded herself as excluded from this state of beatitude. She finally comes—arduously and ambiguously—to an understanding of a different sort by way of her attraction to a third writer, one even less renowned than she: "The lights of earth are all the beings who draw you out from the dark, and are they everyone in your life?"

Gina Berriault's prose is an instrument of great subtlety and perfection, and her powers of observation, psychological and otherwise, are unrivaled in recent fiction. The smallest detail can bring into being a whole personality or a whole society. . . .

The short story is, if anything, an even more congenial medium for a writer who can do so much with so few words, and the twenty-five stories (representing a period of as many years) that Berriault has collected in *The Infinite Passion of Expectation* certainly demonstrate her mastery of the genre. As the title suggests, the main realities of life for the astonishing variety of characters in these stories are hope and disappointment. . . . (p. 124)

Many of the characters have a sense of election, and they are repeatedly facing the disappointment of realizing their own mortality. Others continue to delude themselves. . . . Rare-

ly, and beautifully, the characters rise above their mortality, as in the powerful final story, **"The Light at Birth,"** in which an anxiety-ridden professor shares the dying visions of an old German woman: she is at a garden party, happily attended by the Kaiser and other *Herrschaften* from the world of her youth.

It is to Gina Berriault's credit that generalizations about her work do not come easily. Although certain concerns recur—expectation, disappointment, and transcendence, the ravages of time and guilt, the tension between fame and obscurity—she is not a writer with a program. The main constant in this collection, as in *The Lights of Earth,* is the precise and unflinching psychological and moral exploration of people at important moments of realization, of how they come to terms with their lot, are undone by it, or transcend it. Few of her contemporaries manage these matters so well. (pp. 124-25)

Gary Davenport, "The Blessed and the Forsaken," in The Kenyon Review, *N. S. Vol. VII, No. 4, Fall, 1985, pp. 122-25.*

Lee Blessing

1949-

American dramatist.

Blessing's first drama to be produced on Broadway, *A Walk in the Woods* (1988), is set in Geneva, Switzerland, and details the burgeoning friendship between a young American nuclear arms negotiator and his veteran Soviet opponent. When the two men meet in a park between official sessions, they discuss their country's differences and discover similarities between themselves and their governments. After their joint proposal is rejected for superficial reasons by both the United States and the Soviet Union, the men conclude that their nations purposely evade disarmament issues, for without nuclear weapons the countries are "nothing more than a rich, powerful Canada and an enormous Poland," in the words of the Russian diplomat. Many critics praised Blessing's use of humor and witty dialogue to temper his serious themes. Frank Rich observed: "*A Walk in the Woods* tells us that all people and nations are fundamentally alike, and that all world problems could be solved if only the adversaries might build mutual trust by chatting face to face on a park bench." Blessing has also written the plays *War of the Roses* (1985) and *Eleemosynary* (1986), both of which were produced at the Yale Repertory Theater.

CLIVE BARNES

The phrase "a play of ideas" sounds as cold and dry as dusty charity, but Lee Blessing's *A Walk in the Woods* . . . is just that, yet much more.

Luckily, the playwright is an unusual writer of wit and resource, as well as an artist of considerable technique. The theater should count this singular Blessing as a new potential force. . . .

What makes this nihilistic anecdote for our times dramatically fascinating is partly Blessing's gift for the provocative phrase, such as when his Russian remarks that "History is geography over time," or his epigramatic comment that "Formality is merely anger with its hair combed."

Then there is the playwright's feel for character and its conflict, and, most of all, the chill horror at the base of this situation so urbanely uncovered.

Like the Russian, most in the audience will learn little, for as a civilization we have accepted cynicism as a way of trust, the alternative being too terrible to contemplate seriously.

The disconcerting Russian bear, here ranging from Teddy to grizzled, and the baffled, ugly, well-meaning American basset-hound that Blessing presents as his negotiators, are not so much national stereotypes as our own stereotyped thinking-man attitudes toward nuclear disarmament.

We realize the balance of power, the demands of supernational egos, and that the whole pattern of arms talks has been accompanied by a spiraling arms build-up that seems as inevitable as the stately pavane of the talks themselves.

We know all this. We know that such talks are an end in themselves.

For that matter, we know that the real danger is, as Blessing puts it, that "a computer will declare war on another computer because the computer got nervous," and we identify with Blessing's Russian (cast as rational man as counterposed with the role of emotional man played by his American) when he sums up the discussions by saying: "Our talks together have been a very great failure. But—a successful one."

At the end, when Blessing and his diplomats have led us through the whirligig of our confirmed fears, we rest content at having foreseen the questions, disconsolate that the answers are just as foreseeably dusty.

Although the play may alert us to gentle danger and even provoke us to uncomplicated thought, it is a lovely play that is, above everything, entertaining. The nihilistic pill is sugar-coated with fun—just like our civilization, that could go to the grave chuckling. . . .

A play of ideas, then. I must admit that *A Walk in the Woods* confirms ideas rather than suggests them—that is its own limitation of arms—but it is good to have on Broadway a play that suggests intelligence as well as emotion, and puts a questioning echo where its laugh is.

Clive Barnes, *"Arms & Ideas in the Woods," in* New York Post, *February 29, 1988.*

FRANK RICH

In one of several funny passages that threaten to quicken *A Walk in the Woods* into nearly a trot, a Soviet disarmament negotiator tells his American counterpart that the real blame for their nations' nuclear deadlock belongs to Switzerland. With its bucolic mountains and centuries of peace, Switzerland is so soothing that it drains the urgency from diplomatic talks about Armageddon. "We should put the table at the bottom of a missile silo," argues the Russian, Andrey Botvinnik, to the American, John Honeyman. *"Then* we would negotiate."

It's a smart point, and one only wished the . . . playwright, Lee Blessing, had taken it fully to heart. Like his two characters, Mr. Blessing is an earnest foe of the arms race, frustrated by the intractable political games superpowers play with the destiny of mankind. But as a piece of theater, *A Walk in the Woods* is the esthetic equivalent of Switzerland, and not only because its setting is "a pleasant woods on the outskirts of Geneva." . . . [The play] fudges the distinctions of actual international politics and arms negotiations, choosing instead to telescope the messy, life-or-death conflict into a sentimental relationship between two likable envoys. Because the candied antagonisms of that relationship are more reminiscent of *The Odd Couple* or *I'm Not Rappaport* than harsh reality, Mr. Blessing has made a subject as volatile as the bomb seem as pleasantly cool—and as safely remote—as his neutral forest setting.

The play's premise does spring from recent history. In 1982, the negotiators Paul H. Nitze and Yuli A. Kvitsinsky left the official Geneva sessions for an unofficial "walk in the woods" and achieved a breakthrough, soon rejected by their Governments. As is his right, the playwright has changed more than the names in fictionalizing the events; Honeyman and Botvinnik resemble their antecedents in neither age nor career. But Mr. Blessing's fictional liberties, however welcome an alternative to ersatz docudrama, all seem designed to dilute rather than heighten his fascinating subject. The play's walks in the woods take place in an unspecified year and involve debates over unidentified "tiny points" demanded by unnamed leaders of undefined ideology.

The characters are nearly as generic as their vague negotiating positions. Andre . . . is a jovial, wry, cynical bear of a Russian, with a taste for American pop culture (country-western music, Mickey Mouse) and a desire to personalize the bargaining sessions with declarations of friendship and frivolous small talk. He's as much a cliché of the glasnost Soviet Union as the wily, cold-blooded spy was of the "Evil Empire." . . . John is a formal, humorless, sanctimonious Mr. Deeds—a prissy Felix to [Andrey's] gregarious Oscar.

As is typical of stage pairings of this formulaically symbiotic type, the men must each teach the other a lesson by the time they reach their bittersweet parting: the burned-out old Russian will inevitably warm to the American's youthful idealism even as the American will at last start to lighten up. The men's growing friendship in turn conveys Mr. Blessing's un-

sophisticated, if quintessentially American, political message. *A Walk in the Woods* tells us that all people and nations are fundamentally alike, and that all world problems could be solved if only the adversaries might build mutual trust by chatting face to face on a park bench. The villains are the faceless, self-aggrandizing leaders (of all regimes) who subvert the people's will, insuring that progress in arms negotiations is at best an illusion leading to a new military buildup.

The play's other, unassailable polemical points, whether about the erotic properties of nuclear warheads or the devastation they unleash ("If we fail now, history itself will disappear"), will not come as news to anyone conversant with Stanley Kubrick's *Dr. Strangelove* or the rhetoric of Jonathan Schell. Mr. Blessing does invent his own bright jokes and aphorisms along the way, most of them given to [Andrey]. The Russian defines "formality" in diplomacy as "anger with its hair combed" and notes that without nuclear weapons, the United States and the Soviet Union would be "nothing more than a rich, powerful Canada and an enormous Poland." . . . One only wishes that Andrey's evaporated hope were not symbolized by a dry-tearduct condition calling for the repeated, treacly onstage administration of eye drops.

As his straight man, [John] starts out shrill, with hot-under-the-collar self-righteousness and red-faced slow burns in Act I, leaving him nowhere to go but up (into yelling) in his well-written soliloquy of catharsis in Act II. . . . To this end, the more metaphysical speeches about weaponry are accompanied by wistful background music, and the passing of time is marked by seasonal changes in [the] pretentious set, which frames the forest with what looks like a Holiday Inn conference room. Autumn arrives with an attenuated shower of perfectly shaped yellow leaves, winter with a burning rubber-scented fog effect and then, finally, spring with an abundant sprouting of, blossoms. Like Mr. Blessing, this garden stands for peace, but it typifies *A Walk in the Woods* that the flowers bearing that transcendent hope look all too conspicuously like plastic.

Frank Rich, *" 'A Walk in the Woods': Falling Leaves," in* The New York Times, *February 29, 1988, p. C15.*

ALLAN WALLACH

Theatergoers who buy tickets for *A Walk in the Woods* thinking they're going to see frolicsome fairytale characters are in for a surprise. . . . [Blessing's] two characters are Soviet and American negotiators who are after nothing less than an arms - control agreement to help preserve life on earth.

The second surprise is that Blessing has managed to lighten the life-and-death-of-the-planet debate. Along with the concern we expect from any work about so weighty a topic there is a welcome sprinkling of humor and incisive lines.

Why then did I come away from *A Walk in the Woods* . . . wanting more?

I think it's largely because Blessing asks us to think about the crucial subject matter under discussion instead of feeling something about the two people involved. The negotiators may carry the weight of the world on their shoulders, but they carry little emotional weight. Then, too, disarmament is riddled with so many complexities that no stage treatment can be much more than a brisk stroll to the subject's foothills. . . .

Botvinnik is at first a kidder, his frivolity masking a cynicism instilled by years of fruitless talks. Honeyman, the newcomer, is all get-down-to-business earnestness. Yet it is the Russian who makes the play's deadly serious point. The superpowers don't want real progress on disarmament, he says; there is only "the quest for the appearance of the quest for peace." Knowing that without nuclear weapons they are "nothing more than a rich, powerful Canada and an enormous Poland," the U.S. and Soviet governments follow every limited treaty with precipitous weapons buildups and technological breakthroughs.

"If mankind hated war," the Soviet negotiator declares, "there would millions of us and only two soldiers."

Contrasted with these provocative statements are Honeyman's idealistic platitudes. . . .

If *A Walk in the Woods* has its artistic shortfalls, it also has a bracing willingness to buck Broadway's shallow currents and deal with a subject that's so vital to us all. In a better world the play, despite its deficiencies, would encourage audiences to think and other playwrights to turn to matters of substance. It would also provoke governments to take action on real disarmament. But for that we would need a much, much better world.

Allan Wallach, "A Bid to Humanize Disarmament Issue," in Newsday, *February 29, 1988.*

GORDON ROGOFF

It's an ominous moment when a serious play begins with a joke. Certainly, Lee Blessing's *A Walk in the Woods* finds a surprising amount of laughter in the sour subject of U.S.-Soviet arms negotiations. The long-winded opening joke, however, is a hint that, like diplomatic strategy, the humor is a ploy to seduce an audience not likely to find the issues gripping enough on their own. Who would have thought that the tedious manipulations of governments and the terrifying realities of nuclear bargaining could yield the most charming play of the season?

This isn't a Graham Greene "entertainment," one of those cunning narratives thinly disguising its darker purposes under the cover of chase scenes or sexy diversions. Blessing is more austere: taking his cue from a walk in Geneva's woods by the U.S.'s Paul H. Nitze and the Russians' Yuli A. Kvitsinsky in 1982, when the two negotiators actually returned with a simple agreement later rejected by Washington and Moscow, Blessing presents four walks in the woods, taken by John Honeyman and Andrey Botvinnik, each walk occurring in a different season. In a formal sense, Blessing is setting up what can only be a play of ideas, since his characters exist entirely within the decorously arranged framework of their walks; mercifully, they never refer to wives, kids, or any other life outside their discussions.

Neither, however, do they refer much to the actual content of their negotiations. Blessing gives each character a moment of personal reflection when all the buzz-words are trotted out, not merely to give the play authenticity, but to remind us that this isn't only about two simple men enjoying and disappointing each other. Not unlike *Breaking the Code's* acrobatic

avoidance of the Enigma code itself, *A Walk in the Woods* manages to keep all the "boring" details at bay. Or rather, they're shoved into conveniently forgettable lists—SDI, SALT, human rights, megadeaths, Afghanistan, etc.

In their place is the charm, most of it given to Botvinnik in the play's only flirtation with dangerous politics. A delightful character, quite capable, as he says, of contradicting himself because he'd "go to any length to keep a friend," Botvinnik keeps the play humming with the appearance of maverick ideas. Whether suggesting that they should both be embarrassed to be Russian and American—"the world's fools"—or blaming Switzerland for their troubles, since they ought to be doing business "at the bottom of a missile silo," Botvinnik is in almost complete charge of the best arguments and the play's vitality. For him, Americans and Russians are too alike for comfort, with the Russians just as likely to have murdered the Indians as we were. Where we believe we're idealists, and they believe they're realists, he knows that both are illusionists, better at hiding truth from themselves than from others. All Honeyman can muster against this is the feeble charge that Botvinnik is a cynic.

Now that we've had the Gorbachevs in our living rooms holding hands while swaying through a sing-along, Blessing's Botvinnik assumes a kind of bizarre believability, not least when he's crooning—briefly—"Blue Eyes Crying in the Rain." But it's never clear if Blessing is trying to humanize the Russians or merely saying that sentimentality can redeem us. Both characters are sentimental in their own ways—Honeyman insisting on "hope" as a negotiating tactic, Botvinnik relying on "friendship." The Russian, in fact, gets one of his gentler laughs when reflecting on their rejected proposal, which he liked: "I will miss it," he says, almost as if he wasn't referring to an event that could blow up the world. . . .

For all his good intentions and sprightly dialogue, Blessing is not Shaw, not only because he doesn't turn ideas on their spinning heads, but also because he reveals so few driving convictions of his own. Sure, he'd like to write happier endings than the one here, in which Botvinnik predicts that "talks will go on for hundreds of years—if we're lucky." Where, however, is the imaginative lift that would admit that real negotiators can only be shits?

Paul Nitze was distrusted by Carter and used by Reagan. How in heaven's name could he ever be a good guy? Why trust the evidence of a dramatist willing to confuse the issues by jamming these walks into a single year while pretending that the progression from Brezhnev to Gorbachev actually takes place within the play's time-span? Would these negotiators go on and on without ever naming their bosses by name? What kind of credibility or suspense can there be when we all know that Honeyman wouldn't stand a chance in the company of Reagan's real favorites—North, Casey, and Max Kampelman?

Blessing's fantasy is in good company, if one can include it in the same breath, say, as Beethoven's *Fidelio,* where trumpets announce the last-minute rescue of the prisoners. But let's not kid ourselves that this is history—with or without geography. . . . This is a play that has buried its politics and thought in the treacherous precincts of the well-meaning human heart.

Gordon Rogoff, "Still in the Woods," in The Village
Voice, Vol. XXXIII, No. 10, March 8, 1988, p. 102.

JOHN SIMON

There are a few things wrong with *A Walk in the Woods,* but
let us attend first to what makes it eminently welcome on
Broadway. To begin with, it is not a family play: Nothing has
become so facile and monotonous as the eternal family comedy or drama, usually tailored to the limited talents of some
TV star eager to return to his roots. Even a somewhat different and better family play, e.g., *Fences* or *Woman in Mind,*
cannot quite eradicate the sense that the genre has honorably
earned the right to a rest.

Second, *A Walk in the Woods* is not a play about the usual
issues that have been bombarding us with numbing predictability. It is not about a sensitive, misunderstood soul, often
on his or her way to becoming a writer, coming to terms with
growing up, society, life. I am happy to say that neither of Lee
Blessing's two characters—the seasoned Soviet diplomat Andrey Botvinnik or the American tyro John Honeyman—is
based on Mr. Blessing himself, which these days is a very real
blessing. And the play is not about the problems of maintaining a sexual relationship, although Honeyman and Botvinnik
become something like surrogate lovers in the games they
play with each other—but it's all platonic.

Third, this is not yet another of those the-way-we-yuppies-
live-now comedies . . . that shamelessly proliferate nowadays; nor is it the rural equivalent about good ol' boys booz-
ing or Christering it up in some backwater polluted with cuteness. And, fourth, it is not obsessed with yesterday's crusades
about race, the Holocaust, the Vietnam War, women's lib,
gay lib, etc.—all of which are more than entitled to a hearing,
but not the same one over and over.

No, *A Walk in the Woods* is a political play, and, irresponsi-
bly apolitical as I tend to be, I still recognize the crying need
for the American theater to concern itself with the pressing,
oppressive subject of global politics, because that is a matter
that concerns all of us equally and is too important to be
abandoned to the words of politicians and the minds of journalists. We should ponder, as Milan Kundera does in his provocative new collection, *The Art of the Novel,* that "the history of the planet has finally become one indivisible whole, but
it is war, ambulant and everlasting war, that embodies and
guarantees this long-desired unity of mankind. Unity of mankind means: No escape for anyone anywhere." Blessing ponders this in his play, pointedly, poignantly, wittily—and un-
ponderously.

All right, the defects. The two actual negotiators in Geneva,
on whom the play is remotely based, took one walk in the
woods, reached a sensible agreement, and were promptly
overruled by their respective governments. And whereas the
one-time-only walk of Nitze and Kvitsinsky was an admirable attempt to cut through red and red-white-and-blue tape,
four such walks—one for each season, as in the play—are neither believable nor desirable: A table is required to put your
cards on, in arms conferences as in poker. But let us not deny
the playwright a little poetic or political license. And, yes, it
may be a mite precious to have computerized leaves punctuating the autumn scene as they flutter down in scientifically
random patterns, or to have spring burst out in symmetrical
and plastic flowers, a little too perfect even for the Switzer-

land that the play drolly blames for being so peaceful and
idyllic as to lure arms conferences into going on forever, unresolved but restful.

Those woods may be more of a park, with that nice down-
stage-center bench on and around which the action—or, if
you insist, the talk—of the play circles, falters, hurtles, and
ebbs away. But the play earns the privilege of being a Platonic
dialogue with no other overt action than an unsuccessful
chase after a stray rabbit. For it knows how to turn words
into action as the fatuous but idealistic American, a novice
at life as well as at politics, and the cynical and slyly baiting,
but also relaxedly humane, Russian fence, flirt, tangle, crush,
evade with every form of small and heavy talk, as if badinage
were foils and verbal outbursts sledgehammers. Above all,
as in Shaw but less brilliantly, the dialogue demands a
thinkalong.

Again, one may object that the Russian is too worldly for a
current medium-level diplomat—why, he is almost a cross
between Maxim Litvinoff and Ilya Ehrenburg, and not even
Gorbachev is that dapper and savvy, to say nothing of his
command of Amerenglish. Similarly, the American may be
too naïve even for an untried American negotiator, too un-
versed in diplomatic skills and foreign languages—though
that, regrettably, may be the truth, as may be, in some cases,
the absence of jingoism and skull-duggery. *Grosso modo,* the
pair do manage to represent America and Europe-cum-Asia
in their unending, verbally unequal but militarily matched,
duel.

The subject is not new, but valid and dramatically unexhaust-
ed. First: Peace conferences accomplish very little, mostly
small concessions covering up a proliferating secret arms
buildup. But they keep up appearances, offer hope, and obvi-
ate actual warfare. Second: Individuals from opposite sides
of the East-West fence can come to understand and even
cherish each other, but one superpower cannot afford to trust
the other. Or thinks it can't, which comes to the same. To
dramatize this accurately, playfully, thoughtfully will not
save the world—no play will—but does make for challenging
and pleasurable theatergoing. (pp. 70, 72)

A Walk in the Woods is particularly shrewd in not making
the political issues overspecific, and in keeping its juicy characters dangling on the edge of stereotypes (or, equally prefab-
ricated, antistereotypes) only to achieve last-minute deflec-
tions into genuine sagacious wit. A little too eager to be accessible, to please with dabs of sentiment, this is a play to make
the average viewer enjoy thinking; a footnote in dramatic history, but a minor miracle on Broadway. (p. 72)

John Simon, "Counting Our Blessing," in New
York Magazine, *Vol. 21, No. 11, March 14, 1988,
pp. 70, 72-3.*

ROBERT BRUSTEIN

Some plays are born out of their time, and it is a paradox that
this can account either for a quick demise or a successful run,
depending on what seems dated, the substance or the form.
August Wilson's *Fences* was voted Best Play of 1987 by virtually every award committee extant. But with its tidy structure, linear realism, backyard ferment, and father-son confrontations, it's actually the Best Play of 1947, being a tendril
of Arthur Miller's *All My Sons.* Lee Blessing's *A Walk in the
Woods* might have been a worthy competitor for Best Play

of 1982. But since its political agenda fails to keep pace with current events, it was obsolete before it opened and may not have the stamina to last the course. (p. 25)

The idea of two citizens of adversary nations trying to inject some sense into the official proceedings, before being blocked by cold war politics, has poignant potential; and [*A Walk in the Woods*] proceeds in its earnest, well-intentioned, if plodding, fashion to demonstrate the ultimate ineffectuality of their melancholy labors. But *glasnost* and Gorbachev's surprising capacity to conclude an arms control deal with Reagan, despite the resistance of the president's right-wing supporters and, presumably, his own defense department, consign the play to the historical wastebasket.

Blessing makes little effort to accommodate recent developments, apart from one skeptical reference to "the new openness." It's not hard to see why. He displays an obstinate pessimism about transactions between governments as opposed to the possibility of positive dealings between men of goodwill, perhaps in the liberal delusion that long-standing ideological conflicts are merely the result of misunderstanding or suspiciousness, rather than the consequence of genuine differences: in short, if governments could display the same benevolence toward each other as private individuals, they would quickly resolve the issues that divide them. *A Walk in the Woods* reminds me of all those movies and TV miniseries that conclude with Russian and American citizens ruefully shaking hands while their rulers prepare to press the buttons that will blow them to smithereens.

It is at least possible that ruling systems are administered by the same species of human being as those amiable and judicious creatures who sit on park benches to discuss affairs of state. And if Gorbachev is presently the most interesting figure in world politics, it is because he has demonstrated how a powerful individual can change, even if only temporarily, the inexorable course of history—not through hands-across-the-sea sentiments as much as through recognizing that his system will collapse if it continues on its present course.

Friendship, on the other hand, is the taproot of the relationship between Andrey Botvinnik and John Honeyman, the fictionalized Russian and American negotiators of *A Walk in the Woods.* The play is really a flirtation on a park bench—a solemn and discursive version of *Key Exchange*—where two affectionate characters risk the wrath of their superiors in order to deepen their relationship. . . . Both are charged with the difficult task of keeping our interest alive over the space of two hours, when the outcome of their efforts is foreordained before the curtain even rises.

Blessing is clearly less interested in the details of their proposals than in their courtship. "Do you like me?" asks the Russian, and though the American replies that "I'm here to make a treaty with you, not a friendship," it is their personal interaction that fills the interstices of the play. Botvinnik tries to persuade Honeyman to be more frivolous, to talk about Mickey Mouse or country music, while Honeyman tries to persuade Botvinnik to submit a new proposal to his superiors, saying, "If you don't do this, we will never be friends." Botvinnik agrees and, when the U.S. government rejects it, resigns from the peace table. "Will you miss me?" he asks Honeyman. "The new man will not be you" is the answer. They fail to kiss, but the play concludes with the two men sit-

ting quietly, if hopelessly, in the lap of nature, pledging eternal friendship. (pp. 25-6)

Robert Brustein, "The Best Play of Which Year?" in The New Republic, *Vol. 198, No. 4, April 4, 1988, pp. 25-6.*

WALTER GOODMAN

After seeing *A Walk in the Woods* and reading *The Rise and Fall of the Great Powers,* I attended a performance of *Julius Caesar.* Lee Blessing's Broadway play concentrates United States-Soviet relations in a couple of good-guy negotiators, Paul Kennedy's history traces the destinies of nations to impersonal forces and Shakespeare delivers a momentous period through a clutch of world-class heroes. Their convergence naturally incites thoughts about the part individuals play in struggles for global power, and the approach of a summit meeting with the Russians gives the matter a certain topicality.

A Walk in the Woods, which brings together the sentimental, cynical and quite humorous Andrei Botvinnik and the proper, idealistic, quite humorless John Honeyman, offers a peace marcher's view of the nature of the difficulties between Moscow and Washington: the pacific impulses of decent men on both sides are being frustrated by forces back home seeking national advantages at the expense of the greatest good of all.

Mr. Blessing spares himself the difficulty of grapping with the issue of whether removing nuclear arms might make the world more dangerous or put some wholesome interests and values at risk. Such questions, granted, are not easy to translate to the stage, but lacking them, *A Walk in the Woods* never amounts to much more than an amusing getting-to-know-you romance, a sort of West Side-East Side story.

Walter Goodman, "How Men Shape History, and How History Shapes Men," in The New York Times, *April 4, 1988, p. 17.*

THOMAS M. DISCH

Of the two new plays about East meeting West and the resulting strains, I must confess my preference for the ostensibly less serious, Larry Shue's *Wenceslas Square.* . . . That's not to say that Lee Blessing's *A Walk in the Woods* . . . fails to engage the attention or command respect, but ultimately these simulated meetings between a U.S. and a Russian arms negotiator seemed . . . laboriously contrived and unconvincing. . . .

The problem with *A Walk in the Woods* inheres in its central merit. It is a calm, lucid, nonpartisan scale model of the frustration generated by decades of disarmament negotiations that both the United States and the Soviet Union use as window dressing for the reality of an unstoppable arms race. . . . [Honeyman] is the quintessential Yankee. He rebuffs [Botvinnik's] overtures of friendship, refuses to play trivia games with him and delivers the show's one overt sermon on the horror of the nuclear arms race, a serviceable paraphrase of Jonathan Schell's *The Fate of the Earth.* However, the play's last word on the subject savors more of Samuel Beckett than of any crusader for disarmament. The negotiators' best efforts prove futile, and they part ways (much as the audience leaves the theater), knowing the nuclear night-

mare will go on. Such a muted curse on both superpowers'
houses is probably the most commonly used aspirin for fraz-
zled nuclear-age nerves, and *A Walk in the Woods* has enjoyed a fair success with critics and audiences for saying what
is universally thought but almost always repressed: We all
live in a nuclear submarine.

*Thomas M. Disch, in a review of "A Walk in the
Woods," in* The Nation, *New York, Vol. 246, No.
14, April 9, 1988, p. 510.*

André Breton

1896-1966

French essayist, poet, novelist, critic, dramatist, and editor.

Breton was the founder and primary theoretician of Surrealism, a highly influential literary and artistic movement dedicated to examining the irrational, paranormal, and subconscious aspects of the human mind. Originated in the 1920s, Surrealism sought to replace established moral and ethical concepts with a philosophy of irrationality that Breton described as "exalting the values of *poetry, love,* and *liberty.*" Although particularly noted for his seminal manifestoes in which he defines Surrealism's basic goals and tenets, Breton is also praised for poetry and prose works in which he draws upon socialist politics, the psychological theories of Sigmund Freud, and such mystical phenomena as alchemy and astrology to support his theories.

Prior to his literary career, Breton attended medical school at the University of Paris and became familiar with the publications and ideas of such neurologists as Freud, Jean-Martin Charcot, and Pierre Janet. His psychiatric work in an army medical unit during World War I furthered his interest in subconscious aspects of the human mind. Following the war, Breton became active in Tristan Tzara's movement of Dadaism, a nihilistic philosophy of art and literature that proposed the cynical rejection of all established cultural values, in part as a response to the atrocities of World War I. Although described by Jean-Pierre Cauvin as "frankly terroristic, in the manner of Dada," Breton's first collection of poems, *Mont de piété* (1919), was also compared to the works of nineteenth-century French Symbolist poets Stéphane Mallarmé and Arthur Rimbaud for its inspired, passionate tone. In his verse collected in *Les champs magnétiques* (1920), which he coauthored with Philippe Soupaut, and *Clair de terre* (1923), Breton began to experiment with Pierre Janet's concept of psychic automatism, using a stream-of-consciousness approach known as automatic writing in which random, subconscious responses to self-induced dreams, hallucinations, and trances are transcribed into written form.

While Breton described Dadaism as a "revolutionary necessity," he soon became disenchanted with the limitations and destructiveness of Tzara's reductionist theories and sought to supplant the movement with Surrealism. Although he drew upon Tzara's ideas in formulating his own concepts, Breton hoped that Surrealism would serve as a foundation for human enlightenment and utopian existence. During the mid-1920s, Breton guided the rapid progress of the Surrealist movement, which reached its creative apex between 1924 and World War II. *Manifeste du surréalisme,* contained in *Manifeste du surréalisme, et Poisson soluble* (1924; revised, 1962), establishes the philosophy of Surrealism and relates Breton's belief in psychic automatism and objective chance. By juxtaposing or combining incongruous objects or events in seemingly irrational patterns, Breton contended that such inverse concepts as love and hate could reveal complementary interrelationships that result in a new view of reality. *Poisson soluble* is an autobiographical prose poem intended as a companion text to the original edition of *Manifeste du surréalisme* in which Breton engages in a dialogue with various mythological characters.

This piece demonstrates the application of Freud's theory of free association to poetic narrative.

In his *Second manifeste du surréalisme* (1930), Breton addresses the philosophical implications of the movement, stridently taking issue with fellow Surrealists who disagreed with his theories and endorsing communism as a means to creating an altruistic society. In his manifesto *Du temps que les surréalistes avaient raison* (1935), Breton denounced communism for its tendency to sacrifice artistic freedom to ideological concerns. These and Breton's other statements on Surrealist principles are collected in *Manifestes du surréalisme* (1962; *Manifestoes of Surrealism*). His further theoretical writings on Surrealism include *Les vases communicants* (1932), a work influenced by Freud's *Interpretation of Dreams* that examines the harmonic relationship between the conscious and unconscious mind, and *Qu'est-ce que le surréalisme?* (1934; *What Is Surrealism?*), in which Breton addresses various definitions of the movement. During the 1920s and 1930s, the Surrealist movement was embraced by such important poets as Louis Aragon, Paul Eluard, and Benjamin Péret, as well as painters Salvador Dali, Max Ernst, and René Magritte. Breton's critical essays on Surrealism in literature and the visual arts are collected in *Le surréalisme et la peinture* (1928, revised, 1965; *Surrealism and Painting*). *Les pas perdus* (1924;

revised, 1969), *La clé des champs* (1953), and *Perspective cavalière* (1970) comprise other essays and miscellaneous prose pieces by Breton.

Breton is also noted for prose works that explore notions of love and physical passion. Advocating the creation of "convulsive beauty" in art, Breton theorized that surreal states of consciousness, which he believed were attainable through sexual love, could also be evoked in art by synthesizing opposed symbols representative of both rational masculine and irrational feminine forces. In his first autobiographical novel, *Nadja* (1928; revised, 1963), Breton recounts his love affair with a mentally disturbed young woman. Although initially attracted to Nadja because he views her as embodying Surrealist traits, Breton abandons her upon discovering darker sources of eccentricity that eventually lead to her institutionalization. In his next autobiographical narrative, *L'amour fou* (1937; *Mad Love*), Breton chronicles his relationship to artist Jacqueline Lamba from their first encounter to their marriage and the birth of their daughter. In his last prose narrative, *Arcane 17* (1944; revised, 1947, as *Arcane 17 enté d'ajours*), in which he discusses his separation from Lamba and self-exile in North America during the German occupation of France in World War II, Breton offers a mythic view of women, suggesting that the female might serve as a means for humanity to attain spiritual enlightenment and renewal.

Much of Breton's poetry of the 1930s is written in free verse and makes use of biological and botanical symbolism as well as contrasts between images of light, fire, and darkness. In the complex theatrical pieces collected in *Le revolver à cheveux blancs* (1932) and in the ritualistic and erotic love poetry in *L'air de l'eau* (1934), Breton evidenced a preference for bizarre metaphors and arcane language. The style of his poetic epics *Fata Morgana* (1942) and *Ode à Charles Fourier* (1947, revised, 1961; *Ode to Charles Fourier*) is considered more hermetic and less automatic than that of his early works and expresses in metaphoric and mythological terms Breton's self-exile during World War II. The prose poems in *Constellations* (1959), written in 1940 and collected with drawings by Joan Miró, present images of the poet as craftsman, painter, and magician. *Selected Poems: André Breton* (1969) and *Poems of André Breton: A Bilingual Anthology* (1982) comprise translations of representative verse from Breton's career. Reviewing *Poems of André Breton*, Roger Cardinal asserted that Breton's poetic opus may be viewed as "a single continuum, an integral search for some ultimate experience, whether this be an encounter with 'convulsive beauty,' erotic fulfillment, or some perfect coincidence of fantasy and reality." The first volume of Breton's *Oeuvres complètes* (1988), which features pieces from the beginning of his career through 1930, was praised by Michael Sheringham as containing "varied, inventive, and often brilliant writing, much of it still very fresh. . . . [Breton's] books are like no others, and each seems to have the uncanny property of simultaneously borrowing from an established genre, forging a new one, and somehow subverting both from within."

(See also *CLC*, Vols. 2, 9, 15; *Contemporary Authors*, Vols. 19-20, Vols. 25-28, rev. ed. [obituary]; *Contemporary Authors Permanent Series*, Vol. 2; and *Dictionary of Literary Biography*, Vol. 65.)

ROGER SHATTUCK

The ashes of Surrealism are still warm in 1969, with a few embers glowing beneath. But we can properly speak now about what the movement has left behind: a corpus of works of art—painting, sculpture, poetry, poetic narratives; and a history of recurrent and vehement interventions in French political and cultural life of the twenties and thirties. (p. 4)

The Manifestoes of Surrealism consists of three major discursive texts, plus a bonus. Trumpeting liberation from our materialist and formalist mental habits, the First Surrealist Manifesto proposes three complementary escape routes: retrieval of childhood, dream infused into the waking state, and language exploited as the locus of a revelation called poetry. Breton's hortatory style covers a very loose structure, but this call to artistic arms still has power. We have neither accomplished nor rejected his program.

By 1930 the Surrealists had become notorious and embattled: time for another manifesto. Breton's second document is long-winded, acrimonious in tone and principally concerned with settling accounts with ex-members. Outside of a few visionary or scientific metaphors, the contribution of the second manifesto is its strong affirmation of the redemptive power of Love.

The third major text comes five years later and is really a collection of political speeches Breton gave in 1935, plus one collective statement. At a time when the European intellectual community was all too ready to participate in Communist-organized congresses against fascism and for cultural liberty, Breton took a courageous stand against the Party's massive bad faith.

The other documents included in this volume are minor—except for the bonus: *Soluble Fish.* No tract or position paper, this. Breton misunderstood the meaning of "Défense et Illustration," the title of the 16th-century manifesto of the Pléiade poets. Along with his "defense" of Surrealist principles, he published an "illustration" or practical application. *Soluble Fish* consists of 15 brief dream narratives (or prose poems, or automatic texts) that provide an excellent opportunity to study Surrealism at its source. They embody the fundamental principle of language used not as description of existing reality but as a means of inventing a new reality—unrecognizable yet beautiful.

The three principal doctrinal texts in this collection permit an alert reader to trace across a 10-year period the market fluctuations of cultural stocks like collective games, automatic writing, and *le hasard objectif*. The most revealing touchstone, as might be expected, is Rimbaud. In 1924, he placed high among the 20-odd patron saints: "Rimbaud is Surrealist in the way he lived, and elsewhere." Then, in 1930, Breton virtually spits on him: "Rimbaud was mistaken, Rimbaud wanted to fool us." In 1935, he is back in favor: "Arthur Rimbaud too is there to confront the new-born Commune with all his seventeen-year-old genius." He has become the great double revolutionary. (pp. 4-5)

Roger Shattuck, "Remaining Is a Corpus of Art Works—Painting, Sculpture, Poetry—Still Warm in 1969," in The New York Times Book Review, *July 20, 1969, pp. 4-5, 34.*

SIMON WATSON TAYLOR

In December 1924, the publication by Breton's group of the first issue of *La Révolution Surréaliste* marked both the end of Dada and the beginning of Surrealism as an organized movement.

It was a long way from the dadaists' self-mocking slogans of "Dada is the biggest swindle of the century" and "Dada is always wrong" to the sonorous "We must work towards a new declaration of the rights of man" adopted by the surrealists as the motto for their new review. Breton had already staked out the movement's proposed territory two months previously in his *Surrealist Manifesto,* a fascinating document which is now available in English. . . .

[*Manifestoes of Surrealism*] contains, along with this first and most important of Breton's manifestoes, an assortment of later polemical pieces up to 1953. A comparison of these texts throws a good deal of light on the way Breton gradually built his concept of Surrealism from its diverse origins.

Through a triumph of Oedipean reticence, the still-warm corpse of Dada is not mentioned once in the First Manifesto, nevertheless this is still essentially a neo-dadaist document. Breton consolidates his recent routing of Tzara and his allies by incorporating their "spirit of contradiction" within "serious" theory. In so far as this theoretical argument is sustained at all, it is based rather tenuously on the basic premises of psychoanalysis: Freud's teaching concerning the functions of the dream process is, however, transformed into a grandiose principle of universal application. In particular, the central idea expressed in the Manifesto that the adoption of an hallucinatory psychic automatism would reveal "the actual functioning of thought" must be considered as wholly alien to Freud's own concept of his theories.

Apart from this insistence on "the omnipotence of dream" and the necessity for man to incorporate the dream process into his waking state, the Manifesto remains almost entirely uninformative, in the best Dada tradition. Painting is mentioned just once, in a laconic footnote. As for literature, "if one is to judge them only superficially by their results, a good number of poets could pass for surrealists, beginning with Dante and in his finer moments, Shakespeare." . . . (p. 42)

The striking feature of the First Manifesto is the total absence of politics. None of the later heroes of Surrealism—Hegel, Marx, Trotsky—has as yet appeared. . . . Things have changed, though, by the end of 1928, and the Second Manifesto marks Surrealism's entry into French left-wing politics. The Dada spirit has entirely evaporated, to be replaced by a tone of querulous intolerance as Breton slashes away in several different directions to mark his newly acquired revolutionary consciousness: he settles scores with such old comrades as Soupault, Artaud, and Vitrac who had dropped out or been kicked out of the movement, and he even reprimands figures as near-sacrosanct as Duchamp and Picabia for remaining aloof from active involvement. But, above all, Breton attempts the impossible task of reconciling the surrealists' declared adhesion to the Communist Party's political program with their insistence on retaining freedom to pursue their own spiritual path toward a parallel "surrealist revolution."

The dilemma seems tragi-comic in retrospect. Breton reproaches the communists for doubting the purity of the surrealists' revolutionary devotion, while almost in the same breath he invokes Rimbaud's "alchemy of the word" as a call to arms for "the profound, the veritable occultation of surrealism." Astrology and clairvoyance are to be studied "with a minimum of mistrust," . . . and surrealist "parlor games" will provide evidence of the reality of psychic phenomena. No wonder the communists looked askance at these strange recruits!

The later texts included in *Manifestoes of Surrealism* carry Breton gradually further away from direct political involvement and closer to a platform based loosely on Hegelian philosophy, Freudian psychology, and a curiously unselective mysticism. The 1935 pamphlet **"On the Time when the Surrealists were Right"** fires a final broadside at the Communist Party for "Stalinist conformism," while **"Surrealist Situation of the Object,"** published that same year, introduces into the surrealist enterprise two main planks that are as esoteric as could be desired: "objective humor" (the "dialectical resolution" of "the two forces which by turn tended to dominate art in the Romantic era . . . ; the force that made the accidents of the outer world a matter of interest on the one hand, and on the other hand the force that made the caprices of personality a matter of interest"), and "objective chance" ("that sort of chance that shows man, in a way that is still very mysterious, a necessity that escapes him, even though he experiences it as a vital necessity").

At the end of the 1942 **"Prolegomena to a Third Surrealist Manifesto or Not,"** Breton marks his intrusion into science fiction with a suggestion that beings he calls "the great transparent ones" perhaps exist "above" man, on the animal scale, beings "whose behaviour is as strange to him as his may be to the mayfly or the whale." And by 1953 and **"On Surrealism in its Living Works,"** Breton appears to have jettisoned his Marxist convictions in favor of a return to the harmlessly dotty utopianism of the early-nineteenth century sociologist Charles Fourier. (p. 43)

Aside from the question of intellectual competence, muddled critical writing about Surrealism originates largely in the mistaken view that Breton's Manifestoes and other *ex cathedra* pronouncements can be used as infallible guides to the meaning and purpose of Surrealism's products, its poetry, its imaginative prose, its art. They should, on the contrary, be treated warily. A perceptive comment on Breton's method of developing his ideas has been made by Marcel Jean in his authoritative if over-Freudian *History of Surrealist Painting.* . . . Discussing Breton's 1926 essay *Le Surréalisme et la peinture,* Jean remarks that Breton's "most persuasive 'reasonings' draw their power of conviction from their sheer incantatory quality, from a rhetoric closely resembling the long sentences of [Lautréamont's] *Chants de Maldoror,* and from a syntax which seems designed, curiously enough, to cast a spell over the mind's logical tendencies and to glorify, though surreptitiously, the disorientation of thought-processes."

It is doubtful, for example, whether even the most subservient of the surrealist poets or painters paid much heed to Breton's decree, in the Second Manifesto, that "the activities of the surrealists" shall be motivated solely by "the hope of finding and fixing" a mythical "point of the mind at which life and death, the real and the imagined, past and future, the communicable and the incommunicable, high and low, cease to be perceived contradictorily." Yet this near-meaningless program is constantly being quoted seriously as a valuable pointer to the intentions of surrealist poetry or art. . . .

The exegetes would save themselves a great deal of tortured rationalization if they accepted the fact that the best of the surrealist poets and painters were entirely selective in their attitude to surrealist theory. In general, they retained from the theoretical apparatus, and adapted to their individual requirements, the basic mechanisms proposed by Breton as the means of liberating the psyche from its enslavement to "reason": hallucinatory and irrational thought associations and recollected dream images. But however effective the formulas for "jogging" inspiration, especially—in surrealist poetry and painting alike—the juxtaposition of disparate images, they can only feed an *immanent* inspiration. Only by exercising his intuitive intelligence and innate sensibility can the poet or painter select images whose confrontation will spark the magical transformation into surreality. Second-rate surrealist painting is easily recognizable by the banal or theatrical relationship between its constituent elements. The comparable vice among surrealist poets is a rudimentary automatism, involving the stringing together of endless non-rational associations.

Breton himself, as a poet, made only half-hearted attempts to practice this kind of writing. His 1923 ***Clair de Terre*** comprises exuberant and perfectly conscious exploitations of dadaist inconsequentiality. On the other hand, his only extended exercise in pure automatism is unconvincing: the sixty-page text, ***Soluble Fish,*** which he appended, as a sampler of the riches of automatic writing, to his First Manifesto, is heavy-handed and self-conscious. Although he continued with varying degrees of obstinacy to recommend automatism ("this magical surrealist art") as a sort of universal panacea, Breton preferred to modify his own prosodic habits thereafter. As may be seen from his ***Selected Poems*** . . . , Breton relies mainly, in his post-1930 poetry, on the development of sequences of slenderly related sense-impressions and surprising analogies. At its least successful, this method produces deserts of ponderous syntax. At his most inspired, however, Breton succeeds through the sheer vigor and visual splendor of the images he conjures up: his finest, and most celebrated, poem, ***L'Union libre,*** is a veritable catalog of erotic compliments paid to his wife.

Unfortunately, this catalog method has been imitated endlessly by his epigones, and must be considered the most abused of all surrealist instant recipes. (p. 44)

Simon Watson Taylor, "Liberation Then," in The New York Review of Books, *Vol. XIV, No. 1-2, January 29, 1970, pp. 41-5.*

ROBERT STUART SHORT

'Whoever has truly penetrated into the temple of painting knows that its initiates seldom communicate in words. They reveal themselves very mysteriously, for the profane—at the most by making a particular gesture of the hand around some small portion of the picture and then by exchanging looks of secret understanding.' This caution to silence before the mystery of painting might seem out of place from André Breton who referred more constantly and pertinently to the arts in his writings than any poet since Baudelaire. This selection of his catalogue prefaces and his essays devoted specifically to painting and the object [***Surrealism and Painting***], which he brought up to date in 1965, . . . makes a very substantial volume. However, a glance at any of the texts will show that Breton was not an art critic of the conventional sort. First of all,

Breton wrote only of the painters he loved. He preferred lyrical celebration to denigration or even critical evaluation. Secondly, he was more interested in the spirit which informs a painting than in its formal qualities. He spoke more of the intentions of the painter and of the creative process than of the finished product. He related art less to other art than to the life experience and his essays are full of apparent digressions with extended allusions to myth, poetry and philosophy. Sometimes, instead of analysing paintings, he would create suggestive verbal equivalents to the artist's images. Sometimes, he would use the artist's work as a springboard for meditation on such issues as the relation between perception and mental representation, the immanence of the marvellous, love and eroticism, the revolutionary potential of art. . . .

As the title suggests, this book is about pictorial Surrealism rather than about surrealist painting. Breton wrote as the founder and theoretician of a movement with its own sensibility, ethic and metaphysic—a movement of which painting was only one of many manifestations. Art works for Breton were so many traces left behind in the course of a spiritual quest, evidence of an adventure but not the purpose of it. They were expressions of a theory which demanded, not illustrations, but the complement of action.

Although Surrealism may have risked the complete dissolution of form for the sake of fidelity to the authentic flux of experience and although Breton might dismiss painting as a 'lamentable expedient', a sizeable body of work built up which laid claim to the surrealist etiquette and which Breton had to account for. From 1926 onwards he did so continuously and also subjected art from the past, or with apparent affinities, to examination through the surrealist lens. The question that now arises is whether there is anything more in common between the artists discussed in this book—between Magritte and Gorky, or between Kandinsky and Crépin—other than the fact that their work may have provoked in Breton at one time or another the sensation of 'a great rustling of leaves surging through the poplars of my blood'. Perhaps part of the answer is to be found in the shock-phrase with which the book opens; 'The eye exists in its savage state', which, like Marx's and Engels's 'a spectre is haunting Europe . . .', was not so much a statement of fact as a programme. According to Breton, all the artists discussed here tried to preserve an eye untrammelled by conventional perceptions, whose untamed vision might share in the same freedom that automatism had won for the poet. Surrealism in painting distinguished itself by the 'purely internal models' to which the painters referred; wild landscapes of the unconscious which were the hunting-grounds of the 'savage eye'. For Breton, the surrealist painter was first and foremost a 'seer'; his Surrealism lay not in the operation of his hand but in that of his inner eye. Thus Surrealism in painting could embrace styles and techniques as different as the illusionistic automatism of a Chirico or a Dali and the 'rhythmic automatism' verging on abstraction of a Miró and a Masson. It was immaterial whether the artist painted a dream; what counted was his sharing in a certain mystique.

It is probable that Breton's principal claim to greatness as a writer about art rests on his elaboration and promotion of such a mystique. Thanks to an unequalled intuition, and without imposing himself, he was frequently able to elucidate the meaning of a developing oeuvre to the artist himself and indicate the direction in which it would most profitably lead, thus generating the courage and conviction the artist needed before he could press forward to more daring invention. A reading of *Surrealism and Painting* gives proof, if proof is needed, of Breton's power to inspire new art. . . . Breton's commitment was accompanied by an alertness to innovating genius which seldom erred. Not only was he the first to recognize a multitude of individual talents, he also established the order of expectations with which we still approach their work. It was Breton who first understood the significance of Marcel Duchamp's itinerary and of his ultimate silence, whose interpretation of Chirico remains the most suggestive. With prodigious style, Breton established the metaphysic of the object, drew attention from African to Oceanic art, anticipated Abstract Expressionism in the United States, and offered the most profound analysis of the processes of mediumistic inspiration in art. André Breton was more than an initiate in the temple of painting, he was high priest and fortunately he did not limit his office merely to 'exchanging looks of secret understanding'.

> *Robert Stuart Short, "Savage Eyes," in* Studio International, *Vol. 184, No. 949, November, 1972, p. 204.*

ROGER SCRUTON

The aim of Surrealism, according to its most articulate apologist, André Breton, was "to prevent the domination of the symbol by the thing signified." It was Breton's belief that modern man had found himself in a world of ill-defined and oppressive objects, objects dehumanised in the service of commonplace ideas and materialistic appetites. Art, he supposed, could rescue man from this state of alienation not by 'imitation' (the reproduction of already existing things) but by transformation. Objects must be changed from their habitual forms and remade as symbols; for in order to become visible the world must first become subjective. The accumulated debris of utilitarian matter must be dissolved and held in solution in the consciousness of men.

These ideas—in which a traditional romantic view of the imagination is tinged by the conceptions of Freud and Marx—represent what was serious in Surrealism. Breton was reacting not only against philistine values but also against what he thought of as the swooning defeatism of *fin-de-siècle* poetry and painting, which, with its taste for mere impressions, had allowed material things to dominate the world. For Breton Surrealism presented a direct and serious challenge to materialistic thought. It was a poetry of affirmation and acceptance, whose vision—unlike that of the Symbolists—was directed to the future, not the past.

[*Surrealism and Painting*] consists of a translation of *Le Surréalisme et la peinture* (1928), one of Breton's most famous writings on art, together with all the pieces of art criticism that Breton wished to preserve at the time (1965) when the French edition of this book went to press. . . . [The] only serious criticism is that the book is far too long. It is precisely in reading Breton's criticism at such length that its weaknesses—and the weaknesses of Surrealism as a whole—are most apparent. Although Breton writes brilliantly, with an astonishing gift for paradox, one soon begins to wish for something more substantial, some real indication of why the work of his friends is so wonderful and the work of everyone else so bad. His strange descriptions are often delightful, but it is doubtful that one can be helped to appreciate the paint-

ings of Victor Brauner (surely one of the most banal of all Surrealists) by Breton's eulogy:

> Everything expands, settles again, grows larger. This is the marvellous moment in time when the geometer, his eyes almost closed, walks along the ramparts of Troy and, without either of them knowing it, crosses Helen's path. In the hollow of one's hand, the stars have rescued their courses from the sky. Flame and leaf refashion the form of the heart, the long sought-for quadratix caresses the curves of a lilac blossom.

One would be able to take four hundred pages of this poeticising if there were any indication that its author was a man of judgement. But a critic who can bestow the same order of praise on Picasso and Dali, on Joan Miro and on Marcel Duchamp, must inevitably awake some suspicion. One looks for reasons to support these strange evaluations, but Breton is disdainful of reasons. He prefers witty paradoxes to genuine ideas. For him originality and surprise have become qualities of such value that the ability to apply standards—and hence the ability to think consistently—has been finally put aside. Surrealism presents itself as something altogether new, but it is unable to say in what its newness consists. Self-consciousness exists here untempered by the consciousness of tradition, and as a result it is impossible to be convinced that the artists and the works which Breton describes really have the importance he attributes to them.

In fairness it must be said that Breton attempts to create an *impression* of standards. *Surrealism and Painting,* for example, contains a long diatribe against de Chirico, who was rejected by the Surrealist school as soon as he turned away from the 'metaphysical' painting of his early years. But one has the impression—from the violence of the denunciation, and the purely abstract terms in which it is couched—that the choice of victim is more or less arbitrary, motivated by external interests. (pp. 964-65)

As a poet and an essayist [Breton] is certainly to be respected, but while the poetry of Surrealism represented something genuine, and indeed something more or less traditional, the painting can only strike us now as fatuous and insincere. The poetry of paradox was familiar in France long before Breton's manifestoes. But it is doubtful that paradox can be translated into painting with the same success—certainly not by Dali, Tanguy or Marcel Duchamp. To represent a thing is to represent it as possible: there is no logical absurdity in the fluid watch, or in the table with the head of an angry dog. The supposed "contradictory" parts of the Surrealist effigy are in fact no more than commonplace entities existing happily in a single space. They remain inactive, sterile, unable to lend to one another the vitality and meaning which they separately lack. In this sense the Surrealists achieved no visual equivalent of metaphor; only a concatenation of unrelated fragments. On the other hand there is genuine absurdity possible in the use of words. When Breton (in *The White-haired Revolver*) describes the seasons as *lumineuses comme l'intérieur d'une pomme dont on a détaché un quartier,* he presents an image that could not be painted (although it could of course be *illustrated*). This is genuine metaphor, and to the extent that it is successful it manages to create something vital from the juxtaposition of incompatible ideas. The real equivalent in painting of this startling use of metaphor is not the work of Dali or Duchamp but rather the Cubism that Breton so much deplored. In Cubism we find the attempt to overthrow normal spatial categories, and thereby bring into a visual relation things that in reality *must* remain apart—the face and the profile of a single head, a vase and its own interior. It is absurd for Breton to assume that Dali and Picasso were engaged in a similar enterprise. Picasso's vision was something finer and more profound than anything that could be captured by the grotesque juxtapositions of Surrealism. In itself Surrealism was visually sterile, as [*Surrealism and Painting*] admirably demonstrates. Its products were without visual beauty and relied for their effect on a literary paraphrase, a symbol, or a funny idea (Max Ernst's 'Garden Aeroplane Traps,' Brauner's 'Woman into Cat'). Perhaps the most striking example of this is Duchamp's picture 'Bride Stripped Bare by her Bachelors, Even': Breton's witty commentary (included in the present collection) is indeed a masterpiece of controlled absurdity, beside which the painting appears as a mindless doodle with no visual character at all. The ideas belong to what is said, and not to what is seen.

Even in literature it is doubtful whether Surrealism can lay claim to the novelty that is sometimes attributed to it. True, the images of the Surrealists are more surprising than those of Baudelaire or Verlaine, but from what does this quality of surprise proceed? . . .

The fact is that the great works of modern French literature had already been written—though not by Lautréamont as the Surrealists fondly imagined—and at its best Surrealist poetry was a refreshing and exuberant return to the urbanity of a previous age. (p. 965)

> Roger Scruton, "Roger Scruton on André Breton and Surrealist Painting," in The Spectator, Vol. 229, No. 7538, December 16, 1972, pp. 964-65.

J. H. MATTHEWS

Reconsidered from a comfortable distance, any document of importance in the history of ideas is likely to elicit condescension as often as admiration. Although it does not make the *Manifesto of Surrealism* unique among documents of this nature, one distinguishing feature of the text André Breton published in Paris in 1924 is that initially it succeeded in inspiring, among critics anyway, more condescension than anything else, and continued for the most part to do so for a long time. This fact lends weight to the question with which I should like to begin: Has the moment come at last, fifty years later, when someone who has not participated in the surrealist venture can feel and even confess publicly to admiration for Breton's manifesto?

True, as time goes by we hear praise of surrealism voiced more and more frequently, and from various quarters. Sometimes, though, our impression is that surrealism at last seems to have earned the right to grudging approval because, as everyone knows, it is not in good taste to speak ill of the dead, but nevertheless reassuring, in some cases, to remind oneself of their passing. At other times, it looks as if a number of those who confidently take upon themselves to comment on society and the art it fosters have made the belated discovery of surrealism's presence in the twentieth century and are determined not to give posterity the opportunity to condemn them for having ignored it altogether. Then, too, there are those who, apparently bent on smothering surrealism with their attentions, generously credit it with having touched just about every aspect of our lives. Into this category fall commentators who gravely cap their tribute to surrealism as a

vital force with the supposedly persuasive observation that even the gentle art of commercial advertising betrays the influence of surrealism these days—as though the launching of the surrealist movement, marked by the appearance of Breton's 1924 manifesto, were somewhat comparable to the discovery of electricity.

Exactly because people can get away with this sort of thing, my guess is that the answer to the question I raised a moment ago is probably negative. It is in the very nature of surrealism to draw a firm distinction between initiate and outsider. Hence we cannot hope to appreciate the true significance of the first manifesto without beginning, as I propose to do, by considering what it represents within the context of surrealist aspiration, rather than within that of art and literature, where critics feel entitled to impose their demands and sometimes manage to do so successfully.

Our perspective on the *Manifesto of Surrealism* will be a distorted one, so long as we have failed to see Breton's purpose in writing as to issue a call to arms, not to lay down a rigid battle plan, arrogantly assumed by its author, and those who shared his views, to be equal to the task of coping with any contingency the future might bring. An interpretation that treats the 1924 text as authority for regarding surrealism as a static rather than a dynamic phenomenon is, whether deliberately or not, twisting its meaning, the proponents of such an interpretation being guilty of grave injustice to André Breton, and the ambitions he sought to bring into focus. By the same token anyone who seeks to discredit Breton, his manifesto, or the movement it officially launched, by the expedient of referring to the *Manifeste du Surréalisme* solely with the aim of highlighting departures in later surrealist practice from theory as formulated there (one thinks of vexing questions about the part played by automatism in surrealist creative effort, for instance)—such a person is paying tribute, inadvertently to be sure, to the remarkable vitality from which surrealism has drawn strength.

The first manifesto simply marked the opening of surrealist activities according to a concerted plan. It codified ideas that had been in gestation for up to half a decade, and it gave a sense of unified purpose to forms of protest and exploration, already tried out, projected, or just anticipated. Of course it marked, too, the opening of the surrealist hunting season, which seems likely to continue so long as there are sportsmen to be found blessed with inaccurate aim and blank cartridges.

Although it placed immediate trust in certain modes of inquiry, Breton's 1924 text by no means limited surrealist action to these directions only. Nor did it preclude additional or even quite different methods for prospecting the surreal. Indeed, displaying that noteworthy lucidity for which he has received all too little credit, André Breton himself warned against the dangers of *poncifs*—of creating a surrealist stereotype—at the very moment when, in the interest of uncovering the surreal, he was recommending that the real be approached and handled in certain ways.

One thing the *Manifesto of Surrealism* did very well, so making a serious claim on the attention of its readers in the midtwenties, was focus on several basic human needs, no better satisfied today than then, under the living conditions imposed by western society. At first sight it may appear that the impact made by what Breton had to say came from his proposals for meeting these needs. It takes close acquaintance both with the manifesto itself and with the history of surrealism in the last half century to persuade us that the immediate proposals—including the much debated theory of verbal automatism—have been of less lasting influence than André Breton's insistence that the needs these proposals were designed to help meet are legitimate, and must be recognized as such. The vigor of the first surrealist manifesto owes much to its author's conviction that these needs cannot be set aside as inadmissible and that the individual has the right to seek their satisfaction, together with the privilege of doing so by whatever means he deems appropriate.

The first surrealist manifesto is not a programme for revolutionizing art and literature, but a programme that appeals for a revision of human values. In other words, the treatment it has received from most commentators—more important still, the perspective in which it has been viewed from outside the surrealist circle—limits its scope to the point where its meaning is radically changed. So it is that much that is in the programme Breton wished to outline is lost on those who know no more of his text than that it supplies a conveniently quotable definition, three or four lines long. In fact, the trouble begins with that definition and, more especially, with the narrow interpretation critics have felt free to place on it. The definition of surrealism in Breton's manifesto, so frequently quoted (as though it said all and as though, too, it carried its own refutation within itself) is somewhat like the tip of an iceberg. Its real value is that it marks, above the water line, the presence of something of far greater proportions, beneath the surface.

There are times when it seems especially regrettable that André Breton did not heed Mallarmé's warning about the limitations of naming things. There are moments when—aggravating though the consequences would have been for so many people—one could wish that, while speaking of surrealism, Breton had refused to define it, just as Benjamin Péret refused to define the marvelous, even though he saw it as "the heart and nervous system of all poetry." For what happens, when the *Manifesto of Surrealism* falls into the hands of art critics and literary commentators? Bent over Breton's text, such people give themselves up to examination of a document in which they pay attention to the "letter" of surrealism. Even those who do so in good faith seem reluctant to take the hint from Breton's statement, within the manifesto itself, that Guillaume Apollinaire, to whom he was indebted for the word *surréalisme*, possessed the "letter" of surrealism, but not its "spirit." And yet the message of surrealism is plainly legible only to someone who is willing to seek the spirit behind the letter of its definition.

Now, as Robert Champigny has demonstrated efficiently enough, the definition of surrealism consigned to Breton's manifesto uses reasonable language in a way unreasonable. Cogently argued and objectively formulated, Champigny's objections set off the fundamental difference between the language of criticism, utilized at the highest level of responsibility, and language as surrealism calls for its use. To Champigny, language is an instrument perfected by reason, its application reasonably governed. To Breton and those for whom he spoke in his *Manifeste du Surréalisme*, language employed only within reasonable bounds is language misapplied.

Clearly there is a paradox here, from which surrealism has never escaped altogether. It is a paradox that carries a heavy penalty, as we see whenever the surrealist idea of poetry is confused with literary ideals and subjected to evaluation by

standards in which surrealists have neither faith nor interest. Looking back from his *Second Manifesto of Surrealism,* first published in 1929, Breton was to remark that the public should not be surprised to see that the surrealist revolt had first found expression on the plane of language. But neither in the *Second Manifeste* nor elsewhere was André Breton ever to arrive at a solution to the problem of how to make the public aware of the difference between language used surrealistically and the language of literature.

It was not that Breton knowingly promoted confusion in this respect. On the contrary, some of the far-reaching consequences of the surrealist conception of language can be detected already in his manifesto of 1924, where, I have suggested, the most important aspects of what he has to tell us elude detection by the process of linguistic analysis to which Champigny feels entitled to resort. Here we face another paradox that can hardly escape notice; one that can leave us wondering whether Breton was indulging in a hoax or whether he fell victim to his own system.

In turning to the manifesto form, André Breton was borrowing a mode of verbal communication that supposedly owes its persuasiveness—its very *raison d'être*—to the reasonable clarity of its dialectical presentation. Apparently, then, this is a paradox just as insurmountable as the other. All the same, I believe Breton had more success in dealing with it. Indeed, when addressing himself to the problem he had created for himself, he succeeded in demonstrating, within the manifesto itself, that the message of surrealism owes its force to the spirit rather than the letter of its definition.

True, as we watch Robert Champigny meticulously and expertly uncovering the weaknesses in Breton's logic, the abuses to which he treats deductive language, laying bare the inconsistencies to be noted in the progression of the argument upon which the very idea of surrealism appears to rest, we see in action a rigorously reasonable mind, intent upon demolishing a structure in which it can place no credence. But if this were all there were to it, we should be left with the simple alternative of belief or disbelief—of blind support for Breton's ideas or rejection of them—and this means we should either be lining up behind Champigny or pretending that he had never opened the *Manifeste du Surréalisme.* Confronting Breton's text and Champigny's strictures has something important to show us, however. For we glimpse, when contemplating the unbridgeable distance separating the author of the surrealist manifestoes from his critic, what André Breton really meant, when he affirmed that language has been given man so that he may make surrealist use of it. Without intending to do so, Champigny has done the *Manifesto of Surrealism* a valuable service.

Those weaknesses that reason brings to light, those all-too-evident breaks in logical sequence, are less significant as signs of dialectical inadequacy or muddy thinking than proof that the *Manifesto du Surréalisme* was never intended to measure up to the demands of reasonable argument. Thus the excitement Breton's text is capable of generating in the mind of a surrealist is not stimulated by persuasive deduction at all. It comes directly from the spectacle of successive intuitive leaps, taken with no display of caution—there was in Breton a strange mixture of self-importance and humility—in a direction which that mind, tired of society and its ways (including its literary and artistic ways)—is already predisposed to follow. In a very literal sense, André Breton practiced what he preached. More precisely, he preached by example, not precept, while yet adopting a form of expression that he seemed to have chosen with the relatively uncomplicated purpose of setting forth a theory.

One cannot say, exactly, that the *Manifesto of Surrealism* carries within it its own defense. Such a contention would reduce Breton's achievement to a cleverly conceived plan, quite expertly carried out. But it does seem to me that this is a text which—without even trying—sets itself outside criticism. Generally acknowledged standards of critical appraisal do not apply, being struck with irrelevance. Meanwhile, the appeal the manifesto offers those whom it invites into the surrealist circle is sufficiently compelling to make all reservations appear superfluous.

Examined from this point of view, the first manifesto is not an exception among André Breton's writings. It explores, of course, some of the major themes that its author and others will take up subsequently in the name of surrealism. More than this, though, it illustrates the manner in which Breton invariably will respond to these themes. Perhaps I can make myself clearer by saying that, in the *Manifesto of Surrealism,* Breton really only assumes the posture of someone devoted to the defense of ideas important to him, while in fact he believes these to be self-evident and incontrovertible truths that, so long as they have been firmly stated, need no supporting argument to impress the reader with their validity. In this important respect, indeed, both in quality and character, in tone and mood, Breton's writing in the first manifesto is different in no way at all from that of his *Les Vases communicants* (1932), shall we say, or his *L'Amour fou* (1937). Gravity, a certain weightiness—these characteristic features of his language are not called upon, ever, to serve a carefully controlled argument, painstakingly followed through. Instead, they regularly are placed at the disposal of an intuitive interpretation of human destiny, which no evidence to the contrary can either halt or cause to falter. Breton's grandly structured sentences advance imperturbably across the pages of the 1924 *Manifeste du Surréalisme* just as they will do, twenty years later, in *Arcane 17.*

Are we beginning to wander from the point, to lose sight of the central text that is supposed to be commanding our attention, behind others which followed it? I think not. For Breton's subsequent writings enable us to place the first surrealist manifesto in the light under which surrealists view it.

Benjamin Péret, the greatest of surrealist poets, wrote comparatively little of a theoretical nature on the subject of poetry. To Péret, evidently, creation and commentary were separate activities, exerting unequal attraction. Breton, on the other hand, theorized as he created, and created as he theorized—the idea of diurnal experience and dreaming as communicating vessels, in *Les Vases communicants;* the concept of mad love in *L'Amour fou.* André Breton never felt the need to draw a line between theory and practice, between the language of theory and the language of creative action, even in that initial formulation of basic ideas which he issued as a manifesto.

This is one of the important discoveries the first manifesto has to share with those who really hear its message: the fascination of language lies in its being a less-than-adequate instrument and, at the same time, the most readily available means by which man may assert his freedom from controls, sociopolitical, ethical, moral, literary, and artistic. Obviously, Breton's manifesto was not the first document, nor will it be the last, to celebrate the tantalizing potential of language and its disappointing limitations. Its special value, at least for many of those it has helped recruit to the surrealist cause, lies in the tension it establishes between hope and despair (the fundamental tension on which surrealist effort rests, after all), in the excitement released beneath the surface of a text that, at first sight, looks to be far more indebted to the demands of reasonable discourse—and therefore, in Breton's eyes, condemned to failure—than it really is, and which, then, owes its magnetism to forces that reasonable disputation can do nothing to invalidate. (pp. 1-7)

Today the *Manifeste du Surréalisme* stands, as it did in the twenties, as an act of faith. It still communicates Breton's confidence in the resonance his words can find in the minds of others, in that echo which, in spite of everything, justifies reliance upon words. His trust in the future which, for him, gave meaning to the vanity of believing one can reach a public by means of the written word, is entirely in keeping with Breton's optimistic assurance that surrealism "is what will be." Indeed, as exemplified in the first surrealist manifesto, it clarifies that affirmation by confirming that the full flowering of surrealism is not to be sought in a statement like the *Manifesto of Surrealism,* but in the response it solicits.

Has reconsideration of Breton's first manifesto really done nothing more than bring us up against a truism? One writes, and André Breton freely admitted this, to find an audience. All the same, the distinctive emphasis placed on communication, effected at the extra-reasonable level that surrealism makes its own, saved Breton from self-contradiction, as he published a manifesto while yet firmly believing "it is absolutely necessary to keep the public from coming in." The public, that large majority of the reading population content with life in contemporary society, and with the satisfactions it provides, must be kept at a distance, surrealists have always been convinced; at no less a distance than art critics and professors of literature. To such people the *Manifesto of Surrealism* does have something to say, of course, because its medium is language. Yet we can be sure that, however much admiration or condescension it releases in them, their response will reflect reaction to the letter of the manifesto. To this extent, objections raised, reservations expressed, disagreements voiced appear, from the surrealist point of view, to tell more about the limitations of the reader than about the spirit of the text under criticism. And, as André Breton was hardly the first to point out, it is the spirit that quickeneth . . . (p. 8)

J. H. Matthews, "Fifty Years Later: 'The Manifesto of Surrealism'," in Twentieth Century Literature, *Vol. 21, No. 1, February, 1975, pp. 1-9.*

BETHANY LADIMER

André Breton, Paul Eluard, Robert Desnos, and Benjamin Péret, to mention only a few writers of the early period in which surrealist concerns were clearly defined, explicitly invested in Woman much of their hope for social revolution and profound cultural change. Breton is particularly interesting in this regard, for as leader for many years of the almost exclusively male surrealist movement, he valorized Woman and the experience of love above all other potentially "revolutionary" forces. His veneration of Woman explicitly emphasized what he believed to be her distinctive mode of thought:

The artist should emphasize to the fullest extent all

that falls within the feminine mode of understanding, as opposed to the masculine, and [he should] base his work exclusively on characteristic feminine perceptions: he should exalt and preferably even appropriate for his own personal use everything that distinguishes the female from the male in matters of understanding and volition.

It is apparent that Breton perceived a connection between his personal experience with women, and what he and the other surrealists considered to be the "feminine" experience in our culture: extralogical or extrarational modes of thought, including, as an extreme form, madness itself.

In her book *Surréalisme et sexualité,* Xavière Gauthier presents an enlightening analysis of the contradiction between the official surrealist position on women and social change, and the kinds of roles that women, in reality, were assigned within the canon of surrealist works. The contradiction is in fact both real and overt because these artists frequently declared that women would help effect social change precisely by asserting themselves and insisting on the value of their separate experience, and that they would ultimately find a place of honor in a new society. Gauthier points out that while Breton may have taken a first step toward realizing that society might be transformed by an assertion of the extrarational, and—more realistically for most women—of the value of a different, independent female experience, he failed utterly in recognizing the social and political conditions that are always a necessary preliminary to female self-assertion. He was not realistic about what such social transformation would involve.

Gauthier also stresses that Breton's entire project concerning the study of Woman is in fact undermined by a fundamental contradiction within the general surrealist vision of femininity: "How can the writer at one and the same time exalt the cult of supreme lover, and plead for the unleashing of a completely unimpeded sensuality?" This kind of contradiction, which often leads simultaneously to the sanctification of Woman and to fear and debasement of her, is by no means unique to surrealism. Here, she is seen as "edible, but she devours men; she is angel and demon, fairy and sorceress, salvation and damnation, symbol of purity as well as sin; she is singular and multiple, repose and turbulence, victim and executioner, nurturance and destruction, protector and protected, giver of life and of death, mother and child, heaven and earth, vice and virtue, hope and despair, God and Satan."

Our understanding of men's views of women now recognizes that such extreme polarities often coexist, and we can probably agree that Woman thus perceived is "imaginary" or "fictional," whether or not her "real" counterpart ever actually lived: a character possessed of all these mutually contradictory traits at once could exist only within the male imagination, and nowhere at all in reality. From our present point of view, however, such contradictions are noteworthy, in that they seem to forecast definite obstacles to an open-minded surrealist consideration of a complicated or problematic experience with a real woman.

Although his vision of Woman is certainly colored by all these opposites and extremes, Breton's predominant tendency with respect to this contradiction was toward sanctification, an attitude that grew out of his insistence on the cult of supreme, monogamous love. According to this belief, assumed by the young surrealists to be the complete opposite of "free love" or "unimpeded sensuality," the love of Woman

acquires something of a mystical or divine quality. As the satisfaction of a lifetime quest, it is an ultimate experience which is unique for each individual man, and it is also the *sine qua non* of artistic inspiration. But the cult of supreme love is directly antithetical to the notion of a relationship with a woman as a means of cultural change or liberation because Breton's understanding of exclusive monogamy is in fact the status quo, and his sanctification of the woman strongly reinforces her obligation to maintain it. Some of these artists, and Breton in particular, were in fact simply strengthening a traditional ideal of monogamy. The sanctification of the woman, which appears despite a certain ambivalence in so many surrealist works, is above all a desire and a need to *possess* the woman, and to consider her, in quite traditional ways, as an object to be possessed, rather than as an autonomous being.

Equally important to a discussion of social mutation, especially where male-female relations are concerned, is the fact that Breton, by his own admission, was in search of his missing female "counterpart." According to the Platonic idea of the original androgynous couple, as expressed by Aristophanes in *The Symposium,* each individual seeks his or her "missing half," who will be recognized instantly. The two halves will form a single, reconstituted person in whom *all difference* between the two partners will be dissolved in favor of complete physical and spiritual resemblance, or *sameness.*

In the light of Breton's ideas concerning Woman's participation in extrarational modes of thought, and the suggestion of a certain difficulty he experienced in perceiving in any realistic way her independent, different existence, I propose to reexamine a key text of surrealism, *Nadja,* written in 1928, when Breton was still in search of the "only woman, unique in all the world, who [was] worthy of [his] love." Nadja was a woman who truly existed and was perhaps the most important encounter of Breton's early life. She provided the rigorous and revealing test of reality for Breton's theories and principles concerning love as a predestined, unmistakable encounter, and the extrarational or "feminine" mode of thought, including madness. Breton's account is a somewhat fictionalized, though ostensibly completely faithful diary, of their unsuccessful love affair. I believe it is of special interest to examine this interpretation of a verifiable, lived experience, in order to enhance our understanding of surrealism. For in Breton's attempts to deal with Nadja's "irrationality" and ultimate "madness," much is revealed about the specificity of madness as it occurs among women, and also about a more general masculine refusal to recognize the independent, separate experience that leads to persistent and valuable feminine "difference."

Breton is particularly concerned with the literary representation of this adventure because he believes, as previously stated, that Woman actually represents a system of understanding that could ultimately help him to expand his own. The major problem that Breton discerns is a literary dilemma of textual representation. As a writer, how is he to communicate to his reader just how wondrous the experience with Nadja really was? And how is he to benefit from the greater range of understanding that Nadja seems to offer him, if he cannot really understand her? There are certain elements in Breton's report which, as he is aware, remain elusive to him, and which he can neither interpret *nor* communicate. *Nadja,* as I have suggested, thus becomes above all an investigation of the relationship between the *true* (or verifiable) and the *real* (or plausible and convincing, within the familiar terms of a literary system of representation) in the organized account by a male author of his encounter with a woman.

As Michel Beaujour observes, the experience with Nadja, whose friendship clearly included an exploration of all of Breton's major interests, ultimately *fails,* in that he cannot love or truly understand her, or even interpret his own verifiable experience with her. Breton's dissatisfaction with his written account is emphasized by great concern for the precise verifiable *quality* of the narrative, the abundance of documents and photographs provided—for the book is in part a scrap book—his insistence that nothing was invented, and the elusiveness of the wondrous, mystical sense he is trying to capture without recourse to fiction. Breton may have begun with the assumption that a verifiable experience would surely guarantee plausibility. The problem is that even the verifiable events in a narrative cannot seem "real" without a complementary system of interpretation ideologically, and hence aesthetically, wide enough to include them.

Up to a point, Breton succeeds in representing an enlarged circle of reality, by adopting several literary modes or strategies that *intersect* the stereotype of the "feminine" experience in our culture, i.e., the antilogical and the irrational, as well as some more universal aspects of that experience, i.e., non-participation in work and production, with a consequently different temporal organization and freedom of the imagination. New rhetorical devices are found to represent these new values, which are in revolt against the dominant values of society and which he and Nadja share. Thus we find analogical modes of discourse, constellations and associations which are not linear or "logical," and a disregard for traditional temporal organization of the narrative. . . . (pp. 177-80)

In the end, . . . Nadja and the meaning of his experience with her do elude Breton. Her own words are coopted by his rendering, and the more traditional prose seems to indicate, by a final suppression of the irrational or "feminine" mode, the exclusion of the individual, specific woman from this "feminized" universe. Breton cannot love her because, as he rightly says, he has never known her, and I would be tempted to add, in terms he would doubtless not approve, because she is mad.

Contemporary feminist analysis and criticism offer several possibilities for the interpretation of *Nadja,* which illuminate both the image of the mad woman in literature, and certain representations by male authors of "mad" female behavior as they have, in reality, experienced it. In the case of Breton and the surrealists in general, it is important to distinguish between the madness which threatens, and the "irrational," which is often fascinating and enlightening. The "irrational," even in its extreme or pathological manifestations, is a term describing the clinical basis for the *conscious* understanding of madness. In its more controlled forms, the "irrational" is a viable mode of perceiving the world. This latter variety can be "practiced" by men and by women, and it is what draws Breton to Nadja initially. It actually allows him to accept and to value a certain notion of insanity potentially present in all intelligent individuals.

But according to an *unconscious,* logocentric frame of reference shared by surrealist artists and others, "Woman" in some real sense is already "madness," in that she is the "Other" side of Reason, logic, the known and familiar. Despite this profound and pervasive view of her, Woman is still perceived as "safe" and "normal" as long as she remains squarely within the sex role defined for her by men, in a cer-

tain prescribed relation to masculine values. As long as her characteristics consistently refer back to his, and conform to a predictable principle of *opposition* or of simple *lack* or *absence* of "masculine" traits, her "difference" is safely contained within a system of fundamental "sameness" which, like a mirror, can only reflect the image of the man when he looks to it, and thus can only confirm his masculinity in its central and dominant position. In contemporary French critical terminology, this reassuring definition of femininity as a constant reminder of masculinity is often labeled the "specular" Otherness of woman because it functions as a sort of mirror or reflector.

Shoshana Felman, who has written extensively on the relationship of literature to socially defined madness, offers a lucid discussion of the implications of this basic Western philosophical principle in a recent article entitled "Women and Madness: The Critical Phallacy." It is perhaps already obvious that we are dealing here with a restatement of the Platonic ideal of the reconstituted Androgyne mentioned earlier as an essential part of Breton's concept of love. We may well expect that the failure of his love affair with Nadja results from *her* failure to conform and submit to this "specular" masculine definition of femininity: at a certain point, her madness becomes a hyperbole of feminine difference which Breton finds unacceptable. That is, she is not *Breton's* "Other," reassuringly reflective of him, but she goes off instead into new modes of "different" behavior clearly not prescribed by the masculine norm. Instead of blending with him as his missing half in the "sameness" of the reconstituted androgyne, Nadja becomes quite literally incomprehensible, and therefore "mad."

It would seem most pertinent to investigate precisely *which* elements in Breton's reported experience remain elusive to him, especially those concerning the specific nature of Nadja's madness, and precisely why these are invisible and difficult to interpret. I have already suggested that they are invisible to him, and not simply absent, because they become visible to the reader, provided another system of interpretation is applied that includes the reported facts and Breton's own observations of Nadja's behavior, more completely within the literary reality it seeks to explain. Breton left his book an "open door," literally inviting the reader to pass through and deal with the problem of bringing life and significance to the otherwise flat, empty documents and photographs, by discovering what the "real" experience with Nadja was all about. Thus a feminist interpretation, which includes a social and economic dimension to the surrealist encounter with Woman, is possible: out of Breton's own terms of literary representation ironically emerges a fully "real" image of an oppressed, rebellious, desperate, and eventually psychotic young woman.

In terms of events, *Nadja* is a simple story. It includes a wondrous, chance encounter with a woman, which the surrealists believed was the first sign of the much-sought supreme love. The meeting is a mystical event, for Nadja seems to be "already aware," as though she somehow always knew Breton's past and has divined the future. This sort of signal is particularly meaningful to Breton, who is seeking precise interpreters of what lies beneath everyday banalities. One of these will surely be his "missing half," who is also predicted to appear in an esoterically marvelous way.

Nadja and Breton arrange a series of rendezvous during the weeks that follow; their wandering through Paris, their conversations in cafés, and Breton's meditations on their relationship constitute the action of the story. Although Nadja is certainly an eccentric and charming person, she is also clearly ensnared in several typically female dilemmas that lead to certain estrangements, although Breton at no time interprets their communication problems as sex-related. Finally, Nadja recounts an anecdote involving an act of violence on her part. The friendship between her and Breton collapses, despite her obvious grief, and she is interned soon afterwards in a mental asylum. By the end of the text, an interval of time has passed, during which Breton has found his "supreme love" and "missing half" with someone else, and he reconsiders his experience with Nadja with sincere awe and fascination, but with an even greater perplexity.

The moment of final estrangement, alluded to as a violent point of rupture in the plot, is also the final suppression of the "feminine" mode of discourse and analogy that functions only as long as Breton is able to relate to the woman he is describing. Rarely mentioned by critics of the work, the dramatic incident yields the remaining information needed to interpret Breton's experience and his perplexity, Nadja's "reality," and finally her madness.

Nadja describes an event from her past, which serves to remind Breton of her frightening vulnerability on the one hand, but also her unsuspected capacity for self-assertion and violent expression of refusal and anger on the other. His own violent reactions to the account determine the entire course of their relationship:

> I had a frightfully violent reaction to the excessively detailed account she gave of certain scenes from her past, and I judged, perhaps with too much detachment, that her dignity must have been somewhat impaired by these events. One story about a blow she had received directly in the face, so that she bled profusely, one day in a room in the Brasserie Zimmer, the story of a blow she received from a man whose propositions she had refused with calculated satisfaction simply because he was despicable (and several times she had called for help but had nonetheless taken the time, before disappearing, to bloody his clothes) this story very nearly, in the early afternoon of 13 October, alienated me from her forever. I do not know what absolutely irremediable feeling her derisive, sardonic account of this horrible adventure awakened within me, but I cried for a long time after hearing it, in a way I did not suspect I could still cry.

Breton cries because he knows that such incidents might well occur again, and he lacks the courage to face them. While he has willingly emphasized Nadja's own courage in view of her *vulnerability*, this story would seem instead to point to a strong gesture of *self-assertion* and of *self-preservation*, yet it is nevertheless symptomatic of socially unacceptable or disapproved behavior. Nadja has here become "unrecognizable" in terms of traditional sex-role definitions, and hence "mad" in the terms outlined above. With this anecdote in mind, we are now in a position to assert that the interpretation of Breton's text that we are seeking actually involves a different concept of madness or schizophrenia, related to the specifically female experience in society and characterized above all by a phenomenon called "sex-role alienation." I believe this concept is especially enlightening in view of Gauthier's discussion of Breton's internally contradictory view of women. It is also closely related to Felman's summary of masculine/social suppression of female separateness or "differ-

ence," because an instance of sex-role alienation threatens to prevent a man from finding in a woman his specular "Other," or his "missing half." (pp. 181-84)

I am not suggesting that Nadja herself was other than clinically insane. She was an individual particularly unfit to deal with stress, and above all with the stress inherent in the feminine social condition. But she does represent, in exaggerated form, the essentials of the paradox in that condition, in relation to socially defined female psychosis. Irrationality, unreason, and analogical thinking, while suppressed and devalued by masculine Logic, are not persecuted when they are acted out, up to a point, by men. In fact, although men who choose these modes are likely to be marginal and not very powerful members of society (many poets and artists, for example), they can by these means arrive at awareness and knowledge of both themselves and the universe. In Nadja, these are not freely chosen modes of functioning, but thoroughly conditioned ones. Her somewhat different attempts to realize her Self by breaking away from these social handicaps lead to even greater vulnerability, increased oppression, and ultimately to genuine psychosis, as is shown by her escape into another role from the "recognizable," and, to her, intolerable condition of womanhood.

Breton's insistence early in the text that there is no distinction between a "clinical" and a "literary" account of his experience is a feature of his antifictional bias:

> The tone which I have adopted for this text is an attempt to imitate that of medical observation, especially neuro-psychiatry, which is characterized by a tendency to preserve every trace of evidence which examination and interrogation can yield, but which is not in the least concerned with literary effects of style.

If this distinction, in its traditional acceptance, now seems somewhat blurred or effaced, it is not because fictional devices have not been employed, but because a new, multivalent, and complex relationship between the "clinical" and the "literary" has been established. Something of the clinical description of the trained psychiatrist has in fact entered Breton's system of representation and textual strategy, and we should remember that he received this kind of training during his military service in World War I. But his blindness to the specificity of the female dilemma, and the final interpretation of the text in an attempt to define Nadja within Breton's own terms, rather than as "Other," and different, exemplify the way in which cultural systems of representation can in turn shape "objective" clinical observation.

When thus reconsidered in light of contemporary feminist writing, *Nadja* leads us to a new set of conclusions regarding the true status of the feminine experience within acceptable social and—more surprisingly—artistic modes of expression. Bearing in mind that "feminine" experiences and perceptions intersect those of the surrealist artist at several points, it is evident that only a woman who actively refuses the demands of masculine society could have revealed the true menace to psychic freedom inherent in social oppression. On some level, the Zimmer episode demonstrates to Breton that Nadja's apparent freedom and determination of her own fate are mere delusions. Her doomed attempt at securing true psychic freedom is sufficiently analogous to that of the artist in society and accounts for some of the dread Breton feels.

A fuller understanding of his experience with Nadja would

have allowed Breton to grasp the connections between his methods and values on the one hand, and the exact nature of society's normative, repressive function on the other. At the heart of the individual psychic revolution is the societal truth that conditions it. A mad woman is merely the hyperbole of the specific female experience of oppression, but the lesson she teaches to the artist, or to anyone who would transgress the boundaries of the power structure of patriarchal society, is that the price of transgression may be destruction. (pp. 193-95)

> *Bethany Ladimer, "Madness and the Irrational in the Work of André Breton: A Feminist Perspective," in Feminist Studies, Vol. 6, No. 1, Spring, 1980, pp. 175-95.*

LAURENCE M. PORTER

Breton's ideas reveal striking affinities with Jung's. Woman, as object of his passionate and at times almost mystical adoration, suggests a projected Anima. In *Nadja,* she guides the poet to and through the domain of meaningful coincidence which Breton calls "objective chance." This domain, which resembles closely that of "synchronicity, an acausal connecting principle," in Jungian thought, seems to hold the promise of knowledge which may lead to individuation. Obviously Breton is engaged in an intense effort at psychic development. From a Jungian viewpoint, the question is whether or not his quest succeeds.

During the decade preceding the publication of *Nadja,* André Breton explored the creative potentialities of the unconscious. As a medical student, he had learned of Janet's research on automatic writing, and of Freud's on the interpretation of dreams. When he became an author, he published a collection of automatic writing (*Les Champs magnétiques,* with Philippe Soupault, 1919), and later experimented with hypnotism (observing the trance states of Desnos and Crevel from 1922 to 1924), free association, and collective creation. His aims, however, were almost diametrically opposed to those of Freud. Freud's motto was "where id was, ego shall be." Psychoanalysis aimed to bring the unconscious contents to light in order to neutralize them and assimilate them to ego-consciousness where they could be kept under surveillance and controlled. Breton's long theoretical preface to *Les Vases communicants* in 1932 presented Freud as his main rival, calling him impressive but falsely original (for he did not acknowledge the work of the person from whom he had borrowed most), and secretly inhibited (for he demanded utter frankness from his patients, but censored the sexual contents of his own dreams owing to a bourgeois concern for status). Breton denied that only psychoanalysis could bring the repressed to light, on the logically unconvincing grounds that he himself always had an association with each detail of his dreams and fantasies. He mistrusted ego-consciousness as being only too vulnerable to domination by what Jung would call the "persona": the social mask of conformity which conceals and often stifles the infinite variety and potentialities of the individual. "For surrealism the accent has been on displacing the ego, always more or less despotic, by the id, held in common by all."

Breton therefore sought to apply the notion of a Hegelian dialectic to the opposition between conscious and unconscious. Surrealism would propose the investigation of the unconscious as an antithesis to the thesis of rationality, in hopes of stimulating a higher synthesis: "I believe that in the future these two so apparently contradictory states of dream and reality will be resolved into a sort of absolute reality, of surreality, if one may use the expression." He wished to find an example of this synthesis in his lived experience, since he aspired to think in an intuitive-perceptual rather than in a thinking-judgmental mode.

Breton sought to achieve a synthesis not only of conscious and unconscious, but also of mind and matter, by investigating examples of "objective chance," a concept which for him included premonitions as well as striking coincidences. It suggests an objective correlative of Freudian "free association." (pp. 25-6)

Jung arrived at the concept of "synchronicity" from his studies of the possible relations between mind and matter in alchemy, astrology, and extra-sensory perception. Synchronicity is "a meaningful coincidence of outer and inner events that are not themselves causally connected." Jung first broached the notion of synchronicity in conversation in 1930, but then hesitated for years before discussing it in print. Only in 1946 and 1952 did he reveal his belief that "psyche and matter are two different aspects of one and the same thing . . . the nonpsychic can behave like the psychic, and vice versa, without there being any causal connection between them." Jung insisted that synchronicity was "not a philosophical view but an empirical concept." He established a quaternio (four-part scheme) with two axes, one running between the poles of Energy and the Space-Time Continuum, the other between the poles of Causality ("Constant Connection through Effect") and Synchronicity ("Inconstant Connection through Contingence, Equivalence, or 'Meaning' "). The causeless events of synchronicity are creative acts, "the continuous creation of a pattern that exists from all eternity, repeats itself sporadically, and is not derivable from any known antecedents."

In each person, this pattern can work itself out through the process of individuation. Individuation is Breton's goal in *Nadja.* (p. 27)

Our unconscious personality complements our conscious one, according to Jung. One cannot achieve individuation unless the unconscious is brought to light. Literary works which see the unconscious as a hidden layer embedded beneath consciousness in the psyche tend to adopt the structure of a *monde gigogne*—to create a world of nesting boxes rather than a linear progression. *Nadja* has a structure which can be represented ABCBA. A—the question of personal identity; B—investigations of the influence of the unconscious upon waking reality; C—the catalytic love relationship with Nadja. In terms of specific pages, we have:

A—Who am I?

B—Examples of mysterious coincidence, particularly meetings with people he was to cherish, concluding with a rejection of routine.

C—The relationship with Nadja, creating in Breton a conflict between the values of spontaneity and of dignity. . . .

B—Reflections on madness (the eruption of the unconscious in others' lives), beginning with an impassioned plea not to incarcerate the insane.

A—Confused reactions of mingled hope and despair, ending with the appearance of a new feminine savior.

The unconscious tries to call attention to itself in order that ego-consciousness may help it emerge to awareness. There it may be integrated with ego-consciousness in the synthesis which is the Self, according to Jung. Human beings possess the inherited tendency to represent universal experiences in the form of images which recur from country to country and age to age. These are usually, but not always, the images of persons. Archetypal images may be projected from our unconscious onto real people of our acquaintance, or onto distant figures whom we fear or admire. Because it is our unconscious which does the projecting, we experience ourselves as encountering projections rather than as making them. Until we recognize them for what they are, their fascinating presence blocks psychic development. . . . A person who is suitable for embodying our projected psychic images inspires emotion and serves as the catalyst for a new stage in an ill-defined psychic quest such as the one depicted in *Nadja.*

Certain women, Jung explains, are particularly susceptible to attracting Anima projections. If they are enigmatic, elusive, fairy-like, sexually experienced, childlike and wise, mysterious and unpredictable, then many fantasies can be woven about them. Nadja fits this description well. Breton encounters her by chance in the street and they are immediately fascinated by each other. He never learns her real name. She has chosen "Nadja" because it is the beginning of the word "hope" in Russian, but only the beginning. She is physically frail, theatrically made-up, acutely sensitive, and makes unpredictable, enigmatic remarks. (pp. 28-9)

But the Anima-projection was not complete on Breton's part. He doubts whether he loves her, and fears she may be only an object of curiosity for him. He refuses to reveal himself by playing the game of free associations she suggests, and even in the published text he repressed his reasons for this reticence and his reactions. He finds her alienation from life, and her increasingly abrasive behavior, taxing. He refuses to follow her into madness or death, and cannot bring himself to visit her in the asylum where she has been confined at the end of the story. At the end of *Nadja,* however, Breton addresses a new feminine psychopomp who promises to give rich meaning to his life. . . . This book no longer has a raison d'être, he declares, for Nadja was merely a presentiment of you.

Such an attitude reinforces psychic projections rather than dissipating them. Romantic love is Breton's highest value, and the exclusive object of his worship. . . . Only through uncompromising love, Breton believes, could man receive a guarantee that his earthly endeavors had not been in vain. He admits that love may be incompatible with adaptation to externality. . . . For 20 years after *Nadja,* Breton elaborates and clarifies his ideas about love, but they do not change. Since he persists in overvaluing the love object, he fails to come to a full understanding of himself. (pp. 30-1)

[As Aniela Jaffé], a disciple of Jung wrote, with his editorial approval, Breton's Surrealism was valid insofar as it attempted to reconcile the "apparent antagonism between dream and reality." But, she adds, the procedures Breton used to this end—free association, automatic writing (and, one must add, "l'amour fou")—were bound to lead him astray from the way of individuation, since "the important or even decisive part to be played by consciousness is ignored." Breton's Anima-fixation, dramatized by him as a path toward higher knowl-

edge, actually works against individuation, reinforcing psychic projections and perpetuating the resultant delusions rather than dissipating them. In his personal life, reiterated Anima-projection, each time accompanied by dizzying hopes, led him through passionate affairs and through three marriages without producing greater enlightenment. Nor do any of the resulting paeans to love—*Les Vases communicants, L'Amour fou, Arcane 17*—come close artistically to rivaling *Nadja,* whose chief merit derives from the detachment which provides a relatively clear portrait of the heroine. (pp. 33-4)

Laurence M. Porter, " 'L'Amour fou' and Individuation: A Jungian Reading of Breton's 'Nadja,'" in L'Esprit Créateur, Vol. XXII, No. 2, Summer, 1982, pp. 25-34.

JEAN-PIERRE CAUVIN

Any attempt at defining the poetry of André Breton must begin with mention of a notion for which there unfortunately exists no corresponding term in English, and that is the notion of *dépaysement:* the sense of being out of one's element, of being disoriented in the presence of the uncanny, or disconcerted by the unfamiliarity of a situation experienced for the first time. Without *dépaysement,* there is no *merveilleux,* no encounter with the marvelous, the objective of all surrealist activity. Both terms imply a subversion of accepted norms and values, a reevaluation of reality—at least of reality as defined in Western culture. At its inception and in all its later phases, surrealism aims at revolutionizing our experience of words and of things by stripping them of their conventionality, their banality, and their utilitarian purpose, the better to foster the emergence of the unknown and the unexpected that lie dormant within their everyday appearance. For the surrealists in general and Breton in particular, it is the privilege, indeed the mission, of poetry to liberate the immense potential of the human psyche by repudiating the forces of reason and routine which hold it in check. Poetry is not art, but life itself, life as a constant adventure shepherded by chance, love, and liberty. Life is poetry in practice, the pursuit of adventure "dans le langage, dans la rue, ou dans le rêve" (in language, in the street, or in dreams). Poetry entails a radical transformation of the self and of society. All human concerns fall within its purview: psychological, ethical, and material. Like the alchemical quest, poetry seeks to transmute into the gold of a better life all the elements of mind and matter. The sensuous and intellectual desiderata of traditional poetry—euphony, lyricism, verbal virtuosity, elegance of discourse, taste—and the formal or structural devices it prescribes are, for Breton, the trappings of an outworn literature designed to charm, to reassure, and to please. His disdain for composition, rhyme, and rhythm is matched by his rejection of the poetics of transcendence so prevalent in nineteenth-century literature. In this regard, Breton's loyalties lie with Rimbaud and Lautréamont (Isidore Ducasse), two revolutionaries whose present-day importance can in no small measure be attributed to his lifelong advocacy of their works. Breton's own poetry thus constitutes an anti-poetics, all the more because it unfailingly disregards formal concerns: "La poésie? elle n'est pas où on la croit. Elle existe en dehors des mots, du style, etc." (Poetry? It isn't where you think. It exists outside of words, of style, etc.) The subversion of poetic form is of course a consequence of Breton's war on reason. Because its function is to police and to censor, to reduce and to exclude, reason's participation in the poetic act is negative. By super-imposing form and convention upon the spontaneous and the inchoate, reason conceals. The role of poetry, on the other hand, is to reveal. Poetry is nothing less than the antithesis of repressive reason and the translation of desire (the energizing principle of the unconscious and a key word in the Bretonian lexicon). The surrealist poetic act is not a function of poetics, but of what I shall call *poethics:* it bespeaks a way of life. Inasmuch as art implies premeditation, the notion of literature as art no longer obtains. The overriding objective of surrealist activity is precisely to eliminate any interference by the mind's rational, conscious processes in order to eavesdrop on the unrehearsed murmur of the unconscious. Like Baudelaire before him, Breton believed that the most precious endowment of the human mind was the imagination. The play of involuntary images constituting the language of the unconscious is the most genuine manifestation of the vital forces within us—forces whose inherent logic cannot be equated with that of our conscious intellect. By tapping the wellsprings of the imagination, we can achieve a deeper knowledge—knowledge of the surreal, synonymous with the marvelous. Clearly, the least-expected images are the most "marvelous," as unconditioned spontaneity alone confers significance upon them: . . .

> For me, the strongest (image) is one that presents the highest degree of arbitrariness . . . ; one that requires the longest time to translate into practical language, either because it contains an enormous dose of apparent contradiction, or because one of its terms is strangely hidden, or because it appears to unravel feebly after heralding itself as sensational . . . , or because it derives some ludicrous *formal* justification from itself, or because of its hallucinatory nature, or because it very naturally lays the mask of the concrete upon abstract things, or vice versa, or because it implies the negation of some elementary physical property, or because it unleashes laughter.

Obviously, the formation of figures of speech or tropes is proscribed and, if it occurs, is accidental. Characterized by immediacy and incongruence, surrealist images bypass all willful intellectual controls. They are not subject to interpretation during their creation. Thereafter, interpretation (at least by their surrealist creator) is relevant only insofar as coincidence and happenstance may reveal their hitherto unforeseen significance. The poem **"Tournesol" ("Sunflower")**, written in 1923 but later revealed to have been premonitory, is a celebrated case in point. . . . What I shall call the imagenic process of surrealism not only produces disparate and unanticipated images; it also works to verbalize the unconscious associations which occur in dreams, including those that reason interprets as contradictory. Image incompatibility betokens the disfranchisement of reason. Breton is keenly aware of Freud's discovery that, in dreams, the categories of contradiction and opposition are voided, that the unconscious is blind to negation, and that dreams evince a particular tendency to join opposites together into a unit or to represent them in a single object. In the surrealist perspective, antinomies are never dissolved nor definitively resolved; notwithstanding the tension of desire that propels them toward resolution, they are preserved as dynamic and symbiotic correlatives. Breton derived further corroboration of this view from another quarter: . . .

> It goes without saying that the "point" at which all antinomies that rankle and distress us are destined to be resolved is in no way to be found on a mystical level. There is no need to stress how the idea of overcoming all antinomies is "Hegelian." Unquestionably, it is Hegel . . . who enabled me to perceive this point, to tend toward it with all my strength, and to make of this very tension my life's goal. (. . .) Where the Hegelian dialectic does not function, there is for me no thought, no hope for truth.

The anharmonic bias proclaimed by Breton and evident in his poetry cannot be ascribed only to his tone deafness, admitted by him and confirmed by others; it is wholly consistent with his vision of man and the world. The very word *harmony,* he wrote in 1922, is meaningless. Pleasure is conveyed through accident and surprise, whether discordant or otherwise. (pp. xvii-xx)

Whereas the logical mode sets inflexible limits, the analogical mode allows access to the realm of "absolute possibility." The joy of analogical discovery presupposes a constant receptivity or *disponibilité* to revelatory signs and events, but also an eagerness to invite the occurrence of such phenomena. All of Breton's writings express the anticipation of strange but happy coincidences, the delight provoked by sudden, random revelations born of objective chance (*le hasard objectif*), and the celebration of serendipity. In one of his most important essays, first published in 1934 and later incorporated as the opening chapter of *L'Amour fou* (*Mad Love*) (1937), Breton describes "convulsive beauty," certainly one of the most significant concepts of modern art. Several of its key features may be summarized here.

Breton first posits a relationship between beauty and sexuality. Aesthetic emotion, whether induced by a natural spectacle or by a work of art, is signaled without warning by a feeling of inner disturbance (*un trouble*) or by a shudder (*un frisson*). He adds: "Je n'ai jamais pu m'empêcher d'établir une relation entre cette sensation et celle du plaisir érotique et ne découvre entre elles que des différences de degré." (I could never help establishing a relation between such a sensation and that of erotic pleasure, and can only discover differences of degree between them.) The experience of beauty, animate or inanimate, is thus the fulfillment of desire, of a desire sought and sustained by cultivating "states of perfect receptivity." Aesthetic emotion is of course always characterized by unpredictability and *dépaysement*.

Breton then goes on to define convulsive beauty not as motion proper, but as "l'expiration exacte de ce mouvement" (the very moment at which movement stops), that is, motion in suspension or in repose. Among several examples adduced to illustrate the idea of convulsive beauty, the most striking is that of a high-speed locomotive abandoned for many years in a virgin forest and overwhelmed by an unruly wilderness, an image found in the poem **"Facteur Cheval" ("Postman Cheval")** in *Le Revolver à cheveux blancs*. . . . The image vividly symbolizes the victory of the unconscious over the conscious. The locomotive, as a male symbol, has penetrated the virgin forest, identified with the female principle, and has been absorbed by it. A complex artifact constructed by human ingenuity as a powerful vehicle for the fulfillment of human imagination and desire is assimilated by the raw power of nature.

Breton cites other illustrations of convulsive beauty drawn from the range of natural phenomena: stalagmites, coral, and crystal. Each constitutes, in the realm of nature, "le merveilleux précipité du désir" (the marvelous precipitate of desire). Crystal, a particularly frequent image in Breton, is defined by him as the perfect expression of spontaneous action and creation. The hardness and transparency of crystal correspond to that "moment where the mobile and unceasing activity of magnetism achieves complete repose," a definition borrowed from Hegel and quoted by Breton in a letter written two years earlier. Coral is an example of natural ambiguity and contiguity, the passing of the animate into the inanimate being termed by Breton "tout ce qu'il y a de subtil au monde, tout ce à quoi la connaissance n'accède que lourdement par degrés" (everything that is subtle in the world, everything that knowledge arrives at but ponderously and by degrees).

The four examples of convulsive beauty cited by Breton share certain characteristics. The locomotive trapped in the virgin forest, stalagmites, crystal, and coral—all embody immobilized, frozen motion, motion in seeming suspension, yet ever potential and virtual, a *stasis* subject to imperceptible change. Paradox is an intrinsic element of beauty: arrested motion is susceptible of ulterior development; time is frozen, yet the process of creation, of accretion, and of subsidence is ever implied. Convulsive beauty arises from an exquisite balance between action and inertia, perpetuated by the hidden laws of spontaneity and chance. Breton has clearly refined in this essay his previous definition, stated in *Nadja* (1928), of convulsive beauty as "ni dynamique, ni statique" (neither dynamic, nor static).

Finally, convulsiveness is not an inherent quality of things, but an impregnation brought about by external influences, the result of a dialectical process. The locomotive, stalagmites, crystal, and coral are nothing without the forest, cave, grotto, and ocean in which they are so to speak consummated. The reader cannot but notice that the latter are all feminine symbols, and the former, masculine. Their interplay yields yet another seeming paradox, namely that the feminine principle fecundates the masculine, not vice versa. That Animus fulfills its potential only when it is nurtured by Anima is a constant in the writings of Breton, who elsewhere approvingly cites Goethe's last thought that "the Eternal Feminine is in truth the keystone of the edifice," and the observation by the German physicist and theosophist J. W. Ritter (1776-1810) that "man, stranger on earth, is acclimatized here below by woman alone." To which Breton adds in conclusion: "C'est pourquoi l'amour et les femmes sont la plus claire solution de toutes les énigmes." (That is why love and women are the clearest solution to all enigmas.) Such is, of course, the message later developed in *Arcane 17* (1944) and resumed in *Du Surréalisme en ses oeuvres vives* (**"Of Surrealism in Its Living Works"**) (1953). The reader will perhaps remember that Breton establishes a link between convulsive beauty and erotic pleasure at the beginning of his essay. The very image of convulsiveness is of course sexual. That it constitutes a metaphor for the consummation of desire and for orgasmic fulfillment is implicit in Breton's writings. . . . (pp. xxi-xxiii)

The genesis of poetic imagery and its kinship with the oneiric (or at least unconscious) process is a matter that fascinated the surrealists, who, least of all Breton, never claimed to have found the key to its mystery. Whether word-images translate the imagenic chemistry of the unconscious, or whether dreams are themselves a visual translation of verbal elements, is of course a chicken-or-the-egg dilemma that warrants no discussion here. Like the mystery of love itself, it remains, to

use Breton's admirable phrase, an "infracassable noyau de *nuit*" (unshatterable kernel of *night*). Yet the means by which Breton sought to express the "subliminal message" is one of the most significant—if admittedly imperfect—contributions of surrealism to modern writing. Beginning in 1919, Breton's attention had been drawn to the occurrence of sentence fragments in his mind as he approached somnolence. These sentences had struck him as revealing an unexpectedly rich imagery within normal syntactical patterns. Initially, he felt impelled to consign the most remarkable of these involuntary images to memory. Only later did it occur to him and to Philippe Soupault that similar imagenic states could be reconstituted voluntarily. The outcome was the first "automatic" text, *Les Champs magnétiques* (**"Magnetic Fields"**), a series of prose poems written by Breton and Soupault in eight feverish days and published in 1919-1920. The authors had induced what might be termed self-hypnotic trances, thus enormously enhancing their receptivity to the subliminal messages dictated by their inner voices. In the process, they in effect became the passive scribes of their unconscious. The hallucinogenic impact of such sessions, while literarily fruitful, nonetheless gave Breton pause. An inherent peril lay in the impression that such images could make upon the conscious mind, namely an increasing inability to retain a sense of reality. In a later (1930) commentary on the production of *Les Champs magnétiques,* Breton acknowledged that he had felt at times possessed by the mental images that had emerged from such hypnotic trances, and that madness or even suicide lurked just around the corner. Referring to the image "pneus pattes de velours" (tires velvet paws) in the third poem, **"Eclipses,"** Breton indicated that it had caused him to fancy himself pursued by cats one afternoon when crossing the Place de l'Etoile. Such personal experiences were confirmed by the alarming turn taken during a number of collective sessions devoted to dream narration and automatic writing in 1922. The spectre of violent and self-destructive behavior on the part of the participants led Breton to terminate these sessions, most memorable for the extraordinary streams of unconsciousness that gushed forth from the mouth and pen of Robert Desnos. The pitfalls of automatic writing quickly became evident. The experiment consisted in attempting to capture the continuum of involuntary verbal representation and to set it down in writing without bringing to bear any kind of qualitative judgment. As Breton explained in a revealing essay written in 1933, the intended result was, of course, to "puiser aveuglément dans le trésor subjectif pour la seule tentation de jeter de-ci de-là sur le sable une poignée d'algues écumeuses et d'émeraudes" (to dip blindly into the subjective treasure simply from a temptation to cast here and there upon the sand a handful of emeralds and foam-laden seaweed). His remarks on the nature of verbal inspiration in automatic writing are noteworthy for the light they shed on the surrealist (or at least Bretonian) imagenic process. A critical distinction is established between "verbo-auditory" images and strictly visual images; that is, between images resulting from the spontaneous emergence of words and those that occur without the accompaniment of words in the imagination alone. Purely visual images are deemed to be highly disruptive of the verbal "murmur," less continuous, and much more difficult to capture. In the final analysis, he says, . . .

> I hold . . . verbal inspiration to be infinitely richer in visual meaning . . . than visual proper. That is why I have never ceased to raise my voice in protest against the alleged "visionary" power of poets. No, Lautréamont, Rimbaud did not see, did not enjoy

a priori what they were describing. . . . "Illumination" comes *afterward.*

In sum, words do not attempt to describe visual images; words create them. Words make love; images are born from their latent sympathies and magnetic properties. Like a living organism, language has its own biochemistry, its own metabolism. In reacting to and with each other, words arouse their many reciprocal latencies and expose their hidden complicity. Listening to the words spoken within and transcribing them brought to Breton intense feelings of deliverance and euphoria. The writer's joy is that of being the unwitting but willing agent of happy coincidences, of discovering the marvelous not in oneself but in the images created by the random, unforeseen concatenation of words within orthodox, although often disconcerting, syntactical structures. The latter point is an important, if perhaps surprising one, at least at first glance. In surrealism, linguistic coherence is preserved, for it is not the syntactical or lexical corpus of language that is challenged. Language is, after all, a legacy of the collective unconscious, the result of a complex, age-old, ongoing dialectical process. Automatic writing thus never threatened to disrupt or disregard the laws of language. (pp. xxvi-xxviii)

Language affects, and is affected by, its practitioners. It must be allowed to function, to signify its own desires. T. S. Eliot's observation that the modern poet's job is "to force, to dislocate if necessary, language into his meaning," if subjected to surrealist scrutiny, is susceptible to some dislocation of its own: in a surrealist image, it is language itself that forces and dislocates meaning. . . . Surrealist imagery draws its meaning not from interpretation or explanation but from the immediacy of its illuminative power. Its success is measured by the degree of *dépaysement* it generates. . . . Analysis becomes pertinent only after it has been preceded by spontaneous delight. Knowledge and understanding are ancillary. (pp. xxviii-xxix)

The practice of automatic writing did not yield uniformly "successful" results. Breton, who was the first to acknowledge the occurrence of many a slip twixt the cup, the lip, and the pen, never claimed any surrealist text to be a perfect example of verbal automatism. A minimal degree of authorial guidance subsists, particularly "dans le sens de l'*arrangement en poème,*" that is, in the distribution of sentences into lines of poetry. . . . [Automatism is] evident in the poems of ***Clair de terre (Earthlight)*** (1923) and ***Poisson soluble (Soluble Fish)*** (1924). Thereafter, though its flux never ceases to irrigate Breton's poetry, it becomes less intensive, more intermittent. The imagery nonetheless continues to reflect the dictation of an inexhaustible inner voice. The reader is, of course, not aware of the extent of authorial intervention, if any. As for the first collection, ***Mont de piété (Pawnshop)*** (1919), it belongs to an entirely different phase in Breton's development. Its poems are notable for a high incidence of intertextuality; a number of them include more or less concealed quotations from, or oblique references to, works by other writers (Rimbaud, Mallarmé, Lautréamont, Jarry, Apollinaire, Gide, Valéry). These references are stubbornly, indeed gleefully, cryptic. Their hermeticism is deliberate and their composition exemplifies the most aggressive kind of deconstruction, achieved by means of discontinuity, ellipsis, disharmony, and ambiguity. Their purpose was frankly terroristic, in the manner of Dada. Breton sought to gut the "pohème" from the inside, thus contributing to the death of *ancien régime* art and literature. In this regard, the turn to automatism

was a natural reaction against the highly conscious and intellectual tenor of his first poems. The last major collection of poems, ***Constellations*** (1959), written as an accompaniment to a series of similarly entitled gouaches by Joan Mirò, attests impressively to the felicitous balance between automatism and arrangement that Breton could achieve in his later poetry. These prose poems offer a brilliant array of surrealist images set like jewels in a highly condensed, magnetically charged, often idiosyncratic (but never aberrant) prose.

The reading of any poetic text of Breton is likely to elicit a number of simultaneous, often conflicting reactions. A not inconsiderable effort is required to adjust to a style characterized by the absence of normal logical or rhetorical props, and tending toward syntactical patterns of unusual complexity. The impression of *dépaysement* arises not only from the imagery; it is a function of the very texture of surrealist discourse. It has been noted that in yielding to automatism, Breton's rapid writing mirrors the autistic process, marked by withdrawal into extreme fantasy. Autism expresses itself through undirected thought and daydreaming, both of which surrealism sought to convey verbally. Besides the imagery, the single feature of Breton's style that most appreciably contributes to its power of disconcertion is a highly disjunctive, centrifugal syntax. Beneath the often seemingly hypotactic arrangement of his discourse, the syntagmatic linkage is in fact very loose. (pp. xxx-xxxi)

The syntactical and lexical plays so consistently present in Breton's writings reflect his fascination with chance, manifest not only in automatic writing but also in the extensive practice of graphic or verbal games and riddles engaged in by all the surrealists. The success of such ludic activity was of course measured in terms not of rivalry but of surprise. In the surrealist perspective, games were experiments in chance, not contests. They were intended to elicit a discovery, not a solution. Language itself is a ludic phenomenon, for it is the adventure of words, their chance encounter and association, that reveals and delights. Word-plays issuing from the "lovemaking" of words are constantly encountered in all of Breton's poetry, the attendant impression generated being one of ambiguity and *dépaysement*. Surrealist literary creation does not enact aesthetic concerns, but an adventuresome way of life, a poethics reflecting and affecting all aspects of human existence.

Breton's extraordinary lexicon merits some commentary here. The very high incidence of botanical, zoological, entomological, ornithological, and ichthyological terms is striking indeed. Use of recondite vocabulary becomes extensive in the later works, culminating in the quasi-baroque, *précieux* lexical (and syntactical) richness of ***Constellations.*** Breton's explanation of his use of zoological terminology is interesting: " . . . le bestiaire surréaliste, sur toutes les autres espèces, accorde la prééminence à des types hors série, d'aspect aberrant ou fin de règne comme l'ornithorynque, la mante religieuse ou le tamanoir" (. . . the surrealist bestiary gives preeminence above all species to out-of-the-ordinary types, aberrant or end-of-a-line in aspect, like the duck-billed platypus, the praying mantis, or the great anteater). A revealing statement indeed, summing up as it does what earlier observations have, I hope, served to show—namely that what characterizes Breton's poetry and the surrealist vision is the primary role of the irregular and the anomalous, seen as purveyors of the marvelous within an essentially naturalistic universe. Breton's writings all attest to the profound respect in which he held the world of nature. The animal, vegetable, and mineral kingdoms are repositories of the marvelous, the images drawn from them being always those of a poet

> Aux yeux de niveau d'eau de niveau d'air de terre
> et de feu
> (With water-level eyes the level of air earth and
> fire)
>
> (*L'Union libre*)

Breton's poetry challenges the reader to perform an exacting task. Understanding surrealist discourse does not come easily, even to the initiated, and is often intermittent at best. Its linguistic and cultural content is so extensive, allusive, and elusive as to become hermetic. But that is, so to speak, the very nature of the beast. For the marvelous and the surreal are seldom immediately perceived, let alone understood. It is their irruption into our consciousness, however fleeting, however flickering, that matters. . . . (pp. xxxvii-xxxviii)

> *Jean-Pierre Cauvin, "Introduction: The Poethics of André Breton," in* Poems of André Breton: A Bilingual Anthology, *edited and translated by Jean-Pierre Cauvin and Mary Ann Caws, University of Texas Press, 1982, pp. xvii-xxxviii.*

ROBERT ATWAN

At its best, Surrealist poetry resembles a state of lucid dreaming as the reader plays both actor and director in the drama of our unconscious. At its worst, it sounds like the toneless, disconnected monologues of Thorazined mental patients. What makes this poetry especially difficult to deal with is that the best and worst of it usually occur side by side in the same poem, so that we move uneasily back and forth between moments of astonishing beauty and stretches of impenetrable banality.

The uneven quality of Surrealist poetry is not accidental, but results directly from certain methods of composition insisted on by Andre Breton, the movement's founder and its chief publicist for nearly 50 years. Believing that poetry must invite the "irrational," Breton gladly accepted Rimbaud's conviction that the poet becomes a seer only "through a long, immense, and reasoned derangement of all the senses." Breton laid down "almost all the groundwork of Surrealism" during World War I while he served as a psychiatric intern recording the dream associations of shell-shock victims.

In 1919 Breton began recording curious sentences "stripped of all quality of vocal sound" that drifted involuntarily into his mind just before sleep. These auditory hallucinations were soon augmented by experiments in automatic writing, a method of spontaneous composition that Breton at once made a sine qua non of Surrealist poetics. Pure automatic writing, however, as anyone knows who has tried it, can be hazardous to one's mental health. Frightened by the lingering disassociated states it produced, Breton resorted to a safer method of semiautomatic writing that still permitted the proper combination of disorientation and lucidity.

Though Breton brought Freudian psychology directly to bear on poetic composition, Surrealism is not—as so often thought—a poetry of the unbridled unconscious. In fact, Breton was less interested in exploring the unconscious than in transcribing the interaction between conscious and unconscious thought. That dialectic, Breton felt, yielded a new, disorienting form of consciousness that he considered the prime condition of Surrealism. Much of Breton's work [in *Poems of André Breton*] registers this drama of double consciousness. In **"Vigilance,"** for example, he imagines setting fire to himself in a dream—the transformation takes him to the pure reaches of surreality: "I touch nothing but the heart of things I hold the thread."

One of the most influential personalities of modern French literature, Breton never found the American audience so many of his Surrealist painter friends eventually won over. This is not simply a matter of translation. Breton's poetry seriously lacks the virtues that American criticism has more or less officially endorsed: structural unity, dramatic speech, a tight system of related metaphors. Above all, his poetry lacks the one element perhaps most essential to our standards of close reading—the inclusion of the reader as a necessary participant in the literary act. The point of Surrealist poetry exists in the writing, not the reading; it is a poetry wholly determined by its production, not its consumption. This fact has not endeared it to American criticism, which places supreme importance on purposeful, communicative speech.

To read [*Poems of André Breton*] . . . is to realize how wide a gap exists between modern French and American poetry. Ours is essentially a gestalt poetry, always careful about the meaningful organization of consciousness. French poetry, on the other hand, seems to have followed more radical associations; explosive spurts often shock our holistic and humanistic values. This associationism can be enormously trying: line after line of Breton's poetry seems to evaporate in the very act of reading. But it has its moments. Such works as *Fata Morgana,* **"Unconscious,"** and **"Always for the First Time"** rank among the memorable accomplishments of modern poetry. (pp. 1, 5)

> *Robert Atwan, "Surreality and the Irrelevant Reader," in* Los Angeles Times Book Review, *January 23, 1983, pp. 1, 5.*

ROGER CARDINAL

[*Poems of André Breton*] covers the four decades of André Breton's poetic production, from the self-conscious verbal assemblages of *Mont de piété* (1919) to the hieratic proclamations of *Constellations* (1959). It allows laudable coverage to major collections like *Clair de terre* (1923) and *Le Revolver à cheveux blancs* (1932); although it is disappointing that a relatively trivial grouping like *Xénophiles* (1948) should be reproduced almost intact, while the magnificent *L'Air de l'eau* (1934) is cut from fourteen to eight poems, a harsh reduction of that most organic of sequences.

Within the sphere of Surrealist poetry, one might locate Breton's verse writings somewhere between the polar influences of, on the one hand, Benjamin Péret, the exponent of an integral automatism tending towards sheer nonsense, and on the other, Paul Éluard, the foremost lyricist of Surrealism and arguably its most aesthetically appealing poet. Though receptive to the latter's display of luminous, steady images and formal balance, Breton seems to have been equally taken by the impishly subversive example of the former, to the point of inserting into some of his most fluent and lovely passages certain deliberately unkempt phrasings of an irrational type. It is as if a ragged finish, irritating to the "reasonable" or aes-

thetically responsive reader, were Breton's way of guarantee-
ing the authenticity of Surrealist inspiration and of protecting
his work from any charge of being merely pleasing. "Prête-
moi tes serres vieux délire" ("lend me your claws old delirium") may be taken as the battlecry of an unrepentant autom-
atist.

Breton's poetic style is thus conditioned by his programmatic
pursuit of the Surrealist freedom to "chase real appearances
before me." His striking metaphors—"dans la menthe de la
mémoire" ("in the mint of memory"), "un rideau de rosée
frangée de sang" ("a curtain of dew fringed with blood"), "les
gants de gui" ("mistletoe gloves"), "le gréement des astres"
("the rigging of the stars"), and the irreducible "un ac-
cordéon de chauves-souris blanches" ("an accordion of white
bats")—are but one manifestation of a generalized strategy
of "strangification" which transforms all things that drift into
the orbit of the poem, to the point of denying any sense of security and stability. As one turns the pages, the impression
is of a rushing current which absorbs all disparates, annuls
all accentuations and swallows all shadows within an overall
scintillating light. Breton has developed a kind of verbal ka-
leidoscope that will take in all kinds of words and ideas and
shake them into brilliant and precarious unison.

Skimming over the surface of Breton's work, one can discern
the wide variety of his materials. The poems seem on one
level to sweep up all the flotsam and jetsam of an idle yet re-
tentive memory. One finds a doll with its eyes open or shut,
a magnetic needle, a fragment of moist chalk, a window display of silk stockings, a whalebone sealed in black wax,
Abraxas stones, even the prescription for a potion to soothe
angina pectoris! The effect is that of an eccentric private museum, or perhaps a pawnshop . . . , a *mont de piété* littered
with unclaimed and de-contextualized junk. A fondness for
arcane literary and cultural allusions prompts Breton to
refer, in mid-flight and with no real explanation, to the red
helmet in *The Castle of Otranto,* the glittering handcuffs of
Peter Ibbetson . . . , or the lost shadow of *Peter Schlemihl.*
As Jean-Pierre Cauvin says, Breton can be "gleefully cryptic," and rare words like *bramer* (to cry like a stag in rut) or
coréopsis (a type of thistle) introduce a definite note of preci-
osity, while insistent references to abstruse zoological species—ibis, quetzal, axolotl, platypus—represent so many superfluous markers of the marginal, the marvellous. In short,
the poems foreground their own heteroclite complexion; their
semantic diversity generates, to adapt a phrase of Barthes, a
willful *effet de surréel.*

Many poems seem to be constructed as anti-discourses or
anti-narratives, with abrupt shifts of register, perspective and
tense, implausible juxtapositions and often flabbergasting
non-sequiturs. . . . (pp. 1029-30)

We may surmise that Breton—renowned for the majestic
stride of his prose style—was worried that his verse might become too mellifluous, wished it to remain "raw material"
which would attract yet frustrate reading, stimulate yet nag,
like a broken tooth.

Yet the reward for the persistent reader is the discovery that,
embedded within the skeins of loosely threaded propositions
and surprise effects, are several passages of quite breathtaking
evocation or reflection that provide miraculous pockets of
rest amid the eddies of textual outpouring. Breton's explicit
theme of anxious questing, his bewildered surrender to a Surreal world of hurried marvels, may encourage the reader to

treat the poems as a single continuum, an integral search for
some ultimate experience, whether this be an encounter with
"convulsive beauty," erotic fulfillment, or some perfect coincidence of fantasy and reality. (p. 1031)

> Roger Cardinal, in a review of "Poems of André Bre-
> ton: A Bilingual Anthology," in Queen's Quarterly,
> Vol. 91, No. 4, Winter, 1984, pp. 1029-31.

MATTHEW WARD

Why has it taken 50 years for one of the central texts of Surrealism [*Mad Love*] to appear in English? The title itself is a
clue. *L'Amour Fou* is one of those French titles or rubrics,
such as *Les Fleurs du Mal* or *L'Art Brut,* that become more
than titles, that are absorbed as cultural or artistic concepts,
whole and indivisible, surrounded by an untranslatable aura
of meaning. For Breton love was the gold created by Rimbaud's "Alchemy of the Word." In *L'Amour Fou* he conjures
and quickens all that he has learned of poetry, dream, revolution and love—the great Surrealist subjects. He addresses it
to the artist Jacqueline Lamba and uses their love for each
other to describe the path of "mad love" from an enigmatic
encounter to a voyage through the landscape of amorous apprehension, to discord and peril and, finally, to the birth of
a child, their daughter, Aube. Breton strove to be poet, lover
and madman, and his immodest ambition required that his
always high, lyrical tone be even higher and more lyrical in
L'Amour Fou. The demands of such language are a large part
of the reason why his book has never before been translated
in its entirety.

> Matthew Ward, in a review of "Mad Love," in The
> New York Times Book Review, July 26, 1987, p.
> 17.

LEONARD SCHWARTZ

Fifty years after its original publication, **Mad Love,** authored
by surrealism's prime mover, André Breton, has finally been
translated into English. Coupled with David Gascoyne's
error-filled but important translation of Breton's **The Magnetic Fields** in England in 1985, and alongside the recent publication in America of works by minor surrealists like René
Crevel and Jacques Prévert, it would appear as if there is, precisely now, a resurgence of interest in the root-sources of surrealism. "Why" is an interesting question in and of itself.

It was Breton, born in 1896, who was the movement's ranking writer, ringleader, and chief propagandist, the one person
with the power to embrace other writers or excommunicate
them from the group. It was also Breton who in his **Second
Manifesto** thought to link Marx's revolutionary call of
"Transform the world" to Rimbaud's call for a poetry so
volatilely close to the stuff of human existence that it would
"change life." For Breton, these two dissimilar articulations
of the desire for radical change had something in common—
desire itself. Indeed, lifting desire out of the darkness that envelops it, in such a way as to allow desire to become intelligible and whole, was to become surrealism's primary task.
From there, romantic love, because of its obvious link to desire, could then take on primary importance. . . . **Mad Love**
is the work in which Breton most fully explored these related
ideas.

"Mad love" because unique love, directed toward a unique

object of desire: *amour fou* is in effect a dream of singularity. At the book's beginning, Breton imagines a series of women, all the former lovers of one man, the line they form culminating in "the last beloved face," which is somehow the outcome or sublation of all the others. Opposite them stands another series, this time consisting of all the former lovers the aforementioned man had been, once again culminating in his mediated present, individualized as never before. For Breton, in 1937, the beloved was Jacqueline Lamba, who would become his wife, and to whom *Mad Love* is dedicated and addressed. Their love, or to be more accurate, Breton's own enthusiasms, are here molded into a tiny "phenomenology of spirit" in which subject and object, man and woman, discover their alternatively fiery and crystal-cool common ground. The influence of Hegelian methodology is all-pervasive here, Breton at one point writing that he wants to show "the ruses which desire, in search of its object, employs as it wavers in preconscious waters, and once this object is discovered, the means (so far stupefying) it uses to reveal it through consciousness." While this passage works, Breton's grasp of Hegel at other times seems tenuous, so that many of the "dialectical passages" are painful to read. The deeper question of how Breton might reconcile Hegel's rationalism with his own irrationalism is never broached. Ultimately, one is forced to admit that the French philosophical tradition beginning with Alexandre Kojeve and ending in Jean-Paul Sartre made for better use of Hegel's philosophical wealths than surrealism ever did.

Just before meeting Lamba—who, in her entrance into the café in which Breton was sitting gave off "the illusion of moving about, in broad daylight, within the gleam of a lamp"— Breton had begun writing *Mad Love.* Speaking of his motivations, and of the need for "illogical solutions," Breton writes:

> I have never ceased to believe that, among all the states through which humans can pass, love is the greatest supplier of solutions of that kind, being at the same time in itself the ideal place for the joining and fusion of these solutions. People despair of love stupidly . . . and yet for each, the promise of each coming hour contains life's whole secret, perhaps about to be revealed one day, possibly in another being.

In a passage such as this one, Breton's lyric imagination is at its best, and many of surrealism's central ideas are unveiled. The gradual crystallization of the object of desire truly worthy of love, the very desire to love and be loved: all these find their culmination in "the delirium of absolute presence," as Breton later puts it. But love depends, first of all, on the expectation of something marvelous, a cognition of the wonderful in both its possible and its actual forms. In turn, the marvelous reveals itself only when one assumes an attitude of *disponibilité,* a sort of openness to chance encounters behind which are to be discovered intentional designs, as though through the mediation of another being, chance might turn into necessity. It's as if, for Breton, "one need only advance to live, to go / Straightforward towards all that you love," as if "I was going towards you / I was moving perpetually into the light," as Eluard wrote in his *The Capital of Sorrow.* A beautiful image, but a telling comment in and of itself that I am obliged to turn elsewhere for the more lucid and passionate expression of Breton's ideal.

Indeed, *Mad Love* makes it clear that Breton was neither a great thinker nor a great writer. As I've pointed out, his usage of Hegel is problematic. In addition, there are passages in this book that are extraordinarily stilted, and it isn't the fault of the translator either. At the more general level, surrealism certainly had its naive side in conception and its excesses in execution, from the failure of automatic writing to the turn to astrology and occult mysticism; it also had its long stretches of bad prose. However, this should not obscure surrealism's enormously positive influence; in context, it was for the French a "breaking out" from restrictive aesthetic conventions. And Breton saw the need to bring a philosophy of the self to Marxist thought well before anyone else did. . . . Nor should my criticisms obscure the other important contribution that Breton made at the level of thought, which was that he always clung to a vital, even metaphysical optimism, an optimism which for him spelled out human freedom. Unlike Hegel, Sartre, and the philosophical tradition, the surrealist position grounded freedom in plenitude, not negation. This plenitude translated into a novel potency—there is no "end of art" attitude in surrealist rhetoric or practice, no buried attitude of desiccation—and into the insistence that poetry was an action in the world. As a writer Breton was a master at catching up the tiniest prereflective rays of hope, at illuminating those instants of expectation which in and of themselves can pass over into joy. For Breton, poetry was, in effect, a strategy for affirmation, and surrealism, a complex strategy by which poetry might endure. It is to this optimism, I think, that we are instinctively drawn, and it is by the failure to make this optimism plausible often enough that we are disappointed. (pp. 13, 22)

Leonard Schwartz, "Lifting Desire," in The American Book Review, *Vol. 10, No. 4, September-October, 1988, pp. 13, 22.*

MICHAEL SHERINGHAM

[The first volume of André Breton's *Oeuvres complètes*] takes us to 1930, from the early neo-symbolist poems, via the manifestos of 1924 and 1929, to the remarkable collaborative works of 1930: *Ralentir travaux,* poems written conjointly with Paul Eluard and René Char over a few days in the Vaucluse, and *L'Immaculée conception,* a series of texts in which Breton and Eluard applied some of the main vectors of surrealist writing— *écriture automatique,* systematic *détournement* of canonical writings—to the evocation of a human existence from foetus to cadaver.

The *Champs magnétiques* of 1920, the poems of *Clair de terre* and the essays of *Les Pas perdus,* perhaps above all the prose work *Nadja* (1928), are the peaks; now, however, we see them not as a range of discrete paperbacks but as features of a landscape scarred by the outcrops and blowholes of constant bubblings beneath the surface. Breton collected up some of his shorter pieces, but a great many have remained inaccessible in defunct reviews, or, unpublished, in various archives. The three groups of *Inédits* and *Alentours* into which all this has been divided contain some of the most fascinating material in the volume. . . .

It has long been routine to condescend somewhat to Breton, and to be superior about his relations with the movement he launched and then animated, through thick and thin, for forty years. Surrealism is likened to a banana republic, with Breton as its crackpot dictator, or to a schism with Breton as its heresiarch. These and other tiresome misrepresentations naturally pay little heed to the hundreds of pages of varied, inventive and often brilliant writing, much of it still very fresh, that we find in this volume and look forward to in its successors. Breton can be dull sometimes, as any good writer can, but his books are like no others, and each seems to have the uncanny property of simultaneously borrowing from an established genre, forging a new one, and somehow subverting both from within. The first *Manifeste* mixes the discourses of the essay, the memoir and the scientific treatise, while at the same time purporting to be the preface to a series of poetic texts; *Nadja* is part case history, part diary and part manifesto.

Breton did have a magus side (Maurice Martin du Gard spotted it early and, wittily, called him a "mage d'Espinal"), but it derives partly from the seriousness of his central project, which was to try and make poetic revelation a force to change human existence. In trying to create a movement rather than shaping his own *oeuvre,* and in seeking, out of genuine if sometimes wayward intellectual curiosity, to create a fusion of poetry with psychology, philosophical speculation and politics, while never allowing it to be entirely subordinate to them, he paid a price. He never wanted to be a *littérateur,* and all his work has a provisional, *ad hoc* quality. One of the interesting things about surrealism is its rejection of the cult of form which remained such a massive plank in the modernist programme—Yeats, Pound, Eliot, Joyce, Valéry—but also a beam in the eye when it came to socio-political action. However, Breton's attempts to remake the canon, promoting important writers such as de Sade (but also some duds), while immensely prescient and influential, were also counterproductive since they helped to turn surrealism into a ghetto outside the literary metropolis. It is remarkably difficult to situate Breton *vis à vis* other writers of his generation, and while this is in some measure to his credit, it has not generally been to his advantage.

Breton once observed that surrealism originated in "a wide-ranging operation bearing on language". The latter-day prestige of the movement's visual legacy often obscures the fact that it was as self-professed nominalists, intoxicated by the power of words seemingly to impinge on reality, that the surrealists began writing. Breton always stressed that poetry was aural before it was visual: Rimbaud and Lautréamont listened first, illumination came afterwards. This was initially part of the symbolist bequest which Breton grasped avidly but initially squandered on fey pastiches of Mallarmé and Valéry.

A series of events—the First World War, experience of treating neurological disturbance as a young medic, the Dada movement, the discovery of Freud—added ballast to Breton's sense of the gravity of *la chose linguistique.* The dadaists, sickened by propaganda, had wished to subject language to every indignity, but their varied affronts seemed to Breton to lay bare the remarkable resilience of sense. What he gleaned of Freudian theory at this stage tended to confer ontological prestige on even the tiniest verbal scraps thrown up in our mental lives. "Surréalisme" was initially no more than a name for the method he devised, and first tried out with Philippe Soupault in 1919, for tapping the ceaseless flow of discourse just beneath the surface of consciousness. It was a decisive move to confer honorific status on the products, and to publish it on a par with, if not as, "poetry". This sowed the seeds of much confusion and malpractice, in the face of which Breton was to write some years later that the history of what was by then called *écriture automatique* had been continuous calamity. He came to insist that it wasn't a recipe

for getting poems on the cheap, though part of the impetus had come from a repudiation of the work-ethic poetics of neo-symbolism, incarnated by his erstwhile mentor, Paul Valéry.

Breton's relationship with Valéry cries out for analysis along the lines of Harold Bloom's "anxiety of influence". As late as 1920, the older poet was a witness at Breton's wedding to Simone Kahn; by 1923 Breton had written his epitaph. In a marvellous text, from early 1924, Breton staged a subtle confrontation between his view of the poetic process and Valéry's. The piece consists of the contents of a notebook in which, over a few months, Breton had jotted down addresses, quotations, remarks about other writers (including Valéry), odd phrases and titles, short meditations on chance, memory and so on. Suddenly, after all these stutters, there is a poem, **"La Mort rose"**, bearing a title noted a few weeks earlier. Far from being the product of graft and craft, a "feast of the intellect", a monument to the laborious genesis in which a scaffolding is provided for the meagre "vers donnés", the incoherences of the Pythia, the poem comes in its own due time, a fruit of parthenogenesis, at once quite alien, unprecedented, and redolent of the subjectivity from which it emerges.

Yet, like most of Breton's poems and "automatic" texts, **"La Mort rose",** for all its majestic indifference to what Rimbaud called "current appearances", is riven by anxieties. Typically, the poem is at one level no more than an allegory of its own emergence, the linguistic energies which drive it being personified in the shape of the poetic "I". His adventures—endless scenarios of liberation—form a kind of mental picaresque, as the onward rush of a discourse seeking above all to keep going necessitates new twists and turns of the narrative thread, but at the same time devalues them by revealing intermittently that we are in a wordscape.

Breton saw poetic language as a liberator of desire, and liberated desire as the key to a transformed universe, but he also had a feel for desire's darker side, and the possible collusion with it which an addiction to the verbal might constitute. He suppressed much of his "automatic" writing, and it is amusing to witness the return of the repressed, duly sanitized by the apparatus of scholarship (*Poisson soluble* is here double the familiar length). In a fascinating letter to Jean Gaulmier, Breton admits the feeling of nausea and "écoeurement" which these texts inspire in him. This material is much more personal than it seems, not because it reveals guilty secrets but because even when language insists on its own prerogatives it acts as a channel for desires deeper than self-expression. Reading the poems of *Clair de terre* we can watch Breton, as he spills out his obsessions with things in miniature, with furry woodland creatures, with metamorphosis and surprise, or becomes captivated by a spectral image of himself disseminated in the workings of the language he generates; and we can monitor his addiction to the spasmodic recognitions such writing affords, but also to the equally frequent experiences of exclusion—as he is spurned by the words he spawns.

Nadja transposed these intermittences of recognition and rebuttal into the sphere of lived experience, making the Paris streets, with their signboards, flea markets, haphazard encounters, another sort of text. . . . *Nadja*'s opening question, "Qui suis-je?", is initially reformulated in terms of the ghostly identity that certain uncanny events—coincidences, impulses, unforeseen encounters—seem to portend. By adopting a non-utilitarian, expectant stance during his endless urban perambulations, Breton goes less in hope of apparitions than of signals emitted on his own particular frequency. . . .

Nadja herself, first sighted in the late afternoon of October 4, 1926, in the rue Lafayette, *is* an apparition, and as such she disturbs the euphoric solubility of mind, city and text. Everything about her—. . . her strange utterances, predictive and apodictic, her drawings, her *comportement*—make her an incarnation of the spirit of surrealism: another surface on which Breton can catch reflections of his ghostly countenance. Yet the woman herself, with a sordid past and no future, the vulnerable creature of flesh and blood who will succumb to the madness which Breton, clued-up as he was on this score, failed in his dazzled state to detect, proves insoluble, unassimilable to the manipulative energies of the poet's desires. . . . Breton found he couldn't love Nadja; it is not for us to blame him for that. But when we think of her destiny it is hard not to feel some dismay at the opportunistic way

he ended his book—*her* book—with a celebration of the convulsive beauty of *amour fou,* inspired by what was to be a fairly brief infatuation with Suzanne Muzard. . . .

Yet it would be wrong to see in this the triumph of a surrealist ideology. *Nadja*'s coherence derives from its seismographic sensitivity to Breton's *imaginaire.* As such it is consistent with the way, in Breton, surrealism was not a matter of slogans, or literary terrorism, but an existential project, enacted in remarkably innovatory literary forms, albeit one which, in being pursued in the medium of words, always risked assuring the perpetuation of what it sought to transform—the dogged dominion of things as they are, the selfishness of desire, and literature's easy victories over experience.

Michael Sheringham, "The Liberator of Desire," in The Times Literary Supplement, *No. 4462, October 7-13, 1988, p. 1125.*

Ron(ald F.) Carlson

1947-

American novelist and short story writer.

Carlson earned critical acclaim for his short story collection *The News of the World* (1986), in which he combines humor and pathos to examine the vagaries of suburban domestic life. Several of the stories in this volume make use of informal first-person narration to portray quirky characters who confront absurd and mysterious situations. In "Life before Science," for example, a creatively stifled artist who is unable to produce a child with his wife tries occult remedies to increase their fertility. At the story's end, the artist's creativity returns, suggesting that hope exists for biological conception.

Carlson's first novel, *Betrayed by F. Scott Fitzgerald* (1977), chronicles the adventures of Larry Boosinger, a confused, individualistic graduate student. Disenchanted with academia and eager to realize his romantic aspirations, Larry leaves school and travels to Mexico in search of the inspiration to write a novel. He ends up in prison, however, after being wrongly accused of murder, leading him to conclude that he must moderate his extreme lifestyle. *Truants* (1981) is a picaresque novel that details the attempts of a sixteen-year-old fugitive from a juvenile delinquent center to find his uncaring father. During his travels, the protagonist forms a makeshift family with another teenage runaway and an octogenarian escapee from a rest home. Barry Yourgrau commented: "The situations in *Truants . . .* develop the theme of how—in contrast to this fleeting household—most families, and their surrogates, wretchedly mishandle the business of nurturing and succoring."

(See also *Contemporary Authors*, Vol. 105 and *Contemporary Authors New Revision Series*, Vol. 27.)

RODERICK NORDELL

"And when my mind was ravaged by old movies, a silver screen of ninety heroes, I read the books," says Utah graduate student Larry Boosinger [in ***Betrayed by F. Scott Fitzgerald***]. He is trying to explain his romantic notions à la F. Scott Fitzgerald. He is a bit of a '70s echo of another brash young academic, Kingsley Amis's *Lucky Jim* of the '50s, terribly mixed up himself but clinging to some thread of aspiring integrity.

"Well relax," says the eccentric friend who refuses to publish his novel about Vietnam because he does not want to subject others to his experiences there. "Don't worry. We're the last victims. There aren't any good movies left and no one reads books."

When Larry goes to prison for a crime he didn't commit, he finds it a bore rather than the Big House of Hollywood legend. . . .

The thing is that Larry is a little like Jimmy Carter in Playboy

recognizing the Biblical warning against lusting in the heart as well as more overtly. While author Ron Carlson, alas, uses some of today's license for vulgarity—and the Lucky Jim-like alcoholic haze calls for some pollution control—most of the book is a relief from the familiar blatancy. This is in keeping with such concerns of Larry as that he may deserve punishment even if not for the reason he was convicted.

As a teacher of English, Mr. Carlson cannot be unaware that his swings from amusing intellectual allusions to lyrical nature writing evoke echoes of America's mixed literary tradition. There is a faint bow to Thoreau in "To be like everyone else, yikes; that is the cardinal sin." But Larry's life of unquiet desperation makes him see that he can't live always separately and at a high pitch—though he is reluctant to give up the quest for perfection.

If Larry's story is minor, Mr. Carlson's promise is more than that when his prose ranges from a perfidious woman's apartment, where the cosmetics were "arranged like a minor city on the counter," to the innocent air of the Colorado mountains, where the boulders cast shadows "the size of European countries."

Roderick Nordell, "Questing Hero Is Back," in The Christian Science Monitor, *July 6, 1977, p. 23.*

RICHARD R. LINGEMAN

Ron Carlson's **Betrayed by F. Scott Fitzgerald** is most directly in the coming-of-age tradition, with the contemporary attributes of humor and cool. As the title suggests, Mr. Carlson's hero, Larry Boosinger, a graduate student in Utah, identifies with the romantic egoism of Scott Fitzgerald, as well as a ragbag of images from old movies. Adolescence is part of the problem, but it is a chronic condition: "Perhaps the biggest lie we're told as we enter the inferno of adolescence is that it will pass," says the protagonist.

Larry expects no peace from his glands—"I realized that I didn't understand sex either";—worse, he can't fit into any mold, including marriage with the "perfect" girl, his fiancée, Leonore. He keeps "the edge of noncompromise sharp," cultivates extremes—"the middle ground is so goddamned crowded." He has a skittishness of personality that keeps him glancing off commitments, grown-up jobs. He wears his individuality defiantly, like the bloody bandage of a Fitzgeraldian football hero: "Being told I'm like everybody else is one of a dozen ideas, like the concept of snowmobiles, that simply won't go into my head."

So Larry chucks his Ph.D. studies, climbs in his truck and drives south to Mexico: "I dropped down through the state like a steel ball in a pinball machine." He intends to sequester himself and write some sort of unspecified novel, but he catches nothing but trouble. A girl, not Leonore, turns up at his seaside cottage, and the mix of her, tequila and writing is too volatile. He caroms back north, landing in the student digs he shares with Eldon the writer, a Vietnam vet who is finishing his obligatory war novel, but only to clear his desk, so to speak, so he can write pleasant nature articles for Arizona Highways. Larry puts his wrecked truck in the thrall of the garage run by the sinister Fat Nicky, and pumps gas in part payment for the repairs. Again a mistake: Nicky's gang commits a criminal caper and Larry takes the fall for them, going to prison.

Eventually he regains his lost legal, if not spiritual, innocence, and along the way, with the help of some healing trout fishing, he finds a way back into the main stream. . . .

Betrayed is written in a seriocomic vein, flecked with apt observations, often very funny, though more successful on the comic than it is on the serio side. Life remains different than Larry's Fitzgeraldian romanticism and movie myths; the illusions are the kind to be outgrown—with difficulty—unlike Jay Gatsby's. Larry is more happened to than happening; a humorous counterpuncher to the heavyweight, life. Still I liked him for his unpretentiousness, his wry, caring angle on experience.

Richard R. Lingeman, in a review of "Betrayed by F. Scott Fitzgerald," in The New York Times, *July 14, 1977, p. 16.*

BARRY YOURGRAU

[**Truants**] involves the rite of passage of a boy in trouble. But Mr. Carlson's wistful, tangy picaresque—told in short first-person takes—has the feel of a psychological fable.

Collin Elder, the narrator, is a diffident, hurting, imaginative 16-year-old, who decides after several years in an Arizona home for troublesome juveniles to run off to California to be reunited with his heretofore flagrantly uninterested father. By sheer last-minute happenstance he is joined in flight by a worldly, very appealing but very tough teen-age beauty named Louisa Holz, who is running *away* from her father, a maniacal motorcycle stunt artist.

On the road, the moneyless twosome stumble into jobs at a deleteriously run "rest home." They manage to stir things up for the better before running off again, this time accompanied by a redoubtable, rejuvenated octogenarian named Will Clare. This strange trio detours through Utah and Nevada. . . .

Pointed finally in a straight line for California, Collin momentarily owns up to the true nature of his quest for the elder Elder—whereupon abruptly, with a dismaying, perplexing wrench, circumstances force the road-side break-up of the threesome's enchanted mobile home.

The situations in **Truants** (including highly detailed family histories of its main characters) develop the theme of how—in contrast to this fleeting household—most families, and their surrogates, wretchedly mishandle the business of nurturing and succoring. Mr. Carlson . . . presents all of this in an affecting manner, with a very decent heart and a tart tongue. He practices a kind of wit that is at once tender, canny and vivid, capable of burnishing a passing moment with a quick touch. He has a lot of fun with contemporary Americana. . . . Mr. Carlson is not, however, above the too improbable (the degree of Will's spryness, for example) and a much-heavier-than-air sentimentalism. Also, I'm really not comfortable with the sudden ending he's given **Truants;** but there are numerous small pleasures that appeal about this book. (p. 12)

Barry Yourgrau, "The Wrongs of Passage," in The New York Times Book Review, *February 15, 1981, pp. 12, 38.*

T. O. TREADWELL

Writers cannot be held responsible for the excesses of their imitators; J. D. Salinger's Holden Caulfield is as funny and touching a character as any in post-war American literature, but thirty years after the publication of *The Catcher in the Rye,* the legion of tormentedly sensitive adolescents of which he is the archetype still marches glumly through the American novel.

[In **Truants**], Ron Carlson's example of this type is sixteen-year-old Collin Elder. Having lost his mother in a cutely ironic accident in early childhood, Collin has tried despairingly to earn the attention and love of his indifferent father by frightening away his girlfriends and setting the house on fire. Not altogether surprisingly, the poor man's patience runs out and, committing his son to an Arizona home for wayward children, he heads for California. The novel opens with Collin's decision to abscond from his institution and go off in search of his sire.

Translating his decision into action takes up the first third of the novel, and when the break is finally made it comes as the result of accident rather than will. Collin has a summer job shovelling cutely symbolic cow-dung at the Arizona State Fair, and he becomes interested in Louisa Holz, a girl of about his own age who performs a motorcycle high-wire act with her father. An accident on the wire temporarily incapacitates Louisa's dad (also a monster), and she takes the opportunity to run away, trailing Collin in her wake. Louisa, too, is a sensitive soul, a fact Carlson communicates by giving her a colloquial style of speech consisting largely of expletives— another trick traceable to Salinger.

The two waifs find temporary employment at an old people's home, the hellishness of which they transform through their sympathy and warmth. Here they meet Will Clare, a sensitive, wise, and vigorous octogenarian, with whom they set out on a journey through the western states, their engaging sincerity and freshness exposing the selfishness and hypocrisy of everyone they meet, particularly the middle-class and middle-aged (a category that in this novel seems to include everyone from twenty to sixty-five). . . .

The story is told in the first person by Collin, whose style combines agonized sensibility with that love of baroque imagery which, at this end of the novel-market, is identified with fine writing; the manner is much valued by connoisseurs of the absurd. . . .

Why does this "wise child" school of fiction remain so popular? Perhaps because of the cosily reassuring optimism that underlies its assumptions. Collin and Louisa have had cruel and lonely childhoods, yet they have come through the experience without having been brutalized—even the salt sand of the desert can nourish sensitive plants. Beneath the callousness and ugliness of American life, the theory runs, the old freshness and honesty are being renewed. The past (octogenarian Will) condemns the unfeeling present, but the future (Collin and Louisa) offers a vision of regeneration.

> T. O. Treadwell, "Siring the Wise Child," in The Times Literary Supplement, No. 4121, March 26, 1982, p. 361.

NANCY FORBES

[In the short stories of *The News of the World*], the subject is domestic life, whose secrets [Carlson] tracks like a hunter, flushing them out with paranoid intensity. Most of his narrators are husbands ardently committed to their wives, who are often sexy professionals, and to their children. Even in the comfortable middle-class communities where these families dwell, newsworthy threats invade their bedrooms, their cars, their kitchens. . . . The narrators—wage-earning artists, sheriffs, insurance brokers, gamblers, clairvoyants—all strain after magic, ritual and ceremony, to anchor their precarious world and to ward off the losses risked by simply loving someone. . . . It's not surprising to learn that some of these robust stories with their garrulous Western voices and their mix of the serious and the funny first appeared as performance pieces.

> Nancy Forbes, in a review of "The News of the World," in The New York Times Book Review, January 4, 1987, p. 18.

RICHARD EDER

Ron Carlson sees patterns in lives. He sees love, struggle that is sometimes rewarded and bravery. He also sees love turned cannibal, defeat, poltroonery and the doping effects of contemporary life. But the outcome of his stories [in *The News of the World*], whether upbeat or the opposite, tends to be an outpouring instead of an evaporation of spirit.

So he is a warm writer, and this makes the collection in *The News of the World,* relatively unusual. . . .

In **"Life Before Science,"** a painter who encounters a double sterility in his work and his life—he cannot paint and his wife cannot conceive—makes a double break-through. In **"Half Life,"** a teacher who has remained resolutely suspicious of a slickly assured student—and of his wife's affection for the young man—suddenly moves out of his coldness when confronted by the student's self-doubt.

In other stories, if there is defeat, it is accompanied by some form of lament. The protagonist of **"Orchard Love"** tries but fails to break away from the messy pattern of promiscuous sex that he, his wife and their friends have drifted into. In **"Milk,"** the narrator's brief revolt against what he sees as one more symptom of society's degradation—a neighborhood campaign to fingerprint children in case of abduction— promptly collapses. But in both cases, the message is not, as with a cooler writer: This is how it is, period; but this is how it is, and I detest it. Even foredoomed protest suggests hope.

Is this a virtue? I think so. Partly, because like all literary fashions, even absolute zero comes to seem warmed-over. And still more, because a writer is kept going by his form of engagement with reality, because belief is Carlson's form, and because whatever keeps a writer of such sensibility writing has to be welcomed. (p. 3)

In Carlson's weaker stories, there seems to be a waver. Sentimental is too strong, but there is a suggestion of patness, of arrangement, of an effect imposed at the end which, though thoroughly prepared, may be too thoroughly prepared. Carlson wants to find a design in things, even though this goes against the spirit if not the evidence of the times.

Yet in his best stories, he does find it. And he finds it by a kind of magic, by a *credo quia absurdum* in which the will to believe is suddenly snatched up and transfigured. Carlson's dervish occasionally needs a jump-start, but when it gets whirling, we experience a vision touched by wildness sometimes, by audacity sometimes, and sometimes by the sheer pleasure of inventiveness.

It is at the edge of things that Carlson's power works best. **"The Governor's Ball"** starts with desperate normality. The narrator and his wife live in a Western state—Utah perhaps?—where many of the stories are loosely set. They have some unspecified place in local events; they are to attend the governor's ball. On the other hand, it is bitter January weather and their pipes have burst, flooding their basement.

Winter tends to recur with Carlson; it is a sign of the worlds that lie at the edges of ours. Here, it has conducted a warning incursion. It puts the notion of the ball in a different light. "All that gray cleavage," the narrator thinks as he hauls his frozen, ruined possessions to the dump.

Despite his wife's urgings to get ready for the ball, he makes one last trip with an old mattress. On an elevated highway, it flies off his pickup truck and lands in a skid-row area below. Two derelicts, a man and a woman, help him retrieve it in exchange for whiskey.

In the spectral final scene, the two of them ride through the frozen city lying on the mattress in the back of the narrator's truck. They drink and look up at the winter stars and she weeps because they are beautiful. The freezing water rising in the narrator's comfortable home has forced him out into a wider universe, both abject and exalted.

In **"Mme. Zelena,"** Carlson gives us a different kind of omen. The protagonist is a comfortably middle-class woman, whose second-sight—her ability to see what will happen to people in the future—forces her to leave her pleasant family and take up a wandering life. As a child, her first vision was of a gray whale; toward the end, she sees it again and knows that it will fatally injure her in a freak accident on a Mexican beach holiday.

"I'm looking forward to that trip. I've never been to Mexico. It will be wonderful to see that whale again," she says.

Even in his softer, more contrived stories, Carlson can achieve a rare quality of intensity in his narrators, who are usually men and often fathers. (pp. 3, 6)

The News of the World is an uneven collection. Carlson does not have impeccable taste. We can feel shoved. But quite a few of his discoveries are more than worth the shoving. (p. 6)

> *Richard Eder, in a review of "The News of the World," in* Los Angeles Times Book Review, *February 1, 1987, pp. 3, 6.*

ALAN CHEUSE

The world of Carlson's 16 stories [in ***The News of the World***] shows us mostly that of the nuclear family and its environs. And the news? Domestic love of a very rare homey and affectionate sort is alive and well in the work of a writer who has acquired the technique to depict such values and situations with absolute integrity. No sentimental gushing here, but rather the strictly designed passage of men and women through lives of domestic, though not domesticated, desire.

In, for example, the fine long story **"Life Before Science,"** the failed artist spouse of a woman mayor from a small town in the Northeast gives up on medical advice on how to turn their sterile search for children fertile. He turns to alchemy and magic instead. Babies come forward. In **"Milk,"** too, a man protects his kids with wizardry of a sort.

Carlson seems to use a lot of magic and alchemy himself in most of the rest of these lovely narratives. . . .

> *Alan Cheuse, in a review of "The News of the World," in* Chicago Tribune—Books, *February 15, 1987, p. 6.*

ALIDA BECKER

[Ron Carlson's ***The News of the World*** is] an exuberant, wise and wonderfully inventive evocation of the kinds of love and longing that never really go out of style, no matter how much they're threatened by sentimentality on the one hand and cynicism on the other. Carlson's characters may be *au cou-*

rant lady lawyers and artists and fortune-tellers and teachers—even the unexpectedly funny modern monster, Bigfoot—but they're also just folks. They brood about jealousy and failure, and they're scared about their kids and they chafe in the roles that society sometimes hands them. But they're also believers in the magic of life, in having the smarts to recognize happiness and celebrate it when they can. . . .

[It's] a story like **"Life Before Science"** that conveys best the blend of tragicomedy, sheer optimism, sharp perception, and almost manic energy that makes Carlson's work so distinctive—and so appealing. Here his narrator, a blocked artist who teaches at a small college in Connecticut, starts out telling a clever, slightly world-weary saga of the feats of medical wizardry inflicted on himself and his wife (who happens to be the town's mayor) as they set about the unexpectedly difficult chore of conceiving a child. But quite soon his professional and personal frustrations launch him into an odd new state of mind, "a time when cause-effect would take one new meaning, when order, sequence, science would whirl away." He begins reading occult books, sets himself heroic ordeals, and tacks up 200 pounds of garlic all over the house to induce fertility ("It's a conceptual piece I'm trying," he bluffs bravely to his resolutely sensible spouse). Surprisingly enough, what results is a crazy kind of creativity, a mesh of logic and lunacy that perfectly expresses his dreams and desires—and may just work to boot.

That's because Carlson is the kind of writer who can squeeze the secrets of failed love from something as seemingly insignificant as a game of Donkey Kong or the superstitions that parents hold about their children from a simple picture on the side of a carton of milk. He's a meat-and-potatoes writer, a man who'll entertain you even as he's tricking you into swallowing that extra spoonful of understanding. And he'll never ever let you go away hungry.

> *Alida Becker, "Satisfactions of the Short Story," in* Book World—The Washington Post, *April 5, 1987, p. 6.*

ALICE BLOOM

These stories [in ***The News of the World***] are new, news, and if Carlson started to tell one at that above mentioned party, you'd have the impulse to say let's go around the corner to someplace quiet so I can hear you talk. His stories have something I've been hungry to hear, and his quiet, familiar style is so seductive, convincing, that I am led to believe that his ordinary (wives, husbands, parents, babies, modern Americans) people have elaborate, you could even say baroque, and not minimal lives; and they have speech, too. A kind of friendly, naked, confidential prattle or ramble, not fancy but expressive and wide-ranging, is the characteristic narrative voice. (16 of the 17 stories are first-person narration.) For example, the narrator of **"Phenomena"** is a small-town cop, explaining, as though he were off-duty with all the time in the world, and leaning at you over a table for two in a roadside diner, the weird experience he's just had meeting up with a flying saucer on one of his late-night rounds. (This flying saucer turns out at the end of the story to be an elusive metaphor for the commonplace loneliness, dailiness, and sheer stuckness in the soul of a nice man who's grown old doing his humble duty, but that resonance in the metaphor, along with the suggestion that this man went momentarily crazy, doesn't interfere with the "this was my real life experience" feel of the story.) The rhythm of the way in which moot information is given, especially in country talk—you work *up* to it, circling—Carlson's ear wonderfully catches and mimes. . . . (pp. 323-24)

Another example: a modern man, we've met him about 10,000 times now, in need of world myth, meaning, connection to something enduring, could be presented and certainly has been, in all his absurdity, impotence, disappointment; but in **"The H Street Sledding Record,"** this man is not only content but tickled with his yearly Christmas Eve habit of tossing horse manure up on his roof and letting his child know it's proof of reindeer. In **"Bigfoot Stole My Wife,"** a man patiently explains that exactly this has happened, and here are the reasons why. In the next short monologue, **"I Am Bigfoot,"** Bigfoot just as patiently, plangently explains that this is wrong; he doesn't *steal* wives; he doesn't have to; all he has to do is *call them* and they come. "Things get lovely when I call," Bigfoot explains. In **"Life Before Science,"** a husband who's given up on sperm count tests, thermometers, laparoscopies and the other paraphernalia of modern clinics, gets an old book from the local library, looks up charms related to fertility, orders 200 pounds of fresh garlic and nails it around every opening to his house. At the end, there aren't any children yet, but there are some new paintings of who they might be (the man is also a painter with painter's block), a wife who thinks he's nuts but wonderful, and the feeling in this Common Reader that the garlic just might work. Not that these stories have happy endings (though they do end, and that's sort of new again, isn't it?); they have something better: happy actions in bad times.

The overall effect, however, is not so much that Carlson's plain people are imaginative and high-spirited, but that Spirit has taken up residence in their bodies. They seem gifted or touched, like peasants in old tales who can converse with forest creatures. They see themselves as normal ("I'm not a weirdo") and also see as perfectly normal the fact of their being artists of life, inventors, culture-creators, magicians in some old benign folk sense. Which is to say too, these characters are not stuck in emptiness or longing, or, more fashionable lately, stuck in not knowing they long; and for how many years has fiction been telling us those were the choices, the realistic human lot nowadays. Carlson's characters have a problem—love has failed; God is dead; life is short; things just aren't working out—and, they solve it. Having solved it, and the stories are often a detailed report of how, they stand back and survey their success with unsoured pleasure. So does Carlson. So do we. (pp. 324-25)

Alice Bloom, "Shorted Out," in The Hudson Review, *Vol. XL, No. 2, Summer, 1987, pp. 323-30.*

MARGARET C. BRADHAM

[In *The News of the World*] Carlson includes reports of marriage and family life. He also devotes space to personal accounts of an odd cast of characters who include a psychic, a man whose wife was stolen by Bigfoot and Bigfoot himself. Carlson has chosen to separate his stories into three groups.

The first group of stories is about sharing. In **"The H Street Sledding Record,"** Carlson captures and describes the intensity of feeling that comes from shared rituals. Every Christmas Eve, a husband and wife take their sled up H Street and try to outperform their sledding records of the past years. The narrator tells us that the annual sled ride is the second ritual of their marriage, the first ritual being the word "condition" and "the activities it engendered in our droopy bed." (p. 94)

The good news Carlson brings is that love and tenderness are still alive in the modern marriage. This is not to say, however, that the news of the world he brings is full of happily married couples. He describes relationships in which couples do not share much at all. . . . .

In the second group of short stories, Carlson flexes and gives play to his highly creative imagination. The cast of characters has been enlarged to include a man whose wife was stolen by Bigfoot, Bigfoot himself, a psychic, a woman who has died, a man who videotapes himself sleeping in order to discover how and why his blanket falls off his bed . . . , and a man who has spotted a UFO.

For all of their eccentricities and oddness, some of these characters do offer their own brand of wisdom, and it is a brand of wisdom to which Carlson ascribes. In the first short story of this group, **"Bigfoot Stole My Wife,"** the narrator, Rick, whose wife has been stolen by Bigfoot tells us in the first sentence, "The problem is credibility." He goes on to tell us, "People are always saying: don't believe everything you read, or everything you hear. And I'm here to tell you. Believe it. Everything. Everything you read. Everything you hear. Believe your eyes. Your ears. . . ." . . .

In the third group of short stories, Carlson returns from his imaginative recess and describes with a delicate sensitivity, feelings and emotions which erupt from everyday life. The couples he describes in this third and final grouping are older than the couples of the first group and most have families. In **"Blood and Its Relationship to Water,"** a father who has awakened for the two a.m. feeding of his six-week-old adopted son, Eddie, tells us, "It's funny about love, about how you think you're in love or how you may think you know your capacity for love, and suddenly somebody like Eddie comes along and shows you whole new rooms in your heart."

This diverse collection of short stories reveals not only Ron Carlson's irrepressible imagination but also and more importantly, Carlson's capacity of feeling deeply the special moments of ordinary life and his talent for describing them without losing any of their poignancy and without importing an uncomfortable sentimentality. With the exception of one story, all of the stories are told in a partly conversational, partly confessional, but always honest voice that speaks to us from the first person singular, and it is so personal that the reader sometimes does not even learn the name of the character telling the story. If *The News of the World* has a message, it is Rick's message, the man whose wife was stolen by Bigfoot,—"to believe with our ears and our eyes." This is certainly what Carlson has done in bringing to us this highly original collection of short stories. (p. 95)

Margaret C. Bradham, in a review of "The News of the World," in New Mexico Humanities Review, *Vol. 10, No. 2, Summer, 1987, pp. 94-5.*

Luis Cernuda (y Bidón)

1902-1963

Spanish poet, critic, translator, and short story writer.

Cernuda was a controversial member of the "Generation of 1927," a group of important writers who revolutionized Spanish poetry by introducing innovative approaches and modern techniques to what had become a staid poetic tradition. Throughout his poetry, Cernuda utilized a variety of European literary modes, including classicism, romanticism, symbolism, and surrealism, to express his search for self-affirmation. Described as solipsistic in its incessant self-examination and universal in its moralistic vision, Cernuda's poetry promotes sexual desire, creative expression, and recognition of natural beauty as means to transcend mundane existence and achieve immortality. Spiritually isolated from Spanish society and eventually exiled from his homeland, Cernuda received relatively little recognition during his lifetime. While the complexity of his verse, his homosexuality, and his acerbic personality are considered to have contributed to his obscurity, Cernuda's works have undergone substantial critical reevaluation since his death. In 1964, Octavio Paz asserted: "If it were possible to define in a phrase the place Cernuda occupies in modern Spanish-language poetry, I would say he is the poet who speaks not for all, but for each one of us who make up the all. And he wounds us in the core of that part of each of us 'which is not called glory, fortune, or ambition' but *the truth of ourselves.*"

The poems in Cernuda's first two collections, *Perfil del aire* (1927) and *Égloga, elegía, oda* (1928), reflect his early interest in both symbolism and classicism. While initially dismissed as facile, these works have been reassessed as impressive evocations of ambivalent adolescent emotions. After Cernuda became aware of his homosexuality during the late 1920s, he began to express through surrealist verse the turmoil that he was experiencing. In many of the poems contained in *Un río, un amor* (1929), *Los placeres prohibidos* (1931), and *Donde habite el olvido* (1934), Cernuda utilizes free association of images and events to express particular emotions and to voice his reaction to society's hostility toward his erotic desires. Stephen J. Summerhill commented: "Surrealism 'humanized' [Cernuda's] poetry in the sense that it encouraged him to speak his deepest passions for the first time; and it gave him an artistic form with which to control these feelings, which were always on the verge of being inexpressible."

Influenced by early nineteenth-century German lyric poet Friedrich Hölderlin, Cernuda abandoned surrealism in *Invocaciones* (1934) to present his increasing alienation as a metaphor of the modern human condition. Cernuda's wider scope is further elaborated in *La realidad y el deseo* (1936), which critics term his "spiritual autobiography." Consisting of previously published and unpublished collections, this volume was revised on three occasions and ultimately encompassed nearly all of Cernuda's poetic work. As reflected in the title of *La realidad y el deseo,* which translates as "Reality and Desire," Cernuda's later poetry attempts to transcend reality and to achieve self-affirmation through understanding and fulfilling personal desires. Initially daunted by the homoerotic themes of Cernuda's verse, critics later regarded his exalta-

tion of sexual desire as a means through which he strove to unite with an eternal force that has been labeled "daimonic power." Philip Silver commented: "As Cernuda employs it, *deseo* is *eros,* a 'desirous longing for.' It is the product of the radical solitude, the gesture of seeking to bridge the gulf between the poet and 'otherness,' for to desire is, in Cernuda's vocabulary, to long to be one with, and to *be,* the object of that desire." In Cernuda's poetry, sexual love ultimately gives way to poetic expression and nature as vehicles for eternal transcendence.

The outbreak of civil war in 1936 halted Cernuda's literary career in Spain. Following a foreign lecture tour in 1938, Cernuda lived in exile in Great Britain, the United States, and Mexico for the rest of his life. *Las nubes* (1940), Cernuda's first volume published abroad, chronicles his concerns for Spain and the alienation that he felt as a result of physical isolation from his native country. During his years as an expatriate, Cernuda was greatly influenced by the meditative poetry of Robert Browning and T. S. Eliot. In the collections *Como quien espera el alba* (1947), *Vivir sin estar viviendo* (1949), and *Con las horas contadas* (1956), he increasingly objectifies his search for self-knowledge through alternative voices and colloquial speech free of poetic rhetoric. Cernuda's final collection, *Desolación de la quimera* (1962), reflects his growing preoccupation with death in its summary of his lifelong search for self-affirmation. Critics observed that in these poems the perfect state of desire pursued in earlier collections loses its significance, while the quest itself becomes the primary motivation for Cernuda. Derek Harris asserted: "The resolution with which he pursued his self-analysis, is, in the last resort, more important than his success or failure to find his ideal of harmony between reality and desire. . . . The clash between reality and desire in Cernuda's own life was the stimulus that led him to seek to come to an understanding of himself through his poetry, and by doing this, so to create himself in his poetry."

In addition to his verse, which appears in English translation in *The Poetry of Luis Cernuda* (1971) and *Selected Poems of Luis Cernuda* (1977), Cernuda published several well-regarded critical texts on modern Spanish poetry, including *Estudios sobre poesía española contemporánea* (1957) and *Poesía y literatura* (1960).

(See also *Contemporary Authors*, Vols. 89-92 [obituary].)

OCTAVIO PAZ

[The essay excerpted below was completed on May 24, 1964.]

Cernuda's work is an exploration of himself; a proud affirmation, in the last account not without the humility of its irreducible difference. He said it himself: "I have only tried, like every man, to find my truth, my own, which will not be better or worse than that of others, only different." To serve his memory, it is useless to build him monuments which, like all monuments, conceal the dead, but rather it is necessary to go deeply into that different truth and set it against our own. Only then will his truth, because it is distinct and irreconcilable, come near to our own truth, which is neither better nor worse than his, but our own. The work of Cernuda is a road toward our own selves. That is what gives it its moral value. Because, despite being an excellent poet—or, more accurately, *because* he was one—Cernuda is one of the very few moralists Spain has given us, in the sense in which Nietzsche is the great moralist of modern Europe and, as he said, "its first psychologist." The poetry of Cernuda is a criticism of our values and beliefs; in it destruction and creation are inseparable, since what it affirms implies the dissolution of what society regards as just, sacred, or immutable. Like Pessoa's, his work is a subversion, and his spiritual fecundity resides in the fact that he puts to the test the systems of collective morality, both those established on the authority of tradition and those which social reformers propose to us. His hostility to Christianity is no less intense than the repugnance he feels for political utopias. I am not suggesting that one has to agree with him; but I do say that, if we really love his poetry, we must *hear* what he is actually saying. He does not seek a pious reconciliation with us; he expects of us that most difficult thing: recognition. (pp. 191-92)

I once wrote that [Cernuda's] development was like the growth of a tree, in contrast to the verbal constructs of other poets. That image was only partly just: trees grow spontaneously and fatedly, but they lack consciousness. A poet is one who is conscious of that fatedness, I mean one who writes because he cannot help it—and knows it. He is an accomplice

of his fate—and its judge. In Cernuda, spontaneity and reflection are inseparable, and each stage of his work is a new attempt at expression and a meditation on what he expresses. He never ceases advancing into himself, and at the same time asking himself if he is really advancing. Thus, *La realidad y el deseo* can be seen as a spiritual biography, a succession of lived moments, and a reflection on those vital experiences. Thence his moral character.

Can a biography be poetic? Only if the anecdotes are transmuted into poems, that is, only if the deeds and the dates cease to be history and become exemplary. But exemplary not in the didactic sense of the term but in the sense of "notable action," as when we say: unique example. Or: myth, ideal argument and real fable. . . . The dangers of poetic biography are twofold: the unsolicited confession and the unasked counsel. Cernuda does not always avoid these extremes and it is not unusual for him to stray into confidences and moralism. No matter: the best of his work lives in that real or imaginary space of myth. A space as ambiguous as the very figure it sustains. Real fable and ideal history, *La realidad y el deseo* is the myth of the modern poet. Though a descendant, a being different from the *poet maudit*. The doors of hell have shut, and for the poet not even the resource of Aden or Ethiopia is left: wandering the five continents, he always lives in the same room, talks to the same people, and his exile is everybody's. Cernuda did not know this—he was too intent upon himself, too abstracted in his uniqueness—but his work is one of the most impressive personal testimonies to this truly unique situation of modern man: we are condemned to a promiscuous solitude and our prison is as large as the planet itself. There is no exit or entrance. We move from the same to the same. (pp. 192-94)

All the ages of man appear in *La realidad y el deseo.* All, except infancy, which is evoked only as a lost world whose secret has been forgotten. . . . Cernuda's book of poems could be divided into four parts: adolescence, the years of apprenticeship, in which he surprises us with his exquisite mastery; youth, the great moment when he discovers passion and discovers himself, a period to which we owe his most beautiful blasphemies and his best love poems—love of love; maturity, which begins as a contemplation of earthly powers and ends in a meditation on human works; and the final period, already at the last boundary of old age, his gaze more precise and reflexive, his voice more real and bitter. Different moments of a single word. In each period there are admirable poems, but I prefer the poetry of his youth (**"Los placeres prohibidos," "Un rio un amor," "Donde habite el olvido," "Invocaciones"**) not because the poet is entirely in possession of himself in them but precisely because he is not: a moment in which guessing has yet to become certitude, certitude formula. His early poems seem to me to be an exercise whose perfection does not exclude affectation, a certain manneredness from which he never entirely freed himself. His mature books evince a plaster classicism, that is, a neoclassicism: there are too many gods and gardens; there is a tendency to confuse eloquence with diction, and it is indeed odd that Cernuda, constant critic of that inclination of ours toward the "noble tone," did not perceive it in himself. Finally, in his last poems reflection, explication, and even impertinences take up too much space and displace song; the language does not have the fluidity of speech but the written dryness of discourse. And yet, in all those periods there are poems which have enlightened and guided me, poems to which I always return and which always reveal something essential to me. The secret of that fascination is twofold. We are in the presence of a man who invests himself entirely in every word he writes and whose voice is inseparable from his life and his death; at the same time, that word never renders itself to us directly: between us and it is the poet's face, the reflection which creates distance and thus permits the true communication. Conscience gives depth, spiritual resonance, to what it says; the thinking unfolds a mental space which gives the word seriousness. Conscience gives unity to this vast and varied oeuvre. Fated poet, he is doomed to speak and to consider what he says. For this reason, at least in my reading, his best poems are those from the years in which spontaneous diction and thought fuse; or those of the moments of maturity in which passion, rage, or love give him back his old enthusiasm, only now in a language that is harder and more lucid.

La realidad y el deseo, biography of a modern Spanish poet, is also the biography of a European poetic conscience. . . . Of course the Spanish are Europeans, but the genius of Spain is polemical: it fights with itself, and each time it attacks one part of itself, it attacks a part of Europe. . . . Cernuda chose the European with the same fury with which others of his contemporaries decided to be natives of Andalusia, Madrid, or Catalonia. His Europeanism is polemical and is tinged with anti-Spanish sentiment. Revulsion for the native land is not exclusive to the Spanish, it is a constant in modern European and American poetry. (I think of Pound and of Michaux, of Joyce and of Breton, of cummings . . . the list would be endless.) Thus Cernuda is antagonistic to Spain for two reasons: because of his polemical Spanishness and because of his modernity. As to the first, he belongs to the family of the Spanish heterodox; as to the second, his work is a slow reconquering of the European heritage, a search for that central current from which Spain set itself apart a long time ago. It is not a matter of influences—though like any poet he has suffered many, most of them beneficial—but of an exploration of himself, not now in a psychological sense but of his history.

Cernuda discovers the modern spirit by way of surrealism. (pp. 194-96)

[For] Cernuda surrealism was something more than a lesson in style, more than a poetic or a school of verbal and imagistic associations: it was an attempt to embody poetry in life, a subversion which embraced language quite as much as institutions. A morality and a passion. Cernuda was the first and almost the only one who understood and made his own the true meaning of surrealism as a movement of liberation—not of verse but of consciousness: the last great spiritual shaking-out of the West. To the psychic commotion of surrealism must be added the revelation of André Gide. Thanks to the French moralist, Cernuda accepts himself; from that time on his homosexuality was not to be a sickness or a sin but a destiny freely accepted and lived. If Gide reconciles Cernuda with himself, surrealism will serve him to set his psychic and vital rebellion within a vaster, more total subversion. The "forbidden pleasures" open a bridge between this world of "codes and rats" and the underground world of dream and inspiration: they are earthly life in all its taciturn splendor ("marble members," "iron flowers," "earthly planets") and they are also the highest spiritual life ("exalted solitude," "memorable freedoms"). The fruit these harsh liberties offer us is one of mystery, whose "taste no bitterness corrupts." Poetry turns active; the dream and the word cast down the "anonymous statues"; in the great "hour of vengeance, its brilliance can

destroy your world." Later Cernuda abandoned surrealist mannerisms and tics, but his essential vision, though his aesthetic was different, remained that of his youth.

Surrealism is a tradition. With that critical instinct which distinguishes great poets, Cernuda traces the current back: Mallarmé, Baudelaire, Nerval. Though he kept faith with these poets, he did not stop at them. He went to the source, to the origin of modern Western poetry: to German romanticism. One of his themes is that of the poet confronting a world hostile or indifferent to men. Present in his earliest poems, from **"Invocaciones"** on, it develops with an increasingly somber intensity. The figure of Hölderlin and those of his descendants are his model; soon those images are transformed into another, entrancing and terrible: that of the devil. Not a Christian devil, repulsive and terrifying, but a pagan one, almost a boy. It is his double. Its presence is to be a constant in his work, though it changes with the years and each time its words sound more bitter and hopeless. In the image of the double, always the untouchable reflection, Cernuda seeks himself but he also seeks the world: he wants to know that he exists and that others exist. The others: a race of men different from men.

Beside the devil, the companionship of dead poets. Reading Hölderlin and Jean Paul and Novalis, Blake and Coleridge, is something more than discovery: a recognition. Cernuda goes back to his own. Those great names are living persons, invisible but dependable intercessors. He talks with them as if he talked with himself. They are his true family and his secret gods. His work is written thinking of them: they are something more than a model, an example, or an inspiration: they are a gaze that judges him. He has to be worthy of them. And the only way to be worthy is to affirm his truth, to be himself. The moral theme reappears. But it will not be Gide, with his psychological morality, but Goethe who will guide him in this new phase. He does not seek a justification but an equilibrium; what the young Nietzsche called "health," the lost secret of Greek paganism: the heroic pessimism which created tragedy and comedy. Often he spoke of Greece, of its poets and philosophers, of its myths, and, above all, of its vision of beauty: something which is neither physical nor corporeal and which is perhaps only a musical chord, a measure. In *Ocnos,* when he speaks of "beautiful knowledge"—because he knows beauty or because all knowledge is beauty?—he says that beauty is measure. And thus, by a road which leads from surrealist rebellion to German and English romanticism and from there to the great Western myths, Luis Cernuda recovers his double heritage as a poet and as a Spaniard: the European tradition, the sense and savor of the Mediterranean noon. What began as a polemical and unbounded passion ends in a recognition of measure. A measure, it is true, in which other things—also of the West—do not fit. Among them, two of the greatest: Christianity and woman. "Otherness" in its most absolute manifestations: the other world and the other half of this one. Nonetheless, Cernuda makes a virtue of necessity and creates a universe in which two essential elements are not lacking, one peculiar to Christianity, the other to woman: introspection and the mystery of love.

I have not spoken of another influence which was of the first importance both on his poetry and on his criticism, especially after *Las nubes* (1940): modern English poetry. In his youth he loved Keats and later on felt himself drawn toward Blake, but these names, especially the latter, belong to what could be called his demonic or subversive half: they nourished his moral rebelliousness. His interest in Wordsworth, Browning, Yeats, and Eliot is different in kind: he seeks in them not so much a metaphysic as an aesthetic conscience. The mystery of literary creation and the theme of the ultimate significance of poetry—its relations with truth, with history, and with society—always concern him. In the reflections of the English poets he found—formulated in a way different from or similar to his own—answers to these questions. One evidence of this interest is the book he devoted to the poetic thought of the English lyric poets. I believe I am right in thinking that T. S. Eliot was the living writer who exerted the most profound influence on the mature Cernuda. I repeat: an aesthetic, not a moral or metaphysical influence: the reading of Eliot did not have the liberating effects that his discovery of Gide had done. . . . His encounter with Eliot coincides with the change in his aesthetic; having assimilated the experience of surrealism, he does not bother to seek new forms but rather to express himself. Not a norm but a measure, something which neither the French moderns nor the German romantics could give him. . . . I could not say whether this attitude of return, in Cernuda and in Eliot, benefited or harmed their poetry; in one sense, it impoverished them, since surprise and invention, the wings of the poetry, disappear to some extent from their mature work; in another sense, perhaps without that change they would have become mute or impoverished in a sterile search. . . . In a word, Eliot's poetry and criticism helped Cernuda to moderate the romantic he always was. (pp. 197-200)

Though our poet did not learn the art of the long poem from Eliot—he had written them before reading Eliot, and some of them are among the most perfect poems he made—the English writer's ideas clarified his own and partly modified his conceptions. But ideas are one thing, the temperaments of each another. It would be useless to seek in his work the principles of *harmony, counterpoint,* or *polyphony* which inspire Eliot and St.-John Perse; and nothing could be more remote from the "simultaneity" of Pound or Apollinaire than the linear development, like that of vocal music, of Cernuda's poems. The melody is lyrical, and Cernuda is only, and outstandingly, a lyric poet. Thus the form most congenial to his nature was the monologue. He wrote monologues throughout his life, and it could even be said that his work is a long monologue. English poetry showed him how monody can turn back on itself, unfold and question itself: it taught him that monologue is always dialogue. In one of his studies, he alludes to the lesson of Robert Browning; I would add that of Pound, who was the first to exploit the monologue of Browning. (Compare, for instance, the use of questions in "Near Périgord" and in the long late poems of Cernuda.) (p. 201)

Often it is said of Cernuda, and more generally of the poets of his generation, that they "close" a period of Spanish poetry. I confess that I do not know what this means. . . . Cernuda neither closes nor opens an era. His poetry, unmistakable and distinct, forms part of a universal tendency which in the Spanish language begins, a little behind time, at the end of the last century and which is still not over. Within that historical period his generation, in Latin America and in Spain, occupies a central place. And one of the poets central to that generation is—Luis Cernuda. He did not create a common language or style, as Rubén Darío and Juan Ramón Jiménez did in their day or, more recently, Vicente Huidobro, Pablo Neruda, and Federico García Lorca. Perhaps on this rests his

value and his future influence: Cernuda as a poet is a loner for loners.

In a tradition which has used and abused but seldom reflected on words, Cernuda represents the conscience of the language. A similar example is that of Jorge Guillén, except that while for him poetry lives—to use the jargon of the philosophers— at the realm of being, Cernuda's is temporal: human existence is his domain. In both poets, more than *reflection,* we find poetic meditation. Reflection is an extreme and total process: the word turns upon itself and denies itself a meaning in the world, to denote only its own meaning and thus to annul itself. . . . For Cernuda meditation—almost in the medical sense: to watch—consists of leaning on another mystery: that of our own passing. Life, not language. Between living and thinking, the word is not an abyss but a bridge. Meditation: mediation. The word expresses the distance between what I am and what I am being; at the same time, it is the only way of transcending that distance. (pp. 203-05)

The tension between a life ignorant of itself and conscience of self is resolved in the transparent word. Not in an impossible beyond, but here, in the instant of the poem, reality and desire reach an accord. And that embrace is so intense that it not only evokes the image of love but also that of death: in the breast of the poet, "just like a lute, death, death only, can make sound the promised melody." Few modern poets, in any language, give us this chilling sense of knowing ourselves to be before a man who *really speaks,* effectively possessed by the fatality and the lucidity of passion. If it were possible to define in a phrase the place Cernuda occupies in modern Spanish-language poetry, I would say he is the poet who speaks not for all, but for each one of us who make up the all. And he wounds us in the core of that part of each of us "which is not called glory, fortune, or ambition" but *the truth of ourselves.* For Cernuda the object of poetry was to know himself, but, with the same intensity, it was an attempt to create his own proper image. Poetic biography, *La realidad y el deseo* is something more, too: it is the history of a spirit which, in its self-recognition, transfigures itself.

It is now customary to say that Cernuda is a love poet. That is true, and from this theme all the others spring: solitude, boredom, exaltation of the natural world, contemplation of the works of men. . . . But one must begin by stressing something he never concealed: his love was homosexual and he did not know or speak of any other. There is no possible doubt: with admirable courage, if one considers the Spanish public and literary establishment, he wrote *boy* where others prefer to use more ambiguous nouns. "The truth of myself," he said in a poem he wrote in his youth, "is the truth of my actual love." His sincerity is not a taste for scandal nor a challenge to society (his challenge is elsewhere): it is an intellectual and moral point of honor. Moreover, one runs the risk of missing the point of his work if one omits or attenuates his homosexuality, not because his poetry can be reduced to that passion—that would be as wrong as to ignore it—but because it is the point of departure of his poetic creation. His erotic preferences do not explain his poetry, but without them his work would be different. His "different truth" sets him apart from the world at large; and that same truth, in a second movement, leads him on to discover a further truth, his and all of ours.

Gide gave him the courage to give things their proper names; the second book of his surrealist period is called *Los placeres prohibidos (Forbidden Pleasures).* He does not call them, as one might have expected, *perverse* pleasures. If one needs pluck to publish this kind of book in the 1930s in Spain, one needs still greater lucidity of mind to resist the temptation of adopting the role of ostracized rebel. The rebellion is ambiguous; those who affirm their "wickedness" consecrate the divine or social authority that condemns them; the condemnation includes them, negatively, in the order which they violate. Cernuda does not feel himself to be wicked: he feels excluded. And he doesn't lament this: he gives back blow for blow. The difference between him and a writer like Genet is revealing. Genet's challenge to the social world is more symbolic than real, and thus to make his gesture dangerous he has had to go further: eulogy of theft and treason, cult of criminals. Confronted by a society in which the honor of husbands still resides between the legs of women and in which "machismo" is a widespread disease, Cernuda's frankness exposed him to all sorts of actual risks, physical and moral. On the other hand, Genet is marked by Christianity—a negative Christianity; the sign of original sin is his homosexuality, or, more precisely, through it and in it is revealed the original stain: all of his deeds and works are the challenge and homage that nothingness raises against being. In Cernuda the sense of guilt hardly appears, and against Christian values he sets up others, his own, which seem to him the only true ones. It would be hard to find, in the Spanish language, a less Christian writer. . . . Cernuda's subversiveness is simpler, more radical, more sane.

To recognize one's homosexuality is to accept that one is different from others. But who are the others? The others are the world at large—and the world belongs to the others. In that world with the same fury heterosexual lovers, the revolutionary, the black, the proletarian, the expropriated bourgeois, the lone poet, the half-wit, the eccentric, and the saint are pursued. The others pursue everyone and no one. They are everyone and no one. Public health is the collective illness sanctified by force. Are the others real? A faceless majority or an all-powerful minority, they are a gaggle of ghosts. . . . Between man and what he touches there is a zone of unreality: evil. The world is built on a negation, and institutions—religion, family, property, state, fatherland—are ferocious embodiments of that universal negation. To destroy this unreal world so that at last the true reality might emerge. . . . Any young person—not only a homosexual poet—can (and should) reflect on this. Cernuda accepts that he is different; modern thought, especially surrealism, shows him that we are all different. Homosexuality becomes synonymous with liberty; instinct is not a blind impulse: it is criticism transformed into deed. Everything, the body itself, acquires a *moral coloring*. . . . The affirmation of his own truth makes him recognize the truth of others: "because of my pain I understand that others suffer greatly," he was to say years later. Though he shares our common destiny, he does not propose a panacea to us. He is a poet, not a reformer. He offers us his "true truth," that love which is the only liberty that exalts him, the only liberty worth dying for.

The true truth, his and everyone else's, is called desire. In a tradition which, with very few exceptions, . . . identifies "pleasure" with "agreeable sensation, spiritual contentment, or diversion," Cernuda's poetry violently affirms the primacy of eroticism. That violence grows calmer with the years, but pleasure continues to occupy a central place in his work, beside its opposite-complement: solitude. They are the pair which govern his world, that "landscape of brooding ash" which desire peoples with radiant bodies, beautiful and glowing savages. . . . With a certain laziness one tends to see in Cernuda's poems mere variations on an old commonplace: reality in the end destroys desire, our life is a continual oscillation between privation and satiety. It seems to me that they say something else as well, something more true and terrible: if desire is real, reality is unreal. Desire makes the imaginary real, it makes reality unreal. The whole being of man is the theater of this continual metamorphosis; in his body and soul desire and reality interpenetrate and change, join and divide. Desire peoples the world with images and unpeoples reality at the same time. Nothing satisfies it because it turns living beings into ghosts. It feeds on shadows, or better said, our human reality, our substance, time and blood, nourish its shadows.

There is a point of intersection between desire and reality: love. Desire is vaster than love, but love-desire is the most powerful of desires. Only in that desiring of one being among all others does desire expand to its fullest extent. Who knows love wants nothing else. Love reveals reality to desire: that desired image is something more than a body which vanishes: it is a soul, a conscience. The erotic object turns into the beloved person. By means of love, desire at last touches reality: the other exists. This revelation is almost always painful because the existence of the other presents itself to us simultaneously as a body which is penetrable and a consciousness which is not. Love is the revelation of an alien liberty, and nothing is harder than to acknowledge the liberty of others, above all that of a person who is loved and desired. On this rests the contradiction of love: desire aspires to consummate itself by the destruction of the desired object; love discovers that that object is indestructible . . . and nothing can be put in its place. What is left is desire without love or love without desire. The first dooms us to solitude: those interchangeable bodies are unreal; the second is inhumane: can what is not desired be loved?

Cernuda was very aware of this genuinely tragic condition of love, of all love. In the poems of his youth the violence of his passion blindly collides with the unexpected existence of an irremediably alien conscience, and that discovery fills him with rage and shame. (Later, in a prose text, he alludes to the "egoism" of youthful loves.) In the books of his maturity the theme of Western love and mystical poetry—"the beloved transformed into the lover"—appears frequently. But union, the ultimate end of love, can be achieved only if it is realized that the other is a different and free being: if our love, instead of trying to abolish that difference, turns into the space in which it can unfold. . . . Cernuda always affirmed his different truth: did he see and acknowledge the truth of others? His work provides a double answer. Like almost all human beings—at least, like all those who really love, and there are not that many of them—in the moment of passion he is alternatively worshiper and adversary of his beloved; later, in the hour of reflection, he understands bitterly that if they did not love him as he wanted it was perhaps because he did not himself know how to love entirely disinterestedly. To love we ought to overcome ourselves, suppress the conflict between desire and love—without suppressing either one or the other. Difficult union between contemplative and active love. Not without struggles and vacillations did Cernuda aspire to this, the highest union; and that aspiration indicates the meaning of the evolution of his poetry: the violence of desire that never ceases to be desire tends to develop into the contemplation of a loved person. When I write that down, I am troubled by a doubt: can one speak of a loved person in Cernuda's case?

I am thinking not only of the temper of homosexual love—with its underlying narcissism and its dependence on the world of childhood, which makes it capricious, tyrannical, and vulnerable to the illness of jealousy—but also of the disturbing insistence of the poet on considering love as an almost impersonal, fated thing.

In one poem from *Como quien espera el alba* (1947) he says: "Love and not the beloved is eternal." Fifteen or twenty years earlier he had said the same thing, with greater exasperation: "It is not love that dies, but we ourselves." In both instances he affirms the primacy of love over lovers, but in the poem of his youth he stresses man's death and love's immortality. The difference in tone shows the meaning of his spiritual evolution: in the second text love is no longer immortal but eternal and the "we" becomes "the beloved." The poet does not participate: he sees. He moves from active to contemplative love. What is remarkable is that this change does not alter the central vision: it is not men who realize themselves in love but love which makes use of men to realize itself. The idea of the human being as a "plaything of passion" is a constant theme in his poetry. Exaltation of love and a debasement of men. Our little value derives from our mortal condition: we are changed and we do not resist the changes of passion; we aspire to eternity and one instant of love destroys us. Deprived of its spiritual sustenance—the *soul* which Platonists and Christians gave him—the creature is not a person but a momentary condensation of inhuman powers: youth, beauty, and other magnetic forms in which time and energy manifest themselves. The creature is an apparition and there is nothing behind it. Cernuda seldom uses the words *soul* or *conscience* in speaking of his lovers; nor does he even allude to their particular physical characteristics. . . . In his world the face, mirror of the soul, does not reign, but the body. What this word means for the Spanish poet will not be understood unless it is stressed that in the human body he perceives the code of the universe. A young body is a solar system, a nucleus of physical and psychic irradiations. The body is the source of energy, a fountain of "psychic matter" or manna, a substance neither spiritual nor physical, a force which, according to primitive men, moves the world. When we love a body we do not adore a person but an embodiment of that cosmic force. Cernuda's love poetry goes from idolatry to veneration, from sadism to masochism; he suffers and delights with that will to preserve and to destroy the thing we love, in which consists the conflict between desire and love—but he ignores the otherness. It is a contemplation of *that which is loved,* not of the lover. Thus in the conscience of the other person he sees nothing but his own questioning face. That was his "true truth, the truth of himself." There is another truth; each time we love we lose ourselves. . . . (pp. 205-12)

If loving is desire, no law which is not the law of desire can subject it. For Cernuda love is a break with the social order and a joining with the natural world. And it is a break not only because his love differs from that of most but because all love shatters human laws. Homosexuality is not exceptional; the really exceptional thing is love. Cernuda's passion—and also his rage, his blasphemies and sarcasms—spring from a common root: from its origin Western poetry has never ceased to proclaim that the passion of love, the highest experience of our civilization, is a transgression, a social crime. . . .

Natural passion, revelation of being in the person loved, bridge between this world and the next, contemplation of life or death: love opens the doors to a state which escapes the laws of common sense and current morality. No, Cernuda did not defend the right of homosexuals to live their life (that's a problem for social legislation) but he exalted as man's supreme experience the experience of love. A passion which takes on this or that form, always different and, nonetheless, always the same. Unique love for a unique person—though it is subject to change, disease, betrayal, and death. This was the only eternity he desired and the only truth he believed to be dependable. Not the truth of man: the truth of love.

In a world scoured by the criticism of reason and the wind of passion, so-called values become a scattering of ashes. What survives? Cernuda returns to ancient nature and discovers in it not God but the divinity herself, the mother of gods and myths. The power of love does not proceed from men, weak beings, but from the energy which moves all things. Nature is neither matter nor spirit for Cernuda: it is movement and form, it is appearance and it is invisible breath, word and silence. It is a language and more: a music. Its changes have no finality: it ignores morality, progress, and history; it is enough for it that it is, as is the case with God. And like God it cannot go beyond itself because it has no limits and all its transcendence is endlessly to contemplate and reflect itself, nature is a ceaseless changing of appearances and an always remaining the same as itself. An endless interplay, which means nothing and in which we can find no salvation or damnation at all. To watch it play with us, to play with it, to fall with and into it—that is our destiny. . . . World without creator though breathed over by a poetic breath, something I do not know whether or not to call religious atheism. True, at times God appears: he is the being with whom Cernuda talks when he talks with no one and who vanishes silently as a momentary cloud. He might be called an embodiment of nothing—and it returns to nothing. And yet veneration, in the sense of respect for the holy and divine, which skies and mountains, a tree, a bird, the sea, always the sea, inspire in him, are constant features from his first to his last book. He is a poet of love but also of the natural world. Its mystery fascinated him. He proceeds from a fusion with the elements to a contemplation of them, a development parallel to that of his love poetry. Sometimes his landscapes are arrested time and in them light thinks as it does in some of Turner's paintings; others are built up with the geometry of Poussin, a painter he was among the first to rediscover. Faced with nature, man does not cut a very good figure either: youth and beauty do not save him from his insignificance. Cernuda does not see in our unworthiness a trace of the fall, still less some proof of future salvation. The nothingness of man is without remission. He is a bubble of being.

Cernuda's negation resolves itself into an exaltation of realities and values which our world degrades. His destruction is creation, or better said, the resurrection of occult powers. Faced with traditional religion and morality and the substitutes which industrial society offers us, he affirms the contradictory pair desire-love; faced with the promiscuous solitude of cities, solitary nature. What is man's place? He is too weak to resist the tension between love and desire; nor is he a tree, cloud, or river. Between nature and passion, both inhuman, there is our consciousness. Our misery consists in our being time; a time which runs out. This lack is wealth: because we are finite time we are memory, understanding, will. Man remembers, knows, and works: he penetrates into the past, present, and future. In his hands time is a malleable substance; in converting it into the raw material of his deeds, thoughts, and works, man avenges himself on time.

There are three ways into time in Cernuda's poetry. The first is what is called an *accord,* the sudden discovery (by means of a landscape, a body, or music) of that paradox which is to *see* time hesitate without ceasing to flow: "timeless instant . . . fullness which, repeated through a lifetime, is always the same . . . what most resembles it is that getting inward by means of another body at the moment of ecstasy." Everyone, children and lovers, we have all felt something like this; what distinguishes the poet from others is the frequency and, most of all, the consciousness of those states and the need to express them. Another road, different from that of fusion with the instant, is that of contemplation. . . . The third way is the vision of human works and of the work itself. After **Las nubes** it is one of his central themes and it is expressed mainly in two ways: the double (characters from myth, poetry, and history) and meditation on works of art. This is how he gains access to historical, human time.

In a note which precedes the selection of his poems in the *Antología* of Gerardo Diego (1930), Cernuda says that the only life which seems to him worth living is that of mythological or poetic beings, like the *Hyperion* of Hölderlin. This should not be taken as a challenge or an uncharacteristic statement; he always thought that daily reality suffers from unreality and that the true reality is that of imagination. What makes daily life unreal is the deceptive character of communication between people. Human communication is a fraud or, at least, an involuntary lie. In the world of the imagination things and beings are more of a piece and complete; the word does not conceal but reveals. In **"Dístico español,"** one of his last poems, the real reality of Spain turns for him into an "obstinate nightmare: it is the land of the dead and in it everything is born dead"; he challenges that Spain with another, imaginary but more real, inhabited by "heroes loved in an heroic world," neither closed nor grudging but "tolerant of contrary loyalty, in accordance with the generous tradition of Cervantes." (pp. 212-16)

Who does the poet address when he talks to a hero of myth or of literature? Each of us has in us a secret interlocutor. He is our double and something more: our contradictor, our confidante, our judge and only friend. The man who cannot talk alone to himself will be unable to talk truly with others. When he addresses myth creatures, Cernuda speaks for his own benefit, but in this way he talks to us. It is a dialogue which aims obliquely to elicit our response. The moment of reading is a now in which, as in a mirror, the dialogue between the poet and his imaginary visitor is reflected in the dialogue between the reader and the poet. The reader sees himself in Cernuda who sees himself in a phantom. Each seeks his own reality, his truth, in the imaginary character. Besides figures from myth and poetry, there are historical persons: Góngora, Larra, Tiberius. Rebels, marginalized beings, exiled by the stupidity of their contemporaries or by the fatal course of their own passions, are also masks, personae. Cernuda does not hide behind them; on the contrary, by means of them he recognizes and goes deeper into himself. The old literary device ceases to be that when it is changed into an exercise in introspection. (pp. 216-17)

[The] creations of others bring him to a consciousness of his task: history is not only time lived and died but time which is transmuted into work and deed.

In contemplating this or that creation, Cernuda perceives that fusion between the individual will of the artist and the will, almost always unconscious, of his time and world. He discovers that he writes not only to tell the "truth about himself"; his true truth is also that of his language and his people. The poet gives a voice "to the mute mouths of his own kind" and thus frees them. The "others" have become "his own." But to state that truth it is not a matter of repeating the commonplaces of the pulpit, the public tribunal, the council of ministers, or the radio. The truth of all is not at variance with the conscience of the solitary nor is it less subversive than individual truth. This truth, which cannot be confused with majority or minority opinions, is concealed, and it is the poet's job to reveal it, free it. The cycle opened in the poems of his youth closes: negation of the world which we call real and affirmation that the reality that is real is the one that desire and creative imagination reveal; exaltation of natural powers and recognition of man's task on earth: to create works, to make life out of dead time, to give meaning to blind transience; rejection of a false tradition and discovery of a history which has not ended yet and into which his life and his work are woven as if in new accord. At the end of his days, Cernuda is unsure whether to credit the reality of his work or the unreality of his life. His book was his real life and was constructed hour by hour, as one might raise a building. He built with living time and his word was *scandalstone*. He has left us a body of work which is in every sense *edifying*. (pp. 218-19)

Octavio Paz, "Luis Cernuda: The Edifying Word," in his On Poets and Others, *translated by Michael Schmidt, Seaver Books, 1986, pp. 190-219.*

PHILIP SILVER

At the outset, the unifying concern [in Cernuda's work]—the thirst for eternity—entails the question of the poet's *own* acutely sensed mortality and, ultimately, his lack of Christian resignation in the face of death. No other poet among those of the Generation of 1927, and perhaps no other poet in the history of Spanish literature, has been as explicit in his criticism of Christianity as has Cernuda. But disbelief is, in a sense, one of the most important ingredients of modern poetry, a commonplace, for example, among poets of the English-speaking world, though not among Spanish poets. Cernuda's **"Nochebuena cincuenta y una,"** which bears a marked resemblance in theme and tone to the first of Allen Tate's "Sonnets at Christmas," is a case in point. In its nostalgia for belief it is unlike any other poem of his generation. . . . [In the poem] Cernuda makes articulate modern man's inability to participate in a ritual event which he recognizes as one that should contain a deep meaning for him. But the speaker, lacking the grace of belief, is a nonparticipant who, half sadly, half ironically, exhorts those who had first-hand experience of the miracle, if indeed that was what it was, to do it homage. Neither the world nor the speaker is able to, for their lives contradict the very possibility of such a miracle.

Yet the disbelief implicit in Cernuda's poem is not the disbelief of an atheist. The sad and humble tone and the tentative movement of the discourse bespeak a very real nostalgia for belief. And, indeed, a nostalgia for the security of belief in God, or some Supreme Being, waxes and wanes throughout the course of his poetry, particularly in **Las nubes,** his book of poems written during and immediately after the Spanish Civil War, and in parts of the last section of **La realidad y el** *deseo*. . . . [By] and large, Cernuda has come to see the religion of his birth as a myth or cult demanding a docile resignation in the face of death that is foreign to his nature and with which he cannot comply. He sees Christianity as the worship of death rather than of life. . . . Christianity, and more specifically Catholicism, seems to Cernuda an empty ritual to which society adheres for social and commercial reasons rather than out of any profound conviction. In the section *Invocaciones,* of *La realidad y el deseo,* Cernuda opposes an ideal of pagan abandon and enjoyment of the beauties of the world to a contemporary society shut up in cities and perpetuating its own boredom in children. This is the society that deserves the cult of death that Christianity represents. . . . (pp. 31-2)

The matrix of Christianity, the miracle of Christ's birth, foretold by prophets, awaited by mankind and illuminated by the Star of Bethlehem, is seen in Cernuda's long poem **"La adoración de los Magos"** with strictly secular eyes. There is no miracle that occurs but instead only another birth of a tragically mortal child, destined to die as is the rest of mankind. (p. 33)

There is in this poem that characteristic contradiction between the longing to believe and the dismay of disbelief that colors all the poems that treat Christian themes. For Cernuda tends to portray God as the Creator who now stands aloof from his work, watching with unconcern as it tumbles toward destruction. If God created life, he also created death. Thus, the mindless world presents a panorama of birth and death to the eyes of the beholder. Man is the only one of God's creatures who has been endowed with the awareness of this cycle of destruction, and this is his damnation. Created, placed on earth, and abandoned there, man lives in the anguished knowledge that as his life progresses the worm of time is gnawing away within. Thus, man's burden is twofold: not only must he live with the awareness of his own finitude, but he is also able to conceive of, and hence long for, the one incomparable treasure that God has withheld—eternity. And this is the reason for the poet's disbelief in the face of the miracle, and for his religious skepticism.

That Cernuda has chosen to speak most explicitly of his "thirst for eternity" in those poems which have at the very least Christian overtones is natural and even inevitable. But, when we observe that it is this same concern that provides the dominant note in his mythological poems as well, we are forced to conclude that Cernuda's definition of eternity, although it lends itself to formulation in Christian terms, is one peculiar to himself. . . . However, in order to have a definition on hand—one on which to ring the changes—let us say that Cernuda's "eternity" bears a resemblance to Blake's and the Christian mystics' subjective experience of eternity [as noted by W. T. Stace in his book *Time and Eternity*]:

> It is a commonplace that eternity is not an endless prolongation of time, has nothing to do with time. Eternity is a characteristic of the mystical experience. The word eternity doubtless meant originally endlessness of time, which must count, therefore, as its literal meaning. But in its religious and metaphysical use it is a metaphor for the characteristic of the experience. For in that experience time drops away and is no more seen.

As reference to the prose poem **"Escrito en el agua"** will confirm, Cernuda's is not so much a quest for immortality as it is a longing to be graced with the ability to apprehend the phenomenal world *as eternal* and to dwell within the moment

without an awareness of its passing. Described in this manner, the "ability" Cernuda seeks suggests analogies with God's "view" of the world, as well as with that of the child. As we will see, these are far from chance analogies, for Cernuda, as poet, does approach a godlike view of the world. Not only that, but his poetics can only be fully understood by reference to a desire to experience again the world as the child does, that is, as eternal present. In fact, what the child and the poet share with God—omnipotence—provides a key to the relationship between Cernuda's use of the word eternity and his formulation of it in Christian terms. For, as we observe in the prose poem **"Escrito en el agua,"** it is the poet's awareness of change *together* with his own acutely felt mortality that moves him to cry out for "eternidad." Thus, when Cernuda writes, "Dios!, exclamé entonces: dame la eternidad," it is primarily a plea for the experience of eternity here and now, rather than for a personal immortality. . . . Nevertheless, Cernuda admitted to being favorably disposed toward that survival after death which even Unamuno found more acceptable than eternal death; that is, the sacrifice of individuality and the reabsorption back into some Absolute. In a short prose piece entitled **"Homenaje,"** published during the Spanish Civil War when he was still in Madrid, Cernuda spoke of this minimal survival as an absorption back into Nature. . . . This notion of reintegration into the cosmos is present in 1937, as an answer to the death and destruction of the war. Only later did Cernuda find confirmation for this intuition, surely the result of "wishful thinking," when he read Diel's monumental work on the Pre-Socratic philosophers. Here he became acquainted with the, to him, congenial idea of the cosmos as the eternal interchanging of the four elements which are its substance. . . . [This] Pre-Socratic notion was congenial to his nature because he had earlier had an intuition of it, and because it could be used, and half believed in, to give poetic form to one expression of the thirst for eternity: a desire for personal immortality. (pp. 35-6)

It is [the] failure of the Christian God to grace mankind with eternity, in combination with the poet's blanket rejection of all of society's institutions, that explains his interest in Greek mythology. The gods of Antiquity were Olympian but they were human also. They had not withdrawn and left those who believed in them. They could be invoked and they were not above falling in love with mortals. All this is implicit in Cernuda's poem **"El águila"** based on the myth of Zeus's love for Ganymede, the beautiful shepherd boy whom he made immortal cupbearer to the gods. In other words, what in Christian terms must remain an unanswered prayer to an unknowable God is actually described in terms of Greek myth, that is, realized. Implicit also in this poem is the analogy between Zeus's action and the poet's task. (p. 36)

The poem is a monologue that Zeus directs to Ganymede. If the latter remains on earth, the beauty of his youth will pass. . . . Zeus, and the poet he symbolizes, cannot let this beauty of youth perish, for beauty is a glimpse of eternity in the world, an impossible, momentary ransoming of life from death. . . . But even myths die when they are no longer the property of a community, for belief is a communal enterprise. And, when the union of gods and men is broken, the community perishes also. Thus, today the Greek gods are present only in the form of marble statues relegated to the dusty museums of the modern world instead of worshiped in their own parthenon. . . . Or else the statues of the gods are to be found in the formal gardens of modern cities, exposed symbolically to the destructive powers of the elements which the gods themselves once controlled. . . . Yet if the formal systems of belief, Ancient and Christian, do not now provide man with an ultimate truth, because he *is* man he continues to postulate some "still, unmoving center" that will make life meaningful. This is the impulse behind the Christian and the mythological poems we have examined, as well as others like **"Lázaro,"** and two poems that are structured on beliefs of Aztec Mexico—**"Quetzalcóatl"** and **"El elegido"**—the latter identical in theme with **"El águila."**

But, if there seems to be no fixed point in the universe and everything including the poet himself must perish, the effect upon the poet is to heighten rather than diminish his delight in the beauties of the world. Since the destruction of the world's beauty serves as a mirror for his own tragic mortality, his every creative act is an attempt to stem the rush toward non-being. (pp. 37-9)

In this life and death struggle it is not to God that the poet turns for his example, but to the Zeus of the poem **"El águila"**; like Zeus, the poet seeks to bestow a kind of immortality through the passionate intensity of his love, and failing that, to experience each moment as though it were eternal. This is the supreme measure of the poet's vocation since to succeed would be to become a god in his own right—"Eterno es ya lo que los dioses miran." But, because what the poet attempts is impossible, he is for Cernuda more like Satan, the fallen angel, in the Arabic legend. . . .

And like the Christian Satan the poet's existence is a challenge to God, for if God made man mortal, depriving him of eternity, He also quickened in man the thirst for eternity that makes the poet. And it is with his craft that the poet expresses his refusal to accept mortality and death with Christian resignation. (p. 39)

> *Philip Silver, in his* "Et in Arcadia Ego": A Study of the Poetry of Luis Cernuda, *Tamesis Books Limited, 1965, 211 p.*

ALEXANDER COLEMAN

In 1935, just prior to the publication of the first edition of what was to become his only book of poetry, *La realidad y el deseo,* successively enlarged through the years, Luis Cernuda reluctantly attempted [in *Poesía y literatura*] to define the impulse which governed his poetic instinct. It is an important text, since it describes in simple terms the alienation and solitude so characteristic of the life and poetry of Cernuda, and from this the almost involuntary ferment which brought forth the poetry. . . . [In it, the] poet lies at the center point between contradictory forces, a mediator, so to speak, between the world of things and the soul. How essential it is, then, to retain a balanced middle way, to remain "attached" to the world of objects. It is a fragile relation, because its substance is an emotive force on the poet which Antonio Machado calls a "bond of feeling" (lazo cordial). Cernuda will insist upon the critical and logical faculties of the poet over the dubious gifts of imaginative fancy. The world must not indiscriminately invade the poet. Quite the contrary: the poet must give to the world through his art a new perception of the meaning of reality. . . . Cernuda laughed at himself frequently, but never because of the futility of his mission as a poet. He sensed the need for a bond between the world and the artist, no less than the need to preserve the distance between them. Desire impels us away from

the soul toward reality; the final step in this process is a catastrophic one, oneness with the universe being at the same time an annihilation of the self. . . . But with Cernuda, this distance has implications for society also. Cernuda's world is full of people seen and loved, Society enters rarely, History never. In this he inherits a furtive tradition which he sensed in an intuitive fashion while a child and which was later confirmed by reading Rimbaud and Baudelaire. (pp. 13-15)

Cernuda was a bitter observer of himself, his country, and his contemporaries. His critical faculties, both as spectator of his own inner life and that of others, retain a prejudiced and rancorous acumen which never relents even when directed to himself or his poetry. . . . Cernuda's rancor has had an undue effect upon his literary reputation, a fact that shouldn't surprise anyone who is familiar with the *ad hominem* criticism which has been directed toward Cernuda. There are other factors to consider. Luis Cernuda was born in Seville in 1902, attended the University there, and finally left Spain for England in the heat of the Civil War. In 1947 he accepted a professorship at Mount Holyoke College, where he remained until 1952. At that time he moved to Mexico City where he lived until his death in 1963. This exile from Spain was bound to affect all those who were forced to take it up. But there is another kind of exile, that of the "inner exile," still within the borders of Spain. This was the case with the young Cernuda. His geographical exile was a confirmation in reality of a spiritual state which had already fully crystallized while still a youth in Spain.

Cernuda's poetry is very much one of estrangement, nostalgia, and exile. He was destined to become a permanent stranger to Spain. It is a disservice, however, to reduce his sense of nostalgia to a uniquely geographical plane—narrow and exclusive conclusions about the poetry result all too readily. Cernuda's exile must be seen as incidental, in spite of the shattering effect that it must have had upon his life. His inner self, already so divided from within and divorced from others, underwent only an intensification of the many dualities and contradictions which he carried about him wherever he went. That sense of exile while still in Spain was instinctive at first, but soon his literary readings under the guidance of Pedro Salinas at the University of Seville aided him in a slow process toward a self definition and a justification of spiritual exile, to which he adhered in an, at times, tiresome fashion all through his life. . . . In order to grasp the full stature of Cernuda, he must be taken out of the circumstances which brought him forth. The world is very much present in his poems, but it is there and valid only when it is symbolic of a human situation.

The central issue is still the figure of the poet, his intent, his view of the poet's role in society. (pp. 15-17)

The poet, Cernuda maintains, approaches the Divinity in that he unifies the diversity and flux of the world into a single vision; he senses the acute trials of humanity in any epoch and assumes the burden of expressing the suffering of those who are unable to "speak." . . . Assuming a divine perspective, he views the world in its totality, intuitively grasps the essential themes and preoccupations that are only vaguely apprehended by ordinary man. . . . Poetry must relate to the human condition, although its maker is foreign to humanity: a connection must be found that is central to the reader, a fully rounded human image must arise from the poetry, almost in spite of the tragic isolation of the poet. But he too, like the Divinity, has the obligation of taking on the sufferings of man in spite of the contempt and disdain accorded the poet—this is very much in the order of things. The burden which he carries is consciousness itself, a melancholy watchfulness about the fate of man on earth. Only the artist-poet protests against the injustice of man's condition. . . . [In] the dialogue poem **"Noche del hombre y su demonio,"** [Cernuda] defends his transcendental role against the contemptuous lack of comprehension of the devil-daemon. The poet, in Cernuda's view, can never uphold the values of the ordinary man. He must approach the Divinity with his art, serving as opposite to the moral collapse to which the devil invites him. The poet's superiority has nothing to do with morality—it can almost be described in terms of spatial elevation. He is proud, lonely, above men in the perspectivist sense. He has a broader view while contemplating incidentals. This kind of poet senses the power lines of an epoch, plunges to the essential spirit of the times. It is just this ability to see beyond, this comprehension and expression of a spiritual experience of a civilization that makes of him what he envisions himself to be—a poet. No matter how chaotic or attractive the world, the poet rises above it. His aim is unity and concordance, bringing together those seemingly endless series of opposites which characterize the life of the imagination when confronting the reality of the world. The title, *La realidad y el deseo,* points to one of the most striking polarities that summarizes his ever-present formulative conflicts. Similar to one of Cernuda's preferred philosophers, Heraclitus, the poet has within him a striving toward unity and oneness of the universe as perceived with the aid of the imagination. . . . With change, one becomes what one is not, a being is left behind with a particular set of circumstances, a new being awaits the spirit in another country. . . . The poet is the final result of an artificial consciousness, one that is beyond the capability of singular man; he is a construction of one image and situation after another. Since in Cernuda the personal and subjective perspective is not at all primary, he must represent the outer limit of man's consciousness, he must somehow escape the fixed point of view; . . . the man Cernuda is an omnipresent citizen of everywhere.

The determination to avoid an unexamined and simplistic creative life has led the poet to speak of the need for a certain dynamism with regard to the self—it cannot be static, it must be incessantly in movement toward a further development, another incarnation. The *other* which is still to exist carries out the scrutiny of the being in the present. . . . This endless play of many selves within the self, what might be termed the division of the personality into divergent entities, of the many mirrors within the poet which reflect back upon himself, are all manifestations of the highest degree of consciousness. In Cernuda's poetry, any narcissistic fascination with the self never reaches a mental paralysis brought on by the self immobilized by its own image in the mirror. The symbolist cul de sac, a total stasis of being, is here replaced by a mobile searching for new selves through the use of monologues, *personae* other than the poet, who dramatize and express objectively an inner conflict which was initially subjective.

The role of the self is a recurrent preoccupation in Cernuda's poetry and literary criticism. The problem might be formulated in this way: how can objective validity be gotten from emotive, wholly personal experience? . . . Cernuda insisted upon an escape from the self into other selves and voices, but

his insistence does not mean that this was always achieved. (pp. 17-21)

An *other* is needed. For Cernuda, poetry should not be the monologue of a personality, but a created thing, an artificial poetic voice with which the *persona* may speak. Consciously literary language must be avoided. Cernuda's literary preferences are those which approximate his own ideal of calm, meditative speech. He found this idea in the English Metaphysical poets, in Wordsworth and Browning also. His affinity to spoken language in poetry was at first intuitive; as it was confirmed by his reading, it gradually became his credo as a poet. (p. 22)

This meditative poetry, where the word serves only to express and to limit the thought, found an avid student in the young poet who took up residence in England in 1938. The affinity was a close one. . . . What is striking is the use of elocutionary terminology in referring to poetry. It is indicative of one of Cernuda's many obsessions—poetic language must be very near colloquial speech. In Spanish poetry, Manrique serves as a good example of the laconic and quiet language which Cernuda prefers. . . . The tradition of Manrique and Aldana, Cernuda feels, was revived in Spanish letters by Unamuno. In effect, what Unamuno achieved was nothing less than the return of poetic thought to Spanish verse. To this end he approached the work and the spirit of Leopardi, Wordsworth, Coleridge, Browning and Hölderlin. In this stern brand of poetry, visual or aural impressions are abandoned, the natural world functioning only as a trope to carry the import of the underlying idea.

Thus the radical actuality of physical objects is not presented in an idle or passive way. The presence of things in the poem is the natural basis for the poet's higher ordering of experience. So too for the emotions of the poet. They are not directly, not to say mechanically, transmitted to the page, but transformed, not just "expressed." . . . With unordered and impulsive revelation of the self, a poem is no longer evidence of the unifying powers of the poet's imagination, following Coleridge, but a simple manifestation of chaotic receptive powers. In order to get below the appearances, to relate things within the imagination, the poet must objectify his impressions and emotions. (pp. 22-3)

[Cernuda] advocates a fidelity between the inner man and the poetry, an organic bond between the world observed and the man, and finally a union between the philosophical conceptions of the poet and its expression in poetry. In any case, a sportive wielding of objects or a simple instinctive ecstasy before the world is anathema to him. Poetry is valid only when feeling is subjected to the logical faculty, where the thought expressed relates separate identities, and not just the rich diversity of passive fancy. This notion of poetry brings the world to a single vision; it is a refusal to allow chaos to destroy the effort to pattern and to order experience. The world must be held at a distance. (p. 24)

The objects of the world should never determine the poem, but should be subservient to the philosophical imagination, and not the fancy. The poet envisioned by Cernuda is one who correlates and objectifies. (p. 25)

The language of poetry is governed by the ideal which it serves. An organic bond between thought and feeling dictates, or at least would indicate, the suitability of the plain, flat cadences of ordinary speech. . . . All the poetry of Cernuda orients itself around two poles—the submission of the poetic word to the thought and the equilibrium between spoken language and written language. Although Cernuda's vocabulary is relatively constricted and the poetry itself abounds in flat apthegms and "prosaic" rhythms, the final breakthrough to the colloquial was never accomplished, and perhaps it is just as well. Nowhere in the collected poems can the garrulous and unbridled speech of a Browning be found, even though the latter is often cited by Cernuda as a supreme example of the use of the *persona*.

But what of the poem itself? How does it extend itself from the object observed to an idea? The mental process involved has rightly been termed "meditative poetry" by Louis L. Martz, and his definition applies to Cernuda's poetic practice:

> A meditative poem is a work that creates an interior drama of the mind; this dramatic action is usually . . . created by some form of self-address, in which the mind grasps firmly a problem or situation deliberately evoked by memory, brings it forward toward the full light of consciousness, and concludes with a moment of illumination, where the speaker's self has, for a time, found an answer to its conflicts.

The "problem or situation" is a human one—the poet must speak in human terms to humans . . . to present the world in its disappointing finitude, its plainness, and then bring his imagination to play on what he has perceived. There are no easy ways to insight.

In English and American poetry, we have come to recognize and appreciate a plain, unrhetorical language, exemplifying concision of style which matches the simple naming of unadorned things. The poetic diction is thus severely attenuated—Cernuda has already said in another connection that in his opinion dryness (*sequedad*) is one of the best qualities that a poem can have.

In the regretful questioning of Manrique before the spectacle of the world's mutability, in Unamuno's uncertainty before Velazquez' Christ, in Cernuda's plaintive celebration of the spirit of Greece, we sense the underlying power of a pensive and measured poetic speech which is truly *una honda palpitación del espíritu.* (pp. 25-7)

> *Alexander Coleman, in his* Other Voices: A Study of the Late Poetry of Luis Cernuda, *The University of North Carolina Press, 1969, 185 p.*

DEREK HARRIS

The existential problem of disassociation between self and world, which Cernuda formulates as the conflict between *realidad* and *deseo,* inevitably provokes a dual reaction: the tendency to withdraw from an inimical reality into the hidden garden of dreams and the tendency towards self-assertion within that unfriendly reality. Both of these tendencies are firmly established in the early poetry, although the first is dominant and leads to the theories of **"Palabras antes de una lectura".** The conviction that the tangible world is an illusion hiding an invisible, superior realm of harmony is the philosophical justification for Cernuda's sense of alienation. His longing for a transcendental mode of existence where the division between self and world is healed, is, in fact, a search for an environment where his personality can be fully realised, and therefore a complement to the pursuit of his *verdad del hombre.* The search for the state of bliss he calls the

acorde is Cernuda's primary motivating force, yet, while he never completely abandons the desire to live in a private world tailored to his own aspirations, what becomes increasingly significant is his developing relationship with this ideal as he comes to understand its impossibility. . . . The conflict between dream and reality provides the dynamic for existence and becomes the means by which the existence of the individual in the grip of the conflict is affirmed. Cernuda's poetry is the record of the process by which he comes to understand that what validates his life is not his ideal but the conflict the ideal provokes. The search for the *acorde* leads him to the discovery of himself and then involves him in a struggle to preserve the personal truth he has found. The exercise of integrity, being true to himself, becomes for him an existential necessity.

In **"Historial de un libro"** Cernuda illustrates his attitude to life by quoting Heraclitus's axiom "carácter es destino." The discovery that a man is what he is does not offer a profound insight into the human condition, but what is significant in Cernuda's poetry is the way in which he faces up to this discovery. In the last analysis the exact nature of a man's truth is of little import compared to the integrity with which it is pursued and preserved. . . . On the level of his search for a transcendent reality Cernuda is, in his own terms, a metaphysical poet, on the level of the struggle to affirm and sustain his identity he is an ethical poet. What he is not is the effete *licenciado Vidriera* or the astringent pessimist that so many critics have tried to make of him.

La Realidad y el Deseo is the result of Cernuda's experience of life, the account of the growth of his personality as the experience of life is absorbed and understood. . . . A concern with identity is a common feature of a large part of twentieth-century literature, but unlike authors influenced by existentialist ideas Cernuda knows only too well who and what he is. His problem is that of coming to terms with himself and his situation. Yet while he is seeking to affirm his personal truth, the honesty with which he examines his experience is able to produce a deep insight into the human condition in general. . . . Through the discovery of his private truth [concerning his homosexuality] Cernuda throws into relief the common human truth of his situation; his own sense of estrangement in the world is thus turned into a metaphor for the struggle of any individual for self-affirmation. The contrast between what Cernuda calls his *leyenda* and his idea of the *mito personal* illustrates the existential concern of his poetry and the attempt to produce a universalised statement from his individual experience of life. He uses the term 'myth' in the sense of the embodiment of a truth, which in this case is his own truth pieced together from the analysis of the circumstantial details of his life. His poetry is an act of self-creation and self-redemption. . . . For Cernuda poetry was also a means of resolving the contradictions of his character and of producing a solution to the problems of life. *La Realidad y el Deseo* has the qualities of authenticity and compulsive necessity, the ring of truth. The passionate concern to find and preserve this truth gives to his poetry its ethical character and also a dimension of common human significance. . . . The struggle for self-affirmation makes him into an exemplary figure, in the sense of being an example of an ethical attitude to life.

Cernuda's personal integrity is matched by an equal literary integrity, immediately apparent in the way in which he handles the various influences on his work. From his earliest poems he has a strong tendency to respond only to those influences with which he has an affinity, shunning literary fashion. Yet this careful selection of influences does not lead to an insular attitude avoiding new ideas or new sources of inspiration. The progressive discovery of himself is paralleled by a discovery of that part of the Spanish poetic tradition to which he feels he belongs and also of that part of the corpus of European poetry with which he finds himself in sympathy. Beginning with his reading of Hölderlin before the Civil War and continuing through his concentrated study of English poetry during his exile he discovered and absorbed a tradition of meditative poetry that had had little impact in Spain. As a result Cernuda broke out of the restricted environment of French literary ideas, which have provided the basic influence on Spanish poetry for more than two hundred years, and set an example for the young poets of Spain today, who show interest and awareness for a wide area of foreign literature. Cernuda is now an active influence on a new generation of Spanish poets, and although it is still too early to assess the ultimate effect of this influence, I believe it can only be a salutary one. Cernuda is not a poet who can be imitated, but he is a poet from whom other poets can learn by example, and there is a further dimension to his exemplarity.

The complexity and contradiction of Cernuda's character are reflected faithfully in his poetry, but the poetry itself absorbs these contradictions into an organic unity, just as the figure of Cernuda the man is transfigured by the literary form given to his life. The search for self-knowledge embraces all the multiple facets of his personality. . . . In *La Realidad y el Deseo* the reader is given the opportunity to watch Cernuda's emotional and spiritual development, to watch a man grow in moral stature and self-awareness under conditions of almost constant stress. We are presented with Cernuda's experience, with the effect on him of that experience, and with what the accumulated experience of a lifetime makes of him. In a situation where life, as Cernuda comes to realise, is an odyssey without an Ithaca, he provides an example of how that life can be lived with integrity, and the dignity that comes from integrity. His poetry stands before us like a mirror that reflects his truth and invites us to measure ourselves against that reflection. (pp. 176-79)

Derek Harris, in his Luis Cernuda: A Study of the Poetry, *Tamesis Books Limited, 1973, 188 p.*

C. G. BELLVER

In the early 1920's, as a counterpart to their scorn for the past, the *ultraístas* and those who fell under their influence embraced the city as the home of the modern mechanical marvels and as the epitome of speed, progress, and excitement. Poets such as Alberti, Aleixandre, Lorca, and Cernuda, however, rejected the city as the bitter antagonist of nature and the human spirit. Luis Cernuda sees the city as lonely and oppressive in contrast to nature which represents freedom, beauty, and purity to him. The motif of the city in Cernuda's poetry must be discussed as a concomitant of his perennial theme of loneliness, of his antagonism toward society in general, and of his growing cynical concept of man.

In Luis Cernuda this rejection of the urban environment is closely related to his concept of paradise. Cernuda's paradise manifests the attributes of a timeless Eden of childhood. Physically this garden of Eden is depicted as the enclosed world of an Andalusian patio of the poet's childhood in Se-

ville or as the open, sun-caressed marine environs of Sansueña, his name for the Málaga of his youth. (p. 156)

The driving desire to unite with another being to fulfill physical desires and also to regain the sense of wholeness possible only in a perfect paradisaic state is constant in Cernuda's poetry. When he comes to realize that love provides only temporary consolation and more often deceit and anguish, he turns to nature as the only avenue to the innocence, purity, and timelessness of Paradise. The theme of nature as Eden and the poet's yearning to be one with it unfolds particularly in the poetry Cernuda wrote after the Spanish civil war. Within this notion of paradise, images of the city will be conspicuously absent or whenever present, diametrically opposed to the harmony and peace of Nature.

The city, especially in *Un río, un amor,* emerges as the objective correlative of Cernuda's pervading loneliness. Loneliness is one of the first and most constant themes encountered in Cernuda's poetry. . . . His loneliness is not an abandonment curable by reunion or soothed by nostalgia but the profound inner dilemma of a man who finds himself alone within the universe and before his destiny of nothingness. It is an alienation from others as well as from oneself. Cernuda's solitude is a modern solitude in that it relentlessly pursues and persecutes him irrespective of where he may be or of what he may do. As Octavio Paz has observed [see excerpt above], this solitude is both limitless and confining, a prison without an entrance or an exit, the magnitude of which stretches to include the entire planet. Cernuda's solitude can be defined as a spiritual emptiness resulting from his sense of loss that leaves him in a vacuum characterized by distance, isolation, and incompatibility. Although some would maintain that Cernuda deliberately sought estrangement, Cernuda's intention in his poetry is to convince us of the harsh and absolute alienation imposed upon him by a completely inhospitable world. The city sets the scene for this alienation.

Cernuda views the city from a distance as he does life itself. His poetry often displays the figure of an exile or fugitive who wanders alone in distant and foreign environments. . . . The poet's frequent evocation of far-away places such as Durango, Daytona, Virginia, and Nevada accentuates this sense of distance.

The city not only stands as a distant place, but it also reveals an emptiness that produces an enveloping sense of bleak desolation, which in turn reflects the poet's own loneliness. The motif of the city is introduced in the initial poem of *Un río, un amor,* where from the outset it is portrayed as an empty and inhospitable place through whose streets a human phantom, equally empty and almost invisible, advances like a somnambulant. . . . This human phantom wanders aimlessly among the shadows of the foggy street neither lost nor conscious of any goal, as if suspended in a hypnotic state of nothingness. Cernuda's frequent recourse to the aimless wanderer of vacant city streets with doors closed and "aceras apagadas" is an attempt to capture the confusion and hopelessness that oppresses him. This vacuousness is intensified by the prevailing silence and the sense of continual absence that hover over these cityscapes, adding a note of sterility to them. . . . (pp. 157-58)

The city, especially in Cernuda's surrealist poetry, becomes an objective correlative of the alienation, unfriendliness, and hostility which he senses in the world around him. The "puertas bien cerradas" that divorce him, the nocturnal wanderer, from those anonymous city dwellers sleeping comfortably represent psychological barriers between him and the human warmth he fruitlessly seeks. This exclusion from communion with others expresses in concrete sensations and objects his emotional reality of sadness, disorientation, and that total spiritual fatigue, as he says, "de estar vivo, de estar muerto." The following stanza is significant in this regard:

> Como el viento a lo largo de la noche,
> Amor en pena o cuerpo solitario,
> Toca en vano a los vidrios,
> Sollozando abandona las esquinas.

The unidentified protagonist of the poem, who obviously enacts the poet's psychic states, touches in vain the barrier, the "vidrios" that shut him out from humanity. The tactile sensation of coldness suggested by the windowpane only accentuates the alienating rejection that he experiences. Unreceived, he must withdraw in tears from the crossroads of the city to its peripheries.

The city at times stands as an antagonist not of the poet but of the love he seeks so intensely. The aggressive force and the adolescent restlessness of love are embodied in the surge of the sea, with which the poet identifies his own aspirations. The sea attempts to penetrate the city, but its natural, primitive forces are out of place there and unable to find reciprocation. The forgotten, groaning sea in **"Mares escarlatas"** objectifies the poet's ontological fatigue; and the doors, walls, and "ciudades humeantes" externalize the inexorable obstacles of reality thwarting the realization of his yearning for love, freedom, and an undefined ideal of happiness.

On rare occasions we are allowed to infer that the insurmountable exterior forces are not solely to blame for the antagonism between the poet and the city, but that the personal disposition of the poet himself is at least in part responsible for this alienation. **"En medio de la multitud,"** a poem in *Los placeres prohibidos,* presents a phantom-like being roaming along crowded streets, whose absorption in himself makes him oblivious to the woman kneeling before him and whose detachment from his environment converts him into an invisible, mutilated ghost. The fog that envelops this specter suggests his own spiritual annihilation, and his loss of vigor and of sensory perception serves not as a social comment on the city but as a poetic reproduction of the disorientation and impotence that constitute Cernuda's basic loneliness. (pp. 159-60)

While the motif of the city may translate the poet's predisposition to loneliness, on the whole the city looms in Cernuda's poetry as a culprit of that loneliness. As a conglomerate of people, it epitomizes his estrangement from human affection and recognition, and it incorporates the indifference, ignorance, and oblivion he encounters in the social order. The inhabitants of the city, completely unaware of the poet's existence, do not suspect his presence among the nocturnal mists of their streets. They sleep while the poet endures his destiny. If people once knew him, they have long forgotten him. Poignantly stressing the city's overwhelming indifference, Cernuda employs the image of the wind to universalize the victimization that he himself feels within society. The wind, a foreigner and a fugitive, roams dark streets, as does the anonymous protagonist of so many poems of Cernuda, attempting to seek out human companionship but finding that people are deaf to his knock. Cernuda makes evident his bitter rancor toward an insensitive and indifferent world that re-

jects him and which he in turn shuns. . . . He sees a world of men insensitive not only to him but also to youth, beauty, and love. . . . They are despicable phantoms enslaved within their own inanity. . . . (pp. 160-61)

Cernuda's bitterness toward the city constitutes a part of his contempt for society in general. . . . Cernuda lashes out in his poetry against social conventions and institutions such as marriage, the family, and religious organizations. He scoffs at marriage, scorns the family, and disparages their dwellings. . . . Society of the cities with its closed windows, its walls, and dark streets erects constricting laws that represent to Cernuda prisons for his "placeres prohibidos." . . . In this oppressive urban society the solitary man—the pure soul or the nonconformist—is out of place.

Cernuda hates the world out of resentment for the rejection he experiences. The wounded spirit defends his sensitivity with the harshness of hatred. Society demands spiritual accommodation even from those who are unwilling or unable to prostitute their ideals. Cernuda suffers the irreconcilable conflict between imprisonment in a world of tedium and a constant yearning for some impossible Golden Age of love, beauty, and eternal youth. This is a conflict that encompasses his entire production and fittingly furnishes its title: *La realidad y el deseo.* The city, with its insensitive inhabitants and oppressive conventions, operates as a prevailingly negative force within that reality which antagonizes and ultimately frustrates his desires.

Our discussion up to this point has concentrated on the poetry Cernuda wrote before 1940. In exile, the city no longer appears as an objective correlative reflecting the personal and intimate feelings of the poet but exists for its own sake as an element of the outside world—this is true of London specifically. Despite this shift in poetic perspective, the accent remains somber. In his evocations of the world around him in London, a certain serene, limpid sadness prevails. The empty and darkening streets will now lead him to the silent, cloistered peace of a cathedral at twilight. Although the solitude of a cathedral may instill some consoling peace, the city as a cluster of people continues to emphasize the reality of the poet's misfortune. The congested anonymity of London only allows him to hear the fleeting mention of Spain from a weary stranger who disappears like a lifeless shadow among the gray streets, leaving behind in the poet a disquieting emptiness. The city stands as testimony to the pride of the rich, while demanding from the less fortunate a struggle for livelihood greater than that demanded of ancient heroes who battled fierce dragons.

In contrast to his surrealist poetry with its emotionally charged ambiguous images, Cernuda's postwar poetry displays a direct, unadorned technique of description and enumeration. But the city still signals a reflection upon the indifference of the city dweller. The previous note of romantic disillusion and of melancholic detachment, under the stress of prolonged frustration and the additional burden of exile, evolves into a throbbing cynicism. In one poem he suggests that man's indifference may only be a counterpart of God's disregard. In another poem he perceives in the ruins of a city an affirmation of hunger, hypocrisy, man's folly, and the mortality of all things. The city embodies sterility, vulgarity, and the nothingness of life. . . . We thus see that Cernuda's hostile relationship with the city during the pre-civil war days broadens after his exile to include a negative vision of social reality and of man himself.

No matter whether appearing as a figurative or literal image, the city in Cernuda's poetry signifies a lonely, distressingly hostile place, empty and dark or inhabited by inhospitable and indifferent people who attempt to impose their oppressive conventions on everyone. Cernuda's view of urban society reflects his continual solitude and growing cynicism. The city affords us a glimpse of a hell counterposed to the paradise that Cernuda found in the natural world, and it underlines that irreparable antagonism between "la realidad y el deseo," between the real and the ideal which persecuted Cernuda all his life and manifests itself constantly in his poetry. (pp. 161-63)

> C. G. Bellver, "The City as Antagonist in the Poetry of Luis Cernuda," in Romance Notes, *Vol. XIX, No. 2, Winter, 1978, pp. 156-63.*

STEPHEN J. SUMMERHILL

It has often been pointed out that the poetry of Luis Cernuda manifests a disarmingly simple biographical structure of four basic phases, each corresponding generally to different stages in human life: adolescence, youth, maturity, and old age. Of these phases, Cernuda himself preferred his "mature" period, the works he wrote from approximately 1935 until 1944, when he began to cultivate a deliberately prosaic and narrative style, while exploring the solitude of his many-sided exile: exile from Spain, from God, from childhood, and even it sometimes seems, from life itself. Over the years, it has been this "realistic" Cernuda, with his penetrating analyses of human finitude, and his anguished yet remarkably detached search for meaning in the gardens of the past or the landscapes of England, who has come down to us as the dominant image of the poet; and such volumes as **Las nubes** (1940), **Ocnos** (1942), or **Como quien espera el alba** (1947) have long been recognized as major contributions to the existential trends which emerged in all Spanish poetry after the Civil War.

Prior to developing in this direction however, Cernuda passed through a brief period of contact with surrealism which resulted in two earlier volumes, **Un río, un amor** (1929) and **Los placeres prohibidos** (1931). Traditionally, little importance was ever attached to these works. . . . (p. 131)

Ever since Cernuda's death in 1963, however, and coincident with the recent revival of interest in Spanish *avant-garde* literature, a small but growing number of readers has begun to turn more and more to this earlier poetry. Octavio Paz was the first to point the way in a fundamental essay of 1964 [see excerpt above] where he affirmed that, far from being superficially surrealistic, Cernuda was in fact the only Spanish poet of his generation to have understood and accepted as his own the full implications of surrealism, its goal to be much more than a new technique for poetry by becoming a complete subversion of all things in the name of freedom. . . .

In his source study *Surrealism and Spain,* C. B. Morris describes the poet's motives and expression as "nearer to those of the surrealists than any other Spanish poet of his generation." This of course is not necessarily laudatory since one could imitate quite well without making a contribution of one's own. But in an earlier study, Morris had made his feelings quite clear by stating that **Un río, un amor** was Cernuda's

highest achievement, comparable in excellence to the finest poetry of both Alberti and García Lorca. (p. 132)

It is undoubtedly correct to say that, of all the major figures of the Generation of 27, Cernuda has so far received the least attention, even in the case of his later poetry. This is particularly true in the area of imagery and poetic diction, where much room for investigation remains. (pp. 132-33)

Un río, un amor is an interesting work because it marks the poet's sudden immersion into a whole new set of personal circumstances, and a corresponding attempt to develop a new style with which to express them. It is a kind of leap into the abyss, a rare moment when he let down many of the barriers normally protecting his reserved personality, and decided quite simply to say what was on his mind. At the same time, he did this by resorting much more than usual to imagery, which therefore plays a more central role in this work than in the rest of his poetry. It has frequently been noted that Cernuda was an idea-oriented poet who tended to use a more direct language than many other poets of his era. That is true of all his books except this one, which, without reaching the metaphorical exuberance of Aleixandre's or Neruda's early works, does represent his most sustained effort to speak analogically. It therefore affords us greater than usual opportunity to see him develop in this direction at the same time as it shows him at his moment of greatest passion.

It should be noted that restricting attention to themes and imagery of **Un río, un amor** does not mean avoiding the complex issue of surrealism, but rather, approaching it through the poetry itself. Such a perspective seems appropriate to Cernuda because, in spite of Paz's statements to the contrary, he saw himself as independent of surrealism, and selected from it only what he wanted as he saw fit. As he said many years later, surrealism was for him a "springboard" to something else, and our problem is to determine what that something else was. (p. 133)

Un río, un amor is a collection of thirty brief poems written during four and a half months from April to August, 1929, after a long and frustrating battle on the poet's part to find the kind of language he felt most appropriate to what he calls an "urgency of all my being" burning inside of him. The key factor in releasing these bottled-up feelings was an attentive reading of writers like Aragon, Breton, Eluard and Crevel, who, he tells us, were successful at putting into words a certain "malaise and daring" which he felt corresponded to his urgency. His basic idea then, was to express his inner feelings of agitation under the guidance of surrealistic writings and this no doubt explains the turn to imagery.

But the task did not come to him easily, for he went some nine months without writing anything at all, and even then he found himself capable of composing poetry only by approximating the surrealistic notions of objective chance and psychic automatism in the actual writing of the texts. He tells us that, after this long period of silence, one day he found himself writing poems "dictados por un impulso similar al que animaba a los superrealistas." He started to take external stimuli which he had encountered by chance—the title of a jazz song or of a movie he had seen, for example—, let them expand in his mind until they formed into a poetic statement, and then he would write out what had appeared to him "all at once and without corrections." In truth, this seems less a veritable automatic writing than it does a kind of free inspiration typical of many writers, and similar in fact to a procedure such as Unamuno's "viviparous" writing. Cernuda never cultivated oneiric experience, nor do his texts suggest that he did, though it is also notoriously difficult to know the extent to which the surrealists themselves incorporated that experience in their work. In any case, according to Cernuda, all the poems of *Un río, un amor* were composed in this way, as well as those of the following volume, *Los placeres prohibidos.* But the fact that a gap of some twenty months separates the two volumes indicates that even this first leap into a new style was insufficient to overcome completely the poet's incapacity to write, and that more time would still be necessary to transcend the agitation he was feeling. By the time of *Los placeres prohibidos,* much of the agitation is gone; but not so in *Un río, un amor,* which erupts in the middle of a crisis, one that the poet cannot resolve through the writing process. In this sense, *Un río, un amor* is part of an ongoing search which does not end with this book.

Overall, what we can see in Cernuda's contact with surrealism is a psychological release of pent-up feelings, a general agreement about ideas of agitation and revolt, and an attempt to use certain stylistic features of French poetry, notably metaphor, as a means of self-expression. It is noteworthy that such tendencies work against the theories of surrealism itself in the sense that they maintain the priority of self-expression, and lead ultimately to increasing the conscious control of the artist. Surrealism liked to flaunt its scorn for art and sought to transcend expression, as is well known, through its experiments in automatism. As has often been observed however, Cernuda's approach was basically that of most Spanish poets, who adopted surrealistic techniques in order to channel purely private worlds into more objective form. The difference in Cernuda was his direct knowledge of much surrealist writing, and his tendency to agree with the ideas behind the movement. Whether or not he agreed completely however, is an issue we will consider. . . . (pp. 134-35)

In turning directly to the poetry of *Un río, un amor,* we shall begin by noting that on first reading the volume appears to lack thematic unity. Critics have observed that, though a number of identifiable ideas appear and reappear here and there, there seems to be little direction to any of them, and the whole collection thereby gives an impression of aimlessness, as if unable to communicate a unified group of themes which the poet might have been attempting to develop.

This problem is a familiar one however, and depends upon our capacity to distinguish types of aimlessness and the situation of the poet in respect to his texts. The poems themselves are not without direction or purpose, but the state of mind being presented in them is aimless. In reality, *Un río, un amor* is a deeply unified, very coherent group of poems which present a state of mental or psychological disruption. For reasons that will be discussed momentarily, the speaker of the poems—whom we may safely assume to be Cernuda himself—feels frustrated, lonely, disoriented in his life. He is thus wandering confusedly without knowing where to turn. The result quite naturally is aimlessness, both in his own state of mind, and also in the overall structure of the volume. Each text presents a different "moment" or feeling or facet of the speaker's overall situation, and though we can organize certain ideas since some occur more frequently than others, the whole is meant to lack direction because the speaker cannot find any in his life. However, neither of these two forms of indirection—in the speaker and in the relationship among the

poems—affects the poems themselves, which are nearly always coherent. (pp. 135-36)

The essential theme being developed in *Un río, un amor* is the dislocation caused in the speaker by the loss of a former wholeness. Some shock has upset his life, has transformed him into a mere fragment of his former state, and has now left him wandering in helplessness, frustration and uncertainty. We can detect this shock above all in the temporal structure of the poems, which nearly always describe two times, an earlier time of truth, instinct and desire, and a present time of "mentira," chaos and death. The poems themselves are written from the perspective of the present time, but they constantly allude to that other time as an era of truth which is now gone forever. (p. 136)

It is never certain in *Un río, un amor* exactly what has happened to produce the Fall being presented, though we can infer certain details here and there. The poem **"Todo esto por amor,"** for example, begins by alluding to the destruction of instinct and desire. . . . Various poems allude moreover to love as an experience which has come and gone. . . . At the same time, the destruction of desire and the frustration of love are overshadowed by an all-pervasive awareness of death, which now falls heavily on the speaker and has come to appear as the only thing he knows for certain: "Sabiendo nada más que vivir es estar a solas con la muerte." Everything suggests a personal disillusionment in love which has expanded into a more universal apprehension of human limitation and finitude.

But Cernuda is less interested in accounting for the causes of his failure than in simply presenting with as much immediacy as possible the collapsed state of mind which results from it. If we may continue the analogy of the Fall, we can say that, rather than describing the actual failure while he was in the garden of paradise (a task which would require some capacity to objectify and explain the experience), he is immersing us into those first moments of exile when Eden has just been abandoned. A vast, unfamiliar world lies before him, without his yet knowing how to find his way in it. For this reason, the event itself which caused the Fall is left deliberately vague, enigmatic, like an unsolvable crime which we think was committed though we cannot be certain. (pp. 137-38)

Of the various emotions, ideas and feelings which now engulf the poet because of his loss—remorse, fear, solitude, anger, uncertainty—, two are very prominent, and though far from new in modern poetry, deserve special attention. The first . . . can be described with a variety of terms: fatigue, boredom, *hastío, ennui.* Essentially, it is a feeling of tedium, an oppressive sensation of emotional fatigue and monotony in the face of the sameness of all things. Sometimes it is difficult not to become bored with the theme of boredom, so common is it in post-Symbolist poetry; but what makes it significant in Cernuda is its relationship to characteristic tendencies of his style. Many lines create an atmosphere of weariness and sterility by means of a deliberately heavy, almost "antipoetic" repetition of words and phrases which accumulate in the texts like monotonous dead weights. This can be done in a straightforward manner, by means of a repetition which echoes the sameness being discussed in the lines. . . . Or it can be done with surprising substitutions, where one would expect one word, but the poet instead repeats one already used, as in the expression "desde el suelo hasta el suelo." Here, the second instance of "suelo" takes the place of "techo" or perhaps "cielo" which we would have expected to see in a phrase describing the completeness of a situation: "from the ground up to the sky." By repeating the word "suelo" however, Cernuda both evokes the missing word through the similar rhyme, and emphasizes the collapse of the phrase from the heights to the even more complete monotony of a thoroughly earth-bound existence.

The theme of boredom or fatigue reaches its most complete expression in a few poems where the poet contrasts a striking visionary image to his use of repetition, in order to convey an underlying attraction for difference which becomes drowned in a sea of sameness. Since this involves his use of imagery, we may take a closer look at the procedure in what is probably the most well-known text of the volume, **"Estoy cansado"**. . . . Two things immediately impress the reader of the text, the striking visionary image comparing fatigue to feathers in the first line, and the weary repetition of similar sounds and words, especially in the second and third stanzas. The initial image, though at first obscure, is explained in lines two through four: being tired has feathers in the sense that feathers are synecdochical for a parrot, and parrots are characterized here by the fact that they are always in the same place ("nunca vuelan"), and by the empty repetition of sounds which for them have no meaning. Fatigue is thus a kind of confinement within endlessly repeated sounds, and the poem incarnates this through the many repetitions throughout the text. The whole text clearly shows that state of boredom and monotony which the poet so much loathes.

What becomes significant within the context of Cernuda's style is the contrast here between two ways of speaking, one oriented toward difference, and the other toward sameness. By comparing his fatigue to feathers, the poet at first seems to be attempting to break out of the monotony which surrounds him by creating an image, a transformation through the power of the word, which could hopefully offer a more pleasant alternative to his boredom. When fatigue is described with feathers in the first two lines, it is metamorphosed into something different from it, something apparently unrelated. That this is a fundamentally attractive, positive thing is apparent in the word "graciosas" of line two, where we sense the appealing variety of the multi-coloured feathers of the parrot. Were we to stop at the end of that line, we could not help but be struck by the paradox that an apparently unpleasant state, being tired, is described in such attractive, almost dynamic, terms. Metaphor itself seems to be at stake here as a capacity to offer variety and difference: the unpleasant becomes the pleasant through the creativity of an image.

But the creative, the novel, the diverse and different: none of these can survive for long in Cernuda's world. They are but a weak desire for the visions of metaphor which is soon overcome by what was there all the time, the straightforward and reiterative language of sameness. Already the repetition of "tiene plumas" in the first two lines insinuates the presence of fatigue, and the attraction of the feathers is soon swallowed up in the "balbuceo" of the parrot. The fatigue becomes all the more burdensome because it has drowned the only note of difference, the pleasant feathers, under the monotony of empty sounds.

If it is true that Cernuda tended less to metaphorical language than other poets of his era, a text like **"Estoy cansado"** can perhaps give us one reason why. In effect, metaphor seems here to imply an element of diversity which he was unable to feel within himself, and which he therefore de-emphasized in his work. It is not of course that metaphor

thereby disappears, for the image of the parrot still stands at the end of the poem. Nonetheless, the parrot itself has been transformed from a vision of difference to one of sameness in a general collapse into monotony, and its original appeal has disappeared. Cernuda, we might say, has shown us why he could never have written with metaphorical exuberance: he simply could not escape his overwhelming sense of sameness. At the same time, the idea of metamorphosis or transformation shows us one of the essential directions of his images which we can pursue in more detail.

The subtle interplay between sameness and difference in the theme of boredom leads to a second group of poems in *Un río, un amor,* one where the other dominant feeling of the book is made present. This is the notion of escape, what might be called a desire to find some far off *different* place where despair and anguish would disappear, and the fatigue he feels would be lulled to sleep in the utter sameness of tranquility. In the second poem of the volume, **"Quisiera estar solo en el sur,"** this place is called simply "the south," an undefined location characterized, significantly, by its capacity to create difference, that is, to transform the rain and fog which dominate the present into rosebuds and laughter. . . . (pp. 138-41)

According to Cernuda's own declarations, the name *el sur* came from a jazz song whose title he found in a record catalogue. In its original context therefore, it would have referred to the southern United States, and in this sense, it is exactly the same place as that evoked in other poems which also use American place names to designate that far off place to which the poet would like to escape: **"Nevada," "Durango,"** . . . **"Daytona,"** and **"Colorado."** What is interesting about all these names is their contradictory quality of being specific yet unreal. They suggest a concrete place, yet they are deliberately exotic and remote, not really concrete at all. This paradox underlines the basic contradiction in the whole notion of escape: Cernuda is always aware that he cannot get away even as he longs to, and he ambiguously presents these dream-like regions as both attractive yet likewise buried under monotony. . . . (pp. 141-42)

The poems which use American place names as the remote region of escape appear almost exclusively in the first half of *Un río, un amor.* The longing does not disappear as the work progresses however; it shifts into a related feeling which would later play an essential role in all of Cernuda's poetry. This is the urge to be swallowed up into the utter and complete sameness of oblivion, "olvido." Toward the end of the volume, one has a sense that the poet has given up looking for ideal regions, and now seeks only to enter a realm of nothingness. In the poem **"Nocturno entre las musarañas,"** he tells us that he wants love, not as a means of satisfying pleasure, but because it must necessarily be frustrated, must destroy him, and must therefore drive him toward "olvido." (p. 142)

It would be difficult to overestimate the importance of the idea of oblivion throughout the whole development of Cernuda's poetry. Beginning with the 1934 volume, ***Donde habite el olvido,*** the poet centered more and more upon a longing for oblivion as the only means of preventing the fatal conflict between reality and desire which he saw as both creator and destroyer of all things. What we see here is the beginning of that idea, and though it may have come from one of Cernuda's favorite poets, Mallarmé, it indicates that an understanding of the later poetry is incomplete without reference to this earlier book. *Un río, un amor* is in fact the groundwork for all of the poet's later verse.

It has often been pointed out that *Un río, un amor* was influenced by one of the most outstanding French surrealist poets, Paul Eluard. The sign of this influence would ostensibly lie in the similarity between the title of the volume, and Eluard's *L'Amour La Poésie,* which was published in the same year Cernuda wrote his work. Actually, however, while it is true that the Spaniard admired Eluard and later translated some of the poems of *L'Amour La Poésie,* what we have already seen of his work should be enough to indicate that enormous differences exist between the two poets. Eluard is essentially a poet of fluid, sensuous love for woman. . . . The splendour of the female body dissolves for Eluard the conventions of the outside world, transforms reality into surreality, and creates a poetic universe of perpetual discovery.

If Cernuda was influenced by such a poetry, it could only have been in the sense of seeing in it a vision of the wholeness which he could never possess, and which he therefore had to learn to live without. At most, he gives us only the first half of Eluard's surreal I-Thou relationship, the self without love and poetry, the self of anguish and despair because he cannot find the other who would fulfill him.

In this context, the notion of metamorphosis, which has frequently been pointed out as characteristic of surrealism, and which we have repeatedly seen in Cernuda, should be understood carefully. (pp. 142-44)

[In Cernuda] the entire direction of metamorphosis is different. The loss of love or the imminent sense of death have crumbled his world, and left him wandering in bewilderment. Though he encounters a world without logic, it is this which is precisely his dilemma, for disorder produces anguish not excitement, disorientation not a freedom for re-orientation, destruction not creation. To be sure, such a destructive vision can be seen in many surrealist texts, if not typically in Eluard, but the deepest sense of the movement was to move from disintegration to re-integration, as so many have insisted. Cernuda could not do this, and never would be able to. He had fallen into a chaotic reality and he remained there. Even in his later works, where he elaborated a systematic understanding of the world about him, he simply codified this same perspective into a permanent and unresolvable contradiction between reality and desire. Desire could never become real in his mind because reality inevitably overcame it while leaving him disillusioned and distraught.

To point this out is not of course to criticize Cernuda, but to stress the basic difference between his version of surrealism and the at least theoretical goals of the surrealists who influenced him. *Un río, un amor,* as indeed all his poetry, is cast within the perspective of reality not surreality, and the world of love alluded to in its title is ultimately but the hopeless dream of children, desired but impossible, beautiful but lost forever. (p. 144)

[For Cernuda] the function of the word is not to illuminate the heretofore unseen and unknown, but to reflect what is known only too well already. As he says in the text **"Drama o puerta cerrada":**

> Sólo sabemos contar afirmaciones
> O negaciones, cabellera de noche;
> Sólo sabemos invocar como niños al frío

Por miedo de irnos solos a la sombra del tiempo

The operative terms here are *contar* and *invocar.* Lost and alone in a world which is doomed to disappear, all he can do is to recount the confused comings and goings, the affirmations and negations, of his present state; and to invoke the cold there before him, as if praying for his deepest fears not to come true, all the while believing that they will.

Symbolically, the universe projected in *Un río, un amor* draws so much upon imagery recognizable throughout Symbolist and post-Symbolist poetry, while integrating it so completely into the poet's peculiar understanding, that we are not sure if Cernuda adapted this imagery to himself, or if, as seems much more likely, he in fact adapted himself to it. When reading Cernuda, one is always hearing the voices of other poets, rarely Spanish poets at this stage of his life. . . . He was like a chameleon, now this colour, now that colour, yet always the same. In a very real sense, the world of *Un río, un amor* is like an emblem of many of the motifs and images belonging to the myth of the "poète maudit," and as such, it is built upon literature, not just surrealist literature, but upon that whole line of development extending from Baudelaire into the twentieth century. Cernuda however, lived this myth with the intensity of a deeply felt truth. The result is a poetry alive with his own passion; and at the same time a strong sense on our part of literature's enduring capacity to be taken as real.

The setting of the volume is a world of vast, deserted spaces through which a lonely figure, symbolic of the poet, wanders confusedly. This figure could in fact be called the wanderer, and recalls many similar figures from Romanticism to Surrealism. In Cernuda, however, the wanderer is not the *flâneur* of so much surrealist literature, for there is no sense of the vagabond, the happy-go-lucky type such as the Aragon of *Paris Peasant.* Cernuda's is more openly tragic.

The spaces take various forms: the empty streets of a dark, foggy city; a beach, a desert, the pampa; or even the sea or the sky. All are extensions of an inner emptiness, and connote solitude, monotony, and the sudden openness of the future there before the poet. . . . (pp. 144-46)

Frequently, as the poet-character wanders through the empty spaces, slow moving objects shift in and out of his line of vision, and give an eery dream-like quality to the atmosphere. They are not so much in a dream, however, as in a now deformed reality. For this reason, they are presented with one of the procedures most clearly linked to Surrealism, mutilation. We see decapitated men passing in file with broken chains hanging from their hands. . . . The element present in such scenes is contradiction, here the incomprehensible reality of prisoners with broken chains, that is, men who are free yet who live enslaved to both their middle-class mediocrity, and especially their inevitable imprisonment in death.

It is this contradictory element of existence which has suddenly appeared to Cernuda, and which becomes apparent in every detail of *Un río, un amor.* If he sees "Árboles sin colores y pájaros callados" for example, the absent element of color or song is still making itself felt, undoubtedly as a former presence for which he now longs but which has been cut off, expelled from the universe. (p. 146)

Though the imaginary universe of *Un río, un amor* is one of open spaces, the one object which most frequently appears in it is a wall. This image may have originated in Cernuda's own experience insofar as much of his poetry from *Perfil del aire* (1927) through his works of old age, alludes to the emblem of the garden, with its fountain, tree, and walls. . . . As in Reverdy, the wall in *Un río, un amor* seems capable of taking a variety of forms—closed doors or windows for example—and it functions as a barrier. Unlike Reverdy, however, Cernuda does not construct his wall so as to create an aura of mystery and transcendence lurking behind all things. Consistent with the disillusion governing his work, he presents a wall that has blocked access to love or self-fulfillment at some time in the past, and that now stands there indifferently as a reminder of lost hope and as a warning not to try again. Thus in nearly every instance he depicts the wall with some object or emotion lying shattered at its base, as if a failed effort had been made to find a way beyond it. (p. 147)

On only one occasion does the wall appear weak in *Un río, un amor,* and this is when it is being used in a specific metaphorical context to show the totality of night. The poet tells us that the shadow of night breaks the weak walls ashamed of their whiteness. . . . Here, the wall is still conceived as a barrier, but it is used to give corporeality to the fading light of sundown. This in turn serves to evoke more fully the utter totality of the black which invades the world by knocking down the wall of white.

If the wall is an image of failed desire, it is frequently pictured with a lamp hanging from it. . . . Like the extinguished stars, only reversed, the lamp is a glimmering memory of lost love. . . . In this context, it is interesting that Cernuda in turn compares the lamp to a fan. . . . It is possible that here he is echoing a note from Mallarmé's *éventails,* those delicate objects which seem like fluttering wings flying to the future, yet which lack the strength really to penetrate time. Cernuda too feels the attraction of the lamp, but its weak glimmer, like the delicate fan, is unable to restore light to his world, and really only reminds him of the past. . . . (pp. 148-49)

The symbol of desire lying broken at the foot of a wall leads us to another common series of images in *Un río, un amor,*—the many allusions to beggars, rags and torn clothing. All of these are connected to the notion of an earlier brilliance which now finds itself in ruin and decay. (p. 149)

If we were to seek a single structuring principle running throughout *Un río, un amor,* and capable of explaining both its themes and imagery, it should by now be evident that it would be metamorphosis, that transformation into contradiction and monotony which we have been seeing throughout this study. Change was a dilemma lived in the poet's experience, and it underlies the many contradictory images we have seen: the flower which becomes a fist, the kings who become beggars, or the bird flying beneath the ground. As a final example of the potential subtlety of Cernuda's figurative language, we should like to discuss a particularly interesting image of transformation.

In the poem **"La canción del oeste,"** the poet evokes the world of the Far West and cowboys in order to suggest the remote region to which he longs to escape, the ideal realm of love. At the same time, because Cernuda knows he cannot achieve this realm, he is also showing the destruction of his desire, and the consequent urge for oblivion which he now feels. In order to bring this out, he compares the West to an object which he tried to enfold in his hands as air surrounds and enfolds the moon. . . . But then the moon metamor-

phosed into a hard object such as wood, while his hands became liquefied like teardrops:

> Mas la luna es madera, las manos se liquidan
> Gota a gota, idénticas a lágrimas.

At the outset, this image is built upon an almost ironic contrast: the nebulous element, the West, is given corporeality by being compared to the moon at the same time that the corporeal element, the poet's hands, are emptied of their solidity by being compared to air. Such a coordinate movement of aethereal to solid and solid to aethereal or shapeless, suggests the impossible; and is designed to bring out the poet's inability to grasp that West of his dreams.

Under this light, the fascinating part is the metamorphosis of moon into wood and hands into water. In effect, the word *Mas* suggests that an entirely new or different event then took place: the hands became water and the moon became wood. Yet this had already been achieved by comparing hands to air and the West to the moon. The nebulous air is no more capable of grasping the moon than is the shapeless water of grasping wood. This latter image is therefore not different, and the metamorphosis is apparential or illusory because the idea behind it remains the same. The whole sequence thus turns out paradoxically to be no more than another version of that monotonous repetition which pervades so much of *Un río, un amor,* and creates an overall atmosphere of tedium and futility.

It has been shown that apparential development permeates much of the conceptual structure of *Un río, un amor:* ideas are stated which seem to offer opposition when in fact they all turn out the same. It is the same kind of illusion which we would suggest is present in the image of wood and water. Even as a complex transformation is proposed, there is an underlying repetition which empties it of the very movement being described. Everything looks different, but it is always the same, for difference in Cernuda's world is impossible unless it be no more than sameness. The problem of course, is that life *is* now different from what it was, but at the same time, it is always the same for him; and he communicates this clearly in a contradictory vision of difference and sameness which, ultimately, is the basis of the entire volume called *Un río, un amor.* (pp. 151-53)

Stephen J. Summerhill, " 'Un Rio, Un Amor':
Cernuda's Flirtation with Surrealism," in Journal
of Spanish Studies: Twentieth Century, *Vol. 6, No.*
2, Fall, 1978, pp. 131-57.

GREGORY RABASSA

Luis Cernuda now seems almost like a museum piece, a relic of the generation of Lorca and the young poets who had found their strength just as the Civil War and its foul concomitants festered and broke. Cernuda went into exile and remained there until his death in Mexico in 1963. Even in Spain before the war he had been a "loner," following his own devices, which were more often based on foreign patterns drawn from his knowledge of French, German, English, and American writers, rather than on his own traditions. These latter were not missing, of course; it was just that he was far less parochial than most of his compatriots, who too often lingered too long to savor the superficial past that Spain had created for itself in the nineteenth century. In a sense, Cernuda, with the Civil War, simply turned from internal to external exile. (pp. 140-41)

At an early stage Cernuda saw that poetry (and expression in general) was always trying to reach beyond its means, trying to produce something worthy of Pygmalion:

> He did not speak words
> Merely drew near
> An inquisitive body
> Not knowing that desire is a question
> Whose answer does not exist
> A leaf whose branch does not exist
> A world beneath a nonexistent sky.

> (from *Forbidden Pleasures,* 1931) . . .

In this extremely physical poem

> (Anguish makes its way through the bones
> Rises up along the veins
> Until it breaks the skin
> Fountains of dream made flesh
> And questioning the clouds.)

Cernuda is close to César Vallejo, that other Spanish-speaking poet whose fame languished so long at great remove from recognition except by the likes of Pablo Picasso and others of the elect. (p. 141)

Cernuda's isolation from his fellows was broken when Fascist thugs murdered García Lorca. As Gibbons points out [in his introduction to *Selected Poems of Luis Cernuda*], Cernuda knew his country well enough to see that this monstrous act was not some horrid accident of fate but a reflection of the rancor in the Spanish heart that is so easily transformed into hatred and ultimately someone else's destruction. Cernuda, unlike many others, did not see this trait as the dire obverse of some primitive shield of strength. . . . [He] was appalled by the envious hatred his countrymen bore as they whittled their betters down to their level. His poem to Lorca is in his collection *The Clouds* (1937-1940) and he speaks of how Spain destroys its best, much as Joyce did concerning Ireland. . . . Much later, in a bitter poem done from exile, all hope gone (if there ever was hope in this consummate pessimist) he ends a poem entitled **"Limbo"** and dedicated to Octavio Paz with a searing line that might well include the "occult fire" of the earlier work and calls for the prophetic disaster that James Baldwin has also predicted, "Better destruction, better fire." (From *Your Hours Are Numbered,* 1950-1956). (p. 142)

The word "useless" appears more often than would normally be the case in many poems. The sense of this reaches beyond each time the word is applied and suggests that Cernuda sees Spain in its self-destruction as a useless society, which leaves him in total isolation, and that his own existence is useless or hovers close to such a bleak state. In one poem he speaks of a "Useless stone which no celestial breeze enlivens" (**"To the Statues of the Gods,"** *Invocations,* 1934-1935). This stone would be the earth, often called a cinder, after the destructive fire has done it in. Fire can be cleansing, but what it has cleansed it has also rendered useless. This is the bitter, hopeless attitude of the defeated exile that Cernuda is to become, giving the poem a vatic tone.

The image of the stone brings him close to the Brazilian Carlos Drummond de Andrade, who speaks about "a stone in the road" in an emphatic way as he follows through with his sense of "thingness." Cernuda says "And again he lies like a stone in a path no one walks" (**"Bodies Like Flowers,"** *Forbidden Pleasures,* 1931). Drummond lacks the negative sense of a path no one walks. The two poets have a common reduction of things down to just that, but Cernuda, from an early time, did not feel much more attachment to things than he did to people. Along with Drummond and the Portuguese poet Fernando Pessoa he represents his generation in its isolation, but unlike them the sense of finding other voices is not as strong. The roots of Modernism are also still there as he asks, with Rubén Darío, where we come from and where we are going: "Not knowing where to go, where to go back to" (**"Nocturne Among Grotesqueries,"** *A River, A Love,* 1929). (pp. 142-43)

Gregory Rabassa, "Other Voices, Other Rheums: Three Versions of the Outsider," in Parnassus: Poetry in Review, *Vol. 9, No. 1, 1981, pp. 140-47.*

MICHAEL UGARTE

"No se quede aquí, no se quede aquí." These words were spoken to Luis Cernuda in 1948 when he was suffering through his final days at Mount Holyoke College before a summer in Mexico and well after his departure from Spain, a country to which he would never return. In his autobiography, Cernuda recalls this haunting phrase as somewhat of a moral imperative. Like an echo, it repeats itself. The stress on the final syllable of "aquí" suggests an obsession, an urge, a desire. One familiar with Cernuda's poetry could imagine these words . . . as a line of verse from *La realidad y el deseo.* "No se quede aquí" reveals not only the restlessness of Cernuda's life, but that of his poetry. The speakers in Cernuda's poems always seem to be drawn away from where they stand. Whether in the surrealist stage before the departure, or in the nostalgic verses of *Las nubes,* the lines themselves constantly stray from an initial direction. Cernuda's words wander from conventional meanings to associations to traces of other words. Yet perhaps more important, the moral imperative of departure is the mainstay of one of the most dominant motifs of Spanish literature, and for that matter, of all literature: exile. (pp. 325-26)

Cernuda was most certainly a restless nomad, and his risks, hints, and encounters were his poetry. *La realidad y el deseo,* the title he gave to his complete poems from *Perfil del aire* (1927) to *Desolación de la quimera* (1962), is emblematic of one of exile's most enduring dilemmas: the realization of desire. In Cernuda desire is both a motif and the force which sets his life and poetry into exile, an eternal movement away from a secure home. (p. 329)

The numerous metaphorical and metonymical designations of desire in *La realidad,* "brisa," "rosa," "estrellas," "grito," "extender la mano," "una pregunta," reveal its multi-faceted nature as well as the turmoil it creates. Desire displaces the poet at the outset, for his urge is illicit. Cernuda boldly casts his homosexuality, a condition he never denied, into his book of life poems. Homosexuality defines the nature of his desire as a force unlike that of the mainstream and as an object of society's scorn. The poet's need to transgress, however, asserts itself continuously, not as an apology but as a triumph, proof of his own transcendence of the world's banalities:

> Por ello en vida pagarás largamente
> La ocasión de ser fiel contigo y unos pocos,
> Aunque jamás sepan los otros que desvío

Siempre es razón ante la grey.

Typical of Cernuda's didactic tone, these lines from **"Aplauso humano"** embody a fundamental paradox. What in the eyes of the flock is deviant and repugnant becomes virtuous in the eyes and words of the poet. Homosexuality is both the reason for the harsh price of ostracism and the opportunity to remain loyal to his own nature. It separates him and at the same time renders him complete. The allusiveness of these words, representative of Cernuda's references to homosexuality ("ello," "ocasión," "desvío," "razón mejor"), indicate the taboo associated with homosexual behavior as well as the poet's wish to focus not so much on the act, or even the pleasure of the act, but its motivating force. (pp. 329-30)

Cernuda embraces the uniqueness and aberrance of his own desire and the separation it creates. Yet ironically, the desire of exile is also a yearning for oneness, a home in which love burns perpetually. The irony of Cernuda's love taboo leads to the conceptual and linguistic contradictions in much of his poetry. In *Un río, un amor* desire is a natural force compared to the wind, sea, flowers, clouds, water, and heavenly bodies. The title is a transcription of the singularity of the poet's yearning, a narcissistic desire of desire. Yet the inward direction of this desire, a longing to find the heart of the heart or the home of the home, cannot lead to a sense of wholeness. On the contrary, its end result is a split: the object of desire needs a subject to realize it and vice versa.

Throughout *La realidad y el deseo,* desire is the lens Cernuda employs to view his own present and past experience. The urge to look at himself results in one of the most characteristic features of his exilic desire: an on-going dialogue between the two voices of love, the *yo* and the *tú.* All of love's trials, the suffering, the losses, the separations, and at the same time, the joys and gains, stem from the poet's desire of himself, a want which is as much a pursuit of wholeness as a cause of fragmentation. The dialogue between Cernuda's two selves is a lovers' discourse whose pronouns affirm both the dependence and independence of their referents. The linguistic division, however, between *yo* and *tú,* even though they refer to one person, renders the realization of desire an impossibility. In a sense, Cernuda has been exiled to the paradoxes of poetic language. For him, poetry is a celebration of desire, yet the very language of the lovers' discourse erases the possibility of its fulfillment.

The conceptual conflicts within the realms of desire lead to structural contradictions in Cernuda's poetry. These inconsistencies are further marks of the linguistic manifestations of exile: the text in exile from itself. In the early stages of his career, Cernuda found in surrealism the aesthetic authority to affirm his own poetic incongruencies. The ideas of the European avant garde offered him a vehicle to avoid the simple apprehension of his words, a wish to liberate his language from the constraining forces of meaning. But surrealism went even further in that it provided Cernuda with a partial satisfaction of his wanderlust. The French resonances of the movement, the taste for transgression, and the willingness to allow the text to stray from conventional significations was appealing to this Andalusian poet in search of a home. Desire, the reigning force in Cernuda's displacement, was no less inconsistent with the interests of the Parisian surrealists.

A case in point is **"Como el viento"** from *Un río, un amor.* The word "deseo" never appears, yet the existential and linguistic displacement it engenders is typical of the early poetry. . . . (pp. 330-31)

The poem is structured upon an asymmetrical equation in which one side is absent. The poet's desire (the invisible side of the equation) unmasks its identity purely by suggestion: the repetition of "como" followed by a variety of images associated with the wind. The wind's power arises from its ability to move, to unsettle the world (as the surrealists wished to do) throughout its travels: "sollozando," "gritando," "tristeza errabunda." The poet ascribes these powers to himself. Even before the final verse, human qualities of the wind ("tristeza," "fuga," "llanto") prepare the way for the poet's identification with it. Like the wind, the poet is a foreigner ("extranjero") and a fugitive ("fuga sin objeto"). "Huyo lejos," he declares, since he must act in accordance with the wind's natural laws. Wind, desire, and poet unite to become a life force in their flight away from their present locus.

Yet the most jarring feature of the poem is the last line. Up to this point, all the objects which play a role in the drama of desire are in commotion; but the confusion remains within the poet's (and the reader's) grasp. In contrast, the final verse throws chaos into further chaos by virtue of its language. "Sin embargo" posits a contradiction, a conflict with something that was already in conflict. The preterit "vine" jolts the temporal reference of the poem out of the present in which it comfortably resided, thereby placing the very situation of the poem into question. In contrast to the wind, the appearance of "luz," with its godlike definite article, belies the fragmentation which set the tone for the body of the poem. Typically surrealistic, this last line is marginal; it seems unwilling to stay within the bounds of the poem as a whole. "Como el viento" is a discourse on the asymmetry of asymmetry and, in the last analysis, the exile of exile.

While the later poems of Cernuda are not as radically hostile to interpretation as some of the early ones, the structures remain uneven and at times unveil a series of synthetic contrasts whose illusory unity is another linguistic marker of exilic desire. One case is **"Vereda del cuco,"** one of Cernuda's most extensive reflections on desire. The subject, the poet himself who is once again addressed by the speaker as tú, takes the form of a bird moving along a path in search of water. Past blends with future and present from beginning to end so as to erase any specific time reference. The bittersweetness ("extraño dulzor,") of the past momentary satisfactions of desire intrudes into the present experience of the poet's contemplation of the path. He watches himself battle with a shadow in order to reach a light, at which point he drinks the coveted water. But the liquid does not quench his thirst; on the contrary, it produces an even greater thirst. The lines which treat the risk one must take to satisfy desire ("Para que sea perdido,/Para que sea ganado,") pinpoint the paradox of the poem as a whole: the loss and gain of following one's desire. In this poem, as in many others, the presence of desire reveals itself through absence. To be in exile is to think of oneself both present and absent. The concept of absence and the exile's futile search for presence is a trademark of Cernuda's language and, as I suggested earlier, an inherent feature of language itself. (pp. 332-33)

Memory and its counterpart, oblivion, occupy a primordial place in Cernuda's poetry. Not only do they provide Cernuda with essential components in the interplay between reality and desire, they embody the very act of writing. Just as the tenuousness of reality frustrates the poet at every turn, so memory fills the vacuum of oblivion with imperfect copies in writing of what was once real. . . . To fill the abyss of oblivion with words is no consolation, for the poet is painfully aware that he has not recreated a reality, the ideal for which he thirsts, but has strayed further from it. For one such as Cernuda whose experience of exile is metaphysical, moral, and sexual, as well as political, oblivion is a haunting figure which gives rise to a question without a response. Oblivion is one of the most grueling symptoms of the enfermity of exile; for those afflicted, existence is rooted in an unverifiable past.

In Cernuda's longest sustained discourse on oblivion, the volume titled, *Donde habite el olvido,* the word "donde" signals the geographic importance to the concept of forgetfulness. The first poem in the collection sets the mood and defines the subject matter for the others. "Where" is an anaphoric conceit frequently followed by a plethora of verbs in the subjunctive. The notion of a hypothetical dwelling place of oblivion structures this poem and engenders a variety of images, all of which evoke the nebulousness of oblivion itself. . . . As the speaker confirms through his repetition of the word, "ausencia," the loss of what was at one time a land, a love, a memory, is no longer. Yet the absence is not absolute; it is a "leve ausencia" whose trace is still felt "como carne de niño." The knowledge of the former existence of the forgotten, to know that at one time the forgotten took shape, intensifies the pains of oblivion. In this poem, absence brings on the yearning for an elsewhere: "allá, allá lejos."

Donde habite el olvido is filled with transparent images which come not only from Cernuda's surrealist influences, but as a statement on the formlessness of oblivion. Water, wind, clouds, and shadows occupy the space of forgetfulness in what the poet calls at one point "una verdad transparente." Cernuda sees through the objects in the land of oblivion as he searches for a truth which is itself intangible: "un mar delirante," "aire tranquilo en la nada," "el mar es un olvido." These images coalesce with the phonetic qualities of this collection, especially the echo which appears both as a mental construct ("Soy eco de algo,") and as repetitions of sounds, words, and phrases. The echo, like something forgotten, is a representation doomed to nothingness. In its chain of mimicry, it yearns to duplicate its immediate predecessor, but it cannot. Like the transparent image, the echo must always defer to another entity. It cannot contain its own form. Such is the condition of exile, never complete in and of itself.

Oblivion is also a relational concept, for there is a necessary interplay between the time and space of the present and that of the past. While these relations appear metaphorically in the early poems of *Un río, un amor* and *Donde habite el olvido,* Cernuda's physical departure from his homeland spawned a renewed contemplation of oblivion, this time within unfamiliar surroundings. In the poetry of *Las nubes, Vivir sin estar viviendo, Con las horas contadas,* and *La desolación de la quimera,* objects situations, and occurrences are more easily identifiable than in the early poems. In this later poetry, Cernuda refers to a real geography in relation to one literally left behind. The reader is as mindful in these collections (as the poet seems to be) of exile as a social experience.

The social and political dimensions of Cernuda's later poetry take the form of an attempt to resucitate forgotten objects, people, and events, and further reveal the relational properties of exilic writing. Cernuda's reflections on the surroundings of his new domicile allow him to see only the traces of

things from another time and place. In the new land all seems to point in the direction of a different place, things have their imperfect correspondences elsewhere, and the mediation between the two lands is an arduous process which is never complete. Other flowers, other springs, other winds pervade this poetry so as to create a world in which nothing is whole without a reciprocal entity from a distant land. In **"Otros tulipanes amarillos,"** the recollection of the poet's homeland and a former state of mind is touched off by a glimpse of golden tulips. . . . [They] remind the speaker of similar flowers from a land he once occupied. The image of the other tulips brings to mind the painful process of their remembrance, a longing not so much for the Spanish soil as for the youthful state of mind which contemplated the flowers years ago as the poet does now. The poet realizes that the moment is lost and that its seeming repetition (its remembrance) is illusory. The tulips of years gone by can only come to life with language; the poet must name them, an act which can never recover the tulips as they were. . . . The poem ends on a note of resignation as the poet admonishes himself to cope with his dilemma with silence: "aprende ese silencio." Silence is a skill that must be learned like a language from another land; the linguistic assimilation of the new environment is a necessity. Ironically, however, silence can only lead the poet further into exile.

Cernuda creates a geography of the forgotten in **"Otros tulipanes"** as in many poems written after his departure. One of the most telling features of his creation is the anaphoric use of demonstratives, a feature which further illustrates a relational perception of reality. The land of Cernuda's poems is filled with ambiguous directional signals which provide guidance only through a poly-referential thought process. In the first line of **"Otros aires,"** a poem written at the moment of Cernuda's arrival to the United States, the poet asks, "Cómo serán los árboles aquellos?" . . . The poet gazes out his window and contemplates the trees from a distance, yet they are less remote now than when the question was first asked. As they maintain their illusiveness, the trees in this unfamiliar setting create a series of possibilities for the poet. . . . For an exile, the expectations of the new land bring momentary joy and rebirth. The durability of this instant, however, is nothing more than a hypothesis. . . . Like the land of oblivion, the place called "over there" is unreachable. Similarly, a return from exile, regardless of politics, is impossible. (pp. 333-36)

The realization of desire, along with the losses and gains of oblivion, have political dimensions, yet the tension between social reality and poetic language manifests itself most clearly in one of Cernuda's favorite figures: *tierra.* In the midst of a body of poetry which seems at times indifferent to political forces, the resonances of specific historical polemics within a designated culture echo throughout *La realidad y el deseo.* Cernuda's land is at some points a formless space, yet the persistent use of the word *tierra,* in a variety of contexts (country, climate, earth, homeland, family, exile) underscores a social dilemma which initiated a dispute. His poetry is indeed narcissistic, but self-contemplation divides as well as isolates and thereby creates a dialogue of voices within one. The land, both here and elsewhere, is the ideology and the geography in which a heated dialogue takes place.

In Cernuda's early poems, land has no real geographic referent; it is a land of language. . . . But as Cernuda becomes older, his elsewhere moves closer. In *Invocaciones, Las nubes,* and *Como quien espera el alba* the yearning for the native land is no less evident than in the typically nostalgic poetry of Rafael Alberti. The gardens and oceans of Cernuda's later collections are of a specific time and place. Beaches, castles, and convents take form within an identifiable geography through titles such as **"Un español habla de su tierra,"** as well as natural features which act as emblems for a specific region. . . . In several poems, Cernuda recreates the land of childhood, the memory of which has become bitterly painful. (pp. 336-37)

Yet the nostalgic desire for the setting of earlier years becomes problematic as the social reality of that time invades the privacy of those memories. A case in point is **"La familia,"** a social institution as well as a force in the poet's personal history. Cernuda's memory again comes into play as he recreates his childhood and adolescence. The yearning for the home of happier days does not set the tone of this poem; it is rather a melancholy reflection on the austerity, inhibition, and personal guilt engendered by a hierarchical Andalusian family. The poet does not accuse; instead, he accepts what he has become through familial influences even though there has been a spiritual, social, and geographic falling out, a separation between himself and his kin. . . . The family is another manifestation of the land: "el hogar . . . el nido de todos los hombres." Like the land, the family embodies a paradoxical force which draws and extracts the subject toward and away.

Cernuda's critique of the family is implicit of a larger issue, a historical dilemma which encompasses the complete spectrum of the politics of Spanish exile. The rigidity of the patriarchal family leads to the intolerance, tyranny, and repression of a nation. Spain as a problem pervades *La realidad y el deseo* from beginning to end in much the same way as the theme of cultural identity and national character obsesses so many Spanish intellectuals. . . . While the poet's dialogue with his own cultural tradition at first glance binds him to it, his dissonent and dissenting voice will never allow him to join the group. Cernuda's discourse is different and brands itself as such. . . . Cernuda identifies with no one, except perhaps himself. . . . Cernuda makes a serious attempt to cut off the exchange with his own tradition. His political dialogue ensues outside the familiar milieu, as exile has rendered him eternally other.

The poetry dealing with Spain unveils opposing voices and social postures; it is difficult, if not impossible, to identify a consistent political stand on anything. Cernuda glorifies the history of his land with the remembrance of the Escorial and in another poem, he extolls Philip II in his efforts to create eternal harmony. But in both texts, the poet speaks as an outsider who can admire the virtues of his land only because of his position from without. . . . (pp. 337-39)

Strangely coupled with these admiring odes, is a selection of poems in diametric opposition. The poet lashes out in these lines with a series of invectives, accusations, and curses all directed at the homeland. . . . Cernuda assaults his own nation with a vengeance uncommon to other Spanish intellectuals who deal with similar issues. For Cernuda, the problem is not so much the social errors and injustices of his country, but that he, as a Spaniard by birth, must endure the shame of being Spanish. The attachment to a land is, in this case, not as much a condition but a being, as the title, **"Ser de Sansueña,"** illustrates. Through invectives Cernuda seems to re-

sign himself to the fact that his native being will always provide a link to the Spanish soil, however tenuous, however abhorrent. . . . The Spaniard who wishes he were not, as Cernuda calls himself, responds to the oblivion in which his land has cast him with the vicarious pleasure of deeming that land unreal through poetry, writing the land out of existence. While the land of Galdós is real, the nation that murdered Lorca, the land of the censors and the "terrible Spaniards" is a "limbo." Cernuda wishes destruction and fire on his land at one point, and toward the end of his life seems to write as if the act of annihilation has been carried out: "Soy sin tierra," he declares.

The self-contradictory Spain over which Unamuno, Machado, and others of that generation brooded is not part of Cernuda's scenario, for his land is neither paradoxical to nor self-contradictory. The self-contradiction and ambivalence are not of the land but of the language. Home is no longer subject to change, no longer a region of social conflict and struggle. In the language of exile, time within the land has ceased; everything is as it was. Home is now a metaphor, an eternal force pushing and pulling but never changing.

Cernuda's account of his own land's history does not claim accuracy, nor does it even pretend to offer a penetrating discourse of the ambiguities and tensions of his culture. . . . Rather, it is a self-critique, a rendition of his own life on, through, and away from the land. It is a discourse which constantly turns on itself and questions its own motivations, as politics and social history become faint traces of a past, influences almost lost. Cernuda's introspection seems so pervasive that at times one wonders where the social issues of exile, the concrete conditions which set the process into motion, have gone. But for Cernuda, the language of social history is the language of poetry, and by the same token, the language of verse is the idiom of a fleeting personal history, the "dossier of a book," as he calls his autobiography. (pp. 339-40)

Poetry, defined as the binding and weaving of words, is contrary to the necessarily monological voice of those who must endure the banishment from the group: "the exile is a kind of anti-poet . . . an unbinder, an undoer, an uncreator. Cernuda would indeed fit into this category and perhaps celebrate the term "anti-poet." But his language of self-absorption is by no means monological, and it is precisely the process of unbinding and undoing which splits his voice and creates a dialogue between the two. *La realidad y el deseo* is an exploration of the dynamics of a multifaceted dialogue—between reality and desire, memory and oblivion, the self and the other, the land and its elsewhere, the poet and the text. One could go further and posit exile as the creative activity itself. . . . In being other, the poet welcomes otherness and inconsistency both in himself and in his word, and Cernuda testifies to this linguistic concept of exile. The "I" never speaks in Cernuda without a listening "you." By the same token, the land does not exist without an elsewhere. For Cernuda, the way home is the way of writing, an eternal journey in which finality and origen are one and the same. Cernuda speaks this journey, and in so doing, he speaks to the exile in us all. (p. 341)

Michael Ugarte, "Luis Cernuda and the Poetics of Exile," in MLN, Vol. 101, No. 2, March, 1986, pp. 325-41.

(John) Michael Crichton

1942-

(Has also written under pseudonyms of Jeffery Hudson and John Lange and with Douglas Crichton under joint pseudonym of Michael Douglas) American novelist, screenwriter, director, and nonfiction writer.

A prolific novelist of diverse interests, Crichton combines the taut plot and rapid pace of the suspense thriller with the technical emphasis of science fiction to comment on humanity's self-assured attitudes toward scientific crises and the conflict between primitive natural instinct and rational intellect. Writing in a vivid, clinical style, Crichton often uses such factual and scientific data as graphs, charts, maps, and computer printouts to sustain the realism of his works. Although some reviewers have faulted Crichton for stereotypical characterizations and situations, many have commended his informative and entertaining narrative style and his ability to impart specialized technical information to the uninitiated reader.

Crichton graduated from Harvard University with a bachelor's degree in anthropology in 1964. He then enrolled at Harvard Medical School, where he funded his education by writing suspense thrillers as John Lange. Crichton's works under this pseudonym include *Odds On* (1966), *Scratch One* (1967), *Easy Go* (1968; republished and credited to Michael Crichton as *The Last Tomb*), *The Venom Business* (1969), *Zero Cool* (1969), *Drug of Choice* (1970; republished as *Overkill*), *Grave Descend* (1970), and *Binary* (1972). Although most of his works from this period received scant critical attention, Crichton garnered approval for an intelligent analysis of modern social problems in *A Case of Need* (1968). In this detective novel, written under the pseudonym of Jeffery Hudson, a Chinese-American obstetrician is unjustly charged with murder after performing an illegal abortion on the daughter of a prominent Boston surgeon. After Crichton received his medical degree from Harvard in 1969, he worked briefly as a postdoctoral fellow at the Salk Institute for Biological Studies but decided instead to pursue a writing career.

Crichton established his reputation as an author of bestselling fiction with *The Andromeda Strain* (1969), his first novel published under his given name. Written in the form of a historical journal, this work uses such data as computer printouts, bibliographic references, and fictional government documents to lend authenticity to the story of a deadly microorganism that is collected from the earth's outer atmosphere by a NASA space satellite. The virus is inadvertently scattered over a small town in the southwestern United States, where it kills most of the region's inhabitants prior to being isolated in a secret underground laboratory in Nevada. The remainder of the novel concerns conflicts that arise between the efforts of scientists to resolve the crisis and those of the United States military to procure the microorganism for use as a weapon of biological warfare. Many critics compared Crichton's next major work, *The Terminal Man* (1972), to Mary Wollstonecraft Shelley's novel *Frankenstein*. This book examines the predicament of a paranoid computer scientist who suffers from a brain disorder characterized by seizures during which he unconsciously commits violent acts. By implanting an electrode designed to deliver a mild electric shock

to his brain, doctors seek to abort his psychoepileptic responses. They discover instead that the shocks stimulate the pleasure terminals of the man's brain, prompting his nervous system to initiate more frequent seizures that lead to increasingly brutal crimes.

The Great Train Robbery (1975), for which Crichton received an Edgar Allan Poe Award from the Mystery Writers of America, reconstructs the circumstances surrounding an infamous crime that occurred in England in 1855. The protagonist of this novel is an upper-class confidence man who masterminds an intricate plan to rob a train of a cargo of gold bullion intended for British soldiers fighting in Crimea. Described by Edmund Weeks as "[an] exciting and very clever piece of fiction," *The Great Train Robbery* garnered praise for its authentic recreation of Victorian argot and history. Crichton's first-person travelogue *Eaters of the Dead: The Manuscript of Ibn Fadlan, Relating His Experiences with the Northmen in A.D. 922* (1976) describes the wanderings of a cultured Arab traveler in medieval Scandinavia who helps a group of Norsemen combat a tribe of neolithic cannibals that has been attacking Norse settlements by night. Most reviewers regarded *Eaters of the Dead* as a contemporary retelling of the eighth-century verse epic *Beowulf*.

In *Congo* (1980), Crichton draws on scholarly anthropological tracts as well as the narrative tradition of H. Rider Haggard's novel *King Solomon's Mines* to depict a group of corporate-sponsored explorers who search the rain forests of Africa for the Lost City of Zinj, where a race of hostile apes guards rare diamonds capable of nullifying humanity's need for nuclear weapons and energy. The group's survival becomes dependent on their ability to control Amy, a domesticated gorilla skilled in human sign language who acts as a liaison between the apes and the explorers. Harold Hayes commented: "*Congo* is the result of some serious reading by an intelligent man, reflecting on the endless possibilities and permutations of communication." *Sphere* (1987), which James M. Kahn lauded as "[Crichton's] best work since *The Andromeda Strain*," depicts the efforts of an underwater research team to recover a gigantic alien spacecraft from beneath the Pacific Ocean, where it is estimated to have landed more than three hundred years before.

Crichton has also directed several films for which he wrote the screenplays. Among his numerous productions are *Westworld* (1973), which centers on an American frontier-town fantasy resort where a vacationer is forced to fight for survival against a mechanical gunslinger; *Coma* (1978), a medical thriller based on the novel of the same title by Robin Cook, about a conspiracy to randomly murder hospitalized patients so that their organs may be sold for black market transplants; *The Great Train Robbery* (1978), based on Crichton's novel of the same title; and *Runaway* (1984), in which a police specialist combats a madman who programs robotized appliances to murder their owners. Crichton's nonfiction works include *Five Patients: The Hospital Explained* (1970), in which he uses medical case histories to explore the dynamics of a modern hospital; *Jasper Johns* (1977), a biography of the celebrated contemporary painter; and *Electronic Life: How to Think about Computers* (1983), an introduction to computers for beginners.

(See also *CLC*, Vols. 2, 6; *Contemporary Authors*, Vols. 25-28, rev. ed.; *Contemporary Authors New Revision Series*, Vol. 13; *Something about the Author*, Vol. 9; and *Dictionary of Literary Biography Yearbook: 1981*.)

FRED ROTONDARO

As I looked over *A Case Of Need* I mentally jotted down the main ingredients of the tale. A doctor, a Chinese-American living in Boston, is accused of the abortion-murder of the daughter of a prominent local surgeon. Dr. John Berry sets out to prove his friend innocent and find the real murderer. In the process he discovers the fact that doctors, just like other people, will often turn their backs on truth when their own interests are involved. . . . (pp. 207-08)

It's a great relief to find talent where you expected mediocrity; it's a greater relief to find substantial talent. And that is just what I found in *A Case Of Need.* For despite what appeared to be a very mundane set of fictional elements, author Jeffery Hudson, a pseudonym for a Boston-educated scientist, has managed to tell a fine story and at the same time comment deftly on some severe contemporary social problems. Rather than being bored with insubstantial characters I found myself taken up with the remarkably vivid world the author creates. Boston comes alive; so does the medical pro-

fession. The case for abortion is presented with tact but effectively. At times the author makes those who generally oppose abortion look just a bit too muddle-headed and as one who does oppose abortion I huffed and puffed belligerently on my cigar when I read what a narrow minded guy I was. The author concludes his work with an appendix in which he discusses in an extremely lucid manner such topics as medical terminology, the attitude of doctors toward policemen, and the case for and against abortion. Those of us who oppose abortion come off much better here than in the body of the work.

The novel will—or should—make the best seller lists. And no doubt it will become a movie. But don't wait for the movie version. Read *A Case Of Need* now; it will entertain you; get you angry—it will make you think. (p. 208)

> *Fred Rotondaro, in a review of "A Case of Need,"*
> *in* Best Sellers, *Vol. 28, No. 10, August 15, 1968, pp.*
> *207-08.*

ALLEN J. HUBIN

Though he does not attempt to supply solutions to the impasse of abortion, Jeffrey Hudson provides searching glimpses into the dilemma as viewed by a physician in *A Case of Need.* The pseudonymous Mr. Hudson presents his case (that the situation today is intolerable) within the agreeable framework of a detective story. Dr. Arthur Lee, obstetrician and (because of conscience) active abortionist is arrested for murder when named by a teen-ager dying from the effects of a botched operation he did not perform. . . . Pathologist John Berry's search for the real abortionist airs considerable unlaundered linen in high places—and some well-reasoned deductions finally lead him (after a bewildering change of direction at top speed) to the killer. This breezy, fast-paced, up-to-date first novel, flavored with after-hours medical shop-talk, demonstrates again the ability of detective fiction to treat contemporary social problems in a meaningful fashion.

> *Allen J. Hubin, in a review of "A Case of Need," in*
> The New York Times Book Review, *August 18,*
> *1968, p. 20.*

CHRISTOPHER LEHMANN-HAUPT

Last Sunday night was bad for me. At about 3 o'clock in the morning I got some news that terrified me. I already knew [from Crichton's *The Andromeda Strain*] . . . that the town of Piedmont, Ariz., had been contaminated by a mysterious microorganism borne from the earth's outer atmosphere by a Project Scoop satellite. I knew that the microorganism, code-named Andromeda Strain, had somehow wiped out all but two of the 48 inhabitants of Piedmont and that the two survivors, an old man and a tiny infant, had been taken, along with the lethal satellite, to a secret underground laboratory in Nevada, where a team of top-flight scientists was busy trying to figure out what was what. . . .

What particularly scared me at about 3 A.M. was the announcement by the head of the President's Science Advisory Committee on Day 4 of the five-day crisis that something else besides depolymerized plastic dust had been found in the wreckage of the plane. The examining team had "found a few pieces of bone that have been identified as human. A bit of humerus and tibia. Notable because they are clean—almost polished." . . . Nothing like this had happened until now; the citizens of Piedmont had died in an entirely different manner. The news shook me.

You see, I was taking all this pretty seriously. Tired out by a long day in the country I was awake way past bedtime. My arms were numb from propping up my head. By turning from side to side to relieve the numbness, I had driven the cats from their sleeping place at the foot of the bed, and they were disgruntled. . . .

But I was well into Michael Crichton's science-fiction thriller, *The Andromeda Strain.* And he had me convinced—what with his Harvard medical-school training, with his copies of Government files and memos and computer-base output mapping, with his reference notes to actual scientific papers (not to mention the actual news that the crew members of Apollo 11 will be quarantined after their return from the moon)—that it was all really happening.

So I had kept racing ahead despite fatigue, sore arms, disgruntled cats. I had forgiven Mr. Crichton his irritatingly hokey little asides about how "it was to prove an unfortunate mistake," and how "he could not have been more wrong."

I had waded through his tedious little lectures on enzymes, amino acids and proteins, electron microscopes, bacteriology and X-ray crystallography. And I had held back the knowledge that science-fiction thrillers have to end in one of two ways: either humanity gets wiped out, or the extraterrestrial threat is defeated at the last moment. You see, I figured it was all building to something special—a lovely irony, a chilling insight, a stunning twisteroo. And then there was the gleaming horror of those bones, which served to ignite in me some irrational, nontechnical dread—as all science fiction worth its salt will do. The whole business had to be resolved before I could sleep.

Well, it wasn't worth it, because instead of using all the sophisticated detail and the subtle plotting, Mr. Crichton resolves his story with a series of phony climaxes precipitated by extraneous plot developments—and one huge biological cop-out. And, believe it or not, there isn't another mumbling word about those bones.

So curse you, Michael Crichton. You led me on with a beautiful dud—a chocolate eclair filled with shaving cream. You, with your gibbering, squeaking computers—you stole a night's sleep from me with a fast shuffle. If you don't do better next time, I'll mutate you.

> *Christopher Lehmann-Haupt, "A Hard Five-Days' Night," in* The New York Times, *May 30, 1969, p. 25.*

ALEX COMFORT

Science fiction has undergone an unwelcome change. It used to minister to our need for prophecy; now it ministers to our need for fear. Secure, prosperous people who—atom bombs and race riots notwithstanding—have less to fear from life than ever before frighten themselves silly with carnivorous fungi, germs from outer space, and Martians who make parasites of statesmen's brains. . . .

What I find distressing is that in the public nightmare science has replaced the supernatural, and the scientist is cast in the role of the Faustian black magician. Worse still, we are now using real science as if it were fiction, for the physical acting out of the brainsick matter of such tales. . . .

Which is why Michael Crichton's novel is disturbing. It makes the point, but only obliquely. What raises *The Andromeda Strain* above the tired ranks of books about threats from Outer Space is its use of the nasty apparatus of contemporary play therapy for disturbed adults—e.g., "THIS FILM IS CLASSIFIED TOP SECRET: Examination by unauthorized persons is a criminal offense punishable by fines and imprisonment up to 20 years and $20,000." Who are they hiding it from? And why? Presumably from us, because if we knew about it we would certainly put a stop to this game.

But the author cheats in getting his deadly organism in from Outer Space. An unmanned American space satellite lands on the edge of a small Arizona town, contaminated with a lethal germ strain. Most of the town's inhabitants and the first investigators die grotesquely. Scientists in an underground government lab strive to find a way to combat the deadly invader. At the last moment, only a few seconds from "self-destruct," fortunately . . .

Think for a moment what would really happen if a dangerous organism were to appear. Resources would indeed be mobilized against it. The play therapists would quite possibly exploit the opportunity for dramatics, self-destructs, secret documents, the lot. At the top, a few higher-level play therapists would be concerned to prevent panic and damage, but also to secure the disease and its antidote as one more weapon to Defend Our Way of Life.

If Michael Crichton's story had concerned a virus deliberately rendered virulent by our scientists, rather than one which dropped in from the galaxy, it would have put the cloak-and-dagger stuff, the secret test sites, the self-destruct systems, and the rest of the nasty hardware which so fascinates both readers and the administrators, into their true perspective. It might then have had Wellsian symbolic overtones. The Faustian use of science—the fascination of secrecy, hierarchy and playing with danger—this is the virus that may indeed destroy Man. It is already among us, and its concordance in public policy with the need of an anxious society for a folklore of terror is one of the most dangerous developments in modern social anthropology.

Accordingly, the better Crichton tells his tale, the more tables of amino acids, computer printouts, crystallograms and data he includes, the more upsetting *The Andromeda Strain* is to a concerned scientist. The purpose of science is to save men from the hazards of nature; its subject becomes terror, secrecy and self-destruct mechanism only when its falls into the hands of neurotics and the service of pathology. The author probably knows this, but he doesn't hit us with it. Instead he titillates and scares. This is mere scientific pornography. We run a real risk of dying titillated, through the leakage of fear and fantasy into science and back.

If I am being over-serious about an entertainment, and am failing to do justice to a very skillful and well-observed piece of fake actuality, it is because the self-destruct mechanism bothers me. Apathy and mental disorder could make our science into just that, and cosmic catastrophe scares, however cleverly done, seem to me to belong to that matrix of thinking.

> *Alex Comfort, "When Fiction Invades Science," in*

Book World—The Washington Post, *June 8, 1969, p. 4.*

RICHARD SHICKEL

The Andromeda Strain is the *reductio ad absurdum* of that much discussed sub-literary genre, the non-fiction novel. While I do not like this book very much, I must confess to feeling that Michael Crichton . . . deserves a great deal of credit—if for nothing more than his willingness on the first try to test the outer limits of the logic of his genre. Eschewing the dramatically easier subjects of such writers as Irving Wallace, Fletcher Knebel, or Robert Serling—the Nobel Prize committee, a military cabal, or the possible workings of the Presidential airplane—he has attempted no less than a fictional construction of the world's first biological crisis.

As he is careful to point out to us, scientific crises . . . are increasingly familiar to us. Moreover, it is logical to suppose that the next such crisis will occur in the most rapidly expanding scientific discipline, biology. Finally, he is clever enough to realize that we laymen know even less about that subject than we do about physics or rocketry and that we will, therefore, snap up (as we did *The Double Helix*) anything that looks like a convenient, readable trot on it.

So he has imagined a space shot that returns from outer space contaminated by a deadly bacterium against which man has no natural immunity and which could, if not neutralized or destroyed, wipe out the race. . . . And he gives us an indecipherable blend of true, half-true, and imaginary theories about the nature of the invading organism and the strategies for dealing with it that is fascinating, believable, and seemingly informative—though the problem of what, precisely, to believe does nag at one. Finally, he has found an interesting form for his work, casting it as a journalistic-historical work written a few years after the Andromeda crisis has passed. There are acknowledgments of fictional informants, a made-up bibliography, computer print-outs, and exact typographic reproductions of what purport to be government documents.

Indeed, he has spared no effort in his attempt to make us believe *The Andromeda Strain* could happen here. Except one—the creation of people. Granted the ability of the non-fiction novelist to characterize is not his great strength. Were it, he would not, perhaps, become a hyphenated novelist. But the lack of interest in this matter is, in Mr. Crichton's case, amazing. Perhaps so much creative energy went into imagining his basic situation that none was left for people. Perhaps he is trying to tell us that high-level scientific technicians, obsessed with their work, are, in fact, inhumanly traitless. Still, one would have liked some human quirks to get hold of, if only to help keep the names straight. By the end of the book I would have settled for a few of Irving Wallace's walking clichés, even a few physical descriptions. Just for fun. Or as an acknowledgment of literary tradition and the expectations we still bring to a work that must still be called, for want of the better term that is surely coming, a novel.

> *Richard Shickel, in a review of "The Andromeda Strain," in* Harper's Magazine, *Vol. 239, No. 1431, August, 1969, p. 97.*

ALEXANDER COOK

[*The Andromeda Strain* is] a science fiction novel masquerading as a suspense thriller. Its excellent disguise has fooled a good many already. First of all, it fooled Alfred Knopf, presumably—for whoever heard of his Borzoi imprint going on a piece of sci-fi? And it must have fooled the Literary Guild, too, for had they known what it is they would surely not have sent it out. And by this time, finally, it must have fooled a lot of readers, as well. They must have supposed it just a very up-to-date thriller, since the novel is set in the present, since its space hardware (only incidental to the story in the first place) is of no more than contemporary sophistication, and since the "aliens" who invade the earth are mere microbes.

But nevertheless *The Andromeda Strain* is science fiction. What else are you going to call a novel that begins out on the desert like one of those scary old sci-fi movies from the fifties—*It Came from Outer Space* or *Them*, for instance—with the discovery of a town that has been mysteriously wiped out? The cause is soon made clear: a NASA probe vehicle has returned to earth nearby, been broken open, and an unknown strain of microbes picked up from outer space has infected the small community. The mystery is solved; the panic is on. A team of doctors, biologists, and specialists of every sort is hastily assembled from all parts of the country, and the remainder of the story is an account of their efforts to isolate, identify, and deal with this new strain they dub Andromeda.

Nothing very new in this, of course. The basic plot is one that has been done and re-done innumerable times in science fiction. . . . What is impressive here, however, are the many exact scientific details the author has included and the narrative skill with which it is written. The pace is fast and absorbing; the writing is spare and its quality generally high; and the characters, if not memorable, are at any rate efficiently sketched in and have been given little personal touches of their own.

Does this make it *good* science fiction, as opposed to the stuff you see on your drugstore racks? No, it's not quite as simple as that. For whatever else it may be, science fiction is the last solid redoubt of the imagination. And the writers who command that fort may not always be the most skilled writers of fiction by the usual standards but they are the ones with the most fertile imaginations—the Blishes, the Pohls, and the Heinleins. And while *The Andromeda Strain* may rate as superior in science and as a marked improvement in fiction, it lacks something of the catalytic glow of imagination that under the best circumstances seems to spark when those two disparate elements are conjoined. (pp. 493-94)

> *Alexander Cook, in a review of "The Andromeda Strain," in* Commonweal, *Vol. XC, No. 18, August 8, 1969, pp. 493-94.*

FRED ROTONDARO

If ever a novel was meant for the movies, *The Venom Business* is. It has all the necessary ingredients.

The central character in the tale is Charles Raynaud educated in the Ivy League, a man who has decided that there is more fun and fortune to be made in smuggling than in a standard business position. . . .

Raynaud becomes involved with an old friend, Richard Pierce, a millionaire who is fearful that his business enemies are plotting to kill him. Raynaud, taking a job as bodyguard to Pierce for $500-per-day, comes to realize that Pierce is setting up the suspected murder himself and realizes that Pierce is trying to goad him into killing him. The reasons why this should be begin to prey on the reader's mind as the author skillfully unfolds the base of the mystery. . . .

The final character of note is the stock personage of a rich, idle, young woman, looking for a plaything. Her name here is Jane Mitchell. Her affair with Raynaud entangles an already confusing web of international finance, mystery and death.

John Lange, author of **The Venom Business,** is the pseudonym of an American research scientist who writes "in order to remain sane and to escape the pressure of work." His book is a good one—fast-moving with interesting characters and that almost forgotten device of modern writing, an ending that really does end things.

> *Fred Rotondaro, in a review of "The Venom Business," in* Best Sellers, *Vol. 29, No. 10, August 15, 1969, p. 186.*

CHRISTOPHER LEHMANN-HAUPT

It will be said—in fact I have already heard it said—that "Michael Douglas's" novel **Dealing** is a new breed of book—a unique excursion into Head Country, into the hearts and minds of America's spaced-out youth. And that it's strictly for the lotus-eaters, because its heroes turn on and its villains are narcotics agents, parents and other squares. But I wonder.

Admittedly, the novel has all the scales of Puff the Magic Dragon. Its hero and narrator is a semidropout who earns money in his spare time toting bundles of cash from Boston to Berkeley and running back bricks of Mexico's finest. It is filled with inside news and terminology. . . . When its plot stumbles, or time must be lapsed, it blows out insights on righteous highs; on why the narcs waste America's time, money and moral nerve chasing small-time grass-dealers instead of the big-bad hard-stuff pushers; on why parents just don't understand; and on other artifacts of youthcult. **Dealing** is all the rage.

And admittedly, it is entertaining—slick and cool and savvy. It races along as smoothly as a Flexible Flyer on snow. Michael Crichton . . . has brought to it all the plot-spinning tricks he presumably picked up writing mysteries under the *noms de plume* Jeffrey Hudson and John Lange. And whatever Douglas Crichton, his younger brother (hence "Michael Douglas"), contributed, it hasn't hurt.

But I wonder all the same if **Dealing** is really a drug-culture book, because if you stop and think about it, it's as square as a carton of booze. After all, when the going gets rough and the plot sticky, the characters blow the smoke away and act as tough, vindictive and romantic as Bogie in the 1940's. And when "Michael Douglas" gets down to the fag-end of the plot and has to wind things up, "he" resorts to trumpery straight out of Dick Tracy's Sunday best.

O.K., so it doesn't matter that much. So **Dealing** was only meant to be fun—Heads and Narcs instead of Cops and Robbers. Let's just not pretend it's anything more. And let any Head who digs it realize he's caught in the old, old game of power.

> *Christopher Lehmann-Haupt, "One Drug and a Look at Drugs," in* The New York Times, *February 3, 1971, p. 35.*

SAUL MALOFF

The packaging of this collaborative effort [**Dealing**] by the phenomenal young author of **The Andromeda Strain,** Michael Crichton, and his kid brother Douglas screams of countless hilarities to come: far more than a mere wrapping, the dust jacket is a heady experience of bubbling mirth. On the back, where a photograph of the author usually grimaces or smiles sardonically or looks wistfully into the distance, there is a family-album [photo] of two small boys. The caption reads "Michael Douglas" in quotes; and the credit line, with boyish simplicity: "Mom." . . . Now get this title: **Dealing, or The Berkeley-to-Boston Forty-Brick Lost-Bag Blues.** Oh, wow!

And that's not all, not by a country mile. The usual legal disclaimer is modified to read that any resemblance to real persons is "either coincidental or the result of stoned paranoia" and all of it is dedicated "To the Lawmakers of Our Great Land: Play This Book Out LOUD!" And then, after four epigraphs (Thoreau, Art Linkletter, Billie Holliday and Fats Waller), you arrive, battered, breathless but quiveringly expectant, at the beginning of the novel itself.

Now you may not find any of this ingratiating, but stay a while; for this book wants to tell us something—and it does, though not always what it intends. "Dealing," as any child knows, is trafficking in dope; and here, as the very type-font proclaims, the dealer is Peter Harkness, not only the protagonist-narrator but the hero of his own tale. What's more, square society, with its booze and armamentarium of pills, is represented by the most vicious of cops, a sadistic, corrupt narc named Murph, himself a dealer in soft goods lifted from his victims. Masks in place, the forces of Light and Darkness are thus aligned.

But even masks need a few features, so the authors provide them, beginning immediately with the entire hip lexicon, strung across the opening pages like day-glo baubles, the principle being that those who authentically speak in tongues must be beautiful, especially if they burn their margin of profit by turning on. Naturally the hero happens to pass Sproul Plaza during a demonstration and a police riot. And then there must be a girl, and her name, if at all possible should be Sukie. In fact her name is Sukie. Damn if she hasn't just come from the Sproul Plaza scene. They meet cute. They turn on, again and again and again; and then they are ready. But it is not meant to be: at *the* critical moment, the fuzz break in and bust them. . . .

[Yet, this] turned-on Government major from Harvard is all guts. Under interrogation by the narcs—by the dreaded Murph himself—he more than holds his own, more than stands up, he gives better than he gets. Even when he's kicked in the groin, twice, he doesn't yield an inch. . . .

Not that Peter is political, unless post-political is political. . . . He has some fun early on putting down a Black Power spokesman and a self-designated "Marxist-Leninist." Nor is he into any sector of the peace movement. Dealing is his scene—and scandalizing the bourgeoisie. Back in Cambridge, he goes to a garden party. A garden party, for God's sake! Everyone is dressed as for a garden party—but Peter comes decked out in his credentials, a "pair of greasy blue jeans, a rumpled, plasticly-freaky shirt . . . a tired old blazer, and sneakers." Once there, he amuses himself by spilling numerous bottles of "hooch" all over the lawn, and when the "fun of hassling the old dudes" wears off, he engages in the rich comedy of conning some incredibly square chick into actually believing he's the rock star "Lucifer Harkness." (p. 25)

The boy is as nasty a little prig as you're likely to meet anywhere between Boston and Berkeley, bereft of the smallest redeeming feature or shred of social utility; and yet the authors don't have the slightest doubt that we'll love him as they do, no questions asked. The implied plea (Legalize Pot) is spurious, a clumsy attempt at blackmailing us into assent. We know all about the narcs and the insane laws they execute. And since the book is nothing more than a shoddy plastic construction, whom is it for? . . . [One] must conclude with dismay that there is abroad in this land a vast audience of "young people" of all ages, all of them tuned into the same drummer, all of them decked out in the same plasticly-freaky shirt bought in the same trendy shop who will take any sleazy commodity providing the right signs are flashed, so they know where they're supposed to be at. (p. 25-6)

Saul Maloff, "A Nasty Little Prig," in The New Republic, *Vol. 164, No. 6, February 6, 1971, pp. 25-6.*

EDWARD WEEKS

[In *The Terminal Man,* Crichton] has now written a novel quite terrifying in its suspense and implication. His subject is "mind control," his situation what can happen in the neurological-surgical unit of a university hospital when a paranoid who has been wired with an implant to abort his seizures instead goes berserk.

Harold Franklin Benson, a computer scientist, was healthy until his thirty-third year, when he was involved in an automobile accident on the Santa Monica Freeway. Thereafter he suffered from blackouts preceded by peculiar, unpleasant odors; they often occurred after drinking and as they increased in frequency and duration, Benson would on regaining consciousness find himself with cuts, bruises, and torn clothing but with no recollection of what violence he had been party to. He had been divorced from his wife, and now his seizures cut him off from his remaining friends. A meek, pudgy-looking man with a bewildered air, it did not seem possible that he could have beaten a garage mechanic to a pulp, as the police accused him of doing. The charges were dropped, but they unnerved Benson, and his outbreaks continued until, under police guard, he was brought to the neurosurgeons. They discovered that he was suffering from psychomotor epilepsy, vulnerable to thought seizures leading to violent spells; and that he had a mania about machines, which he believed would ultimately take over the world. He was reassured that the disease could be controlled and was started on a series of drug trials leading up to the operation.

Dr. Ellis is to perform this refinement of brain surgery, and the only one on his operating team with misgivings is Dr. Janet Ross. . . . Ellis goes ahead with the operation in the full blaze of the theater, inserting the tiny electrode with its forty points pressing into the brain, one of which will trace the sources of the disturbance, and placing under the skin of Benson's shoulder a power-packed computer, wired to the electrode, which will deliver an electric shock to abort the seizure. All done in an hour and forty minutes and the patient appears to be doing well.

No one seems to have anticipated that the stimulations might overload Benson, pushing him into seizures which were for a time agreeably sexual, but accelerated into monstrous violence. . . . When he escapes into the maze of Los Angeles, the doctors, already tense, realize that neither talk nor police can turn off the implanted computer: Benson in his alternations between guile and frenzy is a demonic Frankenstein monster, and it is the search for him and his vengeance which make this story such a chiller.

The people are skillfully typed. The nurses supply the essential touch of humor, and the operation is as dramatic as the hunt. In contrast to the vanity and the overconfidence of the surgeons is Janet Ross, the only rounded character, a comely woman whose fatigue and whose fear of the electrically charged guinea pig the reader shares. (pp. 108-10)

Edward Weeks, in a review of "The Terminal Man," in The Atlantic Monthly, *Vol. 229, No. 5, May, 1972, pp. 108-10.*

JOHN R. COYNE, JR.

Michael Crichton has it. His first book, **The Andromeda Strain,** was a splendid suspense novel. But some of us suspected that Crichton might be a one-shot novelist. He was under thirty, and his subject matter, biological science, seemed a bit too specialized to yield up many more plots.

We were wrong. **The Terminal Man** is nearly as good as **The Andromeda Strain,** and that makes it one of the season's best. Again, the subject matter, medical science and mind control, is specialized. But Crichton proves himself capable of making the most esoteric material completely comprehensible to the layman, no small gift in any writer. Even more important, he can create and sustain that sort of suspense that forces us to suspend disbelief. (p. 700)

Crichton writes clean, simple, intelligent prose with a self-confidence that is most common among first-rate British suspense novelists. Few American writers seem capable of it. Perhaps it's the scientific training. Whatever it is, **The Terminal Man** is very nearly the best suspense novel of the year. (pp. 700-01)

John R. Coyne, Jr., "Suspense and Insomnia," in National Review, *New York, Vol. XXIV, June 23, 1972, pp. 700-01.*

THOMAS R. EDWARDS

The Terminal Man, a routine science-thriller . . . , tries to be worried about medical technology. A computer engineer named Benson, who thinks the machines are taking over and who has a way of smashing people about when he's had a drink, is diagnosed as a stage-two (drug resistant) psychomotor epileptic. In spite of the misgivings of his "tall and exceptionally good looking" girl psychiatrist, Dr. Ross, he is given behavior-modification surgery by a research group that's a little too eager to see what happens when you insert electrodes into the brain and hook them up to a chest-implanted minicomputer programmed to stimulate pleasure terminals whenever a seizure begins.

But they forget about autonomic learning—Benson *likes* having his pleasure terminals stimulated, as who wouldn't, and so he involuntarily initiates ever more frequent seizures, like any lab rat, just to get his kicks. Since he also feels, not too unreasonably, that the doctors have turned him into a machine, he escapes from the hospital, kills or mutilates several citizens of Los Angeles, and finally is gunned down by tall, good-looking Dr. Ross . . . when he comes back to get even with the main computer, which has gone a little nuts itself.

The story is pure "Medical Center," right down to the little psychological touches that go out the window when the chase begins—the neurosurgeon who's myopic, balding, and lame (heal thyself, we mutter knowingly), the professional woman who occasionally remembers to resent her male associates, as well as her sporty boyfriend with his enviable Ferrari, because she can't forgive herself for not being the boy Daddy wanted. But Crichton's way of providing a little something for everyone without doing anything with it is an interesting caricature of something good fiction itself requires.

First we get a sober warning that the "shocking or frightening" subject of behavior modification must be faced simply because it's real, like "pollution, depersonalization, and urban blight." Our rage at thoughtless science grows when, during the hunt for Benson, we see Los Angeles as a place where people are indeed being turned into machines, just as poor psychotic Benson insists. Yet he really is dangerous, and we must hope they catch him in time. And science isn't all bad, either—it's fun to watch it do its weird things (the operation is lovingly described). . . .

Certainly Crichton's hope of bringing in all the precincts shows rather too clearly in his presentation of the Computer Problem. At one time he chills us with the news that in July, 1969 ("Watershed Week" to the trade), the "information-handling capacity" of all existing computers passed that of all existing human beings (it will be 50-1 against us in 1975), but later we perk up at hearing that it would take a huge skyscraper and the power consumption of Buffalo to house and run an electronic computer with the "capacity" of a single human brain. Clearly it is rhetorical need, not technical instruction, that determines how words shall be used here.

The Terminal Man, true to its genre, accepts the inertness of fact. Once something has happened, right there on the page, there's nothing to do but have something else happen. The modified Benson, once he exists, becomes an item of police business, and when he's disposed of, nothing remains to say except "You better leave this area," the last spoken words in the book. In a way this is right. If Crichton had not pretended to be warning us against it, we could see and understand better the valueless technological outlook which the tough realism he attempts is meant to express. A more thoughtful and resourceful writer, one less concerned with turning out an attractive commodity, might have made something of this. (p. 20)

Thomas R. Edwards, "People in Trouble," in The New York Review of Books, Vol. XIX, No. 1, July 20, 1972, pp. 20-2.

NEWGATE CALLENDAR

[*Binary*] takes place in San Diego during a Republican national convention. A right-wing millionaire, disgusted at a United States President capable of recognizing Red China,

plans to wipe out him and his entire party—and the city of San Diego along with them. The method: steal a consignment of Chemical Warfare Department nerve gas and disperse it over the city while the President is addressing the convention.

Lange has written more than a down-to-the-wire thriller. He has created a psychological, mind-to-mind encounter rather than a physical, *mano-a-mano* struggle. This is a neat puzzle, in which good and evil, in the form of an introspective government agent and the millionaire, play on each other's weaknesses. The author maintains tension ably to the last chapter, and his postscript is a special dividend. (pp. 26-7)

Newgate Callendar, in a review of "Binary," in The New York Times Book Review, August 20, 1972, pp. 26-7.

DORIS GRUMBACH

Educated readers always have a problem of conscience with crime and suspense stories. They feel guilt at enjoying them so much, and seek intellectual explanation of their appeal to them. Well, they need seek no longer, for Michael Crichton's wonderful crime-suspense-Victorian-cultural history, **The Great Train Robbery** combines the pleasures, guilt and delight of a novel of gripping entertainment with healthy slices of instruction and information interlarded. . . .

[What Crichton] has done in this new book is extraordinary because it is authentic. Anyone who wanted to write a novel based upon England's 1855 train robbery that stunned the Victorians (contemporary accounts called it "The Crime of the Century" and "The Most Sensational Exploit of the Modern Era") could have done so from the court trial records and from a careful perusal of the classic London Labour and the London Poor written by Henry Mayhew in 1861-1862. Indeed I suspect Crichton may have resorted to Mayhew to find some of the criminal class jargon he uses so convincingly. . . .

Having done his research so well, and using it in a way that convinces the reader he knows the culture of Victorian England, he has produced a cannot-put-it-down narrative about all the events that led up to the daring and successful robbery. It is a fascinating crime story during which you are involved in step-by-step strategies of a master criminal, in this case Edward Pierce, upper-class, well-to-do thief, a man of high intelligence, great patience, an infinite capacity for detail. When asked at his trial why he did the robbery, he responded with the simplicity of which only a complex mind is capable: "I wanted the money."

Crichton is talented and canny. He makes no attempt to "analyze" or "understand" his characters. He gives us his thieves, his "skippers" (people who sleep in outhouses and barns at night), his "canaries" and "dolls" straight, letting us listen to them talk in authentic street slang of the time, and educating us, incidentally, in the ways they live and make a living. We do not so much understand them—there is no fakery about the criminal mind or sociological overlay about the terrible effects of poverty on the criminal mind—as we watch them, delighting in their ingenuity, and yes, wickedly urging them on to success.

While we see how it was done, and stand by while it is being done, we learn about such matters as a "carriage fleecement," a trick of using an attractive woman to engage the butler of a wealthy house at the curb with a question about direction while two "lurkers" get into the house, make impressions of keys in wax and slip out again. (p. 30)

The object of the great robbery was the money that was on its way to the Crimea, the army payroll to be exact, during that war. It is "grifted," no, "gafted," no, "tooled." Whatever it is, the "pogue," that is the object of the whole scheme, is a seemingly impossible "lay" (job). But it works; and we are delighted that it does.

You learn more, you find out something about the sporting events of the day, including "ratting sports" in which a "fancy dog" or a most excellent "made dog" is sent into a ring to kill a rat against wagers as to how long it will take. . . . You will be right there, running with the "miltonians" (police), or the "kinchin lay" (robbing children), listening to "beefers" (complainers) who may be "glocky" (crazy) or "lushington" (drunk) with "reeb" (beer), or dressed in "crusher's dunnage" (a policeman's uniform to help along the gaff).

You may have noticed that I have no beef with any aspect of *The Great Train Robbery,* neither the writing nor the research nor the choice of subject. Sure, there is some fiction mixed in with the facts. No one could have known for sure all that Crichton tells us; he has said in an interview that he added to the number of keys required to pull off the pogue, among other inventions. . . . The book will be widely read, much enjoyed, and without doubt make a first-rate adventure movie. (p. 31)

> *Doris Grumbach, "Fine Print," in* The New Republic, *Vol. 172, No. 23, June 7, 1975, pp. 30-1.*

CHRISTOPHER LEHMANN-HAUPT

Well now, it begins to look more and more as though Brian Moore really hit on something with the metaphor of his latest novel . . . , *The Great Victorian Collection.* It would seem that . . . the artifacts of Victoriana do still exert a powerful pull on our 20th-century American imaginations. For hardly had I finished enjoying *The Great Victorian Collection* when I picked up Michael Crichton's *The Great Train Robbery,* a documentary novel about a daring crime that was actually pulled off in England in 1855. And found myself not only captivated because it is Mr. Crichton's best thriller to date (his previous ones were two rather wooden sci-fi adventures, *The Andromeda Strain* and *The Terminal Man*), but also charmed most of all by the story's Victorian style and content.

Not that the crime itself isn't an entertaining one—full of clever twists and turns, surprising reversals and a satisfactory quantity of suspense. A train carrying £12,000 in gold bullion; a daring plot to heist the gold, conceived by a master criminal who lives in high style in Mayfair; four keys to be located and copied so that two safes may be opened; a railway guard to be blackmailed or bribed; an unprecedented escape from Newgate Prison; a fortuitous case of venereal disease—these various elements add up to a plot that, properly told, would hold our attention in almost any setting.

But what gives *The Great Train Robbery* its particular satisfying flavor is the way Mr. Crichton folds in the Victorian ingredients—ingredients such as the Crimean War, to help finance England's share in which the gold is being shipped in

the first place; or the period's penchant for secret hiding places, which helps make the search for and location of the four keys an enterprise of great moment and adventure; or the age's incomplete understanding of a certain law of physics, which helps to explain why the robbery very nearly failed.

Indeed, this is a historical thriller in the truest sense of the phrase precisely because so much that seems implausible at first makes excellent sense once certain background details are filled in. Thus, for example, our credulity may be strained when the need to smuggle a man on board the train is solved by the introduction of a wooden coffin onto the station platform—a coffin, moreover, complete with "several ventholes drilled in the sides" and "on the lid . . . a kind of miniature belfry, containing a small bell." . . .

But our disbelief turns to delight and thence to wonder as Mr. Crichton pauses to discourse documentarily on the 19th-century obsession with premature burial and on the consequent innovation of "the Bateson Life Revival Device," or "Bateson's belfry," as it was ordinarily known. . . . And when the little bell in this particular coffin's belfry actually begins to ring, thus raising hopes for a resurrection and reversing the psychology of the railway guards (for how much deader seems a fake corpse you expect to see alive but find looking dead when you open the coffin, than does a fake corpse you suspect of fakery in the first place)—the whole business seems not only plausible, but is also an absolute stroke of genius in plotting.

Mr. Crichton even uses Victorian underworld argot to embellish his story (or perhaps I should say Dr. Crichton does so, since the author did, after all, graduate from the Harvard Medical School and has here used his knowledge of medicine more cleverly than in his previous fiction). And if I had to register any complaint about *The Great Train Robbery* it would concern the number of times I had to consult Eric Partridge's *A Dictionary of Slang and Unconventional Language* to look up words like "crusher" (a policeman), "flash" (expert), "pull" (an illicit trick or manipulation) and "pogue" (stolen property). But this is not a serious drawback. So compelling is *The Great Train Robbery* and so charming is Mr. Crichton's manner of unfolding it that you can even run across sentences like "Damn me if I'll voker flams at this dead hour. This is no simple kynchen lay tomorrow. It that not plain?" and still somehow draw sense from them. You are *that* caught up by it all.

> *Christopher Lehmann-Haupt, "A Flash Pull for a Fat Pogue," in* The New York Times, *June 10, 1975, p. 37.*

EDWARD WEEKS

From a hilltop in Kent in May, 1854, a tall handsome man in his early thirties with a full red beard observed through his binoculars the morning express of the South Eastern Railway on its way to Folkestone at fifty-four miles an hour. . . .

Twelve months later Red Beard himself, with the aid of his accomplices, was to engineer the successful theft of the same train. . . .

[In *The Great Train Robbery*], Michael Crichton tells this suspenseful story with the cool calculation of the mastermind, disclosing only so much as Pierce himself was willing to confide in his team. Each episode is set against the background of the underworld, the lodging houses in the slums with twenty crowded in one room, the bordellos, the pubs, and the prisons. As the author reminds us, Victorian England in a matter of decades had become "a nation of cities," the first and wealthiest urbanized society on earth, in which criminals preyed on the aristocracy with a skill far beyond the control of Scotland Yard.

Edward Pierce himself was a fascinator and remains a man of mystery. Was he a genius up from the streets or a gentleman turned rogue? He was the owner of pubs and a fleet of cabs that supported him in style; he had a cultivation that passed muster with bankers, and he could drop into the criminal jargon with the men he trusted. They were four in number: Burgess, the burly cabman with a white scar on his forehead; Clean Willy, the most famous snakesman of the century, a former chimney sweep who could wiggle through the smallest space; . . . Agar the screwsman, a specialist in keys and safe-breaking; and, most important, Miss Miriam, the actress who was Pierce's mistress. An exciting and very clever piece of fiction.

> *Edward Weeks, in a review of "The Great Train Robbery," in* The Atlantic Monthly, *Vol. 236, No. 1, July, 1975, p. 80.*

JACK SULLIVAN

Having borrowed motifs from H. G. Wells for **The Andromeda Strain** and from Mary Shelley for **The Terminal Man**, Michael Crichton has now attempted to do the same with medieval sources [in **Eaters of the Dead: The Manuscript of Ibn Fadlan, Relating His Experiences with the Northmen in A.D. 922**]. Taking as his point of departure an obscure 10th-century Arab travelogue by Ibn Fadlan, Crichton's new "sword and sorcery" novel chronicles Ibn's kidnapping by the Vikings and his role in helping them combat a primitive race of cannibals who are devouring the inhabitants of King Rothgar's meade hall. The tale is strongly reminiscent of *Beowulf*: Crichton even names his doomed hero Buliwyf.

Academics sometimes forget that *Beowulf* is, above all, a good monster story. Grendel is a deadly, but undefined personification of evil, a half-human creature with an indeterminate number of limbs, who never speaks. **Eaters of the Dead** experiments with the opposite technique of evoking terror through exact, reportorial detail. The results are diverting but disappointing: Crichton's moribund cavemen are remarkably tame, even for cannibals.

Part of the problem lies in the thinness of Crichton's prose. He warns us in the introduction that his persona's tone "is that of a tax auditor, not a bard; an anthropologist, not a dramatist." This is a cruelly accurate description. Ibn's account of distant travels and Norse mores is so relentlessly prosaic, so devoid of subtlety and imagery, that the reader can only sympathize with Ibn's Viking companions, who continually grumble about his sparse imagination.

As if to compensate for his undernourished style, Crichton stuffs his tale with learned minutiae; we are offered a scholarly introduction, editorial insertions, footnotes, an appendix and a bibliography. A fetish for hardware of one sort or another has always been apparent in his books, and this novel is no exception . . . : he inflates his new narrative with a densely footnoted apparatus of anthropological and literary scholarship. Like the text, the commentary derives from both

real and bogus sources. Footnotes frequently interrupt the tale—occasionally filling half the page. . . . After a while, this straining toward verisimilitude becomes a pedantic mannerism, a puzzle that the reader wearies of piecing together.

Taking his cue from Vladimir Nabokov and John Barth, Crichton sometimes parodies scholarship by concocting exotic sources. . . . Crichton's put-ons, unlike Nabokov's, are rarely imaginative enough to amuse the reader who lacks inside information. They function mainly as padding, a means of making a short story look like a novel.

If Crichton's humor is mild at best, the serious speculation which constitutes the novel's appendix is downright debilitating. Here we find a summary of all the arguments in an "academic debate" over whether the "eaters of the dead" were pristine Neanderthal men or retarded *Homo sapiens*. This long-winded addendum dissipates what little mystery and menace these frustrated creatures are allowed to evoke in the novel. Killed off, in the final chapters by the Vikings, they are finally buried by the academics.

> *Jack Sullivan, in a review of "Eaters of the Dead," in* The New York Times Book Review, *April 25, 1976, p. 22.*

RICHARD R. LINGEMAN

After steeping himself in Victoriana in **The Great Train Robbery** the last time out, Michael Crichton turns to Vikingiana for **Eaters of the Dead.** Mr. Crichton leans heavily on an actual travel journal by Ibn Fadlan, an Arab from Baghdad who traveled through Turkey and Russia in the year 922.

Mr. Crichton involves Ibn Fadlan with a group of brawny, wenching Norsemen he has met up with at a camp along the Volga. It seems that a Norse king is troubled by creatures known as wendols—ugly hairy things that eat the dead—and his son begs Buliwyf, leader of the Norsemen, to break off his own travels and return for a sort of police action. Promised that his name will surely be in the sagas if he undertakes this heroically difficult mission, Buliwyf agrees. . . .

What had been a Marco Poloesque travel journal shifts plot gears into a sort of remake of *The Magnificent Seven,* as Buliwyf's terrible 13 busy themselves fortifying the King's demesne and ultimately engaging their horrendous foe. Mr. Crichton's story jogs along smoothly and mindlessly, narrated in an archaic style meant to suggest the original, consisting mainly of a lot of verilies strewn about. . . . He also appends some mock-scholarly footnotes—to pad out his rather slim tale, truth to tell, but further confusing the reader as to just what is verily Viking and what is verily Crichton.

> *Richard R. Lingeman, "Novels for Our Times," in* The New York Times, *June 4, 1976, p. 22.*

JOHN PYM

[Crichton once] admitted to a particular admiration for the documentary conviction of Len Deighton's novel *The Ipcress File.* Whether or not Crichton would now endorse the extremes of documentary realism espoused by this school of spy/thriller writing, the fact remains that the subtext of scientific fact (or forecast) which forms the basis of his own novels, **The Andromeda Strain, Westworld** and **The Terminal**

Man, has proved the most consistent strength of their subsequent movie adaptations.

Westworld, which Crichton himself directed, was an awkward apprentice movie, but one which was at least partially salvaged by the ingenuity of its script and the feeling that, despite the caper-ish setting, the notion of cognitive robots was certainly plausible. Crichton is a quick student . . . , and *Coma,* only the second film he has directed for the cinema, proves that he has learned from the mistakes of *Westworld.* The new film, adapted by Crichton from a novel by Robin Cook, combines dry humour and documentary realism in an imperilled-Pauline yarn, finely calculated not to overstretch audience credulity.

In a Boston hospital an anaesthetist (played by a genuine doctor) gives a breakneck rundown of an anaesthetic console for the benefit of a couple of medical students. The man rattles on with professional conviction: we may not understand—and it is not Crichton's purpose that we should—all that is being explained, but before the narrative gets under way we are made to believe in the fictional truth of this gleaming modern hospital. During the ensuing operation, all is unhurried, practised dexterity. We are lulled into a state of confidence; there is no goriness, and the feeling of discreet normality is underlined. It transpires, of course, that all is very far from well in this most hallowed sanctuary of American medicine. The patient goes into a coma and dies, supposedly from an adverse reaction to the anaesthetic; and, after the results of the post mortem disappear into the confidential recesses of a computer, the woman's body is taken to the monolithic Jefferson Institute, a government foundation for research into the care of comatose patients.

An exemplary member of the hospital staff, and one who by her diligent seriousness personifies the hospital itself, is our surgeon heroine, Dr. Susan Wheeler. Although she has a lover, Mark Bellows, a doctor preoccupied with hospital politics, Susan is the almost exclusive focus of our attention: probing for the reasons for the death of her best friend during the opening operation, she gradually uncovers a conspiracy to murder a random but steady stream of patients. (p. 193)

The film is admirably plotted. Its climaxes are carefully spaced, with dashes of cathartic humour, such as when Susan escapes from the man sent to kill her in the hospital by burying him under a pile of polythene-wrapped corpses, strung up like sides of meat in a refrigerator. Its punctuating pauses, such as Susan and Mark's brief idyll in the New England countryside, are never unnecessarily prolonged. And its effects are judiciously restrained—a hall full of comatose patients at the Jefferson Institute, suspended aloft by wires, is used specifically as a divergent ploy, a convincing example for a group of visiting doctors that the institute is caring for the chronically sick rather than acting as a conduit for global deals in human innards. *Coma* skims along with an audacious, good-natured artifice, never really threatening us with the proposition that spare-part surgery could in fact lead to a hospital director, frustrated by the legal constraints on euthanasia, losing his reason and murdering appendicectomy cases.

Coma is in some ways a pleasingly old-fashioned movie. It reaffirms the virtues of a logical plot, an identifiable milieu, characters shoe-horned into the action. Without the Hitchcockian concern with psychological motivation, it nevertheless has something of Hitchcock's sleight of hand, something

of his taste for pleasing symmetry. Aiming to please rather than horrify, it can show a pathologist nonchalantly slicing up a human brain as if it were a ham in such a way that it does not turn our stomachs. Talking about the film's making, Crichton said: 'By the time this picture is finished, I will have more than doubled my previous directing experience. . . . I have a certain sense of being in my infancy now—and that's exciting.' *Coma* conveys this excitement. (pp. 193-94)

John Pym, in a review of "Coma," in Sight and Sound, *Vol. 47, No. 3, Summer, 1978, pp. 193-94.*

HARRY M. GEDULD

Edwin S. Porter's *The Great Train Robbery* (1903) was one of the major events in film history. . . . Seventy-six years later, director Michael Crichton has come up with another picture of the same title. Based on Crichton's own novel, [*The Great Train Robbery*] is by no means an attempt to remake Porter's "classic," and there is no likelihood that anyone will consider it a landmark in film history; but it is, in its own way, an intriguing picture that deservedly ranks among the cinema's best offerings for 1979.

Crichton's film can be classified as a caper movie, that is, a thriller in which the commission of a crime (generally a robbery) is treated as a light-hearted escapade. Caper movies are usually concerned with contemporary criminal exploits; but—quite exceptionally—*The Great Train Robbery* is set in mid-Victorian England, and it deals with a theft of gold bullion intended to support the Crimean War. The first half of the picture focuses on the exploits of master-criminal Edward Pierce and his gang in securing wax impressions of four keys that can unlock a Chubb safe aboard a locomotive. The second half concentrates on the actual robbery (supposedly the first to involve a moving train) and its aftermath, in which Pierce is arrested, tried, and sentenced; but then he contrives to make a brilliant daylight escape—to the resounding applause of the London mob.

Visually, *The Great Train Robbery* is sheer delight. It is, unquestionably, the most vivid evocation of Victorian London ever to grace the motion picture screen. This is due partly to Crichton's keen eye for significant detail . . . , and partly to the recurrent and quite deliberate suggestions—in color, composition, and subject—of such Victorian artists as Frith, Landseer, and the Pre-Raphaelites. It would not surprise me in the least if this film inspired a resurgence of interest in the currently démodé painting of that period.

Aside from its stunning decorative qualities, the film holds the attention with several gripping action sequences. In one, an accomplice makes a perilous escape over the high, spiked walls of Newgate gaol while a public hanging is in progress in the courtyard below. . . . [Another] sequence, the most exciting of all, takes place on the moving train when the hero makes his hazardous way to the bullion over a dozen carriage rooftops and under a score of low-slung bridges.

Each of these episodes has a vital place in the overall scheme that Pierce ingeniously and relentlessly pursues, regardless of the many obstacles that are placed in his path. He spares no one, least of all himself, in realizing his objective. Of shrewd intelligence, he operates unscrupulously with skill and determination in a chaotic society that is riddled with hypocrisies and absurdities. In the great age of propriety he has no respect for respectability. "No respectable gentleman can be that respectable," he says in one scene as he proceeds to uncover and exploit the secret vice of a bourgeois victim. Pierce himself never bothers to tell the truth or allows himself to be caught in the act of lying. He has no morals, no values, and no respect for his fellowmen. He operates profitably on the assumption that everyone is corruptible and no one is totally trustworthy. In the face of all this he is cheered by the mob. . . . What enables Pierce to defy the law, to survive, and to flourish, and what most endears him to his followers and admirers are, of course, those very qualities that have turned many power-hungry men into dictators. He is audacious, determined, and totally self-interested. But he has no thirst for power. His motive for the robbery redeems him from fanaticism. For when the judge pompously asks Pierce to confess why he "conceived, planned, and executed this dastardly crime," he makes his one concession to truth and answers with unequivocal simplicity: "I needed the money." In a mercenary world this is perhaps the only motive that could humanize that dubious quality known as singleness of mind.

> *Harry M. Geduld, in a review of "The Great Train Robbery," in* The Humanist, *Vol. XXXIX, No. 3, May-June, 1979, p. 65.*

HAROLD HAYES

[In *Congo*], Karen, Peter, Munro and Amy parachute into the Zaire rain forest in pursuit of diamonds believed to be hidden in the lost city of Zinj. Chased by cannibals, hippopotamuses and an unknown species of gorilla, they find the diamonds only to lose them to the ebullitions of an active volcano, from which they themselves escape inside a makeshift balloon. As plots go, even in the jungle genre for which the rules are not too strict, this one places ahead of *Sheena, Queen of the Jungle,* perhaps, but not by much.

But wait. We know from the jacket that the author holds a medical degree from Harvard, which is more than you can say for the author of *Sheena.* And at the end of *Congo* there is a no-joke bibliography. Moreover, whereas the characters of Karen, Peter and Munro seem to be more or less interchangeable, Amy is a gorilla. So, whatever you may expect from a novel, it is apparent right away that this is intended to be something more than an extended screen treatment floated in hard covers as the first phase in preproduction planning for a wall-to-wall blockbuster.

Congo is the result of some serious reading by an intelligent man, reflecting on the endless possibilities and permutations of communication. If it is language that distinguishes man from beast and makes possible the accumulation of knowledge, what can happen when language is conveyed to nonhuman forms? To apes on the one hand and to computers on the other? And once they begin to talk back, what is the difference between animal intelligence and artificial intelligence? . . .

While literarily vapid and scientifically more anthropomorphic than *Dumbo,* Mr. Crichton's novel tries to get at the ironies of a situation in which three human beings find themselves dependent for their survival upon their resourcefulness in manipulating the cognitive powers of the gorilla Amy through the analytic assistance of a computer. Having con-

trived such a boggler, who has time to worry about character development?

Ferocious animals and human flesh-eaters become necessary props to move Mr. Crichton closer to the meatier questions that intrigue him. If apes can talk to us in our idiom, what can they tell us about their own language? More crucially under the circumstances, if an ape raised among humans and taught to talk by humans finds itself suddenly in confrontation with a hitherto unknown species of ape, which is hostile to humans, where does the first ape's loyalty lie? An interesting and all-new moral choice, particularly in light of the avidity of humans in clearing the world's rain forests, which include the habitats of apes, at the rate of 50 acres a minute. (p. 13)

Still another question raised by this book is why Mr. Crichton would have chosen so puerile a form to explore such matters. Did he need a simple-minded plot to provide room for the play of interesting ideas? Or did his preoccupation with interesting ideas force him into a simple-minded plot? Pretty depressing either way you look at it. The tactic of including so tempting a bibliography—presumably to lend an aura of authenticity to this fever dream—proves a dangerous strategy, too. The tribal sociology comes from Colin Turnbull, Amy from Francine Patterson's Koko, and so on. The books listed in the back are better than the book they are meant to bolster.

But maybe, after all, this book should be read as nothing more than a film-maker's exercise. Turnbull, Patterson, Herman Kahn, E. O. Wilson and the like are, in this case, the entrepreneur's ticket to mystifying, newly opened lines of inquiry, a quick pass at some questions we haven't quite managed to articulate for ourselves. Our uncertainty about these questions makes them all the more compelling. Thrilling, even. *Congo* is Michael Crichton's pop-science offering to Hollywood's World of Tomorrow—to the mythology of a future so close and yet so unsettling as to be perceived safely only through imaginings formed first by comic strips. (pp. 13, 53)

> *Harold Hayes, "If Apes Could Talk," in* The New York Times Book Review, *December 7, 1980, pp. 13, 53.*

JUSTIN BLEWITT

Michael Crichton has done it again. His first novel, ***The Andromeda Strain,*** was an exciting, fast-paced adventure. . . . It rang very true and at the same time was a terrific page-turner. That's a rare combination—as rare as the species of gorillas that dominate his new novel.

Congo contains all the best elements of the earlier book, in a more classic adventure story setting. Here it's a trek to the darkest part of the Dark Continent in search of diamonds and the Lost City of Zinj. Again the heroes are scientists (now that's fiction): Dr. Peter Elliot, a specialist in primate research who brings with him on the journey his laboratory-raised gorilla, Amy, to whom he has taught more than 600 words of sign language, the brainy and beautiful Karen Ross, another Ph.D., who heads the expedition, and the great white hunter, "Captain" Charles Munro. Outfitted with all the trappings of 20th Century Computer Technology, including satellite communications, they encounter everything you'd expect to find in a jungle book, except Tarzan. . . . Fear not, however. For every classic crisis, science has an answer. Join the caravan. It's really a lot of fun. Unless, of course, it really did happen. . . .

Justin Blewitt, in a review of "Congo," in Best Sellers, *Vol. 40, No. 11, February, 1981, p. 388.*

THOMAS A. SEBEOK

Rework *King Solomon's Mines,* the famous "faithful but unpretending record of a remarkable adventure" dedicated "to all the big and little boys who read it", mix in some modern ingredients—hocus-pocus computer gadgetry; Amy, a counterfeit gorilla that habitually uses sign language . . . ; and a mutant gorilla species, as lethal as it is biologically unlikely, a troop of "attack animals, trained for cunning and viciousness"—and you get a commercially viable screenplay (the movie rights were, in fact, sold before Michael Crichton wrote the first word of *Congo*), if hardly more than a pastime novel. In brief, *Congo* is a machine-tooled adventure story, cast in the lurid spirit and manner of Rider Haggard.

The principal characters are a cardboard trio of human protagonists, pitted against the murderous band of gorillas; and the mediating "bilingual" chimera, Amy. These figures are programmed to shove the plot forward, in conflict with a host of human, animal, and other obstacles, at rapid pace; but the story is of a depressing dottiness characteristic, alas, of the kind of science-fiction which is centred on semiotic problems.

There is nothing more significant at stake in this piece of fiction than the doctrine of verisimilitude: Aristotle's concept of *tō eikos,* and the closely related notion of the imitation of nature. Following Chapter Nine of the *Poetics,* it is Crichton's business not "to tell what happened but the kind of things that would happen". The impossible is allowable, so long as it is convincing; and the implausible permissible, since (as Aristotle says in Chapter Twenty-Five) it is probable that some improbable actions will occur. Crichton is licensed to offend against what is known to be known if, and only if, there is some overriding artistic reason for him to do so. Ursula K. Le Guin laid down a pertinent principle of science fiction in ruling that the writer "must not flout the evidence of science . . .". In some quarters, this is known as the "automatic translator" gimmick: if you have to communicate with aliens—or animals—in a hurry, use the Universal Translator, an ad hoc magic coding machine. Amy incarnates one variant of this over-used device.

Crichton has obviously conducted some research into communication, both animal and electronic. He appends four pages of authentic references on these subjects. . . . But it is not clear whether he can evaluate objectively what he claims to have read, and he has not read nearly enough. True, A. F. Dixson's *The Natural History of the Gorilla* appeared too late for him to take into account, but he either misunderstood or preferred to suppress the conclusions in Herbert S. Terrace's works, some of which he does cite, and has completely ignored the by now voluminous and devastatingly critical literature showing that loose talk about ape-talk is based at once on naïve theoretical preconceptions and pathetically poor experimental procedures, the results of which were very largely perpetuated in distorted form and so massaged into the popular consciousness by dint of media hype.

It is not often that a thriller, such as this, gets reviewed in the austere pages of *The Wall Street Journal,* but Raymond Sokolov went to that trouble in this year's January 14 issue, under the title, "Separating Fact from Fiction". . . . Like Sokolov, I was upset by having caught Crichton out as either a sloppy researcher or a perverse prevaricator: once he lets you down on so crucial a figure as Amy, on whose linguistic skill the basic plot hinges, how can you trust his veracity about the rest of the scientific and technological minutiae which he heaps on and on, page after page? These details, in the aggregate, should add up to a convincing, comprehensive view of his imaginary world, but, for me, the magic was dispelled with the early introduction of Amy: not because she is impossible—although that she is all right—but because she is so plainly a phony.

What, then, are Amy's functions in this book? She accompanies an American expedition back to Africa—where she was born, although she was linguistically trained (where else?) in the California Bay Area—in search of a diamond mine (the MacGuffin) in the lost City of Zinj (which Haggard fans will promptly recognize as the Place of Death). Control of the mine will alter the future of warfare. The killer apes that guard the diamonds of Zinj must be got in touch with. Amy serves as a convenient intermediary. She is also one of two heroines in the book. The other, Dr. Karen Ross, is a "genuine mathematical prodigy", "logical to a fault", young and attractive, but glacial and ruthless. Amy indicates on first meeting Karen "No like woman no like Amy no like go away away." . . . The relationship of the two females continues to be tense, but the antagonism becomes strangely muted as the journey progresses into the heart of darkness. At the conclusion of *Congo,* Karen joins the US Geological Survey, Amy joins a Zaire gorilla troop (regulation, not outlaw), and the romance ends with her bearing an offspring whom she appears to be busy teaching sign language in the jungle.

A story-teller may, as Aristotle pronounced, depart from the representation of reality if (among other considerations) he follows "common opinion". In our society, common opinion tends to be moulded by the media, to which Crichton is closely attuned. According to the media, some apes—as well as dogs, dolphins, maybe even horses—can be transubstantiated from the baser metal of which speechless creatures are thought to be composed into the golden endowment which language capacity alone is widely believed to vouchsafe. In the authentic world of science, as opposed to alchemy, no such transmutation has ever taken place, contrary to what you imagine you have learned from doctored films shown on TV, or read in magazines. . . .

Consequently, a literary form has come forth, stemming from an ancient tradition which conjures up talking animals as props in order to actuate the author's narrative intent. . . . The genre I have in mind took a decisive turn towards science-fiction, beginning perhaps with Mary Shelley's *Frankenstein,* whose endearing monster rediscovered the endless delights of semiotics. . . .

[Possession of the science of language] is typically imputed to whatever species of animal is currently the focus of public attention. Thus, throughout the 1960s, porpoises held the centre of the stage, as in Robert Merle's astutely framed *The Day of the Dolphin* (1967). . . . In the 1970s, into the present decade, and who knows how far into the rest of the century, the chosen species has become African Great Apes. Peter Dickinson's elegant detective story, *The Poison Oracle,* appearing in 1974, set a milestone in the development of chatty chimps, as did, in quite another mode and mood, T.

Coraghessan Boyle's short story, "Descent of Man", at once foul and pulverizing.

The first major garrulous gorilla was a Uganda-born male, devised by John Goulet, for his wondrously imagined and brilliantly executed *roman à clef, Oh's Profit* (1975; retitled *The Human Ape* . . .). Goulet's plot is at least as entertaining as Crichton's, but there are also issues of much consequence at stake, among them, human nature and the nature of language. The story of Oh is profoundly moving: it grips while it instructs. Where Amy makes a mockery of authenticity, Oh is true to the essentiality of man. It is a pity that Crichton's gorilla is bound to prevail over Goulet's, and that most people will continue to credit the factitious over the real. As Oh decides midway through Goulet's underestimated novel, "from now on he would not willingly misuse language, lest it misuse him . . .".

Thomas A. Sebeok, "Amy and the Apes," in The Times Literary Supplement, No. 4085, July 17, 1981, p. 802.

MICHAEL COLLINS

[Crichton's] first book, *The Andromeda Strain,* was a best-selling novel about a virulent organism of extraterrestrial origin that threatened life on earth. *Sphere* is similar in that an extraterrestrial presence is again involved, but this one lies 1,000 feet below the surface of the Pacific Ocean, where a gigantic spacecraft has been discovered. The U.S. Navy, by measuring the coral encrustations on it, estimates it has been there for at least 300 years.

A team is assembled to descend to an underwater habitat placed next to the strange craft. In addition to the naval commander and support staff, a group of civilian scientists are included. Ted Fielding, an astrophysicist, seems to worry more about quotable quotes and desirable camera angles than he does his science. Harry Adams, a black mathematician, is cocksure, impatient, arrogant—and very smart. Beth Halpern is a weight-lifting biologist who vacillates between feminist hostility and a kittenish sexuality. . . . But Norman Johnson is our main man, a 53-year-old psychologist not too keen on the idea of being locked up 1,000 feet down. He's a bit too much of a nerd for my taste. . . . Norman starts off as a detached and somewhat supercilious observer, but when the wild things begin, he's forced into the middle of the action.

Unlocking, entering, and searching the spacecraft is like opening a series of nested boxes, each exposing another riddle. The final one is a "large, perfectly polished silver sphere about thirty feet in diameter." How to open it?

Having a spaceship immersed in water gives the author an opportunity to explain the widest range of scientific and technological issues, everything from black holes in space to the effect of pressure on the human body. Crichton is adept at it, especially when he can call upon his medical training, and he uses imagery the lay person can easily follow. (pp. 1, 14)

[Crichton's] details, rather than the characters, make [*Sphere*] seem more believable. Although toward the end I did become sort of fond of old Norman, most of the others seemed cut out of cardboard. In particular, Crichton's treatment of the captain of the habitat annoyed. The man is stupid as an ox and spends most of his time screaming out orders at the top of his lungs. Apparently, all he cares about is discovering a new weapon for the Pentagon. Too stereotypical, not believable.

The plot? Well, that's the key to the enjoyment of this book: whether you can go along with it, or find it just too much. I don't want to tell enough to spoil it, but would you believe that attacks by giant squid are the least bizarre of the fast and furious onslaught of emergencies that confront the four scientists? Early in the book, Crichton leavens it with a bit of humor. . . . But toward the end, there's no time for fun, its all WHAM! BOOM! BASH! for Norman and company.

It's a short book, and the pages turn quickly. For a little while, suspend your disbelief, and put yourself 1,000 feet down. Suddenly, your computer terminal lights up, and there is a message that emanates from the spacecraft: "I am coming," it says. (p. 14)

Michael Collins, "Summer Thrillers from Three Masters," in Book World—The Washington Post, June 14, 1987, pp. 1, 14.

JAMES M. KAHN

[In *Sphere,* an] American sailing vessel laying phone cable in the remote Pacific runs into a snag. Navy exploration reveals, buried on a shelf 1,000 feet beneath the surface, what appears to be a gigantic spaceship—completely intact, showing no signs of corrosion . . . and at least 300 years old. . . .

Startling questions arise from the very beginning: Is the craft alien or man-made? From our past, or from our future? And what is the nature of the mysterious hollow sphere they discover on board?

Crichton keeps us guessing at every turn, in his best work since *The Andromeda Strain.* Each chapter end reveals some new clue or poses some new threat that compels the reader to read on. And each new twist builds the pace with careful precision.

Precision is, in fact, a Crichton hallmark. His works give a sense of meticulous researching—no surprise, coming from a research MD. In *Sphere,* his details range from integral . . . to casual. . . . (p. 1)

But such digressions are not merely entertaining in science fiction of this sort. They are essential to establishing an environment of believability, so that when the inevitable speculative leaps *are* made (and there are a couple big ones here), the reader eagerly tags along. Somehow it's easier to buy the concept of *extraterrestrial* intelligence from an author who shows a little terrestrial intelligence himself.

Crichton shows plenty. Philosophical discussions abound, covering theories of extraplanetary life, black holes, human knowledge and behavior. The latter is actually a recurring theme, explored from the point of view of psychological Norman Johnson—the man who chose the other mission specialists, yet who remains under constant attack by them for being a champion of the "soft science" of psychology, in the face of their death-struggle against the considerably "harder" forces of inexplicable deep-sea monsters. (pp. 1, 13)

Terror—the terror of death, and of the essentially unknowable—is at the core of this book. Terror, and how to confront it. "Understanding is a delaying tactic," muses mission psychologist Johnson. "Only people who are afraid of the water want to understand it. Other people jump in and get wet." So Crichton's academic credentials may be impeccable—but only in letting them lapse does his researcher become a hero in this tale.

There are more than sonar echoes of Verne's *20,000 Leagues Under the Sea* here—and that's another charm of the novel. One of the subliminal ways Crichton achieves this is by titling every chapter . . .—a literary device that is rather out of fashion, and rather evocative of all those grand adventure yarns we read as kids. And, not incidentally, rather effective.

There are some problems with the book: Crichton's dialogue tends to be a bit stilted at times, his characters a bit broad (there is the self-hating feminist; there is the weapon-mongering military man)—but these criticisms seem, at the end, pale in context, the context being that Crichton is a story-teller, and a damned good one. (p. 13)

James M. Kahn, in a review of "Sphere," in Los Angeles Times Book Review, *July 12, 1987, pp. 1, 13.*

ROBIN McKINLEY

Michael Crichton's new novel, **Sphere,** kept me happy for two hours sitting in a grounded plane while the mechanics or whatever they were tried to decide whether the plane would ever fly again. The answer came up no, whereupon **Sphere** continued to keep me happy for another half an hour, standing in line to have my ticket rerouted. No one can ask more of a thriller, except maybe that it be a little longer; this one ran out sometime before my involuntary tour of the major airports of the United States.

Norman Johnson is a psychologist who is occasionally called in by the Federal Aviation Administration to help survivors of plane crashes cope with shock and trauma. He receives a mysterious call from the military and is whisked away to a bit of Pacific Ocean very far from anything. . . .

It's not a plane crash this time—or not exactly. Years ago Johnson had been involved in a top-secret Government program to draw up a plan for dealing with an alien invasion. Johnson needed the money, so he kept a straight face as he wrote a paper called "Recommendations for the Human Contact Team to Interact with Unknown Life Forms (ULF)." But he thought it was a joke. Now he has been dragged to the middle of the Pacific to be a part of a human contact team. . . .

Part of the fun of **Sphere** is that it keeps you going even when you're pretty sure of what will happen next. Suffice it to say that the title comes from a mysterious object that is found inside the spaceship, an object that may or may not contain alien life, and that may or may not be responsible for the sudden, terrifying havoc that is wreaked on the contact team. And, of course, just when things are getting seriously out of hand, a bad storm blows up on the ocean's surface and all the ships have to pull out, leaving our team stranded without recourse 1,000 dark, hostile, claustrophobic feet down, with monsters stalking them.

The novel's point of view is Johnson's and he is perhaps a bit slow about figuring out what the enemy is—but psychologists, like many of us, may have blind spots about answers that cut a little too close to the bone. Johnson's grappling

with that enemy doesn't have quite the climactic excitement that it might. But the suspense is real—they *are* going to make it, aren't they? You *know* they're going to make it. Or do you? The last 10 pages are exactly what they should be. Take this one with you for your next long plane ride.

Robin McKinley, "Anybody Home?" in The New York Times Book Review, *July 12, 1987, p. 18.*

L. J. DAVIS

It is remarkably difficult to dislike a book by Michael Crichton—some would say it is impossible. . . . Although he has never exactly burned the barns of literature, Crichton has a fine hand with pacing and dialogue, plot and detail, and there does not appear to be an ironic bone in his body, neither does there seem to be a mean one. In his potboilers, Michael Crichton gives good value, or at least tries to, and it is a quality not to be sniffed at.

Now, however, Crichton has perpetrated **Travels,** a book whose title is self-explanatory. The real Michael Crichton, not some improved fictional stand-in, has taken some actual journeys and recorded his findings. This is perilous ground. Any experienced travel editor can tell you that such adventures usually fall into two broad categories. On the one hand, there are the oeuvres of those well-to-do citizens who have either killed or neutralized their spouses, filled the ensuing free time with travel, and produced monographs on the subject of the West Palm Beach Nobody Knows. . . . On the other hand, there are those travellers, usually but not exclusively British, who prowl the globe in search of personal enlightenment, exotic locales, and geopolitical and anthropological wisdom. Michael Crichton, like Paul Theroux, falls somewhere between these two stools.

On occasion, Crichton can be insightful. . . . At other times, however, he lapses into the usual bromides about the tension between urban man and the natural order, which is not only tiresome but misleading. Crichton is not Urban Man—any denizen of Chicago or Brooklyn could teach him volumes about handling a street tough he encounters in Jamaica—but Suburban Man, a child of privileged circumstances who did well for himself in later life, and who purchases adventures from travel agents in hopes of adding an elusive dimension to his life. I do not think it churlish to suggest that Michael Crichton could learn vastly more about himself—while vastly expanding his store of useful memories—by volunteering his services at the nearest soup kitchen.

Indeed, this insight takes on the force of prophecy roughly halfway through the book when Crichton more or less abandons his attempts to gain meaningful insights from the deer of Malaysia (and also the bees) and launches himself, all innocence and superficial thinking, into the psychic absurdities of Southern California. There is spoon bending, entertainingly but not insightfully described. There is channeling. There is much talk of auras. Nowhere, however, is there any suggestion that this is the way a civilization ends, with magical thinking and travel agents, amiable chatter and absorption in a self that, alas, asks no serious questions. The address of the soup kitchen will be furnished on request. (p. 6)

L. J. Davis, "Touring the World Mostly on the Surface," in Chicago Tribune—Books, *April 17, 1988, pp. 6-7.*

PATRICIA BOSWORTH

The novelist Michael Crichton toys with all sorts of faiths and superstitions in [*Travels,* a] diverse, more or less chronological collection of pieces. . . . [He] participates in "energy work" at the Institute of Mental Physics in the Lucerne Valley desert in California and discovers in himself a kind of healing body energy hitherto "unknown to medical science."

This energy is a vital force within us, he says, and it is distributed at various points in our anatomy (heart, ribs, forehead). It affects our sexuality, our emotions, our sense of survival. It can be transferred from one person to another by "laying on hands." . . .

Dr. Crichton approaches "energy work" and everything else in this book like a scientist; he once taught anthropology at Cambridge University and is a Harvard-trained physician. As a matter of fact, he spends the first 90 pages of *Travels* reminiscing about his medical school days, and these are among the most startling and informative pages, especially the ones that deal with the doctor-student relationship. You'll learn a lot about sickness and death and the cynical attitude many doctors take toward their patients. (They appear more interested in diseases than in healing.)

I particularly liked the piece that revolves around an autopsy. "It is not easy to cut through a human head with a hacksaw," Dr. Crichton writes, "the blade kept snagging the skin." His descriptions of the competition between medical students are brutal. "In the labs, if you asked the person at the next bench a question, he'd tell you the wrong answer in the hope you would make a mistake, or, even better, start a fire."

Dr. Crichton had the dubious distinction of starting more lab fires than anyone else. . . . Eventually, writing became more interesting to him than medicine. . . . In 1969, while completing his last year at Harvard Medical School, he published *The Andromeda Strain* (about germ warfare) under his own name. It was an instant best seller and sold to the movies. When he subsequently left medicine, one of his teachers commented, "I knew you'd quit. Your fantasies are too strong."

But it was more than that. Dr. Crichton believed that living by his wits would keep him free to change his life whenever he wanted something he could never do if he remained a doctor. He moved to California; he wrote more best sellers, such as . . . *Terminal Man,* and he directed movies like *Westworld* and *The Great Train Robbery* (which he also wrote). By the time he had reached 30, he was rich and famous and confused. Success hadn't made him happy. So he left Hollywood and began traveling to exotic places like Shangri-La and the remote highlands of New Guinea where he sought out "direct experiences." The bulk of *Travels* is an account of these.

Since his is also a spiritual journey, a journey into self-awareness, I was disappointed when Dr. Crichton . . . chose to remain so shadowy and unclaimable on the page. Not only that, but many of the people close to him are mere blurs. . . . For him, thought, not anecdote, humanizes experience. Plenty of conflicts and dramas occur in his life, but very few of them are completely fleshed out. That's disappointing.

However, in spite of myself, I was ultimately swept away, not just by his richly informed mind, but his driving curiosity. Satisfying your curiosity takes guts. Michael Crichton may

be overly detached, but he seems bound and determined to explore every single mystery in the universe.

At first when he traveled, he would hang on to his Walkman, portable computer and notebooks. Eventually he decided to travel unencumbered. . . .

And just as his manner of traveling shifted, so did the focus of his concentration. He grew less interested in the look of the gaudy temples of Bangkok and more involved with their dark silences, the rituals, the prayers. And although he kept notes on his continued need to take risks—diving through clouds of sharks off Tahiti, a nightmare struggle to the top of Mt. Kilimanjaro—his "inner travels"—exploring the psychic and spiritual worlds—took on as much significance: he practiced yoga, went on retreats, meditated, fasted; he experienced altered states.

Everybody, says Dr. Crichton, has a degree of psychic ability. And such experiences, he maintains, can be reproduced by anyone who tries, that it is just another way of saying "I'm not crazy." His ultimate concern is that we recognize why we need the insights of the mystic as much as we need the insights of the scientist.

There's plenty of both in *Travels.*

Patricia Bosworth, "Touring the Altered States," in The New York Times Book Review, *June 26, 1988, p. 30.*

JOSEPH HONE

[Crichton's experiences in *Travels*] are certainly a rich and unusual mix. And with his scientific training what he has to say about psychic phenomena in general is all the more valuable. He was convinced by them because he experienced them. And his accounts of these events . . . are both believable and quite captivating—as when a novice in these visionary matters, and failing to see anything for a long while, he suddenly sees the mountains exploding in "big bursts of orange powder". Thereafter, finding the right attitude of meditative relaxation, he cannot stop seeing things: mysterious energies in the shape of brilliantly coloured sparks, streaks or cotton-wool fuzz. . . .

All riveting stuff, which he sums up in a closely argued postscript (a piece with distinct echoes of C. P. Snow's "Two Cultures" essay) where he says, "These inborn gifts, or trained procedures, lead to other kinds of knowing. . . . And before you dismiss [them] as outright fraud or fantasy it seems useful to experience them at first hand." . . . Fair comment, especially coming as it does from someone so intellectually rigorous, for Crichton thinks and writes in a concise, hardheaded manner—unlike the dreamy, gushy-limp prose which most disciples employ in their testaments on the paranormal.

What he is not so clear about is how all this has helped him. Does he, having crossed into the nether world of the irrational, still suffer from irrational daytime terrors? Probably not, one supposes. Though what he does say on this may be more valuable. From having been a quintessential over-achieving Western man, taught "to control everything around me . . . living in a frantic, active way for 30 years", he comes to accept things as they are, visible and invisible, without frenzy.

His other geographic travels, though told in rather too flashy a style, with something of a Hemingway urge to put hair on his chest, are no less interesting—to a wild tribe in Borneo, to Kenya and a near contretemps with an elephant, dangerous scuba diving over a sunken wreck in the Caribbean. Finally, the long section on his training and career as a doctor in the grim public wards of a Boston hospital—and on why he abandoned this career—is perhaps the best thing in the book: a horrifying account of United States public medicine, with its attendant nightmares of lousy (literally) lying-in hospitals and wards of uncared for, gibbering psychiatric cases.

"It is not easy to cut through a human head with a hacksaw", he writes of one part of his training. Quite so—especially for someone who, as he admits, was terrified of blood. But this is what the book is really all about—discoveries, victories over fear and self, how one scientific, highly successful Western man goes into the human mind, literally and metaphorically, as well as out among the headhunters in Borneo, faces the worst and overcomes it all, finding in the end nothing so remarkable, or valuable, as simple acceptance and peace.

Joseph Hone, "Into the Nether World," in The Times Literary Supplement, *No. 4464, October 21-27, 1988, p. 1168.*

Don DeLillo

1936-

(Has also written under pseudonym of Cleo Birdwell) American novelist, dramatist, and short story writer.

Widely regarded as a preeminent satirist of modern culture, DeLillo depicts American society as rampant with paranoia and malaise and on the brink of chaos. His fiction displays a preoccupation with the overwhelming influence of the American media and the ritualistic qualities of language, the latter of which he considers the only human means capable of imposing order on random events. Favoring episodic narration and disjointed dialogue over conventionally structured plots, DeLillo combines erudition of an array of disciplines, command of jargon, aphoristic wit, and vivid descriptive powers. DeLillo's work is often compared to that of Thomas Pynchon and Kurt Vonnegut for its black humor and apocalyptic vision.

DeLillo's first novel, *Americana* (1971), recounts the bizarre adventures of a television advertising executive who embarks on a cross-country journey to escape an unsatisfying job and marriage and to discover his identity. His second book, *End Zone* (1972), which attracted substantial critical notice, centers on Gary Harkness, a running back on the Logos College football team who is obsessed with the concept and language of nuclear warfare. Chronicling the exploits of Harkness and his unusually philosophical teammates during one season, *End Zone* examines similarities between football and combat and develops the idea of nuclear war as the ultimate consequence of systems of ordered violence. Thomas R. Edwards observed: "[DeLillo] makes us see football as an efficient illusion of order, a perfecting of reality through organized *language* . . . whose complete and antiseptic coherence is the end of civilization itself, goal and cessation at once." *Great Jones Street* (1973) portrays a rock star's retreat from public performance into the drug underworld and his paranoia as he becomes involved in the search for a potent new experimental narcotic. Some critics interpreted *Great Jones Street* as a cautionary tale of the rock and drug subculture of the 1960s.

In *Ratner's Star* (1976), a satirical, quasi-science fiction novel that has been compared to Pynchon's *Gravity's Rainbow* and Lewis Carroll's *Alice's Adventures in Wonderland,* DeLillo portrays a fourteen-year-old mathematics genius who is employed by a government organization to decode messages from space. Asserting that closed systems of energy in physics are related to closed systems of thought in metaphysics, DeLillo postulates that a combination of the two can create a potentially destructive illusion of an ordered universe. This theory is realized at the conclusion of *Ratner's Star* through the depiction of an apocalyptic nuclear war. Paul Gray contended that DeLillo's aim in this novel "is to show how the codification of phenomena as practiced by scientists leads to absurdity and madness." *Players* (1977) and *Running Dog* (1978) focus on decadent urbanites who seek to avert boredom through espionage, pornography, and terrorism. In these novels, DeLillo suggests that the behavior of his protag-

onists is symptomatic of the spiritual emptiness of American society.

DeLillo's next novel, *The Names* (1982), revolves around a mysterious cult that ritualistically kills people whose names bear the same initials as the place where the murders are committed. An American working as a "risk analyst" for multinational corporations in Greece and the Middle East becomes interested in the cult and tries to discover its motives. According to some critics, *The Names* represents DeLillo's most penetrating investigation of the enigmatic nature of language. *White Noise* (1985), which won the American Book Award for fiction, incorporates such concerns as mortality, the numbing impact of the American media, and fatal effects of technology. In this novel, both Jack Gladney, chairman of Hitler Studies at a midwestern university, and his wife, Babette, have an obsessive fear of dying which is exacerbated when an industrial accident releases a cloud of toxic insecticide. While evacuating their home, Jack is exposed to a lethal dose of the chemical. When he learns that Babette has been taking an illicit medication—which she committed adultery to procure—that eliminates the fear of death, Jack undertakes a desperate search to obtain the drug for himself. Richard Eder commented: "[*White Noise*] is a novel of disintegration, of familiar things hijacked and spoiled, of nature, love and civility leached and estranged. . . . It is a novel of hair-line prophecy, showing a desolate and all-too-believable future in the evidences of an all-too-recognizable present."

In *Libra* (1988), DeLillo weaves historical and invented characters and events to explore the life of Lee Harvey Oswald and the circumstances leading to his assassination of President John F. Kennedy. Employing two nonsynchronous narratives—one tracing Oswald's life from childhood to death, the other detailing the development of a conspiracy to murder the president by vengeful right-wing activists—DeLillo illustrates how random factors can propel an individual into history. DeLillo has also authored the plays *The Engineer of Moonlight* (1979) and *The Day Room* (1986) as well as *Amazons* (1980), a farcical novel about the first woman to play in the National Hockey League that was published under the pseudonym of Cleo Birdwell.

(See also *CLC*, Vols. 8, 10, 13, 27, 39; *Contemporary Authors*, Vols. 81-84; *Contemporary Authors New Revision Series*, Vol. 21; and *Dictionary of Literary Biography*, Vol. 6.)

DAVID BOSWORTH

The constant theme of DeLillo's work, the spiritual vacuum of modern life, is common to much American fiction; but no American writer has captured with his flair the flip and, to my mind, more fascinating side of contemporary despair—how meaninglessness stimulates as well as depresses, how it tempts and challenges the modern imagination. Rather than predictably passive and directionless characters, he gives us latterday spiritual questors. In a world bereft of sanctioned holiness, in a world of adamant relativity, they are mad jazz-monks, improvising their own ceremonies, their own strange gods, scratching frantic liturgical graffiti on the face of the Void.

In *End Zone*, for example, DeLillo's haunting and hilarious examination of college football, the hero's team is populated with young men given to odd exercises in spiritual self-discipline—one-arm pushups for the soul. One teammate memorizes poetry in German, a language he doesn't understand. The hero himself takes long walks in the desert and recites to himself the names of Presidents of the United States. That both of these self-created nonsense rituals are dependent on language is no accident; few authors are so obsessed with the religious and anthropological dimensions of everyday speech—language as display, language as social dance, language as koan or mantra, language serving some purpose beyond the meaning of its constituent words.

In particular, DeLillo has an infallible ear for the absurd inflations of rhetoric, that pseudo-knowledge, that verbal plummage, which so often attend the sects and subsets of American life. He has a comic knack for mimicking, whether in a football coach's half-time speech or an Air Force colonel's press release, the way we strangle our syntax with the graceless neologisms of technology, apparently hoping in the process to borrow some of the intellectual authority ascribed to Science, the twentieth century's minimalist god. But the invitation is not simply to laugh at fools, although laugh we do. Behind the satire lies a more serious and universal point: DeLillo's suspicion that *all* language, that of the poet as well as

the pedant, serves the same desperate and self-defensive purpose. The costume we spin to hide ourselves from our nakedness. The pattern we use to fabricate a home, our imaginary womb in the infinite dark.

In *The Names*, DeLillo's seventh novel, most of his previous preoccupations reappear. Again he explores specific aspects of contemporary life, this time international business and cult fanaticism, and again language itself is central to the book's overall theme.

James Axton, the first-person narrator, has taken a job as a "risk analyst" for an international insurance company. An American stationed in Athens, he has accepted the position to be near his estranged wife, Kathryn, who is living with their son on a small Greek island where she works on a failing archeological dig. It is there, on Kouros, through Kathryn's boss, Owen, that Axton first learns of a wandering cult whose sole act of "religious" celebration is the selection and murder of a seemingly random series of victims. Never content to emphasize one plot thread, the novel keeps shifting, then, between these three realms of activity: Axton's life as an expatriate businessman, including a subplot concerning the CIA and Greek nationalism; his attempt to be reconciled to his wife and son; and finally his pursuit, more mental than physical, of the mysterious cult.

As we have come to expect from him, DeLillo uses the occasions of his novel's plot and setting to inscribe for us a multitude of precise and memorable observations—on old age, on Americans abroad, on airports, pleasure, and second wives. (pp. 29-30)

But when we draw back from this busy, varied canvas, with its plethora of small and vivid points, a larger pattern becomes clear. *The Names* is about "naming," about language, about its irrational, emotive, almost mystical power; about how, beneath the pale skin of their meaning, words link up in a kind of geometric abstract art that soothes our deepest fears and satisfies our most urgent need to rescue order from the chaos of our lives. Owen—whose profession is the study of ancient inscriptions and who has become obsessed with the glyphs themselves, the "shapes" of the letters untranslated, apart from any context or explanation—warns Axton when he asks about the cult, "I wouldn't look for meaning, James." . . .

Time and time again, with perhaps excessive thoroughness but undeniable eloquence, DeLillo impresses upon us his view that what matters about language is its "pattern," its deeper rhythms and syntax, the design behind the signs rather than what they signify. His vision is that of an anthropologist, a cultural relativist, who upon surveying the variety of human societies refuses to endorse one system over the others, stressing instead mankind's unique capacity to make systems at all. All answers, he suggests, all explanations are ultimately false. Meaning is eternally elusive, but the search for meaning, the model worlds we continuously make with our words are all that we have to comfort ourselves—lullabies to mask the great white noise of the universe.

And the test case, the most extreme challenge to our talent for turning the entropy of experience into the arabesque of language, is represented in *The Names* by the cult itself. The apparent "senselessness" of its killing appalls and attracts us. Like Axton's, our minds pursue the members of the cult, desperate to find the hidden design that will explain their actions, believing that if we can just classify them, just find a name for what they do, it will somehow tame the horror we feel. But in an ironic twist, when a system is discovered—the cult is simply matching the initials of its victims' names with the initials of the town where they happen to be staying—our horror is not diminished by being defined; it is instead intensified.

"These killings mock us," Owen concludes. "They mock our need to structure and classify, to build a system against the terror in our souls. They make the system equal to the terror. The means to contend with death has become death."

Our means to contend with death, according to DeLillo, is, of course, language. Words are our defense against the one explanation for events we can never accept: randomness. The awful sacrilege of the cult is to use the very instrument of our protection—our names, our naming—as a weapon against us, just as, on a grander scale, the Nazis used all the instruments of higher civilization—medicine, technology, the intricacies of rational social planning—to perform the most monstrously uncivilized of acts, the maintenance of a bureaucracy of death. This profound if simple observation about the nature of terrorism is just one feature in DeLillo's complex metaphorical examination of contemporary life. Indeed, Axton himself can be seen as emblematic of the author's grim view of modern man: a stranger abroad, lost in a sea of incomprehensible signs, without beliefs, without metaphysical answers, forced by their absence to improvise his own theories, to surround the "bare act" of existence with his own "desperate speculations," aware though that these theories are "mainly for his own comfort," illusions to succor, aware that in the end he'll be "left with nothing"—"nothing signified, nothing meant."

Whether we accept this view as fundamentally true, as DeLillo appears to, or merely as an illusion characteristic of the times, it is nevertheless an accurate expression of this century's central spiritual dilemma. And there is much else to admire in this truly contemporary novel beyond the clarity and significance of its theme: a verbal vivacity, an almost effortless flow of witty conversation, an ease in depicting a variety of settings.

But it must be said, too, that *The Names* is a curiously static book. One would never guess that a novel about cult murders and CIA plots, written by a man of DeLillo's obvious gifts, could be a slow read, and yet *The Names* never quite acquires the pace or urgency its subject matter would seem to guarantee. Only the tension between Axton and his wife is rendered dramatically with emotional as well as intellectual resonance—and then, too abruptly it seems, Kathryn leaves. The cult, which is more a cerebral puzzle than a physical threat, more reported to Axton than experienced by him, and the CIA-terrorist subplot, which is evolved too late and indifferently paced, are strangely unexciting. They seem too frail a narrative skeleton, thin-wired hangers, upon which to drape the heavy flesh of DeLillo's theme. The author's talents, I think, undo him here. A lesser writer could not hold our attention, as DeLillo does with his sentence by sentence virtuosity, without more carefully attending to the theatrical rhythms of the novel's plot. But in *The Names* we read on anyway, tempted by the author's well-turned phrases, unusually lucid observations, gradually aware, though, that this performance, for all its flair, is somehow less than satisfying. . . .

It is possible, I suppose, that the book's slow pace is a con-

scious strategy: that matching style to theme, DeLillo is striving to carve a kind of fictional glyph: a stately, static, abstract pattern, one of those "letter shapes" which so fascinate Owen. . . . Ideas, if they are central to a novel's existence, must come into being; they must develop for the characters and for the reader with a growing sense of discovery, carry the force of a revelation. The ideas and analyses in *The Names,* despite the wit and cogency of their exposition, are less compelling because they are not successfully dramatized, because they are not developed so much as described . . . and described . . . and described again. . . .

To capture somehow the confusion and despair of contemporary life without in the process submitting to them, without committing the esthetic sin of the "imitative fallacy," is one of the most urgent challenges confronting fiction today. Because Don DeLillo dares to track the deepest sources of our discontent rather than merely to record its mannerisms, he has always seemed to me uniquely qualified to meet this challenge. If he hasn't yet, his failure arises from the difficulty of the task and not, as with so much fiction of the day, from an inexcusable lack of effort. Here is a man whose books should be read. A novelist of high purpose, of rare ambition, whose ongoing examination of our present-tense lives amuses and astounds us even as it educates. To say we expect more from him is an implicit if impatient compliment—a measure of this writer's special gifts. (p. 30)

David Bosworth, "The Fiction of Don DeLillo," in Boston Review, *Vol. VIII, No. 2, April, 1983, pp. 29-30.*

BRUCE BAWER

[Most of Don DeLillo's novels are] born out of a preoccupation with a single theme: namely, that contemporary American society is the worst enemy that the cause of human individuality and self-realization has ever had. In one semi-surrealist opus after another, DeLillo has told the story of a conspicuously successful American who jumps off the assembly line and, in one way or another, tries to—well—"find himself." *End Zone* (1972), for instance, is the story of Gary Harkness, a college football player who is revolted by the doctrine of "team spirit"; America, he says, is "becoming a nation devoted to human xerography," and he wants to be more than a photocopy. So he leaves a promising gridiron career at Penn State and ends up playing ball at an obscure college in west Texas. *Great Jones Street* (1973) is about a rock star, Bucky Wunderlick, who, convinced his fans are not responding to him as individuals anymore but simply as a mob, drops out of his band in the middle of a successful tour and moves into a seedy East Village flat, where he becomes the focus of a bizarre drug plot straight out of Thomas Pynchon's *The Crying of Lot 49.* In *Players* (1977), a young stockbroker named Lyle Wynant leaves Yuppiedom behind when his fascination with a murder at the Stock Exchange leads him to become involved with terrorists. In *The Names* (1982), James Axton, an international businessman disenchanted with the life of a corporate jet-setter, is intrigued by an unusual series of cult murders in Greece and the Mideast; like Wynant, he becomes increasingly obsessed—and, ultimately, involved—with the killers.

One thing that these novels all share, aside from the goodbye-American-dream motif, is a stunning implausibility. Representation of reality is not DeLillo's strong suit. It's hard to accept most of his characters as living, breathing human beings, or to conjure up a clear picture of Logos College in *End Zone* or the huge, futuristic scientific institute called Field Experiment Number One in *Ratner's Star* (1976), or to believe in the existence of all these cliques, clans, and cabals . . . . (pp. 34-5)

But then, these novels are not meant to be true-to-life tales. They are tracts, designed to batter us, again and again, with a single idea: that life in America today is boring, benumbing, dehumanized. Not only has the American system robbed us of our individuality; the era's despicable technological innovations have afflicted us all with a dreadful condition known as "sensory overload"—a term introduced by a character in *Great Jones Street:*

> A man in Missouri spent a hundred and sixty-one days in a deep cavern. . . . He ate canned food, he drank water, he burned over nine hundred candles. He said it's the first time in his life he wasn't bored. Sensory overload. People are withdrawing from sensory overload. Technology. Whenever there's too much technology, people return to primitive feats . . . .

Return to primitivism: this, in different ways and to varying degrees, is what the protagonists do in most of DeLillo's novels. Harkness's tiny Texas college, Wunderlick's East Village flat, Wynant's terrorists, and Axton's cult are all versions of the Missourian's cave—they are places to escape to, refuges from a technologically overdeveloped society whose major achievement, DeLillo would have us believe, is to have dragged us further and further away from our true selves.

And what *are* our true selves? DeLillo's answer to that question is clear. To DeLillo, to be human means to be, at heart, a primitive beast; those of us who live in high-tech America are, therefore, more out of touch with our humanness than any humans who have ever lived. To "find oneself" one must, like the Missouri caveman, return to primitivism; and in the world according to DeLillo, returning to primitivism means, in essence, entering into a community, conspiracy, or subculture governed largely by primitive violence. In DeLillo's overly diagrammatic world, savagery is the only alternative to depersonalization by means of sensory overload; only through a pure, brute physicality can one reclaim one's selfhood. . . . At the heart of each of DeLillo's novels is the assumption that, deep down, all human beings long to wreak havoc, to run wild, to kill. . . . [To] DeLillo, art—in present-day America, anyway—has got to confront the primitive yearning, deep inside every human soul, to kill, maim, and destroy.

Why? Because if you don't, you're denying your humanness. It's better, DeLillo seems to say in one novel after another, to be a marauding, murderous maniac—and therefore a *human*—than to sit still for America as it is, with its air-conditioners, assembly lines, television sets, supermarkets, synthetic fabrics, and credit cards. At least when you're living a life of primitive violence, you're closer to the mystery at the heart of it all. That's what life is to DeLillo: a mystery, an enigma. His books are full of codes, ciphers, secret names and places and organizations. Most of the books take the form of suspense stories (why is the cult murdering these people in *The Names*? what do the conspirators want with Wunderlick in *Great Jones Street*? what's the meaning of the interplanetary radio signal in *Ratner's Star*?) but—significantly—the clues never add up to much of anything. By the end of the typical DeLillo novel, in fact, things are hovering pretty near the point of utter incomprehensibility. What is always clear, however, is that one is supposed to come away from these novels convinced that life is a teleological puzzle that no novelist (or scientist, for that matter) is ever going to piece together—a mystery that technological advances can only serve to distance us from. (pp. 35-6)

White Noise represents yet another go at these rapidly aging nihilistic clichés. This time around, the passenger on the Primitivism Express is Jack Gladney, professor of (like it or not) Hitler Studies at a large Eastern college. Though, like all DeLillo heroes, Jack is a connoisseur of destruction, and though he starts making gibes about our stifling assembly-line culture on the first page of the book, it takes an "airborne toxic event" in his hometown to make him truly frantic about his mortality and the unrelieved emptiness of his life. It doesn't help any, either, when he discovers that his wife Babette, a teacher of posture, has slept with another man, a quack doctor who claims to have developed a drug that eradicates the fear of death. Though it is less surrealist than any of his previous novels, *White Noise*—as is par for the course with DeLillo—grows steadily darker, more fantastic, its direction less and less clear. Jack, like Axton in *The Names,* grows obsessive, loses touch with his family, breaks out of his structured existence. He learns from his colleague Murray that "there are two kinds of people in the world. Killers and diers. Most of us are diers" (mainly, it seems, because we don't have the guts to be killers). "Violence," Murray explains, "is a form of rebirth," murder a means of self-liberation. Jack decides he is a killer. He starts carrying a gun with him to school; eventually he steals the neighbors' car and, rod in tow, seeks out the quack doctor.

There should be profound emotions at work here, but *White Noise* is, like its predecessors, so masterfully contrived a piece of argumentation that believable human feelings and actions are few and far between. There is hardly a natural moment in the whole book. Characters do not think, they cogitate; they do not talk, they engage in dialectic and deliver endless monologues about the novel's major themes. It is often difficult to tell them apart when reading a stretch of dialogue, because they all sound exactly alike. Indeed, with rare exceptions, they all *think* exactly alike. When they are not pondering the significance of one contemporary American phenomenon or another (e.g., supermarkets, TV commercials, the *National Enquirer*), they are contemplating life, death, and the cosmos. And when their mouths open, they produce clipped, ironic, self-consciously clever sentences full of offbeat metaphors and quaint descriptive details. (pp. 36-7)

Life—life itself, that queer entity that Flaubert and Tolstoy and Thomas Mann somehow never grew tired of describing—does not interest DeLillo at all; for him, life seems to exist so that we can theorize about it. He never leaves anything alone and just lets it *be*. His narrator and characters, in *White Noise* as elsewhere, are always knee-jerk generalizers. The introductory description of Babette, for instance ("Babette is tall and fairly ample . . . . Her hair is a fanatical blond mop"), turns within a couple of sentences into a broad, seemingly frivolous general statement, the only apparent purpose of which could be to reduce Babette to a stereotype: "If she were a petite woman, the hair would be too cute, too mischievous and contrived. Ample women do not plan such things. They lack the guile for conspiracies of the body." Later in the novel, Jack observes that his teenage son's hairline is receding, wonders guiltily whether he might be at fault ("Have I raised him, unwittingly, in the vicinity of a chemical dump site . . . ?"), and before you know it has happily found himself a suitable generality: "Man's guilt in history and in the tides of his own blood has been complicated by technology, the daily seeping falsehearted death." DeLillo's, quite clearly, is a mind that lets itself be violated by any old idea that happens along.

If you like your novels studded with these kinds of Philosophy McNuggets, you'll love *White Noise.* Lead a character in this novel into a supermarket, bank, or kitchen, and—presto!—he launches, unbidden, into an impromptu interpretive essay, the thrust of which is that deep beneath the surface of our plastic culture lurk the manifold mysteries of human existence. (pp. 37-8)

Of course, supermarkets and banks and kitchens can hold symbolic meanings for people. But why, pray tell, must those meanings be talked about endlessly, with such awesome banality and at such tiresome, unrevealing length? DeLillo's purpose in having his characters carry on about supermarkets and banks, of course, is chiefly ironic: to him, such phenomena are paramount signs of the dehumanization of America. He is, as might be expected, especially devoted to the tiredest of all contemporary clichés, the one about the tyranny of television. In *White Noise,* as in *Players* (at the beginning of which Lyle Wynant is a cathode-ray addict of psychotic proportions), DeLillo portrays the American mind, high and low, as being haunted constantly by sounds and images from the tube. At times, to be sure, he comes close to a perceptive characterization of the role that commercial slogans, jingles, and brand names play in some TV-centered American households, interpolating, for instance, stray sentences from the Gladney family's television set into the stream of dialogue. But DeLillo defeats any hope of verisimilitude by going way overboard. During the "airborne toxic event," he has Jack describe the huge black cloud of poisonous Nyodene gas (the novel's major symbol) as "resembl[ing] a national promotion for death, a multimillion-dollar campaign backed by radio spots, heavy print and billboard, TV saturation." This description does not help the reader to see the cloud, or serve to consolidate its symbolic preeminence in the book; it tends, rather, to diminish it. It is inconceivable that a man whose family was threatened by a cloud of toxic gas would describe it in such a way. The simile is an utterly contrived one, dictated not by the author's intuitive gift for imagery but by his polemical motives, his obsession with commercialism. The only image it fixes in the mind is one of DeLillo himself, sitting at his typewriter, mechanically tapping out his book. (pp. 38-9)

DeLillo's people don't talk about things, if they can help it; they talk about the *nature* of things. Jack's smug, brainy fourteen-year-old son Heinrich (the successor of obnoxiously brilliant adolescents in *The Names* and *Ratner's Star*) likes to expatiate upon the nature of modern knowledge: "What good is knowledge if it just floats through the air? It goes from computer to computer. It changes and grows every second of every day. But nobody actually knows anything." Murray, for his part, discourses pretentiously about "the nature of modern death": "It has a life independent of us. It is growing in prestige and dimension . . . . We can take cross-section pictures of it, tape its tremors and waves . . . . But it continues to grow, to acquire breadth and scope, new outlets, new passages and means. The more we learn, the more it grows."

The less DeLillo's characters have to say, the more they talk. (p. 39)

Perhaps the most disturbing aspect of *White Noise* is Jack's fascination with Hitler. The dictator is the subject not only of his professional research but of his private obsessions. He has hitched his wagon to Hitler because, as Murray tells him, "You thought [Hitler] would protect you." Jack admits as much when he explains why he named his son Heinrich: "I thought it had an authority that might cling to him. I thought it was forceful and impressive and I still do. I wanted to shield him, make him unafraid." He tells his daughter Denise:

> "There's something about German names, the German language, German *things.* I don't know what it is exactly. It's just there. It's in the middle of it all is Hitler, of course."
>
> "He was on again last night."
>
> "He's always on. We couldn't have television without him."
>
> "They lost the war," she said. "How great could they be?"
>
> "A valid point. But it's not a question of greatness.
>
> It's not a question of good and evil. I don't know what it is. Look at it this way. Some people always wear a favorite color. Some people carry a gun. Some people put on a uniform and feel bigger, stronger, safer. It's in this area that my obsessions dwell."

Keep in mind that this is DeLillo's idea of a sympathetic character. Indeed, we are clearly meant to see Jack as the archetypal twentieth-century victim—a victim whose sense of helplessness is so profound that he cannot help but succumb to the temptation, shocking but psychologically understandable, to identify with the aggressor; and since Jack is the archetypal twentieth-century victim, whom else could DeLillo have him identify with but the century's premier aggressor, Adolf Hitler?

White Noise is not, as it happens, the first DeLillo novel in which Hitler has made an appearance. Quite the contrary. Germany, Nazism, Hitler haunt DeLillo's novels the way Maud Gonne haunts the poetry of Yeats. The reason is obvious: Hitler is the ultimate example of twentieth-century man reverting to primitivism. If the nature of humanity is essentially a dark mystery, Hitler is the murderous monster at the heart of that darkness. He is (so DeLillo seems to feel) all of us writ large. This, presumably, is why there is a rock group in *Great Jones Street* named Schicklgruber and, in *End Zone,* a character named Hauptfuhrer; it is why, in the latter novel, there is a student who wants to "get my hair dyed blond so everybody will think I'm one of those small blondie boys with that faraway look in their eyes who used to be so big on the Himmelplatz three or four decades ago." It's why the putative pornographic film at the thematic center of *Running Dog* turns out to be not pornography at all but a film of Hitler, in derby, wing collar, baggy pants, and boutonniere, doing an imitation of Charlie Chaplin. It's why, in *White Noise,* Jack and Murray compare notes on their respective scholarly subjects, Hitler and Elvis, and discover that the two men were really very much alike. DeLillo's point, throughout, is unmistakable: Hitler was just like us. We are all Hitler.

Am I alone in finding this whole business extremely offensive? DeLillo's offense, to my mind, is that he refuses to make distinctions. To him, as to Jack Gladney, the question of Hitler is simply "not a question of good and evil." Nor, it is clear, do moral considerations enter into his appraisal of any human act. A craving for primitive destructiveness dwells deep in all our hearts, DeLillo's books insist; it is what makes us human. But is DeLillo honestly interested in what makes us human? I submit that he is not. His characters are little more than authorial mouthpieces, all but interchangeable with one another. And what makes human beings fascinating, and worth writing novels about, is their differences. Real people talk differently and think differently and have different interests and tastes and fears. None of this is reflected in DeLillo's novels. It is impossible, in the end, to accept his characters as human beings, or to take his novels seriously as representations of reality. All they amount to, really, is documents in the history of nihilistic chic.

But it is probably *déclassé* of me to try to discuss DeLillo's novels as representations of reality. "Surely," I can hear DeLillo's devotees saying, "you realize his true subject is not 'real life' at all, or even *ideas* about life, but words, words, words—language, codes of every kind, the whole question of signification?" Very well, it's true: DeLillo's narrators and characters *are* constantly talking about language. Football, Harkness tells us in *End Zone,* "is the one sport guided by language, by the word signal, the snap number, the color code, the play name." The murders in *The Names* are likewise guided by language: Axton's cult chooses its victims by their initials. DeLillo's characters are, as a rule, unusually sensitive to words, often worrying, in casual conversation with friends and family, about whether they've used *le mot juste.* (pp. 40-1)

Words—the very sound or look of them, utterly divorced from their meanings—alternately hurt and comfort these people. (p. 41)

Though DeLillo's philosophy of language is not perfectly coherent or consistent, it is clear that his preoccupation is not with language as a means of communicating sophisticated ideas and complicated feelings, but with language as ritual. The ultimate purpose of language, DeLillo seems to feel, is not to convey meaning but simply to affirm one's existence. Language—especially language freed of the rhetorical trappings of "civilization" and the illusion that scientific progress leads to greater understanding—is, simply, the cry of human identity. This idea dominates the end of *The Names,* when James Axton, at the Parthenon, is surrounded by people speaking a variety of tongues and realizes that "[t]his is what we bring to the temple, not prayer or chant or slaughtered rams. Our offering is language." The fundamental importance of language as a ritual of identity is likewise suggested toward the end of *White Noise,* when Jack wonders: "Is there something so innocent in the recitation of names that God is pleased?"

One cannot deny that all this is at least theoretically interesting. And it is certainly conceivable that a compelling novel of ideas might be built on an intellectual foundation much like the one I have outlined. DeLillo, however, has yet to write it. Though his preoccupation with the philosophy of language occasionally yields thought-provoking, or at least memorably expressed, observations (e.g., "Mathematics is what the world is when we subtract our own perceptions"), it generally results in little more than one discouraging bat-

tery after another of pointless, pretentious rhetoric. He does not develop ideas so much as juggle jargon.

What makes the case of Don DeLillo especially unfortunate is that he does have real talent. He has always had a flair for humor—dark humor, naturally, of the Vonnegut-Heller sort—and that gift, in particular, is demonstrated in *White Noise* more abundantly than in any of DeLillo's previous books. But his continuing lack of interest in developing his characters and ideas, and his stubborn adherence to a stylish, schematic view of modern America as a great big xerox machine, continue to cripple DeLillo as an imaginative writer. It's ironic. While those of us who live in the real America carry on with our richly varied, emotionally tumultuous lives, DeLillo (as *White Noise* amply demonstrates) continues, in effect, to write the same lifeless novel over and over again—a novel constructed upon a simpleminded political cliché, populated by epigram-slinging, epistemology-happy robots, and packed with words that have very little to say to us about our world, our century, or ourselves. If anyone is guilty of turning modern Americans into xerox copies, it is Don DeLillo. (p. 42)

Bruce Bawer, "Don DeLillo's America," in The New Criterion, *Vol. III, No. 8, April, 1985, pp. 34-42.*

PICO IYER

The DeLillo universe is an ordinary world transfigured by extraordinary concerns, a quotidian place seen in the terrifying white light of eternity. Thus *White Noise* is furnished with all the suburban props of the all-American novel: an amiably rumpled middle-aged professor, his plump earth-motherly wife, bright children from scattered marriages, a nuclear family in a pleasant postnuclear home. Their story is unlikely, however, to be mistaken for a fifties sitcom. The academic, Jack Gladney, teaches Advanced Nazism at the College-on-the-Hill; the matriarch leads adult education classes in posture; Gladney's three ex-wives all have ties with the intelligence community; and the fourteen-year-old eldest child of the household, Heinrich Gerhardt, has both a receding hairline and a philosophical bent—on his first appearance in the novel, he solemnly proclaims, "There's no past, present or future outside our own mind. The so-called laws of motion are a big hoax. Even sound can trick the mind."

Nothing in DeLillo's world is casual, nothing free of occult significance. Dark forces swirl around the bright, plastic artifacts of Anytown, U.S.A., and the country seems nothing but a gleaming library of portents. Bills, bank statements, the brand names of cars are recited as if they were mantras; tabloids are read as fragments from an American Book of the Dead; the television is consulted as a mystic oracle in the dark. The very title of the book, we learn, refers to death: the static of our lives is thus the sound track of our dying.

Yet of all the subversions of the everyday, the nightmare turns on the American Dream, the most unnerving comes when the Gladneys pile into the family station wagon and head off on what resembles a picnic. It is in fact a nuclear evacuation. The huge cloud of escaped poison gas that drifts through the novel's central episode as symbol, prophecy, white whale and man-made black death all in one seems at first to be the stuff of routine sci-fi apocalypse . . . . Yet the effect of the rogue chemical is almost entirely internal. In the wake of the fugitive cloud, Gladney brings up pulsing stars on a computer. What does that mean? The poison has entered his system; he has come to incarnate death.

It is said that DeLillo is funny, but his is the funniness of peculiarity, not mirth. It is, more precisely, the terrible irony of the lone metaphysician, rising to a keening intensity as he registers the black holes in the world about him. In *White Noise,* as in all his novels, DeLillo absorbs the jargon of myriad disciplines and reprocesses them in a terminal deadpan. His is a hard-edged, unsmiling kind of satire. It is not user friendly. . . . DeLillo has no time for anarchic pratfalls, Aristophanic gambits, non sequiturs. His humor is pitch black. (pp. 292-93)

Just as DeLillo's characters are often not people so much as energies or eccentricities with voices, just as his suburbia is a crowded set of signs fit for a moonlighting Roland Barthes, so his speech is not normal discourse as much as a kind of rhetoric pitched high, a collection of phantom sentences, a chorus of texts without contexts. And his (charnel) house style has the cool metallic sleekness of a hearse: it is all polished angles, black lines, sunless planes. No wasted motion. No extraneous matter. No scraps of the regular world. Words in DeLilloese are stripped dry, sheared clean, given a deadly precision:

> "Am I going to die?"
>
> "Not as such," he said.
>
> "What do you mean?"
>
> "Not in so many words."

It is this stark tonelessness that accounts for the terrible beauty of much of his writing. DeLillo does not put spin on his words; he leaves them hanging—weightless, somber things full of density and gravity. Disconnected, theirs is the kind of bare, brooding blankness that suggests not numbness so much as mystery, a world not empty of meaning, but too full of it, electrically supercharged. The most conspicuous tic in a DeLillo novel, indeed, is to end chapters with a paragraph consisting of nothing but a single sentence. . . . (pp. 293-94)

DeLillo's other characteristic device is to put together words and rhythms into patterns, sequences, escalating cadences that build a mood and gather momentum and pick up in time a hypnotic and heart-stopping intensity. They turn into riffs, disquisitions, revved-up harangues. They move with the even, pounding purposefulness of footfalls down an alleyway.

This dazzle of Promethean language is largely consecrated to a single driving theme: the rising struggle between tribalism and technology. DeLillo's novels worry and worry at humanity's fight with science; DeLillo's characters are caught between the spirits of their ancestors and the gods of their computer world. The courses in "Eating and Drinking" he satirizes are no idle joke; in Gladney's world, primal instincts are threatened by a conception of progress that would transform men from animals into machines. "The greater the scientific advance, the more primitive the fear," Gladney tells his wife. Science and fear, those are the antagonists in *White Noise;* we need our fear to defeat a science that tries to conquer fear. And the most potent instrument in this contest, the original—and aboriginal—martial art, is language. DeLillo is fascinated with the ways in which language creates and recreates the world. Names nail down slippery identities; chants mass together crowds into forces stronger even than

technology; language is a way, perhaps the only way, of making connections, an ordered system that can withstand the entropic pressure of the world at large. (Like Pynchon, DeLillo everywhere seeks out networks, circuits, codes, connections; and, like Pynchon, he knows that the man who finds connections everywhere is a paranoid.) Words, in the end, make up the fabric of our beings (and so the assurance that Gladney is not dying "in so many words" knells with particular plangency).

Above all, language, for DeLillo, is like fear: it is all we have of certainty, and of humanity. In this novelist's (largely verbal) universe, words are treated as archaeological fragments that can help us recover something of a more primitive and so more human past. Words are runes, atavistic relics, talismans with something of the sacred about them. Language is ritual; language is liturgy. . . . At his most reverberant DeLillo at once explores and embodies the power, the fear of sound: recitation, repetition, incantation, words as rough magic, a way of making spells.

At times, perhaps inevitably, DeLillo's rhythms overpower him, acquire a life of their own, race so fast that they overthrow the meaning they are meant to carry. The minute Gladney is given a gun, he thinks of it as "a secret, a second life, a secret self, a dream, a spell, a plot, a delirium." Also concealed in the runaway rhetoric is the deeper liability of seeing eternity in a grain of sand: DeLillo and his characters are so eager to read the world, to invest it with significance, that they come on occasion to seem overanxious. . . . His atmospherics stronger than his aphorisms, DeLillo occasionally builds up menace without meaning, is about profundity rather than full of it, becomes—in a word—portentous. The price he pays for his hubristic ambition is an intermittent bout of pretension; manuals for Zen and the art of emotional maintenance, his books mass-produce fortune cookies along with their koans.

Perhaps the oddest and most enduring mystery of DeLillo's remarkable novels is that, though preoccupied with plotting, they are themselves ill-plotted; portraits of a mind as searching, driven and ceaselessly vagrant as the voice in a Beckett novel, they have trouble with resolutions. Such, perhaps, are the treacheries of a Melvillean course. For DeLillo is determined to take on inquiries that cannot be concluded, to make challenges that cannot be met (just as Gladney resolves to wrestle with the riddle of the Holocaust while his colleagues content themselves with deconstructing detergent jingles, soda bottles, and bubble gum). Writing of the unspeakable, DeLillo is fascinated with the unanswerable. "Is a symptom a sign or a thing? What is a thing and how do we know it's not another thing?" "What is electricity? What is light?" "What is dark?" "How does a person say goodbye to himself?" The questions keep coming and coming, pushing the reader back to metaphysical basics, mocking the answering machine, refuting artificial intelligence, mimicking the manner of a child who goes instantly to the heart of the matter, and with it the heart of darkness.

Next to DeLillo's large and terrifying talent, most modern fiction seems trifling indeed. A connoisseur of fear, his novels leave a chill in one's bones. At the same time, however, it is always difficult to tell what he is about, beyond fear, emptiness, the dark. He knows his data cold; he addresses the great themes with uncommon courage (and so, at moments, heroic presumption and folly); his skills are astonishing. But where is he going, what can he do, with them? Imprisoned, it sometimes seems, within the four walls of his obsessions, he keeps on, in a sense, writing the same book, simply carrying his medicine bag of tricks and themes into a different genre, a new language, with every novel: college football or rock-'n'-roll, science fiction or international business or the academy. Thirteen years ago, his second novel *End Zone* sounded many of the same notes of foreboding that toll through *White Noise:* film clips of hurricanes and tornadoes; some all-American boys with names like "Hauptfuhrer," others burdened by an obscure need to master German; the consoling, earth-bound magnetism of the fat; classes in "the untellable."

For all that, however, *White Noise* remains a far greater book than *End Zone,* in large part because it is something more than cold and curious reason; it offsets its existential shivers with a domestic strength that is touching and true. (pp. 294-96)

Pico Iyer, "A Connoisseur of Fear," in Partisan Review, Vol. LIII, No. 2, 1986, pp. 292-97.

JOHN SIMON

What a way with words, you think as you try to absorb Don DeLillo's *The Day Room* and laugh quite a lot during its first act. It begins with two patients in a semi-private (an oxymoron, as one of them points out) hospital room. There is Budge, an elderly widower who may or may not have serious health problems but whose most urgent need is to talk to someone, and Wyatt, an affluent yuppie father in for a routine, somewhat hypochondriacal checkup, who, not being good at talk, is eager to be left alone. One of them is not what he seems.

Nor, alas, is *The Day Room* the easeful absurdist comedy it starts out as. Absurdist, to be sure, it remains; more and more so, in fact. But it becomes less of a comedy, to say nothing of easeful. Still, Act I manages to maintain a decent quota of tickling verbal conceits and dizzying sight gags. We have here an extended hospital—and, in the adjoining and overflowing wing, madhouse—joke: blackly beautiful humor about physical and mental patients, demented doctors and nurses. If you like that sort of thing, you can float blissfully on the darkening tide of the wit, relieved by lighter whimsy and some grimly compelling wisdom.

Running through the first half is a paean to talk, the art of language deployed in the act of conversation, words used with sensuous joy, preferably artfully, but, at the very least, enthusiastically. As the author stimulatingly notes, talk becomes more alive and essential the farther east one gets from America, where it hardly matters or exists at all. This notion is developed with great baroque glee, but it is, ultimately, a novelistic development. DeLillo, a fiction writer of distinction, is using prose more bookishly than dramatically. Mind you, he doesn't commit the obvious errors of neglecting action and stichomythia, two essentials of theater. Yet there is a proclivity to let long speeches get out of hand—or, rather, out of our ear too quickly, as old tenants are importunately crowded out by new ones before we get a chance to savor them. . . .

Rather sophisticated witticisms—many flawed, many sound—come at us at tremendous speed, and the stage action bunches up in certain places like an ill-fitting suit, not necessarily polyester, and not nearly so effective as were it more evenly distributed. *The Day Room,* in short, suffers mainly from the wrong rhythm, although in Act II the author's invention, on top of that, overreaches and underachieves. Representing the idiot box—especially in the day room of a loony bin—with a live actor . . . is a superb idea, marvelously developed. But now several kinds of strain set in: for more bizarre concepts, more rarefied humor, more elaborate and more symmetrical plotting. The strain rubs off on us, and nascent laughter stops dead.

In fact, the imbrications and encapsulations of the two acts are devices more appropriate to modern fiction. . . . There are a lot of good lines, and there is an idea here; I am not sure there is a play. (p. 45)

John Simon, "Methods of Madness," in New York Magazine, Vol. 21, No. 1, January 4, 1988, pp. 45-6.

MIMI KRAMER

The Day Room isn't a play so much as an essay, a metaphysical speculation on the themes of madness and theatre. Its spiritual setting is neither the hospital room where the first act takes place nor the motel room where we find ourselves in Act II but another place entirely—a mental ward that may or may not exist somewhere offstage—and its spiritual hub is Arno Klein, a character we may or may not ever see. The hospital room—occupied by Budge and Wyatt . . . is said to be adjacent to the Arno Klein Psychiatric Wing. As characters in Act I prove not to be the patients, doctors, and nurses they seem to be but lunatics who have wandered in from the Klein wing, it becomes less and less clear to the audience who the real doctor is. In Act II, "the Arno Klein wing" has become "the Arno Klein group," a touring theatrical company that Gary and Lynette . . . have come in search of. But the Arno Klein group turns out to be as difficult to locate as the Arno Klein wing. And as characters in the second half wander into the motel room babbling about the elusive theatrical troupe it becomes less and less clear who the real audience is. Are these actors or madmen, we wonder. Are they performing for us? For each other? For themselves?

If all this sounds faintly pretentious and irritating, that's probably because *The Day Room* is a slightly pretentious and, at times, irritating play. Long stretches of it sound as though they were written by a precocious high-school student who had recently read *Rosencrantz and Guildenstern Are Dead* for the first time—a play that *The Day Room* in fact resembles in many ways. Of course, Stoppard's play took stock of itself in relation to its own literary tradition (Molnár, Pirandello, and Beckett as well as Shakespeare); DeLillo's play doesn't: it seems unaware of the whole history of absurdist drama. . . . Actually, if you can get past the preciousness of some of DeLillo's dialogue *The Day Room* turns out to be entertaining. This is due largely to the comic flair of its director, Michael Blakemore, and a first-rate cast . . . transforms DeLillo's rather bloodless play into a metaphysical farce in which mistaken existence takes the place of mistaken identity. It's mostly a question of orchestration. *The Day Room* is about the degree to which we make epistemological judgments on the basis of what we think is plausible behavior. (pp. 74-5)

The Day Room may not make any discoveries about the nature of theatre or of existence—it's too far removed from realistic, consequential action to be anything but mute about the human condition. But it does provide a kind of comic therapy. And it comes up with some lingering images: the television as lunatic; the elusive theatrical company as an expression of that transforming aesthetic experience we're all looking for. (p. 75)

Mimi Kramer, "Who's the Boss?" in The New Yorker, *Vol. LXIII, No. 47, January 11, 1988, pp. 74-5.*

CHRISTOPHER LEHMANN-HAUPT

It's obvious even before the story begins that Libra must be Lee Harvey Oswald, President John F. Kennedy's assassin. There he is on the dust jacket of [*Libra*], in the famous backyard photograph, dressed in black and holding his rifle and his revolutionary magazines. . . .

And it's apparent soon after the story starts how the plot of *Libra* is going to work. As the omniscient narrator jumps around in time, we learn that shortly after the failed Bay of Pigs invasion, unhappy Central Intelligence Agency men begin working on ways that Fidel Castro and Cuba can be made the targets of official American hostility once again.

> "We need an electrifying event," their leader, Win Everett, tells a small gathering of the conspirators. "We want to set up an attempt on the life of the President. We plan every step, design every incident leading up to the event. We put together a team, leave a dim trail. The evidence is ambiguous. But it points to the Cuban Intelligence Directorate . . . We script a person or persons out of ordinary pocket litter. Shots ring out, the country is shocked, aroused. . . .

> "But we don't hit Kennedy. We miss him," Win says.

So there's not really that much suspense to *Libra*—only the puzzles of how Oswald will link up with the C.I.A. plan, to what extent Jack Ruby will become involved, whether there will be another assassin on the grassy knoll, and why J.F.K. will be killed instead of spared.

Instead, the novel is like the acting-out of some ritual, an anti-passion play, a pilgrim's regress, a station of the crosshairs: Oswald in the Bronx, Oswald in Moscow, Oswald in Dallas, Oswald in the window of the Texas School Book Depository. . . .

Why then, lacking great surprise or tension, does the novel eventually work so powerfully, starting slowly, almost tediously, but gathering momentum like thunder from a far horizon that finally splits the sky?

Part of the answer is in the details: Oswald's Soviet interrogator explaining how Hemingway's writing style always makes him hungry; Marina Oswald astounded at seeing herself on television in a store window; Jack Ruby driving his white Olds around Dallas, "bottles and jars" rolling "across the floor of the car"; Oswald in prison, after he has shot the President, hearing his name on the radios and televisions. . . .

Another part of the answer is in the seamlessness between the known and the unknown, between the actual record and what Mr. DeLillo has invented. In the foreground are all the facts that those who lived through that traumatic ordeal know as well as their autobiographies, from the roses that lay on the car seat between Jack and Jackie, to the whining non sequi-

turs of Marguerite Oswald, Lee's mother. In the background lie every rumor, shadowy figure and crackpot theory, from Jack Ruby's mob connections to Judith Exner; and Clay Shaw to the proposition that there were many Oswalds. All together they add up, at least to an imaginative whole.

Two threads help to knit them together. One of them is the character of Oswald, specific enough to accommodate all psychologies—the dyslexic truant, the fatherless son, the alienated defector, the castrated husband—yet general enough to stand for all who dream of merging with history. . . .

What Lee Harvey Oswald will do—and why—hangs in the balance throughout the space-time of Mr. DeLillo's book, which is why Clay Shaw identifies him as a Libran, the Scales, and says: "Easily, easily, easily influenced. Poised to make the dangerous leap. Either way, balance is the key."

The other thread is the conspiracy theory. The historian Branch, "a retired senior analyst of the Central Intelligence Agency, hired on contract to write the secret history of the assassination," sits in "the room of theories, the room of growing old," meditating on "the death rate among those who were connected in some way to the events of November 22," on all the accumulating evidence that he has come to think of as "the Joycean book of America . . . the novel in which nothing is left out."

What he concludes is: "If we are on the outside, we assume a conspiracy is the perfect working of a scheme." But in fact, "the conspiracy against the President was a rambling affair that succeeded in the short term due mainly to chance. Deft men and fools, ambivalences and fixed will and what the weather was like."

Are we meant to take all this literally? In an eloquent concluding author's note, Mr. DeLillo writes that *Libra* is "a work of the imagination" that to some may seem "one more gloom in a chronicle of unknowing." But, he adds, "because this book makes no claim to literal truth, because it is only itself, apart and complete, readers may find refuge here—a way of thinking about the assassination without being constrained by half-facts or overwhelmed by possibilities, by the tide of speculation that widens with the years."

We do. We most gratefully do.

Christopher Lehmann-Haupt, "A Pilgrim's Regress in Dallas, November '63," in The New York Times, *July 18, 1988, p. C15.*

ANNE TYLER

Don DeLillo has produced nine novels in the past 17 years, and by now his admirers have learned to expect almost anything. His central character may be a rock music star or a child math genius; his setting may be a remote Aegean island or a college football field. Certain preoccupations, however, tend to reassert themselves: the assassination of President Kennedy, the labyrinthine underworld of spies and terrorists and (most notably in *White Noise,* which won the American Book Award in 1985) the pervasive effect of the modern American news media.

These three subjects come together in *Libra,* his latest and richest novel. It is also his most complicated, with a dual slate of characters and a plot line that might be described as herringbone-shaped. Apparently unrelated events slant forward from distant sources to be channeled into a single moment in history: six seconds in Dallas on Nov. 22, 1963.

What if, Mr. DeLillo asks, the assassination was a C.I.A. conspiracy? What if agency operatives, disgusted by the Bay of Pigs debacle and alarmed at signs of growing rapprochement between Kennedy and Castro, schemed to stage an unsuccessful attempt on Kennedy's life that would implicate Castro supporters? And what if they seized upon Lee Harvey Oswald—a onetime defector to Russia, sole member of his own unauthorized branch of the Fair Play for Cuba Committee—as the man to shoulder the blame? And finally, what if they decided in the end that a successful attempt would be even more effective than an unsuccessful attempt?

Other people have asked these questions before, of course, but never so provocatively. For one thing, that herringbone plot line serves to make the most humdrum occurrence seem suddenly meaningful, laden with dark purpose. The book begins with Lee Oswald as a boy in the Bronx—a misfit, a chronic truant, sharing oppressively close quarters with his mother. Then there's a brief intermission: a glimpse into the book-filled, document-choked study of Nicholas Branch, who is writing a secret history of the assassination of President Kennedy. This is followed by our introduction to Win Everett, a C.I.A. man now semiretired, so-called, on account of his overzealousness in the matter of Cuba. It is April 1963, and Everett has just begun to frame his plan for an "electrifying event" that will bring the anti-Castro movement back to life.

Oswald will reappear as a high school dropout in New Orleans, as a marine at a U-2 base in Japan, as a factory worker in Russia and finally as an order filler at the Texas School Book Depository in Dallas. Win Everett will reappear surrounded by more and more associates—first the two former colleagues he trusts most and then other men less predictable, less controllable, as his plan takes on a life of its own. Nicholas Branch will reappear only rarely, sinking ever deeper in a morass of eyewitness accounts, hair samples, chemical analyses, then the accounts of the *dreams* of eyewitnesses and then 25 years of novels and plays and radio debates about the assassination. He's not really part of the story, but he plays an important role nevertheless. He reminds us of the broader view; he casts the light of history over the other characters' most commonplace moments.

It's in those commonplace moments that Mr. DeLillo reveals his genius. After all, he must have had the same source materials available to anyone else—the Warren Commission report, the usual newspaper articles and court proceedings. But he takes the stale facts and weaves them into something altogether new, largely by means of inventing, with what seems uncanny perception, the interior voice that each character might use to describe his own activities. (pp. 1, 22)

At what point exactly does fact drift over into fiction? The book is so seamlessly written that perhaps not even those people who own both upstairs and downstairs copies of the Warren report could say for certain. Oswald's mother, for instance, with her nonstop, plaintive, sometimes unwittingly comic stream of talk, was probably willing to speak to any newsman who poked a microphone in her face; and therefore Mr. DeLillo had merely to transcribe her long-ago monologues. Or did he? Other voices are equally convincing, and yet obviously not all of those could have been taped. . . .

He knows the elliptical style people use when they've fallen

into certain conversational grooves together. . . . As in real life, non sequiturs startle us at every turn. . . .

But *Libra* is not merely lifelike; it is also, in the best sense, novellike. It tells a story, and it tells it skillfully, with much attention to character. . . .

And how about the most important character of all? Lee Harvey Oswald has always seemed both much, much too familiar (his rabbity, weak-jawed face staring out of the grimmer sections of every city in America) and endlessly mysterious. To Mr. DeLillo's credit, that ambiguity is kept alive in *Libra.* It may even be heightened, because the portrait is so intimate— Oswald washing dishes, Oswald playing with his baby, Oswald cuffing his wife—and yet still he manages from time to time to surprise us.

Oswald is a loser, a loner, pathetic and self-aggrandizing, one of those people who seize crazily upon the significance of every insignificant coincidence. He tries to shoot the right-wing general Edwin A. Walker but hits Walker's window frame instead; he tries to renounce his United States citizenship but it's early-closing day at the embassy; he tries to defect to the Russians but they're not so sure they want him. Still, sometimes when he's discussing his dissatisfaction with the inequities of capitalism, or his extensive readings in Marxism, you catch a glimmer of intelligence. "I'm not an innocent youth who thinks Russia is the land of his dreams," he tells one Russian. "I look at this coldly in the light of right and wrong. . . . How would I live in America? I would have a choice of being a worker in a system I despise or going unemployed."

Finally, what emerges as most central to Oswald's character is this: His picture of himself seems to have been taken by a television camera. He seems to have viewed his life in terms gathered from second-rate newspaper reporters and excited telecasters. Even when he lies bleeding from a suicide attempt, his thoughts are oddly nonprivate in tone: "I won't answer questions about my family but I will say this for publication. Emigration isn't easy. I don't recommend it to everyone." His main ambition is "to be a short story writer on contemporary American life," and he keeps what he calls his Historic Diary in order to reveal "the fears and aspirations of a man who only wanted to see for myself what socialism was like." (pp. 22-3)

Whether or not the C.I.A. conspiracy actually happened— and we end up persuaded that it could have—the book's most compelling point is Oswald's curiously external view of himself. He seems to have lacked an inner core, an absolute and unalterable sense of his own character. It's easy to imagine such a man committing murder almost at random. Maybe the assassination was not so much a scheme as a long, helpless, headlong plunge downward.

In **"American Blood,"** an article published by *Rolling Stone* magazine in 1983, Mr. DeLillo suggested that the John Kennedy assassination was a story about our uncertain grip on the world—a story exploded into life by a homeless man who himself could not grip things tightly and hold them fast, whose soul-scarred loneliness and rage led him to invent an American moment that echoes down the decades. That Mr. DeLillo has been able to make his readers see the story the same way—that finally we're interested less in the physical events of the assassination than in the pitiable and stumbling spirit underlying them—proves *Libra* to be a triumph. (p. 23)

Anne Tyler, "Dallas, Echoing Down the Decades," in The New York Times Book Review, *July 24, 1988, pp. 1, 22-3.*

JONATHAN YARDLEY

[*Libra*] is presented as a work of fiction, but it is more accurately described as fanciful journalism: a retelling of the story of Lee Harvey Oswald in which, among other things, DeLillo has attempted to invent solutions to the many lacunae with which that story is riddled. It is a book to which readers are likely to be drawn both because DeLillo has now quite inexplicably acquired a substantial literary reputation and because Oswald's story—like those of Marilyn Monroe and James Dean and other 20th-century misfits—continues to fascinate us. But there is in truth precious little in *Libra* that illuminates and much that offends; it is, in the end, an act of exploitation.

No doubt *Libra* will be lavishly praised in those quarters where DeLillo's ostentatiously gloomy view of American life and culture is embraced. Like Robert Stone and Joan Didion and Russell Banks and others less prominent, DeLillo looks out from the comfortable vantage point of the literary hothouse and sees a country teeming with maniacal imperialists, right-wing zealots and unhinged CIA operatives, and he populates his novels accordingly. For this he is applauded by those of like views, who manage to overlook his novels' many shortcomings as fiction so as to be able to celebrate the rectitude of their politics. . . .

[DeLillo] is a writer of skill, wit and ingenuity, but he employs these considerable gifts in the evanescent craft of pamphleteering rather than the durable art of fiction. Never has this been more so than in *Libra,* which by contrast with DeLillo's previous novels is notable for its lack of interesting prose, its deficiency of wit and—this, perhaps, most surprising of all—its failure of the imagination; in *Libra,* that is to say, DeLillo offers no pleasures or surprises to compensate for the tedious predictability of his politics.

Leaving aside for the moment the problems inherent in fictionalizing the actual, the greatest disappointment of *Libra* is that DeLillo does not come within shouting distance of making a plausible or interesting character out of Lee Harvey Oswald. This strange, unknown and perhaps unknowable man was the instigator of what DeLillo calls "the seven seconds that broke the back of the American century," yet here he is portrayed as little more than an anonymous American of "mixed history" who sees himself as "a zero in the system" and longs "to reach the point where he was no longer separated from the true struggles that went on around him."

Who longs, that is, to be a part of history and to separate himself from the crowd. But is that really the best, the most inventive, that DeLillo can come up with? The image of the assassin as loner and victim is by now a commonplace, in large measure because what we know of the actual Oswald has made it so. My hope had been that DeLillo somehow could get past the received wisdom into a new understanding of Oswald, but this he fails to do. Instead he gives us little more than a cliché—a man for whom we clearly are intended to feel sympathy, but who does nothing to earn it because he never is shaped into a flesh-and-blood character.

He is, rather, a cat's-paw: not merely for the disgruntled CIA operatives, Cuban exiles and right-wing crazies whom DeLillo imagines—does this come as any surprise?—to have been the architects of the assassination, but also for DeLillo's own politics. Oswald killed John F. Kennedy, this book argues, not by his own volition but as the unwitting agent of forces too large and malign for him to identify or comprehend. . . .

Oswald is a Libra, poised on the scales between "the positive Libran who has achieved self-mastery" and "the negative Libran who is, let's say, somewhat unsteady and impulsive." The question is which direction his "dangerous leap" will take him, but the answer, DeLillo would have us believe, is that his course is beyond his control: he will go in whichever direction "they," who "were running messages into his skin," choose to take him. "They," of course, are the CIA and the FBI and the John Birch Society and the Cuban exiles and the Mafia and all the others whose invisible hands, fiction such as this insists, control not merely Lee Harvey Oswald and his ilk, but all of us.

Yes, what we have here is a conspiracy theory, though DeLillo does back far enough off it to suggest that "the conspiracy against the President was a rambling affair that succeeded in the short term due mainly to chance." This conclusion is reached by Nicholas Branch, who is assembling a "secret history of the assassination" for the CIA and who senses that it is a history so permeated with blood and death and mystery that its true ramifications can only be speculated upon. But this, again, is neither surprising nor interesting, merely a slight variation upon what the paranoid left has feasted on for a quarter-century.

In the end DeLillo says, "Because this book makes no claim to literal truth, because it is only itself, apart and complete, readers may find refuge here—a way of thinking about the assassination without being constrained by half-facts or overwhelmed by possibilities, by the tide of speculation that widens with the years." In fact, though, *Libra* is merely another ripple in that tide, precisely because it so clearly is not "apart and complete" within the literature of the assassination. Rather, in the guise of fiction it offers only still more "half-facts," presented through the eyes and actions of a cast of characters not a single member of which ever comes to life—precisely because each character is not a person but a representation of one point or another on DeLillo's political compass.

Jonathan Yardley, "Appointment in Dallas," in Book World—The Washington Post, *July 31, 1988, p. 3.*

RICHARD EDER

Libra, a novel about the assassination of John F. Kennedy, is built upon the particular practice of "deniability." From that administrative virus, invented to dissolve the constrictions of the old rule that "who wills the end, wills the means," DeLillo cultivates a moral and political pandemic.

Although the author seems to be averse to the term, *Libra* is a form of fictionalized history. It has some of the form's disadvantages, which I will get to, and the strengths, as well. In the hands of a writer of DeLillo's fierceness and subtlety, the strengths are supercharged.

It has an additional advantage, owing to its subject. We have no solidly accepted factual history of Kennedy's killing, though we have an infinity of facts. One of the best things in

Libra, and one of its central symbols, is the wryly drawn figure of a man hired by the CIA to write the "secret history" of the assassination. . . .

Using real figures, and others more or less invented to fill out his plot, DeLillo chooses and elaborates one frequently suggested version of the conspiracy theory. Simply put, the killing of Kennedy is the work of assorted anti-Castro activists who, by disguising it as a Cuban-backed effort, hope to provoke an American response more concerted and effective than the Bay of Pigs venture.

That is putting it simply, and DeLillo does not. The plot is at least two plots, piggy backing upon each other. Those involved include some dissident middle-level CIA officials heavily involved in the Bay of Pigs, and unable to accept the subsequent U.S. toning-down of the anti-Castro campaign, right-wing mercenaries, armed Cuban exiles, a former New Orleans police official, a Mafia overlord aiming to control gambling in a post-Castro Havana, and assorted odds and ends.

The oddest of these is Oswald, who comes drifting through in his balloon of self-exultation and misapprehension, intersects the various plots, and fits in perfectly with all of them. He is a nebulous leftist, a vociferous admirer of Castro, and has spent several years in the Soviet Union in protest against his own unprivileged portion of the American way of life.

Having, in his peregrinations, brushed up against several different intelligence agencies—the CIA, the FBI and the KGB—it is not hard to devise a confected paper trail linking him to the Cubans. As for enlisting this unstable man, who rather admires Kennedy, it is enough to convince him that the U.S. government is making plans to assassinate Castro.

DeLillo disassembles his plots with the finest of jigsaw cuts, scrambles their order and has us reassemble them. As the assorted characters go about their missions, we discern them more by intuition than by perception. The chronology goes back and forth, disorienting us. We do not so much follow what is going on as infiltrate it.

The author has constructed the shifting segments of a conspiracy that changes shape as it goes along. The original notion, devised by a disaffected CIA man on extended leave for excessive zeal, would have had the assassin miss. An associate, directly in charge of the operation, as he was at the Bay of Pigs—and therefore more bitter about the "betrayal"—simply switches the arrangements.

DeLillo's paranoid grid is much larger. The operatives may be "renegade" CIA men, but the agency has its own contacts with an armed exile group that is also planning a Kennedy assassination. At the same time, the FBI is working to frustrate the exiles' activities. (p. 3)

The picture, once the pieces drift together, is of a wavering line leading from the top of the government to the intelligence agencies, down through a morass of white, gray and black operations, out into assorted extremist groups and individual nut cases, and finally to the demented, oblivious figure of Oswald himself.

Things are set in motion, contacts made, plans bruited. A policy may be changed or canceled—or seem to be—but its segments have acquired a life of their own. DeLillo's stunning portrait is a schema of the methods and consequences of deniability as governance.

Top-level government committees meet and adjourn after setting general policies; one or two members of the committee meet with an operations committee whose discussions are more concrete; one or two members of *this* committee meet a lower-level, still more concrete, and proportionately bloodier committee, until the exploding cigar and botulism-tipped needle is arrived at.

The higher you are, the less you are to know. "Knowledge was a danger, ignorance a cherished asset," DeLillo writes. Senior officials "expected to be misled; they counted on it." Deniability is alluring and effective until something goes wrong; then it goes fearfully, uncontrollably wrong; and its dementia, which has already sickened the processes of government, assassinates them.

Chilling and penetrating as it is, and for all its fascination, *Libra* has its defects. Some of the characters may be invented, and the real ones may have fictional attributes; still, they all must schedule themselves to the demands of the real as against the fictional event. It is like touring Paris with so many appointments to keep that the sense of travel is curtailed.

Most of the figures in *Libra,* however suggestive when we first meet them, fade into their functions. There are exceptions. Jack Ruby, expansive and crooked, exploiting his friendships—largely imaginary—in the Mafia and the police, is a beautifully written sketch, as beguiling and sickening as junk food. Oswald's wife, Marina, drawn with the lightest of strokes, has a persistent life to her. Oswald is the most haunting of all. Alternating with segments of the plotting, we follow his zigzag life in detail. Poor, uneducated, incompetent, he is moved by a burning need to achieve something against the grain of wherever he finds himself. He studies Marx and Engels despite his reading difficulties, enters a vague arrangement with a Soviet agent while working as a radar operator in Japan, moves to the Soviet Union, becomes frustrated there, turns Trotskyist, tries to go to Cuba. (pp. 3, 8)

Oswald comes to us as a white whale mutely signaling his lifelong mission to bring down Ahab. He is a ghostly prodigy whose instincts and compulsions are faintly recognizable, as belonging to a fellow mammal, but also remote and unfathomable, as suited to the submerged white form and the cold depths and fishy companions he frequented. (p. 8)

> *Richard Eder, "Imagining the Kennedy Assassination," in* Los Angeles Times Book Review, *July 31, 1988, pp. 3, 8.*

ROBERT TOWERS

In *Libra* DeLillo turns back a quarter-century to the double event that fixed death most intimately in the collective consciousness of America: the assassination of John Kennedy and the incessant replay, on TV, of the murder of his assassin. Lee Harvey Oswald's death was also the event that gave rise to the most feverish outburst of conspiracy speculation in American history, far exceeding that following the death of Lincoln. In this exceptionally interesting novel, which uses real names and repeatedly anchors itself in recorded fact, DeLillo imaginatively traces the lines of force converging to produce those echoing shots that "broke the back of the American century."

In a note at the end, DeLillo insists that *Libra* (the title refers to the astrological sign under which Lee Harvey Oswald was born) is a work of imagination that aspires "to fill some of the blank spaces in the known record. To do this, I've altered and embellished reality, extended real people into imagined space and time, invented incidents, dialogues, and characters." DeLillo has, then, written a historical novel that ideally one should be able to approach as one does *Ivanhoe* or *I, Claudius*—with a degree of aesthetic detachment and without excessive concern for historicity so long as the "feel" of the period is communicated and blatant anachronisms are avoided. But here, the events narrated are too recent, too awful, too raw. Readers over thirty-five will remember not only the major events narrated but their own reactions and thoughts concerning them. Some will want to compare DeLillo's fictional account with the other countless published speculations, and that way madness lies, as well as contamination of the critical process.

For those who have followed different conspiracy theories of the assassination I will only say that *Libra* does not maintain that the Lee Harvey Oswald who defected to Russia was replaced by a second Lee Harvey Oswald who fired at the President. It does assume a second assassin (a Cuban exile) who was firing from the "grassy knoll"; and the portraits of Lee Oswald, his bewildered Russian wife, Marina, and his egregious mother, Marguerite, are in substantial (though not total) agreement with those drawn by Priscilla Johnson McMillan, Jean Stafford, Robert Oswald (Lee's brother), and by Edward Jay Epstein in his several books on the subject. It also assumes Jack Ruby's shooting of Oswald is linked to Ruby's indebtedness to the New Orleans Mafia, which is in turn linked to the Kennedy assassination plot. DeLillo makes extensive (though selective) use of the now thoroughly discredited charges by the demagogic district attorney of New Orleans, Jim Garrison, connecting Oswald with the bizarre ex-airline pilot David Ferrie, the businessman Clay Shaw, and the homosexual underground of New Orleans.

How does DeLillo go about transmuting such explosive and clearly intractable material into a work of fiction? He begins the novel with an evocation of the brief period in the 1950s when Lee, aged thirteen, and the garrulous and complaining Marguerite Oswald are living unhappily in the Bronx. The dyslexic, lonely, frequently teased boy has already come to the notice of psychiatrists and social workers because of his truancy and other disturbed behavior. (p. 6)

Libra then leaps forward to the present, and we find ourselves in the fireproof study of a retired senior analyst of the CIA, Nicholas Branch, who has been hired to write the secret history of the Kennedy assassination—a project on which he has already spent fifteen years, with no end in sight. . . . As the author's alter ego, Branch makes only a few appearances in the novel, mainly to discuss the self-reflexive nature of conspiracies and to lament, wearily, the overkill of documentation, much of it of dubious relevance. . . .

Three (invented) CIA agents meet in a small Texas town to listen to a plan to undo the disaster of the Bay of Pigs. Two of the agents, Win Everett and Larry Parmenter, are in disgrace with the agency for their overzealous involvement with anti-Castro Cuban exiles after the Bay of Pigs. The third, T.J. Mackey, is described as "a cowboy type to Win's

mind . . . , a veteran field officer who'd trained exiles in assault weapons and supervised early phases of the landings." By staging an assassination attempt on President Kennedy with a carefully manufactured trail leading to Fidel Castro, Win Everett believes that they can provoke the United States into a full-scale second invasion of Cuba. . . . Mackey's assignment is to find a model for the gunman whom Everett plans to create out of ordinary pocket litter. Unfortunately, Mackey, who is more of a "rogue agent" than the others realize, has secret reservations about Everett's plan for a "surgical miss" of the President and, without telling his two colleagues, sets about planning a real assassination in conjunction with the anti-Castro Cubans in Miami.

DeLillo organizes his complex novel along two separate narrative tracks, each having its own time sequence. One follows the haphazard and dispiriting career of Oswald from his boyhood to his death, lingering over his Marine Corps experiences in Japan and defection to Russia, his return with Marina to Texas, and the confusing period in New Orleans when he was passing out leaflets for the Fair Play for Cuba Committee. The other track, which is presented in chapters alternating with Oswald's story, covers a time span of only eight months. It deals with the progress of the conspiracy and the ways by which Mackey subverts Win Everett's original plan. When the conspirators hear (by way of the mysterious White Russian émigré George de Mohrenschildt, a "real" person who had befriended Oswald in Dallas) of Oswald's failed attempt to shoot the right-wing General Edwin Walker, it occurs to them that the young defector may be exactly the man they are looking for. Thus the two tracks are linked, and in the final chapters of *Libra* the time sequences more or less converge.

The reader of *Libra* is confronted with two plots of great intricacy that shadow each other: the plot of the novel itself and the plot of the conspirators. DeLillo is a master of dovetailing. Employing rapid shifts of scene and voice, he creates the novelistic equivalent of a Sixties European film by, say, Godard or Antonioni, although without Antonioni's loose ends. One is dazzled by the virtuosity of *Libra*'s construction, by the pungency and ellipses of the dialogue, and by the descriptive brilliance with which the lowlife characters materialize before one's eyes. (pp. 6-7)

There is a price to be paid for all of this staccato vividness. One hardly has time to become absorbed in a particular episode before there is a sudden cut to a very different, equally spotlit scene. The result is a fragmentation of the reader's attention and a consequent diffusion of emotion. No doubt this effect is deliberate—one has encountered it before in DeLillo's fiction, notably in *Running Dog*. It suggests that the author intends to create a kind of Brechtian alienation, to put a distance between the reader and such highly charged material in order to focus on the more abstract or ideational elements of the case. DeLillo's preoccupations with secrecy, conspiracy, and death are threaded thematically throughout the novel. . . .

The fragmentation is particularly characteristic of the sections dealing with the conspirators. The Oswald scenes tend to be longer, more leisurely in their pacing, fuller in their detail. Oswald himself occupies much of the novel's space, and DeLillo handles him almost cautiously, with a minimum of melodrama. The fatherless boy who rages at his overwhelming mother; the alternatively arrogant and defensive loner with his tight little smile; the Marxist autodidact and half-baked ideologue; the inept worker who can't keep a job; the needy, sometimes loving, often violently abusive husband who tries to keep his wife dependent by refusing to let her learn English; the compulsive liar who litters his trail with odd aliases ("Hidell," "Hideel," "Drictal"); the grandiose dreamer with his mail-order weapons—this is the figure made familiar to us by witnesses and biographers, and this is essentially the figure that DeLillo presents to us as his antihero. He is the man who drifts into the toils of conspiracy, who may or may not, as he listens with seeming impassivity to the devilish temptations of Mackey and Ferrie, decide to tip the scales of history. Though DeLillo animates Oswald's history in a score of handsomely executed small scenes, he never quite manages to extricate him from his life's record and to launch him as an autonomously functioning and convincing figure in fiction. The Oswald of *Libra* remains as incoherent as was the Oswald of real life: we learn a lot about him but in the end he is still more a case than a character.

The emptiness at the center is damaging but by no means fatal to DeLillo's achievement. *Libra* should be read for the boldness of its enterprise, its unflagging liveliness of surface and pacing, the engaging idiosyncrasy of its style, and, above all, for its vision of an outlaw element in American life devoted to the well-oiled mechanism of sudden death. (p. 7)

> Robert Towers, "From the Grassy Knoll," in The New York Review of Books, Vol. XXXV, No. 13, August 18, 1988, pp. 6-7.

TERRENCE RAFFERTY

"The best things shimmer with fear," says David Ferrie, one of the many dangerous American brooders whose voices echo in Don DeLillo's novel *Libra,* about the life of Lee Harvey Oswald and the assassination of John Kennedy. Statements like Ferrie's come at us from all directions. In this book of loners and conspirators, everyone is an artist of paranoia, defending himself against the chaos of the world by firing words, ideas, and bullets at it in elaborate patterns, and De-Lillo's novel is like a stop-motion frame of the crossfire, a still picture of an awful moment, in which the deadly trajectories have a seductive clarity, and even, shockingly, a kind of beauty—we're almost dazzled enough to take it all as truth. But it isn't truth, of course. DeLillo says, in a note at the end of the book, that his work "makes no claim to literal truth," that "it is only itself, apart and complete." What we mistake for truth in *Libra* is only the shimmer of a fear that has been hoarded, cared for, lovingly developed, polished with a fetishist's single-minded devotion. *Libra* isn't for assassination buffs, though in some strange way it's about them. It is, like all DeLillo's novels, about how we nurture and stroke our dreads in solitude and then, with ferocious intensity, project them into the world. It's his best novel, because it goes right to the source—to Dallas in November, 1963, the primal scene of American paranoia. (p. 108)

The novel leaves us feeling spooked, and vaguely guilty over our enjoyment of it, and thus identifies us both with DeLillo, the self-spooked author of this fantasy history, and with the character he has invented as the author of the assassination plot. This is a semi-retired C.I.A. man named Win Everett, a kind of intelligence-community visionary: he dreams up a scheme to fake an attempt on the President's life—"a surgical miss"—whose artfully constructed trail would lead investigators back to the object of his own private fears and obsessions,

Fidel Castro. Everett, according to DeLillo, intends to conjure an assassin out of the thin air of his own mind: "He would script a gunman out of ordinary dog-eared paper, the contents of a wallet." He and his fellow-conspirator, an Agency man named Parmenter (disgraced, like him, by the failure of the Bay of Pigs operation), want their shooter to be only "a name, a face, a bodily frame they might use to extend their fiction into the world." Everett's sense of his mission, his view of the true meaning of intelligence work, verges on the mystical. . . .

Win Everett is a frightening man, a quiet monster of inwardness, and his creator understands him scarily well. DeLillo's prose has—has always had—a quality of demented lyricism, a tendency to trance out on mystery, hidden meanings, intimations that someone is coding our experience in ways we aren't meant to crack. His home turf is a realm of indeterminacy, unknowability, half-apprehension, a nightmarish connectedness that either is showing us the way things really are or is simply a shimmering mirage, just another deceptively suggestive metaphor. When he's in this territory, his sentences sing with an epic vagueness: "We were all linked in a vast and rhythmic coincidence, a daisy chain of rumor, suspicion and secret wish." And even when he's not, when he's describing what history has recorded for us, he seems most interested in capturing the blurs and shadows of events, the moment when the evidence of the senses is at its most tenuous and most contradictory, when it's closest to the beautiful abstractions of memory . . . The writing in *Libra* is enthralled, as weirdly eroticized as prisoners' poetry. The ghostly figures that glide through these pages seem the products of a consciousness drifting toward the ecstatic, inducing visions as a form of self-stimulation: the grave, solitary play of the confined.

This is the kind of consciousness that Win Everett has: he's turned on by playing with phantoms and flirting with danger. And his project is to create a reality, apart and complete in itself, whose ambiguity is bottomless—a plot in which fiction and fact mate unnaturally and make a creature that devours the minds of those who gaze on it. The hero he wants for his story is to be "a self-watcher, a man who lives in random space"—a man, that is, much like him, a man sitting in a room and thinking and waiting, dreaming the convergence of his vivid private world and the hazy, threatening world outside. "There is a world inside the world" is a refrain that runs through *Libra.* At times, this seems to be DeLillo's credo; at times, we believe it ourselves. But DeLillo is aware, as Everett isn't, of the perils of becoming carried away by visions of worlds inside worlds; he might almost have written this novel to exorcise his own tendency toward paranoid mysticism, to take a clear look at the nature of the thrill he gets from conspiracy. In isolation, Everett's plot is beautiful, elegant; escaped from his mind, running loose in the world, it's a catastrophe. One of the renegade Bay of Pigs veterans who take part in carrying it out says to himself: "Everett's obsession was scattered in technique. The plan grew too twisty and deep. Everett wanted mazes that extended to infinity. The plan was anxious, self-absorbed. It lacked the full heat of feeling." . . . The people who carry out Everett's hermetically perfect plot more than compensate for its chilliness. They have feeling to burn; they intend to make this shadow play real—to shoot to kill, not just to confuse. They have too much reality, too much life, themselves to fit comfortably into Everett's mazy, solipsistic plan; and their unpredictability enriches DeLillo's work too—rescues it from self-absorption. In *Libra* he's a self-watcher in the process of transcending himself.

DeLillo manages to break out of the conspiracy junkie's cell by constructing what seems to be an unusually complex arrangement of mirrors: there's never only one angle on events, always another eye drawing a bead. While Everett, Parmenter, and the other disgruntled spooks (all characters invented by DeLillo) are refining their secret designs, illuminating the sacred text of their conspiracy, the life of Lee Oswald is being laid out for us in a kind of mocking, parodic counterpoint. He's as paranoid as they are, but his madness lacks the pure, ascetic, aestheticized dimension of theirs; it's messy, incoherent, needy, a state of mind created not by a runaway sense of empowerment but by squalor and oppressive enforced loneliness. "His space," DeLillo tells us, "had been nothing but wandering, a lie that concealed small rooms, TV, his mother's voice never-ending." Oswald thinks of himself as "a zero in the system," feels at peace only when he's riding the subway in New York . . . , and caroms like a pinball from one home to another, from one set of beliefs to their opposite. DeLillo tracks Oswald through all his small rooms— from the ones where as an adolescent he sits alone, reading about Communism and imagining himself borne along on that great tide of history, to a cell in a military brig, to hotel rooms in Moscow where he's confined after his defection, to a crummy house in New Orleans, to the sixth floor of the Texas School Book Depository, and to yet another cell, in the Dallas Police and Courts Building. Oswald's is a life that refuses to make sense, in part because he's obsessed with self-definition: he's constantly, restlessly searching for a system he isn't a zero in, for a context to explain, and enlarge, him. The horrible joke of *Libra* is that this random particle named Lee Oswald attaches itself to the grand structure of the intelligence mandarins' plan. He appears out of nowhere, as the living confirmation of a theory, the embodiment of Everett's abstractions. (pp. 108-09)

DeLillo's portrait of Oswald is unexpectedly touching. It's what gives *Libra* the full heat of feeling. We sense in it (as we do in Conrad's *The Secret Agent*) the intensity of the writer's belief that he can illuminate the world by striking match after match at its dark margins. For the first time, DeLillo's work has the incendiary concentration of great fiction: his writing about Oswald is a long fuse that seems to lead straight to the heart of things. DeLillo uses Oswald's miserable story to show us a kind of American life that can't be imagined by lofty manipulators like Everett and Parmenter (who think of themselves as "alone in a room that was itself alone, a room that hung above the world")—a life of pain and degradation and aching alienation, a life in which paranoia is visceral, not intellectual, and resolves itself in violence. Everett's plan goes wrong (and the novel goes right) because Oswald, and his mother, and Ferrie, and Jack Ruby were *real,* and ultimately unassimilable by even the most sophisticated paranoid art. They're too volatile to be simply used: the behavior of the newly discovered particles is unpredictable, and everything blows up, and real people die, and something toxic is released and spreads indiscriminately, uncontrollably, without mind.

There's another line of development in *Libra,* alongside the progress of the assassination and the sordid biography of the assassin, and this line has a cautionary tone. DeLillo has created, as an instrument of self-reflection, an investigator named Nicholas Branch, a retired C.I.A. man who has been hired to "write the secret history of the assassination." Inundated with data (sent to him by someone known as the Curator), Branch sits alone in a "room of dreams, the room where it has taken him all these years to learn that his subject is not politics or violent crime but men in small rooms." The description links him with that other solitary dreamer, Everett, and also with DeLillo, the brooding writer, the man who's trying to make all the right connections, to find the pattern in the chaos of crude facts and refined deceptions. Branch's project, and DeLillo's, is a constant struggle against the seductions of solitude: the temptation to wipe out the mess of traumatic experience by the pure exercise of intellect, to abstract everything in a grand and perfect metaphor, something that can be held in the mind, apart and complete. Branch's investigation—itself a metaphor for our shifting reactions to the assassination over the past twenty-five years—takes him through despair, solipsism, poetic reverie, deep paranoia, sorrowful anger at his own limitations: his method is a kind of creative drift, an unfocussed receptivity. . . . Branch ends up with an interpretation that is partly theoretical, partly not, a half-abstraction that acknowledges its inability to satisfy the paranoid mind: "The conspiracy against the President was a rambling affair that succeeded in the short term due mainly to chance. Deft men and fools, ambivalence and fixed will and what the weather was like." And DeLillo concludes *Libra* with the image and the voice of Marguerite Oswald, the "mother in history," standing over her son's grave (marked with a fictitious name) and ranting incomprehensibly, inelegantly, howling with animal confusion. Her presence, like her son's, is an unbeautiful anomaly in the world of patterns and conspiracies, and it gives us a less pleasurable tingle than the glimpses of the "world inside the world." It's an intimation of the more terrifying world without. (p. 110)

Terrence Rafferty, "Self-Watcher," in The New Yorker, *Vol. LXIV, No. 32, September 26, 1988, pp. 108-10.*

CECELIA TICHI

[In *Libra*], DeLillo works the kind of territory exploited by Truman Capote's self-styled nonfiction novel, *In Cold Blood,* and Norman Mailer's *The Executioner's Song.* **Libra,** like them, concerns actual killers and victims, though DeLillo's characters are not the anonymous murderers off the interstate and their "ordinary" prey. Because this novel deals with Lee Harvey Oswald's assassination of President John F. Kennedy, its protagonist is a public byword from the outset, and DeLillo sets himself the task of making fresh characters who are already notorious in the public mind, giving suspense to a narrative already detailed in various post-assassination reports, depositions, and journalist accounts.

DeLillo foreswears the Faulknerian or Joycean interior monologue, evidently believing such a form to be impossible in the age of the multi-media information explosion. Data ("data-spew," he calls it) has overwhelmed the individual consciousness. "The Joycean Book of America . . . the novel in which nothing is left out" is no longer feasible. The very idea of comprehensiveness has become, of all things, the fiction of the historian.

And DeLillo does challenge the prerogatives of the historian whose facts, he argues, threaten to be chimerical when computers can tell us everything about our bank transactions and yet leave matters as seemingly simple as a hat size or time of day indeterminate. Embedded in *Libra* is the parable of the mute historian, a retired CIA senior analyst assigned to write the definitive account of the assassination. In the fifteenth year of his task, he works in a room overflowing with "an incredible haul of human utterance," witnesses' names, hearing transcripts, polygraph reports, canceled checks, tax returns, the grisly material of ballistics tests conducted on goat carcasses, human skulls, blocks of gelatin. Devoting his life to understanding a moment that "broke the back of the American century," he has yet to write a word. His data "lies so flat on the page . . . lost to syntax and other arrangement, that it resembles a kind of mind-spatter." The novelist, on the other hand, can spend a few weeks at the local library shelf on the Kennedy assassination and find the random points of light that will become a fictional constellation. . . .

DeLillo essentially pits the novelist against the historian, which is to say fiction against nonfiction.

Indeed, to dip into volumes on the assassination is to see how closely DeLillo sticks with the published material. . . . DeLillo amalgamates the conspiracy theories developed in the aftermath of the Warren Commission report (which Norman Mailer called "a congeries of evasions"), basing his own theory on findings of the 1970s Congressional House Assassinations Committee, which expressed "suspicion" that elements of the Mafia and/or anti-Castro activists may have taken part in the plot.

Libra is also indebted to the BBC journalist Anthony Summers's book *Conspiracy,* which argues the possibility that "a renegade element in U.S. Intelligence manipulated Oswald."

DeLillo constructs exactly that scenario with fictionalized CIA men moved by zeal and greed. But DeLillo also questions the nature of conspiracy itself, presenting it on the one hand as "the perfect working of a scheme, a cold and certain game [by] silent nameless men with unadorned hearts" who find "coherence in some criminal act"; on the other, as "a rambling affair that succeeds in the short run due mainly to chance," a convergence of "deft men and fools, ambivalence and fixed will and what the weather was like." This latter may suggest the reason for DeLillo's preoccupation with conspiracy in virtually all his novels.

Libra is loosely biographical, following the episodes in Oswald's life that weave into the convergent conspiracies. . . .

Readers of DeLillo can certainly take pleasure in *Libra.* The characteristic barbs are here: "All over [the CIA] they were formulating plans to hit Fidel. It was an industry like wood pulp or shoes." And no one writing today so well sees the metaphysical in the American mundane, or so clearly recognizes loneliness as the great American subject. . . .

Libra, moreover, continues its author's ongoing meditation on the mass media, especially television which virtually brackets the novel. In contrast to the rosy nostalgic fictional TV moments recalled in a number of recent novels, the boy Lee, sequestered in a forced, suffocating intimacy with his mother, watches the filter-tinted "blue heads [that] spoke to them from the TV screen." Later we see Marina enraptured by an erotically televisual President Kennedy, and finally Lee's detached sense of his televised death at the hand of Jack Ruby, which he watches onscreen: "He could see himself shot as the camera caught it. Through the pain he watched TV. . . . The only thing left was the mocking pain, the picture of the twisted face on TV."

Yet *Libra* pays a high price for these fictional moments. The usually ebullient and bold DeLillo so curtails his range of language here that he competes, unsuccessfully, with his own sources. Too often we get paraphrase instead of the imaginative depth the novel at its best affords. *Libra* is too much a novelization, too little the kind of novel we have come to expect from DeLillo.

Cecelia Tichi, "Walking the Line," in Boston Review, *Vol. XIII, No. 3, October, 1988, p. 16.*

GREG TATE

It seemed inevitable that DeLillo would one day write *Libra,* his new novel about Lee Harvey Oswald and the CIA. Not just because he's fascinated with the conspiratorial bent of the human species, but because in DeLillo's fiction Everyman is as culpable for the state of things as the monstrous secret agencies of power. DeLillo's books don't read like "moral fiction"; he doesn't write moralizing prose. But his fictional worldview has always implied a moral taxonomy unblinking enough to lump the sins of the lowly in with those of the Feds. . . .

For DeLillo's small-time operators, history is a wilderness waiting to be conquered by sheer force of personality. The construction of a false persona—which looks like their shot at immortality—instead becomes the arena for a bumrush on insignificance. Hot in pursuit of the neuroses of lost souls, DeLillo subjects their ethical blind sides to the same condemnation he puts down on the powerful. Condemnation, however, is too inelegant a word for the way ethical lessons are handed out in DeLillo's books—mainly in one scintillating sentence after another. The epigrammatic rush of his sentences suggests a prose ménage à trois of Chandler, Sartre, and Barthes. Surgical and shamanistic, a DeLillo sentence mixes existentialism and deconstruction in a style charged with the cool vernacular zing that Crane, Twain, and Hemingway brought into the language and that Chandler made sing like guttertalk.

Like Chandler, DeLillo loves an epiphany as much as he loves a mystery, and in Oswald and the CIA he's latched on to subject matter that allows him to toss some combination lallapaloozas. While other DeLillo novels have read like metafiction whodunits, *Libra* shrewdly involves us more with the mystery of Oswald's being than with why Kennedy was assassinated. On the sly, *Libra* performs a service to popular history by putting to rest the notion of Oswald as a lone gunman who popped out of nowhere.

The weight of facts supporting the argument that Oswald was a pawn or creation of U.S. intelligence—at the very least well known to them long before November 22, 1963—is overwhelming. In Oswald, after all, we have a Marine who defects to Russia after receiving security clearance at a U2 spy-plane base in Japan, goes to the American embassy in Moscow and throws down his passport, belligerently declaring himself a Marxist. He leaves Russia married to the niece of a Russian colonel. Upon his return to the U.S., he's visited by FBI and CIA operatives and pumped for information; soon he's seen passing out pro-Castro literature in Miami.

As DeLillo runs his version, the assassination plot is hatched by the CIA masterminds Kennedy betrayed when he refused air support for their anti-Castro operatives during the Bay of Pigs. In planning an assassination attempt they hope to blame on Castro, these agents concoct an imaginary assassin. The joke is that if Oswald hadn't existed, the CIA would have invented him.

Libra reaches fuguish complexity in floating every possible source for a Kennedy assassination plot you've ever heard—Oswald as lone gunman, Mafia, pro-Castro and anti-Castro operatives, Russians—while clearly settling on a CIA conspiracy. Through narrative legerdemain and a sense of detail bordering on the cartographic, DeLillo doesn't close the door on any of the suspects, even as he's narrowing it down to his chosen ones. . . .

Libra stretches credulity with a string of coincidences that can make even synchronicity diehards beg for relief. Were DeLillo not such a spooky writer, the novel might collapse beneath its parallel narrative shafts and converging plot lines. DeLillo doesn't just invent characters; he possesses them, inhabiting their personas, like a vampire or psychotherapist. His social range, always vast, has never seemed so preternaturally knowledgeable. When he takes you inside the head of Jack Ruby or a Russian intelligence man or Oswald's mama, you feel like a telepathic and unrepentant voyeur—or a gatherer of covert information. Same difference, and another metafictional effect: DeLillo replicates the very thing he's deconstructing.

Geographically and structurally, the novel roams with Oswald all over space and time: Texas, the Bronx, Dallas, Miami, Japan, Russia. It also takes place in the present: Nicholas Branch, a retired CIA historian, has been assigned the fool's task of writing an account of the assassination. (p. 39)

Libra is most obsessed with the Spook Mind, the psyche of the secret police set loose upon the world by the powerful. The bulk of the book's characters are spies—Ivy League spooks and aristocratic émigré operatives, anti-Castro spooks and spies who moonlight with the John Birch Society, Russian intelligence men and Japanese double agents, U2 pilot Francis Gary Powers. The cult of secret intelligence is rendered as a faith, the men in it driven less by purpose than by fear of being left out in the cold. Behind the freebooting adventurism is the anxiety of being turned out of the warm womb of the national intelligence apparatus.

While the Kennedy assassination has been seen as the harbinger of things to come in the '60s U.S. of A., prelude to an era of shocking political violence, through DeLillo we come to see the Bay of Pigs and the many failed plots against Castro as the era's true preview—the first inkling that the American imperialist monster might not be such hot shit after all. The CIA cowboys who had to live with the Bay of Pigs disaster had failed the macho credo of the patriarchy. In *Libra,* we come to sense that the defeat embarrassed their culture, and they decided to place the blame on Kennedy's head.

Oswald and the renegade spooks become, in DeLillo's hands, case studies of the white supremacist male as Other, as a species flailing against the reality that history is moving so fast their only hope for survival is going undercover—plotting and scheming against the world because subversion has become the last refuge of their dying doctrine. As with all DeLillo novels, *Libra* is also fiction about the making of fiction, and about those fictionalized versions of the facts that we call history. DeLillo's reconstruction of Oswald from the data that has his CIA historian Branch in a tizzy is a satirical cele-

bration of the freedom of fiction makers to play around with the facts.

The most poignant reward of DeLillo's fiction is being seduced by the pity and compassion he showers on the cold-blooded monsters among his characters. I'm thinking of a scene involving the most ruthless of DeLillo's CIA cowboys, T-Jay Mackey—though dozens of other close-ups on the domestic lives of spies in *Libra* illustrate the same point. . . . (p. 40)

It's DeLillo's portrayal of Oswald, though, that nearly makes you want to cry. Oswald comes on the set star-crossed, fucked from birth. His daddy dies of a heart attack before he's born, and he and his mother spend most of his childhood living at the poor-house gate. The relationship between Oswald and his mom is claustrophobic, spiteful, and unrooted. In Texas, to which he will one day return on his mission, his Bronx accent gets him figured for a geek. Oswald is no nerd—he's just consumed by the belief that he's destined for something more than routine white-boydom. (pp. 40-1)

Like several other DeLillo protagonists, Oswald has a problem with language and verbal communication, possibly in the form of dyslexia.

> Always the pain, the chaos of composition. He could not find order in the little field of symbols. . . . [T]he language tricked him with its inconsistencies. He watched sentences deteriorate, powerless to make them right. The nature of things was to be elusive. Things slipped through his perceptions. He could not get a grip on the runaway world. Limits everywhere. In every direction he came up against his own incompleteness. Cramped, fumbling, deficient. He knew things. It wasn't that he didn't know.

DeLillo might well be alluding to his own tortured creative process—to the burden of needing infinite knowledge to write his kind of books. Not only does he need to know Oswald; he needs to know the Oswald others know. In the metafiction that is *Libra,* every other character seems to be creating a fictitious Oswald, preying on Oswald's impassioned sense of self-destiny and limited self-knowledge—even Oswald, who endlessly invents and reinvents his own myth. But in a sense he remains an enigma to himself. The voice that lays claim to knowing the *real* Oswald belongs to Oswald's mother, who throughout his life is forever negotiating to get him a better deal from fate. She may be the most berserk stage mother ever encountered in literature. As Oswald stumbles toward his destiny, she's always one step behind, attempting to explain the plot that's been in effect against her son's life from birth. And in seeking some plot, any plot, she scrambles and rambles out a first-person history as overbaked with irrationality as the Official Story.

Against DeLillo's observation that all plots, and hence all narratives, inevitably end in death, Oswald's mother's narrative is the unhinged and chaotic narrative of life, the force that goes on and on beyond the power of the machinations of men to contain it, control it, silence it, deny it, and ultimately to historicize it. DeLillo makes us remember that even Lee Harvey Oswald had a mother and, therefore, once upon a time, an innocence. Through Marguerite Oswald's arguments, DeLillo demonstrates that the God-novelist not only has the power to peek into his neighbors' skulls and pass judgment, but to listen intimately, to record the fragility and folly of that absolving mechanism figuratively known as the human heart. . . . (p. 41)

Greg Tate, "White Magic: Don DeLillo's Intelligence Networks," in VLS, *No. 68, October, 1988, pp. 39-41.*

Rick DeMarinis

1934-

American novelist and short story writer.

In his fiction, DeMarinis often creates unsettling comic situations to illustrate the distorted values and psychological perversions of his characters. Utilizing such devices as parody, satire, and black humor, DeMarinis frequently concentrates on the theme of moral disintegration in contemporary society. Although some critics have faulted DeMarinis's development of subject matter, many commend his inventive approaches to fiction. Joanne Wilkinson observed: "DeMarinis writes in a beautiful and languorous style about unrelentingly grim subjects. His technical virtuosity . . . never masks his high emotions; he is alternately angry, compassionate, and darkly humorous."

DeMarinis's first book, *A Lovely Monster: The Adventures of Claude Rains and Dr. Tellenbeck* (1975), burlesques Mary Shelley's classic novel *Frankenstein* and its well-known cinematic adaptations. Created in Dr. Tellenbeck's condominium, the monster, Claude Rains, is a benevolent being who enjoys crafts and painting and yearns for love and kindness, which his insensitive master is unable to provide. In *Scimitar* (1977), DeMarinis satirizes both the American military industry and humanity's desire for immortality. This novel centers upon an employee of an aerospace corporation who is wrongly accused of murder. His attempts to vindicate himself, however, carry bizarre and dangerous consequences. A story of suspense and adventure, *Scimitar* was praised for DeMarinis's adept parody of the rhetoric and techniques of science fiction. *Cinder* (1978), a reworking of the tale of Aladdin and his magic lamp, focuses upon an elderly man who becomes the reluctant master of a genie. The protagonist's hesitancy to wield his new power provides much of the story's comic irony. *The Burning Women of Far Cry* (1986) is a psychological chronicle of small-town Americana that is related by Jack, an adolescent boy. Referring to the women in Far Cry as "burning" because of their fervent comprehension of life's oppressiveness, Jack observes and comments upon members of his family, in particular his domineering and embittered mother. Jack's flight from her hostile dominion lends the story a hopeful conclusion.

DeMarinis's short stories reflect the thematic concerns of his novels. His first collection, *Jack and Jill* (1979), consists of two novellas and a short story examining the spiritual peace that can be attained when people relinquish illusions and confront reality. *Under the Wheat* (1986) focuses on protagonists with distorted perceptions of society. The title story, for example, features a character whose only view of the world is from the bottom of a missile silo. The stories in DeMarinis's recent volume, *The Coming Triumph of the Free World* (1988), concentrate on individuals whose sense of humor enables them to cope with a decaying, corrupt society. Elizabeth Tallent stated: "[These] tales imply a chilly, brilliantly lit world on the brink of absolute darkness, chronicled with speedy, black-hearted elan."

(See also *Contemporary Authors,* Vols. 57-60 and *Contemporary Authors New Revision Series,* Vol. 9.)

RICK DeMARINIS

[With *A Lovely Monster*] I wanted to write a Frankenstein novel from the point of view of the monster. It occurred to me that a creature made up of a variety of donor organs would first of all not be in robust health. In novels of this kind, the monster is usually endowed with terrifying physical strength right from the outset. That has never seemed plausible to me. Therefore, my monster, 'Claude,' begins life in a post-operative twilight: weak, dazed, frightened. He also starts out a terrible hypochondriac. That too seemed probable to me. After all, his survival depends on the successful interdependence of many organs, each alien to the other. The danger of massive rejection is ever-present. Claude does become powerful and a bit frightening, but only after he takes up a regimen of jogging and weightlifting. Thus, his strength is never super-human even though it is formidable. Other things occurred to me: the monster would be motherless. His 'father,' Dr. Tellenbeck, is a bachelor scientist who created Claude in a spare room of his condominium. There are no women in Tellenbeck's life, and he shows no patience or understanding for the monster's esthetic inclinations, as a sympathetic mother certainly would. (The monster takes up macramé and oil painting.) This absence of feminity in his early life leads him to dream of a giant female who loves him at the risk of offending her giant husband, a gross figure at the bottom of Claude's worst nightmares. The images from this recurrent dream come from the monster's reading of the fairy tale, "Jack and the Beanstalk." In the dream, the monster sees himself as Jack—a Promethean commuter between the intolerable real world and the terrifying world of fabulous discovery. All this gives a strong Oedipal thrust to the novel, as well. Finally, another theme suggested itself to me: just what is human and what is truly monstrous? This led me to juxtapose certain recognizable character types, the satiric content of which is apparent: the monster is closer to being 'human' than most of the humans in the story. (pp. 1851-52)

> *Rick DeMarinis, in a review of "A Lovely Monster,"*
> *in* Library Journal, *Vol. 100, No. 17, October 1,*
> *1975, pp. 1851-52.*

ROBERT J. FLYNN

Will the real Claude Rains please stand up? The fact of the matter is that a return to life by the late, great film actor would be infinitely easier to accept than his fictionalized namesake, a casserole creation of renowned biochemist Kraft Tellenbeck. Or would it? For one wonders if the imagination of first-time novelist Rick DeMarinis conjures up more future fact than fiction [in *A Lovely Monster*].

Tellenbeck has fabricated Alpha Six. This is the lovely monster of the title, an amalgamation of other creatures' spare parts . . . fingers and eyes, bits of bones, brains and pieces of brains, nervous systems and fragments thereof. Included in this humanoid potpourri are the startling genitalia of a shetland pony and a mountain gorilla, not for scientific sensationalism but for external proof positive of experimental validity.

That's the lovely Claude, the name Alpha selects after his favorite late-night TV movie star. He grows in wisdom, grace, and artistry, not to mention sexual proclivity, super strength, and hair-trigger sensitivity. It is the last three conditions that complicate his "life." Everything seems to overwhelm . . . nubile women, a boozy condominium life, barroom brawls, and the ultimate betrayal by Tellenbeck of his cellular paste-up before a symposium of biochemists.

The emotional conflicts between Claude and Tellenbeck, and between Claude himself and society, are monumental. The novel is not.

Or is it? In an emerging age of transplants, bionics, test tube babies, and predetermined sex, author DeMarinis may be alarmingly clairvoyant.

> *Robert J. Flynn, in a review of "A Lovely Monster,"*
> *in* Best Sellers, *Vol. 36, No. 2, May, 1976, p. 37.*

PUBLISHERS WEEKLY

DeMarinis's second novel [*Scimitar*] is quite something: a dazzling piece of serious fun, a futuristic romp that uses some of the techniques and vocabulary of SF to go beyond SF and provide a biting satire on military-industrial technocracy. Middle-aged Arjay Ponce, a technical writer for a giant California-based aerospace corporation, is promoted, rather surprisingly, to be manager of a new, Arab-financed super strategic weapon project, "Scimitar." Then his wife deserts him for an athletic and sinister guru and his girl friend is strangled. Forced into hiding, he tries to substantiate his hunch that the guru is the real killer. Clues lead him to a desert retreat run by an ultra technocrat and monster . . . who makes some astonishing revelations: as to why "Scimitar" is being sabotaged, for instance, why Arjay was framed for murder and how he can win eternal life. It's all splendidly funny, energetic and inventive.

> *A review of "Scimitar," in* Publishers Weekly, *Vol.*
> *211, No. 1, January 3, 1977, p. 60.*

CHRISTOPHER LEHMANN-HAUPT

[Hilarity is] the quality celebrated in the dust-jacket kudos that appear on Rick DeMarinis's *Scimitar.* But it was less amusement that kept me reading this second novel by the author of *A Lovely Monster: The Adventures of Claude Rains and Dr. Tellenbeck* than it was fascination with the cruelty of the novel's characters, the garishness of its prose, and the comic-book excess of the imagination that created it.

Like Mr. DeMarinis's captivating first novel, *Scimitar* is also about monsters, only here, instead of a sensitive human constructed from spare parts, we have the American military-industrial complex and an ancient billionaire, Skylar Blue, who has reconstituted himself by attaching his head to a mechanical spider run by computer. The story the novel tells doesn't cut very deep as a satire of defense spending, international finance, technological jargon, and the Southern California ambience. Nor does it impress particularly with its originality, deriving as it seems to do from a combination of Thomas Pynchon, William Hjortsberg, Don DeLillo, and Joseph Heller.

Still, my attention was held throughout by the story, which is told from the point of view of a schlemiel named Arjay Ponce, who is forced to clear himself of a murder he didn't commit. And the scenes in which Arjay confronts the creature behind it all—Sky Blue, the billionaire spider—are in themselves outlandish and funny enough to make the whole effort worthwhile. Also *Scimitar* is sufficiently different from *A Lovely Monster* to suggest that Mr. DeMarinis has a number of strings in his bow. This would seem to make him a writer worth continued watching to see what unpredictable thing he will attempt next.

> *Christopher Lehmann-Haupt, in a review of "Scimitar," in* The New York Times, *May 11, 1977, p. 31.*

PUBLISHERS WEEKLY

A bravura performance, DeMarinis's third novel [*Cinder*] is a sustained blend of raunchy comedy and pathos. Ulysses Cinder, a lonely widower, tells about happenings in his 70th year when a gigantic stranger, Sadass, enters his life. Cinder thinks his guest is looney or lying when the giant says he's a genie, at his host's bidding. But the first proof of magic, a humdinger, makes the old man a true believer. Cinder makes several wishes that are granted. One instance results in a disaster, another ends in a grotesquely funny situation and one (a reunion with Cinder's dead wife) is painfully disillusioning. Then Sadass and Cinder become condors for a few exultant hours, soaring all over California. In the end, the old man's good sense and humanity impel him to make a touching last request. The story is entrancing, and it also points to the plight of the aging among us.

A review of "Cinder," in Publishers Weekly, *Vol. 213, No. 26, June 26, 1978, p. 100.*

JEFFREY BURKE

[In *Cinder,* a] likably crusty old fellow named Ulysses Cinder one day finds himself in possession of a genuine genie. More power to him. He's able to spend his remaining days doing some good here, some mischief there, visiting his dead wife, flying around as a condor, and—his last wish—building a nice old-age home for himself, where a pretty nurse gives him peristaltic massages when Cinder isn't busy composing the memoir in which this novel is cast. Most of the book's action and irony derives from Cinder's reluctance to take advantage of his power, a caution accompanied by a lot of moral justification and the kind of no-nonsense philosophizing that bartenders and cabdrivers are famous for.

As in his two previous books, *A Lovely Monster* and *Scimitar,* Rick DeMarinis prefers to tell his truths slant—Emily Dickinson's direction—through satire and a fantastic premise; but he does not, continuing the poet's prescription, "dazzle gradually" in *Cinder.* The initial surprise of Aladdin-revisited plays out quickly, and Cinder's voice, as carefully and imaginatively drawn as it is, too soon makes deaf ears of tired eyes.

Jeffrey Burke, in a review of "Cinder," in Harper's, *Vol. 257, No. 1540, September, 1978, p. 94.*

KIRKUS REVIEWS

The Fisherman and His Wife, novella number one [in *Jack and Jill*], is straight cartoon. A nuclear scientist is about to leak secrets to the Japanese in 1940; an oafish giant named Child Monza is hired under false pretenses to help stop this, and finds himself caught up with the scientist's beautiful wife. There's a Japanese jazz clarinetist who gives out constantly with Forties hipster lingo. The only lift to this jerry-built genre piece is its own archness. The companion novella, *Jack and Jill,* bears down a little harder—but not much. Jill and Jack meet at a West Coast health spa. She's a traumatized ex-Air Force nurse, Jack's an engineer courting breakdown as he rushes to beat the Japanese to the first self-learning robot. Soul and science hook up—and it's really quite deft the way DeMarinis leads the story on into disaster. But still you get the feeling that pet themes are being idly toyed with here, not driven to the wall. The short story, **"Medicine Man,"** illustrates, though, how good—and spooky, and inventive—DeMarinis can be when he really bears down and concentrates. An Indian medicine man in the contemporary West can cure anyone but himself; he goes through magics like a man rifling a desk drawer to find an important paper. The story is dry and tight and vivid—which makes the slack noodling of the novellas that much more unsatisfying.

A review of "Jack and Jill: Two Novellas and a Story," in Kirkus Reviews, *Vol. XLVI, No. 22, November 15, 1978, p. 1262.*

SUSAN FROMBERG SCHAEFFER

In Rick DeMarinis' world of bizarre events, exotic characters come and go, and the rational is expected. DeMarinis tells his stories like a man used to sitting in bars and spinning tall tales, and, in [*Jack and Jill*], all three of his tales affirm the existence of a transcending peace which either comes after illusions of the world are cast off, or after one understands that there is a controlling harmony in the universe which includes and requires such opposites as comedy and tragedy, confusion and clarity.

In *Jack and Jill,* DeMarinis plays entertainingly with the idea that "nothing ever really ended and what seemed finished would often fool you and more often than not start all over again with only minor changes for the sake of variety." A life is, in other words, finite in time, but infinite in combination. Everything that happens recombines previous events and personalities.

There is nothing new in this idea, and in *Jack and Jill,* DeMarinis' success depends upon how well he can play theme and variation upon this basic melody. "Life," as DeMarinis repeatedly observes, "is tricky." For the author, the trick is to present his theme in new and entertaining guises. For the reader, the trick is to discover the point of view that provides a pattern in the mosaic of the tale.

Of the three tales, the first, *The Fisherman and His Wife,* is probably the least successful. This tale bears little resemblance to the one from which it takes its name, but there are enough associative links between the two to justify the notion that, in his, DeMarinis is writing a further fable for our time.

In DeMarinis' version, a scientist named Fardell does not want to be Pope, but he does want to buy a kingdom for his wife. The magic passport to this kingdom is not a flounder (Fardell catches the flounder and eats it), but his knowledge of nuclear fission, the secrets of which he intends to sell to the Japanese. . . .

As Fardell and his wife, Beatrice, move through espionage and counterespionage accompanied by an ugly, benevolent giant, a government agent who is also an albino, and a tiny Japanese man who hides in the cars he rents, they are more and more in "complicity with the heartless world." This complicity gives only one of them, Child Monza, a greater understanding of life. He begins to sense that something unites all creatures on earth, and, soon after, understands that "his essence" cannot be imprisoned within his physical body. His feeling of entrapment has been illusory. . . . Monza understands the nature of his freedom: "My freedom. It existed by itself, for itself, and it always would regardless of my mistakes, my fears, or my entangling passions."

Of course the notion that man is as free as he thinks he is has been stated before, notably by all the existentialists. But *The Fisherman and His Wife* fails to make this truth self-evident. If we want to believe that Monza is right, we simply have to take his word for it.

The obsessions of *The Fisherman* are shared by the next story, **"The Medicine Man."** Its central character is a healer who believes, among other things, that "the universe was nothing more than a bundle of close lines." When prevented from healing a dying friend, he becomes obsessed with the inevitability of death. His dreams haunt him with white, dead soapbodies falling from the clouds. He heals a half-dead dog, but to its owner insists that it is "already dead" because he knows it soon will be. His knowledge of death brings a gift for seeing into the future, and he is soon telling people things they do not want to hear. Eventually, he finds a cure for his melancholy in jimson weed, which is known to cause madness. His madness proves curative, and, once again, he becomes the admirable medicine man. . . .

In the novella, *Jack and Jill,* DeMarinis' preoccupations are the same; unlike the first two stories, the obsessions of this one lie close to the surface, although at first they are stated parodically. "The central problem," thinks Jack, the engineer who invents and then tries to perfect his servant robot, "was with the central intelligence." Everyone in *Jack and Jill* is afflicted with this brand of intelligence, and the novella charts many hilarious attempts to deal with it.

Doctor Narian, who practices "Rectification Therapy" at the Waters of Life Spa where Jack and Jill have gone to relax, preaches that pain and anguish comes from misperceived reality. "Rectify the misapprehension," he says, "dissolve the anguish." This turns out to be impossible, since illusions cannot be dismantled "in two stages," as one of the characters had hoped. Illusions, Jill concludes, "were not mortal, and life was probably not possible at all without them. Life was illusion." But if intelligence cannot "dismantle illusion" and "rectify the misapprehension," "ancient principles" deep within the person (better known as instincts) can guide one to the true perception which can then "dissolve the anguish."

Only Kakashi Kioka, a Japanese poet, reincarnated as a robot in the midst of the novella's events, and Jill, who finds her "inner animal," escape the bounds of their artifical intelligence; at least, they see the harmony that orders all things in nature. . . .

As the characters of *Jack and Jill* move to their destinies, they reach the conclusion that forms the volume's epigraph: "Out of this world we cannot fall." In this world, there is order and harmony, perception of which brings peace, light, and freedom. "OM," as the dying scientist says, unaware of the word's meaning, or that, in dying, he is reaching peace.

Rick DeMarinis' *Jack and Jill* will certainly please readers of Vonnegut, although his often witty tangling of theme and form may irritate a reader who had come to like such tangles when tied by Nabokov. His characters often fail to come alive, as if powered by defective batteries, and frequently, the seams in the story are left showing. Nevertheless, this is an innovative, interesting, and highly imaginative book.

> *Susan Fromberg Schaeffer, "Three Fables for Our Times," in* Book World—The Washington Post, *January 21, 1979, p. 1.*

JANET SHAW

When a frightened housewife tells the door-to-door salesman peddling the Farrago Cyclops peephole that it distorts her vision, he explains, "It's the lens, ma'am. Fish eye. It puts a bend in the world, but you get to see more of it that way." In *Under the Wheat,* a collection of powerful, irreverent short stories . . . , Rick DeMarinis puts a bend in the world

to give us a long hard look at characters who embody on a grand scale the psychological and spiritual deformities in our culture. In **"The Smile of a Turtle"** the Cyclops salesman seduces and intimidates women in order to sell them self-protection; in the title story **["Under the Wheat"],** a man charged with watching ICBM missile sites doesn't *see* his wife go crazy and vanish; in **"Life Between Meals,"** the huge obese "Commodore" selects young women with enough self-destructive potential to join him in his sex-and-food orgies.

What is the author's attitude toward this bizarre menagerie? Here's one clue: another salesman asks his young apprentice in the soul-deadening arts of sleazy manipulation, "You think the human condition is a form of entertainment for us less unfortunate citizens, amigo? . . . Remember, 'There but for the grace of God go I.' " The young man, Jack, who despises his employer's hypocritical self-righteousness, answers, "Sometimes it's entertaining as hell."

Jack shows up again as the narrator of the novel, **The Burning Women of Far Cry,** which opens with engaging humor. It's the 50's, Jack and his sister, LaDonna, are young teen-agers, and his twice-widowed mother has married Gent Mundy, owner of Mundy's Old Times Creamery. . . . The house Gent moves them into has no secrets Jack can't solve—he's a spy in his own childhood. He discovers that everyone, except Gent, is obsessed with sex; although Gent has a collection of quaint pornographic photos, he's obsessed with *love,* and in the grim world depicted in Far Cry, that's suicide.

Mr. DeMarinis is writing farce, and the characters quickly become cartoons. Spencer Ted, the enormous, retarded baby, roughs up Mom like a stevedore while she flirts with her lover, Guy, who delivers milk for Gent's creamery. LaDonna sleeps with local boys, and Jack is introduced to cigarettes, booze (no drugs, this is the 50's), sex, deception and self-deception. After Jack grows up and leaves home, these episodes are strung together in no discernible order, like box cars on a freight train.

By Part Three, the tone of the novel is as loud and aggressive as a mean drunk. The deft and ironic touch of the opening has become a fist. And how about the gentle Gent Mundy? Beached up in a loony bin, he believes he *is* the saxophone he used to play to ward off despair. Jack imagines Gent blowing "Yawnk dun dun dunna yawnk bleeropp," a sound that captures the mood of Mr. DeMarinis's dark humor.

> *Janet Shaw, "Yawnk Bleeropp," in* The New York Times Book Review, *December 14, 1986, p. 26.*

JOHN CLUTE

Rick DeMarinis started his first short career as a writer about a decade ago. Before the 1970s were out, he had published one fine collection of stories and three novels, of which *Scimitar* (1977) is the most striking. But the world did not sit up and take notice. His fables of moral convulsion and comic despair in the sunrise states may have seemed too much like science fiction for some readers, too unconsolingly bleak for others. Whatever the reasons, DeMarinis published no books after *Jack & Jill* (1979), and seemed to have quit the battle. Until this year.

Like Antaeus, he has returned, and in a very real sense it is as though something in his native soil has energized and transformed his work. Without abandoning the acid rampageousness of the fabulist, he has magically expanded and deepened his version of America. Where in the 1970s his characters performed dances of estrangement and alienation through the duplicitous paradise of Southern California, they are now locked into the hard limitless land that gave them birth.

Set in the small city of Far Cry, somewhere in the High Plains, deep in the heart of the Eisenhower years, *The Burning Women of Far Cry,* his fine new novel, runs its adolescent hero through a phosphorescent rite of passage. Much of *Under the Wheat,* a collection of stories, . . . takes place in the same American heartland, where the dreams start. It too is merciless, irradiated by DeMarinis' cruel intelligence. It too is filled with the textures of love.

Young Jack tells his own story of growing up in Far Cry. His father has shot himself. His mother's new husband soon jumps off a bridge into heavy rapids. The next victim of her burning psyche marries her, watches her cuckold him in his own kitchen, gradually falls through cellars of unendurable despair into lunacy. But Jack's mother is only one of several women in the book who are so cursed with consciousness of the mortal trap of their world that they seem literally to burn. DeMarinis' portrait of her is relentless and moving, and makes deeply plausible the intoxicating effect she has, not only on other men, but on her son as well. That Jack manages to survive his mother's scalding self-knowledge is central to the extraordinary sense of triumph the reader takes away from the final pages, when he has become an unmonstrous man.

It is not an easy accomplishment, for in DeMarinis' world true adulthood is clearly a goal few achieve. Cuckolded, bewildered, infantile and bulimic, the third husband Gent Mundy fills Jack's early adolescence with images of man's impotence to fashion a tolerable life out of the hard facts of the world; DeMarinis' rendering of the man's long despair is at times almost unreadably accurate. . . .

But Jack does grow up. After the ordeals depicted in the first third of the book, he begins to escape into an existence less implacable, less exorbitant, and *The Burning Women of Far Cry* loses some of its fiery grip on the reader. Episode succeeds episode in a fashion almost dilatory, until Jack, after a terrible accident, returns home. . . . Without allowing him to break into undue articulacy, DeMarinis makes it clear that Jack, having seen all, is beginning to know what he needs to know. He earns a living. He meets a girl who has not yet begun to burn. It looks as though she may stay sane, as Jack may, in the world they are about to enter.

One of the less successful sequences in the novel follows Jack into a stint as a door-to-door photographer under the tutelage of Jack Billetdoux, pronounced Billy Ducks, a desultory scam-artist who nearly always sabotages his own successes. In shorter form, and much more effective for the trimming, "Billy Ducks Among the Pharaohs" closes off *Under the Wheat,* a collection of stories of almost unfailing excellence. Embalmed in material goods, the wealthy suburbanites of America may be like Pharaohs, but for Billy Ducks the world itself is ancient Egypt, and the people of the world are unknowable and dread. You can fool them and cheat them, but you cannot penetrate their mystery. At the end of this superb tale the unnamed narrator is about to be initiated into the Circean depths of that mystery. . . .

In "Weeds," perhaps the finest story in the book, "Jack and

the Beanstalk" is recast into an apocalyptic fable about mortality, the ecological destruction of the American heartlands, and the end of the world. Every word counts. *Under the Wheat* is a short collection which lasts long in the mind's eye. DeMarinis has the fabulist's wit, the grave muscle of Antaeus. Taken together, his two new books are a literary event of real importance.

John Clute, "DeMarinis: The Return of a Writer," in Book World—The Washington Post, *January 11, 1987, p. 6.*

GREG JOHNSON

[The seven stories in *Under the Wheat*] seem deliberately arranged . . . to illustrate the author's technical virtuosity, progressing from the brooding realism of the title piece to the surrealistic comedy of **"Billy Ducks Among the Pharaohs,"** which concludes the volume. **"Under the Wheat"** explores the effect of subterranean nuclear missiles upon farming people in North Dakota, and is followed by **"Good Wars,"** which traces the military buildup of the twentieth century as it affects an ordinary, bewildered protagonist; an ambitious, coolly rendered story, it explores the patriarchal drive for power and domination, as when the child Bernard hears the following advice from his mother's boyfriend: "No matter what the enemy does to you, . . . you must refuse to submit. His techniques may be subtle, and you may be tempted to bend to his arguments, but you must hold yourself apart from him. Deep within you there is the unviolated place of refusal. You must preserve this, under torture, under bribery, under his vile promises." If the man sounds like a 1950's version of G. Gordon Liddy, the boy is nonetheless "very impressed." Like other stories here, **"Good Wars"** is a wayward yet believable narrative, and it fully achieves the broad social and political relevance implied by its oxymoronic title.

As if to suggest that considerations of powermongering and nuclear war lead naturally into surrealism, farce, and other forms of whimsical abandon, DeMarinis' other five stories view "reality" from artfully distorted perspectives, evoking the comic madness and absurdity of the contemporary world.. . . . In **"Life Between Meals,"** a tremendously funny story, the narrator's own body suggests a grotesque distortion of vision. Disdaining thin people, whom he calls "nibblers," he celebrates the glory of overeating and the beauty of fat women: "That summer I reached a happy three hundred. I felt good. Antoinette was only one-ninety, but she was coming along fine. . . . 'Come over here, you lovely dumpling!' I'd command, and the walls of the condo would shake." Finally the narrator's infatuation with food suggests a pathological hunger for power and control, which he hides in the guise of common-sense philosophy: "Everything is either inside or it is outside. Make no mistake. If it is inside, it is being eaten. If it is outside, then it is either eating or waiting to eat. That is all anyone can say about it. The rest is manure."

Though such stories ultimately make a serious point, they are reminiscent of the postmodernist fictions of Barth or Barthelme in their flamboyance, playfulness, and self-conscious artifice. Likewise, **"Blind Euchre"** implicitly compares fiction to game-playing, and **"Billy Ducks Among the Pharaohs"** gradually shades from comic hyperrealism into unbridled fantasy. DeMarinis, unbound by conventions or any particular notions about audience, has let his materials dictate his method. Although it is conceivable that a metafictionist would scorn the earnest solemnity of **"Under the Wheat"** and a neorealist would dismiss **"Billy Ducks"** as a flight of irresponsible self-indulgence, readers of any persuasion will admire the versatility and technical skill that characterize this volume as a whole. (pp. 409-10)

Greg Johnson, *"Short Fiction in the Eighties," in* The Georgia Review, *Vol. XLI, No. 2, Summer, 1987, pp. 409-14.*

KIRKUS REVIEWS

DeMarinis explores no new territory in [the stories in ***The Coming Triumph of the Free World***], most of which are as derivative (of DeLillo especially, who does the same but better) and as mean-spirited as much of his past work. But there's also an appealing darkness and cynicism in the best stories here—they're manic tales full of consumer-culture slapstick, and of the "warpage" and "wobble" that define life in the Nuclear Age.

The weakest pieces in this uneven collection take virtuoso turns: **"Romance: a Prose Villanelle"** not only repeats key sentences, but does so in flawless imitation of bodice-ripper prose as it tells of a bored suburban housewife from the East who takes a job out West as head cook at a cattle ranch. . . . **"Queen,"** simply the worst of the bunch here, is a too-spare exercise in repetition, involving a muted romance between an elderly woman and a middle-aged man. In a quartet of stories, all funny for their admitted excesses, an unemployed fellow suffering from "severe, broad-spectrum anxiety" copes with his own twerpdom: in one, he won't shoot the dog (barking under the bedroom window) that keeps the bread-winning wife awake (**"The Handgun"**); in the title piece [**"The Coming Triumph of the Free World"**], he discovers our failure as "social animals" while shopping among psychotics, winos, bag ladies, and bikers. . . . Two other imitative stories here capture the essence of Pynchonesque paranoia; a few strike at suburban malaise and modern culture shock; and a couple even seem to suggest the possibility of "optimism and decency in a toxic-waste-dump world."

Amidst all the "defeat and degradation," then, some important truths, however vitiated by DeMarinis' perverse sensibility.

A review of *"The Coming Triumph of the Free World," in* Kirkus Reviews, *Vol. LVI, No. 9, May 1, 1988, p. 640.*

ELIZABETH TALLENT

The writer, with a cheerful lack of fastidiousness, sweeps everything into a heap—the grim bits, the ironies, hilariousness and shock, the more dismal human passages of illness, insanity, fakery and remorse, and presto!, Rick DeMarinis has written the 14 stories in ***The Coming Triumph of the Free World.***

By a certain lack of discrimination and an avid willingness to pounce, comedy, like a magpie's nest, is enriched: Oddities are allowed that would never survive a more miserly parsing of America. Thus an ominous Disneyland crops up in these stories, dirty Polaroids, a South Sea Islander who discourses on *It's a Wonderful Life* and the deleterious effects of "profound Big B Boredom Himself" on housewives, a farcical

range called the Y Bar Y, and a vivid witch out of Grimms' by way of Donald Barthelme, and you get first sentences like these: "The grizzled psychotic entered Safeway laughing," or "I lie on the nail-bed of my life still believing I am a good-hearted, sensitive man who would never beat his wife"— sentences bristling with bitter possibilities.

Possibilities, in the stories DeMarinis writes, are made to be enlarged upon, exaggerated, unrolled so that every minute ridiculousness may be examined. Here, a narrator contemplates Hopper's paintings:

> I'm looking for Edward Hopper's sense of the *thing.* How the *thing* exists for itself and itself alone. How it produces instant feelings of irrelevance in the viewer. A world of unmoving solids has no place in it for that drifter, the soul. Hopper is one of the dangerous ones. (Countertop cafe pie can leave you feeling abandoned. Curtains blowing in a dark hotel window will give you bad dreams. A gas station in Iowa can stun you to your knees.

The reader, guessing that DeMarinis would like himself considered another of the dangerous ones, does suffer acute feelings of irrelevance as the narrative torrent pours over her head.

In the collection's weaker stories, the momentum is purely verbal and only slenderly coupled to plot, while in the stronger tales it's all one thing, the voice revving a flattish story into startling verve. **"Your Story,"** narrated—intermittently and subversively—by the Grimms' witch, is a frightening thing, a fairy tale about abandoned children with elements of *In Cold Blood,* the nightly news and that post-modernist fiction that reflects on its own devices, and it works with an eerie unsettlingness on the reader's peace of mind, disquiet being a quality DeMarinis prizes in a reader. A nervous reader is a thinking reader, he implies.

A satisfied reader is a witless one, he further insinuates, in **"Romance: A Prose Villanelle,"** which adroitly parodies those paper romances containing sentences the clones of these:

> If this was not meant to be, then nothing was meant to be. Sometimes when two strangers meet they feel they've known each other forever. The tall man in cowboy regalia was such a person to Marianna. She quivered involuntarily, like the delicate needle of a compass, before the quiet magnetism of his male presence.

This story, too—a villanelle in its repetitive, back-tracking formality, by which entire annoying paragraphs are simply repeated, the funnily seductive plot bumps and grinds along, and Marianna realizes that "No Man Can Provide My Identity"—pauses to reflect on itself. . . . (pp. 1, 9)

Entropy, the silence lying in wait, "Big B Boredom Himself," the gray that is the color of the walls, the desks and the carpeting in the offices of a minor defense contractor, are the enemies here. DeMarinis takes them on with panache. He's especially good at eliciting the intolerant intimacy of groups, the way the odd individual suffers as eccentricity and privacy are abraded by the group's vigilance. **"The Flowers of Boredom"** is a psychological portrait, not of its main character Lamar, but of the vast industry that employs him. . . .

"The Flowers of Boredom" ends with a memory of missiles on huge transport vehicles slipping out of a black building into a rainy night. The mechanical-malevolent is in evidence in other stories, as well. In **"The Handgun,"** the gun has "a tight, self-satisfied sheen, like a deceptively well-groomed relative from a disgraced branch of the family," having infiltrated the home of a jobless narrator who is rapidly losing his hold on life and over his remote wife, who, despite having "the long-muscled legs of a Zulu princess" and lovely eyes, is an increasingly menacing figure: " . . . the gun had summoned . . . real changes in Raquel."

In **"Red Chair,"** an old woman is tormented into disorientation by the intrusion of an enormous, hellishly red recliner into her pastorally brown-and-green private room in a nursing home for the elderly. While the old woman's disturbance is painstakingly detailed, she is so eminently dislikable and petty that the reader, in order fully to collude with the writer, must condescend to her bewilderment.

If the collection's lesser stories seem more vehement message than complex interpretation, the problem seems to be that the writer, while hyperalert to the ludicrousness of the world, shows little actual fondness for anything about it except a splattering of brand names and the occasional reifying dose of sex, and so his indignation, even when it flares most incandescent, seems cold, cannily cerebral, disinterested. . . . In 1900, the critic, Henri Bergson, wrote in *Le Rire,* "[Art] has no other object than to brush aside the conventional and socially accepted generalities, in short, everything that veils reality—from us, in order to bring us face to face with reality itself." The reality one is left facing in *The Coming Triumph of the Free World* is unconvincing; perhaps the depths cannot prosper when the surface is so manic. When Raquel, the Zulu-legged wife, is informed by her husband, "Love is not harmless," the claim is interesting; given the story's unfolding context, it is at once confession and threat. But her answer, "Jesus, *listen* to what you are saying for once" remains meaningless, except as callously casual rejection. In these stories, emotion is casually rejected, brutalized, or allowed to degenerate into slapstick. Taken together, these tales imply a chilly, brilliantly lit world on the brink of absolute darkness, chronicled with speedy, black-hearted elan. (p. 9)

> *Elizabeth Tallent, "Tales of Manic Light on the Brink of Darkness," in* Los Angeles Times Book Review, *August 7, 1988, pp. 1, 9.*

RUSSELL BANKS

[*The Coming Triumph of the Free World*] is so consistent, original, seductive and delightfully sad that Rick DeMarinis can afford to save his best piece for last, a thing rarely done these days. The story, **"Medicine Man,"** is longer than the 13 others and perhaps for that reason accomplishes more, but even so it's only 25 pages. It is large, however, because, among other things, its ambition is immense, which is also rare these days. In **"Medicine Man,"** Mr. DeMarinis aims to give us not just a portrait of a wise man (who, typically, as in a Sufi tale, is found in a most unlikely place, a dive in a small town in Montana), but a vision of the wise man's wisdom. That is, the story intends to convey wisdom itself. And it succeeds. One has to go back almost to Flannery O'Connor to find a story that so deliberately, methodically and with such brave comedy transforms ordinary life into the sublime.

A synopsis won't say how, any more than a synopsis of one of O'Connor's stories can say how, dross gets spun into gold,

but it might give a reader insight into Mr. DeMarinis's methods and conventions. The narrator is an old fellow, a barfly, who believes in the healing powers and universal wisdom of Louis Quenon, a man who, other people say, is "trouble in the long run. You'll hear it said he'll drink a week and disappear for two. They'll tell you he's a Feejee Indian from Africa. They'll call him a breed, oily customer, quack, boomer, con man, crook." (p. 7)

It's clear, however, that Louis Quenon is a miracle worker: he cures fainting spells with snails, mint and fennel cooked in the milk of a red cow; he gets rid of a melanoma with a yellow paste; he dissolves blood clots with a blue unguent. Louis is a white man, huge, bearded, "only a fraction Assiniboin," and though his great-uncle was a medicine man, Louis insists that what he knows, which is mostly about white man's diseases, he learned when he was a medic in the United States Army stationed in Sicily and North Africa. "For the white man's diseases," he explains, "you've got to go to the roots of the old white world and find the ancient remedies."

Soon Louis runs afoul of medical authorities and the law: he tries to remove, with his hands, after elaborate spiritual preparations, a hospitalized man's stomach cancer and is stopped by the doctors just as he's about to yank out what looks like an "oblong head of lettuce." . . . Louis is tossed in jail, Moley dies (the "lettuce eel" having slipped back into his stomach) and "Louis got the blues after that episode."

His decline begins. The middle part of the story is taken up with an account of Louis's withdrawal from the secular world, as it were, his wandering in the land of dreams and self-mortification, his denial of his own powers, as if in order to test those powers. It is a pure harrowing, described by the puzzled, trusting narrator with the anxiety of a disciple whose own faith is threatened. In the final section of the story, Louis returns from his wandering in the wilderness (most of it spent holed up in an abandoned mine shaft), larger and more powerful than ever, and takes the narrator, and the reader, on a metaphysical journey that would make Carlos Castaneda quake.

The trick, Mr. DeMarinis's trick, is that this is done with enormous affection and without irony: it is pure and ancient comedy. We who have identified with the narrator join him on his amazing journey: he has become for us a reliable witness to a ridiculous, utterly unbelievable series of events composed of the details of everyday life, the same details that make the stories of Richard Ford and Raymond Carver, for example, so believable. But while their stories, like Hemingway's, so often leave one face to face with the everyday and loving it mainly for its esthetic possibilities, Mr. DeMarinis leaves one facing that same humdrum reality filled with belief in one's ability to transcend it.

Perhaps Mr. DeMarinis is a contemporary avatar of that tradition in American short story writing that, by way of Hawthorne, Melville, Faulkner, O'Connor, Welty and Cheever, is essentially religious and, because rooted in the everyday, comic. His language is demotic: he has a gifted ear for American speech, a crush on all kinds of slang, and usually relies on a first-person narrator. He has a wry appreciation of brand names, the detritus of contemporary life, but unlike the so-called minimalists, he refuses to use them as a shorthand method for characterization and instead uses them to show how his characters are diminished by their material lives. Most of his characters in *The Coming Triumph of the Free*

World are lower middle class, out of work and marginal, which he regards not as merely amusing or as a sad sign of the times but as a personally felt affliction, a significantly crippling form of alienation that, faced with humor, patience and mother-wit, makes his characters as close to heroic as we are likely to find these days. . . .

Now in his 50's, Mr. DeMarinis writes slowly but carefully, so that he comes to us meaning every word he says. Yet the world he writes about is as contemporary and high-tech, as shockproof and bland as the world we learned about from last season's laid-back brat-packer. The difference is rage: Mr. DeMarinis refuses to give in to "chronic sulkiness." "We're all shockproof these days, even the priests," says the narrator of a fine story, **"The Swimmer in Hard Light."** "Nothing is profane enough, nothing blasphemous enough. The bodily humors barely raise a smile. It follows then that we have entered a new age of innocence. Our ancient power to shock each other has been canceled. We are naked again, reborn in a high-tech Eden, watched over by disinterested electronic gods." It's this nakedness, this innocence, that is Mr. DeMarinis's subject, and he regards it with a protectiveness that is never sentimental and always fierce. His art, then, is comedy of a very high order, the comedy of a decent heart enraged. (pp. 7, 9)

Russell Banks, " 'We're All Shockproof These Days'," in The New York Times Book Review, *October 30, 1988, pp. 7, 9.*

Ralph (Waldo) Ellison

1914-

American novelist, essayist, short story writer, critic, and editor.

Ellison is considered among the most influential and accomplished contemporary American authors for his highly acclaimed novel *Invisible Man* (1952), which affirms the need for the individual to advocate humanism and attain self-awareness. Honored with the National Book Award for fiction, *Invisible Man* is regarded as a masterpiece of twentieth-century American fiction for its complex treatment of racial repression and betrayal. Shifting between naturalism, expressionism, and surrealism, Ellison combines concerns of European and African-American literature to chronicle the quest of an unnamed black youth to discover his identity within a deluding, hostile world. Although critics have faulted Ellison's style as occasionally excessive, *Invisible Man* has consistently garnered accolades for its poetic, ambiguous form, sustained blend of tragedy and comedy, and complex symbolism and characterizations.

Born in Oklahoma City, Oklahoma, Ellison was raised in a cultural atmosphere that encouraged self-fulfillment. After studying music from 1933 to 1936 at Tuskegee Institute, a college founded by Booker T. Washington to promote black scholarship, Ellison traveled to New York City, where he met Richard Wright and became involved in the Federal Writers' Project. Encouraged to write a book review for *New Challenge,* a publication edited by Wright, Ellison began composing essays and stories that focus on the strength of the human spirit and the necessity for racial pride. Two of his most celebrated early short stories, "Flying Home" and "King of the Bingo Game," foreshadow *Invisible Man* in their portrayal of alienated young protagonists who seek social recognition. "Flying Home" is set during World War II and depicts a young black pilot whose obsessive desire to rid himself of stereotypes causes him to become contemptuous of his own race. After his airplane crashes, he is nursed back to health by a group of farmers who awaken his sense of cultural kinship and self-esteem. The anonymous protagonist of "King of the Bingo Game" is desperate to save his dying wife and enters a bingo tournament hoping to win enough money to hire a doctor. As the tournament proceeds, the bingo game becomes a symbol of his inability to control his destiny.

Although he originally envisioned writing a war novel, Ellison instead began work on *Invisible Man* following his honorable discharge from the United States Merchant Marines in 1945. Ellison's initial intention, which was to show the irony of black soldiers fighting for freedom who return to a civilian life of oppression, developed into a broader psychological study of the individual in society. Most critics consider the unspecified action of *Invisible Man* to take place between the early 1930s and 1950s. The novel's picaresque hero is often compared to Voltaire's Candide, who remains optimistic despite enduring betrayal, manipulation, humiliation, and the loss of his illusions. Narrating his story from an underground cell, the anonymous protagonist explains in the prologue that he is involuntarily invisible, since society sees his social stereotype rather than his true personality. Establishing the

novel's themes of betrayal and anonymity, the narrator recalls how he was raised in the South, named valedictorian of his high school graduation class, and invited to recite a speech for the community's prominent white citizens. This episode, which critics often refer to as Ellison's "battle royal" chapter, was originally published as a short story entitled "Invisible Man" in *Horizon* magazine. Among other degradations, the protagonist and several other black youths invited to the meeting are forced to participate in blind boxing matches and to crawl for money on an electrified carpet. Only after he has suffered these humiliations is the narrator allowed to recite the speech that he assumes will express his personal views to the white community. Although largely ignored by the drunken gathering, Ellison's hero is presented with a college scholarship and assumes that education will help overcome the racial problems he encounters. The evening's brutality convinces him that he will be rewarded if he does what white people expect, and this naive assumption provokes an identity crisis.

While attending a Southern college that strongly resembles Tuskegee Institute, the protagonist is assigned to chauffeur Mr. Norton, a white philanthropist, and innocently takes him to visit Jim Trueblood, a disreputable sharecropper whom Norton believes to be a colorful storyteller in the folk tradition of Uncle Remus. Upon hearing Trueblood's account of incest with his daughter, Norton is both horrified and fascinated by the indulgence in moral taboos that he himself has secretly considered transgressing. Many critics concur that this episode contains some of Ellison's finest dialogue and characterizations. By evoking society's reactions to Trueblood, Ellison refutes stereotypes of ethical, principled whites and decadent, unscrupulous blacks. Following Trueblood's revelation, the narrator takes Norton to a saloon called the Golden Day. The saloon's title refers to the Era of Reform between 1830 and 1860, during which many citizens entertained idealistic hopes of social reform that were thwarted by industrialism and materialistic values. Norton's visit occurs at a time when the saloon is crowded with American veterans of World War I who, after fighting overseas for the freedom of others, were institutionalized for refusing to conform to segregational laws. One patron, a brilliant brain surgeon, later gives the narrator advice for his future: "[The] world is possibility if only you'll discover it." The narrator contemplates the surgeon's comment as he travels north, a move reminiscent of the Great Migration of the 1920s, when displaced southerners journeyed to the industrialized northern United States to obtain employment.

Expelled from college for his misadventure with Mr. Norton, Ellison's protagonist travels to the Harlem district of New York City in search of a job. He possesses sealed letters of reference from Doctor Bledsoe, President of his former university, that are later revealed to contain character defamations. The narrator nonetheless obtains employment with Liberty Paints, a company that creates white paint to be used in the bleaching of national monuments. As the result of an accident for which he is held responsible, the protagonist is hospitalized and receives a form of electroshock therapy intended to reproduce the effects of a lobotomy. Although desensitized, he vividly recalls the folklore of his Southern boyhood and emerges with a new sense of racial pride, while the superficiality of his previous experience is erased. For the first time he is unashamed of his background and asserts his disdain for servile blacks by dumping a spittoon on a man whom he mistakes for Doctor Bledsoe.

Following an impromptu speech that he delivers on a street after discovering that an elderly couple have been evicted from their home, the narrator of *Invisible Man* attracts the attention of the Brotherhood, an organization that critics generally equate with American Communist associations of the 1930s. After briefly embracing the group's utopian ideals, he discovers that the Brotherhood merely feigns interest in civil rights while actually working to repress blacks and deny their individuality. The chaos that ensues in the black community following the frenzied exhortations of a fanatic nationalist develops into a hallucinatory treatment of the Harlem race riots of the 1940s and culminates in the protagonist's final rejection of false identities. Wright Morris asserted: "Mr. Ellison handles this surrealist evening with so much authority and macabre humor, observing the forces with such detachment, that the reader is justified in feeling that in the process of mastering his rage, he has also mastered his art." Upon escaping the uproar of the riots, the narrator accidentally falls into a coal cellar that leads to the cell where he eventually achieves self-definition. Although he succumbs to anger by stealing electricity from the local power company, he deduces that his experiences have made him a unique indi-

vidual. Despite his invisibility, the protagonist realizes that he must accept social responsibility and face the world.

Although attacked by black nationalists for lacking stringent militancy toward civil rights issues, *Invisible Man* garnered laudatory reviews immediately following its publication and has continued to generate scholarly exegeses. Many critics have commented on how the book's dexterous style, dense symbolism, and narrative structure lend intricacy to its plot. The narrator, who reflects on his past experiences, is observed as both an idealistic, gullible youth and as an enlightened, responsible man who actively addresses problems that may result from social inequality. Timothy Brennan declared: "[The] language and methods of the protest tradition are wielded by Ellison with an ambiguous voice, never finally pronouncing or judging, but building to a culmination of alternating hope and bitterness, rebellion and despair."

The foremost controversial issue of *Invisible Man* involves its classification as either a work particularly for blacks or a novel with universal import. Critics who insist the book strictly concerns black culture maintain that the experiences, emotions, and lifestyles described could not possibly be simulated by white authors, while supporters of the more prevalent view that *Invisible Man* transcends racial concerns contend that the protagonist's problems of illusion, betrayal, and self-awareness are experienced by every segment of society. Ellison asserts that *Invisible Man* is a novel that attempts to provide a portrait of the American individual who must define his values and himself despite a transitory existence. Jonathan Baumbach observed: "Refracted by satire, at times cartooned, Ellison's world is at once surreal and real, comic and tragic, grotesque and normal—our world viewed in its essentials rather than its externals. Though the protagonist of *Invisible Man* is a southern Negro, he is, in Ellison's rendering, profoundly all of us."

Ellison is also highly regarded for his accomplishments as an essayist. *Shadow and Act* (1964) collects twenty-two years of reviews, criticism, and interviews concerning such subjects as art, music, literature, and the influence of the black experience on American culture. This acclaimed volume is often considered autobiographical in intent and is noted for its lucidity and insights into *Invisible Man. Going to the Territory* (1986), which contains speeches, reviews, and interviews written since 1957, echoes many of the concerns of *Shadow and Act.* Making use of ironic humor in the manner of *Invisible Man,* Ellison reflects on personal influences and pays tribute to such creative mentors as Richard Wright and Duke Ellington. Ellison's short stories remain uncollected but are anthologized in such volumes as *A New Southern Harvest* (1957), *The Angry Black* (1962), and *Soon, One Morning: New Writing by American Negroes, 1940-1962* (1963; published in Great Britain as *Black Voices*). The latter book contains "Out of the Hospital and under the Bar," a noted excerpt deleted from *Invisible Man.*

(See also *CLC,* Vols. 1, 3, 11; *Contemporary Authors,* Vols. 9-12, rev. ed.; *Contemporary Authors New Revision Series,* Vol. 24; *Dictionary of Literary Biography,* Vols. 2, 76; and *Concise Dictionary of American Literary Biography: 1941-1968.*)

WRIGHT MORRIS

The geography of hell is still in the process of being mapped. The borders shift, the shore lines erode, coral islands appear complete with new sirens, but all the men who have been there speak with a similar voice. These reports are seldom mistaken as coming from anywhere else. As varied as the life might be on the surface, the life underground has a good deal in common—the stamp of hell, the signature of pain, is on all of the inhabitants. Here, if anywhere, is the real brotherhood of man. . . .

[The title character of Ellison's *Invisible Man*] lives, he tells us, in an underground hole. To fill this dark hole with light, he burns 1,369 bulbs. He burns them free. A fine Dostoevskyan touch. In his *Notes From the Underground* Dostoevsky says: "We are discussing things seriously: but if you won't deign to give me your attention, I will drop your acquaintance. I can retreat into my underground hole."

The Invisible Man is also discussing things seriously. His report in this novel might be subtitled, "Notes From Underground America," or "The Invisible Black Man in the Visible White Man's World." That is part of his story, but the deeper layer, revealed, perhaps, in spite of himself, is the invisible man becoming visible. The word, against all of the odds, becoming the flesh. Neither black nor white flesh, however, for where the color line is drawn with profundity, as it is here, it also vanishes. There is not much to choose, under the skin, between being black and invisible, and being white, currently fashionable and opaque. . . .

[The Invisible Man's] report begins the day that rich men from the North, white philanthropists, appear on the campus of a Negro college in the South. They are there for the ceremony of Founders Day. The Invisible Man, a student at the college, is chosen to act as the chauffeur for one of them. He shows him, inadvertently, the underground black world that should not be seen. Before the day is over, both the millionaire and the student have been disillusioned, and the student, expelled from the college, leaves for New York.

In the city he becomes increasingly invisible. Hearing him rouse the crowd at the scene of a Harlem eviction, a key party bigwig sees a bright future for him in the brotherhood. The mysteries of the Order, revealed and unrevealed, as they fall to the lot of the Invisible Man, have the authentic air of unreality that must have bemused so many honest, tormented men. The climax of the book, and a model of vivid, memorable writing, is the night of the Harlem riots. Mr. Ellison handles this surrealist evening with so much authority and macabre humor, observing the forces with such detachment, that the reader is justified in feeling that in the process of mastering his rage, he has also mastered his art. . . .

The reader who is familiar with the traumatic phase of the black man's rage in America, will find something more in Mr. Ellison's report. He will find the long anguished step toward its mastery. The author sells no phony forgiveness. He asks none himself. It is a resolutely honest, tormented, profoundly American book.

"Being invisible and without substance, a disembodied voice, as it were, what else could I do?" the Invisible Man asks us in closing. "What else but try to tell you what was really happening when your eyes were looking through! And it is this which frightens me: Who knows but that, on the lower frequencies, I speak for you?"

But this is not another journey to the end of the night. With this book the author maps a course from the underground world into the light. *Invisible Man* belongs on the shelf with the classical efforts man has made to chart the river Lethe from its mouth to its source.

Wright Morris, "The World Below," in The New York Times Book Review, *April 13, 1952, p. 5.*

GEORGE MAYBERRY

To paraphrase Graham Greene's already classic remark, "I am not a Catholic writer, but a writer who happens to be a Catholic," it can be said of Ralph Ellison that he is not a Negro writer, but a writer who happens to be a Negro. The parallels between these otherwise dissimilar novelists are that each within a brief space of time has written a book concerned with his dominating stigmata, semi-autobiographical, in the first person singular and yet in each instance the work of a writer whose writing as such overrides his preoccupation with, in Mr. Green's case, religion, and in Mr. Ellison's, race. In addition, both are masters at catching the shape, flavor and sound of the common vagaries of human character and experience.

Here the resemblances cease, and it is up to one's approach to fiction which author comes off on top. For Greene, who has it over Ellison in age and experience, is perhaps the finest living writer of the well-made book in which every word, sentence, paragraph and chapter is a dependent and contributor to a perfected whole. Ellison, whose first novel this is, although he already exhibits considerable technical maturity, has not yet achieved the integration of skill, experience and view of life necessary to the seriously ambitious novel. But in a time when the poles of fictional success have been reached by tidy little bundles of nothing and sprawling monsterpieces which appear to have gone directly from an adolescent's typewriter to the printer without benefit of editorial midwifery, it is a joy to encounter a vigorous, imaginative, violently humorous and quietly tragic book that is informed with far more than the rudiments of the novelist's art. . . .

[*Invisible Man*] is the story of one man, born in the American South, whose exceptional abilities brought him educational opportunities and later in the North social and cultural "advantages" denied the vast majority of his race. It is a story told accurately and with a redeeming hilarity of a pensive disillusionment. On the road to invisibility, our pilgrim encounters the Southern small businessman, the Uncle Tom educator, the Northern do-gooder, the Negro military racist, the Harlem messiah with a sideline in numbers, the socioscientific, highly organized Brothers whose Sisters most frequently discussed the dialectic in the boudoir, a journey that would have left Bunyan's Christian without care or hope for redemption. Ellison's solution, with a little aid from Dostoevsky and Kafka, is ingenious and original—perhaps a little too much so of both.

Invisible Man is a book shorn of the racial and political cliches that have encumbered the "Negro novel." It firmly establishes Ellison with that small group of writers—William Faulkner, Bucklin Moon, J. Saunders Redding—as an artist in handling his given material. The bane of the problem novel, in particular the "Negro novel," in America is that the cart of the subject has preceded the horse of artistic sensibility. Having given ample proof of the latter, it can be earnestly hoped that from the underground to which history and human frailty has driven him, Ellison can emerge to write of other places.

George Mayberry, "Underground Notes," in The New Republic, *Vol. 126, April 21, 1952, p. 19.*

T. E. CASSIDY

You meet the hero of [*Invisible Man*] in his underground home. Then you go back to whence he came. He is the off-spring of a Southern college for Negroes. He has left there, though he loved it, because he took Mr. Norton, a benevolent white trustee, around the region and showed him that which he should not have seen: the seamy, dreadful slums and bums of his race. . . .

He is bewildered and befriended, in rapid succession. Mary, a benign elderly lady, takes him in. When he finds his work in the factory, he is set upon by his surroundings and his fellow men. Then, one day, he witnesses an eviction of some old people, his own black people. He finds out, when he bursts out in angry speech at this outrage, that he is powerful and persuasive. . . . He is pursued by 'Brother Jack' of the 'Brotherhood,' signs up, goes in training, and returns to the beginning of triumph and horror as a member of the movement, a Brother in the Brotherhood, and a leader who discovers that his power is an overwhelming, obsessive tumult. (p. 99)

Ralph Ellison's invisible man is really many men. He is not only the embodiment of the Negro race. He is the conscience of all races. He is the result of both conscious and unconscious torture, one man to another. He is the horror of history, the triumphant yell of bitter fate. He is blasted hope, and he is also the revived spirit. He is the mad leader and the blind follower. He is rampant, and his rampage starts in the sky and ends in a coal pit. His light is the light of God, and the light of 1,369 bulbs, stolen from Monopolated Light and Power. He, himself, is pure power and smashed power. And he is probably, in some way, you.

This is a novel of violence, to be sure. It is a novel written with force and fire, but it is a novel, too, that sputters sometimes, almost as if the author were unwilling to write well when his invisible man shows signs of becoming visible. It has surging scenes and fantastically detailed characterizations. Even when the man leads in the Brotherhood, *he* is the driven. In public meetings and in committee meetings, he is the blisterer, but also the blistered. He drifts back and forth, in and out of the movement—at its core and at its fringes. He has great theories and insane practices. And the violence erupts regularly, be it in the form of special self-torture through the mind, or in the madness of the scene in which the man is disgusted and degraded by an invitation to rape, or in the almost epic proportions of the final riot in the book.

One might select a continual underlying theme: betrayal. The man is betrayed at the very beginning by his own blacks and by whites, to whom he is an object to be either eliminated or used for fun. He is betrayed by his college president and by the trustee. He is betrayed by the factory bosses and the workers, and, most blazingly, by his Brothers. Yet all the time, he is the one who is accused of being the betrayer—just as he has always been the driven. Perhaps this is the greatest single moving feature of this sprawling work: the invisible man's inability to belong, visibly, on any level of existence. He is always forced to dig in, to fight, to hide, to pretend to be another, and finally to disappear. But despite everything that happens he is willing, at the end, to reappear.

Ellison stands somewhat alone as a novelist. He is not a Richard Wright yet, but really he is quite different. He is more diffuse, more introspective, but somehow less powerful. He is more dramatic, perhaps, but less compelling. He blends the weird and the warm, the grotesque and the appealing, often with fine effect, so that if your attention wanders, it always comes back. You must call him, finally and simply, dynamic. (pp. 99-100)

T. E. Cassidy, "A Brother Betrayed," in The Commonweal, *Vol. LVI, No. 4, May 2, 1952, pp. 99-100.*

ANTHONY WEST

Ralph Ellison's first novel, **Invisible Man,** is an exceptionally good book and in parts an extremely funny one. That is not to say that it is without defects, but since they are almost entirely confined to the intolerably arty prologue and epilogue, and to certain expressionist passages conveniently printed in italics, they can easily be skipped, and they should be, for they are trifling in comparison with its virtues. What gives it its strength is that it is about being colored in a white society and yet manages not to be a grievance book; it has not got the whine of a hard-luck story about it, and it has not got the blurting, incoherent quality of a statement made in anger. What gives it its character is a robust courage; it walks squarely up to color the way seventeenth-century writing walks up to mortality and death, to look it in the face as a part of the human situation that has to be lived with. Mr. Ellison's hero is a Negro of the South who starts out with the naïve illusion that what stands between him and the whites is a matter of education. He is given a scholarship to a Southern college that has been endowed by Northern philanthropists, and he goes to it in great delight, thinking that what he will learn there will pare away all his disabilities and disadvantages. He finds that the college cannot do that for him and does not even try to do it; it is concerned only with helping him make realistic adjustments to things as they are. He gets into a mess of trouble and is expelled. Before expelling him, the dean tells him just what the facts of colored life are:

> You have some vague notions about dignity. . . . You have some white folk backing you and you don't want to face them because nothing is worse for a black man than to be humiliated by white folk. I know all about that too. . . . But you'll get over it; it's foolish and expensive and a lot of dead weight. You let the white folk worry about pride and dignity—you learn where you are and get yourself power, influence, contacts with powerful and influential people—then stay in the dark and use it!

He is too young and too nobly stubborn to believe that this is the best that can be done with his life, and the rest of the book deals with his attempts to force the world to accept him on a pride-and-dignity basis, and with his final realization that he has to stay in the dark as an invisible man. This could easily be a glum and painful performance, but Mr. Ellison has the real satirical gift for handling ideas at the level of low comedy, and when he is most serious he is most funny. The technique is that of which [Voltaire's] *Candide* is the supreme example, but there is nothing archaic about the writing, which has an entirely contemporary vitality and a quite unexpected depth.

The first chapter is a little slow, but the second and third, which describe the trouble that leads to the hero's expulsion, convince one that Mr. Ellison is a writer with much more than promise. (p. 93)

A good deal of [*Invisible Man*] is concerned with penetrating to the unease and self-consciousness that underlie a great many earnest white progressive approaches to The Question. After the student is kicked out of college, he goes North to try to make his way in New York, and his adventures are told in a highly imaginative, picaresque story, but, though the storytelling is excellent, in the end the impressive thing is the analysis of attitudes that rises out of each situation; there are always such sharpness of observation, such awareness of shades of feeling, at work. The hero is caught up in what is clearly an agit-prop apparatus of the Communist Party (Mr. Ellison does not, though, give it that name) that is exploiting the color situation in Harlem. He is a natural speaker and he is made use of in campaigns as a front for the white committee. There is not only perceptive writing about the feeling between Negro and white in this part of the book but there is also perhaps the best description of rank-and-file Communist Party activity that has yet appeared in an American novel. . . . At last, the hero discerns the rank stink of falsity in the Party line about color, partly through catching on to the way in which a white Comrade who has married a colored girl makes play with the fact to strengthen his hand in policy discussions of district tactics, partly through a realization that the white Comrades have used him as a lure, as a Negro gull to gull other Negroes. He sees that his district leader, Brother Jack, is just as much Marse Jack as a field boss in a white-supremacy state. The description of his disillusion with the Party, a true agon, which is also his final understanding that there is no external machine that can produce any ready-made solution either to the color problem or to his own perplexities, is as moving and vivid a piece of writing on this difficult subject as one could wish to read.

The book ends with a . . . tour de force. . . . The Party has lost control of its agitation campaign as a result of what at first seems to the hero to be a typical tactical blunder, and the mass support that it has won drifts over to a straight anti-Communist and anti-white agitator called Ras, whose wild speeches bring on a wave of rioting and looting. The drift into disorder and the spread of violence are astonishingly well described in realistic terms, and through it all Mr. Ellison never loses touch with his gift for comic invention. As the riot builds up, the hero realizes that not only have the Communists an unfriendly interest in him but that he is due for unpleasantness from Ras's strong-arm men. . . . The hero's evasions as all Harlem comes apart have a real nightmare humor. And in the middle of it all, as the riot squads and the mounted police move in and shooting begins, he suddenly sees what is happening. The Party has not made a tactical blunder at all; it has deliberately surrendered its mass following to Ras in order to provoke violence, so that colored martyrs, shot down by the police, can be exploited in the next phase of agitation in the district. The hero emerges in his own identity to warn the innocents he has helped to fool what is being done to them. But Mr. Ellison has a tight grip on his satiric comedy, and he is not going to let his buffoon hero escape into tragedy; martyrdom is not to be *his* fate. A gang of white looters chase him up a dark street, and he falls through an open manhole into a coal cellar. The whites, enraged by this surprising vanishing trick, slam the manhole cover down and leave him lying there helpless while the riot burns itself out above.

Few writers can have made a more commanding first appearance. Up to a point, *Invisible Man* resembles Céline's *Death on the Installment Plan.* Its humor recalls the jokes that hang on Céline's fraudulent scientist, with his ascents in worn-out and patched balloons, his absurd magazine, and his system of electromagnetic plant culture, but Ellison's jokes are on the whole funnier, and his satire is much more convincing because there is clearly visible behind it—as there is not in Céline—a positive alternative to the evils he is attacking, the knowledge of a better way without which all satire becomes merely an empty scolding. It is a pity that Mr. Ellison's direct statement of the better way takes the form it does in the prologue and the epilogue, since they are the two worst pieces of writing. But the ideas toward which they fumble are as dignified as they are impressive, and it is perhaps unnecessary to have this direct statement; as they are so plainly implied in the rest of the book. It is not merely the Negro who has to realize that the only escape from the rattrap of worry about what one is or is not is to abandon the constant tease of self-consciousness. The Invisible Man of Mr. Ellison's title is the unattached man of Aldous Huxley's Perennial Philosophy, the man with courage to be utterly indifferent to himself and to his place in the world, the man who is alone free to be fully a man. (pp. 94-6)

Anthony West, "Black Man's Burden," in The New Yorker, *Vol. XXVIII, No. 15, May 31, 1952, pp. 93-6.*

MARCUS KLEIN

Invisible Man is a novel of extraordinary weight, precisely as it bears the history of Ellison's own strenuous adventuring in the definition, as it were, of himself. . . . (p. 84)

The large action of *Invisible Man* is all a circular voyage, consisting of four prominent adventures. It begins with a ritual of the hero's initiation, a test of his bravery, of his knowledge of caste, and of his sexuality, and it ends in failure, with the hero castrated, presented with proofs of his cowardice and ignorance, in a condition prior to his initiation. He is at the end back in the underworld from which he had tried to emerge, with this difference only, that he has illuminated his underworld and he now knows where he is.

That is the great irony the novel deliberately plays on itself—the world moves, the hero tells us in almost the first words of the Prologue, not like an arrow, nor in a spiral, but like a boomerang; his end, he says, is in his beginning. And it should be said immediately, the novel's great fault is in the fact that its end *is* its beginning. The novel is a furious picaresque which plunges the hero forward through a series of violences. Moreover, it is *all* an initiation rite. . . .

[The hero moves] through what seems at all points a linear exploration of the "Negro problem," through ideologies by which it might be approached, and beyond that, through what one of the symbolic structures of the novel suggests is an exploration of some one hundred years of American history. But for all that multiplicity of parallel actions, the novel has no real progress except that at each stage it clarifies and reinforces the hero's dilemma.

" 'Ah,' I can hear you say," the hero says in almost the last words of the Epilogue,

> "so it was all a build-up to bore us with his buggy jiving. He only wanted us to listen to him rave!" But only partially true: Being invisible and without substance, a disembodied voice, as it were, what else could I do? What else but try to tell you what was really happening when your eyes were looking through?

But the witness is not here being responsive to the witness against him. This appeal is a last-ditch attempt to rescue the book from what must have seemed to Ellison its strategic error. The amount of clarity the novel finally comes to is enormous, and so much clarity is shocking, but still it is a clarity without any further effect. The novel doesn't finally go anywhere.

It is a fault that apparently led Ellison to the desperate, empty, unreasonable, and programmatic optimism of the last few pages of the novel: ". . . we [Negroes] were to affirm the principle on which the country was built. . . ." We "were linked to all others in the loud, clamoring semi-visible world. . . ." ". . . I've overstayed my hibernation, since there's a possibility that even an invisible man has a socially responsible role to play." One asks this hero how he is to come out and be socially responsible? Upon what ground in reality can he affirm *any* positive principle? Just what is he going to do? Everything in the novel has clarified this point: that the bizarre accident that has led him to take up residence in an abandoned coal cellar is no accident at all, that the underworld is his inevitable home, that given the social facts of America, both invisibility and what he now calls his "hibernation" are his permanent condition. And really his only extension into the upper world can be in negative acts and fantasies of vengeance—which do indeed make up another ending to the novel. (pp. 107-09)

[The protagonist of **Invisible Man** is transported] through adventures in the typical ways Negroes and whites manage, or don't manage, to live together in America. He is moved in each case to the point where all relationships disappear in an explosion, from the way of the caste system of a Southern town to that of the subtler caste system of the Negro college created and endowed by whites, the caste inherent in latter-day abolition, to that of the factory in the industrial North, to that of the dogmatic brotherliness of the Brotherhood, finally to the ultimate extension of all these ways: the race riot with which the action proper of the novel ends. And the issue of each of these adventures is a race riot of one dimension or another, and that is the point of them all. An earnest, yea-saying young man reluctant to be a saboteur explores the typical relationships between Negroes and whites and finds them charged with incipient violence, needing but the slightest accident to set them off. The hero moves from one episode to another because in every one an accident happens.

The accident is always just a slight and unavoidable lapse from the propriety he struggles to maintain. In the first episode he delivers his high-school valedictory address. It is a speech on the proper subject—humility is the secret and the essence of progress for the Negro—addressed to the Southern town's most prominent white citizens, who are drunk at this moment and who pay no attention to him. Benumbed by the

noise, the smoke, and the reek of the stag dinner for which he is a part of the entertainment, he speaks the words "social equality" for "social responsibility," and by his slip he springs from the crowd a moment of sudden, terrifying silence. (pp. 113-14)

At college, next, with all proper respect he chauffeurs a visiting Northern trustee, Mr. Norton. He takes Mr. Norton to a place Mr. Norton wants to visit, the cabin of a local share-cropper, and discovers himself in a double accident. The sharecropper tells a story of incest and Mr. Norton suffers a heart attack. Still properly deferential, the hero takes Mr. Norton to a local saloon, which unfortunately this day is entertaining the Negro veterans from the local madhouse, and he deposits him into the middle of a riot. The adventure ends with his being expelled from college because, so the college president tells him, he has actually obeyed the wishes of a white man and not merely seemed to. Then in the North, as a laborer in a paint factory, he stumbles into a union meeting and, earnest to please everyone, he finds that because he is a Negro, he is a scab, and as such a catalyst to violence. Then as a favored recruit in the Brotherhood, he takes a single step on his own authority: he organizes a public funeral for a Brother shot by the police, which results in the riot in Harlem that is his last adventure. It is his one lucky accident that in that riot he tumbles into an open manhole, leading to his coal cellar.

The lesson in his accidents is, of course, the instability in all typical relationships between Negroes and whites in America, and the impossibility for a Negro of propriety enough. There is always a boomerang somewhere. Beyond that, these accidents function to reveal to the hero that he is not a person in his relations with whites, but a role, and furthermore they serve to reveal to him the kind of role he plays. It is always the same. The end of the novel is finally his ironic acceptance of his role. . . .

His whole fate is present, though the hero is not allowed to know it, in that first adventure the climax of which is his dreadful slip of the tongue. A great part of the novel, indeed, is in that initial episode. (pp. 114-15)

[In] this first adventure [the protagonist] is clearly threatened but not actually punished for his slip of the tongue. . . . He and his friends are [forced] to stage a battle royal. . . . They are herded before a magnificent, stark-naked blonde, and threatened if they look and threatened by the crowd if they don't. They are held there, made to suffer sexual embarrassment becoming sexual torture, and made to participate then vicariously in the lurching obscenities of the town's ranking citizens. (p. 116)

It is to this crapulous mob, in this coliseum, that the hero then talks about "social equality." The episode is a sustained orgy. It not only mocks the hero's earnest dogma of pacific humility, and it not only baptizes him in the terror that, he will find, lurks in all adventures of Negroes among American whites. There is no telling what craziness and what brutish violence lie at any next step. More than that, the episode concentrates, brilliantly, and it exposes at the pitch of a ritualistic frenzy the interior facts of caste, not only its mechanism of economic exploitation (the hero tries to make a deal with one of his schoolmates and is rebuffed, division has been effectively imposed upon them), but all its deeper exploitation of the Negro as a ritualistic scapegoat.

The hero is not only discriminated against. The politics of

this system goes much deeper. In fact, he is coddled by that white man, the school superintendent, who has most immediate authority over him—the school superintendent presents him for his speech with a pat on the back, a brief case, and a scholarship. He and his schoolmates are not without honor. These whites use them in ways curiously like love. It is the function of this caste system to suppress a great deal more than the Negro, and it is the lesson of this episode that these Negroes incarnate for these whites everything that they suppress. The Negroes are made by them into the bacchants they themselves dare not be. (pp. 116-17)

The battle royal is an extraordinarily compressed piece of work, and its one fault is that it is both more intensely maintained and more exhaustive than anything else in the novel, and so the hero's adventures hereafter become more or less adequate echoes of it. But in any event it does contain, both in its significances and in its form, the most of the hero's career. The same chaos of appetites and guilt that is the real, hidden nature of Negro and white relations is exploded at the hero in each of his subsequent accidents.

That same chaos is what is revealed in the double accident of the Mr. Norton episode. The sharecropper, upon command, *lures* Mr. Norton to a heart attack. His story of incest has a truth of blood in it—his name is "Trueblood"—a truth that Mr. Norton, a New England gentleman and a latter-day, declined Calvinist, cannot in any other way accept. He is fascinated, as it were, into a heart attack which is the equivalent of the townsmen's orgiastic smoker. . . . He acts out a scapegoat ritual with Trueblood and then he gives Trueblood money. (p. 118)

As the hero moves north, madness, confusion, violence, the bursting of the irrational, are always the last and the purest expressions of the relationships between black and white. He has been warned by Southern Negroes—by one of the crazy veterans, and then by his college president. His advisers have told him that he is invisible, and they have echoed his grandfather's advice. His proper life is a war, at least a guerrilla action. In the North of industry and labor unionism, then, he finds that black is a disturbing secret of the white social fabric, a secret which has been tucked almost out of sight by a stated ideal of liberty, a secret which to his peril he unwittingly springs. He becomes a laborer in a paint factory called Liberty Paints whose pride is its Optic White, a paint that will cover just about anything. The paint is so very white, he discovers, because it is made with a dash of black dope. But it must be the right dope, and when he mixes into it a little other dope that looks and smells the same, the paint turns gray. The action is of course the hieroglyphic of the episode. He is not the right dope. He is an innocent who cannot quite meet the precarious propriety established in the industrial North between black and white. (pp. 118-19)

And he lets loose a riot. In his simple need for a job he stumbles on the complicated fact that industry uses Negroes as scabs. The plant has typically been hiring Negroes in order to undersell its union labor, and so the hero is caught in a contest between labor and capital which has become another contest between white and black. The conflict in this episode is between the local union and the plant's representative Uncle Tom, the right dope. The hero is an innocent who in his innocence will choose neither side. He is therefore a traitor to both sides, and so he brings about an explosion. The plant's Uncle Tom, threatened by this traitor and in an insane need to preserve his place, traps the hero in the boiler room and throws the switches that will blow it up.

It is a Negro who throws the switches, but the explosion is, for all that, the race riot that is always the hero's lesson. . . . That it is a Negro who tries to destroy him—he has just a moment before been feeling an inflation of racial pride—is another harsh irony. (pp. 119-20)

Then the Brotherhood, with its doctrinaire idealism that it wears as a mask, is still another. The hero wanders into it because at this time in history it is present, because he and the Brotherhood have use for one another. The hero has verbal powers for sale, and the Brotherhood offers him not only a job but a platform, leadership and spokesmanship. The Brotherhood, moreover, is obvious about its brotherliness. But then the Brotherhood is not brotherly at all. It uses the hero in order to manipulate Negroes to its own ends of sabotage and disruption. (p. 120)

The Brotherhood is the ultimate of the hero's social experiences, the climax of his maturity and of his trek north. It is the society that is completely rational, scientific, the final expression of the historical dialectic, and it is the society in which the irrationality of race warfare should disappear. It is, as it were, the Enlightenment itself, but then the hero finds when he is in it that it has a disturbing ambience, that the lights flicker, that there are ominous rustlings and furtive sounds. And when the explosion that completes his engagement with it comes, what is revealed is neither the Red menace nor the fate of a dogma, but that this last hope of a society *too* is an unstable composition of guilt and patronage and perverted sexuality, that it is as unknowledgeable about the Negro as any other society, and that it *too* exploits him, and for reasons that are irrational.

As he joins the Brotherhood, the hero glimpses for the first time "the possibility of being more than a member of a race." But the joke is on him. It is precisely a Negro that the Brotherhood wants him to be. It fixes his place. (p. 121)

What the Brotherhood would have him be is presented to him in the crazy, bitter self-destruction of another Negro Brother, Tod Clifton. The hero discovers him on Forty-second Street, [where Clifton gives him a Black Sambo doll]. . . . [Though] the hero doesn't know it, it is presented to him by Tod as a portrait of the hero as the Brotherhood's Negro.

The hero doesn't realize until later that the doll has a grin on both sides of its cardboard head, and that has something to do with . . . his coming descent into the underworld. But meanwhile the doll comments on the brotherliness of the Brotherhood, and the racial content of this perfectly rational society. . . . Through the movement the hero comes upon the factions of Negro politics and particularly upon a fanatic nationalist who calls himself Ras the Exhorter, who calls the hero a traitor. Somewhere inside, the hero knows that Ras is right, that in this enlightened, this light, white society, black men and white men aren't brothers. There is division that isn't healed by the scientism of the historical dialectic, and more than that, the Brotherhood has set him against his brothers. . . . (pp. 122-23)

[The hero] comes to realize, before he goes underground, that the historical dialectic is "a crummy lie they kept us dominated by," and that he is not included in it. He resolves, precisely, to yes the movement to death—but not before it has made him the unwitting instrument of a riot in Harlem that is the battle royal all over again. Brother Tod is shot on Forty-Second Street by a white policeman—Tod's *Tod* is the hero's own and Tod precedes him into the underworld. The hero, acting as the spokesman he has become, on his own authority organizes a public funeral for him. He brings Harlem to a fever of generalized protest, and then he finds that the Brotherhood, far from leading that protest to practical action, condemns him as a racist.

But he has started something. The fever in Harlem climbs to a confused, bloody riot. The riot is on the one hand a revel. . . . And it is on the other hand an orgy of self-destruction. . . . [The] chief politics of this mob is that it engages Negro against Negro. The hero is pitched against Ras, who with this opportunity has mounted a black horse, taken the costume of an Abyssinian chieftain, and become Ras the Destroyer, urging the crowd to what can only be suicide. It will be a suicide for which the Brotherhood is responsible, the hero now realizes, because at the crucial moment it abandoned leadership. . . . But the Negroes in the crowd don't see it, it isn't clear, and they move to—lynch him!

The hero runs, pursued by the Destroyer's destroyers, and a moment later, having eluded them, in this nightmare he is then pursued by a couple of white men armed with baseball bats, until he plunges in a fortunate fall through an open manhole into his coal cellar. The cellar will be his home and, finally, it will be his political position. (pp. 123-25)

The speeches of Ras are, it happens, far more eloquent than any made by the hero. It is clear that Ellison found it easier to be eloquent in Ras's behalf. His hero, who, we are told, strangely moves crowds by the secret power in his speeches, doesn't really orate very well. Ras on his black charger does have excitement and nobility about him. But Ras, and the nationalism he represents, *are* suicidal, and they are vulnerable to exploitation. (p. 125)

The hero is then, at the end, back where he began, before all his political experiments failed him, without doctrine. None of these political positions he has tried has met the reality of American life for Negroes. They have all, to the contrary, been only different ways in which the complicated exploitation of the Negro takes place. And the hero, after he has outfitted his coal cellar, commits himself only to the role he has always had. He will be a something hidden and deeply disturbing in American life, constantly felt and never seen. Committing himself to the role, he has become a thief—he steals light and power from Monopolated Light and Power—and a saboteur.

It is just the same negative resolution that confirms him as an invisible man, because all his adventures at the same time as they have had political significances, have been a search as well for personal identity. More than for others, because as a Negro he is more than others a political fact, as his politics ends up negative, he is negative, invisible. All of his voyages are from point zero to an adequate politics. All of them bring him back to his beginning. In the same movement they each take him from invisibility toward anticipated visibility and then back to zero. At the end, having been frustrated in every promise of visibility typically offered a Negro in America, he ominously accepts the identity that has been given him, one that is negative but that is an identity none the less. (p. 126)

As the Brotherhood is [the hero's] ultimate adventure in self-definition, it most elaborately prepares his descent back to himself. In his initial meeting with Brother Jack, he is told that his past, his "old agrarian self," is dead. "*History* has been born in your brain." He is given a new name by the Brotherhood, to honor and protect this birth. When he addresses his first mass meeting, he declares that he has found his true family, people, country, and he glimpses the possibility of being more than a member of a race. But throughout his engagement with Brotherhood, at every inconvenient moment, he has a persistent consciousness of a self within him that is racial and that is not dead, that this new identity does not incorporate, that it costs him always a greater effort to suppress. (p. 129)

He is not one of the Brothers. His own history is active in him, and it is not theirs. His history is, to the contrary, that of the Brotherhood's enemy, Ras the Exhorter—"Brothers are the same color," says Ras, and he knows where the hero comes from. . . . Tod tells the hero, prophetically, that it is "on the inside" that Ras is strong and dangerous, and he tells him that "('sometimes a man *has* to plunge outside history.' " (p. 130)

The climax to his engagement with Brotherhood and history, and to all his attempts at self-definition, is [the protagonist's] own accidental plunge into the void—which is Negro-ness. Before he falls into his underground, he falls, through some bizarre circumstances, into the Harlem underworld—into, as it were, the underlying Negro experience. It is where he has all along been heading, or, alternatively, where he has always been. Through all his adventures he has felt a tug to simple racial identity. (p. 131)

Invisibility is the lesson in his penultimate fall into the Harlem underworld, into, as it were, the heart of darkness. Pursued, ironically, by Ras's black legions, the hero puts on a pair of dark glasses and a wide-brimmed hat, and in that disguise he makes a discovery of identity. He has lost the identity he has thought he has had. Ras's legions don't recognize him. But he has unwittingly put on the uniform of a man named Rinehart, for whom he is everywhere mistaken. Rinehart, by that accident, becomes the last of his tutors, and the significant thing about Rinehart is that he has no positive identity, only a shifting appearance. (pp. 132-33)

When he reaches his Epilogue, the hero abruptly dismisses Rinehart as a personal possibility, apparently because Rinehart is antisocial. Rinehart is another of the victims of Ellison's abrupt affirmativeness. But even so, at the end he sets it down as one of the hero's ironic lessons that his world is possibility—and it would appear to be the case that Ellison, at this desperate point turned to optimism, refuses to see that Rinehart has made the world-as-possibility identical with the world-as-chaos. Rinehart is, in fact, the novel's most convincing end. The hero's progress has throughout been repeated lessons in the fact that the world, so far as he is concerned, is not fixed. It provides him with a nonidentity. After much boomeranging, he discovers that he is essentially invisible, and Rinehart is the incarnation of the invisible.

Rinehart is the culmination, too, of the historical process the hero has been in all his adventures tracing. Rinehart is the underground, the secret of Harlem, the complicated city. He is a master of its latest inventions: he drives a Cadillac and at his religious meetings he uses an electric guitar. The secret he incarnates is chaos, an ancient secret, but he has learned to manipulate it. By accepting its lessons, he has given a final formulation to the history of Negroes in America, and so he has mastered his and the Negro's history. (pp. 133-34)

[The hero is first initiated into radical politics] by coming on what may be taken as the Great Depression's most conspicuously typical event, a tenement eviction. . . . [He] makes a speech to the crowd and is on the spot recruited by the Brotherhood. There is seeming opportunity in the Brotherhood, of course, because it seems brotherly, because it is active, because it seems to make the Negro's cause its own. Beyond that, it imposes on the hero a version of his racial history that unites him with the majority, thereby eliminating the war that he has borne in his secret consciousness. The evictees for whom the hero has just spoken are, Brother Jack tells him, "agrarian types" who are being "ground up by industrial conditions," and so, all Brotherhood doctrine would seem to say, the race war is subsumed by and solved by the class war.

To wage the class war instead is not only the way toward freedom, but it is freedom itself. Like other Negro intellectuals during the Great Depression, the hero accepts this unique promise provided by the Great Depression. There is an alternative only in the futile nationalism of Marcus Garvey, for whom, in the novel, Ras the Exhorter-Destroyer stands. But then the Communist Party did not secure its promise, and so neither does the Brotherhood. It abruptly withdraws its concerns for Harlem—and the hero comes on the fact that the race and the class wars are not identical. Furthermore, he discovers that he is bound to maintain the race war within the ranks of the Brotherhood. . . . The Brotherhood's version of history is arbitrary and does not include his history. And therefore the hero is forced back to the version of reality that at bottom he knows—which is, it turns out, Rinehart's, and which is in the image of chaos.

Rinehart is what this history comes to, and he is its hero. He is the climax of the progress up from slavery. Chaos is his freedom. He moves easily in it. He secures his living from it, and if he has been condemned to it, he takes from it also the implements of his revenge. He has made chaos a base of political action. He is a thief, a rascal, an underground man engaged in the subversion of society. Like Melville's hero, he undermines confidence, and thereby the very foundation of society.

The hero's last adventure, in the Epilogue, in his hole in the ground, serves to confirm and to deepen Rinehart, and Rinehart, the underworld man, is the last of a series of puns for the "underground" which now, in a last shift, is to become actual. The hero's progress has been a series of boomeranging reversals, and he returns now to the most final reversal of all. In every instance when he has thought he has been moving upward, he has been moving down. (pp. 139-41)

But his descent into the underground is the climax to still another set of implications in his adventures, and his return now to his beginnings is a full and stable resolution to all his adventures. With this final reversal, his reverses have come to an end because, like Rinehart before him, he now accepts reversal as the positive law of his being. It is his metaphysics. He is an invisible man in a world without form—but that, his underground adventure, like the Rinehart episode, goes to prove, is something. He does have an identity and a place, only they are contrary. There is a paradox in the fact that the hero's place in the world is underneath the ground, out of the world, but then the paradox is twisted again when the hero converts his hole in the ground into a home. His coal cellar,

Ellison has himself pointed out, is not a sewer, but a source of heat and light and power. The hero converts all his losses to assertion. In fact he has found his politics and his person, and he has made sense out of his history, and so in his fall there is finally an ascension—which Ellison ultimately blurs by his promise that the hero will someday rise to do good among men. (p. 142)

The invisible man's end is in the embrace of his diabolism— diabolism is his politics, his identity, his history, and his metaphysics. And his future is to be Satan's—treason, violence, revenge. These are the normal activities now of his underground life. (p. 144)

[Yet] the hero is turned, in any event, at the very end, to a staccato of abrupt affirmations—of democracy (" . . . we, most of all, had to affirm the principle, the plan in whose name we had been brutalized and sacrificed"), of love (" . . . in spite of all I find that I love. . . . I *have* to love"), of the mind, of social responsibility, and of the immediate prospect of his emergence. It must be said that Ellison is to be seen at the very last moment trying to take back the book he has written, or at the very least muffling all its severities, and that is unfortunate. But then it should be said as well that lacking some such attempt, there will be nothing more for Ellison ever to say.

The constant technical flaw in *Invisible Man* is that it so frequently comes to an end, and Ellison is put at every point to a greater muscularity to make the next scene more intense, more thoroughly revealing of what has already been largely revealed. It is the concomitant of that flaw that *Invisible Man* is a death-driven novel. Its movement is to confirm again and again that the hero doesn't exist, and Ellison's difficulty, to put it another way, is to resurrect the hero for each subsequent adventure. The novel's series of ironic negations is, after all, a series of negatives. It can and does reach its last possibility. Ellison will be left with only stale repetitions of the act of dying unless he can in fact assert social responsibility and mind and love—and, because the "Negro problem" is entirely an American problem, democracy. That is the only way he can keep possibility open.

That is to say that the end of *Invisible Man* is the beginning of another novel, one that will draw the complicated positive engagement of the hero in this life, specifically this American life. It is the huge achievement of *Invisible Man,* meanwhile, that it has got a vastness of experience as Negroes particularly must know it—there can be very little that it has left out— into a single meaning. The novel creates a negative metaphor, invisibility, that is fully analytic and fully inclusive, that does hold together for a moment the long experience of chaos that has met Ellison's vision. (pp. 145-46)

Marcus Klein, "Ralph Ellison," in his After Alienation: American Novels in Mid-Century, *1964. Reprint by Books for Libraries Press, 1970, pp. 71-146.*

GENE BLUESTEIN

[*The essay excerpted below was originally published in* The Massachusetts Review, *Autumn, 1967.*]

[Ralph Ellison's *Invisible Man*] defines the ideological and technical possibilities of American Negro materials more accurately and effectively than any work in our literary history. (p. 124)

To begin with, it is important to recognize that Ellison does not conceive the book as a "Negro novel" in any sense of the term. What he has learned from Faulkner is that the relationships between black and white are central to the meaning of *American* development. That does not prevent him from understanding the unique qualities of Negro life and culture, but it does mark him from the tendency discernible in some Negro writers to associate themselves with separatism or Black Nationalism. (pp. 124-25)

Ralph Waldo Ellison is a lot closer politically and esthetically to his namesake than he has admitted. More importantly . . . , he has given us a major illustration of how the American writer uses folk materials to create a distinctly national expression which yet speaks in broadly human rather than racial or regional terms. . . . Ellison not only brings us up to date; he is an effective and impressive heir to what has gone before, filling in outlines of crucial areas that had only been sketched earlier.

Ellison's central concern in **Invisible Man** is to provide a portrait of the American. . . . The American is conceived to be a man without a past or anterior folklore which will serve to define his national values and literary expression. If this is true for the American in general, it is especially true for the Negro—and Ellison's point is that his situation is the same as his white counterpart's. But the circumstances of his attempt to define his identity will be framed by his relationships to the white world, which functions in relation to the Negro as the European world operated in regard to the white American. The hero, in short, is *peau rouge* whatever the actual color of his skin. And he is also the American barbarian, although the source of barbarism in this case is not the frontier but the jungle heritage of Africa. In the face of this collection of stereotypes, the hero assumes the mask as a means of undercutting the assumptions of his adversaries. The next step is predictable: as the American in general needs to show that his tradition is rich and meaningful, so the American Negro needs to convince himself and his critics that black folk tradition is more than the mumbo-jumbo or the cacophony that jazz is usually taken to be. The dynamic of the novel stems from the hero's struggle with himself to acknowledge the legitimacy of his heritage in the face of constant attacks by the white community or its allies in the society of Negroes. Nothing is simple and the virtue of Ellison's comic strategy is that it cuts both ways, undermining the stereotypes of the whites and exposing the insecurities of the Negroes. But the progression of values is clear: in order to acknowledge his existence as a man, the hero must first accept the folk legacy of his people; having attained this position, he will discover his identity as an American; but then he must move to the next stage, which expresses the universal values of humanity. The progression is from folk to national and finally international values.

But everything depends on the identification of the folk culture as rich and sufficiently sophisticated to pass the test of the self-appointed culture which judges it to be innately inferior. In order to satisfy these demands, Ellison must first establish the legitimacy of black folk tradition, and his argument runs along lines already familiar to us. The anterior folklore of the Negro (like all folklore) is not simpleminded or barbaric but operates on a level very close to that of formal art. The central question can be resolved in terms of the rich-

ness of folk diction, and Ellison gives us several scenes which make the point well. After the narrator arrives in New York he encounters a junk man one morning singing a blues as he pushes his cart along: "She's got feet like a monkey / Legs like a frog—Lawd, Lawd! / But when she starts to loving me / I holler Whoooo, God-dog! / Cause I loves my baabay, / Better than I do myself. . . ." The junk man asks the narrator if he's "got the dog," and the narrator plays "The Arkansas Traveler," pretending he doesn't understand the reference:

> I laughed nervously and stepped back. He watched me out of shrewd eyes. "Oh, goddog, daddy-o," he said with a sudden bluster, "who got the damn dog? Now I know you from down home, how come you trying to act like you never heard that before! Hell, ain't nobody out here this morning but us colored—why you trying to deny me?"

The narrator is uncomfortable in the face of this attempt to make him acknowledge his country background, but he cannot resist the junk man's spiel and his relish for language: . . .

> "All it takes to get along in this here man's town is a little shit, grit, and motherwit. And man, I was bawn with all three. In fact, I'maseventhsonofaseventhsonbawnwithacauloverbotheyesandraisedonblackcatboneshighjohntheconquerorandgreasygreens—" he spieled with twinkling eyes, his lips working rapidly. "You dig me, daddy?"
>
> "You're going too fast," I said, beginning to laugh.
>
> "Okay, I'm slowing down. I'll verse you but I won't curse you—my name is Peter Wheatstraw, I'm the Devil's only son-in-law, so roll 'em. You a southern boy, ain't you?" he said, with his head to one side like a bear's.
>
> "Yes," I said.
>
> "Well, git with it! My name's Blue and I'm coming at you with a pitchfork. Fe Fi Fo Fum. Who wants to shoot the devil one, Lord God Stingeroy!"

This is only one of several scenes in which the issues of identity, name, and black tradition are brought together. (Joyce has a similar motif in *A Portrait of the Artist* in which a play of language is associated with Stephen's name and relationship to Ireland.) Ellison's nameless narrator is prodded by the junk man to acknowledge his roots as a Southern Negro and though he has been trained to look down his nose at the country people and their culture, he has nevertheless intimations that there is something rich and valuable in their expression. The combination of blues and folk speech appears in several other sequences where the same point is made.

The Jim Trueblood episode, which is one of the best drawn scenes (and to judge from the critics, one of the most problematical) moves along similar lines. . . . [Trueblood is] a sharecropper "who told the old stories with a sense of humor and magic that made them come alive. He was also a good tenor singer, and sometimes when special guests visited the school he was brought up along with members of a country quartet to sing what the officials called 'their primitive spirituals' when we assembled in the chapel on Sunday evenings." Ellison's handling of this situation reveals how well he can utilize the materials of folk tradition to expose the full range of their ideological and technical meaning. To begin with, it gives him a chance to undercut the conventional image of the

Negro folk character whose major reference for most readers is the kindly Uncle Remus. Norton is ready to receive the impression of a fascinating spinner of tales in the quaint and curious diction of the country folk. What he gets is Trueblood's devastatingly effective recital of incest. (pp. 127-30)

Having punctured the stereotype of the kindly folk character, Ellison pursues the implications of the scene. Like many of Ellison's characters, Trueblood's name carries much of the meaning. Incest is literally being true to one's blood and though Trueblood does not know it, the practice is an ancient and often honorable one, reserved indeed for the aristocracy. It is, in short, an old folkway and Ellison can thereby indicate his rejection of the sentimental notion that folklore will reveal the naiveté and innocence of the common people. The white trustee anticipates a version of pastoral innocence and agrarian antisepsis, quite unaware that for the Negro, pastoral would carry major associations with the horror and brutality of slavery. . . . What counts most heavily is Trueblood's [unconcerned] reaction after his sin—and after he barely manages to escape the wrath of his wife. (It is true that sex figures prominently in certain areas of Negro folklore, but that should not lead to the dangerous and erroneous conception that Negroes are generally promiscuous—a point made by Trueblood's wife with an axblade!) The old man is rejected by his family, his preacher, and the Negro community but the whites take a great interest in him, encouraging him to tell the story over and over again. . . . It will take the rest of the book for Ellison's hero to learn the lesson, but ultimately he comes to the same understanding that "a man ain't nothin' but a man." Unlike Norton, who represses the knowledge of his deep instinct, Trueblood owns up to his sin—it is another sense in which his name is symbolic. But it is important to emphasize that the catharsis occurs through [Trueblood's decision to express his feelings in song], a creative act which Ellison accurately relates to a black folk tradition, the blues. As much as the spirituals, the blues is susceptible of ideological interpretation, though its definition was much later in coming. Yet the form easily takes on esthetic, political, and historical meanings. As one of the major forms of black music, the blues has defined a central tradition in American music at large. (pp. 130-32)

[The blues] suggests sadness, an awareness of trouble or a general lament, and that meaning of the term goes back to Elizabethan usage. The poetry of the blues reveals the ability of the folk to create striking and impressive imagery and in this case it exposes the remarkable range of black folk expression. The themes are often love, death, the sense of loss and at the same time a hope for release and fulfillment. The imagery is often frankly sexual but in highly metaphorical terms which contribute a joy in language and the possibility for a witty humor based on *double-entendre*. Ellison's definition of the blues expresses succinctly and effectively the ideological implications of the form: "the blues is an impulse to keep the painful details and episodes of a brutal experience alive in one's aching consciousness. . . . As a form, the blues is an autobiographical chronicle of personal catastrophe expressed lyrically." We can see how far this is from earlier conceptions of black music as an expression of hopelessness and chaos. What emerges is an artistic form that makes possible the catharsis we usually associate with tragedy. Ellison pointedly emphasizes that the blues does not skirt the painful facts of human experience, but works through them to an artistic transcendence. . . . Ellison recognizes both the force of folk tradition and its close relationship to a sophisticated literary

expression. Inevitably such an approach will move against the idea of isolated literary genres (such as tragedy) and in the direction of those mixed modes which seem to define American literary tendencies. The blues is not the "power of positive thinking" but a transformation of catastrophe through the agency of art. . . . And because of its close association with black folk culture, it is an esthetic which will also resist a movement toward expression for its own sake. There is, in short, that same balance of natural facts and spiritual truths which pervades a good deal of the literature in America that has been influenced by the Emerson-Whitman tradition.

This is precisely what Trueblood accomplishes with his blues. But Ellison extends this possibility to jazz as well, for if, on the one hand, the blues is a stage forward from earlier black musical expression (work songs, field cries, and spirituals) it is also a major link with jazz; and Ellison's use of jazz as a literary theme is one of his most impressive accomplishments. He raises the issue first in the Prologue: . . . "Nor is my invisibility exactly a matter of a bio-chemical accident to my epidermis. That invisibility to which I refer occurs because of a peculiar disposition of the eyes of those with whom I come in contact. A matter of the construction of their *inner* eyes, those eyes with which they look through their physical eyes upon reality." The mass of men are blind to the spiritual truths, and Ellison's narrator explains that "without light I am not only invisible, but formless as well; and to be unaware of one's form is to live a death." To be free is a function of the awareness of form, that is to say, it is closely related to the creative act, and the analogue of that combination is best defined by jazz:

> I'd like to hear five recordings of Louis Armstrong playing and singing "What Did I Do to Be so Black and Blue"—all at the same time. . . . Perhaps I like Louis because he's made poetry out of being invisible. I think it must be because he's unaware that he *is* invisible. And my own grasp of invisibility aids me to understand his music. . . . Invisibility, let me explain, gives one a slightly different sense of time, you're never quite on the beat. Sometimes you're ahead and sometimes behind. Instead of the swift imperceptible flowing of time, you are aware of its nodes, those points where time stands still or from which it leaps ahead. . . .

Appropriately it is a jazz performance of a blues that the narrator responds to and it is not accidental that the selection has strong social overtones. (pp. 132-34)

In more positive terms, jazz provides one with a new sense of time; . . . there is always the offbeat, or offbeats, which are characteristic of jazz style. . . . [Jazz] demands an awareness of the nodes, those moments within the heart of pulsation which are static or which provide the occasion for a leap to another level of rhythmic awareness. This is an effective description of those essential qualities of jazz syncopation which are difficult to notate but which we recognize as fundamental to the jazz performance. But the rhythmic awareness that Ellison is concerned with also provides an analogy to the recognition of spiritual truths, the opening of the inner eye. The musician slips into the breaks and looks around; he enters into the center of meaning and creates his own statement, which is precisely what the jazz soloist must do. (p. 134)

[Yet] if jazz provides an outlet for individual expression it also demands an allegiance to the group as well, and Ellison employs this circumstance thematically as a way of defining the relationship of the individual to his society, thus raising the issue from a purely esthetic to a political level as well. It seems to me the best explanation for the denouement of the book in which the narrator affirms his resolve to emerge from underground: "I'm shaking off the old skin, and I'll leave it here in the hole. I'm coming out, no less invisible without it, but coming out nevertheless. And I suppose it's damn well time. Even hibernation can be overdone, come to think of it. Perhaps that's my greatest social crime, I've overstayed my hibernation, since there's a possibility that even an invisible man has a socially responsible role to play." (p. 135)

[After he has emerged from the underground], the narrator of *Invisible Man* is finally able to unravel the meaning of his grandfather's advice: "I want you to overcome 'em with yeses, undermine 'em with grins, agree 'em to death and destruction, let 'em swoller you till they vomit or bust open." At first he takes this to mean accepting the values of the white world, playing the good Negro, all the while making the most of his opportunities for himself. But ultimately he understands that the grandfather's plea for affirmation was toward something else: "Could he have meant—hell he *must* have meant the principle, that we were to affirm the principle on which the country was built and not the men, or at least not the men who did the violence. Did he mean say "yes" because he knew that the principle was greater than the men, greater than the numbers and the vicious power and all the methods used to corrupt its name?" . . . For all his awareness of evil and his contempt for an easy optimism, the narrator reveals himself to be essentially an Emersonian "yea sayer." He has tried all the versions of the American dream, beginning with the tradition that hard work and prudence will lead to material success. . . . This is essentially what one strand of Emerson's thought has come to suggest—that the reality of our life needs to be held constantly to the demands of the American dream; and when it fails to measure up to the standard, it is the individual's responsibility to say so. . . . The principle that Ellison's narrator affirms is best defined as nonconformity. . . . (pp. 137-38)

The narrator will not give up his color because that would mean rejecting as well the heritage of black culture which, as Ellison has argued, is a major contribution to America as well. But the force of black culture (in folklore and jazz) is to remind us of the principle especially appropriate for American development—that the roots of high culture lie in the expression of the common people. Ellison modifies the optimism of Emerson's ideology with his blues formulation; it is what he means by "continuing to play in face of certain defeat." . . . What Ellison has in mind in his formulation of equality recalls Herder's conception of the equal validity of incommensurable cultures. The aim is not to make the Negro white, or the white Negro, but to allow for the fullest development of each strand which will ultimately contribute to the definition of a black *and* white America. It is not black nationalism Ellison is after, but American nationalism as the Emerson-Whitman tradition had defined it. For the Negro it means first accepting his folk heritage in order to be an American; then he can acknowledge his status as a man. (pp. 139-40)

Gene Bluestein, "The Blues as a Literary Theme," in his The Voice of the Folk: Folklore and American Literary Theory, *University of Massachusetts Press, 1972, pp. 117-40.*

EDWARD MARGOLIES

[It] was not until the 1920's that Negro authors seriously attempted to deal with the folk materials in their culture. And when they did, the authors of the Harlem school treated Negro life self-consciously, as if somehow Negroness and poverty produced a superior kind of humanity, given to song and dance, and to a primitive, noble, exotic happiness as opposed to the corruption and neurosis of the surrounding white civilization.

The stark years of the thirties forced the Negro author to take a more realistic assessment of his situation. Frequently he labored under a structured ideology not altogether suited to his problems, but in any event he was required by this kind of discipline to relate what was unique in his culture to a broader over-all concept of history. During the first half of the decade the Communists appeared to champion an independent state located somewhere in the South, but after 1934 more and more stress was laid on full-fledged assimilation and integration into American life. This forced Negro intellectuals to examine even more closely their own ambivalent assimilationist and separatist views.

One of these was a young college student, Ralph Ellison, who came to New York in 1937 and began writing under the guidance and encouragement of a confirmed Party member, Richard Wright. Wright himself had written about the problem of Negro cultural identity and its place in a pluralistic society. Ellison almost immediately took up the dilemma, and in a sense devoted all his energies to its pursuit. (pp. 128-29)

No one could have been better suited, by virtue of his training and upbringing and experience, to undertake the challenge. Born in Oklahoma City in 1914, when caste lines were not yet so rigidly drawn as in other parts of the South, Ellison enjoyed a freedom to partake of the various crosscurrents of American life that were still sweeping across that near-frontier area. Not only did he encounter in his day-to-day experiences persons of different backgrounds, but he learned their songs, dances, and literature in the public schools. Moreover, he attended films and theater and read books avidly, and none of these suggested to him the "limitations" of Negro life. (p. 129)

He knew best, of course, his Negro culture, and he projected on his vision of the outside world the specificities of a Negro outlook. . . . [Jazz] and especially blues provided him with the greatest sources of satisfaction. In his growing years, Kansas City jazz attained its ultimate refinement in the environs of Oklahoma City, and figures like Jimmie Rushing, Hot Lips Paige, Charlie Christian, and others became heroes to hosts of Negro boys. And if jazz was not regarded as being quite respectable in the schools he attended, he was given a rather impressive training in classical music so that he could make comparisons and perceive relationships. Thus for Ellison it was not simply a case of Negro culture standing apart, but a convergence in which Negro culture maintained its separate identity in a wider spectrum.

Not surprisingly, Ellison's understanding of his early life corresponds to his definition of Negro jazz. And ultimately it is jazz, and blues especially, that becomes the aesthetic mainspring of his writing. . . . [Music], however tragic its message, is an affirmation of life, a celebration of the indomitable human spirit, in that it imposes order and form on the chaos of experience.

The delicate balance struck between strong individual personality and the group . . . was a marvel of social organization. I had learned too that the end of all this discipline and technical mastery was the desire to express an affirmative way of life through its musical tradition and that this tradition insisted that each artist achieve his creativity within its frame. He must learn the best of the past, and add to it his personal vision. Life could be harsh, loud and wrong if it wished, but they lived it fully, and when they expressed their attitude toward the world it was with a fluid style that reduced the chaos of living to form.

(pp. 129-31)

The hero of *Invisible Man,* in the course of a journey from the deep South to Harlem, assumes a variety of poses, most of which he believes in at the time, to fit the white man's definition of a Negro. But each of these roles fails him, and a kind of chaos ensues . . . , for no one of them takes into account the fluidity and complexity of his individual being. At the end of the novel, hidden away in a forgotten basement room in an apartment building, the hero comes to no true resolution of his dilemma except the realization that his humanity is invisible to most persons, Negroes as well as white, and that he must discover for himself what he thinks, feels, and is. Yet the mere act of telling his story in novel form has given order to the meaninglessness of his experiences, and has thus become an affirmation, a celebration of life. He intends, he says, to ascend to the surface soon, to have another "go" at the world.

The novel is no more than a recapitulation of the pain the hero has suffered in his twenty or so years—the telling of which is its own catharsis. No social message, no system of beliefs, no intellectual conclusions arise from his tale other than his own consolation in telling it. Yet in the telling, he cannot but see the comically absurd aspects of his existence, of all Existence—and his narration is therefore not without humor. (Ellison told one interviewer that he thought he had written a very funny book.) *Invisible Man* is tragic in the sense that it celebrates the hero's capacity to endure, comic in the sense that he avers the fecundity of life, the wealth of the possibilities he may choose (and he often chooses wrongly) amidst the abundance of chaos.

Ellison has several times described this view of life as blues. In 1946 he wrote:

The blues is an impulse to keep the painful details and episodes of a brutal experience alive in one's aching consciousness, to finger its jagged grain, and to transcend it, not by the consolation of philosophy but by squeezing from it a near-tragic, near-comic lyricism. As a form, the blues is an autobiographical chronicle of personal catastrophe. . . .

Ellison also sees the blues as serving a ritual function.

The blues speak to us simultaneously of the tragic and comic aspects of the human condition and they express a profound sense of life shared by many Negroes precisely because their lives have combined these modes. . . . This is a group experience . . . and any effective study of the blues would treat them first as poetry and ritual.

Invisible Man opens with a prologue in which the hero, in his secret basement room, announces he is about to recite the catastrophic events of his life. . . . He has been playing a Louis Armstrong record, the refrain of which runs: "What did I do / To be so black / And blue?" In a sense, this refrain implicitly follows each of the major episodes of the novel. As his attempts to play out the roles that whites have assigned him (each of them different, but all of them dehumanizing, like variations on a theme) meet with disaster, the hero in effect asks himself Armstrong's punning question. He has tried to play the game according to the rules but has each time discovered himself more bruised. Thus each episode serves almost as an extended blues verse, and the narrator becomes the singer. The epilogue brings us back to the present; the reader is returned to the basement room, and the hero tells us that despite his psychic wounds (he has dreamt that he has been castrated), he has not yet given up on life. Hence the novel ends as it had begun, just as the last verse of a blues is frequently the same as the first.

Since the blues, according to Ellison, is by its very nature a record of past wrongs, pains, and defeats, it serves to define the singer as one who has suffered, and in so doing it has provided him with a history. As the novel develops, the hero takes on the role of a Negro Everyman, whose adventures and cries of woe and laughter become the history of a people. As a high-school boy in the South, he is a "Tom"—little better than a darky entertainer; in college, a Booker T. Washington accommodationist. When he moves North, he works as a nonunion laborer and then flirts for a while with Communism. Finally, he becomes a Rinehart, Ellison's word for the unattached, alienated, urban Negro who deliberately endeavors to manipulate the fantasies of whites and Negroes to his own advantage. But besides being a kind of symbolic recapitulation of Negro history, the blues structure of the novel suggests a philosophy of history as well—something outside racial determinism, progress, or various ideologies, something indefinably human, unexpected and perhaps nonrational.

In one sense the Negro since Emancipation has telescoped the American experience, passing from an agrarian existence to a highly industrialized urban life. In another sense this history is enigmatic—not only invisible but unformed—a history in which chance and accident act as principles in a designless universe. So long as men demand predetermined patterns of their universe, in order to reassure themselves that existence is not chaotic (which it is), they will demand that Negroes play out certain roles to conform to these patterns. But there is an issue of "necessity" involved. The Negro, like any other man, is unresolved nature, mysterious and complex, and cannot by the very exuberance of his being long play out these roles. When this occurs, illusion is then momentarily stripped away and chaos is seen for what it is. But the white man, terrified at these realities, proceeds to force upon the Negro still another role to suit yet another fancied pattern of existence. Does this mean that history and life need be perceived as unmitigated purposelessness? In effect Ellison never truly resolves the question aesthetically. But he seems to be saying that if men recognize first that existence is purposeless, they may then be able to perceive the possibility of shaping their existence in some kind of viable form—in much the same manner as the blues artist gives form to his senseless pain and suffering. (pp. 131-34)

As the novel proper opens, the hero recalls his grandfather's dying words: "I never told you, but our life is a war and I have been a traitor all my born days, a spy in the enemy's country ever since I give up my gun in the Reconstruction." He goes on to advise, "I want you to overcome 'em with yeses, undermine 'em with grins, agree 'em to death and destruction, let 'em swoller you till they vomit or bust wide open." These then will be the tactics the Negro will employ for survival in years to come. He will pretend to agree to his invisibility until reality strikes down the white man for his obdurate blindness. The novel then proceeds to record the hero's various initiation rites into invisibility wherein the white man accords him several identities—none of them human. Ultimately his is a journey into self-recognition. He recognizes first that he is invisible—and second, that he is a man. (pp. 134-35)

The tone of the first half of the novel is that of an almost Gulliverlike innocence. [The hero] relates objectively how "sincerely" he attempts to fulfill his roles, how deeply he believes in them. As a high-school graduate, he is invited to deliver his valedictorian address on humility as being the "very essence of progress" to a smoker of the leading white citizens of the town. . . . The hero is finally allowed to give his speech (at first scarcely anyone appears to be listening), but there is very nearly an explosive situation when, by a slip of the tongue, he mentions social equality. At the end of his speech, he is given a briefcase in which, during the course of his subsequent adventures, he will place tokens and mementos of the various identities the Negro has assumed during his history.

The second major episode takes place in a Southern Negro college whose buildings and environs—magnolias, honeysuckle, moonlight—the hero describes in glowing (faintly satirical) terms. The college has been endowed in large part by Northern liberals who, since Reconstruction, have endorsed Booker T. Washington's twin principles of equality and castle submission—not only a logical contradiction, but, again, a kind of blindness to reality. But here Ellison is suggesting as well that the Northern white liberal philanthropist demands the invisibility of the Negro no less than his Southern racist counterpart, in order to conceal from himself his ancestors' complicity in Negro slavery. Ellison, in this portion of the novel, employs, in addition, constant allusion to Negro history as a means of discovering the Negro's present invisibility. The hero relates, for example, the presence on the campus of a statue of the Founder, a former slave, who is removing (or placing?) a veil from (or on?) the eyes of a kneeling Negro. Was Negro enlightenment simply another guise of keeping the Negro in the dark, invisible from himself?

There are mellow scenes of students assembled in chapel singing symphonic and devitalized slave spirituals for white patrons. Or a moving and eloquent address by an ancient Negro minister rehearsing the life, trials, and achievement of the Founder. The Founder's immense sacrifices, the students are told (probably for the thousandth time) in wonderful old-fashioned ringing rhetoric, have made possible the progress and happiness they enjoy today. At the close of his speech, the minister stumbles as he leaves the rostrum and the students suddenly realize that the minister is himself blind.

Some of the best passages in the novel occur when the hero, an honors student, acting as chauffeur to one of the white patrons who has been visiting the college, inadvertently drives him beyond the picturesque manicured environs of the college campus past the old slave quarters. This is a part of the countryside Mr. Norton has never before seen and he is met with reality for the first time. The habitations are unchanged since ante-bellum days and the Negro peasants living thereabouts are regarded as little better than barbarians by the middle-class college community. Norton talks to one of

them, Jim Trueblood, who recounts the fantastic events relating to his incest with his daughter, which has made him a celebrated figure among the whites in the county. (Respectable Negroes are ashamed.) . . . At the close of Trueblood's story, Norton apparently suffers a heart attack, and the hero takes him to a Negro roadhouse, the Golden Day, in order to revive him with whisky. As luck would have it, they arrive at about the same time as a group of Negro mental patients, shell-shocked veterans of World War I, who pay periodic visits under guard for a respite of drinks and disreputable women. A wild riot erupts and Norton is hurt and hustled out, but not before one of the veterans tells him that for all his vaunted philanthropy, the Negro is not a human being but a "thing," a cipher to satisfy his guilt and his cravings for adulation and love.

Here Ellison suggests the results of a hundred years of white liberal patrimony of the Negro. Large financial donations may afford the givers some illusion of having fulfilled their moral obligations, but failure to recognize the Negro's humanity has produced only a worsening of pain. . . . Although Norton would like to believe the college is a monument to his efforts, in reality the maddened rioting veterans of the Golden Day are his true fate. They represent the logical absurdity of his dream, for they are not, like Trueblood, Negro peasants bound to the soil, but testimonials to Negro progress—doctors, lawyers, teachers. Thus has Ellison married elements of the Negro's invisible past to the Negro's invisible present: slavery (Trueblood), Reconstruction (the college campus), philanthropy (Norton), and World War I (the veterans)—all resulting in a chaos called The Golden Day. (pp. 135-38)

[As the novel ensues], Ellison moves from the white-Negro Southern power structure to the Negro's Northern plight. Bledsoe has ostensibly suspended the hero for the summer months but has provided him with letters of identity to important New York capitalists who might employ him. The journey North has a blues ring, especially when the hero discovers that Bledsoe too has deluded him with false promises. But the hero does manage to find work at the Liberty Paint Company, whose motto reads, "Keep America Pure with Liberty Paints." His first task is to infuse ten drops of a blackish substance into buckets of a white base liquid and stir, the result being a product called Optic White which is used in repainting national monuments. Here Ellison's allegory becomes a little too obvious.

The hero is next assigned to work at the furnaces of a basement, three levels underground, with a strange little Negro foreman named Lucius Brockaway. It develops that Brockaway, who has charge of all the immensely complicated machinery below ground—boilers, furnaces, cables, pipes, wires, and so on—is indispensable in running the plant. Efforts to displace him with white engineers have resulted in a total breakdown of production. . . . From simple allegory Ellison has moved to a more subtle kind of symbolism. Somewhere beyond the narrative level, he is saying that America has depended from the start on the unacknowledged skills and sacrifices of Negro labor.

But if Brockaway is the indispensable man, he is also the white capitalist's man as well. He is fiercely opposed to labor unions, and when he learns that the hero, during his lunch hour, inadvertently stumbled onto a union meeting (in which, incidentally, a discussion had been proceeding regarding the employment of nonunion Negro workers), he accuses the hero of treachery and betrayal. He attacks the hero and the two wrestle weirdly in the underground chamber—a Northern echo of the battle of the boys at the white citizens' smoker. Just when the hero believes that Brockaway has finally reconciled himself to his presence, a boiler explodes and the hero awakens to discover himself in the plant hospital. (pp. 138-40)

The hero is released from the hospital and dismissed from his job ("You just aren't prepared to work under our industrial conditions"), after an operation intended to produce in him a new and more docile personality. . . . Yet the operation does not altogether remove his identity. He remembers snatches of folklore and songs his grandmother had sung to him as a child which seem strangely applicable to his situation. The past lives on, then, in the present, and whatever else urban life and the Depression may have done to him, they have given him a greater sense of pride and an awareness of his history.

The hero now strides through the streets of Harlem somehow reassured by the swarming black life about him. He eschews the black middle class that hopelessly and ludicrously models itself on the white bourgeoisie—his first place of residence, Men's House, is a haven for such persons—and lives in a boardinghouse run by Aunt Mary, a formidable mother-earth figure who cares warmly for the lost and bewildered children of her native Southland. Nor is the hero any longer ashamed of Southern Negro foods that identify him with a slave and peasant ancestry. On one occasion he stops to purchase a yam from a Southern street vender. "I am what I am," he says as he bites into the hot buttered delicacy.

But if urban life awakens the hero to emotions of a specific Negro historical identity, . . . the Depression expands these feelings to include an active sense of social responsibility the hero now shares with many other city Negroes. And the latter part of the novel deals with some of the forces that endeavored to make political use of the new awakening in Negro communities.

Black nationalism, the first of these, is represented in the figure of Ras the Exhorter, an exotic West Indian extremist. The hero sees Ras violently addressing a street corner gathering when he first arrives in Harlem from the South. He pays little attention at the time but when he later involves himself with the Brotherhood (the Communist Party), Ras and his followers play a distinct role in his experiences. Ras, who suggests something of the colorful Marcus Garvey, preaches a doctrine of complete black virtue coupled with an utter distrust of the white man. (pp. 140-41)

The hero is recruited by the Brotherhood when, after witnessing the physical eviction of an elderly Negro couple from their tenement, he delivers a fiery speech protesting the injustice of it all to a gathering street crowd. Even here, Ellison suggests the specific Negro history that has ultimately placed the unhappy pair on the dreary Harlem sidewalk. He cites the pathetic paucity of personal effects they are allowed to keep, among them a small Ethiopian flag, a tintype of Abraham Lincoln, a manumission paper dated 1859, a pair of "knocking bones" used in minstrel shows, some faded and void insurance policies, and a "yellowing newspaper portrait of a huge black man with the caption: 'MARCUS GARVEY DEPORTED.'" (pp. 141-42)

Ellison perhaps devotes too much space proportionally to the Communist wooing of the Negro, but these are experiences he knew, after all, firsthand, and the Marxist emphasis on Negro history as being part of a larger dialectical process must have appealed to Ellison's ingrained aesthetic sense. In any event, his hero's Communist experiences are too complicated to chronicle fully. He becomes an authentic Harlem "spokesman," but even when he is most blinded by his Marxist rhetoric, there persist in the marrow of his being some suspicious regarding the relevance of his Negro experience to the notions of history he publicly upholds. Indeed, Ras's violent and chauvinistic opposition to Brotherhood ideals is closer to what the hero knows to be true. What he finally learns in the course of his radical adventures is that even for the Brothers, the Negro is a thing, an object, an instrument of power politics and of preordained historical design, rather than a divinely complex and complicated human mystery. (p. 142).

Yet his experiences as a radical are not a total loss. For one thing, the hero, like his author, has acquired an education of sorts regarding the Negro's role in history. If what the hero learns is at considerable variance from what the Brotherhood wanted him to learn, he does nonetheless take away with himself an added sense of his own importance. Second, and possibly more important, is that in making him a Harlem leader, the Brotherhood has unwittingly given him access to his fellow Negroes on a level he had hitherto seldom achieved. He discovers to his astonishment (and to the chagrin of the Brothers) a bond of love and shared experience that the outside world can never know.

In one of his first performances for the Brothers, he addresses an assembly of Negroes on the question of rent evictions. (pp. 142-43)

As a result of his speech, his reputation is established. He begins to campaign against rent dispossessions, but then quite unexpectedly he is transferred downtown, ostensibly for further indoctrination. Upon his return several months later, he learns that the agitation he had begun so successfully has lost nearly all its momentum and that the community has become hostile to the Brotherhood for its betrayal. . . . His anxieties are further aroused when he learns that Tod Clifton, his closest Harlem comrade and a Brotherhood lieutenant, has vanished. . . . Later the hero witnesses Clifton being shot to death by a policeman who had been trying to arrest him.

On his return subway trip to Harlem, the hero ponders Clifton's death, and then as he observes a trio of zootsuited adolescent Negro boys sitting quietly in front of him, he realizes that:

> They were men out of time—unless they found Brotherhood. Men out of time, who would soon be gone and forgotten. . . . But who knew (and now I began to tremble so violently I had to lean against a refuse can)—who knew but they were the saviors, the true leaders, the bearers of something precious? The stewards of something uncomfortable, burdensome, which they hated because, living outside the realm of history, there was no one to applaud their value and they themselves failed to understand it. What if Brother Jack were wrong? . . . What if history was not a reasonable citizen, but a madman full of paranoid guile and these boys his agents, his big surprise! His own revenge? For they were outside, in the dark with Sambo, the dancing paper doll; taking it on the lambo with my fallen brother, Tod Clifton (Tod, Tod) running and dodging the

forces of history instead of making a dominating stand.

Here then is the blues theme as applied to history. The accidental, the unplanned, the unforeseen variables of history are symbolized by the presence of the Negro, who because of his invisibility should not logically exist, but who nonetheless endures and may, on some future occasion, transform events overnight. And the mere fact of his survival, despite sufferings, defeats and repressions, represents an affirmation of life that undercuts any "system" of history. Because human beings are involved, history, like blues, records only the possibilities of existence.

The hero organizes a huge procession for the dead Clifton on the streets of Harlem. . . . The Brotherhood at once makes plain its opposition to the hero's militancy and he is now finally convinced he has once more been betrayed. He intends as vengeance to delude them as they had all along been deluding him. He will follow his grandfather's advice: "overcome 'em with yeses, undermine 'em with grins" until the entire Harlem community erupts in their faces. He will pretend to them that their more pacific plans to organize the community are eminently successful, while in reality he knows that Harlem seethes with social and racial tensions, not the least of which are aimed at the Brotherhood.

Since much of the hostility of the community is directed toward him as being an instrument of a white man's organization, the hero determines to take a new identity. He settles for a wide-brimmed white hat and dark glasses—but the disguise works only too well. He is constantly being stopped on the street by persons who mistake him for someone named Rinehart. But on each occasion they know Rinehart as possessing a different occupation. . . . The hero is thus reborn as Rinehart, whose "world was possibility . . . [a] vast seething hot world of fluidity" in which Rinehart plays many roles. For the real Rinehart had evidently perceived the Negro's world as an undesigned Chaos in which he could have as many images as he wished. Is this not the white man's world as well, the hero wonders, since no understanding of history can have any validity if it fails to recognize the Negro's existence? Here Ellison and his hero stand at the brink of existential despair, where values such as love, honor, and integrity have no meaning.

But before he can resolve his disturbed vision, the hero is pulled back into a Harlem uprising of destruction and violence for which he is in part responsible. . . . [Pursued by a pair of white hoodlums he] dives into an open manhole and ultimately finds his way into the discarded basement room which will become his home.

In the basement room the hero decides that he has all along been invisible. But before he can determine who he is, Ellison makes his discard the contents of the briefcase he has been carrying ever since the night of the smoker. In the course of his life he has collected a number of objects which he has "unthinkingly" stuffed in his briefcase. In effect these represent not only his past identities but the roles the Negro has played in history. At one time or another, the briefcase has contained a small antique cast-iron bank for coins molded in the figure of a red-lipped, minstrel Negro (economic exploitation), a leg shackle (peonage), his high-school diploma (his Jim Crow education), Clifton's Sambo doll (his minstrel role), a letter from Jack identifying him as a Brother, and his dark Rine-

hart glasses. In jettisoning these, as it were, the hero can come to a true recognition of himself.

In isolating the historical theme of Ellison's blues, one does not, of course, begin to do justice to the novel. The narrative pace is swift and engaging, and the hero's adventures possess their own intrinsic interest. Moveover, Ellison's symbols seldom intrude as they explain, and yet are quite as original as they are functional. Nonetheless, splendid and ambitious as Ellison's novel is, it does not quite succeed. Perhaps one reason is that his hero, owning no identity or at best an invisible one, does not create in the reader any real empathy. He is not a lovable rogue, nor a goodhearted innocent, but merely a passive figure who, for the most part quite mindlessly, allows things to happen to him. This was of course Ellison's intention, but given the sustained length of the novel and the colorlessness of the protagonist, the reader is made more and more aware that he is reading a book. There is simply too much distance between the reader and the hero and one finds oneself subconsciously congratulating the author for the deftness with which he moves his character along, rather than paying attention to his troubles or his meaning. Secondly, there is a singleness of theme—the hero's invisibility—and episode after episode plays variations on this theme. It is as if one were compelled to listen to a marvelous blues extended to symphonic length. One may admire its various parts, but wish after a while for a different kind of movement—to catch oneself up in surprise or elation or another level of comprehension.

In all fairness, Ellison attempts to do this. The tone of the hero changes from that of a gullible innocent in the beginning to that of a straightforward narrator somewhere midway in the novel, to that of a somewhat more sophisticated observer of himself later on. And Ellison himself has said of his novel that it moves stylistically from naturalism to expressionism to surrealism—all of which is true. But these are, after all, effects, and the single idea still dominates. One somehow expects more, for all its richness, and the "more" is seldom forthcoming.

Which brings us once again to the thematic weakness of the novel. For Ellison's hero simply has nowhere to go once he tells us he is invisible. He does indeed, in the Epilogue, say that he intends to rise again and try his hand at life, that he has faith in democratic principles, and that life itself is its own excuse despite the blows it has dealt him. But there is no evidence in the text to fortify his beliefs. The blues singer has depths of feeling to begin with, but Ellison's hero has just begun to learn to feel as the novel ends. (pp. 143-48)

> *Edward Margolies, "History as Blues: Ralph Ellison's 'Invisible Man'," in his* Native Sons: A Critical Study of Twentieth-Century Negro American Authors, *J. B. Lippincott Company, 1968, pp. 127-48.*

THOMAS A. VOGLER

There is a standard psychological experiment known to produce neuroses and psychopathic behavior patterns in most domestic or trainable animals. In an experimental environment that bears a striking resemblance to the world of the novel, the animals are trained to react in certain ways to certain stimuli, and then placed in a situation in which the reactions are impossible. The animal then makes what attempts it can to go on acting as it has been trained to do, but with continued frustration a nervous collapse of some kind inevitably follows. With some, the reaction is solipsistic—they refuse to mix with other animals even for eating. Others react by batting their heads against the walls of their cages until they die or are too exhausted to continue. The equivalent experience of conflict between expectations and reality has produced what Ellison calls "the American Negro impulse toward self-annihilation and going underground," which can only be overcome by "a will to confront the world, to evaluate his experience honestly and throw his findings unashamedly into the guilty conscience of America." His *Invisible Man* is a record of that agony, and of the discovery of the realities that must be faced before a genuine identity can be achieved. (p. 66)

In the novel we see the kind of training the invisible man is subjected to most clearly in the chapel scene in Chapter 5. Here are Barbee's concluding remarks, holding up Bledsoe as the pattern for the hero to follow:

> His is a form of greatness worthy of your imitation.
> I say to you, pattern yourselves upon him. Aspire,
> each of you, to someday follow in his footsteps.

In the next chapter, Bledsoe tries to explain to the invisible man what he calls "the difference between the way things are and the way they're supposed to be," but it is a lesson he is not yet prepared to learn. The invisible man, like most of us, is living in a culture whose incentives, rewards and punishments prevent the development of the kind of personal standards which the public ideals demand for a feeling of self-respect. He is in the situation Paul Goodman describes in *Growing up Absurd,* where the only truly healthy response is to reject those parts of society that threaten his own possibilities for self respect. But he cannot reject them without knowing what they are, and they are built in so that he is himself responsible for much of what he must go through.

To call a novel a protest novel at this point of history is inevitably to call back the thirties and the great American discovery of social injustice. . . . The war experience was another catastrophe, piled on top of the depression, which the American novelist had to cope with in his attempts to find a view of his place in society. Another discovery during this period—and a much belated one—was of the extent and complexity of the social problems of the Negro, and of the essential part these problems took in any attempt to achieve an overall view of American society. The development of the Negro problem is not adequately explained by a theory of growing liberalism, or a shedding of prejudice which now makes white readers willing to read books they know were written by Blacks. . . . What is clear is that in the 20th century, as in the 19th, the position of the Black citizen in our society is the *focus* of social and ideological polarities that go far beyond the question of race relations. It is also the focus for many of the neurotic fears and desires that are an inevitable part of our gross national product. From Richard Wright's first novel on, the movement has not been a shedding of prejudice, but a growing awareness, in writers and readers alike, of the essential centrality of the Black problem to any adequate view of American society.

> Negro life is a by product of Western civilization, and in it, if only one possesses the humanity and humility to see, are to be discovered all those impulses, tendencies, life and cultural forms to be found elsewhere in Western society.

It is in this way that Black writers have been developing and expressing an awareness of the universal significance of their position, as Faulkner had earlier found in a single southern county all the elements necessary to an understanding of human nature and the movement of history. Ellison is like Faulkner in seeing the South as a land doomed by the curse of slavery, yet still with a vestigial aura of Edenic simplicity. But Ellison follows his Black hero out of the South, as Wright had done, and is much more concerned than Faulkner with a direct consideration of the relationship of the civil war to all aspects of contemporary society, both North and South.

It would be too simple a view to consider the function of the Black protagonist as merely that of another outsider who can serve as a foil to define weaknesses in the social structure. The situation of the Black, like that of the writer, is a part of the society and reveals important things about it.

> Anyway, in the beginning I thought that the white world was very different from the world I was moving out of and I turned out to be entirely wrong. It seemed different. It seemed safer, at least the white people seemed safer. It seemed clearer, it seemed more polite, and, of course, it seemed much richer from the material point of view. But I didn't meet anyone in that world who didn't suffer from the very same affliction that all the people I had fled from suffered from and that was that they didn't know who they were. They wanted to be something that they were not. And very shortly I didn't know who I was, either. . . . In short, I had become an American.

The final test of the mastery of illusion and reality, and the discovery of an identity, is the ability to *tell* it. This is not the novelist's prerogative, as the examples of Malcolm X and Eldridge Cleaver show, and as Ellison suggests in Brother Tarp's recognition of the "signifying" embodied in his chain link and his pleasure at finally being able to communicate his story to the invisible man ("I'm tellin' it better'n I ever thought I could!"). If Ellison has entered the mainstream of modern art, it is through his fusion of the problems of his Black protagonist with those of the writer, whose search for form and reality is the central problem of most serious writers of fiction in the last 100 or so years. In an eloquent mood, Ellison has spoken to the best hopes of most novelists of whatever color:

> Life is as the sea, art a ship in which man conquers
> life's crushing formlessness, reducing it to a course,
> a series of swells, tides and wind currents inscribed
> on a chart. Though drawn from the world, "the organized significance of art," writes Malraux, "is
> stronger than all the multiplicity of the world; . . .
> that significance alone enables man to conquer
> chaos and to master destiny."

Invisible Man is not 'just' a Negro novel, then, and Ellison has been very careful throughout to avoid this tempting limitation, even while giving us a very comprehensive view of race relations in both the South and the North. Look for a moment at Tod Clifton, remembering that it is no accident that *Tod* in German means "death." Tod is part black, part white, symbolically gray like the "Liberty Paint" that goes out of the factory to decorate some important national monument. Tod's death is one of the key turning points of the book, forcing the invisible man to the recognition that we all shall die, leading finally to the recognition that, in an absurd society, it is an error to cater to any but one's own unique absurdity. His reflections on Tod's death are a turning-point from which he intensifies the exploration of his own identity and begins to recognize more fully the possible identities of others. . . . The specific racial killing of a Black man becomes more than the death of an individual caused by social injustice. It is the death of the best parts of the individual caused by the worst parts of society; it is "OUR. HOPE SHOT DOWN," for on the lower frequencies Ellison has been speaking for us all.

In *Invisible Man* we have a full portrait of the element of despair and of the destructive element forced on the Black, the writer, and on us as well if we go along. The question we are deliberately left with, in the end which is also a beginning, is the constructive use to which these elements can be put—the role for the self which has at last been recognized and accepted, the kind of life one can live in a realm of absurdity which is also a realm of possibility. The problem of how all this negation can be put to use is already answered in part by the very existence of the novel. It is emphasized in the beginning and end that the protagonist of the book is also its creator, and that the writing of the book is itself part of the experience, and of the discovery of an identity, which is the subject of the book. What is affirmative in both the structure and the existence of the book is that the invisible man does survive through turning his experience into art. In the same way, the ordinary Black in a hostile society has been able to turn daily injustice and suffering into the folk art of the blues. The novel, like the blues, offers a way of standing apart from one's experience without losing its intensity or its meaning. . . . The blues recognizes both the painful and contradictory aspects of experience, turning them into something like a joke. "There is a mystery in the whiteness of blackness, the innocence of evil, and the evil of innocence, though, being initiates, Negroes express the joke of it in the blues." (pp. 66-9)

[The] discovery of the potential for self discovery in the blues, or in a novel which approaches them in spirit, comes on the invisible man almost unawares, in spite of the more literary and more conscious quest for identity that he has been pursuing before. Sooner or later it seems that almost every modern work can in some way be read as a search—or more typically a "quest"—for a father or a mother. The two concepts are not interchangeable; they offer primitive but different solutions to man's basic need to reach beyond his own mind and find some fixed point around which to orient his own existence. The search for a father is almost always for a principle of authority, a lawgiver of some kind, even if it is the stern inscrutability of some abstract principle of necessity. In the earlier part of *Invisible Man* we find figures like the Founder and Bledsoe, and the great white father figures of Norton and the other trustees. Even the Brotherhood, at first felt as a fraternity of equality and freedom, is finally seen to be dominated by a harshly paternal theory of history, and Brother Jack turns out to be a disguised father masquerading as a brother. The mother figure typically offers an alternative orientation for experience, and has something that is always missing or of lesser importance in the father figures. The strictness of the father is replaced by the all-embracing acceptance of the mother, who refuses to reject her child no matter how poor, weak or sinful he has become. In *Invisible Man* the landlady Mary who takes up the hero and keeps him and feeds him is such a figure. He is trying to reach Mary's when he falls down the hole at the end, and it is to Mary's that his feet had unconsciously taken him earlier in the book. . . . The recognition that he can't return to Mary, that the alternative she suggests,

with all its religious overtones, is as unattainable as that offered by the series of fathers, is paralleled by the tone and structure Ellison uses to handle the theme in the novel. The invisible man's search for a father or a mother is a reflex in him, and therefore an inevitable part of his experience and a necessary part of the novel. But if the novel must go through the quest because its protagonist must go through, it can at least do it in a different way. Ellison has pointed out that "When you are influenced by a body of literature or art from an earlier period, it is usually the form of it that is available to you," and he has openly acknowledged the high degree of literary self-consciousness manifest in the novel. "Let's put it this way—I'm a highly conscious writer. I know what's been done because I've read the books, I've studied them." The consciousness of form and archetype leads to a deliberate and parodic use of such patterns in Ellison's work, and contributes to its enlightened literary humor. The invisible man may be duped into questing after unattainable or irrelevant goals, but he will not let his novel make the same mistake. The more innovative quest in *Invisible Man* is not that for a father or a mother, but the search for a group, a fraternity, a brotherhood of fellow humans in which the invisible man can find his identity and achieve the freedom and dignity which are the real goals of his quest. The final irony of this quest is that the real brotherhood, that of all humans facing death and oppression, can be joined only by renouncing all fictitious bases of brotherhood. (pp. 70-1)

Until he finds [his identity] the invisible man is like a cup of water without the cup; he takes on his identity from whatever shape his environment offers until, finally, he realizes that his once new and clean briefcase, now battered and dirty, is symbolically the container of all the clues that are essential to finding his true identity. This chameleon-like flexibility is one of the most typically American features in the whole book, and it is perhaps our best clue to Ellison's identity as an American writer. From the legendary versatility of Benjamin Franklin, through innumerable characters in Irving, Hawthorne, Melville, Whitman and Twain, there is the concept of a character who can move from one identity to another without effort, preparation or reflection. This concept is so basic that it turns up both in the traditions and idealized national myths—characters like Franklin and Alger—and in the works of writers like Ellison who are rebelling from the hypocrisy of those ideals while still realizing that metamorphosis is a basic fact and possibility of existence. It can be a debased, almost subhuman instrument of survival, as in Faulkner's Snopes family, or it can be a social triumph as in the legendary founder of the invisible man's college. It can be the source of humor, as in *Huckleberry Finn,* or the more cosmic and ironic humor of Melville's *Confidence Man.*

At a crucial point in the novel the invisible man "discovers" this principle of metamorphosis which has been there all along. At first, he is impressed by the world of possibilities opened up before him. . . . So he tries to Rinehart it; he will find a woman in the Brotherhood and use her to gain inside information about their plans. Unfortunately for the invisible man he picks Sybil for his informant, and she has the enthusiastic frenzy but lacks the information he is looking for. Instead, she merely gives him another lesson in his invisibility. She looks through him and sees nothing but her own fantasy of the Black phallus, the Negro rapist. And since he is now "doing a Rinehart" as he puts it, operating in the world of possibility, he can convince her—or let her convince herself—that she was raped without actually doing it. "SYBIL,

YOU WERE RAPED BY SANTA CLAUS SURPRISE" he writes on her bare belly. And the image is a perfect one, for her fantasy of him is no more real than the child's fantasy. She has been taught to believe in the Black sex fantasy as the child is taught to believe in the great magic gift-giver.

There is an interesting example of the precision and economy of Ellison's characterization in this episode. There are two sexual adventures in the book, and they both serve distinct functions. The first adventure occurred when the invisible man was sent down town to lecture on "The Woman Question," only to find out that the real question was the one Ras had asked earlier, when trying to understand what could move a Black to join the Brotherhood. What is it, Ras asks, money or women, that is confusing the invisible man's ideology. The woman who seduces him in her apartment is confusing the concept of brotherhood with biology, offering in fact still another alternative that he must try and then reject during the novel.

> Why did they have to mix their women into everything? Between us and everything we wanted to change in the world they placed a woman: socially, politically, economically. Why, godammit, why did they insist upon confusing the class struggle with the ass struggle, debasing both us and them—all human motives.

This is the other side of the confusion that Ras showed on the woman question. They both attribute a sexual motivation to a drive to attain social equality and human dignity.

The principle of invisibility and projected fantasy which we have seen operating in these episodes—and which the invisible man is gradually discovering—was announced on the first page of the novel. It is "a peculiar disposition of the eyes of those with whom I come in contact. A matter of the construction of their *inner* eyes, those eyes with which they look through their physical eyes upon reality." The consequence of this disposition of the inner eye for the invisible man is not that people see nothing at all when they look in his direction, for they know that *something* is there. What they do is look through that something at what they expect to see, what they think is there—the inner eye sees a fiction that it has itself created. The first concrete example of this error of vision comes in the Prologue, when the invisible man bumps into a tall blond man who insults him and curses him when asked to apologize. In the fight that follows the white man is almost killed, but not by the invisible man. "Something in this man's thick head had sprung out and beaten him within an inch of his life," and that something was the man's own prejudiced concept of the Nigger which he had insulted and cursed.

The Prologue also introduces the problem of names which the reader encounters with almost every character, and the critic suffers while trying to write about the nameless protagonist of the novel. Thoreau once wrote an essay largely devoted to praising the system of naming practiced by the American Indians. What Thoreau admired about the system was the idea that everyone had to wait until he had earned a name through some significant action, or until he had revealed enough of his basic personality for a name to be chosen that adequately reflected his individuality. The "invisible man" is an earned name in something like the same sense, as "Jack the Bear" is his underground name because he sees his underground time as a period of hibernation. Most of the names we are given for characters in the novel are also earned names, or names which serve as clues to the character's na-

ture or his function in the novel. Sometimes these names are symbolic, like "Tod" Clifton or "Mary." More often they are not so much directly symbolic as suggestive.

For example, when we look at Brother Jack, we should remember that a common slang meaning for "jack" is money. The name emphasizes the financial element in the relationship between the invisible man and the Brotherhood. When Ras ("race") the Exhorter asked whether it was money or women that could blind a Negro to his racial identity, the invisible man was outraged that his purity of motive could be questioned. But the whole scene takes place in front of a garish sign that says 'CHECKS CASHED HERE." Brother Jack first showed up when the invisible man was out of money, and his first reason for joining the Brotherhood was for the pay they offered. (pp. 72-4)

Rinehart is another significant name, but it can be misleading if one looks to the German *rein* ("pure") for help. "Rind" (or "rine" in the pronunciation of the novel) is a good American slang word. If a person has a lot of rind, it means he has a lot of nerve. If he *is* a rind, it means he is thick-skinned in a sense ranging all the way from not caring what other people think to not caring what happens to them. This is the rind in the Rinehart in the novel, and the invisible man points to it just before hunting up Sybil:

> Now I recognized my invisibility. So I'd accept it, I'd explore it, rine and heart. I'd plunge into it with both feet and they'd gag. Oh, but wouldn't they gag.

As it turns out, however, it is the invisible man who gags on the rind, for he is not cynical enough to keep up the role. "Such games were for Rinehart, not me," he says, and he washes off the lipstick inscription he had meant to leave behind. Meanwhile, by doing a Rinehart, by pretending to agree with the Brotherhood in order to undermine it, he does in effect agree, and becomes a betrayer of the Harlem Brothers while working in his own interests. The irony of this role is that in the very moment of seeing Sybil's fantasy of the Black rapist he is himself attempting to live one. (p. 74)

"Emerson" is another important name in *Invisible Man,* and one Ellison is acutely aware of as that of his own namesake. He deliberately uses it to undercut the conventional liberal attitude towards race relations, when the *son* of old Emerson (to suggest the historical continuity) tries to befriend the invisible man. Young Emerson tries to find him a place in the great Liberty Paint company just as Norton had tried to help him find a place in the American society, but both Norton and Emerson have an image of *the* Negro which limits their possibility of sharing any kind of reality with the invisible man. Emerson even wants to find a place for him in his own confused private life; after announcing that he had "a difficult session" with his analyst the evening before, Emerson goes on:

> "Some things are just too unjust for words," he said, expelling a plume of smoke, "and too ambiguous for either speech or ideas. By the way, have you ever been to the Club Calamus?"

> "I don't think I've ever heard of it, sir," I said.

> "You haven't? It's very well known. Many of my Harlem friends go there. It's a rendezvous for writers, artists and all kinds of celebrities. There's noth-

ing like it in the city, and by some strange twist it has a truly continental flavor."

The fey tone of this speech alone is enough to destroy what little respect we might have had for Emerson, but the Calamus Club reference takes it a bit further. The allusion is to the group of Whitman poems commonly called the Calamus Poems and dealing in a subtle but unmistakable way with the theme of homosexuality. In other words, here is still another fraternity or Brotherhood that is being offered the invisible man, and as the historical Emerson's ideas are debased in his 20th-century "son," Whitman's androgynously cosmic appetite is reduced to a stylish sexual mystique. Emerson makes it even more explicit later, when he says ". . . I'm Huckleberry, you see. . . ." in hopes that the invisible man will be another Jim. . . . (p. 75)

Characters' names, and the club names, and the names of factories, places and institutions—even the names of things, like the Sambo doll—can be explored indefinitely in this novel. The Brotherhood has its parties at a place called the Chthonian Club, which is a classical reference comparable to that of the Sybils. The Chthonian realm belonged to the underground gods and spirits; and true power for Ellison is an underground influence as we learn from seeing Bledsoe and Brockway and Brother Jack in action, as well as the invisible man writing in his hole. Where does Ras get his name, with its vocal nearness to "race?" He gives it to himself, as the invisible man gives us the name we must call him by if we are to know him for what he is.

The invisible man in action is an image collector or symbolist, gathering up into his briefcase all the concrete emblems and reminders of his experience that can serve as clues to finding his real name and identity. The book itself is for the reader a similar container of images and clues expanded into actions and events. The first example of an action-as-image after the Prologue is the battle royal scene which opens the story. If we explored this scene far enough, we could find in it a prefiguration of almost everything else in the novel. (pp. 75-6)

In the first few pages of the book, this scene seems to be primarily a description of what happened to a few people at a particular "smoker" in some small unidentified southern town. But as we read through the book, with this scene planted in our memories, we gradually realize that in it is condensed the whole world of the novel and almost all of the American society. The final scene, the race riot in Harlem, is in large part a repetition of the beginning scene, but one which we can more easily relate to the larger context it represents. Instead of the coins on the electrified rug, there is the safe on the third rail showering the streets with sparks. Instead of control being in ordinary citizens, it is in Brother Jack who represents their interests in controlling the Blacks. Instead of Tatlock and the invisible man battling it out at the end for supremacy, we have Ras and the invisible man, finally silencing his fanatic appeal to race by throwing a spear through his jaws. The riot is probably the most impressively sustained section of the whole novel. It is still carefully kept to the elements already prefigured in the brawl, yet expanded into a comic apocalypse of enormous proportions. It begins as a drunken orgy of consumer wish-fulfillment which is a fantasy Christmas ("At St. Nicholas the street lights were out.") and Fourth of July combined. At the peak of their frenzied rebellion the looters are still being controlled and manipulated by society's official symbol-makers. . . . Even Ras, who now calls himself the "Destroyer," has made him-

self up from the scrap heap of cultural detritus as Quixote made himself up from scraps and pieces of the old Romances. He is a composite of cowboy and African movies, equipped with stage-prop lion skin, spear and shield, "one of the kind you see them African guys carrying in the moving pictures. . . ." Although they are rioting against society, no one knows how the riot got started, and the only damage they do is to themselves, in the pathetic burning-down of their own tenement. The only difference, save that of scale, is that at the end the invisible man does not step forward and give a speech prepared for him by the cultural myths, but instead disappears down his hole and creates a book which could only be written after he had recognized his invisibility.

On a smaller scale we can see the same kind of significance at work throughout the novel. In fact, there is a whole scale of images at work at almost every point in *Invisible Man.* Small ones, like the statue of the Founder removing the veil from the slave, but seen in such a way that it is impossible to tell whether it is being removed or put more firmly in place—echoed later by the invisible man's spotlight blindness as he makes his first official Brotherhood speech. (pp. 76-7)

Some of these images seem to be quite clearly intended for the reader alone. Although they are registered through the eyes and consciousness of the invisible man, they are not noted by him as containing any special significance. In the El Toro bar, there are two bullfight posters which are described matter-of-factly along with the other miscellaneous contents of the room. The first poster shows a large black bull, being skillfully controlled by the matador. The other poster shows the tables turned, the bull finally discovering the illusion of the cape and tossing the matador high into the air. . . . [The bullfight posters] are a silent comment on the discussion going on in the bar between Brother Jack—who is trying to discipline him—and the invisible man. They are also a prediction of the outcome of the contest which will be fulfilled later in the novel. (pp. 77-8)

Although some of these images are like guideposts for the reader, reminding him of the larger pattern of the novel, the larger ones are all in some degree meaningful to the invisible man, and there is a consistent pattern in his reaction to them. After each significant event, he gives a speech which summarizes his state of development as of that moment in the novel. The most naive speech is the one he gives after the brawl. In each succeeding recognition he is at least potentially more aware of who he is and what his experience means until the point where he is able to summarize the whole in a book which *includes* the other speeches. (p. 78)

Most of the actions and images I have been discussing have a plausible existence in the real world, and the important thing is the sensitivity of vision we bring to them. No matter how subtly calculated we can afterwards see the effect to be, there is always the impression of a real event while we are reading. There are places in *Invisible Man,* however, where the action seems decidedly secondary to the ideas Ellison is trying to convey, where the priority of the ideas dominates so that we can't read without the attempt to translate the action back into the ideas. In these cases Ellison seems to share Ishmael's attitude towards what he calls "hideous and intolerable allegory," not believing in it at all, yet unable to resist the comic indulgence of his appetite for it.

The clearest example here is in the factory hospital scene, where the doctors try to remake the invisible man into the mechanical man he had been before, the subservient southern Negro who died when he attacked Brockway in the boiler room. When he wakes in the hospital his mind is a blank, and he only gradually becomes aware that the doctors are trying to achieve a machine-induced prefrontal lobotomy that will return him to his previous state. . . . "You're a new man," the doctors pointedly tell him. On the way home from the hospital the "new man" is metamorphosed into *the* new man, the Biblical Adam, who even predicts his own fall. "And I felt that I would fall, *had* fallen," he says, and then looks across the aisle of the subway car to see "a young platinum blonde nibbling at a red Delicious apple."

The same serio-comic intent is behind the 1,369 light bulbs that are made so much of in the Prologue. The light bulbs are his means of fighting the Monopolated Light and Power Company, and Ellison's way of illustrating the effects of a self-recognition on the power struggle that occupies most of the novel. After first finding his own light by burning the papers in the brief case, he can begin to take revenge on the power monopoly that he has suffered under for so long. He is finally out of their control. He can't overthrow them, but he can undermine and weaken them by draining off part of their power. No writer would go to this extent for the sake of an idea alone, and there is a very pointed humor in much of Ellison's "allegory." The ironic, joking tone of the blues is continually showing through, as well as the pleasure Ellison obviously gets from the virtuoso manipulation of words. . . . Ellison is a fierce punster, and he can't always restrict himself to the obvious level of "I yam what I am," or turning Brother Tobitts into two bits.

He is also a prophetic writer, and that is why I must conclude with the envelope or frame which makes up the novel's beginning and end. The Prologue gives us a picture of the invisible man after he's finished writing the book, a picture of his present state. He has discovered that he is invisible, and taken the first step that he must take after the discovery. He has preserved his anger and his suffering by embodying it in art, and has even more fully grasped his identity in the process. But what is he to do with his identity after this, and after all the emphasis in the Epilogue on "the possibility that even an invisible man has a socially responsible role to play." We know that he is in hibernation, and we can't help wondering with him whether he will come up to find the smell of death or the smell of spring in the outside air. The invisible man doesn't know; he is prepared for a rebirth, and a new life, but has not yet been born into it. (pp. 79-80)

> *Thomas A. Vogler, " 'Invisible Man': Somebody's Protest Novel," in* The Iowa Review, *Vol. 1, No. 2, Spring, 1970, pp. 64-82.*

WILLIAM W. NICHOLS

As many teachers of American literature have discovered, Ralph Waldo Emerson's "The American Scholar" provides a useful framework for discussing the protagonists in much American fiction. Emerson's Scholar is, in some ways, an allegorical figure, an ideal American hero who is creatively and harmoniously related to nature, the past, and the worlds of thought and action. He has a kind of integrity in his relations with society that an Ishmael, a Huck Finn, a Nick Adams, or an Augie March can only struggle toward; and the struggles of such characters often take on additional meaning when they are considered in the light of "The American

Scholar." There are, in addition, more compelling reasons to consider the relation between Emerson's Scholar and the protagonist of Ellison's *Invisible Man.* First of all, there is Ralph Waldo Ellison's sense of his own special relation to Emerson, his namesake. . . . More importantly, in the novel itself there are explicit references to Emerson and his relation to black Americans; for example, Ellison's nameless narrator-protagonist (hereafter referred to as N) is told by a Northern businessman early in the novel: "I am a New Englander, like Emerson. You must learn about him, for he was important to your people." Along with this kind of allusion, there are interesting parallels between the influences which educate the American Scholar of Emerson's address and the terrifying forces which initiate Ellison's N into a knowledge of his invisibility. My purpose is to suggest that these parallels set up a pattern of irony in Ellison's novel and that an awareness of this pattern is helpful in attempting to understand the rather difficult Epilogue.

Emerson's treatment of the Scholar places immediate stress on setting: "The first in time and the first in importance of the influences upon the mind is that of nature. Every day, the sun; and, after sunset, Night and her stars. Ever the winds blow; ever the grass grows." As usual in Emerson's work, the setting is essentially pastoral; and when the nightmarish landscape of *Invisible Man* is compared with it, the discrepancies are so great that they produce an ironic dimension in simple descriptive passages. Ellison's novel begins and ends in a hole where the sun never shines, the winds never blow, and no grass grows. The most acceptable environment which N can find, this hole is a measure of the failure of the pastoral dream in the world of the novel. . . . The hope of pastoral immediacy is discarded as fatuous myth in *Invisible Man;* what Ellison calls "mid-country peace" is either a facade erected by white society to hide reality from Negroes or it is the terrifying deprivation of the "field nigger."

The "beautiful college" which N attends, for example, is such a triumph of landscaping that at first he understands his expulsion as a loss of Eden. . . . But from the beginning the illusory quality of the college landscape is apparent in the descriptions with their jarring alternation between an antebellum, agrarian beauty and signs of human degradation. N follows in his mind's eye the road which leads through the beautiful campus "past the buildings with the southern verandas half-a-city-block long, to the sudden forking, barren of buildings, birds, or grass, where the road turned off to the insane asylum." As N recalls that fork in the road, it is clear that he can never regain the dream of a peaceful, cultivated agrarian world. When later, in Central Park, he is tempted to dream of "mid-country peace," he reminds himself that "somewhere, close by in the night, there was a zoo with its dangerous animals."

If the idea of pastoral immediacy is treated as a bitter joke in Ellison's novel, the Emersonian promise that the self-reliant Scholar can make creative use of the past is shown to be a fantasy as misleading as the Horatio Alger myth. For Emerson, of course, the past need not be at all restrictive. (pp. 70-1)

[Throughout *Invisible Man*], N's attempts to find meaning in the past or to extricate himself from it are painfully unsuccessful, and the failure is most apparent in his inability to understand his grandfather's deathbed advice to his father about dealing with the white world. . . . Until he has accepted his grandfather's premise that a black man's life is a war against white people, N is troubled in his relations with the white world by a sense that his friendliest overtures are weapons that he does not understand. After a series of bitter experiences with white people leads him to accept his grandfather's war premise, N momentarily believes that he can successfully confront and control his past: "And now all past humiliations became precious parts of my experience, and for the first time . . . I began to accept my past. . . ." But N soon discovers that he has not really learned to use the past at all. When he tries to apply his grandfather's advice by agreeing with the white leadership of the Brotherhood, the result is the death and destruction of Negroes in the Harlem riot, a catastrophe which had been planned all along by the Brotherhood as a propaganda device. N is forced to conclude that either his grandfather was wrong "or else things had changed too much since his day." In either case N's heritage is worse than useless, and in the Epilogue he is still trying to understand his grandfather's advice, this time as an affirmation of "the principle on which the country was built and not the men, or at least not the men who did the violence." That voice from the past continues to echo through his consciousness, but ultimately he is not convinced that it has any meaning for him when he concludes "I can't figure it out; it escapes me."

One reason for N's inability to use his past creatively is that he can never separate himself from it. Like a fetter from his slave ancestry, it oppresses him so that he can never view it with detachment. Freedom to turn one's back on the past, implied in Emerson's admonition to Americans to stop listening to "the courtly muses of Europe," simply does not exist for N. Significantly, it is the ideologically blinded Brotherhood that preaches the necessity and the possibility of breaking with the past. . . . The Brotherhood's doctrine of history, however, denies black men any meaningful selfhood. Ras the Exhorter, a black nationalist leader in Harlem, explains this to N and his co-worker, Tod Clifton, in a grim metaphor: " 'What is your past and where are you going? Never mind, take your corrupt ideology and eat out your own guts like a laughing hyena.' " Unlike Tod Clifton, who understands Ras and ultimately dies when he tries to "plunge outside history," N tries to accept the Brotherhood's vision of the past. But whenever he tries to act as though he has indeed shed that "old agrarian self," he is brought up short, as he says, "by the sense that I had somehow been through it all before."

If nature and the past do not offer N anything like the kind of fruitful education that Emerson promised, experience is no better teacher. Again, the Emersonian promise is extraordinarily hopeful:

> So much only of life as I know by experience, so much of the wilderness have I vanquished and planted, or so far have I extended my being, my dominion. . . . The true scholar grudges every opportunity of action past by, as a loss of power. It is the raw material out of which the intellect molds her splendid products.

In this relationship between ideas and action, N feels that he has "learned some things," but Ellison's whole novel denies N's optimism about his education.

Perhaps the most fully developed example of N's inability to translate experience into knowledge is found in the series of episodes which focus upon the sexuality of Negroes and their imposed invisibility. There is, first of all, the smoker at which N expects to play the dignified role of a "potential Booker T.

Washington" only to find that he must participate in a humiliating battle royal with nine of his schoolmates. The scene becomes a psychic emasculation when N and the other young Negroes are forced to stand helplessly before a naked blonde dancer. N watches Tatlock, the biggest of the group, guiltily try to hide an erection and beg to go home; and he sees another member of the group faint. N himself experiences the kind of intense conflict of emotions—fear and desire, hatred and guilt—that produces impotence; and he witnesses the frenzied reactions of respectable white men to the combination of blonde sexuality and black humiliation. The next episode in the novel is really a variation of the first, exploring more terrifying dimensions in the relationship between black and white sexuality. This time N observes Mr. Norton, the millionaire Bostonian, as he listens fervently to a Negro sharecropper tell how a dream in which he fled terrified from sexual contact with a white woman led to an actual incestuous union with his own black daughter. As in the battle royal scene, the white man here pays the Negro for accepting sexual humiliation and for inflicting violence on people of his own color. (pp. 72-3)

N's one complete sexual experience in the novel, which is with a white woman, is rendered deeply traumatic by his fears of the white world's reaction, and the psychic cost is so high that he avoids all further contact with white women who wish to test his expertise as the Brotherhood specialist on the "woman question." Finally, when the frustrated wife of one of the white Brotherhood leaders asks N to reenact upon her a Negro's rape of her friend, "a lovely girl . . . with a complexion like strawberries and cream," he finds that he is impotent. And ironically, although he can understand the white woman's desire for him in a society which teaches her to fear his potency, N cannot understand his own response to her. At the end of the novel, N's awareness of the white world's willful suppression of his sexuality remains unconscious—figured in a terrifying dream of his castration by the Brotherhood. Unlike Emerson's Scholar, for whom experience, at first a part of the "unconscious life," ultimately "detaches itself from the life like a ripe fruit, to become a thought of the mind," Ellison's N can only transform his experience into haunting nightmares. Despite his participation in a pattern of parallel action structured to reveal the inevitable entrapment of black men in America, N never sees the pattern clearly. He gains only a vague sense of *déja vu*.

Although N is unable to avail himself of the resources promised in the Emersonian version of the American Dream, he does maintain in the Epilogue, as I have said, that he has learned something. And part of what he understands to be his new knowledge is framed in language that echoes Emerson at his most optimistic:

> I believed in hard work and progress and action, but now, after first being 'for' society and then 'against' it, I assign myself no rank or any limit, and such an attitude is very much against the trend of the times. But my world has become one of infinite possibilities. . . .

There is, of course, bitter irony in a phrase like "infinite possibilities" within the context of *Invisible Man,* where the young hero is ultimately not allowed to realize even the most limited possibilities of American life; and the irony can be underlined with a final quotation from "The American Scholar." Emerson is discussing the duties of the Scholar, which he says, "may all be comprised in self-trust":

> . . . the instinct is sure, that prompts him to tell his brother what he thinks. He then learns that in going down into the secrets of his own mind he has descended into the secrets of all minds. . . . The poet, in utter solitude remembering his spontaneous thoughts and recording them, is found to have recorded that which men in crowded cities find true for them also.

N's life in the dark hole of the Prologue and Epilogue is a metaphor for Emerson's self-reliant descent into the secrets of the Scholar's mind. Of course, N has not chosen this self-reliant stance; he has been, as he admits, "clubbed into the cellar." But once he is there, he attempts, despite the chaos of the external world, to probe his own deepest instincts and emotions; and his final conclusion is that, beneath the racial conflict which he has described, there may be a possibility for human communication: "Who knows but that, on the lower frequencies, I speak for you?"

The discrepancy between this fragile possibility and the promise of "The American Scholar" sets up the most bitter irony in the novel. N's vision of the future is finally apocalyptic and impersonal. While Emerson never gives up the conviction that his American Scholar represents the limitless potential of the individual who will transform society, Ellison's N seems at the last to see himself as a pawn in an inevitable social revolution. There is a personal fatalism like that found in some of the apocalyptic prose of black revolution when he says: "You won't believe in my invisibility and you'll fail to see how any principle that applies to you could apply to me. You'll fail to see it even though death waits for both of us if you don't." Despair is part of that prediction, and N's decision to end his "hibernation" seems to be posited more on a sense of death than of rebirth as he continues his discussion of the future:

> There's a stench in the air, which, from this distance underground, might be the smell either of death or of spring—I hope of spring. But don't let me trick you, there *is* a death in the smell of spring and in the smell of thee as in the smell of me. And if nothing more, invisibility has taught my nose to classify the stenches of death.

N has, in short, become a specialist in death and violence. His emergence from the dark hole will not be an Emersonian metamorphosis of butterfly from larva but the potentially violent awakening of "Jack the bear" from hibernation. Early in the Prologue N tells of having almost knifed a white man who was unable to see him as a human being. Subsequently, he decides that his own restraint was an act of cowardice; he should have killed the man "to protect the higher interests of society." This is the final promise of the Epilogue and the implication of the whole novel—that a society might be awakened and purified by violence and that the value of an individual human life may have to be subordinated to that awakening. Such a conclusion carries with it the frightening implication that the Black American Scholar may inevitably be forced to follow Ras the Exhorter turned Destroyer. (pp. 74-5)

William W. Nichols, "Ralph Ellison's Black American Scholar," in PHYLON: The Atlanta Universi-ty Review of Race and Culture, *Vol. XXXI, No. 1, first quarter (Spring, 1971), pp. 70-5.*

F. H. LANGMAN

Ralph Ellison's *Invisible Man* has suffered some fierce attacks, survived, and seems now to be taking its place as a classic. The attacks on it have been usually for bad reasons, misreading and the misapplication of dogma; but it has been defended for reasons often equally bad. Much of the dispute has shown not the irrelevance to literature of the clamour for social relevance but its sometimes stupefying shallowness and lack of focus. Critics on both sides have used the novel as a pretext to affirm their own preconceptions, slogans, and wishes. But others who have tried to lift the debate to a level more technically sophisticated, more literary in a restricted sense, have generally done no better. If anything they have done worse, because they have obscured the ways in which a concern with literary quality can show itself through serious, exacting assessment of the claim to social significance in such a work. . . .

Like much else in the intellectual fiction of its period (1952), *Invisible Man* puts itself rather self-consciously at the service of a criticism specializing in elaborate mechanical analysis. Its reward has been high praise, but the praise seldom touches the life of the book. Thus critics have been able to trace through it a complex pattern of symbols and motifs; images of sight, of the visible and the invisible, of black and white, dark and light, have been counted through, assembled, interpreted. . . . To recognize these patterns has some point: they are certainly present. Yet to accept them as significant grants far too much. The kind of organization they represent is inadequate, without further development, to mediate deeper understanding, to give substance to the novel's key inter-relationships, or to pull the whole work together in a meaningful way. Beneath the intricate surface pattern, the novel may remain unrealized and incoherent. (p. 114)

Invisible Man is clearly a novel into which a good deal of impassioned thought has entered. It seeks to take a position, it formulates and reformulates a persistent problem, and by the fabling, allegorical cast of its narrative it invites interpretation in depth. Critics have pointed to the universality of the book's preoccupations. Although it tells the story of a black man's search for himself—his name is never given—it represents more than the quest for black identity. It is at once more specific, a very individual story, and more general, dramatizing the identity-crisis of a whole society. The case of the hero is seen not as unique but only as heightened by his blackness, made more dramatically explicit. He is seen as a quintessential American, trying to find his real nature through the succession of roles he is called on to play, trying to restore the traditional values his society professes but disregards, trying to reaffirm his personal innocence while caught up in the corruption of history. To recognize all this is to become aware of what the novel undertakes, of its scope and serious intent. It would be a mistake, however, to suppose the undertaking significant merely because of its scope, or to take it seriously because of its earnest ambitions. Even at the high level of generality prompted by thematic interpretation, where almost anything can be made to seem important, the novel's main conceptions may appear as facile as they are familiar. The necessary critical question is whether these conceptions are adequately realized in the novel, brought convincingly to life and mastered.

The answer is that the manifest intentions of *Invisible Man* remain largely embryonic. It is a novel of patches, a few of them brilliant, but as a whole deeply unsatisfying. Part of what makes it so unsatisfactory is the evidence it contains of how good it might have been. At its best the novel races along, vivid, funny, thoughtful, powerful; but it quickly flags, time after time. Then the meanings become forced, the comedy wilful, the judgments perverse or confused.

In form, *Invisible Man* is picaresque. That accounts sufficiently for its loosely episodic sequence, and enables it to accommodate the inset tales which provide its main strength. But it is riven by kinds of confusion and indeterminacy more fundamental than such considerations of form can explain. The narrative moves through a variety of styles, not in a controlled and cumulative development but, it seems, according to the fluctuations of merely local impulse, passage by passage. Documentary literalism alternates with surreal nightmare, farce with rather precious lyricism. The trouble is not that these modes are intrinsically incompatible, or could not be unified by ironic counterpointing: it is that the novel as a whole lacks orchestration. In addition, Ellison's success in each mode is unsustained, fragmentary. The novel reads as a succession of improvisations, often weakly derivative and eclectic in their models. Thus the abounding verbal quibbles and attempts at lyrical fine-writing carry strong but pointless (and damaging) reminders of James Joyce. (pp. 114-15)

Like the unaccountable changes in style, the passages of pastiche and imitation can be taken as signs of technical immaturity, but it is difficult to separate that from an immaturity of conception. Wavering between parody and simple attempts to emulate, they indicate an author unsure what effects he wants to produce and from what moral position he writes. Similar indications occur elsewhere, in fact almost everywhere in the texture of the prose: an uncertainty of touch is in the grain.

At its best the prose has remarkable vigour and sweep. It is contemporary, fluent, figuratively rich, rhythmically apt and various. . . . (p. 116)

More typical of the prose—the novel has a multitude of sentences and extended passages like it—is this passage:

> Shuddering into motion, the machine gave a sudden scream like a circular saw, and sent a tattoo of sharp crystals against my face. I moved clumsily away, seeing Brockway grin like a dried prune. Then with the dying hum of the furiously whirling drums, I heard the grains sifting lazily in the sudden stillness, sliding sand-like down the chute into the pot beneath.

This is characteristic in its fresh, vivid particularity; characteristic too in its weaknesses—the use twice in three sentences of "sudden" (one of Ellison's most overworked words), the intrusive alliteration, the straining for effect. The sense of strain, of an attempt to force words to do what the imagination has failed to do, is endemic in the novel. It comes most often from the extended comparisons, the paradoxes, the sheer violence of expression in sentences like this:

> I had to take myself by the throat and choke myself until my eyes bulged and my tongue hung out and

wagged like the door of an empty house in a high wind.

What makes that example particularly telling is its emptiness of reference in the context. The protagonist is describing the outrage done to his own feelings on the occasions when he had tried to justify and affirm the mistaken beliefs of his friends, "saying 'yes' against the nay-saying of my stomach". The realities of experience to which that would correspond are simply not in the novel. The convictions of the protagonist have been too nebulous, his conscience too opportunistic, to provide concrete instances of the self-suppression the quoted sentence lays claim to. (p. 117)

[What saves *Invisible Man* from dismissal is] Ellison's gift for writing set pieces, those self-contained episodes and passages in a special style which display his considerable gifts at their best. Some readers have found the first of such pieces, the account of the battle royal, so effective that the remainder of the novel seems one long anti-climax. But the best single sequence, the one in which the author's urbane sense of complexities and his powerfully aroused emotions are held together in full equipoise, is Jim Trueblood's story.

Faulkner provides the model here. We catch his note in the sly humour, the idiom, the long, additive, conversational sentences. But whatever Ellison has learned from Faulkner he here makes his own, and the character of Trueblood—abject, proud, calculating, naive, sardonic, stoical, loving—is created with economy, insight, compassion and zest.

Trueblood's recollection of the time in his young manhood when he would lie in bed with his girl on summer nights and listen to the boats moving along the river establishes the moral ground of the tale. In his evocation of sounds and sights, the sensations of encroaching sleep, the multiple blended enjoyments of repose, companionship, spectacle, there is a human reality, and a sense of the deep satisfyingness of life, which transform the raw farce of his disgrace. His shameful act itself comes to seem an outcome of his innocent capacity for the enjoyment of life, and leaves untouched the fundamental self-respect to be felt here:

> They used to have musicianers on them boats, and sometimes I used to wake her up to hear the music when they come up the river. I'd be layin' there and it would be quiet and I could hear it comin' from way, way off. Like when you quail huntin' and it's getting dark and you can hear the boss bird whistlin' tryin' to get the covey together again, and he's coming towards you slow and whistlin' soft, cause he knows you somewhere around with your gun. Still he got to round them up, so he keeps on comin'. Them boss quails is like a good man, what he got to do he *do*.

The first-hand quality of the observation here, and above all the authenticity of the feeling—the huntsman's respect for the bird, amounting almost to empathy with a worthy opponent—warrant the idea of a standard implied in the last sentence. Trueblood's conception of what makes a good man grows directly out of experience. With this passage, his own claim to be a man becomes charged with a kind of moral force. His affirmation of that force is there in his account of responsibility: "a good man, what he got to do he *do*". (pp. 119-20)

In his frank enjoyment and his strong sense of mutuality, Trueblood possesses a more complete identity, is more fully a man, than any other figure in the book. In contrast with the puritanical self-suppression and sublimation of Mr Norton, the white millionaire, Trueblood's self-acceptance makes him whole yet keeps him from the chaos that Norton fears. This completeness transforms his act of shame into something approaching a triumph. It happens because of the strength of life in him, not because of perversity or deprivation. And it begins in the innocence of sleep. Matty Lou, his nubile daughter, lies close beside him for warmth, and blends in his fading consciousness with the girl he has been remembering from his long-gone youth. He falls into a dream of elemental images, unmistakably suggestive to the reader yet strange enough to keep the dreamer from seeing through their disguise to the real nature of what he is doing. Were it left here, though, were it simply a matter of something done in sleep, the act would have only the moral quality of an accident. But Trueblood wakes up, and the act isn't over. He is still, so to speak, fixed in his predicament. As he puts it, "once a man gits hisself in a tight spot like that there ain't much he can do". Either to move or to stay would be sin: "There was only one way I can figger that I could git out: that was with a knife". The scene has become farce; another page and it becomes knockabout, when his wife wakes up and has to use several kinds of violence to dislodge him. Even in the account of these wild moments, Trueblood preserves some dignity beneath the absurdity. He likens himself in that hair-raising situation to a man whom the police had besieged, and who continued to shoot at his assailants "until they set fire to the house and burned him up". "So like that fellow", he says, "I stayed, I had to fight it on out to the end. He mighta died, but I suspects now that he got a heapa satisfaction before he went". (pp. 120-21)

[While making Trueblood admirable in some respects], Ellison avoids sentimentalizing him. The comic treatment of his tale helps to ensure this, although humour in such a case could seem defensive and dishonest. Trueblood is not reduced to a clown or a grotesque. He is given a human complexity sufficient to prevent his example from being shrugged off or laughed away. The very verve with which he tells his story testifies to his integrity; and then another side to his character peeps through—he half-enjoys the story and the effect it invariably creates, and his manner of telling it is not without artifice and creative pride. (p. 121)

It would be tempting to suggest that the comic treatment is what saves this tale from the over-insistence and obscurity which mar comparable things in some other parts of the novel, but it wouldn't be quite true. Elsewhere the humour too can seem forced or disproportionate; and on the other hand some of the best things in the book occur in quite other kinds of narrative. In certain scenes of anger, fear or pain there are flashes of impressive moral insight. One of the finest is in the description of the blonde dancer at the battle-royal:

> The hair was yellow like that of a circus kewpie-doll, the face heavily powdered and rouged as though to form an abstract mask, the eyes hollow and smeared a cool blue, the colour of a baboon's butt.

At this stage the hero does not see the significance of this picture. He is too fiercely caught up in the turmoil of his own emotions, but the very ambivalence of his feelings—"I wanted . . . to caress her and destroy her, to love her and murder her"—indicates what she has been made into: her vulnerable humanity is at once exposed and depersonalized. She is turned into something less than human—beast, mask,

object. And in this ghastly subjection what she undergoes is a telling counterpart to the depersonalizing of the hero himself. At first he fails to see it: regarding her as an object (the definite articles instead of pronouns in the passage quoted help to indicate this—the hair, the face, the eyes), he is unable to think of her as capable of suffering. He speaks of her "impersonal eyes". Later, when she is roughly manhandled, he does make the connection: "above her red, fixed-smiling lips I saw the terror and disgust in her eyes, almost like my own terror."

Another such moment, though somewhat less persuasive, occurs during the first party of the Brotherhood's. A drunken guest makes remarks about the musicality of Negroes that sound offensively patronising. He is ejected from the party for "unconscious racial chauvinism". Afterwards, the hero is disturbed by a new reflection:

> Shouldn't there be some way for us to be asked to sing? Shouldn't the short man have the right to make a mistake without his motives being considered consciously or unconsciously malicious?

At such moments the novel cuts not only through the familiar forms of racial prejudice but also through the complementary prejudices of enlightenment. It shows how even supposedly benevolent attitudes in a polarised situation force people into predetermined roles, denying their individual humanity. These insights intimate what the novel might have achieved. They are too isolated and undeveloped, intermixed with too much that is inferior or even morally oblique, properly to justify the novel's theme. But at least they show an awareness of what might have been done with it. And in the treatment of the central character, too, there are signs of the clarifying honesty the whole conception of the book required. Invisible to others because never seen simply as himself, seen always in the garb of their own preconceptions, he is also invisible to himself. He cannot know himself because he is altogether too ready to try the roles he is offered, especially the role of leader of his people. If the character of the invisible man seems sketchy, elusive or inconsistent, this is surely part of the meaning of the novel. The absence of recognition in the world around him deprives him not only of visible identity but also of a stable inner sense of self.

And yet, granting the importance of this conception, I think we have to demur. Much in the presentation of the character troubles me, and I'm troubled still more by the willingness of critics to accept an estimate of his moral claim more generous even than his own. If he does not fully know himself, it's not clear how certainly the author knows him either. The author's attitudes and purposes waver, he treats the character sometimes as spokesman, sometimes as uncomprehending victim, and fails to create for him a distinctive voice. This happens partly because Ellison has not mastered the perils of first-person narration. The method creates peculiar difficulties in the control of distance, tone, and irony, and requires considerable definiteness of purpose and attitude. Lacking sure control, the novel frequently leaves us uncertain how far to accept the hero's valuation of himself or others. In consequence, no strong sense of a central personality can be created, and it is not surprising that the novel seems to break up into fragments of variable quality.

The same kind of uncertainty appears in the novel's attempts at direct handling of its social and political materials. The hero's relationship with the Brotherhood provides the main test. Because his own values remain unclear—because it is frequently difficult to tell whether he is offered as victim or villain, satirical butt or prophetic spokesman—his hostility to the organization remains unfocused, seems merely personal and arbitrary. (pp. 122-23)

The Brotherhood is blamed for cynically manipulating the people of Harlem, and the hero indignantly tells himself that they must be made to pay for the betrayal. Yet precisely how and where the committee perpetrated this betrayal, and what they could hope to achieve by it, never appear. On the contrary, the riot in Harlem occurs only because the hero himself had chosen, without instructions and as it turns out against the committee's wish, to stir up the people. By his speech at Tod Clifton's funeral he exacerbates their feelings, but as he has neither programme nor principle to put before them it's no wonder that what they are moved to ends in bloody and pointless riot.

There is a still deeper anomaly. Although the hero is outraged by the cynicism of the Brotherhood, his own cynicism is as great. He exploits the Brotherhood without caring for its policies, and the people of Harlem without offering any tangible reforms. His own driving concern has never been the welfare of his people. It has been the fulfilment of his own ambitions. He goes to New York to prepare himself for personal success. At first, he sees himself as Dr Bledsoe's successor. . . . His cynicism towards his own people is thorough: "I would have one way of speaking in the North and another in the South. Give them what they wanted down South, that was the way". As the book goes on, he modifies his ambitions but not his attitude. Instead of wanting to join Bledsoe, he hopes to succeed through the Brotherhood. . . . When he has worked for the Brotherhood, studied its ideology, and made himself (unbelievably) the leading figure in Harlem, his real motives remain unchanged. He seeks self-advancement: "I could reach the very top and I meant to get there". . . . When he plans the public funeral for Tod Clifton, it is neither out of homage to his dead friend nor in the belief that the people of Harlem need this means of expressing their grief and outrage. He sees it as a way of restoring his own political fortunes, regaining his prestige: "I seized upon the idea now as though it would save my life". My life! Given this motive, it is difficult to accept his sense of moral betrayal when the Brotherhood refuses to endorse his action and sustain the campaign in Harlem. Still less is it possible to believe in the protestations of injured innocence he is made solemnly to utter. Of all things, he prides himself on integrity in his dealings with the Brotherhood: "I'd tried to build my integrity upon the role of Brotherhood and now it had changed to water, air."

As such examples accumulate, they prompt the question of whether the novel has been misread by a generation of admirers. Perhaps its main purpose is to satirize political demagogues and charlatans, with the nameless hero as archetype of the breed. At times such a reading does seem plausible. In the Epilogue, for example, Ellison has the protagonist confess that he finds "the utmost difficulty" in being honest. Commenting on the novel, in *Shadow and Act,* Ellison describes as "the major flaw in the hero's character" his "unquestioning willingness to do what is required of him by others as a way to success". That, however, is ambiguous testimony: it's not clear whether the "flaw" should be understood as the desire for "success" or merely as the "unquestioning willingness". It looks unhappily like the latter, since Ellison adds

that "this was the specific form of his 'innocence' ". And in much of the novel itself the hero is presented as naive but honest victim. This makes the moral drive of the book peculiarly disturbing. . . . It is not true that what he wants is what Harlem wants. He wants personal power, prestige, admiration; by the end of this very paragraph he is again shown to be concerned simply with salvaging his "career". It would be comforting to think that Ellison saw the hero's claim to be a spokesman for Harlem as a contemptible rationalization, but the novel gives no sign of that. What it shows instead, time and again, is an uncertainty about his motives and actions amounting, in places, to self-contradiction. (pp. 123-25)

The worst confusions in the novel, however, seem to me to lie in its treatment of white women. Except for the one moment of clear sight with the terrified dancer, it subjects white women to a kind of indignity essentially similar to what the hero is supposed to suffer. It sees them as stereotypes. There is something extraordinarily obtuse and unpleasant in the way they are reduced to the role of bitch on heat. By what I take to be an inadvertent though also inexcusable irony, these women are shown as projecting their fantasies of sexual fulfilment on to the black hero while the novel itself conjures them up out of fantasy just as gross and untrue. The writing in these episodes becomes intolerably trashy: "in one swift motion the red robe swept aside like a veil, and I went breathless at the petite and generously curved nude". It also becomes cruel: "she was a leathery old girl". But the ugliest quality of these scenes is their self-righteous moralizing. The hero has made up to the woman called Sybil solely in hope of extracting information about the Brotherhood from her. He is unashamedly ready to exploit, and in that way dehumanize, the sexual relationship he fully expects to have with her. When she makes an obscene proposal he is horrified. With no awareness of using a double standard, he thinks of lecturing her "on the respect due one's bedmate in our society". These scenes are meant to be comic, and the hero's ineptitude as a seducer is offered as something to smile at, but this is another way of trying to make him seem innocent.

At the end of the novel, the hero decides to come out of hibernation. He affirms his belief in the "possibility that even an invisible man has a socially responsible role to play". It is a hollow gesture, and critics have been rightly troubled by it. But their attempts to explain what is wrong with it seem to me disastrously wrong-headed: they put all the blame on to the world outside the hero. . . . Marcus Klein argues that there is no positive principle on which the hero can come out and act responsibly, since "given the social facts of America, both invisibility and what he now calls his 'hibernation' are his permanent condition". Against that, one has to say "the social facts of America" are not "given". They are not given in the sense that the novel does not persuasively render and interpret them: apart from a few intense and well-realized scenes, the social setting remains vague or factitious. But in a larger sense, too, the social facts are not "given". The stultifying assumption made by both critics, and attributed by them to the novel, is far too easy. Social attitudes are not immutable, meaningful action is not inconceivable, the novel has merely failed to conceive of it, and its satire on political activists has been directed against men of straw. The invisible man's affirmation at the end is meaningless, not because the novel has shown the impossibility of responsible action but because he has no specific idea of what a responsible role might be. (pp. 126-27)

F. H. Langman, "Reconsidering 'Invisible Man',"
in The Critical Review, *Melbourne, No. 18, 1976,*
pp. 114-27.

PHYLLIS RAUCH KLOTMAN

The Running Man in literature is recognizable in his most simple state as the protagonist who rejects the values of the culture or society in which he finds himself by birth, compulsion, or volition, and literally takes flight. During the nineteenth century when he attempted to escape the tentacles of an inimical society, he could still run away *from* but also *to* something: from the settlement to the frontier (Cooper), from slavery to freedom (the slave narrative), from land to sea (Melville), from society to the river (Twain) or to the Pond (Thoreau). Often romantic, his flight was rarely abortive. He was, then as now, a critic of his time and place. Twentieth-century society, however, in effectively depriving him of his goal, has forced his very act of running to assume complex shades of ambiguity. (pp. 3-4)

Ralph Ellison's *Invisible Man* is the culmination of the Running Man metaphor, the electric "umbilical cord" connecting the running men of the past with those of the present. In no other single work is the metaphor as central to the meaning and significance of the artist's overall conception; in no other work is the ambiguity so consistently sustained. Indeed, running gives shape and unity to the novel. While the prologue and epilogue are static—in both sections the protagonist is immobilized, even though the epilogue intimates a change—the central section is a series of spasmodic movements in flight.

Unlike the slave, who exercised volition in his desire and decision to escape, Ellison's protagonist is essentially a runner by coercion, precipitated into flight by some unwitting but irrevocable blunder. His *faux pas,* though seemingly self-initiated, are for the most part governed by those all-but-invisible puppet strings, manipulated by the forces of power in whatever form they manifest themselves: the southern white power structure, the black college, the factory system, industrial unionism, the Brotherhood. Running, then, as revealed in the dream quotation, is a negative uncontrolled response to a metaphoric cattle prod used by others to shock the Invisible Man into random, indiscriminate movement, leaving him impotent, without control over himself or his environment (symbolized specifically in the "hospital" scene, which is ambiguously rebirth *and* the partial death of emasculation). The protagonist never controls his environment—that great Hemingway ideal—until he stops running *physically* and is alone, reflective, visible at least to himself. (p. 71)

The major part of the book is an account of the narrator's life: the first half, an escape from various unsatisfactory social identities, leading to the climactic death-and-rebirth section; the second half, the quest for a new identity, and in common with Harry Angstrom and Holden Caulfield, the search for an "environment in which he can perform at his best," the result "a painful contemporary odyssey." The epilogue rounds the work to a finish with an indication of renewed activity: "Without the possibility of action, all knowledge comes to one labeled 'file and forget,' and I can neither file nor forget." True, there is no final resolution; the Running Man metaphor remains ambiguous, because running for Ellison as for Thoreau is striving, and therefore a function of life. The narrator, like Thoreau, absents himself from society for

a time, although not initially by choice—the black experience in America has a way of eliminating free will. *His* Walden is not a pond but a hole; he has not walked out to it of his own volition, but fallen *into* it while attempting to escape with his life. (pp. 72-3)

Once "clubbed into his cellar" and losing the world, the Invisible Man learns the difficulty of looking into one's self:

> When one is invisible he finds such problems as good and evil, honesty and dishonesty, of such shifting shapes that he confuses one with the other, depending upon who happens to be looking through him at the time. Well, now I've been trying to look through myself, and there's a risk in it.

At risk may be more than being hated when trying to be honest, or liked when dishonestly affirming someone else's mistaken beliefs; the risk may be the trauma when one is confronted . . . with the specter of a formless self and the incumbent responsibility, albeit opportunity, to shape one's own identity. . . . The protean quality of Ellison's protagonist is symbolized by the namelessness of the character and is artistically related to the Running Man metaphor, for each time he takes flight his identity is subtly altered or drastically changed. As one critic has pointed out, "If you are no one, you are at the same time potentially everyone."

To Ellison, Proteus is both America and "the inheritance of illusion through which all men must fight to achieve reality." The writer must

> challenge the apparent forms of reality—that is, the fixed manners and values of the few, and . . . struggle with it until it reveals its mad, vari-implicated chaos, its false faces, and on until it surrenders its insight, its truth.

Isn't this also the struggle of the nameless narrator in *Invisible Man?* The forms of reality with which he struggles stubbornly refuse to reveal their truth, so that he himself takes up the masks, the false faces, that reveal only chaos. Ironically, he is both Proteus, struggling and turning into diverse shapes, and the grandson of Proteus, holding and pressing the past so that he can achieve reality in the present.

The first identity the narrator assumes is conventional for a bright southern Negro boy: he imagines himself another Booker T. Washington. . . . Only the dream, ineluctably linked to the stolid black peasantry of his past—symbolized by his grandfather—mocks his false face and sets him mentally on the road. The white-man's-black-man identity fades into unreality when his next irrevocable error threatens the myth so carefully nurtured by the southern black educator. Dr. Bledsoe makes a reality of the nightmarish dream. Because the young idealist hasn't learned "to act the nigger," Bledsoe propels him onto the road North, ostensibly because "the race needs good, smart disillusioned fighters," but actually because his own position of power depends upon the docility and blindness, or covert compliance, of the young.

Bewildered by his loss of identity—"here within this quiet greenness I possessed the only identity I had ever known, and I was losing it"—the protagonist runs North with "letters of recommendation" from Bledsoe, honorably unopened in his treasured briefcase, a gift from the good white citizens in the distant past of his white-man's black-man identity. But the letters, one for each day in the week, open no doors, and he begins to feel that he is playing a part in some scheme he cannot understand. No matter how he wrings his mind, the scheme will not reveal its truth. What is his role, his new identity? Who assigns the roles—northern whites or southern black educators? He doesn't find the answers to all of these questions but he desperately tries to prove his "identity" to the disenchanted son of his seventh and last hope. This liberal son of a northern industrialist lives in his own masquerade world and offers the confused narrator a more sophisticated role in his version of an old classic: Huck and Jim at the Club Calamus. But the young narrator doesn't understand the double entendre and keeps insisting that he has another identity. " 'Identity!' 'Huckleberry' Emerson cries, 'My God! Who has any identity any more anyway?' " Then he reveals the information that impels the protagonist again to flight. " 'I beg of you, sir,' Bledsoe says in his letter to Emerson the father, 'to help him continue in the direction of that promise which, like the horizon, recedes ever brightly and distantly beyond the hopeful traveler.' " Nowhere is there a more sardonic treatment of the Emersonian style of northern intellectual, the man who deals in instant self-reliance; obviously Ralph Waldo Ellison has a special antipathy for the type.

As hopeless traveler and black pariah, the protagonist blunders into the role of union scab at Liberty Paints, artfully conceived as a microcosm of both American society and the industrial complex. A neophyte laborer, he commits an unpardonable error in paint mixing by exceeding the ten black drops that assure pure American whitewash. This blunder reveals the invisible contributions of black people to America (as did his off-campus error of exposing atavistic Trueblood of the black past to the delicate white sensibility), and projects him into an abortive conflict with Brockway, who represents the black foundation on which society and industry rest. The importance of outside pressure (the gauges) is forgotten as the two men lock in a black-against-black struggle (comparable to "battle royal") while the factory explodes, at least in the protagonist's mind. " 'I seemed to run swiftly up an incline and shot forward with sudden acceleration into a wet blast of black emptiness that was somehow a bath of whiteness." He is thus projected, like human fallout, into the climactic hospital scene, which symbolizes both death and rebirth. Immaculately conceived by the machine (age), the protagonist is reborn without identity, individuality, or background—the proper moment for his re-conception, when he no longer knows his name, where he was born, who he *was*. (pp. 73-5)

One flaw mars the machinery, however; it cannot turn out a completely computerized (non)man when even the most minuscule amount of humanity remains to touch him into life. This is much better illustrated in the original section deleted from *Invisible Man* and published separately as **"Out of the Hospital and Under the Bar"** in *Soon, One Morning* (1966). In an "Author's Note," Ellison explains:

> For those who would care to fit it back into *Invisible Man* let them start at the point where the explosion occurs in the paint factory, substitute the following happenings, and leave them once the hero is living in Mary's hope.

Mother Mary of Harlem, who finds the young man staggering out of the subway, springs rather unsatisfactorily from nowhere into the novel, but she helps him achieve rebirth in the original episode. . . . Without real knowledge of the machine's complexity, she partially releases him and restores his strength with a foul-tasting home remedy: "That stuff'll make a baby strong." Through Mary and her urbanized black folk world, the protagonist moves toward an identity based on his gradual acceptance of the realities of the past: swallowing the past, no matter how galling, makes the present possible. The overtones of emasculation are still there, for it is quite clear that to Ellison this is the essence of the black experience in America.

"Out of the Hospital and Under the Bar" is one of the most effective, densely symbolic scenes Ellison has written and the exigencies of publication should not have forced its excision. It is similar but superior to the Golden Day episode and foreshadows the running riot scene that returns the narrator to his underground womb. In a Freudian serio-comic nightmare, the naked narrator runs and is chased through the labyrinthine passages of his mind, until he bursts newborn from the subterranean womb into Harlem:

> I rolled, looking into the faces of two women dressed in white.
>
> "Police! A naked man, a naked. . . . !" the woman screamed. "Police!"
>
> "Oh no! No!" called a woman who crouched against a building front. "Not naked! Is he, Sis Spencer? Let's us be sure 'fore we call the cops. Wait'll I change my glasses."
>
> "As ever he was born in the world!"

Two nurse-like women attend this birth, but the protagonist himself has been the most active, experiencing the pangs of passage, expelling himself from the symbolically ambiguous orifice—a manhole—naked into a new world of consciousness. But he has run a long way, leaving behind bodies deadened by the machine (age); shocking whites with his nakedness; encountering another basement black whose life is a perpetual gamble; and slipping away from the straitjacket-bearing attendant who tries to fit him with an adjustable identity—"It'll fit, all right, it's endlessly adjustable." The naked narrator, however, has slipped off *all* identities, theirs and his own, and is racing toward some intangible hope, the possibility of perception:

> And I was conscious of being somehow different. It was not only that I had forgotten my name or that I had been processed in the machine, or even that I had taken Mary's medicine—but something internal. My thoughts seemed to be the thoughts of another. Impressions flashed through my mind, too fleeting and secretly meaningful to have been my own—whoever I was. And yet somehow they were. It was as though I had become capable of new powers of understanding.

But the cellar of his mind is still cluttered with old memories, all of which he must traverse before he can be free. . . . (pp. 76-7)

"Out of the Hospital" is almost completely a running scene, but for the first time the protagonist has an awareness of the meaning of running. The runner is in a flight that has the dreamlike quality of double vision: standing back, he watches himself running through his own history, which is, in a sense, a history of the race in microcosm. The hospital scene in the novel has this quality, but with little of the dramatic impact of the deleted section. Ellison sustains this motion and suspense, reminiscent of the excitement of escape in the slave narrative, even to the inclusion of the pursuing hound. When the narrator finally arrives **"Under the Bar,"** he blends into the blackness—"nigger in the coal locker"—until the dog and the men at his heels force him to thrust himself through the manhole. The section ends with the protagonist deciding to find "Old Mary," but in the meantime he has had an important encounter with a blind man in Harlem who bears a startling resemblance to his grandfather (from whom he cannot escape), and who also reminds him of Bledsoe, the briefcase, and part of his still undigested past: "Well, a young fellow has to keep moving. . . ."

"Out of the Hospital" is an artfully executed recapitulation section that will be used later, not so much as a structural device, but as contrast. The protagonist's running in the simulated riot is realistically, almost naturalistically, described and the outcome is reversed. The runner drops back through the manhole into the womb of the earth to be born again or finally buried. In this earlier episode, however, he is reborn into the bosom of the folk with a beginning recognition of and pride in his origins—essentially a new identity reshaped from the old. The old remedy, put together from herbs and recipes of the past, has given him strength to force himself out of the mechanical womb of an automated society that seeks to make automatons of men and to exploit their strength for its perpetuation. When he finally comes up for air, from the underground of past feelings and experiences, he finds himself in Harlem, the promised land that will not yield its promise. This he has yet to experience; now he is without fear, but also without illusions. (pp. 77-8)

Ironically, the Brotherhood thinks of him as a new "Booker T. Washington," but he has already shed his illusions of ever assuming such an identity: "To hell with this Booker T. Washington business. I would do the work but I would be no one except myself—whoever I was." He finds, however, that his role of "Brother" carries with it ill-fitting masks that are repugnant to him: he is an Uncle Tom to Ras, a black stud to Emma, an opportunistic plotter to Brother Westrum (Rest Room), and eventually a traitor to the people in Harlem who trusted him. The latter mask he tries to rid himself of when Ras the Destroyer's men attempt to track him down. The Hollywood disguise he thinks he is assuming with shades "of a green glass so dark that it appeared black" metamorphoses him into Rinehart, a confidence man in the Melville tradition, a "confidencing sonofabitch." . . . (p. 78)

Ellison sees Rinehart's nonidentity as a negative perspective for his protagonist. The epitome of the happy Proteus, his invisibility is essentially egoistic, conscienceless, asocial if not antisocial. He is a gambler, a briber, a lover (roles the protagonist will never master), a man who can cope with the shifting realities of the times because his own identity is fluid, unimpeded by the barriers of a functioning superego. Running is a way of life for him and invisibility his natural dress. (p. 79)

Running has become a way of life for the narrator, too, but its meaning remains ambiguous. Because he has neither a "smooth tongue" nor a "heartless heart," he is not at home in Rinehart's "hot world of fluidity," in the confidence game of life even though its potential seems limitless. . . . Knowing of Rinehart's existence, however, is a salutary experience, and the narrator even thinks for a time that he can put it to use. But the Rinehart mask he dons, fortuitously does not fit when he tries to act the role. Rinehartism, which he finally equates with cynicism and charlatanism, is not his way and eventually he rejects it. What he does learn is that "some-

where between Rinehart and invisibility there were great potentialities."

Rejecting Rinehartism as an identity does not mean that the protagonist embraces invisibility. That final role is forced upon him by the blindness of others: Bledsoe, Norton, Emerson, Kimbro, Brockway, Jack, Hambro, even Mary. It was his role in the beginning ("the end was in the beginning"), only he did not recognize it. He *was* and yet *was not,* and somehow his recognition of nonbeing moves him toward a state of definition:

> I was my experiences and my experiences were me, and no blind men, no matter how powerful they became, even if they conquered the world, could take that, or change one single itch, taunt, laugh, cry, scar, ache, rage or pain of it."
>
> (pp. 79-80)

Ellison's protagonist has no martyr complex. He is not a godlike, heroic figure ready to sacrifice himself for the sins of humanity, black or white; he is unheroic modern man, fleeing from chaos toward a rational sense of order, which if it does not exist in the world, can exist at least in his own mind. When he returns to his underground womb (a circular journey if we include the **"Out of the Hospital"** sequence), it is to escape irrational forces in the shape of two white men armed with a baseball bat who want to wrest from him all that he has gained in experience—his briefcase. He alone can divest himself of those past identities, and he does, one by one, lighting his way to his underground future. But the underground life is not permanent: "Thus, having tried to give pattern to the chaos which lives within the pattern of your certainties, I must come out, I must emerge." His hibernation is over, the narrator tells us, the immobility that can be like death—total inaction, final invisibility. He does not know whether he will find death or life aboveground, and he is braced only by the certainty of his invisibility and the possibility of ours.

That possibility, and the narrator's sense of social responsibility, makes Ellison one of the few black writers whose Running Man most clearly reflects both positive *and* negative aspects of running, and whose protagonist epitomizes the experiences of both the black and white Running Man of the twentieth century. For Running Man *is* twentieth-century man, fleeing from invisibility (nonidentity) toward a visibility (identity) which he has at least some role in shaping. Invisibility in Ellison's novel is due not only to color, or its absence, but to the fact that such is the human condition, the fate of man impotent in the face of the powerful dehumanizing forces of contemporary society. (pp. 81-2)

If Ellison's Running Man is modern man, speaking in a generalized way for all of us, how can he also speak in a particularized way for the Afro-American, whose experiences we know are unique? For one thing, his flight is a creative recapitulation of black history in this country. His roots are in the plantation South; his aspirations move him toward the black southern college for "good niggers"; his move North parallels the Great Migration of the twenties and is fraught with disillusionment. Second, the reality of his life in America, especially his heritage of slavery, has made the experience of running not merely a gesture toward freedom but a flight for his life. This is literally true for Ellison's protagonist during the riot scene—a contemporary development—where he is hounded not only by whites but also by bellicose blacks.

Third, his area of choice is severely limited. Unlike the runners in Fitzgerald, Salinger, Kerouac, and Updike, who, no matter how limited they are psychologically or monetarily, freely make the decision to run, the Invisible Man is usually precipitated into running by some "sin" he commits against the system. It is a satiric comment on the black man's experience in America, on the negative alternatives rather than clear choices with which he is usually confronted. (p. 83)

Is the ending of *Invisible Man* completely negative, as many critics have suggested? Only if we consider all flight negative. The protagonist's last venture into himself, like Thoreau's, is a successful leap into perception, a perception of his own identity and his own reality. What he has begun to learn above ground—that he could not return to Mary's, to the campus, to the Brotherhood, or home—he has assimilated emotionally during the hiatus underground. The knowledge needed to resume action has finally been exhumed to the level of consciousness, and he is ready to leave his hibernation—to return, as Ishmael does, to the shore—with his conflicts but also with his sense of humanity restored. (p. 84)

> *Phyllis Rauch Klotman, in an introduction and "Ellison: 'Keep That Nigger-Boy Running'," in her* Another Man Gone: The Black Runner in Contemporary Afro-American Literature, *Kennikat Press, 1977, pp. 3-9, 71-84.*

LAURENCE B. HOLLAND

It is possible that the vogue of 'the Black Aesthetic' in the United States which arose in the sixties could have pushed Ralph Ellison's *Invisible Man* deep into a limbo of inattention which it did not deserve, while throwing a lurid light on the announcement of Ellison's appointment to an Albert Schweitzer Professorship, which carried with it hugely visible amounts of prestige and of money for projects under his direction. Such academic prominence scarcely seemed healthy to Imamu Amiri Baraka (LeRoi Jones), at least, who already in "Philistinism and the Negro Writer" complained that Ellison was 'fidgeting away in some college'. And Jones's concession then that *Invisible Man* was a 'most finely constructed archetypal, mythological novel' . . . has not often been repeated by those black writers who claim, with Ishmael Reed, a 'marked independence from Western form'.

To invoke archetypes and myths in Ellison's defence, however, may be no more to the point than to demonstrate their appearance in the writings of the same black writers who disown the traditions of English and Western literature that Ellison has been happy to acknowledge. What should engross our attention still is the way Ellison treats at once the matter of 'invisibility' and the form of his 'finely constructed novel'. Ellison's own criticism remains the most probing exploration of the fact that 'invisibility' is a complex and at least partly metaphorical reality, and that his novel is presented as what we may call a 'confessional form'.

'Confession, not concealment' is the tactic of his Protagonist, Ellison has written, but in declaring this and referring to *Invisible Man* as the Protagonist's 'memoir' Ellison is far from suggesting that the book is, on his or his protagonist's part, autobiographical in any literal sense. (Though of course Ellison has drawn upon his own experience, he has denied that the book is literally autobiographical in a well-known interview). Neither is the mode of 'confession' to be defined simply as the explicit 'long, loud rant, howl and laugh' that Ellison

declares the 'memoir' to be in the same breath, for the usual formalization and reluctance or hesitation associated with confession consort oddly with naked ranting. Nevertheless, Ellison's term 'confession' is illuminating when considered in connection with his comments on the novel form and when we recognize that the Protagonist's account—his 'memoir', his novel—is intimately related to his concern about irresponsibility, his search for an identity, and to his 'invisibility'. The issues are puzzling but inescapably important for understanding Ellison's formal strategies, and they are brought into focus in the Prologue when the Protagonist speaks of his 'urge to make music of invisibility' while both comparing and contrasting the aim for music to the novelistic 'compulsion to put invisibility down in black and white'. The 'music' of invisibility and the 'black and white' of its imprint are in problematic relation, and in Ellison's phrasing the 'black and white' of American racial identities are linked inseparably to the conventional black print on the conventionally white pages in our novels. Some attention to Ellison's critical comments on the novel form and on the problem of identities should clarify the Protagonist's position at the opening of the book.

Ellison's critical writings have made clear that the novel is 'a literary form which has time and social change as its special province' and that it takes precedence over archetypal and folklore traditions by absorbing or encompassing them, and moreover he associates the adoption of the form closely with crises of personal transcendence. The 'restlessness' of his Protagonist, he has declared, is a function not of his particular social predicament as a Black nor of any despondency. Nor is it a function only of the fact that he is an American. It is a function more particularly of the fact that he 'appears' *in a novel.* . . . As a Black whom Ellison has called a 'displaced person' of American Democracy, without such 'institutions to give him direction', finding that 'his world and his personality are out of key', the Protagonist is committing himself to the novel as a form of *activity* that is more 'intimate' than the techniques, important though they are, that he acquires to implement it. It is an activity through which 'he comes to possess and express the meaning of his life' but which more importantly entails the creation of the self: a writer did 'not so much create the novel', Ellison has written, 'as he was created *by* the novel'. Accordingly the novel is a defensive protection, but it is also an activity that has a shaping impact on the self of the writer, and the form brings an increment of freedom, indeed it becomes the writer's 'greatest freedom'.

The novel form makes possible the achievement for the self of something like the performance of jazz, as Ellison understands jazz, enforcing the recognition of one's limitations and his membership in the group, while nonetheless liberating the soloist's ingenuity and defining his 'identity', producing 'an art of individual assertion within and against the group'. The problem for Ellison's protagonist, however, which complicates the confessional impulse behind his prose, is that the voice which seeks an outlet in music, and the 'compulsion' to get 'invisibility down' in the novel-memoir, are somewhat at odds—the novel seeks to encompass the tactics of music through emulation and rivalry—and that the identities of the Protagonist are not in complete harmony with the self that eludes, while seeking expression, recognition, and self-definition through those identities. (pp. 54-6)

Ellison's 'confessional form' has . . . [much in common] with pleas of guilty before a priest or bar of justice, because his aim is as much a declaration of faith (in brotherhood, in communion, in the novel) as it is a revelation of complicity. And 'to confess' is to occasion and to hear a declaration by someone else (as in the case of a priest or 'Father Confessor'), as well as to disclose information and feelings to a licensed listener (as in the case of a penitent sinner): the summons and listening, and the revealing response, are combined in an act of confession. Reluctance (whether to hear or to speak) and willingness (to listen or to utter) are conjoined in the confessional exchange, which can be as dependent in its formalization on tacit and implicit communication as on explicit statement. The very process rests, as the Latin roots of the term suggest, on mutual acknowledgement or shared recognitions. It is such a mutual engagement with his readers that Ellison's Protagonist initiates in the Prologue, where the 'ritual understructure' and the 'action' that Ellison has stressed in his commentary on his novel are launched. The ritual action is the confessional enactment that transforms the Protagonist 'from ranter to writer'.

The brash and candid assurance of the Protagonist in the Prologue simply throws into relief the ambivalence of feeling to which he lays claim and the anxious concerns that agitate him when he boasts of the basement refuge he has improvised after escaping from the black nationalist orator, Ras the Exhorter, during the Harlem riot. He tells with undisguised relish of his brutal assault on a white man who is lost in the 'dream world' of the white power structure that excludes Blacks, who had called him an outrageously 'insulting name'. But he discloses also that he was 'disgusted and ashamed', then 'amused' after realising that his verbal assailant, blinded by stereotypes, had not even seen him, and after holding back from murdering him with the knife the Protagonist had drawn for that purpose. But if he is ashamed for the brutality of his assault, he later confesses his cowardly 'irresponsibility' in not committing the murder that the white man's outrages called for. And he associates the irresponsibility with the 'invisibility' that he alternately acquiesces in, welcomes as a refuge, and boasts of. The temptation to murder and to self-definition through violent assault remain, even after his failure to carry through with them, and moreover the question of whether to act at all and whether to act in other ways is one he is reluctant to resolve. 'I believe in nothing if not in action', he declares, but he fears the call to action that he hears in Louis Armstrong's blues, much though he envies that artist's power to make 'poetry out of invisibility' and enviously wants himself to 'play the invisible music of my isolation'. Particularly he fears the experience he knew once of hearing the blues when under the influence of a reefer: he descended to depths of 'unheard sounds', an 'under-world of sound' where he 'discovered unrecognised compulsions of my being' and could not only '*see* around corners' of his mind but 'hear around them', and the shattering experience appears dangerous because it both demands action and 'inhibits action'. He fears both the drug-induced trance that frustrates action and the blues whose deeper rhythms embarrassingly demand it.

Nevertheless the Protagonist's account discloses a commitment to a pattern of action that remains implicit in his definition of his retreat as an hibernation, a 'covert preparation for a more overt action'. The pattern is adumbrated in the hallucination he has experienced under the influence of the reefer, when he heard in the 'underworld of sound' a voice like his mother's and saw the woman's 'ivory' body on the auction block; he learned that she both loved her white master, who had fathered her sons, and had poisoned him, substituting the chemistry of poison for the lacerating knives her sons had prepared for his murder. In the hallucination one of the sons attacks the Protagonist but finally releases his hold on his throat. Likewise the trumpet of Louis Armstrong that the Protagonist emulates translates violence into sound, 'bends that military instrument into a beam of lyrical sound'. The pattern is that of the Protagonist's own assault on the white man. . . . (pp. 59-61)

The effect of the Prologue—with its problematic connections among seeing, hearing, and writing, the racial identities of black and white, and the release and the moderation of violence—is to enforce the excitingly experimental but tentative, insubstantial basis of the main incidents of the memoir proper, including some of the most powerful and convincing as well as some of the less successful which deal with the Protagonist's career as orator in the Marxist Brotherhood. The reader is induced to respond to the succeeding incidents in their immediacy but also in the light of the fact often confessed only tangentially at the time, that they have only problematic validity. All the sections have indeed the 'expressionistic' and 'surrealistic' dimensions that Ellison claims only for later parts, for, while the dreams and hallucinations invoked in the Prologue and later chapters deepen the significance of the novel their authority is not differentiated from that of the objective narration; they are parts of the same fictive context. The racist 'dream' of the Protagonist's white assailant in the Prologue, which stereotypes and excludes Blacks and provokes disclaimers of responsibility and mutual violence, has the same compelling but dubious force as the black farmer Trueblood's later dream, which he makes the basis for his disclaimer of responsibility for incest and which provokes the violence of his wife that he narrowly escapes. The drug-induced hallucination that probes beneath Louis Armstrong's blues to reveal mixtures of black and white, love and hate, erotic love and violence, leads into the Protagonist's accounts later of relations with white women and his eventual encounter with the black separatist, Ras the Exhorter. All of the dreams give point to the Veteran's declaration that Harlem, the Protagonist's destination, is 'not a place, it's a dream'. The self's struggles with its identities are conducted in arenas that are both social and psychic, and his dilemma is nowhere more dramatically rendered than in the episode following the explosion in the paint factory when he is subjected to electric shock therapy in the factory hospital. There is forged for him a fusion of identities that is the culmination of his career up to that point and that continues to agitate him for the rest of the novel.

In the nightmare of his treatment the patient is held not in the glare of electric lights but in the pulsating grip of an electric machine. . . . (pp. 62-3)

[Following his emergence from the machine, the Protagonist's self is] re-born in the process of discovering that its identity has been defined and imposed by black folklore and by the dominant white culture that provoked and still manipulates that folklore, and that the resulting fusion of black and white racial identities is both inescapable and perplexing.

He feels that he had 'been talking beyond myself, had used words and expressed attitudes not my own, that I was in the grip of some alien personality lodged deep within me', but he feels also that 'perhaps I was catching up with myself and had put into words feelings which I had hitherto suppressed'. The precise relation between the self and its identity, the 'alien personality', remains unresolved and subject to change. But the self is strengthened in its invisibility and the new fusion of its identities is subject to manipulation through language as the Protagonist demonstrates when leaving the hospital. He speaks with a new irony and forced sophistication, defining both his blackness and his whiteness in his negotiations with the white world, saying 'It's been quite pleasant, our little palaver, sir'. His use of language soon proves to be the basis of his career as orator, but his exhilaration as he enters that career is countered by the recognition which his novel-memoir has already confessed: that his exercise of power is dependent in part on an 'alien personality' implanted in him, and that in the catharsis of living out his career as orator he will deliberately abandon that role.

His new career is launched when he encounters an ageing couple being evicted from their tenement, with their belongings piled on the sidewalk, and the buried memories and resentments that rise up as he explores 'around a corner into the dark' are of 'remembered words, of linked verbal echoes, images, heard even when not listening at home', including the image of his mother hanging out laundry with her hands whitened by the raw cold. The speech he improvises on that occasion—he later says he was seized by the words, 'I had uttered words that had possessed me'—is the first of his own that is given in detail in his account. (pp. 63-4)

[The Protagonist's] speeches at the eviction and later for the Brotherhood are at once effective and controlled. Yet even the eviction speech, which protests the common 'dispossession' of all Blacks, does not escape from the rhetorical strategies that were displayed in Dr. Barbee's chapel speech and that have been shaped by decades of racial suppression and exploitation. The images of parents and grandparents that the orator evokes from the plight of the elderly couple are authentic but sentimental. Moreover the refrain he improvises by appealing to long-suffering black Americans as a 'law-abiding, slow-to-anger bunch of folks' is one of the 'shock-absorbing phrases' which he musters to moderate and channel the mounting violence which he fears from himself and from his listeners. He does channel their protest into the gesture of returning the belongings to the flat, but the demonstration is ineffectual before the police who fire over the heads of the crowd and force the Protagonist to flee. His escape is supervised by white members of the Marxist Brotherhood who have been observing his performance, and soon the voices and designs of their white world have overcome his reluctance, enrolled him as a salaried member, and issued his 'new identity' in a 'white envelope'.

From then on the burden of the narrative is to acknowledge tacitly the tentative, preparatory, uncertain status of the Protagonist's career in the Brotherhood without utterly discrediting the career and the Protagonist's feats of oratory, over which the novel lingers. At his initiation into the organisation, the remoteness of his invisible selfhood from the role defined for him to play is underscored. . . . [His] first appearance on the speaking platform is presented as an agony like that of the shock therapy, producing at once a transformation of the self and a new identity that threatens his very being and frustrates his efforts to join in a community with his audience.

The naked light bulbs in the dressing room where the Brotherhood spokesmen wait their turn recall the glare of the lighted basement, the hibernation, in the Prologue, and the sheer experience of being 'the focal point of so many concentrating eyes' yields glimpses of his transformation into a new person,

but the process demands that he suppress the 'dissenting' and 'observing' self watching from 'a point deep within me' and keep it at the remote distance in memory to which he relegates the crucial incidents of his earlier life—'the campus, the hospital machine, the battle royal', which were so conspicuously subject to pressures from the white world. But the novel confesses that the significance of those early episodes cannot be obscured. . . . When finally he must deliver his speech he resorts to tried-and-true Southern political routines and under the careful surveillance of the Brotherhood he rises to the pitch of confessing his personal transformation and declaring that he and each of the others has been made 'new' in the community of the Brotherhood. But while he makes this peroration with the glare of their 'black and white eyes upon me', and feels the pressures of the hospital machine, he has been virtually blinded, like the Establishment's Dr. Barbee who was literally blind, by the glare of the spotlight; he stumbles afterward as if 'in a game of blindman's bluff'.

The flow of words has compelled him to confess things the Brotherhood's handbooks had not prescribed, that he had not intended to speak and knows he 'shouldn't reveal', but beneath his plea that his inter-racial audience 'reclaim our sight . . . and spread our vision', and beneath the applause that greets his triumph, is the fact that the experience renders his audience invisible to *him*. Before he takes the microphone he reports that the 'light was so strong that I could no longer see the audience, the howl of human faces' whose applause suggests that they respond 'without themselves being seen'. When he reflects on the experience afterward, exploring the meaning of his own words, lured by the prospect of sharing in the exercise of power and the 'possibility of being more than the member of a race', he acknowledges that the people he is growing fond of comprise a 'blurred audience whose faces I had never clearly seen'. Moreover, phrases that the novel hurries over but presents none the less carefully confess the telling facts that he was not so much a member as an acquisition of the Brotherhood—'I belonged to them'—and that his audience recognised not himself but his language—'they had recognised my words'.

Accordingly, the novel reveals the occasion to have been a compound of rhetorical achievement, authentic commitment, and delusion that marks a crucial development in the Protagonist's career by defining more sharply, rather than resolving, his position in society and his facility with language. The experience prepares him to recognise the invisibility of others and to communicate with an audience that cannot be directly seen—the very condition he will face literally as a novelist—while suggesting that his new role in the inter-racial movement, and his oratory, are not as completely severed from the traditional patterns and exploitive manipulations of his society as he thinks at the time. The ground is prepared for his break with oratory when he discovers that the Blacks' predicament is callously exploited by the white leaders of the Brotherhood and that the explosive oratory in the speech of a black nationalist threatens the black community and the Protagonist himself with destruction.

The power of eloquence is polarised in the later part of the novel, divided between the Protagonist and the black nationalist, Ras the Exhorter. For all the Protagonist's commitment to 'climbing a mountain of words' and his faith in the 'magic in spoken words', he records next to nothing in his novel of his own later speeches in the cause of black rights (or women's rights after his Brotherhood assignment is changed). He chronicles instead the tactical struggles within the Brotherhood bureaucracy and his relations with white women in the movement. (pp. 65-7)

[The example of Ras is] a tempting challenge to the Protagonist after his discovery that the white leadership of the Brotherhood, as Ras had warned, had no genuine interest in black people and intends to sacrifice them to the ideology and historical mission of the revolutionary movement. And this challenge does not inhere simply in the fact that Ras himself instigates the self-consuming violence that the white world will exploit and that threatens the Protagonist with lynching, nor simply in the fact that the Protagonist discovers in the final crisis that he prefers 'the beautiful absurdity' of his 'American identity', which he shares even with the Whites who ignore and repress him, to the racial identity proclaimed by Ras. The ritual action that emerges in Ras's attack on the Protagonist during the Harlem riot, and culminates when the Protagonist strikes Ras in retaliation with Ras's own spear, reveals that there are bonds between the two as well as antagonism. Though their attitudes toward Whites and violence are different, both are genuinely interested in advancing the cause of black people, both are themselves black, and both are orators or spokesmen: as the Protagonist recognises, Ras's destructive fanaticism is but one step behind the insight he himself has gained since the 'stripping away of my illusionment'. The bizarre violence of the Protagonist's attack with the spear is intimately connected with his oratorical prowess and constitutes a ritual transformation, an act that appropriates and aims for a transformation of that power.

Just before ordering his supporters to seize and 'hang' the Protagonist, Ras hurled his spear into one of the white, 'Hairless, bald and sterilely feminine' department store mannequins hanging from a lamp-post. The spearing of the white female dummy is a nightmarish image both of Ras's intentions against the white world and of their futility, for he strikes not at Whites but at their possessions and at the mere simulacra or substitutes, the dummies or racist stereotypes, generated by his society. But the Protagonist's appropriation of Ras's weapon is even more significant. He reaches up in an 'oratorical gesture of disagreement and defiance' and it is thanks to this oratorical gesture that he accidentally seizes the spear. Then in the face of Ras's resistance to his argument he finds that he has 'no words and no eloquence' and he hurls the spear instead. His eloquence thus translated into action, he feels as if he has 'surrendered my life and begun to live again' while the spear cuts off Ras in the middle of a shout, 'ripping through both cheeks' to lock the orator's jaws. The Protagonist's act of violence—seizing the spear and hurling it—aims to extinguish the rhetoric of violence while appropriating its force, and to prepare for its transformation, its conversion into the rhetoric of fiction. Ras the Exhorter, in what is left of his Abyssinian regalia, disappears into the riot, and the Protagonist soon falls into the coal pit that becomes his temporary refuge. (pp. 69-71)

The Epilogue simply confirms the significant features of the Prologue, and the main orientation of the fiction's movement that culminated in the attack on Ras the Destroyer, while bringing it to no completion other than that of an anticipatory and novelistic form. The effect of the form is to suggest that the action even at the end is mediatory and preparatory, not the consummation or fulfilment of the plot, and to define the ambiguities of the Protagonist's situation as well as his commitments.

He has rejected the tempting refuge of mere masking identities (the facades of a Rinehart behind a white hat and dark glasses), and he affirms, instead of that 'chaos', the 'infinite possibilities' of 'imagination'. Along with this commitment to the imagination he affirms the principles of American democracy. But the very movement of his progress toward creation of the self is compounded of incompletion and unresolved ambivalence. (p. 71)

Where earlier he associated 'invisibility' with 'irresponsibility', he now insists that he will be 'no less invisible' even while assuming the burden of responsibility for his fate, and his new birth leaves the self vulnerable as well as renewed. As he gratuitously assumes partial blame for his invisibility, standing 'naked and shivering before the millions of eyes that look through you unseeingly', he acknowledges feeling like those black men who suffer 'that strange disease' which turns them from 'black to albino, their pigment disappearing as under the radiation of some cruel, invisible ray'. In these phrases he confesses at once his willingness to accept the responsibility and his shame in conceding the scarcely natural whiteness for which recent black critics have scorned Ellison. The Protagonist is ready as before to attack and 'denounce', but he confesses being also 'prepared to defend' because the very effort 'to get some of it down' in writing has brought the discovery that 'I have to love', revealing that the cost of 'infinite possibilities' is both involvement and unpredictability. The writing of the novel entails those victories that the Protagonist claims at the end, which are his triumphs *qua* writer. Encountering white Mr. Norton in New York, long after the incidents at the Trueblood farm and the Golden Day, he can boast that he knows that white man because as novelist 'I made you'. As novelist he can echo Whitman's longing, at the end of "Song of Myself", for communion as a 'disembodied voice' with his readers, voicing the closing sentence that asks: 'Who knows but that, in the lower frequencies, I speak for you?' But the fiction that enables the Protagonist to create himself, prepare for an active role, and forge the bond of communion with his reader, provides no clear blueprints for his later conduct, and this discovery about the resources of his fiction—its mediating power and its disarming limitations—is confessed in black and white by Ellison in *Invisible Man*. (pp. 71-2)

Laurence B. Holland, "Ellison in Black and White: Confession, Violence and Rhetoric in 'Invisible Man'," in Black Fiction: New Studies in the Afro-American Novel since 1945, edited by A. Robert Lee, London: Vision Press, 1980, pp. 54-73.

ROBERT G. O'MEALLY

Published in 1952, Ralph Ellison's *Invisible Man* has been acclaimed by a growing line of commentators writing in diverse critical tongues: formalists, structuralists, psychological critics, folklore and myth critics. Despite the high-beamed scrutinies, however, *Invisible Man* retains its mysterious power to rock us with laughter and terror. As if in defiance of the single-minded critic, Ellison drew symbols and rhetorical schemes from any and every source he felt would enrich the texture and meaning of his first novel's prose. Sophocles, Homer, Dostoevsky, Bergson, Freud, Jung, Raglan, Burke, Eliot, Joyce, Wright, and Malraux; spirituals, blues, and minstrels' jokes; personal experiences rendered symbolically—all figure in *Invisible Man.* Some allusions and symbol clusters trail off like wistful jazz riffs; some recur and provide the novel with structure. No one formula, though, can explain this capacious novel, which owes as much to the symbolist tradition of Melville and Hawthorne as it does to the vernacular tradition of Mark Twain and Hemingway. Without seeking, then, to unfasten every trapdoor of *Invisible Man,* I would like to examine an important aspect of the book, an aspect treated fleetingly by even Ellison's most apt critics: its uses of black American folk art.

An intricate pattern of folk forms is woven through the fabric of *Invisible Man.* Ellison makes use of a Mother Goose rhyme, "Who Killed Cock Robin," transforming it into a mock dirge, "They Picked Poor Robin Clean." "Three Blind Mice" appears in a Brotherhood political speech, and "London Bridge Is Falling Down" and "Hickery Dickery Dock" also turn up. Archetypal tricksters and heroes are stretched and mocked. By using these varied sources, Ellison makes the point that black Americans have an extraordinarily broad cultural heritage that expands beyond political and social boundaries in sometimes surprising ways. (pp. 78-9)

Verbal games abound in the novel. Critics have noted that the snappy patter of the blueprint carrier who claims to be "Peter Wheatstraw the Devil's Son-In-Law" is framed in the form of an American boast, a folk form as old as the roaring of such ring-tailed folk heroes as Boone, Crockett, and Mike Fink: half-alligator, half-bulldog, half-rattlesnake. It should be noted too that Peter Wheatstraw, whose name, like that of Stakolee and High John, associates him with black folk heroism, appears in *Invisible Man* as a uniquely black badman whose language and style of performance transmute his American boast into an Afro-American one. Some attention has been given to Ellison's uses of the "dozens" and "signifying," those games of verbal competition in which one's opponent and, in the case of the dozens, one's family (especially one's mother) are assaulted with polished insults. (p. 79)

Invisible Man is built on folk foundations. Furthermore, the Invisible Man's gradual move from innocence to experience and from repression to expression is spurred by folk forms. His acceptance of black folklore keeps him from losing touch with his identity in the fast and maddening world of the North. In time he sees that without his folk tradition, without the "mother wit" inherited from the past struggles of black Americans, he truly is an Invisible Man, a calculation rolling helter-skelter in social space.

The use of black folklore enabled Ellison to achieve the "magical" stylistic effects he had been seeking in his fiction for ten years. Not only did the folkloric allusions provide the work with a richness of texture and a solid structure; they also propelled its themes and images into a swirling dream world beyond that of social realism. (pp. 79-80)

Ellison employs several folk motifs to give structure to *Invisible Man.* The Invisible Man's archetypal movement from darkness to light is treated ironically by the author who, in an interview, says:

> In my novel, the narrator's development is one through blackness to light; that is, from ignorance to enlightenment: invisibility to visibility. He leaves the South and goes North; this, as you will notice in reading Negro folktales, is always the road to freedom—the movement upward. You have the

same thing again when he leaves his underground cave for the open.

Underlying the black-white motif is a play on the notion of blackness as evil, whiteness as good. The twist here is that the Invisible Man finds his enlightenment as he finds his blackness; his "movement upward" is also a plunge into a dark manhole. According to black folklore and history, though, this underground trail does lead to freedomland.

The rhyme from black Americana and from vaudeville recurs in the novel: "If you're white, you're right; if you're brown, stick around; if you're black, get back." The veteran from the Golden Day warns the Invisible Man against believing in this terse refrain, but Bledsoe tells him that white *is* right and he had better not forget it. [Lucius] Brockway, the old badger-faced black man, wins a special bonus for thinking up the motto for the Optic White Paint Factory, "If it's Optic White, it's the right white." Ellison also plays with the idea, based on a standard joke, that one reason people keep bumping into the Invisible Man is that in the dark the black boy is just too black to see. And this despite the notion that blacks were "perfect slaves" because their skin color made for "high visibility."

Symbolically, the novel involves a series of elaborate green-horn's initiations that test and temper the Invisible Man for black life in America. Thus he suffers the battle royal where, as in many folktales (as well as in black fiction, autobiography, and biography), black boys are pressed into fighting one another for the amusement of white men. This nightmarish game not only highlights the caste lines in the segregated South, but prepares the greenhorn Invisible Man for the unpredictability and viciousness of American life. Thus, too, he is victimized by the cynical college president [A. Herbert] Bledsoe who, after requiring the Invisible Man to leave school, gives him sealed letters of recommendation secretly asking potential white employers to "help him continue in the direction of that promise which, like the horizon, recedes ever brightly and distantly beyond the hopeful traveler." This classic "fool's errand" is foreshadowed in the young man's earlier dream about his grandfather, who tells him to read aloud the gold engraved words in a letter he has been carrying: "To Whom It May Concern: Keep This Nigger Boy Running." The greenhorn's initiation is universal; it was part of the stock in trade for the Yankee humorists of the eighteenth and nineteenth centuries. In an Afro-American context, however, the razzings of the black yokel assume special meanings: they teach him to brace himself for the foibles and caprices of humankind—and especially for those city slickers or country sharpies who hate his race. Enfolded here too . . . is a crucial survival lesson: learn to read! (pp. 80-1)

During his reefer-inspired dream in the prologue, the Invisible Man encounters a woman moaning and singing. She stops her song to tell the young man her story. She was a slave who bore her master several sons. Loving her children, she came to love their father, even though he never made good his promise to set them free. One day, when she realized her sons were angry and old enough to kill their father, she poisoned him and he withered away "like a frost-bit apple." This story is based on the "folk secular" sometimes called "Promises of Freedom." . . .

Another folk character dating from slavery days, Brer Dog, also shows up in the novel. In Afro-American lore the dog is an enigmatic and deceptive fellow who is usually outdone by the rabbit, his natural enemy. In the novel as in the folk-lore, the dog may earnestly pledge to be the rabbit's friend, but the careful rabbit is never convinced. (p. 82)

[Throughout] the novel the dog is a threatening figure who nonetheless can be overcome. Brother Tarp, we are told, is guarded on the chain gang by a team of dogs, but gradually he befriends them and is able to escape.

The dog has made his way north too, it appears. Peter Wheatstraw, singing "Feet Like a Monkey Blues" on the street in Harlem, hollers about his woman with legs "like a mad bulldog." Furthermore, the Harlem dog is on the prowl and dangerous. In part of a ritual of recognition, Wheatstraw, sensing the Invisible Man is from the South, says, "What I want to know is, is you got the *dog?*" . . . When finally the Invisible Man remembers his lines and says, "No, not this morning," a grin spreads over Wheatstraw's face. Then discoursing on Brer Dog and Brer Bear, Wheatstraw gives the Invisible Man his view of the way things are in Harlem:

> "Damn, man! I thought sure *you* had him," he said, pretending to disbelieve me . . . "Well maybe it's the other way round," he said. "Maybe he got holt to you."
>
> "Maybe," I said.
>
> "If he is, you lucky it's just a dog—'cause, man, I tell you I believe it's a bear that's got holt to me . . . Hell, yes! *The* bear. Caint you see these patches where he's been clawing at my behind? . . . Man, this Harlem ain't nothing but a bear's den. But I tell you one thing . . . it's the best place in the world for you and me, and if times don't get better soon I'm going to grab that bear and turn him every way but loose."

Harlem may be a bear's den or a mad dog's house but, naturally, "Peter Wheatstraw the Devil's Son-In-Law" knows that he will get by as long as he has "a little shit, grit and mother-wit." Having remained conscious of his southern folk roots, he is well prepared for Harlem's bears or "dog-days."

Waiting to give his first address as a Brotherhood spokesman, the Invisible Man recalls his own experience with Brer Dog. As a child he stood outside a chicken-wire fence watching Master, the bulldog, and was afraid to touch him even though, panting in the heat, the dog "seemed to grin back at me like a fat good-natured man, the saliva roping silvery from his jowls." Master was a likable but untrustworthy old fellow: he wore the same expression and growled the same low note whether calmly "snapping flies" or "tearing an intruder to shreds."

Brother Jack, who at the end of the novel our hero calls "Marse Jack," is as much the *dog* as he is the rabbit of Afro-American folklore. Accordingly, Jack the Dog seems to be peaceful and trustworthy, but is not. Early on, the Invisible Man senses that Brother Jack was "in some ways . . . like a toy bull terrier." Here is a warning, submerged in folklore, that our hero, who has repressed his "mother-wit," does not comprehend until very late in the game. (pp. 82-4)

In their discussions of ***Invisible Man***'s folk allusions, few critics have included spirituals and gospel music. Like the blues allusions, the many subtle references to sacred folk music serve to enrich the weave of the novel's prose. Church forms also dominate certain scenes. As with the blues, the hero starts out ashamed of the "primitive" sacred forms and is not

freed of his illusions until he recognizes their beauty and wisdom and their value as a bridge to the past.

The Invisible Man's dream-vision between the "Black and Blue" notes that sound through the prologue takes him to a place where a black woman sings a somber spiritual. Her song reflects the "hybrid" (though black American) nature of the singer's and culture of her style of singing; the spiritual is "as full of Weltschmerz as flamenco." Singing it grants a certain freedom, she explains to our hero. *"Old woman,"* he asks her, *"What is this freedom you love so well?"* It lies in loving, not hating, she says, and also in the power of self-expression: *"I guess now it ain't nothing but knowing how to say what I got up in my head."*

The young man is most ashamed and contemptuous of black church music while he is in the South. At school, during spring festival when the white millionaire trustees descend to be courted and ceremonialized, the sacred forms are exploited as entertainments. As the Invisible Man moves toward his chapel seat, he hears voices "mechanically raised" in song by students with faces "frozen in solemn masks." Purged of genuine emotion, the hard-faced singers answer the powerful whites' demand for a sign of black docility. Like the songs performed at minstrel shows, the spirituals seem to constitute "an ultimatum accepted and ritualized, an allegiance recited for the peace it imparted." To that extent, says the narrator, the songs were loved by the students, "loved as the defeated come to love the symbols of their conquerors. A gesture of acceptance, of terms laid down and reluctantly approved." Thus in tribute (or mock tribute) did Bledsoe strike up his favorite spiritual, "Live-a Humble." For the benefit of the rich white guests the students stiffly sing, "Lead Me To a Rock That Is Higher Than I," again seeming to conform to the minstrel-show idea that blacks are contented and self-effacingly humble.

Jim Trueblood and his country quartet of gospel songsters, brought forward to entertain white guests at the school, also cause the students to wilt with shame. The collegians hold Trueblood and all the local "black peasants" in strict contempt but tolerate their "primitivism" on occasion for the good of their school's coffers:

> We were embarrassed by the earthy harmonies they sang but since the visitors were awed we dared not laugh at the crude, high, plaintively animal sounds Jim Trueblood made as he led the quartet . . . How all of us at the college hated the black-belt people . . . during those days! We were trying to lift them up and they, like Trueblood, did everything it seemed to pull us down.

At times, even in the presence of the white financiers, the meaning of the sacred music penetrates the congregation. Though repressed by the upward-bound blacks, the folk music continues to have a grip on their imagination. Before Homer A. Barbee's chapel address to the students and millionaires, a thin brown girl serenades the gathering *a cappella*. Beginning softly, the girl appears possessed by her song, her voice "a disembodied force that sought to enter her, to violate her, shaking her, rocking her rhythmically, as though it had become the source of her being, rather than the fluid web of her own creation." Before the eyes of the congregation, she appears as a vessel of "contained, controlled and sublimated anguish," expressing the bottled-up feelings of her black classmates. While the words of the song reverberate indistinctly in the chapel air, the song's impact on the hero is definite; it expresses a mood that is "sorrowful, vague and ethereal." Like certain spirituals, her song "throbbed with nostalgia, regret and repentance." At its conclusion, the Invisible Man sits with a lump in his throat as even the white guests exchange smiles of appreciation. (pp. 92-4)

Overwhelmed with grief at his dismissal from the college, the Invisible Man rushes from the auditorium. Dvorak's New World Symphony is played by the school orchestra. And although he has been ashamed of the gospel music and spirituals performed there, he dimly senses that out of these folk forms come symphonies, novels, and dance suites. In New World Symphony, the hero "kept hearing 'Swing Low Sweet Chariot' resounding through its dominant theme—my mother's and my grandfather's favorite spiritual. It was more than I could stand." Hearing strains of the spiritual also makes him feel guilty since, by his blunders, he has smashed his family's hope that he would finish college. (pp. 94-5)

Not until Tod's funeral does the Invisible Man become fully conscious of the transcendent value of black sacred folk music. As he speculates whether or not the crowd gathered around Tod's casket is moved by love or hate or political militancy, he hears two men spontaneously lifting a spiritual, "Many Thousand Gone." The song's words contain a stern renunciation of slave life, described in the starkest of terms. . . . (p. 96)

For the first time, he is conscious of the wonder and depth of feeling conveyed by the spiritual. And although the song speaks of redemption from the evils of slavery, somehow it transcends the particular moment. He contemplates his own response and that of the crowd:

> I was listening to something within myself, and for a second I heard the shattering stroke of my heart. Something deep had shaken the crowd, and the old man and the man with the horn had done it. . . . It was not the words, for they were the same old slave-born words; it was as though he'd changed the emotion beneath the words while yet the old longing, resigned, transcendent emotion still sounded above, now deepened by that something for which the theory of the Brotherhood had given me no name.

He looks around: even the whites are singing.

The song's emotion frees the Invisible Man from his self-alienation and fortifies a sense of continuity within his tradition. Moreover, it aids him in realizing that within himself and within his tradition there are forms of expression to which all men may respond. Significantly, though the Brotherhood terms the funeral for Tod a "circus side show," the Invisible Man, for once, defends his true feelings about the event. He sees at last that in a guise of objectivity and political scientism, the leaders of the Brotherhood (like Bledsoe and the college trustees) despise the blacks whose interests they pretend to serve.

As in many major American novels, the sermon plays an important part in **Invisible Man.** In the prologue, the Invisible Man hears a black preacher sermonizing at high pitch. Choosing as his sermon topic "The Blackness of Blackness" (echoing the Bible), the preacher shouts, *"Now blackness is . . . an' blackness ain't . . ."* He continues, chanting, *"Black will git you . . . an' black won't . . . It do . . . an' it don't."* Conjuring and then undercutting the biblical story of Jonah (echoing the theme of several spirituals as well as

the sermon used by Melville in *Moby Dick*), the preacher says that black *"will get you, glory, glory, Oh my Lawd, in the WHALE'S BELLY."* *"Preach it, dear brother,"* the congregation answers. *"An' make you tempt . . . Old Aunt Nelly! . . . Black will make you . . . or black will unmake you."* Here, as in many fables and myths, magic words (like those of the narrator's grandfather) confound our hero. What, given all these contradictions and ironies, *does* blackness mean? For the Invisible Man part of the answer lies, as we have seen, in his acceptance of the black folk form in which the question is posed.

Though no other sermons per se exist in the novel, in several instances characters employ the styles of black preachers. Homer A. Barbee claps his hands and chants in sermonic style. And inevitably, when the Invisible Man begins making public addresses for the Brotherhood, he uses black church techniques. His improvised speech on the steps of the dispossessed old couple's apartment house rings with the spirited repetitions of the sermon. In his first speech as the Brotherhood's Harlem leader, he depends on shouted responses from the audience, as a black preacher does. Most tellingly, in this speech, again improvised, he gives an eloquent testimonial:

> "May I confess?" I shouted . . . "You are my friends. We share a common disinheritance, and it's said that confession is good for the soul . . . *Something strange and miraculous and transforming is taking place in me right now . . . as I stand here before you! . . .* Let me describe it. It is something odd. It's something that I'm sure I'd never experience anywhere else in the world . . . I feel . . . I feel . . . I feel, I feel suddenly that I have become *more human . . .* I feel that after a long and desperate and uncommonly blind journey, I have come home."

And although the home he speaks of is, on one level, the political one, the Brotherhood, his style of speech recalls the home of the spirituals: a heavenly home or a state of mind that brings peace. The hero's conversion to the Brotherhood is stated in terms often used to describe spiritual salvation.

Folk forms also permeate the scene in the factory hospital where the narrator's sudden remembrance of a spiritual shields him from the planned annihilation of his identity. As he strains to recall who he is, the words of his grandmother's mock spiritual also come back to him:

> Godamighty made a monkey
> Godamighty made a whale
> And Godamighty made a 'gator
> With hickeys all over his tail.

The doctors, after examining the young man, believe that their dehumanization process (which, like the program of the Brotherhood, is designed to nullify his past and individual will) is a huge success. Though he says nothing, the Invisible Man thwarts their plan as he remembers another childhood rhyme. . . . He also remembers Buckeye the Rabbit, a familiar figure in black folklore the doctors have only the vaguest knowledge of. Brer Rabbit, of course, could escape from the silly machine with no difficulty at all. . . . In a flash, the Invisible Man feels that somehow he is the folkloric rabbit, able to escape the modern-day briar patch of the hospital.

The dozens also save the Invisible Man from destruction in the factory hospital. At a time when he seems able to remember neither his own name nor his mother's, the game of the dozens places him on the correct track. "WHO WAS YOUR MOTHER?" the doctor inquires. "Feeling a quick dislike," the Invisible Man thinks, "half in amusement, I don't play the dozens. And how's your old lady today?" When the examiner asks, "BOY, WHO WAS BRER RABBIT?" the reply rushes to the hero's mind, "He was your mother's back door man." The doctors interpret the young man's silence as total success for the machine. In truth, however, the Invisible Man does not lose his identity; he falls back upon it in wonderment.

Throughout the novel, as the hero grows in self-awareness, his use of signifying and dozens multiplies. At first he hurls stylized insults (he signifies) at his foes only in his imagination. In his mind's eye, he sees himself watching President Bledsoe in New York, then advancing upon the pompous "educator" to accuse him of eating chitterlings in private. He would snatch out "a foot or two of chitterlings, raw, uncleaned and dripping sticky circles on the floor" and shake them in Bledsoe's face, shouting insults: "Bledsoe, you're a shameless chitterling eater! I accuse you of relishing hog bowels! Ha! And not only do you eat them, you sneak and eat them in private when you think you're unobserved! You're a sneaking chitterling lover! I accuse you of indulging in a filthy habit." (pp. 97-100)

As he walks the streets in Harlem, the Invisible Man's southern politeness and meekness gradually dissolve into the dozens and signifying. When he throws the Sambo bank-doll into a trash can, a light-skinned black woman, revealing extreme prejudice against her southern cousins, rudely tells the young man to fetch it and move on. "You field niggers from the South . . . are ruining things" for better colored people, she tells him. Steeped in good home training, the Invisible Man protests politely and then, with disgust, reaches through the garbage to retrieve the bank. "It serves you right," the woman says. This time, signifying words are on his lips. "That's enough out of you, you piece of yellow gone to waste . . . I've done what you wanted me to do; another word and I'll do what *I* want to do." (p. 100)

When [Lucius] Brockway, the paint factory Uncle Tom, insults the Invisible Man and even bites him on the shoulder, the younger man jumps on him with a few old, signifying insults he has heard his grandfather use: "Why, you old-fashioned, slavery-time, mammy-made, handkerchief-headed bastard . . . Does this paint go to your head? Are you drinking it?" In disgust, he looks at the greasy old man with his pockets slicked shut with black slime and thinks, Tar Baby!

The heated differences between the Invisible Man and the other members of the Brotherhood, particularly Brother Jack, break into swift dozens and signifying play. At the meeting where Brother Wrestrum . . . accuses him of treachery, the Invisible Man asks if the organization truly believes the absurd charges. "Is everyone reading Dick Tracy these days?" demands Jack. "Oh, yes," says the Invisible Man. "Yes, I am. I'm interested in all manner of odd behavior." In the climactic confrontation with Brother Jack, in which the Invisible Man perceives that the group's leader is coolly willing to sacrifice the black community in behalf of "larger interests," dozens crackle from the hero's end of the table. Paralleling the southern town leaders who at the battle royal challenge the Invisible Man for a slip of the tongue, "social equality," Jack questions the hero's assertion of "personal re-

sponsibility." Jack is answered—or nearly so—in the language of the dirty dozens:

> "We went ahead on my personal responsibility," I said. Brother Jack's eyes narrowed. "What was that?" he said. "Your what?"
>
> "My personal responsibility," I said.
>
> "His personal responsibility," Brother Jack said. "Did you hear that, Brothers? Did I hear him correctly. Where did you get it, Brother?" he said. "This is astounding, where did you get it?"
>
> "From your ma—"I started and caught myself in time. "From the committee," I said.

Realizing that talking about Jack's mama would be misunderstood and unappreciated, the Invisible Man holds off. "Wouldn't it be better if they called you Marse Jack?" he says.

As this brisk exchange proceeds, white Brother Tobitt gets into the act and is also confronted in dozens terms. Why, he asks, was Tod eulogized by the Invisible Man at "that side show of a funeral"? The hero forces a harsh smile and inquires, "How could there be a side show without you as the star attraction, who'd draw the two bits admission, Brother Twobitts?" Challenged further by Tobitt about the funeral, the Invisible Man asks: "And what is the source of your great contribution to the movement, Brother? A career in burlesque? And of your profound knowledge of Negroes? Are you from an old plantation family? Does your black mammy shuffle nightly through your dreams?" Learning that Tobitt has "a fine Negro" wife, the Invisible Man says his source is too narrow.

The hero goes on to tell Tobitt what he himself has learned at great pain—that for anyone to know what is happening in the black community, he must check with ordinary community people. He advises: "Ask your wife to take you around to the gin mills and the barber shops and the juke joints and the churches, Brother. Yes, and the beauty parlors on Saturdays when they're frying hair. A whole unrecorded history is spoken then." The Invisible Man speaks here from the experience gained after Tod's death. In one of the novel's most powerful scenes, he ponders the importance of black folk art and ordinary blacks he has forgotten and taken for granted. He sees some black boys in a subway station and considers their styles and habits.

> Yes, I thought, what about those of us who shoot up from the South into the busy city like wild jacks-in-the-box broken loose from our springs—so sudden that our gait becomes like that of deep-sea divers suffering from the bends? What about those fellows waiting still and silent there on the platform . . . standing noisy in their very silence; harsh as a cry of terror in their quietness? . . . Walking stiffly with swinging shoulders in their well-pressed, too-hot-for-summer suits, their collars high and tight about their necks, their identical hats of cheap black felt set upon the crowns of their heads with a severe formality above their hard conked hair? It was as though I'd never seen their like before.

The Brotherhood has taught him that such men are "out of time," unimportant. Suppose, though, that such men were of supreme value? (pp. 100-02)

The Invisible Man's realization of the value of the black masses is important in several ways. It is in line with the democratic ideal that people have fundamental rights, including that of participation in the political process. No downtown Brotherhood (however left-wing) has the right to make categorical decisions for the people uptown. The Invisible Man also sees that black people, though ignored and abused by the majority, have managed to maintain their own unique sense of life and integrity; he has no reason to be ashamed of his grandparents. Finally he understands that he is one of the "jacks-in-the-box": he is an individual but connected to a tradition. By the end of the novel he is moved by a spiritual ("Many Thousand Gone"), quotes a blues ("Buddy Bolden's Blues"), and talks in the language of the dirty dozens. He sees at last that he is one of "the bearers of something precious." He feels "as though I carried a heavy stone, the weight of a mountain on my shoulders." True to this image, the novel ends with the Invisible Man's conscious need to play a heroic role, to help blacks "move on up a little higher."

Invisible Man is not a historical novel, of course, but it deals with the past as a burden and as a stepping stone to the future. The hero discovers that history moves not like an arrow or an objective, scientific argument, but like a boomerang: swiftly, cyclically, and dangerously. He sees that when he is not conscious of the past, he is liable to be slammed in the head with it again when it circles back. As the novel unfolds, the Invisible Man learns that by accepting and evaluating all parts of his experience, smooth and ragged, loved and unloved, he is able to "look around corners" into the future. . . . (pp. 102-03)

At the beginning of the novel, the Invisible Man presents himself as a kind of Afro-American Jonathan, a "green" yokel pushed into the clownhouse of American society. He starts out ignorant of his society, his past, himself. By the end of the book he accepts his southern black folk past and sees that ordinary blacks like his grandfather, Trueblood, Mary, Tarp, Dupre, the unnamed boys in the subway, and himself are of ultimate value, no matter what the Bledsoes and Jacks say. Jarred to consciousness by folklore (among other things), the Invisible Man realizes that the tested wisdom expressed in spirituals, blues, dozens, and stories is a vital part of his experience. At last he comprehends that whatever he might do to be "so black and blue," he is, simply, who he is. (pp. 103-04)

> *Robert G. O'Meally, in his* The Craft of Ralph Ellison, *Cambridge, Mass.: Harvard University Press, 1980, 212 p.*

TIMOTHY BRENNAN

No black American author has been so showered in glory as Ralph Ellison. Awards, honorary degrees, and committee chairs followed the publication of *Invisible Man,* winner of the National Book Award in 1952. On the merits of this novel alone, a poll of the literary community in 1965 ranked Ellison the sixth greatest American author since the War. And yet the unprecedented acclaim has more or less based itself on the fiction of a continuous Ralph Ellison, obscuring the novel's tension between public and private, oration and dream. The clenched fist has been submerged beneath the bended knee of a spiritual suffering, distorting a perceptual ambivalence in Ellison on the nature of racism and culpability.

Only a small group of dissenting critics has hinted at the dichotomy in Ellison's career between a Wrightian protest apprenticeship and a later affinity to the ritualist and symbolic schools of Stanley Hyman and Kenneth Burke. The new emphases which surface in a comparison of a 1945 essay like **"Beating that Boy,"** and a typical post-*Invisible Man* essay like **"Hidden Name, Complex Fate,"** describe an evolution from the world of physical conflict to the world of unity in diversity. The former condemns the "ethical schizophrenia" of the white world in disregarding racism; the latter speaks of "the diversity, fluidity and magical freedom of American life." Composed between 1945 and 1952, roughly the period in which his essays show signs of the change, *Invisible Man* is in part a document of Ellison's pilgrimage from one view to the other.

The novel's stylistic virtuosity and its immense erudition have directed the attention of friends and foes alike to its unique "sophistication" among black novels, which had always more or less meant kinship with a white European literary tradition. Many enthusiastic admirers have therefore foolishly encouraged what they saw as Ellison's rejection of racial themes at the same time that they praised his high technique, seeing the one as part of the other. His detractors, on the other hand, have scoffed at Ellison's remarkable poetic finish in the apparent belief that a racial theme can be handled only with the grunts and blunts of "realistic" narrative. If one looks at American literature as a racially integrated totality (which is how Ellison saw it), neither of these views grasps the point.

On the one hand, the admirers refuse to consider Ellison's didacticism—his concern not only with portraying the black man in historical anguish and human triumph, but with a fullness demanding empathy from a white audience. For Ellison, black characterization simply had to transcend *both* the conditioned responses of the black protest school *and* the racist caricatures of its white forebears. . . . The enormous excitement of Ellison's admirers with his technical achievements, his employment of myth and ritual, and his incorporation of the blues is thoroughly apt, but unfortunately has been used as a shield of insulting disregard for his ambitious attempt to solve an old American literary problem: how to find a fictional form that might embody the immense diversity of American life. (pp. 162-64)

On the other hand, his detractors have been unable to move beyond the esthetic of the protest school. They have equated Ellison's "reactionary" conclusions with his sensational plot devices, his employment of various styles, and his literary allusions, all of which they have seen as commercially minded sensationalism or self-conscious snobbery. In fact, these elements are all corollaries of a symbolic elaboration of his early work which these critics, often without saying so, associate with Ellison's "cop-out."

Neither side is able to draw a connection between Ellison's eventual loyalty to a symbolic structure and his evolving views on the historical question of black liberty. They are too busy evading the half of Ellison they find offensive. So while *Invisible Man* has either been faulted on political grounds or praised on esthetic grounds, no one seems to have traced in the pages of the text a tangible flaw. This can only be done by investigating the novel's operative thematic threads. For when Ellison seeks to translate his evolving views into the form of his novel, the writing of his apprenticeship continues in a vestigial form and is forced to the surface by the nature of his material. It is this expression of the material forcing it-self to the surface which is the crucial point. Consequently, the novel is unable convincingly to develop its view of the primacy of self-awareness and "possibility" as unifying factors because of its inadvertent portrayal of a specific and mutable oppression. The problems of identity, the assimilation of tradition, and social involvement are so closely patterned after the specific historical experiences of the American Negro that their claims to universality are destroyed. The bridge from black to white experience collapses with them, ruining Ellison's chances to realize his maxim, "one, and yet many." In its place, and with soggy props, is placed a bridge of solipsism. (pp. 164-65)

Invisible Man can be seen as an attempt to synthesize two "realities": a white, which represses guilt by denying the existence of the black as human; the black, which, insisting upon its separateness, cultivates it, wallowing in a blind rage against an inequality which becomes alibi. In the sphere of culture, this divergence has taken the form of two recognizable traditions which are ostensibly pure but secretly miscegenational. For Ellison, the two "realities" are surmountable, just as their two cultural strains have long since grown together, although they are never expressed with equal force, and though the two deluded sides refuse to admit the other's influence.

Among so many other damaging effects, this division in American society has created a barrier to the writing of an inclusive American novel. Although the nineteenth-century American masters had progressed in this direction by using the Negro as the symbol of Man, they could not create characters with the sensitivity required for a believably human portraiture. Ellison's answer is to symbolize black experience itself, so that the travails of the American Negro reappear as a manifestation of a larger human condition, thus creating a common ground for white and black.

Between 1945 and 1952, however, his views on the culpability of racism (the major issue of his novel) significantly shift. In the pre-1946 Ellison, the problem is that writers have pushed the issue of racial conflict underground after the Emancipation, buried it in the depths of their consciences, and subsequently ignored it. The suppression of the issue has shrivelled the writer's creative energies because it has given him the habit of "living and thinking in a culture that is opposed to the deep thought and feeling necessary to profound art." The argument is that "there is . . . an inescapable connection between the writer and the beliefs and attitudes current in his culture." If one pretends that something vital in one's culture does not exist, one is doomed to produce 'literary offspring without hearts, without brains, viscera or vision." (pp. 167-68)

The early Ellison mercilessly condemns the same kind of fiction he later tries to create in *Invisible Man.* In 1945, the practical result of the white writer's willful blindness to racism was an inferior literature. The so-called "Negro Problem," he says, is a "guilt problem charged with pain. Just how painful might be judged from the ceaseless effort expended to dull its throbbings with the anesthesia of legend, myth, hypnotic ritual and narcotic modes of thinking." He goes on to complain of how "serious literature . . . [has] been conscripted . . . to drown out the persistent voice of outraged conscience." (pp. 168-69)

In the course of the evolution from protest to poetry, two

enormous efforts become congealed in a single project: to portray the black man in his human fullness and to find a common theme for white and black. On the one hand, Ellison investigates Negro history, psychology, and everyday life. In respect to the novel, this entails a treatment of the historical crises of the black past—the period of slavery, the Emancipation, the migration North after the First World War, the era of Garveyite nationalism, and the peak of Communist Party influence. In this mode, the language and methods of the protest tradition are wielded by Ellison with an ambiguous voice, never finally pronouncing or judging, but building to a culmination of alternating hope and bitterness, rebellion and despair.

On the other hand, Ellison undertakes the effort to abstract from the black experience a common ground. The black is not free, but no one is "free"; the black must hide his true emotions to advance in business, but the working world demands everyone's duplicity; the black is cut off from his African origins, but the white, too, is a loner in the New World. In this second mode, the problem becomes volitional. And the tension we referred to in the opening paragraphs arises here, pulling at either end of the major theme until the whole is placed into a box which is the human mind. (pp. 169-70)

"Invisibility," as it appears in the novel's Prologue, is an unwanted state imposed from without:

> I am invisible, understand, simply because people
> refuse to see me. . . . When they approach me they
> see only my surroundings, themselves, or figments
> of their imagination.

The avoidance of guilt for "the Negro Problem" which Ellison had described as a form of mental suppression is converted here into literature as visual metaphor—the black man, who is a "man of substance, of flesh and bone, fiber and liquids," is made invisible by a willful myopia. One sees a Negro; one feels then either irrational hatred ("blond man"), paternalism (Mr. Norton), myth-based and insulting admiration (Emerson), or the assumption of ingrained rebellion (Jack). But one does not see a person, as you or I are persons; one sees a member of a race. . . .

[The white] world is hostile to blacks; the protagonist, already in the hibernation with which the novel ends, appears ready to set about describing how, as a black man, he has learned to deal with this hostility. The response is sure to coincide with the prevalent feelings of indignation and resistance—of refusing to pay "outrageous rates" to a monopoly, of "striking out with your fists," of refusing to "ignore the violence of [our] days." (p. 170)

But the "invisibility" image undergoes a similar mutation. The Prologue has been speaking of the poor inner vision of others—"you often doubt if . . . you aren't simply a phantom in other people's minds." In the Epilogue, however, although in the same novel-time as the Prologue, this colloquial irony departs, and "invisibility" becomes something indeed of the mind—the evanescent "failure to assent to [one's] own humanity." The social shortsightedness of the beholders of the Negro has become the moral failing in the Negro himself, to the point where the protagonist can speak even of Mary Rambo, the shelterer and mother figure, as guilty of the blindness which has made him "invisible."

So, too, in the Golden Day episode a thematic confusion prevails. As the hero enters the bar with his white benefactor,

Mr. Norton, one of a group of black war veterans grips him by the arm and coldly prophesies:

> It will occur at 5:30 . . . the great all-embracing absolute Armistice, the end of the world.

Looking around at the drunk and lascivious black veterans—insane asylum patients on leave—the hero realizes that appearances lie. The vets, whom the hero first describes as a chain gang, are actually a broad cross section of the black community:

> Many of them had been doctors, lawyers, teachers, Civil Service workers; there were several cooks, a preacher, a politician and an artist. . . .

The Golden Day itself, a tavern and whorehouse, attains a historical-mythical stature. . . . [Its clientele] suggests a collectivity of black experience. The intermittent allusions to a selective American history reinforce this idea as they contribute to a broader picture of Ellison's insight into a trauma of the Negro past, namely the redefinition of racial identity which followed the Negro's participation in the First World War. The taste for freedom acquired overseas in a Europe without Jim Crow, and the victory of "democracy" implicit in the War itself, helped to motivate the migration Northward in the post-War years, along with the aspirations of social improvement which accompanied it. (pp. 170-72)

Seen in this light, the irony of the lives of the imprisoned black veterans begins to take shape. The nature of their "madness," their relationship with the white world, and their responses to a degrading incarceration begin to reveal themselves. Beneath the "insanity" lies a ubiquitous proof of accomplishment. (p. 172)

Finally, and predictably, the "madness" of the vets is associated with political rebellion of a primitive form, mirrored both in the chiliasm of the prophet of "absolute armistice" and in another vet, a "student of history," who proclaims:

> The world moves in a circle like a roulette wheel. In the beginning, black is on top, in the middle epochs, white holds the odds, but soon Ethiopia shall stretch forth her noble wings.

Ellison is here developing a coherent argument for his theme of racism, first introduced in the concept of "invisibility." Despite the acidity of his irony and what may appear in this explication as the transparency of its form, the passage retains an elaborate rhetorical depth. Ellison is not content to leave the story on this level alone. To express the actual containment and suppression of black rebellion, Ellison allows the Golden Day to assume still another symbolic identity—that of the Negro mind. Supercargo, the veterans' guard and overseer from the asylum, becomes the "superego" of Ellison's symbolic architecture. He is described as a "stool-pigeon" and a "kind of censor," bellowing "I WANT ORDER" from the top of the stairs and kicking the vets back as they rush up to the whores' rooms, mimicking the act of mental suppression.

If Supercargo is the symbol of psychic order, he is also the representative of the white's mental manipulation of black aspirations. For he wears a "white suit" and "white shorts" and, when white folks are in the house, "[he] wan's *double* order." Talking to Mr. Norton after Supercargo has been beaten into submission by the increasingly unruly crowd, one vet doctor explains:

> The forces of destruction are rampant down below. They might realize you are what you are, and then your life wouldn't be worth a piece of bankrupt stock.

Supercargo's role is to keep the blacks from rebelling.

In Ellison's allegory, images of psychological suppression mingle confusingly with references to physical oppression. Is the entire Golden Day episode simply an allegorical recreation of the white's suppression of "the Negro Problem" and their subsequent forcing of it into the unconscious? Or is it a parody of the blacks' damnable gullibility before the talismans of white domination? On the broadest level, Ellison portrays the vets as a fearful swarm of undifferentiated sparks to the black unconscious. In this scheme, patterned after the psychical symbolism of the early sequence, Mr. Norton is merely a "trustee of consciousness"—a figure whom blacks deceive themselves into finding a "great white father . . . [or] the lyncher of souls," the alternate poles of security and fear delimiting choice. For Mr. Norton and the hero, in an upstairs room above the commotion, learn from the doctor vet that the others "know nothing of value" without Supercargo. In accordance with Ellison's revised terms of "invisibility," the trauma of post-War black America is volitional. (pp. 172-74)

One is constantly given the sense of a rending quality to the torturous path that Invisible Man travels in the course of the novel. Given the abruptness of the novel's change in the Epilogue, one feels that Ellison has been driven into a solution that abolishes contradiction by fiat, and into a literary strategy in which the products of American diversity can survive on a technical level, if not on an organic. Dream-symbolism, pastoral poetry, "hard-boiled" naturalism, and ghetto slang all meld into a unity whose boundaries are the ego. Unable to find a viable common ground for the white and black in his vision of American experience, driven by the logic of his own protagonist's descent into hell, Ellison reverts to a unity which no longer would exist in a common recognition of unity in diversity, but on the level of consciousness alone—the precise opposite of what he had set out to do. The work, in other words, tends toward a kind of solipsism.

The post-Invisible Man Ellison manifests the shift: "Good fiction is made of that which is real, and reality is difficult to come by. So much of it depends upon the individual's willingness to discover his true self." The notion that reality is somehow dependent upon one's knowledge of self, that the external world relies upon a subjective ordering becomes the fundamental principle:

> I whipped it all except the mind, the *mind*. And the mind that has conceived a plan of living must never lose sight of the chaos against which that pattern was conceived.

History is chaos, not only nature, but society, too, demands the discipline of the solitary will:

> I carried my sickness and though for a long time I tried to place it in the outside world, the attempt to write it down shows me that at least half of it lay within me. . . .

Looking closely, we watch a dialectic of will and determinism unfold. Freedom changes imperceptibly from the recognition of "possibility" to the recognition of necessity. We have travelled from an impassioned voluntarism to a nightmarish sense of inevitability.

Imagination, discovery, order—all these blossom from within, conferring enormous importance on the pre-existing order within. It is only natural, then, that a search for identity would become paramount. This is why the search for "freedom" (in the old protest sense) with which *Invisible Man* tentatively began, transmogrifies in the final pages to an equation with "identity gained." Translated to the specific world of the novel, this general idea (in retrospect) becomes the novel's moral core:

> It is what the hero refuses to do in each section which leads to further action. He must assert and achieve his own humanity; he cannot run with the pack and do this. This is the reason for all his reversals.

But, again, still taking the novel on its own terms, this can only be a half-truth. The evolution from throwing angry truth "into the guilty conscience of America" in 1945, the evolution away from "the will to confront the world" to the world of self-knowledge, describes a journey onto a terrain where the contradictions between American principles and racial inequality, between "high" and "low" culture, between social responsibility and spiritual fulfillment, can be collectively worked out.

By the terms Ellison originally laid out, we cannot help finding in this solution to the American synthesis and the inclusive novel a peculiar failure. . . . Unlike the earlier white writers who themselves were ill-equipped to portray the black man in the flesh, Ellison is unable, in practice, to see the black man any other way. The specific manipulations, injustices, and opportunism suffered upon the narrator are too concrete, too clearly a part of a common social understanding of a specific social oppression with localized perpetrators.

The novel's closing words raise in full force the problem of whom the work is addressed to: "Who knows but that, on the lower frequencies, I speak for *you?*" (emphasis added). Apparently, it is the "you" of humanity. However, it arises in an Epilogue which establishes in the immediately preceding pages a "we" of unmistakeable Afro-American identity. (pp. 177-79)

In the recognition of racial divisions, Ellison seems to reach out to whites in *Invisible Man*'s final words as if to say, "We have similar feelings and aspirations; we are human too." The concept is active; as he wrote in his review of *The American Dilemma*, it is to use "the Negro's strongest weapon in pressing his claims: his hold upon the moral consciousness of Northern whites." The very creation of a fully rounded black character would then itself be a kind of imaginative propaganda for the recognition of the harm of racism. This would be consistent with what he seemed to think in 1945 was the way to achieve the great synthesis.

As we saw at that time, he tried to portray a debilitating doublethink still identified with the whites' refusal to reconcile "the Negro Problem" with their own principles of freedom. In his acceptance speech for the National Book Award, Ellison locates the chief significance of *Invisible Man* in its contribution to the creation of a "personal moral responsibility for democracy."

But in the Epilogue in which blacks become as culpable as whites for their own alienation (in the old protest sense), it is no longer a question of recognition for a minority, of the great and noble unity in diversity, but of atomized individuals equally "invisible" to one another. Since the conscious suppression of the black problem (as Ellison had described it) changes in the era of *Invisible Man* to the "symbol [of the] underground aspect of human personality," the *primum mobile* of the novel has become centered in a dilemma specific to white consciousness. For this process of burying the facts of racism and inequality in the underground of the personality is a process peculiar to white consciousness; the black man lives, not only witnesses, his experience. Consequently, Ellison's transference of a social apprehension located in the unconscious to a symbol of that same unconscious, ostensibly forming the bridge between whites and blacks on the level of mental processes, seems in fact to abandon the journey to the black frontier.

In his acceptance speech mentioned above, Ellison explains his avoidance of understatement in *Invisible Man* because "understatement depends . . . on commonly held assumptions, and my minority status rendered all such assumptions questionable." In other words, the artist is responsible not only for the literal meanings of his text, but also its connotations, and these are shaped differently from subculture to subculture. When he admits the separation existing between the two halves of his audience, he shows the necessity of finding a metaphor which can communicate with both. The question is whether his symbol (both personal and American) for alienation—the agony of black experience—can accomplish this. (pp. 179-80)

For the Negro, the vividness of an actual racism along with Ellison's evocation of its terrible immediacy, burdens the transcendence of the symbol with the weights of a reasoned bitterness. For the whites, the "Negro Problem" (as Ellison himself had pointed out) is too uncomfortable a part of the national memory for them to decline Ellison's invitation to dissolve race in an exultation of the individual. . . . Under the centripetal pressures of solipsism, hope mutates into the stark and taunting picture of what cannot be. (pp. 180-81)

Timothy Brennan, "Ellison and Ellison: The Solipsism of 'Invisible Man'," in CLA Journal, *Vol. XXV, No. 2, December, 1981, pp. 162-81.*

THOMAS SCHAUB

[In *Invisible Man,* Ellison's protagonist] appears to struggle with two ideas of reality: one that portrays a solid social world in which he wishes to play a part, and one that renders the depth of that social world as mere surface, in which no action short of charlatanism seems possible. In both ideas, however, reality remains merely external, and it is this epistemological naiveté that Invisible Man must outgrow. This naiveté is in part the understandable result of the protagonist's exclusion from society, but in Ellison's vision his character can fit himself for that social reality only by first coming to terms with the chaotic fluidity of existence itself. This decision was part of Ellison's effort to locate some ground of commonality outside the conventional terms of social discourse (of visible class and race), which tended only to perpetuate the absence of such community. Ellison thus twists his novel in a spiraling curve that elevates his character above and outside the theater he took to be real, until—having traveled through the ether of absurdity—he rediscovers the justification of social diversity and unity, and is thus in a position to suggest a more ambivalent (and benign) social order. (pp. 128-29)

To define Invisible Man's experience as an education in looking beneath the surface is, paradoxically, to frame the novel within the characteristic claim of realism, one of the forms that Ellison was at pains to amend and abridge. Within the abstract generality of this claim—to expose the way things really are—*Invisible Man* may be termed *realistic,* for it attempts to offer an expression adequate to the experience of living. But this realistic quality is achieved in the novel with techniques—not only of symbolic and surrealist presentation, but of self-conscious form—that violate the habitual decorum of realist conventions, especially as they were understood by the critic and writer in the forties.

The central device by which Ellison educates his character to the self-consciousness that defines the novel's reality is the image and idea of the mask. Images of the mask cluster about the intimations of political and sexual power, and, like words themselves, are a source of ambiguity revealing as much about their interpreter as about the realities they appear to conceal. As we shall see, in fact, the masking and unmasking in which Invisible Man participates parallels the mask of language that constitutes his world. This paralleling is a political element in the novel because the inherent ambivalences of language have calcified—in the society to which Ellison was addressing his fiction—into a system of associations that excluded and imprisoned black reality within white stereotypes. Thus it was Ellison's strategy to submit not only Invisible Man, but the author and his reader as well, to the discipline of the mask.

When Invisible Man remembers himself standing before the statue of the college founder, whose hands are "outstretched in the breathtaking gesture of lifting a veil," he cannot "decide whether the veil is really being lifted, or lowered more firmly into place; whether [he is] witnessing a revelation or a more efficient blinding." Clearly, the ambiguous gesture is fatal ("breathtaking") as well as awe-inspiring, for Ellison's use of the "veil" alludes to [W. E. B.] DuBois's attack on Booker T. Washington and reappears throughout *Invisible Man* as an image of false revelation. One of the most compelling lures of the Brotherhood is its promise of powerful insight: "I had the sense of being present at the creation of important events, as though a curtain had been parted and I was being allowed to glimpse how the country operated." This promise helps sustain the hero's naiveté even when he is demoted to lecturing on "The Woman Question": "Now was certainly no time for inactivity; . . . not at a time when all the secrets of power and authority still shrouded from me in mystery appeared on the way toward revelation."

Like all the other falls Invisible Man suffers in the novel, this one is fortunate and helps propel him toward the realization of the "lie that success is a rising *upward.*" Moreover, by means of this demotion, Ellison moves his novel toward the final but ironic union of power and sex when Invisible Man attempts to seduce prophecy from Sybil, a wife of one of the Brotherhood. (pp. 136-37)

The figure of the veiled alluring white woman recurs again and again in *Invisible Man,* but the symbolic associations that encircle her figure—so that it arouses both desire and guilt—are firmly established by Ellison's use of the character Mr. Norton. Norton, the white philanthropist and trustee of Invisible Man's college, is not merely a veiled allusion to Charles Eliot Norton and to white trustees everywhere, but is also a figure for the liberal, governed by too simple an idea of control, and whose good intentions disguise—especially from themselves—the persistence of racist assumptions. (p. 138)

To Norton, his daughter was "a being more rare, more beautiful, purer, more perfect and more delicate than the wildest dream of a poet," and her death—which thwarted the best that "medical science" could do for her—has driven him to his "first-hand organizing of human life," to reaffirm the order threatened by the chaos of death. His daughter is the immaculate vision that holds up the entire edifice of civilization, so it is no wonder that the white woman, bearing these associations, should inspire both love and hatred in the black hero, whose pigmentation makes him the figure of chaos. With comic irony directed at both of the men in the car, Ellison alludes to the parallel between the garish dancer [at the battle royal] and Norton's sacred girl when Invisible Man thinks, "I seemed to remember her, or someone like her, in the past. I know now that it was the flowing costume of soft, flimsy material that made for the effect."

That these associations are internal, psychological realities and compulsions is reinforced by their recurrence in Trueblood's dream, which follows closely upon the exchange within the car. (pp. 138-39)

Trueblood, as his name implies, lives by his own tempo and tells his own story; for his dream images graphically depict the displaced and incestuous eros implicit in Norton's adulation of his daughter. . . .

Trueblood is willing to take responsibility for the incest in which this dream culminates ("I makes up my mind that I ain't nobody but myself") and returns to face his wife and daughter, but both Norton and Invisible Man are horrified by his story. Invisible Man is worried that Trueblood will reflect negatively upon himself and the school, but underlying that fear is the one he shares with Norton: that reality and dream are not distinct realms after all, and that the dream of controlling reality is one for which—as the hero has learned by the time he writes the Prologue—"all dreamers and sleepwalkers must pay the price." . . . (p. 139)

Trueblood's self-reliance and his mesmerizing storytelling ability are inseparable elements of his unified being and differentiate him from both the white Trustee and his black sycophant. The larger significance of this integrated being will not become apparent to Invisible Man for many pages, yet it is the key to Ellison's sophisticated handling of structure and language in this novel, as well as the answer to Invisible Man's search for pattern and meaning.

Ellison is willing to suggest that such pattern exists, but only within experience, not in the reification of a symbolic world supposed to exist beyond or behind experience. Thus, when Invisible Man travels North from school, Ellison purposely floods the description of his departure with every literary, mythic, and symbolic trope he can muster:

> In less than five minutes the spot of earth which I identified with the best of all possible worlds was gone, lost within the wild uncultivated countryside. . . . I saw a moccasin wiggle swiftly along the gray concrete, vanishing into a length of pipe that lay beside the road. I watched the flashing

past of cotton fields and cabins, feeling that I was moving into the unknown.

Ellison exploits these echoes of literary and mythic understandings of human experience not only to emphasize that Invisible Man is recalling his feelings as the maudlin reflections of an earlier self—since this "spot of earth," earlier identified explicitly as "Eden," is no more known to him than the metropolis he is about to enter—but also to call attention to the fictive structures by which we interpret our experience. This is the kind of doubleback joke that runs throughout the entire novel—as when Invisible Man feels a "sudden fit of blind terror" at being blindfolded: "I was unused to darkness," he says—and that the novel itself as a self-conscious fiction enacts.

Thus, much of the novel's overt symbolic texture is not only an expression of the hero's present understanding being exercised at his own expense, but is doubly exploited by Ellison to dramatize the ambivalence of the word and its power to subordinate experience to symbolic correlative. The high visibility of the novel's symbolic texture should alert us to the amused distance that Ellison keeps from his own story, which, like Trueblood, he has learned to tell so well. Control comes from power over language, but this power defeats itself unless it is employed with knowledge of the distance that always exists between ideas and experience. In such passages as the preceding one, Ellison is not merely inverting white tropes, drawn from Milton and Voltaire; he is exploiting them *as* tropes, converting them into self-conscious, ironic fictions. (pp. 140-41)

Such comic distance always qualifies, for example, Ellison's use of myth to structure his novel, for the ultimate use of that structure is to return the hero to the embodiment of myth in experience. "I knew that in both *The Waste Land* and *Ulysses*," Ellison said in *The Paris Review* interview, "ancient myth and ritual were used to give form and significance to the material; but it took me a few years to realize that the myths and rites which we find functioning in our everyday lives could be used in the same way." Ellison's use of these materials doesn't point toward a transcendent order of art or religion, but down to the "abiding patterns of experience which . . . help to form our sense of reality and from which emerge our sense of humanity and our conception of human value." From Ellison's point of view, Eliot had replaced one narrative with another, but Ellison was trying to tell a story that would convey the reality of black life without at the same time appearing to fix the nature of reality or limit its permutations. Such a narrative would have to be, in some sense, an antinarrative, just as the visible form of its speaker is his invisibility.

Mythic order in *Invisible Man* always remains subordinate to the uses that it may have, just as narrative never acquires a reality beyond its purpose, both private and social, as a means of self-definition and renewal. In these terms, Invisible Man may be seen as a man determined to locate the material solidity of the narratives that entangle him; as a result of this naiveté, he remains divorced from experience and continues to think of the veils, curtains, and gowns of the novel as surfaces outside himself that—once parted—will reveal the reality and power he seeks.

We can measure how little Invisible Man has advanced by his reaction to the next incarnation of the white woman who haunts his waking nightmare. After his first lecture on "The Woman Question," one of the Brotherhood's wives seduces him, provoking in him the same ambivalent reactions that the blonde nude had inspired four hundred pages earlier: "I wanted both to smash her and to stay with her and knew that I should do neither." When he demands "What kind of game is this?", she expresses the reader's own amazement: "Oh, you poor darling! It isn't a game, really you have no cause to worry, we're free."

Here, too, the vocabulary embodies the ambivalence and contradiction that are the governing principles of the novel's expression, for although the woman's invitation is not a game (nor are they free), Invisible Man's acceptance of it would be a large step toward learning how to "play the game." This latter contest is the game the black doctor refers to when counseling our hero, but Invisible Man cannot play along because he is unwilling to discard his superficial narrative of how things operate: "my mind whirled with forgotten stories of male servants summoned to wash the mistress's back. . . . Pullman porters invited into the drawing room of rich wives headed for Reno—thinking, But this is the movement, the Brotherhood." (pp. 141-42)

The white woman ceases to unnerve him only when the veil of associations and expectations with which he surrounds her begins to part, and his experience in being mistaken for Rinehart is the necessary prelude to that revelation. In that experience Ellison dramatizes most explicitly that our sense of reality is illusion—*though none the less real for that.* Invisible Man has persistently sought to distinguish between reality and illusion, to pierce the surface to find the substantial depth beneath, but he misunderstands the black doctor's advice and begins to intuit this fact only when he dons the dark green glasses that cause him to be confused with Rinehart. For the first time in the novel he is trying not to be seen, but this too is a joke, since he has been invisible all along. This irony is underlined by Invisible Man's unintentional echo of the veteran's declaration, "You're hidden right out in the open—that is, you would be if you only realized it." His green glasses do hide him "right in front of their eyes," but they conceal another mask, not a true self that is invisible without them. (p. 143)

Since one of Ellison's purposes in writing the novel was to take issue with those prevailing descriptions (and their ideological assumptions) that served the white world as images of the real, his own narrative had to avoid the same error of assuming a material, absolute reality to which his language might refer. At the same time, Invisible Man *does* experience the reality of his encounters with the world around him, and that reality—though different for each man or woman—is the psychological relation shared by all, which Ellison sought to express. That this relation may be either imprisoning or liberating is part of the social and political power latent in the ability to tell one's story, and accounts again for Ellison's insistence upon the ambivalence and power of masks.

Despite the apparent insight informing his rage, Invisible Man is not yet entirely free of the naive model of reality that keeps him blind. The fundamental lesson he has drawn from his Rinehart experience is that it is possible to be invisible; although he has been living this fact all along, it is only when he consciously conceals himself that he experiences his invisibility. He determines to make use of this new knowledge by deceiving the Brotherhood. Ellison's control in this latter section of the novel is brilliant, for it appears that Invisible Man has at long last touched down; but when he asks, "now that

I had found the thread of reality, how could I hold on?", he shows that he is still securely lodged in the double frame of his own (and his author's) irony.

The actions that follow upon this determination demonstrate that Invisible Man reads the syntax of his phrase "the thread of reality" to emphasize possession and control, which assume a center of authority at the heart of the labyrinth. By following the "thread of reality" he hopes to learn "what actually guided their operations." In his mind, reality is still distinct from his own existence, and finding it is merely a "problem of information." His first efforts to employ this naive idea of action—offering the Brotherhood false membership lists—work almost too well, for they are received and made use of without the blinking of an eye: "Illusion was creating a counter-illusion." But when he seduces Sybil, one of the "big shot's wives," in the hope that she will prove to be an oracle and give him access to the Brotherhood's plan, he is once again rebuffed.

Secure in the knowledge of his invisibility, Invisible Man enters upon his evening with the last avatar of the novel's white goddess, but in this scene Ellison shows the goddess to be a figure existing only in the psychological territory of the novel's deluded characters. Throughout the book, she has been thought of as the sexual power at the center of all control and planning; but Sybil is no oracle, source neither of information nor of revelation. Like Norton in the Golden Day, she is just a human being. When Invisible Man says to her, "Tell me about George. Tell me about that great master mind of social change," she expresses disbelief: "Who, *Georgie?* . . . Georgie's blind'sa mole in a hole'n doesn't know a thing about it." This itself, of course, is a partial revelation; additionally, Sybil's own humanity finally impresses itself on him despite her failure to see him: "What had I done to her, allowed her to do?" Having learned to use his mask of invisibility, he now learns the responsibility of masks. Though invisible, he is not without the power to affect others.

By this point in the novel, readers may have become impatient with the failure of Invisible Man's recurring insights to pay off in strategic dividends, but this final gambit is rendered ineffective because Ellison is trying to bring down bigger game than the Brotherhood, and *his* strategy is the progressive disillusionment of his character. Each disillusionment involves the removal of another mask, revealing the successive surfaces of the world—instead of discovering an origin of power and reality outside himself. Within this larger context, the Brotherhood—most narrowly, a parody of the left in the United States during the thirties—is only a figure for the force that the veteran refers to as "They": "the same *they* we always mean, the white folks, authority, the gods, fate, circumstances—the force that pulls your strings until you refuse to be pulled any more."

The veteran's words should remind readers of the "doll's mask" of the nude dancer, first of the novel's puppets, and they point to the fact that so long as Invisible Man imagines that reality is to be found at the end of Ariadne's thread, he too will be only a doll. The complex significance of the phrase "thread of reality"—anticipated in the dancer's motions and the vet's figure of speech—thus involves the relations of mask, reality, and power; and those relations are most fully dramatized in the scene of Tod Clifton's demise.

Tod Clifton, we may recall, has been the handsome face of the Brotherhood (just as Invisible Man has been its eloquent spokesman). When Invisible Man discovers him peddling Sambo dolls, he is stupefied that Tod should have chosen to "fall outside of *history*," for "only in the Brotherhood could we make ourselves known, could we avoid being empty Sambo dolls. Such an obscene flouncing of everything human!" Invisible Man is unwilling to admit that Tod has recognized his identity as a doll of the Brotherhood, and prefers to make a living by manipulating a mask rather than be the manipulated face of the Brotherhood.

This scene is another example of the novel's precise ambivalence, for Tod's peddling is both an allegory of manipulation and a model of reality as the relationship between the private self and its public mask. Ellison's tripartite model—self, thread, and mask—allows him to maintain a connection between formlessness (of self and world) and order (of the public mask operating within social form). The connecting thread can be manipulated from either end: One may choose the mask by which he makes his way in the world and thus participate in constituting his reality, or one may accept the mask he is given, in which case his strings are being pulled by a power that remains hidden, "out there." Though Invisible Man at first fails to see the connection between Tod and the dancing dolls, he later finds the "fine black thread" that had made them move. This connecting thread, moreover, had been "invisible," and these two characteristics—connectedness and invisibility—are the central qualities of the phrase Invisible Man later misinterprets, "the thread of reality."

The discovery of the black thread enables Invisible Man to make the doll come to life, to maintain an erect, "taut" posture, for this thread is the invisible connective on which life itself depends. The thread of reality joining self and mask is also that invisible present connecting future possibility with past form, so that the idea of the mask in Ellison's thinking is central not only to the self but to the development of social identity as well. (pp. 144-47)

The relations of personal and social identity, implicit throughout the novel, are made explicit in the final scene of the story Invisible Man has to tell. Ellison's emphasis upon reality as process leads him to submit his character to a final disillusionment—necessary to complete the dematerialization of Invisible Man's assumptions—which occurs in the castration dream that closes the interior narrative. In addition to providing a kind of curtain call for all of the novel's major figures and dramatizing their sustained manipulation of Invisible Man, this scene emphasizes the transient relationship of the individual body to the process of the social organism. Having castrated him and tossed his parts up onto the Washington Bridge, Brother Jack asks, "How does it feel to be free of one's illusions?" Typically, Ellison's ambivalent language cuts at least two ways, for Jack's question assumes, on the one hand, that Invisible Man is now faced with reality, whereas, on the other, it points to the idea that reality is made of illusion; and it is this illusion-making power to reproduce that Invisible Man—in his dream—has lost. But in his lost seed, Invisible Man sees a waste not only of personal but of social possibilities as well. The Washington Bridge, which leads from black Harlem to white Jersey, becomes for him an image of humanity's effort to overcome the flow and diversity of life: *"the bridge seemed to move off to where I could not see, striding like a robot, an iron man, whose iron legs clanged doomfully as it moved."* Moving off to where he cannot see, the bridge suggests a sterile, white, machinelike future. Invisible Man's response (*"No, no, we must stop him!"*) calls for collective action because he realizes that personal and social development are inseparable, that both the body of the self and the body politic have substance only in what gives them body, which is the power to embody, to generate and create continuity.

The body, then, is a kind of mask, participating in a succession that is reality. This is not a denial of masks but an affirmation of their inevitability and necessity. One of Invisible Man's college teachers—revising Stephen Dedalus—had suggested as much, but at the time he hadn't understood: The problem of the black man is that of "creating the uncreated features of his face. . . . We create the race by creating ourselves." Ellison insists only that such masks be worn with a degree of irony, for "the mind that has conceived a plan of living must never lose sight of the chaos against which that pattern was conceived. That goes for societies as well as for individuals." This requires developing a tolerance for contradiction and ambiguity, and thus for a complicated idea of freedom and action; but without this tolerance human action—liberal, as well as fascist or communist—remains a kind of sleepwalking, "making a mess of the world."

Not only is the mask the inescapable means by which we have being in the world and are enabled to act, but the mask—as it was for Yeats—is also an instrument of imagination and change. As Invisible Man's closing admonition makes clear, this capacity has ramifications for both individual and national identity. Ellison found a familiar passage from Yeats's autobiography useful for explaining this dual importance of masks:

> There is a relation between discipline and the theatrical sense. If we cannot imagine ourselves as different from what we are and assume that second self, we cannot impose a discipline upon ourselves, though we may accept one from others. Active virtue as distinguished from the passive acceptance of a current code is therefore theatrical, consciously dramatic, the wearing of a mask. It is the condition of arduous full life.

Ellison finds Yeats's view especially appropriate for describing the experience of Americans, who, by throwing off their identity as colonials, had necessarily assumed the discipline of a second mask in order to invent for themselves a new identity. This is the particularly American "joke" that always lies between appearance and reality, and this is the joke whose dynamic ironies are the reality of *Invisible Man,* peeking out from behind every ambivalent surface of the novel.

Invisible Man is thus a novel whose imaginative project involves an act of leadership, for its hero's education requires that he imagine himself as other than what he is taken to be, and that education—dramatized as the novel—is an invitation to reconstitute the American experiment in equality and diversity. Ellison has said that while he was writing the novel he was "speculating on the nature of Negro leadership in the United States" and its failure to offer an alternative image of the black man. The novel offers the alternative of an articulate consciousness from its opening self-assertion, "I am an invisible man," and expresses Ellison's determination to "explore the full range of American Negro humanity and to affirm those qualities which are of value beyond any question of segregation, economics or previous condition of servitude"—which is to say, beyond those "deterministic" terms

that whites and blacks alike have used to interpret black culture and identity.

However, given both the context of his time—in which collective action seemed at best inept and at worst totalitarian—and the vision of existence that underlies his conception of identity, Ellison found it necessary to frame his portrait of leadership in negative terms. Throughout the novel Invisible Man has wanted to be a leader, but the paradoxical dilemma that increasingly paralyzes him is the question of how to be a leader without by that very act falsifying his mission, how to accept a position from the world he is trying to change without also undermining any hope of credible leadership. All of his efforts have brought him into contact with the major institutions of society and their corrupt leaders: school (Norton, Bledsoe), industrial capitalism (Emerson), political parties (Brother Jack), and race organizing (Ras the Exhorter). Thus, Invisible Man is able to lead only when he conceives of his project negatively. Facing Ras the Exhorter and his men, Invisible Man "recognized them at last as those whom I had failed and of whom I was now, just now, a leader, though leading them, running ahead of them, only in the stripping away of my illusionment."

This negative leadership has led several readers to conclude that *Invisible Man* fails to mend the divisions it dramatizes and so falsifies the hero's closing affirmations. In this view, Invisible Man ends as paralyzed as Trueblood says he had been, left on the verge of a "second self," which Ellison seems unable to invent. Instead, Invisible Man has been reduced to a disembodied voice. All else, we are given to understand, is illusion. . . . Ellison seems to have cut the ground from beneath him, for how can a disembodied voice be "socially responsible"? The social reality upon which the novel is so evidently predicated has had its apparent depth gutted by the hero's penetrating insight, and the hero—having accepted his invisibility—has only partial, inadequate being, seeming to hanker for activity on a stage of social theatrics in which he no longer believes.

Invisible Man overcomes these reservations only when the novel's existence is granted reality as the embodiment of its invisible hero. If the language of the novel is viewed as a transparent medium through which we "see" Invisible Man, then the character at the end of the novel is in fact without full being. He is only a voice in need of a body in order to exist in historical social time. Prior to such incarnation, Invisible Man doesn't exist except as a kind of absence or negativity, but this negativity is the very source of his existence for us—present only as the language that gives him being in our world. This is the far end of the logic with which Ellison has pursued the idea of the mask, for just as the wearing of a mask is the enabling discipline of self and society, so is the act of narration the means by which the speaker acquires a second self. (pp. 147-50)

Certainly, Ellison's novel may be read as a story about the world of a character whom we know as Invisible Man, but the novel fails to substantiate its own vision unless we shift our attention from the reality the story is "about" to the reality of the story. Even as a story "about," of course, the novel is a reflection only of a fictional world, but that world, already past, is only a stage in the process the novel enacts. Invisible Man has prepared himself for his next "role" by telling us his experience, but this act of self-generation (by which he becomes, as the vet had advised him, his own father) is a succeeding experience that exerts its influence in turn. In this way, the form of the novel is not merely that of a framed tale, but one that continues to outstrip itself in a spiraling motion. Closing with the hero's incipient emergence—like Thoreau leaving Walden—emphasizes the border between chaos and order as the complex territory of human ambiguity and keeps the novel in motion, faithful to its vision of a world no longer solid. Invisible Man continually renews his relation to the world, and from this standpoint his story about himself describes a prior, accumulated reality that he now sheds ("I'm shaking off the old skin," he says), exchanging one mask for another, an exchange that evolves, appropriately, from within.

This Emersonian, expressive idea of reality is radically allied in the novel with the example of Frederick Douglass—whose portrait hangs in Brother Tarp's office and whose doctrine of leadership was based upon self-assertion. It is within this tradition that Invisible Man finally places himself, and his self-assertion within the novel coincides with the anterior act of authorship executed by Ellison himself. The novel, thought of as enclosing the narrator, who encloses his own story, is another mask through which Ellison acquires a public identity and exerts his leadership. This autobiographical aspect of the novel-as-mask, everywhere implicit, is subtly confirmed by the number of lights that line Invisible Man's den. The peculiar specificity of the number—1,369—accords well enough with the hero's desperate frame of mind, but because these lights are an image of self-awareness, it is not surprising that in them Ellison should have coded his own initials. At the time he completed the novel, Ellison was thirty-seven years old; by squaring that number, we find the number of lights that give Invisible Man his form. Perhaps Ellison's use of the exponential figure is a metaphor for the power of reflection; a thirty-seven-year-old in the act of writing brings to his work the experience of his thirty-seven years, and the fitting result of his effort is not a sum, but a square. "Fiction," Ellison wrote, "became the agency of my efforts to answer the questions: Who am I, what am I, how did I come to be?"; and the answer his hero finally declares is that he is all that he has been: "I saw that they were more than separate experiences. They were me; they defined me. I was my experiences and my experiences were me." (pp. 151-52)

This reality is implicit in the novel's first words, "I am an invisible man," which announce the phenomenological status of all printed voices; but here, with their defiant self-assertion (as words), they insist upon a rejection of any reference to a bodily form other than their own. Any socially responsible role the voice might play depends upon that rejection and its effective autonomy, for this is the source of its integrity and its capacity to lead. The imagination of the novel's voice, then, is not only the genesis of its self-identity (being, as it were, all imagination) but is also a means of renewing America's dream of equality and diversity. "I learned very early," Ellison said in an interview, "that in the realm of the imagination all people and their ambitions and interests could meet." Without this common ground, the culture is in perpetual danger of hardening about an idea it mistakes for reality, and thus exerting a repressive conformity upon all invisible men. This is the universal truth expressed by the novel's autonomy. Only in that sense is the voice that speaks to us a mimetic device, calling attention to an invisible reality recognizable to all. (pp. 152-53)

Thomas Schaub, "Ellison's Masks and the Novel of Reality," in New Essays on Invisible Man, *edited by Robert O'Meally, Cambridge University Press, 1988, pp. 123-56.*

Shusaku Endo

1923-

Japanese novelist, dramatist, short story writer, essayist, and biographer.

Regarded as one of Japan's most important contemporary novelists, Endo explores themes relating to conflicts between Christianity and the Japanese temperament, Eastern and Western morality, and belief and skepticism. A Roman Catholic in a largely Buddhist country, Endo frequently draws on personal experiences as a member of a minority faction to dramatize what he considers modern Japan's spiritual indifference. Often compared to such Catholic authors as Graham Greene and François Mauriac, Endo writes passionately moral fiction in a realistic style that he frequently embellishes with lyricism and humor.

Born in Tokyo, Endo spent his early childhood in Manchuria before returning to Japan and moving with his mother into the home of a Catholic aunt after his parents separated. Strongly influenced by the aunt, Endo's mother soon converted to Catholicism, and she pressured her son into being baptized. Endo has described his baptism as the critical event of his life. Because he believed that religion had been thrust upon him, Endo was uncomfortable with Catholicism for many years and responded with shallow commitment, which in turn fueled feelings of guilt over disappointing his mother. Gradually, however, Endo came to accept Catholicism. Endo studied French literature at Keio University and later became one of the first postwar Japanese students to attend a foreign school, enrolling in the University of Lyon in 1950 to pursue his interest in twentieth-century Catholic fiction. Endo's first novel, *Shiroi hito* (1955), won the Akutagawa Prize, an award for promising young Japanese writers.

Chinmoku (1966; *Silence*), Endo's first novel to be translated into English, is considered by many critics to be his finest work. A fictionalization of the initial seventeenth-century Christian expeditions to Japan, during which Italian and Portuguese missionaries and their followers were persecuted, *Silence* focuses on Rodrigues, a young Jesuit evangelist who voyages to Japan to learn why his former mentor has apostatized rather than endure martyrdom. Soon after arriving, however, Rodrigues is captured and forced to witness the torture of native converts, which will stop only if he publicly renounces Jesus Christ. Rodrigues initially prepares for martyrdom but capitulates after realizing the selfishness of the alternative. Jean Higgins observed: "*Silence* concerns itself with the theological question of the image of God, Eastern and Western. Yet it does so without dogmatizing or indoctrinating." *Umi to dokuyaku* (1958; *The Sea and Poison*), also based on historical fact, concerns the illegal vivisection of American prisoners by Japanese doctors during World War II. In this novel, which is written as a detective story, Endo subtly compares the lack of conscience of the doctors to the attitude and actions of Nazi soldiers and activists during the same era. *Kazan* (1959; *Volcano*) focuses on a scientist who has devoted his life to monitoring a long-dormant volcano that once threatened a city. His prediction that the volcano will remain inactive conflicts with that of an unfrocked French priest, who expects an eruption in retribution for the evil inherent in the world.

In *Obakasan* (1959; *Wonderful Fool*), Endo blends broad humor and social realism to portray a naive French priest whose determination to gain complete faith in the people he meets in Japan is tested by their taunts, deception, and violence. After he drowns, his exemplary life inspires the Japanese to reassess their spiritual insensitivity. *Kuchibue o fuku toki* (1974; *When I Whistle*) deviates from religious concerns using parallel narratives to compare generational differences between Ozu, an inept businessman who represents pre-World War II Japan, and his son Eiichi, a callously ambitious surgeon who symbolizes modern Japan. The stories converge when Eiichi treats his father's former lover, a terminal cancer patient who personifies the deterioration of morals in Japanese society. *Samurai* (1980; *The Samurai*), based on historical fact, depicts a Japanese warrior's trip to the West to establish trading ties in the seventeenth century. Advised by the shogun to fake conversion to Christianity if it will aid their cause, the samurai does so against his will. When he returns to Japan five years later, the country's political regime has changed, and he is deemed a state enemy. Through the torment that he experiences, the samurai comes to empathize with Jesus Christ and becomes a true Christian. Van C. Gessel noted: "Thematically *Samurai* is on one level an implicit critique of the enclosed Japanese society. . . . Yet in a broader sense the novel takes aim at all man-made institutions—whether political, social, or even religious—that seek only their own preservation and thereby undermine the humanity of the individual."

In Endo's recent novel, *Scandal* (1988), a distinguished Japanese Catholic novelist finds his reputation threatened by allegations that he has engaged in sordid sexual activities. The author, who bears many similarities to Endo, believes that an impersonator is trying to humiliate him but realizes after investigating Tokyo's bordellos that he has been concealing his depravity behind a facade of virtue. Endo's short stories collected in *Juichi no iro-garasu* (1979; *Stained Glass Elegies*) examine themes similar to those of his novels, in particular the problems Christians confront in Japan. Endo has also written the play *Ougon no Ku* (1969; *The Golden Country*) as well as *Iesu no shogai* (1973; *A Life of Jesus*), a study of Jesus Christ and the New Testament.

(See also *CLC*, Vols. 7, 14, 19; *Contemporary Authors*, Vols. 29-32, rev. ed.; and *Contemporary Authors New Revision Series*, Vol. 21.)

KUNIO FRANCIS TANABE

The atrocities took place at a medical school in southern Japan a few months before the end of the Second World War.

> Eight captured American airmen had been used for medical experiments. In general the purpose of the experiments had been to obtain such information as how much blood a man could lose and remain alive, how much salt water in place of blood could safely be injected into a man's veins, and up to what point a man could survive the excision of lung tissue. There were twelve medical personnel involved in the vivisections, two of them nurses. The trial opened in Fukuoka but was later transferred to Yokohama.

I had never heard of such a story until I recently read Shusaku Endo's fictionalized version of this gruesome episode in *The Sea and Poison.* The case is probably news to most Americans since the trial took place 32 years ago in occupied Japan, and the newspapers here did not publicize the event then—partly because the "Class A" war criminals such as General Tojo were being tried in Tokyo at around the same time. *The New York Times* of March 12, 1948, buried a short article with the sensational headline: "Cannibalism Laid to High Japanese: Thirty Go on Trial on Charge of Using Eight U.S. Fliers for Vivisection Experiments." According to this article, "five of the thirty accused ate bits of the liver of one American flier at a party." In Endo's novel, there is such an episode.

The Sea and Poison begins with a prologue, written as if the author stumbled onto the case. In a faraway suburb in Tokyo, he finds a surgeon, Dr. Suguro, who, though a bit strange and taciturn, proves to be unusually adept at treating his lung. By chance at a wedding reception in Kyushu, he meets a physician who knew of Suguro's dark past. The narrator becomes curious and digs up old newspaper clippings on the case and is astonished. . . .

Endo takes us back to the scene of the crime—Fukuoka in 1945—when the city "was more than half burnt out with all the air raids. . . . The exploding anti-aircraft shells kept up a constant chatter, and in the lead-coloured sky the lazy drone of the B-29s went on interminably." It was a time when "no one any longer paid much attention to whether people lived or died." The author maintains this dark, ominous tone throughout the novel.

Endo focuses on three participants who played minor roles in the vivisection: Suguro, an intern at the time, dedicated and obliging to his patients but a coward easily swayed by his superiors, with no control over his own destiny; Toda, a ruthlessly ambitious intern, lured onto the team with promises of promotion; Ueda, a nurse embittered by a failed marriage, jealous and contemptuous of the chief surgeon's German wife, gleeful that she is ignorant of her husband's participation in the evil act. "This is for your country's sake," a doctor tells Nurse Ueda. "They've all been condemned to death anyway. This way they can do some good for the advancement of medical science."

The grievousness of the crime is clear enough. What preoccupies Endo in this novel is not so much the obviously villainous but someone with a touch of humanity like Suguro who becomes entangled in a vicious web. He is not merely a victim of circumstance but through his moral cowardice and later his apathy, he becomes just as guilty as the more willing participants. He could have blown the whistle, or at least have refused, but Suguro no longer cared. And repeating the leitmotif of his moral fiction, Endo probes into the question of the Japanese conscience: Are we not a bit like Toda who fears "disapproval in the eyes of others" rather than in the eyes of God? And when that disapproval becomes weak and murky as during those dark days when they were under the pressure of the military henchmen and the steady barrage of bombings, would our conscience too fail? (p. 3)

Kunio Francis Tanabe, "Facts and Fiction of a Japanese War Crime," in Book World—The Washington Post, *October 12, 1980, pp. 3, 14.*

GARRY WILLS

In the post-Mishima era, perhaps only Kobo Abe's and Kenzaburo Oe's novels are more respected than those of Shusaku Endo. The other two writers are radical in their politics and their literary technique; but Endo writes old-fashioned novels strongly influenced by François Mauriac, and identifies himself with the theologically conservative Catholic church in Japan. Since Catholics make up only half of one percent of the Japanese population, he begins as an exception, and presents himself as something more than an anomaly, almost as an absurdity. In his play *The Golden Country,* he argues that Japan can never accept Christianity, since the country lacks a sense of God, a sense of sin, and a sense of death.

Why, if Christianity and Japanese culture are so hopelessly at odds, has Endo devoted a very active career to exploring the hopelessness of it all? The best place to seek an answer may be the recent American edition of *The Sea and Poison,* the 1958 novel that gave Endo his first experience of fame and controversy. . . . Though he claims the Japanese have no sense of sin, this novel describes the growth of that sense in a doctor who was guilty of war crimes. Christianity plays no part in **The Sea and Poison,** but its protagonist recognizes his guilt. . . .

The sin of the novel is taken from history. Japanese doctors subjected American POWs to vivisection in experiments meant to establish the limits of lung surgery and the tolerance to certain injections. It was as monstrous as some things done in Europe's death camps; yet, like those acts, it was not necessarily performed by monsters. Endo creates the hospital world of sterilized ambition and corporate blame-shifting that domesticated, gradually, the unthinkable as the merely unpleasant, that masked war crimes as a grim war duty. And recognition of the crime psychologically cripples the one doctor who holds back. Guilt does not redeem among the Japanese; it is so alien that it paralyzes.

The story is told as a kind of detective tale. Most such stories begin with a crime and look for the criminal. But this story has a criminal at the outset, but no crime. We meet Dr. Suguro through the curiosity of a bored patient, who notices the seclusion of this skilled doctor, abandoned by his wife and shunning all other company. Given the chance to check on Suguro's background (through the certificate on his wall), the self-appointed detective begins to uncover Suguro's crime—and so Japan's, and so the detective's. By understanding the doctor too well, the patient threatens his own bored security.

It is a novel with powerful scenes, but it has a disjointedness that comes from the Japanese practice of publishing novels serially. . . .

The novel by which Endo is best known, both in his own country (where it was made into a movie) and abroad, avoids plotting difficulties by a great simplicity and intensity of linear narrative. **Silence** is based on another historical scandal, the defection from Christianity, in the seventeenth century, of a Jesuit superior. The missionary, Father Christovao Ferreira, married, became a Buddhist scholar, and helped to examine those suspected of Christianity. In Endo's novel a young Portuguese admirer and ex-student of Ferreira seeks him out and joins him in his apostasy. Again, a detective comes to understand his prey too well and repeats his crime.

Since the translation of **Silence** into English (in 1969), Endo has been repeatedly, tiresomely, compared to Graham Greene, who warmly praised the book. And some of the criticism directed at Endo by Japanese Catholics resembles early Catholic attacks on Greene, who was accused of glorifying sinners and mocking the pious. But Greene's fascination with sin and guilt looks very tame when put beside Endo's. The whiskey priest of *The Power and the Glory* does not defect or lose his faith; he maintains a priestly ministry despite his own unworthiness, which partially qualifies him for serving other weak people. Endo explores a more interesting paradox; his priest does defect, not from weakness but from love, to spare Christian converts the persecution mounted against them.

John Updike, pushing the comparison with Greene in his review of **Silence** in *The New Yorker,* said a weakness of the novel was the clear resemblance of Kichijiro, the man who informs on the Christian converts, to the mestizo informer in *The Power and the Glory.* Greene's priest conquers his last bit of pride when he confesses a shared weakness with the man who betrayed him—a conventional enough Christian theme. But Endo's priest finds that he needs Kichijiro as an alter ego, that the two have been indissolubly linked in a cross-cultural mismatch, a marriage of the minds that can bring nothing but

misunderstanding, yet that neither can surrender without giving up his own identity. Endo later suggests that this was the relationship between Christ and Judas. The union of Japan and Christianity is doomed, but so are all meetings of man with God; and they go forward nonetheless. . . .

A more interesting comparison of Endo with Greene would consider the former's **Wonderful Fool** (*Mr. Fool* in Japanese) and *The Quiet American.* There is no question here of direct influence. Instead, one finds parallel themes looked at from two cultures. The Western "innocent" tries to grasp Oriental "doubleness," which is not always duplicity, but is that too. The innocence is in both cases destructive, but Endo's French fool comes to *be* destroyed and Greene's American comes to *do* the destroying. (p. 21)

[In **Wonderful Fool**], Bonaparte blunders about in a picaresque series of urban misunderstandings, some of them rather predictable (the brothel he thinks a hotel). Endo must have seen some Monsieur Hulot films in Paris. But then the blunderer is drawn into a gang slaying (the murderer is called Endo). As the murderer pursues his quarry, the fool pursues the murderer, the one trying to move with stealth, the other banging into garbage cans, as it were, pleading with the slayer not to kill—for his own sake. This weird pursuit of the pursuer is enough to drive anyone to murder, but Bonaparte-Neyrand actually saves the well-deserving victim, by getting in the way and dying for his intrusiveness. East has met West again, and the West has lost. But the two superficial young people on whom Bonaparte was foisted have, strangely, become embarrassed about their embarrassment over him. East has met West, and these two are no longer fully Eastern. Guilt is stirring.

Endo nurses the tiny embers of guilt he finds in Japan, blowing on them through his laughter in novel after novel. In his 1974 book, **When I Whistle,** he suggests a reason for guilt about Japan's present as well as its wartime past. The protagonist, Ozu, remembers his own prewar youth as he watches his son's bustling rise in the medical world. A central character in the earlier scenes is Ozu's repulsive friend "Flatfish," who is madly in love with an unattainable beauty. . . . Traces of Huck Finn idleness touched the young Ozu's comic and aimless days; yet he cannot think why his mind returns so compulsively to a misfit and sadsack like Flatfish—until his son's fierce and narrow aim tells him why. (pp. 21-2)

Japanese ways of evading reality amuse and haunt Endo, and he gave over one novel to that theme. In **Volcano,** the action all takes place in the shadow and on the flanks of an extinct volcano which has shown signs of reawakening. To live with impending disaster—by earthquake, typhoon, tidal wave—the Japanese have acquired the trick of preparing for disaster without letting themselves actually *think* about it. Endo traces this psychic mechanism in a place where bureaucratic careers are made or broken by predicting an eruption or declaring it impossible. Fortunes can be acquired by building on the volcanic slopes. A Christian priest makes providence the guarantor of his Church's safety, while an apostate priest hopes (because he cannot pray) that the volcano will erupt, break through the surface pretense of those around him. As is often the case with Endo, the evil man sees more than the others, yet twists himself in the process.

This may be Endo's technically most satisfying novel. He solves his difficulties with plot by turning them into advantages. Nothing happens in the book. The eruption impends without ever occurring; its whole meaning is as a threat. . . . Private to each [character], the thing locked up inside is both *the* volcano and something different. Though Endo was addressing Japanese concerns of many different kinds, and there is nothing so obvious as allegory in the tale, an American is bound to think of the Bomb in whose shadow we live by carrying it inside us. (p. 22)

Garry Wills, "Embers of Guilt," in The New York Review of Books, *Vol. XXVIII, No. 2, February 19, 1981, pp. 21-2.*

GEORGE KEARNS

The moral problem examined by Shusaku Endo in **The Sea and Poison** might have provided material for Ibsen. The central figure, Dr. Suguro, a young intern in a Japanese hospital during World War II, is drawn into a plan to perform unnecessary experimental operations upon American prisoners of war in behalf of the Japanese military command. It is a comment on our times that as a moral problem it is at once complex and trite. Exactly where does individual responsibility rest when an immoral act, an atrocity, arises not from the mind of a single "evil" person, but from a multitude of interacting pressures: sheer tiredness and mental confusion, self-preservation, personal and organizational allegiances, confusing lines of authority, actions shared and endorsed by a "group" or by "society," patriotic appeals, and the difficulty of knowing in modern warfare or politics where the battlefield begins and ends. Dr. Suguro knows, or thinks he knows, as we often tell ourselves, that his solitary protest would be quixotic, that no action of his, no refusal to participate, will stop "society" or the "organization" from proceeding. Moreover, no one expected the operation to turn out so badly, for the prisoner has died. Endo's moral stance—the vivisection was *wrong*—is unequivocal. His young intern is only slightly less certain: "I shut my eyes in there today. I don't know what to think, even now. . . . Still, some day we're going to have to answer for it." A more cynical colleague replies: "Answer for it? To society? If it's only to society, it's nothing much to get worked up about." . . . For me, **The Sea and Poison** is interesting for the odd experience of seeing the War through Japanese eyes, and for glimpses of life in wartime Japan and after.

George Kearns, in a review of "The Sea and Poison," in The Hudson Review, *Vol. XXXIV, No. 2, Summer, 1981, p. 310.*

VAN C. GESSEL

[**Samurai**] is a remarkably faithful account of a voyage to Mexico and Europe undertaken in 1613 by envoys of the powerful Sendai daimyo Date Masamune. . . . The chief Japanese ambassador, Hasekura Tsunenaga . . . , 1571-1622, was a low-ranking vassal who obediently submitted to his lord's command and made the arduous journey to the West, guided by an ambitious, zealous Franciscan friar. In the novel, Hasekura's only concern is to open trade relations with Mexico as he has been ordered; Velasco, the priest serving a different lord, is eager to be appointed Bishop of Japan so that he may win the hearts of the Japanese people.

Despite the dynamic potential of the plot, Endō's purpose in re-creating Hasekura's life is to provide a record of the spiritual voyage that takes place within an individual's soul.

Readers who expect the novel to portray nothing more than a temporal journey are, if you will, all at sea. It is the finely tuned apposition of rapid surface movement across oceans and continents in the outer world, and the almost imperceptible stirrings of faith within Hasekura's soul that gives **Samurai** its tension, its richness, and its power. This contrast is reflected in the narrative structure. As with **Chinmoku,** Endō employs both first-person and omniscient narrators to tell the story of this voyage. But in **Samurai** he has two main characters instead of just one, and for this reason the dual-voice technique works even more effectively. The first-person narrator in **Samurai** is the self-asserting priest Velasco, and the close proximity between storyteller and listener etches the sharp outlines of Velasco's personality in the reader's mind. Because this Franciscan is a dominant—even domineering—actor in the drama, the immediacy of his actual presence as he plots stratagems, pursues ambitions and parries opponents is heightened by having him serve as one of the narrators. We respond to the dramatic moments that he instigates, and we recognize him as a vibrant, combative human force. He is, in short, the very embodiment of aggressive Western Christianity.

When the samurai takes to the stage, however, the narrative voice in the novel retreats to a more subdued, passive position. The elevated perspective of the narrator here allows the reader to share in the gradual changes that take place within the samurai. At first Hasekura registers no reaction at all to the crucifixes and images of Christ that he sees all around him; they have no significance for him. But when thirty-eight of the Japanese merchants in the entourage are baptized in Mexico City as an obviously hypocritical means to further their financial interests, Hasekura begins to view these images with contempt.

Yet as the external narrative surges forward under Velasco's guidance, embroiling the envoys in violent struggles (with political and religious institutions working against them in both Japan and Europe), the samurai and two of his fellow ambassadors are persuaded that baptism as an expediency is the only practical means to accomplish their mission successfully and return to Japan with honor. They submit to a spiritually meaningless baptism.

When the embassy fails in its purpose and the envoys return dejectedly to Japan after several years, however, they find that the political climate has undergone many changes, not the least of which is the strict ban on Christianity. After his return Hasekura is increasingly isolated from any source of sympathy or understanding. His experiences in the West have torn him away from family and friends in his tiny, insular marshland, and the shogunate forbids him to associate with his other comrades who have converted to the proscribed faith. He is left without anyone who can offer comfort or compassion. The relentless political wheels still grind forward, and the domainal authorities conclude that the samurai's very existence is an intolerable affront to their anti-Christian policies. When Hasekura is summoned before the Council of Elders, he knows that he will be ordered to atone for his crime of conversion.

Deprived at this point of every recourse of human empathy, Hasekura embraces the still cloudy yet constant image of another Man who was 'despised and rejected of men'. The samurai's final scene in the novel strongly yet subtly suggests the ultimate spiritual change that has come over him. (pp. 445-46)

The reader is left with the strong impression that religious conviction faces its most formidable challenge when an individual is hovering at the brink of death. At the moment when life itself is about to be snuffed out, it is the faith which lies at the core of his existence that sustains the samurai and transforms his miserable death into a kind of martyrdom. And his sole companion as he makes the final journey of his life is the Jesus who met with similar rejection in the world of men.

This image of a wretched but sympathetic Christ is a familiar one in Endō's literature: it is the same forgiving Christ who urged Rodrigues to trample on the *fumie* . . . in *Chinmoku.* In *Samurai* it is this encounter with faith at the very instant of death that unifies the external and internal narratives which have been so carefully woven together over the course of the novel. A clear commentary on Endō's metaphysical aims in writing the book is the fact that his original title was to be [*A Man Who Met a King*]. The Hasekura of both fact and fiction had the opportunity to meet many of the kings of the earth (including Philip III of Spain and Pope Paul V); but only when he stands before an abyss of despair and death does he encounter a King who can salve his wounds and lessen his torment. It is when Hasekura meets and embraces this pathetic King that his own sorrows become endurable, and his abortive life's journey is transformed into a spiritually significant success.

Unlike Shiina Rinzō, who accepts *prima facie* the liberating elements of Christianity and extolls them in his fiction, Endō has had to grapple with the Japanese resistance to the monotheistic exclusivism of his adopted religion. In his earliest works this conflict between Eastern and Western theologies was presented as a struggle in which there can be no victors. Thus the anguish over sin that fills *Shiroi Hito,* a novel about betrayal in the French Resistance, is conspicuously absent in the companion work set in Japan, *Kiiroi Hito.* This dichotomy of beliefs continued to shape the major themes of Endō's fiction for some time, and the dialectical juxtaposition of East/West, pantheism/monotheism made for novels as ideologically discomforting as Shiina's early Christian writings. Endō declared a tentative truce between the two battling cultural camps in *Chinmoku,* but there is still a lingering sense in that novel that Japan cannot absorb Christianity until the religion is altered to suit the local climate. Conversely, the faith of Rodrigues and his companions has to be stripped of its cultural trappings before they can comprehend the true nature of Christ. Only when he rejects his image of a stern paternal judge and clings to the forgiving, motherly companion of the Japanese faithful is Rodrigues able to hear the voice impelling him to perform the sacrificial act of love.

Thus, while *Chinmoku* is certainly a turning point of Endō's work, not until *Samurai* does his thematic vision mellow to the point that he no longer need be dogmatic about the conflicts of faiths and cultures. In the present novel he awards the palm of victory to neither side, or perhaps to both sides. Velasco, once he has cast off his unseemly pride, is allowed to worship and serve his image of a glorified Christ with a rational and aggressive faith. Captured when he returns to Japan following Hasekura's death, Velasco is burned at the stake; his martyr's death becomes an unsullied reflection of his dynamic, Western beliefs. Hasekura, by contrast, accepts the companionship of Jesus almost passively. His faith is pri-

marily non-rational and thoroughly internalized, and the blurred intimations of his death are a fitting representation of a conviction different from—but no less valid than—that of the Spanish missionary. Endō in *Samurai* grants both men a place in the eternal mansions of heaven.

Samurai is an intricately crafted novel. The carefully balanced interweaving of plot lines with the ever-shifting narrative voice; the array of contrasts between East and West, faith and unbelief, fervor and passivity, flesh and spirit, victory and defeat, the Council of Elders in Sendai and the Council of Bishops in Madrid; the abundant use of nature imagery, shifting between land and sea, and setting the soft, hazy-white images of snow associated with the samurai against the vibrant, fire-like images that surround Velasco; the journey motif, sustained in both the physical and spiritual threads of the narrative; the gradual shift in focus from the vast external world to the private recesses of the samurai's heart; the use of *makura-kotoba* . . . like phrases in the novel's diction; and the contrasting deaths at the end that function as coda-like refrains—all these elements converge to make *Samurai* read very much like a *chōka* . . . , the long verse form of the *Man'yōshū* . . . age.

Thematically *Samurai* is on one level an implicit critique of the enclosed Japanese society, for Hasekura has to break out of the tiny microcosm of his marshland and encounter Christ before he can find someone to comprehend and soothe his private torment. Yet in a broader sense the novel takes aim at all man-made institutions—whether political, social, or even religious—that seek only their own preservation and thereby undermine the humanity of the individual, discarding him as a mere cog in the works when he ceases to be of use or becomes a threat to the integrity of the system. In such a world, Endō asserts, the individual must look beyond human sources for the sympathy and love which he must have to survive. He must turn to the realm of the spirit; when death looms near, only a spiritual power can offer consolation and courage.

On a final level, *Samurai* also functions as a sort of I-novel. Endō was one of the first Japanese to travel abroad for study after the Second World War, and a number of the ocean scenes in the novel are re-creations of that experience. But the book is autobiographical in more than just the externals of a voyage to Europe. The feelings of incomprehension and even revulsion that Hasekura experiences as he gazes at the many images of Christ are not unlike the emotions which Endō has ascribed to his own youth. The scene in which Hasekura is baptized in Madrid is an eerily accurate reproduction of the ceremony in which Endō participated at the age of eleven. Like the samurai, Endō did not choose Christianity of his own volition, but initially had it thrust upon him, and for some time he felt distant from it. Only when the trials of his life's voyage—particularly his battles with illness—brought him to a point where he could 'meet a King' did he, like his novel's protagonist, come to terms with a religion no longer foreign, but intensely personal. (pp. 446-48)

Van C. Gessel, "Voices in the Wilderness: Japanese Christian Authors," in Monumenta Nipponica, *Vol. XXXVII, No. 4, Winter, 1982, pp. 437-57.*

NOEL PERRIN

In 1613, Japan was ruled, under the shogun, by about 200

feudal lords called *daimyo,* each with his own domain. One of the greatest of these *daimyo* was Date Masamune, the one-eyed Lord of Sendai. Though not a Christian himself, he was a protector of Christians at a moment when most of the lords were briskly helping the shogun to stamp Christianity out.

All during 1613, Lord Date was working on a quite extraordinary project. He had as refugees in his domain the crew of a wrecked Spanish ship. With their assistance, he had a galleon built, far larger than the usual Japanese junk. Then he sent it off on a combined trading mission and embassy to Mexico. As ambassadors he sent four of his low-ranking samurai and (to be their interpreter) an ambitious Franciscan monk named Luis Sotelo. The chief of mission was a middle-aged samurai named Hasekura Rokuemon, an obscure rural squire with an income of 60 *koku* a year. By contrast, Lord Date himself had an annual income of 625,000 *koku.*

The embassy accomplished little or nothing in Mexico—the viceroy said he had no power to make a treaty with Japan—and eventually it went on to Madrid and then to Rome, where Hasekura had an audience with Pope Paul V. He didn't get back to Japan until 1620. . . .

[In *The Samurai*], Endo has done far more than write a historical novel about an early and odd encounter between East and West. Taking the history of Hasekura's embassy as a mere base, he has written a really quite profound religious novel.

One of the oddities of that voyage was that all of the Japanese on it (except some of the sailors) converted to Christianity. None of them, however, did so sincerely. They were just infiltrating. The merchants on the galleon converted first, because they believed, correctly, they couldn't hope to trade in Mexico unless they did. Anything for profit was their motto, and they were quite open about it. (Endo makes some sly parallels with modern Japan here.)

The four samurai ambassadors converted much later, in Madrid, and *they* did it because they were persuaded they couldn't hope to accomplish Lord Date's mission otherwise.

As it turned out, they couldn't accomplish it anyway—the whole seven-year trip was a failure—and even if they had, it wouldn't have mattered. By the time they got back to Japan, the shogun had gathered nearly all power into his own hands, and Christianity was totally forbidden in all domains. Even for their seeming conversion, they wound up being severely punished. Sotelo, who returned to Japan separately, was caught and executed.

To this already ironic history, Endo adds another and supreme irony. He has Hasekura become genuinely a Christian *after* his return to Japan. But not the kind of Christian the bishops in Madrid thought they were baptizing—that is, a promising colonial convert. Throughout the novel, Endo gradually distinguishes two kinds of Christianity. The first hint comes when the envoys meet a renegade Japanese monk living in a remote Indian village in Mexico. . . . They are astounded to find that the former monk is still a Christian. "I believe in my own Jesus," he tells them. "My Jesus is not to be found in the palatial cathedrals. He lives among these miserable Indians."

At the time Hasekura is totally unimpressed. If anything were to attract him to Christianity, it would *be* the palatial cathedrals. He is attracted to power and resplendence, not to the "ugly and filthy" figure he sees hanging on those omnipresent crucifixes in Mexico, Spain, and Italy. . . .

But by the end of the book, Hasekura is a secret Christian, dying for the faith Lord Date doesn't even know he has. And Father Velasco, no longer dreaming of a bishopric, has also become an "ugly and filthy" Christian. Against all canon law, he has administered the last rites to one of the envoys who, when he realized the mission had failed, committed *seppuku* (better known in America as *hara-kiri*). He has collaborated in a small way with Buddhism. He has ceased to think he has special access to God's will. He has died a failure in nearly all eyes but his own. And at the end the two men are alike, and are heroes.

If all this makes the book sound gloomy, it isn't. It is calm and understated and brilliantly told. Simple on the surface, complex underneath. Something like a fable from an old tapestry. Endo does wonders at evoking the early 17th century, as it was both for Japanese and for Europeans. . . . He uses, and effectively, the kind of repetition, almost a refrain, that we associate mainly with the chorus of a song, or perhaps with Homer and his wine-dark sea and rosy-fingered dawn. At first it seems odd in a novel, but it works. He alternates sections in the samurai's mind and sections in Father Velasco's (first-person for Velasco, third-person for Hasekura); and this duality of vision is what works best of all. Van C. Gessel's translation is fully worthy of all this.

If you're interested in how East and West really met, forget Kipling. Read Endo.

> Noel Perrin, "How East and West Really Met," in Book World—The Washington Post, *October 24, 1982, p. 6.*

GEOFFREY O'BRIEN

Shusaku Endo is a Japanese Christian, an identity whose contradictions define the dynamics of his fiction. Whether in an austere historical drama like *Silence* or a glum modern fable like *Volcano,* his characters invariably confront—or refuse to confront—notions of sin and redemption which are seen as inimical to a moral complacency at the heart of Japanese culture. That this conflict is very much Endo's own story can be gleaned from the fact that he first became a Christian not through conversion, but as a young child obedient to his mother's wishes. The hero of *The Samurai,* similarly, receives baptism out of loyal compliance with his feudal lord's political maneuvering.

The Samurai's point of departure is a Japanese mission to Mexico and Europe that set out in 1613, a final effort at establishing international trade relations before the closing-off of the country in 1633. Unknown to the four low-ranking samurai chosen as envoys, government policy is reversed when they are on the first leg of their journey; by the time they get back to Japan five years later, they will be treated as state enemies for their politic adoption of Christianity. . . .

What with highly colored images of 17th century samurai disembarking at Acapulco, enduring Indian attacks and storms at sea, and becoming embroiled in ecclesiastical intrigue in Madrid and Rome, there is plenty here to occupy the reader unmoved by Endo's spiritual scenario. The sense of cultural insularity felt by the samurai, their confusion at the sudden influx of new information about the world, mirrors both a fundamental Japanese preoccupation and Endo's specific discomfiture as one of the first of the postwar generation to study abroad. . . .

Some may find the dramatization of issues too schematic. Like many novelists of ideas, Endo makes little room for accident, and it sometimes seems as if every character who strays into his narrative does so to represent a particular point in the spiritual spectrum. Credibility falters a bit when the envoys discover a renegade Japanese Christian living in a Mexican village, preaching a very up-to-the-minute Liberation Theology in the era of Pope Paul V. What saves Endo from arid abstraction is a tremendously lyrical sensory imagination. He gives us the temperature of the samurai's marshland domain, the effect of ocean and desert on eyes seeing them for the first time, the sound of snow falling off a roof in the silence after a political edict. The place in which his characters undergo their transformations is made tangible. This sense of physical reality carries over to the interior domain of faith and terror which for Endo is the real scene of the action.

Those for whom modern Japanese fiction means the mandarin limpidities of Kawabata, or Mishima's hall of self-reflecting mirrors, may be surprised to discover in Endo a writer of straightforward technique in the service of a passionate conscience. Irrevocably enmeshed in Japanese culture, he is also by virtue of his religion irrevocably alienated from it. The writing in which he expresses again and again the nature of that double bind goes well beyond the parochial in its ramifications.

> *Geoffrey O'Brien, in a review of "The Samurai," in* The Village Voice, *Vol. XXVII, No. 46, November 16, 1982, p. 52.*

ALAN CHEUSE

In *Wonderful Fool,* the Western reader, like the Catholic missionaries who arrived in Japan in the 16th century to convert the Japanese to their faith, may at first find a lot of material that can be fitted into familiar paradigms. Gaston Bonaparte, a hulking, horse-faced Frenchman, a former seminarian and the "wonderful fool" of the title, certainly plays a role we've seen before—the innocent, virginal, redemptive and even Christ-like interloper who appears in the midst of a decadent but probably salvageable society. Gaston, the longtime pen pal of a young Tokyo clerk named Takamori, arrives by ship in postwar Japan to visit him and his sassy sister, Tomoe. Life is never the same for these polite but befuddled siblings or a number of other characters, including a French-educated hit man suffering from the last stages of tuberculosis, whom the novelist ironically names "Endo"; an avaricious land surveyor from the north called Kobayashi, who, as it turns out, is a war criminal with a great deal to hide; and even a stray dog the gentle Frenchman adopts.

Gaston slowly discovers his true motive for traveling fourth class on the good French ship Vietnam to the distant country he has known only through Takamori's letters. And while he's floundering in the vastness of Tokyo, sometimes in the company of his host and hostess, sometimes with his dog or alone, he becomes a vehicle for the novelist's satirical presentation of Westernized Japanese society. Whether he is in a car, the streets, a neighborhood restaurant, a brothel on the seamy side of town or a pachinko parlor, where rowdy young customers play a sort of horizontal pinball game, Gaston

gives Mr. Endo a chance to present the ordinary from a fresh and often comic point of view. Tomoe, for example, thinks that the foreign visitor might enjoy a cafe that specializes, the author tells us, "in a kind of ersatz French atmosphere," a place where Japanese Francophiles gather, "berets on their heads and French books tucked under their arms . . . to sigh over French *chansons.*"

As even this brief moment in Gaston's tour suggests, those of us who have no reading knowledge of Japanese can still enjoy the gawky pilgrim's progress against the backdrop of modern Japan in Francis Mathy's translation. But to read the novel as a sort of *Gulliver's Travels,* as a reader who goes through it too quickly might, would be to surrender to the lazy impulse of a tourist for whom the foreign must be rationalized and thus rendered harmless. Once Gaston becomes familiar with the strange country he is visiting, this mysteriously resonant novel reveals there are more things in Mr. Endo's fiction than Western philosophy or even the author's Catholicism can immediately explain.

We begin to get an inkling of this while Gaston roams the streets of the nighttime city, his gaze switching back and forth between the stars above and the passing crowds, yearning somehow to do something to alleviate the "many misfortunes and hardships and causes for grief scattered about the earth." Then he runs into Endo the gunman, a former classmate of Takamori's, who kidnaps him to use in an assassination plot with personal as well as historical dimensions and who is then stalked by Gaston, who goes along with the plot to try to foil it. In a narrative of great charm and intensity, the gunman heads north to the Tohoku region, "open country" as opposed to the cramped spaces of the city, and we follow him to the castle city of Yamagata, a place "of ancient camphor trees and the remains of old stone walls covered with moss, and old houses reminiscent of the samurai houses of former ages."

At this point the novel itself becomes "open country," its overt themes—the dialectic between East and West, Shintoism and Catholicism, tradition and modernity — continuing to unfold against the broad horizon evoked by its violent climax in the Big Swamp outside Yamagata. Here, legend has it, a samurai named Fujigoro quieted the waters stirred up by a dragon god and rescued a maiden who had appeared to him in a dream. And here Gaston, the Frenchman with the as yet to be realized vocation, thwarts the evil intentions of several lesser human beings and wins the affection of the fickle Tomoe. . . . Then he disappears from the swamp, possibly transformed into a lonely egret, "flying across the rice fields, and slowly and gracefully climbing into the blue sky." (pp. 13, 21)

> *Alan Cheuse, "Gaston Goes to Tokyo," in* The New York Times Book Review, *November 13, 1983, pp. 13, 21.*

MARY JO SALTER

Wonderful Fool, with its postwar setting and the bright tone of Francis Mathy's admirable translation, may seem to share little with last year's grim historical novel, *The Samurai.* But a postscript to that tale of Christian persecution in seventeenth-century Japan provides an oblique autobiographical link to *Wonderful Fool.* "I was the first Japanese to study abroad after the war, the first to travel to Europe," Endo remarks, suggesting an affinity with the samurai-protagonist and his fellow envoys to the New World. Endo, who converted to Catholicism in childhood and later traveled to Paris to study the French Catholic novelists, has explored time and again in his work the alienation of the Christian in Japan, and his sorrow that Christianity as the West knows it has not taken root in his country, which he repeatedly likens to a swamp. In *Wonderful Fool,* these familiar images and autobiographical details appear—indeed, the climactic action of the novel takes place in a swamp, and one of the principal characters, a former student of French embittered by the war and now a tubercular gangster, is actually called Endo.

But one might also see autobiography in the portrait that Endo, erstwhile foreigner in France, makes of the "wonderful fool" of the novel's title, Gaston Bonaparte, who shores up unexpectedly in Yokohama harbor. "Gas," as his former pen pal and first host, Takamori Higaki, rather foolishly nicknames him, is a descendant of Napoleon. Ancestry figures so large in the Japanese imagination that Takamori and his shrewish sister Tomoe are continually, comically mystified that anyone of Gaston's lineage could be so clumsy, naive, ill dressed, and ineffectual. Surely much of the humor of Gaston's initiation in Japanese ways—his wearing boots with a kimono, for instance, or mistaking a man's loincloth for a table napkin—must derive from the young Endo's embarrassing experiences in France. But Gaston, as is probably clear much earlier to a Western than a Japanese reader, is descended not only from his creator and from Napoleon but from another great conqueror, Christ, whose victories were also mysterious and unlikely.

The essence of Gaston's success as a character, and as an exemplar of Christian meekness and trust, is paradox. So cowardly he won't even defend himself in a fistfight, heroically he takes it upon himself to try to prevent Endo the gangster from killing three men, and in effect to save Endo's soul. Just as Christ's message is foreign to Japan (and by larger implication the entire modern world), his spokesman can barely speak Japanese—is little more, by his own admission, than someone to dog the heels of those who don't want him. And so he is likened, a little too obviously and often, to the street mongrel he picks up and names Napoleon. If it seems odd that we should accept Gaston as part Endo the novelist, part Christ, and part dog, he is also likened variously to a Sumo wrestler, a horse, a monkey, a potato, a popeyed goldfish, and a hippopotamus. He may, or may not, actually turn into an egret. For all the gravity of his mission, one might read Gaston not as a person at all, but as a protean cartoon character.

Curiously, Endo's least convincing character is his namesake, who vacillates between black-and-white villainousness consistent with the comic-strip tone of the novel and a heavy-handed psychoanalytical approach to his own failures: "I don't trust [people] because I've been made not to trust them," he confides to Gaston. Throughout the novel it is Takamori who serves more effectively as the novelist's pagan and instinctive interpreter of Gaston's apparent foolishness: "But for such a man, a man both weak and cowardly, to bear the burden of his weakness and struggle valiantly to live a beautiful life—that's what I call great," he proclaims in one such feat of insight. (It is a conviction familiar to readers of other novels by Endo and by his mutual admirer, Graham Greene.) Chotei Kawaii, a fortuneteller Gaston befriends, serves as another mouthpiece for Endo: "Purity of heart . . .

young Japanese have no use for it. . . . It's in the spirit that Japan is poor."

Ultimately it is the novelist's humor—slapstick, corny, irreverent—that permits him to moralize so openly, to instruct as he entertains. . . . The humor in *Wonderful Fool* is so broad, in fact, that one sometimes feels one is reading the screenplay of a screwball comedy. When Gaston, unaware of the Japanese custom of bowing, greets Tomoe by offering her his hand, she "was put out, but she could not very well refuse his gesture. So she handed him instead her handbag. He opened his large mouth and smiled with great joy." (A nice touch, that: in Endo's world view, it is the young Japanese who is crassly materialistic, the Westerner who is endowed with inscrutable spirituality.) (pp. 36-8)

Just as Endo has lamented throughout his oeuvre what Christianity has lost in translation to Japan, it may prove difficult for a Westerner—Christian or not—to be sure of reading Endo in the appropriate spirit. That Gaston considers himself an unofficial Christian missionary, for instance, so soon became obvious to me that it seemed virtually a premise of the novel; and yet when Endo makes this explicit at its end, he clearly expects his Japanese readers to experience a revelation. Japanese readers' lesser familiarity with Christian teachings may also allow them to sit still for the sermonizing with fresher interest. And yet as so often, and so fascinatingly, occurs in a Japanese novel, the faintly irritating hammering of certain themes and images is counter-balanced by an elusiveness of plot (does Gaston turn into an egret and fly away?) or character (is Endo the gangster perhaps not meant to be funny at all?) which, I suspect, a Japanese would understand or at least accept more comfortably. It is the awareness of ourselves as foreigners to Japanese sensibility in *Wonderful Fool* that doubles Endo's challenge to English readers, and that adds to this funny, offbeat novel yet another layer of depth. (p. 38)

Mary Jo Salter, "Jesus in Japan," in The New Republic, *Vol. 189, No. 26, December 26, 1983, pp. 36-8.*

LOUIS ALLEN

Stained Glass Elegies, a group of eleven short stories put together from two Japanese collections, deals with themes familiar from *Silence* and *The Samurai;* and others strangely and startlingly different. Most of the "heroes" are Catholics, not convinced believers, but hangers-on to an etiolated set of beliefs and practices inherited from their mothers.

"A Forty-Year Old Man" undergoes lung surgery and asks his wife to bring a myna bird to the hospital. He is visited by his sister-in-law, who has been his mistress and has aborted his child. He remembers going to confession to a foreign priest whose breath was as foul as the myna bird's cage; just as the cage's gridwork recalls that of the confessional. He tries to teach the bird "Good morning", but the bird cannot say it, any more than he could bring himself to confess the adultery and abortion. Egi, "The Despicable Bastard", lives in a Christian student dormitory in war-time Tokyo. A group of students visits a leper colony to entertain the patients. The visit ends with a baseball game in which Egi, who has a gash on his knee and is terrified of being infected, sprints to base and is halted in his tracks by the thought of colliding with the leper baseman. The leper sees what is going through his mind and says softly, "Go ahead. I won't touch you". In **"My Belongings"**, Suguro is baptized because his aunt thinks it's a good idea. Instead of shedding Christianity in adult life, he finds that his internal Christ takes on with him "the sunken grizzled face of middle age". Suguro, who has married unromantically, tells his wife he never really wanted her, and as he watches the tears streaming down her face he discovers behind it the face of "that Man". He will never leave her, and for the same reason never leave his Christ: "I have tormented you the same way I have tormented my wife. I'm not at all sure that I will not go on abusing you as I do her. But I will never cast you off utterly."

The stories are peopled with self-indulgent moral weaklings, afraid of physical pain, accustomed (like Endo himself) to massive surgery and long bouts in hospital, remorseful and Christ-haunted. They are not lapsed Catholics, they are inadequate, rather, and the sense of their inadequacy is pointed up by Endo's fascination with the Christian martyrs of sixteenth-century Japan, who stand out in sharp contrast to the timid apostates of their own day and the flaccid half-believers of the present.

The hero of **"Mothers"** has been brought up by a woman abandoned by her husband (there is autobiography here, too) and one day arrives home to find his mother dead. He had been delayed on the way, scrutinizing a friend's pornographic photos. He visits the remnants of early Catholic settlements on the fringes of Southern Japan, the islands off Kyushu where "hidden Christians" (*kakure Kirishitan*) survived persecution by outwardly conforming, but hid statues of the Virgin Mary behind the family Buddha and observed the Christian festivals as well as compulsorily attending the local temple. These people still live as outsiders. The local Catholics have little to do with them, and they shun newcomers, refusing to marry outside their own kind, and claim their brand of Catholicism to be the true one. But it is not their stubborn endurance which interests him; rather the fact that they are the offspring of apostates: "Like their ancestors, they cannot utterly abandon their faith; instead they live out their lives, consumed by remorse and dark quiet and shame."

Louis Allen, "Hangers-On," in The Times Literary Supplement, *No. 4256, October 26, 1984, p. 1223.*

JEAN HIGGINS

In and through historical and contemporary fictional characters, Endo's writings restage his own problematic encounter with Western culture and its conception of God. The encounter under question, then, will be presented here not in abstract analysis from one or the other specific perspective, but in and through the concrete life-experience of a Japanese convert to Christianity, whose creative works address themselves to the problem of understanding and reconciling the gulf between East and West, between the Japanese and Western understandings of self and God.

To be the *locus* of an encounter of this nature is to be vulnerable to psychological, spiritual and, by extension, physical suffering. Endo's life has been marked by these. It has also been molded by them. The experience of prolonged internal conflict between his Japanese and Western sensibilities, while painful, has nevertheless served him well as a creative writer. This "cross," as he has termed it, has hollowed him out, creating room within him for an understanding of similar suffer-

ings on the part of his fellow-Japanese. The works of Endo Shusaku speak out of life-experience. They speak to life-experience. (p. 414)

Before turning to Endo's works, a few words on a theme that intimately links *the* crucial event in his life—baptism—and his writings. That theme is betrayal. The theme of infidelity or betrayal which is found in all of Endo's serious works has its roots in his rote baptism as reflected upon in adult life. The betrayal first of all is of his mother. Not unlike Augustine's mother, Monica, Endo's mother bore her son twice: in physical and in spiritual birth. She had high hopes for the spiritual life of her son, which were not to be realized in her lifetime. For the sake of his mother, and in sincere effort to fulfill her hopes, Endo goes through the motions of being a believer. But his heart is not in it. In this he feels he has betrayed his mother. Yet despite his betrayal, he feels the presence and love of his departed mother as a constant reality. He reads this as her forgiveness.

The betrayal, secondly, is of Christ. The soullessness of his baptismal commitment haunted Endo increasingly as he matured. Yet paradoxically it was this very soullessness, reflected upon, that kept Christ constantly in and on his mind. A spent-faced Christ is met again and again in Endo's works in the image of Love constantly betrayed yet constant in his forgiveness of the betrayer, even of the apostate. Concern for the weak, which is characteristic of Endo's writings, arises out of his personal sense of infidelity and betrayal (whether or not such a sense is justified). It is this that urges Endo to let the weaklings of the faith, the rejected apostates of the age of persecution in Japan, come to voice in his historical novels. The same sense draws him to the *kakure* (crypto-Christians) whom persecution forced into a double life of public denial and penitential private affirmation of Christ and Christianity. And, above all, this experience and understanding of human weakness drives him to question the image of a judgmental, paternal Christian God which earlier and later Western missionaries had brought to Japan.

While still a student at Keio University, Endo published an essay entitled **"God and gods,"** in which he discusses the opposition between the "pantheistic blood of the Japanese" and the "monotheistic blood of the Christian West." After a three-year stay in France, Endo returns strengthened in his conviction of the incompatibility between the cultures of Japan and the West. In **"Christianity and I"** he speaks of the two cultures as totally other, as *boko* (concave) and *deko* (convex). The Japanese *boko* world is blissfully unconcerned with the existence or non-existence of God. The Western *deko* world is eternally preoccupied with God, whether in affirmation or denial of his existence. The implications of these two stances with respect to the image of self and world clearly indicated the unbridgeable gulf which Endo knew well from personal experience. This "gulf between the Japanese on the one hand and Christianity and Europe on the other" becomes theme and focus of Endo's writings.

From 1955 through 1966, all of Endo's serious works (*junbungaku*) treat in one way or another of this issue. Setting, theme, and character of the novels of this period are so constructed as to bring Japanese and Western (Christian) worldviews into confrontation. As if to emphasize the personal nature of the theme he is pursuing, Endo employs images drawn mainly from the human body: eyes, skin, blood, and, above all, face.

The novel *Kūroi hito (Yellow Man)*, written in 1955, brings into contrast the sensibilities of the "yellow" and "white" protagonists—Chiba, a Japanese Christian student, and Father Durand, a fallen French priest—particularly with respect to consciousness of sin. In this story, Endo makes skillful use of the imagery of eyes as mirrors of the soul. The leaden, impassive, expressionless eyes of the yellow man create problems for the Westerner's understanding of the Oriental, even when both are Christian. These eyes reflect a threefold insensitivity to those issues which are of utmost concern to the white man: sensitivity to God, to sin, and to death. The murky color of the yellow man's skin likewise suggests an imperviousness, an apathy to these three issues which plague the conscience of the Westerner in general and the conscience of this fallen priest in particular. Chiba, confessing to another French priest, says, "a yellow man like me has absolutely no experience of anything so profound and exaggerated as the consciousness of sin which you Caucasians have."

In *Nanji mo mata (And You, Too)*, written in 1965, Endo dramatizes the encounter with the West of a Japanese professor of literature doing research in France. The professor, Tanaka, has set himself the task of understanding and assimilating the alien culture of Christian Europe. Like his friend, Mukaizaka, who has returned home to Japan because of poor health, Tanaka had at first been impressed with certain similarities between European and Japanese culture. This comforting illusion gradually becomes disillusion. Depressed and oppressed by the unassimilable weight of tradition-laden European culture, he comes to share the view of Mukaizaka "that there is after all an unbridgeable chasm between the cathedral of Chartres and the Horyuji temple in Nara."

Tanaka himself falls ill, defeated in body and spirit by the impossibility of bridging the gulf. As his ailing friend Mukaizaka wrote to him of his own lost battle, "It isn't surprising that I should be worn down, since I tried to make my own in one or two years the culture that this country has taken two thousand years to build up. Tanaka, this illness is the pitiful outcome of my losing my fight . . ." The striking image of blood transfusion is used in this novel to underline the incompatibility of the two cultures: "the blood that produced the two was of altogether different type . . . We are unable to receive a blood transfusion from a donor with a blood type that differs from our own."

During this same period, the image of "mudswamp" is a frequent theme. It symbolizes the threefold insensitivity to God, sin and death; the moral and spiritual apathy of which Endo wrote in *Yellow Man.* He speaks of Japan as a swamp that eats away at the roots of Christianity, making it impossible for that faith ever to flourish in Japan. In his early works the "mudswamp" appears unconquerable. But as Endo gradually progresses in his understanding of the conflicting cultural mentalities, he constructs novels in which a solution to the "mudswamp" mentality is at least indicated.

In his half-in-fun, wholly-in-earnest novel *Wonderful Fool (Obakasan)*, published in 1959, Endo introduces a Westerner as a Christ-figure of sorts. In and through the profound compassion and self-sacrificing love of this "fool," certain "swamp-dwellers" he encounters in the Tokyo area are led to an awareness of their moral and spiritual insensitivity. The possibility of reform is opened up. The closing scene of the novel takes place in a real swamp where a murderous criminal (named Endo!) is moved to repentance by the persistent and forgiving love of the "fool." In the novel *Hechima kun*

(Mr. Gourd), 1963, Endo turns the tables and presents a Japanese Christ-figure, another wonderful fool who manages to communicate with some of those caught fast in the swamp. Through love and compassion he too arouses in them some awareness of their morally apathetic condition.

The "mudswamp" mentality is found also in *The Sea and the Poison (Umi to dokuyaku)*, published in 1958. This novel is based on an actual incident of the use of a captured American airman for scientific experimentation involving vivisection. While Endo here highlights the absence of a sense of sin, indicating thereby the absence of a sense of an Absolute, he nevertheless portrays a growing awareness of guilt in the novel's protagonist, a doctor involved in the experiment. One of the characters speaking of delivery from moral apathy and insensitivity, says, "We would have to give the name of God to anything that could set [us] free [from those forces of evil]."

In novel after novel from 1955 through 1965, Endo resembles a scientist at work experimenting, puzzle-solving, constructing one model after another in his quest for a solution to the problem of the incompatibility of Japanese and Western cultural—particularly religious—sensibilities. It is of interest to note that the emphasis in this period is on the image of the self, on the moral-religious characteristics of the "white" and the "yellow" man in a universe with or without God. Of the image of God, little is said.

Yet it is precisely on the basis of new insight into the image of the Christian God that the ten-year quest for an understanding of conflicting sensibilities finds partial resolution. The novel, *Silence* . . . successfully identifies the root of the problem: a Western, paternalistic image of God, unacceptable to Japanese religious psychology.

Silence is an historical novel set in the seventeenth century, toward the end of the period of Japan's first encounter with Christianity (1549-1650). This setting affords Endo the possibility of observing from a distance and recreating from a twentieth-century perspective the first clashes of Western and Japanese worldviews. The theme of this book is the shifting image of self and God in the mind and heart of a dedicated young Jesuit missionary. The hero, Rodrigues, has entered Japan at literal risk to life and limb in disregard of the Tokugawa regime's prohibition against foreign missionaries. His concern is twofold: the plight of the priestless Japanese Christians, and the unbelievable report of the apostasy under torture of his revered theology professor of seminary days, Christovao Ferreira.

The story is told in the form of a journey, both physical and spiritual. The physical journey takes Rodrigues initially to a hiding-place in the mountains and to restricted though joyous ministry to the Christian peasants. Before long, near-discovery demands flight. His physical journey follows a pattern of gradual descent from mountain, to lowlands, to sea-level, and, finally, to prostration in a confined prison cell. His spiritual journey follows a similar pattern of descent; from exalted sense of self, of mission, and of triumphal God, down through the valley of diminishing spiritual strength and questioning of the silence of God, to the final betrayal of his priestly self, his faith, and his God, in humbling apostasy.

Silence dramatizes two models of understanding self and deity. The first is found in what we may call the "Rodrigues of the West," the young missionary who comes to Japan with dedicated aggressiveness, bearing in heart and mind the image of a transcendent God of power and might. The image of Christ constantly before his mind's eye is that of the risen Christ, serene in conquest; a Christ of glory, whose example calls for heroism in his followers, for fidelity unto death, even in martyrdom, if such must be. Rodrigues' God is a judgmental God. (pp. 417-21)

The second model of understanding self and deity, found in the "Rodrigues of the East"—transformed through exposure to the spiritual climate of Japan—presents not an exalted but a kenotic God. The face of the *fumie* (the bronze plaque upon which Christians were obliged to trample when renouncing their faith) reveals a weak and powerless Christ who shows himself understanding of the weak, who has compassion with the betrayer, who knows well the pain in the foot of the apostate who tramples upon his face. (p. 421)

A glorious martyrdom, so desirable to the "Rodrigues of the West," is of no account in the light of this new image of God. When Rodrigues, at Christ's invitation, apostatizes in order to spare Japanese Christians further torture, he renounces all that was previously meaningful to him: his mission, his priesthood, his membership in the Church, his membership in his own religious order, his good name, his Western self-image, his Western conception of God. He, too, practices kenosis.

What Rodrigues has found, after physical and spiritual anguish, is what Endo sought in all his own years of probing: an image of the Christian God which was not judgmentally paternal but compassionately maternal; an image, in other words, acceptable to the Japanese, responding to "what is most essential in all Japanese religion, devotion to Mother."

Silence concerns itself with the theological question of the image of God, Eastern and Western. Yet it does so without dogmatizing or indoctrinating. To register the shift that takes place in the hero's conception of God, Endo employs with remarkable skill the image of "face." From serene, powerful and heavenly to harried, weak and earthy, the face of Christ tells the tale of Western transcendental triumphalism and Eastern all-assimilating, all-embracing immanence. (pp. 421-22)

[*Silence*] definitively locates the heart of the problem of gulf in the lack of an image of God which speaks to the religious psychology of the Japanese. *Silence* also provides a rough sketch of what Endo considers an acceptable image. The God that emerges in *Silence* is clearly a God more of act than of word, but act that is expressive of quiet, meek, co-suffering rather than power and might. Endo, in fact, makes his point in paradox: the power of Christ lies in his very powerlessness, his fullness in his nothingness.

But can Endo's Christ of the *fumie* be justified from the sources? On completion of *Silence,* Endo undertakes intensive study of the New Testament with the intention of uncovering the true face of Christ. He explores the Christian sources to convince himself and his readers that the image he sketched is a true picture of the Jesus of the gospels. In the results of his study, *A Life of Jesus,* Endo shows that the essential experience of Jesus' first followers was that Christ was for the weak, that he understood and forgave the betrayer. After Christ's death, what moved his disciples to unshakeable faith was the realization that even though they had betrayed him, he still loved and accepted them as his own. (pp. 423-24)

In the writing of *Silence* Endo made the journey with Rodrigues from image to image, from face to face. With the com-

pletion of *Silence,* the gulf begins to close. The research and writing of *A Life of Jesus* assures him that he can be both Japanese and Christian without internal warring. But Endo's "anguish of an alien" was not at an end.

Endo's most recent novel, *The Samurai* (1982), carries his search one step further toward mature completion. *The Samurai,* like *Silence,* is a spiritual journey framed within an actual historical journey. The traveller this time is not a Westerner journeying to and in Japan, but a Japanese samurai travelling West as envoy to kings, lords and prelates of the Christian Europe, and being received royally by them. For mercenary reasons, the samurai agrees to be baptized, espousing himself spiritually to a "lord" who appeared anything but lordly: ". . . ugly and emaciated . . . with outstretched arms and drooping head." To the samurai this "lord" was "much like the vagabonds who sometimes came begging in the marshland" back home. His baptism was a mere formality, and he thought little of it while being heralded and hosted in Europe.

During the samurai's absence, the tides turned in Japan. His glorious mission as envoy to the West is now a liability. Japan has closed its doors to the West and is vehemently engaged in the persecution of Christians. The samurai returns to a life lived under a cloud, and out of the depths he begins to understand the "lordship" of Christ; he begins to see that the beauty of this emaciated man lay in his life and co-suffering with the weak and wretched. Though he had not known it at the time, the samurai had, indeed, met a king in Europe, a king who took espousal seriously and would never abandon one who bore his name. In *The Samurai* we have a Japanese hero, baptized without conviction, who gradually internalizes his faith in a thoroughly Japanese way around an image of God like the one Endo provided in *Silence* and defended in *A Life of Jesus.*

The samurai's journey is Endo's spiritual journey come full circle. The Japanese Endo, in and through his serious writings, restaged his problematic encounter with Western culture and its God-image and arrived at peaceful resolution. What was originally an alien religion put upon him like a suit of clothes has been personally appropriated. The Western suit which his creative writing retailored is Christianity, or, more precisely, Christ himself, who will not be discarded but humbly permits reshaping of his image to conform to the religious sensibilities of all believers. Endo's conviction all along had been that Christianity did not belong only to Europe. In *The Samurai,* he has a Japanese convert to Christianity say: "I have finally been able to grasp an image of Him that conforms to my own heart"—Endo's own sentiments. (pp. 425-26)

Jean Higgins, "The Inner Agon of Endo Shusaku," in Cross Currents, *Vol. XXXIV, No. 4, Winter, 1984-85, pp. 414-26.*

JOHN B. BRESLIN, S. J.

God and death, the ineffable and the irrevocable, haunt these stories [in *Stained Glass Elegies*] as they do the more well-known novels of Shusaku Endo. . . .

Endo published a collection called *Elegies* in 1965 and another called *Eleven Stained-Glass Segments* in 1979. The twin spectres of war and disease hover over the former, while in the latter contemporary experience merges with accounts of the martyrdom of early Japanese Christians. But as a composite title, **Stained Glass Elegies** has the merit of revealing that God and death are not so neatly divisible in Endo's universe as the original titles might suggest.

For the martyrs, death in great agony presented the ultimate trial of their belief in the Christian God. Endo's 20th-century characters—believers, half-believers, and non-believers—are alternately fascinated and repelled by accounts of the martyrs' suffering. "Yet he could not rid himself of the feeling that the martyrs were far removed from his own life. Only those, like them, who were strong and specially appointed could carry out such superhuman acts. They lived on a higher plane than the one where he subsisted." Ironically, the young student who makes these reflections is at that very moment standing on a former execution ground next to a despised European monk (known as "Mouse"). By the end of the story ("Fudano-Tsuji"), the man makes two discoveries at a class reunion years later: first, that Mouse had sacrificed his life to save another man at Dachau, and, second, that heroism flows out of love, not physical stamina, and is as uncommon in the 20th century as in the 17th. . . .

This quest for heroism in the face of pain and death, like the quest for God, takes place in these stories in most unpromising circumstances: the tedium of hospital rooms, the depression of wartime cities, the isolation of mountain villages. Hating themselves for their lack of courage or love or both, Endo's "heroes" find consolation only in the sad-eyed creatures around them: a myna bird, a dog. But when the sorrowing eyes belong to human beings, they trouble as well as console.

In **"Mothers,"** the most successful fusion of the era of persecution and the present, the main character, a writer, travels to a remote island to visit descendants of 17th-century Christian apostates (*kakure*), who have maintained their own idiosyncratic and syncretistic version of Catholicism quite distinct from that of the Roman Church. What he finds is a religion built on shame that focuses devotion on the merciful Mother of God who offers hope of winning pardon from a stern Father for their infidelity. In counterpoint to this theological theme, the writer thinks and dreams regularly on the island of his own mother. Gradually he realizes that the image he has formed of her ("with her hands joined in front of her, watching me from behind with a look of gentle sorrow in her eyes") derives not from actual memories of her but from a statue of the *Mater Dolorosa* she kept in their house. . . .

All the sad eyes of these stories—of birds and animals, of lepers and draftees—find their origin in the sorrowing glance of the Mother, even the eyes of her son, "that Man," as Endo's alter ego, the novelist Suguro, is driven to call God in **"My Belongings."** This is a vision of religion, and of human life, as far away from "happy talk" theology as could be imagined. Significantly, the most positive statement in these stories (and the last) belongs to a man who has known great suffering personally. Fr. Bosch, an aging French priest imprisoned and tortured in Japan during World War II, and thus a modern analogue of the early missionary martyrs, turns aside his former students' concern for his health by saying, "I only feel pain in the winter when it is cold. When spring comes, I am fine again. That is the way it always is." If Endo's thoughts are never far from Good Friday and the *Mater Dolorosa*, it is comforting that—in his more recent stories at least—he is not unaware of Easter.

John B. Breslin, S. J., "Shusaku Endo: Martyrs and Moralists," in Book World—The Washington Post, *June 23, 1985, p. 10.*

A. N. WILSON

W. H. Auden defined the novelist as one who must, "in his own weak person, if he can / Dully put up with all the wrongs of man." Such qualities of unsentimental sympathy, though, are rare in any but novelists of the highest rank. Shusaku Endo has them in full measure.

In **"The Day Before,"** one of the 11 short stories in **Stained Glass Elegies,** the narrator is having an argument with a Catholic priest. Why did Christ give the sop to the traitor, Judas, and say, "That thou doest, do quickly"? Why didn't He stop Judas from perpetrating this act of terrible betrayal? The priest replies that Judas was an old friend of Christ and that in His human nature Christ hates being betrayed. But the narrator's view is different. "That thou doest, do quickly" is not really a command. "It's like He's saying, 'You're going to do this anyway, I can't stop you, so go ahead and do it.' . . . Christ knew all the desperate acts of men."

This exchange lies very close to the heart of Mr. Endo's portrayal of the human condition in his novels and stories. Very often merciless to himself, he has a sort of shrugging acceptance of imperfection in others. It leads him to select strange models for sympathy and identification. In the story **"Despicable Bastard,"** the title refers to himself. But he is inspired to identify himself with a group of lepers who manage to turn their appalling degradation into something like strength.

The point is made most vividly in the best story in this volume, **"Mothers."** (In fact, it is one of the best things Mr. Endo has ever written.) Two things are going on in this tale. On the one hand, the narrator is thinking about his own mother. When she is betrayed by her husband and left to bring up her child alone, she becomes almost fanatical in her Catholic devotion. The narrator, looking back, is wistfully grateful to her, but during childhood and adolescence the rigor of her religion was almost intolerable. It led him to form deliberately an unsuitable friendship with a boy whose father ran a brothel. The fact that the pleasures enjoyed with this companion—surreptitious visits to the movies or furtive glimpses of photographs of naked women—were mild in their sinfulness did not and does not minimize his guilt about the pain they inflicted on his mother. She died of heart failure, knowing he was with this boy. As it happened, her death occurred at the moment her son was peering at some markedly explicit pornographic material. . . .

Mr. Endo's art always reminds us that certainties and loyalties are more fluid than we should perhaps like them to be. But in exploring the limits of loyalty, he does not forsake it. He remains firmly Catholic in spite of guilt and doubt, and for all his divided feelings about East and West, he remains firmly and mysteriously Japanese. In the end, his most impressive quality as a moralist is his silence.

In **"Old Friends,"** the last story in this volume, the narrator attends the anniversary mass of a friend who has been a priest for 25 years. He and a few Christian friends look back to the days of the war, when their fellow citizens regarded them as traitors for following a Western religion. Among those friends is a French priest who alone of these suffered torture in a Japanese concentration camp. He survives, still French, still in Japan, still a priest. The narrator has just returned from Europe, where he met a victim of Auschwitz who told him she would never forgive her tormentors—it was an impossibility. But the priest is silent about his sufferings. We do not know if, like the Auschwitz victim, he feels unable to stop hating or whether he has achieved a serene forgiveness. He is silent. For us and for Mr. Endo, this silence emphasizes the extraordinary gulfs that would have to be spanned if the word "forgiveness" had any meaning, gulfs even larger than those that divide Japan from the West or our own generation from that which suffered in the war.

A. N. Wilson, "Firmly Catholic and Firmly Japanese," in The New York Times Book Review, *July 21, 1985, p. 21.*

LOUIS ALLEN

Scandal has echoes of Camus's *La Chute* (and also of *The Ordeal of Gilbert Pinfold*), not for the first time in Endō's work. Suguro, a Japanese Catholic novelist in his mid-sixties, whose creative life has been devoted to exploring the Christian past in Japan, is pestered by a journalist who is convinced he has seen him in the shadier parts of Tokyo, engaged in highly un-Christian pursuits. A girl artist at a prize-giving ceremony says the same, and claims to have painted his portrait in a sleazy hotel. The portrait is recognizably Suguro, but the face is sordid and cruel. In pursuit of this Jekyll-and-Hyde schizophrenia (or what he takes to be an unscrupulous double), Suguro makes contact with the group of street portraitists. One of them, Motoko, has a friend, Mrs Naruse, with whom her relationship is not merely lesbian but sado-masochistic. Fearful yet fascinated, Suguro is drawn into the world of Mrs Naruse's erotic confidences. Her husband has committed atrocities as a war-time soldier, and she derives sexual ecstasy from his narration of them, just as Motoko derives hers from being strangled. A masterful and elegantly attractive woman, with instincts of loving kindness, Mrs Naruse gives Suguro a Life of Gilles de Rais, strips the Christian surface from the bewildered novelist, and shows him that the man he takes to be his double is himself, and that neither his Christianity nor his art is capable of shielding him from the volcanic magma or "rage" which is hidden in every human being. It is not merely sex, but the urge to possess and destroy, ecstasy pursuing pain pursuing death.

Side by side with this revelation of his inner being runs Suguro's life with his tender, solicitous wife. They make a trip to Nagasaki, whose early Christian community has been Suguro's source of literary inspiration (as, of course, it has been Endō's). But even here, even in her company, Suguro is aware of the horrifying link in his mind between Motoko's sexually motivated suicide, the atrocity-induced ecstasies of Mrs Naruse and the tortures of the persecuted Catholics in sixteenth-century Kyushu. The sure grip Suguro thought he had on his world is gradually prised loose. His relation to his wife is falsified, and his art is seen to be built on self-deception. He realizes that "sin" and the salvation which can arise from it are somehow shallow and superficial things. The reality is the magma which erupts and alters everyone's personal landscape for ever. . . .

There are many autobiographical traces in *Scandal,* and the name Suguro is one Endō has used before when he has needed a figure mildly or apathetically clinging to vestiges of an etiolated Catholicism. But the shift of the central figure from his

foundation of custom and intellectual comfort is stronger here. It has links with a Lawrentian life-force, and with de Sade's unleashing of appetite. But what strikes in *Scandal* is the awareness that this volcanic power which appropriates the individual is not the trite Christian "sin" (something containable), or even the sense of betrayal so deeply etched in *Silence* or *The Samurai,* but an irresistible flood of evil, a demon rather than a daemon, which leaves Suguro's past life like a pale abandoned shadow.

Louis Allen, "Stigma and Magma," in The Times Literary Supplement, *No. 4439, April 29-May 5, 1988, p. 471.*

J. THOMAS RIMER

Shusaku Endo, long a novelist involved in chronicling the unsettled state of the Japanese soul, past and present, [in *Scandal*] presents one of his most absorbing views to date of human spiritual darkness.

Some of Endo's most successful novels, such as *Silence* and *The Samurai,* dealt in their own ways with some of the same themes now taken up in *Scandal.* In these earlier books the historical trappings, with their exoticism, led to a certain romanticism, at least for Western readers. *Scandal* provides no such agreeably distancing frame of reference. Here Endo's explicit reference points—Dante's *Divine Comedy,* Thomas Mann's *Death in Venice*—show just how much the modern Japanese milieu has become our own. . . .

Endo is a superb storyteller. If the pace of the novel suggests a detective story, the concerns that drive it are far more spiritual, and considerably more frightening. In one sense, the subject of the novel is death. At the beginning of the book, Suguro knows that he is not well. By the end of this macabre adventure, he knows that he is lucky to be alive at all. The proximity of death forces him to a relentless self-scrutiny, one that allows him to grasp at last the difference between that bureaucracy of sin charted by all organized religions (in this case, the Catholic church) and the real, animal evil that, for Endo, lies at the heart, and in the guts, of every human being. (p. 3)

Finding, sensing the real truth, is one of the oldest virtues in the classical Japanese literary canon. This same venerable search surfaces here, even if Christ and Freud, both quoted, have replaced Buddha. The questions raised about the nature of man and what he can know about himself place *Scandal* in a line of strong descent from many a classic pilgrim's diary.

However serious Endo's concerns, it would be a mistake to find his cautionary tale merely grim. *Scandal* is filled with wry observations of contemporary Japanese society. Some of his minor characters, ranging from a pious priest in Nagasaki to a buck-toothed nurse in the hospital, are sketched with a highly deft and loving pen. Nevertheless, Endo is resolved to tell the truth as he sees it. And the truth hurts. That is surely why *Scandal* is so painful, and ultimately so enlightening, to read. (p. 13)

J. Thomas Rimer, "Endo's Divine Comedy," in Book World—The Washington Post, *August 14, 1988, pp. 3, 13.*

CHARLES NEWMAN

"None of you has any idea how difficult it is for a Christian to write fiction in Japan" is the silent assertion of the distinguished novelist Suguro, as he receives his latest award at the age of 65. "Within every sin," says the critic who introduces him, "lurks the desire of men to find a way of escaping from the suffocating lives we lead today," sardonically implying that the theme of salvation may produce interesting writing even while it posits an unknowable, troublesome foreign god and a concept of sin at once alien and shopworn. That such themes appear early in Shusaku Endo's *Scandal* is hardly surprising. They are familiar ones in his earlier stories and novels. And it is significant that the aging writer in *Scandal* is, like Mr. Endo, a man of many literary honors and, like him, a Roman Catholic and the author of a life of Christ.

The harmony Suguro feels he has finally achieved between his life and work is shattered at this reception, however. A drunken woman accosts him, accusing the venerated writer of frequenting the brothel district of Tokyo. In fact, she tells him a portrait of his degenerate self now hangs in a gallery there. And a journalist, Kobari, a dabbler in literature and Marxism who is intent on exposing the hypocrisy of this Catholic convert and celebrated artist, forces Suguro to pursue this allegation.

Suguro suffers all the doubts of the established contemporary writer, equally bemused by critics who reduce his work to a "position" and fans who find his fiction a prescription for living. Only the writer knows his ideas are neither a priori events nor post hoc justifications of action; they are simply the residue, an afterimage, of his struggle with his work, and only the writer knows how far he has fallen short of the mark. In short, art is religious, but it is not religion.

Suguro's quest for what he supposes is an impostor takes him through the seamier parts of Tokyo, where among "blatant imitations of European and American avant-garde works" he does in fact find his portrait, a lewd likeness distinctly at odds with the face he shows to his audience or his family. The trail Suguro leaves looks very much to Kobari like corroboration that the face of the portrait and that of the writer are one and the same, whereas Suguro suspects they are wholly different but somehow otherwise entangled—a nice juxtaposition of the journalistic and novelistic minds. And when Suguro befriends a teeny-bopper, Mitsu, and discovers that his very loathing of her nature actually arouses him sexually, he begins to realize that the dirty old man of the portrait is no stranger.

This is confirmed to him by the best-drawn character in the novel, a middle-aged widow, Mme. Naruse, who lives an openly double life. By day she is a saintly volunteer nurse at a children's hospital, by night a devotee of extreme sadomasochism, and the lover of the woman who painted Suguro's portrait and later commits suicide. . . . Eventually, Mme. Naruse arranges for Suguro to meet his double. Through the peephole of a brothel room, he watches his "ghost" defile a drugged Mitsu. Then the line between reality and illusion blurs. Does he merge with his double, the erotic impulse merging with the murderous?

Kobari has followed him, of course. As Suguro and Mitsu leave the hotel, he photographs them, and Suguro's publisher is obliged to buy the negative to save face. As the certainty of death approaches, Suguro is left with a knowledge more complex than that of a moral hypocrite and more human than that of a writer who had commonly confused the esthetic with the spiritual. For his acceptance of the neat dualism of sin and salvation has blinded Suguro to the possibility of multiple selves and allowed him to avoid the irreducible evil at the core of his own character, the evil that is in fact an essential component of his adopted religion. (pp. 15-16)

It is interesting to note that the very worst writing always has to do with the description of interior states, surely suggesting problems of linguistic and cultural transmission, but the effect is to empty what is billed as an intellectual psychological thriller of both psychology and intellect.

Nevertheless, the central problem of the novel can hardly be attributed to the translator when the narrator apparently believes that the debate between appearance and reality was begun only in the last few years, and insists on illustrating his protagonist's every insight with banal citations of the most obvious Western classics—Dante on that well-worn path lost in the wood, King Lear on age and rage, Poe on perversity and Baudelaire on madness. One might think this is a parody of literary intellectuals, or perhaps a satire on the Japanese desire for things Western, but not after we have to endure a Japanese Freudian analyst giving us, in case we have missed the double motif, a full disquisition on the doppelgänger phenomenon and other out-of-body experiences (not to mention the use of a PEN club executive meeting as a dramatic setting, which admittedly is something of a first). Kobari is a shallow fellow, but one can sympathize with his aim—to expose "the epitome of the pseudo-literati in Japan."

There are serious and strange themes in this murky suspense novel—a committed Christianity without a sufficient sense of evil, a doctrinaire Freudianism that denies any therapeutic function to the superego and a naïve attempt to order the world in literary terms. But *Scandal,* in its English version, can only finally invite a querulous incredulity. (p. 16)

Charles Newman, "A Portrait of the Artist as a Dirty Old Man," in The New York Times Book Review, *August 28, 1988, pp. 15-16.*

Louise Erdrich

1954-

American novelist, poet, and short story writer.

In her fiction and poetry, Erdrich draws upon her Chippewa heritage to examine complex familial and sexual relationships among midwestern Native Americans and their conflicts with white communities. Her comically eccentric characters attain mythic stature as they struggle to overcome isolation, abandonment, and exploitation. Erdrich's evocation of a particular American region through multiple narrative voices and striking imagery has prompted comparison to William Faulkner's creation of Yoknapatawpha County, Mississippi. Jean Strouse asserted: "Louise Erdrich has been populating a specific place—the Chippewa Indian reservation and its North Dakota-Minnesota surround—with characters as strong and original, as funny and tough, as furious and vivid as any who have recently graced the American literary landscape. Her sure sense of the way people think and talk keeps it hard to remember she is making them all up, and her lithe, athletic prose makes wildly improbable events seem as natural as the weather."

Erdrich's first published volume, *Jacklight* (1984), is a collection of poems that garnered praise for infusing ordinary American Westerners and everyday situations with mythic qualities. Her initial novel, *Love Medicine* (1984), for which Erdrich won the National Book Critics Circle Award, gathers fourteen interconnected stories related by seven different members of the Kashpaw and Lamartine families of the Turtle Mountain Chippewa community. Although several reviewers expressed confusion with Erdrich's use of alternating narrators, others commended the lyric quality of her prose, which emphasizes the beauty and universality of the Native American experience.

In *The Beet Queen* (1986), Erdrich continues her portrait of the Turtle Mountain Chippewa but shifts her focus to the community outside the reservation. In this novel, a woman orphaned in childhood settles into middle age in the small fictional town of Argus, North Dakota, while her brother, a traveling salesman, repeats the familial pattern of manipulation and abandonment before fathering Dot, a character in *Love Medicine*. While faulting the conclusion of *The Beet Queen* as contrived, most critics lauded Erdrich's humorous yet powerful portrait of misshapen lives and unfulfilled relationships. Dorothy Wickenden observed: "[Erdrich] has conveyed unforgettably the mixture of the prosaic and the uncanny that informs the lives of dreamers and plodders alike. And she has endowed all of her characters with an idiosyncratic trait that both isolates them and allows them to survive: the energy and ingenuity to grapple with the terrors of intimacy."

In Erdrich's recent novel, *Tracks* (1988), a Chippewa elder and an abusive young female of white and Indian heritage relate the exploits of Fleur Pillager, a destructive yet magical woman who is an ancestor of several characters from *Love Medicine*. Critics generally praised Erdrich for a balanced presentation of the struggle of Native Americans to reconcile their culture with the encroaching white world. Jean Strouse commented: "[Ms. Erdrich passes] along not only everything

her characters know, but the story of the stories as well. Giving life and shape and sense to what's happened, she lets the designs spring clear."

(See also *CLC,* Vol. 39 and *Contemporary Authors,* Vol. 114.)

CAROLYNE WRIGHT

Obscurity is emphatically not one of the traits of Louise Erdrich's first volume of poetry [*Jacklight*]. Her work is so clearly rooted in its setting and milieu as to enable her to achieve access to the invisible: the realm of myth, which must always be grounded in the actual and tangible. Erdrich's mythmaking is based on the lore of her Native American and German immigrant origins. To attain to the enduring and universal via the minute particulars of individual and community experience has been a stated aim of poetry written in English since Wordsworth's Preface to the *Lyrical Ballads*. Erdrich's poetry responds to this aim by finding in the patterns of the visible world of nature and the received legacy of family and tribal history a vast fund of material, and she transmutes its wealth to her own unique vision. (pp. 120-21)

[Erdrich] does not concentrate solely on the Native American branch of her family; she devotes the book's longest section to a series of dramatic monologues in the voices of her (paternal?) grandmother, Mary Kröger (**"The Butcher's Wife"**), and Mary's neighbors, would-be lovers, and the other Mary—Mary Kroll, her "mislaid twin," who was Otto the butcher's second wife after the first Mary died. The series has a strong narrative impetus that carries us from Mary Kröger's girlhood to the widowhood of Mary Kroll, and it presents to us characters with memorable names (**"Step-and-a-Half Waleski"**) and stories (**"Leonard Commits Redeeming Adulteries With All the Women in Town"**). But for all their earthy sensuality, these personae are able to attain to the stature of Teutonic myth. . . . (p. 121)

Erdrich also tells, or retells, versions of her Chippewa ancestors' stories—of the **"Strange People"** (the antelope); the evanescent **"Whooping Cranes"**; the dreaded **"Windigo"**; and, in a delightfully humorous series of short prose narratives, the life of Potchikoo, the potato boy. In all his impetuosity and lustiness, Potchikoo embodies the humorous vein of Native American storytelling. . . . Erdrich also treats contemporary reservation life with humor and no-nonsense compassion, as in her portrayals of Raymond Twobears, of teenage braves watching a racist shoot-'em-up Western at a drive-in, of girl runaways from the Indian boarding school:

> Home's the place we head for in our sleep.
> Boxcars stumbling north in dreams
> don't wait for us. We catch them on the run.
> The rails, old lacerations that we love,
> shoot parallel across the face and break
> just under Turtle Mountains. Riding scars
> you can't get lost. Home is the place they cross.

                    (**"Indian Boarding School: the Runaways"**)

With its largely pentameter line, its series of short declarations, its evocations of emotive touchstones—home, sorrow, dreams—its landscape of isolation and regret, the poem is reminiscent of the work of the late Richard Hugo.

The occasional tendency to write beyond its energy or ending, and thus to dilute a poem's strength, is one fortunately minor liability of this poet's narrative and mythic orientation; and *Jacklight* on the whole is one of the most refreshing and absorbing new books to appear recently. (pp. 121-22)

> *Carolyne Wright, "Women Poets: Seven New Voices from Small Presses," in* Northwest Review, *Vol. 23, No. 1, 1985, pp. 118-33.*

VERNON SHETLEY

Louise Erdrich's rough-hewn poems view the American West they inhabit under two contrary aspects: as wild, daemonic nature or as landscape of human loneliness, whose physical correlatives are on the one hand forest and plain, and on the other roadside and small town. In the former mode, she seeks what was once called the "deep image," a logically inexplicable but archetypally resonant cluster of language meant to liberate an elementally powerful emotional response. While her reading has probably included W. S. Merwin and Galway Kinnell, she may have gone back beyond those practitioners of the style to some of its sources;

the quest for the deep image was significantly informed by the poetry of oral cultures, and Erdrich (as the book jacket [to *Jacklight*] informs the reader) "belongs to the Turtle Mountain Band of Chippewa." Erdrich achieves some fine, spooky effects; **"The Woods,"** with chilling terseness, rewrites the Daphne myth in the terms of a Native American animism. . . . But this is an inherently chancy mode, which depends heavily on the poet's "ear," her ability to distinguish the genuinely striking from the merely portentous. Erdrich at times is betrayed by the speed with which the mysteriously evocative language of one moment flattens into the cliché of the next; when she writes "Husband, by the light of our bones we are going," one reflects that bones have already shed rather too much light on the landscape of American poetry, and that no one is likely to find much new ground by that source of illumination.

More frequently, Erdrich takes as her subject everyday life, though the everyday life of those who are in some way marginal, exploited, isolated. A colloquial plain style, enlivened by an eye for irony and a sense for speech-rhythms, serves these poems well. The series of dramatic monologues gathered in the sequence **"The Butcher's Wife,"** written in the personae of various inhabitants of a small town in the early twentieth century, stand out as probably the volume's best work. Erdrich dwells on the loneliness of the characters she creates, their double estrangement in a vast, empty landscape and in their isolation from one another. . . . As a sequence, **"The Butcher's Wife"** relies less on Erdrich's uncertain talents as a coiner of epithets and more on her ability to build a fictional world through an accumulation of vignettes. While the notion of a sequence like this might seem alarmingly like another cruise up Spoon River, Erdrich shows a flair for imagining the texture of other lives. One is not surprised to find out that she has also published a novel recently. Variety and scope are goals as worthy as compression and power; Erdrich pursues the former a good deal more comfortably and effectively than the latter. Indeed, her gifts seem to lie more in narrative than in lyric, and her growth as a poet will likely depend on her finding ways to embody in poems her talents as a narrator. (pp. 40-1)

> *Vernon Shetley, in a review of "Jacklight," in* Poetry, *Vol. CXLVI, No. 1, April, 1985, pp. 40-1.*

MICHAEL LOUDON

Designating someone's "first book of poems" as such is typically an apologetic strategy. For Erdrich, "first-rate," "first ground," and "first light" are more descriptive of the forty-four poems of *Jacklight.* I felt early in the reading the same narrative force, precise images, and complex characters that eventually found full expression in her celebrated novel *Love Medicine,* but the poems are far from mere exercises on the way to a novel. They are first-rate poems: the language again and again sings to its own vision. An ordinary event in the cycle of seasons, the falling of blossoms, becomes "White crowns of the plum trees / were filling the purple throats of the iris"; or consider the reflection of parents: "We are alone here on earth / with the ragged breath of our children / coming and going in the old wool blankets." I am humbled before a committed language expressing courage tempered by fear.

The ground of Erdrich's poems is the region of the Turtle Mountain Chippewa reservation in North Dakota, but political boundaries alone cannot suppress the fragmentary cultures of the Chippewa, Cree, French, English, Scottish, and German legacies of the people who stand in the midst of degradation, rejecting self-pity and improvising their strength from whatever is around them. Repetitions (evoking the mythic light upon which she draws throughout the book) and stunning images (Neruda and James Wright resonate within them) build the insistent will of characters who continue when "everything around . . . is crying to be gone." Such a character, "who drank Vitalis [and] Sterno" but "is the green light floating over the slough," in the haunting **"Rugaroo,"** is one of many that "will not let you sleep." . . .

[From the oral tradition], Erdrich's poems reach first light. Her last section weaves myth and memory, the Windigo and the White Roach Bar, toward a moving eulogy for her grandfather; yet the eulogy becomes affirmation for all humanity. . . . Each of us coming to these poems will have the jacklight turned upon himself (*jacklight:* any light used to lure game in night hunting—usually "illegal"). Each of us will have to find his way "forward alone."

Michael Loudon, in a review of "Jacklight," in World Literature Today, *Vol. 60, No. 1, Winter, 1986, p. 159.*

MICHIKO KAKUTANI

"Where did everything go?" a character named Mary in **The Beet Queen** wonders as she and a friend drive home across the windy fields of North Dakota. . . .

What Mary—and the rest of the people in this fiercely lyrical new novel—see receding before their eyes are not just their shared memories of a particular time and place, but also their private dreams of unconditional family love. Just as the land about them succumbs to the impatient flow of history . . . so too are their bonds of marriage and friendship subjected to the centrifugal spin of time. In the course of Louise Erdrich's novel, brother and sister, husband and wife, children and parents—all run, drift or turn away from one another, leaving behind only fractured memories and a craving for some kind of connection.

With her first novel, **Love Medicine,** published in 1984, Ms. Erdrich announced herself as an immensely gifted young writer. Drawing upon her own family's American Indian past, she delineated the intertwined fates of two families living in and around a North Dakota Indian reservation. And in doing so, she mixed up the mythic and the naturalistic, the mundane and the magical, to conjure up a world that bridged the small-town America of Sherwood Anderson and the deracinated new America of Bobbie Ann Mason and Marsha Norman.

The Beet Queen not only uses the same method of multiple perspective narration used in that earlier book . . . but it also evinces similar qualities: passages of shimmering, poetic description; startling sequences of physical and emotional violence, and a cast of characters, at once ordinary and strange like eccentric folk-art figures. The overall effect is . . . a beautiful yet unsentimental evocation of a particular time and place.

In **Love Medicine,** we were introduced to a huge, irritable woman named Dot, who "moved loosely among the dangerous elements" in town; and in this volume we learn how the

teen-aged Dot came to be crowned Beet Queen of Argus, N.D., and how her family history unraveled.

It's a peculiar story, Dot's, full of emotional loops and coincidences, and it begins with an extraordinary act of abandonment, committed by her grandmother many years ago. Poor and despairing, forsaken by the father of her children, Adelaide Adare glimpses a chance for a new life one day at the county fair. Seeing the Great Omar, who's flown into town to perform his tricks in the sky, she runs over to his plane, jumps inside and flies off for good, leaving behind three children—Karl, Mary, and a baby boy. The baby is promptly kidnapped by a childless couple, and Karl and Mary jump a train, traveling west to seek refuge with their aunt in North Dakota. Although their paths quickly diverge . . . their fates will crisscross one another's, tangling up, in the process, the lives of many others.

In fact, Ms. Erdrich quickly sinks us into the social matrix of the entire town of Argus, efficiently sketching in the ties of sympathy, jealousy and betrayal that bind members of the Adare family and their neighbors together. Her portraits tend to have a powerful afterlife, for her people glare out at us with the peculiar off-kilter gaze of distant ancestors found in old daguerreotypes—they seem familiar but somehow dangerous in their hidden passions. . . .

As for Mary and Karl themselves, these two orphans, who had hoped to begin new lives in Argus, discover that they're doomed to retrace their mother's patterns of cruelty and loss. . . .

At times, Ms. Erdrich dwells a bit too insistently on the darker aspects of Mary's and Karl's personalities . . . and as a result, a portentous gloom occasionally clouds the lucidity of her prose. The final pages, which bring together all the people we've met, also smacks of artifice: we're left not with the sense that character and fate have led to an inevitable end, but with the suspicion that the author has been laying time bombs in her plot all along—with the intention of setting them all off in a single grand finale. It's unfortunate that **The Beet Queen** ends the way it does, for it's a conclusion that diminishes the impact of what is otherwise a remarkable and luminous novel.

Michiko Kakutani, in a review of "The Beet Queen," in The New York Times, *August 20, 1986, p. C21.*

ROBERT BLY

Midwestern writers have to do the best they can with their inheritance of flat rhythms. . . . It is hard to write poetry or fiction with the worm of flatness coiled around the house since childhood. In **The Beet Queen** Louise Erdrich plays well with the demon of flatness and often wins. . . .

She does not settle for satire. Instead, keeping short sentences and characteristic pitch sequences, she adds the original image, the revealing blast of light, and opens a channel that allows dangerous impulses from beneath to flow to the surface. Her genius is in metaphor. She gives short sentences to wild-boned characters, some of them Indians not yet pressed to death under bushels of wheat, and brings life to the kind of tales that so often become tedious in memoirs and the work of lesser novelists.

Ms. Erdrich's second novel, **The Beet Queen,** is a book of power and precision. Like her first, *Love Medicine,* it is set in North Dakota, near the Indian reservation where she grew up. A few characters in *Love Medicine* reappear. . . . *Love Medicine* jumped off the page—its characters vividly alive, outrageous, both Indian and white. The Indians in particular were more funky, more wild in their failures, more frank about their uncontrollable minds than most characters, Indian or white, in American fiction.

The Beet Queen circles around the adventures of Mary Adare, whose father is dead and whose mother abandons her and her two brothers at a circus by flying off with an aviator. It is 1932, and the 11-year-old girl takes a freight to an aunt and uncle who are butchers in North Dakota, and lives after that with them and her cousin Sita and a friend of both, Celestine. Years later, her older brother Karl turns up in the town, and eventually fathers Celestine's daughter, Dot, who becomes as the novel closes the queen of the sugar beet festival.

Characters in *The Beet Queen* show a convincing ability to feel an image with their whole bodies. . . .

After visiting her brother, now crippled by a stroke, his mind empty, Celestine asks, "Where did it go?" Mary, who has since become a butcher, says to herself:

> In my line of work I've seen thousands of brains that belonged to sheep, pork, steers. They were all gray lumps like ours. Where did everything go? What was really inside? The flat fields folded, the shallow ditches ran beside the road. I felt the live thoughts hum inside of me, and I pictured tiny bees, insects made of blue electricity, in a colony so fragile that it would scatter at the slightest touch. I imagined a blow, like a mallet to the sheep, or a stroke, and I saw the whole swarm vibrating out. Who could stop them? Who could catch them in their hands?

That is good writing, and to do it requires attention not to fact or the way we all speak—although Ms. Erdrich pays sharp attention to that—but to private perceptions and bizarre images appearing from so far down that they arrive in their own fresh rhythms, not dancing, but at least walking, and walking confidently.

The Beet Queen brings forward four main female characters who differ greatly in their responses to society's demands on them. Mary's mother, Adelaide, leaves with the pilot and lets others raise her children. Sita, obsessed with social climbing, a "practiced voice" and "careful slenderness," ends connected to the world only through remote control devices for television and radio. . . . Mary, by contrast, reads tarot sticks and spits on a brick to see calendar dates, as if adhering to a community of matriarchal intuitives. She and Celestine, who has thick arms and a "common sort of fierceness," raise Celestine's baby without wishing the father to be present at all. He agrees to stay away.

The men in the book do not have any channel to inner power as clear as Mary's and Celestine's. Russell Kashpaw, a soldier who has served in Germany and Korea, is badly shot up and becomes an exhibit propped up for parades. The two white men who are the most prominent male characters, Karl and Wallace (a businessman deeply involved with Karl and Dot), belong to salesmanship, small-town exploitation, sexual confusion and boosterism.

Ms. Erdrich's method of telling a story is to choose a few minutes or a day in 1932, let one character talk, let another talk, and a third, then leap to 1941 and then to 1950 or 1964. In *The Beet Queen* the main characters talk often in their own voices; then in other chapters a narrative voice describes their adventures and feelings as well as the adventures of lesser characters. One sees the men and women when they are young, and when they are old—and Ms. Erdrich notices the losses. Few characters live out a chosen pattern, but instead some harsh pattern lives them out.

What we primarily remember are certain powerful scenes in the novel, pungently visualized, suggesting the stark grotesquerie of Günter Grass, and we remember the noisy, direct voices talking. . . . Celestine notices a strange sight one night while nursing her infant daughter . . . :

> Celestine noticed, in the fine moonlit floss of her baby's hair, a tiny white spider making its nest. It was a delicate thing, close to transparent, with long sheer legs. It moved so quickly that it seemed to vibrate, throwing out invisible strings and catching them, weaving its own tensile strand. Celestine watched as it began to happen. A web was forming, a complicated house, that Celestine could not bring herself to destroy.

I let that passage stand to represent the intelligent, alert writing of Louise Erdrich that I so much admire. *The Beet Queen* seems more fragmentary than *Love Medicine,* and the characters here carry less vital feeling than the predominantly Indian characters in the previous novel, but the two books together provoke in me amazement and gratitude at this splendid, feisty talent, capable of bizarre comedy, ordinary Midwestern facts and vigorous tragedy.

> *Robert Bly, "Another World Breaks Through," in* The New York Times Book Review, *August 31, 1986, p. 2.*

DOROTHY WICKENDEN

There are two sorts of people in [*The Beet Queen*]: dreamers who are barely able to cope with the false promises and humiliations of daily life, and plodders who merely wring out a grim satisfaction from surviving. The dreamers are driven to an existence of perpetual drifting or madness. The plodders periodically take them in, offering a granite will in exchange for the opportunity to patch up someone more battered than they are. Erdrich's novels have little in the way of traditional plot or character development because her characters have already been marked indelibly by fate. What she brings to *The Beet Queen,* as she did to *Love Medicine,* is a prose style of ringing clarity and lyricism, and a shrewd vision of the pathos and comedy that characterize provincial lives.

In *Love Medicine* Erdrich deftly cut open the closed world of two families on a North Dakota reservation. Part Chippewa herself, she managed to evoke at once the traditions of Anglo-American realism and Native American mysticism in a story about the weird permutations of love. In *The Beet Queen* she moves just outside the reservation to a small, unsophisticated town called Argus, inhabited by whites and a scattering of Chippewa. Erdrich brings with her the same narrative method, themes, and even a few characters. Once again she takes on several generations of an extended family, allowing each member to narrate periodically. . . . And here too she creates a matriarchy composed of women with extra-sensory powers and men with ineffectual longings.

But in *Love Medicine* the generations were cast in an erratic time frame, and the characters jostled for the reader's attention. *The Beet Queen,* another composite of unsettling vignettes, has an assured, polished quality that *Love Medicine* lacked. Erdrich centers the story on a fragmented white family, and she has dropped the dreamlike connections between characters and events in favor of an unconventional narrative of a more sculpted kind. . . .

Erdrich is an economical writer. She allows her characters neither lingering introspection nor excessive sentimentality. From the opening pages she sharply etches the incongruities between the stolid Mary and the delicate Karl, and lays out the pattern that will determine the rest of their lives. . . .

In the course of the novel, Mary's hardened heart and Karl's pained restlessness come to shape—and misshape—the lives of each of their friends and relatives. Mary grows up behind the butcher shop with their cousin, "the beautiful Sita," a girl with aspirations for a life of romance and success whom she torments over the years and slowly drives insane. Karl eventually makes his way back to Argus as a slick traveling salesman, and in a short-lived affair with Mary's only friend, Celestine, fathers a child, Dot. . . .

It is Dot who inadvertently unites the discordant clan. This glowering, aggressive child, who is "either lit up by her imaginary future, or depressed, a dark lump, by what she saw as her life's realities, harsh and awful," brings unreasonable hope into the lives of Celestine, her aunt Mary, her "uncle" Wallace, and even her absent father, Karl. (p. 46)

Erdrich's characters inevitably find sexual love (if they find it at all) furtive and disappointing, family love fierce and destructive, and friendship stolen and betrayed. Yet *The Beet Queen* is a comic novel. It is not pity that Erdrich seeks to elicit on her characters' behalf, but amused sympathy with their fumbling quests for happiness. . . .

[These] moments are conveyed in the melodic rhythms of Erdrich's prose and the brisk, atonal frankness of Western speech. The effect, both eerie and utterly matter-of-fact, gruesome and funny, can border on the surreal. (p. 47)

There is no disputing the grace with which Erdrich skates across the surface of unhappy lives. And she has created an unusual balance between humor and poignancy that allows her to make full use of her poetic turns, her observant eye, and her fascination with the haphazard and the coincidental. But there are inevitable problems in a narrative that is punctuated by a series of extraordinary scenes rather than sustained by an evolving plot and characters that grow and change. In her determination not to linger over any character or scene, or to lose the comic effect, she relies too heavily on caricature. Mary becomes cartoonish, and rather tiresome, in her role as the spinster aunt and town eccentric, with her hideous cut-rate dresses, the grisly satisfaction she derives from others' misfortunes, her ersatz talents as a fortuneteller.

Erdrich has chosen a form that allows her talents to shine but necessarily limits what she can do with her fictional family. The coming together of all the characters and themes at the beet festival—complete with Dot's dramatic reliving of her grandmother's flight—is a contrivance, not a natural culmination to the drama. It is a device that Erdrich clearly hoped

would help dramatize her themes and effectively join the realms of fantasy and realism. Instead it simply draws attention to the novel's mechanics.

Still, these imperfections hardly spoil the novel. . . . [Erdrich] has conveyed unforgettably the mixture of the prosaic and the uncanny that informs the lives of dreamers and plodders alike. And she has endowed all of her characters with an idiosyncratic trait that both isolates them and allows them to survive: the energy and ingenuity to grapple with the terrors of intimacy. (pp. 47-8)

Dorothy Wickenden, "Off the Reservation," in The New Republic, Vol. 195, No. 14, October 6, 1986, pp. 46-8.

LINDA SIMON

Before she won the 1984 National Book Critics Circle award for her novel *Love Medicine,* Louise Erdrich already had gained acclaim as a poet. . . . *The Beet Queen* is very much a poet's novel, and the texture of the prose finally is more seductive even than the movement of the plot. It is a novel that throbs, at times, with the intensity of its small vignettes. . . .

The novel itself reveals a complicated web of relationships from which no character can extricate herself. The men and women who people *The Beet Queen* are bound by ties that they only partially understand, and they live out patterns that seem unalterable.

Mary Adare and her two brothers are orphaned when their mother abandons them by flying off with a carnival stunt pilot. The three children, one an infant, set off for their aunt's house in Argus, North Dakota. . . . Only Mary arrives, telling her improbable tale. She is welcomed by her aunt and uncle, but resented by her cousin Sita, who even as a child has aristocratic pretensions and little tolerance for other people.

Mary, Sita, and their friend Celestine James are the focus of this novel, and we follow their lives from 1932, when Mary comes to Argus, to 1972, when Celestine's daughter, Dot (fathered by Karl Adare), is named Beet Queen during a local festival. . . .

When Celestine says of Mary that she "tries to get her imagination to mend the holes in her understanding," she could well be referring to any of the three women. Not given to reflection, trusting in a visceral response to the world, they seek signs and portents to guide their lives. Mary, most overtly, believes in forces that defy human intervention: she reads palms, spits on bricks to determine dates of future events, and dreams ominous dreams.

Despite the often grotesque events in their lives . . . , the women are unremittingly prosaic. Having a child and naming her, Mary remarks about Celestine, "was the first thing Celestine ever did out of the ordinary," and apparently the last. For these women, "out of the ordinary" means "as an act of free will." They seem bound by fate, and so do their men.

Karl, Celestine's friend Wallace Pfef, and Russell Kashpaw, an Indian who fought in the Korean War and now, a quadriplegic, who wastes away in a wheelchair, also seem characters to whom life happens. Small gestures of individuality help them to survive, but do not alter the patterns which they find themselves enacting. (p. 565)

Within these bleak lives, however, there are luminous moments. If the characters cannot probe their own personalities and motivations, they eagerly render for us the power of the physical landscape. Here is Mary, for example, describing the North Dakota winter:

> My fruit trees suffered. The snow came so high that rabbits gnawed the trunks and upper limbs, girdling them completely so that even spring, when new buds should have shown, was a time of death. In the shelterbelts, I came across more of the deer's frail hulks and the banks of the river stank of bleached carp. An old man was found, one who for years had lived alone. He was curled in a large drift beneath his clothesline and his arms were full of towels.

The Beet Queen is filled with such passages, which convey a palpable reality of the midwest at its most grim and forbidding. Yet despite Erdrich's striking skill and imagination, her characters keep the novel from being totally satisfying. In the end, the distinct narrative voices of Mary, Sita, and Celestine blur, and our sympathies with them cannot go far enough. Yet Erdrich is a writer who has been justifiably lauded, and even with its weaknesses, *The Beet Queen* stands as a product of enormous talent. (pp. 565, 567)

Linda Simon, "Small Gestures, Large Patterns," in Commonweal, *Vol. CXIII, No. 18, October 24, 1986, pp. 565, 567.*

JOSH RUBINS

Louise Erdrich's *Love Medicine* was a commanding first book of fiction, but not necessarily the announcement of a major novelist's arrival. Winner of the National Book Critics Circle Award for Fiction in 1984, the book consists of fourteen short stories about life on and around a North Dakota reservation in the decades since 1934. . . . Recurring characters, repeated themes, and entangled bloodlines offer bridges from one tale to the next. Nonetheless, the traditional novelistic devices—narrative shape, momentum, suspense—play almost no part in the book's modest cumulative effect. Instead, the stories in *Love Medicine* remain stubborn little islands of image-charged prose, often painfully beautiful (and occasionally comic) as they juxtapose the harsh specifics of these Native American lives with the emotional strength, even grandeur, derived from family bonds and mystical beliefs. The parade of oddly neutral first-person narrators, the often confusing crowd of interrelated characters, the seemingly haphazard shifting of close-ups—all these suggest documentary, *cinéma vérité*, rather than full-length fiction. In fact, Erdrich's first "novel" seems deliberate, *faux naif* perhaps, in its asymmetrical patchworking, almost as if a structure would be out of place in such a stark amalgam of poetry and sociology.

As *The Beet Queen* makes clear, however, Erdrich has nothing against—and hardly a thing to learn about—large-scale storytelling. Not since Philip Roth's *The Ghost Writer* has the first page of a novel so authoritatively invited this reader into a fictional world that's about to expand naturally and easily, in all directions. Two quasi orphans, eleven-year-old Mary Adare and her older brother Karl, come to Argus, North Dakota, on a cold spring morning in 1932, arriving together as boxcar stowaways on a freight train; within six short paragraphs, the siblings, chased by a large dog, will be running in opposite directions—Karl back to the departing boxcar, Mary to a new life in Argus with Aunt Fritzie Kozka and Cousin Sita. Immediately, then, a narrative arc, taut with Dickensian possibilities, takes shape, along with the sense of an unabashedly conscious craftsman at work.

Just as quickly, Erdrich also lets us know that her embrace of old-fashioned narrative in no way involves a retreat from the stylistic and tonal complexity that distinguished *Love Medicine.* There's that riskily lyrical imagery, too, in the near-melodramatic opening sequence—when Karl's dreamy fascination with an Argus tree in blossom leads him fatefully astray: "His cheeks went pink, he stretched his arms out like a sleepwalker, and in one long transfixed motion he floated to the tree and buried his face in the white petals." Here, however, and throughout *The Beet Queen,* the poetry never stalls the developing action, or becomes an end in itself, as it sometimes does in *Love Medicine.* And if the contrast between hard facts and sweet music can make *Love Medicine* seem self-consciously literary (a "poet's novel," for better or worse), the use of heightened language remains unobtrusive in *The Beet Queen,* generating a fine subliminal tension—just one of the balancing acts that transform a doleful scenario into an airy, even jaunty, novel.

In outline the five-decade saga of Mary and Karl Adare is a dreary litany of abandonment and loss, of emotional stunting and atrophy. (p. 14)

Played as melodrama, such an unrelievedly calamitous family saga would probably collapse into bathos. A naturalistic approach might easily have reduced the dispossessed, neurotic Adares to chapters of clinical case history. Unlike *Love Medicine,* however, which draws much of its intensity from the shared culture of a Native American community, *The Beet Queen* leapfrogs around and beyond any sociological pigeonholes. . . . Nor, despite the precise evocations of snowbound childbirth and convent schoolrooms and bleak parades, is this a "midwestern" novel in any limiting sense. Erdrich's Argus, North Dakota, is real enough to ground the social comedy that she so consistently, surprisingly, pulls up from those unpromising, grim materials; yet it's also enough of a nowhere place to melt away obligingly whenever *The Beet Queen* turns operatic, mysterious, or fablelike.

Erdrich is hardly unique, of course, in using comedy to circumvent sentimentality, playing against the pathos of derailed lives. Few writers, however, have managed to maintain so much respect and compassion for a cast of frail souls while making the farcical most of their eccentricities. Mary Adare's cramped spirit may transform her into a monstrous, hilariously meddlesome aunt—misguidedly assaulting Dot's grade-school teacher, or storm-trooping the fun out of a kiddie birthday party until the other adults feel compelled to slip her a Mickey Finn. But none of her misadventures reduces Mary to a mere figure of fun, viewed under glass or at a distance; she is always capable of unexpectedly grabbing a more heroic role or exposing a "sudden blue pang" of vulnerability—especially since, like the other five principal characters here, she is given several opportunities to address us directly. (The plain, largely undifferentiated narrative voices in *Love Medicine* serve no apparent purpose in the book's overall scheme; in *The Beet Queen* that same grave neutrality seems to work as a buffer against caricature.) Similarly, a single scene—Wallace Pfef, jealously eavesdropping on an erotically charged moment between Karl and Celestine, is attacked by mosquitoes—registers simultaneously as slapstick and empathic psychodrama. And in a single outrageous utterance—"Even thinking about her strange Jell-O makes me furious," says Celestine of her irritating soul mate Mary—absurd domestic satire and oddball Greek tragedy can cheerfully coexist.

This tragicomic complexity—the ability to project each of six narrator-protagonists as a sad case, a buffoon, and a hero all at once—wouldn't be possible without the plain yet poetic prose that unobtrusively steadies and suspends *The Beet Queen*. . . . Even more crucial to the novel's buoyancy—and even more delicate—is the playful balance between sincerity and artifice in Erdrich's orchestration of an elaborate, often far-fetched plot. While verisimilitude and sympathy remain on some level intact, the reader is gently, frequently reminded that the story he has entered is also a conscious creation: most specifically, a wry set of variations on the "foundling fiction" genre of Fielding and Dickens.

Those orphaned, isolated Adare children, for instance, would, by convention, be expected eventually to find their way to dramatic reunions, to the familial recognitions that unleash joy and terror on Oliver Twist or Ralph Nickleby. Erdrich teasingly encourages these expectations, with missed connections, letters fatefully mislaid, and highlighted clues. . . . When Mary and Karl meet again, however, twenty years after their childhood separation, it's a nonevent, worthy of no more than a brief second-hand report from Celestine. . . . A momentary chance encounter between Karl and his long-lost little brother, circa 1948, is even more sourly anticlimactic. . . . So the youngest Adare sibling, now a fledgling priest, never learns his real identity—not even when, twenty-five years later, he makes an outlandishly coincidental appearance in the novel's final set piece, which blatantly arranges the intersection of (among other things) the redemptive return of wastrel Karl, the black-comic demise of Cousin Sita, and the rigged election of sullen Dot Adare as the 1972 Beet Queen of Argus, North Dakota.

Unlike the comparable stratagems of such writers as Joyce Carol Oates and Mark Helprin, Erdrich's departures from conventional realism—stylized language, constant shiftings of tone and viewpoint, elements of parody and knowing artifice that verge on "metafiction"—don't undermine the story's forward momentum and emotional conviction. Carried along by the Adares' thorny vitality and their unpredictable maneuvers within confining circumstances, we barely notice the author's manipulations, hardly realize how they lend a shimmer to otherwise earthbound events. This is a rare second novel, one that makes it seem as if the first, impressive as it was, promised too little, not too much. (pp. 14-15)

Josh Rubins, "Foundling Fiction," in The New York Review of Books, *Vol. XXXIII, Nos. 21 & 22, January 15, 1987, pp. 14-15.*

THOMAS M. DISCH

Louise Erdrich is the first novelist of her generation—she was 30 when her first novel, *Love Medicine,* appeared in 1984—to have achieved front-rank writerly stardom. While her peers were writing just those novels that the young are expected to write, chronicling their first dates and drug busts, Erdrich lighted out into the territory of Literature, working on a scale, and with an artistry, that simply dwarfs her contemporaries. One must reach for names like Balzac and Faulkner to suggest the sweep of her three interlocking novels, which already constitute a *comédie humaine* of some 800-plus pages, a North Dakota of the imagination that, like Faulkner's Yoknapatawpha County, unites the archetypal and the arcane, heartland America and borderline schizophrenia.

Tracks, the third novel of this world-in-progress, is chronologically the earliest, being set from 1912 to 1924, and its main characters are members of Chippewa families, weakened by starvation, decimated by plagues and being slowly bulldozed from their treaty lands by the white men, whose tawdry triumph was chronicled in Erdrich's *The Beet Queen* (1986). There's no question on which side of the racial divide the author's sympathies lie . . . ; the Chippewas of *Tracks* and *Love Medicine* are noble and anything but savages. But her novels never slip into the tendentious tone of the minority spokesperson; Erdrich never preaches, never even appears to be much concerned about the ways in which her Indian characters are being given a raw deal. The injustices of history are simply part of the landscape she paints.

Tracks is about survival. It begins in 1912, after two epidemics—the "spotted sickness" and consumption—have wiped out whole families in the densely packed reservations/prison camps of North Dakota. The story is narrated alternately by two survivors of those plagues: Nanapush, an old man whose many bereavements have dulled neither his sense of humor nor his sexual appetite, and the ineffably demented Pauline, an orphaned waif who blossoms into the kind of monster you love to hate. (Readers of *Love Medicine* already have encountered her as the older but ever-malevolent Sister Leopolda.) The tale these two narrators tell centers around the love of Fleur Pillager and Eli Kashpaw (both of whom had cameo roles in the earlier novels); but "love" doesn't quite convey what passes between this pair, while "passion" calls to mind the guff of conventional bodice-ripping fiction. The love that Erdrich celebrates is simply the fuel of the process of survival.

Yet it may be that the secret of Erdrich's success is the way she spins the straw of conventional women's romance novels into the gold of literature. . . .

One reason for this may be that she is able to write about erotic matters convincingly from a male point of view; her male characters never have the unreal shimmer of wish-fulfillment that so often sets the TILT light to flashing when Sex A is writing about the sex life of Sex B. And one reason for this clarity of gender may be that her novels have been, by her own report, an enterprise she shares with her husband, Michael Dorris. However she does it, or they do it, the scene in which Eli Kashpaw and the nymphet Sophie Morrissey are bewitched into having sex verges on the Wagnerian in its delectable suggestiveness. (p. 1)

A rarer virtue still, Erdrich can communicate what is unique and terrific about Indian culture and character without piety or scolding. . . . She gets us inside her character's skins by tailoring them so artfully they slip right on.

None of the above explains why Louise Erdrich's books, though written in prose that Ph.D. candidates can purr over, are sure-fire best-sellers. The reason is (as usual in such cases) that she knows how to plot. With almost each new chapter, her readers will be amazed, confounded or enlightened by some new swerve of the story. Those who can't do this sort of thing are prone to dismiss it as 'mere' cleverness; those who can do it . . . enthrall vast audiences, sell millions of copies and still carry off literary prizes. Louise Erdrich can do it in spades, for not only are each of her novels cannily and precisely plotted, but, as their several strands interconnect, there are further "Oh-hos" and "Eurekas" for the attentive reader. Thus, readers of *Tracks* will discover that one of the romantic couples in *Love Medicine* actually was committing incest. They'll find out more about the dead man Lulu discovered in the woods, and his murderer, and who their daughter was. For this reason I urge readers who've not yet read *Love Medicine* to do so before they begin *Tracks*. . . . Readers who have read *Love Medicine* will need no urging. (pp. 1, 6)

Thomas M. Disch, "Enthralling Tale: Louise Erdrich's World of Love and Survival," in Chicago Tribune—Books, September 4, 1988, pp. 1, 6.

PATRICIA VIGDERMAN

Louise Erdrich's 1984 novel, *Love Medicine,* takes its strength from the matter of fact way her characters take their shape from the present moment, yet are still overlapped by the past, the land they live on, the others around them. They are modern day Chippewa, living as they can on what's left of their tribal inheritance. . . . However, their sense of themselves is carried on the thread of group memory, the mystery of Chippewa history. Sexy Lulu Lamartine has eight sons, all by different fathers, but what is important about Lulu is less her loose ways than her rightful connection to the earth. . . . Lulu's history and that of the other characters unfolds in a series of linked stories, told by different voices and moving backward and forward in time. The "plot" is subordinate to the sense of a powerful fate working in multiple lives.

In Erdrich's new novel, *Tracks,* she goes even further back in time to tell the story behind the stories. The earliest episodes in *Love Medicine* are dated 1934; *Tracks* takes place between 1912 and 1924. The story is told in alternating chapters by Nanapush, a tribal elder who has watched the Chippewa lose their land and culture, and Pauline Puyat, part Canadian, part Chippewa, whose creepy psychology blends primitive magic, sexual obsession, and Catholic superstition. Unlike *Love Medicine* the stories in *Tracks* are required to move along a single plot, a humdrum task that drains them of some of their effect. Not only must they mix light-of-day personalities and unorthodox beliefs, but also explain the demise of a tribeful of characters.

The audience for Nanapush's tale is none other than the young Lulu, his adoptive granddaughter. At the center of his story is the girl's mother, Fleur—both the source of Lulu's later sexual powers, and the crucial counterweight to Pauline. Fleur's powers are directly connected to the natural world—to the lake, the forest, the clouds—to the old ways. When the land is all lost to white loggers, she disappears into the forest with a cartful of symbolic possessions. The final solution for Pauline is to deny her Chippewa origins and finally to take the veil.

Pauline's narrative erupts from the war inside her, from her loneliness, cowardice, and desire. Her story is told to whoever will listen; it pours out in a desperate stream, a tumble of sex and salvation. . . .

The novel evokes a world in which human and nonhuman nature overlap, share power. Thus in a winter of famine the starving Nanapush lies down in his cabin, calls on his "helpers," and follows in a vision young Eli Kashpaw as he hunts a moose, bringing him home safely through the snow with the meat strapped to his body like armor. Thus Fleur, gang raped by her co-workers at the butcher shop in the nearby town of Argus, calls down from the summer sky a tornado whose devastation includes the imprisonment of the low fellows in a meat locker where they freeze to death. And thus Pauline, tormented by sexual need, frustrated in her desire for Eli, whose passion is only for Fleur, works a cockamamie and complicated piece of black magic involving crushed roots and fingernail clippings baked in a loaf of bread.

Meanwhile, the tax collector is selling off the Indian land to the lumber companies. Smallpox and consumption have thinned the Chippewa, snow and government papers and the mixed-blood collaborators in their midst are starving those who remain. Those who seem to have any spiritual power express it through sex. (p. 22)

So it makes sense that Pauline might be confused about sexuality and spiritual power. Her confusion, in fact, has made her a kind of evil spirit, part of the force that blocks the natural powers. When sex doesn't work out for her, she embraces increasingly bizarre mortifications of the flesh as if they were money in the bank—the price of a ticket to heaven. She is the one whose supernatural mischief drains the connection between Fleur and Eli of its lifegiving power, and turns the mixed-bloods firmly against the Indians. And it is just her importance as a plot mover that makes *Tracks* a less satisfying book than *Love Medicine.*

In the earlier book, each story has its own mixture of ordinary human motivation and mysterious forces. The result is often comic, as when a boy tries to use frozen turkey hearts from the Red Owl supermarket in a love potion that calls for wild goose hearts. Oddly enough, though, the universal forces seem less powerful and important when the strictly human stuff isn't in command of its full powers. In *Tracks* the human comedy, even in Nanapush's stories, is overcast by Pauline's craziness, and the ancient, mysterious waters of cause and effect seem muddied rather than deepened by that shadow. (pp. 22-3)

Patricia Vigderman, in a review of "Tracks," in Boston Review, Vol. XIII, No. 3, October, 1988, pp. 22-3.

JEAN STROUSE

Ever since her first novel, *Love Medicine,* appeared in 1984, Louise Erdrich has been populating a specific place—the Chippewa Indian reservation and its North Dakota-Minnesota surround—with characters as strong and original, as funny and tough, as furious and vivid as any who have recently graced the American literary landscape. Her sure sense of the way people think and talk keeps it hard to remember she is making them all up, and her lithe, athletic prose makes wildly improbable events seem as natural as the weather.

Ms. Erdrich, herself half Chippewa . . . , has said that her favorite authors are Faulkner, Eudora Welty and Toni Morrison. That admiration shows as she gives imaginative life to a world many of us would not otherwise see. It is a world of haunting texture and detail. . . . Ms. Erdrich's novels, regional in the best sense, are "about" the experience of Native Americans the way Toni Morrison's are about black people, William Faulkner's and Eudora Welty's about the South, Philip Roth's and Bernard Malamud's about Jews: the specificity implies nothing provincial or small.

Ms. Erdrich's characters tell their stories in the first-person singular, and out of these shifting points of view a larger tale takes shape and organically grows. As the saga goes on over many generations and from one novel to the next, chronologic matters less than the integrity of the voices: an ancillary character in *Love Medicine* comes up at the center of *The Beet Queen* (1986)—and now *Tracks* gives the cycle another deft turn, going way back to the parents and grandparents of people in the first two books. (pp. 1, 41)

The novel opens in the bitter winter of 1912: the Chippewa, their ranks already diminished by smallpox, fevers, forced migration and exile, now get nearly wiped out by a raging TB epidemic. "Our tribe unraveled like a coarse rope, frayed at either end as the old and new among us were taken," says a foxy old survivor named Nanapush.

Nanapush is one of two storytellers who narrate and play key roles in what follows. He knows the "old" ways. . . .

Also telling the story, alternating chapters with Nanapush, is a young woman named Pauline from a family of "mixed-bloods, skinners in the clan for which the name was lost." . . .

What Pauline and Nanapush recount, from these starkly different perspectives, is the mysterious story of a young woman named Fleur Pillager, the last of a clan "who knew the secret ways to cure or kill." Nanapush finds Fleur, that devastating winter of 1912, alone in a cabin deep in the woods, raving and starving. . . . He takes her home and nurses her back to life. Cured, Fleur returns to live in the Pillager cabin on Lake Matchimanito, where she hunts, fishes, dresses like a man, studies old tribal medicines and excites plenty of curious talk. She "messed with evil," reports Pauline, and any man who messed with Fleur ended up dead. . . .

In the summer of 1913, Fleur takes off for Argus, N.D. (the setting of *The Beet Queen*), and gets a job cutting meat for a butcher. Pauline, already there sweeping floors and being ignored . . . , attaches herself to Fleur, feeling the older girl's sexual power with the avid hunger of the outcast. Yet it wasn't, notes Pauline, just that Fleur was a Chippewa, or "that she was good-looking or even that she was alone that made [the white men's] brains hum. It was how she played cards." How Fleur plays cards brings her a lot of money—and a nightmare of rape and revenge, described with hallucinatory intensity by Pauline. And when Fleur walks back onto the reservation that fall with something—money? a baby?—under her dress, people hum with gossip.

Speculation grows louder when a young loner named Eli Kashpaw follows a gutshot deer out to Fleur's cabin and falls in love. . . .

Ms. Erdrich's women are for the most part fiercer, nastier, more powerful, effective and inexorable than her men—and for sheer demented malice Pauline takes the prize. The mission-Catholic girl, "stark and bony" as a starved cow, hangs around watching Fleur and Eli with predatory prurience. . . .

Enraged with envy and desire, Pauline turns desolation into

a weird kind of power—part pagan hex, part devious Christian mysticism. Ms. Erdrich has said that she had a "Gothic-Catholic" childhood, and Pauline's lust to be chosen by God is nothing if not Gothic. . . . [There's] nothing amusing about the damage Pauline does as her hysterical martyrdom ratchets up—as she meets mercy with destruction, dispenses pain instead of love, and step by self-deluding step helps force the Chippewa off their ancestral land.

That other tragic story—of incomprehensible taxes and allotment fees, government treachery, church collusion, liquor, the dollar, the loss of the "old" life and powers and finally the loss of the land—runs all through the tales Pauline and Nanapush tell. And the saddest part isn't in the machinations of some far-off bureaucracy: it's in the way these changes bring on the betrayal of one Indian by another, in shocking abdications of love.

With all three books Ms. Erdrich artfully sifts the miraculous through the mundane: people see God(s) where they want to, in a wounded hand, a smashed pane of ice, an owl, a bear, a convent kitchen stove. Her stories reflect on various kinds of power—spiritual, sexual, emotional, political—and on the nature of stories themselves. If knowledge is a kind of power, stories preserve and pass it along, tracking, shaping, trying to make sense of what happens. (p. 41)

Some storytellers, generous and supple, pay a special kind of attention to what they see. Like Nanapush, they are imaginative reporters . . . , able to follow the ineffable tracks of what goes on. Others, like Pauline, are at such odd, rigid angles to the rest of the world that they distort and try to control the things they see, leaving their own tracks all over the story as they remake what's happened into something they can bear.

This novel feels a bit more didactic and wrought than Louise Erdrich's previous books: good and evil play out their parts somewhat too schematically, and the politics that previously came alive through the characters themselves sometimes seem imposed with a heavier hand. However, the story of the Chippewas' losing struggle to preserve their land and culture *is* inherently more political than the stories set later in the 20th century, more about radical innocence up against ravenous greed. It has a mythic force, and Ms. Erdrich is, as always, the generous kind of storyteller, passing along not only everything her characters know, but the story of the stories as well. Giving life and shape and sense to what's happened, she lets the designs spring clear. (p. 42)

Jean Strouse, "In the Heart of the Heartland," in The New York Times Book Review, *October 2, 1988, pp. 1, 41-2.*

ROBERT TOWERS

Louise Erdrich's first novel, the prize-winning *Love Medicine* (1984), presents, as through rifts in a smoke screen, lurid glimpses of the struggle of a group of Chippewa and mixed-blood Indians to cope with a life of poverty, alcoholism, and general demoralization on or near a reservation in North Dakota. The treatment is somewhat confusingly episodic, the prose poetically charged with imagery of exceptional vividness. Her second book, *The Beet Queen* (1986), deals primarily with the inhabitants of a small North Dakota town in the 1950s and only peripherally with the reservation Indians. Even more episodic in structure, it lacks, I think, the power of its predecessor. Now we have *Tracks,* which, we are told, is chronologically the first in a projected cycle of four novels. Set between 1912 and 1924, it evokes a brutal period of harsh winters, raging epidemics, famine, and expropriation, and it goes a long way toward accounting for the demoralization and uprootedness that prevails in *Love Medicine*. . . .

Rape, murder, vengeful tricks, spells, hideous starvation, bloody childbirth, weird practices both Christian and Indian—these elements of what might be called Native American Gothic occur on almost every page. Though there are moments of grotesque comedy and wry humor, especially in the [sections narrated by Nanapush], the prevailing tone is rhetorically exalted and solemn, often portentous, and occasionally pretentious. The forest and the lake, haunted by the spirits of tribal ancestors, are endowed with mythic and symbolic properties, while the devastating advance of the developers and land-grabbers is attributed to the powerlessness of the old magic—personified in the indomitable Fleur Pillager—to protect the sacred places. . . .

Louise Erdrich's gift for vivid descriptive writing is everywhere in evidence, and many of the episodes are almost blinding in their hallucinated brilliance. But the novel has, I think, serious problems in addition to its rhetorical inflation. For one thing, the narration of events is kept at such a pitch that finally one wishes to stop one's ears. Credence is exhausted. This is indeed too bad, for *Tracks* contains not only much information about the history and culture of the Indians that is interesting in its own right and little known to most readers but also the potential for a powerful narrative. While Louise Erdrich reveals the terrible privations endured by her characters and the heartless exploitation to which they were subjected by official policy and private greed, she allows the tragedy of the Indians to be overwhelmed by the sheer volume of sensational detail—giving rise to the suspicion that the author herself was determined to exploit its exotic and bizarre aspects for all they are worth. The characters—even the wise old Nanapush—are melodramatically conceived, and tainted with speciousness. Fleur, the ostensible heroine, becomes, hardly less than Pauline, the figment of a nightmare. The reader is sometimes reduced to a horrified onlooker, unable to identify with or care much about the characters. (p. 40)

Robert Towers, "Roughing It," in The New York Review of Books, *Vol. XXXV, No. 17, November 19, 1988, pp. 40-1.*

Jessie Redmon Fauset

1884?-1961

American novelist, editor, short story writer, critic, essayist, and poet.

An integral figure of the Harlem Renaissance, a period of great achievement in black American art and literature that took place following World War I, Fauset earned recognition for her work on the *Crisis,* a progressive magazine published by the National Association for the Advancement of Colored People. As literary editor of the *Crisis,* Fauset discovered and published early works by such authors as Langston Hughes, Jean Toomer, and Claude McKay. She also wrote short stories and novels that were originally categorized as romantic melodramas but are now regarded as pioneering advocations of feminism and civil rights. Tracing the lives of upper middle-class black families, Fauset often centers upon a light-skinned heroine's efforts to gain economic security and social status by passing for white. Many of Fauset's protagonists subsequently suffer anguish as a result of bringing false values upon themselves and their families. Fauset challenged conventional literary portraits of females by featuring women who actively pursued careers and sought equality in their relationships with men. Although critics have noted limitations involving Fauset's themes and subject matter, her discussions of racial and sexual discrimination are considered to be sound and insightful social commentaries. Joseph J. Feeney declared: "Miss Fauset's novels picture a mixed world of romance and prejudice, success and humiliation. . . . There is also a strong, underlying social purpose: to portray the educated black middle class and thereby uncover American racial prejudice."

Fauset's first book, *There Is Confusion* (1924), was inspired by T. S. Stribling's *Birthright,* a highly regarded novel of a half-black, half-white Harvard University graduate's inability to refine the residents of his Tennessee hometown. The success of *Birthright* encouraged Fauset to further illuminate the realities of black life to white audiences and offer a perceptiveness and insight into racial issues that she believed white authors intrinsically lacked. In *There Is Confusion,* Fauset depicts two wealthy black Philadelphia families who are brought together by the marriage of their children. Instead of focusing on the differences between black and white society, however, she attempts to portray their similarities. While some critics faulted the book for an enigmatic narrative and melodramatic dialogue, the numerous characters, storylines, and details in *There Is Confusion* prompted William Stanley Braithwaite to describe Fauset as "the potential Jane Austen of Negro literature." Carolyn Wedin Sylvander observed: "By taking the traditional *Bildungsroman* and family novel patterns and adapting them to study the peculiar confusion, learning, and ultimate understanding of American Blacks, Fauset has revealed insight into the human experience."

Fauset's second work, *Plum Bun* (1929), is regarded as her finest literary achievement. Illustrating the conflict between the aspirations of blacks and the realities of a society dominated by whites, this novel portrays the consequences of Angela Murray's decision to advance her artistic career by passing for white. Although Angela's strategy proves successful,

she becomes embarrassed by her deceptive actions and angry over society's unequal treatment of women. Fauset contrasts the emptiness of Angela's life with that of her sister, who embraces her black heritage by marrying a dark-skinned man and becoming a teacher in Harlem. When Angela is awarded a trip to Paris for her artistic accomplishments, she seizes the opportunity to proudly reveal her racial identity to a group of reporters. In *The Chinaberry Tree: A Novel of American Life* (1931), Fauset explores the psychological consequences of racism within the black community. This book revolves around three characters of mixed racial ancestry who are denied respectability by narrow-minded residents of a small town. While Fauset's blend of tragedy and romance garnered complimentary reviews upon the novel's publication, later critics have noted numerous plot deficiencies while identifying *The Chinaberry Tree* as her weakest work.

In Fauset's final novel, *Comedy, American Style* (1933), the theme of passing is implemented through the character of Olivia Cary, whose pathological desire to be white alienates her entire family. After her light-skinned husband refuses to pass, Olivia emotionally destroys her daughter by forcing her to marry an insensitive white professor and leads her dark-complexioned son to suicide by masquerading him as a Filipino houseboy while entertaining white friends. Phebe, Olivia's daughter-in-law, serves as the antithesis of Olivia's obsession with skin color. Although blond and blue-eyed, she is passionate about her black heritage and refuses to marry a rich white man whom she does not love. The novel ends with a miserable and isolated Olivia successfully passing in Paris. The ironic title of *Comedy, American Style* provoked several critics to connect the despondent conclusion of Fauset's book with the decline of the Harlem Renaissance and with the general literary movement away from genteel novels of manners that was precipitated by the popularity of social protest fiction.

(See also *CLC,* Vol. 19; *Contemporary Authors,* Vol. 109; and *Dictionary of Literary Biography,* Vol. 51.)

HIROKO SATO

In 1892, when the first novel by a black writer after the Civil War came out, the author, Mrs. Frances Ellen Watkins Harper, added the humble statement at the end of the novel, *Iola Leroy, or Shadows Uplifted:*

> From threads of fact and fiction I have woven a story whose mission will not be in vain if it awakens in the hearts of our countrymen a stronger sense of justice and a more Christian humanity in behalf of those whom the fortunes of war threw homeless, ignorant and poor, upon a threshold of a new era. Nor will it be in vain if it inspires the children of those upon whose brows God has poured the chrism of the new era to determine that they will embrace every opportunity, develop every faculty, and use every power God has given them to rise in the scale of character and condition, and to add their quota of good citizenship to the best welfare of the nation. There are scattered among us materials for mournful tragedies and mirth-provoking comedies, which some hand may yet bring into literature of the country, glowing with the fervor of the tropics and enriched by the luxuriance of the Orient, and thus add to the solution of our unsolved American problem.
>
> The race has not had very long to straighten its hand from the hoe, to grasp the pen and wield it as a power for good, and to erect above the ruined auction block and slave pen institutions of learning. . . .

Thirty-five years later, young artists like Langston Hughes, Zora Neale Hurston, Gwendolyn Bennett, Aaron Douglas, and Wallace Thurman got together and published a magazine, *Fire 11.* In the "Foreword" of the magazine they wrote:

> FIRE . . . weaving vivid, hot design upon an ebon bordered loom and satisfying pagan thirst for beauty unadorned . . . the flesh is sweet and real . . . the soul and inward flush of fire. . . . Beauty? . . . flesh on fire—on fire in the furnace of life blazing. . . .

What had happened between the timid and humble statement of Mrs. Harper and the bold declaration of the young artists was the explosion of the black energy called the Harlem Renaissance. (pp. 63-4)

Of course, this flowering of the black arts did not come as

suddenly as it seemed. The war and the great migration of the black people to Northern cities had something to do with it. . . . In a way, the Harlem Renaissance and the literature of the so-called Lost Generation came from the same social situation—the breaking down of the old ideals and sense of value. Those young artists, black and white alike, widened their world into that of physical sensations. Also, while the whites exiled themselves to Europe and looked back toward their homeland and tried to find its meaning, the blacks turned their eyes to Africa and tried to find their ties to the vast continent. . . . With the widening of the horizon of the black world of America, it seemed to some of the black people that the boundaries of American consciousness as a whole were enlarged. W. E. B. Du Bois proudly points out:

> We black folk may help for we have within us rare new stirrings; stirrings of the beginning of a new appreciation of joy, of a new desire to create, of a new will to be; as though in this morning of group life we had awakened from some sleep that at once dimly mourns the past and dreams a splendid future; and there has come the conviction that the Youth that is here today, the Negro Youth, is a different kind of Youth, because in some new way it bears this mighty prophecy on its breast, with a new realization of itself, with new determination for all mankind.

This movement was the restoration of "some of the things we thought culture had forever lost." There was no longer the need to be "over-assertive and over-appealing." The black artists felt that the American public had to acknowledge their full share in the world of art. (pp. 65-6)

Among those who helped this movement was Jessie Fauset, the literary editor of *The Crisis* from 1919 to 1926. . . . Though she did "a yeoman's work for the Negro Renaissance," most of her own literary activities were done during the period of the Harlem Renaissance. And the significance of the fact that her first novel, *There Is Confusion,* came out in 1924, almost simultaneously with Toomer's *Cane,* will be discussed later.

The publication of her first novel was a memorable event in the Negro literary world. W. E. B. Du Bois greeted its arrival with the following words:

> The novel that the Negro intelligentsia have been clamoring for has arrived with Jessie Fauset's first novel, *There Is Confusion.* What they have been wanting, if I interpret rightly, is not merely a race story told from the inside, but a cross section of the race life higher up the social pyramid and further from the base-line of the peasant and the soil than is usually taken.

William Stanley Braithwaite comments: "Miss Fauset in her novel *There Is Confusion,* has created an entirely new milieu in the treatment of the Race in fiction. She has taken a class within the Race, given it an established social standing, tradition, culture, and shown that its predilections are very much like those of any civilized group of human beings."

This statement coincides with the author's attitude expressed in the preface to her third novel, *The Chinaberry Tree.*

> I have depicted something of the home life of the colored American who is not being pressed too hard by the Furies of Prejudices, Ignorance, and

Economic Injustice. . . . And behold he is not so vastly different from any other Americans.

As it has become clear from these statements, Jessie Fauset's novels can be regarded as novels of manners of the Negro upper class, and her attitude is to emphasize the similarity between the blacks and the whites, rather than the difference. Yet the words in the same preface, "To be a Negro in America posits a dramatic situation," cannot be ignored. (pp. 66-7)

Several reasons can be given why Miss Fauset chooses the people of her circle for the characters of her novels—tales of the "non-cabareting, churchgoing Negroes, presenting in all their virtue and glory and with their human traits, their human hypocrisy and their human perversities glossed over." The first one is, of course, that these are the people she knows best; secondly, according to her own words, the publication of T. S. Stribling's *Birthright* in 1922 stimulated her into fiction writing. This novel about a mulatto boy, a Harvard graduate, who, with an idealistic ambition, tried to improve his own people in a small town in Tennessee and failed, was considered as "the most significant novel on the Negro written by a white American" at the time of its publication. However, the techniques are poor and ideas about the race questions are stale. In an interview Jessie Fauset tells what she thought of the book at its publication: "A number of us started writing at that time. . . . Nella Larsen and Walter White, for instance, were affected just as I was. We reasoned, 'Here is an audience waiting to hear the truth about us. Let us who are better qualified to present the truth than any white writer, try to do so.' " Whether or not this kind of novel was what the audience of the time had been waiting for becomes clear if we consider the difficulties Miss Fauset encountered in her efforts to find a publisher for her first novel. Publishers rejected her manuscript because "it contains no description of Harlem dives, no race riot, no picturesque, abject poverty." This shows the real attitude of the white world to the blacks.

Jessie Fauset's four novels have a similar plot—the heroine's pursuit of happiness. At the beginning of each novel the heroine has a rigid idea about the means to attain what she thinks to be happiness. The story evolves around the idea and a reader is told how her experiences in life affect and change it, or if not, what consequences the rigidity of her attitude has brought to her. In her first novel, *There Is Confusion,* the heroine, Joanna Marshall, was haunted with the idea of greatness. Even before she was five she determined that she would be someone great. . . . Joanna tried her best to be a great singer and dancer, but in spite of her extraordinary talent, she could attain only a mild success because of her color. She forced her sweetheart, Peter Bye, who had the tendency to be easily discouraged, to be a surgeon, the hardest road to take. Joanna even interfered with her brother's marriage to Maggie because Maggie was poor and without any family connections. Finally Joanna came to realize her mistake— that greatness, fame, and material success were not happiness. The most important thing was love. She and Peter were united in marriage and the novel ends with Joanna's declaration, "My creed calls for nothing but happiness."

Of course, this novel has more than this story. As Robert Bone severely says, "*There Is Confusion* is nothing if not well titled" [see *CLC,* Vol. 19]. The author puts too many events in the novel to give it an artistic unity and coherence. There is the whole history of the white and black Bye family, with the story of miscegenation and exploitation, which explains Peter's subdued temperament. This story comes to its climax at Peter's encounter with his white kinsman, Merriwether Bye, on the boat to France, at Merriwether's death in the war, and with it the extinction of the Bye family on the white side, at Merriwether's grandfather's wish to acknowledge the son of Peter and Joanna as his heir, and their proud refusal. There is also a story of a short engagement of Peter and Maggie while both of them were separated from their true loves. A brief but moving tale is about Vera Manning, who could pass, and her lover, Harley, who could not, and their final separation. When William Stanley Braithwaite calls Jessie Fauset "the potential Jane Austen of Negro literature," the comparison seems well taken. The subject matter is the same, and the social status of the characters is the upper middle class. But when we think of what creates the dramatic situations in the fiction of these two writers, we come to realize the vast difference between them. In Jane Austen's case, what moves the plot is a certain temperament created in each character by the manners and morals of the class he or she belongs to. In Jessie Fauset's case, though she chooses a certain class of Negro people, what really moves the story is not what is inherent to that class and hence to the character but what is imposed upon the person from outside. Miss Austen looks into the character's mind and creates humorous situations contrasting various temperaments and prejudices. In the Negro writer's novels the author's concern tends to be not psychological but social; and all the situations are serious. In a sense, Jessie Fauset's novels are those of social protest. (pp. 69-71)

In her next novel, *Plum Bun,* there is a great improvement in technique: William Braithwaite calls this novel "her most perfect artistic achievement." If we regard this novel as a melodramatic story of a girl who searched for a true love, fighting against adverse fate, it is the best conceived among Miss Fauset's four novels. She forms her novel around the nursery rhyme:

> To Market, to Market
> To buy a Plum Bun;
> Home again, Home again,
> Market is done.

She divides the novel into five parts, "Home," "Market," "Plum Bun," "Home Again," and "Market Is Done," to express the five stages of the heroine Angela Murray's ambition to attain happiness through passing, acquisition of wealth, her realization of the falseness of her idea, and the final happiness with her true lover. (p. 72)

To the parents, Junius and Mattie Murray, "who had known poverty and homelessness, the little house on Opal Street represented the *ne plus ultra* of ambition." But to the elder of their two daughters, Angela, the house seemed "the dingiest, drabbest" place. Angela thought that the shortest way to "the paths which lead to broad thoroughfares, large, bright houses, delicate niceties of existence" is to cross the color line and to live as a white girl. After her parents' death she cut off her family ties and even denied her only sister, Virginia, who showed color. She came to New York from Philadelphia and studied painting. The reason she chose art was not that she was interested in painting but because, through her study of art, she could meet interesting and wealthy people who would serve her purpose. She was gifted but "her gift was not for her the end of existence; rather it was an adjunct to life which was to know light, pleasure, gaiety and freedom." She found out that the surest way to accomplish her ambition was to marry a rich white man. She met a very wealthy young man, Roger Fielding, and tried every means to attract him and make him love her, though she was attracted to a quaint fellow student at Cooper Union, Anthony Cross. However, the result was that Roger only made her his mistress, because he did not care to marry a poor girl, and eventually threw her away when he was tired of her.

As a subplot, Miss Fauset describes the contrasting life of Angela's younger sister, Virginia, who came to Harlem and found happiness in teaching music to black children and in her marriage to Mathew Henson. Angela thought, "Jinny had changed her life and been successful. Angela had changed hers and had found pain and unhappiness. Where did the fault lie?" Miss Fauset seems to say that the fault lies in the fact that Angela used everything, her family, her friends, her profession, for the sake of her pursuit of happiness—she exploited everything, while Jinny always tried to serve others. This preaching of Christian virtues of service and sacrifice seems a little strange, but quite acceptable, for Miss Fauset's novels are in the tradition of the eighteenth- and nineteenth-century novels in subject and technique. However, the explanation she gives for Angela's selfishness surprises a reader:

> In all her manifestations of human relationship, how selfish she had been! She had left Virginia, she had taken up with Roger to further her own interest. . . . She had been too intent always on happiness for herself. Her father, her mother and Jinny had always given and she had always taken. Why was that? Jinny had sighed: "Perhaps you have more white blood than Negro in your veins." Perhaps this selfishness was what the possession of white blood meant: the ultimate definition of Nordic Supremacy.

This stereotyping of the white race as a kind of white fiend startles us when it comes from an intelligent person like Miss Fauset. Yet she never blames Angela for her most significant act—passing—for she knows the meaning of the expression "free, white and twenty-one." Also, though Harlem is gay and full of life and energy, it is "after all a city within a city." The problem of crossing the color line has been treated by several black writers before her: Frances E. W. Harper and Charles Chesnutt are among them. Mrs. Harper's attitude toward this question is that the near-white people have to cast their lot with their Negro race. Miss Fauset's attitude to the race solidarity is ambivalent. (pp. 72-4)

She even tries to describe the difference which the black blood made to people like Anthony and Angela—the near-white people. Yet when it comes to the question of the black intellectuals' role in the advancement of their race, her attitude becomes skeptical. She clearly shows the idea of the talented tenth, and treats the less fortunate of her race as if they were an inferior kind. Van Meier, one of the characters of *Plum Bun,* said: "Those of us who have forged forward, who have gained the front ranks in money and training, will not, are not able as yet to go our separate ways apart from the unwashed, untutored herd. We must still look back and render service to our less fortunate, weaker brethren." The standard of her judgment is that of the white world. Miss Fauset fails to present a new aesthetic peculiar to her own race.

Her third novel, *The Chinaberry Tree,* is considered by many critics as the weakest among her four novels. . . . This novel deals with the narrow-mindedness of a black community in a town in New Jersey, Red Brook. The story evolves around the huge chinaberry tree that Colonel Halloway brought

from the South for his lifelong lover, Aunt Sal, his mother's maid. Though he could not marry her because of her color, he did everything possible for Aunt Sal and their beautiful daughter, Laurentine. Aunt Sal was contented with her life, though she suffered a great deal from the prejudices of the white people and the moral accusation of the black people, for she knew what love meant to her. . . . Yet the black community of Red Brook regarded her as a degenerated woman and treated her and her daughter as pariahs. They said the strange family had bad blood. The most galling experience to Laurentine happened when she was a little girl. One of her friends stopped playing with her all of a sudden. Seeing the friend playing with other girls, Laurentine went up to her and asked the reason.

> Lucy stared at her, her eyes large and strangely gray in her dark face. "I wanted to Laurentine," she answered, "but my mumma say I dasn't. She say you got bad blood in your veins." Abruptly she left her former friend, ran to the table and came back with a tiny useless knife in her hand. "Don't you want me to cut yo' arm and let it out?"

Through her twenty-four years of life, Laurentine came to have an indelible complex about her birth, and every time something went wrong with her life she put the blame on it, and most of the time she was right. She wanted, above anything else, security in life. She tried in vain to make Phil Hacket, the richest Negro youth of the town, with a political ambition, marry her. Phil could not because he knew her strange parentage would be an obstacle to his career. Laurentine finally found her happiness with Dr. Denlaigh. As usual, Miss Fauset uses a subplot in this novel, describing the life of Melissa Paul, Laurentine's younger cousin. If there is anything to blame in this novel, it is this artificial subplot of incestuous love—obviously influenced by Greek tragedies—between Melissa and her half-brother, Malory Forten.

The main point of this novel, however, is to show a reader why colored people had to be rigid with their moral code and how Laurentine and Melissa, though in different ways, had to suffer from it. Though full of descriptions of elegant lives of wealthy colored people, we cannot help feeling what a strong influence the problem of race has had in forming black people's mentality. One example of this is, when black boys started to fight at a skating carnival, the minister complained: "Now boys, boys, don't start nothin'. Too many white folks here for that. We don't want this kind thing closed to us." They have to be decent and moralistic to avoid the deprecating criticism of the whites. In spite of the unfavorable criticism, this book presents a deeper and subtler problem—the impact of the racial discriminations and prejudices by the whites on the black society in the long run.

Her last novel, *Comedy: American Style,* is a curious one. So far as the techniques are concerned, this is the most elaborate of Miss Fauset's novels. . . . The first two chapters show us the family background, social circumstances, and so forth, concerning the heroine, Olivia Cary, her children, and their friends. Olivia, who firmly believed that every advantage in the world can be attained only through the possession of white skin, forced her two older children, Chris and Teresa, to pass. Chris rebelled against her and, ignoring her wish, found his happiness with Phebe, a Negro girl with white skin and golden hair who remained faithful to her mother's race. But Teresa, after she was forced to denounce her handsome but brown-skinned lover, Henry Bates, came to realize that she was too much of her mother's making to rebel against her. When confronted by Henry as to whether she would choose him or her mother, she almost unconsciously said: "I was thinking, I was wondering—your Spanish, you know. Couldn't you use it most of the time and . . . and pass for a Mexican? In that way we could avoid most inconveniences. . . ." This suggestion for passing hurt Henry deeply and their relationship ended. Teresa succumbed to her mother's wish and married a petty and miserly French linquist, Aristide Pailleron, in Toulouse, and led a miserable life. Oliver, the youngest and most beautiful child, had brown skin. His mother never showed him love and somehow contrived never to be seen with him on the street. When she had white women for tea at home—Olivia herself had passed into the white world—she treated the child as if he were a houseboy. When he found out that his mother thought that he was an obstacle to the happiness of other members of the family, he killed himself. Even after this tragedy Olivia was adamant in her belief. Finally, she went away to France, and the book ends with a picture of Olivia, bleak and lonely, living in a dingy Paris pension. When we finish reading the book, Olivia's coldness toward her family is unbelievable. Also, there are some unnatural situations: How could Olivia hide that she and her family were Negroes, when her husband, Dr. Cary, was practicing in the black community in Philadelphia, even though he had white skin? Yet a reader somehow is made to feel that the blame should not be placed totally on Olivia. All through this novel sufferings of the gifted and brilliant young people, like Phebe, Chris, Nicholas, and their friends—prejudices and discriminations in education, in profession, and in human relationships—are shown. You are almost convinced that you have to have white skin to enjoy living. I think the author's intention lies there, judging from the ironical title of the book.

This is the only book among her four novels with a depressing ending. Except for one slight light of Chris and Phebe's life, everything is under a dark shadow. Olivia, trying to cheat the world, cheated herself, her husband, and her family. In spite of many unnatural situations in the novel, a reader will readily accept William Braithwaite's comment on Olivia:

> She is the symbol of a force that must ultimately be acknowledged and discussed frankly by both races in America and when that discussion takes place there will be concessions and revisions on the part of white Americans which will make it possible to draw her like again as a warning.

And it seems symbolic that Jessie Fauset ended her literary career with this tragic portrayal of Olivia Cary.

Jessie Fauset is not a first-rate writer. First of all she failed to attain what Alain Locke called "the buoyancy from within compensating for whatever pressure there may be of conditions from without," though she was not unconscious of what was happening in the Negro world of the 1920s. Her appreciation of Negro musicals like *Shuffle Along* shows that she was aware of the new stirring of the black energy. . . . Yet this is a far cry from the younger artists' positive affirmation of the blackness. (pp. 75-9)

In a way, she shows the tragic situation which faces many of the black intellectuals: they are making too much of the white world, so that they can never escape its influence. Even if they try to create works unique to their race, they do not possess means to express them. They are deprived of the black soul. Jessie Fauset has never known the life of the black people of the rural South, nor the ghettos of the Northern cities. She came from a well-to-do old Philadelphia family, was educated at Cornell University, where she majored in French and was elected a member of Phi Beta Kappa. She did her graduate work at the University of Pennsylvania, and had been to France three times by the time of the publication of her first novel. The only thing she could do as an artist was to produce "uniformly sophomoric, trivial and dull" novels with almost painful persistency, to show the world the goodness of the black people and to ask justice for the race. In her ideas she belongs to the older school of black writers like Mrs. Harper and Mrs. Hopkins, who wrote novels to "raise the stigma of degradation from [my] race." (pp. 79-80)

Miss Fauset does not have anything to do with "the investigation of the human soul" and her interest lies solely on the social level, yet there is one saving grace: the soundness of her judgment on racial situations in this country.

When we reflect upon the fact that her four novels came into the world between 1924 and 1934, and that the final picture she presents is the tragic product of the society of the white supremacy—Olivia Cary—we cannot deny that Miss Fauset had never drunk of the heady illusion of the Harlem Renaissance that affected many young blacks: the whites were accepting the black primitivism as a part of their civilization and hence the blacks as their equals. It was just a fad, exploited by commercialism, which came to its sudden end with the financial crash of 1929. Langston Hughes writes as follows:

> We were no longer in vogue, anyway, we Negroes. Sophisticated New Yorkers turned to Noel Coward. Colored actors began to go hungry, publishers politely rejected new manuscripts, and patrons found other uses for their money.

Jessie Fauset's observation on the social scene of the United States of the time is sane and sound. (pp. 80-1)

At the beginning of the discussion of Jessie Fauset's novels I said that the fact that Jean Toomer's *Cane* and Jessie Fauset's *There Is Confusion* came into the world almost simultaneously was important. What I mean is that the kind of novels Jessie Fauset wrote could have been nourishment and root for the flowering of quite different kinds of works represented by *Cane,* until these two tendencies are united in one and bring about the establishment of the black culture. Unfortunately, the white world took up only one side, because it coincided, in a way, with their conception of the black people, and ignored the other. This pattern in the treatment of the black arts has been repeated again and again, and the black arts have had several false flowerings without bearing any fruit. (p. 82)

> *Hiroko Sato, "Under the Harlem Shadow: A Study of Jessie Fauset and Nella Larsen," in* The Harlem Renaissance Remembered, *edited by Arna Bontemps, Dodd, Mead & Company, 1972, pp. 63-89.*

JOSEPH J. FEENEY, S.J.

Writing in 1949, a critic complained that "contemporary Negro fiction, though it follows a darkly tragic pattern, bears no resemblance to classical Greek tragedy." He found that modern Black novels emphasized blood and killing and lacked Greek composure and universality. But in 1931 a Black woman published a novel which had indeed used many techniques of Greek tragedy to add a dimension of universality and bloodless horror to a story of love and domestic life among comfortable Blacks in a small north Jersey town. The novel was Jessie Fauset's *The Chinaberry Tree*.

The book told the love stories of two middle-class black girls, one eighteen and one well into her twenties, in the fictional town of Red Brook. One of these stories, that of the young and vivacious Melissa Paul, combined a suspense novel and a Greek tragedy; Miss Fauset tried to keep the reader in suspense about the ending and at the same time have him experience the inevitable doom of a classic family curse. To a surprising extent she succeeded in maintaining the Greek tragic mood despite the suspense and happy ending, but some sense of the plot—or at least Melissa's part in it—is necessary to understand the writer's accomplishment.

Two young cousins, Laurentine Strange and Melissa Paul, were both illegitimate. Laurentine knew her parentage—she was the child of a black mother and a white father who had a deep and warm love affair in Red Brook—and felt herself the innocent victim of this "bad blood," a family curse. Melissa, however, believed that she had been legitimately conceived and born in Philadelphia, far away from the family problems in Red Brook. But in reality Melissa's mother, staying with her relatives in Red Brook, had become the mistress of a man named Forten and Melissa was, in fact, Forten's child; Melissa's mother, becoming pregnant, had immediately left Red Brook, gone to Philadelphia, and married Mr. Paul. For eighteen years there had been little contact between the Philadelphia Pauls and the Red Brook relatives until, at the beginning of the novel, Melissa came to live with her aunt and cousin in Red Brook. Then in the course of the novel Melissa met, fell in love with, and almost married young Malory Forten, her own half-brother. Only at the end of the book, in a series of recognition scenes, did Melissa and Malory discover their blood relationship and the horror of their love. The reader, like them, does not discover the incestuous dimension until the end of the book.

Miss Fauset maintained suspense, then, by withholding from the reader the knowledge of Melissa's and Malory's parentage; by withholding this information Miss Fauset gained her suspense at the cost of that Greek sense of horror in which the reader (like the Greek audience) would watch the characters discover the truth which the onlooker already knew. For this suspense, too, the novelist traded most of her opportunities for irony. Yet Miss Fauset still managed to keep many aspects of Greek tragedy: a family curse, a sense that fate ruled events, a tragic inevitability, and the use of recognition scenes. (pp. 211-12)

Some of the actions of these families, in consequence of the family curses, seemed to be designed and ruled by fate. The developing love of Melissa and Malory, especially, seemed fated. The narrator spoke of "this year in which fate showed itself at its sorriest" and the Teiresias-like Mr. Stede, a wise, old friend of the Stranges, commented that "things don't happen, e'fects don't happen because a man sez this or that. They jist happen because this is for you and thet for me." . . . As the love between Melissa and Malory developed and they began to make wedding plans, Mr. Stede groaned, "God, You know, that hadn't oughta happen." Finally, Malory, after he had discovered the horrible truth, raised his arms to "the blazing, pitiless sky" and cried, "Oh God, how could You do it? You knew I loved her . . . You knew I wanted her . . . and she's my sister!"

Through the use of the family curse, fate, and careful plotting the reader senses an impending doom, a tragic inevitability. Because Miss Fauset maintained the suspense of a conventional novel and did not indicate the incestuousness of the young people's developing love, the reader does not know just what the doom will be. But Miss Fauset was careful, especially toward the climax of the novel, to communicate the sense of at least some impending doom. The various neighbors' comments on the love of Melissa and Malory were almost sibyllic. . . . Even Melissa herself noticed a change in the townspeople, "a queer aloofness that had in it something different from either meanness or malice, something faintly terrifying." (pp. 213-14)

Sensing the arrival of fate and destruction of love, the reader is prepared for the book's several recognition scenes. Mr. Stede was the first to recognize the connection between their secret love and their lineage, and "he sat up straight, his faded eyes at last scared and miserable." Calling on God, he said that Malory had to give up Melissa, for he knew that Melissa's mother and Malory's father had been lovers and that the two young people were quite possibly sister and brother. He told a mutual friend, Gertrude Brown, so that she could handle the situation; her recognition made her pale, frightened, and tearful. Gertrude's sister, Kitty, next found out and she wondered how God could permit such a love to develop; implying the Aristotelian "fear" of tragedy, Kitty cried, "That poor girl! . . . You know for the first time I'm really afraid . . . I'm afraid of life." Malory, prevented by his mother and sister from bringing Melissa into his home, was told the truth in his turn by his wraithlike mother and sister who "told him what he had to know . . . told him why they were always so sad." (p. 214)

Miss Fauset's use of these Greek elements—the family curse, the notion of fate, the inevitability of some doom, the recognition scenes—provided the substantial imitation of Greek tragedy; a few images and verbal touches underscored the Greek tone. In a recurring nightmare Melissa was terrified by the Greek comic and tragic masks, especially by the leering laughter of the comic mask. . . . [The] novelist occasionally (and rather artificially) mentioned the muses, the gods, Fate, Chance, the Furies, and the maenads.

In commenting on *The Chinaberry Tree* as a Greek tragedy, I do not mean to suggest that the Greek framework is woodenly imposed on Miss Fauset's story; the opposite is the case. The reader is first interested in the story of Miss Fauset's characters, before he recognizes the Greek dimension. He feels the fated inevitability before he consciously reflects on the artistic parallel. The American Black men and women are not turned into Greeks, but Miss Fauset treats her characters as contemporary Americans, middle-class Blacks, who remind us of Greek tragic figures.

Does *The Chinaberry Tree* succeed as a Greek tragedy? On the plot level it does, for the reader is interested in the developing doom and feels the hopeless situation of Melissa and Malory. But there are several problems elsewhere. The novel does not share in the religious beliefs and philosophical undercurrents of the Greeks; thus the role of fate or of a family curse is not as strong as for the Greeks. Further, the love story of Laurentine takes up a good part of the book and prevents a focus on the central tragedy. Finally, the book remains at heart a domestic novel. At the end Melissa goes back to an old beau, Malory is removed from the picture, and in a closing scene the Strange family all share in happiness as they enjoy a picnic under the old chinaberry tree. There remains a memory of tragedy, but the novel ends happily as Laurentine's fiance reflects (a bit obviously), "There actually is such a thing as Greek Tragedy even in these days. . . . We were almost swamped with it. But the wave missed us." There is Greek tragedy in *The Chinaberry Tree* but it is alloyed with much conventional sentiment. (pp. 214-15)

Joseph J. Feeney, S.J., "Greek Tragic Patterns in a Black Novel: Jessie Fauset's 'The Chinaberry Tree'," in CLA Journal, Vol. XVIII, No. 2, December, 1974, pp. 211-15.

AMRITJIT SINGH

In America a fairly rigid caste system defines the status of blacks. "Being colored is like being born in the basement of life, with the door locked and barred—and the white people live upstairs." Using a caste framework to explain black status in America originated with W. Lloyd Warner and his associates in the thirties and forties, and, when applied to Americans of African origin, is a useful conceptual tool. Middle-class blacks might have life-styles and values parallel to their white counterparts, but they nonetheless share with the lower-class blacks certain limitations on their "life-chances." Despite increasing desegregation and the new opportunities for middle-class blacks during the last two decades, the color caste persists.

Although biological theories are used to justify the artificial division into black and white, Afro-American writers have always exposed the dilemmas arising from the classification of individuals according to caste. In this tradition the Harlem Renaissance writers insist that caste is a matter of social designation; it is not based on scientific evidence. (pp. 89-90)

Passing as a theme in literature or as a happening in real life could not have taken the twenties by surprise. But disappearing into the white world is more than an Afro-American phenomenon; immigrants of different backgrounds have accelerated their social mobility through assimilation. For a black, the risks in passing have always been higher, but the possibilities that lie beyond have been more tempting. For obvious reasons, individuals from white ethnic groups find it easier to assimilate, but even in cases where it proves difficult, they have advantages over their black counterparts. For one thing, they were not humiliated by a legally and socially sanctioned system that segregated them on the basis of their ethnicity. Moreover, even when the hyphenated Americans were discriminated against, they always had the dubious freedom of feeling superior to American Negroes.

But blacks did not have such options. They either grudgingly accepted their subservient status, or tried to maneuver themselves onto the other side of the fence. (pp. 91-2)

The three major Renaissance novels of passing—[Walter White's] *Flight,* [Jessie Fauset's] *Plum Bun,* and [Nella Larsen's] *Passing*—all reflect the same pattern in their octoroon heroine's life—yielding to the temptation of passing as white, living as mistress or wife to a bigoted white man, and finally returning to the fold of black life when she begins missing the warmth, the color, the vivacity of black life. The three books are set in different cities for the early portions of their heroines' careers, but in each case the lure of Harlem plays a part in the heroine's decision to return to black life. Like other novels dealing with the lives of middle-class black Americans, the novels of passing "portrayed people, who, while black by the definitions imposed in America, looked and behaved very much like whites." Thus, at one level there is an attempt to delineate a dimension of culture and values which the middle-class blacks shared with white Americans. At the same time, these novels inform white readers that middle-class blacks have no intention or desire to relinquish the joy and abandon of black life for the dullness of the white bourgeoisie. The fleeting but exaggerated pictures of the lower-class black, who enjoys himself in spite of his problems, indicate the magnetic pull that brings the heroines back to black life. (pp. 93-4)

[Jessie Fauset] emphasizes the social and economic aspects of the passing theme in *Plum Bun.* Fauset's approach to passing is well expressed in the nursery rhyme epigraph that supplies the titles of her novel's five sections:

> To Market, to market
> To buy a Plum Bun
> Home again, Home again
> Market is done.

The heroine, Angela Murray, passes as white to seek greater opportunities for herself as a young girl and artist. Although the unfolding of Fauset's thesis in *Plum Bun* runs parallel to White's in *Flight,* Fauset shows a finer craftsmanship in anticipating the turns and twists of her plot and manages to write a story whose exploitation of the black-white ironies in American life parallels that of Mark Twain's in *Pudd'nhead Wilson.* A successful device is the presence from the beginning to the end of Virginia Murray, Angela's brown sister, a perfect foil to the heroine. Fauset also avoids the cluttered multiplicity of interests that had plagued *There is Confusion* and tries to concentrate on related aspects of one significant theme; *Plum Bun* is easily her most successful novel.

Angela and Jinny grow up in a small house on Opal Street in Philadelphia where their honest and hardworking parents shower warmth and affection on both. Yet the two sisters are as different as can be. Jinny has a simple ambition in life—to be able to keep house like Mattie, her mother, for a man like Junius, her father. Angela, restless and ambitious, feels cramped in the drab little house. With her mother, she passes for fun in downtown restaurants and theaters. But although her mother never gives thought to serious passing, Angela is fascinated with the idea of taking a short cut to "the paths which lead to broad thoroughfares, large bright houses, delicate niceties of existence." When Junius and Mattie both die within days of each other (Fauset is good at getting rid of people who have served their purpose for the plot—sometimes two or three characters die on a single page), Angela decides to take her share of the estate and disappears into the white world as Angèle Mory.

Arriving in New York, Angela admits that she is breaking with her family and race to seek greater opportunities less as an artist and more as a young white girl. . . . Failing to invite serious matrimonial interest from the rich and suave Roger Fielding, she overcomes her "fastidiousness" to become his mistress. Even though she does not love Roger, she develops in time "a beautiful feeling" for him. For a while, she even forgets her intention of marrying in order to secure her future. She and Roger both know that "her surrender was made out of the lavish fullness and generosity of her heart." Yet Roger deserts her abruptly and she turns in her loneliness to Anthony Cross, her classmate from an art class at Cooper

Union, whose earlier attentions she had politely ignored. In a curious turn of events, Anthony reveals that he is part Negro and that he is already engaged to Jinny, even though still in love with Angela.

Meanwhile, Angela analyzes her career to date and comes to accept what her mother and sister have always understood—that "when one is taken up with the problem of living, with just life itself . . . being colored or not is just one thing more or less you have to contend with." She realizes that she has been selfish in her pursuit of happiness and learns to appreciate close family connections and the warmth of black life. She fights her new malaise with inspiration from the values of black life in America, particularly the endurance blacks have long shown in the face of heavy odds. Now she begins to see blacks "as a people powerfully, overwhelmingly endowed with the essence of life. They had to persist, had to survive because they did not know how to die." (pp. 95-7)

Some early reviewers justifiably denounced the excessive use of coincidence in the book—especially in the hackneyed device by which Anthony Cross and Angela Murray are both shown to be of the "same race"—they also gave the author due credit for her remarkable restraint in the treatment of a potentially sensational subject. Her interest is primarily sociological rather than psychological, in situation rather than character, and she uses it in *Plum Bun* to her maximum advantage. She does not allow genealogy, glimpsed briefly in the case of Anthony Cross, to overwhelm *Plum Bun* as it had *There is Confusion*. She draws both her black and white characters clearly enough as individuals to meet the demands of her theme and weaves their reactions to passing into the general pattern of the narrative.

Fauset introduces protest without resorting to pages of introspection or self-pity. Angela's black friend, Rachel Powell, along with Angela, is granted a fellowship to study at the Fountainebleu School of Fine Arts near Paris in an open competition; but the award to Rachel is withdrawn when the Selection Committee learns of her racial identity. A committee of concerned citizens meets at the house of Martha Burden, Angela's white liberal friend, to fight on behalf of Rachel, who refuses to take part in any such effort. Anthony Cross dramatically announces his racial identity and justifies Rachel's attitude by emphasizing that blacks sometimes "have to stop their fight for the trimmings of life in order to hang on to the essentials which they've got to have and for which they must contend too every day just as hard as they had the first day." Anthony's revelation of his racial background causes confusion among his white listeners, many of whom are shown to harbor deep prejudices behind their liberal postures. However, it is Angela who must rescue the beleaguered Rachel from a horde of journalists eager to exploit her story for sensation. Pestered by questions from newsmen and frustrated in her attempt "to explain to these smug, complacent people Rachel's ambition . . . her only too obvious endeavour to share their training and not their friendship," Angela announces that she is turning down the American Committee Fund grant for the same reason. In absorbing the reactions of her white friends to her avowal of black ancestry, Angela discovers how Rachel Salting, the Jewish girl of high ideals, hurt deeply over anti-Jewish prejudice, is herself full of antiblack sentiment; how the rich and lonely Mrs. Denver finds the courage to continue her friendship with Angela, and

how Elizabeth and Walter Sandburg, the young white couple, pass the test as genuine friends of the Negro. (pp. 97-8)

The near disappearance of the passing novel during the last three decades is partly a measure of the inadequate objectives that the earlier black novelists wanted to convey through their near-white protagonists and partly a reflection of the changes in America during the same period. Contending that mulattoes have never really been representative of black people, Blyden Jackson argues that since the forties, the black novelist has come to find the tragic mulatto protagonist "inadequate for his larger hopes." Some Renaissance novelists, especially Jessie Fauset and Walter White, did use their mulatto heroines to bear the weight of racial protest. White and Fauset moved away from the earlier novelists' misdirected sympathies in dealing with the tragic mulatto as someone isolated from both races and provided a nonbiological motivation for their main characters; they followed the lead of James Weldon Johnson's *The Autobiography of an Ex-Colored Man* and foreshadowed later sociocultural and literary Afro-American developments. (p. 104)

> *Amritjit Singh, " 'Fooling Our White Folks': Color Caste in American Life," in his* The Novels of the Harlem Renaissance: Twelve Black Writers, 1923-1933, *The Pennsylvania State University Press, 1976, pp. 89-104.*

BARBARA CHRISTIAN

[Jessie Fauset] was one of the intellectuals who "midwifed" the Harlem Renaissance, to which end she wrote articles covering a wide range of interests, from Pan-Africanism to blacks in the American theater. Her article **"The Gift of Laughter"** is an incisive analysis of the black actor as the "funny man" of America. She quickly grasped in this article the paradox of this gift of laughter that the American Negro is contributing to the American theater:

> In passing one pauses to wonder if this picture of the black American as a living comic supplement has not been tainted in order to camouflage the real feeling and knowledge of his white compatriot. Certainly the plight of the slaves under even the mildest of masters could never have been one to awaken laughter. And no genuinely thinking person, no really astute observer, looking at the Negro in modern American life, could find his condition even now a first aid to laughter. That condition may be variously deemed hopeless, remarkable, admirably inspiring, depressing; it can never be dubbed merely amusing.

Yet, although she knows the image of the laughing Negro to be partly a ploy, she does not discount the quality of zest and the love of life that the black actor brings to the stage:

> The remarkable thought about this gift of ours is that it has its rise, I am convinced, in the very woes which beset us. Just as a person driven by great sorrow may finally go into an orgy of laughter, just so an oppressed and too hard driven people breaks over into compensating laughter and merriment. It is our emotional salvation.

Fauset, however, seldom mentions the depressing conditions under which most turn-of-the-century blacks lived in her novels. Her fiction is peopled by characters who are "trying for a life of reason and culture," culture in this case being

Western refinement. Her novels insist that the upper-middle-class Negro has the same values as the upper-class white. This indeed may be true, and a presentation of upper-class Negro life is certainly interesting material for fiction. The problem with Fauset's novels is that she gives us this particular Negro exclusively and as the representative of what the race is capable of doing. "She records a class in order to praise a race." Her Negroes become apologists for the race, indicators of the heights of refinement blacks might attain, given the opportunity. (pp. 41-2)

Jessie Fauset could certainly write with authority about the upper-middle-class Negro of the day. She herself came from an old Philadelphian family and, in contrast to most black women of the day, received an extensive formal education. . . . She traveled extensively in Europe and was as aware of the European culture as she was of upper-class American Negro life. Nor was she a "puff" of refinement. . . . She wrote consistently about the problems and aims of the Negro, translated poems of French West Indians into English, and was committed to the betterment of the race. She was in many ways a fine example of W. E. B. Du Bois's "talented tenth." (pp. 42-3)

[Fauset] had at her disposal, because of her intimate knowledge of her class and because she was not fooled by the fad of primitivism, unique and significant subject matter. But because she was so conscious of being an image maker and because she accepted wholesale American values, except on the issue of race, her novels hardly communicate the intellectual depth that some of her articles do. Her fiction does not capture the essence of the upper-middle-class Negro society, a subject that certainly would show the relationship of class to race in America, because her characters lack critical insight and complexity, and because her plots seldom rise beyond the level of melodrama. In other words, her stories become bad fairytales in which she sacrifices the natural flow of life to the thesis that she feels she must prove—that blacks are as conventional as whites. Upper-middle-class blacks may have been as conventional, but Fauset's novels are so conditioned by her narrow mind set—the glorification of this position—that she does not allow her characters to become themselves.

Given her orientation, it is not surprising that Fauset's novels accepted the literary conventions of the nineteenth-century black novel. Her heroines are proper light-skinned women who unquestionably claim propriety as the highest ideal. They pursue the values of material success through marriage and inevitably believe that refinement is a reflection of spirituality. As a result, her heroines, like Laurentine Strange in *The Chinaberry Tree* and Angela Murray in *Plum Bun,* suffer crises because of a social mishap, either of birth or deportment. Nor does Fauset exercise any critical distance toward the unimportance of her heroines' major crises. She, too, believes that not being able to take up with the "right people" is a tragedy.

Her heroines, of course, are always beauties, according to the norms of the day. Light-skinned, long-haired, fine and graceful, they resemble princesses from a children's story who but for the complications of haphazard Negro birth would live happily ever after. *The Chinaberry Tree,* for example, is the story of Laurentine Strange, who is unfortunate enough to be the daughter of an ex-slave, Aunt Sal, and her former master, Captain Halloway. Far from having a primarily physical relationship, her parents were passionately in love with each other. "Halloway was a lad of serious bent but of tearing ty-

rannical passion. He loved her . . . he could not marry her." Aunt Sal, a straight, brown-skinned woman, lives in the glow of her memorable passion, the only traces of which are her daughter Laurentine and her house protected by the chinaberry tree. The tree is ever present throughout the novel as comforter and solidifier until one wonders if Captain Halloway's spirit has entered it.

Although Aunt Sal might have been a woman of passion, her mulatta daughter Laurentine is a lady, except for her manner of birth and the strained strangeness that seems to come from her mixed blood. Appropriately, she is the finest beauty in the town, who except for the sordidness of her birth would have few social difficulties in life. But Laurentine Strange's background alienates her from upper-middle-class society to which, by virtue of shade and taste, she rightfully belongs. The novel is, to a large extent, the measure of her ability to step softly and straight, so she might be admitted into its shelter.

Fauset's novels also employ the theme of "passing," a phenomenon that exemplifies the shakiness of the upper middle class. If upper-middle-class blacks could successfully compete with whites, why then would they have to resort to passing? Ironically, passing is a major theme of the 1920s when race pride was supposedly at a peak. One might at first think that this theme fed into the American belief system that it is better to be white than black. In actuality, the theme, as it was presented in the twenties, heightened the white audience's awareness of the restrictions imposed upon talented blacks who then found it necessary to become white to fulfill themselves. Talented blacks, however, in the novels of Walter White, as well as Jessie Fauset, are the mulattoes, who are distinguished from other blacks by their restiveness and frustration, a motif reminiscent of the rebellious mulattoes of the abolitionist novels. Inevitably, though, in Fauset's novels as well as in most novels of the Renaissance, the passer returns to her race convinced that her loss of identity, as well as the values she must adopt to be in the white race, are too high a price to pay. Assailed by passion, the taint or glory of her black blood, depending on your point of view, these mulattas also resemble the tragic mulattas of antebellum novels.

It is significant, too, that the passer is often a woman who believes that through her marriage to a wealthy white man, she might gain economic security and more freedom of mobility. The process of passing could have peculiarly feminine overtones, for a woman can often cement her future according to the man she marries. This theme is so inordinately prevalent during this period, engaging the attention of black writers and white writers alike, that one is tempted to wonder if it offered vicarious wish fulfillment, as well as amusement for those blacks who would pass if they could, and titillating drama for a largely white reading audience. Sterling Brown summarized the characteristics of the passer in the Harlem Renaissance novel, underlining the difference in interpretation, according to the novelist's race:

> We have thus seen that the mulatto who "passes" has been a victim of opposing interpretations. Negro novelists urge his unhappiness, until he is summoned back to his people by the spirituals, or their full-throated laughter, or their simple, sweet ways. . . . White novelists insist upon the mulatto's unhappiness for other reasons. To them he is the anguished victim of a divided inheritance. Mathematically they work it out that his intellectual strivings and self-control come from his white

blood, and his emotional urgings, indolence and potential savagery come from his Negro blood. Their favorite character, the octoroon, wretched because of the "single drop of midnight in her veins," desires a white lover above all else, and must therefore go down to a tragic end. The white version is nearly a century old; the negro version sprang up recently.

In spite of their many social traumas, Fauset's heroines have great faith in America and in the American dream—that through hard work you can achieve equality. They even go one step further. They accept the precept that blacks must be superior to whites in their accomplishments to qualify. For what do they qualify? They qualify for freedom, yes, but not the freedom to experiment or experience. They want the highest of all American values: security. (pp. 43-5)

We must remember that Fauset exemplified the dominant position of the Harlem intellectuals of her day. Her works were praised by critics and her images exalted. However, her values also posed a serious threat to the New Negro Philosophy. If blacks were culturally no different from whites except when downtrodden, how could anyone posit a unique Negro genius, a specifically different culture? If Fauset's novels were to be believed, the Negro's peculiar contributions to America were a result of oppression rather than the consequence of a different cosmology or tradition. Also, what should one do with the issue of class? Why should lower-class Negroes rise up and change their situation if they only replaced one master with another, black like them, but master nonetheless. Fauset's novels indirectly pose the question of whether one could really be conservative about all things except race unless one were sitting in a position of relative comfort. (p. 47)

> *Barbara Christian, "The Rise and Fall of the Proper Mulatta," in her* Black Women Novelists: The Development of a Tradition, 1892-1976, *Greenwood Press, 1980, pp. 35-61.*

DEBORAH E. McDOWELL

[The essay from which this excerpt is taken was originally published in Afro-Americans in New York Life, *July, 1981.]*

Jessie Fauset's novels are generally read as novels of manners of the black middle class, the refined intelligentsia, written to emphasize that, except for the biological accident of color, blacks are no different from whites and should therefore enjoy all the rights and privileges that whites enjoy. . . . [She] was traditional to some extent, both in form and content, but as Gary de Cordova Wintz rightly observes, "in spite of her conservative, almost Victorian literary habits," Fauset "introduced several subjects into her novels that were hardly typical drawing room conversation topics in the mid-1920s. Promiscuity, exploitative sexual affairs, miscegenation, even incest appear in her novels. In fact prim and proper Jessie Fauset included a far greater range of sexual activity than did most of DuBois's debauched tenth."

When attention is given Fauset's introduction of these challenging themes, it becomes possible to regard her "novels of manners" less as an indication of her literary "backwardness" and more as a self-conscious artistic stratagem pressed to the service of her central fictional preoccupations. Since many of Fauset's concerns were unpalatable to the average reader of her day and hence unmarketable in the publishing arena, the convention of the novel of manners can be seen as

protective mimicry, a kind of deflecting mask for her more challenging concerns. Fauset uses classic fairy tale patterns and nursery rhymes in a similar fashion; however, although these stratagems are consciously employed, they are often clumsily executed.

In addition to the protective coloration which the conventional medium afforded, the novel of manners suited Fauset's works in that the tradition "is primarily concerned with social conventions as they impinge upon character." Both social convention and character—particularly the black female character—jointly form the nucleus of Fauset's literary concerns. The protagonists of all of her novels are black women, and she makes clear in each novel that social conventions have not sided well with them but, rather, have been antagonistic.

Without polemicizing, Fauset examines that antagonism, criticizing the American society which has institutionalized prejudice, safeguarded it by law and public attitude, and in general, denied the freedom of development, the right to well-being, and the pursuit of happiness to the black woman. In short, Fauset explores the black woman's struggle for democratic ideals in a society whose sexist conventions assiduously work to thwart that struggle. Critics have usually ignored this important theme which even a cursory reading of her novels reveals. This concern with exploring female consciousness and exposing the unduly limited possibilities for female development is, in a loose sense, feminist in impulse, placing Fauset squarely among the early black feminists in Afro-American literary history. It is this neglected dimension of Fauset's work—her examination of the myriad shadings of sexism and how they impinge upon female development—that is the focus of this discussion. A curious problem in Fauset's treatment of feminist issues, however, is her patent ambivalence. She is alternately forthright and cagey, alternately "radical" and conservative on the "woman question." On the one hand, she appeals for women's right to challenge socially sanctioned modes of feminine behavior, but on the other, she frequently retreats to the safety of traditional attitudes about women in traditional roles. At best, then, we can grant that Fauset was a quiet rebel, a pioneer black literary feminist, and that her characters were harbingers of the movement for women's liberation from the constrictions of cultural conditioning. (pp. 86-8)

[Fauset's short story] **"The Sleeper Wakes"** is crucial to an understanding of [her] concern with female psychology and socially-conditioned female role patterns. In this story Fauset sets the pattern that she will return to, in varying degrees, in each of her novels. She positions her major character in the adolescent stage . . . to demonstrate that her possibilities for development and attainment of freedom, well-being, and happiness are sorely limited in range. These limited possibilities are due both to how she perceives herself, based on socialization, as well as to how society perceives her. This early protagonist, like those to follow, aspires to "grow up" and marry, an orthodox female vocation, but she has extremely romantic notions not only about marriage, but also about life and human relationships in general. To dramatize her character's romanticism, Fauset uses patterns and imagery from classic fairy tales.

It is apparent even as early as 1920 that Fauset was aware of how folk literature—particularly fairy tales—serves to initiate the acculturation of children to traditional social roles, expectations, and behaviors, based on their sex. Marcia Lieberman has cogently explored this concept in " 'Some Day My Prince Will Come': Female Acculturation Through the Fairy Tale," where she outlines the fairy tale patterns and demonstrates how they condition women to limited roles and expectations. Lieberman points out that central to the fairy tale is a beautiful girl who is finally rewarded by marriage to a handsome prince. . . . Lieberman concludes that "since girls are chosen for their beauty, it is easy for a child to infer that beauty leads to wealth, that being chosen means getting rich." Thus "the system of rewards in fairy tales . . . equates these three factors: being beautiful, being chosen, and getting rich." These fairy tale patterns clearly operate in **"The Sleeper Wakes,"** which Fauset modeled on the classic tale, "Sleeping Beauty," for Amy, the protagonist, exists in a state of suspended animation, passively waiting for her prince to come. Unlike the classic Sleeping Beauty, however, Amy's "prince" does not bring her a "happily-ever-after" existence, but only the temporary illusion of happiness. Fauset inverts the classical ending to demonstrate that women's traditional attitudes and expectations about marriage are romantic and impractical. Moreover, the corresponding marital role-playing dictated by convention keeps women in stasis preventing their development of independence and autonomy.

When the story opens, Amy, a mulatto foster child, is growing up with the Boldins, a black family of modest means. She is youth personified, associated predominantly with the color pink, a symbol of innocence and femininity. We first see her in a dress shop, arrayed in a pink blouse, about to try on an apricot-colored dress. Her face is a "perfect ivory pink," highlighted by her "smooth, young forehead. All this made one look for softness and ingenuousness." Amy's physical appearance mirrors her perceptions. She sees life through the proverbial "rose-colored" lens, living totally in the realm of fantasy, fed by fairy tales, "the only reading that had ever made any impression on her," and movies of poor, beautiful girls who married "tremendous rich" men who gave them everything. Mr. Boldin's warning to Amy that "pretty girl pictures are not always true to life" does nothing to shake her persistent belief that "something wonderful" will happen to her, a belief that demonstrates a passive ("female") rather than active orientation. Following her talk with Mr. Boldin, Amy goes upstairs to her room for her flight into fantasy. She "lit one gas jet and pulled down the shades. Then she stuffed tissue paper in the key hole and under the doors, and lit the remaining gas-jets. The light thus thrown on the mirror of the ugly oak dresser was perfect. . . . In the mirror she apostrophized . . . the beautiful, glowing vision of herself." The passage is important for exposing Amy's tendency to refract the harsh light of reality (suggested by the "ugly oak dresser") through her romantic imagination (suggested by the light from the gas jets). Amy believes that this image of herself reflected in the mirror will bring her happiness. . . . Deciding that her home environment with the Boldins is stifling, Amy runs away to New York, "Altogether happy in the expectation of something wonderful, which she knew some day must happen."

At the end of her second year in New York, Amy meets Zora Harrison; their developing friendship is a study in contrasts, a technique Fauset uses in each novel. The developing protagonist is foiled by more sophisticated characters who introduce her to alternative ways of thinking and behaving. While Amy is soft and pliable, Zora is hard and callous. Amy's "blonde, golden beauty" contrasts with Zora's dark beauty. Amy is passive and naive, Zora, active and worldly. In other

words, while Amy is content to be more acted upon than acting, Zora actively goes after what she wants in life with a selfish and hardened determination. She first encourages Amy to marry the wealthy Stuart James Wynne (his name has a regal sound) and then to divorce him should she become dissatisfied. A retired and wealthy stockbroker of fifty-five, Wynne is instantly attracted to Amy. She "seemed to him everything a girl should be—she was so unspoiled, so untouched." He proposes marriage and Amy accepts, thinking that he is her prince, her "dream come true."

In her marriage Amy is nothing but an adornment, a doll for Wynne's amusement. (It is obvious that Fauset is also adapting Ibsen's *A Doll's House* to the special problems of a black woman.) . . . Their relationship is founded on inequality, analogous to that of vassal and lord, child and parent. Her sole activities are reading to Wynne and affecting her " 'spoiled child air,' as he used to call it. It was the way he liked her best." Amy is perfectly content to act as a spoiled child, fearful of upsetting her placid, "doll house" existence, ruffled only by Wynne's coarse insults to their black servants. Although Amy is passing for white, she intensely identifies with the servants and finally begins to wonder how Wynne would react should he discover that she is black. She confidently assures herself that her beauty has an unshakable hold on him. . . . Amy's assurance and security are soon shattered, however, for in a violent argument between Wynne and one of the servants, Amy confesses her blackness. To her chagrin, her beauty is not a stay against her husband's consuming racial prejudice, for he wants to divorce her immediately after she reveals her heritage.

Amy moves to New York and is supported by Wynne's alimony payments, but her financial ease does nothing to assuage her feelings of emptiness and loneliness. . . . Amy's solitude precipitates a period of introspection during which she reviews her past and slowly rejects her lifelong assumption that her beauty was her pass to a world of infinite possibilities. Admitting to herself that "amazingly [her] beauty availed her nothing," she begins to make plans for her future as a woman single and alone. She contemplates going to Paris to try her hand at dress designing.

One afternoon while she works on a design, Wynne comes to visit. In his characteristic manner, he commands that she come back to live with him, attempting to entice her with jewels as he had before. Amy mistakes his gesture for a marriage proposal but he quickly explains that he merely wants a mistress. . . . Thus Amy, the sleeper, wakes to the harsh reality of a "prince" transformed into a consummate racist and sexist. Having discovered that Amy is black, Wynne—consistent with the white male's history of sexual exploitation of black women—regards remarriage to her as unthinkable. His attack reveals Fauset's understanding of a sexist society that often makes a marriage a form of prostitution, a vulgar financial arrangement that rewards women for being creatures of artifice and ornamentation and forces them to assume degrading forms of behavior.

With Wynne's insults Amy wakes from her romantic illusions about men and marriage, and to a realization of her own resources kept in dormancy by the dictates of convention. Whereas she had stifled the talent that would earn her a livelihood while relying instead on the supposed advantage of her beauty, Amy vows never more "to take advantage of her appearance to earn a living." She then releases her servants, refuses any more alimony from Wynne, and begins work as a dress designer to pay back all money received from Wynne to this point. When she has paid the sum in full, she feels "free, free! she had paid back her sorry debt with labor, money and anguish. From now on she could do as she pleased." Amy's freedom from monetary debt parallels her psychological freedom from her former slavish conformity to society's most invidious assumptions about blacks and women. Consistent with that nascent freedom, she makes plans to visit the Boldins, finally recognizing that they represent the regenerative virtues and riches of the black experience which she had rejected in pursuit of what was only a figment of happiness. More importantly, however, she makes plans to establish her own business, the returns on which will be not only financial solvency, but also the beginning of the self-reliance and autonomy that is impervious to society's assault. Fauset has thus inverted the classical fairy tale ending. "Happily-ever-after" is not marriage to a handsome, wealthy prince but realization and acceptance of the virtues of the black cultural experience as well as a realization and rejection of conventional social relationships that are injurious to the growth of selfhood.

Early in her career, then, Fauset is challenging sexual stereotypes and criticizing the conditions that give rise to them. In tracing Amy's growth from a fantasy-orientation to a realistic one, Fauset challenges some of society's most cherished sexist beliefs that women have bought wholesale, beliefs that have insured their marginality in society. Amy's story is a criticism of women who rely preeminently on beauty, which requires nothing of them, save for sitting and looking pretty. In so doing, they reinforce and perpetuate conventional stereotypes of women as passive sexual objects. Moreover, Fauset criticizes a society that encourages women to dissemble, to assume, uncritically, insulting and degrading forms of behavior in exchange for the so-called privilege of marriage. For all women who feign childishness and frivolity, who repress their talent and intelligence out of deference to an ideal of woman which men have largely created and maintained, Fauset has a message. These masquerades, she makes clear, are performed at great price. Stereotyped sexual roles, by their very nature, deny human complexity and stifle growth, completeness of being, a state toward which Fauset aims all of her women characters. Inasmuch as this role-playing is, more often than not, a prerequisite to marriage, as well as a requirement during marriage, Fauset questions an institution that demands that women remain locked in growth-retarding roles. Therefore, at least in its more conventional forms, marriage can work to limit women's possibilities for self-realization and autonomy, a position that Fauset curiously repudiates in her first novel, *There Is Confusion.*

There Is Confusion chronicles the development of the protagonist, Joanna Marshall, tracing primarily her ambition to become a stage success as a singer-dancer and the trials she encounters in the process. (pp. 88-93)

The multiple stylistic weaknesses of *There Is Confusion* . . . are somewhat compensated for by its strengths in content. As usual, critics have missed the essential point of the novel, reading it as a formulaic apology for the black middle class and a plea for acceptance by whites. These critics ignore Fauset's continued exploration of the circumscribing effects of sexism on women.

Throughout the novel Joanna is described as self-assured, cool, practical, egotistical, and independent. It seems evident from the beginning of the novel that she has neither desire nor intention to accept or conform to conventional images of women, an option encouraged by the general run of the Marshall household where Joanna's mother "insists on each child's [girls and boys] learning to do housework." The female-related fixation with physical beauty and the cosmetics that are so-called beauty aids is equally unappealing to Joanna. Rather, "she had the variety of honesty which made her hesitate and even dislike to do or adopt anything artificial, no matter how much it might improve her general appearance. No hair straighteners, nor even curling kits for her." Even dolls that have traditionally oriented female children toward roles as wives and mothers fail to appeal to Joanna. Her dolls were usually in her sister Sylvia's care while Joanna was "reading the life of some exemplary female," "notable women of color." Reading of these important women inspires in Joanna a "fixity of purpose." (p. 93)

Although Joanna is inspired by the notable examples of her female ancestors, she is initially unaware that racist and sexist practices, deeply entrenched in the social structure, work to frustrate her ambitions. Her father's success as a caterer has instilled in her the American success ethic, and she mistakenly believes that any ambition is realizable if one is diligent and industrious. The success ethic doesn't work for all, Joanna soon discovers, for when she isn't plagued by occupational barriers because of her race, she is because of her sex. Her perennial struggles finally convince her that "it was women who had the real difficulties to overcome, disabilities of sex and of tradition." . . . Fauset is suggesting that sexual discrimination, more so than racial, is responsible for Joanna's occupational difficulties.

Joanna's ambitions, her fixity of purpose, are in sharp contrast to those of her boyfriend Peter Bye, who aspires to be a doctor, but whose awareness of racial prejudice paralyzes him and renders him temporarily incapable of fighting to reach his goals. Thus Joanna's and Peter's turbulent relationship, her struggle to help him overcome his inertia, form the second plot of the novel. From the beginning, Joanna places her relationship with Peter second to her career ambitions. Although "she had a very real, very ardent feeling for Peter . . . it was still small, if one may speak of a feeling by size. Her love for him was a new experience, a fresh interest in her already crowded life, but it had not pushed aside the other interests. At nineteen she looked at love as a man of forty might—as 'a thing apart.' " . . . (p. 94)

Joanna's verbal sparring with Peter, her strong and critical objections to love and marriage, are extraordinary and antithetical to those of other young women her age who are predominantly shallow, unambitious, and consumed with thoughts of marriage. Peter is "pleasantly struck" by their "apparent lack of aspiration. . . . They seemed to be pretty well satisfied with being girls. A few were able to live at home, many sewed, a number of others taught. There was no talk of art, of fame, or preparation for the future among them." One, Arabelle Morton, explains to Peter, " 'Well, of course we want to get married, and we're not spoiling our chances by being highbrows. . . .' "

Like Arabelle, Maggie Ellersley has been conditioned to repress any ambition and intelligence for fear of threatening potential mates. Maggie's aspiration for social respectability via marriage constitutes still another plot line. Fauset sets Maggie and Joanna up as antitheses to dramatize differing perceptions of self between women and corresponding behavior patterns and expectations. The poor daughter of a working class woman, Maggie is drawn to Joanna and her family because of their financial success and their status as "Old Philadelphians." . . . Maggie sees marriage to a prosperous and respectable man as "one avenue of escape" from her "dreary existence." Men "were stronger than women, they made money" to support women. Joanna's brother, Phillip, conforms to Maggie's ideal, but Joanna breaks them up because she considers Maggie's social status "beneath" Phillip's.

Her plans to establish a relationship with Phillip foiled, in desperation Maggie begins seeing an older man, Henderson Neal, a boarder in her mother's house. Fauset provides an ironic twist to Maggie's story, for unknown to her, he is a gambler, exactly opposite to her wishes for a socially respectable man. (p. 95)

Although she doesn't love Neal, Maggie marries him, rationalizing that at least the marriage "represented to her security, a home for herself and her mother, freedom from all the little nagging worries that beset the woman who fights her own way through the world." . . . When Maggie learns that Neal is a gambler, she divorces him and begins to support herself. The reality of confronting the day-to-day exigencies of living, however, does not abate Maggie's still-thriving romantic desire to marry a respectable man. This time she sets her sights on Peter, who is a penniless medical student, but who "boasted a long, a bonafide ancestry." "She saw herself suddenly transformed in this inhospitable snobbish city from Maggie Neal, alone and déclassé, into Mrs. Peter Bye, a model of respectability. That he had no money, no accepted means of making a livelihood she understood would mean nothing. He was a Bye and she as his wife could go anywhere. . . . And afterwards when he got his degree!" Maggie's romantic reasoning is typically "female"; her strategies to win Peter's affections are equally consistent with traditional female behavior patterns. (pp. 95-6)

Maggie's overwhelming attention is especially noticeable compared to Joanna's chronic inattention, and because he is conditioned as a traditional male, Peter temporarily welcomes Maggie's domesticity. He boasts to Joanna that Maggie does not resent doing "women's work," that she freely waits on him. Joanna's adamant refusal to submit to woman's work, as well as her stringent demands on Peter, create tensions that steadily mount until they break their engagement. Maggie's fawning passivity, her dependency, provides temporary relief from Joanna's exacting demands. He becomes engaged to Maggie who promises to "be as unlike Joanna as possible." . . .

Like Amy in **"The Sleeper Wakes,"** Maggie has capitulated to social pressures to play dependent roles and to forego self-actualization and self-sufficiency in exchange for marriage and its spurious rewards. Peter is soon bored of that dependency and wants to be free of Maggie, but she pleads, " 'Oh, Peter, can't you see I want to be safe like other women, with a home and protection.' "

Joanna's reaction to her breakup with Peter is diametrically opposed to Maggie's. Although Joanna is initially disappointed and reveals a side of her character never before seen, her remorse is shortlived, for she has begun to realize some stage success. She therefore channels the energy of her agony over Peter into her work. . . . (p. 96)

Joanna finally decides, however, that her work is unable to fill what she describes as a gnawing sense of emptiness, a feel-

ing that her life is a "ghastly skeleton" that the "garish trappings of her art" cannot clothe:

> It has not occurred to her that [her art] would be the only thing in her life. . . . She had expected her singing, her dancing—her success in a word— to be the mere integument of her life, the big handsome extra wrap to cover her more ordinary dress—the essential, delightful commonplaces of living, the kernel of life, home, children, an adoring husband.

While Joanna is changing to a more traditional orientation, Maggie reverts to one somewhat less conventional. Narrowly missing death at the hands of her ex-husband, she takes stock of her life while she is recovering. She begins to examine and then criticize her blind acceptance of the middle-class fixation with "proper" marriage, social mobility and respectability. She decides, rather, that respectability, in its truest sense, is neither passed on from generation to generation nor conferred on a woman by a man in marriage. She decides, moreover, that her dependent personality is not conducive to developing a healthy relationship with a man. Described throughout as a yellow calla lilly—suggesting fragility and pliability—Maggie begins to contemplate the virtues of independence. (p. 97)

Maggie seizes the outbreak of World War I as an opportunity to test her budding self-sufficiency. She goes to France to help nurse wounded soldiers, and, while there, makes plans to inaugurate a chain of beauty shops once she returns to America. . . . In another of Fauset's embarrassing fictional coincidences, Maggie and her first love, Phillip, are reunited in a hospital ward, where she is assigned to nurse him. They eventually marry and she nurses him until his death. The consciousness with which Maggie enters their marriage is substantially altered from her earlier days, however. Although vestiges of her domestic sentimentalism surface in her treatment of Phillip, it is evident that Maggie is a much stronger, more self-reliant individual with more realistic perceptions of marriage.

Fauset continues to tie up the loose ends of her narrative by reuniting Joanna and Peter, who also marry. Their marriage, however, means an end to Joanna's career. Unlike the Joanna who dominated throughout the novel with her stubborn independence and indifference to marriage, she now becomes absorbed in the traditional role as wife and mother, abandoning altogether her earlier passion for a career. . . . Thus, Joanna unconvincingly settles for biological rather than artistic creativity and, true to the feminine ideal, sacrifices her own career and further development, and defers completely to her husband.

By having Joanna and Maggie trade places in a sense, Fauset is suggesting that each represents the extreme of independence and dependency, extremes that need to be tempered. This position is not unreasonable in and of itself, but it is Fauset's final statement on her joint protagonists that creates problems. In her depictions of Maggie and Joanna, Fauset must be finally seen as a traditionalist regarding women's roles. Both characters, to varying degrees, accede to male-determined roles for women. Joanna's accession is most dramatic, for she has to resolve the classic female conflict between marriage and a career, an either-or proposition historically forced on women by men. Although Fauset herself combined a marriage and a career, she demonstrates in her characterization of Joanna that the two roles may be incompatible. Given Joanna's mindset throughout the novel, Fauset's ending seems forced and inconsistent, not growing organically out of the novel, but rather, "tacked on" to it. Notwithstanding the novel's focus on characters who must all grow and alter their perspectives in some way, Joanna's growth from stubbornly independent careerist to dependent, self-abnegating wife rings false. What accounts for Fauset's retreat to a traditional value system after clearly promising the opposite? A brief look at the peculiar network of social, economic, and literary circumstances under which she composed can help to answer that question. (pp. 97-8)

Fauset admitted to an interviewer that she began earnestly to write fiction to counteract T. S. Stribling's novel *Birthright* that had failed, in her estimation, to depict blacks authentically. She, along with Nella Larsen and Walter White, reasoned, "Here is an audience waiting to hear the truth about us. Let we who are better qualified to present that truth than any white writer, try to do so." Thus Fauset's mission was reconstructive in a word.

Concomitant with wanting to tell the truth about blacks, Fauset also set out to tell the truth about women, who had been similarly the victims of literary misrepresentation, a reflection of dominant social attitudes. Fauset's mission was necessarily fraught with uncertainty, ambivalence, and fear, for not only was she challenging prominent literary images of women, but she was also challenging traditional expectations of women in the social sphere. She was writing at a time when social definitions of womanhood were in flux. There was a tremendous ferment of ideas concerning sexuality, sex roles, marriage and family, observable in social and political thinking and in literary culture. Fauset was unsure of what road to take. She herself had defied the cult of domesticity by remaining unmarried for an unusually long time and by insisting upon maintaining an active career when she did marry. To transfer that personal, democratic style of life into her writing was not easy. From various ranks within society she invited reprisals for exploring concerns outside the realm of the traditional, reprisals that she, a fledgling writer, would ironically fear and defer to in subtle ways. A perpetual source of fear was the major publishing firms that Fauset continually battled and that stifled her freedom of expression and directness by prescribing and proscribing her literary province. "White readers just don't expect Negroes to be like this," wrote the first publisher to see and reject the manuscript of *There Is Confusion*. Censorship and rejected manuscripts were what she came to expect, and thus, Fauset had to develop strategies to offset rejection, strategies that frequently took the form of indirectness. (p. 99)

Fauset's awareness that the publishing and critical arenas were essentially male preserves may well have pressured her into deflecting her dissenting statements through "safe" literary mediums if not falsifying them altogether. Thus the indirectness of **"The Sleeper Wakes"** and the curious and unconvincing resolution of *There Is Confusion* are not without explanation.

Fauset's oblique and ambivalent treatment of women's roles in **"The Sleeper Wakes"** and in *There Is Confusion,* respectively, is less apparent in her next three novels, *Plum Bun, The Chinaberry Tree,* and *Comedy: American Style.* She continues her exploration of women's roles, their lives' possibilities, and her criticism of social conventions that work to restrict those possibilities by keeping women's sights riveted on men, marriage and motherhood. These domestic and bio-

logical facets, Fauset suggests, while important, are just one dimension of a woman's total being, one aspect of her boundless capacities and possibilities. Seen in this light, then, fairy tale illusions about life give way to mature realities, and women, instead of waiting for their imaginary princes, aggressively take charge of their lives and move toward achieving authentic selfhood.

The idea of Fauset, a black woman, daring to write—even timidly so—about women taking charge of their own lives and declaring themselves independent of social conventions, was far more progressive than critics have either observed or admitted. Although what Fauset attempted in her depictions of black women was not uniformly commensurate with what she achieved, she has to be credited with both presenting an alternative view of womanhood and a facet of black life which publishers, critics, and audiences stubbornly discouraged if not vehemently opposed. Despite that discouragement and opposition, Fauset persisted in her attempt to correct the distorted but established images of black life and culture and to portray women and blacks with more complexity and authenticity than was popular at the time. In so doing, she was simultaneously challenging established assumptions about the nature and function of Afro-American literature. Those who persist, then, in regarding her as a prim and proper Victorian writer, an eddy in a revolutionary literary current, would do well to read Fauset's work more carefully, to give it a more fair and complete appraisal, one that takes into account the important and complex relationship between circumstances and artistic creation. Then her fiction might finally be accorded the recognition and attention that it deserves and Fauset, her rightful place in the Afro-American literary tradition. (pp. 99-100)

> *Deborah E. McDowell, "The Neglected Dimension of Jessie Redmon Fauset," in* Conjuring: Black Women, Fiction, and Literary Tradition, *edited by Marjorie Pryse and Hortense J. Spillers, Indiana University Press, 1985, pp. 86-104.*

CAROLYN WEDIN SYLVANDER

Comedy: American Style zeroes in on the ironies of American Black life with more directness and less sentimentality than any of Jessie Fauset's novels. This last of her longer published works takes most of the major and minor thematic elements of her first novel and intensifies them in various ways. White racial discrimination faced by Northern urban Blacks in *There Is Confusion* is essentially internalized into the Black characters themselves in *Comedy: American Style.* The range of characters and actions possible given the realities of discrimination is narrowed historically and by introducing fewer characters in the final novel than in the first one. Limited alternatives available to women generally and to Black women particularly as shown in *There Is Confusion* become in *Comedy: American Style* a concentration on the powers wrought by mistaken, misled mothers. Fauset in the final novel includes new 1930s slants on the race issue, slants stemming from insights gained through the controversies of the Harlem Renaissance period. The dominant theme which emerges from these exploratory themes is not so different in the final book as compared to the first. Both novels place emphasis on the importance of human relationships and the attaining of happiness through those relationships; life and the plot of the two novels are a working out of this understanding of essentials. Where the final novel does finally differ from the first, however, is in its unstinting depiction of the characters who fail to attain true understanding as well as of characters who succeed.

The meaning of race discrimination for Fauset was frequently expressed in terms of its being a burden added to the ordinary trials of living. "Life is hard for everyone, but to ordinary difficulties are added intangible difficulties in the case of the Negro. For him life is very uncertain. He's never sure what sort of break he may get. . . . It would seem that my people are cut off from advantages exactly in proportion to their color." This statement from a Fauset interview differs only in emphasis from the understanding of American life that Teresa Cary of *Comedy: American Style* gains as a college student. . . . The irony of Teresa's life is that no white person destroys it for her, at least directly. No white person keeps Teresa from marrying the man she loves. No white person denies her the career which seems later to be her only possible source of happiness. No white person pushes her into a senseless hateful marriage with a man she grows to despise. No white person forces her beautiful, talented, much-loved younger brother to commit suicide. All these destructive acts come not from a white American, but from Teresa's own Black mother, Olivia Blanchard Cary.

In the character Olivia Cary Fauset has achieved "the most penetrating study of color mania in American fiction," a successful "analysis of psychopathic Aryanism," according to Hugh Gloster. Though critics would often have one believe otherwise about the customary class of Jessie Fauset's fictional characters, Olivia Cary is her only central character who comes from the highest class of Black women. . . . Significantly, Fauset's most caustic criticism of a Black character is of Olivia ("blanched") Cary, a woman of this essentially parasitic class and life style.

All of Olivia's motivations are from her desire to be white, her hatred of Black. Superficially she justifies her actions in relation to her marriage, her social life, and her children by saying that it is for their own good. Sending away one of young Teresa's dark-skinned friends, she tells her, " 'You don't understand these things yet, Teresa. But you will when you're older . . . and you'll be grateful to me. I just don't want you to have Marise and people like that around because I don't want you to grow up among folks who live the life that most colored people have to live . . . , narrow and stultified and stupid. Always pushed in the background . . . out of everything. Looked down upon and despised!' " In action, though, Olivia Cary does nothing in the best interests of her family. She is indeed a deceived character who is never in the course of the book undeceived.

Fauset is not totally convincing in explaining what kind of sources such color mania as Olivia Cary's is likely to have. Early in the book the reader learns a great deal about her mother, Janet Blanchard, who is very class-conscious but not at all color-conscious, so family heredity or environment is not passed off as the source. We learn that Olivia was a very odd child from babyhood on in not displaying any evidence of affection for other humans, including her parents. (pp. 210-13)

If the delineation of sources for Olivia's mania is weak, the depiction of the negative power she wields over the lives of her husband and children is not. Two things only get in the way of Olivia's plans and form the conflicts in the plot line. First, the man she marries, Dr. Christopher Cary, while light

enough to "pass" does not care to, and continually frustrates Olivia's pretenses of being white by bringing home obviously colored friends and by doctoring colored patients. Through his sensible efforts of accepting his racial inheritance and of teaching them of Black history and biography, the older two children, Christopher and Teresa, are raised free of their mother's dominating concern. The second barrier to Olivia's goals is even more difficult to overcome. Olivia anticipates the birth of her children happily only because she expects them to be white. Her third child, she tells big Christopher, would be a boy. . . . Olivia's third child is just as she predicted: the handsomest and most attractive of them all, and named Oliver after her. He is also, like Olivia's father, obviously Negro.

The pathological extent of Olivia's fixed idea is shown in her treatment of Oliver. He is exceptionally attractive, personable, intelligent and loving—but his mother can't stand him. She pretends she does not know him when he runs up to her on the streetcorner where she is talking to her white lady friends. She sends him away for long periods to live with his two sets of grandparents. Ultimately, she dresses him up as a Filipino servant to wait on her white guests. Family and friends keep Oliver from knowledge of the reason for his mother's disgust, but he accidentally discovers the reason in a letter she has written her husband from France. " 'If you and Chris would come and settle down over here we could all be as white as we look . . . if it just weren't for Oliver. I know you don't like me to talk about this . . . but really, Chris, Oliver and his unfortunate color has certainly been a mill-stone around our necks all our lives.' " Others can understand and scorn Olivia's madness, but when Teresa fails him, too, young Oliver has no defenses against rejection by his mother of the one thing about himself he cannot change. He shoots himself. (pp. 213-14)

Three of the Cary family are destroyed by color mania. Oliver dies physically. Teresa dies mentally, emotionally. Olivia lives on in isolation and poverty. Only young and old Christopher overcome and survive, with much intermittent pain. . . . In its picture of American race discrimination *Comedy: American Style* is thorough in showing a certain kind of Black prejudice against Black. The thinking reader must of course look beyond that portrayal to sources in the society, probably to conclude with Kenny Williams that "Fauset ultimately does not blame her characters for their own weaknesses, rather she blames American society which so emphasized the differences between the two races that these characters become victimized by it." But within the novel itself, concentration is on what internalization of race discrimination does to the Black character and the Black family.

Having said that there is much direct negative criticism of color-struck Blacks and indirect negative criticism of prejudiced whites in *Comedy: American Style,* one must then go on to point out that it is not in Fauset's nature here or elsewhere to write pure protest fiction. She presents alternative solutions to race relations in the United States in characters contrasted to Olivia Cary and in quick but perceptive references to positive traits of Black culture and history.

Christopher Cary, Sr. is a quiet antidote to his wife's disease. Christopher Cary, Jr. is able to resist his mother's domination in a way that his less aggressive sister finds impossible. But it is in a woman outside the family that the primary contrast to Olivia Cary is given. Phebe Grant is a very light skinned Black; in fact she is blond and blue-eyed. Her light skin and hair come from her runaway white father—she is illegitimate. Her mother is of the lowest class of Black women, having marginal employment and income with a white family. Phebe herself by her responsibility and cleverness rises from seamstress with that white family to shop-owning modiste. More significantly, Phebe plays no games with her racial inheritance. . . . In direct contrast to Olivia Cary's school-girl choice, Phebe makes clear her race mixture and her race preference.

Phebe is offered the prize Olivia craves for her daughter—marriage to a rich white man, Llewellyn Nash. As soon as she discovers Nash's intentions, Phebe, however, tells him of her racial mixture. Nash can marry a poor girl, a shop girl, an illegitimate girl, but he cannot marry a girl of invisible Black blood, though he does offer Phebe a permanent mistress-ship in his life. Phebe sends back the proposition and its envelope—a huge floral box full of paper money. Again in direct contrast to Olivia, Phebe refuses a life based on deceit, no matter how attractive its other foundations.

As a final contrast to Olivia, Phebe is absolutely loyal, though severely tested. She marries Christopher Cary long after the real love of her life, Nicholas Campbell, has left her and has married her friend Marise. In *Comedy: American Style* as in *There Is Confusion* Fauset spends some time depicting the trials of marriage even for responsible, mature, deromanticized adults such as Christopher and Phebe. Phebe is still working in her Philadelphia shop. She is nursing Christopher, Sr. back into health. She is the sounding board for the complaints of her mother about Olivia, since the two extended families are living together in the rooming house which Phebe had originally purchased for her mother and herself. Phebe is coming home from work exhausted; her husband is coming home from his infant medical practice exhausted; and their life in their bedroom once they get there is not thrilling.

Nicholas contacts Phebe from New York, with a pertinent, tempting suggestion, for he is also a bit disillusioned with married life. The temptation is carefully great, and Phebe's yielding very near when her loyalty to Chris is reasserted. (pp. 215-17)

Phebe triumphs over temptation and is rewarded upon her return to Philadelphia by Chris, Jr.'s new attentions, Chris Sr.'s healthy demeanor, and Olivia's recent and permanent absence. For these struggling characters—Chris Jr., Chris Sr., and Phebe—there is a kind of happy ending, at least a temporary victory over their trials and an increased strength from having overcome. There is no easy way of dealing successfully with life or race in America, Fauset reminds us, but there are alternatives to Olivia Cary's imitation white life. Phebe Grant's alternative is acceptance of her inheritance, hard work, unswerving loyalty and honesty. (p. 217)

More so than in her previous three novels, Fauset in *Comedy: American Style* presents positive aspects of Black culture that further suggest alternative to white imitation or assimilation. Sprinkled in the earlier books are brief suggestions of this positive alternative: Laurentine in *The Chinaberry Tree* feels a oneness in a Black crowd at the Lafayette Theatre; Angela notices the same thing at the Van Meier lecture in *Plum Bun;* Virginia in that book expresses the belief that Black people are happier and less selfish than white. In *Comedy: American Style,* however, the discussion of positive Black culture

is wider and more clearly influenced by the many race discussions coming out of the intense Harlem Renaissance period.

In Teresa Cary, Fauset creates a character handicapped by lack of a race identity. . . . Teresa's situation is different than that of a character like Angela Murray in *Plum Bun,* who chooses to "pass." With a mother who tries to make her white and a father who assumes her Blackness, Teresa has no clear identification in her own mind, either to accept or to rebel against. She is the eternal miserable observer, the eternal drifter. Other light-skinned Blacks, with Black identity, carry on the "gesture of whiteness with pride, with amusement, with a sense of perpetrating a huge joke. But to this eighteen-year-old girl the process had already brought misery, embarrassment and the hint of future wretchedness."

Since Fauset spends much of the novel on the unfortunate fate of a character without a racial birthright, she must also suggest the characteristics of that birthright. Elsewhere, outside her novels, Fauset has spoken of the Black birthright as being a "spontanaeity of humor, mellow understanding, tolerance, warmth of fellowship that is beautiful." As the race "suffers, so does it rejoice. Target of the slings of fate, it learns the art of interpretation." She has also stated the relevance to American literature of depicting that birthright. "I see sometimes the colored man as the last stronghold of those early American virtues which once we fought so hard to preserve—integrity, pride, indomitableness and a sort of gay hardihood. . . . A pity to let the archives of America build up without a record of the deeds and thoughts of these people, so brave and grave and gay. So I have tried to set them down."

In *Comedy: American Style,* Fauset succinctly explores the Black birthright which Teresa has been denied through insights of various characters. Belief like Olivia's that the white race was created superior is denied by the fact that "there were more unwhite than white people in the world." The slave history of the American Black "had not been a special curse visited upon a special people. . . . It had been a cause to produce an effect, a necessity to permit a certain group of people an opportunity to glimpse and adopt another kind of civilization." The essence of American Black history is survival. (pp. 218-20)

But the time for adoption of "white is beautiful—exclusively"—is past. Teresa thinks of the fallacy of white denial of Black beauty in observing "how earnestly and deliberately Americans every summer exposed themselves on shore and water to the burning sun in order to obtain the effect which, when natural, they affected so to despise." *Comedy: American Style* dwells on the particular beauty of certain shades of Black people. (p. 220)

Fauset's ideal Black person as suggested in *Comedy: American Style* is the one who has gone through acceptance and respect for racial inheritance to a confident but unchauvinistic awareness of human worth. Young Christopher Cary is described as such a post-Renaissance person. "He was entirely without the slightly self-righteous attitude which characterized so many young colored people of his day and station. Christopher never talked about 'my people,' never mouthed pompous phrases pertaining to 'the good of the race.' He was in this respect the forerunner of the modern young colored man who takes his training as a matter of course for himself primarily and for the race next." Alicia Barrett is another such person. Her "whole attitude said serenely: 'Here I am, the best of my kind, and I am perfectly satisfied with my kind.' Thus she arrived at a *ne plus ultra* at once personally satisfying and completely baffling to all conjectures on superior bloods, racial admixtures, hybridizations and all the sociological and biological generalizations of the day." The ultimate teaching is that which Grandfather Cary tries to give Oliver—"that greatness knew no race, no color; that real worth was the same the world over; that it was immediately recognizable and that it was a mark of genuine manhood to know no false shame." Thus, Fauset tells us, a racial birthright is essential to a healthy emotional development, but exclusive racial identification is not the ideal goal of the mature adult.

One feels the greater difficulty of obtaining happiness and full, honest human relationships in *Comedy: American Style* than in Fauset's previous three novels, though those goals are the same in all four books. In this final novel, there are central characters who don't succeed in reaching those goals. It is not true, however, that most of the characters "are ultimately frustrated, ill-adjusted and doomed, . . . victims of their own desire to deny their race, and of the cruelty, prejudice and lack of understanding by which they are surrounded." Most of the characters are not doomed, but some of them are. In that realistic assessment of Black life in America Fauset concludes her long fiction. (pp. 220-21)

Carolyn Wedin Sylvander, in her Jessie Redmon Fauset: Black American Writer, *The Whitston Publishing Company, 1981, 275 p.*

JOSEPH J. FEENEY, S.J.

With Nella Larsen [Jessie Fauset] ranks as the major novelist of the middle class during the Harlem Renaissance, and—except for *The Chinaberry Tree,* which takes place in a small New Jersey town—she writes about black urban life in Philadelphia and New York from 1900 to 1930.

In her novels happy families enjoy Sunday morning in turn-of-the-century Philadelphia, and sophisticated artists and intellectuals talk and drink together in the Greenwich Village of the twenties. There are lively street cries in Harlem, successful doctors in West Philadelphia, trips to City Island in the Bronx. Bronze dancers cavort on a Broadway stage while black theatregoers have to sit in the balcony. Light-skinned young blacks "pass" but have to reject their families. A Du-Bois-like leader speaks out for justice.

In short, Miss Fauset's novels picture a mixed world of romance and prejudice, success and humiliation. Sometimes the romance ends happily, other times prejudice stunts a career or drives a young black to suicide. In these novels one finds racial pride, proper middle-class English, Ivy-League educations, cultured "old Philadelphians"—but Miss Fauset's picture of her race's middle class hardly indicates unmixed optimism.

There is also a strong, underlying social purpose: to portray the educated black middle class and thereby uncover American racial prejudice.

The critics of Miss Fauset's novels generally dismiss her as a conventional middle-class novelist. . . . [Most] current critics—both black and white—consider her books as, at best, good examples of the conservative middle-class novel.

At worst they consider her romantic, melodramatic, and excessively genteel.

Robert Bone's *The Negro Novel in America* even calls her a dull "novelist of the Rear Guard" whose "literary aspirations were circumscribed by her desire to convey a flattering image of respectable Negro society" [see *CLC,* Vol. 19]. Only the rare commentator recognizes her social criticism and notes how her talent ranges from comedy of manners through romance to tragedy. (pp. 20, 22)

[Yet] her novels are not simply romances but have a two-fold structure and a complex tone. What appears on the surface to be a conventional romance stands also as a novel of betrayed hope or near-tragedy or sardonic "comedy." And her allegedly pleasant pictures of the comfortable middle class mask a world of pain, prejudice, suicide, unfair choices, and stunted careers.

Miss Fauset is angry and disillusioned, as well as fastidious and cultured. "To be a Negro in America posits a dramatic situation," she wrote in the preface to *The Chinaberry Tree,* and her novels dramatize black anguish and indict White America. She does love romance and feel racial pride, but she also feels a "bitter peace" since blacks in America are not free to aspire.

"If you're black in America," says one character, "you have to renounce." Her fiction portrays this conflict between a black's just hopes and limited possibilities and, as a result, Miss Fauset's four novels are both angrier and more interesting than critics have recognized.

Miss Fauset is also interesting as an early black feminist—an aspect unnoticed by critics. Her principal characters are generally women, and either the narrator or her characters often discuss the role of women in America.

Speaking with the post-war freedom of the twenties, they indict the double standard of morality, criticizing the "typical male defense" of this standard and noting the black male habit of arrogantly demanding a ridiculously careful virtue of their women. Men have a much easier life, they argue, and Miss Fauset ironically describes a woman whom "her husband considered a perfect woman, sweet, industrious, affectionate, and illogical. But to her he was God."

Some men simply do not like a capable woman; others want a woman to surrender herself completely in marriage. A woman in the novel *Plum Bun* summarizes the female dilemma: "If we don't give enough we lose them. If we give too much we lose ourselves."

To cope with such prejudice and such demands, various solutions are offered: do not marry at all; have a profession which will offer a woman shelter in a storm; or simply refuse to let femininity stand in the way of what a woman wants. And in these novels women want much and accomplish much.

There are female dancers, singers, painters, teachers, even successful planners of a peace conference. Granted, some of Miss Fauset's women are quite happy and satisfied with motherhood and family life, and Miss Fauset and her characters enjoy clothes and beauty and the great diversity of skin shades among blacks.

But if a black woman wants to be different, she should not be limited to conventional feminine roles and tastes. She should not be subordinated to men. And in *Plum Bun* Miss

Fauset expressly recognized the terrible parallel: being a woman is like being black, for opportunities and choices are grossly limited by prejudice.

Her novels spoke for the freedom of women as well as for the freedom of blacks.

It is surely time . . . to celebrate Jessie Fauset: her life, her work for *The Crisis,* her novels, her passion for the freedom of blacks and of women. This passion was usually expressed in a low-keyed voice in both her novels of romance and her smoothly crafted prose. But below the calm surface was genuine passion as well as breadth of vision. (p. 22)

*Joseph J. Feeney, S.J., "Jessie Fauset of 'The Crisis':
Novelist, Feminist, Centenarian," in* The Crisis,
Vol. 90, No. 6, June-July, 1983, pp. 20, 22.

Natalia Ginzburg

1916-

(Has also written under pseudonym of Alessandra Tournimparte) Italian novelist, short story writer, critic, essayist, biographer, autobiographer, journalist, and dramatist.

A major Italian novelist of the post-World War II era, Ginzburg examines the difficulties of maintaining interpersonal relationships in contemporary society. Writing in a reserved, understated prose, Ginzburg often utilizes small but significant details to develop the crises of her characters. Ginzburg's early works depict individuals whose ambitions are stifled by marriage and familial restrictions, while her later writings explore problems caused by the disintegration of the family unit. A reviewer for the *Times Literary Supplement* declared: "At first sight [Ginzburg's] writing seems throwaway, so inexplicit, so easy does it appear; at a second look its artifice and intricacy begin to be seen—the unity of thought and expression, the comedienne's sense of timing." Ginzburg's minimalist style and compassionate evocation of the frustrated lives of her protagonists have elicited comparisons to the works of Anton Chekhov.

Ginzburg's first major works of fiction are narrated by young women who are disappointed in love. The heroine of *La strada che va in città* (1942; *The Road to the City*), which Ginzburg published under the pseudonym of Alessandra Tournimparte, successfully manipulates a wealthy young man into marrying her but realizes afterward that she has sacrificed her relationship with the man she really loves. *È stato cosí* (1947; *The Dry Heart*) features a woman who murders her husband as a result of his neglect and infidelity. Ginzburg's first full-length novel, *Tutti i nostri ieri* (1952; *A Light for Fools,* also published as *Dead Yesterdays*), chronicles the experiences of a family that opposed Italy's Fascist government during World War II. This novel's young heroine marries a Resistance fighter who is murdered by the Fascists. Marc Slonim commented that in *A Light for Fools* Ginzburg "succeeds in drawing a picture of Italian society between 1934 and 1944 and in revealing the hidden connection between the fate of individuals and the pressure of the times."

Several of Ginzburg's early novellas present a bleak yet often humorous view of domestic life. For example, *Valentino* (1951) concerns a promising young man who disappoints his family by marrying an unattractive but wealthy woman, and *Sagittario* (1957; *Sagittarius*) depicts an eccentric woman's disastrous attempt to win favor among a local artistic circle while neglecting her sick child. Ginzburg returned to the theme of frustrated love in her next novel, *Le voci della sera* (1961; *Voices in the Evening*). This work concerns a young woman whose love affair with a neighbor's son is destroyed by the interference of her overbearing family.

While Ginzburg's early works portray the family as a source of personal suppression, they also emphasize its importance as a stabilizing social force. Her later writings decry the effects of divorce and the growing alienation between generations. In the novel *Caro Michele* (1973; *No Way,* also published as *Dear Michael*), Ginzburg centers on the last days in the life of an exiled activist through a series of letters writ-

ten by his estranged parents and friends. Michael emerges as a symbol of hope for the other characters, whose fragmented lives become whole after his death in a political demonstration. Tragedy and sudden death, common elements in Ginzburg's fiction, are the subjects of the novellas *Borghesia* and *Famiglia,* published together as *Famiglia* (1977). Both works concern middle-aged characters who unknowingly suffer from terminal cancer. The fate of the female protagonist of *Borghesia* is foreshadowed by the mysterious deaths of her pet cats, while the hero of *Famiglia* confronts his mortality through a melancholy reassessment of his past.

Ginzburg's next novel, *La città e la casa* (1984; *The City and the House*), reflects her growing pessimism over the possibilities of establishing relationships within fast-paced, superficial urban conditions. This work is related through letters exchanged between a middle-aged widower and his married ex-lover who is about to be divorced. Their unfulfilled yearnings for love and security are symbolized by the comfortable country homes they abandon to live in the alienating environment of the city. Liz Heron described the novel's epistolary form as "the perfect vehicle for [Ginzburg's] impressionistic patterning of life's hurts, softened through mutual trust and the shared intimacies of words and gestures, objects and places."

Ginzburg has also earned critical recognition for her autobiographical and biographical writings. *Lessico famigliare* (1963; *Family Sayings*), a memoir of Ginzburg's life from the 1920s through the 1950s, features a laconic, conversational style reminiscent of her fictional narratives. *La famiglia Manzoni* (1983; *The Manzoni Family*) chronicles two hundred years in the family history of eighteenth-century Italian poet Alessandro Manzoni. Each of this book's eight sections focuses on the experiences of a particular family member through the transcription of actual letters and a novelistic recreation of events. Filippo Donini observed: "Italian biographies have only rarely reached the level of works of art, but *La famiglia Manzoni* is one which does."

In addition to her fiction and biographical writings, Ginzburg has published numerous articles and critical essays. These pieces are collected in *Le piccole virtù* (1962; *The Little Virtues*), *Mai devi domandarmi* (1970; *Never Must You Ask Me*), and *Vita immaginaria* (1974). In her review of *The Little Virtues,* Kate Simon commented that Ginzburg's essays treat "a variety of subjects close to her memory and the realities of her life, all of them carrying her signatures—the clear, direct eye, the firm moral stand eased by a sympathy that flows from intimacy with the human condition." Ginzburg has also written several plays, including *L'inserzione* (1965; *The Advertisement*), *Fragola e panna* (1966), and *La segretaria* (1967).

(See also *CLC,* Vols. 5, 11 and *Contemporary Authors,* Vols. 85-88.)

ANN SCHAKNE

[*The Road to the City*] is Mrs. Ginzburg's first book to be published in this country, although, as her publishers note, her literary reputation in Italy, where she lives, was established before the war. Both novelettes, **The Dry Heart** and **The Road to the City,** are written in the first person, and in each a girl tells the story of her marriage.

The Dry Heart is the more effective story. It opens baldly with the heroine stating that she has shot her husband between the eyes, and then goes back to tell the story of her meeting and unfortunate marriage with Alberto, the birth of their daughter and the baby's death a year later, and, finally, the murder. If there is no great emotional impact to the story, the reader does feel the weight of neglect and callousness growing more intense until, for the narrator, it becomes intolerable.

The heroine of **The Road to the City,** Delia, is an empty-headed country girl living on the fringes of a city where, for her, all that means glamour exists—food and clothes and fun. She is as much in love as her calculating heart will permit her to be with a cousin named Nini, but she lets herself be seduced by the doctor's son because of his more elevated social standing. Eventually she marries the seducer and goes to live in the city. Delia is not an interesting figure and there is not warmth or local color to make the story of much consequence.

Ann Schakne, "Two Novelettes," in The New York Times Book Review, *August 21, 1949, p. 20.*

JOSEPH G. HARRISON

The Road to the City comprises two short novels, **The Dry Heart** and the title piece. Natalia Ginzburg is an Italian writer; yet her atmosphere is Latin and continental rather than national: and the period, though it is presumably postwar, is never clarified, nor is it material to the book.

For these two stories are essentially excursions into feminine psychology. Technically superb, they ultimate in an effect of negativism and pessimism, for they present a society in which women are, overwhelmingly, still pawns. . . .

On the book page of *The Christian Science Monitor* of May 26, 1949, there appeared a "Letter From Rome," in which it was indicated that since writing these novels, Mrs. Ginzburg has joined the Italian Communist Party. During the German occupation, she carried on active clandestine resistance, and her husband died a civil prisoner. Shortly after joining the party, the "Letter" continues, Mrs. Ginzburg published an article condemning the degenerative feminine habit of introspective and intuitive thinking, and establishing the necessity—for women generally and for writers like herself—of concentrating upon "the hard realities of life," upon "all the important and serious things of the world."

While **The Road to the City** hardly deals with eternal values, it does present with very considerable relative truth and artistry some aspects of human living. Yet, for reasons valid to herself, Mrs. Ginzburg is driven to repudiate even this insight in favor of the predetermined stereotypes of communistic art. It seems a misguided, even a tragic, decision, illuminating afresh the dilemma of the European who believes himself to possess only two alternatives, reactionary stagnation or communistic dogma. Whether in hope or in despair, Mrs. Ginzburg has declared her allegiance to an externalized, arbitrary, wholly materialistic concept of life. It remains to be seen if and how, as an artist, she can handle this concept.

Joseph G. Harrison, "Some Books Lately Out of Italy," in The Christian Science Monitor, *September 22, 1949, p. 11.*

ISABEL QUIGLY

Dead Yesterdays is written in those short sentences, loosely joined by a lot of casual commas, so beloved in Italian writing today, and beautifully translated into a rather monotonous, sing-song English that perfectly suits the atmosphere by Angus Davidson. For the life it conjures, rather than describes—though youths may blow their brains out on park benches, and schoolgirls become pregnant, and people may be shot as hostages by one side or have their heads shaved for collaboration by the other—is, in fact, characterised by monotony, by that peculiar temperamental gloom, that domestic greyness and uneventfulness and general air that nothing will ever happen so pleasant for an Italian provincial fortnight, so terrible for a year. Inevitably, Chekhov comes to mind: not only because the long summer days, the endless agreeable but unrewarding chat, the whole provincial-intellectual set-up, recall him, but because the Italian charm, and volatility, and loquacity, and unselfconscious egocentricity, and inability to move out of grooves . . . that Miss Ginzburg so brilliantly captures, are all Chekhovian qualities. Her story of two neighbouring families, small-scale liberal-intellectuals, ending on exactly the right post-war note, part-hopeful, part-diffident, is the most illuminating study of this *milieu* I have yet come across: she has an extraordinary gift for what you might call cumulative characterisation—a method that dispenses almost entirely with description and builds up solid and memorable people by the gradual mounting up of small actions, oblique glances, other people's opinions. A serious, subtle, and very entertaining book, [*Dead Yesterdays*] has something of Pavese's sad invocation of far-flung events to illustrate personality: but better organised; to my mind, more forceful.

Isabel Quigly, in a review of "Dead Yesterdays," in The Spectator, *Vol. 197, No. 6687, August 24, 1956, p. 269.*

MARC SLONIM

Natalia Ginzburg belongs to the post-war generation of Italian writers who were instrumental in the recent revival of native arts and letters. . . .

A Light for Fools (published in England as *Dead Yesterdays*) . . . has all the characteristics of her genuine literary gift. Its heroes are teen-agers, four boys and three girls of two well-to-do families who live on the same street in a provincial town of Northern Italy. Ippolito, Giustino, Concettina and Anna are children of a widowed professor who is writing a denunciation of fascism and of Socialist turncoats. His book, however, does not satisfy him and the disappointed old man burns the manuscript and dies shortly afterward. The orphans, brought up by an old aunt, become intimate friends of Amalia, Emmanuele and Giuma, children of a late factory owner who left a substantial fortune to his flighty second wife.

The lives of the boys and girls get all entangled and intertwined. Each of them is a distinct, separate individual but they all breathe the same artificial air of Mussolini's dictatorship, and their personal destinies are determined by the social forces of the era. . . .

Vivid and often brilliant characterizations are not the only merit of this family novel. Through hints and intimations, the author succeeds in drawing a picture of Italian society between 1934 and 1944 and in revealing the hidden connection between the fate of individuals and the pressure of the times. The narrative has force and directness and there are delicate, impressionistic touches which remind us of Chekhov. Natalia Ginzburg is at her best when dealing with detail, and her descriptions of children and adolescents have a definite poetic flavor. Most of the incidents and characters are seen through the eyes of an adolescent, and the book has much of the naïveté and charm of a child's vision. This "point of view" in the Jamesian sense gives a unity of diction to the whole narrative.

Another element of unity in this terse book, which shies away from eloquence and literary ornamentation, is Natalia Ginzburg's attitude toward her heroes. She loves them, and she talks about them with such warmth and sympathy that her reader gets emotionally involved in the lives and dreams of her young protagonists.

Marc Slonim, "Wreckage of War," in The New York Times Book Review, *January 6, 1957, p. 5.*

R. G. G. PRICE

If it were set in England, *Voices in the Evening* might seem rather small beer, all the smaller since, by making each sentence into a separate paragraph, a longish short story is turned into fifteen-shillingsworth of book. But gossip about Italian families in Italian towns has everything on its side. The British love affair with Italy needs to be fed with every scrap of information which can add to understanding of the infinite strangeness of the beloved. I was not aware of any great universal significance in these dark chronicles of unhappy marriage and political disintegration; but anybody who has loitered outside shuttered villas with terracotta roofs and little gardens on top of the high walls wondering what makes the inhabitants tick will be grateful for a degree of illumination that, shone on English families, might be unimpressive. (pp. 247-48)

R. G. G. Price, in a review of "Voices in the Evening," in Punch, *Vol. CCXLV, No. 6414, August 14, 1963, pp. 247-48.*

THE TIMES LITERARY SUPPLEMENT

The Italian women novelists lack the power and energy of the men, but, generally speaking, they also lack the temptation of falling into certain almost adolescent sexual exuberance. Natalia Ginzburg is one of the best of the women, and when it comes to disentangling delicate feelings in what seems a quite effortless way she has no rival. Sensitive understatement is the rule with her, with irony almost completely under the surface. And her technique of repeating "he said" or "she said" in continuous short paragraphs is more than a way of conveying reflective conversation. It also somehow suggests the passage of the scythe of time over life and the slight melancholy and "tears of things" which is her particular tone.

Voices in the Evening is just the right title for this chronicle of a family of factory owners with socialist inclinations and their circle of friends who pass through the Italian version of the vicissitudes of life and death—with the complications of Fascism and war. There is no central character, for the narrator, Elsa, with her hypochondriac gossipy mother, eclipses herself in telling the story of the Balotta family, as she eclipses herself—sadly but not despairingly—in bringing her engagement with one of the Balotta sons to an end. . . . In spite of its shortness, this novel is, in its way, a saga of those aspects of Italian life that Natalia Ginzburg knows best.

"Italian Overtones," in The Times Literary Supplement, *No. 3213, September 27, 1963, p. 729.*

OTIS K. BURGER

The style of this small Italian novel [*Voices in the Evening*] is both extremely bare and full of feminine detail. It records the life of a remote, ingrown Piedmont village, chiefly through dialogues and brief biographies.

The book begins (and ends) with a monologue, directed at Elsa, by her gossipy, hypochondriac mother, who worries over her daughter's unmarried state. "I am 27," Elsa explains to the reader, and goes on, with a similar flatness, to describe the village. "The whole neighborhood lives by the factory. The factory produces cloth."

The factory was begun before the war by "old Balotta" de

Francisci. Old Balotta is now dead. His five children are totally inefficient. . . .

The reason for telling these life-stories (and for Elsa's intimate, semi-humorous, but coolly bitter matter-of-factness) is revealed only halfway through the book. Elsa is having an affair with Tommasino, the youngest of the Francisci. She loves him; he, like his brothers, is unable to love, but lets himself be drawn into a betrothal. The scenes between the engaged couple and Elsa's relieved mother are comic, and stifling. The engagement finally breaks up, through the sheer claustrophobic pressure of small-town past and present upon the weak Tommasino.

Miss Ginzburg has been attracting attention in the literary world of Italy—and this novel tells us why. The style of *Voices in the Evening* is crisp, brittle, entertaining and skillfully informative, and the book is nicely framed in its tone-setting monologues. The plot is slight, and revealed rather late, and the characters are too inactive and emotionally passive to be genuinely interesting. The very coolness of the style tends to defeat the subtle theme of the death of a family (and a love) through sheer lack of gumption. The brevity of the book and its semi-comic treatment of a muted tragedy come to seem, not a strength but part of the general, fatal weariness. The "voices in the evening" tend to cancel each other out—succeeding only too well in presenting people who, pallid to begin with, end as mere phantoms.

Yet the heroine, her mother, the whole tone of small-town domestic concerns, have a curious, attenuated resemblance to characters in the work of Elizabeth Gaskell, or even Jane Austen. It is as if a whole set of inquietudes, hidden in these earlier women authors, had come briefly to the surface; not to be allayed by happy marriages or even by the pleasure of accurate, small observations but merely to be seen and endured. This generic resemblance and the skillful style lend depths to a tale which studiedly remains on matter-of-fact surfaces.

> Otis K. Burger, "Muted Tragedy, Framed in Tone-Setting Monologues," in The New York Times Book Review, October 6, 1963, p. 38.

THE TIMES LITERARY SUPPLEMENT

The Italian *bella figura* is a concept hard for outsiders to understand, for it has to do with pride as well as swank, with self respect as well as arrogance. Roughly, it is what we call "face". At its most obvious, it appears in dress and social habits; but in subtler ways it sneaks into outlooks and attitudes of every kind, and shows itself in style and temperament and where the emphases in life are placed. Not to have a sense of it is to be, in an important way, un-Italian, its antithetical qualities being irony and unpretentiousness, the result of which, in any form of expression, is understatement.

Understatement, indeed a curious technique of omission, of felicitous gaps, is Natalia Ginzburg's most obvious characteristic out of a number too disconcerting and bizarre to be exactly labelled. A brilliant eccentric, she is almost certainly Italy's best woman writer today, but for reasons of temperament she will probably always be (or seem to outsiders to be) underrated in her own country. Her style, in so self-consciously stylish a country, is a non-style, and this applies to her manner, her whole way of looking at the world, as well as to style in the ordinary literary sense. She writes conversa-

tionally (some say chattily), with an apparent simplicity that is in fact dense and suggestive; what she says seems transparent, but when you peer through it you find implied an almost disturbing richness. It is in this capacity to mean much while saying little—a kind of poetic compression, or metaphorical outlook, using the plainest, most "antipoetic" language—that her quality and above all her originality lie.

When *Lessico famigliare,* now translated as *Family Sayings,* first appeared in Italy nearly four years ago, opinion was divided sharply between those who thought it mere chitchat and those who thought it a great deal more. The authoritative Strega prize, which it won, seemed to support the latter party, and certainly Signora Ginzburg's reputation has been, as it were, expanding these last years. But the book understates its purpose too much, perhaps, for Italian taste. Its scope is wide, its accomplishment in applying the techniques of fiction to biography and autobiography a triumph; yet a description makes it sound like a book of nostalgic reminiscence and family jokes.

The family sayings are, of course, those phrases that mean nothing to outsiders but to members of the clan open up a whole world. The world in this case was that of the Levi family in Turin, from 1920 onwards; Natalia was the youngest of five children of a Jewish professor of anatomy; a brother married Modigliani's daughter, a sister Adriano Olivetti; Natalia's first husband, Leone Ginzburg, died of torture near the end of the war in Rome (but characteristically, the large events get a sentence apiece: "We got married, Leone and I, and went to live in the apartment in the Via Pallamaglio"; and later: "Leone was conducting a secret newspaper and was always out of the house. They arrested him twenty days after our arrival, and I never saw him again any more"). They were a hardy, individualistic lot, and the family habits, at least, have a familiar ring—yoghurt and cold baths, hobnails and mountain holidays, a total spurning of fashion and frills. But even in Turin there were enough like-minded others—the unfashionable, unbelonging antifascists of the early years, the fighters or exiles of the 1940s, the postwar intellectuals—to fill the book's large canvas. Treated with fictional frankness and freedom, but marvellously solid and alive, these characters wander in and out of the story only when they are wanted, as in a novel.

From Turati to Pavese, the names are distinguished and foreseeable; but what makes this unlike other books of memoirs is the way in which they are treated—with an impartiality that gives them all the same weight and attention as the other family people. . . . Indeed, the whole book is comedy of a high, sad sort, in which themes and people recur in a musical way; nothing is wasted, nothing stressed. It seems to give biography a new dimension, new possibilities, and the tired old form of the family chronicle an aspect that is entirely new.

> "Un-Italian Activities," in The Times Literary Supplement, No. 3391, February 23, 1967, p. 149.

HERBERT MITGANG

"He used to read Heine to her and taught her to love violets." This paradigm line illustrates the faraway world created by the modern Italian novelist Natalia Ginzburg in *Family Sayings.* It is a factual book wrought by a literary stylist; the facts are sublimated by mood and significance. Out of the despair and rising fury of the Fascist years, she has devised an anachronistic *belle époque* about her family and the intellectual community in Turin and Rome.

Readers familiar with Miss Ginzburg's fiction—*A Light of Fools, The Road to the City, Voices in the Evening*—will discover here the background not only for her own stories but those of Cesare Pavese, Carlo Levi and other political activists who fought with pen and gun as partisans. Again and again, in spite of the author's self-effacing manner, the reader surmises that brutality, not clownishness, prevailed during the Mussolini era, that exile or death, not just castor oil, was the price paid for writing and publishing freely. . . .

Some of the events in *Family Sayings* seem too cool, too Proustian. The author married Leone Ginzburg, an expatriate teaching Russian in Turin, and the couple were sent to restricted residence in the Abruzzi. Later he edited an anti-Fascist paper, was arrested, and died as a result of torture by the Germans in Rome. After the war the author married Gabriele Baldini, who teaches English Literature at Rome University. But about these family events concerning herself, the author is reticent. As a result, the reader is sometimes left dangling.

Family Sayings does in nonfiction what Giorgio Bassani's marvelous family novel, *The Garden of the Finzi-Continis* achieved in fiction. Both cover minor dynasties in the Italian-Jewish community in northern Italy under Fascism. Miss Ginzburg's Turin is not too far from Bassani's more imaginative ducal town of Ferrara.

> Herbert Mitgang, "Private Lines," in The New York Times Book Review, April 30, 1967, p. 42.

THE TIMES LITERARY SUPPLEMENT

Natalia Ginzburg is undoubtedly the most interesting woman writer in Italy today, and unlike many, perhaps most, modern Italian writers she translates pretty well into English. For her style is transparent: it is her manner, her personality that must be caught, and occasionally is. The manner is disconcertingly simple, the personality disconcertingly deep. Words she uses decorously, unrhetorically, and so personally that they seem like stones held in a hand and warmed there. At first sight her writing seems throwaway, so inexplicit, so easy does it appear; at a second look its artifice and intricacy begin to be seen—the unity of thought and expression, the comedienne's sense of timing.

Her categories overlap but the manner pervades them all, the strong but hardly describable personality setting its stamp on essay, short story, novel, review, article. One of these may seem much like another, or like the rest; sometimes you can hardly tell whether a piece is fact or fiction, short story or article; the same "I" character appears in nearly all of them, the same apparent simplicity, actual intricacy, conversational tone, delicate placing of apparently artless words. In everything there is the same gentle detachment that makes *Mai devi domandarmi (Never must you ask me)* so good a title for this collection of short pieces. They are self-explanatory or they are nothing; you do not probe or argue with them; like poetry, they say what they have to say in just those words and no others.

Most of them are articles—a few pages on this or that, the kind that perhaps more than anything reflect the quality of a writer's mind: whether it trivializes, or whether it turns the trivial into something. And everything Natalia Ginzburg touches she turns into something, with a kind of visionary concentration, a quite unordinary eyesight.

> "An Art Concealed," in The Times Literary Supplement, No. 3597, February 5, 1971, p. 149.

THE TIMES LITERARY SUPPLEMENT

In a kind of introductory blurb on the jacket of *Caro Michele,* Cesare Garboli compares Signora Ginzburg with one of those outsize biblical women whose families were not small units as they are today but tribes, desert wanderers over whom plagues and calamities, fire and slaughter, every kind of accident and upheaval could pour without overwhelming the everyday life that had to continue, the processes of birth and death, the slogging heroism of survival. This rightly suggests her stature but makes her seem too domestic. The idea of her surviving earthquake or air-raid and making soup for the survivors in a crater is convincing enough; the idea of an earthy, kitchen-sink mother (which it also suggests) is not. She is an intellectual by birth and background and marriage, above all through her interests, her cast of mind; in an Italy that often seems full of fanatical housewives her stories suggest a healthy disregard for the details of hearth and kitchen, an eye fixed on wider horizons, and a total lack of interest (clearly passed on by the parents of her autobiographical *Lessico famigliare*) in keeping up with the Joneses, socially, domestically, culturally. This is one of the things that make her characters, selfish and feckless though they generally are, often endearing.

Caro Michele is her saddest, chilliest novel but perhaps her best. Without noticeable effort, it is carefully structured and satisfactorily balances ideas and action, feelings and behaviour. Much of it is written in letters . . . , the rest in narrative. By the end, the many aimless-seeming lives have achieved a pattern of sorts and a kind of compactness; the ideas, mostly unformulated, have made their point obliquely. An extraordinarily strong sense of the characters' presence comes across, one feels one has lived among them and shared a past, that one is open to their personalities, hears their voices. Signora Ginzburg has been compared with Chekhov and this is perhaps her most Chekhovian work, not just in atmosphere and in its characters but in the pathetic hope of some distant happiness unattainable in the present, or by present-day souls, minds, outlooks. . . .

Within the context of Italian middle-class life, in which mood and weather are suggested with marvellous subtlety and economy of words, and action seems haphazard yet in fact is tied in strange patterns to the past (a Spanish anti-fascist song runs through it, for instance; a theme of joy and idealism, yet never explicitly so), much is said about communication, the generations, the footloose young, this or that way of life; but mainly about sadness, loss, loneliness, solitude and death; said sidelong, not outright.

> "The Unenchanted," in The Times Literary Supplement, No. 3719, June 15, 1973, p. 661.

VALENTINE CUNNINGHAM

The epistolary novel didn't last, perhaps because there's nothing inevitable about letters as modes of communication: just as readily as they annihilate the gulfs between people they can simply confirm distance and distantness. Intent on revelation, Richardson's *Pamela* soon gave up the tussle with the ambivalence of epistles, quickly settling for proceeding 'journal-wise'. And the success of Natalia Ginzburg's use of letters in *Dear Michael* rests heavily on the recognition of their elements of effective non-communicativeness. Adriana, Michael's mother, rambles on to her son rather endearingly about his father's illness or about feckless Mara's baby (it might be Michael's) or about what Oswald says, but these important items, the meat of the novel's plot, only get granted the importance afforded the milkman's present of rabbits. Michael's accounts of his trip to England and his marriage to a nuclear physicist are, even at their most confiding, reticent, not to say mendacious.

And the letters resemble the novel: it's about friable links, and continually distracted by trivia—bogged down in the inevitably messy particularities of family life. To be sure, Michael's is a particularly unhumdrum family, with a painter father and a novelist aunt, and Michael is into the even more exciting business of some mysterious leftish crusade. When he quits Rome there's a submachine-gun for his sister to chuck into the Tiber, and he's finally knifed by a fascist in a demo in Bruges. But in the end the novel brings home the overwhelming significance of the inescapably humdrum. *Dear Michael* offers no saving glosses on its people's lives: but it does make Mara's jacket with dragons on it, Michael's German stove, his father's cashmere scarf and the snatches of an old anti-fascist song matter memorably.

> Valentine Cunningham, "Griding Mistress," in New Statesman, *Vol. 89, No. 2293, February 28, 1975, p. 284.*

ISABEL QUIGLY

Take the subjects of the essays in *Vita immaginaria,* and they suggest what anyone with a claim to what is called "informed opinion" might turn out. Books, films, plays, current happenings, well-known people, all made short pieces in the past five years for *La Stampa* and the *Corriere della Sera,* which sound like the sort of thing you might expect from someone with a column to fill and a full life (present and past) from which to fill it. Take their spirit and style, though, and their treatment of these quite ordinary subjects, and it is clear that "informed opinion" is the last thing Natalia Ginzburg would lay claim to: information does not particularly concern her, and the state of being well-informed sounds hilariously unsuitable, applied to her brilliant oddity.

Writer of novels, short stories, memoirs, plays and unclassifiable writings like these, she is not—because she happens to write for newspapers—at all what one thinks of as a journalist. Style, voice, manner, cast of mind, a vision of the world that, for all its lack of spiritual side (or smugness, portentousness, pretensions), seems direct and complete, make everything she writes seem part of a whole: the novels read like memoirs and the memoirs like novels, the plays like conversations and the essays like letters to a friend. Once the cadences of her writing are familiar they seem hypnotically suitable, for all their apparent casualness unalterably right and precise. With passion and intuition she writes *around* whatever subject she chooses, circling it, stalking it, watching it from unexpected angles and in the end often pouncing, with some

piercing insight, her tone halfway between triumph and dying fall.

"Fine writing" is as foreign to Signora Ginzburg as rhetoric, that windy quality much prized in Italy during her formative years; so that most of her writing is even, light, fast-moving, apparently effortless, with a liberal use of repetition and everyday words. But sometimes (indignation is generally the catalyst) it swells into grandeur, and instead of flowing briskly becomes sonorous: a wonderful description of Pavese, all strenuously long sentences and powerful adjectives, is inspired by hatred of a play about him. Likes and dislikes are powerful factors in everything she writes, in fact, quickening or dampening her style, inspiring her to make what sometimes seem inspired exaggerations.

Her last book of essays like these was called *Mai devi domandarmi (Never must you ask me),* a title that well suggested their self-contained quality, their impenetrability to questioning or argument. She fastens on some aspect of a situation, a character, a work of art—some aspect of its spirit, as a rule, often secret and unexpected—and ignoring the obvious rest explores it. This makes for lopsided criticism very often, but for intuitions and surprises.

> Isabel Quigly, "Beyond the Obvious," in The Times Literary Supplement, *No. 3812, March 28, 1975, p. 344.*

ROSETTA D. PICLARDI

Anyone writing about Italian women novelists cannot help notice their much larger number in our century in comparison to their nineteenth-century counterparts. Due to many social and literary barriers, Italy did not produce in the last century a George Sand or a George Eliot. But today, managing to break down many of these barriers, women writers in Italy have come into their own. Novelists such as Gianna Manzini, Elsa Morante and Natalia Ginzburg, to name a few, have expressed with individual style and with authentic voice their personal view on life and reality. By and large their search has been for a coherent identity, and their attacks have been at outgrown social and psychological stereotypes. Never at odds with their most intimate affinities, never uncertain how or whether to be themselves, they have chronicled family life, the female condition, the anarchy of human emotions. In doing this from a particular point of view, they have produced a body of work which, even if eluding immediate categorization, is implicitly feminist. (p. 585)

Natalia Ginzburg has established her identity and her independence in a muted manner, aiming the complexities of her art at producing a series of novels that find their most appropriate measure in a brief, tight narrative not so much interested in facts and events as in capturing moments and meanings in the lives of a small group of figures who share with their author a precarious sense of human existence. This restriction on the range of the novels has been accompanied by the verbal and structural economy that Natalia Ginzburg is famous for. Yet it is precisely in this reversed chic of the novels, in their measured expression, in their tendency toward understatement and in their surplus of potential meaning that we find the roots of poetic tension and esthetic clarity.

While these premises can serve as an introduction to Natalia Ginzburg's fiction, simply to list the qualities of her prose and construction can be an empty exercise unless it leads to the analysis of specifically imagined and specifically constructed entities. Identification of narrative devices, always an epistemic even if unconscious choice on the part of an author, can lead to understanding the nature and meaning of the texts themselves. In *È stato cosí* (*The Dry Heart;* 1947), one of Ginzburg's first works, the monologue of the main character and first-person narrator can thus be fruitfully examined. A perfect example of the sustained point of view, it is the chief means of structural and thematic delineation. The book is made up almost entirely of the monologue-justification of the protagonist, who has just shot her indifferent husband to death and is about to drift into the silence of her own suicide. In fact the use of the isolated "I," a somewhat detached, almost disincarnate voice that presents facts and figures as if through a prolonged aside, is a favorite device of this author, reflecting as it does the resigned impassivity of her characters. Most often the voice we hear is a feminine one. At the very beginning of her career, in the two short stories **"Un'assenza"** (1933) and **"Casa al mare"** (1937), Ginzburg used a male protagonist. She has done so again in *Famiglia,* one of the two short novels that make up her latest book by the same title. . . . In *È stato cosí* the units of dialogue are imbedded in the narrator's monologue, the linear, persistent strain in which all else is absorbed and which is sustained throughout by the character's lucidity and controlled despair.

In *Le voci della sera* (*Voices of the Evening;* 1961) the straight chronological line of the narrative is broken up by a series of flashbacks made up in large part by juxtaposed blocks of brief, sketchy dialogue interwoven in the narrator's monologue. There are six major flashbacks, each a portrait of a member of the De Francisci family, owners of a textile factory in a small town on the outskirts of Turin. In the close perimeter of this provincial environment moves a small cluster of individuals interrelated by marriage, friendship, business association. Elsa, the narrator, is one of them. She is the young daughter of the factory's chief accountant and the lover of the youngest of the three De Francisci sons, Tommasino. Each portrait is set in the same locale and covers the same period from immediately before World War II to the narrator's present. Echoes of the war are heard as it touches the lives of the characters, but indirectly and at second hand. The portraits deal essentially with the same material: the disintegration of personal relationships, including that of Elsa and Tommasino.

Le voci della sera is a book of endings, a recurrent theme in Natalia Ginzburg's fiction, where there are no happy endings. Written during the author's stay in England of 1960-62, the book has all the nostalgic and elegiac tones of a *piccolo mondo antico.* Looking at the way that she has fashioned this microcosm, we could speak of Ginzburg's "crepuscolarismo." Actually the selective realism of this prose has none of the self-indulgence of the *crepuscolari.* Enumeration and accumulation of physical details, special care given to objects and space do not strike here a sentimental note. Images of houses being abandoned that mirror the theme of endings create most of all a sense of physical and psychological reality that is attended to with the most veiled irony. (pp. 585-86)

Connected with the theme of endings are two other thematic interests of Natalia Ginzburg. *Famiglia* and *Borghesia,* the two separate titles of the two short novels that make up her latest book, *Famiglia,* point in 1977, as *Le voci della sera* did in 1961 and *Caro Michele* did in 1973, to the author's preoccupation with the crisis in our time of an institution and of

a class. The merit of this author is not to have dealt with her concerns in an abstract manner. In her novels there is no abstract analysis of the feelings and motives of the characters. Through the narrator's monologue of both *È stato cosí* and *Le voci della sera* we are not seized by the force of an argument but by that of a felt reality. And it is through the perceptual field of the narrator in both books that the psychological dimension of the novels is created. In *Le voci della sera,* while the climactic moments in the sequence of events shift from one portrait to the next, the same events and characters appear and reappear in each. This counterpointing of presences, voices, gestures does not slacken throughout the book. And in a work that presents different pictures of the same problem, such repetition does give the fixity of icons to the figures in it. They become as such the prismatic complements of Elsa's account of her own story; they give symbolic extension to her monologue. All the voices we hear find a common denominator in her voice, the explicit, identifiable narrator who plays the motive role in the novel. (p. 586)

Many critics have remarked on the even, monochord, unruffled manner of Natalia Ginzburg's prose. Most recently, in her review of *Famiglia* for the *Times Literary Supplement,* Isabel Quigly has said much the same thing in pointing out that in Ginzburg's fiction "birth and death, love, relationships, separations, the large matters of personal life, are given the same amount of space on the page, the same weight in the telling, as the supposed trifles; enormities and banalities balanced in a serio-comic mixture of mood and attitude that recalls (inevitably, given their remarkably similar social settings and attitudes) Chekhov." An appropriate comparison with an author whom Ginzburg has professed to admire very much, and one which could provide the basis for a study of its own. Both authors feel intuitively that life is accessible to art only when caught in its most prosaic, mundane flow. Accident is for both writers a given of reality, a given that is made a thematic and formal element of their art.

As the monologues in both *È stato cosí* and *Le voci della sera* are the live, connective tissues of the space and time dimensions, so is the letter in *Caro Michele,* a novel that is for the most part epistolary. Here the letter as a structural device allows the novelist to make use of both multiple monologues and multiple points of view. Written after a twelve-year hiatus from the novel, *Caro Michele* shows the influence of the theatre (a genre to which the author had dedicated herself during that time) in its concern with presenting many characters who speak in the first person instead of a single dominant voice. While a strict linear chronology is kept by the dating of the letters from December 1970 to 1971, the total effect of the book is of a spiral set in motion and kept up by the exchange of letters and by the current of feelings passing among those engaged in the correspondence. With the various narrators inside the story, with the story moving along through the characters' perceptions, Ginzburg works out an ironic construct that allows the reader to see through its surface rigidity to the inner emotional chaos it contains. The elliptical effect of the letter device, which makes for built-in transitions, creates and sustains the quick tempo of the narrative.

Set in a contemporary context, *Caro Michele* reflects some of the social unrest of Italy in the seventies. Michele, a young Roman from an upper-middle-class family, must leave Italy for England to avoid arrest as a political activist. After a series of episodes that include a short-lived marriage to an American physicist with a drinking problem, he is killed by a fascist group during a student demonstration in Bruges. But it is not his political activity nor his death that is stressed in the book. Tragedy and violence in Natalia Ginzburg's fiction come always as an overlay. If it is true that their sudden appearance has the effect of bringing into sharp focus all the other elements in the book, they are also pointers to the deep inner personal disorders that have unconsciously led to them. *Caro Michele* is no exception; in this book, as in all Ginzburg's novels, the crisis is one of response. Not that the characters are inarticulate, for quite the opposite is true, judging from the letters they write. They are keenly aware of their feelings and of the feelings of others. But in the end they fail to capture the meaning of their own experience. They write to each other out of a need to communicate and to put on paper what they feel and think. With the urgency of the damned, they try to exorcize the empty space they feel growing around themselves. So the beautiful aging mother Adriana writes to her son Michele fretting about his well-being while mourning the end of a love affair. So does his sophisticated, dutiful sister Angelica; so does his sometime girlfriend Mara, a flower child Italian style, whose infant son could be Michele's.

Most of the thirty-six letters are addressed to Michele, who answers them in brief, sometimes cryptic terms. As the central character of the novel, he remains an ambiguous one. His motives are explored with tentativeness; he remains a minimal presence, an enigma. In his physical and emotional remoteness he is a typical male character of Natalia Ginzburg's fiction. It is surprising to see how she succeeds in giving a tragic dimension to such a cast of passive characters who do not derive any sense of personal order from their world and who have no will to impose themselves on it. Yet she succeeds in the same way that Ivy Compton-Burnett does, by creating close-knit domestic worlds whose members are joined in a vortex of emptiness and frustration. Natalia Ginzburg's work does not possess the fierceness of Compton-Burnett's, suffused as it is by a mitigating *pietà*. Still it too is controlled by the dominant idea of a fundamental organic disturbance in the relationship of the members of that social nucleus we call family. The novels of both writers are miles away from those domestic novels that portray the family as a secure natural domain.

With her latest books, *Caro Michele* and *Famiglia,* Natalia Ginzburg's fictional world has not changed. Relationships, family situations, the theme of endings are still there. If any change at all is to be noticed in relation to her previous work, it is in a certain crispness of movement and detail, in the effective portrayal of contemporary urban background, say in the manner of a Lessing, a Spark, a Rhys. In *Famiglia* there is also a more consistent overlay of the symbolic dimension, an element of unity that remains nonetheless tenuous and understated. In this book the author has chosen to deal with the most irrevocable of endings, death. The two stories that make up the text, *Famiglia* and *Borghesia,* are linked by the same subject, the sudden illness and impending death of their respective protagonists Carmine and Ilaria. Not that they are consciously aware of the fate that awaits them. Yet in their detachment from life there is an insinuation, a prefiguring of last things. Throughout the development of *Borghesia* a recurrent event takes on a symbolic dimension when a number of household cats, all Siamese, die or disappear as if vowed to a dark necessity. Their passing scans the novel like a beat, a beat that the main character Ilaria, the middle-aged woman who owns them, progressively hears and recognizes as a call:

"Ilaria said that she did not know how to explain why, lately, when she looked at her cat Ninna-Nanna, she thought of her own death. It seemed to her that it was due to a faculty to guide her thoughts in an unknown direction."

Carmine, the main character in *Famiglia,* has come to realize that he can only know life when he is no longer living it. Not that he treasures memories; certainly he does not sentimentalize them. However, an unhappy married man, an indifferent architect when we meet him right before his death of cancer at forty, he finds contentment only in the little meal, the quiet evening shared with his past lover Ivana: "He thought that Ivana, and all that surrounded her, was the best part of his existence, and the only zone from which came to him something that made him more intelligent, stranger and stronger."

As always, Natalia Ginzburg knows exactly how to make a technical tool yield the very texture of experience. In *Caro Michele* the revolving monologues/letters had been the means of organizing experience and of attempting to make sense out of it. Here in *Famiglia* a very skillful manipulation of the point of view and the use of indirect discourse are the strategic narrative modes. (pp. 587-88)

Since Natalia Ginzburg's main concern is condition and not action, the story line moves once again more through the characters' perceptions of the physical reality around them than through plot, which in her novels is practically nonexistent. As such, the material world is given high specificity in her fiction. Things are very real and very present, and they remain wholly concrete and wholly themselves. But where does all this contingency lead to? Does attention given to physical reality yield a cognitive dimension, say in the line of Proust, who saw through perceptions and emotions a way to metaphysics? This would seem to be the case, for through the taking in of impressions Ginzburg seems to want to lead us to read contingency for meaning. Through things characters get in touch with the world around them and, most of all, with themselves in a kind of mystical contingency that can be taken as the key to her art. And yet truth ultimately eludes her, as it does the characters in her novels. Her loyalty of vision, her fundamental honesty in attending, in being a witness, does not allow the emergence of a clear-cut message. Montale, in speaking of Natalia Ginzburg's fiction, has said it best in observing that when reading her work "we are in front of the acceptance of an intelligent animal who gathers his little happiness wherever he finds it, but who knows that happiness is short-lived and that the meaning of life is all in living it without asking oneself why."

The specific clarity that Ginzburg's art gives to life is the awareness that we are what we learn, and what we learn is our limitations. There is no vantage point in this world for anyone, and experience most often leads only to dead ends. In *Famiglia* Carmine's last memory is an incidental one. One cannot be satisfied with this ending, but that is precisely the point. Destinies are irrelevant. Shaped by change, they have no meaning. The question of why things happen or fail to, echoed throughout her books, only finds the most abiding silence. This is Natalia Ginzburg's perspective, her philosophy and therefore her manner. It is well represented in her novels, where meaning is reached through a process, not a statement, a process wherein words and structures, forms and figures all become relevant signs. (pp. 588-89)

Rosetta D. Piclardi, "Forms and Figures in the Nov-

els of Natalia Ginzburg," in World Literature
Today, *Vol. 53, No. 4, Autumn, 1979, pp. 585-89.*

FILIPPO DONINI

Neither Manzoni's life nor that of any member of his family
contained many elements that may strictly be called "romantic". This most homebound of all Italian poets did nothing
adventurous; with the exception of a few visits to Paris,
Turin, Genoa, Pisa and Florence, his life was spent entirely
in Milan and Brusuglio, his country-house, and can be accurately described as uneventful. The great historical upheavals
of his times affected him deeply (he fainted on hearing of the
death of Napoleon; he wrote the most moving lines of any
poet about the Risorgimento) but neither wars nor revolutions caused any serious loss or trouble either to him personally or his family or his property. The one mystery in his life
concerned the identity of his father, but it is doubtful whether
he himself ever suspected he might not be the legitimate son
of Count Pietro Manzoni.

Yet Natalia Ginzburg's book [*La famiglia Manzoni*] is more
fascinating and gripping than any work of fiction. No doubt
the fact that every single story in the book is true has something to do with it, but that is so with all the best biographies.
So how is it that in this case one simply cannot put the book
down, even if one knew before opening it that Manzoni's first
wife would die young, that he would remarry but only to become a widower again, and that of his nine children only two
would survive him?

There is only one explanation, and it lies in the book's authorship. Italian biographies have only rarely reached the level of
works of art, but *La famiglia Manzoni* is one which does. Natalia Ginzburg is at her best when writing about families, either relating her personal memories (*Lessico famigliare*) or
in her stories (*Le voci della sera, Caro Michele*). The Manzoni family obviously attracted her as it would attract anyone
with literary inclinations, but it is also interesting in itself,
being full of remarkable characters who are rewarding objects of study as individuals, and who, as a group, form an
outstanding collection of different, sometimes conflicting,
personalities. . . .

[Letters] are the substance of this book: the letters written by
the numerous members of the Manzoni family to one another, as well as letters to and from friends. Long excerpts from
this correspondence give the ring of authenticity to each episode of the story Mrs Ginzburg has to tell. Her supreme
achievement lies in the way she has joined these fragments together so as to give the impression of a story that develops
naturally by itself, smoothly but implacably. The book is divided into eight chapters, each bearing the name of one of the
eight members of the Manzoni family who follow one another
chronologically as the protagonists. Giulia, Manzoni's mother, is followed by Enrichetta, his first wife. Then come Giulietta, Teresa (his second wife), Vittoria, Matilde and Stefano,
the stepson who survived them all: he died in 1907, at the age
of eighty-eight. The only outsider is the French writer Claude
Fauriel, who is inserted between Enrichetta and Giulietta: his
inclusion is more than justified by the warm friendship that
both Giulia and Manzoni professed for him, and by the unbounded devotion of his god-daughter, Giulietta. His own
letters, and those of Manzoni and Giulietta to him, are
among the best in the book.

Although Giulia, Enrichetta and all the rest are brought in
succession to the fore, and given temporary precedence, the
character who dominates the book from beginning to end is,
of course, Manzoni himself. We follow him from his dissipat-
ed youth to his troubled, tormented maturity, from the frivolity of the Paris *salons* to the discovery of God and his consequent total submission to the commandments of an austere,
perhaps too gloomy and ruthless religion. There is his progress too in the study and practice of literature, his work on
his poems and plays, his great novel, his solitude at Brusuglio,
which slowly becomes peopled by the heroes of his imagination. What is disconcerting, alas, is his seeming lack of humanity in his dealings with his children: his beloved Vittoria
sent to a convent-school at the age of nine, his cruelty towards Enrico and Filippo in their troubles, his unforgivable
neglect of the dying Matilde. On the other hand he embraces
in rapture a small girl because she resembles Vittoria, and
there is ample evidence of his tender heart. One cannot escape
Manzoni's charm; perhaps the most sensible reaction to him
was that of Mary Clarke, Fauriel's English lover, who said
of him: "His charm is supreme: I wanted to roll on the
ground in front of him, like a cat in the sun."

Short of doing the same in front of Natalia Ginzburg, let me
say that she has written a wonderful book.

Filippo Donini, "A Novelist and His Brood," in The
Times Literary Supplement, *No. 4186, June 24,
1983, p. 680.*

OLGA RAGUSA

It took today's Italian novelist of family life (most recently
in *Caro Michele,* 1973, and *Famiglia,* 1977) to discover, lying
at hand and already "told," the chronicle of what happened
to a famous but by no means exceptional Milanese family between 1762 and 1907: 1762, birth date of Giulia Beccaria,
Manzoni's mother; 1907, death date of Stefano Stampa, Manzoni's stepson. [*La famiglia Manzoni*] reads like a novel, although it is almost entirely composed of letters or parts of letters, the published correspondence of the historical persons
involved. Ginzburg has first of all translated the many letters
originally written in French; she has supplied the connective
narrative, provided a genealogical table and selected illustrative material from the different Manzoni archives, and she
herself has discreetly withdrawn—as is her usual habit—to
let the story tell itself.

What must most strongly strike the Manzoni scholar already
acquainted with much of this material is the removal of the
great writer and venerated spiritual leader of Risorgimento
Italy from center stage, the pushing to the side of the literary,
religious, intellectual and political concerns for which his biography normally serves only as background. They continue
to be present but are muted, in no sense more important than
the births and marriages, the illnesses and deaths, the visits
and changes of residence, the children's lessons and games,
the financial problems and the getting in of supplies, the apologies for letters delayed and the expressions of joy over letters
received that crowd in upon these pages. The bibliography of
works consulted by Ginzburg brings a surprise and an illumination: here are many of the titles that recent literary criticism has disdained; but the musty volumes on the shelf have
their own survival power, and like the reconstructed rooms

in Casa Manzoni in Milan, they give back the flavor of life as it was once lived.

Olga Ragusa, in a review of "La famiglia Manzoni," in World Literature Today, *Vol. 57, No. 4, Autumn, 1983, p. 621.*

WILLIAM WEAVER

Natalia Ginzburg has been publishing since the 1930's, when she was in her teens. But the list of her books is not long—perhaps a dozen titles—and it gives only a partial idea of her significance in the Italian cultural panorama. . . . Because of her Jewish background Mrs. Ginzburg had to publish her first novel under a pseudonym. Her husband's political activity earned him *confino,* a Fascist punishment involving forced residence in a remote village (in the Abruzzi, in his case). Then in 1944 he was arrested by the Gestapo, tortured and killed. Other friends of Mrs. Ginzburg fought with the partisans, and some suffered imprisonment and death. . . .

In Mrs. Ginzburg's latest novel, *La Città e la Casa (The City and the House)*, which has just appeared in Italy, one character says about another character's book: "Too many descriptions; I can't bear descriptions in novels." And in this most recent work, in fact, descriptions are few. . . . The book is in two parts. The first takes place in an unnamed northern town that has some factories (it could be Ivrea, headquarters of Olivetti; Adriano Olivetti was for a time Mrs. Ginzburg's brother-in-law). The second part is set in the south, perhaps in the Abruzzi, where she lived with her husband during his *confino.* The reader is never nudged; things are never underlined in the novel. But the difference between life in the industrialized North and the peasant culture of the South is vividly suggested.

Terrible things happen in Mrs. Ginzburg's novels—suicide, murder, death from lingering or swift illness, air raids and bombings. But less awesome events like a family quarrel, an adultery or a deception are given equal space and importance, as if to say that to the victim adultery and an air raid can be equally maiming. Mrs. Ginzburg does not exclude the larger picture, the world context, but it appears in her novels only as it is seen by her characters.

A decade after *All Our Yesterdays* appeared, Mrs. Ginzburg published an autobiographical work, *Family Sayings,* a wry, affectionate memoir that indicated, to some extent, the sources of this novel. There are no exact correspondences (the A of real life is not the B of *All Our Yesterdays*); but the atmosphere and the quirks often coincide. Mrs. Ginzburg is good with families, as another recent work, *La Famiglia Manzoni,* demonstrates. Imaginatively using a store of documents, she re-creates the family life of Italy's great 19th-century writer with an immediacy that grips even one who has read little or none of the work of Alessandro Manzoni. The book cries out for translation, and so does *La Città e la Casa.*

The success of these two latest books in Italy has led to a wider recognition there of Mrs. Ginzburg's position as one of the country's leading writers. There are, and have been for years, some dissenting voices. A while back, the critic and occasional novelist Oreste Del Buono wrote a carping article on Mrs. Ginzburg entitled "La Finta Tonta," ("The Fake Simpleton"), criticizing her narrative detachment, her refusal to pontificate, calling it all a pose. Mrs. Ginzburg, obviously, is

no simpleton; her simplicity is an achievement, hard-won and remarkable, and the more welcome in a literary world where the cloak of omniscience is all too readily donned.

William Weaver, "War in Classical Voice," in The New York Times Book Review, *May 5, 1985, p. 39.*

P. N. FURBANK

There is an initial adjustment that English readers have to make to Italian writing, which so often strikes their ear as rhetorical, even oratorical. The novelist Natalia Ginzburg is, in fact, well known for a certain narrative dryness and understatement, a Hemingwayesque quality. Nevertheless, she too impresses one as, indirectly, a very rhetorical writer. It comes out not in the texture but in the form of her novels, which depend in a high degree on what you might term 'time-passing' effects. 'Then they had children. A boy was born and then a baby girl and then a boy again'; 'It was October once again': such sentences, with their repetitionary flavour, are the staple, for instance, of her *Voices in the Evening (Le Voci della Sera)*.

To exploit the pathos of time, including the time it takes to read a novel, is a favourite trick of the early 20th-century novelist (Arnold Bennett occasionally, and Galsworthy almost always, seem to be doing little else); and I have some suspicion of it. But at least Natalia Ginzburg's essays [collected in *The Little Virtues*] (which have been splendidly translated by Dick Davis) amount to a powerful plea in its justification. I am thinking especially of the long essay, written in 1953, entitled **"Human Relationships"**. This takes the form of a sort of "Seven Ages of Man", a conspectus of human life from the aspect of changing attitudes to human relationship. . . .

This cycle, culminating in an 'awareness of things', is presented as a generalisation about life but, we perceive, is actually a generalisation about art; and as such, in its didactic way, it is not unimpressive. I like what it says about the art of speech. 'Finding the words for our vocation' is equated with 'finding the words for our neighbour'; and in another rather fine essay, **"Silence"**, Ginzburg castigates silence (and regarding our own thoughts as unutterable) as a sin, a perverse regression to childish sulks and contempt for our parents' 'public' language. It is a congenial view, and certainly preferable to that of critics, like Alvarez and George Steiner, who ask us to admire poets for going silent—which is not a wish that anyone can properly have on someone else's behalf.

Here in these essays, at all events, is a convincing rationale for Ginzburg's own school of novel-writing, which, for all its understatement, is essentially voluble and is all about growing up and growing old. Here is an art which loves to fall into the rhythm of the seasons. The autobiographical essay **"Winter in the Abruzzi"**, in the present collection, has just the same seasonal shape as her fiction. It perorates: 'There is a kind of uniform monotony in the fate of man. Our lives unfold according to ancient, unchangeable laws, according to an invariable and ancient rhythm'—and this, one feels, is less a conviction about life than a wish, or voluntary determination, on the part of a novelist.

The title of her essay **"My Vocation"** could really serve for her whole collection; and this essay, too, has some salutary and even inspiring things to say. Typically, Ginzburg anthropomorphises her calling. 'My vocation has always rejected me, it does not want to know about me. Because this vocation is never a consolation or a way of passing the time. It is not a companion. This vocation is a master who is able to beat us till the blood flows . . .' She also explains very convincingly why hoarded observations 'crystallise' and lose their value. Parsimony, she argues, is the trait most fatal to a writer, who, when he writes a story, must 'recklessly throw the best of everything into it, the best of whatever he possesses and has seen'.

I am not sure, in fact, if observation is Ginzburg's own strongest card. Even in 1961, when she wrote **"England: Eulogy and Lament"**, I can hardly believe that English railway stations were smothered in coal-dust, or that English people never tasted wine. Certainly she is quite funny about the melancholy English relationship to food; but that is a large target, not too easy to miss.

P. N. Furbank, "Time Passing," in The Listener, *Vol. 114, No. 2919, July 25, 1985, p. 31.*

DICK DAVIS

Natalia Ginzburg is famous for being able to communicate, with a subtlety and realism that few other novelists approach, what it is to be part of a family, "to live together, to sit at the same table, to have the same walls and furniture around one . . .". In her new novel, *La città e la casa,* she examines what happens when families go to pieces.

La città e la casa is an epistolary novel; in this it resembles her earlier *Caro Michele* (there are also resemblances of plot between the two works) and her group biography *La famiglia Manzoni,* though neither relies exclusively on letters as *La città e la casa* does. The central characters are Giuseppe, a widower, and Lucrezia, a married woman with five children; the two have just finished having an affair when the novel opens, and Giuseppe leaves for America, where he lives with his brother. Lucrezia is still clearly half in love with him and has another affair out of boredom and pique; this turns out disastrously but by the time she has realized her mistake her long-suffering husband has finally left for good. Giuseppe's brother dies, Giuseppe drifts into a marriage with his brother's widow and then proceeds to fall vaguely in love with his new wife's daughter by a previous marriage. Other relationships, equally unsatisfactory, equally shot through with boredom and bad faith—between Giuseppe and his homosexual son Alberico, whom he had ignored as a child and with whom he cannot make contact as an adult, between Alberico and Nadia, a girl whose illegitimate child Alberico adopts in a moment of impulsive generosity—form a background to Giuseppe's and Lucrezia's long-distance bickering about the past and what went wrong.

At the edge of the novel are people unable to form any sustained or sustaining relationships; Serena, whom loneliness has made stupid and bitchy; the sensitive, intelligent Albina whom loneliness makes pathetic and despairing and whose story, lightly touched in as it is, is perhaps the most affecting in the book. All these characters, and many others including Piero (Lucrezia's husband) and Ignazio Fegiz (her second lover) are beautifully and very economically realized; they have the force of truth, we recognize them and feel irritation and sympathy for them.

The title indicates the journey taken by the book's characters, from the familiar comfort of a house, a home where they are welcome and part of a group, to the aimlessness and anomie of the city. "The City" is Rome, and an act of spectacular, random violence in its back-streets (which it would be unfair to potential readers to describe in more detail) brings the book to its sudden and grim end. . . .

Ginzburg's style, an understated blend of tragedy and comedy (in an early essay she said that she discovered how to write when she realized that people in fiction should be "comici e un po' miserevole") and her subject-matter, the relationships of well-meaning but ineffectual middle-class characters, have meant that she has been compared to Chekhov. Certainly the vacancy and sense of impotence at the heart of many of Chekhov's creations are recognizable in her work, and nowhere more so than in this new novel. But her writing has become much more sombre, less comic, less optimistic; the triumphant will to live, to continue against all odds, which characterized her early work, is very muted in *La città e la casa;* there are some comic scenes (chiefly at the expense of the ineffably silly Serena), but her characters are now much more "miserevole" than "comici". They seem almost incapable of taking part in life other than selfishly; the unselfish characters are peripheral, their function is largely to see that the central characters do not give up on life altogether. . . .

This is an excellent novel and a dispiriting one; dispiriting because the reader recognizes the desolate truth of the life the author describes. It is not, however, equally convincing at all points: the older generation (Giuseppe, Piero, Lucrezia, Albina) is much more solidly and persuasively portrayed than the younger (the film director Alberico—who is perhaps distantly modelled on Pasolini—Nadia, and their friends). This younger generation is presented as a mystery, from the outside—a recognizable mystery, but a mystery none the less, as much it would seem to its author as to the reader; whereas the older generation is presented with full knowledge, from the inside, and is thus the more convincing. A second slight problem of belief is the very large number of deaths in the novel, three of them violent (unexpected violent deaths, together with a memory of a lost, shared Eden hardly appreciated while it was present, are not uncommon in Ginzburg's work, perhaps in part because of the death of her first husband at the hands of the Nazis, a death that seems to re-echo throughout her writing). And there is, too, a stylistic problem; the author's prose style is very distinctive—clipped, deadpan, clear, seemingly impulsive but in reality extremely controlled and sure of its effects. Though the characters of her novel write their letters in recognizably distinct styles many of them tend to write like their creator for much of the time.

But these are minor cavils to set against the strength of her achievement, which is to have given us a chillingly accurate picture of human relationships in decay, of a life in which "everything is breaking up here, the whole house is going to pieces".

Dick Davis, "At the Breaking-Point," in The Times Literary Supplement, *No. 4305, October 4, 1985, p. 1115.*

GABRIELE ANNAN

All Our Yesterdays first appeared in Italian in 1952 and in English [as *Dead Yesterdays*] in 1956. *Family Sayings* was published in Italy in 1963 and in translation in 1967. Now comes *The Little Virtues,* a collection of essays written between 1944 and 1962. It makes a useful gloss to the novels which, for all their sober realism, are somewhat inscrutable in intention, written through clenched teeth, as it were, giving away as little as possible. Ginzburg is the least garrulous of writers.

Most realist fiction has its feet in psychology or sociology. Ginzburg despises these ways of interpreting life, bringing them on like clowns, only when she is out to entertain. Her comedy plays on psychological and sociological problems. She is particularly funny about adolescent malaise and bourgeois social anxiety, mocking the first and even the second with affection; it is only social pretension that turns her humor savage. But all this is merely a sideshow. She interprets behavior in order to judge it. She judges with understanding and pity, but her understanding and pity are metaphysical, not the social worker's or analyst's. In fact, the essay **"Silence"** (1951) in *The Little Virtues* can be read as an attack on psychoanalysis. Silence, she says, is the vice of our age; it "should be called by its true name"—which is not, presumably, lack of communication or alienation. . . .

From the two reprinted novels—both autobiographical—one gets the impression that among the seven deadly sins, acedia is the one Natalia Ginzburg understands best, her own besetting sin. It may even account for her unmistakable tone of voice, for she is one of those writers whose voice is immediately recognizable, even in translation. It has a dying fall, a dry cool despondency, which goes with her personality as she describes it: inept, disorganized, dejected, shy, lazy, withdrawn, she is held together, it seems, only by her obedience to truth and moral rightness. It sounds a bleak combination, and it is; but there is also something irresistibly appealing about the struggle from weakness toward goodness, especially when she looks at her younger self with a kind of comical deprecation as though it were a baby toad in the palm of her hand.

All Our Yesterdays, with only a few actual characters and events transposed, seems about as autobiographical as a novel can be until you get to *Family Sayings.* This belongs to a genre all of its own, a sort of autobiographical "faction" in reverse. Faction is facts with extra tension, drama, and emotion pumped in. Ginzburg scrupulously siphons them out, like the blood from a rhesus negative baby. So there is an apparent bloodlessness, a grayness deliberately chosen in the cause of total veracity. Not in the early part of the book with its engagingly funny accounts of family idiosyncracies and where affection manages to worm its way past the writer's guard. But as the story gets grimmer with the spread of Fascism, the outbreak of war, and natural and unnatural deaths among family and friends, so emotion is more and more rigorously suppressed until by the aftermath of the war the stony evenness of tone and tempo begins to anaesthetize you. Sometimes it feels almost like boredom. But when you put the book down you realize that under the anaesthetic you have sustained a trauma. The shock of truth, perhaps. (p. 29)

The Italian title [of *Family Sayings*], *Lessico Famigliare,* unlike the English, does not suggest that the sayings are proverbial or wise. It just means a dictionary of family expressions—though it could also mean a dictionary for family use. Either way, the sayings stand for the people who used them; in reality or in memory, they are what is left at the end of a life, the solid sediment at the bottom, however much it has been shaken up.

Superficially, the earlier *All Our Yesterdays* seems more pulled together, with more plot, structure, and overt purpose. It is a *Bildungsroman* with Natalia's alter ego, Anna, learning how to break out of the "silence" of her adolescence and "connect." She learns through harrowing experiences. At fifteen she becomes pregnant by a schoolboy who abandons her. She is rescued from her predicament by a friend of her dead father's, an eccentric, middle-aged philanthropist who marries her and takes her to his home in the deep south—a culture shock for her—where he champions the peasants against the landowners. When the Germans march in he dies a martyr's death, giving himself up to be executed in another man's place.

After the war Anna returns north with her child and finds an intimacy she had never known before with her surviving brother and her dead brother's friend:

> And they laughed a little and were very friendly together, the three of them, Anna, Emanuele and Giustino; and they were pleased to be together, the three of them, thinking of all those who were dead, and of the long war and the sorrow and noise and confusion, and of the long, difficult life which they saw in front of them now, full of all the things they did not know how to do.

The elegiac ending seems to carry in it some kind of good resolution, which gives it a faint upbeat. Ten years later, in *Family Sayings,* what minimal optimism there was has so shrunk that it could be expressed in Pushkin's lines:

> Habit to us is given from above.
> It is a substitute for happiness.

Another ten years on, in *Dear Michael,* the melancholy has grown impenetrable, with the most sympathetic character concluding: "One gets used to anything when there is nothing left." On the other hand, this pitch-black tragi-comedy has a formal perfection which comes as a surprise after the deliberate randomness of the other novels. Perhaps one should interpret that as a determination not to let go. (p. 30)

Gabriele Annan, "The Force of Habit," in The New York Review of Books, *Vol. XXXII, No. 17, November 7, 1985, pp. 29-30.*

NICHOLAS SPICE

All Our Yesterdays and *Family Sayings* will not be read fast. Finishing these books is, appropriately, a matter of weeks or months, not hours. Each is a family history—*Family Sayings* autobiographical, *All Our Yesterdays* a novel. The stories they tell, they tell simply, in the past tense and without dramatisation. *All Our Yesterdays* has no dialogue, only reported speech, and in *Family Sayings* the exchanges between characters are given as examples of general habits of communication—they are not vehicles for a drama or plot. The structure of these histories is undiscernible, or rather it is simply the structure they have, as if they had been set down without the slightest re-arrangement. They proceed from start to finish on one level, without increase or decrease in pace, every event, both significant and insignificant, trivial and tremendous, receiving equal treatment, equal weight. Narrative phrasing rarely extends over more than a paragraph, and mostly it is confined to single sentences. Ginzburg's grammar is simple and rhetoric is banished from her style.

At its purest, her writing reads with the intensity of philosophical logic, where every stage is carefully and clearly established before we move on to the next. Yet apart from what her characters indulge in, there is no argument, discourse or commentary in these books. They are not 'about' anything. Even the humour and irony that flicker across them appear to be released of themselves by the characters and events, without the author pointing them up.

Family Sayings was first published in Italy in 1963. It is not really an autobiography, since Natalia Ginzburg herself figures in it as only one of the many individuals whose stories she has set out to tell. In the author's preface she describes the book as 'the record of my family'. It begins with her childhood in Turin and closes with her second marriage in 1950. Her first husband was Leone Ginzburg, a Russian Jew. He worked in a small anti-fascist publishing house and died in the custody of the Nazis in 1944, after only a short time together with Natalia, which she speaks of elsewhere as an especially happy period in her life. The passage in *Family Sayings* which treats Leone's death is typically taciturn:

> Leone was running a secret newspaper and was always out of the house. He was arrested 20 days after our arrival, and I never saw him again. I rejoined my mother in Florence. Misfortune always made her feel very cold and she wrapped herself in a shawl. We did not exchange many words about Leone's death.

All Our Yesterdays is unmistakably the fictional prototype for *Family Sayings.* It tells the story of a family from a small town in Northern Italy, in the time leading up to the outbreak of war, through to 1945 and liberation. It concentrates on the lives of four children: Concettina, Ippolito, Giustino and Anna. Their father dies early on in the book, their mother before the book begins. Half-way through, attention focuses on the youngest of the family, Anna. At 16 she gets pregnant by her boyfriend Giuma. Giuma abandons her, after giving her the money to have an abortion. War has broken out. Her brother Ippolito shoots himself. She is rescued from all this darkness by Cenzo Rena, an extravagant and eccentric friend of her father's who turns up out of the blue and offers to marry her on the spot. She accepts, and despite the disapproval of the rest of her family, who are unaware that she is pregnant, she leaves with Cenzo Rena to go and live in his village in the South. The second half of *All Our Yesterdays* is about their life together there and about Cenzo Rena's death. This part of the book draws directly on Natalia Ginzburg's own memories. During the war, she and Leone were sent to live in a village in the Abruzzi, and she describes what it was like there briefly in *Family Sayings,* as well as in an essay called **"Winter in the Abruzzi"**, one of 11 miscellaneous essays written between 1944 and 1960, and published now for the first time in English as *The Little Virtues.*

All Our Yesterdays and *Family Sayings* stand very close on either side of the line that divides fiction from fact. This is a distinction which makes Natalia Ginzburg uneasy (or, at any rate, it used to make her uneasy), as the preface to *Family Sayings* shows. Every detail in her book is true, she says. She has invented nothing. Nonetheless, we are to read *Family Sayings* 'as though it were a novel, that is . . . without demanding of it either more or less than what a novel can offer'. The equivocation here points to a dilemma at the heart of Ginzburg's career as a writer. She distrusts fiction, but knows that, since there can be no direct access to reality, fiction is in a sense all there is. To invent is to lie, but to claim to tell the truth can be a greater lie.

For Natalia Ginzburg the problem of writing is a moral problem and the attempt to be a good writer, as opposed to a wicked or pernicious one, engages her in a fierce internal struggle, where philosophical, emotional and psychological forces meet. Her greatest enemy in this struggle is silence. To begin with, there was the silence induced by war, by suffering on a scale that had struck Europe dumb, an experience of evil and pain that was literally unspeakable. Natalia Ginzburg saw breaking this silence as a duty, to bear witness to the suffering and to establish whether it could again be possible to say something true. But the silence she most deplored was of a different kind and origin. In an essay called **"Silence"**, published in 1951, a year before *All Our Yesterdays,* she identifies this silence as a characteristic condition of her generation and 'amongst the strangest and gravest vices of our time'. The essay, however, is too sententious to be illuminating. We must go to the novel to understand more clearly what she means. There, silence is shown to be a failure to speak out about what is inside us, and a failure to find out from others what is inside them. It is associated with darkness, emptiness and death. Silence is an index of the slow gathering of despair in Ippolito. No one troubles to find out why he is silent, and then it is too late: 'Memories, also, were searched for words that he had spoken. But he had spoken so few words. It seemed impossible now that nobody should have asked for a few more words . . .' After Ippolito's death, Giustino and Anna cry until 'they had nothing left inside them but amazement and silence.' At moments during her secret pregnancy, Anna is able to imagine what it will be like to have a real baby, but she cannot hold onto the idea, 'and the real baby disappeared with a plunge into darkness, and nothing but fear and silence was left inside her, the baby was again nothing but darkness inside her.' The relief that Cenzo Rena brings Anna is not so much the relief of being able to keep her baby, but the relief of at last being able to break out of her silence. Cenzo Rena himself is a great and wonderful talker. His capacity and willingness to talk is a symptom of his generosity of spirit, his embracing magnanimity. It is a sign of life. When Cenzo Rena gets ill with typhus and almost dies, he stops talking. Giuma too, the boy who jilts Anna, is a talker. Like so many of the men Ginzburg describes, he is a holder-forth. His boyish utterances may be absurd and self-important, but they express his personality artlessly, and that in itself is good. People, these books of Ginzburg's declare, are what they say and how they say it. That is what we remember of them when everything else is gone.

The character who has most trouble talking in *All Our Yesterdays* is Anna. At 14, she is described as 'a plump girl, pale and indolent', and Cenzo Rena delights in calling her an 'insect', and she is recognisably akin to the author as she presents herself in *Family Sayings,* where, by virtue of her position as chronicler, her own sayings are not recorded. The strictly limited self-portraiture in these books is fully corroborated by their style, and we leave them with a definite sense of who Natalia Ginzburg is, which is ironic, in view of her evident distaste for talking about herself. Saturnine, self-critical to a fault, perfectionist, fiercely moral: these are the attributes which dominate in her, and they do so with a rod of iron, so that one is left wondering what it is in Natalia Ginzburg that needed such tyrannical government. She gives our speculation most to feed on in an essay called **"My Vocation"**, dated 1949. There she speaks of the 'grave dangers' which threaten writers when they write a page. For example: 'There is the danger of suddenly starting to be flirtatious and of singing.' She reflects: 'I always have a crazy desire to sing and I have to be very careful that I don't.' She doesn't say why. But the answer seems to lie two paragraphs back. Her vocation, she says, in a metaphor quite untypical of her style as a novelist, is

> a master who is able to beat us till the blood flows, a master who reviles and condemns us. We must swallow our saliva and our tears and grit our teeth and dry the blood from our wounds and serve him. Serve him when he asks. Then he will help us up onto our feet.

No wonder she does not dare to flirt or sing. The figure of the capricious male, father or husband, whose moods the women of the household must humour, whose anger they must placate, and who rewards obedience with flashes of kindness and a guarantee of structure and support, is to be found throughout Natalia Ginzburg's fiction. Her own father, most obviously, as she describes him in *Family Sayings*, but also Anna's father in *All Our Yesterdays*, and even in a much softened form Cenzo Rena, are versions of the type. And here, grotesquely exaggerated, he turns up again as Ginzburg's muse, now internalised as a cruel censor of everything she writes. Obedience to this master generates in her, not surprisingly, a fair degree of anger, which she turns upon herself, and which, in the essays, she is apt also to turn upon the world—on her contemporaries and on us. This harshness towards herself and the rest of us is reflected in the burning integrity of her prose style, where every word seems to have been chosen from millions that were found wanting. But it is not redoubled in her treatment of her characters. On the contrary, she does not judge them at all, but cares for them with a compassion which teaches us a far deeper lesson than anything she arraigns us with in her essays. In *All Our Yesterdays* and *Family Sayings* Natalia Ginzburg puts into loving practice her dictum, formulated in **"My Vocation"**, that men and women in novels should be neither good nor evil, 'but funny and a little sad'. (p. 18)

Nicholas Spice, "Ashes," in London Review of Books, *Vol. 7, No. 22, December 19, 1985, pp. 17-18.*

RITA SIGNORELLI-PAPPAS

Natalia Ginzburg has once again cast a novel in letter form [*La città e la casa*], but she has vivified the style of the letters more successfully than in her earlier epistolary novel, *Caro Michele* (1973), allowing the writers to shed their coyness and reveal themselves with a wry, engaging candor. At the center of this colorful coterie of letter-writing friends is the middle-aged Giuseppe, who leaves his home and newspaper job behind in Rome to go live with his brother in Princeton, New Jersey. Quirky and agoraphobic, Giuseppe restricts contact with his Italian friends even before he has left Italy. Once in America, he shuns the telephone, becomes a passive househusband to his brother's widow, and never actually sees his friends again, not even when he makes a swift return visit to Italy for his son's funeral. He is a classical figure in the Ginzburgian repertoire: lonely, alienated, yet curiously lacking in self-pity. Ginzburg's characters have always possessed an

odd, haunting balance of detachment and loyalty; though they limit communication with each other, the bonds that they form endure.

The story that the letters tell is not a happy one: husbands and wives abandon each other; young people are shot randomly in the street, and apparently healthy, carefree adults die unexpectedly from sudden and—as Flannery O'Connor would say—"dread" diseases. Ginzburg has never had a sentimental view of modern life, and over the years she has preserved her capacity to present its homely essence in a language that captures the cryptic, staccato rhythms of real human speech. She has preserved too her manner of artistic compression and reaches with the poet's deft extension for the range of limpid images that unify her narrative.

Rita Signorelli-Pappas, in a review of "La città e la casa," in World Literature Today, *Vol. 60, No. 1, Winter, 1986, p. 89.*

ANNE-MARIE O'HEALY

Although in recent years Natalia Ginzburg has declared herself opposed to the women's movement, there is a contrast between her current denial of feminist sympathies, and the sensitive portrayal of the alienation of women found in her early novels. Few writers have described as poignantly as Ginzburg the situation of women as "outsiders" in the traditional Italian family, and the feminine internalization of patriarchal norms. This inspiration which dominates her first six novels, has, however, been discarded in recent years. (p. 21)

Although Ginzburg, during the past decade or so, appears to have abandoned her interest in the problems of women, her fascination with the institution of the family still persists. The household looms large in all of the author's writing. It is the uncontested given which provides the parameters of her fictional world. . . . Even important events of history—the rise of Fascism, the Second World War and the terrorism of the 1970s—are glimpsed only to the extent that they impinge upon the lives of a particular household. Yet two quite different attitudes towards the family prevail in Ginzburg's writing: the first, an increasingly critical view, is expressed in the novels which precede the autobiographical *Lessico famigliare* (1963), and the second, characterized by a profound nostalgia for the disciplined stability of the patriarchal family, is voiced implicitly or explicitly in most of the works she has written since that time. Both attitudes are pessimistic, but in the early period the author's pessimism is alleviated by a mood of gentle irony or melancholy, whereas in more recent years this mood has given way to an unrelenting despair.

All of Ginzburg's works preceding *Lessico famigliare* evoke a dismal picture of traditional family life and offer an implicit condemnation of family relationships. The chief focus of this subtle attack is parental insensitivity towards the needs of the younger generation, particularly towards those of the daughters. Within the traditional family which she depicts daughters are discounted or exploited, and all expectations of achievement are invested in the sons. Both daughters and sons grow up to form unhappy, uncommunicative marriages, and so, it is implied, the cycle is perpetuated from generation to generation. Yet, despite the bleak moral implications which this pattern conveys there is no overt demonstration of malice in Ginzburg's families (with the exception of the brutish father in her first novel, *La strada che va in città,* published in 1942). Alan Bullock has justly pointed out that the author's characters are never the victims of active forces directed against them, but are essentially the casualties of passive indifference or good—willed incompetence.

In the six novels which precede *Lessico famigliare* it is always through a daughter's perspective that the varied results of parental repression are demonstrated. All but one of these works are related in the first person by a submissive, self-effacing young woman. In a short story written in 1948, however, a different narrative strategy is used with very effective results. The story, entitled **"La madre,"** recounts the events which lead to the suicide of a young widow, and is narrated through the combined consciousness of her two small boys. This is one of Ginzburg's most chilling portraits of a woman's alienation within a traditional, conformist family. The ironic distance obtained by the unusual narrative strategy reinforces the theme of the widow's isolation. The boys relate their impressions of their mother with a mixture of bewilderment and shame, for they have absorbed the stereotypical prejudices of the grandparents with whom they all live. The mother's "sin" is her failure to conform to the traditional idea of motherhood. The children, like their grandparents, identify this flaw and openly resent it. The grandmother indicates that the mother's principal mark of strangeness is that she lacks a husband. The boys observe that she also lacks the opulent physique of a "real" mother, and they find it more likely that they might have originated within the body of the grandmother of the housekeeper than within their own mother's thin and wiry frame. In addition she has the strange habit of sobbing herself to sleep, and this behavior, far from inspiring sympathy, serves only to increase the sons' sense of disgusted alienation. . . . The mother's final depression and suicide (which follow a disappointing love affair) are summarily indicated by the children who have no comprehension of her anguished state of mind. Even at her most vulnerable and pitiable state they remain unsympathetic, seeing only an odd, puppet-like exterior, rendered even less human by the ravages of despair. Throughout the story the language is kept within the limits of the young narrators' psychological perspective, and the reader is able to reconstruct from the jumble of misconstrued information which the boys assimilate the unspoken complexity of the woman's unhappy life. (pp. 21-3)

In the world of Ginzburg's early novels young women are brought up to assume that they are without worth and without identity. They most often seek to fill the void of their ambition with the elusive, destructive quest for romantic love. This is a dominant theme in five of her first six novels, where she shows how women's misguided pursuit of an amorous illusion leads either to painful rejection, or, much more often to lonely, disappointing marriages. In *È stato così* (1947), Ginzburg's most dramatic study of obsession and repressed identity, it leads even to murder and suicide.

The author's consciousness of the subtle tyranny of family relationships receives its most complex and eloquent expression in *Le voci della sera* (1962). This novel gives an intimate portrayal of the lives of two middle-class families: that of Elsa, the narrator, and that of Tommasino, her lover, over a span of several years concluding with the post-war period. Here we find a group of female characters who embody with great subtilty the "feminine" or potentially feminist themes of the earlier novels. In this work, however, the desolate plight of unfulfilled young women is linked with the desolation of their male counterparts, who are seen as fellow victims of parental insensitivity. This is the first novel in which we find a strong authoritarian father: Balotta, the socialist factory owner. Yet, despite this man's enlightened principles in business and in politics, he treats his family with a gruff off-handedness, and is ruthlessly critical of his sons and daughters as they grow up. All three sons, of whom Tommasino is the youngest, manifest the typical traits of Ginzburg's male characters: they are rich in potential but, because of intolerable domestic pressure, are disappointing in achievement. It is Tommasino who suffers the collective burden of remorse for the wasted existence of the young generation and its unwillingness to follow the example of a highly energetic father. . . . Tommasino's inability to free himself from his family, his past and the prying provincial community eventually invades and destroys his delicate relationship with Elsa.

Ginzburg herself considers *Le voci della sera* to be an important turning point in her work. In the two previous decades of her fiction she had made a declared effort to exclude from her narrative any material which might have been prompted by intimate personal memories, for fear of becoming what she described as "sticky and sentimental". . . . It was during a two-year stay in London in the early 1960s that she consciously overcame this inhibition and decided to allow autobiographical inspiration a free rein. (pp. 24-5)

The sense of exuberance which Ginzburg reports having experienced when she finally allowed personal reminiscences to flow freely into her writing prompted her, a short time after the conclusion of *Le voci della sera,* to begin the autobiographical *Lessico famigliare,* which would win the Strega prize in 1963. This work is preceded by a foreword in which the author makes the rather extraordinary request that her story should not be read as autobiography, but as fiction. . . . This seems to be a warning to those readers who might have hoped to find in *Lessico famigliare* an accurate documentary of one of the most turbulent and interesting periods in recent Italian memory; an insight into the relationships which the author has enjoyed with people who had since passed into history, and also, perhaps, a glimpse into the mind of the author herself. Such expectations were bound to be disappointed, for Ginzburg totally rejects conventional biographical methods, and her reminiscences unfold in a haphazard, dream-like sequence, where the author appears primarily as the captive observer of others, rarely emerging to the center of the stage.

This work is not merely an account of the author's own family. It is principally an idealistic, yet occasionally ironic, celebration of family life in general, and the power of its affections and its special language (the *lessico*) to overcome all vicissitudes. It is the only optimistic work that the author has ever written, despite the many allusions to the troubled historical period in which the story of the Levi family unfolds. This family, in the portrait drawn by its youngest member, is solidly bourgeois and patriarchal, but it is depicted in a far more positive light than any of her fictional families.

The evocative power of the *lessico* is not the exclusive experience of the author-narrator, but is shared by all other members of the family, for whom it revitalizes the past, creating a sense of identity and continuity through the mutual recognition of a shared set of values and rituals. The particular jargon and minutiae of everyday domestic life thus prevails as the foundation of familial solidarity. (pp. 25-6)

Ginzburg's father, Giuseppe Levi, dominates the book, and

his loudly intoned sayings remain the most memorable part of the domestic lexicon. He emerges as an aggressive, eccentric and intolerant paterfamilias, and it is his presence which gives thematic focus to passages which at first might seem to have little connective logic. His powerful personality is seen as the great shaping force in all attitudes and customs observed in the household, and all "deviant" tastes held by other family members are kept secret to avoid his displeasure. Although his egocentricity and arrogance are treated by the adult narrator with affectionate irony, it is clear that the child, Natalia, as well as her brothers and sister, regarded him with a mixture of terror and awe.

Despite the many graphic details of the character of Giuseppe Levi which are glimpsed throughout *Lessico famigliare,* the reader is never permitted to perceive him, or indeed any of the other members of the household from a truly adult viewpoint, for the author's childlike essentially two-dimensional characterization of her family prevails right to the end, and contrasts sharply with the more complex character portraits of some adult friends introduced in the latter half of the narrative. This strategy caused a number of critics to find fault with the work. Several reviewers objected specifically to Ginzburg's manneristic characterizations, as well as to her cursory treatment of the historical background. (p. 27)

The author's decision to write this story seems to have been prompted by the need to formulate a personal myth which would act as an antidote to the traumatic events of history. In her reminiscences she purposely created an enchanted domain where the kind of self-revelation which might result in acknowledging and reliving the painful experiences of life's vicissitudes is either minimized or excluded. In the face of the chaotic cruelty of public events she thus chose to exalt the stability and predictability of traditional family life. It is a passionate nostalgia which inspires her mystification of the Levi household and causes manneristic distortions in character portrayal. The same nostalgia inspires her refusal to openly acknowledge the injustices inherent in her family's rigorously patriarchal principles, of which she herself was so obviously a victim. *Lessico famigliare* might be considered as Ginzburg's epitaph to bourgeois family life, and it is possible that it was in the very act of writing it that she realized that the kind of family she had set out to remember and to celebrate had disappeared permanently from the face of the earth.

An unrelentingly pessimistic tone characterizes the author's work since the composition of *Lessico famigliare.* This pessimism reflects her negative reaction to the historical and social changes of the 1960s and 1970s, it is often accompanied by an explicit yearning for the many traditional values and customs which previously gave meaning and direction to the life of the individual. One of the first direct statements of the author's malaise is an essay written in 1969 and entitled **"La critica".** In it she mourns the loss of true critics in modern society, and the terms in which she expresses this are quite unique. Her delineation of the ideal critic whom she describes as aloof, stern, yet sometimes compassionate, possesses the traits of the patriarchal father and is clearly reminiscent of the description of her own father in *Lessico famigliare.* Good critics, she says, are as strong and as protective as good fathers, and both are equally absent from the world of today. . . . In this essay she also formulates a perception of contemporary human-kind as orphans in quest of a father, a theme which prevails in all her subsequent writing. . . . Another pessimistic essay from the same period as **"La critica"** is **"Sul credere o non credere in Dio",** which is prefaced, significantly, by Simone Weil's statement that "the God whom we must love is absent".

The eight plays Ginzburg wrote between 1965 and 1971 closely mirror the pessimism of her essays written for the *Terza pagina.* Although some themes from her previous works continue to find expression here, a number of new thematic preoccupations begin to appear with insistent frequency. Chief among these are the disintegration of marriage and the family, as well as the absence of moral responsibility, emotion, memory and hope in the world of today. The later plays in particular focus on the purposeless, unhappy and often parasitic behavior of the new generation. Although these plays, like Ginzburg's novels, often unfold against the background of domestic life, the features of the household have changed utterly. Gone are the solid middle-class structures suggested in her earlier fiction. The new characters inhabit instead rented or borrowed accomodation, sometimes in a state of disrepair and lacking the most basic amenities. Occasionally there is heard an explicit lament for the older, supposedly saner, order of things, now thought to be permanently inaccessible. (pp. 28-30)

Although the theme of women's destructive social conditioning, so prevalent in Ginzburg's early novels, recurs occasionally in her plays (*L'inserzione, Fragola e panna,* and *La segretaria,* all provide examples of women's masochistic dependency on the men they love) it is now subordinate to the author's existential vision of a "fatherless" world. (p. 31)

"The end of fathers in our world" is also the theme of *Caro Michele,* published in 1973. This novel, written largely in the epistolary mode, gives an emblematic account of the moods and vices of our age. Central to the story is Michele, whose mysterious flight to England provides a focus of attention for the other characters, principally as a pretext for communication with each other. All the characters, including Michele and despite his superficial involvement in left-wing politics, are without conviction, commitment or hope. They seem to be oppressed by an overwhelming sense of isolation and unhappiness. Many express a rebellious attitude towards the institution of the family, yet at the same time all are nostalgic for it. The novel traces four marriages in various stages of collapse, and yet, despite the discouraging evidence of reality most characters continue to believe in marriage as a possible solution to their existential anguish.

Ginzburg's preoccupation with the demise of the traditional family is fundamental to the inspiration of this work. At the beginning of the story a baby is born, and, although at first it is suspected to be Michele's child, the question of its paternity remains unanswered in the end. It is also significant that Michele's own father dies early in the narrative, and that his voice is never heard in the epistolary exchange. The only men who do contribute to the correspondence are Michele and his friend Osvaldo, both of whom are believed to be homosexual. For some of the characters in *Caro Michele* Michele had represented a secret hope for a strong male figurehead, who might be expected to rescue his disintegrating family from anguish and despair. During his lifetime they avert their eyes from the difficult truth, for all but his sister, Viola, refuse to acknowledge his homosexuality. His eventual assassination by a band of right-wing terrorists means the death of hope for the rest of the family, and they numbly survive the loss, continuing their daily existence like sleepwalkers.

The author's latest narrative works, *Borghesia* and *Famiglia,* published in a single volume in 1977, re-explore the themes of *Caro Michele. Borghesia* is related through the perspective of a middle-aged widow (whose husband has died by suicide), and the other story, exceptional in Ginzburg, through that of a forty-two year old man. Both protagonists are, unknown to themselves, terminally ill with cancer. The theme of death in each story is thus intricately interwoven with the two themes suggested in the titles.

We are presented in each story with what at first seems to be a conventional middle-class household, where different generations of the same family live in separate units of the same building. Yet there is no evidence of warmth or genuine communication between the various family members, many of whom lead alienated, unhappy lives. Both protagonists, however, manage to find some small measure of solace outside family relationships. For Ilaria, in *Borghesia* it is the company of her cats. For Carmine, in *Famiglia,* it is his friendship with a former lover, Ivana, whose apartment provides a haven for his unhappy spirit. In both stories we are presented with a frenetically unsettled world where couples come together, separate, and pair off in new combinations with a surprising rapidity. Both Ilaria and Carmine are parents of children with whom they fail to establish effective communication. Both are also examples of squandered talent and potential, for neither has lived up to the promise of youthful achievement.

Thus in her works of the 1960s and 1970s Ginzburg has abandoned the potentially feminist and controversial direction of her earlier works for an inexorably pessimistic view of the world. She now shows both men and women as the victims of an identical existential unhappiness. In an orphaned world where the present is meaningless and the future does not exist, many of her recent characters turn their gaze to the past. Memory is an important theme in these works: in the end it is the only value that is salvaged. At the conclusion of *Caro Michele,* Osvaldo, a close friend of the dead youth, laments, as he gathers a ragged undershirt left behind by Michele, that many of the younger generation fail to grasp the value of memory. For Osvaldo only the remembrance of the past can exorcise the traumatizing reality of the present, and he believes that nothing in our current existence measures up to the moments and places encountered in memory. . . . At the conclusion of *Famiglia* the dying Carmine suddenly experiences this therapeutic power which can provide (or so Ginzburg believes) some "strange, icy consolation" in the midst of hopelessness. The final paragraph evokes Carmine's reunion through remembrance with his peasant origins, from which he had long been separated by education, profession and marriage. . . . Gradually there unfolds a series of hitherto forgotten memories of family happiness: trivial, fragmented details of an outing in the country, which, much to Carmine's surprise, re-emerge with vivid precision after so many years of oblivion.

Ginzburg's insistence on the function of memory is indicative of her profound historical pessimism. In *Caro Michele* we find her clearest statement of the necessity to reject the present, and the implication that the only mode of survival in an otherwise intolerable world is to regard each moment of actual existence as the material of future reminiscence. This self-conscious standing-back from the present realities of life is,

in itself, a strategy of emotional and social alienation and seems to indicate that nothing can be done in the face of the fortuitous violence which permeates our "orphaned" world. On the positive side, however, the theme of memory is a vindication of the inner, "spiritual" life of the individual, and the resourcefulness of the human imagination in the face of suffering. (pp. 31-4)

> *Anne-Marie O'Healy, "Natalia Ginzburg and the Family," in* Canadian Journal of Italian Studies, *n.s. Vol. 9, No. 32, Spring, 1986, pp. 21-36.*

KATE SIMON

[Natalia Ginzburg's *The Little Virtues*] treats of a variety of subjects close to her memory and the realities of her life, all of them carrying her signatures—the clear, direct eye, the firm moral stand eased by a sympathy that flows from intimacy with the human condition.

Another Ginzburg magic is the utter simplicity of her prose, suddenly illuminated by one word that makes a lightning streak of a plain phrase, a prose whose poetic economy suggests large landscapes. **"Winter in the Abruzzi,"** for one, gives us in a few short pages not only the exile's inner life ("Sometimes it was even pleasant . . . slightly intoxicating. . . . Sometimes our homesickness was sharp and bitter, and turned into hatred") but, as well, the poverty, the premature aging, the superstitions and tribal fears of the villagers, sketched in a few angry and deeply pitying phrases.

Profound homage and the gentlest of criticism color the memory of a dead friend, the poet Cesare Pavese. "His unhappiness seemed like that of a boy—the absent-minded, voluptuous melancholy of a boy who has not yet got his feet on the ground and who lives in the sterile, solitary world of his dreams." And yet, in the company of this unformed boy, "we became more intelligent; we felt compelled to articulate whatever was best and most serious in us, and we got rid of commonplace notions, imprecise thoughts, incoherent ideas."

A stunning tour de force is a listing, much of it in the simplest of declarative sentences—"He always feels hot, I always feel cold. . . . He speaks several languages well; I do not speak any well"—that opens the essay **"He and I."** It continues in that vein of discord to expand, still in the same deceptively flat manner (touched, however, with subtle, telling grace notes), to become a full, rich portrait of a man and a woman and the indulgences, the resistances, the meshwork of complexities that weave a marriage that is both singular and a reflection of yours and mine.

One indelible word, "exile," understandably appears and reappears in several contexts, as in an essay that describes the constant unease of harsh memories that cast their shadows on present uncertainties. It is dispelled in a love letter to her vocation as a writer of stories, the one steady refuge in a disrupted life. "When I write stories I am like someone who is in her own country, walking along streets that she has known since she was a child, between walls and trees that are hers." That same essay wittily explores early attempts at devoutly wrought, later embarrassing, poetry and romances and the emergence, ultimately, of a fully accomplished work whose strength lay in a distinctly Ginzburg talent: "And the man and the woman were neither good nor evil, but funny and a little sad" (a reminder, incidentally, of the pathetic, bizarre protagonist of a masterly novella, *Sagittario*).

"Human Relationships" is a moving exploration of our lives with others, as children with incomprehensible parents, as adolescents forcing our foolish, showy ways among our peers; trying on people and discarding them to follow the avid, restless search for the one person who "has an infinite capacity to do to us everything that is good and everything that is evil. And yet we feel infinitely calm," a calm that leaves with the birth of children. "We did not know that there could be such fear, such frailty, in our body: we never suspected that we could feel so bound to life by a chain of fear, of such heartrending tenderness."

The last essay, **"The Little Virtues,"** is a credo of undaunted idealism. As direct and clean as if it were carved in stone, it yet speaks thoughts of the heart. We are to teach our children "not thrift but generosity and an indifference to money; not caution but courage and a contempt for danger; nor shrewdness but frankness and a love of truth; not tact but love for one's neighbour and self-denial; not a desire for success but a desire to be and to know."

The essay, of course, goes on to explore phases and details of this credo, leading us to a renewed admiration of the steady, full, sympathetic gaze; the lucid thoughts, the absence of cant and the adroit prose, seemingly simple but enriched, to use two of the author's favorite words, with the quiet shimmer of "secrets" and "silences."

> *Kate Simon, "A Contempt for Danger," in* The New York Times Book Review, *November 16, 1986, p. 15.*

MAUREEN FREELY

Strictly speaking, Natalia Ginzburg's *The Manzoni Family* is not a novel at all, but a biography of Alessandro Manzoni, author of the nineteenth-century Italian classic, *I Promessi Sposi*. If she insists that it be read as one—'without demanding more or less of it than a novel can give'—it must be partly because she has a horror of footnotes. Although the book consists largely of excerpts from letters, nowhere does she reveal her sources. 'It is a story,' she states baldly in her preface, 'that is scattered in various books, most of them unobtainable in bookshops.'

It is a strange story, too. Manzoni's father was a dull landowner, his mother an aristocrat who abandoned infant Alessandro to live in stylish sin in Paris—only to fall in love with him when he tracked her down as a young man. She lived with Alessandro for the rest of her life, following him back into the church and seeing him through two wives (both handpicked by her) and 11 children. But they never quite learnt how to be mother and son, and this led to gaps in his own understanding of how to be a father.

Anyone else might have seen this as raw material for a costume drama of Risorgimento Italy. Not so Natalia Ginzburg, who is interested in destroying the distance and security we are accustomed to enjoying when reading about the nineteenth century. And so she dispenses with overviews and interesting theories, swamping us with an endless stream of births, deaths, marriages, and illnesses, the treadmill of domestic life.

The method is interesting in retrospect, suffocating in prac-

tice: there are times when you feel as if you're sitting in the bottom half of an egg-timer. You cannot help but think that much is lost on the English reader, who would not have been force-fed Manzoni in school. But even for the novice, the book evokes the obsessions of the age with a terrifying vengeance.

> *Maureen Freely, "To Hell with the Men," in* The Observer, *August 2, 1987, p. 21.*

ANN CORNELISEN

Over thirty years ago the Spanish Steps were the campsite of hundreds of scruffy, self-proclaimed "Existentialists," not all Italian, of course, waiting for something, anything to happen. They did not add much to Rome, which was, then, one of the most beautiful and, what is now harder to believe, most manageable of the world's cities. They did not detract much either: they were simply there, waiting. And complaining. The young have lolled there ever since, waiting and complaining—the "Hippies," the non-militant mass of the " '68ers," the . . . who remembers?—while their meeker brothers, sisters and cousins plodded to school and plodded on into jobs, not jobs they cared about, just jobs they could get, and into marriages that bored them to people who bored them and eventually left them. Nothing is wrong, but nothing is quite right. . . .

[Natalia Ginzburg] is fascinated by these quiet ones, the disaffected, apathetic, rather whiny members of the middle class and has, indeed, explored the emotional everglades of their lives in many of her books, including her latest, *The City and the House.* They are safe. They are not poor, certainly not rich. They live in respectable neighborhoods, neither oldinteresting, nor new-gaudy. Still, nothing is quite right.

The tenuous strands of affection that tie families and friends together dissolve, slowly, slyly, like surgical stitches. Their love affairs collapse. Even restaurants and cafes they have patronized, for no better reason than they were familiar and right across the street, suddenly close. Everything dissolves, slips away.

They sense life should offer more—not the more of their noisier brothers, sisters and cousins, who early put their confusions about life on public display. *They* managed with surprising ease to fade back into their part of the jungle and acquire the proper spots, the designer suits, the mink coats that the climate does not warrant and the Mercedes and the Volvos that the traffic cannot digest. The quiet ones are not jealous of them. They are too conscious of themselves for envy, too conscious of the loss of something they never had. What was it? Where can they find it now? Inevitably, if they break away from the inertial drag of every day and dare to search, they are frustrated by fate or circumstances or bad judgment. Again nothing is quite right.

Unfortunately, as in *Caro Michele* (published here in 1974 as *No Way*), Mrs. Ginzburg has lumbered herself with an awkward device: the story is told entirely through letters. The limitations of the form are obvious and irritating enough, but 10 ruminant correspondents, some related, others friends, who all write in exactly the same, flat style, stretch probability and patience a bit far.

Giuseppe, a Roman journalist who has decided to sell his apartment and go to live with his brother in Princeton, N.J., writes, ostensively saying good-bye, to Lucrezia, the lady of the country house in the title. He has seen her the day before, in fact stayed at her house, but goes to great lengths to describe to her his affair (long since over) *with her* and, if that were not enough of a burden, moves on to describe his wife, their separation, her death, his son Alberico's youth with a maternal aunt, his son's homosexuality, etc. Lucrezia, when her turn comes, fills in the details. She herself says, "I fall in love easily." (To help the reader keep them straight each character has such a tag, repeated regularly by all the others. Or could the tags be symbolic? People are reduced to encapsulated personalities?) . . .

Literary gray is not *necessarily* drab—or dull. Barbara Pym's world shimmers in pearl. Louis Auchincloss's is neatly tailored in flannel and grace. Joyce Carol Oates's, even when gritty, has a mica glint. But Natalia Ginzburg's is the opaque gray of postwar Italian "realism." Forty years ago it brought the shock of recognizable truth that saddened. Now it seems a waste of compassion. Too much has changed. Worst of all, she forgot Henry James's dictum: the "only obligation to which . . . we may hold a novel [is] that it be interesting."

Ann Cornelisen, "The Ties That Bind Dissolve," in The New York Times Book Review, September 13, 1987, p. 30.

KATE KELLAWAY

Natalia Ginzburg's fine novellas **Valentino** and **Sagittarius** were both written in the 1950s. Valentino is a pampered dandy who marries the rich and impossibly ugly Maddalena—so ugly that Valentino's family go into mourning for him. But Ginzburg insists that we see Maddalena as impressive: a manager of others and of her farm, a tractor of a woman. Valentino's story is told in a grave tone by his sister. Her reserved narration heightens the comedy and deepens the sadness.

Ginzburg employs the same device in **Sagittarius,** where a quiet daughter feels compelled to tell the story of her noisy mother who, like Maddalena, is powerful but unprepossessing, a compulsive talker with a sweet tooth and unrealisable dreams. Both women are destroyed when love turns out to be a confidence trick. The endings are painful and not quite predictable. About betrayal Ginzburg writes with absolute authority.

Kate Kellaway, "Thaw Out," in The Observer, November 8, 1987, p. 28.

RITA SIGNORELLI-PAPPAS

In the late sixties, when I announced my intention of writing a thesis on the fiction of an Italian woman writer named Natalia Ginzburg, my thesis advisor was surprised and sceptical. His response was not unusual; like most female Italian writers, Ginzburg's published work had not received wide critical attention. When they reviewed her books, the critics were often unkind, faulting her style for its naive simplicity and her characters for their childlike primitivism. Now, almost two decades later, Ginzburg's unusual style, with its haunting staccato rhythms and disarmingly direct tone, is finally being understood as the sophisticated formal experiment it always

was, and she is considered—by both male and female critics—to be the most important woman writer in Italy today.

When it was first published in Italian two years ago, [**The City and the House**] met with instant praise. Though hardwon, the acclaim is richly deserved, for Ginzburg has fashioned a remarkably moving, powerful story within the provocative, technically elliptical epistolary form. An earlier novel, **Caro Michele** (1973), was an imaginative mix of narrative and letters, and **La Famiglia Manzoni** (1983), a biography about the family of the great nineteenth-century Italian writer Alessandro Manzoni, is a similarly inventive blend of narrative and epistolary conventions. But it seems to me that by limiting **The City and the House** to letters only, Ginzburg achieves effects of poetic condensation and tension that surpass the earlier works and carry more potent suggestive force.

The background for these letters is divided between two continents, Europe and North America. The novel opens with long exchanges between a middle-aged journalist, Giuseppe, and his former mistress Lucrezia, mother of five children, who is married to Giuseppe's dear friend Piero. Having sold his house in Rome, Giuseppe methodically bids farewell to an offbeat but loyal coterie of friends before leaving to go live with his brother Ferruccio, a biology professor at Princeton University. So insistently self-absorbed are Giuseppe's letters throughout the book that it is sometimes difficult for the reader to remember that this is not the voice of an adolescent but of a man close to fifty. What is his motive in crossing the Atlantic? In part it is a stereotypical response to the apparently indestructible myth that life is better in America, where, he tells Lucrezia, "I shall give Italian lessons in small schools. Teachers are well-paid in America. And then my brother is well-off and has no problems." But his decision to leave is also colored by a submerged longing for order and stability. His older brother has "all the qualities I lack," and lives in a storybook clean, quiet American town that seems to embody the order Giuseppe feels has eluded him in his frenetic life in Rome.

The forlorn Giuseppe is not the only character in the novel hungry for human warmth and security. Everyone in the tightly-knit group of friends he leaves behind in Italy suffers to some extent from uncertainty and a pervasive narcissism that arrests their advance into mature love relationships. Bonds between lovers, siblings, parents and children, husbands and wives, intensify and evaporate, only to form once again.

Relationships are, in fact, the real subject of this novel. Maintaining a vibrant human relationship is a process that never really ends, for all enduring relationships contain mysteries that are never wholly revealed. And even shattered human intimacies have the power to inflict pain. When Lucrezia and Piero's marriage breaks up, a close friend observes, "I thought that it is very difficult to dissolve a marriage, there are always scattered bits of it lying about and every now and again they give a twitch and draw blood." The flux of the letter form, with its sudden time-shifts, flickering backdrops and changing idiosyncratic voices, is a perfect match for the central theme of anguished relationships that continually break and renew. As in Ginzburg's previous novels, form is always a faithful mirror of content.

The personal solitude that deepens whenever a search for human companionship fails is conveyed with metaphoric force by the emblem of the empty house. Like human bonds, houses offer us the dream of a full, satisfying life, a vision of order and stability. But unlike people, bricks do not disappoint. When Giuseppe sells his house in Rome, his cousin Roberta deplores his foolish mistake: "Never sell bricks and mortar, never. You have to hang on to bricks and mortar for dear life." There are a great number of houses in this novel, houses bought, sold, remodelled, deserted and reclaimed. It is the mystique of the house that survives, gaining poignancy and power as human connections in the book continue to fragment and crumble. . . .

Although critics are fond of classifying Ginzburg's fiction as postwar Italian neorealism, the fact is that her highly individual style places her more in the area of the abstract. An experimental craftswoman, she has always been preoccupied with structure and form. Over the years she has developed a concentrated, oblique style that is at once translucent and solid, static yet in motion. By keeping the surface of her work so calm and still, she allows us to see directly through it, to advance beyond what is clearly visible to all that is omitted and implied. Her novels slowly reveal their meaning, creating a sense of echoing immensity as they unfold.

While Ginzburg deliberately keeps description to a bare minimum, her narratives have great poetic force because the few images she does select are precise but highly evocative. In *The City and the House,* for instance, there is a limpid pattern of hand imagery woven through the letters: both Giuseppe and his son Alberico are known for their cold hands, even in hot weather, and the flamboyant art restorer, Ignazio Fegiz, who seduces and then deserts the confused Lucrezia, is said always to keep one hand behind his back, as if he were hiding something. Only in the closing pages of the book does that hidden hand come forward and open, as the disenchanted Lucrezia at last perceives the futility of their affair. "There is nothing in that hand," she bitterly reflects, "Nothing."

In a recent interview Ginzburg was asked how deeply her differentiation of characters—was affected by her being a woman. She responded that in her own country she has seen a clear progression in the roles that men and women play in modern life; whereas men previously occupied a central, more visible, position, they have become increasingly remote, while women have emerged from the shadows and are now more visible and more vocal. Certainly this progression is apparent in her novels, where the quiet, self-deprecating females of her early fiction have over the past decade been replaced by bold, exuberant women. (The obstinate mother in *Caro Michele* and the effervescent Teresa Borri in *La Famiglia Manzoni* come to mind.)

In *The City and the House* the emergence of females from subordinate roles is striking. In this novel it is the reticent male characters—Giuseppe, his quirky son Alberico and the gentle Piero—who are happiest staying indoors in their houses, while the restless women prefer to test their inventiveness outside the home in careers as diverse as real estate sales and theatre or movie production. That pattern of both domestic and professional visibility is printed too in Ginzburg's own life: she has been a mother, a novelist, an editor, a translator, a journalist, a playwright and, most recently, a member of Parliament as well.

Rita Signorelli-Pappas, "Lives in Letters," in The Women's Review of Books, *Vol. V, No. 3, December, 1987, p. 14.*

DANIEL HARRIS

To say that Natalia Ginzburg, Italy's pre-eminent woman novelist, is excellent and interesting, and home-grown American minimalism bad and boring, is to overlook some of the things they share. In regard to subject matter, Ginzburg and her American counterparts write a literature that takes place behind closed doors, comprising emotions and memories from which all concepts and commentary have been deliberately excised. In regard to rhetoric, there are striking similarities as well. American minimalists such as Anne Beattie or Frederick Barthelme are an editor's holiday, paralyzingly coy in matters of style. Ginzburg, by contrast, is not so much coy as indifferent, making the austerity of minimalist prose look, if not purple, then black and blue. Minimalist prose is clean; Ginzburg's, immaculate.

Given their remarkable affinities, it's odd that I find the one so anesthetizing and the other so exhilarating. The refrigerated chic of American minimalism with its constriction of subject matter is the aesthetic outcome of a rigorous political agnosticism. Imprisoned in an unreflective present, minimalist heroes are too blue to have convictions, too blah to take decisive action.

Although Ginzburg, at present a senator in the Italian Parliament, claims that "the only thing I know with absolute certainty is that I know nothing about politics," her fiction is, in contrast to the woolgathering of American minimalists, virulently political; politics hover over her narratives, which, in response, clutch to their chins the protective covers of a fastidiously rendered domesticity. Social upheaval appears in her novels as something that annihilates privacy, separates families and erodes the perfect insularity of the household. In *Voices in the Evening, A Light for Fools, Family Sayings* and *No Way,* the incursion of the state into private life elicits an unlikely political response: an attempt to shore up impregnable barriers of memories and personal ties, to fetishize the family and all the idols of the tribe, in order to guard against the divisive forces of politics. In her earlier novels, World War II and the role her very political family played in it as premature anti-Fascists represent snakes in the garden, threats to domestic life, and more recently in *No Way* and *The City and the House,* terrorism and crime have filled this narrative role. The domesticity that is static and complacent in American minimalism is thus tortured and obsessive in Ginzburg.

In art if not life, Ginzburg is covertly political: Her novels attest to the disruptive power of ideological unrest. In itemizing the everyday details of her characters' lives, she means to suggest their passionate involvement with their environments, and the obsessive emotional engagement which ultimately encumbers them with the ballast of private jokes, family sayings, mementos and memories. The flood of gratuitous detail in minimalist fiction, by contrast, suggests only fashionable anomie.

As a rule, Ginzburg writes stories from which the narrator seems to have evaporated, leaving behind just a naked record of incident. The following passage from her most conspicuously narrated novel, *A Light for Fools,* shows her at her gaudiest. It is the climactic moment of the story, the execution of two main characters by the Fascists, and yet it passes with virtually no rhetorical fanfare, blending like camouflage into an unmarked, undifferentiated, unsubordinated rush of events:

> And later they were taken out into the village square, and Franz was seized and flung back against the wall, the order was given to fire and Cenzo Rena covered his face with his hands. And he too was flung against the wall and he felt his head bang against the wall and heard bells and voices. And so they died, Cenzo Rena and Franz.

Ginzburg's gestures at this crucial juncture are, if not imperceptible, minute: the repetition of "against the wall," the whining, chaotic parataxis and then, in the final sentence of the passage, a characteristic move—the simple, if supererogatory, naming of proper names, Cenzo Rena and Franz, a gesture at once rhetorically chaste and extraordinarily intimate. I let the passage stand as representative, not only of the gorgeous poverty of her style but also of her whole conception of narrative, which is for her an act of recording and remembering in which events are considered sufficiently valuable in themselves and therefore in little need of decoration and arrangement. The absence of stylistic flourish and direct commentary in her books is essentially a tribute to the worth of the incidents they record—the naming of names, the transcription of events being in itself a passionate if nearly indiscernible form of rhetoric.

As a consequence, her novels, while conservative in form, are often inadvertently stylized. She evades commentary, indeed the whole business of narration, and moves irresistibly toward the pure voice of her characters, as in the most idiosyncratic of her novels, **Voices in the Evening,** which consists almost entirely of its characters' hauntingly discrete statements, along with a rickety, paratactic skeleton of events. The logical outcome of this narrative evasiveness is the epistolary form, and it therefore is no surprise that over the years Ginzburg has resorted more and more to what now seems a dilapidated anachronism. Letters allow her to create an unnarrated voice, but at the same time they deprive her work of her electrifying signature: her athletic resistance to the limitations—for a writer as disquietingly intimate as she is—of the omniscient point of view. In the past, the more she obliterated herself in her stories, the more her magnificent narrative presence was felt. But now that she seems to be turning away from objective narration, she has in a sense withdrawn and become a hidden artistic force in work that once bristled with the stark, self-effacing virtuosity of her unintrusive style.

The Manzoni Family, her latest epistolary experiment, is really fiction *manqué,* an immense novelistic pastiche of the correspondence of Alessandro Manzoni, the author of *The Betrothed,* and several generations of his distinguished nineteenth-century Italian family. More than just a biography in letters, it's a vast cultural archive that documents in excruciatingly punctilious detail the lives of a sprawling diaspora of talented hypochondriacs, from Manzoni's cultured and (in her youth) libertine mother to his two wives, ten children and umpteen grandchildren.

Ginzburg arranges their biography around a rudimentary alphabet of domestic situations—a marriage, a birth, a death, a will—giving the book the emotional kemptness and clarity characteristic of her fiction. As in her novels, she makes the narrator less a commentator or interpreter than an epistolary emcee who, providing only meager context for the letters, introduces them with austere tags such as "Enrichetta to Vittoria" or just plain "Father." Her elusive presence is, in fact,

the source of the book's highly individual strength. The Manzoni family's squabbling, eating, disinheriting, dying, taking cures, attaching medicinal leeches, separating, hating and writing great nineteenth-century Italian novels is all set down with a pitiless equality of emphasis, with no subordination of event and no chiaroscuro, every detail illuminated with the same flat, frontal light. Ginzburg's adoration of Manzoni and his achievement is studiedly implicit so that one is never distracted by the cloying reverence which nags at the reader in many literary biographies.

And yet Ginzburg ultimately leaves an enormous vacancy in her narrative by failing to intervene and comment on the events that she painstakingly documents. Readers accustomed to the seductive informality of the essays collected in **Never Must You Ask Me** or **The Little Virtues,** with their cavalier, unbuttoned dilettantism and their Saxon directness of address, are bound to be disappointed here by her impenetrable reserve. Refusing to give opinions, interpretations, summaries and précis, she often retails with reckless abandon flaccid banalities from her subjects' domestic lives. . . . (pp. 686-87)

[**The City and the House**] is Ginzburg's first complete epistolary novel (**No Way,** the American translation of her 1973 **Caro Michele,** combined letters and third-person narration). Although vastly superior to **No Way** and of the same high quality as her earlier novels, to which I am, admittedly, partial, it presents a real farrago of unsubordinated events—six separate deaths (including three murders), several separations, a divorce and a whole brood of children marked with the bar sinister. . . . If there's a thread running through what is otherwise a narrative helter-skelter . . . it's Ginzburg's brief for the family, her profound, deeply conservative fear of the havoc wreaked by the loss of one's moorings in family and friends.

But as is so often the case with Ginzburg, **The City and the House** derives its strength and passion less from its story than from her tone of intimate address. And thus her attraction to the epistolary form, in which she circumvents what is for her the disagreeable and uninviting prospect of third-person narration—and the necessary disengagement from her characters that it entails—for the illusion of quiet, passionate colloquy. And yet as a genre, the epistolary novel seems a quaint, faintly ridiculous non sequitur in the world of telegraphs and telephones and televisions. Especially in a book as compositionally busy, as crowded with stage business as this one, it's an unusually maladroit contraption for exposition. In my own letter to Natalia Ginzburg, I would tell her that I admire her third-person narration in which she is so splendidly herself and hope that she returns to it soon. (pp. 687-88)

Daniel Harris, "To the Letter," in The Nation, *New York, Vol. 247, No. 17, December 5, 1987, pp. 686-88.*

LIZ HERON

In Natalia Ginzburg's writing there's a certain claustrophobia that's an intrinsic part of its strength. Here, as always, she writes about the family, neither quizzing its place in the social scheme of things nor drawing it as a template for domestic normality. She just closes in on the messy connectedness between people who live together or are tied by blood, marriage, sex or emotional need. And she seems to insist that, whatever is happening outside the door, it's what goes on in the four walls of these intimacies that's at the heart of everything.

These two novellas [*Valentino* and *Sagittarius*], written six years apart in the 1950s, are not only swathed in the same family atmosphere but carry the same fatal motifs of vanity and ambition. In each there's a bossy matriarch and a gloomy, inauspicious wedding, which in itself confirms the flawed nature of family delusions. Far from being a haven, a place of certainties, the family and its consolations are insecure, impermanent. Yet Ginzburg suggests that there's no freedom from all this, unless it's in the utter selfishness of a Valentino.

Handsome, lazy and narcissistic, Valentino remains oblivious to the sacrifices made for him so that the hazy promise of a medical career might be fulfilled. Parental hopes are dashed when he announces marriage to a woman ten years older. She's ugly and overbearing, but rich. His parents accuse him of marrying for money, overlooking his chronic incapacity to love at all. (p. 30)

All of Ginzburg's characters have something to redeem them; even Valentino is less to blame than others for their expectations of him. Self-deception blurs vision everywhere. If its penalties seem well deserved by the pretentious mother in *Sagittarius,* the narrating voice reserves some sympathy behind its critical detachment. It is, after all, the voice of a daughter, one who has escaped the family home and her mother's selfish management of all those in it. The worst casualties are the other daughter, frail Giulia, who has missed out on a moneyed marriage, and Chaim, the refugee doctor she had to settle for as a husband.

There's the same hurried inevitability to events. In pursuit of her ill-considered plan to open a gallery, the narrator's mother gets conned by the tackily arty Scilla, whose transparent phoniness is only partly obscured by the cosy domestic familiarities of their friendship. The sheer ordinariness of Ginzburg's characters and situations makes them all the more painful; the ill-invested emotions, the neglect and unfairness in family relationships is nowhere better expressed than in her delicate passing vignettes.

Valentino takes dramas in its rapid stride; the long chronicle of marriages, deaths and births in its 53 pages unfolds smoothly, evanescent like a fable, a tragic fable of families rather than the tale of one in particular. Its narrator, thoroughly embroiled in the family fates, concludes in a doomed present tense that seals off her life. *Sagittarius* ends, less suffocatingly, in the past, at a backward-looking distance from its narrator, a more off-stage character altogether, independent, paying for her studies with teaching, sharing a flat with a good and close friend.

But the friend gets married and is missed; and the narrator sometimes wonders if she'll find someone too. The family is no *bildungsroman;* it just goes on and on. (pp. 30-1)

Liz Heron, "All in the Family," in New Statesman, *Vol. 114, No. 2959, December 11, 1987, pp. 30-1.*

PETER BRUNETTE

Having outlived any possible rivals, Natalia Ginzburg is at 71, the undisputed doyenne of contemporary Italian letters.

Both a successful playwright and essayist, in addition to being an acclaimed translator of Proust and Flaubert, she has also become, through a steady outpouring of quietly memorable fiction over the last four decades, a world-class novelist. She is not yet nearly as well known in America as she deserves to be, but this will change as her books continue to be translated. Unfortunately, *The Manzoni Family,* a nonfiction biographical study of the famous 19th-Century Italian novelist Alessandro Manzoni and his family, will not do much to further her reputation in this country.

Manzoni, the book's central figure, is the author of *I promessi sposi* (*The Betrothed*), a long historical novel first published in 1828. Though perhaps seldom read outside of Italy, it is universally recognized as a masterpiece of European Romanticism and, in terms of its influence, occupies roughly the same position in Italian literature as, say *War and Peace* does in Russian. Ginzburg's group portrait of Manzoni's colorful extended family begins in 1762, with his formidable mother Julia, and continues to the death of the last of his children in 1907. The entertaining and highly individualized cast of characters includes hypochondriac wives, spendthrift sons, and sickly daughters—enough fascinating human raw material, in other words, to make the book much better than the severity of Ginzburg's method ever lets it become.

Her intent is clear. By quoting almost exclusively from the participants' letters and memoirs, she is able to impart a vivid sense of the mundanities of daily life in early 19th-Century Europe, now of course grown delightfully strange to modern readers. The amount of detail is in fact overwhelming at times, but only through such apparently "irrelevant" information can the portrait of an age be rendered in three-dimensional terms.

In spite of these often fascinating external particulars, however, the reader finally comes to feel starved for substance, for inner life. The problem is that Ginzburg's method never allows her to probe deeply enough into the characters to make us care about them; the figure of Manzoni himself gets completely lost amid the debris of domestic history. And her decision to rely primarily on letters results in our being subjected to an inordinate amount of the banalities of existence—house moving, travel, vacation plans, home remedies, and so on—the stuff of most correspondence, surely, but only the merest surface of lives.

Actually, the most powerful thing in the book is the constant presence of illness and death (most of Manzoni's children and even some of his grandchildren die before he does), a fact of life in earlier centuries that is fortunately alien to most modern readers. Horrible to say, when the deaths start coming thick and fast in the second half of the book, one's interest picks up dramatically.

Ginzburg's fiction is noted for its laconic style, full of thudding short sentences that have a powerful cumulative effect, suggesting a whole world never directly expressed. In her recently translated novel, *The City and the House,* in fact, this effect is quite brilliantly accomplished solely through a series of letters. The heavily rhetorical mode of the letters offered in *The Manzoni Family,* however, quickly tires the contemporary reader with a surfeit of religious piety and polite sentimentality. The difference of course is that in fiction, such letters can be imaginatively and consciously crafted so as to resonate far beyond what they seem to be saying on the surface.

In a work of nonfiction, however, the writer must be faithful to the historical record.

For reasons of her own, Ginzburg indulges only intermittently in her own analysis of character motivation, preferring, apparently, to let the letters speak for themselves. Sometimes they do, of course, and quite eloquently. Most often, however, they don't, and, instead of offering her own views, Ginzburg limits herself to the deadening task of providing enough of the requisite factual details to insure that the letters make sense on a literal level. Conveyed in her typically sparse style, these details quickly dull the reader's sensibilities. . . . In short, Ginzburg seems to have assembled the materials for a biography without actually having written one.

A final, virtually insurmountable difficulty for American readers will be the lack of a proper cultural and historical context for understanding and appreciating this book. A great deal of the interest for an Italian reader presumably lies in the portrayal of the domestic life of a famous literary figure. For Americans, however, this motivation will largely be lacking. Nor does Ginzburg or her translator provide much assistance beyond a somewhat helpful but sketchy list of characters at the end. Since the book also assumes a reader completely familiar with *I promessi sposi,* no description or critical overview of it is ever given, apart from the sales it enjoyed. And when such prominent Italian men of letters as Massimo d'Azeglio and Giuseppe Giusti appear, the typical American reader will not understand what the fuss is all about. Non-Italians will also be thoroughly bewildered by the legendary complexities of Italian political history during the period of the Risorgimento, dealt with near the end, nothing of which is ever explained.

Peter Brunette, "Natalia Ginzburg Defeated by the Manzoni," in Los Angeles Times Book Review, December 27, 1987, p. 13.

ANNAPAOLA CANCOGNI

At the age of 72, Natalia Ginzburg has devoted her entire literary career—almost half a century of it—to the family. Her ear is tuned in to the subtlest frequencies of domestic life, its accents, its gestures, its ups and downs and constant contradictions.

As she has said time and time again, with a modesty verging on coyness, she is a "small, small writer" who needs to feel at home with her material—literally. She does not like to venture outside the known, the familiar. Nor does she like to linger on the more dramatic aspects of a life: its larger crises, such as love, death or war. She acknowledges their occurrence, then lets them fade out into the background and quickly turns her attention to more tangible, if seemingly more banal, concerns: the tilt of a beret on graying hair, the weight of a thin hand on one's arm, the imperious recurrence of household chores—the stuff daily life is made of. The language she uses is also pared down, naïve, colloquial, not to say familial. In other words, deceptively plain. . . .

"I lived with my father, mother and brother in a small rented apartment in the middle of town. Life was not easy. . . . My brother was studying medicine. . . . My father believed that he was destined to become a man of consequence." Thus begins *Valentino.* There follows a terse account of how the brother, Valentino—far from becoming a man of consequence—after the failure of his marriage to a very ugly and very rich woman, winds up strutting his life away in the town square with his sister's blessing. The main character of *Sagittarius* is a mother, a middle-aged widow with one more dream and enough vanity to go after it. With her savings, she wants to open up a small art-gallery-cum-literary-salon, where the most exciting people in town will gather to drink her tea and relieve her boredom. By the end of the novella, she will lose both her savings and her dream, as well as her favorite daughter, whose sad, consumptive smile she has only just begun to understand.

These are stories told by a more or less self-effacing, more or less anonymous sister-daughter (a familiar figure throughout Natalia Ginzburg's fiction), impotent witness and willing victim of her family's hopes and failures. Hers is the plain talk, the shoulder to cry on, the anger and the pain of loss—the real story her own words try to hide.

Valentino and *Sagittarius* . . . are characteristic of Ms. Ginzburg's earlier work, culminating in *Family Sayings,* the autobiographical novel that earned her the Premio Strega in 1963. Whereas in her later work—her plays and the so-called Roman novels—the emphasis would radically shift to the disintegration of the family, its loss of a common language and shared memories, here the focus is still family cohesion, that espirit-de-corps whose tribal tongue allows its members to withstand the pressures of the outside world and to recognize one another, as it were, "in the darkest cave, in the midst of millions of people," for better and for worse.

Annapaola Cancogni, "A Widow's Dream," in The New York Times Book Review, June 26, 1988, p. 31.

A(lbert) R(amsdell) Gurney, Jr.

1930-

(Has also written as Pete Gurney) American dramatist, novelist, and scriptwriter.

The 1987 recipient of the Award of Merit for Drama from the American Academy and Institute of Arts and Letters, Gurney is best known for his witty, mildly satirical portraits of upper middle-class New Englanders. While Gurney's works are often compared to those of short story writer and novelist John Cheever for evincing an insider's view and a strong identification with the white Protestant communities in the Eastern United States, his plays are contrasted with the works of Philip Barry and S.N. Behrman, who wrote from the perspective of outsiders and viewed the community as a permanent institution. Depicting this society as gradually losing its once formidable power and privilege, Gurney blends affectionate descriptions of their manners and foibles with poignant social criticism. While many of his plays have received mixed reviews, Gurney has earned a reputation as a gifted and important contemporary dramatist.

Born into an affluent family in Buffalo, New York, Gurney began writing plays and musical revues while a student at Williams College and Yale University. His early plays include musicals and such one-act dramas as *The Bridal Dinner* (1962), *The Rape of Bunny Stuntz* (1964), and *The Golden Fleece* (1968). Gurney's first major off-Broadway production, *The David Show* (1966), is a political satire that transplants figures from the biblical story of King David into a modern television studio. Since writing his first two-act play, *Scenes from American Life* (1970), which traces the social elite of Buffalo from the Depression to the near future, Gurney has concentrated primarily on full-length dramas. During the 1970s and 1980s, he wrote an average of one play per year, and his works were produced in regional, off-Broadway, and London theaters.

Gurney achieved his first significant critical and commercial success with *The Dining Room* (1982). This play consists of interconnected episodes dramatizing the traditions of upper middle-class Northeasterners and their reactions to the changing manners and morals of American society over several decades. In *The Perfect Party* (1986), Gurney employs a deliberately artificial, farcical style similar to that of Oscar Wilde's play *The Importance of Being Earnest*. Gurney imparts a dimension of allegory to his story by comparing an arrogant university professor who attempts to create "the perfect party" to a dramatist longing to stage the perfect theatrical event. Frank Rich noted: "Mr. Gurney's point may not be startling. . . . But this play's declaration of artistic freedom is given added buoyancy by the fact that its author is practicing what he preaches, offering surprises and laughter in equal measure." *Sweet Sue* (1986) concerns a middle-aged woman who becomes infatuated with her son's college roommate. Each character is portrayed by two actors who appear onstage simultaneously. In *The Cocktail Hour* (1988), Gurney details the life of a disillusioned playwright who decides to write a drama based on his affluent but emotionally hollow family.

Although Gurney is best known as a comic playwright, reviewers praise his ability to create affecting dramatic situations. In *Children* (1974), his adaptation of John Cheever's story "Goodbye, My Brother," Gurney examines tensions underlying family relationships as well as the powerful emotions beneath the reserved exterior of the New England aristocracy. His recent play, *Another Antigone* (1988), addresses such issues as academic freedom and bigotry. This piece focuses on a classics professor who refuses to accept a student's updated version of Sophocles's tragedy *Antigone* as her term paper for his class. The professor becomes the center of controversy when the student, who is Jewish, accuses him of anti-Semitism and attempts to produce her play on campus. Jeremy Gerard observed: "If *The Dining Room* marked a bemused farewell to the cultural values of a white Protestant elite, so *Another Antigone* does the same to academic standards whose roots were shaken in the '60s and barely had time to recover in the '70s."

In addition to his plays, Gurney has written several novels. *The Gospel according to Joe* (1974) is a contemporary retelling of the story of Jesus Christ; *Entertaining Strangers* (1977) is a comic examination of academia; and *The Snow Ball* (1985) resembles Gurney's dramas in its satirical portrait of a group of elderly socialites who attempt to revive their opulent lifestyle by sponsoring a formal dinner-dance.

(See also *CLC,* Vols. 32, 50 and *Contemporary Authors,* Vols. 77-80.)

FRANK RICH

In comedies such as *The Dining Room* and *The Middle Ages,* the playwright A. R. Gurney Jr. has claimed John Cheever's territory for the stage. With rueful humor, if not exactly regret, Mr. Gurney writes about the decline and fall of the hapless white Anglo-Saxon Protestant in the second half of our century. But while there's much more to Cheever's fiction than artful social reportage, Mr. Gurney's plays have been a shade cautious. His writing, highly polished and enjoyable, has often seemed as polite as his characters are—at least until they knock back their requisite double martinis. Mr. Gurney has given us the telling details of reality without always finding a larger truth of his own.

It's in this context that the playwright's new comedy . . . , *The Perfect Party,* is a daring leap forward. While this work is still set in Cheever land, a WASP enclave in East Coast suburbia, it distorts that milieu in a manner that sometimes recalls the surreal Cheever (of "The Swimmer" or *Bullet Park*) but more often suggests the emergence of a new and inventive Gurney style. *The Perfect Party* is hardly perfect— it lacks an ending, for instance—but it is surely Mr. Gurney's funniest, meanest and most theatrical play yet. What a pleasure it is to watch a veteran writer step out, at some risk, into the unexpected. . . .

[The play's] setting is a lifelike study—previously a den and family room, it's anthropologically explained—complete with back issues of American Heritage, a VCR and Claude Bolling on the stereo. Mr. Gurney's protagonist, Tony, is a 50-year-old professor of American studies, all dressed up in a tuxedo as he prepares to give "a perfect party" for nearly everyone he's ever known. Like past Gurney heroes, Tony is of two minds about his patrician lot and prerogatives. If he truly believes that "people look and act their best in evening dress," he also cracks that his party may be the first major Protestant contribution to American culture "since Cole Porter wrote *Kiss Me, Kate.*"

Yet Tony and his party are not nearly as straight as they first seem. A woman named Lois arrives, announcing that she is a critic who has come to review the festivities for the Arts and Leisure section of "a major New York newspaper." Given to grand pronouncements, Manhattan chauvinism and clipped diction, she declares that the party may be an attempt to "recreate the multiplicity of America under one roof." Soon everyone joins her in speaking in highly lacquered epigrams that depart from the more naturalistic dialogue of past Gurney plays. Tony's wife announces that if the WASP ruling class "can no longer lead America," it must "at least teach it how to entertain." When the party finally gets under way (offstage, in Act II), it proves a Wagnerian social event that is variously likened to everything from *Gatsby* to *Citizen Kane* to "civilization itself."

Mr. Gurney, however, has his own ideas. If his characters see the perfect party as a metaphor for the American dream or idealism (or its collapse), *The Perfect Party* seems a metaphor for the relationship between a playwright, his audience and his critics—with a strong statement about esthetics thrown in. As Lois notes early on, she hears not only "the themes and rhythms" of Cheever and John Updike in her host's "casual discourse" but also "the insidious influence of Oscar Wilde." . . .

While the playwright isn't Wilde, his lines often have the whiplash snap of S. N. Behrman's, whether the subject be Meryl Streep or the role of cultural critics. What's more, Mr. Gurney's jokes build to a point. Though this writer is, as usual, charting the erosion of a privileged class in *The Perfect Party,* he is also championing the democracy that has followed in WASP society's wake. Mr. Gurney pleads for what he calls a "generous perspective" in all of American life, from foreign policy to the pursuit of success to the practice of theater. Just as the perfect party may not be an elaborately planned soiree but an impromptu get-together over takeout food, so Mr. Gurney argues for a theater liberated from any hidebound standards that might prohibit the mingling of styles and concerns as diverse as Wilde's and Updike's.

Mr. Gurney's point may not be startling, and it doesn't need to be spelled out repeatedly, as it is in the weaker second act. But this play's declaration of artistic freedom is given added buoyancy by the fact that its author is practicing what he preaches, offering surprises and laughter in equal measure.

Frank Rich, " 'Perfect Party', New Gurney Comedy," in The New York Times, April 3, 1986, p. C20.

JOHN SIMON

It all depends on how you feel about "almost." A. R. Gurney Jr.'s *The Perfect Party* is an almost clever idea, almost well written, and almost perfectly produced. It has almost enough funny lines, almost enough amusing characters, and it almost makes a useful point. It does, however, belabor that point heavily and unremittingly, and it's not one that will bowl you over with its novelty. Still, the overeagerness with which the hero, Tony, attempts to give a perfect party; the lengths to which Lois, the society columnist of New York's leading paper, will go to review this out-of-town event that may give her the chance of a snotty lifetime; the changing reactions of Tony's wife, Sally, and the couple's best friends, Wes and Wilma; and the way it all staggers on . . . these things form a nice metaphorical commentary on the life of the theater, and a somewhat less apt one on the status of this nation in the eyes of the world. The ending goes particularly soft, but up to then it is a dependably "almost" kind of play. . . .

What Gurney has done is to write a two-act play entirely in *New Yorker*-cartoon captions. Either a perfect cliché is presented in its purest, quintessential form with a seriousness and intensity to make it explode; or else a cliché is teased or manipulated, compromised or belied by the drawing above it, to make it slip on an existential banana peel. Often this involves the euphuism of advertising copy or the parody of some other brand of verbal speciousness. The trouble, despite Gurney's acumen, is that what diverts for some two dozen cartoons involving, say, four dozen characters does not hold up as a two-act play involving no more than five or six. The party palls.

Yet there is incontestable, though intermittent, wit and much neatly parodic writing. Unfortunately, Gurney's satire grows in precision at an inverse ratio to the importance of its target—is, in fact, best with trivia: "At least you don't have to make much effort at the movies." "Except with Meryl Streep—you never know what accent she's doing." "If she ruins one more book for me! . . ." "Was she in *The Color Purple?*" That is dead-on, but on the subject of the ship of state, Gurney is rather off course. (p. 109)

John Simon, "Pieces of Five," in New York *Magazine, Vol. 19, No. 15, April 14, 1986, pp. 109-10.*

EDITH OLIVER

Mr. Gurney has been trying throughout his playwriting career to make a statement, to draw some conclusions, about America, and [in *The Perfect Party*] this is his most direct attempt yet: Lois, reading the guest list, realizes at once that what she has been handed is "a spectrum of America in the closing years of the twentieth century." I think he did far better through indirection, in *Scenes from American Life* and *The Dining Room* and, above all, *The Middle Ages.* This play is a fable whose themes and seriousness have become overt. Tony's obsession with perfection—he has resigned his job and would like to become an expert on perfection, preferably on a TV talk show—is compared with this country's insistence on inflicting its ideas about perfection on the world. Mr. Gurney's own ideas are certainly sound, but somehow his seriousness does not work—dramatically, that is. There is, on the other hand, plenty to enjoy in *The Perfect Party.* Mr. Gurney is one of our wittiest writers, his ear sharply attuned to fatuities, and he is almost always very funny when he tries to be. For all my reservations—during the first act I feared his tongue might become permanently embedded in his cheek—I seldom stopped laughing. (p. 86)

Edith Oliver, "Imperfect," in The New Yorker, Vol. LXII, No. 8, April 14, 1986, pp. 85-6.

WILLIAM A. HENRY III

Playwright A. R. Gurney Jr. is a cocktail party charmer—funny, deft with words, genially self-mocking and ever ready to step in before the discussion gets too heavy. His best plays, *The Dining Room* and *The Middle Ages,* have been set at social events and have had the rambling, episodic quality of witty but wayward conversation. Not surprisingly, a fiftyish college professor who fancies himself capable of shaping an ideal evening is at the center of Gurney's sprightly new puzzle box of a play, *The Perfect Party.* . . .

In pursuit of his ambition, the mild-mannered host squabbles with his wife, snubs friends, forces drinks on the unwilling, tries to orchestrate the tempo of encounters, wages war against spontaneity. His every move is being judged by a remorselessly bitchy critic from a newspaper resembling the New York *Times.* Her very presence indicates that Gurney has metaphors in mind. Other hints include references to Oscar Wilde, whose epigrams the characters mimic, and a mounted portrait of Hawthorne, master of allegory. . . .

The play closes in a Shavian debate about a larger theme that resonates through all of Gurney's work: America, he says, has lost its sense of absolutes and faces the painful task of living with ambiguity. Striving for perfection in any endeavor signals an inability to cope with an unsettled world. This pas-

tiche, conveying more than a casual cocktail notion, could easily be pretentious. Gurney makes it sly.

William A. Henry III, "Puzzle Box," in Time, New York, Vol. 127, No. 15, April 14, 1986, p. 103.

CLIVE BARNES

The new play by A. R. Gurney, Jr., **Sweet Sue,** . . . is undeniably sweet. It is also undeniably slight.

The heroine is Susan. She is middle-aged, but defiantly undefeated. Deserted by her husband, she has raised her family by herself, making her living as a freelance artist for Hallmark greeting cards.

Here—if you have not read the advance publicity—comes the surprise. Susan is played by Mary Tyler Moore. And Lynn Redgrave. Together. Both. On the same stage at the same time.

The hero is Jake. He is 23 years old, the roommate of her son at Dartmouth. He is also made into a doubleheader, played by [two actors]. Anyone for schizophrenia?

The time is summer. Jake is staying at Susan's home, while he makes a few bucks painting houses in the neighborhood. She also is painting, rather more seriously, for she is hoping to escape from her greeting card formulas and to produce one genuine picture.

However, Susan—a paragon of apparent common sense who sees her home as "an oasis of decency in a world gone absolutely haywire on the subject of sex"—now finds Jake the surprising object of her matronly desire.

Nothing much happens between curtain rise and curtain fall, but that nothing much is cheerfully provided with a certain style and wit.

And, as a basic story line, Jake learns a few lessons in praise of older women—and takes a rather long time in learning them.

Movie buffs might scent in this scenario a mingling of an updated *Summer of '42* with a down-numbered *Three Faces of Eve*—the generation gap meets the split personality.

But, unfortunately, the meeting never takes place. Having stated his theme and unleashed his dramatic device of a twin heroine and twin hero both jabbering in friendly counterpoint, Gurney sits back and does remarkably little, apart from writing in his customary civilized and urbane fashion.

If you had been expecting a frantic debate between the id and the ego, desire and conscience (possibly one of those graphic cartoon angel-and-devil battles), you would be disappointed.

Occasionally, Gurney does use his duality of protagonist to have his heroine edit herself a little, or even more daringly, to fantasize on what she might have said rather than what she already had said.

After all, as Susan tries to promise us, she is "of two minds when it comes to most things." Unluckily for both us and Gurney, she really isn't—the two selves have what even Susan describes as a "good working partnership with themselves."

Thus, there is no real conflict, no dramatic need for two selves at all and nothing for us in the audience but to sit back and watch while Susan finally has her way with the young man, with modestly predictable results.

So the play is slight, so slight that it would make a souffle seem like a bagel by comparison. However it is still sweet, and I suspect that a lot of people could find its ingenuous charms sufficient.

Clive Barnes, "Two Susans & Two Jakes: One Thin Plot," in New York Post, January 9, 1987.

ALLAN WALLACH

Sweet Sue is a duet for four.

Essentially a two-character play, it utilizes two actors for each role, a device that does a bit for theater employment without doubling the fun or our understanding of the characters. The play remains slight and conventional.

To tell the story of Sue, a middle-aged woman who falls in love with Jake, her son's college roommate, A. R. Gurney Jr. came up with the idea of having two Sues and two Jakes. This injects some clever interplay but not much point. Because Gurney has made each second self a replica of the first, we don't see a contrasting alter ego that would make each character more nearly complete, more complex. . . .

However attractive, four actors are a bit much for an exiguous story (even if Gurney did suggest to an interviewer that he was retelling the tragedy of Phaedra and Hippolytus). Sue, a successful greeting-card illustrator whose husband has run off to a Vermont commune, suddenly discovers that Jake, her son Ted's Dartmouth roommate, is moving in with her for the summer while he and (the unseen) Ted make money painting houses.

Before long, Sue and Jake are admitting mutual infatuation, and each is manifesting jealousy over the other's dates. Jake refuses to pose nude for his hostess, who wants to outgrow her prudish Sweet Sue upbringing, because he fears it would turn him on (although we see a different Jake posing—rear view—at the beginning of each act as part of Sue's wish-fulfillment reverie), and the closest they come to consummation is a dance and chaste kiss.

Whatever different colors the split characters have are painted in by the performers rather than the author. Unlike such playwrights as Brian Friel (in Philadelphia, Here I Come!) and Peter Nichols (Passion), Gurney doubles characters only for emphasis and efficiency. (Already in place, a second team can begin a new scene while the first is exiting.)

All sorts of cross-conversations spring up among the four actors—sometimes as discussions, sometimes as interior monologues. A good deal of this is amusing. Gurney all but winks at the audience when one Sue suggests seeing a psychiatrist and the other ripostes, "He'd probably charge us double." . . .

Though the director and cast embellish the material, they can't disguise the thinness of its texture. The two characters are pleasant enough company, but their not-quite-romance is the stuff of sitcom rather than the passion suggested by talk of Anna Karenina. For that we'd need Tolstoy Too.

Allan Wallach, "Four Hearts Beating in One Infatuation," in Newsday, January 9, 1987.

WILLIAM A. HENRY III

Is [the] quirky storytelling device [in Sweet Sue] meant to lend intellectual gloss to an apparently slight tale? Is Playwright A. R. Gurney Jr., whose works (The Dining Room, The Perfect Party) are often short on incident but long on sly allusion and will-o'-the wisp charm, once again slipping away from consummation of a plot? Beneath the winsome comedy, Gurney is playing with the Whitmanesque notion that each man contains multitudes. When the two Sues contemplate a nude sketch of the boy—all that lingers from the maybe affair—what they term "very good" is not just his lithe body or their rendering but the feeling of being finally at peace within one's own mind, that house of many mansions. For an artist and perhaps for everyone, Gurney implies, building a relationship with oneself is at least as crucial—and as complex—as coming to terms with the world. . . .

[Sweet Sue] is the play Gurney's fans have been waiting for him to write, funny and inventive but also bravely expansive in scope. Gurney once described his comic gift as "dancing in chains." In Sweet Sue he breaks free.

William A. Henry III, "Double Profile," in Time, New York, Vol. 129, No. 3, January 19, 1987, p. 77.

MICHAEL FEINGOLD

A. R. Gurney Jr. writes two kinds of plays. The good kind is dedicated to memorializing ideas that no longer exist, like the family solidarity and noblesse oblige celebrated so charmingly in The Dining Room. In the bad kind, unfortunately, Gurney doesn't just pay tribute to dead ideas, he attempts to resuscitate the old-fashioned stage genres through which the WASP ruling class of bygone days used to reaffirm them. A piece like The Dining Room, starting from the assumption that the notions it hailed were already dead, could query and critique, even while praising, them; underneath the nostalgia and the old pieties, it laid a disruptive structure of jagged, modernistic querulousness, the essence of the real Gurney's sensibility. But in his bad, old-clone scripts, the situation is reversed: Under a slick veneer of ostensible modernism, what we get is the dead old form, with the idea it once embodied now sticking deadly out of it, like a fossilized fern.

In Gurney's latest play, Sweet Sue, the dead old form is the female-star-vehicle-with-blighted-love-affair. You know, the kind where the heroine responds to the thwarted lover's last passionate declaration by turning downstage, right arm quiveringly raised, and gasping, "Oh, don't, don't!" This particular gasp is so old, I can't remember when I last heard it gasped. . . . [Hearing it the other night], I wondered if I hadn't gotten trapped in a time machine. Partly, the shock came from Gurney's having disguised his dead dramatic content so ingeniously under modernist bric-a-brac: The sexually conflicted heroine and her impassioned young suitor are played by two performers apiece, though not for any reason I could discern—except perhaps to get the playwright the bargain of two top stars at the cost of one slender characterization. . . .

In the playwriting of any country but ours, sex between Susan and Jake would be the beginning, not the end, of the matter, and the failure to have it would never be treated as half a tragic frustration and half a hairbreadth escape. But of all the older women who have slept with younger men in plays since Jocasta decided the boy from Corinth was a hot number, the only American on the list is Blanche Dubois, who was run out of Laurel, Mississippi, for it. Twenty years after the Sexual Revolution, New York is a little more sophisticated than pre-World War II Mississippi, so one may be forgiven for gaping at Gurney's Susans as creatures slightly akin to prehistoric monsters in their repressedness.

Even more annoyingly, Gurney attempts to make Susan an artist-figure. Since her divorce, she's paid the family's way by designing greeting cards. Jake's presence inspires her to try to get up-to-date by putting social significance in them (!), which costs her job (has Gurney seen what's being sold in New York card shops these days?), and ultimately drives her back to real art. Moral: Less sex means more creativity. The artist's vision is just a sublimated id. Of evidence that the Susans might have genuine creative power, Gurney doesn't offer a shred; their dialogue is relentlessly priggish and hectoring when not pudding-bland. The Jakes, who alternate blurted stock phrases with magical accessions of articulateness, aren't much more convincing.

The script's tiresome prissiness is a real disservice to one of Broadway's more charming casts. . . . Too bad such an appealing crew had to be wheeled out before us on this broken-down, old-fashioned gurney.

> *Michael Feingold, "Sue-Perfluities," in* The Village Voice, *Vol. XXXII, No. 5, February 3, 1987, p. 88.*

LEO SAUVAGE

The "double" device employed [in *Sweet Sue*] is usually exploited by making one member of each pair the repository of temptation, the other of inhibition. Gurney, who obviously wanted to avoid this cliché, managed to come up with something almost as hackneyed and much more confusing: having the good and the not-so-good impulses (nobody is *bad* in a Broadway moral tale) constantly shift quarters between the two Susans. The same sort of vacillation goes on with the two Jakes, but it is not so pronounced, the young man seeming to be less troubled by lusty urges than his friend's mother. In neither case, though, does Gurney's writing endow the doubles with personalities of their own—hence they add little to the characters, who are pretty short on personality to begin with.

As you might expect, it is easy to get lost in *Sweet Sue.* Whatever Susan or Jake says might just as well be said by their "Too" counterparts (they even finish each other's sentences). With the young man I was often at a loss to tell who was speaking. . . .

Gurney leaves the ending open. If you feel like it—I didn't—you can speculate whether Susan slept with her son's friend at the end of the summer, or whether they simply had a beer together before he left. Art, however, furnishes a more lofty resolution. Being a creative type, a professional designer of Hallmark cards, Susan has Jake pose nude for a drawing. There is no sexual innuendo to it—Susan/Susan Too scrutinizes the naked Jake just as an artist does a model, carefully. After he leaves, both Susans examine the sketch and pronounce it "very good." So whatever has happened or not happened in the oft-discussed double bed, that special suburban

summer has brought about at least one positive result: Susan has become a better greeting card designer. (p. 18)

> *Leo Sauvage, "Midseason Potpourri," in* The New Leader, *Vol. LXX, No. 2, February 9-23, 1987, pp. 17-18.*

HOWARD KISSEL

If truth in advertising were an important criterion for judging playwrights, few would get higher marks than A. R. Gurney. He calls a play *The Dining Room,* and it is about just that. He calls another play *What I Did Last Summer,* and delivers just what he promises.

The title of his new play is *Another Antigone,* and again that says it all. Gurney even provides a knowing criticism of his work early in the play. His most interesting character, an uncompromising classics professor in a university beset by trendiness, is given a play a young woman wants to submit in place of a term paper on Greek tragedy.

He looks at the title page and, in a voice wry and weary, reads, "Another *Antigone?*"

She is, it turns out, one in a long line of students who have been inspired by Sophocles' *Antigone.* The theme of a young woman who risks her life to honor values she considers more important than those of the state, the prof tells his student, has always been appealing.

He has seen *Antigone* updated to address McCarthyism and Vietnam, and her version, in which Jane Fonda will battle Ronald Reagan over nuclear proliferation, does not excite him. Nor, he points out, is it genuinely tragic, which is what his course has been about.

Though Gurney seems aware of the perils of paralleling Sophocles, even apologetic about doing so, he has not been able to resist the task. As if his own play and the young woman's were not enough, he throws something else into the package. The young woman is Jewish, and the rigid professor is thought to be anti-Semitic.

This undercurrent, though Gurney tries to rationalize it with lofty speeches about the conflicts between Athens and Jerusalem, ultimately undercuts the play. It is really a red herring that complicates an already complex subject.

> *Howard Kissel, "Oh, Yes, It's 'Another Antigone',"* in Daily News, *New York, January 15, 1988.*

FRANK RICH

Somewhere—even if it's only Hollywood—there must be a school where all the teachers are as inspiring as Mr. Chips, Miss Brooks, Miss Jean Brodie, Professor Kingsley and those other lovable fictional educators who lecture so often on screen or stage but somehow always seem to be on sabbatical in real life. If so, that institution should offer a tenured post to Henry Harper, the classics professor who is the hero of *Another Antigone,* the new play by A. R. Gurney Jr. . . . Harper is crusty yet passionate about learning, a determined foe of academic fads and inflated grades, a mesmerizing lecturer who can make throwaway jokes about the Bacchae. In the age of word processors and punk rock, Harper is a true defender of Western civilization—and he wears bow ties, too.

Of course, when there's a teacher this noble at center stage, the easiest way to construct a play is to surround him with heathens who want to topple him. So it goes with *Another Antigone.* In Mr. Gurney's version of the formula, Harper's tormentors include a budget-fixated provost determined to cancel high-minded, low-attendance courses in the humanities and, more prominently, a straight-A senior named Judy Miller who raises hell with a grievance committee when Harper rejects her term paper on Greek tragedy. Instead of choosing an "assigned topic" for an essay, Judy has written her own updated tragedy, another *Antigone,* to express her views about the nuclear arms race. Such arrogant flouting of the rules threatens to delay, if not necessarily inhibit, Judy's planned career as an investment banker.

Mr. Gurney wants to write another *Antigone,* too—but not Judy's. Like Harper, he views the student's play as an unacceptable diminution of Sophocles: "a juvenile polemic on current events" that has less to do with tragedy than the stirring up of "cheap liberal guilt." It's one of the playwright's (and Harper's) several laudable principles that a banal play about the Soviet-American arms race deserves no extra credit for serious intentions in the classroom or the theater. But if Mr. Gurney hasn't written Judy's middlebrow *Antigone,* his own variant seems scarcely more lofty. The Creon-Antigone-like clash between Harper and Judy is more a juvenile war of stubborn wills than a battle royal over communal obligation and private conscience.

To try to pump up the debate's gravity, Mr. Gurney eventually turns to a melodramatic trick from Lillian Hellman's *Children's Hour:* He has Judy, who is Jewish, join others in tarring Harper with accusations of anti-Semitism. But it's patently obvious that Harper is no anti-Semite, and Judy's enrollment in the smear campaign only destroys her integrity as a character. Even without her participation in a witch hunt, the heroine is hardly another Antigone . . . , she is not the blossoming idealist and rebel Mr. Gurney seems to intend, or even a narcissistic Jewish American princess from Philip Roth's suburbia, but merely a bratty know-it-all of the sort that used to drive Dobie Gillis crazy.

As was also apparent in last year's *Sweet Sue* . . . , Mr. Gurney is not at his most fluent in writing contemporary college-age characters. Judy has a boyfriend even shallower than she is. . . . The two adults fare better. The scenes between [Harper] and the likably sardonic [Diana Eberhart], a feminist scholar turned battle-scarred dean, feature witty observations from the front lines of those American universities now more preoccupied with fund raising and job placement than with the old verities of a classical education.

Such passages remind us that Mr. Gurney is the author of such incisive comedies of manners and society as *The Dining Room* and *The Perfect Party.* The rest of *Another Antigone,* for all its literary baggage, recalls the bad sitcom habits of *Sweet Sue,* from the excess of off-stage characters and contrived plot twists (also mainly offstage) to the substitution of an anticlimactic string of ill-motivated capitulations and reversals for the full-scale intellectual showdown the audience has been primed to expect. Though Mr. Gurney has Harper rail against a culture that imposes "happy endings" on tragedy, the playwright flirts with the same. "You and I are basically very much alike," is how Judy puts it to Harper late in

the evening. Are they really? Maybe no one cares. In the theatrical era of *I'm Not Rappaport* and *Driving Miss Daisy,* a playwright apparently can't go too far wrong by unearthing the common humanity of a pair of cultural opposites. . . .

Another Antigone may still not deliver the night in the theater its title promises, but I dare say one could do a lot worse in many classrooms.

Frank Rich, "By A. R. Gurney, 'Another Antigone'," in The New York Times, *January 15, 1988, p. C3.*

ALLAN WALLACH

The Professor of classics gazes sadly at the student's term paper, an updated version of a Greek tragedy, and sighs, "Another *Antigone.*" Surprised, the student asks, "Did someone else write one?" Yes, she's told, Sophocles. Not to mention the students in other semesters who turned *Antigone* into modern plays about such issues as race and politics.

From this playful beginning, A. R. Gurney Jr.'s *Another Antigone* goes on to become yet another *Antigone,* a quite serious updating of Sophocles' play about a woman who defies the king of Thebes to bury her slain brother. The student, who'd written her Antigone to resemble Jane Fonda and King Creon as Ronald Reagan, is herself a latter-day Antigone as she fights to have her play considered a term paper. The professor is an equivalent of Creon, adamantly refusing to accept her "juvenile polemics" about the nuclear-arms race in a college course on Greek tragedy.

This sounds a bit contrived and academic, and at times it is. But Gurney has given *Another Antigone* a dimension that lifts it beyond contrivance and classroom dust. As written by Gurney . . . , the professor, Henry Harper, becomes an immensely moving figure.

Harper's antagonist, Judy Miller, is not fleshed out nearly as well. She does change during the course of the intermissionless play, deepening her modern *Antigone* and altering her views about her country and her future. But Judy Miller's change seems dictated from outside by Gurney. . . .

Gurney has given the professor what might loosely be considered a tragic flaw: He is perceived by some students to be anti-Semitic. His purported anti-Semitism is a matter of random remarks and lectures on two disparate cultures, Athens and Jerusalem. As Judy Miller, who is Jewish, proceeds to rehearse her play (offstage) along with fellow students, including her boyfriend, the Antigone evolves into herself and the Creon into an anti-Semitic professor who is unmistakably Harper.

Harper is asked by his friend, the dean of humane studies, to give Miller a B grade for her play. Not only is the university provost concerned about Judy Miller's grade in light of the bigotry charges, she warns, but he's also considering dropping Harper's courses because of pitifully low enrollment.

In an age when college must be "relevant" for employment, the professor has become an anachronism. . . .

The dean is little more than a device for providing information. . . . The same is true for a fourth character, Judy's boyfriend David Appleton. . . . Dave is the play's most contrived character; though a chemistry major, he is, fortuitously, a classics buff who can ghost an estimable term paper on *Antigone.*

Another Antigone, though, is Henry Harper's play. . . . Harper is at first slightly ludicrous with his dry, professorial jokes and faded courtliness. Later, threatened with the loss of his courses, he exclaims, "I have to teach . . . I'm only good when I'm teaching." . . .

Harper resembles somewhat the classics master in another long one-act play, Terence Rattigan's *The Browning Version.* Like him, Harper's private life is a shambles and his teaching is derided. By the end, it becomes unimportant that Gurney's parallels to the Sophocles play are somewhat forced. His professor is not King Creon with a tragic flaw but a flawed human being who matters a great deal to us.

        Allan Wallach, "An 'Antigone' in an Academic Setting," in Newsday, *January 15, 1988.*

JOHN SIMON

A. R. Gurney Jr.'s *Another Antigone* has a number of good basic ideas, reasonably smooth dialogue laced with pertinent impertinence, an aura of civilizedness, and plentiful guts. Why, then, did it have me frequently scrutinizing my watch during its 100 continuous minutes? Why doesn't it work at all? Because when it comes to specifics, none of them is believable. (p. 71)

The themes are worthy and provocative: Hellenism versus Hebraism, America's fatal lack of a tragic sense of life, the tyranny whereby minorities can bring down innocent parties with trumped-up charges of discrimination, the terrible permissiveness in our colleges, the survival and reenactment of myths in the very society that ignores them, and (though I'm not quite sure to what extent Gurney intended this) the unpleasantness of heroic figures in everyday intercourse. The trouble begins right here: The author is crowding too much into a short play; there is even a formerly aborted and almost renewed romance between the professor and the dean, not to mention private and professional disasters heaped on Henry's head. With merely four characters, Gurney gives us enough plot to keep a Greek trilogy going; why should Judy learn from Sophocles if Gurney can't?

Peripeteia piles up precariously. Every character undergoes at least one major and a couple of ancillary reversals. Judy recognizes in herself an anti-Gentilism no better than anti-Semitism; she also becomes self-destructively disillusioned, for hazy reasons, when she is most ahead. Henry Harper, the unwavering idealist, turns, under pressure, into a pitiful compromiser. Dave, who begins as a seeming illiterate about Greek drama, is suddenly revealed (to even his girlfriend's surprise) as a dedicated crypto-classicist, pulling both an academic and an emotional switcheroo. Diana commits a strategic error bordering on imbecility; she also shifts allegiances and resigns her deanship with, at best, nebulous motivation.

But I disbelieve the characters and situations fundamentally. Henry is not only ignorant of the outside world, he also knows little about how his, or any, college functions. Though he has an extensive education, he is unaware that his "original" ideas have become, since Arnold's *Culture and Anarchy,* commonplaces. And he goes around dropping classical quotations and allusions like dandruff. A professor of drama offers Judy an A in a course she didn't take, and no one chal-

lenges this. (Yet the way our colleges are going, that may not be so preposterous.) A chemistry student can write a brilliant and flawless paper for a classics course he has never taken. Most incredible of all, two of today's students speak in perfectly structured sentences and paragraphs. The one time Judy says "That's cool," she is being ironic.

And Gurney deliberately fudges issues. The end points toward a tragic mutual destruction of a latter-day Creon and Antigone, yet everything is left comfortingly vague. Even about Judy's play, Gurney remains noncommittal. It is one thing to leave it to us to judge its merits, quite another to send out willfully contradictory signals. (pp. 71-2)

        John Simon, "Endangered Classics," in New York Magazine, *Vol. 21, No. 4, January 25, 1988, pp. 71-2.*

HOWARD KISSEL

For some time, A. R. Gurney, the author of **The Dining Room,** has been the token WASP of the American theater. This is not an easy role when, as Jean Shepherd observed many years ago, "WASPs are the only minority in America that you can attack with impunity."

In his delectable new play, **The Cocktail Hour,** Gurney has an openly autobiographical character, a man who writes plays about WASPs, comparing himself with a medieval stone cutter toiling in the cellar "while everyone else is outside enjoying the Renaissance."

Gurney examines all the ramifications of the cocktail hour, which, the writer's father maintains, "kept all of life in an amazing state of suspended animation." Gurney knows that it was a charmed time but also one when the truth, normally kept at a distance, might unexpectedly emerge.

He makes a potentially old-fashioned play "modern" by the self-conscious device of having the writer explain what he's doing, like a magician who can do his tricks even while he appears to tell the audience his secrets. The effect is witty and joyous. . . .

The world of the WASPs and the theater that described it are endangered species. Having grown up in a Midwestern suburb, this world was enchanting to me. So was this theater. Maybe that's why, when I watch Gurney at his best, as he is here, I laugh through tears.

        Howard Kissel, " 'Cocktail Hour': A Highball," in Daily News, *New York, October 21, 1988.*

FRANK RICH

"Nobody goes to the theater anymore," says Bradley, the well-off 75-year-old WASP father who presides over **The Cocktail Hour,** the new A. R. Gurney comedy. . . . As far as Bradley and his wife, Ann, are concerned, modern plays contain too much screaming and disrobing to lure them to Manhattan from their home in upstate New York. But this couple can still remember a distant time when "wonderful plays" regularly visited their local Erlanger Theater. A wonderful play was one featuring an attractive, "very sophisticated" couple—invariably the Lunts—a "minor indiscretion" and a happy ending. A wonderful play gave the audience something "to celebrate at the end of the day."

What Ann and Bradley fear is that their very own son, a full-time publisher and sometime dramatist named John, has written a brutal autobiographical diatribe in the post-Lunt-Fontanne theatrical style. John's play, described as hitting "pretty close to home," is called *The Cocktail Hour,* and he has traveled to his parents' house at cocktail hour to ask their permission to proceed with it. The audience watching Mr. Gurney's *Cocktail Hour* never finds out exactly how inflammatory John's *Cocktail Hour* is, but if the two plays are at all alike—which, of course, they must be—the parents needn't worry. The author of *The Dining Room* and *The Perfect Party* is not the sort to turn an evening of martini-fueled drawing-room banter into a truly drunken *Long Day's Journey Into Night. The Cocktail Hour* is a play its own characters would find pretty wonderful, if not entirely so. . . .

[The] entire production might well be a replica of a fizzy, between-the-wars star vehicle. While the author does have his darker aspirations—which remain unfulfilled and prove a serious drag on the second act—he is at the top of his form when being unapologetically anachronistic and letting the zingers fly. Even at this late date, Mr. Gurney still has new and witty observations to make about a nearly extinct patrician class that regards psychiatry as an affront to good manners, underpaid hired help as a birthright and the selling of blue-chip stocks as a first step toward Marxism. . . .

While the mother has narrow notions of domestic decorum and little use for intimacy, she somehow emerges as generous and vulnerable. . . . What might have been a New Yorker caricature is instead a complex illustration of how both nurturing affection and punishing neglect can co-exist in reticent parents of the breed Mr. Gurney describes. . . .

[The] stiff patriarch, a snobby clubman whose mustache seems to do the bristling that his bald pate cannot, is a made-to-order foil. . . . Funny as [Bradley] is when decrying Roosevelt or apotheosizing golf, he is also touching at that one moment when remembered pain briefly causes his austere facade to crack. As his offspring, [John and Nina] are attractive as only middle-aged malcontents to the Philip Barry-manner born can be. Though [Nina's character] is billed as minor—to her frustration, both in her family's priorities and in her brother's play—she still captures both the resilience and anguish of a perfect daughter, wife and mother who sublimates life's disappointments into a curious obsession with seeing-eye dogs. . . .

[If] John makes less of an impression, it's not the actor's fault, but that of Mr. Gurney's play. [Nina] describes John as "a mess" and presumably he is a troubled man, driven to write his autobiographical *Cocktail Hour* to try to come to terms with his unhappiness. But except for a stirring moment at the end of Act I . . . , the character, as written, remains opaque: a blank journalistic interlocutor gathering research on his parents rather than a playwright urgently sifting through his past to achieve an emotional or artistic reckoning.

After intermission, when John takes over center-stage for a series of one-on-one confrontations, he becomes the vacuum that saps the play's vitality. We don't know him well enough to care about his plight: the deficiencies he cites in his play become signposts that point to the shortfalls in the play before us. Once John tries to nail down the family secrets, big

scenes and final curtain that might bring his *Cocktail Hour* closer to the truth, Mr. Gurney leaves pure froth behind to try to provide those elements in his own *Cocktail Hour.* He doesn't succeed. Every surprise seems contrived and hollow, including a long, supposedly revelatory monologue . . . and the reconciliation that provides the unconvincing, albeit happy, ending. The canned familial insights don't compensate for the punch lines they supplant. By the time the family leaves behind the cocktail hour for the dining room, one is still waiting for Mr. Gurney to push his characters beyond the circumscribed limits of *The Dining Room.*

As if to head off his own critics, the playwright gives [Ann] a speech in which she accuses her son's reviewers of panning his plays because they resent his WASP characters. "They think we're all Republicans and all superficial and all alcoholics," she says. Though it's a funny line (followed by a funnier one), it begs the issue. It isn't Mr. Gurney's characters who are superficial but, in the final clutch, his presentation of them. Not that audiences should mind. Until it turns sober, *The Cocktail Hour* is about as entertaining as superficiality in a theater without the Lunts can get.

Frank Rich, "Light Banter and Dark Feelings in Gurney's 'Cocktail Hour'," in The New York Times, *October 21, 1988, p. C3.*

LINDA WINER

So the family guilt trip is an equal-opportunity oppressor. As A. R. Gurney tells us in *The Cocktail Hour* . . . , "Tradition!" is not the exclusive cry of fiddlers on the roof, and Portnoy is not the only grown man with parental complaints. . . .

Much of *The Cocktail Hour* is a conventional play about people for whom convention is the mechanism used to save them from their feelings. The liquor table is the "well" to which John's parents have returned for 50 years, and drinking—"never before six, never after dinner, never alone"—is the approved anesthetic.

Much of *The Cocktail Hour* is also very funny—an affectionate behavioral satire that . . . peels away a class of social shells without bruising too much flesh. Gurney's techniques flirt dangerously with sitcom conventionality here and the plot does creak. Nevertheless, Gurney's virtuosity on the WASP stomping ground, not to mention his analytic passion for the theater, brings us closer to both of these specialized, elusive worlds.

What does not work, unfortunately, is Gurney's attempt to combine his social study with a serious family exorcism—to find a *Long Day's Journey* within the structure of a drawing-room comedy. John wants to know why he always felt like a foundling, why Pop doesn't love him, what "went wrong when I was very young." His psychological insights are Mickey Mouse Freudian, and the sibling rivalries could have been taken from a psych workbook.

Gurney makes a little playwrighting joke by having John "write" the play as he is living it. But when John reaches for the "twist at the end of the first act," the twist has little tension. When he demands the "obligatory scene with mother," the scene is mild, not brutal. When he goes for the "kicker" that will tie everything up, there is not much kick. Like the kind of plays his family used to love in the old days, this one sends us home with nothing raw or messy to embarrass the sensibilities.

That's a nifty technical trick, considering the theme, but we do not get the feeling that Gurney wants to leave us unmoved. "Feelings," [John's] mother laments, "I never could get the feelings right." What does move us, however, are Gurney's layers of telling and detailed humor, and the humanity behind these performances. . . .

Perhaps most affecting of all is the voice of the playwright, explaining why he is "trapped" in the artifice of something as "medieval" as the theater, "restrictive beyond belief," besieged with critics, while others are writing for TV and movies and "having fun in the renaissance." The artifice in *The Cocktail Hour* cannot handle the deeper ambitions here, but Gurney, a deft craftsman who has been turning out a play every season these days, is a bit of a renaissance himself.

Linda Winer, "A Family on Show in 'The Cocktail Hour'," in Newsday, October 21, 1988.

JOHN SIMON

The dramatic career of A. R. Gurney has proceeded in reverse order from challenging to promising, and some time ago entered its third phase: spent. Though appreciably less offensive than his recent *Another Antigone* and *Sweet Sue* (even the title, happily, does not alliterate), *The Cocktail Hour*, which drowns in its own blandness, can most charitably be described as insipid. It is not, to be sure, in Wyndham Lewis's 1921 phrase, one of "the worst insipidities of our degenerate stage"; assiduously likable and occasionally mildly amusing, it is one of 1988's better insipidities.

This is unabashed autobiography, Gurney's own crossbreeding of *Long Day's Journey Into Night* and *Broadway Bound*. But—as in that celebrated and perhaps apocryphal reply of Shaw's to a famous actress wanting to bear his child, "What if it inherits my looks and your brains?"—the play is heir to O'Neill's wit and Neil Simon's depth. It is one of those how-to-tell-the-truth-about-everyone-without-offending-anybody works, in which the three walls of the stage seem to be covered with hooks from which no one is hanging. For a family to be interesting, it must have either arresting problems or mundane problems arrestingly dramatized. Gurney and his folks fall into that category of happy families that, as Tolstoy told us, are all alike.

Bradley, the father, a middle-class chap who married rich and forthwith proclaimed himself upper, is in a business that allows him to spend more time at lunch and at golf than in his office, and enjoy an extensive cocktail hour (the present one lasts two hours) with his wife and however many of his three children happen to drop in. Ann, his wife of 50 years, was extremely rich, once harbored literary ambitions, and is, like him, in the mid-seventies, which is also the period of the play; the place, as usual in Gurney, is his native "Upstate New York."

Nina, the eldest, lives in the same city, has a good husband and children but cares mostly for dogs, and dreams of going to Seeing Eye–dog–training school in Cleveland. . . . The elder son, John, a playwright who gets his bread and butter from a publishing job (Gurney was a professor—so much for strict truthfulness), seems to have regular productions and a no less regular family; yet he tells us that he is on the wagon because he is "an angry drunk," and he is in psychiatric treatment. It seems he was insufficiently loved by his parents. The younger son, Jigger, the apparent favorite, is doing well in New York City, but, as is his wont, doesn't make it to the family reunion. Instead, he phones for advice about whether to take a less lucrative job in California that would allow him to indulge his lifetime dream of building ships.

Bradley has leukemia and keeps talking (as he apparently has been for years) about dying, though he is in a state of remission and, as Ann assures us, in no danger of death: There are no mortal illnesses in Gurney, except, perhaps, boredom. Ann's only notable problem is that she has had to hire a temporary maid who cannot cook and whose name is caught differently by each of the four dramatis personae as Cheryl Marie, Sharon Marie, Shelley Marie, or Sheila Marie. This, along with references to T. S. Eliot, supplies the play with one of its several running gags. The dinner, fraught with delays, is yet another of these, allowing the eponymous cocktail hour to stretch to the point where everyone ought to be smashed but, unfortunately for the play's comedic value, isn't. . . .

Where, then, is the drama? John has come upstate to ask permission to put on his play, *The Cocktail Hour*, which tells all about him and the family. Father won't hear of it and offers a $20,000 bribe for its postponement. Mother, for her part, would much prefer it to be "a nice, long book," because books are quieter and mostly unread. Sister approves, but strongly resents being a minor character. . . . Jigger's opinion is not solicited, presumably because of the long-distance rates. Since we know that *The Cocktail Hour* will be produced in 1988, the pressing problems of the play are: Will Jigger go down to the Pacific in ships? Will Nina go to the dogs in Cleveland? What really was that maid's name? (p. 105)

John Simon, "The Family Communion," in New York Magazine, Vol. 21, No. 43, October 31, 1988, pp. 105-06.

Gert Hofmann

1932-

German novelist, dramatist, short story writer, and essayist.

Winner of Germany's prestigious Alfred Döblin Prize for his novel *Auf dem Turm* (1982; *The Spectacle at the Tower*), Hofmann is respected for bizarre, fabulistic works of fiction that have been compared to those of Franz Kafka and Günter Grass. Best known in West Germany as an author of radio plays, Hofmann did not publish fiction until 1979. His first novel to be translated into English, *The Spectacle at the Tower,* is a first-person, present-tense narrative of an unhappily married couple's nightmarish experience in a squalid Sicilian village. Led by an eccentric tour guide, the protagonists witness horrific rituals in which children are sacrificed for the entertainment of sightseers. The plight of the children forces the couple to reassess their own troubles.

In *Unsere Eraberung* (1984; *Our Conquest*), Hofmann portrays the strange adventures of two boys in a ravaged German town on the day following the Allied victory in World War II. Narrated in an unspecific first-person plural form, this novel, according to James A. Snead, "shows how children can distill wonder from the dregs of war." In *Der Blindensturz* (1985; *The Parable of the Blind*), Hofmann attempts to imagine the thoughts of the six blind vagrants depicted in Pieter Breughel's sixteenth-century painting *The Parable of the Blind.* Hofmann again makes use of the first-person plural viewpoint, as he describes from the perspective of the blind men the hardships that they endure while posing for Breughel's painting, which he envisions as a definitive statement on the wretchedness of the human condition. *Veilchenfeld* (1986) concerns the persecution and suicide of an eminent Jewish philosopher and the moral insensitivity of his fellow citizens. Hofmann avoids ethical judgment by establishing as the novel's narrator the young son of the doctor who treats the title character. Stella P. Rosenfeld observed: "[Indirectly], Hofmann powerfully indicts all those who simply 'went along' with the immorality of the Third Reich." The collection *Balzac's Horse and Other Stories* (1988) illustrates Hofmann's skill at combining humor and grotesquerie to examine the nature of life and the function of art. Phillip Lopate noted: "[Hofmann's] sentences . . . coax a comedy out of the distance between their high-spirited energy and the miserable straits in which his characters invariably find themselves."

THOMAS H. FALK

The plot of this hauntingly powerful novel [*Die Fistelstimme*] is easily recounted: a new German instructor arrives in Ljubljana, Yugoslavia, presumably to begin his career as a language teacher at the university. He meets a student, Herr Ilz, who acts as an interpreter, guide and even host during the two days he is in that city. Although arrangements for an apartment had been made for him, he has an argument with his landlady, abandons the place on the day of his arrival and spends the night with Herr Ilz. On each of the two days he

has a meeting with the dean at the university, which results in his not being hired because he has falsified his past record. On the second day he returns to Germany.

A basically very simple story told by the narrator in the form of a moment-by-moment, thought-by-thought chronicle. The most detailed linguistic train of thought with every conceivable deviation is presented in an effort to clarify the narrator's view on any given issue. He explains his effort by suggesting that if he could do as he really wishes, he would write only one infinite sentence in which everything is contained. But that only leads to his realization of the impossibility of such an effort.

Portions of the narrated experience lead to an absurd but most humorous situation. After the narrator meets the student Ilz, a Slovene studying German at the university, he makes every effort to be understood. Frequently he inquires whether Ilz knows the exact meaning of each word. After a while he even thinks he has befriended Herr Ilz, only to be told that perhaps Ilz was doing nothing other than practicing his German with the new language instructor. But this possibility—as well as many others—is shrouded in linguistic ambiguity.

Some parts of the novel remind the reader of episodes in the work of Franz Kafka. (pp. 303-04)

But this novel by Gert Hofmann should not be seen as an imitation of Kafka. With all the apparent absurdities, Hofmann seems to be concentrating on the potential destructiveness of the thought process. The narrator's constant effort to be understood in a world that never understands him is the agonizing message which is, however, presented in a very clear and powerfully understandable manner. (p. 304)

Thomas H. Falk, in a review of "Die Fistelstimme," in World Literature Today, *Vol. 55, No. 2, Spring, 1981, pp. 303-04.*

WES BLOMSTER

Words are easily bent today; it is reassuring to encounter a collection of novellas which meet the demands of the concept. Each of the narratives offered [in ***Gespräch über Balzacs Pferd: Vier Novellen***] grows out of "an unheard-of event"—to use Goethe's coinage—involving one of the four writers here studied.

Students often grow weary of the German writer's preoccupation with writers; therefore there is something particularly affirmative about Hofmann's ability to involve himself with understanding sympathy in the lives of past authors. He performs this task with no indication of narcissistic identification, nor does any of the stories seem to present a Tonio Kröger in another guise. . . .

Beyond the fact that they were indeed writers, there is little apparent common ground between Lenz, Casanova, Balzac and Robert Walser, the four authors around whom Hofmann here weaves fictive biography. Their relationship lies in the endangered restlessness of their lives—the factor which explains their appeal to their contemporary colleague. The novellas are not an exercise in creative biography; it is the creative impulse itself which stands at the center of each story, and this in turn accounts for the difficulty and hopelessness in which each man finds himself.

> *Wes Blomster, in a review of "Gespräch über Balzacs Pferd: Vier Novellen," in* World Literature Today, *Vol. 56, No. 3, Summer, 1982, p. 505.*

DENNIS MUELLER

[The radio plays in *Die Überflutung: Vier Hörspiele*] cover a wide range of topics and are testimony to the author's versatility. **"Autorengespräch,"** which opens the collection, has a publisher and his director conversing with a successful writer. The author does not speak a single word throughout the play, and yet we know from the words of the other two what he feels about their capitalistic aims in trying to motivate him to start writing again. In the end we, the listeners, are compelled to share the author's aversion to the capitalistic methods of the publisher and his director and can well understand his tacit refusal to continue writing for them.

"Schmährede des alten B. auf seinen Sohn" gives us an insight into the generation conflict between a conservative father and his terrorist son. Although the setting is prerevolutionary Russia, the subject matter is as relevant today as ever. **"Der lange Marsch"** is set in revolutionary China and gives witness to the hardships encountered by Mao and his followers on the famous Long March. It is not Mao, however, who is the center of the piece, but a young soldier who suffers his way through the mountains and deserts and is one of the few who reaches the final destination. Gert Hofmann shows us how the little man can be a victim in the grand political machinations, even when the plan is successful.

The last play in the collection is the one that gives the book its title, **"Die Überflutung."** This is a monologue by a survivor of the last days of the war in Berlin when thousands of people were trapped and killed by a flood that inundated the subway tunnels. The narrator remembers the terrible massacre even though it occurred twenty-five years earlier. The real tragedy is that the narrator is alone with his memory and cannot communicate his grief to anyone. (p. 680)

> *Dennis Mueller, in a review of "Die Überflutung: Vier Hörspiele," in* World Literature Today, *Vol. 56, No. 4, Autumn, 1982, pp. 679-80.*

HARRIETT WATTS

A car whose occupants are the hostile partners in a failing marriage stalls in a crumbling, poverty-ridden village in the remotest, scorched hinterlands of Sicily. The name of the village, Dikaiardeia, means "city of the just." The smell that permeates every aspect of this scene is a sweet, inescapable stench of carrion. The narrator of Gert Hofmann's **Spectacle at the Tower** steps out of the car into this *zona morta* and into 20 hours of a guided horror tour. It is a tour he agrees to take and he subjects his wife to it as well.

A sleazy, German-speaking native who is called only "the supervisor" accosts them at lunch. He seems impossible to

shake off, and he proposes the day's itinerary. It includes a visit to an apparently deserted house in which they discover withered, catatonic old women perched on an iron rod; a trip to the Foundlings' Home, where all superfluous children are stuffed headfirst through a hole in the wall, and finally a stop at the tower, fantasized by the narrator into what should be the one monument of note in the town, but which proves to be a 19th-century eyesore, a squat rotting water tower with the obligatory cafe for tourists. This tour of the village is highlighted by a round of sacrifices staged throughout the day, beginning with the noontime slaughter of a goat by village children for the two visitors and concluding with the main tourist attraction, a ritual suicide leap from the tower by a child at sundown.

As the sun finally sets on a day of sightseeing in this village of the dying and the dead, the narrator finds himself, with his wife, in the cafe at the foot of the tower. They await the spectacle of the suicide leap, which has attracted tourists from around the world, all of them eating, drinking and taking photographs in restless anticipation of the evening show. The world condenses to a present moment of impending disaster.

At dead center of these events is the narrator, who records every detail in a first-person, present-tense account that allows no pause for breath or reflection until the final page, when he has completed his task of rendering palpable every instant and impression of those 20 hours as "the story of the present moment."

> "In brief," he says, "we can't be concerned anymore with our own problems, so we can't talk about our separation or even think about it on this hot, now less hot than oppressive steamy early September afternoon in this putrid village of D., which has quite imperceptibly become a steamy, oppressive, breathless and speechless early September *evening* in D. The open blaze of the noontime has given way to suffocating closeness. The evening heat, perhaps even worse than the heat of noon. And I'd be lost if I didn't . . . And that's how I always do it: In such circumstances I always tell myself *the story of the present moment,* whether I'm lying sleepless in bed or waiting in despair for a phone call, or, as now, seated grudgingly in a basket chair with my wife and the other person."

That "other person" is the supervisor, the enigmatic, repulsive, insistent guide who has been leading his accomplices through their day in hell, a figure who might easily be dismissed as a stock figure were he not presented in such immediate, unpredictable detail by the narrator. The same is true for numerous confrontations in the novel, situations which border on the clichéd archetypal but which are rescued by the narrative acuteness with which they are reported and particularized into discrete, unforgettable life. The narrator is alert to what is essential in these particulars. "Yes, indeed, I stuff the most trivial things into my story *At the Foot of the Tower,* for these trivial things alone make it into a story, they alone."

The barrage of trivia demands sentences which can order and transmit detail at the same speed with which the narrator perceives his situation and wants to convey it. Here Mr. Hofmann succeeds brilliantly. The telling of every moment is a tour de force. The trivia itself is the amassed tedium of one person's life with another that erupts at midnight into a third sacrifice—the wife's miscarriage, which is precipitated by the heat, the ghoulish images and the spectacle at the foot of the tower. Or is the miscarriage "achieved," as the narrator puts it, by his insistence that evening that his wife perform a sexual act with him after he has attempted to draft a letter disavowing her and the child she bears? . . .

The novel, known as *Auf dem Turm* in German, has been admirably recreated in English by Christopher Middleton in all its sustained, furious detail.

> Harriett Watts, "Filling the Day with Death," in The New York Times Book Review, *May 20, 1984, p. 41.*

[JULIE SMITH]

The unbearable mixture of dread and insight peculiar to nightmares permeates this surreal story [*The Spectacle at the Tower*]. . . . The narrator is an unhappy German vacationing in Sicily with his unhappy wife. She has just confessed that she may be pregnant and he has just confessed to fathering a bastard son when their car breaks down outside a "disease-ridden, filthy, fly–blown, rat-scuffling place" called D., where they are obliged to book a room for the night, and where a sweaty creature called "the supervisor," who happens to speak German, drags them off to witness a rite that Kafka and de Chirico might have conjured up. This is a story about unwanted children—and, by extension, about cultural corruption—and therefore about cruelty and depression. (pp. 131-32)

> [Julie Smith], in a review of "The Spectacle at the Tower," in The New Yorker, *Vol. LX, No. 14, May 21, 1984, pp. 131-32.*

JAMES A. SNEAD

[In *Our Conquest,* Hofmann] shows how children can distill wonder from the dregs of war. *Our Conquest* places the children of the Imbach family in an apocalyptic setting. The narration, using an intentionally unspecific "we," provides a child's-eye view of defeat, as seen in a small Saxon town on May 7, 1945, the day after the Allied conquest of Germany. Oddly, Allied forces are completely absent from this tale. Rumors of gunfights and exotic black American soldiers abound, but "there's no trace of our conquerors." When the children's mother sends them to search for leftover bacon fat at a slaughterhouse, they undertake a bizarre daylong odyssey during which they try to acknowledge a censored German past, seeking atonement through ritualistic remembrance. . . . Christopher Middleton's translation does justice to Mr. Hofmann's precise style, which seems slow at first but soon absorbs the reader in its breathless cadences. At the outset the title seems to refer to the German defeat, but by the last page it attests to the tougher triumphs of "our" mind over a fractured past.

> James A. Snead, in a review of "Our Conquest," in The New York Times Book Review, *April 14, 1985, p. 26.*

GRACE INGOLDBY

The Spectacle at the Tower is set in Dikaiarcheia, a desolate and unpleasant little spot. X and his wife, already on the point of separation, are forced to spend the night in this poor, apparently almost empty and miserably squalid Sicilian village when the transmission 'goes' in their car. What happens in their 20 hours in this neighbourhood of 'perishing theatricality' is horrifying because it is not quite beyond belief.

Dikaiarcheia is very grim, a place without tourist potential, its tragedies rendered superfluous because no outsider ever witnessed them. 'They don't know what a guest is,' exclaims X, but the village supervisor, a fat and sweaty man in a black coat, necktie and crimson sash, knows exactly what a guest is and gets his hooks into this unsuspecting and unhappy couple straight away. For the supervisor has studied the 20th-century public, a public brutalised by over-exposure, a public without imagination, spoiled, demanding, a public which needs to see personally, to touch, hear and smell, and the spectacle at the tower is all his own idea. A spectacle that is original and that can't be copied, an idea to bring the money in, an idea that will turn Dikaiarcheia into a veritable tourist trap.

Relentlessly the supervisor 'talks the tower into the middle' of the couple's lives; in this blazingly hot and awful place he stages, among other things, a demonstration against death so that, after just one night in the village, X and his wife are emotionally and physically drained, rendered incapable of protest. . . . This is an extraordinarily striking novel, tense, horror with a breeze of humour, almost embarrassingly honest and frank. The landscape, 'the pointy faces' of the people in the processions are brilliantly evoked. (p. 25)

> Grace Ingoldby, "Horror Stories," in New States-man, *Vol. 110, No. 2838, August 9, 1985, pp. 25-6.*

LEIGH HAFREY

[In *The Spectacle at the Tower* and *Our Conquest*], as in the rest of his fiction, Mr. Hofmann's characters—particularly his narrators—seem ready to sink beneath the weight of the gruesome, often ambiguous information they are asked to convey. The action suggests frenzy even when the motive for such a state is not evident; the dialogues are a mass of sentences broken and then fleshed out by environmental noise, like the soundtrack of a Robert Altman film in transcription. Mr. Hofmann's narration becomes an explication of the unsayable as he fills the gaps left by these failed attempts at communication.

So it is a pleasure to pick up his most recent work, *The Parable of the Blind,* and find it not only short, like the best of Mr. Hofmann's fiction to date, but written in deliberately short and yet complete sentences that invite the reader's confidence. The subject is Bruegel's painting of the same name. . . .

For Bruegel there were six blind men, winding their way across a sere landscape dominated by a village church and a stream into which they topple one after another. Mr. Hofmann gives four of them names: Ripolus, the leader, who can see just well enough to tell light from darkness; Slit Man, blinded for stealing; Bellejambe, once a soldier; and Malente, who at odd moments begins to sing the praises of the Lord who allowed him to go blind. In the middle are two unnamed figures, the narrative "we" of the story, who are at once themselves and all six blind men and—in the universalizing style of parables—mankind at large.

For if Bruegel's blind men are alone in the landscape, Gert Hofmann's canvas is crowded with people. His six figures are not on an abstract journey; they are roused from sleep on the day they are to be painted by the artist, who wants, as we learn late in the book, to have one last try at putting "everything he had to say about the world" into a single picture. The six men are fetched from the barn where they've been dreaming by a man called "the knocker," led to breakfast by "the child," cleaned up after their meal by "the woman" Lise, and watched off and on throughout the day by a host of others, named and unnamed, whom the blind men cannot see but of whom they are always uncomfortably aware.

The human community is to them a fading reality, a world that demands too much of them in their handicapped state. They want to let go. . . .

In the interim, though, Bruegel wants to paint them. Intent on realism, he has them practice walking to the creek that runs by his house and, as they begin crossing the bridge, has them fall, screaming, into the water, still icy from the winter. Eager to catch the desolation he sees as intrinsic to the human condition, he has them go through the motions over and over until he gets the pink of their distended mouths just right.

The paradox is evident, and conveys the paradox of Gert Hofmann's own work. If he chooses to talk, in *The Parable of the Blind,* about a failure of perception and the evanescence of language, he does so with an acuity worthy of the Flemish master himself. There is an earthiness to this book, an immediacy of sensory impression that is enhanced by the continuing, very cerebral meditation on the contradictions of art, and that comes through in the smallest details: the squealing of a stuck pig, the saltpeter sweating from the walls of Bruegel's house in the spring floods. . . .

Mr. Hofmann displays the linguistic concision of a poet here, and develops a dramatic tension lacking in his other novels. But if this short book marks a turning point in his fiction—the blind men speak at one point of standing where "one region of the world ends and goes over into another"—it is not merely a stylistic change. The "we" so freely used by the narrator includes the reader, after all, as well as the artist, a kind of deity who presides both in and beyond the work. Within this community (at its worst called complicity), the grotesque turns spiritual, revealing the oxymoronic potential of the phrase "blind faith."

> Leigh Hafrey, "Eyeless with Bruegel," in The New York Times Book Review, *January 26, 1986, p. 27.*

FREDERICK R. LOVE

Best known until recently for his radio plays . . . , Gert Hofmann, in [*Der Blindensturz*], his free reconstruction of the genesis of Brueghel's *Parable of the Blind,* has retained much of the special atmosphere of a *Hörspiel.* Its narrative voice emanates not from the sphere of the artist but from the midst of the group of blind outcasts who become the human subjects of the artist's statement. The physical world has to be reconstructed from fading memories, their verbal signifiers, and the acute nonvisual sensitivities of the blind subjects. There is an overwhelming sense of six marginal existences uncomplainingly awaiting total oblivion under the snows of time. Isolation, hunger, useless travail, and exposure to the unconcern of nature (and most humans) cycle endlessly. Human impermanence is starkly complemented by the painter's esthetic vision, in which the anguished cries of poor

wretches in extremis are preserved in graphic terms (in this the artist seems a misplaced expressionist).

Having no function other than awaiting the Lord's time while they hold on to shreds of some earlier existence, the blind men respond almost happily to their abusive exploitation as study subjects for the artist caught up in a rush of renewed creative passion. . . . I have no satisfactory rationale for the composite narrator—he accounts for the two middle figures in the painting, whereas the other four have names and, in some sense, biographies—except in expanded auditory powers as a possible key to the narrator's ability to convey the somewhat intricate dialogue between the painter and his "good friend" inside the next building. Hofmann makes no attempt to incorporate the traditional thesis that Brueghel was expanding the parable from Luke 6:39 about the blind (mis)leading the blind. His artist wants to capture the terror in the faces (and voices) of those who *know* they are about to suffer indignity.

> Frederick R. Love, in a review of "Der Blindensturz," in World Literature Today, *Vol. 60, No. 2, Spring, 1986, p. 304.*

D. J. ENRIGHT

Gert Hofmann's novel, *The Parable of the Blind,* is [a] triumph of technique over matter, insofar as there can truly be any such triumph. It is an account, at close quarters, of a day in the life, or half-life, of six blind beggars. Awoken from their dreams in a barn, in the unspecified but presumably Flemish village of Pède-Sainte-Anne, they are given a substantial meal, and in due course—having been led and misled on the way—they reach the house of a painter. The latter, who provided their breakfast, is going to paint them—not sitting, but walking and stumbling and falling, and also screaming.

We learn next to nothing about the blind men. They talk repeatedly of birds, and of their having been blinded one hot evening, while sitting under a cherry tree, when the crows or ravens came down and pecked out their eyes. This serves as a cover story for them all, in the form of a nursery-rhyme legend. Each of them has his own name, and they have a nominal leader, called Ripolus, not because he is of any use but simply because someone has to walk in front. But they are not individuals so much as one ill-controlled body, lurching along hand in hand like "a deep-sea monster, a general, noiseless, dark, laboriously shifted thing." The narrator, one of the six, refers to himself in the ambiguous plural: "ourself," thus avoiding the distinguishing "my" and ironically favoring the royal "we."

Cut off from external reality, and with little memory of that reality left in their heads, their thoughts revolve in a narrow circle, as for much of the time their bodies do, too. . . .

As they remark, they have their dignity. They are the Lord's elect, if only because those whom He loves He punishes. "Even if His Love goes a bit too far, sometimes, we're thinking." (p. 37)

We see no more than they do of the painter himself, and hear only what they hear as he talks to his friend. He declines to look at them until he's ready to paint, for he might put himself in their place, and he doesn't wish to be moved except in his art. His ambition is to portray convincingly the human scream: this would be a "concluding and ultimate picture," containing everything he had to say about the world. "So that they (we), who are always being ignored," the narrator remarks, "will finally be seen for once, and people will know what a human being is, what being human is about." (pp. 37-8)

Bruegel's painting of 1568, *The Blind Leading the Blind,* part of which is reproduced on the jacket of the novel, shows a church in the background; and, while the biblical parable was then a commonplace emblem for human folly in general, it is possible that Bruegel also had in mind contemporary controversies over the forms and observances of religion.

We are virtually bound to surmise a parable or allegory of some kind in Gert Hofmann's novel, and not only because of its title in English. (The original is neutral translating as *The Fall of the Blind.*) Since we are not told how the men actually came by their blindness, whether through accident or as punishment for wrongdoing, the parable cannot well pertain to human folly, though the story answers as a somewhat conventional illustration of human misfortune. Another conceivable interpretation relates to art and the coldbloodedness, more politely impersonality, of the artist. Here the painter admits that it is probably more important to live than to capture life, yet "in his case, painting, even just the thought of it, kills all thought of anything else in the world." The blind men are repeatedly lined up and sent through the routine of walking, stumbling, and falling as slowly as possible into a stream. Never mind that they are bruised and bleeding, or that the day grows hot and they start to sweat: the painter won't allow them to unbutton their smocks or take off their bonnets. He is determined to get it right. What occupies him is not their fate but the fate of man, and when he has finished, "Stop now, he shouts, take them away." The callousness, not to say unscrupulousness, of the artist in action is another well-worn theme.

The Parable of the Blind possesses a number of negative virtues: absence of corn, and of porn, no striving for effect, no trite or portentous pleas for the underprivileged, and none of the longwindedness often taken for profundity. And it conveys, all the more persuasively for its matter-of-factness, a sense of what it is to be sightless—a prey to flood and fire and precipice; at the mercy of malicious jokers, and likewise of the well-disposed who almost choke you by pouring milk down your throat; and afflicted by the consciousness of having forgotten what the most ordinary things are like. Perhaps we should be content with that. (p. 38)

D. J. Enright, "Special Subjects," in The New York Review of Books, *Vol. XXXIII, No. 13, August 14, 1986, pp. 37-8.*

STELLA P. ROSENFELD

Gert Hofmann's [*Veilchenfeld*] tells the story of the persecution and suicide of a once-renowned Jewish philosopher and professor, Bernhard Israel Veilchenfeld, and of the moral capitulation of his fellow human beings (even the "best" of them), of their indifference and callousness, and their tacit acquiescence in his victimization. . . .

The story unfolds by bits and pieces, as it is seen and experienced by the narrator, the young son of the doctor who treats Veilchenfeld and shows at least a measure of concern and compassion for the old man, although significantly, he too

proves to be as prone to the same indolence of the heart as everyone else. In keeping with the sensibilities of a naïve observer, through which the world of *Veilchenfeld* is filtered, the story contains no analyses or interpretations of events, and no moralizing; nor does it employ shadings of tone that might differentiate events of existential consequence from daily trivialities. Hofmann sustains this narrative mode throughout, and the resulting juxtaposition of the inscrutably sinister and the all too familiar lends his story an atmosphere of the unreal and the uncanny. While the boy never quite grasps the significance of what he sees and hears, the reader, of course, does, and moral judgment is left to the latter. Thus, indirectly, in a muted, understated way, Hofmann powerfully indicts all those who simply "went along" with the immorality of the Third Reich; at the same time he compellingly and movingly portrays in one individual fate the tragedy of the Jews in Hitler's Germany.

Stella P. Rosenfeld, in a review of "Veilchenfeld," in World Literature Today, *Vol. 61, No. 1, Winter, 1987, p. 91.*

ANDREW SMITH

Early in Gert Hofmann's *The Spectacle at the Tower* there is an episode which brings together several strands of the novel. . . . The narrator sits with his wife in a hotel diningroom in a remote corner of Sicily and reveals to her the existence of a son by another woman. As he slowly utters phrases, "fatal, probably, to our marriage", he watches handsome, filthy children tormenting and killing a goat. Domestic crisis, murderous in its own way; a different, public kind of violence; the separate world of children; an exotic location—there are extreme effects here, and this is only the beginning. One of those children will die in public self-destruction, the wife will miscarry, and between the death of a goat and the death of a boy the couple, led by a sinister, relentless local guide, will traverse a landscape blasted by heat and poverty, peopled by the dead and the half-alive. It is a world where nothing gladdens the eye, where even the window-openings are "like scoured eye sockets goggling at us". It is, moreover, a world where places and objects are more vivid than people, because the people, even indeed the Strindbergian couple at the heart of it all, are at least as much spectators as actors in the drama. The result is closer to symbolism than to domestic drama. Shadowy persons are enacting vivid rites at a grotesque, macabre remove from reality.

Attempts to read more precise themes—tourism, the Third World, German versus Italian—into the sharply drawn horrors have been made, but they seem wide of the mark. If there is in fact a precise theme it centres in the narrator's own continuous presence: he, half-victim, half-manipulator, is full of a dead-pan despair about "what's called a human life".

The lack of an obvious purchase on topical issues may be one reason why German critics have had difficulty with Hofmann. His is not, however, a private, encoded world—urgent, perhaps even topical questions are being asked, but Hofmann chooses oblique angles on them. His most recent work, for instance, *Veilchenfeld* (1986), takes a familiar subject, the persecution of the Jews, in this case one solitary Jew, Veilchenfeld, seen and only dimly understood by two children. In *Der Blindensturz* (1985)—the title is that of Brueghel's picture, "The Parable of the Blind"—it is the blind beggars in the painting who speak, epitomes of the exploited.

The blind are at an extreme point on the scale, but they are of a kind with the children or with the German couple half-blinded in their marital rage, since all share an impeded vision on a cruel world. That same theme—and a similar approach to it—is central to *Our Conquest*. . . .

Again, locations are determining the narrative rather than characters and motives, and on this occasion, because the journey is less climactic, its stages seem to follow a more accidental sequence and the novel seems correspondingly less taut. The children keep this looser structure together, giving the novel an ambiguous centre. They are by turns wide-eyed and knowing, victims and victors—the double meaning of the title suggests as much—and they are an enigmatic presence to the end, separate and yet having a curiously single voice. . . .

> *Andrew Smith, "The Blighted and the Blind," in* The Times Literary Supplement, *No. 4389, May 15, 1987, p. 524.*

PHILLIP LOPATE

In Gert Hofmann's short-fiction collection [*Balzac's Horse*] we are dealing with writing of such sustained excellence it is a question of deciding which stories are masterworks and which merely accomplished virtuoso pieces. . . .

The temptation in speaking of a foreign writer who has not been given the full promotional treatment is to place him within a thicket of more familiar names. And indeed, Gert Hofmann's work does evoke a certain grotesque strand of imaginative German fiction: there are echoes of Kafka's anxious fables about performers (especially "Josephine the Mouse Singer" and "The Hunger Artist"), Robert Walser's spasmodic, excitable lyricism, Günter Grass's savage worldliness and Thomas Bernhard's hyperrationalizing syntactical tapeworm. Mr. Hofmann seems as idiosyncratic as these, if not yet as original. His sentences, which give great pleasure, coax a comedy out of the distance between their high-spirited energy and the miserable straits in which his characters invariably find themselves.

Some of that flavor may be detected in the opening lines of **"Casanova and the Extra,"** the longest and perhaps best story in *Balzac's Horse:* "In a recently discovered letter to the Portuguese ambassador Da Silva, the Prince de Ligne (1735-1814) writes concerning his friend Giacomo Casanova (1725-98), inter alia, that at a certain point in his life Casanova had an uncanny encounter, which would certainly have changed his life, if at that point his life could have been changed." For the next 25 pages the anonymous "we" narrator (like Kafka, Mr. Hofmann is a master of group narration) plays cat and mouse with the reader, promising to deliver the uncanny encounter and then drawing it back. Meanwhile we get a vivid picture of the celebrated roué in his declining years, exiled, poor, banished from one town after another, no longer attractive to women (or particularly excited by sex) but unable to give up his buffoonish compulsion to seduce. One would think that a figure like Casanova would be fictively exhausted for us; yet the story brings him alive by dwelling on the details of his humiliation, a strategy that tickles our contemporary

sense of justice while awakening twinges of sympathy for the old debauchee.

In any event, the uncanny encounter finally occurs: Casanova trails a woman in the street who seems "to possess one of those ample but firm behinds which he prizes so highly," and who turns out to be his mother. Having swallowed this Oedipal embarrassment, Casanova repairs with his mother to her room for a long chat, their first in decades. She demands that he give an accounting of his life. He replies defensively that he has tried to make his life into a work of art. She is openly contemptuous of her son for acting like "the biggest pig in Europe"; moreover she knows what she is talking about, having secretly followed him for years, gathering the complaints of the women he has left behind. With a reversion to the child's fear of his parents' omniscience, he "blushes . . . at the thought that his mother could have seen everything he's done in his life." He is also surprised to learn that his formerly stay-at-home mother has become an actress with a traveling troupe—more an extra than a principal. The "extra" may also refer to the superfluity of this one woman with whom Casanova may not have sex, and who therefore appropriately becomes his judge.

The author teases us, perhaps gratuitously, by leaving a doubt in our minds as to whether the woman is indeed Casanova's mother or an actress playing the part. On the other hand, Mr. Hofmann is so preoccupied with performance and role-playing that the added element of artifice may be justified. As it stands, the author is performing his own version of Casanova, the woman is performing Casanova's mother (and may well be Casanova's mother), and Casanova has turned into such a parody of himself that he is reduced to performing routines that he assumes the public still expects of him.

A number of the other six stories as well are about historical personages: Balzac and Tolstoy's son. There are obvious risks in such a gambit: the reader brings such a surfeit of background information that the text is in danger of being flooded by it, and the characters reduced to wooden overachievers. Mr. Hofmann surmounts these risks by two devices: catching the famous person at a point of declining celebrity, which shifts the focus away from genius toward human ruin; and dramatizing the process by which character becomes rigidified into performance, especially under the stress of renown. . . .

The title story, **"A Conversation About Balzac's Horse,"** is a vivid if nasty tour de force in which the ailing novelist, about to suffer a debacle in the theater, is shown as an egomaniac given to boastful bombast, the point of which he keeps forgetting. His patient listener, Mr. Brissot, inspector of the sewers of Paris, gradually turns the tables on him by bragging that his own "spectacles," of a more ferocious nature, have lured the audiences away from Balzac's tamer bourgeois entertainments. The story evolves into two parallel monologues, with each self-important speaker interrupting the other. The description of Brissot's sewer performances is Bruegelesque in its powerful imagery; a horse is set upon and eaten by rats, which in turn are ravaged by dogs, and so on.

If I have one objection to Mr. Hofmann's manner, not only here but in several less successful stories in the collection, it's that there is something unpleasantly didactic and mechanistic in his need to keep demonstrating that bestiality must in the end triumph over civility, or that human growth is a fiction, or that people are locked into benighted selfishness. Against the cold glee of these "proofs," I prefer those stories where he allows some real communication to occur between the characters, like Casanova and his mother, who do care, however reluctantly, about each other's opinion.

Phillip Lopate, "Casanova's Big Night," in The New York Times Book Review, *May 8, 1988, p. 9.*

ADAM LIVELY

The imagination of German writer Gert Hofmann was clearly seized by the sixteenth-century painting, "The Parable of the Blind" by Pieter Brueghel. Reproduced on the cover [of *The Parable of the Blind*], it depicts, in grotesque, almost cruel detail, the passage of six blind men as they stumble and fall, hand on the shoulder of the one before, through the countryside.

What Hofmann has attempted to do is reconstruct the experiences of that group of blind men, bound together by their misfortune, during the momentous day on which their sufferings are recorded for posterity. They wake in a barn, and are brought out to feed and empty themselves. Then they find themselves deserted, and have to grope around the village, walking into marshes, bitten by dogs, to find the painter's house. There they are paraded up and down, made to stumble and fall again and again, while the painter sketches them from the window of the house.

All this Hofmann narrates in the collective voice of the blind men themselves. Voices from the outside intrude, bringing the tart mixture of kindness and callousness of the villagers, but there is little to mitigate the suffocating blackness and confusion of not seeing. It would be interesting to hear the opinions of blind people of this novel, but from the outside I found Hofmann's evocation of blindness terribly convincing. Convincing, too, was the critique implicit in the book of the way art can cold-bloodedly milk the misfortunes of others. Hofmann uses pathos subtly, so that when, the painting done, the blind men are simply sent packing, to go on suffering whatever the world throws at them, it is all the more affecting. (p. 28)

Adam Lively, "Under Evil Eyes," in Punch, *Vol. 295, No. 7701, August 12, 1988, pp. 28-9.*

(John) Robinson Jeffers

1887-1962

American poet, dramatist, essayist, nonfiction writer, and short story writer.

Jeffers is an important figure in twentieth-century American poetry whose prophetic admonitions against modern civilization and human introversion have attracted both critical censure and admiration. He is perhaps best known for long dramatic narrative poems in which he combined violent imagery with a somber tone and dense syntax to explore unsettling topics. Guided by his philosophy of inhumanism, which he defined as "a shifting of emphasis and significance from man to not-man; the rejection of human solipsism and recognition of the transhuman magnificence," Jeffers contrasted the strength and enduring beauty of nature with a tragic vision of human suffering and inconsequence. Incorporating structures and themes from Greek drama, the Bible, and Eastern mysticism, and influenced by such thinkers as Lucretius, Arthur Schopenhauer, and Friedrich Nietzsche, Jeffers drew upon science, history, nature, and contemporary events for subject material. Jeffers was also inspired by the landscape and legends of Southern California's Monterey coast, where he lived throughout his adult life.

The son of a Presbyterian preacher and theologian, Jeffers was born in Pittsburgh, Pennsylvania. He was tutored by his father in various languages, the classics, and the Bible before being sent to boarding schools in Switzerland and Germany. Following his graduation from Occidental College in 1905, Jeffers earned a masters degree in literature from the University of Southern California; he later spent several years studying medicine at USC and forestry at the University of Washington. After a modest inheritance freed him from the necessity of earning a living, Jeffers and his wife settled on an isolated plot of coastal land in Carmel, California, where he built a stone house and tower overlooking the Pacific Ocean. This rustic setting and Jeffers's ensuing austere lifestyle suggested both the dominant imagery and tone of his poetry.

Jeffers's first two books, *Flagons and Apples* (1912) and *Californians* (1916), are generally considered conventional and undistinguished. In the poems collected in these volumes, Jeffers employs traditional structures, rhyme schemes, and diction, using the natural world as a backdrop for his semiautobiographical lyrics of frustrated love. *Roan Stallion, Tamar, and Other Poems* (1925; revised, 1935), which was originally published at Jeffers's own expense as *Tamar and Other Poems* (1924), exhibits a significant advance from his earlier work. Eschewing traditional modes, Jeffers utilizes simple, declarative, and often colloquial language, as well as long narrative forms, while exploring sexual themes that display the influence of Sigmund Freud, Carl Jung, and Havelock Ellis. "Tamar," for example, illustrates the folly of incest through a tragic tale of sexual passion between a sister and her brother. Based upon a story from the second book of Samuel, "Tamar" combines California locales with biblical diction and themes. "Roan Stallion" centers upon a woman whose abusive husband is killed by her horse when she flees to the animal for protection. After slaying the horse in retaliation for the death of her husband, the woman realizes that she has

destroyed the embodiment of her freedom. Her subsequent anguish symbolizes the suffering that humanity inflicts upon itself when it squanders opportunities for change and improvement. "The Tower beyond Tragedy" is drawn from Aeschylus's *Oresteia*, in which Orestes kills his mother to avenge her murder of his father, Agamemnon. In his version, Jeffers focuses on the character of Cassandra, whom Agamemnon obtains as spoil from his victory at Troy and who prophesies many of the grim events that follow. Jeffers's Cassandra foretells not only the fall of old empires, as in the Greek myth, but that of future civilizations. Some of the shorter lyrics in this collection describe Southern California's terrain and display Jeffers's knowledge of biology, astronomy, and physics.

The Women at Point Sur (1927; revised as *The Women at Point Sur and Other Poems,* 1977) is an ambitious and complex dramatic narrative poem that is considered one of Jeffers's most controversial works. Described by Dwight McDonald as "a witches' dance of incest, suicide, madness, adultery and Lesbianism," this piece relates the story of Barclay, a Christian minister whose disillusionment with the war that claimed his only son turns him from theology. Abandoning his wife and church, Barclay withdraws to the Carmel coast, where he seeks to establish a new religion based upon the external world. He is distracted from his intention, however, by overbearing narcissism and lust for his daughter. Barclay eventually goes insane, and following an orgy of destruction, he wanders off to die in the hills. Modern in its use of science for poetic material and its candid, realistic concern with sex, *The Women at Point Sur* satirizes human self-importance and explores harmful aspects of civilization.

Cawdor and Other Poems (1928) is regarded by some critics as Jeffers's finest single volume. The title poem of this collection is based upon the plot of Euripides's *Hippolytus,* in which Hippolytus is cursed by Aphrodite with the physical love of Phaedra, his stepmother. When Phaedra hangs herself in grief over her stepson's resistance to her advances, Hippolytus is driven from Athens by his father, whose prayers are fulfilled when his son is dragged to death by his own horses. This book also contains several short verses in unrhymed forms that focus upon the benefits of death over life. The title piece of *Dear Judas and Other Poems* (1929) dramatizes the crucifixion of Jesus Christ by adapting elements of Japanese Noh theater. Narrated by the ghosts of Jesus, the Virgin Mary, and Judas, "Dear Judas" exhibits Jeffers's most sustained concern with human emotion. Stage adaptations of "Dear Judas," first produced in 1947, have been banned on various occasions for allegedly sacrilegious subject matter. This volume also includes "The Loving Shepherdess," a dramatic narrative about a long-suffering young woman who roams the Southern California coast through settings reminiscent of those in other works by Jeffers. During her travels, she encounters a friendly vaquero to whom she relates the events which have led to her tragic predicament. *Descent to the Dead: Poems Written in Ireland and Great Britain* (1931) contains sixteen short poems written in stately verse that feature a wealth of local color and lore. In the title piece of *Thurso's Landing and Other Poems* (1932), Jeffers recounts the tale of an unhappily married couple whose passion is unable to save them from misery and confusion. In *Give Your Heart to the Hawks and Other Poems* (1933), Jeffers presents a psychological portrait of a strong-willed man who is driven insane by remorse for the murder of his brother. This volume also includes several short pieces that are predominantly concerned with themes of death and resurrection, poems from *Descent to the Dead,* and "At the Fall of an Age," which concerns the death of Helen on the island of Rhodes twenty years after the fall of Troy.

In *Solstice and Other Poems* (1935), Jeffers presents a modern version of the Greek legend of Medea founded upon an account by Euripides. This volume also contains the long narrative "At the Birth of an Age." Derived from the final sections of the Teutonic epic the *Nibelungenlied,* this poem portrays a petty argument between three sibling leaders of a small Germanic tribe and their sister that contributes to the defeat of Attila and the Huns during an invasion of Europe in 451. Jeffers overshadows the individual personalities of his characters by emphasizing the enormous consequences of their small-minded conduct. The title piece of *Such Counsels You Gave to Me and Other Poems* (1937) features a modernization of a traditional Scottish ballad in which the protagonist's medical acumen provides Jeffers with a vehicle for demonstrating his knowledge of science. Also included in this volume are short poems concerning Jeffers's refusal to align himself with any particular economic, social, or political movement, a position for which he was frequently criticized. *Be Angry at the Sun* (1941) contains several controversial portraits of Adolf Hitler, whom Jeffers considered historically

necessary and simultaneously fascinating and disgusting. In *The Double Axe and Other Poems* (1948; revised, 1977), Jeffers utilizes elements of Eastern ideology to convey the alienation and hatred experienced by many veterans of war. The title poem of this collection is a tale of a young soldier who returns from the dead to confront and kill his father, who had sent him into battle during World War II. This volume also features the philosophical poem "The Inhumanist," in which Jeffers expounds his fundamental convictions. In the final collection published during his lifetime, *Hungerfield and Other Poems* (1954), which was inspired by his wife's death in 1950, Jeffers portrays death as a welcome respite from life's distress.

Several compilations and posthumous publications of Jeffers's poetry have been issued, including *The Selected Poetry of Robinson Jeffers* (1938), *Selected Poems of Robinson Jeffers* (1963), and *Rock and Hawk: A Selection of Shorter Poems* (1987). *The Beginning and the End and Other Poems* (1963) collects verse that Jeffers composed following *Hungerfield,* while the works assembled in *The Alpine Christ and Other Poems* (1973) were written between 1916 and 1924. The longest single poem that Jeffers composed, "The Alpine Christ," opens with a conference in heaven during which Satan compliments God for allowing World War I to exceed the horrors of hell. As a result, Jesus Christ returns to earth to redeem humankind but is unsuccessful and departs as the war continues. *Brides of the South Wind: Poems, 1917-1922* (1974) gathers verse that Jeffers composed immediately after the publication of his first two books, and *What Odd Expedients and Other Poems* (1981) contains many pieces concerning war.

Jeffers adapted several of his long dramatic narrative poems for the theater. The title character of *Medea: Freely Adapted from the Medea of Euripides* (1947) is a woman of elemental passions whose tendency toward violence illuminates humanity's need to surmount the limitations of mere emotion. *The Tower beyond Tragedy* (1950), like Jeffers's poem of the same name, is a rendering of Aeschylus's *Oresteia* in which Orestes rejects vanity and identifies himself with the divine nature of all things. In *The Cretan Woman* (1954), the text of which is included in *Hungerfield and Other Poems,* Jeffers borrows from his poem "Cawdor" to rework the plot of Euripides's *Hippolytus.* Although Jeffers wrote little criticism, he occasionally composed pieces that endeavored to express or clarify his beliefs. *Poetry, Gongorism, and a Thousand Years* (1949) was originally published as an essay, and *Themes in My Poems* (1956) was written to promote a lecture tour. Much of Jeffers's personal correspondence is compiled in *The Selected Letters of Robinson Jeffers, 1897-1962* (1968).

Critical reception of Jeffers's work has fluctuated greatly. During the 1920s and early 1930s, Jeffers was hailed as among the greatest living American writers; *Time* magazine, which is often considered a barometer of popular achievement, placed him on its cover in 1932. During subsequent years of the Depression and World War II, however, Jeffers suffered a reversal of literary reputation that critics variously attribute to his unpopular social and political views and the diminishing quality of his verse. Since his death in 1962, Jeffers's work has undergone extensive reevaluation, and several of his shorter poems, including "Shine, Perishing Republic," "Boats in a Fog," and "To the Stone-Cutters," remain essential to anthologies of American verse. Mercedes Cunningham Monjian concluded in 1958: "Whatever the future holds for this poet, our own age is still awed by the magnificent talent and effort of a burdened mind struggling to free humanity from the shackles of an impoverished self-love, and the myths to which he believes it gave birth."

(See also *CLC*, Vols. 2, 3, 11, 15; *Contemporary Authors,* Vols. 85-88; and *Dictionary of Literary Biography,* Vol. 45.)

ALFRED KREYMBORG

If we look upon Whitman as the last figure in the first half-century of American poetry, we may look upon Jeffers as the last in the second half—a view not strictly mathematical. Walt may also be called the dawn of the latter half. Quite aside from any arbitrary scheme, Whitman and Jeffers afford parallels and antitheses to the student of the American race. Both men are prophets; both write in the grand manner; and each reflects his own period. Whitman, the sprawling, gabby tramp of Manhattan, embraced as much of the universe as his great heart could gather. Jeffers, the aristocratic hermit and bacteriologist, finds the human race, and especially the American, inimical. (p. 624)

[Jeffers'] first two books, *Flagons And Apples,* 1912, and *Californians,* 1916, now out of print, are overshadowed by the books of recent years: *Roan Stallion And Tamar, The Women Of Point Sur, Cawdor,* and the forthcoming volume, *King Judas.* Each huge volume is composed of long narratives and shorter poems. The fragments contain the gist of Jeffers; they are keynotes to the narratives. And after reading one narrative—"Tamar" by preference—one has virtually read them all. The later narratives are extended variations of the earlier: the Greek "Tower Beyond Tragedy" and the American "Tamar." I have been unable to finish *The Women Of Point Sur,* and prefer its prelude to what I have read of the body of the poem. After incest has been piled on incest, one takes further incest for granted. "Cawdor" is a much finer narrative. The figures of old Cawdor, of the passionate girl-wife, Fera, of Cawdor's son, Hood the hunter, hunted by Fera, of the childish Michal Cawdor, of the eagle captured for her by Hood, of the squirrels she traps for the eagle—bloodshed on bloodshed—these figures are dynamic; their tragedy has a relentless drive. Somehow, the figures, especially Fera, who does most of the talking, are helpless puppets for Jeffers' philosophy. He is a splendid novelist, dramatist and moralist by turns. Whenever the moralist emerges, he writes fiery speeches and makes the actors recite them. These are not the moments of a supreme dramatic artist. And the scenes he invades with explanatory monologues belong even less to the classic dramatist. The Greeks assigned such commentary to the traditional chorus. Jeffers' commentaries are stirring, but they have the air of circumlocution. If characters do not completely reveal their relations to a given situation, revision is imperative. The playwright should ring down the curtain, send the audience home, revise his script, remove his own person and then raise the curtain in earnest. Jeffers' disdain for humanity involves as great a disdain for readers and spectators. Such an attitude may not be fatal to a lyrist or philosopher, but it is fatal to a dramatist or epic poet. Jeffers has it in him to become a dramatic poet of a high order. His achievement falls short of his major intention. He has a glorious imagination; his dithyrambs have the range and movement of the tides he worships; his people throb and bleed with

reality; the California background is Olympian. But the artist backstage lacks the hard integrity of his Greek masters. His fingers "had the art to make stone love stone," but not the art to make every word love every word. His love of language makes speech run in torrents; his contempt for language fails to control the streams and guide them seaward. Two men, two wrestlers, two serpents, are at odds in the poet: the lover and the hater, the human and the hermit, the man and the superman. The shorter poems impart a clue to the dual temper of this pantheist.

In "**Granite And Cypress,**" he wonders "why tree-tops and people are so shaken." "I have granite and cypress, both long-lasting." "Like me they remember old wars and are quiet." He scorns our new arts. "The restlessness of talent runs over and floods the stage or spreads its fever on canvas." His own work has the "coldness and the tenor of a stone tranquility." Here we perceive the desire to become like stone, the desire without the power, a power reserved for stones. In "**Shine, Perishing Republic,**" the poet derides our vulgarity, "heavily thickening to empire." He instructs his children to "keep their distance from the thickening center . . . when the cities lie at the monster's feet there are left the mountains." . . . Wise men should not envy "the little people making merry like grasshoppers," who "dance, talk, dress and undress," and who shrill: "What does the future matter, we shall be dead?" . . . "Our people are clever and masterful . . . but at present there is not one memorable person, there is not one mind to stand with the trees, one life with the mountains." These are the people the poet has fled. . . .None the less, he itches with another fable. Though Nature makes him "ashamed to speak of the active little bodies, the coupling bodies, the misty brainfuls of perplexed passion," though "humanity is needless . . . culture's outlived, art's rootcut," he sits down to another fable, hating the word. And it is the longest fable of all. He is not only a witness, but a part "of the world's deadly and wonderful destinies." He cannot resist the vestiges of his former humanity. . . .The yearning for stony silence finds relief after stormy passages, through tales of the utmost terror in which everything is violated: people rending each other like beasts, members of the same family destroying each other through passion and incest, murder and bloody fire laying waste to the final scene.

Jeffers found his grandest models in the incestuous house of Agamemnon. But "**The Tower Beyond Tragedy**" is more than a revival of Electra's revenge on her mother. The visionary Cassandra, cursed with the gift of prophecy, sees not alone the fall of old empires and rains curses on future Rome, Spain, France, England. "There remains a mightier to be cursed and a higher for malediction when America has eaten Europe and takes tribute of Asia, when the ends of the world grow aware of each other and are dogs in one kennel, they will tear the master of the hunt with the mouths of the pack." Like Jeffers, Cassandra chants: "Death, make me stone, make me air to wander free between the stars and the peaks; but cut humanity out of my being, that is the wound that festers in me." Electra, having goaded Orestes to the murder of Clytemnestra, in vengeance for the murder of their father, urges her brother to ascend to Agamemnon's throne. When Orestes refuses, she woos him with her virginal body. But her brother refuses her. He recalls a vision of their intricate human family. Man pursued woman and woman clung to man,

> Strained at each other in the darkness, all loved or
>   fought inward, each one of the lost people
> Sought the eyes of another that another should

praise him; sought never his own but another's;
   the net of desire
Had every nerve drawn to the centre, so that they
   writhed like a full draught of fishes, all matted
In the one mesh; when they look backward they see
   only a man standing at the beginning,
Or forward, a man at the end; or if upward, men
   in the shining bitter sky striding and feasting,
Whom you call Gods . . .
It is all turned inward, all your desires
   incestuous . . .

This magnificent passage reveals the whole of Jeffers. Orestes continues: "I have greater kindred than dwell under a roof." "I have cut the meshes and fly like a freed falcon." The pantheistic youth feels in himself "the great life of the ancient peaks, the patience of stone . . ."

                      and I was the stream
Draining the mountain wood; and I the stag drinking; and I was the stars,
Boiling with light, wandering alone, each one the
   lord of his own summit; and I was the darkness
Outside the stars, I included them, they were a part
   of me.

Electra, threatening to die because she has lost her brother, accuses him of madness: "This horror draws upon me like stone walking." Orestes agrees, the image describes him exactly, and adds in Jeffers' own guise: "What fills men's mouths is nothing; and your threat is nothing; I have fallen in love outward." That one line—"I have fallen in love outward—" hammers home the poet's ideal, the sum of his superhuman effort. Electra clings to "the honor of the house." Orestes forsakes the family, and the family of the whole human race. Later hearsay reports "that a serpent killed him in high Arcadia." (pp. 625-29)

Whitman, falling in love inward and viewing the race through himself, embraced humanity. Jeffers, falling in love outward, embraces mountains and the sea. His early training in bacteriology caused him to view mankind as biological microbes rending each other incestuously. Walt's love and Jeffers' hatred have been reared on a monumental scale. Obviously, both elements, on a grand or smaller scale, reside in every being, human or superhuman. So far as one can limit any age to its leading characteristic, one might say that Whitman's age was all for love, Jeffers' all for hatred. The Whitman period, stemming from Emerson, believed in the virtues of the race; the Jeffers period believes in its evils and vices. (pp. 629-30)

Alfred Kreymborg, "Shine, Perishing Republic," in his Our Singing Strength: An Outline of American Poetry, 1620-1930, *Coward-McCann, Inc., 1929, pp. 624-30.*

LAWRENCE CLARK POWELL

Nineteen-twelve was a momentous year in our literature. Seed sown a half-century earlier by Walt Whitman was about to germinate from the soil of the midwest. A realistic poetry, born from life not literature, waited in manuscript for publication. Vachel Lindsay's *Rhymes to be Traded for Bread* was privately printed by the author. In October appeared the first issue of Harriet Monroe's *Poetry, A Magazine of Verse,* a monthly that was to introduce and champion the work of hitherto unknown poets, schools and movements.

In December of this same year came . . . a thin volume of thirty-three poems by John Robinson Jeffers, which bore the title *Flagons and Apples.* Unconcerned with the realistic, anit-bookish movement then beginning to stir American poetry, this first volume by Jeffers was inspired by the poet's personal experience rather than by any contemporary group-movements. The lyrics, in conventional forms, are in dispraise of a frustrated love.

Whereas Jeffers' college verse owed its inspiration to the "young Spartan's" love of nature, and bore such titles as **"The Lake," "Mountain Pines," "The Fox," "The Condor,"** the poems in *Flagons and Apples* show him come into a painful, romantic young manhood; and though nature is not forgotten, it is the poet's heart that concerns him most. (pp. 31-2)

In spite of an Epilogue, in which the poet denies that he has written autobiographically, there is too close a parallel between the facts of his life during the period 1907-1912, as we know them, and the story in these verses, to allow one to view them as objective exercises in versification. If there is not present the close-knit drama of *Modern Love,* neither is there the enigma of Shakespeare's sonnet sequence.

Taken separately, these poems are for the most part undistinguished, though they do exhibit a promising gift of prosody and a feeling for form. It is, however, as a whole that I judge them finally; for this is no ordinary first volume of love-poems. Its chief virtues I find to be an emotional intensity and a passionate lucid sincerity—qualities which combine with originality in Jeffers' later work.

Nature appears in *Flagons and Apples* as background for the poet's passion and solace for his pain. Jeffers is too intent on linking his own emotions with the vaster aspects of nature— dawn and sunset, night and the stars, seasons and winds—to give attention to less obvious natural phenomena such as flowers and trees and birds. Though passionately subjective, these poems are not the work of a morbid introvert, nor do they smell of the lamp. They were written chiefly at Hermosa Beach, and the ocean is in many of them: tides and watery sunset, fogs and surf-worn shingle, remembered days on the Palos Verdes cliffs and beaches with his love "Helen," solitary night-walks on the sand: there is hardly a poem in which the sea is not present, either as background or as figure. Thus originates the bond between this poet and the Pacific Ocean, a bond that deepens as the years pass.

Although Jeffers was a good student of the classics, these early lyrics do not reveal him a bookworm, escaping from the present to the antique past. In classical allusions there is evidence simply of the poet's familiarity with the old poets of Greece and Rome: **"Nyassa"** recalls a Dionysus legend; **"To Canidia"** evokes Horace; **"To Helen Whose Remembrance Leaves No Peace"** is prefaced by a line from Archilochus— *Dystenos egkeimai potho.* A taste for modern languages appears in the title **"Morgengabe";** in the epigraphical Italian folksong; and in a poem of the Los Angeles *plaza* with its sprinkling of Mexican oaths.

Flagons and Apples reveals its author, in spite of his religious training, unorthodox in his view of God. Jeffers' father was an extremely liberal theologian who never attempted to foist dogma on his son. In fact, Jeffers did not attend Sunday-school, and was taught the Bible by his father as Oriental literature, not as divine revelation. But in these poems, Jeffers does not share his father's ultimate faith in a God of Love, nor has he succeeded in establishing the impersonal Power-God of his mature years. He wavers between a "wild and cruel and occult God"—a thundering Jehovah—and the many gods of classic antiquity. (pp. 32-3, 35)

Not only is he sick of love, but he is troubled as well by a conflict between his reason and his inherited religious faith. (p. 35)

With the publication four years later, in 1916, of Jeffers' second volume, *Californians,* this dilemma is resolved, doubt dispelled, and the poet rests firmly upon a consistent metaphysic. (p. 36)

After eliciting two brief reviews and having one of its verses reprinted in a magazine, *Californians* went quietly out of print. . . . [This] is not hard to understand; for the book is written largely in "poetic diction" and devoted to such quaint archaisms as *terza rima,* the Spenserian stanza and regular blank verse.

If, however, the diction is traditional, the themes are not antique or bookish, and they show their author to be keenly aware of the present, though less obviously so than the realistic reporters of the midwest school. The contents of *Californians* may be divided into three general groups: (1) Narratives of Californian folk, (2) Descriptive songs of nature, (3) Odes and other long poems addressed to people.

Jeffers' development in the four-year period separating *Flagons and Apples* and *Californians* is remarkable. His own emotional life being happily resolved by marriage, he is free to explore the external world for the stuff of poetry; and the beautiful coast on which he lives forms an ideal décor for his passionate imagination.

Written in the first flush of maturity, *Californians* is Jeffers' most optimistic book. "Ode on Human Destinies" expresses the poet's faith in mankind and his determination to celebrate its glories in verse. . . . (p. 37)

In this book the European war, two years advanced, troubles him, but he nevertheless welcomes it as a housecleaner. The homely virtues of the coastal folk are sufficient proof to Jeffers that man is an essentially noble creature. Though several of the shorter narratives are not tragic, the longer, more pretentious tales end on sombre tones. Often the tragedy arises from a conflict between the simple country-folk and the wicked city-dwellers.

Jeffers' love for the Pacific coast is expressed through one of the characters, who

> . . . had wandered our whole coast, and knew it
>   well,
> San Diego to Vancouver. All the forms
> Of nature, every promontory and bay,
> Mountain and valley and gorge and stand of trees.
>   **"Maldrove"**

This attachment to the west coast, which, as we have noted, appears in *Flagons and Apples,* is intensified in this second volume, and calls forth one of the book's most successful poems—the **"Invocation"** of the evening star, in which Jeffers wonders at the future now that the westward migrations that were drawn out of "huge Asia, northward of cloudy Caucasus" have come to a halt at the continent's end. And

in **"Dream of the Future"** he visions a solution, in which the race leaves the earth in the newly-invented airplane to colonize Venus and Jupiter!

Jeffers' God is increasingly unorthodox. Resolution of his philosophic dilemma came with maturity. Thus the philosophy of *Californians* is affirmative. The poet finds immortality a deceitful dream. The rewards of life are to be found in life itself, in strength, love and freedom. There is a "universal Power" that endures forever, from which man gains dignity because he is a part of it. The poet's faith is essentially non-human . . . [and] fatalistic. . . .(pp. 38-9)

To me the most moving piece in *Californians* is the long ode, **"The Year of Mourning,"** in memory of the poet's father, and a daughter who died the day of her birth. In the tradition of Moschus, Milton and Shelley, this poem has a lofty beauty which derives from its exalted language and restrained passion. (p. 39)

If *Californians* took no part in the reawakened pageant of American poetry by being neither imagistic nor realistic, and if it is not free from the influence of Shelley, Wordsworth and Milton on philosophy and diction, it is nevertheless a book of rich melody and emotional intensity, which shows its author determined to make poetry from the contemporary scene. Though a volume of tender maturity and apprenticeship, it is none the less a great advance from the verses of four years earlier and gives abundant promise of the poetry to come.

Eight years passed before Jeffers' next book appeared. In 1924 *Tamar and Other Poems* was printed at the author's expense, and in the following year was reissued, with the addition of new poems, by a New York house, under the title of *Roan Stallion, Tamar and Other Poems.*

Between this volume and *Californians* stretches an eight-year period, during which the war was fought and ended, and the poet's mind came to full maturity. In the later book not only does Jeffers abandon rhyme for an original system of accentual prosody, but he disposes as well of traditional diction—the "ye's" and "thee's" and "thou's"—and employs a simple, declarative, and at times colloquial, manner of writing.

The contents of the *Roan Stallion* volume include narratives of the Carmel coast, lyrics, and a long dramatic narrative, **"The Tower Beyond Tragedy"** which is a Jeffersian version of two plays of Aeschylus, the *Agememnon* and the *Libation Bearers.* From rural idylls ruined by city-dwellers, the narratives become stark, realistic tales of morbid psychology and the emotional aberrations of the coastal ranchfolk. In his frank use of sexual themes, Jeffers profits by the freedom from Victorian prudery, pioneered in literature by Zola, Hardy and George Moore, and Dreiser in America, and given a scientific basis by such men as Havelock Ellis and Freud.

And in the extent to which the poet occupies himself with his characters' dreams and symbolical nightmares, it would seem that he had familiarized himself with the work of Freud and Jung and other dream-psychologists.

Incest as theme was used in *Californians* in a mild, Shelleyan way, but in the long narrative, **"Tamar,"** the Biblical story is transplanted and adapted in such realistic fashion as to frighten the timid.

The poet's unsocial way of life is complemented by a definitely unsocial philosophy: not only are cities to him evil and full of vice, but the fact that they exist is taken by him as a sign that our civilization is decadent. His earlier faith in the nobility of mankind, which rings through *Californians,* is replaced by this surprising utterance from **"Roan Stallion":**

> Humanity is the start of the race; I say
> Humanity is the mold to break away from, the
>   crust to break through, the coal to break into
>   fire,
> The atom to be split.

I look upon the war of 1914-1918 as responsible for Jeffers' disillusionment. That time of folly, when the human race butchered ten million of its members, killed idealism in many a young artist's breast . . . and Jeffers did not escape. His first reaction to the war was a romantic one, and we have seen that he even sought to enlist. In retrospect, however, he saw the insane horror of it, and as the smoke of propaganda cleared, the futility of the struggle became apparent.

This volume reveals the intensely religious nature of Robinson Jeffers . . . but his is not the religion of his fathers. In him appears in prophetic fervor the accumulated zeal of generations of devout Calvinists. From the modern sciences, biology, astronomy and physics, he formulates an impersonal Deity, a God "whose essence and end is beauty," whom he worships passionately.

And the verse in this and subsequent volumes is a strong blend of two elements, the religious and the erotic. Jeffers is a twentieth century, post-war Puritan, in whom mingle the twin streams of passion and humility. He is, in some ways, a modern Milton.

The poems in *Roan Stallion, Tamar and Other Poems* are not of uniform quality; some of them are too manifestly transitional work, necessary experiments in Jeffers' modulation from the unoriginal style of *Californians* to the decidedly original accents of his mature verse. But the later verses, such as **"Tamar," " Night," "Continent's End," "Gale in April,"** etc., are among the best examples of this poet's genius. The foreword to the Modern Library edition of *Roan Stallion* (1935) is a delightful essay on the torments suffered by Jeffers when, at the age of 27, he realized that his first two volumes were only imitative, and wondered how he was to attain the originality that distinguishes a poet from a versifier. Asked by his publisher if he wanted to revise anything for the new edition, Jeffers thought in a kind of a panic, "Of course I ought to revise, but how terrible! for it is a pleasure to write, but after a thing has been written I hate to see it again; poems are the sort of children that it is delightful to beget, dreary to educate." Instead of revising, Jeffers wrote the introduction, "a mere conscience-penny," he termed it.

In 1927 appeared Jeffers' fourth volume, *The Women at Point Sur,* a single narrative, with a prelude, of 175 pages. It is the most ambitious thing he had yet attempted, and is so fraught with horror that [Dwight McDonald] said of it, "Not since the later Elizabethans has there been such a witches' dance of incest, suicide, madness, adultery and Lesbianism."

It is the story of a Christian minister, Barclay, who, disillusioned by the war (which claimed his only son), cuts adrift from theology and, abandoning his church and wife, comes to the Carmel coast where he seeks to build a new religion from the external world. He is, however, seduced from a non-anthropomorphic view of the universe by desire for disciples among the ranch-folk and by lust for his daughter. Insanity breaks his mind, and after an orgy of destruction, he wanders off to die in the hills.

Of all Jeffers' work, it is this long and complex poem which most puzzles the general reader. Certainly it calls for careful reading. Like Browning, Jeffers does not intend his poetry as a substitute for an after-dinner cigar or a game of checkers. Thoroughly modern in its use of science for poetic material and in its frank, realistic concern with sex, *The Women at Point Sur* is evidence of the poet's intention to put his world into a poem, as Dante did.

In a letter to a critic who had asked for an explanation of the poem, Jeffers replied that he had tried "(1) To strip everything but its natural ugliness from unmoral freedom; (2) To show in action the danger of that *Roan Stallion* idea of 'breaking out of humanity,' misinterpreted in the mind of a fool or a lunatic; (3) To attempt to uncenter the human mind from itself; (4) To present a tragedy which would be a study in morbid psychology, a partial and fragmentary study of the origin of religions, a satire on human self–importance, and a judgment of the tendencies of our civilization."

Someday someone will do with Jeffers' poetry what Professor Lowes did with Coleridge's—investigate the processes and materials which went to the building of the poet's work; then will be revealed the scope of this long poem which distils beauty from such widely separated sources as the Old Testament, Shelley, Terence, the destruction by fire of the oil-tanks at Monterey, and the coastal earthquake fault.

The poem's weakness, as I see it, lies in its lack of balance: climaxes of lust and terror are superimposed, until the reader's sensibilities are nearly benumbed. The symbolical Prelude, however, is a fine achievement, complete in itself; and the poem is strung on a loom of beautiful language which, at times, rises to exalted heights.

This same year brought forth fifteen short poems which appeared in *A Miscellany of American Poetry,* a symposium conducted by Louis Untermeyer, certain pages of which were allotted to each of a group of contemporary poets to fill as they pleased. Jeffers' fellow contributors included Robert Frost, Carl Sandburg, Vachel Lindsay, Conrad Aiken, Archibald MacLeish, Edna St. Vincent Millay and Elinor Wylie.

In this year, 1927, Jeffers was 40 years old. Standing at the midpoint of life, he gazes back the feverish slope of youth, before turning his eyes ahead to what, for him, has become the crown of life: Death. These poems are restrained, sober expressions of belief, and they form a marked contrast with the exciting *The Women at Point Sur.* They are among the most significant poems Jeffers has written.

In 1928, three volumes of poetry by Jeffers appeared from three different presses. A small privately printed edition of a single short narrative, *An Artist,* came from Austin, Texas; in addition to the poem itself, the volume is interesting because it reprints a letter from Havelock Ellis in praise of Jeffers.

The Book Club of California issued a small edition of sixteen poems, with an introduction by a professor at the University of California.

Cawdor and Other Poems was printed by the poet's regular New York publisher. In addition to the title-poem, a long narrative, this volume contains sixteen short verses, all in unrhymed forms, most of which were reprinted from the two smaller volumes of the same year.

This is, in my opinion, Jeffers' finest single volume: the verse in it is on a consistently high level. Whereas some of the narratives in the *Roan Stallion* volume are overburdened with doctrine, and *The Women at Point Sur* is loud with the horns of prophecy, "Cawdor" is a tale told for the telling; and though very serious in tone and marked by awful, violent acts, it is free from themes of incest and sexual perversion. Unlike the mad minister of *The Women at Point Sur,* the protagonist Cawdor is consistently sane. His tragedy, which proceeds inevitably from the postulates, is not one of abnormality, and hence is more likely to be appreciated by the general reader.

In this narrative-poem the painful suffering of life and the relative peace of death are twin themes which possess Jeffers; and he assumes place as one of the few poets of all time who has exalted death without denying life. The beautiful passages on the chemistry of death are, to my knowledge, unique in literature.

In a note to his publisher, Jeffers wrote of "Cawdor": "I think of "Cawdor" as making a third with "Tamar" and *The Women at Point Sur;* but as if in "Tamar" human affairs had been seen looking westward, against the ocean; in *Point Sur* looking upward, minimized to ridicule against the stars; in "Cawdor" looking eastward, against the earth, reclaiming a little dignity from that association."

In three of the shorter poems in this volume, "Soliloquy," "The Bird with the Dark Plumes" and "Meditation on Saviors," there is evident a conflict between Jeffers' cold, objective, unsocial intellect and his warm, pitying heart which goes out to all suffering things. But nowhere is the warm side of the poet more manifest than in the poem to George Sterling, whose suicide in 1926 preceded the publication of his last work, a passionate championing of Jeffers. Other writers had harsh things to say of Sterling's weaknesses, but Jeffers proved himself a true friend, in this and other poems and prose, by seeing that the weary Bohemian's good qualities were not interred with his bones.

Dear Judas and Other Poems appeared in 1929. In addition to the title-poem, a dramatic passion-play of the Crucifixion, there is a long Carmel narrative, "The Loving Shepherdess," and a few shorter verses. (pp. 39-46)

These poems suffer in contrast with those in the preceding volume. Jeffers' Jesus is a continuation of the madly possessive Barclay—both serving as symbols for the poet's belief that religions derive from a "private impurity" in their founder. "Dear Judas," as well as the earlier "The Tower Beyond Tragedy," suffers by not having the Carmel coast as setting.

"The Loving Shepherdess" is more successful. That other keeper of sheep, Clare Walker, tender with all creatures, is a new addition to Jeffers' band of tragic protagonists. With child, the birth of which will mean her death, she wanders the coast from below Point Sur, past Point Lobos and up the Carmel River valley to the far San Joaquin, passing in turn settings which evoke memories of Barclay, Cawdor and Tamar Cauldwell. It is a simple, moving tale, and, with the exception of an interpolated astro-physical picture of the universe, simply told. Most of the action passes in retrospect, as Clare Walker recounts to a friendly vaquero the events which

have led to her tragic predicament. It is a tale of pity rather than of terror.

Jeffers' next book appeared in a limited edition in 1931: *Descent to the Dead,* sixteen short poems, written in Great Britain and Ireland. This is the fruit of the poet's 1929 trip; and, in a way, it is Una Jeffers' book, for she induced her husband to go to the British Isles, declaring that she would show him there abundant material for poetry.

I find the chief interest of these verses to be a wealth of local color and Celtic lore. Jeffers' *genius loci* is transferred from Carmel to County Antrim with such success that one who knows Ireland wrote of these poems, "No living Irish poet, not Yeats himself, could have made them more authentic. The Irish weather is in these poems, the black stones and the gray waters, and the dead that live."

The poet found the lands of his ancestors teeming with ghosts, and was fascinated by the many cairns, cromlechs and dolmens scattered over the Isles. The steep unconsciousness of the earth is deified by Jeffers, and death, which permits suffering flesh to dissolve into the matrix, is praised in stately verse.

Thurso's Landing and Other Poems was published in 1932. ["Thurso's Landing"] is, in its intensity and relative objectiveness, on the same high level set by "Cawdor"; and it continues the strain of humanism which appeared in that poem and in "The Loving Shepherdess." The poet seems to have less need to express, as he often does in the earlier narratives, his own philosophy through puppet-like characters. (pp. 47-8)

The title-poem of *Give Your Heart to the Hawks and Other Poems* (1933) is a tragic narrative of the Carmel coast. A robust tale of adultery, fratricide and suicide—crime and self-punishment—it is also a study of the morbid psychology of a strong man driven half-mad by remorse for the murder of his brother.

With "Cawdor" and "Thurso's Landing," "Give Your Heart to the Hawks" forms a trilogy: all three tragedies portray ruthlessly, among other things, the downfall of strong-willed men, seduced by the desires of passionate, equally strong-willed women. And ever present as background for the human drama is inhuman Nature, vast, inscrutable and beautiful, the sky, the hills, the ocean, all of which Jeffers worships, beyond humanity, as "part of the great and timeless excellence of things."

This last volume also contains two shorter coastal narratives, a few lyrics, the poems from *Descent to the Dead,* and a Greek narrative, "At the Fall of an Age," of which the poet writes: "The story of Achilles rising from the dead for love of Helen is well enough known. That of Polyxo's vengeance may be less familiar; it can be found in Pausanias' *Description of Greece,* explaining the Rhodian worship of Helen as Dendritis, the tree-goddess." These shorter poems are progressively concerned with the death-and-resurrection theme.

Solstice and Other Poems (1935) has for title-poem a thoroughly modern version of the Greek legend of Medea. The heroine, Madrone Bothwell, is one of the poet's typical untamed coastal women. Whereas the murderess Medea fled in a dragon-drawn chariot, Madrone, after cutting her children's throats to keep them from being taken from her by a court order, makes her escape driving her own automobile.

"At the Birth of an Age," the longest poem in the book, is derived from the closing chapters of the Nibelung Saga. Jeffers believes that the seeds of this age—of which we are now reaping the poisoned harvest—were sown when oriental Christianity tamed the western barbarians and the Gothic cathedrals were flung skyward. He has wrongly been called an escapist. It is rather his very preoccupation with the present which from time to time leads him back to a poetic study of our origins. (pp. 48-50)

Such Counsels You Gave to Me and Other Poems (1937) is not highly lyrical. Nearly all of the twenty-two shorter poems seek to clarify and justify Jeffers' aloofness from the various schools of economic and social thought which the prolonged and world-wide depression brought into prominence. They form a continuous *apology* for his refusal to align himself with any group movement. (p. 50)

Jeffers is blamed by the radicals for having no economic panacea to offer. That is not his mission, and he knows it. He has shed the illusions of some of the younger men who believe that a world-wide communist state is the only remedy for impending race suicide. He should be regarded not as a savior but as a seer. Poets of less character climb the ivory tower, flee into the past, or magnify the trivial fugitive mood. It was no coincidence that during the year 1937 the three American poets who are perhaps most representative of our time gave warning in their books of imminent social disaster—Jeffers in **"Such Counsels You Gave to Me,"** Millay in *Conversation at Midnight,* and MacLeish in *The Fall of the City.*

"Such Counsels You Gave to Me" is a typical Jeffersian modernization of that wonderful Scotch ballad *Edward,* which has long been one of the poet's favorites. In making his protagonist a medical student Jeffers creates an ideal opportunity for the transformation of biological data into poetry. (p. 51)

The volume of *Selected Poetry* which was published in 1938 is prefaced by an essay in which Jeffers speaks of three principles which underlie his work: a reclamation of some of the power and reality being surrendered by modern poetry to prose; a concern with "permanent things and the permanent aspects of life . . . poetry must deal with things that a reader two thousand years away could understand and be moved by"; a decision not to tell lies in verse—"not to feign any emotion that I did not feel; not to pretend to believe in optimism or pessimism, or unreversible progress; not to say anything because it was popular, or generally accepted, or fashionable in intellectual circles, unless I myself believed in it; and not to believe easily."

Thus, in summary, Robinson Jeffers' work may be divided into three periods: (1) Early love-lyrics; (2) Idealistic poems of early manhood in praise of rural life and in worship of beauty in nature; (3) Post-war poems of full maturity, which treat sex frankly in regional narratives, and draw upon science, history, nature, and contemporary events for material. The war bred in Jeffers an acute sense of the painful tragedy of existence, but as he leaves the struggle behind in memory, he regains, in place of pre-war idealism, a grave, detached sympathy for humanity. His mature work is a skilful blending of the familiar and exalted, which suits the changed temper of a new day that is repelled by mere heroics yet craves a lift above realism. (p. 52)

Lawrence Clark Powell, in his Robinson Jeffers:

The Man and His Work, *revised edition, San Pasqual Press, 1940, 222 p.*

AMOS N. WILDER

The satisfaction that men take in evidences of the life of nature and especially in its power, and above all in surpassing manifestations of that power, is one of the perennial roots of religion. If it has been the ground of world-wide primitive religion, or one of its grounds, we may be sure that it reappears today among sophisticated minds. And this especially where such minds turn from habits of intellectualism or mechanism to rediscover vital moods. (p. 141)

It is some such sense of the greater and more elemental forces of nature which supplies one of the most powerful attractions in the work of Robinson Jeffers. . . . [It] is in the elemental and untamed in nature that he finds the clues of salvation, of what lies behind and before the human consciousness.

Here, then, he rejoins the tendency . . . to seek out and beyond the human for a solution, and to find the symbols for this in those apparitions of nature that are most alien. . . . One may not speak finally about any particular credo of this poet. There is occasional contradiction of his themes, but the ones we stress will be found to recur.

Apart from the lyrics the work of Jeffers consists of narrative poems of some length written in a Whitmanesque line presenting dramas or rather melodramas of more than usually violent and repellent character. Often the characterization and action is cloudily presented and the style loose, but in the best poems, **"Roan Stallion," "The Tower Beyond Tragedy," "Cawdor," "Give Your Heart to the Hawks,"** these become sharper and more powerful, and one recognizes in any case that the poems are not to be judged first of all as narratives. (pp. 142-43)

The literary interest of the poems is comparatively minor. It comes out occasionally in the eloquent passages on nature or comparing nature and man, or in the occasional lyric philosophy, or in the powerful utterances of remorse and alienation. But the chief interest of the work is its philosophical attitude and for this purpose much is of interest which is poor literature. The case is much the same with D. H. Lawrence, not to say Walt Whitman, though the credos are different. The question is asked, Why should a person with an allegedly "normal" view of life be interested in the view presented by Jeffers? The only answer can be that whole races of men have thought and felt similarly, that many of our own time undoubtedly have hauntings of this kind, and that nothing human is alien to us. Moreover if we would change such a world view we must understand it.

The reason for the repellent themes of crime and incest is found stated in a passage from **"Roan Stallion."** It is indicated that revelation and clues of the superman come not from the usual and conventional experiences but from the exceptional and rebellious. We are reminded of Rimbaud's search for illumination, and can recognize a kind of travesty of the myth of Prometheus or the doctrine of the Cross. . . . (pp. 144-45)

The theme is that man has a best chance often to be stung awake by experiences that force him beyond himself. To create situations that present this kind of possibility Jeffers recurs to the drastic experiences of unnatural crime, incest or matricide, and to their consequences of remorse and the struggle with remorse. Only so does he come to the frontiers of the nonhuman, realizing the insignificance of man, reason, conscience and law. He apparently has an acute sense of the horrible sufferings that can be occasioned by blame, by the sense of guilt, and he would relieve men of that. . . .

Jeffers gets his sense of the comparative inconsequence of man particularly from the contrast with nature to which we have referred. Living in his stone tower over Monterey Bay he has before him the Pacific Ocean, on which, as he says, a thousand-mile hurricane is only a shadow. About him are the crags of the shore and behind him the austere granite ranges. (p. 146)

But men are not only insignificant, they are corrupt. Despite the occasions when a doctrine of moral equivalence appears to be taught, those that argue original sin will find their testimony here as in other of the new poets. The human heart is vile, the human mind is a spider weaving treacheries. Man has corrupted himself in his societies, in his taboos and in his laws. . . .

Thus for every reason death or the discovery of the sense of death in nature is to be desired. It is to life as "heaven over deep hell." Who once being dead would rise again? . . .

The positive teaching of Jeffers offers an escape for man from this condition into a nihilist Nirvana—a return through the original fountain. Nature is only a symbol for that which is not consciousness, not mind, not man. We are . . . on the ground of the Upanishads in the aspect described. The Sierras and the stars and prehistoric cromlechs of Ireland and the life of the eagle have signified to him that there is an "unstated being" in the universe that is everything that man is not. (p. 147)

Jeffers' conception is represented very often in terms of the life of wild creatures as well as of inanimate nature. . . . The mystery of life is often felt with peculiar force in these creatures that live, but that live in ways so alien to men and often so independently of men. This thought is stressed in the speech of God in the climax of the Book of Job, to bring home to him that "the Eternal hath his own purposes" and that existence has other concerns than human. Of course in the Book of Job important complementary attributes of Deity are assumed which give a totally different final picture of him.

But Jeffers not only recurs again and again to these creatures; he seems to have a perverse interest in showing them under torture. A deer caught in barbed wire, a rabbit aflame from the prairie fire, lobsters cooking alive, a wounded Cooper's hawk fighting a gamecock to death, a coyote caught in two steel traps at once so that it cannot stand or lie, a yearling colt swollen with the sting of a rattler—we are apt to say masochism or sadism and satisfy ourselves with that. There is probably no one writing today that is so cruel, with the possible exception of Faulkner. But Jeffers is at least consistent. For his conception of life is of a prodigiously beautiful force that makes its way through shining and splendid creations (man apart), but bleeds as it goes. . . . It is never safe to pin this writer down to a given sentiment as is so unjustly done. . . . But it can be concluded that there is a disgust with man and an exaltation of that which is beyond life which leaves him "numb to the intricacies of human feeling," which as [Yvor] Winters says is a limitation of all mystical poetry. The person who is concerned with ethical and personal values will query

as to the conditions that lead our contemporaries to such misanthropy. (pp. 148-49, 151)

Amos N. Wilder, "The Nihilism of Mr. Robinson Jeffers," in his The Spiritual Aspects of the New Poetry, *Harper & Brothers Publishers, 1940, pp. 141-52.*

ROBERT GORHAM DAVIS

[Jeffers] represents to a far more extreme degree than Pound the human moral failures, the arrogance, the egotism, the limitation of intelligence, the youthful hardness that prevent a genuine imaginative development. Jeffers uses poetry simply to express an attitude; therefore the attitude has never changed. In Jeffers' successive works we have no sense of the way in which a poem, a true poem, once created, becomes a fact, a reality, and consequently falls into dynamic relationship not only with other existing poems, but with the kind of actual events it refers to, the ideas it affirms or denies, and with privacies of the poet's conscious and unconscious mind. These privacies the poem not so much expresses as shapes into a meaningful combination which is a discovery, and a point of departure for new discoveries. The direction of future discovery is determined by the tensions, the coherences and incompatibilities which the preceding poems, by their very existence, have brought into being for the poet. This is the experimental sequence which explains the creative development of most of the major writers.

Jeffers, however, in his youth, accepting both the cosmos of nineteenth century materialism and the theological warning of the human consequences of such an acceptance, could get out of his dilemma only by rejecting human values and human history in favor of the hawks and the hills. He was still a part of humanity and history, though, and wrote about them. Moreover, he remembered that Nietzsche said, "The poets? The poets lie too much," and he determined to tell the truth. This did not mean a constant search for truth, in which one can go only a little way in a lifetime, but speaking the truth he thought he already had. He had rejected the historic, philosophic or religious values by which his truths could be measured, modified or developed. And so they degenerated into mere reflexes, into the truths of the *Chicago Tribune*, into something far uglier, far grosser politically than the truths of Ezra Pound. Without tensions and pressures to form them, the verses are lax in poetic line and journalistic in phrasing. Above all, since Jeffers has separated man from nature and himself from society, truth does not include for him the fact that his attitudes, like the attitudes of other men, have a determining social and psychological history. His tales of murder, torture, necrophilism and incest sound more and more like sexual fantasies which have ceased to excite because of too unvaried repetition. Nothing could be more wearily, uncreatively determined than the image of "Vere Harnish / Kneeling against the bed beside her mother's half-naked body, pumping a pen-knife into it." Marx and Freud, wherever their insights have been separated from their dogmas, have freed the younger poets from this kind of fatuity and self-betrayal. They are far better acquainted with the complexities of truth, and more humble in its presence. (pp. 1222-24)

Robert Gorham Davis, "Pound, Jeffers, and Others," in Partisan Review, *Vol. XV, No. 11, November, 1948, pp. 1219-25.*

HENRY STEELE COMMAGER

Finding their intelligence enslaved," wrote George Santayana in that remarkable essay on the "Intellectual Temper of the Age" which indicted alike evolution and pragmatism, determinism and irrationalism,

> our contemporaries supposed that intelligence is essentially servile; instead of freeing it, they try to elude it. Not free enough themselves morally . . . they cannot think of rising to a detached contemplation of earthly things, and of life itself and evolution; they revert rather to sensibility, and seek some by-path of instinct or dramatic sympathy in which to wander. Having no stomach for the ultimate, they borrow themselves downwards towards the primitive.

It was a just indictment of the irrationalists and the primitivists, of that whole school of thought and emotion represented variously by Sherwood Anderson and Ernest Hemingway, Gertrude Stein and Ezra Pound, Henry Adams and Robinson Jeffers. (p. 120)

The sources of the new irrationality were largely modern and exclusively European, and it is suggestive that where American literature was most derivative it was least articulate and where it was least mature it was most decadent. It owed something to the French—to the Symbolist poets, Mallarmé, Verlaine, Rimbaud, Valéry, Laforgue, and Paul Fort, to critics like Rémy de Gourmont and philosophers like Henri Bergson with his apotheosis of the *élan vital*, to novelists like André Gide and, above all, Marcel Proust. It owed more to Freud of Vienna and Jung of Zurich and the Russian Pavlov who made the western world not only conscious but self-conscious of the subconscious. It owed most of all—doubtless through the accident of language—to the philosophers, poets, and novelists from the British Isles: pioneers in the scientific study of the psychology of sex like Edward Carpenter and the magisterial Havelock Ellis; novelists like the indefatigable Dorothy Richardson and the brilliant Aldous Huxley and the brooding D. H. Lawrence and Virginia Woolf, not only practitioner but critic; the Irish experimentalists, William Butler Yeats and George Moore and Oscar Wilde and, above all, James Joyce, most successful of all those who floated their literary barks down the stream of consciousness.

What were the stigmata—for we can scarcely use the term principles for a persuasion that rejected the very concept of principle—of the new school? First, the rejection—on pseudoscientific grounds—of reason, meaning, normality, morality, continuity, and coherence, the rejection of civilization itself as eccentric and decadent. Second, a passionate interest in the subconscious and the unconscious and an enthusiasm for emotion rather than thought, instinct rather than reason, anarchy rather than discipline. Third, an obsession with sex, especially in its abnormal manifestations, as the most powerful and pervasive of all the instincts and the interpretation of all conduct in terms of sex. Fourth, a weakness for the primitive, for primitive people such as Africans, Indians, peasants, and children, for primitive emotions and activities—eating, drinking, sleeping, fighting, making love—and closely connected with this a predilection for violence in all forms. Fifth, the unqualified repudiation of all orthodox moral standards, all conformities and conventions, and acquiescence in a perverse amorality in which submission to instincts became the highest virtue. And, finally, the formulation of a new language and a new grammar to express more faithfully the fitful impulses emanating from the subconscious. (pp. 121-22)

The cult of irrationality was, from the beginning, doomed to self-destruction, for no literature built upon the quagmire of futility can survive. The attack upon reason, which flourished so furiously in the second and third decades of the [twentieth] century, was designed to pronounce the ultimate degradation of man—a degradation which reduced man, in the end, to gibbering. It carried to logical conclusion the findings of the naturalists and the determinists and revealed, more dramatically than any other inquiry, the bankruptcy of determinism. It was nihilism, but it was nihilism which proved its impotence by its very proclamation. It was the palpable insincerity of the revolt against reason which was, in the end, its most encouraging feature, for revolt is an act of will—even of free will—and those writers who engaged in it confess their inconsistency. They confess faith in their own reason by the act of composition, social consciousness by their appeal for a hearing, and recognition of a moral order by the establishment of standards, however eccentric, and the insistence upon values, however esoteric.

Robinson Jeffers is peculiarly the victim of this paradox, though his statement of it is more eloquent and more dignified than that of most of the irrationalists, as his logic—or his illogic—is more thorough. The most uncompromisingly scientific of the literary spokesmen of determinism, Jeffers is, at the same time, the most romantic. Trained to medicine, familiar with psychiatry, biology, geology, and physics, living, by choice, close to nature and acknowledging no obligation but to nature, his affluent poetry is a scientific as well as a philosophical commentary on the life of man.

So completely does nature fill his poetic vision that man is scarcely admitted even as a part of nature. The men and women who infect his pages are so vile and perverse that they seem to contaminate nature herself. For aeons nature did not know man, and in a short time she will forget the stain he has put upon her. . . . For man is born to pain, as are all living things, but man alone adds moral depravity to physical torture: human beings alone are inhuman. (pp. 128-29)

From *Tamar* to *The Double Axe* Jeffers spreads before us such a pageant of violence, cruelty, bloodshed, depravity, and perversion as we have not heretofore encountered in our literature—not even in Faulkner or Caldwell. He violates our innocence and confounds our philosophy with a picture of unmitigated evil, or of evil mitigated only by endurance. Life is one long agony of pain, interrupted by pleasure that is fleeting and ecstasy that turns upon us and wounds us. . . . Only Nature is worthy of our contemplation, for only Nature has beauty and endurance. . . . The mountains, the sea, granite boulders, the redwood and the cypress trees, the eagle and the hawk—give your heart to these, says Jeffers, but not to men. (pp. 129-30)

What we have here, to be sure, is a scientific version of the Christian view where every prospect pleases and only man is vile. And for all his desperate repudiation of orthodox religion, there is a strain of religious mysticism in Jeffers. He, too, lifts up his eyes unto the hills from whence cometh his help; he confesses, on behalf of ruined man, that we have followed too much the devices and desires of our own hearts and there is no health in us. The mortal flaw, the fatal stain, is introversion—"man regarding man exclusively, founding his values, desires, his picture of the universe, all on his own humanity." . . . And it is as a symbol of this suicidal introversion that he uses incest again and again.

Yet for all his scientific and psychiatric vocabulary, Jeffers lingers in the romantic tradition, closer to Wordsworth and Arnold than to Haeckel or even to Freud and Jung, whose books, we are assured, adorn his shelves. What could be more romantic than this passion for the mountains and the sea and for granite boulders? For to impartial nature the loftiest peak of the Sierras is no nobler than a ditch, or the heaving Pacific than a stagnant pool, and in the long catalogue of time Hawk Tower will have no more permanence than a soap bubble. So, too, with the habit of ascribing dignity and nobility to birds and beasts; the concepts themselves are but tributes to man. Mankind, says Jeffers, has turned inward, and is corrupt. But what more shameless conceit than to ascribe human values to the works of nature, what more extreme introversion than to subject the universe to man's secular judgment?

Romantic though he is, Jeffers does not permit himself the recourse of earlier romantics, of Shelley whom he imitates or Arnold whom he recalls. There is no room in his cosmic philosophy either for Promethean defiance or for escape. Death alone can solace man, death and annihilation and the assurance that this is the fortunate destiny of all living things. (pp. 130-31)

This is nihilism, and it is a logical conclusion to scientific determinism, its consistency flawed only by the subjective view of nature that permeates every line and—it must be added—by the particular inspiration for the outbursts of despair. Thus, apropos the American participation in the second World War—Nazi guilt gave him no concern—Jeffers tells us that

> . . . the whole human race ought to be scrapped
> and is on the way to it; ground like fish-meal for
> soil-food.
> What does the vast and rushing drama of the uni-
> verse, seas, rocks, condor-winged storms, icy-
> fiery galaxies,
> The flaming and whirling universe like a handful of
> gems falling down a dark well,
> Want clowns for?
>   (**"The Inhumanist,"** *The Double Axe*)

With Jeffers, the philosophical reaction to the world of science opened up first by Darwin came full circle. Man, the last born of nature's long travail, was seen not as her chiefest glory but as her most cruel blunder, because having endowed man with the critical faculty, she enabled him to realize the futility and horror of his existence. (pp. 131-32)

> *Henry Steele Commager, "The Cult of the Irratio-
> nal," in his* The American Mind: An Interpretation
> of American Thought and Character since the
> 1880's, *Yale University Press, 1950, pp. 120-40.*

MERCEDES CUNNINGHAM MONJIAN

Radcliffe Squires suggests indirectly [in his book *The Loyalties of Robinson Jeffers*] that Jeffers is more philosopher than poet when he says that the present need in critically examining Jeffers' narratives centers "in their philosophical texture, in the relationship of idea to idea rather than the relationship of word to word, nuance to nuance" [see *CLC*, Vol. 11]. If this is so, and this essay agrees that it is, Jeffers' philosophy has greater potential significance than his expression. Of the

critical materials read for this essay, very few emphasized Jeffers' methods. They concentrated on what his belief is, on the symbols, and on the conflicts that emerge from his poetry. Of course, the nuances are not baffling, since the poetry is not built upon shadings and complexities of diction, and thus need less critical examination for understanding. Jeffers reverses the usual poetic relationship of words to ideas, using his beliefs about man and the world as the substance of his poetry. The memorable lines from a Jeffers' poem are often not dependent upon felicity of language, imagery, or rhythmic effects, but on a conceptual statement that stands out boldly. . . . His philosophy seems to encompass him with such force that he neglects to enhance it with poetic form, resorting to colloquialisms . . . which jar us with their slangy laxness; however, if we do not remember the . . . words as poetry, we will not easily forget their meaning as an assertion in Jeffers' creed. I do not intend to offer for comparison the touchstones of Matthew Arnold, but when most of us think of the lines that have been significant to us for their poetic glitter, they often have no message for us except the beauty of their words in combination. On the other hand, . . . going to Shelley (Shelley's influence on Jeffers as a young man has been noted), who believes that the poet's function is to be a legislator of laws and philosophy, we cannot deny this right to Jeffers any more than we can to Sophocles. The point here is that the philosophy sometimes lacks valid poetic expression which leaves the message, rather than the essence, in predominance.

In the early narratives, which gave him recognition as a world poet, going beyond Aeschylus, Euripides, Sophocles in [what Louis Adamic in his *Robinson Jeffers: A Portrait* termed] "style and form as well as in the dreadfulness of his themes," Jeffers worked to heighten his philosophy with magnificence of language. The results are explicit in a belief and simultaneously manifest in poetic sound and imagery:

>   Humanity is
>   the start of the race; I say
> Humanity is the mould to break away from, the
>   crust to break through, the coal to break into
>   fire,
> The atom to be split.

It is not surprising that these lines [from **"Roan Stallion"**] appear in so many critical essays about Jeffers, not only because they are the beginnings of his creed, but because they have grandeur. But when a poet spends hundreds of lines in reinforcing one idea, it is conceivable that many of the succeeding lines will not have the inspirational vigor of the first even though the philosophy gains in momentum. In *Poets at Work,* a book dealing with the process of poetic creation, Donald Stauffer mentions one way a poet works toward his goal as a "continuous struggle to strip off rhetoric" for economy, as opposed to extravagance. This observation could apply to one of Jeffers' shortcomings, his inclination to over-write. When this happens, we are conscious of redundancy and a lack of discipline that channels and focuses both experience and language into a unique poetic fusion. Such a tendency seems to be due to the unyielding grip Jeffers' philosophy has upon him, subjecting his poetry to idea and to an urgency to be heard and heeded. If this is true, then Jeffers may rightfully be seen as a poet dominated by his philosophy.

Then what is our response to this philosophic poetry? Are we swayed through Jeffers' eloquent execution to a sympathetic understanding of his doctrine? Are we convinced, at least during the time of reading, that Jeffers' conception of how to conquer humanity's dilemma is so artistically satisfying that it is also intellectually and emotionally compatible? These responses would seem to be the test of the success of much of this poetry that is grounded solidly in an effort to instruct. Inhumanism, like other disillusioned philosophies, is aimed at freeing man from myths, superstitions, the fear of death, and at giving him a code by which to live. Similar attempts to disenchant man are evidenced as early as "The Song of the Harper," an anonymous poem written by an Egyptian more than 1600 years before Ecclesiastes, another disillusioned work trying to enlighten man. The *Rubaiyat* by Omar Khayyam follows in this tradition nine hundred years later; in the eighteenth century Voltaire used biting satire to project his bleak message in *Candide.* So we are reminded that many authors have succeeded in making their cheerless philosophies felt and remembered because their artistic performances have qualities to insure lasting appreciation. Then it follows that Jeffers' ultimate achievement rests on his ability to enamour us through his poetry, regardless of the antipathy or affinity we may feel toward the philosophy. When the philosophy becomes the major issue . . . without adequate poetic support, we may react indifferently to what he says if we cannot agree with the concept. (pp. 79-83)

Jeffers chose tragedy as the genre preferred by him. As he explains in Lawrence C. Powell's book [*Robinson Jeffers: The Man and His Work*], it is most often selected by the poets "because pain, being more intense than pleasure produces stronger emotions." All of his narratives can aptly be called tragedy, as opposed to comedy, if only for the reason that they all end in death and destruction. Yet death and destruction can produce merely the terrible and the shocking if they do not perform an artistic function. Since many of Jeffers' tragedies are rooted in Greek tragedy, it seems evident that he admires these great plays from which Aristotle made his observations. And therefore it seems justifiable to apply some of Aristotle's derived principles to the dramatic narratives. Considering character and its necessary function in true tragedy, Aristotle says that "Tragedy is an imitation of persons who are above the common level," who should be "true to life and yet more beautiful." And he concludes with, "The poet, in representing men who are irascible or indolent, or have other defects of character, should preserve the type and yet ennoble it." On Aristotelian terms Jeffers does not succeed. His one-sided personalities, which do not develop with the story, seem more like flat types or abstractions of passions, so unreal do they appear against the stark realism of their environment. Their unreality makes it difficult for us to identify ourselves with these characters so that pity and fear result.

When Fayne Fraser climbs the cliff from burying her suicide-husband, we do not vibrate to the great strength of a noble woman bearing her sorrow, because her inhumanism should save her from experiencing a deep grief for the husband upon whom she brought disaster. She, herself, is beyond pity, because we have been conditioned to know that she will survive as the bitter victor in any situation. When Howard Howren goes back to take the punishment for murdering his father because "There are certain duties / Even for . . . what did you say? . . . modern man," we do not feel relief that the protagonist is fulfilling his duty by possible sacrifice of his life, because he had never valued life highly, contemplating suicide from the beginning. Margrave's inhumanism parallels Raskolnikov's superman attitude in *Crime and Punishment*

only in the initial stage, for while the young Russian suffers and repents so that at the novel's end he shines forth a finer-edged human being, Margrave doggedly believes in his murder's justification until he hangs himself to spare himself.

If we measure the narratives' impacts by the fear and pity they arouse, we find a certain lack. It is hard for us to fear because of the intangible quality of these people. It is hard to experience a deep pity because the characters are alien to us, seldom pausing to wrestle with a moral decision. And the hoped-for katharsis, the cleansing and purifying of mind and emotion that is essential to Aristotle's final definition of tragedy, is only vaguely produced. Denying the importance of plot in *Oedipus Rex* and the *Agamemnon* series, Jeffers writes . . . , "What makes them noble is the poetry, the poetry and the beautiful shapes of the plays, and the extreme violence born of extreme passion." Jeffers says nothing about characters contributing their nobility to the plays. He is conscious, however, of the added attraction of morally responsible characters when he says of **"Thurso's Landing"** that it "seems to me to be the best thing I have written . . . the persons seem to me to be a little more conscious of the moral implications of what they do." In a review of Jeffers' last book [*Hungerfield and Other Poems*] Horace Gregory writes that **"The Cretan Woman"** is more successful than **"Hungerfield"** in which the figures "are less heroic, and of a nearly sub-human world." But it is this sub-human world in which Jeffers has specialized from the beginning, this world of passion without control, of supernatural communings with spirits, of hopelessness and sickness, of misery for the living. The characters involved are sucked under by the dreadfulness of their fate, seldom resisting for the good cause, or for abstract virtue. They are not tragic if we are looking for the element of nobility in them.

But one point relating to Jeffers' intention should be mentioned here: his statement about the great poet's concern being to "habitually address" future audiences. Those audiences may have an entirely different attitude toward this poetry. If Jeffers is writing toward a time in which he believes inhumanistic values will have replaced our present ethics, it is conceivable that his characterizations would receive greater sympathy—if sympathy is still permitted—than we can extend. The characters' merits would depend on their ability to reject such human "frailties" as grief, compassion toward mankind, sacrifice of one for another. Under this naturistic and mechanistic banner, Jeffers' radicalism would prevail as the new vision of temperance, and his characters would emerge as noble figures, or as Jeffers would prefer, realistic ones, at least. He is not a flatterer of humanity, as we have seen, and disparages the illusory ideals others have attempted to bestow upon it. . . . In this same vein Jeffers, addressing himself in **"Soliloquy,"** says:

> August and laurelled have been content to speak
>   for an age, and the ages that follow
> Respect them for that pious fidelity;
> But you have disfeatured time for timelessness.
> They had heroes for companions, beautiful youths
>   to dream of, rose-marble-fingered
> Women shed light down the great lines;
> But you have invoked the slime in the skull,
> The lymph in the vessels.

So we must not mistake the fact that Jeffers is unaware of what he has done or what he hopes to accomplish: "to disgust and shock," in order "to turn humanity outward from its obsession" [**"Fourth Act"**]. Even though we know Jeffers' intention, in trying to make a critical observation about the dramatic poems, we have only the critical tools of this age with which to work. And we are still under the impression that all art accomplishes its function only when it creates beauty and order from disunity or chaos. Beauty and order are hard to perceive in Jeffers' characters as they fulfill their place in the narratives.

Although the defective characters contribute to a dissatisfaction with the truly tragic quality of the narratives, there are other factors to be considered, structure and mood being two I shall touch on here. Herbert Read tells us [in his essay "The Structure of a Poem"] that the distinction between the major and minor poet is in their ability to write a long poem successfully. The ideal, as he conceives it, is a structure which carries the poet on from word to word, line to line, stanza to stanza, and book to book. Otherwise, a poem loses its original inspiration. When inspiration lags, either of two effects may occur. Either the "pure poetry" overwhelms the forward motion, so that we are constantly looking for threads to hold the poem together, or the story usurps the poetry with over-emphasis on what Mr. Read calls "prose padding." Jeffers does not write much "pure poetry"; he seems to be prompted mainly by the action of the poems which carries him along on the circuit of inspiration. When the action rises to one great climax, falling rapidly afterwards, we have a classic development, as in **"Roan Stallion."** The unity of the style, rhythm, and structure produces its most dramatic impact so that the reader does not wander from its forward-moving energy until the last lines are read. Whatever we may personally think of California, we have been brought close to understanding her through the poetic experience. When themes as desperate as Jeffers' are presented, they need concentrated power of expression to sustain the reader to the ending lines. This is especially true in some of the longer poems which are treated in chapters that linger and digress at the expense of forward continuity.

This kind of amorphous structure is used for such poems as **"Thurso's Landing"** and *The Women at Point Sur.* When these digressions, or series of small climactic actions, occur, Jeffers' readers have time to pause and consider whether they can further pursue the suffering and self-inflicted agonies. Conversation, such as "Nobody else / Seems to have kept them down in my absences" [from **"Thurso's Landing"**], frequently interrupts, and again we lose the essence of poetry. Such "prose padding" accounts for much of the narratives' lengths, which means that we continue reading for meaning and plot rather than for poetic effects. Nor can rhythm add much to the intensification of the material, since it, also, is of a nebulous nature. So the structural unity is often disrupted, and we step into the bordering realm of prose. This criticism can be applied to many long poems, other than Jeffers', because it is so difficult for poets to sustain images and action over many pages. Yet it is a fault, since [according to A.E. Housman] verse can be "superior to prose only in the comeliness of that form itself, and the superior terseness which usually goes along with it."

If complete unity of structure seems to be lacking in the narratives, unity of mood and atmosphere does not. Here Jeffers is a master. From the first to the last lines we are immersed in a tragic world, dream-laden with violence and anguish. As Dostoievski depicts a gray Russian world, Jeffers draws his with blood-images against fogs and treacherous promontories. Only occasionally are we allowed a glimpse of a happy,

normal way of living. Even in the kitchens, where warmth and family love are usual conventions, Jeffers uses attempted suicide and book-burning to overcome any presupposed idea about the friendly family hearth. The background of raging nature, together with the distorted lives of the characters merge in turbulent images. All are underscored by the heavy, sometimes ponderous meter that supplies the muffled rhythm. Few readers of Jeffers can forget the oppressive mood he generates. It is a mood of black romanticism which brings into focus the doctrine as well as the dourness of tone, and we may be convinced, as Jeffers wants us to be, that life needs a reevaluation if things are really so bad. Through this depressing convergence of image, setting, subject, and tone, Jeffers comes closest to achieving his purpose, and we begin to believe [as Jeffers states in **"Carmel Point"**] that "We must uncenter our minds from ourselves" to escape catastrophe. If we could feel a strong sympathy toward the characters and could be carried forward on a highly stabilized plane of poetic expression, Jeffers, through his able creation of mood, could doubtless enmesh us in his way of thinking.

Remaining to consider are the short poems, the psalms to nature, in which the poet praises the strength, the endurance, the perennial beauty of his land. These are the poems which may survive, if we were to take a long-range view, long after the narratives have been forgotten. Jeffers' voice is raised in tribute to the cypresses, granite, the night, the sea, and the "Earnest elements of nature." His philosophy in these poems becomes secondary to the language and the imagery which use nature as a mirror to reflect more intensely our own blemishes. Robert Penn Warren believes that his short poems "tend to be fragmentary comments, gnomic utterances without adequate context." Many do lack sufficient form; they fall short of a complete unity. But this critic's statement is not applicable to all. Just because a poem is not built around a metaphysical conceit or is without a key metaphor to guide its form are not reasons why it is not a good poem. These short poems of Jeffers are simple and forthright, charged with electric word-power, and could speak to generations to come as they could to our early civilizations. They are primitive in their expression, but so is "The Song of Deborah," *The Bhagavad-Gita,* and the Psalms. The following poem [**"To the Stone-Cutters"**] is selected as an example of one of Jeffers' poems which has attained and should continue to maintain distinction. Its language grinds and chips like the chisel; "splits," "Fall down," "Scale," "wear," "blotted out," "die," "blacken" press in until no life is left. The motion is sweeping downward, and we are without hope until the rescuing "Yet" appears. Following the polar comparison between poet and stone-cutter, the tension is released and the poem ends on a wistful note of half-hearted consolation, even though a time limitation of a thousand years is the best the poet can offer:

> Stone-cutters fighting time with marble, you fore-
> defeated
> Challengers of oblivion
> Eat cynical earnings, knowing rock splits, records
> fall down,
> The square-limbed Roman letters
> Scale in the thaws, wear in the rain. The poet as
> well
> Builds his monument mockingly;
> For man will be blotted out, the blithe earth die, the
> brave sun
> Die blind and blacken to the heart:

> Yet stones have stood for a thousand years, and
>   pained thoughts found
> The honey of peace in old poems.

This poem, **"Night," "Hurt Hawks," "De Rerum Virtute,"
"Continent's End," "Granite and Cypress," "The Cruel Falcon,"** and many others are such poems, controlled, powerful, reverent. They not only adhere to Jeffers' three prerequisites for survival: permanence, nobility of poetry, and the avoidance of epoch confusions, they are more. They are little dramatic structures that transcend his philosophy of inhumanism and stand free of doctrine. They are artistic entities in themselves, not involvements in rhetoric and idea, only. In them Jeffers does not deviate from the tone, the imagery, the urgency of the narratives, but he is able to sustain his lyrical mood, without interruption, until the last line is read. This concentration, often dependent upon paradox ("bright power" and "dark peace," **"Granite and Cypress"**) is the central difference between the artistic quality of the short poems and the narratives. It is this kind of communication to which A.E. Housman has reference when he writes [in *The Name and Nature of Poetry*], "I think that to transfuse emotion—not to transmit thought but to set up in the reader's sense a vibration corresponding to what was felt by the writer—is the peculiar function of poetry." Because of the concentration, we are caught up in an emotional experience that surpasses the creed. The poem, itself, becomes the end rather than the means for writing.

If we could look ahead as Jeffers says the great poet must in **"Poetry, Gongorism, and a Thousand Years,"** we may perhaps find some of those poems listed above lending their "honey of peace" to the "pained thoughts" of those years. We may discover that Jeffers, like Lucretius, has gained new appreciation. Or we may find no trace of him except in tomes on the history of American Literature. Whatever the future holds for this poet, our own age is still awed by the magnificent talent and effort of a burdened mind struggling to free humanity from the shackles of an impoverished self-love, and the myths to which he believes it gave birth. (pp. 83-92)

Mercedes Cunningham Monjian, in his Robinson Jeffers: A Study in Inhumanism, *University of Pittsburgh Press, 1958, 103 p.*

HORACE GREGORY

The initial advantage of rereading Jeffers' poetry now is that it can be approached without the formulas of critical fashions ringing in one's ears. Since 1925 he has published more than fifteen books of verse—a quantity of poetry which resembles the production of his ancestors, the romantic poets of nineteenth-century Britain. Rereading his poems, one finds them falling into three divisions: the Southwestern narratives with their richness of California sea-sky-and-landscape; the shorter poems which are largely conversation pieces—for Jeffers is not a lyric poet—and a fine group of elegies, his *Descent to the Dead,* the result of a visit in 1929 to the British Isles; and the semidramatic poems inspired by Greek themes and overlaid with Nietzschean and twentieth-century philosophies.

It is best to begin when and where Jeffers' earlier reputation began; the time was 1925 and the place was New York; and credit for the publication of *Roan Stallion, Tamar, and Other Poems* should be given to James Rorty, a writer who met Jeffers during a stay in California and with selfless enthusiasm persuaded New York friends to read **"Tamar,"** to write about it, to make the presence of Jeffers known to New York publishers. Although Jeffers never shared the excitements and diversions of literary circles on the Atlantic Coast, the moment was prepared to receive his semi-Biblical, semi-Sophoclean American Southwestern narratives. Discussions of Steinach operations for restoring sexual vitality were in the air, and so were questions from Krafft-Ebing, Freud, and Jung; D. H. Lawrence's *The Rainbow* was in print as well as Sherwood Anderson's *Dark Laughter.* If a post World War I urban generation had not discovered sex, it had learned to talk loudly and almost endlessly about it. Nothing was easier than to apply cocktail conversations to Jeffers' **"Tamar"** and **"Roan Stallion,"** which at first reading—and particularly to those who lived in cities—held the same attractions as an invitation to a nudist colony on the Pacific Coast.

Yet it was not without self-critical discernment that Jeffers gave first place to **"Tamar"** when he prepared his *Selected Poetry* in 1937. For whatever reasons his public had accepted it twelve years earlier, at a time when he had passed the age of thirty-five, the poem has all the merits of a style that he had made his own. As early as 1912 he had paid for the printing of a first book, *Flagons and Apples;* in 1916 a second book, *Californians,* had been published . . . ; and neither, aside from the praise of a small group of friends, had received encouragement. His friendships, which included the long-sustained devotion of his wife, Una Call, also embraced the good will of George Sterling, who had known Ambrose Bierce, Joaquin Miller, and Jack London, and who was one of the few to see promise in Jeffers' early books of poems. Like Jeffers, who had been born in Pittsburgh in 1887, Sterling, a native of New York State, had become a converted Californian. Sterling's own verse had been inspired by the pages of *The Savoy* and *The Yellow Book* as well as by readings in Oscar Wilde and Ernest Dowson. "Poetry . . . ," he said, "must . . . cherish all the past embodiments of visionary beauty, such as the beings of classical mythology." Sterling's last work, shortly before his suicide in 1926, was a pamphlet written in praise of Jeffers. No doubt Jeffers had been made aware of the presence of evil through his wide readings, but it was through the loyal patronage of Sterling that he became an heir of "Bitter" Bierce. To the general reader, however, Jeffers' first two books offered little more than glimpses of a belated debt to Dante Gabriel Rossetti in *Flagons and Apples,* and a Wordsworthian manner, which included hints of pantheism, in *Californians.*

Before Jeffers met his wife and Sterling, he had an unusual education. He was the precocious son of a teacher of theology at Western Theological Seminary in Pittsburgh. His father taught him Greek, Latin, and Hebrew; and when the boy was five and six, took him on trips to Europe. For three years, between the ages of twelve and fifteen, his father sent him to boarding schools in Switzerland and Germany; and at fifteen, Jeffers entered the University of Western Pennsylvania. The next four years were spent in Occidental College and the Universities of Zurich and Southern California, and these years included studies in medicine and forestry. All this would be of no importance if it did not throw light on the individual ranges of Jeffers' poetry, his familiarity with Greek and Roman and Biblical themes, with German philosophy, with medical terms and semiscientific details, and—since he read French with facility—his possible knowledge of the writings of Sade. Certainly his education provided reasons for an affinity with Sterling, whose idea of poetry embraces, however vaguely, "beings of classical mythology." At the very least, Jeffers is a writer whose early years had prepared him for more than a regional view of the world and its affairs.

A second reading of **"Tamar"** reveals it as a Biblical story in Californian undress. Characters in Jeffers' Southwestern narratives, from **"Tamar"** to **"The Loving Shepherdess,"** from **"Give Your Heart to the Hawks"** to **"Hungerfield,"** are often lightly clothed and are subject to the wind, sun, and rain of Californian climate. Chapter 13 of the second book of Samuel is one source of Jeffers' parable, which contains the story of Amnon's love for his sister Tamar. Other associations taken from the two books of Samuel permeate the poem, for the sons of Samuel "walked not in his ways, but turned aside after lucre and took bribes, and perverted judgment," a statement which is appropriate to Jeffers' view of America and Western civilization. As a parable the poem acquires the force of a Calvinist sermon from an American pulpit, yet it also carries within it echoes of Nietzsche's speech of Silenus, "What is best of all is beyond your reach forever: not to be born, not to *be*, to be *nothing*," and behind these words Sophocles' remark, "Not to be born is best for man." In Tamar's words the echoes are clearly heard: "O God, I wish / I too had been born too soon and died with the eyes unopened. . . ." Jeffers also puts into the mouth of Tamar a remark which has its origins in the doctrines of Sade "we must keep sin pure / Or it will poison us, the grain of goodness in a sin is poison. / Old man, you have no conception / Of the freedom of purity." And as Tamar speaks she has given herself over to unchecked forces of evil. In Sade's novel *Justine*, his heroine is tortured because she fails to purge her taint of goodness; as the poem nears its end, the whipping of Tamar by her brother is the last love scene between them.

This is not to say that Jeffers by voicing echoes of Sade's doctrines had advanced them as examples for Californians to follow; it is rather that he has given the forces of evil a well-established voice of authority, but in doing so he has succeeded with such vehemence that he might be misunderstood by a careless reader. Even at this risk, he has also succeeded in giving the unleashed forces of hell refreshed reality. In his poem, the house of David, Tamar's father—and Tamar is the daughter of King David in the second book of Samuel—is destroyed by fire which in its first association creates a literal image of hell and, in its second, of the funeral pyres of the Romans.

So far I have mentioned only the principal elements of **"Tamar,"** its Californian setting, one of the sources of its story, and a few of the concepts which are made relevant to the retelling of the story—but these do not complete the list of associations that the poem brings to mind, for **"Tamar,"** beneath the surface of a swiftly moving plot, has a richness of detail which rivals the complex fabric of Elizabethan dramatic verse. In the Biblical story the seduction of Tamar by Amnon is scarcely more than an invitation to come to bed; in Jeffers' version the seduction scene has an Ovidian ring; a hidden stream, a pool tempts brother and sister; naked, they enter it and one recalls Ovid's stories of Narcissus and Echo, Hermaphroditus and Salmacis, and by association there is a particularly Roman touch, a glimpse of Phoebus' chariot wheel, from a window of David's house overlooking the Pacific. . . . (pp. 4-9)

It is this kind of richness that places **"Tamar"** among the major accomplishments in twentieth-century poetry. And what of the ghosts that haunt the house of David in

"Tamar"? They are very like the images of guilt that invade the darkened walls of Macbeth's castle. An idiot sets fire to David's house, and one thinks of the line " . . . a tale told by an idiot, full of sound and fury." In this instance, an idiot hastens the end of sound and fury.

How deliberate Jeffers was in making a highly individual combination of Californian locale, Biblical and Graeco-Roman themes, Elizabethan richness of detail, plus Nietzschean ethics and Calvinist denouements, it is impossible to say. The great probability is that, having a deeply felt desire to warn the world of the dangers of its involvements in world wars, Jeffers brought all the resources, conscious or hidden, of his imagination into play. To Jeffers, World War I was a warning of weaknesses inherent in a civilization that permitted mass murders and a situation that approached total war. War, by example, creates a precedent for violent action; and in **"Tamar"** that conclusion is shown by the desire of Tamar's brother to leave his father's house to go to war, not merely to escape the consequences of evil at home, but to plunge himself into scenes of mass destruction. Private violence and public warfare are mutually influential—and the essential sin was not to walk in the ways of Samuel.

Whatever else may be said of Jeffers' beliefs and opinions as they appear with marked consistency throughout the various poems he has written, he has gone to war in the cause of peace; and it should also be said that Jeffers' emotional fervor, his honesty, and his lack of personal vanity strongly resemble the evangelical passion of his Protestant heritage: his image of Christ is always divine. His poem to America, his **"Shine, Perishing Republic,"** has that fervor, its eloquence, its nobility, its protest against earthly tyrants. . . . (pp. 9-10)

But before one considers the merits of Jeffers' best writings, one should spare breath for certain of their failures, for Jeffers is a poet of large flaws and no weaknesses—and the flaws are often easier to see than his larger merits. In the great army of characters that his poems present to us, one has yet to discover a wholly admirable or completely rounded human being—the nearest approach, and her virtue is one of courage, is the heroine of **"Give Your Heart to the Hawks,"** a woman who attempts to save her husband from suicide and fails. An impatient reader of Jeffers, overwhelmed, yet half attracted, and then rebelled by the scenes of overt Lesbianism in *The Women at Point Sur* and by the sight of a mother offering herself, half naked, to her son in **"Such Counsels You Gave to Me,"** would conclude that the poet kept bad company and was himself "immoral." The same reader would also find difficulties in fully accepting Jeffers' beautiful pastoral, **"The Loving Shepherdess,"** which may have been written with a memory of the Elizabethan John Fletcher's *The Faithful Shepherdess* in mind. The witless little shepherdess, dressed in the fewest of rags, is open to all men, young and old; and it is as though she had obeyed Sade's instructions to little girls [in his *La philosophie daus le boudoir* (1795): "The first stirring of desire that a girl feels is the moment that Nature means her to prostitute herself, and with no other consideration in mind, she should obey Nature's voice; she outrages Her laws if she resists them."]. Whenever in Jeffers' poetry one finds a possible echo of Sade's doctrines, the mind, if not the blood, runs cooler. . . . Jeffers' desire to deal solely with elemental passions tends to mislead the reader into the colder regions of hell which are a paradox of romantic agony: the reader is repelled.

Another reader, equally impatient, finds something ridiculous in Jeffers' scenes of sexual violence; since no comic relief is given to the reader in Jeffers' Californian narratives, the reader is forced to supply that missing element in the progress of the story—and sex viewed from a point outside the scene itself always has a touch of the ridiculous in it; if it did not there would be no moments of relaxation in the stories that used to be told in smoking cars. It is almost gratuitous to say that Jeffers' characters lack humor, which is a flaw that Jeffers shares with Wordsworth; and in the progress of his more violent scenes of action, a need is felt for a drunken porter to cross the stage in *Macbeth.* This does not mean, however, that Jeffers lacks ability to write of drunkenness; few scenes in contemporary fiction can equal the vividness of the drunken party which is prelude to the story of **"Give Your Heart to the Hawks"**; in poetry, and in its own grim fashion, its veracity equals the mild, half-melancholy scene of E. A. Robinson's "Mr. Flood's Party." (Robinson, by the way, is one of the few elder American poets for whom Jeffers has expressed firm admiration.) **"Such Counsels You Gave to Me"** must be counted as one of Jeffers' more conspicuous failures: the bare bones of the "Oedipus complex" shine too brightly through it. As the story opens one knows only too well that the weak son is fated to poison his red-faced, hard-drinking father; since 1900 this situation has been the stock property of countless novels and plays; a sinister yet charming hero-villain disposes of a father who is overweight or a rich aunt who spikes her tea with whisky. But in Jeffers' case these flaws are not those of a small-minded writer or a minor poet.

Jeffers' merits as a poet are less well known than the flaws which I have just enumerated. From **"Roan Stallion"** and **"Tamar"** onward, Jeffers' technical contribution to twentieth-century poetry has been the mastery of alternate ten and five stress lines in narrative verse; in some of his shorter poems and in passages of some of his dramatic sequences, he employs a five and three stress variation of his narrative line. In this particular art no living poet has equaled him, and no other poet in America, from Philip Freneau to E. A. Robinson, has developed a narrative style of greater force, brilliance, and variety than his. While reading one of Jeffers' poems one never falls asleep; although there are times when his moral fervor is overweighted and has results which seem far from his stated intentions, he has never committed the greatest of all literary crimes—dullness. Among his shorter poems, his conversation pieces have contained prophecies which at the moment of publication seemed wrongheaded, probably mad, or willfully truculent. Time has proved Jeffers right more frequently than his adverse readers had thought possible; although the poem is too long for quotation here, the thoughtful reader cannot fail to be impressed by his **"Woodrow Wilson (February 1924)"** today. Wilson, the nearly tragic American hero, has been and still is the most difficult of all public figures to write about, yet Jeffers has succeeded in doing so. (pp. 10-13)

Jeffers' opinions (which are less political than colored by his hatred of war, his adaptation of Nietzschean ethics, and non-churchgoing Christianity) occasioned his publishers, in a recent book of his poems, *The Double Axe,* to disclaim responsibility for them. Jeffers had strange things to say of World War II and its aftermath, which he had predicted long before they arrived; he was much too familiar with the scene to be tactful; in another ten years he will probably be found less far from the truth than the majority of his contemporaries. There has been considerable misunderstanding of Jeffers' portrait of Hitler which he included in *Be Angry at the Sun* in 1941; his

Hitler was a figure not unlike Macbeth, a Macbeth who had also become the hero of a Wagnerian opera; his doom was accurately foretold; yet at the time Jeffers' poem appeared many thought that Jeffers had praised Hitler, or at least had made him seem too powerful. There is less doubt today that Jeffers' portrait needs no retouching to give it greater veracity.

Of the shorter poems, his volume *Descent to the Dead* is among his masterpieces; it includes his lines on **"Shakespeare's Grave," "In the Hill at New Grange," "Ghosts in England," "Iona: The Graves of the Kings"**—all memorable poems. It is impossible for an anthologist to make a neat selection of Jeffers' poems and then bind them shrewdly between the poems written by his contemporaries. It so happens that Jeffers has never written an "anthology poem"; he is best represented by his *Selected Poetry* which shows the range of his narratives tempered by his elegies, self-critical comments, and occasional observations; many of them may be read as footnotes to his longer poems. Selections of his shorter poems by anthologists distort the essential qualities of his poetry. (pp. 14-15)

Jeffers' success in reviving Greek themes through Nietzschean and even Wagnerian interpretation has also been a source of annoyance to those who hope to read their classics in "pure" translations. The "pure" translation of Græco-Roman classics do not and cannot exist in English; and it is a truism that absolute translations of poetry from one language into another cannot be made. The best that can be hoped for is that the translator has a more than literal understanding of the poetry he translates and that he has the genius to convert his original sources into poetry in English. Jeffers' re-creations of ancient stories, particularly the plays of Euripides into English dramatic verse, have never pretended to be more than adaptations of situations, scenes, and characters. Actually, his performances are as far removed from their original sources as Shakespeare's adaptations from Plutarch's *Lives* in *Julius Caesar* and *Antony and Cleopatra,* as far as Jeffers' **"Tamar"** is from the second book of Samuel in the Old Testament. In his own way he has applied to ancient writings Ezra Pound's rule, "make it new." Like W. B. Yeats, Jeffers was not "a born dramatist"; as Yeats was essentially a lyric poet, so Jeffers has been a distinguished writer of contemplative and narrative verse. As Yeats's adaptation of *Oedipus at Colonus* reflects Irish seascape in a Dublin accent, so Jeffers' adaptations from the Greek are never far from the climate of the California Pacific Coast.

If Jeffers, even more than Yeats, is not a professional dramatist and is far removed from those who can be called "men of the theater," there are times when his poetry reaches high levels of dramatic power. This has long been evident in his variation of the Orestes cycle in **"The Tower Beyond Tragedy"**; and its concluding statement of how Orestes "climbed the tower beyond time, consciously, and cast humanity, entered the earlier fountain" (walked then, as Nietzsche would say, beyond good and evil) places the poem among the major accomplishments of our time. The same power enters his poem **"At the Fall of an Age,"** with its story of the death of Helen on the island of Rhodes where she was worshiped as a tree-goddess, twenty years after the fall of Troy. The two speeches of Achilles' Myrmidons, risen from the dead, have all the accents of living yet timeless verse. . . . (pp. 16-17)

Jean Cocteau once wrote that a true poet writes to be believed, not praised, and in these lines [of Achilles' Myrmidons] Jeffers' art of persuading the reader is unquestionable.

Nor is he less convincing in the writing of Aphrodite's speech in his recent play, *The Cretan Woman,* a play inspired by and not a translation of Euripides. . . . (p. 18)

The quality of this speech equals the speeches in the plays of the Greek dramatists, but it is also singularly modern poetry; the quality of its language is direct and unstrained—no irrelevant effort at meaning is forced into it: the poetic nature of the speech is *there,* and for its purpose cannot be said in any other way; it is evidence enough of the genius of the man who wrote it. *The Cretan Woman* is a far more successful play to read than Jeffers' *Medea;* for his *Medea* opens with a flood of emotional speeches that cannot be sustained throughout the first act, therefore the play is top-heavy, and his readers as well as his audiences are likely to be exhausted long before the final curtain falls. Jeffers' version of Euripides' *Hippolytus* reserves its strength for the last scene and agony of Theseus; and at this conclusion, one believes that Jeffers has lost none of the mastery that he acquired thirty years ago, rather he has set himself the further task of transforming his narrative genius into writing verse for the stage, or perhaps television.

Robinson Jeffers' accomplishments and the modesty of his private life, now saddened by the death of his wife, should serve as an example to the present as well as the next generation of writers. Within the last thirty years he has made no compromise with the changing fashions of the day. For some readers Jeffers' attitude, which is not unlike the positions held by William Faulkner and W. B. Yeats, has always seemed too aristocratic. Even now I can hear someone saying, "Jeffers loves nothing but rocks and stones; I love mankind." But those who love abstract mankind too feverishly deny the rights of individual distinction and all the choices between men of good and bad, and by implication they also deny the right of the artist to be himself. Jeffers has re-established the position of the poet as one of singular dignity and courage. He is neither voiceless nor without his readers; and he is not without wisdom in seeming to await the verdict of posterity. (pp. 19-20)

Horace Gregory, "Poet without Critics: A Note on Robinson Jeffers," in his The Dying Gladiators and Other Essays, *Grove Press, Inc., 1961, pp. 3-20.*

DIANE ACKERMAN

Something elemental in Robinson Jeffers qualifies him as the near-perfect embodiment of the American poet, a certain type of it, anyway. Unworldly, unconniving, at odds with society both as he found it and foresaw it, he fits an apocryphally definitive idea of the American mind: close to nature, to the universe, closer to them than to fellow-humans, and inclined to prize in himself elements held in common with galaxies, rocks, stallions, or cormorants. He takes the big-sky idyll to an extreme and he achieves—drives his mind incessantly toward—an empathy writ so large that in the end the only quality that pulls some readers into his poems is the manner and tone. He talks preachily to himself. He is a born explainer, even going so far as to prefer definitions of words to words themselves, which is another form of being candid or unsurreptitious. No jokes, no skittish asides counterpoint the earnestness of his vision which, methodically and acutely visual, seems to give off exhortatory vignettes. His poems *feel* illustrated, although there are no pictures in the margins, and the reader feels "got at" on several levels: seduced by the visuals, half-persuaded by the down-home spell-it-out-for-you

that doesn't hesitate to repeat itself or, in the well-tempered onrush of declaration. . . . (p. 16)

If he seems to plod, it is to keep us from being glib or from thinking too soon we know what's going on. If he repeats, it's because this massive transhumanance (or trans-simiance) merits more than a mere lingering look. And what an insidious style it is, as good for dense and almost seismic narrative poems of atavistic violence and blood-letting as for awed renderings of the science to be found in natural objects.

But the style is something else too: not just a badge or an emblem, but (at least in the poems that instruct us in the holy impartiality of the universe) a rhythm of discovery, a cadence to peer through a microscope or telescope by; it's as if he had his hand on some cogged wheel or other, slowly twisting givens into focus; it's what he says while doing something else. The talky intermittance of a wholly occupied mind, it works on us in a special way, so much so that not only what he is saying matters, but also the how of it. Murmur gently along with him as he plies his investigative trade, and you find yourself taken over by a sound in which the clinical, the reverential, the obstinate combine, attuning your mind to teacherly gradations. . . . Each line somehow suggests a capacity for infinite range . . . through a conjuring trick of the voice—an apperceptive voice which intones "This line may never end," a voice which embodies a reverence (and a sometimes itchy or querolous one at that) independent of all severance, sustaining the cumulative insight until it dwindles out.

Such behavior in verse is unique with Jeffers. He doesn't mind doing it, he doesn't worry about lines so long they have to double back twice. . . . Not that he isn't a phrasemaker, a devotee of the concise; he is, as a few phrases taken at random prove—"the prone ocean," "The honey of peace in old poems," "wet and worn out, like an old womb"—but that is his subordinate mode, and anyone casting around in his work (as I here) for a *phrase* that catches the idiosyncratic gist of the man finds the odds loaded the other way. It's easier to provide six-line chunks of autonomous-feeling ruminance. I mean the movement of his mind is toward amplification: to him an epigraph is a challenge to go on exploring, not an exploration summed up and irrefragably neat. His epiphanies are slow-motion ones. They don't zap you and pass, they hang around in the poem, unfolding and peeling, as in this:

> . . . our bones, ours too, would make
> Wide prairies white, a beautiful snow of unburied bones:
> Bones that have twitched and quivered in the night of love,
> Bones that have been shaken with laughter and hung slack in sorrow, coward bones
> Worn out with trembling, strong bones broken on the rack, bones broken in battle,
> Broad bones gnarled with hard labor, and the little bones of sweet young children, and the white empty skulls,
> Little carved ivory wine-jugs that used to contain
> Passion and thought and love and insane delirium, where now
> Not even worms live.
>
> **("Passenger Pigeons")**

Donne is there, but also the American tradition's fondness in prose for successive *ands* (as if to make the sequential the simultaneous by making everything a list). What isn't there is the phrasemaker's willingness to gamble all on five-syllable blaze that announces *Finis* or "material exhausted." Jeffers in fact advances by feeding on what he has already put into the poem, and he doesn't hesitate to reach back over the terrain he's made in order to pick up a resonance, a tune, an epiphany that he's not quite yet treated in the round.

If all this makes him sound laborious, I have done him a disservice. He spreads himself out because he is utterly at home with the imagery of science and doesn't take line after line to domesticate the stuff; it's there in his gut and brain, and he doesn't feel self-conscious about it. He knows the size of Antares ("The Earth's orbit doubled would not girdle his greatness") and works it into the poem as part of the natural gait of his mind. . . . This poet, as each and every line makes copiously clear, is utterly at home in a universe he admires for its persistence, although he resents its ability to go on using his detritus long after he is dead (he'd like a clean and final end, with nothing left). I'm not saying he achieves a perfect harmony, but he does rise to an accommodation more comprehensive than you find in most twentieth-century American poets. His mind is ultra-permeable. He isn't quite sure where the line of division is between what's in his head and what isn't (can a pantheist have dichotomies?). And he perceives in the most contributive manner imaginable, without ever seeming to labor, to grind, to breathe heavily. He has almost no humor, of course; I imagine it's because a mind so holistic is ill-attuned to the absurd, and what he *does* find absurd—the technological suicide of *homo sapiens*—he is too busy denouncing to find ludicruous. It's as if some almost extinct network of nerves survives in Jeffers, the housing of an atavistic skill we may well need to teach ourselves all over again. His world is his and ours as well, more than ours is even ours.

Jeffers is obviously not a poet of categories; instead he is a poet, perhaps even *the* poet—of suffusion, gamut, and total spectrum. "Erase the lines:" he writes in **"Monument,"** "I pray you not to love classifications." Use them if you have to, but don't convert them into a fetish.

> The thing is like a river, from source to sea-mouth
> One flowing life. We that have the honor and hard-
>   ship of being human
> Are one flesh with the beasts, and the beasts with
>   the plants
> One streaming sap, and certainly the plants and
>   algae and the earth they spring from
> Are one flesh with the stars. The classifications
> Are mostly a kind of *memoria technica,* use it but
>   don't be fooled.
>
>   **("Monument")**

Of course, it is one thing to be told this, to accept it, and quite another to feel it, to achieve his own extraordinary sense of the concurrance of things. He himself can feel it only by downplaying the human role in the scheme of things, as if being born human were merely a convenient means of acquiring enough intuition to put mankind in its lowly place. Time and again Jeffers reminds us how marginal we are, how trivial; the Earth will "flourish long after mankind is out" (note the image of the inning) and "Man's life's / Too common to be lamented." Such a chastening view requires of its proponent a sense of expendability that applies to his own work too, and Jeffers has it in abundance. He seems less intent on converting readers to any large view of *his* than on scratching his witness on some available rock and leaving things at that. How impersonal he can be: as conduit, as a reflex from the human sensibility *per se,* not from that of Robinson Jeffers in particular. As a result, his poetry could have been a mere ca-

talogue, a bill of goods, an anonymous primer in humility; but it isn't, mainly because, whatever he professes on the level of rational, discursive thought, he is idiosyncratic enough to come through anyway: the magistral, plane-spotting, star-watching, ancestor-hunting recluse with a knack for twisting what's taken for granted into a didactic device.

Let me pursue this a little further. In the epic writings, he twists the notion of incest to signify that the human race is too much involved with itself. It's not a matter of local taboos having to do with consanguinity; it's a matter of cosmic decorum, having to do with our minor place in the league of things. In fact, his incest implies narcissicism or masturbation, and only in the delirium of self-engrossed passion can we sustain the fiction of our own importance. It is a view found elsewhere, in the poems of Aldous Huxley, for instance, but mostly an unpopular one because it junks the glad humanism of the Renaissance, flouts some of the cherished precepts of democracy, and bypasses the view held by certain religions that the individual is paramount. In effect he says that the "good life," "the pursuit of happiness," et cetera, are beside the point, as is the idea of the absurd, predicated as it is on unjustifiable assumptions about the universe, the galaxy, the solar system, nature, chemistry, the lot. What Edna St. Vincent Millay called the "terrific implications" of his poetry dismiss both nihilist and hedonist, not because deep down Jeffers doesn't care about the quality of the individual life—his own, his wife's, his granddaughter's, but because he has a grand-mindedness which transcends everything else. So, while he can write of his granddaughter Una, . . . his mind invokes other things, especially "the beauty of *transhuman* things" (italics mine). It is not one view shoved into another's place; it's the view that underlies and complements all views, maybe akin to the wise passivity of Wordsworth, but altogether more bristling with the cytological and the galactic. And its effect on the reader is similar, perhaps, to that of the blood-sacrifice images in his longest poems: eluding logic rather than transcending it, working on the mind when the mind doesn't know. (pp. 16-17)

Of course, the human mind being what it is, the more we break out of our humanity (as Jeffers recommends), the more it comes after us. The mode of breakaway reinstates us and the only gain—reviewed by Jeffers over the long run of history, done with censorious impartiality—is the self-knowledge that comes from a tradition of repeatedly failing to assume a god-like stance. Inhuman as our race has tried to be, whether through Naziism or the Inquisition, through logarithms or the social security number; we have, nevertheless, humanized the non-human more than we have inhumanized the human. Those are the odds against which he sets his credo: "The pallid / Pursuit of the world's beauty on paper," which he finds "a pitiful pastime." All he can do is "write and be quiet."

I must now confess that some of his long works, say **"Tamar," "Cawdor," "The Tower Beyond Tragedy," "Thurso's Landing,"** have not worn well and, oddly enough, seem too humanized themselves, as if Jeffers had been trying to broaden, in terms both ephemeral and anthropomorphic, a vision better left in either of two forms: the medium-length poem, such as **"Margrave,"** or the lapidary short-short, such as **"To the Stonecutters."** Perhaps the strain of being inhuman in tight, starched little poems, which have no other faces or voices in them, is too much. Perhaps we assimilate dogma best from dramatized lengthiness rather than from aphorism or proverb. Perhaps Jeffers felt that, talking to himself all the time in short poems, he was only committing his own specialized notion of incest! At any rate, he manufactured a good deal of soapy talk which no doubt appealed to a generation unready for scientific apocalypse. At random in **"Tamar"** I find:

> Lee, Lee,
> Come. He has come." "What? Now," he said. "I
>   have told Lee.
>   I was sick, he was sorry for me, he is going
> To camp tomorrow, he wants to see you and say
>   good-by."

It does not exactly linger in the mind or provoke an impetuous lunge to the next few lines. Such lines may come into their own again when TV puts on Jeffers's talkier pieces; I cite them here only to suggest the other side of Jeffers who, not content with the mundane and the banal, makes club-sandwiches out of it in the interests of a flagellation scene or that of a head hammered to pulp. Why? Because "the beauty of transhuman things," intellectually more worthwhile than anything else, demands of the mind and senses, a self-denudation, a self-occlusion, impossible even for Jeffers who, irate over taxes, complains in the *Carmel Pine Cone* "I believe that the Carmel Sanitary Board is acting illegally. . . .it is ridiculous to assess us more than six thousand dollars" (July 20, 1949). . . . (p. 17)

[Such distractions], "Like insects back of a searchlight," demand his attention and remind him in his poetry of the principle of clash: the world as an arena of dissonance. The irony, for such a transhumanist as Jeffers, is that the very things you don't heed, or don't want to heed, get in your way more than anyone else's. No wonder he developed a special kind of imagery with which to mimic this sensation; his commonplace things are always extraordinary, eerie, startling. The evening is "leopard-footed." Old cypresses have "deep-sea knots." Decomposition begins to "pick and caress the unstable chemistry / Of the cells of the brain." There are not many poets who can, in this way, metamorphose the hard times and heartaches of daily living into key-signatures of cosmic variety, but he does it with near-choreographic bitter-sweetness.

These things said, one returns to the image of Jeffers as some kind of life-force, quietly overpowering everything within reach:

> He brings the world to focus in a feeling brain,
> In a net of nerves catches the splendor of things,
> Breaks the somnambulism of nature. . . .

Yet he never exclaims "Man is magnificent!" or "What a piece of work is a man . . . !" His work is less histrionic, less that of impresario than of a gentle ecumenical eroder who so much esteems "the splendor of things" that he falls into step behind sleepwalking nature itself, mesmerizing himself into a vicarious non-humanity. (pp. 17-18)

> *Diane Ackerman, "Robinson Jeffers: The Beauty of Transhuman Things," in* The American Poetry Review, *Vol. 12, No. 2, March-April, 1983, pp. 16-18.*

ROBERT IAN SCOTT

How can a poet with a new or unpopular view write so vividly that we see the world his way and thereby change the way we behave? Book 22 of Aristotle's *Poetics* says that "by far the greatest ability" a poet needs is "a command of meta-phor," the ability to see resemblances and other connections between apparently unrelated things. Jeffers had that ability. Having said in **"The Answer"** that we need to know that "however ugly the parts appear the whole [universe] remains beautiful," he gives a vivid example of an ugly human part, a severed hand. We may shudder as we imagine such a hand, may wonder what disconnected it and how much that hurt, and so turn to the world as a whole with a sense of grateful relief, as the poem says we should.

Ezra Pound said poets should make us react by making their subjects and language seem new, as if seen for the first time, in part by leaving out every word not needed. He saw poetry as the art of condensing the most meaning into the fewest words. But that otherwise admirable advice can prove self-defeating when it leaves a poet with no subjects but disconnected emotional words and moments. (p. 25)

Jeffers saw modern poetry as suffering from such disconnections and deliberately decided not to be that sort of modern poet. Instead, as he says in his introduction to his **Selected Poetry** in 1938, he decided to write narrative poems (which means connecting words together into plots, connecting causes with results and characters with situations) and to write poems that express scientific and philosophical ideas (*philosophical,* I think, was Jeffers' safer way of saying *religious*).

We cannot have ideas without connecting something. The American philosopher C. S. Peirce defined three types of signs and meaning by the type of *connection* each makes:

1. **Icons** (such as images and maps) *resemble* what they mean. Metaphors suggest mental images, as Jeffers did by describing the universe as all one net or organism, which may encourage us by making it seem understandable. By contrast, *The Waste Land* describes the world (or rather Eliot's emotional state—he ignored most of the world) as bewilderingly disconnected, disgusting, dying, which may leave us too discouraged and confused to do much but feel sorry for ourselves.

2. **Indices** (such as symptoms and clues) *result* from what they mean, as red spots do for measles. In Jeffers' poem **"The Loving Shepherdess,"** her distraction and delusions indicate how much she has already suffered, which may make us feel sorry for her (a less egotistical reaction than the one *The Waste Land* provokes). Possibly as a result of his training in medicine, his poems often describe and diagnose symptoms.

3. **Symbols** (such as words) *remind* someone of something. Probably no two of us have precisely the same reaction to any word, which explains why we so often misunderstand what others say. Eliot used disconnected fragments, expecting us to react to them as he had. He had great faith in words or the capital-*W* Word as magic, a faith common among poets and possibly one reason why Jeffers thought poets "lie too much" and so decided to be skeptical himself. He saw language skeptically, as a by-product of evolution, as inevitably only approximate at best (see his poem, **"Love the Wild Swan"**), as only what we write or say—a scientifically accurate and modest view. He seems to have felt that helping his readers mattered. He wrote clearly by using all these types of meaningful connections. For a man who hated writing letters, Jeffers was remarkably generous in explaining the point of view his poems expressed to readers who wrote him. Eliot, however, repeatedly refused to explain his poems, though they are so puzzling that explaining them has become an academic

industry. . . . Eliot wanted his readers to react emotionally but not to understand his subject, himself; Jeffers wanted his readers to understand his subject, the world's connections.

We also have three more types, to which I give negative numbers because they reverse the connections of the first three:

–1. Rather than resembling what they mean, as icons do, sets of **opposites** *contrast with* each other, as in such reciprocal relationships as those described by laws of physics—such as "the higher the fall, the more violent the result." This is also a part of the sense of tragedy basic to Jeffers' narrative poems and many of his short poems. The moral here is that we should avoid even wanting too much success.

–2. Rather than resulting from and revealing past causes, as indices do, **omens** *cause* results and let us foretell them. For example, the loving shepherdess's distraction and delusions are omens as well as indices. We can predict that they will help cause her death, and they do. Any morality more intelligent than that of blindly following rules depends upon our ability to predict the results of what we might do. This suggests another moral of tragedy. We should know what we and our circumstances are so we can make responsible choices by making accurate predictions. In this way, we can obey that first moral of tragedy, to avoid such dangerous extremes as too much success. To know who we are, we must know the world which limits us, because those limits define us. Thus, we need to take the world seriously—as God. As Jeffers saw it, the world has the traditional attributes of God: it is infinite, eternal, all-powerful, what created us, what can save us from ourselves, what we should love as beautiful, and what does correct us by limiting us—through the laws of physics and chemistry. (pp. 25-6)

–3. Rather than depending upon whatever emotional reactions each individual happens to have, as symbols do, **examples** *give* us *samples* of their subject, which stubbornly remain whatever they are whether or not they remind anyone of anything; Jeffers liked granite boulders as examples of the world in general. But we do react to some examples emotionally, such as the severed hand in **"The Answer."** That hand seems to be an example of both humanity in general and the atrocities humans commit, such as severing hands and heads.

Science uses factual examples as both the source of its ideas and the way it tests them. So did Jeffers. When philosophers told Galileo that he couldn't possibly have discovered that Jupiter has moons, he said, "Look for yourself." (Most of the philosophers refused.) Jeffers' poems also invite us to look at particular places and events as examples of the world. These include discoveries made by Galileo and other scientists, such as that other planets are also worlds and that the salts in our blood indicate that life began in the ocean. If we don't believe him, we can look at the planets through a telescope and see for ourselves or taste blood and find that it tastes salty.

By seeing these connections—(1) icons, (2) indices, (3) symbols—and sets of (–1) opposites, (–2) omens, and (–3) examples, we extend and correct our understanding of the world.

The more unexpected, complexly accurate, and wide-ranging the connections, the greater the intelligence of the scientist or poet, and the greater the effect on the reader. Much modern art and poetry seems intent on producing gaudy but trivial effects with few meaningful connections, often as self-advertising or as a form of protest. For example, during World War I, the Dada artists said that since politicians had made nonsense of history it was the artists' patriotic duty to make nonsense of art, and they promptly did by producing such incongruous combinations as the fur-lined teacup. Such combinations are the method of Pound's *Cantos* and Eliot's *Waste Land,* also often understood as protests against that war or against an even more general decline and fall of western civilization. Such combinations may surprise us, may suggest that the poets find what they notice of the world disgusting, but they remain only emotional reactions with few meaningful connections. By contrast, Einstein's $E=mc^2$ includes so much with such unexpected, important, and often painfully vivid results, that it proves profoundly meaningful and no joke, unlike fur-lined teacups. World War I also affected Jeffers, and, like Einstein's formula, all but his earliest poems consider the universe as a whole and quite impersonally, and find some unexpected, important, and often painfully vivid connections. (pp. 26-7)

Jeffers said he began writing poems by imitating Thomas Campbell and Dante Gabriel Rossetti. The result, the naively self-centered poems of Jeffers' first book, *Flagons and Apples,* published in 1912, soon made him wish he could take back every copy and have them all pulped to make more paper and save a few trees. His second book, *Californians,* published in 1916, imitated Wordsworth through its descriptions of country people and places, some in southern California and some on the Sur coast; he moved to Carmel in August 1914 instead of to England because by then World War I had begun. William Everson has found poems Jeffers wrote between *Californians* and his next book, *Tamar,* published in 1924, the one which made him suddenly famous. They include the longest poem Jeffers ever wrote, the 227-page **"The Alpine Christ."** Like *Paradise Lost,* it starts with a conference in heaven in which Satan compliments God for letting World War I outdo the horrors of hell. As a result, Christ returns to earth to save humankind from itself again, only to vanish having saved nothing. It is as if by writing the poem Jeffers discovered that, unlike Milton, he could not believe Christianity helped and that, unlike Shelley's *Prometheus Unbound,* which seems to have been Jeffers' other model at this stage, he could not promise any happy ending.

Like Buddha, Jeffers was nearly thirty when he realized how much so many humans suffer. **"The Alpine Christ"** goes on for page after page describing examples of senseless violence and misery in the war, showing how much they preoccupied and upset him. Then, in handling the granite boulders which went into the building of Tor House in the summer of 1919, Jeffers came to admire their steadfastness and the beauty of the universe, the more so because he felt so upset himself. As a result, he came to see human suffering as often caused by such egotistical reactions as our delusions of importance—the basic point of Buddhism, identified by Buddha in about 528 BCE. (p. 27)

When Jeffers put together his *Selected Poetry,* he put the poem **"Theory of Truth"** at the end—he may have written it for that purpose—as if he meant it as the book's moral. The poem says he rejected Christianity, Taoism, and Buddhism because they take egotistically narrow views of the universe. Buddha did so by being so hurt by human suffering that he wanted to "annihilate . . . the earth and stars, life and mankind, to annul the suffering." If that could be done, it would be in Jeffers terms the ultimately egotistical and presumptuous denial of God, as well as suicidal. Jeffers defined his view as precisely the opposite. In *Themes in My Poems,* he said:

"The outer world is real and divine; one's soul might be called an illusion, it is so slight and transitory." At the end of ***The Tower Beyond Tragedy,*** Jeffers' character Orestes has such a vision and so escapes any further tragedy. Alan Watts and Gary Snyder, both admirers of Jeffers, told me that *nirvana,* the goal of Buddhism, does not mean "oblivion" but its opposite, an utterly unselfish, undeluded view of everything, a view quite compatible with science (as Fritjof Capra shows in his 1975 book, *The Tao of Physics*).

Scientists, of course, generally assume that the universe they study really does exist and that we exist as parts of it. Notice the resentment engendered by scientific discoveries which reveal our place as parts of the universe, discoveries Jeffers used repeatedly:

1.   That we are not the center of the universe. Galileo was threatened with torture for saying so and, even after officially denying it, spent the rest of his life under house arrest. Even now we talk of "conquering" space and of the moon as "outer space."

2.   That we are not biologically unique but merely one of many products of the evolution of life. Fundamentalists deny and try to suppress that discovery for egotistical reasons ("Who, *me?* Related to a monkey? *Never!*").

3.   That we are material, mortal, and subject to the same physics and chemistry as the rest of the universe.

In about 55 BCE, Lucretius anticipated the second and third of these discoveries in his poem, "De Rerum Natura" (which means "On the Nature of Things"); its survival in a single copy suggests a certain lack of popularity. Since then, apparently, only Jeffers has made these discoveries a part of his poetry. If a poet cannot be original (Jeffers said he asked himself this about 1914), why write? He found something new to say by seeing the world as God in terms of these discoveries. In effect, he was reinventing Buddhism even as he thought he was rejecting it. He replaced its mythology (which would have puzzled western readers) with these discoveries.

In looking beyond himself for his subjects, Jeffers also went back to almost the earliest known beginnings of western literature. By 1918, he had already gone back from Rossetti to Wordsworth to Milton—from 1870 to 1789 to 1667. After **"The Alpine Christ,"** Jeffers went back four centuries before Christ to the Greek tragedies for the form and plots of most of his long poems, as Robert Brophy has shown in his book, *Robinson Jeffers.* From pre-Christian culture also came such beginnings of science as the view that we are not the center of the universe and that the universe and ourselves are all changing structures of atoms in space. Both views see the world as beautifully complex in its connections and reassuringly predictable.

On January 9, 1926, the San Francisco newspaper *The Monitor* warned of a pagan horror in Carmel who was "intrinsically terrible" because he had "the power of Aeschylus" and "the subtlety of Sophocles," apparently without noticing that terror may have a moral purpose or result and that many would see that comparison with Greek tragic poets as a compliment. Since then, other critics have attacked Jeffers for his use of science. H. H. Waggoner claimed that because Jeffers used such scientific words as *electron* his poems must all be meaningless and dull—as if perhaps twenty such words, some of them used only two or three times, could have so drastic an effect on more than two thousand pages. In fact, these words represent discoveries about the world and have become widely used because the public has begun to understand what Jeffers described twenty to sixty years ago. The icon of atoms as tiny solar systems with their electrons in orbits has become a standard illustration in science books for children. Science has enormously extended the range and accuracy of our perceptions. When space probes sent back those astounding images of the cloud belts and moons of Jupiter, I found myself wishing Galileo and Jeffers could have seen them; both seem to have been delighted by the sheer variety and beauty of the universe. Jeffers' descriptions of such discoveries are unfailingly accurate, clear, and vividly put in terms of what we see, hear, smell, taste, and feel.

Another critic, Yvor Winters at Stanford, claimed Jeffers' poems are incoherent and his characters all amoral puppets because the poems use scientific discoveries to explain why his characters act as they do—as if only ignorance makes us organized, free to choose what we do, and moral. But those causes exist whether or not we talk or know about them. In fact, ignorance often increases human helplessness and misery. Other reviewers have called Jeffers sadistic because his poems object to such misery rather than ignore it and because his poems tell no such flattering lies as that our culture or species will live forever. (pp. 28-9)

[Jeffers] made the universe's total interconnectedness vividly clear by describing it as all one net—an icon he might have learned from his college astronomy textbook's description of Newton's law of gravity, which says that every particle in the universe affects each other, or from the Hindu and Buddhist metaphor of Indra's net, in which every world and atom of the universe is a jewel reflecting and affecting all the rest, so every act has many results. Of course, the world's net holds us all, but Jeffers thought every individual was more or less tragic, at least at the end, and deserving of compassion and understanding. Despite what critics and reviewers say—that Jeffers was a terrible pessimist who hated humanity—he objected to what we all ought to object to: needless suffering and the way we litter and poison the planet we inhabit (in Jeffers' terms, that means desecrating a part of God). In his forty-eight years in Carmel, Jeffers saw what happens to even so lovely and out-of-the-way place as this in a state which keeps doubling its population every nineteen to twenty-two years. He knew that in the evolution of life on Earth other species' populations climbed steeply, as they seemed to triumph, only to vanish totally.

In most tragedies and disasters, someone survives and may even benefit. The Renaissance may have happened because of the Black Death, the plague which killed a third of Europe. As a result, individual lives suddenly became much more valuable. The worse the tragedy or the disaster, the more it may encourage the survivors, because they see what not to do, discover they can survive, and see how bravely people can behave in such awful circumstances. They may also feel less anxious because at least they have discovered how people and the world behave—though not all of these apply in every case. Jeffers' tragedies let us see what happens to some remarkably egotistical fools. As a result of feeling fear and pity for tragic figures, we can temporarily exhaust our ability to feel those emotions and so enjoy a liberation from blind self-pity and paralyzing fear. When we do, we may extend our moral imaginations by feeling how someone else might feel, and so become more able to follow the Golden Rule—again, the escape from egotism. . . . (pp. 29, 46)

As for indices and omens: Jeffers described places, people, and events in terms of their causes and results—a scientific as well as poetically perceptive habit, and a moral one. If we understand why someone acts as he or she does, we may be more compassionate and more able to help. If we predict results accurately, we can make morally responsible choices. The accuracy of our predictions also tests our understanding of situations, as Jeffers knew from his scientific training. Possibly no other poet has done so much to diagnose our culture's symptoms nor made so many accurate predictions. For example, **"The Bowl of Blood"** shows Hitler in April 1940 as so worried that his invasion of Norway will fail that he consults a fortune teller. The bowl of blood is a part of her paraphernalia as well as a reminder, a symbol, of how bloody history is. We now know that Hitler did consult astrologers then, and for that reason, but ignored their advice.

By Buddhist standards, the most admirable are not those who merely save themselves but those who take the trouble to help others. Jeffers did this by writing his poems. He knew that in so enormous and complicated a world no one sees the whole truth or has the last word. Others will reach different conclusions, science will continue to discover more, but Jeffers' vision of the universe as all one connected net, a living and sacred organism, will remain a valid metaphor and morally inspiring. . . . His subject is not himself but the universe as the beautifully visible God he loved. (p. 46)

Robert Ian Scott, "The Great Net: The World as God in Robinson Jeffers' Poetry," in The Humanist, *Vol. 46, No. 1, January-February, 1986, pp. 24-9, 46.*

Tadeusz Konwicki

1926-

Polish novelist, short story writer, filmmaker, and journalist.

A leading literary figure in post-World War II Poland, Konwicki examines the grim realities of modern Polish life, particularly the devastating effects and lingering memories of the war and the subsequent Soviet domination of his homeland. Focusing on what he has termed the "Polish complex," a state of alienation and despair in which individuals are haunted by both the romantic idealism and the tragic events of Poland's past, Konwicki assesses his country's history as a series of failed attempts to gain freedom and independence. In his fiction, Konwicki combines elements of satire, irony, and surrealism while engaging in political analysis, philosophical rumination, and observations and interpretations of actual events. Jaroslaw Anders commented: "[Konwicki] is interested in the subjective reality of a people crippled by their historical fate, banished from the world of normal social pursuits and achievements into the domain of dreams, myths, and futile expectations. Using his own biography and the experience of his generation, he watches how Poles create, transform, and destroy their symbols, how they change their weaknesses into strengths, and their strengths into weaknesses."

Konwicki was born and raised in northeastern Poland near the city of Vilnius. During World War II, he fought with the Polish underground Home Army and helped liberate Vilnius from Nazi occupation. When Soviet troops approached the city and joined the conflict, the Polish guerrillas were arrested, deported to Russia, and imprisoned. Konwicki escaped deportment and rejoined those units of the Home Army that continued opposing the Soviets. In 1945, however, after further resistance proved unsuccessful, the unit disbanded, and Konwicki resettled in central Poland, where he attended Jagellonian University in Krakow and later pursued careers in journalism and literature.

Despite his anticommunist past, Konwicki attempted to reconcile himself to Poland's new Soviet-sponsored regime. His early works followed the official model of socialist realism, a Marxist theory that advocates the didactic use of literature, art, and music to cultivate social consciousness in a developing socialist state. The short story collection *Przy budowie* (1950) and the novel *Władza* (1954), both of which exalt heroic workers who support socialism, gained critical acclaim in Poland. Like many of his contemporaries, however, Konwicki soon became disillusioned with this movement, and in the novel *Rojsty* (1956), he abandoned the principles of socialist realism. Written in the late 1940s but not published until after the death of Joseph Stalin, when state-imposed restrictions on literary content were gradually eased, *Rojsty* is a satire based upon Konwicki's experiences with Poland's resistance army. Depicting the actions of a young man who desperately desires to become a hero but dies anonymously while attempting to impede Soviet aggression against Poland, this novel examines concerns and motifs that Konwicki explores in his subsequent work, including themes related to banished hope and vain ambition.

Konwicki achieved international recognition for his novels

Sennik współczesny (1963; *A Dreambook for Our Time*) and *Kompleks Polski* (1977; *The Polish Complex*). *A Dreambook for Our Time,* which Reuel K. Wilson described as "a montage of apocalyptic events seen and relived by an obsessive and guilty imagination," portrays an individual's futile attempts to come to terms with his past. Alternating between the narrator's random, blurred memories of his war experiences and the dreamlike events of his present life, this novel offers a bleak vision of a fragmented and patternless existence. Czeslaw Miłosz remarked: "[*A Dreambook for Our Time*] is a novel about guilt, and since the feeling of guilt oppresses men with distorted, even monstrous recollections, everything bathes in an aura of torment; situations, people, landscapes create a nightmarish web of metaphors." *The Polish Complex,* which was officially banned by Polish censors and later published in the underground literary magazine *Zapis,* revolves around a group of Poles waiting in line for a shipment of gold jewelry from Russia. These characters represent various personality types, and their situations reflect diverse states of life in contemporary Poland. The image of the queue in this novel has been interpreted as symbolic of the passive faith of the Polish people in an idealized homeland and of involvement in an organized process of victimization and oppression. Konwicki's historical digressions, which include accounts of previous failed political uprisings, reveal an unending cycle of thwarted ambitions. Critics have generally praised *The Polish Complex* as a powerful indictment of the degrading effects of totalitarianism and as a poignant analysis of the Polish condition.

In his next major novel, *Mała apokalipsa* (1979; *A Minor Apocalypse*), Konwicki focuses on a middle-aged writer who aimlessly roams the streets of Warsaw after being urged by Polish dissidents to set himself afire in front of the Communist Party headquarters in protest of the Soviet domination of Poland. Utilizing such surrealist techniques as dream sequences and interior monologues, as well as satire, irony, political rhetoric and analysis, and commentary on actual events, Konwicki evidences his belief in the futility of protest and the improbability of change within an autocratic state. Although some critics faulted Konwicki for lacking political understanding and underestimating the power and determination of Polish workers, Maciej Karpinski stated: "*A Minor Apocalypse* offers readers a vision of slavery under a totalitarian system of government. . . . [Konwicki] has given us a grotesque parable that probes to the core of the absurd." In *Wschody i zachody księżyca* (1982; *Moonrise, Moonset*), Konwicki presents a fictionalized diary containing autobiographical anecdotes, historical reminiscences, and political polemic and reflection. Concentrating mainly on the years 1944-1945 and 1980-1981, Konwicki recalls events of World War II and the postwar Polish underground resistance as well as the rise of Solidarity and the government's subsequent imposition of martial law during the early 1980s. This book also contains a fragment of Konwicki's unpublished second socialist-realist novel.

In addition to his fiction, Konwicki has directed and written scripts for several films. *Ostatni dzien lata* (1966; revised, 1973) collects several of his screenplays.

(See also *CLC*, Vols. 8, 28 and *Contemporary Authors*, Vol. 101.)

DAVID CHEEZEM

A Minor Apocalypse, published in 1979, the fourth of [Konwicki's] novels to appear in English translation, is too human to appeal to the part of us that wants to believe in heroism, in the capacity to transcend the mundane and somehow improve it. And Konwicki's characters are plagued by too many questions, too many doubts to measure up as heroes. Their questions are perennials—the meaning of identity, freedom, and purpose. Yet they are posed in this very personal novel with a fresh, earthy eloquence. This text reads like a grim daydream, with the author imagining for himself a melodramatic ending. But Konwicki is never entirely beguiled by his little dream. Everything about his unnamed central character is self-depreciating, uncertain. It is this naked honesty that makes the novel worth reading.

The central question of the work turns out to be the meaning of character and its value in a world of endless lines at shops, decaying buildings, censorship, and harassment of free thinkers.

In a typical brooding aside, Konwicki's protagonist throws out an idea, possibly to bait readers:

character has outlived its day. In ancient, primitive times, when biologically weak man struggled against omnipotent nature, character was useful, beneficial. . . . In today's ambiguous world, character means despotism, tyranny, absolute intolerance. At last it is time to admire a lack of character, inner weakness. Our epoch is that of noble doubts, blessed uncertainty, sacred hypersensitivity, divine wishy-washiness.

Set in the future, the novel opens on what might be the anonymous protagonist's last day. Early one morning, this middle-aged former writer (who seems very much like Konwicki himself) is approached by his old dissident cohorts and urged to mount the ultimate protest against the Soviet domination of Poland by setting himself on fire in front of Communist Party headquarters. He tentatively agrees, and decides to spend the day roaming the streets and taverns of Poland, carrying his gas can, in the company of a pesty young poet-cum-KGB agent and a stray dog. As he tugs the can along, he observes with overwhelming bitterness the decaying grey city of Warsaw. . . .

As the protagonist approaches the moment of decision about seeing his protest through to its fiery conclusion, he reflects: "I beg for justice, but how many times was I myself just? I cry out for moral order, but for how many years have I been trampling it myself?"

Because of such self-questioning, Konwicki's work is disturbing. . . . [He] is determined to make us wriggle.

> *David Cheezem, "Polish Novelist Konwicki Explores the Meaning of Character," in* The Christian Science Monitor, *October 13, 1983, p. 26.*

IRVING HOWE

[*A Minor Apocalypse*] came out in Poland just before the upsurge of Solidarity, and to some Polish readers during those great days it must have seemed excessively sour, even defeatist. For despite its bouncy absurdist surface, *A Minor Apocalypse* is a novel saturated with weariness—weariness with falsity, weariness with having constantly to expose falsity, weariness with continuing nevertheless to live in a world of falsity. Now that Solidarity has been suppressed, Konwicki's book again seems urgent, perhaps even in some grim sense "vindicated." "Here comes the end of the world" is its first sentence. Here comes the breakdown of Poland.

What follows is a string of quasi-picaresque adventures leading to the climax of K.'s self-immolation, prefigured but not portrayed. Often with verve but sometimes with a sinking recognition of how futile K.'s act will probably be, indeed how futile it may be even to write about it, Konwicki uses many different modes to recount his experiences: surrealist episodes, brute factuality, high intellectual chatter, malicious epigrams, touches of fantasy, dream sequences, and a lot of rhetoric. (p. 19)

Clever and painfully amusing as many of these episodes are, *A Minor Apocalypse* seems to me very uneven. Konwicki writes out of a rage that's probably beyond the ability of any writer to control—the rage of impotence which now and again slips into self-disgust. Witty one-liners and passages are made to do the work that only an integrated narrative structure could. Sometimes, as in Kundera's fiction, there is a sudden, curious drop into a tone of adolescent silliness, a half-voyeuristic, half-nasty toying with sexuality. At one point K. makes out his last will and testament—a prescription for treating dandruff and a specific for constipation. A culture in which people can't escape from public falsity must become a culture in which personal relations, even impersonal sensuality, are also contaminated.

The excellent translator Richard Lourie remarks in an introductory note that the book contains some satiric thrusts at Andrzej Wajda, the film director, and Jacek Kuron, the leader of the oppositionist KOR. . . . Throughout the novel Konwicki seems to be settling personal or factional scores, and when one remembers that Kuron has now been in prison for over a year and still faces the prospect of a trial for his "subversion," then the effect is decidedly unpleasant.

Two questions remain. If, with all due allowance for the privileges of fiction, the Poland Konwicki draws has any resemblance to the Poland we have recently been watching, then it becomes very hard to account for the upsurge, only a few months after his book's publication, of the energy and hope embodied in Solidarity. But if nevertheless Konwicki's bleak sense of things has been vindicated and the Solidarity people shown to be mistaken or naive, then one can only wonder what a novelist can draw upon—what events, themes, voices, tones—in the wretchedness of the Poland that remains.

A Minor Apocalypse can't, by its very nature, offer answers. But it has its own wracking and bitter authenticity. . . . (pp. 19-20)

> Irving Howe, "No Exit," in The New York Review of Books, *Vol. XXX, No. 15, October 13, 1983, pp. 19-20.*

MACIEJ KARPINSKI

A Minor Apocalypse by Tadeusz Konwicki, one of Poland's foremost writers, is a vision of the slow death of a world. The narrator watches his native city decay; houses and bridges collapse, friends die, and he himself prepares for his own death. . . .

The novel's world is Poland. The city that falls is Warsaw. Mr. Konwicki's description of it is so meticulous that the narrator's journey can be followed on a real map. Sometimes, however, this Warsaw suddenly dissolves and changes its shape; opening the door to a restaurant, a character might find himself in a police station or a banquet hall for party officials. The world of the novel becomes its own cosmos, in which time and space are shrunk to the size of the author's private hell.

Mr. Konwicki portrays everyday life in a totalitarian state: The police scour the streets; shops that may or may not open the next day are besieged by lines of people; stray dogs lurk in the ruins. At the same time, the city is in a feverish mood: Restaurants are crowded; people drink vodka sitting around bonfires lit in the city's squares. Then there is the party congress at the Palace of Culture, which results in a solemn declaration that Poland has been given the honor of applying for membership in the Soviet Union. That announcement, the narrator's last love affair and the importance to the plot of the Palace of Culture (built by Stalin as a token of Russo-Polish friendship) combine to make Poland's love-hate rela-

tionship with the Soviet Union one of the book's major motifs.

A Minor Apocalypse has elements of satire, nightmare and profound political analysis based on authentic situations. But Mr. Konwicki also mixes crude humor with a lyrical love plot, solemnity with revels, irony with pathos, and realistic observations with philosophical ruminations.

One could read *Minor Apocalypse* as a *roman à clef* with characters bearing some resemblance to well-known personalities of Polish cultural and political life. Thus a reader might link a film director in the novel who oscillates between revolt and submission to the regime with the film maker Andrzej Wajda. Or he might wonder whether an enigmatic leader of the opposition might not actually be Jacek Kuron, one of the founders of the dissident group K.O.R., and whether a dignitary who turns into an artist is not Wlodzimierz Sokorski, once Poland's Minister of Culture and now a novelist. Such a reading, however, might be misleading. Even taking the narrator, a misanthrope and martyr, as a satirical portrait of Mr. Konwicki himself is too simple. His intention is not to meddle with the petty rumors of Warsaw high society but to describe his vision of the end of the world.

Mr. Konwicki wrote this novel in the late 1970's. When the Solidarity movement was growing in power, his predictions of horror seemed too extreme. But the imposition of martial law in December 1981 proved his vision a gloomy reality. The resemblance of events in the novel to those in the real world of Poland is alarming; the soaring prices of consumer goods, treated here as preposterous, have become all too real. Viewed from one perspective, Mr. Konwicki's novel is less satire than prophecy.

A Minor Apocalypse offers readers a vision of slavery under a totalitarian system of government. Mr. Konwicki's view may not be as epic as Aleksandr Solzhenitsyn's or as rationally realistic as Milan Kundera's, but he has given us a grotesque parable that probes to the core of the absurd.

> Maciej Karpinski, "Immolation Day in Warsaw," in The New York Times Book Review, *October 23, 1983, p. 13.*

JAROSLAW ANDERS

A Minor Apocalypse is one of the most powerful, artistically accomplished, and gloomy literary reports to come recently from the twilight zone of Eastern Europe. It is also a cryptic testimony whose real message is buried in the sequence of bizarre events, symbolic characters, and confused internal monologues of the main hero, the narrator who is endowed with the author's own name, appearance, and memory.

Tadeusz Konwicki was born in 1926 near Wilno in what was then Polish Lithuania. He grew up in a country still engulfed in the pastoral past, whose folklore and collective memory reached back to the Middle Ages. Like his older countryman, Czeslaw Milosz, whose autobiographical novel, *The Issa Valley,* he managed to film shortly before the declaration of martial law in Poland, he inherited an acute sense of historical destiny, a belief in the magical power of national dreams, and a taste for visionary realism. In his early youth he fought in a guerrilla unit of the Home Army against Soviet troops, which took over Wilno after chasing out the Germans. Later, when Lithuania was incorporated into the Soviet Union, he moved to Poland and finally settled in Warsaw.

Despite his anticommunist past, Konwicki followed the same path as many in his generation in trying to reconcile himself with the new regime. He even became a member of a group of young literary enthusiasts called "the pimpled ones." His first stories and articles exalted the heroic workers involved in the "construction of socialism," and his first published novel, *Power* (1954), followed the official model of Socialist Realism. Like the majority of his contemporaries, however, he was soon disillusioned. As a writer, he decided to follow his own vision—more personal and much more complex—of the times he had witnessed. In 1963 he published *A Dreambook for Our Time,* a novel that established his literary reputation in Poland. It is a story of a man mysteriously saved from death, who then escapes into death at the end of the book—a pattern that would recur more than once in his later fiction. Konwicki's last three books, the novels *The Polish Complex* (1977), and *A Minor Apocalypse* (1979), as well as a literary journal, *Moonrise, Moonset* (1982), were published outside the reach of state censorship by the independent and clandestine Polish literary magazine *Zapis.*

A Minor Apocalypse is a futuristic yet strikingly familiar fantasy. The place is unmistakably Warsaw; the time, some indefinite future, although we are allowed to guess that we are well beyond 1984. The world is falling apart both physically and morally. Houses and bridges collapse, shops are empty, money loses value, cars run on buttermilk. Even time deteriorates. There are no calendars, so nobody can tell the date. Seasons of the year blur and merge. Life is a grotesque, sometimes hilarious, yet always terrifying spectacle of decay and degradation. The process evidently has been a long and gradual one, since nobody seems to notice or care. In fact, people have adapted to their subhuman condition pretty well. Even a diminishing group of "dissidents," disillusioned about their activities, manipulated and corrupted by the regime, provides little hope for the future. (p. 43)

When the novel was first published in Poland, it was met with bewilderment and more than a few voices of opposition. *A Minor Apocalypse* is a roman à clef portraying, in a thinly veiled way, well-known figures from the official as well as the "underground" culture and politics. Many people took personal offense. Konwicki seems determined to settle accounts with just about everybody: the Russians, the West, the government, the opposition, the intellectuals, the artists, and his own countrymen in general. Konwicki's fantasy was interpreted as a report on the present state of things. As such it was obviously too negative and one-sided. Some critics pointed to his lack of understanding of the real political mechanisms and his underestimation of the power and the determination of Polish workers—objections that were suddenly confirmed by the popular protest of 1980 which transformed the apathetic society.

But such an approach to the author of *A Minor Apocalypse* misses the point. Konwicki is not a political writer. He is an explorer of the subconscious, though the subconscious in a special, collective sense. He is interested in the subjective reality of a people crippled by their historical fate, banished from the world of normal social pursuits and achievements into the domain of dreams, myths, and futile expectations. Using his own biography and the experience of his generation, he watches how Poles create, transform, and destroy their symbols, how they change their weaknesses into

strengths, and their strengths into weaknesses. The characters that appear in his novels are real people, as well as phantoms from the narrator's past and emblematic figures from the Polish collective consciousness. "The boy from the provinces" who accompanies the protagonist, and who turns out to be a police informer, may also be the author's alter ego (his name is also Tadeusz) or his lost youth. The famous writer and Konwicki's master, Jan, who almost reached Parnassus, and now is drinking himself to death in his Warsaw apartment, represents the Polish striving to be admitted to the family of great European cultures. There is also a paralyzed soldier of the Home Army, a survivor of the great war, who watches the disintegration of his country on a TV screen, and a mysterious Russian girl, Nadezhda, who stands for Poland's secret fascination with her neighbor and oppressor.

History in this world is experienced as a repeated disaster or a continuous ending. Konwicki's heroes see their universe evaporating into nothingness, and they in turn are forced out of the familiar domains. By placing his story in an indefinite future, where time has almost ceased to exist, Konwicki captures this repetitive character of the Polish drama, giving us not Poland in a particular moment but a summa of Polish history. What we see is happening right now, has happened before, and will happen again. History confirmed Konwicki's predictions when the military crackdown of December 1981 destroyed all hopes for a major political breakthrough.

Yet there is something much more ominous and terminal in the world of *A Minor Apocalypse.* The novel is also a vision of totalitarianism in the final stage of its decay, which may be, as the author seems to suggest, its final and permanent accomplishment. The most terrifying aspect of this kind of totalitarianism is its almost absolute transparency—"slavery covered by a sloppy coat of contemporary polish," as Konwicki's hero remarks. Those who insist on measuring oppression by the number of political prisoners, the degree of police coercion, and the effectiveness of government control, would find there little reason for indignation. True, there is poverty and corruption of grotesque proportions, yet they are hardly restricted to the totalitarian world. There is also the secret police, which tortures the main hero in a highly inventive and sophisticated way. Still, it looks almost like a relic from the good old days of real struggle and sharp divisions between "us" and "them." The regime itself has grown senile and weak. Its functions have become merely ritualistic. People are mostly left alone, allowed to pursue their petty ambitions. Watched from some safe distant place, they may seem almost free. They make money, have good times, sign petitions and protests; like Rysio, they even write plotless allegorical novels that use neither punctuation nor dialogue. Yet they are slaves, and their slavery has an utterly unprecedented dimension. There is a lot of movement in their world, yet there is no progress. The slavery in Konwicki's novel results from the fact that some great, universal dream of adventure and perfection that has accompanied humanity throughout its history, has irreversibly ended.

The secret power of totalitarianism, Konwicki tells us, is its tremendous inertia, which is released by some historical mistake, and which drives the system to its grim conclusion. Its ultimate result may be the death of history itself, the living death of the world that nobody notices. "This city is the capital of a people evaporating into nothingness. Something needs to be said about that, too. But to whom?"

The world has gotten used to much more spectacular visions

of the apocalypse, and Konwicki, like so many writers from the communist world, warns us that the true apocalypse comes in the form of " . . . an Antichrist diluted, broken into bits and granules," which can be easily overlooked. *A Minor Apocalypse* is clearly an exercise in extreme pessimism, but even Konwicki stops short of total hopelessness. . . . Konwicki's protagonist clings to the belief in the immortality of the world, and this belief makes him accept his own, seemingly absurd death as the only human conclusion of the day of humiliations and reckonings. Yet is he merely dying along with *his* world, Poland, which he has known and which is to be no more, or is his death a real act of sacrifice meant to redeem and save some value for the future? The hero with his irony and taste for dialectical negations and counternegations does not have a clear answer. He climbs to his stake as confused and doubting as when he left home in the morning. Yet his act assumes a larger meaning. The ultimate goal of slavery is to deprive the slave of his subjectivity, make him dissolve in the self of the master. The same can be said about totalitarianism, even though, as Konwicki argues, it is a slavery without a personal master. Every rebellion of a slave, even a hopeless and self-destructive one, is a confirmation of the slave's will to maintain his separate personality. It binds the master and deters his final victory.

A Minor Apocalypse is more evidence that the independent writing from Eastern Europe is taking its place in contemporary world literature. History—cruel to the people who write it—graced it with a subject that Western writers seem to be seeking in vain. Paradoxically it is there, in the oppressive and claustrophobic world, that basic values and ideas of human destiny are undergoing the most thorough examination. If only for that reason, voices like Konwicki's, or Kundera's, or Konrad's, should be listened to today with special attention. (pp. 44-5)

> Jaroslaw Anders, "Not with a Bang," in The New Republic, *Vol. 189, No. 21, November 21, 1983, pp. 43-5.*

JOHN UPDIKE

Tadeusz Konwicki is a Polish writer and film director, born in 1926, who has gone from being an officially approved Socialist Realist to being a dissident whose fiction can be published only in the underground magazine *Zapis* and in the West. A previous novel, *The Polish Complex,* appeared here last year; *A Minor Apocalypse* extends its predecessor's jaunty, picaresque manner deeper into desperation. In both novels, Konwicki's heroes have his name and personal history, as if to say the times are too ramshackle and weary for the conventional concoction of an alter ego. "Weariness and powerlessness were overcoming me. My life was repeating itself and I was repeating myself. . . . My art, like my life, could be sliced like a sausage." (p. 89)

Like such other anarchic spirits as Flann O'Brien and Céline, Konwicki has a lovely light way of writing, which never clogs chaos with self-pity and bestows upon the direst pages sentences of casual magic. He is especially good with women, to whom all sorts of delicate fragrances cling. Here is Nadezhda, being seduced:

> She smelled like water that had been warmed by the sun, and she also had the sharp, enticing aroma of birch leaves . . . We could hear the desperate pounding of each other's hearts and the polyphonic

cry of the birds, like some rising reminder. . . . She had closed her eyes so tightly the lids had turned white. Sharp, predatory teeth gleamed in the heathery pinkness of her mouth.

Konwicki is effortlessly witty, and dizzies the Western reader with the convolutions of the vitiated Polish situation as it drowns in its ironies. A Marxist philosopher explains to the author that Communism has saved Poland from being absorbed by a vital, enterprising Russia: "You should pray every day and thank your gods that the Russians have been rendered inert by that idiotic doctrine, depraved by that ghastly life, exhausted by that moronic economic system." A Party official, Comrade Kobialka, who renounces his career by undressing at a televised Party celebration, appears no less absurd than the televised embrace of the two all-powerful Secretaries: "Two fat men were kissing each other on the mouth." The peculiar demeaningness of television has crept into Poland; all political gestures are aimed toward it, while it turns every event into a trivial flickering. Misery becomes trite, and happiness is absurd, whether it is Kobialka's happiness as he is hauled in a padded straitjacket to the security of the state insane asylum or that of the lusty retired minister, now a painter of nudes, as he rushes off to the outer regions where "you can still find girls who'll put out for good old Polish zlotys" (as opposed to the Warsaw whores, who demand hard currency). Even interrogation by torture is farcical; the police inject Konwicki with a drug that makes him so sensitive he can be agonized by the snap of a fingertip and the battering of a paper ball. At his ordeal's end, he thinks, "Some sort of confused play was over." That Communist governments are atrocious is familiar news; less familiar is Konwicki's repeated point that dissidence, too, has something weary, corrupt, and pointless about it. By now, in Poland, evidently, the motions of opposition, like those of governing, are a kind of sleepwalking. A race has grown up of "dissidents with lifetime appointments. The regime has grown accustomed to them and they've grown accustomed to the regime." Konwicki notices of his young fellow-conspirators that "they were all small, thin, shaggy. But it was in them alone that any resistance to the authorities had smoldered. Over the years, the authorities had grown ugly, too, but in a different way—they had turned into fat, growing sideways; they had become womanish."

No Americans are seen in this long Warsaw day—a blend of Bloomsday and, the reader is often reminded, the Stations of the Cross—but a "senior journalist with the Associated Press" telephones toward evening, saying, "I wanted to ask what was going on in Warsaw today." Konwicki tells him, "Nothing too interesting. The usual holiday commotion." The answer is accepted. The West in general, far from being seen as a superior system to that decaying in Poland, is involved in the same entropic deterioration. Kobialka claims, "The West . . . started running away when we started chasing them, and then they slowed down when we eased up. They're exhausted, too. They're straddling the fence, too." As of 1979, from the Polish slant, we are neither innocent nor dynamic. In regard to the captive plight of Eastern Europe, the free world has proved helpless; capitalism has become not Poland's savior but her creditor. In Paradyz, "the disabled veterans' cooperative band was playing a medley of American tunes but, to disguise them, was playing them backward so they wouldn't have to pay any royalties in hard currency." Poland can only afford to import black humor. Instinctively, Konwicki assumes the tone of absurdist fiction, that tone which says "This happens, that happens, don't expect me to make much of it, because life is meaningless; don't expect me to work you, gentle reader, up into much of a tizzy of caring, either." When, at the very end of *A Minor Apocalypse,* we are expected to care, the rhetoric embarrasses us, so thoroughly have our expectations been lowered by the deflationary slapstick of Konwicki's hopeless world. (pp. 89-90)

John Updike, "As Others See Us," in The New Yorker, *Vol. LIX, No. 46, January 2, 1984, pp. 87-90.*

GERARD T. KAPOLKA

Mala Apokalipsa (*A Minor Apocalypse*) appeared in Poland in 1979 as a publication of the underground journal *Zapis.* But the pessimistic vision of this book was soon overshadowed by the early successes of "Solidarity." Even after the imposition of Martial law, when pessimistic visions again seem appropriate, this book still seems a bit out of place. It is the "minor" aspect of the book, rather than its "apocalyptic" aspect that now seems out of place. Paradoxically, however, this seeming irrelevance can almost serve to emphasize one of the critical aspects of this book. For the protagonist here is indeed isolated from the society in which he finds himself. In addition, this book is much more than a political satire on the Poland of 1979. On one level, it reflects a feeling of frustration that the means taken by the intellectuals to oppose the government are both insufficient and unsatisfying. On a more abstract level, it reflects the more universal feeling that, put crudely, no matter what one does in today's world, nothing much will come of it. Characters of tragic proportion find no place in this book. As the narrator says, "In today's ambiguous world, character means despotism, tyranny, absolute intolerance. Our epoch is that of noble doubts, blessed uncertainty, sacred hypersensitivity, divine wishy-washiness." (p. 107)

The combination of ordinary and exceptional qualities [portrayed in this book] . . . helps to explain the title, *A Minor Apocalypse.* As the protagonist says, "The world can't die. Many generations have thought the world was dying. But it was only their world which was dying." It is precisely the protagonist's world that is dying, quite literally falling apart around him as he goes about his day. And he has no pretensions about a major apocalypse, a catastrophe that would somehow purify the sense of decay. Throughout the novel, the course of events constantly robs the protagonist of any grandness in his impending fate. . . . We are never quite sure whether he has accepted it or not. It is delivered to him as an assignment or a mission, in a manner consciously reminiscent of an order given by a war-time partisan superior officer. This seems to be an indirect allusion to Andrzejewski's *Ashes and Diamonds;* and one of the characters who delivers these orders to the protagonist seems to represent Andrzejewski himself. Like Maciej in *Ashes and Diamonds,* the protagonist is caught between two worlds. He is out of place both in the new opposition and certainly with the establishment. (pp. 107-08)

The structural similarity of *A Minor Apocalypse* to *Ashes and Diamonds* is more than superficial, although the tone of the two books could not be more different. This causes me to view *A Minor Apocalypse,* in large part, as a parody of *Ashes and Diamonds.* . . . The parody is not effected to repudiate *Ashes and Diamonds.* This work has already been repudiated

by Andrzejewski himself, and there really would be no need to take such a step. Konwicki has borrowed some of Andrzejewski's images and brought them up to date to create a new type of hero, equally doomed, but far less grand. Furthermore, and this is extremely important for determining its role in Polish literature, *A Minor Apocalypse* departs from the prototype followed in *Ashes and Diamonds* and, for that matter, in Konwicki's own *The Polish Complex,* the prototype established by Wyspianski's *The Wedding,* of presenting a microcosm of Polish society through its collection of characters. If this book presents Polish society at all, it does so only incidentally. Instead, it concentrates all of our attention on the narrator-protagonist. Polish literature has rarely, if ever, produced so introspective a novel.

A Minor Apocalypse is a disturbing book, even an irritating book, one that makes you squirm. The atmosphere throughout is that of the hangover that the narrator complains of several times. Its annoying tone and several other aspects make this novel comparable to Dostoevski's *Notes from Underground.* First of all, the protagonist here is a kind of "superfluous man," that creature very familiar to readers of Russian literature, but who seldom makes an appearance in Polish literature, which is usually more concerned with presenting an individual as an intrinsic part of society rather than an appendix to it. Secondly, just as in Dostoevski's disturbing work, we are taken so deeply into the mind of the protagonist here that we begin to feel all of his annoyances and begin to believe in the impossibility of continuing to live in such a ludicrous manner.

Certain similarities can be seen in Konwicki's three major novels, *A Dreambook of Our Time, The Polish Complex* and *A Minor Apocalypse.* Though only the first of these is called such, they are all dreambooks. Each has its own, rather fluid dream logic. But this technique is used very subtly, so that we are always left to wonder whether the presumed reality of the novel is only a dream or not. The author plays little tricks on us to accomplish this effect. To give a few examples from *A Minor Apocalypse,* we see inconsistencies in Nadezhda; at one time she is a virgin, at another she has had three husbands. Also, no one in the novel knows the date, and the seasons keep changing, even though the action takes place in about 12 hours. But Konwicki's dream-realities are all too similar to the real world. His absurdities always parallel the absurdities in our own world of appearances.

Here too, as in the other two novels, the protagonist is strongly identified with the author himself. He is a writer with Konwicki's exact background. I do not call the protagonist Konwicki himself even though the author seems to have done everything he could to remove the distance between himself and his protagonist. What he has done instead is very interesting; he has used various literary devices to distance everything around the protagonist from the real world in which the author himself lives, while creating a presumably accurate picture of himself, of his deepest fears and thoughts, in the protagonist. Perhaps this is all just an extension of the dream world which the author has created. The protagonist is the one mainstay in the novel. His thoughts and feelings are real, but his surroundings are draped in illusions and artifices. Many of the characters in this novel can be readily seen as representing specific, prominent Polish figures, but all of them appear under pseudonyms. This is not an autobiographical novel at all, it is rather the converse of an autobiographical novel. For in such a novel an author usually describes events in his life but puts another name on the character who experiences these events, and distances that character from himself and changes him, if only slightly. Here the author presents himself as the main character, but all of the events he experiences are fictions, illusions. There is no doubt that the author is here presenting his personal vision, nor that he is baring his soul to us. Yet the fantasy of the events described here make it very important for us to distinguish Konwicki the author from Konwicki the protagonist.

In conclusion, I must say that although I am quite impressed with this book, I do not think that it is as well crafted nor as moving as *The Polish Complex.* I found myself occasionally tired of the narrator's ramblings. The author does seem to bare his soul through the narrator-protagonist, but I, at least, wonder if he was not a bit too self-indulgent. (pp. 108-09)

> *Gerard T. Kapolka, in a review of "A Minor Apocalypse," in* The Polish Review, *Vol. XXIX, No. 3, 1984, pp. 107-09.*

MICHAEL SZPORER

Already widely acclaimed as a classic, *A Minor Apocalypse* is a fine example of the evolving conspiratorial style that parodies the allegorical parabolizing of contemporary history and the political allusiveness characteristic of the Soviet bloc mentality shaped by the elaborate system of censorship ingrained in the intellectual subconscious. Although *A Minor Apocalypse* invites subversive allegorizing, the social subtext is politically illusive and meticulously textured. Konwicki's subterranean thinking is calculated to force all that is underground above ground. Dreaming about the future for good or ill, in view of the "post-Marxist" experience, has become an anachronism, an expression of intellectual mediocrity hopelessly lost in an uneventful present.

The alternative is neither the left nor the right in the traditional political sense. Konwicki satirizes dystopian brooding about the impending totalitarian nightmare. The run-down imagination of *A Minor Apocalypse* evokes the atmosphere of George Orwell's *1984*. Its victim-hero, Konwicki himself, suffering from an unrelieved hangover, moves from one savagely absurd adventure to another in a dingy world of a deteriorating Eastern European metropolis. He is never really sure about the purpose of his final journey to set himself on fire, presumably as a protest against the regime. While he wanders about the streets and back alleys of crumbling Warsaw, he dodges drunken demonstrators who are uncertain why they are parading about; meets disgruntled politicians who publicly divest themselves of their dogma as well as of their clothes; and makes love among the ruins of *Szpilki* (a magazine specializing in political satire) to Nadiezda, his Russian Hope. He is followed everywhere by his faithful dog and Tadzio, a provincial literary groupie with a gas can who turns out to be a secret police spook.

It may not be surprising that Konwicki, an auteurial film-maker in his own right, has more in common with Jean-Luc Godard's "science fiction" vision in *Alphaville* with its deflated sensibility and sobering irony than with the intellectual angst of postrevolutionary apocalypses such as Zamyatin's *We,* Capek's *RUR,* and Orwell's *1984.* It is the present and not some distant future that overwhelms, terrifies, is inescapable. The future is now. Konwicki's fantasies are real enough. What seems like nonsense twists and turns around facts: On

16 January 1969 Jan Palach, a twenty-one-year-old student at Charles University publicly burned himself to protest the Soviet invasion of Czechoslovakia, sparking a demonstration of more than 100,000 people gathered at Wenceslas Square to commemorate his burial four days later. Little more than a month later, on February 25, eighteen-year-old Jan Zajic burned himself, arousing little public concern. Palach was seen as a martyr and was compared with Jan Huss, the Protestant reformer burned at the stake in 1415. Subsequent public burnings, however, were attributed to mental disturbances and alcoholism.

The most he can bequeath to posterity to redeem himself as a writer and to be of some use to the reader, Konwicki tells us in his will in *A Minor Apocalypse,* is a homey remedy for dandruff, a prescription to relieve constipation, and a handy trick to win at twenty-one. His apocalyptic end by self-immolation to protest Sovietization in Poland is a rather feeble, half-hearted affair of no real consequence. This personal protest, authentic only in the sense that Konwicki himself carries it out, is a hopeless gesture without any apparent significance. In fact, it may not even be a protest but a plot instigated by the secret police. And it probably will not be noticed or taken seriously by anyone because no one really cares, except perhaps the agent personally assigned to him, Nadiezda, and Konwicki himself.

Why then the sacrifice and for what purpose? To conquer the absurdity of history? To fight nonsense with nonsense? Perhaps it no longer matters what makes sense and what does not, whether you have gained or lost. You simply do what you must, what impels you. Not even Konwicki is certain about the occasion for his protest or where the burning should take place. (pp. 89-91)

No one in *A Minor Apocalypse* is really sure about dates or places, about motives or intentions—neither the author nor his friends in the opposition, neither the socialist East nor the capitalist West. Accurate calendars are unavailable anywhere, perhaps because of censorship, perhaps because of defects in socialist production. And, even if Swedish matches are more dependable for a public burning than Polish ones, socialist disorder, we are told, has demoralized capitalism. The entire world is becoming more and more Soviet. Ideologies catch up with one another, surpass one another, become confounded together in an awful nightmarish blur from which it seems impossible to awake. All that we know, in the end, says Konwicki, is that we have invented God in our own inept image, that we have made it all up to give us strength in the course of human history. And, for this reason alone, this fantasy must burn. It must sacrifice itself for us because it is us. And, if we could burn up our private fantasies, perhaps some truth would remain, a miracle might happen.

Fictions conspire against history. To maintain their integrity, they have to find their symbolic meaning in ordinary lives and commonplace experiences. More inspiring ideals, more utopian hopes would only further contaminate our already unreal sense of reality and deform our already deformed sense of history. Ideological revisionism is not the answer because history has been so falsified by its own self-image that it no longer matters. . . . All we have is self-sacrificing contemporaneity ideologically striving for a better future while everything is in fact running down to the ground. (pp. 91-2)

In contrast to the other apocalyptic futurologies, *A Minor Apocalypse* does not lament the passing away of revolutionary hope nor does it relentlessly bemoan the false consciousness the proletariat seems incapable of overcoming. For it seems that the ideological crisis in our time has been falsely reduced in these essentially revisionist "red nightmares" to the impotence of intellectuals, which renders them unable to bring about humanistic changes in the bureaucratic Party apparatus, or to some futile longing for liberalization of totalitarian thinking. Perhaps this is why Konwicki is politically painful to come to terms with for a Western liberal intellectual, for here progressive thinking cancels itself out in idealistic routines that get our minds off real history. How relieved we feel with the self-consuming politics of Orwellian fiction!

The intellectual landscape of *A Minor Apocalypse* is without reason, without any Big Brother to speak of. In Konwicki's world, reason does not triumph over the vestiges of irrational humanity because (in pseudo-Hegelian terms) reason has never really entered history. What rules post-Marxist social reality is a fiction, a supreme fiction perhaps. Of course, this is not to suggest that Konwicki himself is ideological or even antisocialist. "I will not be very happy about the fact that the experiment begun by two German scholars ended in a fiasco," Konwicki cautions in *Moon Rises and Sets.* But the alternative is not wholeheartedly to espouse free enterprise of egoism and greed. "How great that communism has lost. How sad that communism has lost."

Clearly Konwicki must be read in the context of the Polish crisis and with the subtle and complex understanding of the ideological struggles affecting contemporary post-Marxist social reality in the Soviet bloc countries. The publication of *A Minor Apocalypse,* rebounding off the Seventies and the *embourgissement* that characterized the Gierek years, looks forward to the rise of Solidarity. It may well be (as Irving Howe has suggested) [see excerpt above] that Konwicki's grim "here comes the end of the world" thinking has been vindicated by the sudden collapse of the workers' movement, which in its heyday organized about a third of Poland's population with well over ten million members in its ranks. The absurd world of *A Minor Apocalypse* indeed turns out to be more real than the real world. Konwicki himself admitted as much in his journal *Moon Rises and Sets,* written during the apocalyptic year of the Solidarity crisis of 1980-1981: "Out of despair I made up several feeble mind games in my books and my serious and obstinate countrymen are making my mind games come true." Just how real the absurd can become is perhaps best illustrated by Konwicki's own martial law experience. Apparently, he was interrogated and asked to sign a loyalty oath by a Tadzio-type right out of his own novel.

However, to characterize this underground classic as yet another invective against a corrupt and impersonal social apparatus that has maligned all that was once human, meaningful, and true, as Howe has done, is to underestimate the author's political sophistication. By the same token, such a reading seems to romanticize Polish political realities and seriously misreads the world historical significance of the Solidarity movement. We are not simply talking about misguided "proles" and disheartened intellectuals for whom communism was the God that failed. *A Minor Apocalypse* self-consciously identifies itself with the collapse of ideological discourse. The West like the East relies on worn-out slogans for self-understanding. It forgets that only personally experienced history makes us comprehensible to ourselves.

Konwicki's Poland no longer appears to be willing to settle for "Marxism with the human face." The emerging political consciousness has grown tired of ideology and weary of slogans. The past cannot be rectified. It will not be contented with (to use the Czech novelist Milan Kundera's metaphors in *The Book of Laughter and Forgetting*) the original photograph of the past before it was carefully airbrushed by the censor. Konwicki is not particularly interested in restoring the past or in legitimizing personal memories that ideological history has doctored. The frequent personal reflections about his youth in Lithuania, about his activism in the nationalist underground during World War Two (in *Moon Rises and Sets*), or, for that matter, about earlier Polish struggles against oppression (in *The Polish Complex*) are weapons aimed at an uncertain future. For in Poland after martial law, the only future that makes sense, as the Solidarity pragmatist Adam Michnik has suggested, is personally initiated permanent conspiracy working toward the inevitable disintegration of the power structure. As Konwicki proposed somewhat ironically in *A Minor Apocalypse,* the only audience in post-Marxist Poland that guarantees the writer an honest reading is the secret police. The secret police mentality is the latent imagination of the Polish writer. The recognition of this, his political unconsciousness, transforms the writer into a co-conspirator, into a clandestine accomplice.

Why flirt with "the headless regime"? To worry about the censor is, in a sense, to continue to legitimate the system, to deal with its shortcomings cosmetically. In Konwicki's world, the power structure no longer pretends to be legitimate, nor does it even care about being accepted or tolerated. The political apparatus has deteriorated totally. The Bureau of Internal Security makes you eternal, and not actually even the Bureau as a social institution but the specific agent assigned to your case. In the course of an interrogation in *A Minor Apocalypse,* the agent tells Konwicki that everyone in Poland, including the Party Secretary and himself, has joined the opposition. Apparently the only difference between them is in the manner of opposing: he is positive, whereas Konwicki remains stubbornly negative. The different styles go along with their respective jobs. So think positively, the agent tells him. Do not waste your time writing for the censor; write for me:

> —A propos. Why aren't you writing?
>
> —Do you think that it's worth writing?
>
> —The egg heads say, it's not. But if the egg heads say so it means that it's worth it. I even have an idea. You should write for a specific reader, that's always best. Me, for example. Forget censorship, whether the state is just or not, all the fears, and write like a free man to free men. You were always precious but never vain. The size of the edition does not seem to matter much to you. Better one intelligent reader with real literature in hand than ten thousand jellyfish grasping for toilet paper. Your book is safe with me. Only in my hand do you stand a chance of enduring—of achieving eternity.

Why go against the current? Why contest the powers that be in a hopeless struggle that will inevitably end in ruin and accomplish nothing? This seems to characterize the typical Polish dilemma in Konwicki's earlier novel *The Polish Complex.* Is Konwicki's sacrifice then a vestige of romanticism, of that very Polish tendency to dare fate? (pp. 92-4)

It is true (as his readers both within Poland and outside have noticed) that Konwicki for some time now has been railing against the falsities of his world, wracking his brains to find something authentic in it. But he is not just a pessimist over-indulging in some existential angst or suffering from a heavy overdose of Polish romanticism. At the very most, the meta-physical and otherworldly concerns are for him a means of insubordination—a weapon against the sociologizing of facts, against the local yokel canons of social determinism. Kon-wicki's prose overwhelms us with its irreverent running com-mentaries, digressions, and critical asides about the ideologi-cal, moral, and intellectual deterioration of the regime; about the imminent breakdown of the Soviet state; about the rather provincial goings-on in the "Duchy of Warsaw." It spares no one, neither the regime nor its opposition, neither the East nor the West.

In *Moon Rises and Sets* Konwicki tells a cocksure professor who has read *A Minor Apocalypse* and found it a totally un-acceptable portrayal of contemporary Poland that he has missed the point. The defeatism is only half-true, like every-thing else; the dung heap that is his world is worth sacrifices. In *A Minor Apocalypse* Konwicki portrays himself as a mod-est, amateurish, would-be savior riddled with uncertainty about things to come. The underlying message, if any, is that the writer (or any thinking individual for that matter) should step out of his role and reclaim himself. A glimpse of the ordi-nary, at oneself, is beyond truth or falsity.

Most often, Konwicki seems to be cautioning us against being dead certain—against rationalizing literature, history, events. For such pseudo-intelligent and hyperideological to-talizing forms the mindset of social fascism that results in gulags and worse. The recent Polish crisis was not—he re-minds us in *Moon Rises and Sets*—the uprising but one more in a string of uprisings: 1956, 1968, 1970, 1976, 1980; and these uprisings were more psychological than bloody, welter-ing up from the unconscious, "uprisings in the nervous net-work of the libido."

Konwicki imagines himself, somewhat ironically, as the Freudian conscience of his day, as the subliminal collective fantasy deepened by fact. His semijournalistic and counterfic-tional assaults on ideology recall avant-garde writing of the Twenties, especially the antisocialist realist factographies and pseudonovelistic memoirs of an early Soviet dissident, the much-misunderstood Victor Shklovsky. In *A Sentimental Journey,* Shklovsky, then a political refugee essentially left-wing and sympathetic to the revolutionary cause, confronted the communist (Bolshevik) tribunal in Moscow with his own marginalism—with his peripheral, autobiographical social conscience. He wanted to expose the dark underside of his time—which he ironically referred to as Red Restoration—to bring to light its political unconscious. Much like the "disillu-sioned" Shklovsky, Konwicki portrays himself as an ideolog-ical burnout, weary of symbolism. And I would say that it is precisely this weariness, this fuzziness, this seemingly ran-dom and impulsive minoritarianism that makes him the most farsighted, the most thoroughly political writer in "the other Europe."

That struggle to reclaim oneself, to become ordinary, is not hopelessness. Konwicki may well be laying his claim to an an-archistic earthiness and human familiality expressed in litera-ture that seems to transcend frontiers and national identities. Ironically, in *A Minor Apocalypse* Nadiezda recognizes this motif as that typically "Russian" quality of his writing. Kon-wicki, in other words, wants to enmesh the whole world in his Polish complex. Not only Poles but everyone today seems

to suffer from the overindulgence in one's own self-esteem, from being aroused by one's own significance. It makes us mediocre and incapable of wishing and doing for others what we would wish for and want to have done to ourselves. In Konwicki's world everyone, including the author himself, seems incapable of freeing himself from his own mendacity. Hence the question for the future may well be not so much who controls the truth as who is in charge of fiction and what unreal purposes does fiction serve. (pp. 94-6)

Michael Szporer, "Beyond Aesthetics of Censorship: Tadeusz Konwicki's Ordinary Politicking," in Mod-ern Fiction Studies, *Vol. 32, No. 1, Spring, 1986, pp. 89-96.*

WALTER GOODMAN

Labeled a "real-life novel," **Moonrise, Moonset** lurches along from reminiscence to diatribe to confession to lamentation. The autobiography is entangled with politics; there are fre-quent pauses for reflections on Poland's grim history, subject always to the power of its big neighbor: "For centuries now, the Poles have been sentenced by Moscow and Orthodoxy to death, the death of the Polish state and nation." Mr. Kon-wicki, a prominent novelist, screenwriter and director in his own country, seems to be struggling in what he thinks of as his old age (he is only 61, but physical ailments are accumu-lating) to get at the crux of his own past and that of his unfor-tunate country.

As a teen-ager during the German occupation in World War II, he fought with the Polish Home Army against the Ger-mans, and when the Russians moved in at the war's end, he found himself briefly fighting against them as well. Then, for 15 years, he belonged to the Communist Party and supported the regime imposed on Poland by Moscow, a period that he recalls with shame: "My friends dragged me into it, as if it were a beer house or a brothel." For the past decade, his work has been published by the underground press. Yes, he is bit-ter—but what other emotion, he seems to be asking, can be expected from a writer and patriot in the grip of an alien power. . . .

What the author calls his "grotesque journal" is full of anec-dotes, some about his rivalries with writers who have made their peace with the authorities; most of the names ring no bells, and he seems to be straining to make private grudges matters of public import. His comments on better known writers whom he admires, such as Mr. Milosz, Adam Mich-nik and Stanislaw Lem, are not all that interesting. Mr. Kon-wicki seems to know when his memoir is not working. Now and then, he expresses exasperation with his "clogged, lopsid-ed, slipshod" writing.

The more compelling anecdotes, culminating in portions of a novel with which **Moonrise, Moonset** ends, come out of his memories of the war years, especially the Home Army rising against the Germans in 1944 and the arrival of Russian troops not long after ("The first evening of free slavery or slave freedom"); the comradeship with young men who were killed by the Germans or the Russians and his brief ro-mances.

What holds one, intermittently, is the passion of a writer whose hopes seem to have died 40 years ago and who has had to live and work in a society that he despises. He asks whether some future reader will find "a sort of spiritual and intellectual affinity—if only in the sense of humor—with some man by the name of Konwicki, an ex-socialist realist, ex-conformist, ex-oppositionist, ex-pen pusher, envier and sex maniac?" He doesn't make it easy, but like him or not, it's hard to remain unshaken by the strength of his writing, . . . or the depth of his pain over the horrors of his country's history.

> *Walter Goodman, in a review of "Moonrise, Moonset," in* The New York Times, *August 13, 1987, p. 28.*

EWA KURYLUK

Tadeusz Konwicki's **Moonrise, Moonset** is neither a piece of fiction nor a memoir. At times, it seems to become a novel within a diary, or a diary within a diary—one concerned with the author's present, the other with his past. However, this book of loose reflections on God and the world, on Poland in the days of Solidarity and Poland emerging from the bloodshed of World War II, is really about memory—about the way memory comes into being as bits of the present tense solidify into the past; about the way memory works, as those bits are assimilated and the past is mirrored in multiple looking glasses. . . .

In **Moonrise, Moonset** Mr. Konwicki has set himself the modest goal of narrating such phone calls, and many other casual and trivial instants when a name, a word, an image give a kick to the memory and the past begins to unfold, either as an ocean of voices and visions merging into one another or as a staccato of noises and details popping up and disappearing. There is nothing new in this method. It goes back to Dostoyevsky's seismographic recording of psychological and linguistic polyphony, to Edouard Dujardin's inner monologue in the 1888 *Les Lauriers Sont Coupés* (*We'll to the Woods No More*) to Arthur Schnitzler's explorations of the stream of consciousness around 1900 and to the prose of James Joyce. . . .

Mr. Konwicki is well aware that diaries and other mixed and ephemeral forms of literature and art may be regarded in the future as the most interesting and moving testimonies of the 20th century, and he realizes that today we can reach into the inner depths not so much by enlarging as by reducing our scope. Paying homage to his friend Mieczyslaw Piotrowski, a complete outsider not only to the international but even to the small Polish world of arts and letters, Mr. Konwicki speaks with admiration about a draftsman who, instead of moving on as others did, "kept withdrawing . . . abandoning the richer lines, ornament, the decorative element, and color . . . slowly giving up everything, even what is commonly known as beauty or loveliness." The nearly imperceptible art and the hermetic writings of this strange man, whom contemporaries ridiculed or ignored, will, Mr. Konwicki believes, be discovered one day as a "fresco capturing our time in an intellectual and aesthetic pattern."

However, the author of **Moonrise, Moonset** acknowledges, and not without a certain pride, that he himself does not belong to the Piotrowski type of artist or writer. Mr. Konwicki sees himself as an outsider, but he is an outsider to a point only; he does not disregard fame, nor is he unable to strike a compromise. Thus, on the one hand, he is proud of having rejected the temptation to write a novel, something popular with the public; on the other hand, he repeatedly deplores the state of mind that renders him incapable of writing one. After

the success of **A Minor Apocalypse,** which lifted Mr. Konwicki to the stature of a prophet, Polish readers have been waiting for another novel. And Adam Michnik, the glory of Polish dissent, went so far as to commission a book about the young Konwicki's participation in the anti-Nazi underground, the Home Army, which at the end of the war fought the Communist regime imposed by the Soviet Union. . . .

Wishing to preserve in **Moonrise, Moonset** at least some elements of a novel, Mr. Konwicki gives his partisan memoir a slightly fictional character. This is both a weakness and a strength. Narrated in more conventional terms, Mr. Konwicki's youth appears more stereotypical than his adult years. However, one could argue that youth as such is characterized by conventionality, and that fictionalization lies at the very core of everybody's perception of youth and childhood. In Mr. Konwicki's narrative the old and the young selves observe each other like two strangers who were once close friends—with surprise, disbelief and the desire to come to terms with each other, by interweaving life's two threads into one fabric.

Sarcastic, witty and full of self-irony, Mr. Konwicki's semi-conventional prose might nevertheless have had difficulties holding the reader's attention throughout the book had the author not selected an attractive subject as well. The present-tense narrative begins in the autumn of 1980, shortly after the official recognition of Solidarity, and ends with the introduction of martial law in December 1981—and with questioning of the author at police headquarters. The narrated past covers mainly the years 1944 and 1945, but it offers a few glimpses of Mr. Konwicki's childhood in Lithuania and of the postwar period in Cracow and Warsaw, and finally includes fragments of his second novel, written when he was 22. Thus real fiction is added to the half-fiction of youth. (p. 3)

The title, **Moonrise, Moonset,** seems to evoke the tides as well as the cycle of a man's moody soul swinging back and forth between depression and exhilaration, boredom and irritation. This book about abandoning the novel and deploring one's desertion is also a book about growing old, about the present falling to pieces and the past assuming an ever-greater significance. With the body breaking down and the mind dwelling on remembrances, the novel cannot but dissolve. Physiology blends with esthetics in an uneasy text, but it is one that has to be considered Tadeusz Konwicki's best book. (p. 31)

> *Ewa Kuryluk, "A Seismograph in Poland," in* The New York Times Book Review, *August 30, 1987, pp. 3, 31.*

J. HOBERMAN

Say this for the Polish novelist and filmmaker Tadeusz Konwicki—neither Western fame nor national renewal, neither age nor historical perspicuity, has mellowed him. On the contrary. [In his pseudo-diaristic **Moonrise, Moonset**], Konwicki has kept his bitterness as translucent and unalloyed as the most downtrodden adolescent's. . . .

Blind hideousness must be a corrective to the radiant optimism of Konwicki's early, sanctioned novels. Like **The Polish Complex** and **A Minor Apocalypse, Moonrise, Moonset** was first published in the unofficial quarterly *Zapis;* as in the two previous books, Konwicki invents himself as a character—cranky, cynical, perverse. "I seem to be writing out of spite," he says, echoing the inhabitant of Dostoyevsky's mousehole. . . . "Konwicki" remains aloof from Solidarity: "Today everyone's trafficking in national devotional articles." Rather than join the processional, he exaggerates his infirmities and indulges in intimations of obsolescence: "I'll go looking for a country with censorship, where I can write modern allusive prose for the rest of my days."

Although *Moonrise, Moonset* is scarcely allegorical, there's no shortage of cryptic allusions or reflexive gossip. A memoir, a rant, a home for chunks of unfinished novels (inserted into this "prose diary the way you slice a little stale kielbasa into a soup"), the book is overtly, and sometimes tediously, self-serving. "The prophecies I made in *A Minor Apocalypse* have long since come true," Konwicki boasts. . . . As a writer, Konwicki thrived on the fertile disorder of the late '70s, the period of Edward Gierek's corrupt, catastrophic attempt to simultaneously modernize, Russify, and placate Poland. *Moonrise, Moonset*'s funniest setpiece is a left-handed tribute to Gierek as the key historical figure who "made Communism look ridiculous." Unfortunately, Konwicki devotes far more space to locating himself in Polish literature and even more to settling old scores.

Konwicki is a master of insult humor—"The Poles are the most seasoned slaves in Europe . . . perhaps it is our destiny to destroy Communism"—but his evaluations of star writers Stanislaw Lem, Witold Gombrowicz, Czeslaw Milosz, and a dozen lesser-known figures are mostly a bore. Sardonic as he is, Konwicki lacks a genuinely underground self-absorption. His eye is on the audience—his self-disgust is less a pathology than a pose. He's too anxious a name-dropper. . . .

Moonrise, Moonset is the least of Konwicki's recent novels (particularly in the phantasmagorical light of *A Minor Apocalypse*), but even at his least, Konwicki is a tonic writer. When he recounts "a long and dangerous journey through the steppes of Warsaw, the terrible wilderness of our capital city" or remarks that the hookers hanging around the nightclub in the monstrous Palace of Culture "seemed to be from some cosmopolitan paradise where the Communists had been in power for a week," he reveals a disillusionment so total it suggests a new genre of political science fiction struggling to be born.

> J. Hoberman, "Spite and Polish," in The Village Voice, *Vol. XXXII, No. 37, September 15, 1987, p. 58.*

NEAL ASCHERSON

[*Moonrise, Moonset*] is a work hard to classify. It is not a journal like the *Warsaw Diary* of Kazimierz Brandys, although it was written during the same period, ending in 1981, and has entries about contemporary public events and scenes. Neither is it a notebook or a log of reflections, although it has qualities of both. It is a darting, constantly changing mixture of different elements: autobiography, criticism, self-criticism, fiction, gossip, both benevolent and malevolent, history, anecdote, and fierce moral polemic.

It may appear shapeless, but it is not. Konwicki records a remark made of him by the writer Jerzy Putrament: "You know, Konwicki pretends to be poorer than he is; *pribednayetsya,* as the Russians say." Konwicki comments that this was the language of a sadistic Chekist (Putrament went on to suggest peeling layers off him like an onion to see what was

inside). But there is something in it, as a literary judgment. Konwicki, in this sort of work, shows a self-deprecating—almost slapdash—surface. It is contrived. What is really taking place is a complex but carefully planned process of self-exposure, culminating when, near the end of the book, Konwicki reproduces a long selection from a novel written just after the war and never published, which is scathing about some of those who opposed "the People's Power." (p. 44)

Anybody who hopes that this strange book is the result of exorcising a bad conscience, however, is mistaken—and in danger of grievous mental injury from Konwicki's often murderous wit. Certainly, *Moonrise, Moonset* is at one level a presentation of evidence to show how he came to write as he once did, although that unpublished novel written in his early twenties seems to me, on the basis of those extracts, a brilliant piece of fiction that requires no apology. But in all the facets of the book, in the lyrical passages about his home countryside and the Wilno Rising of 1944, or the irritable, aggressive sketches of some contemporaries, there is reflected a search for solid values. He returns constantly to the writing of Gombrowicz, and his doctrine—a simple and sometimes arrogant one—of the superior and the inferior. It is recognizable in people, in institutions, in art. "Gombrowicz of course loved the superior and paid it homage, tried to apotheosize it. But we shall be more restrained." Konwicki is arguing that the ability to identify quality, and the will to respect it, form the only reliable guide.

Throughout his book, Konwicki returns to the theme of Russia, wrestling and cursing at the knot of hatred and love within him. He is an Eastern Pole who had Russian classmates, whose territory spawned the most intense anti-Russian romantic nationalism, and whose countrymen in what was once the Grand Duchy of Lithuania experienced Russian brutality at its worst and Russian culture at its most brilliant. Sometimes he falls into wild abuse, and not only of Soviet communism. But he can also write that

> I am a hideous hybrid formed at the boundary of two worlds. The boundary of Polish life and Russian life. The mind of the Roman Pole chatters in me, making judicious calculations, and the wide-open steppe of Russian Orthodoxy howls in me. In the morning I run my fingers down Johann Sebastian Bach's harpsichord, but by evening time I'm dead drunk in the gutter. . . . Yes, I love what is deceitfully Asiatic in Russia, but I long with all my might for what is rational and European in it.

(pp. 44, 46)

It has to be said that *Moonrise, Moonset* will often be very hard going for a Western reader who does not know much about Poland, as most do not. It is a book written mainly for Polish readers, full of allusions, references to Polish history, and to personalities in Polish culture and politics. Why not? But books like this set problems for publishers in the West. Konwicki becomes unreasonably truculent on this point, complaining of the "offensive compassion" of foreign publishers who worry that his references will escape their readers "as if we were, objectively speaking, snarled, obscure, lacking contour, inarticulate, a subspecies, on a different wavelength, with a different biology, a different brain."

That view is misconceived. To point out that an American reader won't know that Spatif is a club, or who General Dowbór-Musnicki was, or why Soviet troops were arresting Polish partisans in Lithuania, or that the exclamation "Renewal, Renewal, why do all the fine young men run after you?" dexterously mixes together a 1980 Party slogan with a prewar officer's song, is not to denigrate Polish culture as provincial but to raise pertinent practical questions. Either you don't publish the book in English at all, or you equip it with an introduction explaining the episodes of history to which the work refers—the Second World War in Poland and Lithuania, and the Solidarity years—and with proper footnotes—the present edition provides only about three. The decision to publish **Moonrise, Moonset** was the right one. Although it is certainly more "difficult" (*pace* Konwicki) than his novels, Konwicki's importance is such that no book of his should remain unpublished; judgment should be left to readers. But by dumping this work on the public without interpretation, the publishers seem to lack the courage of their own convictions, and to show disrespect to readers and author alike. (p. 46)

Neal Ascherson, "Polish Nightmares," in The New York Review of Books, *Vol. XXXIV, No. 20, December 17, 1987, pp. 44, 46, 48.*

D. J. ENRIGHT

Again [in **Moonrise, Moonset**] Tadeusz Konwicki is failing to write a novel and offering a mixture much as before: a "layer cake" consisting of the author's thoughts on ways and means of writing a novel, on the secrets of the literary trade ("The age of self-service literature is approaching": we shall all do our own writing, and then read it with delight), on God (*absconditus*), on films (*Ashes and Diamonds* did well both at home and abroad because it was "somehow reminiscent of the Western manner", it was based on political science fiction), on Russian literature (a splendid thumb-nail sketch, emblematic of his love-hate feeling for the country). Also stirred in are memories of his childhood and of a partisan attack on a German armoured car in the Wilno area in 1944, and sizeable fragments of a novel written some forty years ago. And much more, a good deal of it distinctly cantankerous.

One novel Konwicki had intended to write was about the eroticism of age, old people surreptitiously in love and trying to hide it from the young. This "sneering piece of trash" would have made his fortune, he says, but fury with the idiotic system he lived under got in the way. In his own country he reckons himself a sort of *Gastarbeiter,* currently running into difficulties while making a film of Czeslaw Milosz's *The Issa Valley.*

Anecdotes are the plums in this barely digestible cake. When he was no more than a young poet and writer of lyrical prose, Stanislaw Lem asked his publishers for an advance to buy a car, on the grounds that penury had robbed him of the strength to walk. (Now he'd be able to afford his own spaceship; Konwicki awaits in vain the day when Lem will return from the dubious heights of science fiction and "speak our language".) In Washington in 1980, Konwicki was to meet Zbigniew Brzezinski, President Carter's adviser, but somehow "Zbig" couldn't find the time. This was unwise of him, since as a consequence Carter lost the election to Reagan. "It's really a terrible thing to possess the sort of passive power

I possess. A power which brings me no benefits but harms people who come my way, or who refuse to come my way out of rash arrogance." Harm very nearly befell Milosz too, who wasn't exactly keen to see him in Berkeley but, being a fellow Lithuanian, had the sense to patch things up—when lo and behold! along came the Nobel Prize.

At length this chutzpah grows wearing. "I am deafened by egocentric pain", and so are we. Konwicki calls himself "a café politician", able to understand and foresee, unlike the professionals. "Take off your hats, grimy from constant, obsequious doffing, and listen to my feverish delirium, which contains an infinitude of accurate diagnoses and wonder-working prescriptions." He could be thought to bear out Milosz's warning against irony as conducive to nihilism. How many pinches of salt are we to take with each mouthful of cake? That his books are officially unpublished in Poland isn't likely to be due to any such uncertainty on the part of the censorship. The first Polish edition of the present book was published in London in 1982.

As already envisaged in Konwicki's **The Polish Complex,** doom is to be virtually universal. The Poles are "the most seasoned slaves in Europe", and the Western world unconsciously "fantasizes about being raped by the Russians". He is on nobody's side, because all sides are disreputable, more or less, including the "martyrish opposition", who were afraid to talk on the phone not long ago but are now calling for a war against Communism. When he gives with one hand he commonly takes away rather more with the other. But he has his particular admirations: most unreservedly and affectingly, the man who couldn't be broken under torture in prison because his captors made a mistake and told him, with the intention of breaking his spirit, that his wife and daughter were dead. So there was no one to jeopardize, he was utterly alone, and hence knew himself a free man.

"I seem to be talking nonsense", Konwicki remarks, "degrading one thing or another, deriding this or that, ridiculing one person and instructing another from on high." But appearances are deceptive, and in truth "yet another childish creature is beating his breast here before you". That's because he was brought up on Hollywood, and is enraged that in real life good can't conquer evil and the villain gets the better of the hero. Possibly one condition the history, the fate, of Poland can lead to is chronic cantankerousness.

Is there—to quote an earlier appearance of Konwicki's—some sense to all this senselessness? Some plain speaking among this seeming irony? Polish society is divided into two parts, he says at one point, the mass of the nation and a scattering of "foreign agents": it reminds him of the mouse who tried to copulate with an elephant. Poland will regain its freedom only when the Soviet empire collapses, and "Poland, among others, will be the cause of that monster's demise". We must have patience, he adds, for the death throes of a colossus are bound to be colossal. "So let's wait, five years, ten, a hundred at most."

D. J. Enright, "Taking a Beating," in The Times Literary Supplement, *No. 4451, July 22-28, 1988, p. 802.*

Pär (Fabian) Lagerkvist

1891-1974

Swedish novelist, short story writer, dramatist, poet, critic, essayist, scriptwriter, nonfiction writer, autobiographer, and memoirist.

Regarded as one of the foremost Swedish literary figures of the twentieth century, Lagerkvist displayed throughout his career a concern with metaphysical and moral issues arising from conflicts between science, religion, and human conduct. He explored themes related to the nature of good and evil, the correlations between the physical and spiritual realms, and the function of skepticism and faith in human existence. Influenced by innovations in French modernist painting, as well as by the evolutionary theories of Charles Darwin and the expressionist techniques of dramatist August Strindberg, Lagerkvist's work often incorporates elements from folktales, fables, and myths and is characterized by obscure symbolism, abstract imagery, and simple, unadorned language. The recipient of the 1951 Nobel Prize in Literature, Lagerkvist was praised by the Swedish Academy "for the artistic power and deep-rooted independence he demonstrates in his writings in seeking an answer to the eternal questions of humanity."

Lagerkvist was born in the city of Växjö in the southern Swedish district of Småland. Although raised amid an atmosphere of provincialism and religious orthodoxy, Lagerkvist rejected these values, and in 1913, following a year of study at the University of Uppsala, he traveled to Paris, where he became acquainted with the Fauvist, Cubist, and "naivist" movements in the visual arts. Impressed with both the intellectual discipline and aesthetic innovations of these groups, Lagerkvist issued the theoretical pamphlet *Ordkonst och bildkonst* (1913), in which he contrasted the "decadence of modern fiction" with the "vitality of modern art." Calling for a renunciation of the realistic methods of nineteenth-century Naturalism, Lagerkvist endorsed an authentic, inspired, and simplistic style that was modeled after the forms of classic Greek tragedy, Icelandic sagas, and the Bible. Lagerkvist applied these principles in the novella *Människor* (1912), the prose poems of *Motiv* (1914), the short stories in *Järn och människor* (1915), and the harsh and strident poems collected in *Ångest* (1916), which has been called the first expressionist work in Swedish literature.

During most of World War I, Lagerkvist lived in Denmark, and his writings of this period have been characterized by Holger Ahlenius as "one single cry of despair over the bestiality of man." His first play, *Sista människan* (1917), is an apocalyptic vision of the extinction of human life and demonstrates Lagerkvist's ardent interest in the dramatic works of August Strindberg and the principles of German Expressionism. In the essay "Modern teater: Synpunkter och angrepp" (1918; "Modern Theatre: Points of View and Attack"), which was originally published in *Teater: Den svåra stunden* (1918) and translated in *Modern Theatre: Seven Plays and an Essay* (1966), Lagerkvist furthered the antinaturalist theories that he presented in *Ordkonst och bildkonst,* advocating the portrayal of spiritual, intellectual, and emotional experience through dreamlike imagery, allegory, and symbolism. In *Den svåra stunden* (1918), a related cycle of three one-act plays,

Lagerkvist utilizes intense lighting effects and inventive stage settings to depict a character's hallucinations at the moment of death. In the play *Himlens hemlighet* (1919; *The Secret of Heaven*), the text of which originally appeared with a selection of stories and poems in *Kaos* (1919), he offers a fantastical representation of a brutal and hopeless world of illusory love.

Following World War I, Lagerkvist displayed a more tempered literary outlook while maintaining a fervent concern with metaphysical subjects and a dedication to the precepts of his theoretical writings. In the novella *Det eviga leendet* (1920; *The Eternal Smile*), a group of souls in purgatory seek answers to the mystery of existence when they undertake a journey to meet God. The poetry volume *Den lyckliges väg* (1921) exhibits Lagerkvist's direct and simplistic verse style, and the drama *Den osynlige* (1923) employs the abstract characterization of the medieval morality play to examine the relationship between the natural and spiritual worlds. *Gäst hos verkligheten* (1925; *Guest of Reality*), an autobiographical work, and *Det besegrade livet* (1927), a book of philosophical meditations and aphorisms, are frequently cited as central to the development of Lagerkvist's aesthetic. These volumes expound a militant idealism, emphasizing faith in both the indelible spirit of humanity and the triumph of good over evil.

265

Other works composed during this time include the short story collection *Onda sagor* (1924), the love lyrics contained in *Hjärtats sånger* (1926), and the drama *Han som fick leva om sitt liv* (1928), in which Lagerkvist implemented more realistic theatrical methods.

During the 1930s, Lagerkvist focused his art upon international social and political developments that threatened global stability. *Konungen* (1932) is a symbolic drama set in Asia in which two protagonists debate the ultimate triumph of good over evil. Holger Ahlenius observed: "The moving and earnest dialogue between [the characters], which is the inner melody of the drama, is really carried on in the mind of the author in which faith in and doubt of the reality and power of the spirit alternated." The specter of spiritual repression and violence is portrayed in the novella *Bödeln* (1933; translated as both *The Hangman* and *The Executioner*), which was also adapted for the stage. A didactic and macabre satire set in a nightclub in Nazi Germany, this piece features symbolism, allegory, and fabulistic techniques through which Lagerkvist transforms direct social and political commentary into metaphysical observations on the fundamental role of evil in history. *Mannen utan själ* (1936) and *Seger i mörker* (1939) are allegorical plays that express Lagerkvist's faith in the moral superiority and eventual conquest of the humanist tradition. *Mannen utan själ* is a study of a cynical political terrorist who is transformed by the love of a woman into a champion of democratic ideals, while *Seger i mörker* depicts a struggle between a humanitarian statesman and his demagogical twin brother who together symbolize the dichotomous aspects of an individual soul in conflict. Lagerkvist's other works of the 1930s include the poetry volumes *Vid lägereld* (1932) and *Genius* (1937), the short story and prose collections *Kämpande ande* (1930) and *I den tiden* (1935), and *Den knutna näven* (1934), an edition of philosophical essays inspired by his travels to Greece and Palestine in which he affirms his humanist ideology.

During the 1940s and 1950s, Lagerkvist continued to produce works in a variety of genres. *Sång och strid* (1940) and *Hemmet och stjärnan* (1942) are collections of patriotic verse that were prompted by the Nazi invasions of Norway and Denmark. *Låt människan leva* (1949) is a drama that depicts a number of historical figures, including Jesus Christ, Socrates, and Joan of Arc, who share a common fate as victims of prejudice and inhumanity. Lagerkvist's first full-length novel, *Dvärgen* (1944; *The Dwarf*), is among his best-known works of this period. Set in Renaissance Italy, this allegorical novel is narrated by a court dwarf who functions as a symbol of the malevolent forces within all people. While the protagonist regards human nature as wholly evil, Lagerkvist reveals that the dwarf's perspective is a distortion wrought of his own depravity and contrasts the title figure with Bernardo, a character resembling Leonardo da Vinci who is capable of cruelty and insensitivity but whose concurrent understanding and artistic temperament embodies human duality.

In his later years, Lagerkvist devoted himself primarily to writing the novels for which he is perhaps best known outside of Sweden. Beginning with *Barabbas* (1950), and including *Sibyllan* (1956; *The Sibyl*), *Ahasverus död* (1960; *The Death of Ahasuerus*), *Pilgrim på havet* (1962; *Pilgrim at Sea*), *Det heliga landet* (1964; *The Holy Land*), and *Mariamne* (1967; *Herod and Mariamne*), Lagerkvist assembled a cycle of narratives that continue his examination of humanity's unending quest for meaning. Focusing on what Winston Weathers has

termed the "Lazarus archetype," which functions in various guises as the main character in these novels, Lagerkvist explores the nature of spiritual death and resurrection. According to Weathers, "Lazarus, in the pentalogy, is the representation of the living-dead—and hence is the representation of modern man. Displacing the orthodox concept of Lazarus as the fortunate man snatched from the jaws of death, Lagerkvist presents, rather, a Lazarus who is [a] victim of survival, the man dragged back into existence to dramatize the very meaninglessness of that existence." In *Barabbas,* Lagerkvist depicts the spiritual tribulations of the condemned thief whose place Jesus Christ assumed on the cross at Calvary. Desperate to discover meaning in his newly regained life yet incapable of faith or love, Barabbas hurls himself into sexual promiscuity, thievery, and murder but remains disillusioned and spiritually confused. One of Lagerkvist's most acclaimed works, *Barabbas* was adapted for both the stage and film. His next novel in the series, *The Sibyl,* focuses on the biblical character Ahasuerus, who refused to allow Christ to rest at his door on the way to Calvary and was consequently condemned to roam the earth forever. While seeking his fortune from a profaned Delphic priestess, Ahasuerus is told a fantastical tale of myth and sorcery in which the oracle illustrates the existence in God of both good and evil. In *The Death of Ahasuerus, Pilgrim at Sea,* and *The Holy Land,* Lagerkvist employs vivid description and an austere prose style to relate the pilgrimage of a skeptical yet dedicated drifter to the Holy Land. Through his blending of myths from paganism and primitive Christianity, Lagerkvist declares the need of individuals to affirm faith in religion and humanity. When the drifter dies after reaching the Holy Land, his death is shrouded in an atmosphere of uncertainty, suggesting that the success of his journey is less significant than the quest for understanding. In his final novel, *Herod and Mariamne,* Lagerkvist reemphasizes the existence of both virtue and wickedness in human experience.

In addition to Lagerkvist's other works, two translated collections of his short fiction, *The Eternal Smile and Other Stories* (1954) and *The Marriage Feast and Other Stories* (1955), have been published. A volume of Lagerkvist's notes and journals, *Antecknat: Ur efterlämnede dagböcker och anteckningar* (1977), was edited posthumously by his daughter, Eliu Lagerkvist.

(See also *CLC,* Vols. 7, 10, 13 and *Contemporary Authors,* Vols. 85-88, Vols. 49-52 [obituary].)

CHARLES MADGE

In this fantasy of the dead [*The Eternal Smile*] one is made to feel the presence of millions of souls: a concourse as innumerable as that of the endless pine-forests of Northern Sweden. And yet all the characters in this book strike one as being Swedes. The dead men who sit and talk endlessly about their lives are those who within or near the Arctic circle sit up all night talking and drinking Schnapps. Night there is a long twilight. Waking and sleeping states are merged; and life and death easily enough become confused. *The Eternal Smile* professes to be a story about the dead; but equally it is a story about the living, in that half-state between death and life which is characteristic of the northern meditative mood. For such a mood, life seems merely to be waiting for death; and death is to usher in another endless period of waiting, apparently for nothing.

Freud has said that the fear of death is in reality a concealed fear of life. The author of **The Eternal Smile** is continually telling himself and his readers to escape from this fear, and accept life. To a neurotic temperament the effect of the book might well be the reverse, and one can only say that the writer makes his nightmare so convincing that his final moralistic advice fails to dissolve it. These meditations on life and death obviously leave room for all the devils of mediocrity to rush in. They are all too familiar properties in the welter of suburban "philosophy." Homer or Tolstoy can speak on matters like these with impunity; of Pär Lagerkvist one can justly say that the style and spirit of his fantasy are those of a man who is aware of difficulties. . . . The English outsider will probably get much pleasure from this vista of the shadowy world within whose remote depths is God, an old man ceaselessly sawing wood.

Charles Madge, "Between Death and Life," in The London Mercury, *Vol. XXXI, No. 185, March, 1935, p. 490.*

I. M. PARSONS

[Let] me say at once that, apart from **The Eternal Smile,** I have read of Lagerkvist's works only **The Hangman** (a play) and a miscellaneous collection of tales and sketches—all in translation and for the most part in manuscript. So that it is only certain aspects of his work that I am at all qualified to discuss. What makes me think these aspects perhaps important is that they reveal qualities common to all three of the books which I have read.

Most remarkable of these qualities, or the most likely to impress itself first on the general reader, is Lagerkvist's predilection for a particular literary form—a blend of allegory, folktale and direct narrative. Referring to it in a note on the wrapper, the translators speak of his 'vivid sense of the detail of living experience combined with his freedom from the restrictions of realistic convention.' It is an apt description, the more so because it indicates both the strength and, to my mind, the weakness of Lagerkvist's writing. In the exact and careful observation of nature, in the highly selective use of material, he certainly displays 'a vivid sense of the detail of living experience.' In **The Eternal Smile,** particularly in those parts where the Dead recall incidents of their lives, there are passages of great descriptive beauty whose variety and clarity of image compel one's admiration. But the use of detail, even the exact, economic and sensitive use of it which Lagerkvist exploits so admirably, is not in itself the sum of good writing. There must be something more, some kind of imaginative experience ordering the process or the result is better only in degree than the unselective, photographic realism of a Galsworthy or a detective novel.

It is just here that the question of form, and Lagerkvist's particular method of presentation, is significant. For though it is perfectly true that his peculiar blend of fact and fancy, of exact detail and exotic fable, does provide an escape from 'the restrictions of realistic convention,' there is a price to be paid for this freedom. Moreover Lagerkvist, one has to remember, is not the first, particularly among Scandinavian writers, to exploit such a method of treatment. The counterpointing of

fact and fable, 'romantic realism' as one might call it, has a tradition of its own, in which only the greatest have achieved success. For it is one thing to create a world in which the facts of normal experience are transcended; it is quite another to justify this by the revelation of some imaginative truth. Yet without the latter no literary 'form,' however adroitly conceived and used, is worth more than an acrostic. And it is in this respect that I seem to find Lagerkvist ultimately unsatisfying. After so much preparation, so elaborate a literary ritual, the mysteries, I cannot help feeling, should be a little more impressive than they turn out to be. And the difference between the expectation and the event is the measure, it seems to me, not only of one's disappointment but of the artist's failure to justify his pretension. (pp. 82-4)

I. M. Parsons, in a review of "The Eternal Smile," *in* Scrutiny, *Vol. IV, No. 1, June, 1935, pp. 82-4.*

NORMAN SHRAPNEL

Here [in **Guest of Reality**] are three short novels which give English readers a chance of scrutinizing Lagerkvist's work on, as it were, three landing-stages of development. **The Eternal Smile,** which [previously] appeared separately . . . , dates back sixteen years. **Guest of Reality,** a very different experiment in direct narrative, was published in 1925; and **The Hangman,** with fascist violence as its theme, in 1933. The task of valuation has to face at the outset the fact that the landing-stages are set along no discernible route. (p. 186)

About **The Eternal Smile** one cannot agree with the dust-cover that it is 'a truly memorable work of art.' It is an allegory about life, death and God, and since it doesn't add anything to our relevant experience about life or death or God it must be said to have failed as art. The style succeeds in filling its folk-narrative dress with body and vitality, but there is something curiously unsatisfying in its very virtues; it is strenuous, but its activity often seems to be in a sub-normal channel, like a highly active brain dreaming. The dream imagery in the narrative is probably deliberate and is quite consistent with the idea of the dead recalling their earthly lives, and yet it is not easy to get away from the feeling that there has been a certain amount of angling after that 'something rich and strange' (dust-cover) which is not really, after all, very close to Hans Andersen.

The prose virtues are better seen in **Guest of Reality,** which tells without stridency or emotional indulgence about a sensitive boy's realization of youth as 'the most wretched age of man.' The narrative and descriptive passages are loaded with detail which in the hands of a less competent writer—half a dozen photographic 'realists' spring to mind who have attempted this sort of thing badly—would make for unconscionable tedium. Here it is always kept in check, subordinated to the main design. The work of a cultivated and alert mind, functioning at an even if not an exalted level, this novel is as far as it goes the most successful of the three. But, also by a long way the least ambitious, it doesn't go very far.

It is to **The Hangman** that we come for the big guns (appropriately enough its date is that of Hitler's rise to power). The whole thing is in fact a thunder of indignation, too vociferous and laboured to be successful satire, too well-planned and powerful to be unimportant. The frame-work is good; particularly well done is the shifting of the scene from a mediaeval tavern with its grim but essentially human associations to a modern night-club where the brutal happenings of the story seem in no way out of place. There is every excuse for making National-Socialism the villain of the piece, but there doesn't seem much point in holding up the Hangman, symbol of bloodshed through the ages, as a kind of mystical hero. The trouble with this, as with *The Eternal Smile,* is that it protests too much. Most of the Hangman's interminable harangue, like that of the Leader in the earlier story, is as gratuitous as a Shaw preface. But *The Hangman* is the most interesting work of the three, and seems to achieve the most in spite of its failures. (pp. 186-87)

Norman Shrapnel, "Lagerkvist," in Scrutiny, *Vol. V, No. 2,* September, 1936, pp. 186-87.

DOROTHY PAGE

To any reader in search of an anodyne for world-weariness, *Guest of Reality* is apt to prove an irritant, and he will probably finish the book with a sense of having been badly ruffled and with no very clear idea as to what should be done about it. Writing in pursuit of a philosophical idea, Mr. Lagerkvist turns and doubles adroitly through a Strindbergian complexity of thought, but the reader who can keep pace is forced to admit he knew where he was going all the time.

The three stories which make up the volume are linked by a common theme, the inevitability of suffering and death. In *The Eternal Smile,* a convocation of the dead in search of God, the author uses pageantry with types ranging from Caliban to Christ in stating his thesis: That the individual's spiritual awareness is only valid when it can be resolved into conscious identification with a universal life force. *Guest of Reality* is concerned with the child Anders and his emergence from childhood into the first idea of death, a motif that is increasingly persistent, and ends with the young man's realization that his painfully acquired realism is to be shortly terminated by disease and the final reality. In *The Hangman,* attention is focused upon a multiplicity of patterns shifting from darkness into the fire-stained light of superstition, culminating in what might be called a paraphrase of the Nietzschean cry, "Man is the cruelest animal" and the symbolic Hangman's passionate protest at being the eternal expression of man's cruelty.

The book is a disturbing one; and if the subtly obvious style leads the reader to think he is about to swallow a limpid draught of fantasy and he finds it to be neat realism, he can but await Mr. Lagerkvist's next book as a "control" test for his sensations. (pp. 29-30)

Dorothy Page, in a review of "Guest of Reality," in The Canadian Forum, *Vol. XVI, No. 189,* October, 1936, pp. 29-30.

HOLGER AHLENIUS

Two central experiences form the point of departure in the authorship of Pär Lagerkvist: one, the conflict between the Christian and the scientific-naturalistic views of life; the other, the World War, which seems to have made a deeper impression upon him than upon anyone else in neutral Sweden. He was not able to share the Christian faith of his pious parental home, and yet he writhed in agony under the yoke of the naturalistic doctrine. The World War seemed to confirm that idea of man as a beast of prey which is inherent in the naturalistic conception of the universe, and Pär Lagerkvist's youthful works are one single cry of despair over the bestiality of man. This mood dominates his first, very imperfect drama *Sista mänskan (The Last Man,* 1917), a vision in lyrical-oratorical form of the extinction of human life on earth. It is a perspective framed on the naturalistic theory of evolution and rendered timely by the slaughter of humanity then taking place. In form, however, it shows the influence both of the Greek choral drama and of the Christian medieval play.

Even as early as this, Pär Lagerkvist, following the model of the German Expressionists, had learned technique from Strindberg's *A Dream Play.* This is still more evident in *Den svåra stunden (The Trying Hour,* 1918) containing three short one-act plays in which the dreams and visions of the moment of death are compressed. They are marked by a decidedly conscious art which utilizes the intense lighting effects and suggestive stylized decorations of modern theatrical mechanism. Using the same technique, the author achieves a more genuinely artistic effect in *Himlens hemlighet (The Secret of Heaven,* 1919), a cosmic vision of a fantastic and ghostlike world. The orb of the earth rises on the stage, and upon it sit, lie, or crawl strange human wrecks, creatures who are crippled in mind and body, each one despairingly alone with his fate, brooding over the lack of meaning in existence. All is contempt, mockery, and hatred. Only for a moment the power of love sounds a note that makes the world beautiful and human beings kind. But it soon dies away. Love is only a fleeting dream, an illusion, and the next moment everything is just as dark and hopeless as before.

This deep pessimism is the last work in the youthful dramas of Pär Lagerkvist. But the metaphysical problems, the great life riddles, never ceased to engross this visionary and brooding genius, and the brief revelation of love in *Himleus hemlighet* was a foreshadowing of how the author was to conquer naturalism.

Love, sublimated into a Christian-Platonic mysticism, gradually transformed Pär Lagerkvist's realism, poured new life into it, and lifted it above the animal. The separation of the animal in man from that which is human in a higher sense, between that in our being which is determined by nature and that which lies on a loftier plane than mere nature, has been the theme of his later works, whether prose or poetry. The faith in something in man higher than mere nature is crystallized also in the play *Den osynlige (The Invisible One,* 1923), built up like a medieval morality play with all the actors embodying certain powers in life. A super-earthly origin is here attributed to the spirit of man. It is a heavenly being which has descended to earth and assumed human form. Itself invisible, it is present wherever men fight against earthliness and evil, but it must descend into the valley of the shadow of death, into the lowest depths. Though the temple is burning, though death is gathering its harvest, and life must be destroyed, yet the eternal *quand-même* of the human spirit, which is revealed in love and heroic deeds, nevertheless rises toward heaven. Death has no power over the human spirit, which will go on living after man has passed away. In spite of its noble fervor, its wonderfully beautiful lyric passages, the drama is one of the weaker in Pär Lagerkvist's production. It is too declamatory, too slow in its tempo, and altogether too vague in thought and form. In a later prose work the author has found much more striking and organic expression for the relation between the natural and the spiritual, comparing them with the roots and crown of a tree—the chief emphasis laid on the latter which "at least strives toward the sky."

At the same time he began to adopt a more realistic technique and a much simpler everyday language, related to naïvism in the art of painting, and this language he has continued to use, although it retains a mystic undertone, as of a double sounding board. In this style the author has written one of his most important dramatic works, bearing the title *Han som fik leva om sill liv* (*He Who Lived His Life Over Again,* 1928), in which the visionary element appears only as a background in the form of a few significant incidents revealing the former self of the main character, once in warning and once in reproach. The spirit of man has found a dwelling-place in a simple shoemaker and its unequal struggle against the animal and the sensual is fought out against the background of a detailed, realistically described milieu of ordinary plain people. The temptation which in his former life had made Daniel a criminal he is now able to conquer, but in the repleteness of his happy and comfortable old age he fails to comprehend the suffering of his own son and thereby drives the youth to his death. In vain he has lived his life over again—he has once more become a murderer. He who does not see his fellowmen as people like himself, who does not find the same elevation and tragedy in their lives as in his own, has not comprehended the essential in the fate of humanity. This demand for human sympathy and understanding, together with a pessimistically clear view of how limited is the power of love and goodness, is the closing note in the drama which, as an acting play, is remarkably strong and vivid.

To the after-War period of doubt and seeking belongs also the symbolic drama *Konungen* (*The King,* 1932). The background is a colorful Asiatic fairy tale milieu. Outwardly it is a drama about social revolution: the old hierarchic, authoritarian State is replaced, after bloody convulsions, by a popular government. Both parties use force and release the animal in man, but better than the stench of corruption and decay is nevertheless the smell of fresh blood over the earth— declares the deposed monarch Amar-Azu. It is not, however, the social and political problems that are the most important, but, as always in Pär Lagerkvist, the metaphysical. Amar-Azu personifies the spirit which has despaired after seeing the bondage of humanity under instincts and passions, and which therefore longs to be released from earthly fetters. His companion, Nadur, is his own youthful self, the spirituality which still has faith and hope and which still wants to serve humanity in the new State. The moving and earnest dialogue between Amar-Azu and Nadur, which is the inner melody of the drama, is really carried on in the mind of the author in which faith in and doubt of the reality and power of the spirit alternated during those years like high tide and low.

Pär Lagerkvist himself stems from the common people and has, to a certain extent, been able to make allowances for the violence that is practised in the service of democratic progress. But the reactionary violence which, since 1933, has been elevated to the position of highest principle in a great European State, moved him from the first moment, to pained, indignant protest. Confronted with the revival of barbarism and the degradation of humanity in the decade of pogroms and concentration camps, his faith in love and in the spirit of man has flamed up with renewed intensity, in Promethean defiance against the reigning god of the age. It is against this background that we must see his last two plays. They are both ideological, realistic dramas in contemporary dress and show him at the height of his powers.

The protagonist in *Mannen ulan själ* (*The Man Without a Soul,* 1936) is a sensitive youth, of a type not uncommon in our day, who is moved by a sick desire for revenge on a world that has no place for him, and who therefore throws himself into political street fights and sadistic hunting down of all who have different opinions or are differently made. The subject of the drama is a man who loses the world but gains his own soul, thanks to the love which, here as in earlier works of the author, is allowed to vitalize the dead mass of reality. When we first meet the man he has just taken part in an act of political terror. Cold and cynical, he scorns all talk of the soul or of religion. But there is a woman who becomes his refuge from the police and from loneliness. She is about to become a mother, to bear the child of the man he had helped to murder. How love conquers him, and how he longs to atone for his crime, is the subject of the drama. The woman dies in childbirth, but when the man's companions jubilantly go to war, he steals quietly to the graveyard to visit both his dead. He has found a new and greater power than that of his former leaders and to this power he yields allegiance, while he bravely meets his punishment, which is death as a deserter. He has not attained to faith in a true sense, but at least to a longing for peace and an understanding that a human being must have something else within him besides his own self. Love and the pangs of conscience have together done their work, and have made him into a human being in a higher and truer sense. Even though the line of psychological development is not always clear, the drama as a whole conveys a serene, almost a devout picture of a deep transformation in a human being. It is the particular gift of Pär Lagerkvist to fuse the timely and the timeless. The frame and external conditions furnish the timely element, but the recreative power of love is eternal. Although the words Nazi and Communist seem to be in the air, they are never spoken.

In a similar manner a theme of today has been lifted to universal significance in the latest work of the dramatist, *Seger i mörker* (*Victory in the Dark,* 1939). The twin brothers Gabriel Fontan and Robert Grant, who are here presented in tragic contrast, are in the deepest sense the two beings who dwell within us, both the self of day and the self of night, the one ruled by reason and the other ruled by passion. The author has set out to show how sinister the consequences may be if the innumerable threads that bind the brothers together are severed, if the self of reason refuses to acknowledge kinship with the self of passion. But above all he wants to show how the latter, if it is let loose, will be a destructive power, while the former, with the help of love, can even render death impotent because it represents devotion to an idea or to a cause that survives ourselves. The external events center on the struggle between a democratic statesman who is the advocate of humanitarian ideals and believes in the goodness of man and the corrupt demagogue who is deliberately playing on the irresponsible elements in the community, appealing to the lowest passions and seeing in them the real nature of man. On the face of it, the latter wins out. After Fontan in a very fine philosophic speech tries to engage the armed forces on the side of righteousness and humanitarianism, his fate is sealed. He and the system he represents are carried away in the deluge. But, on the other hand, he regains the love of his wife, which he had forfeited, and together they face the firing squad, strong in their love and serene in their faith that right will prevail, that no violence can kill forever the cause they have striven for. Grant, on the other hand, is agonized by his sense of impotence under the responsibility his fellows have laid upon him, which he—the irresponsible—is unable to bear. This mighty drama, which so vividly bodies forth the deepest problems of our time and is instinct with human pathos, is so far the last word of the author.

The nightmare dream of the human beast which was created by the World War became in Pär Lagerkvist's hands expressionistic experimental drama in the style of Strindberg's later works. Then the author's world was illumined by love and he began to see the spiritual in man. The human spirit was given divine attributes and eternity in the high-pitched, lyrical-oratorical medieval play **Den osynlige;** assumed lifelike and fragile everyday shape combined with visionary strength in **Han som fik leva om sitt liv;** was torn between resignation and hope in the low-toned conversations against an orgiastic oriental background in the fairy tale drama, **Konungen.** Steeled and strengthened by persecution, it rose again to a more definite though more circumscribed existence in the two great dramas of ideas in the Thirties; grew into the power of love to recreate even the violent mentality of these latter days in **Mannen utan själ;** and fought its apparently desperate fight against passions let loose in **Seger i mörker,** achieving victory in defeat, because—no matter what its origin and nature may be—it enlists us in the fight for ideas that have a longer span of life than we ourselves.

Pär Lagerkvist has not attained to a final clarity in the metaphysical problems or to a religious faith firmly based on dogma. First and last, he is a seeking and a thirsting spirit and, not least in virtue of that, is a true spokesman of his age. His never resting Jacob's wrestle with the great riddles of humanity can be traced in his creative writing, which is in its feeling the most deeply religious, the most fervid and most profoundly human in our recent literature. (pp. 301-08)

> *Holger Ahlenius, "The Dramatic Works of Pär Lagerkvist," in* The American Scandinavian Review, *Vol. XXVIII, No. 4, December, 1940, pp. 301-08.*

THOMAS CALDECOT CHUBB

[*The Dwarf* is] the autobiography of the twenty-six-inch tall favorite of an anonymous Italian prince who has stepped straight from Machiavelli. As such, it is one of the bitterest books that this reviewer has ever read. Even Swift's baleful passages about the Houyhnhnms hardly surpass it. But it is much more than that. It is a dwarf's-eye view of the Rinascimento. In a sense, it is also a dwarf's-eye view—seen from the vantage point of Sweden—of the whole story of human sham and greed.

In its former capacity it marshals up all the conventional paraphernalia of cloak-and-dagger romance. It deals with love, lust and the desire for power. It brings in war and treachery. There are poisonings and there is rape and slaughter. Among its characters are an innocent (for a while at least) daughter, a handsome stripling prince, a lewd and aging princess, a pock-marked captain of mercenaries, a kind of twisted Mercutio, and finally—and best drawn of all—an artist named Bernardo who is so obviously Leonardo da Vinci that one regrets that the author did not give him his right name.

As for the plot, it is drawn from the most violent of the Elizabethan dramas—and from *Romeo and Juliet.* The moral tone is that of a warped Aretino. But it is not for its plot that one

must recommend it. One recommends it rather for its unerring if one-sided psychological report upon a great era—for its penetrating if one-sided comments upon man himself.

> *Thomas Caldecot Chubb, "Dwarf's-Eye View of the Renaissance," in* The New York Times Book Review, *November 25, 1945, p. 4.*

HENRY B. KRANZ

We know that the dwarfs at the Italian courts of the Renaissance were buffoons. Not so is Pär Lagerkvist's hero who tells [in *The Dwarf*] of his life, his sufferings and his hopes in the form of a diary against a background of war and passions, murder and plague, love and treachery. He is a symbol of the evil which through the ages has tried to destroy beauty and goodness in this world. Pär Lagerkvist's dwarf hates all men. "I have nothing against belonging to a different race from the present one," he writes, "and showing it on my person." He adores his master, the Prince, but he hates him too. He thinks he is part of the Prince and "represents his noble person"— always when his master's evil spirit has the uppermost. He no less hates the lascivious mode of life of the Prince's wife, Theodora, though serving her too with loyalty, and he poisons Don Riccardo, the Princess's lover, at an opulent banquet as coolly as he strangled the dwarf Jehoshaphat so that he could be the only dwarf at the court.

The Dwarf is written by a realist of pessimistic outlook and blends together tragedy, high comedy, and farce. The subtlety with which the author has created his atmosphere is admirable. His style, colorful and lucid, reminds one of the historical works of Strindberg and Lagerlöf. The story itself holds you by the sheer beauty of the telling. But unfortunately we have here rather a long short story than a short novel; we hardly learn enough about the hero to understand this misshapen creature's bitterness, and when we leave him all we know is that he is thrown into a dungeon by his Prince. "I sit here in my chains and the days go by and nothing ever happens!" Perhaps Pär Lagerkvist wanted no more than to prophesy in an allegory the continuous resurrection of evil when he ends the story "If I know anything of my lord he cannot spare his dwarf for long. I reflect on the day when they will come and loosen my chains, because he has sent for me again." Yes, indeed, his lord has sent for his dwarf many, many times since the days of the Renaissance. And we hope the reader will not overlook the symbolic comparison of those times and ours. . . .

> *Henry B. Kranz, "Evil versus Beauty and Goodness," in* The Saturday Review of Literature, *Vol. 28, No. 48, December 1, 1945, p. 74.*

RICHARD B. VOWLES

What reputation Pär Lagerkvist, 1951 recipient of the Nobel Prize in literature, has in the United States—and it is slight— derives from two novels, two plays hidden away in collections, and a handful of poems printed in the quarterlies. But in Sweden he is the grand old man, if somewhat austere and remote. His position among Scandinavians is Olympian.

Lagerkvist's service to Swedish letters began before World War I. In 1914, three years before Eliot's "Tradition and the Individual Talent," and at roughly the same time Pound was arguing Yeats into a new kind of poetry, he stated his own program for a new poetic form. For the drama he provided a comparable rejuvenation of spirit. In both genres, as well as in the novel, he has demonstrated the kind of disciplined fecundity that seems more and more part of the past. Lagerkvist is neither the parsimonious poet nor the spinner of frail and occasional drama. Nor are his novels the fatty regurgitations of experience that we have accustomed ourselves to in the United States. Lagerkvist has moved facilely among forms, with some of the versatility of a Dryden, and made each work a stage in a career of high literary and moral purpose.

Pär Lagerkvist comes from a lower middle-class home in the province of Smaland. . . . His early life was simple, severe, and tragic, if one can accept the evidence of the semi-fictional *Guest of Reality.* After a year at the University of Upsala he traveled to Paris for a visit which was, as it has not been for many young men, the making of him.

Once back in Sweden Lagerkvist wrote a review of Apollinaire's *Les peintres cubistes* and issued a pamphlet called *Word Art and Picture Art,* which together set the stage for modern poetry in Sweden. He urged the application of cubistic principles of design to poetry, a reduction to the abstract which would result in a "taut, nicely calculated architectonic composition." One turns to Lagerkvist's poetry of the period to see just how these principles are executed, and is disappointed. The artist's design has not curbed the early, harsh Wertherism.

Although there appears to be more genuine form to the unabashed lyricism of some of his more traditional verses, Lagerkvist accepts the conventional stanzaic patterns, opening them sufficiently to impart something of what Eliot has called "the condition of speech"; there is a certain sustained harmony even as the shades of the prison house darken. Lagerkvist's is a dark, somber poetry of fine modulations, but it does not provide much excitement—none of the sweet surprises of Yeats nor the intellectual legerdemain of Eliot, and nothing that bears the sure, dynamic imprint of cubism. One cannot find Lagerkvist's claim to critical attention in his poetry.

Lagerkvist's three novels—*The Executioner, The Dwarf,* and *Barabbas*—are masterpieces of classical severity. Here the novel is not the successor of the epic, but a kind of monodrama, sculptural in its outlines, centered on one figure of symbolic reference. In brief, these novels are Lagerkvist's judgments on the brutal, the twisted, and the loveless in modern man.

The Executioner, published in 1933, may have its setting in a medieval alehouse, but it is, or was, of contemporary moment, appearing as it did in the early days of the Third Reich. The ominous figure of the executioner, in blood-red cloak, sits silent in the midst of the human comedy. Men come and go, now whispering curiously, now stopping to make obeisance. A well-fed dowager pauses suddenly on the way to the lady's room and exclaims: "Well you don't say! It's the executioner! Wait till I tell Herbert about this. My son is simply mad to meet you. Dear child, he loves bloodshed so!"

Finally the executioner, symbol of violence, steps forward, a *fuehrer* among *heils,* to proclaim the terrible truth of his mission: "Again you call me, and I come. I survey the land—a land lying feverish and hot—and in the air I hear the screams of sick birds. It is the rutting hour of evil. It is the executioner's hour."

The Dwarf, published in 1944, also treats the bestiality of man, but here the central figure is commentator, a court retainer on the Renaissance scene. Lagerkvist's style has never so effectively demonstrated the naked thew and sinew of the Swedish language; his irony has never been more chilling and Swiftian. There is, for example, the dwarf's record of a torture victim's suffering: "He was not in the least heroic—about average."

And yet we are not likely to assume the dwarf's angle of vision, though we must accept his claim: "Nobody else can see through people and unmask them as I do." We are not inclined to honor the twisted commentary of one who finds laughter "unlovely and disfiguring." The attack fails for lack of an adequate spokesman and we may find the novel something short of satisfying, may even reject it for the "little exercise in hair-raising" that Hamilton Basso found it to be. Yet in purity of form and economy of statement it is admirable.

Barabbas, published in Sweden in 1949, is a sadder and profounder moral tale. Throughout his writing Lagerkvist has circled the figure of Christ to discover a saving grace for modern man. Now he approaches the very scene of Calvary in the person of the shadowy Biblical character who was reprieved that Christ might have his cross. Barabbas, as Lagerkvist creates him from the least of materials, is a selfish, restless, loveless man who stands for all of us who linger on the periphery of Christianity, wondering how it could be that one man—and a poor figure of a man at that—could die for another. So Barabbas peers at the dying Christ from a protective screen of bushes, turns away to seek the bed of his fat mistress, commits an impulsive murder out of a confusion of motives, and tries repeatedly but apathetically to accept the testimony of Christ's death. When he finally dies, a martyr by accident, whispering "I entrust my soul to thee," we wonder if he addresses God or Death. The ambiguity is intentional, for Lagerkvist can supply no easy Christian solution.

It is as dramatist that Pär Lagerkvist is most highly regarded in his native Sweden. No writer of popular realistic drama however, he has never seriously deviated from his personal manifesto of 1918, the essay **"Modern Theatre"** prefaced to three one-act plays. Here Lagerkvist explicitly rejected the naturalism of Ibsen and the pretentious interior decoration of the Craig-Reinhardt school for "a simpler, more expressive form," one that liberated the playwright from the past and present and rendered the area of fantasy more accessible—and more reasonable.

The source of Lagerkvist's inspiration is clear in his first stage success, a one-acter called *Heaven's Secret* (1919). It was no accident that it was produced at the Intimate Theatre of Strindberg's founding; nor that Harriet Bosse, Strindberg's third wife, took the one feminine role. The whole play is deeply imbued with the spirit of Strindberg's Inferno-period. The scene is "an enormous blue-black sphere"; on it God is represented by an old man sawing wood, Love by a distraught Ophelia playing a stringless guitar; the stage is further peopled with the grotesques of our modern waste land: an apelike executioner in flesh-colored tights, busy decapitating a heap of dolls; a fawning dwarf in oversize clothes; and others simply crippled or aged. The result is less a play than an oratorio on the theme of meaninglessness.

From Strindberg-inspired nightmare Lagerkvist moves to lyric fantasy cut from the same cloth as Shelley's "Prometheus Unbound." In *The Invisible One* (1923), least successful of Lagerkvist's plays, the unknown god is protagonist and a moody, ectoplasmic Oversoul he turns out to be. The play is notable in introducing Lagerkvist's preoccupation with the afterlife of the soul, with a kind of transcendent humanism that is couched in poetry of real dignity and moment.

But Lagerkvist had fled too far into the realm of fantasy for even the best of expressionistic stagecraft to help him. He resorted to the homely idiom of the people in *The Man Who Lived His Life Over Again* (1928), the parable of a shoemaker who, by supernatural agency, gained reprieve from death for a murder he had committed in a fit of passion. Just as it appears that this self-willed, impulsive tradesman has lived his life over into ripe old age and family tranquility he causes the suicide of his son, in effect repeats his life in much the same pattern. The fusion of fantasy with documentary treatment of a tradesman's life created what is perhaps still the most effective of Lagerkvist's theatre.

Lagerkvist's next two plays, *The Man Without a Soul* (1936) and *Victory in the Dark* (1939), have the surface appearance of realism, but it soon becomes apparent that morality play has been distilled from the substance of polemic drama. Political parties are never named; indeed the characters themselves, in the earlier play, are not named but merely identified as the Man, the Woman, the Beggar—in the manner of the German expressionists from whom Lagerkvist gained many lessons in technique. The "man without a soul" is a febrile sort, a political extremist who finds himself in the complicated situation of loving the mistress of the political opponent whom he has murdered. Love in part resolves the conflict but the soulless chap, who is condemned to death for draft evasion in this unnamed country, goes to the gallows with nothing to assuage the anguish of heart but the priest's doubtful assurance: "Perhaps God has need of you."

In *Victory in the Dark* Lagerkvist again concerns himself with the twilight of the soul as it implicates itself in political revolution, but the moral intent is clearer. The combatant individuals, Fontan and Grant, turn out to be more than benevolent despot and snivelling revolutionary. They are the good and evil of internal conflict translated into the action of the stage. When Fontan walks out into a hail of bullets from the insurgents he is, quite simply, goodness triumphing in death.

If Lagerkvist cannot come to terms with God or man, he can find consolation in the ultimate triumph of the soul. A new optimism is reflected in the title of *Let Man Live* (1949). Lagerkvist has never been hampered by the restrictions of time and here he accentuates the eternal by bringing together the martyrs of history in a short but magniloquent oratorio. There is Jesus; Joan of Arc; and Joe Brown lynched in Columbia, South Carolina, in 1922; there is Socrates; Giordano Bruno; and Richard who operated a make-shift transmitter behind some iron curtain—all dedicated to some sustaining value. Finally there are Paolo and Francesca, caught up in the transcendent love, a love which is for Lagerkvist the rebirth of the soul into the infinite.

In Lagerkvist, then, we have to settle for a transcendent belief in the human soul. Happily the author's sense of form gives substance to this near-Christian Platonism. Lagerkvist is always the artist, seldom the philosopher; and his is a kind of art that we could well afford to know in America. If he is not so robust as Bunyan, nor so brilliantly forensic as Swift, nor as fantastic as Strindberg, caught in the spindrift of his visions, Lagerkvist partakes of the moral and artistic intensity

of all three. He is a giant of modern classicism. (pp. 15, 54, 56)

Richard B. Vowles, "Pär Lagerkvist: Dramatist of the Soul," in The Saturday Review of Literature, *Vol. XXXIV, No. 48, December 1, 1951, pp. 15, 54, 56.*

LARS ÅHNEBRINK

[Pär Lagerkvist] is primarily a seeker, a metaphysician, who, with subtle artistry and never failing insight, probes into vital questions in search of a valid meaning, attempting at the same time to formulate a synthesis of our existence. The following is an attempt to trace the author's development as a writer.

Lagerkvist was born in 1891 in the city of Växjö, located in the province of Småland in south Sweden, where he lived until he had passed his student examination in 1910. . . . Lagerkvist's parents, descendants of farmers, were of a hardy, God-fearing stock. His father was a foreman at the railway station, and the family, consisting of the parents and seven children, of whom Pär was the youngest, lived quietly on the second floor of the noisy station restaurant building, which the author has so admirably described in his semi-autobiographical *Guest of Reality* (*Gäst hos verkligheten*). Although the home was poor, it was eminently respectable, for the Lagerkvists were pious people who read their Bible and went regularly to church. They wanted to give their children the best education they could afford, and Pär, who was a shy boy keeping mostly to himself, was sent to the secondary school, where the records show him to be a student of average ability. Although his essay for the student exam on "The Swedish Hymn-book" did not give evidence of the future writer, it contained an idea which recurs in his later works. "Religion," he argued then, "should be seen as an expression of man's striving for something higher and of man's belief in the good and the beautiful."

Although Lagerkvist grew up in an atmosphere of religious piety, he was destined to outgrow the religion of his parents. There was nothing extraordinary about this, for Lagerkvist shared in the revolt against the old religious belief with many of his generation. He lived in a period during which the State Church was slowly losing its grip, particularly on the minds of the young people. Moreover, Free-Church and Salvation Army activities helped to break down the dominance of the State Church. New ideas, gradually invading the tradition-bound little city, reached the younger generation through various channels. One was the theater, for which the city was justly famous. During his school years Lagerkvist could attend plays by Shakespeare, Strindberg, Ibsen, Björnson, Wilde, Shaw, Sudermann, Maugham, Goethe, Tasso, and Maeterlinck. Another way to the new thought was the school. Through his teacher of biology Lagerkvist came into direct contact with the evolutionary theory propounded by Darwin and his followers. In *Guest of Reality* he referred to Darwinism as "the new doctrine which I absorbed and which swept away God and all hope." By this time he had developed into a rebel, as far as religion and politics were concerned. His radicalism and his socialistic tendencies came to the fore in the secret anarchistic meetings of the members of "The Red Ring," where such questions as the nature of man, the meaning of life, and the existence of God were discussed with fervor.

With such radical experiences outside the family circle, it was but natural that Lagerkvist should feel restless and unhappy in the conservatively religious home, the peacefulness of which he experienced so much more strongly, since it afforded a violent contrast to the clacking of the trains which passed by his window. There was an atmosphere of close austerity in his home which he felt as a band of iron cast around his breast. In addition, he suffered from frequent attacks of anguish, an emotion which dominated his early career. He often fancied that he or somebody else was going to die. . . . When his grandmother died, his fear of death shook him like a leaf. Death and the horror of death had something inhuman about it, he thought later on.

With a feeling of relief mingled with regret Lagerkvist left his home city for Uppsala, where during 1911-12 he followed courses in the humanities at Uppsala University. He also contributed articles and poems to socialistic newspapers and periodicals. At the age of twenty-one he published his first book, entitled **People** (*Människor,* 1912), a narrative of the *Sturm und Drang* period of a young student, like the author himself, alone and rootless in a university town. The book is interesting mainly because of its use of violence and its symbolic interpretation of reality. The hero, Gustav Mörk (*mörk* meaning dark), was part of the darkness which surrounded him; he was at once a demon and a sensitive, frustrated student with an intense craving for life. With its biological determinism and delight in violent details it recalls the brutality of Zola's *Thérèse Raquin.* Later in life Lagerkvist was to say that youth was "the most gruesome of the ages of man," for it was false and unreliable in the extreme, and "those who had not discovered that, had been so false that they had deceived even themselves." In his first book the author had emphasized how disjointed and confused life really was, and how people were prone to live their lives in part only.

Lagerkvist's visit to Paris in 1913 formed a milestone in the development of his artistic creed. There he came under the direct influence of cubism and expressionism. About 1910 new ideas concerning literature and art began to claim his attention. France led the new trends in art. In 1912 Guillaume Apollinaire brought out *Les peintres cubistes,* and his futuristic manifesto of the following year found many followers. The new literary tendencies were felt in several countries almost simultaneously as an attack directed largely against romantic and naturalistic literature. In England and America the Imagists became spokesmen for the new thought. In Germany such periodicals as *Der Sturm* and *Der blaue Reiter* became important forums for the young radicals, whereas *La nouvelle revue française* played a similar role in France. The new artists and writers rebelled against the old tradition by creating a new form, *un art pur,* the significant elements of which were artistic seriousness and simplification.

Lagerkvist's artistic manifesto, **Verbal and Pictorial Art** (*Ordkonst och bildkonst,* 1913), with its characteristic subtitle "On the Decadence of Modern Literature. On the Vitality of Modern Art," must be viewed against the background of his contact with France and should be looked upon as a link in a larger chain of movement toward a new art. The twenty-two-year-old author was filled with a youthful enthusiasm for cubism and a boisterous contempt of modern Swedish literature, which, as he saw it, did not reflect the view of life of modern man. For Lagerkvist the writer's chief aim was to try to explain his own age, to find the artistic expression of his time, for he believed that the characteristics of a given age were best mirrored in its literature. Modern literature was decadent, he argued, because it had become a commodity, and the market was flooded with cheap best sellers. Moreover, the books produced were either psychological investigations or endless descriptions of environment. They excelled in tiresome depictions of the unwholesome, the oversensitive, and the volitionless. The heroes of these books were mostly tired, storm-tossed *fin-de-siècle* men, longing for death. But our age, Lagerkvist maintained, following Bergson, was virile, sound, even brutal.

What in modern literature was lacking Lagerkvist found in modern art. Particularly in cubism he felt a logical clarity and admirable precision, also to be found in primitive art. Since it was an expression of our time, our literature ought to be guided by modern art, he observed. It should be built around more constructive and architectonic ideas. A poem, for instance, should be like a mathematical problem, logically built up in every detail, as Poe, whom Lagerkvist quoted extensively, had shown in his famous analysis of "The Raven." To achieve his aim the author must have a right to construct freely, to recreate reality in order to accomplish artistic effects. But in so doing he must be propelled by an artistic seriousness, coupled with a search for beauty and simplicity. It is true that Lagerkvist's aesthetics came close to that of the *ars gratia artis* school, but there was one important difference. He believed that there must be a definite purpose behind all creative art; it must be the artistic expression of the age, which it should help to synthesize, to explain. For, to Lagerkvist, art was "reality itself, only in other forms; the proportions are magnified, the material is ennobled, but its inner expressive force is the same; it is the same blood, but there are other limbs, a new and nobler creature." Art should be intellectual, precise, even austere, "but at the same time romantic." Ideally it should be, as evidenced in most of the author's writings, a fusion of classicism and romanticism, expressing the temper of our time.

In any discussion of Lagerkvist's aesthetics mention ought to be made of the little volume called **Theater** (*Teater,* 1918), a more mature book than **Verbal and Pictorial Art.** Simplicity of form, coupled with imaginative richness, was his ideal for the drama. He wanted more freedom of imagination, more lyricism, and more poetic ecstasy. He admired Shakespeare, Yeats, and, above all, the later Strindberg, whose influence on Lagerkvist is obvious. He felt akin to the romantic temper of Hoffmann, Kleist, and Poe, maintaining that the world was to him but "a wonder, a ghost, a torture room, where supernatural passions and terrors were ravaging." In the drama he cared less for factual truth than for expressivity and wanted the inner conflict or emotion to be expressed in the outer form. He attacked Ibsen whose plays were merely words on a bare stage; instead, he thought the theater ought to make full use of all modern technicalities and light effects in order to express the violent and sudden contrasts and the "complex, confused, and fantastic elements of modern life."

Lagerkvist wrote this when World War I was still ablaze, and few writers felt the war as intensely as those of his generation. It shattered his mental stability and left indelible marks on his mind. Realism and naturalism, he thought, no longer sufficed to give artistic expression to a world in which old values had crumbled and brutality reigned supreme. His own state of mind and that of many others of the period he brilliantly characterized in the following passage: "In its lack of balance, in its heterogeneousness, and through the violent expansion of mutually conflicting forces, our age seems absurd, fantastic—even more fantastic than naturalism is able to describe it. The feeling of security for existence, which the naturalistic form gives, we do not possess, but rather a burning desire to try to find expression for all the anguish with which life, such as it rolls in upon us, fills our souls."

In the collection of poems entitled *Anguish* (*Angest*) the author interpreted his own feelings in the time of World War I. A personal crisis, too, may have given added force to the emotional depth of the poems. The book, which came out in 1916, is a landmark in Lagerkvist's production, and it is significant also in the history of Swedish literature as the first major experiment in expressionism. This movement took its violent contrasts, its brutality, and its lacerated form from the chaos of modern wartime. It did not try to be an analysis of the inner drama, or a minute photograph of physical reality, but an expression of the author's own intense feelings, a superb vision, and an artistic synthesis of life. (pp. 400-05)

Anguish and the bestiality of man were the recurrent motifs of the author's first experimental play, *The Last of Mankind* (*Sista mänskan,* 1917), which gave evidence of Lagerkvist's debt to Strindberg's *A Dream Play.* The end of the world was near; the sun was about to be extinguished. The few people who were still alive were cold and hungry and filled with hatred. Eventually there was only one survivor left, a blind man who in a last effort had strangled the woman he once loved. In this drama there was no hope for humanity, for love was lacking; everything was darkness and frustration. Pain, terror, and loneliness were the emotions which dominated the author's vision. He saw no meaning in life as he experienced it in his own heart, and as he witnessed it in the world at large. Everywhere coldness, bitterness, and brutality had the upper hand. Not only among the living but also among the dead he found the same terror, darkness, and suffering, as can be seen from the three radical one-act plays, entitled *The Trying Hour* (*Den svåra stunden*), included in *Theater.* The people could do nothing but suffer; they lacked volition and a purpose in life; they were shut up in their own dead, icy souls.

The stark pessimism of these plays gave apt expression to what Lagerkvist felt during those catastrophic years. In 1918 the mood of despair was particularly emphasized in Spengler's *Der Untergang des Abendlandes.* And in the following year Lagerkvist brought out a book with the symbolic title *Chaos* (*Kaos,* 1919), containing some of his finest lyrics. A prose poem describing a broken pot, which symbolizes the world raped by war, is of particular interest. The pot could not be repaired, for the world lay in fragments and its people were both spiritually and physically invalids. The book also contained a remarkable play, *The Secret of Heaven* (*Himlens hemlighet*), the scene of which was a section of the globe. The people were Lilliputian marionettes, who strutted for a while on the surface of the earth, brooding in vain over the riddle of the universe. They were ridiculous, but the author felt sympathy for them. The drama was largely a pantomime, in which the characters tried to express their inner emotions by means of movements and actions.

Into this somber drama there came a flickering ray of light in the form of love, and life began to take on meaning. After World War I Lagerkvist managed to liberate himself from the pessimism and determinism which had dominated his view of life for several years. In 1918 he had married a Danish

girl, but their union was of brief duration. A feeling of hope and a reverance for life came also to the fore in some of the poems in *Chaos.* He made an endeavor to throw off the shadow of anguish and to find a way out of darkness. This shift of attitude must, of course, also be observed against the background of the world scene, where hope of recovery was felt after the end of the war. Life was no longer a mud heap or a cave of torture, where the human beasts were doomed to suffer and die, but could occasionally be beautiful and noble.

Tendencies toward a more hopeful view of life were also discernible in painting about 1920. It has rightly been said that Lagerkvist's own naïve feelings for nature about this time recalled those of the naïvistic painters. In *The Eternal Smile* (*Det eviga leendet,* 1920), a volume of meditative prose, in which in a personal way the author renounced Christianity, as he was to do later on in *The Hangman* and *The Clenched Fist,* Lagerkvist narrated in a remarkable episode how the dead marched, in an endless procession throughout the centuries, up to God in order to find out what His reasons were for creating them and that mysterious thing called life. Finally they reached God, a crooked old man sawing wood. Somewhat puzzled He said to them: "I am a simple man. I have worked untiringly. I have stood at my job day after day as long as I remember. I have demanded nothing. Neither happiness nor sorrow, neither belief nor unbelief, nothing. I intended only that you were never to be satisfied with nothing." Amazed at this paradoxical answer they showed Him the children. "As regards these I had no intentions," He said. "At that time I was only happy." Thereafter the millions who had gathered in front of the old man felt an internal peace, since they knew that there was no preconceived notion of existence, for happiness lay in everyday work and the love of man. (pp. 406-08)

The change of attitude to a more positive outlook on life noted after 1920 was also seen in the modern morality play, *The Invisible One* (*Den osynlige*), which came out in 1923. The method used in the earlier expressionistic plays, wherein everything was consciously chaotic, bizarre, wherein the scenes shifted frequently and were meant to express not the outer milieu but the inner conflict, now gave way to a more harmonious and somewhat realistic form with emphasis on the spoken word. The play, which has been called a lyric oratorium, showed the eternal battle between life and death, good and evil. The hopeful tone found in [a previous volume of verse], *The Path of the Happy Man* (*Den lyckliges väg,* 1921), was here marred by queries, doubts, and resignation. The Invisible One, whose role in the play was entirely lyrical, represented the Spirit of Man, a godlike being, who, having assumed human form, would never be annihilated in the struggle with the forces of darkness. For the author then began to see the importance of higher ideals and to believe in the existence of the indestructible Spirit of Man. The drama ended on a note of hope with the Spirit of Man singing alone surrounded by light. The beast in man was almost conquered in Lagerkvist's world.

The tendency toward realism noticed in this play was more marked in two retrospective books of high merit, *Evil Sagas* (*Onda sagor,* 1924) and *Guest of Reality* (1925). The last-mentioned book, with which all readers of Lagerkvist should begin, is a key to much of the author's thought. He describes in a remarkably lucid and simple style his childhood and early youth, the period which ended in "dissolution, disorder, and chaos."

A second marriage called forth a new collection of love poems, *Songs of the Heart* (*Hjärtats sånger,* 1926). From then on, Lagerkvist became more and more a militant humanist. He reviewed his life in *Life Vanquished* (*Det besegrade livet,* 1927), and was able to see not only thorns but also roses. The purpose of existence was to win victory over life, to strive for things unattainable. He maintained, moreover, that what was purest and best in man would leave its earthly prison and rise toward ideal regions. Furthermore, he preached veneration for man and belief in man, at the same time attacking violently Freudian primitivism. Our duty was not to probe into what was the basest and most animallike elements of man but to find what was the most supreme, the most divine phase of mankind. Man should not relapse into the animal state but fight for humanity and believe in the ideal destiny of man, for in him was righteousness and love. Lagerkvist did not have faith in a creative God, but he believed in man's divinity and in man's ultimate victory over material forces.

The metaphysician and the humanist meet in most of his later works, such as the visionary play, *The Man Who Lived His Life Over Again* (*Han som fick leva om sitt liv,* 1928) and in the symbolic drama, *The King* (*Konungen,* 1932). Lagerkvist saw clearly the looming catastrophe of nazism, against which he rose in immediate and titanic defiance. In 1933, the year of Hitler's rise to power, he brought out the long short story *The Hangman* (*Bödeln*), symbolizing the new cult of violence and barbarity. The story was later dramatized and successfully played throughout Scandinavia. Nazism became to him the incarnation of all the evil of mankind, which had to be opposed to the utmost if our civilization were to remain. The powers of darkness, the enigma of evil, absorbed Lagerkvist's mind, as it had that of Melville and Hawthorne and the Swedish poet Tegnér. The Hangman became ultimately the symbol of the evil forces within man which seem indestructible. Two plays, *The Man Without a Soul* (*Mannen utan själ,* 1936) and *Victory in the Dark* (*Seger i mörker,* 1939) were also concerned with Hitlerism.

Lagerkvist's credo and militant humanism were perhaps best expressed in the travel book covering his trip to Greece and Palestine, *The Clenched Fist* (*Den knutna näven,* 1934), in which he maintained that the clenched fist of our culture was stronger than military force and barbarity. The principles on which Western civilization was based were freedom, peace, and humaneness. These were the everlasting values and must be fought for. In a time of growing darkness and individual subjection Lagerkvist went to the Acropolis, which he saw silhouetted like a clenched fist against the sky, in search of light and freedom, to him the dearest symbols of our culture. The *mystique* of the author's philosophy of life was embedded in the faith that what was best in man would always fight for those values on which our civilization rested.

The outbreak of World War II did not come to the writer as a shock. He had witnessed the gathering of the clouds and knew that it was inevitable. His creative energy was in no way slackened; instead he strung his harp in defense of humanity and spiritual values. In two collections of poetry, *Song and Strife* (*Sång och strid,* 1940) and *The Home and the Star* (*Hemmet och stjärnan,* 1942), Lagerkvist attacked such ideologies of force as nazism and bolshevism.

He returned to the problem of evil in *The Dwarf* (*Dvärgen,* 1944), which is one of his masterpieces. Like the Hangman, the Dwarf was meant as an incarnation of evil, that force which lay hidden in every human breast. It lay there, perhaps nailed to the wall of the darkest chamber in man's soul, prepared to come forth at his bidding. It represented hatred, death, evil, and destruction. In World War II all the dark forces of man were again unleashed, all the concealed hatred had once more come to the surface. The evil, as Lagerkvist saw it, would always remain, for it was indestructible, immortal like the Dwarf in the novel.

The author's latest novel *Barabbas* (1950) is perhaps his most profound as well as his most widely read book. It is an imaginative tour de force comparable to Sienkiewicz' *Quo Vadis? . . . Barabbas* is the author's attempt to penetrate into the workings of the mind of the man who was liberated instead of Christ and who wanted to believe but was unable to do so. But Barabbas is fundamentally a symbol: he is modern man in search of a meaning and human relationship in a world of force and enigmas.

As a writer Lagerkvist is primarily idealistic, with strong Platonic affinities. Although he is robust, even brutal, he shows warmth and pathos for man's suffering. As a personality he is reserved, keeping mostly to himself like a hermit, and refraining from commenting on his work. His struggle for recognition has been long and hard. It needed another war to give this often misunderstood and exclusive writer a universal hearing and final recognition. His rich output falls during the two world wars, the violence, chaos, and frustration of which he has keenly experienced and artistically interpreted in poems, plays, short stories, novels, and meditative writings. Even in translation his simple, colorful style retains its undertones and ambiguities. With its paratactic constructions, short sentences, and brief, everyday words it has the flavor of the old Icelandic sagas. It is also characterized by the frequent use of such contrasts as life and death, light and darkness, belief and doubt, dream and reality. Lagerkvist is primarily a symbolic writer whose most recurrent symbol is blood. His characters form a gallery of strange creatures, distorted fragments of a race of lacerated, suffering individuals.

His work has welled forth like a rich stream, sometimes violent, sometimes quiet, but always as if from an inner compulsion. It is born of the tension between his agony over death and his craving for life, between the forces of darkness within man and man's strivings for higher ideals. But the period of nightmare is over, at least for the present; for the sixty-one-year-old writer, in the fullness of his creative powers, has found faith in man and in eternal values. He is, in his own terms, a "believer without faith," a "religious atheist," a Hellene with strong roots in classical ideals, a brooding visionary whose artistic integrity and searching penetration into the universal problems of modern man will leave no reader indifferent. (pp. 409-12)

        Lars Åhnebrink, *"Pär Lagerkvist: A Seeker and a Humanist,"* in The Pacific Spectator, *Vol. 6, No. 4, Autumn, 1952, pp. 400-12.*

VIVIAN MERCIER

Let's face it: it's not desperately hard for a competent Swedish writer to win a Nobel Prize for Literature. Mr. Lagerkvist has been a member of the Swedish Academy, which awards the prize, since 1940; it would be foolish to say that this fact has hindered his recognition when we note he is at least the fourth Swede to win the award since 1901. Most people have heard of Selma Lagerlof, but who now recalls Verner von Heidenstam or Erik A. Karlfeldt, two other Swedish winners? Mr. Lagerkvist's poetry may possibly overwhelm the reader in the original Swedish, but the evidence provided by *The Eternal Smile and Other Stories* does not suggest that he is one of the great prose masters, though the works in this selection have presumably been chosen to show him to the best advantage. (pp. 346-47)

Most of the work in the new volume—all of which dates from the period 1920-35—classes Lagerkvist with the German and Central European "Expressionist" movement which had its heyday around 1910-25, though it stemmed from the later work of Strindberg, who died in 1912. . . .

The Expressionists were more interested in the abstract than in the concrete, in ideas than in phenomena, in Man than in men; hence their characters, and Lagerkvist's, are all too often walking abstractions—He, She, The Dead. The Expressionists, too, were great seekers after God, and unfortunately they usually managed to find, not Him, but someone made in their own image whom any self-respecting theologian could demolish in about five minutes. Kafka, and Kafka alone, having lost the God of his fathers, was profound enough not to "find" one of these custom-made deities. Having apparently rejected Lutheranism in his adolescence, Lagerkvist seems to me to waver between a humanism that is worthy of respect and a deism that is but a bloodless Lutheranism. . . .

In general, I would warn readers who do not take kindly to the Scandinavian twilight against most of the longer pieces in this volume—especially *The Hangman* and *The Masquerade of Souls*. As *The Eternal Smile* contains a surprise or two near the end and may be considered Lagerkvist's most interesting foray into pseudo-theology, perhaps these impatient readers should struggle through it anyway.

To my mind, Lagerkvist's symbolism is most effective when rooted in explicit realism. The little story **"Father and I"** evokes a boy's walk with his father along the railroad tracks—such a walk being safe and pleasurable in rural Sweden, as in rural Ireland—and many of its vivid details reminded me of similar walks with my own father. Thus I tended to be highly receptive to the symbolic—or allegorical—element when it appeared. An unscheduled train, without lights, suddenly roars past, nearly running down father and son: "That was how this world, this life, would be for me; not like Father's, where everything was secure and certain." Admittedly this passage beats the reader over the head with an idea that is trite enough, but the short story as a whole stands up, even under a critical eye. So do such bits of realism as **"The Marriage Feast,"** where simple goodness is shown to be as real as evil is, and *Guest of Reality,* probably in part autobiographical, which tells of a death-obsessed boy's ultimate rejection of the stifling, though loving, constriction of a Lutheran home where the Bible is the parents' constant and only reading.

Professor Vowles is right [in his introduction] in describing **"The Children's Campaign,"** a short satire on war, as "Swiftian" in its deadly irony and meticulous documentation of a fantasy world. One of the briefest sketches, **"A Hero's Death,"** deserves to rank with the best of Kafka's *Parables,*

but some others just as short would not be out of place in a high-school yearbook.

Marianne Moore once asked of poetry that it "present for inspection imaginary gardens with real toads in them. . . ." Par Lagerkvist can produce imaginary gardens all right, but they do not usually convince us, because the real toads are missing; at other times he supplies the real toads without the gardens; only on a few occasions does he manage to blend the observed particular and the imagined generality in a compelling unity. (p. 347)

Vivian Mercier, "No Toads," in The Commonweal, *Vol. LX, No. 14, July 9, 1954, pp. 346-47.*

TOM FITZSIMMONS

There is a vast range [of styles in *The Eternal Smile and Other Stories*]—from extended anecdote to novelette, from fantasy to a conventional medley of realism and symbolism. **"Love and Death"** is one paragraph long; **"The Masquerade of Souls"** 80 pages. There is anger, satire, tenderness, love, sometimes sentimentality, and often a fine, wry humor. (p. 18)

Lagerkvist is best as a weaver of parables. In these he is not concerned with "real people," but with a sweep of action and a revelation. Then his style, his use of symbolism, his whole manner works a magic of atmosphere. And an American reader is reminded of how strictly we have come to limit our definitions of the "short-story" and the "novel," and what short distances our writers stray. But once having read the whole book in all its variety, the same reader is likely to wonder why some of it is so very good and some so bad.

Lagerkvist is interested in human desire and fear, consequent good and evil, the causes of these, the questions, the answers, the contradictions which men shape as they try to relate their lives to the lives of others and to the reality containing them. Happiness to him is the acceptance of the *actual*—in its diversity and paradox. The attempt to deny some part of that reality, to reject it, leads to confusion and misery. And love adds a dimension to the acceptance, making it positive and joyous.

But he is concerned with all this in its trans-personal aspect first. *The Eternal Smile,* for example, treats of human nobility and absurdity, love, hatred, satisfaction, frustration, as these cut across and through the lives of a great mass of people. Swift, superbly drawn vignettes catch these elements of reality at work in an individual life; but the focus is never the *individual,* it is the forces that work upon and through the person. In stories like this Lagerkvist is strong—unencumbered by detail, he invents and weaves and appears as a wise, sensitive, delightful man whose sense of the tragic although profound never excludes joy, and, I suppose, his faith in life. Such tales make up about half of the collection.

When he does focus on one or two people, tries to write a conventional story, there is neither sweep nor revelation, everything grinds. Nothing happens. He simply tells the reader about the people and what they do and why they do it. It is description from a distance. **"The Masquerade of Souls"** is not much longer than *The Eternal Smile,* but it seems to take an eternity to read. Two people, young, meet, love, marry, drift about in a universe of love, come to want a child; the son is killed in childbirth to save the mother, she retreats into neurosis, the man suffers; as they enter middle age she is discovered to be hopelessly ill, their love once again becomes everything, she dies, he tries to live, cannot and kills himself to join her. We are with these two people a long time, yet they are never real for us, as they must be since this time the story is about them, their love and not love itself. We are never even allowed to approach them, the author holds us off, tells us about them and explains. What he tells us is well said. But here the kind of conception and the techniques which are the strength and flavor of the trans-personal tales work to defeat him. It is as if he has never really *seen* how individuals live those forces he can isolate so well in fantasy. And this impression is encouraged by a confusion of intent and attitude in the story. We are told that the lives of these two people have been immeasurably enriched by their love but it is clear that they have so immersed themselves in that love that they cannot deal with the rest of reality and are destroyed. What the author thinks about this kind of loving, the basis on which he organized the story, is never clear—he drifts toward irony, then pulls back almost to sentimentality, then drifts toward irony again.

One story, however, does stand between what Lagerkvist does excellently and what seemingly he cannot do. In **"The Marriage Feast,"** fantasy and realism are blended into a beautiful, controlled whole. Love and the rest of reality are juxtaposed meaningfully. The theme is one of the author's favorites: the humble, the crippled, the simple in spirit sometimes rise to a happiness, find an accord with reality which we all must envy; and they do it despite us.

These are the people Lagerkvist seems to *see* best—perhaps he trusts them more—and is most willing to present without comment. He is content to let his attitude be implicit in what they do and in the sequence of their doing.

A distinguished artist, Lagerkvist is here in his strength and in his weakness. Since that strength is in an area seldom explored now, it is doubly valuable. (pp. 18-19)

Tom Fitzsimmons, "Strength Where Needed," in The New Republic, *Vol. 131, No. 2, July 12, 1954, pp. 18-19.*

AGNE BEIJER

The dramatist who figures most often in the Swedish repertoire is still August Strindberg. His chief works are as pertinent to our problems now as they were when they were written. . . . In 1917, Pär Lagerkvist, who in the 1920s was to step forward as the most representative and profoundly original dramatist of his generation, asserted in a pamphlet against naturalism in the theatre, his belief in Strindberg's intimate technique as the only possible form for a renewal of drama.

When he later tried to realize this ideal in his own earliest plays it of course implied something more than a mere experiment in dramatic form. Like the whole generation then living through crucial years and reaching out for something to hold on to, he was hurt to the quick by the war and its aftermath. He felt a need to shriek aloud. Here in Sweden, as in other countries, above all in Germany, this shriek developed into expressionistic drama, a direct, immediate, and burning reaction to contemporary events.

Pär Lagerkvist's first play to be performed in a public theatre, the one-act **Heaven's Secret** (1921), was printed in a collection of poems and prose poems entitled **Chaos.** In 1917 he had published a more ambitious five-act drama, **The Last Human Being,** and in 1918 three short one-act plays under the title **The Difficult Hour,** together with the dramatic manifesto referred to above. It would be a mistake to regard his dramatic productions during these years as primarily experiments in form. With all his interest in art, Lagerkvist is far from being an aesthete. The question he asked himself was this: Is there any meaning in all the suffering that has overtaken humanity? Must we human beings be tortured in this way? Is life radically evil? This is the problem which constantly recurs in his work. His preoccupations are those of a non-Christian theologian.

The expressionistic form, which he has never since adopted so consistently, came to his aid, tending as it does away from the individual and subjective towards the supra-individual and objective. The form was thus a logical consequence of the content. What seemed to him his most important task as an expressionist was the reduction of human problems to their prime factors, the finding of a pattern in a haphazard and chaotic tangle of threads.

In a formal sense, Lagerkvist took his cue from expressionistic painting, and so initiated the age of theisms not only in stage-settings but in drama itself. It was not for nothing that he became, and remained all his life, a friend of Per Lindberg, the foremost champion of expressionism among our stage producers. But at the same time he went further back, to the greatest individualist in the history of drama, Strindberg, to whom, as we have seen, he unreservedly acknowledged his debt. He has something in common with Strindberg more essential than mere form however, and that is his shattering experience of suffering, though nothing so well illustrates the difference between them as their respective defences against it. Strindberg endows suffering with meaning by giving it a moral import, by presenting it in terms of crime and punishment and fitting it into a religious view of existence. In this way suffering acquired both metaphysical significance and a dramatic tension fundamentally identical with that of classical drama. In Strindberg the powers of destiny pervade human life, as they did in Aeschylus, in Racine and even—though less perceptibly—in Shakespeare. For Lagerkvist this view was not possible for he acknowledges no supernatural powers. At the core of his anxiety is the discovery that human beings are evil and do each other evil apparently for no reason, simply because they are born wicked and cannot help themselves. What is horrible in evil is its senselessness. Lagerkvist does not judge; he simply cannot escape the facts. His pessimism is radical. His earlier one-act plays, in their artistic concentration perhaps the most perfect things he has produced for the stage, are a kind of vision of life's miseries projected in the form of anecdotal sketches, imprinted on the retina with marvellous sharpness. The terse, colloquial dialogue releases, as it were, the scenic image which is felt throughout as the primary element.

The title figure of his next play, the **Invisible One,** who for a long time remains an obscurely symbolic figure, is in the final scene identified with the human spirit itself, which suffers and is degraded with the humanity it represents.

One might also give the invisible one another name: good will. For the human spirit, which is itself not permitted to guide men's destiny, does nevertheless know good and evil and has good will. In the assurance of the indestructibility of good will we find the polarity which gives Pär Lagerkvist's work its dramatic tension and replaces Strindberg's formula of crime and punishment. We find it in its pure form in his next drama: *The Man Who Was Given His Life to Live Again* (1928).

The Man Who Was Given His Life to Live Again deals with ordinary simple people in modest circumstances, a shoemaker and his wife, who strive to do their duty so far as they are able, and to defend the happiness which is the reward of modesty, faithfulness and good will. Their home life is an idyll. But they themselves are only guests in the idyll. The fence which good will has built for them as a protection against the powers of evil, against the wild beast in human nature, is infinitely fragile. The mild and faithful Daniel is granted the grace of living his life over again, as he would have lived it if the powers of evil had not overcome him in an unguarded moment, and made him a murderer. Before his new life is ended, however, some harsh and thoughtless though well-intended words to his son result in the latter's suicide. Good will has no power over the negative forces of evil in us, which play heads and tails for our happiness. Yet it exists and is the only thing we have to hold on to. Here, as in several other of his works, Lagerkvist's thought borders on a religious view of existence, without actually crossing the line. He exposes to us the psychological prerequisite of such a view: the recognition of our own insufficiency. But there he stops.

What stamps this play, more even than the fundamental view upon which the drama is based, is the dramatic form in which Lagerkvist has clothed it. The hard, tense, harshly trenchant element which gave to the earlier purely expressionistic plays their suggestive intensity is absent. The dialogue is low-pitched and everyday, sometimes even to the point of commonplace. But on the stage it comes to life, taking on shades of meaning that are imperceptible until it is spoken. Everything in this dialogue is genuine, even circumstantially. For circumstantial reasoning is the only means by which a man poor in words may grope his way towards the expression of his thoughts, when the thoughts themselves are no longer commonplaces of the workaday world.

This approach is possible only to a great poet. But Lagerkvist is a great poet, even in his drama. A poet perhaps rather than a dramatist, at least in the traditional sense.

In *The Man without a Soul* (1936), Lagerkvist returned to an everyday milieu, but with a realism even more subtle, elusive and spiritualized than that of *The Man Who Was Given His Life to Live Again.* Though the drama is played against a background of obstreperous contemporary reality, it has a very characteristic point of departure and tries to offer the solution of its problems.

"The Man" has been enrolled in a revolutionary movement akin to Nazism in its earlier stages: he shoots an adversary and immediately afterwards meets a woman who has been abandoned by his victim. He has worshipped action and the brutal struggle of power and life and death; he now realizes that there is something more important. What? He does not exactly know, he knows only that he must get away from this external reality and find this other thing which is more important, and of which he has received an inkling through this quite ordinary woman, who has loved and been abandoned. He becomes a deserter from "action" and is condemned to the firing squad by its henchmen. Will death perhaps reveal this other thing which he is seeking, this thing which would give life a meaning? Once more Lagerkvist stops short on the

threshold of religion. The spirit of this peculiar drama is not easily captured, either by the actors who have to interpret it, or by the audience who have to take it in. But it has a spirit, and is perhaps the most personal of all Lagerkvist's works.

The title of his next play, *Victory in the Dark,* epitomizes the author's fundamental theme: the victory of good will through the death of its bearer. The form of the play is traditional and Lagerkvist is not entirely at home with it—he has gone outside his own domain.

In *Midsummer Night's Dream in the Workhouse,* a blind pauper becomes in imagination king of a realm of joy and in his dream-court fails to recognize his fellow wrecks from the workhouse. He invokes the powers of poetry and imagination against ugliness and sin. This, too, is a victory in the dark. But the victory is not merely one of imagination, it is also a triumph of goodness. For if Jonas had not been such a thoroughly kind person Lagerkvist would never have made him blind, in order that he should escape seeing evil. Nor made him a poet. Nor put into this play about him a side of his own nature that he had never previously revealed: a playful, friendly, conciliatory humour.

The scene of Lagerkvist's last play, *The Philosopher's Stone* (1917), has a colourful Renaissance setting—a period with which he had made himself familiar in the course of preliminary studies for his remarkable *Dwarf.* The chief character is an alchemist obsessed with searching for the philosopher's stone, or the truth about life. Nothing else has any reality for him. He does not notice, refuses to notice, that his experiments in alchemy can only be financed by money which his daughter earns as mistress of a Duke. A political storm breaks out in his native town and in his own house which smashes the outside world for him. His only friend, the wise patriarch Simonides, is driven into exile by anti-Jewish persecution and his son Jacob, caught in the toils of a romantic passion for the Alchemist's fallen daughter, is condemned for murder. The Alchemist himself is forced to submit to that external reality which he has hitherto denied. But in the final scene we find him once more bent over his furnace, about to light it afresh. Once more the same theme: the unquenchable thirst to understand that which cannot be understood. Lagerkvist has here given the theme a counter-motif in the person of the Alchemist's Christian wife, who does not require to understand and condemns his heretical broodings, yet does not abandon him. She represents the unmitigated aspect of goodness, just as the Alchemist represents the unmitigated craving for truth.

Lagerkvist has since dramatized the novel which made his name abroad: *Barabbas.* The dramatization adds nothing essential to the novel, though in my opinion it renders the essentials of the book infinitely better than the film which has also been shown abroad. It is fascinating to observe how in this work Lagerkvist bores even deeper into, and finds new ways of expressing, the problem which has obsessed him all his life: the anxious search for that simple trust in life which religion affords to those who have faith. (pp. 14-21)

Agne Beijer, "Two Swedish Dramatists," in World Theatre, *Vol. IV, No. 2, 1955, pp. 14-26.*

ROBERT GORHAM DAVIS

[*The Sibyl*] is a kind of companion piece to *Barabbas.* Those who were fascinated by the enigmas of the earlier work will certainly want to read this one. There is more beauty in it, and more love. The religious paradoxes, however, which have always fascinated the author, seem now rather to control the events than be implicit in them.

Barabbas was the story of the man released from prison instead of Jesus. He witnessed the crucifixion, and underwent complex and profoundly troubling relations with Christian believers through the rest of his life. The present novel, ***The Sibyl,*** also begins with a man who saw Jesus on the way to Calvary. He is the famous Wandering Jew who would not let the suffering Savior rest at his door, and was condemned by Him to roam through this world to all eternity.

Lagerkvist brings this blighted wanderer to Delphi, to ask the Pythian oracle, the Pythoness, what his destiny will finally be. When the priests refuse to admit him, he seeks out, high on the mountain, a renowned former Pythoness. Her story, as she herself relates it to him, is the major part of the novel.

Her parents are peasants, working land owned by the priesthood of Apollo. As the daughter enters adolescence, inner voices speak to her, and she has periods of religious ecstasy, which bring her to the attention of the Delphic authorities. Chosen as Pythoness, she is wedded to the god. She serves him not in the beautiful temple of light above ground, but in a dark cave beneath, amid snakes and goats and vapors rising from clefts in the earth. Here possession by the god occurs, just as Vergil describes it in the Aeneid. She utters the dark prophecies that the priests interpret to inquirers from all over the Mediterranean world.

On a visit to her parents, she falls lyrically in love with a young soldier. Becoming pregnant, she is driven from Delphi as one who has betrayed her god-husband. There is mystery, however, about the species of passion that has produced this pregnancy.

Both the Pythoness and the Wandering Jew have had their lives blasted by a god. Lagerkvist's ***The Sibyl*** is testimony to the incalculableness and indefinableness of the divine. The non-human is necessarily the inhuman. The Pythoness speaks of God's cruel love almost in the words of Graham Greene. But knowing God also gives her moments of happiness passing all understanding.

The Wandering Jew thinks that he hates the divine for its arbitrary injustice. He protests that he was only an ordinary man, loving his wife and child, and no more wicked than the next man. The end of the book suggests that he may learn to appreciate his special "chosenness." In any case there is no escaping the curse and blessing that comes from God. Whatever men may believe or disbelieve, the prophetess says, "their destiny will always be bound up with God."

In its mingling of psychological, pagan and Christian elements, ***The Sibyl*** resembles C. S. Lewis' *We Have Seen Their Faces.* In that novel, too, a young girl was wedded to a god. Lewis' novel, however, possessed dramatic and imaginative unity, which Lagerkvist's lacks. The narrative sequences in ***The Sibyl*** are written with a lucid simplicity that comes through well in translation. Still there is something artificial in bringing together the Wandering Jew and the Pythoness. They speak in each other's presence, but have no real relationship.

When the Pythoness speculates about the Virgin Mary, who also bore God's son, the book is closer to an essay in compar-

ative religion than to directly felt experience. What gives the novel unity is Lagerkvist's dramatic but not fully dramatized sense of the Divine, all-demanding, enigmatic, inescapable. (pp. 5, 25)

Robert Gorham Davis, "A Sense of the Divine," in The New York Times Book Review, *January 12, 1958, pp. 5, 25.*

ANTHONY WEST

[***The Sibyl***] is a conversation piece set in the interior of a hut on a rocky hillside above Delphi, in Greece. Through the doorway, one sees a temple in the valley below. The setting is simply constructed of a few clichés: there is a "sacred way" along which "pilgrims pace solemnly;" a youth "strewing fresh laurels from the god's grave" in a court through which a priestess, dressed "as god's bride," passes, "attended by two priests." Turning from this slipshod background, which has nothing of either the intense beauty or the archeological interest of the actual place, we come to the three figures in the foreground. A man whose face shows that he has suffered talks to a woman "with old eyes" while an enigmatic male figure with a remote, otherworldly smile listens to them.

What goes on? Well, the woman with the old eyes is a priestess of the Delphic oracle who has been dismissed from her post for committing the indiscretion of bearing a child to the god, and her companion is none other than the Wandering Jew. Naturally, they have a great deal to say to each other, and when they have said it, a miracle is found to have occurred. The smiling figure, who is none other than the god's son, has vanished. He has slipped out of the hut, and after walking uphill, shedding his clothing piece by piece, he has (in a manner carrying one back to an episode in Hemingway's *Torrents of Spring*) taken off, not far above the snowline, into the wild blue yonder. Distressed rather than gratified by this convincing display of supernatural powers in her child, the mother delivers an unenlightening statement about man's relationship to God. This does not reflect anything in the nature of religious experience, but it anticipates the sort of thing said by modern theologians of the liberal variety whose utterances are concerned more with being inoffensive than with expressing any particular convictions. " . . . I know enough," she says,

> of the life of mankind and can glimpse enough of the road that lies before them to know that they can never escape the curse and the blessing that comes to them from god. Whatever they may think and do, whatever they may believe or disbelieve, their destiny will always be bound up with god.

If the quality of the Sibylline wisdom is depressing, the conversation leading up to its disclosure is even more so. In its course, the Sibyl confesses that she had enjoyed an affair with a one-armed man before the god favored her with his attentions. Her account of it is not inspiring; it recalls in its style and content the trundling narratives that fill the confession magazines. It is, for instance, her mother's death, and its effect upon her father, that makes her realize how much of Life she is missing as a temple virgin. ("Strangely enough we never talked much of Mother, though we both thought of her constantly.") Toward the end of her affair with the mortal, he forces his way into the inner precinct of the temple, where she is carrying out her mediumistic duties. "I remained alone with my conflicting thoughts. Why had he come? I did not

understand. What reason had he? Could it mean that somehow he—that he cared about me?" The unpleasing prurience
that goes with the author's banality of feeling and of expression comes out most plainly in the description of the Sibyl's
erotic experiences, which culminate when the god, taking the
form of a black goat, possesses her. There is no classical authority that says this is the kind of thing that went on at Delphi, and the notion appears to have found its way into the
story simply for its own horrid sake. And there seems little
better warrant for the inclusion of a clinical account of the
sex life of the Wandering Jew. As a character, this unlovely
invention is a product of the degraded popular Christianity
of medieval times; it was created as an embellishment to the
Gospel story to justify and to promote anti-Semitism. The
Wanderer is supposedly cursed with eternal life and eternal
restlessness for his refusal to allow the condemned Christ, on
the way to the Crucifixion, to lean for a moment against the
wall of his house. As this story, to be true, would require God
to be an ill-natured and malignant demon, it reflects small
credit on the twisted Gothic mind that conceived it in the first
place, and, one would think, less on any mind willing to give
it a moment's thought today. But Mr. Lagerkvist not only
asks us to consider the situation of this nonentity as if it were
worth thinking about but even attempts to persuade us that
it is so by equipping it with a case history of psychological
maladjustment. The Wandering Jew is seen going to bed with
his wife and failing to satisfy the expectations he has aroused.

This business of letting the left hand fiddle round the subject
of sex while the right leaps through the Gospels is not new
for Pär Lagerkvist. He was at the same game in his earlier
novel **Barabbas,** in which the released thief, having attended
the Crucifixion, hurries off to an athletic night of love with
a fat lady whose necrophilic appetites have been awakened
by her narrow escape from the cross. The story suggests that
Barabbas is being tormented to the end of his days—when,
through a specious irony, he receives martyrdom as a Christian—by a desire to believe that is exactly balanced by an inability to do so. The matter is left in doubt until the book
ends, with Barabbas's death:

> Only Barabbas was left hanging there alone, still
> alive. When he felt death approaching, that which
> he had always been so afraid of, he said out into the
> darkness, as though he were speaking to it:
>
> —To thee I deliver up my soul.
>
> And then he gave up the ghost.

André Gide professed to be impressed by the subtle ambiguity of this, and by the idea that the "as though" created a
question whether Barabbas had surrendered his soul to the
darkness or to the light. The profound lack of reality, and the
absence of any vital interest, in this false problem is made
clear by Lagerkvist's frantic efforts to import substance into
it, both by being "frank" about Barabbas's sex life and by
elaborating his experience with a great deal of excess baggage.
It is perhaps legitimate for Barabbas, after he has seen Christ
die, to encounter Lazarus alive. But it is a luxury of coincidence that St. Peter should select Barabbas as his confidant
and tell him, on the morning after the Crucifixion, how
dreadful he feels about having denied his Master. When Barabbas attends the stoning of one of the first of the Christian
martyrs (Mr. Lagerkvist runs true to form in choosing a
young girl with a harelip for the victim) and murders one of
the responsible officials into the bargain, it becomes obvious

that anything and everything can be expected. Nobel Prize
or no Nobel Prize, Pär Lagerkvist's work belongs in the section of the library that houses such works of classical scholarship and religious feeling as *The Last Days of Pompeii, Quo
Vadis?,* and *Ben-Hur.* (pp. 135-36, 138)

Anthony West, "Dusty Answer," in The New Yorker, Vol. XXXIV, No. 1, February 22, 1958, pp. 135-
36, 138.

ROBERT DONALD SPECTOR

For Pär Lagerkvist fiction is not so much a means of artistic
expression as it is a device for philosophical probing. The
Swedish Nobel Prize winner has for years been carrying on
a dialogue about the nature of man's soul and the meaning
of existence. . . . While the problems he has raised are in
themselves seemingly insoluble, Lagerkvist has never tired in
his effort to resolve them, and in the process he has revealed
all the anxieties, perplexities, and pretenses common to modern man.

In *The Death of Ahasuerus,* the dialogue continues. The new
work is a novella that brings to a close the agony of the Wandering Jew, condemned—so legend would have it—to eternal
life because of his refusal to comfort Christ. Lagerkvist is
never content, however, with either the Biblical or Apocryphal versions of history, but rewrites them for contemporary
significance. By terminating the sentence of Ahasuerus, he
provides what he believes to be the only faith available today.
It is not a reliance on traditional religion, for Ahasuerus at
death is no closer to accepting Christianity than he was earlier to accepting Christ. What it does amount to is an acceptance of man's fate—an insistence on dealing with things as
they are and life as it is.

To be sure, there is no such bald assertion in the story, for
Lagerkvist, despite the surface simplicity of his narratives, is
a complex writer. He masks his message behind seemingly
artless fable-like quality. But there is scarcely a line or character whose symbolism does not challenge a multiplicity of
meanings.

Against a vague medieval setting he throws his Wandering
Jew together with a company of pilgrims assembled at an inn,
preparing to make their journey to the Holy Land in order
to satisfy their individual selfish needs. Ahasuerus singles out
two, Tobias—a former soldier who has mystically found religion—and a woman the soldier calls Diana because he discovered her in a state of virginal bliss in the forest. They are
former lovers because Tobias in removing Diana—a pagan
goddess—from her natural surroundings has ruined her.
When Diana gives her life to save Tobias from an arrow, it
is as though ancient religion has sacrificed itself for Christianity. Ahasuerus, the skeptic, cannot accept this, but he does
learn his lesson from Tobias' death, suffered through the soldier's need to continue his pilgrimage even without knowing
why he is making it. That for Ahasuerus is the meaning of
life—to act according to what one feels must be done, regardless of whether it makes sense beyond the moment.

Perhaps such a conclusion is no solution after all. Perhaps,
too, Lagerkvist's literary methods will annoy readers seeking
a didactic statement or bewilder those concerned only with
the surface narrative. But for many others it will be an honest
effort of a serious contemporary writer to present dramatical-

ly man's predicament in trying to find faith in a seemingly hopeless world.

Robert Donald Spector, "Medieval Fable by a Nobel Prize Winner," in Books, New York, February 18, 1962, p. 6.

EDMUND FULLER

[*The Death of Ahasuerus*] is provocative, interesting, but ultimately disappointing. Its vivid descriptions of scenes, short, sharp vignettes of character, and occasional powerful episodes have not been wrought into a satisfactory whole. . . .

The setting is somewhere in Europe, conceivably near a pass through the Alps. We are not told and do not need to know. In medieval times, a large company of pilgrims is bound for the Holy Land; a train of harlots, ruffians and outlaws mingle with them as with an army. Standing apart from the crowd is a man named Tobias who has lived through war and plague, and who has been an outlaw. He is not truly a pilgrim, but is following under a compulsion because of a dead woman he had found in a deserted village with the stigmata upon her body. For her, he is going. Her half-starved, pitiful dog trails along with him. Tobias is a disturbed man, resisting the Crucified One, yet driven on his errand, and asking, "What's one to live *for?*"

Trailing him is the ruin of the once handsome woman whom he had met and taken in the forest, long ago. They lived a brief idyl, and he called her Diana, the meaning of which she did not know. She has since become the common woman of outlaw bands, yet still feels bound to Tobias.

Joining them is Ahasuerus, the Wandering Jew, who appeared in *The Sibyl,* and who still awaits release from the curse of life. An impulsive act of brutality turns Tobias, through remorse, into an actual pilgrim. Diana gives her life for his in a mysterious manner. Ahasuerus sees Tobias, who has missed the pilgrim ship, entrust himself and his money unquestioningly to a band of ruffians who agree to take him to the Holy Land in their small vessel, but are unlikely to do it. The wanderer finds his long-craved death, sometime after this, in a monastery.

These scenes of the Middle Ages, and many of their episodes, are extraordinarily similar in quality and tone to Ingmar Bergman's tremendous medieval films. The weakness lies in the relating of Ahasuerus' death to what has gone before; also in the mystical murkiness of the dying man's conclusions. Why he is granted the release at this point is not clear. It is not a question of agreeing with the author's theological speculations, but a question of what he intends. Various possibilities suggest themselves that would need long discussion.

Presumably, Ahasuerus had first to see the strange death of the woman, Diana, and understand that it was a means of granting her a happy death. He had to see Tobias brought to a faith in something so important that it would be better to lose life than lose that faith. Then Ahasuerus is given the gift he does not understand himself, in which he is received into the "holy land" of death by that same God whom he thinks he has "conquered." Lagerkvist has worked too cryptically, I think, for the maximum effectiveness of his book. But it is well worth pondering.

Edmund Fuller, "A Parable of Death and Transfig-

uration," in The New York Times Book Review, April 1, 1962, p. 40.

THE TIMES LITERARY SUPPLEMENT

Pilgrim at Sea is the third in a sequence of short novels—following *The Sibyl* and *The Death of Ahasuerus*—and avoids, even more carefully than before, any specific historical signposts. There are pirates, sailing vaguely in the direction of the Holy Land, and there is an outsider, Tobias—the mercenary of the earlier story—who has missed the regular pilgrim ship and given the pirates all he possesses to take him to his destination. Appalled by the brutality he sees when the captain orders his men to loot and murder a wrecked shipful of merchants, Tobias cannot understand why the dark, brutal-looking fellow who talks mystically of the holy peace of the sea should choose to live on such a ship. Giovanni then tells his story—a familiar enough tale of the pure young priest suddenly consumed with desire for the veiled woman behind the confessional grille, exposed as a lecher and unfrocked. A connexion is established in Tobias's bemused mind between this man's sacrificial love, the dream which did not survive except in the symbol of an empty locket, and his own dream of the unattainable Holy Land, a destination beyond the indifferent sea which even if it is as empty a symbol as the locket, is too precious to lose sight of.

The pearl of great price? Or the Prodigal Son? Mr. Lagerkvist has his own paradoxical view of salvation as some kind of accidental discovery made only by those prepared to accept all experience in surrender to an arbitrary, violent God who despises the judgment of men. Undoubtedly his message of needful suffering remains forcibly in the memory, and he has the true teacher's talent for prowling round a question, emphasizing first one, then another angle just long enough to make one reread and compare. His language . . . , is clear and emphatic and perfectly chosen. But simple, homely, or relevant to the predicament of twentieth-century readers? These Mr. Lagerkvist fails to be; there is a vague, Ibsen-like preoccupation with the dark side of mystical experience which will surely sound unrewarding to all who have outgrown solemn faith in euphonic phrases, and the subjectivity of his various visions of pilgrimage makes each of his characters too small and particular for their purpose as symbols.

"Whither, O Splendid Ship?" in The Times Literary Supplement, No. 3232, February 6, 1964, p. 101.

HOLGER LUNDBERGH

It is in a mood of less bitterness and greater serenity that Pär Lagerkvist in [*The Holy Land*] . . . resumes his search for the meaning of life, for a deity able to sustain, for a distant peace behind the clouds of fear and disbelief. Recalling similar quests, in earlier novels such as *Barabbas* and *The Death of Ahasuerus,* the reader finds that the tone is now more muted. The tempests have died down, and the skies have achieved a brilliant transparency.

Bound for the Holy Land on a pilgrim ship, Giovanni, the infidel, the defrocked priest, is set ashore on an alien coast. His friend Tobias accompanies him. They find shelter in a ruined temple. A group of shepherds gives them food. "Is this the

Holy Land?" Tobias asks them. They have never heard of such a place.

One day the herdsmen take Giovanni and Tobias to a hut in the hills, where an infant child reposes on a bed of straw. At the sight of the babe the natives fall on their knees and worship him. Later, Giovanni is stricken with a fatal illness. As he lies dying, a woman appears, bearing a poisonous snake in a basket. She takes from Giovanni's neck a silver chain and locket he has always worn and gives it to Tobias. She knows that the locket (which Giovanni once received from a woman he loved) is empty, but she urges his friend to wear it. Tobias describes to her the baby in the mountain hut and learns the child is dead, bitten by a viper.

After he has buried Giovanni, Tobias sets out on a pilgrimage, in search of he knows not what. As he pushes on, in an atmosphere heavy with dusk, he comes upon a Golgotha, with three bare crosses against the sky. Then, at a fork in the road, he finds a wooden statue of the Virgin. When he lies down to sleep, the figure of the statue approaches him and tells him she will walk with him.

He does not know whether she is the Holy Mother or a woman he has once wronged and deserted. He seeks forgiveness, charging himself with terrible sins, and laments that he will never reach the Holy Land because it does not exist. The vision at his side gently explains that there is a Holy Land—indeed, that this is the Holy Land. She tells him not to despair, for even the one he has betrayed speaks kindly of him. An enormous fatigue suddenly seizes Tobias, and he lies down on the grass. The woman carefully slips the silver chain from his neck and whispers, "Sleep now and rest." And in death "his face seemed full of peace."

It has been said of Lagerkvist's most recent novels that they constitute his farewell to the Christian religion. I have never been able to share this view; his metaphysical thinking is too deep for that. As long as he pursues his quest for religious truth, how can it be claimed that he has come to the end of the road of his belief?

In fact, in *The Holy Land* he seems to me to have come closer to an understanding and a capitulation than ever before. Tobias's vociferous claim that salvation for him is impossible is another version of Jacob wrestling with the angel. Tobias at last is convinced, overcome; mercy and pardon are for him, too. For the first time in his life he is at peace, relieved not only of his doubts and fears but also of the empty locket, the symbol of worldly passion, hollow and meaningless.

Pär Lagerkvist's deliberate tempo is well-suited to his theme; his backgrounds, his descriptions of landscape in its changing moods are superb. The scenes around the temple ruin, with its gnarled trees, the goats, and the knot of herdsmen have the quality of a 15th-century Italian painting, and the picture of the woman who walks the path with Tobias is unforgettably lovely.

> *Holger Lundbergh, "The Pilgrim and the Infidel," in* The New York Times Book Review, *May 22, 1966, p. 5.*

MELVIN MADDOCKS

[*The Holy Land*] is the final work in a related series including *The Death of Ahasuerus, The Sibyl,* and *Barabbas.* It is the briefest and quite possibly the most somber fable of this sequence, with the peculiar Arctic-midnight gloom which can hang like a frosted pall over Swedish Protestantism. (That Swedish clergyman's son Ingmar Bergman would know just how to film Lagerkvist, one suspects.)

Yet there is nothing passive, nothing predestined about Lagerkvist's parable. It pulses insistently, almost angrily with the passion of search. It has finally the positive thrust of a major question. . . .

Lagerkvist's modern version of pilgrim's nonprogress is not without its literary and theological clichés. One begins to anticipate those sips at the symbolic spring, those encounters with the mysterious babe, the mountain climbs—more haze than visibility—and the statues with enigmatic smiles who pop up on cue in subsequent dreams. There is even a certain reversed conventionality to Lagerkvist's conclusion: that the pilgrimage is its own destination, the question is its own answer. The paradox no longer seems so ingenious as it once did.

But what does hold up—under the symbols and theological ploys—is an unmistakable wholeheartedness in Lagerkvist's questing that makes *The Holy Land* less allegory than the masked autobiography which, in fact, all the best allegories may be.

> *Melvin Maddocks, "His Questions Pass for His Answers," in* The Christian Science Monitor, *May 26, 1966, p. 11.*

WINSTON WEATHERS

Pär Lagerkvist, the Swedish author and Nobel Prize winner, has crowned his literary career with the recent completion of a pentalogy of novels dealing with man's unending quest for a meaningful life reconciled with a universe of mystery. With the publication of *The Holy Land* (1964), Lagerkvist brought to a close the tale he began in *Barabbas* (1950) and continued in *The Sibyl, The Death of Ahasuerus,* and *Pilgrim at Sea.*

Behind the pentalogy (Lagerkvist's major literary production since World War II) lies, of course, a significant body of preparatory work. Lagerkvist began his career (with the exception of some early social-protest poems) with the publication in 1912 of a romantic narrative called *People,* the inevitable story of a young, sensitive university student, alone in the world and yearning for the real experience of life. But after an eventful trip to Paris in 1913 and an encounter with the French art world, Lagerkvist was awakened to richer, more original, more creative literary possibilities. (p. 171)

Lagerkvist, perhaps more than any other twentieth century author, has dealt consistently and artistically with the truly eternal questions: What is the meaning of life? Is there a God? What is death? What is the rationale of existence? What should man be doing? In the course of dealing with those questions, Lagerkvist has moved from an earlier alternation between a joyous, almost ingenuous acceptance of life and a bitter awareness of evil, to a more profound and ambiguous philosophy of pilgrimage and quest. Lagerkvist has more and more described a quest and pilgrimage *away* from that which is totally unacceptable in human experience *toward* states of mind and experience that man can structure for himself in spite of the mysteries and enigmatic forces surrounding him. Always the agnostic, Lagerkvist modified and qualified his agnosticism as the result of the horrors of the Nazi experience in the thirties and forties; and in the fifties he emerged a more complex, but no less controlled or compelling, metaphysician than before.

And it is as a literary metaphysician, as a religiously oriented writer, that Lagerkvist has written, in the pentalogy beginning with **Barabbas,** a slender but provocative myth of resurrection. Writing in a century in which cultures, nations, and people have survived vast physical destruction, in a century in which the death of six million can be followed by rebirth into nation and state, Lagerkvist explores the very meaning of *thanatos* and escape from *thanatos,* not simply on the ordinary level of flesh but on the more refined level of spirit, not simply in the ordinary terms of personal or corporate existence but in the greater terms of transfiguration.

Lagerkvist's pentalogy is, quite simply, a challenge to the secular, rational evaluation of survival, a challenge to a modern world dedicated to, and increasingly skillful in, survival techniques—miracle drugs and heart transplants—yet faced with the problem of properly using the survival it manages to achieve. (pp. 172-73)

No matter how far one stretches the boundaries of mortal existence, one has not necessarily solved the problem of human life, its meaning and its significance. Lagerkvist therefore must bring us to his simple question: Is there some way man can move from the limited miracle of physical survival to a greater miracle of spiritual transformation?

One of the principal literary devices used by Lagerkvist in his study of death and transfiguration is the Lazarus archetype, the man returned from the dead to the realities of this world. To a certain extent, the entire pentalogy is a study of the Lazarus figure, not simply the prototypal Lazarus who appears in **Barabbas,** the first novel of the series, but the various Lazarus figures who are the main characters in all the novels.

Lazarus, in the pentalogy, is the representation of the living-dead—and hence is the representation of modern man. Displacing the orthodox concept of Lazarus as the fortunate man snatched from the jaws of death, Lagerkvist presents, rather, a Lazarus who is [a] victim of survival, the man dragged back into existence to dramatize the very meaninglessness of that existence. Lazarus lives on his mountainside outside Bethany, lives alone and alienated from his society, lives on bread and salt, cares nothing for anyone or any event, is the perfectly disengaged and ultimately estranged human being. Lagerkvist's depiction of a melancholy and passive Lazarus emphasizes two of Lagerkvist's observations of the human condition: the intolerableness of simple existence and the over-evaluation of that existence by mankind at large; Lazarus knows the "nothingness" of his survival, but the Christian community assumes that his survival is his most precious gift, indeed a divine reward and blessing.

And Lagerkvist's depiction of a hollow-spirited Lazarus is his most radical demonstration in the pentalogy that death and resurrection must be more than physical events, more than a dying to the physical world followed only by a rebirth into the world, that death and resurrection must finally be events of a higher and different order—if modern man genuinely desires any sort of meaningful accommodation to the eternal mysteries that confront him, or if he genuinely desires his days to be more than a dull and paralyzing stretch of time.

Lagerkvist's Lazarus-truth is further dramatized in the pentalogy by a number of other survival heroes, all of whom have similar experiences of "dying" and escaping from their "deaths" back into an inadequate world. Barabbas, with whom the pentalogy begins, is—in an exchange with Christ—saved from the death-like existence of his prison-grave and is returned to existence in Jerusalem, only to find that he, like Lazarus, is confronted with meaninglessness. (pp. 173-75)

Barabbas finds no joy in his recovered life, can only act out the tawdry role of contemporary man: he hurls himself into sensuality, thievery, murder in a desperate struggle for meaning, only to remain forever disillusioned and spiritually confused. And more than once he acts out the ersatz death-and-resurrection of modern man: He is buried in the grave of the Roman copper mines as a slave; he is resurrected into the dull, pointless routine of serving a Roman master. He "dies" into the confusion of the labyrinthine catacombs of Rome; he is "resurrected" into a night filled with darkness and deception. Yet we are told that he always had death "inside him, he had had that inside him as long as he had lived." Barabbas, modern man, is "immured in himself, in his own realm of death."

Ahasuerus, the wandering Jew (appearing in *The Sibyl* and *The Death of Ahasuerus*) is also burdened with survival. Having refused to let Christ, on the way to the cross, rest against his wall, Ahasuerus is cursed with eternal life, eternal survival, and becomes a haunted man. Given pure, unadulterated absolute survival, he loses the essence of life—he loses wife and child, he loses identity, he loses community, he loses pleasure, he loses his humanity. (pp. 175-76)

And there are others: Tobias, in *The Death of Ahasuerus, Pilgrim at Sea,* and *The Holy Land,* is the man who has survived the wars and the social upheavals of his day, whose life is saved when Diana, the woman who loves him, steps in front of the murderous arrow meant for him. Giovanni, in *Pilgrim at Sea* and *The Holy Land,* has survived his own violation of the codes and taboos of an ordered civilization and survives the brutal world of the pirate ship. Yet all of Lagerkvist's survival heroes are unhappy and alienated men—they survive, but they are sullen, staring, antisocial men, living on their own Lazarus forms of bread and salt, increasingly unconcerned with the world and its nothingness. All of Lagerkvist's survival heroes are frustrated and confused, burdened with their own spiritual emptiness.

The inadequacy of simple survival is underlined by Lagerkvist in his use of two supernatural events—the resurrection of Christ from the tomb and the assumption of the god Apollo from Mount Parnassus. Lagerkvist uses Christ and Apollo—not in any literal acceptance of their supernatural nature—but as literary symbols to disqualify any less magnificent form of survival in this world. In **Barabbas,** Christ ascends from his rocky grave, and in *The Sibyl,* Apollo escapes from this world on a cold winter's night back into the mysterious regions of his deity. Both events are demonstrations of what man's easy, too-available survival simply is not. Lagerkvist uses the mythic tales of Christ and Apollo to make certain the contrast with all the Lazarus resurrections that human beings settle for. In the myths of Christ and Apollo, the resurrections are "out of this world," the escape from death is into a new dimension—and though man may not be expected to achieve the miracle of the gods, man need not settle either for the ordinarily human. Christ and Apollo are used by Lagerkvist to remind us that man must not be saved simply for a renewed ordinary perception, but must be saved out of that perception into new realms of life, beyond the grave of living-death that the contemporary secular world inevitably is.

With Lazarus on the one hand, Christ and Apollo on the other, Lagerkvist moves to the question, Can man progress from one nature to another? He presents his discussion of hoped-for transfiguration in a myth of perception. He develops at length, in the pentalogy, the dilemma of modern man in terms of his capacity to see—although limited vision is typical of all his survival heroes. Lazarus is described as "sitting . . . gazing straight out into the room . . . He seemed not to notice them" with his "pale, lack-lustre eyes . . . queer, opaque eyes that expressed nothing at all." The condition of the eyes for Lagerkvist is the condition of the soul, seeing but not seeing, living but not living.

The discussion of man's inner vision in terms of man's real eyesight is not new in literature, of course. Tiresias says to Oedipus that, in effect, he has eyes but cannot see, and in a more modern literature, T. S. Eliot, discussing the same contemporary condition that Lagerkvist is analyzing, says that the modern hollow man, surviving in the dead land, is "Sightless, unless / The eyes reappear," and dwells in a condition wherein "The eyes are not here. . . ."

Barabbas, perhaps Lagerkvist's most complete presentation of secular man, has "eye-sockets expressionless." And the first mention of Barabbas, at the very beginning of the pentalogy, is that he was "a man standing with his eyes riveted" on the crucified Christ. Lagerkvist declares at once that his tale is a tale of perception, and he also declares that Barabbas—the survival hero—has "eyes too deep-set, as though they wanted to hide."

Looking upon the world with eyes that want to hide, or with Eliot's eyes that are not here, can Lazarus-man see the Christ or the Apollo? Lagerkvist suggests that secular modern man does have within him the capacity to envision the signs of inner transfiguration, to see the possibility of transformation within himself—but man denies his own vision, rejects what is apparent before him. Looking at the dying Christ, Barabbas *thinks* (and where else but in our thinking does our transformation begin or end?) that the Christ is "surrounded by a dazzling light." But his own reaction to his "first glance," his own intuitive realization of transfiguration, is to rationalize the dazzling light: "It must have been because he came straight from the dungeon and his eyes were still unused to the glare. . . . Soon afterwards the light vanished . . . and his sight grew normal again." (pp. 176-78)

Yet Barabbas, torn between desire for a transfiguring vision and desire for a comforting blindness, is haunted by the problem of his eyes: "Perhaps something had gone wrong with them during his time in prison?" When he is confronted with the ultimate sign of transfiguration, when he has the choice to make—to see or not to see—he stares, Lazarus-like, true survival-hero, upon the event of blinding light and Christ's emptied tomb and sees nothing, sees nothing and rejoices: "Deep down inside he thought how very pleased he was not to have seen it. It showed that his eyes were all right now, like everybody else's eyes, that he no longer saw any vision but only reality itself." While the hare-lip girl, also a witness at the resurrection, has "eyes radiant with the memory of what she had seen," Barabbas rejoices at his spiritual blindness—and his normality.

The denial of vision is not, however, easy for man. Barabbas

is burdened with the knowledge that others do "see." The hare-lip girl's last words in life are, "I see Him. I see Him." And Sahak, Barabbas's fellow prisoner in the copper mines, is resurrected from the depths, not to an ordinary world but a world that causes the slave to cry, "He has come! He has come! Behold, his kingdom is here!" And at life's end, when Barabbas wanders in the maze of the catacombs, glimpsing a distant light—the distant light of that "other world" into which true resurrections take us, "He puts his hand to his head. To his eyes. Whatever kind of light was it he had seen? Wasn't it a light? Was it only imagination, or something funny with his eyes? . . ."

If Lagerkvist had ended his myth of death and resurrection with the story of Barabbas, we would have a striking denunciation of secular man and a great expression of the denial of vision and what vision symbolizes: man's transformed situation. But Lagerkvist pursued the matter further and brought his myth to a more hopeful conclusion.

The wandering Jew, Ahasuerus, is also a survival hero and like his companions in secular existence, "would often stand staring in front of me, or out of the window, with empty eyes, seeing nothing. . . ." Yet Ahasuerus is different from Barabbas, for Ahasuerus, when confronted with the miraculous ascension of Apollo ("Now he has thrown off the garments in which he hid, his earthly husk, and became again what he really was") does not deny what he has seen, but accepts his vision as valid, and allows himself to begin the progress from one world to another within his own identity.

The progress is not easy. It is not instantaneous. But Ahasuerus moves in the direction of Lagerkvist's holy land, and comes at last to the escape from mere survival and existence. His own real death is evidence, within the terms of his particular myth, that his Lazarus days are over, that he has come to that new vision, that transformation, that will allow him to step out of the Lazarus-world into another state of being. (pp. 178-80)

Barabbas fails. Ahasuerus succeeds. Lazarus remains Lazarus, or he enacts within himself the "spiritual ascension" of Christ and Apollo. Modern man is presented with the choice of emulating one or another, although Lagerkvist does not suggest that man will inevitably do so. Not everyone in Lagerkvist's novels reaches a holy land, but some do, and that is the hopeful aspect of Lagerkvist's moral essay. It leads Lagerkvist to a consideration of the nature of the holy land, the nature of "spiritual ascension within," to a consideration of the quality of our vision, and the modes of our perception that identify our transformations.

In the last two novels of the pentalogy, *Pilgrim at Sea* and *The Holy Land,* Lagerkvist accompanies two more representatives of contemporary man—Giovanni and Tobias—on their journey to the holy land, where they do achieve transfiguration prior to their physical deaths. Tobias, a man in the turmoil of postwar existence, has, like Barabbas and Ahasuerus, had his opportunity to know about transformation: he has seen in the ravaged village a dead woman with the sign of the stigmata upon her, and this is his epiphany. Death, but a miracle upon it. More like Ahasuerus than Barabbas, he responds to the epiphany and does not deny his having seen it. Moved by this "sudden glimpse" he struggles to achieve the complete escape from blindness, the true awakening, that he can anticipate. Joining with Giovanni on the pilgrim ship, he comes at last to the holy land where the final stages of his true perception are to occur.

For Lagerkvist, the holy land is the land of potential symbols. It is a haunting landscape: ruined temple, simple herdsmen, divine baby, snake-woman, three crosses, river of death, white goddess. All these artifacts are spread out before Tobias and Giovanni in what is the manifestation of that final and ultimate state of mind wherein man encounters the basic realities, freed from the blindness of secularism. Giovanni comes to the holy land literally a blind man, yet he comes, we are told, with "better knowledge"; though his eyes are now "empty and expressionless," they are at least not falsely open, pretending to see while not seeing, as do the eyes of Lazarus and Barabbas. Indeed, Giovanni, blind to the secular world, now "sees" a symbolic world, the world that we create in our minds or, in a Platonic sense, discover in the heights of our minds where our "spiritual ascension" has taken us.

Lagerkvist's holy land is the same holy land that Rilke urges upon us when, in the *Duino Elegies, IX,* he speaks of an invisible earth ascending in us; when he asks the Earth if its imperative to us is not indeed "transformation." Lagerkvist's holy land—the final place of vision, the place where we truly see—is cerebral and archetypal, a psychologic *aftonland,* that condition wherein man, in his own creative capacity, walks through a transfigured state of being. Lagerkvist's holy land is one that frequently begins, as it did for Ahasuerus, in the experience upon Mount Parnassus—that mountain of poetry and art and creativity.

Indeed, as Lagerkvist has written and published the novels of his pentalogy, it has been increasingly evident that he himself, in his art, has been moving from a literal level maintained rather consistently in **Barabbas,** to a symbolic level hinted at in **The Sibyl,** and brought closer to the surface in **The Death of Ahasuerus** and **Pilgrim at Sea.** In **The Holy Land** the ascension of the symbolic is completed.

It is from the perspective of this total symbolism of **The Holy Land** that we see the solution to the problem of Giovanni's empty locket: perhaps the crucial problem in our comprehension of Lagerkvist's message about human life.

Long ago, as a young man, Giovanni had taken from the woman he loved a locket, a locket without a picture in it but which, nevertheless, Giovanni kept all his life. It has become for him a symbol—and like all symbols it need not be something literal within itself. Its entire value as a symbol is that it has meaning, rather than content. It is an object which Giovanni himself invests with meaning. Lagerkvist would seem to suggest that all "things" are empty in essence: that even such a thing as the Eucharist, for instance, though demonstrated to be scientifically empty, may yet function in the religious life because it has meaning. Lagerkvist would seem to suggest that indeed all the artifacts of this world, all objects and persons and events are, in the holy land of the transformed mind, the potential recipients of our investment, and that it is by our investments that we achieve our new world, our new life.

It would be wrong, however, to read Lagerkvist as a traditional Transcendentalist. He is not suggesting that transformed man now has the visionary capacity to read *through* a secular world into a supernatural truth. Rather, transformed man has the visionary capacity to see new meaning in this world, to find in the secular world, with all its physical and material manifestations, what the visionary poet Walt Whitman also found in the tangible things he called "you dumb, beautiful ministers." They are ministers in that they reflect upon us whatever visionary light we cast upon them from within ourselves.

Tobias, the last of Lagerkvist's survival heroes, a man who begins as a Lazarus but who is able by inner will to come to vision, walks up and through the mountains of the holy land, at the pentalogy's conclusion, encountering the signs, artifacts, and archetypes that confront all men in the journey of life. He confronts them in their nudity, their expectancy. He finds the three crosses upon Calvary—but they are empty crosses. They are to mean whatever man would have them mean. They are not messages waiting to be read; they are tablets upon which man is to write. If a man is transformed, if he is more than Lazarus and Barabbas, he will write the message that will make his life meaningful. Tobias is able to do that, and by so doing he reconciles all the loose ends of his life, transforms all the old "blood memories" of ancient loves and ancient guilt into penance and salvation. He can end his life "full of great peace."

Lagerkvist's pentalogy thus concludes with a magnificently effective "acting out" of an ultimate state of mind that—for the Christian humanist that Lagerkvist finally is—represents the holy land of accommodation to life, an accommodation achieved by escaping our Lazarus existence and seeing life truly from the perspective of spiritual resurrection, "in this world but not of it," touching with our minds those transcendental and archetypal realities that are knowable beneath and above the secular glare, and seeing all things of this world with new eyes, with eyes truly open, making their investment in the nature of things.

Lagerkvist believes certainly in dying to this world and in being reborn. But he questions always a rebirth into the same limited mind and perspective. He finds modern man, blind and groping, quite the master of existence, but not the master of life. He calls for modern man to open his eyes into a creative vision that will transform the world in front of him.

Lagerkvist goes no farther than that. He takes his survival heroes to their real and physical death, but he does not step over into the question of immortality or eternity. He neither accepts nor rejects the metanatural possibilities. He remains ambiguous about things beyond our time and our space. Lagerkvist believes in God—but the divine is forever *deus absconditus.* What concerns Lagerkvist primarily is the achievement of a spiritual life here and now, the achievement of a spiritual life that will permit us to come to real death with peace and serenity, that will permit us to die saying that we have truly lived.

All in all, Lagerkvist offers one of the great spiritual challenges of modern literature. He challenges man to a spiritual perception of life. In so doing, he is hopeful without being sentimental. He avoids the pitfall of seeking final answers, and he speaks tellingly and profoundly to a disturbed, myopic, and anxious world. (pp. 180-84)

Winston Weathers, "Death and Transfiguration: The Lagerkvist Pentalogy," in The Shapeless God: Essays on Modern Fiction, *edited by Harry J. Mooney, Jr. and Thomas F. Staley, University of Pittsburgh Press, 1968, pp. 171-84.*

ROBERT DONALD SPECTOR

Like the large body of his poetry, drama, and novels, Lagerkvist's short fiction, published between 1912 and 1935, presents an odd combination of limited range in subject matter or areas of interest and a remarkable variety of literary techniques even within a particular form. To be sure, over the years, Lagerkvist's short fiction, like his work in other genres, has shifted its emphasis and adjusted its moods according to changing conditions in the world and in his personal life, and there has been a deepening philosophical understanding as he has developed as a writer. Nevertheless, the focus has remained essentially unchanged.

Undeniable stylistic differences separate his earlier stories from those beginning with the novella *Det eviga leendet* (*The Eternal Smile,* 1920). In *Människor* (*People,* 1912), *Två sagor om livet* (*Two Tales about Life,* 1913), and *Järn och människor* (*Iron and Man,* 1915) the esthetic ideas expressed in *Word Art and Picture Art* are most clearly in play. The darkly pessimistic mood is conveyed in a style—although by no means identical in all three works, as *Iron and Man* certainly indicates—characterized by the "raucous symbolistic experiments" resembling Edvard Munch's paintings and the works of cubist and German expressionistic artists. The more mature fiction of *Onda sagor* (*Evil Tales,* 1924), *Kämpande ande* (*Struggling Spirit,* 1930), *I den tiden* (*In That Time,* 1935), as well as such novellas as *The Eternal Smile, Gäst hos verkligheten* (*Guest of Reality,* 1925), and *Bödeln* (*The Hangman,* 1933), display Lagerkvist's control of his technique, his ability to range through a greater emotional scale by use of "subtle undertones and irony" in a style that has, at least superficially, become greatly simplified.

Nevertheless, neither this stylistic development nor the clearer emergence of "the warm humanitarianism of his message" should obscure the sense of continuity and the feeling of unity that mark Lagerkvist's short fiction as much as they do the entire body of his writing. Even in style, this sense of continuity and unity remain. (pp. 19-20)

In his prose fiction from the outset Lagerkvist opposed the sociological and psychological conventions that governed the work of contemporary realists. Throughout his writing Lagerkvist has expressed his interest in the themes of man's problems with identity and the individual's struggle to maintain or discover his essence in face of the social and metaphysical forces that impress upon him his insignificance or indeed nonexistence in their overwhelming vastness and seemingly total disregard for any particular man's physical and psychic needs. Otto Oberholzer's discussion of Lagerkvist's work, although making the author seem a kind of twentieth-century Thomas Carlyle who plays between saying "yes" and "no" to life, demonstrates the continual weighing and balancing of varied attitudes that mark his fiction early and late. It is a weighing and balancing concerned with the mysteries of existence, the investigation of the dualities of life, and the constant probing into the nature and relationship of good and evil. Like the rest of his work, the short fiction provides no ultimate and simple answers, moving instead from one point of view to another and playing out a debate that in its entirety may very well be called an unending dialogue of the soul.

The range of subject matter in Lagerkvist's short fiction, inescapably, is narrow, but the varied literary treatment—although Lagerkvist maintains a fundamentally fabulist role throughout—has made its fictional possibilities appear un-

limited. That literary treatment has kept critics searching for an appropriate nomenclature to describe some of its forms. (p. 20)

From the point of view of general form, however, and for the sake of examining Lagerkvist's ingenious technical variety, it is possible to group his short fiction into three rather distinct categories: the fable, the short story, and the novella. The first stresses a particular moral point; the second, a sudden insight or a character assessment; the third devotes itself to an explication of a way of life, a philosophical or social problem, or a question about the relationship of illusion and reality. Within these groupings, Lagerkvist's infinite variety of treatment is striking.

Even in the fable, where it would seem that the fictional possibilities are most limited, Lagerkvist proves inventive. **"Paradiset"** (**"Paradise"**), a brief narrative, does have the pronounced qualities of a parable, concluding with man's exile from Eden and God's luxuriating beneath his best-loved tree of knowledge after man's ouster. Yet the form itself combines parable and parody, in some ways foreshadowing Lagerkvist's technique in his later biblical-historical novels: appearing to retell a biblical or historical episode while altering its meaning as well as its details. For Lagerkvist, God is not omnipotent. Even as in *The Eternal Smile,* the novella, God announces his own limitations in such phrases as "as best I can"; "I hope you will like it"; and "the best I could do."

Lagerkvist's God does not prohibit man from eating the fruit of the tree; indeed, He urges it as the means for man's becoming sensible, and what enrages Him is man's inability to use his knowledge constructively. The message is hardly derived from the Bible, but instead is consistent with Lagerkvist's own philosophy that fixes upon man the responsibility for the way he lives his life.

Parables like **"Äventyret"** (**"The Adventure"**) and **"Experimentvärlden"** (**"The Experimental World"**) do not have a moral tag, but briefly outline Lagerkvist's vision of man's failures as being no more than attempts at finding the right way to exist, holding out the prospect of further opportunities despite the errors. These are not developed narratives, but rather abstract comments or aphorisms on the nature of mankind. Their tone is straightforward, but the details are vague, their characters abstractions, maintaining the qualities necessary for the effect of a vision. (pp. 21-2)

But Lagerkvist's little fables are also capable of richly ironic tone. In **"Kärleken och döden"** (**"Love and Death"**), a single paragraph, Lagerkvist introduces a Cupid who is "a large man, heavy and muscular, with hair all over his body," and the arrow that strikes the lover does not unite him with his sweetheart, but leaves him lying pathetically behind her, his life's blood oozing, as she walks on. In the same way, in **"Den onda ängeln"** (**"The Evil Angel"**), an angel, fettered for centuries in a village church, escapes and warns the town's inhabitants that they are to die, but the warning is to no avail, no more than an anticlimax, since it is something they have always known.

Only occasionally does Lagerkvist pursue the traditional form of the fable, using the formulaic "Once upon a time" and pointing his moral. (p. 23)

[In **"Myten om människorna"** (**"The Myth of Mankind"**)], Lagerkvist uses the formulaic "Once upon a time," . . . to recreate the story of Genesis in his own terms. His unnamed characters visit a strange world, intending to remain briefly. The strange world attracts them because it makes something special of their love for each other. They have children and remain in the world; the children, not aware of any other home, are disturbed when they are finally told about it, and the death of a young child serves only to underscore the difference between the two worlds. When the parents grow old and die, the older sons go forth, feeling free of the ties to their parents' other world. Although here Lagerkvist never makes his moral explicit, it seems quite clear that he is rewriting orthodox religious expression in his own idiom and from his own point of view. (pp. 23-4)

In **"The Myth of Mankind,"** as in all his work, Lagerkvist clearly seeks a form that will best express what, despite differences in changing circumstances, remains his basic attitude toward man and his experiences. Yet the possibilities for him even within a particular form may be observed in Lagerkvist's use of the fable for purposes that are less concerned with man's metaphysical problems and more intent upon dealing with social matters. Lagerkvist writes fables that have nothing to do with this vague fairy-tale world about men in some bizarre locale or princes and princesses or biblical settings. These are tales firmly rooted in contemporary events, concerned with modern materialistic greed, ludicrous patriotism, and inane warfare. (p. 24)

Written during World War I, **"The Fragments"** is a grim fairy tale not only of the war's horrors, but of the effect upon the decency of mankind. No dialogue, no truly developed dramatic incidents, but the quiet, almost unnatural, voice of a narrator characterizes Lagerkvist's method of presenting the ugly detail. For Lagerkvist, life, even without the war, is no idyl, but rather the quiet, hard-work, and routine existence that ordinary survival demands. Arnold and his sons labor in factories without complaining, finding their happiness in tending their small vegetable gardens or enjoying their families.

Even their modest demands on life, however, are altogether denied with the outbreak of war. Arnold's five sons go off to battle, and the pregnant wives of his two eldest come to live with him. First his twins, having gone into the navy, are killed at sea. Then his youngest, hardly mature, falls in the fighting. Finally, the report of the deaths of his remaining sons leaves Arnold a shattered man. Actually, that is not quite the end; the son's wives, broken by their experiences, die.

Lagerkvist relates this tale in measured tones. He describes calmly Arnold's responses to the deaths of his children—responses of increasingly desperate efforts to produce munitions more deadly than those already in use, munitions that will avenge his sons' deaths by tearing asunder his enemies. When the mines, filled with fragments by Arnold and his co-workers, destroy an enemy submarine, and the bodies of its sailors, not yet dead, are washed ashore, Arnold pulls the fragments from the wounds of the dead and dying. With quiet reportorial understatement, Lagerkvist emphasizes the brutalizing effects of war as he describes Arnold's treasuring the shell fragments and hoping to use them again. Lagerkvist's journalistic prose conveys the full horror of Arnold's bearing the bloody mess home to the young children.

Lagerkvist uses nature itself to comment ironically on what man makes of man. He surrounds Arnold with nature's fresh beauty: a benign morning sun and sweetly scented flowers.

Arnold places the fragments with torn flesh before the children and explains his triumph. As they return to their beds, they have lost their innocence—the odor of man's inhumanity clings to the sensitive membranes of their nostrils. (pp. 24-5)

"Det lilla fälttåget" ("The Children's Campaign") and **"Det märkvärdiga landet" ("The Strange Country")** exemplify Lagerkvist's most sustained use of the fable in his short fiction. In **"The Children's Campaign,"** his Swiftian irony about a children's army that gains national prominence as it successfully wages the country's war requires no moral tag. Instead, Lagerkvist achieves his moral through the device of irony and through the rhythmic repetition of phrases. Scaling down the sizes and ages of his warriors, Lagerkvist has no need to make a direct statement about their symbolic representation of real soldiers involved in real warfare. When he remarks on how children are naturally suited to the pursuit of war, it becomes a comment on the nature of war itself. His report on the battle casualties on both sides, setting the figure precisely at "12,924" for each, ridicules the statistical game that converts human lives into abstract figures. Lagerkvist derides the rhetoric of war by calling his infants "men" and turning the cliché "armed to the teeth" into "armed to the very milk teeth."

Beyond the fantasy of Lagerkvist's story stands the actuality of the youth movements in Mussolini's Italy and Hitler's Germany. The allusion itself acts as a moral comment. The love of spectacle in the parades of those totalitarian nations becomes the object of ridicule in Lagerkvist's repeated use of "unforgettable" to describe the horrifying spectacle of children in arms, children at war, children mutilated and returning to march before an enthusiastically applauding nation.

Like **"The Children's Campaign,"** with which it appeared in the same volume, **"The Strange Country"** takes a great part of its effect from contemporary events. The totalitarian world that was threatening in the 1930's becomes in Lagerkvist's terrifying fable the entire world, or at least so dominant that the enclaves of freedom exist only as the oddity of a tourist attraction. In his fabulist voice, Lagerkvist presents his narrative using the inhabitants of the world of the new order as his narrative point of view. (pp. 27-8)

Lagerkvist's irony in **"The Strange Country,"** as in **"The Children's Campaign,"** is scathingly Swiftian. However, even more significant is his attitude toward evil as it emerges from these stories. Lagerkvist never seems appalled by sin, for that he regards as a necessary part of the human condition. Like William Blake, however, he cannot abide what for him is the true evil, that which denies man's humanity, that which stifles the human spirit. In the totalitarian threat to Europe and indeed the world, Lagerkvist found the real evil, and in his fiction he was one of the first major writers to oppose it.

Lagerkvist's fables are clearly the work of a moralist, whether they are cast in the forms of visions, parodies, or satires, but just as his moral code is no mere copy of orthodoxy, neither is literary technique bound to the conventional. What is true of the fables is equally true of his short stories, which retain his fabulist's mannerisms, eschewing modern naturalism and psychologizing, while refusing to fall into traditional patterns. (p. 29)

In **"Hissen som gick ner i helvete" ("The Lift That Went Down into Hell"),** Lagerkvist . . . displays the complexity of his technique. The story combines harsh reality with fantasy in sending adulterous lovers down into Hell, confronting them in their sordid surroundings with the bizarre figure of the woman's husband, who has just committed suicide. Another modern writer might have concluded his narrative at that point, depending on the epiphany for his shocking effect. Lagerkvist, however, proceeds to a deliberate anticlimax, allowing the illicit lovers to return to their customary behavior as they ascend to their own world. It is the fabulist's rather than the modern short-story writer's technique, but again Lagerkvist creates his own form, for, instead of adding the moral tag himself, he allows the action to become the comment on their conduct. Indeed, throughout the work, he has combined the simple narrative development of the fable with a subtle set of ironic contrasts in detail and a continual word-play on their visit to Hell, both devices natural to the short-story form. (p. 30)

"The Basement," too, depends for its effect on the contrasts that provide the structure of the story. While the narrator appears to be recounting the story of Lindgren, a beggar with withered legs, whom he accompanies home, the major concern is with the character of the narrator himself. The deformed beggar has adjusted to life; the seemingly healthy narrator suffers from spiritual malaise. Walking behind Lindgren, the narrator mentally notes his movements, and while apparently praising the cripple, uses language that patronizes and makes metaphorical comparisons in animal imagery. And yet, Lindgren is more a man than the narrator.

Lagerkvist employs an epiphany to drive home the point of his story. Leaving Lindgren's apartment, the narrator observes that only the cripple's light burns, and rather despairingly he remarks, "it lighted me nearly all the way home," indicating still the despair within himself. Coming as it does after a series of descriptions in which the cripple's determination to give balance and meaning to his life hints continually of the narrator's own inadequacies, the epiphany underscores Lagerkvist's intention. The epiphany here . . . serves instead of a moral tag, but Lagerkvist remains the fabulist even though the form masks the allegorical character of his preaching.

Add to these varied stories and fables, the complexity of Lagerkvist's forms in the novella, which are equally the work of a fabulist and moralist, and the technical virtuosity that he achieves in treating similar materials is truly remarkable. For Lagerkvist, in fact, the genre of the novella seems a particularly appropriate form. He is not generally concerned with providing the kind of sudden illumination characteristic of the short story. What happens along the way in his fiction is as important to him as his conclusion; and, indeed, the endings of his narratives, often as not, do not provide resolutions so much as they do harmonizings of the ambiguities that make up the substance of his content. His major themes in his longer fiction do not vary greatly from those in his short stories and fables; they are, to repeat, a concern for the mysteries of existence, an investigation of the dualities of life, and a constant probing into the nature of good and evil. These require a careful and detailed examination: exposition, analysis, and illustration. The process is far more natural to the novella than it is to the short story, and even Lagerkvist's familiar fabulist technique—his authorial voice offering moral comment—seems more suited to the longer fictional form.

Most readers might be inclined to describe even what are called his novels—the fiction from *Dvärgen* to *Mariamne*—as novellas, and at least superficially they are. Yet on closer examination, those works, compared to the four examined here, prove more complex in their structures and effects than at first appears—complex in their depth of characterization, in their philosophical ramifications, and in their use of rhythm to provide unity and develop extended meaning. Not that any of the four novellas studied here is simple or lacking in development; it is rather a matter of comparative complexity.

These novellas are not only complex themselves, but show—as even his short stories do—Lagerkvist's surprising variety in treating a relatively limited range of subject matter. Whatever form he uses, Lagerkvist manages to maintain the unity of his own fictional world, with its own value system and its particular preoccupations, and yet he offers a variety of literary treatment that makes each work distinct from the others. Here, within four novellas so obviously a part of that fictional world and so clearly concerned with the moralizing characteristic of the fabulist, he offers four very different uses of the form: the autobiographical probing of *Gäst hos verkligheten* (*Guest of Reality*); the philosophical quest of *Det eviga leendet* (*The Eternal Smile*); the idyllic romance of *Själarnas maskerad* (*Masquerade of Souls*); and the social commentary of *Bödeln* (*The Hangman*).

Critical interest in *Guest of Reality* runs high, for the autobiographical suggestiveness of the novella offers something unusual in Lagerkvist's work. Although Granlid's warning about using the novella as any reliable source for Lagerkvist's life is well taken, it is clear that the author has turned fact to useful fictional advantage, and critics have made the most of their opportunities. (pp. 32-4)

Yet ultimately the value of *Guest of Reality,* like that of all important literature, is greater than its autobiographical revelation. What truly matters is what Lagerkvist has done with the facts of his life, how he has rendered them in fictional form. (p. 34)

Guest of Reality is a novella, and Lagerkvist needs the form to cover a sufficient time span, to include a variety of experiences, and to take some philosophical by-paths in covering his material. It would be possible, for example, to think of the first major portion of the novella as the material for a short story. The fear and confusion of the hero—a little boy awaking to the terrors of death—culminate quite naturally in the scene in which he lies alongside his grandparents, uncertain whether they are sleeping or dead. Lagerkvist clearly regards it as a unit, for the next scene skips to the boy's twelfth year. Yet, if it were a short story, what would have to be done with the earlier material? Instead of the very first scene, devoted to expository details of the boy's home, parents, and their values, the fourth scene—Anders's visit to his grandparents' farm—could have provided the starting point. All that emerges from the scene itself, however, is the sense of the boy's "confusion," only one element in the culminating epiphany.

The epiphanies in *Guest of Reality* do not exist for themselves, but contribute rhythmically to the overall conclusion in the final line. The scene in his grandparents' bed anticipates the actual death of his grandmother in the seventh scene. In between, Lagerkvist describes the boy's own terror of death, his taking to relieving his anguish at a "prayer stone" during a rainfall. That material, in turn, provides a counterpart to Anders's looking through the window and watching his grandfather pray after the death of his wife. And so it goes, each epiphany tying in with the others to inform the whole.

Guest of Reality requires the slow development through time of Anders's character: from childhood to earlier manhood. But Lagerkvist's concern is with the emotional and spiritual changes, which particularly require fictional time to develop. To cover that time, Lagerkvist uses summary expressions to convey a mode of life, rather than the details of every event. He makes explicit the values of home and society that Anders rejects at the conclusion. To convey the duality of Anders's experience, Lagerkvist needs considerable expository material. All of these are characteristic of a novella—a form that borrows some of the qualities of a novel, some of the short story, and combines them for its own purposes.

Contrasts between the values of two generations, between faith and skepticism, between the security of childhood and the freedom of maturation, these are Lagerkvist's main concerns. At the heart of these is the relationship of illusion and reality. Although it is particularly apparent in the boy's inability to distinguish between his grandparents' sleeping and their being dead, it is more fundamental than that in the novella. It makes up the very structure: whether Lagerkvist is describing the household, that is, the physical circumstances of Anders's family (peasants who have moved to town, an apartment over the railroad restaurant, never quite the right size for their needs); or he is contrasting the outward calm and inner turmoil of Anders's life; or he is comparing the sense of security in the one-armed Jonas with the insecurity of the physically sound Anders. None of these stands apart from the rest, and the combination requires the development of a novella, a form which also permits Lagerkvist to offer moral comment in his characteristically fabulist manner.

Lagerkvist's *The Eternal Smile* is a remarkably different kind of novella. A kind of frame story, it uses a bizarre narrative quest of souls in limbo—seeking the answer to the mystery of existence in a journey to God—to present a variety of examples of the human condition. Despite critics' suggestions that the work concludes with a philosophy that willingly accepts life as it is, Lagerkvist's technique of presenting a multiplicity of enigmatic revelations allows for no such easy solution. His artistic principles in the novella develop his earlier ideas in *Word Art and Picture Art* and show the continuing influence of cubist painting on his literary experimentation, an influence that extends to even his latest novels. While the simplicity of his prose style follows the primitivistic works he had admired in his essay, his deliberately ambiguous meaning results from a literary cubism that offers a variety of perspectives to the reader without ever fixing upon a single point of view. (pp. 35-7)

As each of the souls in Lagerkvist's limbo recalls his experience, it reveals a particular insight. Some suggest how they have allowed their individual deformities to become so all-consuming that it is their total meaning of life. Yet these small epiphanies merge into a larger as one character remarks: "It is a fact that a hunchback is born into the world every minute. It seems, therefore, that there exists in the race a definite need to be in part hunchbacked." That revelation, too, becomes part of the concluding epiphany of life's being "the one thing conceivable among all that is inconceivable." Life, in all its elements and divergencies, makes up the nature of human existence. The anguish of deformity is no more than another part of the human condition. (p. 38)

Like *Guest of Reality,* then, *The Eternal Smile* seeks its effect through all of its parts and not through its ending. His story's structure is gradual: building up the separate speakers and their individual voices and revelations in choral fashion, each voice insisting on its apartness, its own note. To what might be called the thesis of their individual concerns, however, he ultimately juxtaposes the scene in which the multitude loses all sense of its individuality and merges into one to become the human condition itself. . . . This is Lagerkvist's antithesis to all that has gone before. In itself it is no resolution, but together the parts are like the two voices in Hebrew antiphonal poetry in which the meaning comes out of the harmony of the whole.

Although the form of *The Eternal Smile* has been labeled in many different ways, it is surely a novella, one which demonstrates by comparison with his other works in the genre, the great variety in his technical achievement. Here he has used it for the philosophical probing of the mysteries of existence. The form seems ideally suited to his needs as a moralist, and it allows him to maintain a narrative voice of a fabulist, a voice that persists throughout much of his work.

Through long stretches of summary, punctuated by informing scenes, the novella form in *Masquerade of Souls* allows Lagerkvist to cover a way of life over months and even years. He needs the genre to enable him to move at an easy pace, to create an idyllic mood, against which the force of reality can provide a crushing contrast. His contrasts between illusion and reality, the latter coming in brief denuding comments, cannot be wrought swiftly for Lagerkvist would then seem to be describing a momentary oddity rather than his theme: the difference between the illusory desires of humanity and the actuality of human experience.

Individual episodes in Lagerkvist's story build to present this theme. No part of his narrative about a couple whose souls bring them together and cause them to seek a life apart from society, a happiness in their merging existence, is intended to stand on its own. The opening and closing episodes, in themselves the material of short stories, illustrate Lagerkvist's process. In the first scene, the hero and heroine meet, talk, and find the union of their souls amid the usual occurrences of a fashionable dinner party. It concludes with their going together toward the door, "she in front and he a few steps behind her." He pauses for a moment, his attention "drawn to something," and then he observes: "She was lame." It could be the epiphany of a short story, although not a particularly striking one. In fact, its very conventionality serves Lagerkvist's purpose: pricking the illusions of romanticism. More importantly, it sets the stage for Lagerkvist's mode of handling his material throughout the novella. (pp. 39-40)

Like the first scene, the last is functional, not an end in itself. Lagerkvist, unconcerned with providing a witty comment on life or seeking a small sensationalistic shock, focuses on the relationship between illusion and reality. Everything in the novella reinforces the duality. His hero's desire for complete absorption in his love conflicts with the need to carry on the ordinary business activities of the world. When the couple seem most at ease with each other, the outside world does not, after all, dissolve. It enters their consciousness with the woman's desire to have a child. The incompleteness of that world of illusion is expressed by her physical need. When her anguish at not being able to conceive is finally resolved in her pregnancy, Lagerkvist punctuates the idyllic with reminders of her physical condition, a warning of threatening reality.

Her physical deformity, overlooked when the husband has been absorbed in her soul, cannot be dismissed after the child has died and reality has so entered their lives that her handicap becomes spiritual decadence. With disintegration of her spiritual strength, Lagerkvist says, she becomes "more of a woman who was lame." (pp. 40-1)

The choice of the novella form for *Masquerade of Souls* provides another example of Lagerkvist's concern for the expressive ideal in his work. To be sure, it would be possible to condense the novella so that several opening episodes would become one, or the scenes about the stillborn birth would not afford the same detail, or the concluding portions on the coarseness of Parisian life could be narrowed in its summary; but effectiveness in probing character, exploring theme, and creating tone would suffer. Even Lagerkvist's use of a fabulist's frame serves in its philosophical comment to underscore his theme. It seems a proper part of the mood of the novella when he twice declares that the soul has its own land, "And in that land there is always festival. There it is always masquerade."

The novella form in *The Hangman* is unlike any that Lagerkvist uses in his other stories. To be sure, the fabulist narrator is present, but his function is extremely restricted, providing atmosphere and symbolic detail for what is essentially a two-part drama. He sets the medieval scene in part one, placing the hangman apart from society even when functioning as part of it. Within the tavern, the hangman sits at a "dimly-lit table," separate from the others, marked off by his "blood-red uniform," and inspiring terror in the girl who waits upon him. Throughout the medieval scene, the silent hangman remains a presence by the authorial comments on the manner in which he evokes the anecdotes of the others.

Again in the second scene, the narrator provides the setting through what amounts to stage directions in the details of a night-club in Nazi Germany—the "people in the night-club, milling around in the half-light among the sounds of voices, laughter, and the clinking of glasses; in the middle of the room couples . . . dancing slowly to soft music under the dim greenish and violet light cast by the slowly revolving globe in the ceiling." Once more, the hangman—at least until the final moments—remains silent, but his presence emerges from the consciousness of others and the relevance of their horrible actions to his being there.

Lagerkvist's technique, limiting the fabulist's voice and choosing a dramatic device to cover a time span of centuries, results from his awareness that the story is formidably didactic and from his desire to turn particular social commentary into larger observations of the role of evil in mankind's experience. On one hand, *The Hangman* stands as the most didactic of his novellas, as the first attack by a major Swedish author against Nazi totalitarianism—a forerunner of Eyvind Johnson's *Night Training* (1938), *The Soldier's Return* (1940), the "so-called Krilon novels" (1941-43), and Vilhelm Moberg's *Ride This Night!* Yet the first scene and the hangman's concluding speech indicate the meaning beyond contemporary comment.

No more than the major action of the second scene—*sans* the hangman himself—would have provided the attack on Nazi evil. The specific attack stands clear in its brutal action. The true believers of Hitler's Germany are intent upon making the world acquiesce or on wiping out the doubters. (pp. 41-2)

But Lagerkvist's purpose, as his first scene indicates, goes beyond this. As the hangman sits in a medieval tavern, surrounded by, though apart from, the ordinary customers, his presence evokes speculation about a forthcoming execution and various superstitions connected with the executioner. Individual anecdotes suggest the hangman's important role in society and show the close relationship of good and evil in man's experience. One particularly stresses the tie between good and evil as the speaker describes a childhood experience in which, by touching the executioner's sword, he had been forewarned of his evil destiny and could only be saved by the executioner's ritualistic purging of his fate. Another argues the persistency of evil through a story of a hangman whose love for his victim temporarily gains her pardon, but who eventually must bury her alive for having strangled her child born with the gallows' mark that had been burnt into the mother's forehead. And finally, Gallow's Lasse, who boasts of having bound himself to evil by digging up the mandrake root under the gallows, serves to argue the unending role of evil in society, an episode which ties together the two parts of the novella.

Lagerkvist's larger theme is made explicit in the hangman's final speech. A spectator to centuries of man's evil and a character in Lagerkvist's story, he can speak dramatically in protest and explanation without seeming didactic. He recounts the scapegoat role he has played in mankind's history, serving to carry the burden of evil, removing the guilt from mankind and allowing that evil to lead to man's more positive achievements. Mankind's guilt becomes his burden, and while he suffers its "lust for blood," man is permitted to enjoy, as he cannot, "the beautiful meadows with their flowers and trees in the magnificent, peaceful stillness of the evening. . . ." Life itself, as he notes, "can be so beautiful."

For the executioner, bound to man's evil, Christ's crucifixion and death are his own experience; Christ is no son of God, but "just an ordinary man," no savior, but a victim. The executioner is that part of mankind not to be released from the evils of this world, a part of man's experience that will continue for as long as man exists.

And yet, Lagerkvist does not see this evil as the whole of man's experience. If for the executioner, there is Good Friday, for mankind there is also Easter Sunday. Even here, as in all Lagerkvist's work, the obverse side of man's evil is love, a saving grace in the human experience. Describing the woe of the executioner, Lagerkvist presents the woman who awaits his return, who is there for him to rest his head in her lap, to kiss his "burning forehead and wash the flood from [him]."

The Hangman, like all Lagerkvist's work whatever its immediate purpose, does not offer a one-sided argument. Damning the evils of totalitarianism, it does not despair of humankind. Its dramatic structure successfully links the evils in the long history of man, but its ultimate didacticism insists that evil is not the only role in that history. (pp. 43-4)

Robert Donald Spector, in his Pär Lagerkvist, *Twayne Publishers, Inc., 1973, 196 p.*

Norman Levine

1924-

Canadian short story writer, novelist, autobiographer, poet, and scriptwriter.

Levine is known for highly autobiographical fiction that draws upon his experiences as a Jewish youth growing up in Canada and as an expatriate writer living in St. Ives, a rural community on the Cornish coast of England. While often focusing upon themes related to alienation and materialism, as well as loss, loneliness, and disillusionment, Levine's writings express longing and affection for his native country yet convey a cynical opinion of Canadian society. Frequently described as a minimalist, Levine employs a sparse, laconic style and an emotionally detached authorial viewpoint. Maurice Capitanchik concluded: "Mr. Levine's quiet, unpretentious talent is more subtle, more truly serious, and more honest, than much writing which makes greater claims; he deserves his growing reputation."

Levine's first novel, *The Angled Road* (1952), which recounts an unnamed protagonist's desire to escape his oppressive surroundings, is based upon Levine's upbringing in a lower-class Jewish neighborhood in Ottawa, Ontario. While serving with the Royal Canadian Air Force in England during World War II, the central character of this book decides to leave Canada permanently. *Canada Made Me* (1958) documents Levine's experiences during a journey across Canada that he undertook after living in England for several years. Contrasting the sordid, deprived lives of the people he encounters with their illusory expectations of happiness and prosperity, Levine offers a bitter indictment of what he perceives as the amoral materialism of Canadian society. *From a Seaside Town* (1970), another installment in Levine's fictionalized autobiography, centers upon Joseph Grand, an impoverished young Canadian writer who lives in Cornwall with his English wife and children. In a detached, self-deprecating narrative, Grand reflects on the boredom and frustration that he feels in his present situation and comments on the lives of friends whose similar dissatisfaction is not abated by their materialistic success.

The autobiographical themes of Levine's novels are also evident in his short fiction, which is collected in such volumes as *One Way Ticket* (1961), *I Don't Want To Know Anyone Too Well and Other Stories* (1971), *Selected Stories* (1975), *Thin Ice* (1979), *Why Do You Live So Far Away?* (1984), and *Champagne Barn* (1984). A number of pieces, including "Boiled Chicken" and "Ringa Ringa Rosie," describe the hardships Levine endured as a struggling writer during the 1960s, while others examine the creative process and the lives of fellow writers. For example, "Thin Ice" relates the story of a successful author who is treated like a vagrant while stranded without money or identification in a small Canadian town, and the novella *The Playground* depicts eccentric, self-destructive residents of an artists' colony in St. Ives. The theme of memory also plays an important role in Levine's stories; his narratives often involve recollections of past occurrences or a journey to the scene of an earlier experience. "In Quebec City," for instance, compares Levine's impressions of a Jewish family that he met before World War II with

the knowledge he gains about them on a visit several years later. "In Lower Town" contrasts his memories of the neighborhood where he lived as a child with the changes he observes upon his return as an adult.

In addition to his stories, novels, and nonfiction works, Levine has written several volumes of poetry, including *Myssium* (1948), *The Tightrope Walker* (1950), and *I Walk by the Harbour* (1976). He has also contributed screenplays to both Canadian and British television.

(See also *Contemporary Authors,* Vols. 73-76 and *Contemporary Authors New Revision Series,* Vol. 14.)

ALICE EEDY

[*The Angled Road*] is the story of a boy who grows up hating the cramping environment of his small-town home setting, made more unpleasant by his parents' conflicts in their struggle for social betterment. His loneliness, which becomes more articulate as he carries it into the world and his relations with other people, determines the angle of vision which sharpens around scenes, narrowly lighting up corners of his experience in a sort of match light, opening vistas of streets printed with a live precision of detail. Drab outlines of the Dorset Street world are glimpsed, with its boredom of verandah rockers, sad-colored houses, decaying cartons of garbage. . . .

Faced by the return to Canada, the boy's conflict is movingly sharpened in an imaginary dialogue which takes place during a last flight out to sea, when he confronts with courage, the need not to be submerged, the needs of his parents, and what they have done for him.

Unfortunately the struggle for a solution in himself is not pursued with the same honesty following his return. There is the same dimness, a myopic intensity of seeing for details "in small." But in the final scenes this seems an oblique exploring of sensations for its own sake, when what is wanted is the effect of a photographer's exploding flash bulb. The effect of the last scenes is one of flat autobiographical echoes with cloudy talk of "pushing away the old self," and returning to the sun and soil. More power, more light is needed, one feels, to release him from the confines of his own narrowness, Dorset Street from its shadow. The reader is left with a feeling of loss. It is a disappointing experience to turn the last pages in this book by a writer of such fine perception, committing himself to an important, yes, Canadian subject.

Alice Eedy, in a review of "The Angled Road," in The Canadian Forum, *Vol. XXXIII, No. 393, October, 1953, p. 163.*

HECTOR G. KINLOCH

[*Canada Made Me*] is not a travel book and certainly not a traveller's guide; yet Norman Levine describes a trans-Canadian journey. It is not an analysis of Canadian mores; although in every chapter Canadian stones are overturned to see what pathetic, self-centered, ugly little creatures are crawling underneath. There is historical reminiscence, reportage, autobiography, social comment, literary portraiture, down and out philosophy and, throughout, images of the furtive sexual delights of repressed adolescence. Perhaps a psychologist would be best fitted to decide the correct shelf on which to place this repulsively fascinating soul-baring of a professional odd man out fleeing through the mammon-choked sewers of Canada from his *bourgeois* tormentors.

Whatever the shelf, the historian of the Canadian cultural scene cannot ignore *Canada Made Me.* It is a social and literary document. For all its schoolboyish concentration upon cultural genitalia, it is a revealing, although distorted action-shot of a shapeless nation whose constantly changing pattern is to be seen in the cycle of immigrant arrival and tourist departure: the immigrant, unlovely and boorish, in search of a prosperous future; the tourist crazily chasing an unrecoverable, plumbingless past.

Nostalgically and vindictively, with love and with hate, Norman Levine scents out decadence, futility, hypocrisy, social pretentiousness, and human foibles wherever he can find them—on board ship, in fifth-rate hotels, in fashionable synagogues, in slaughter-houses, in strip-tease joints and brothels, and even in the private homes of his Canadian hosts. Bewailing a Canadian quality of "sameness," he contrasts the dullness and boredom of a small town nation with his rich, fertile,

earthy, rural paradise in the English countryside where the inscriptions on public lavatories are more literate.

This self-portrait of a Canadian writer, who has half-turned his back even on those parts of Canada which appear to be dearest to him, is also significant as a mirror of certain aspects of the Canadian literary scene. This book was published in London, not in Toronto. Canada for such an author as Levine seems to contain nothing but fatted calves, and certainly no literary heroes. This emotional expatriation is seen even in his style which is a blending of Isherwood, Henry Miller, and Nathanael West. His not very probing vignettes of Montreal Babbitry are imitative and reflective of the reigning literary lights of the twenties and thirties; whereas they could and should have been contemporary critiques of the culture of 1958. (pp. 75-6)

Hector G. Kinloch, in a review of "Canada Made Me," in The Canadian Historical Review, *Vol. XLI, No. 1, March, 1960, pp. 75-6.*

DESMOND PACEY

Norman Levine is a young writer who appears to be finally coming into his own. His first two books, *The Tightrope Walker* and *The Angled Road,* were of the type we usually call "promising": they revealed sensitivity, a gift of observation, and some sense of style, but they were tentative, exploratory, deficient in power and authority. His third book, *Canada Made Me,* was more penetrating, but had about it a sour grapes flavor: much as I enjoyed the book for its unusual acerbity in the treatment of the Canadian scene, it struck me as the work of a disappointed man who felt that he had not realized his own potential and was eager to blame his native country for his failure. Happily, its relative success (most of the reviewers attacked it, but most readers quietly enjoyed it) seems to have given Levine the self-confidence he needed. The short stories in this book [*One Way Ticket*] are excellent—detailed and evocative in setting, clear and yet subtle in characterization, crisp and clear in style. . . .

Desmond Pacey, in a review of "One Way Ticket," in The Canadian Forum, *Vol. 41, March, 1962, p. 285.*

DONALD STEPHENS

Levine's stories are not associated to a larger scheme as are those of many short story writers (Katherine Mansfield's New Zealand stories are an example of this). Rather, when his stories are finished, he has said all that he feels is necessary. Finely wrought, carefully explained, Levine's stories are complete; the reader does not wonder what happened before the action began, or what will occur in the future. There is never a vagueness about the stories; never is the reader left in obvious doubt. This certainty, or lucidity, in his work, is his most compelling quality, the factor which makes Levine a distinguished writer among the many new Canadian writers. He is a sincere and simple teller of tales; in an age which boasts of being astute and knowing in experience, Levine's unsophisticated stories appeal, if only because they are always readily understood and unequivocal.

Levine does not experiment with the story form, as a novelist frequently does. Nor does he develop and strengthen the theme as the story progresses; it is completely thought out before he begins. In *One Way Ticket* there are eight short stories and one long one, each dealing with a number of journeys. The long story is the poorest, where the focus is more on character and the episodes are selected to display the character's personality. In the others, however, the character is selected to point out a significant episode. It is hoped that Levine will stay with the story form, for this collection indicates that if he were to write a novel the quality of sustainment would be lacking, as it is in this book in *The Playground.*

The title of the book is misleading. The publisher tells us, on the jacket blurb, that these are stories where the narrator holds a return ticket; it is the other people who have to remain where they are, who have only 'one way tickets' that the book is about. But even the narrator at times has a 'one way ticket'. He seems to want to leave what he finds, but he never does; he finds similar things each time.

There is, however, a diversified picture of life in Levine's stories; he moves from one extreme to another in attitude and is careful not to merge these into an ineffectual medium. On one level his stories are complete with strong realism, ordinary simplicity of common men, and graphic actual description. On the other level there are the fantasy and psychological studies, as in *"Ringa Ringa Rosie"*, interspersed with lyrical passages and subtleties which are interesting in themselves.

Levine is a sincere author who writes stories showing a unique ability to tell a complete tale. Showing does not necessarily mean displaying. Levine's stories, indeed, make little obvious display at all. That, perhaps is why many people would prefer the stories of a Lawrence or a Huxley. Levine's work is free from affectation. His full appeal is not immediate. The reward with the stories of Norman Levine lies not merely in the number of separate examples of fine stories in this volume, but in the way that they go so well together to produce a wonderfully rich and varied picture of ordinary people. (pp. 70-1)

> *Donald Stephens, "Ordinary People," in* Canadian Literature, *No. 12, Spring, 1962, pp. 70-1.*

THE TIMES LITERARY SUPPLEMENT

One of the most pleasing things about the self-investigatory tone of *From a Seaside Town* is the air of wry apology with which it is assumed. Joseph Grand, used to making a more than reasonable living from travel-writing, finds himself cut off from both loot and the world at large when one of his most lucrative markets founders. Trapped in Carnbray by the terrible inertia that poverty so often brings, he is obliged to look closer to home for his material; he turns to autobiography with enough healthy misgivings to provide the narrative with a sardonic unease, which manifests itself in the fussy, over-informative footnotes and the sometimes curt, counteractive style which, together, lend the impression of someone treading carefully on unfamiliar ground. At the same time because he is fully aware of the risks he takes with this unaccustomed approach, Grand is careful to temper his autobiographical delvings with some unflattering views of himself. . . . His insights into an imperfect marriage and ambivalent relationships with parents and with friends who are making it are those of the professional observer who has caught himself in the act of observing. It is this air of faintly shocked, mildly

amused recognition which makes Grand the disarmingly honest, thus likeable, character that he is.

> *"Turned in," in* The Times Literary Supplement, *No. 3574, August 28, 1970, p. 941.*

PHYLLIS GROSSKURTH

Now that we no longer live in a world of definable certainties I suppose we might as well call Norman Levine's *From a Seaside Town* a novel. Its narrator is named Joseph Grand, but the facts of his life bear so close a resemblance to the biographical blurb about Levine on the dust-jacket that the author seems to be having a little private joke about his fiction. (p. 36)

From a Seaside Town is about a writer's block. But the writer's block is a symptom of a deeper malady—middle age, with all its frightening realizations that there isn't going to be much more. In making the decision to move to England, Grand believed that he was taking a step toward a more expansive life. Now, in his shabby restricted house, hounded by creditors, he sits idly before his typewriter wondering how he has trapped himself. This stock-taking involves exploring his relationship with his wife, a few eccentric or colourful friends who lead rather improbable lives, an abortive illicit passion, a brief success as a writer—and that's all. At one point, on a visit to Canada, he realizes that this is where he really belongs, ugly and dull as it is, but he also sees that if he had remained here he would have been caught in only another form of self-destruction.

It's not a cheery theme, and Grand is unable to find significant pattern or triumphant defeat in his life—or in life in general, for that matter. The tone never varies in its monotony—brief snatches of commonplace dialogue, glimpses of passing encounters with people on his walks or occasional forays into London. Nor do we ever get much of an insight into Grand himself beyond the fact that he is laconic, ineffectual, and utterly boring in his paralyzed inertia. The town had once appealed to him for its picturesqueness, but now the landscape is a sombre *grisaille,* the weather a perpetual winter.

One could praise a book like this by describing it as low-keyed, unpretentious, and perhaps an honest self-assessment. But I have the romantic notion that a good novel should be something more than a depressed description of menopause. (p. 37)

> *Phyllis Grosskurth, "Paralized Inertia," in* Saturday Night, *Vol. 85, No. 12, December, 1970, pp. 36-7.*

THE TIMES LITERARY SUPPLEMENT

Norman Levine's closely integrated, carefully weighted stories [in *I Don't Want to Know Anyone Too Well and Other Stories*] reflect the reticence of the collection's title. All but two of the fifteen have first-person narratives, but in each of them there is a studiously fostered sense of natural reserve. The intention here is not to tease, but to instil in events modestly stated a real sense of depth by using what amounts to a kind of extended meiosis, thus causing the reader to take a closer interest in occurrences which, in other hands would have served as little more than fictional kinetics; as a means to push the story along from beginning to end. In this case, the stories' essence lies precisely in what appear as small events, and the technique serves not only to underline their importance, but also to provide us, by implication, with a good deal of knowledge about the character behind the narrative.

A story called **"The English Girl"** is one of the most notable for its reserve. It tells of a short affair, and is narrated, like many of the stories, by a Canadian (who is usually studying at McGill, or has just left there) using the basically short, declarative sentences which are common currency throughout the book. Conspicuous by its absence is any description of the sexual details which are implied (not in any sense coyly), but taken for granted. The effect of this is to engage the reader more than usually; there is a feeling of fragility about the relationship intentionally incurred which relies on the tenuous note which comes as a direct result of things omitted; as a result, that is, of avoiding any close analytical run-down on the way things were between the lovers.

In the same story, and throughout the book, there is a pervasive nostalgia; not for things lost, that would be too strong a definition, but simply for things past. In many of the stories, the protagonist returns, after a briefly noted absence, to look things over, to remember what happened, not with any sense of regret, but with a fond curiosity. . . .

In a way, the very triviality of the events recorded is an essential part of the total effect. Looked back on, they represent nothing intrinsically important, but are, for all that, the source of a vague regret: time passing, acquaintances dying, the strangeness of what was once so immediate having become irretrievable. It is an emotion that crops up again and again: a minor incident, distanced by a brief description of the intervening circumstances, recalled during a return to the place or the people concerned. In one instance, the narrator, stationed in a strange town, is befriended by a Jewish family who make a habit of cultivating young officers in an attempt to find a husband for their daughter. The encounter is brief, friendly, a little strange. The war forces separation; and then, years later, there is the journey back, almost by chance, to find things changed (the daughter married, the mother dead) but not so changed as to be unrecognizable. The important fact is that it's the reader who finds himself wondering how things might have been if. . . . The narrator simply recounts the facts. It's a masterly and greatly rewarding touch, scarcely ever overplayed; and despite his reliance on the art of exclusion, Mr. Levine is never prevented from endowing the stories with a gentle humour, or an atmosphere of sympathetic concern.

"Small but Significant," in The Times Literary Supplement, *No. 3640, December 3, 1971, p. 1497.*

MAURICE CAPITANCHIK

As a writer about Cornwall, Norman Levine has been compared to Virginia Woolf and D H Lawrence; this, in itself, is remarkable, as Mr Levine is not Cornish, nor even English, but a Canadian who first came to this country as a young RCAF officer during the War, and who returned to stay. Unlike Henry James, who perhaps knew more about Americans in Europe than he knew about them in America, Mr Levine contemplates his Canada and his England with equal comprehension, the one throwing a revelatory light on the other. In his sad and comic vision, time is a betrayer, dreams lead

to disillusion, happiness can't endure; yet, outright failure is better than overt success, for in that we retain our humanity. In Cornwall, the tourist trade rubs out the old, rooted life; in Canada, where the children of poor immigrants may become millionaires, squalor is exchanged for the smart and the brash, at the price of insensitivity and dullness. Mr Levine is a master of the delicate suggestion; within his deceptively simple style, in brief incidents, he can imply complex meanings; his remarkably acute eyes and ears enable him to achieve vivid pictures of people and the world, which have been compared with those of painters, notably Monet. . . .

Feeling a need to 'make a reconciliation' with his Canadian background, Mr Levine made a journey home during the fifties; the result was the autobiographical tour-de-force, *Canada Made Me.* As with the Irish, Canadian writers tend to find their home environment narrow and provincial, and to go into exile; but, again like the Irish, they cannot quite leave it behind. Mr Levine found much to hate and to love, and much that had changed. His father, a poor immigrant, had been a fruit-pedlar; his generation, now old and worn out, and uncomprehending of their successful children, have been replaced by a new breed of immigrant, many of them Displaced Persons: 'What I admire about them' (the fruit-pedlars), says the author,

> their gaiety, their jokes, their obscenities, their gesture of going against the grain, was gone. And it left in its place a doddering uncertainty . . . a community that human injustice had thrown together was breaking up; by dying out. And those who replace them—the immigrants since 1945—come to Lower Town better equipped. They are old hands at survival . . . Murray Street is only a stopping-off place for them: one of many.

Poverty and failure had given a richness to life that the modern, more ruthless world has lost. (p. 32)

In *From a Seaside Town,* too, poverty is thwarting and money, corrupting. Joseph Grand, a Canadian travel-writer, is tied to the Cornish town of Carnbray by his need for a stable home-life with his wife and three daughters, and by lack of money. He feels isolated, but the rich friends he compulsively visits in London are even more alone than he is. Albert, an eccentric would-be writer, spends his time making notes and visiting his parents' graves, and Charles, a successful painter, is a homosexual who indulges in endless casual relationships. In a short story which is inserted into the book, in which Joseph Grand's name is changed to Gordon Rideau, Gordon meets an old college friend in Piccadilly, and is invited to a reunion. His former friends are now successful, and as the only writer among them he is lionised, until each discovers he has scrounged money from the other. Gordon Joseph, as his wife tells him, enjoys being poor; the harm that poverty does is repaired by the next cheque, but wealth trivialises all but the strongest.

This deceptively modest tale about an intelligent fidget is notable for the fact that Grand weaves his despair at his fate as a slightly successful writer into a convincing individual vision—artists (represented by Charles), he implies, are inevitably alone; the concerns of the human community are footling. Poor Joseph is somewhere between, gently agonised and acutely aware. His real trouble is that he cannot find sufficient excitement in his warm family circle, to which he is actually devoted: it is one of the simple, deadly problems of life. Although the single note of the narrator's predicament renders his story repetitious, and the tone is dangerously near self-pity, there is a rare honesty and genuine simplicity about this sad, funny, and economically written novel.

I Don't Want to Know Anyone Too Well consists of 15 cameos about the ways in which people are thwarted by life and time. Here, to return to the past is merely to discover that people have got older, or have died, or that a dream has been destroyed. A meeting results in disappointment or betrayal; journeys end in disillusion, and poor old Hugh-Mannity is always ridiculous, generous, funny, selfish and infinitely sad. . . .

Mr Levine's quiet, unpretentious talent is more subtle, more truly serious, and more honest, than much writing which makes greater claims; he deserves his growing reputation. (p.33)

Maurice Capitanchik, "Canadian in Cornwall," in Books and Bookmen, *Vol. 17, No. 12, September, 1972, pp. 32-3.*

BARRY CAMERON

All but one of the nine stories gathered together in [*Selected Stories*] are drawn from Levine's two previous collections of stories, *One Way Ticket* (1961) and *I Don't Want to Know Anyone Too Well* (1971), and from his loosely structured novel, *From a Seaside Town* (1970). Despite the apparent variety in subject matter and theme exhibited by the range of such a selection, the sense of a common voice and a continuity of style, particularly in its stark or austere qualities, unify all the stories. There are presumably several different narrators in these stories, but behind each story lies a controlling voice with a unifying tone that transcends the distinctness of any one narrator; and that unifying, shaping vision is most evident in the common characteristics of Levine's style and in its rhetorical implications that emerge in each story. Levine's tendency to rework details from one story into another, despite a changed narrative context, also contributes to this sense of continuity.

The fictional structure of all Levine's stories is autobiographical; the least satisfying stories in the collection are those that tend to drift away from an autobiographical mode—the only two stories written in a third-person point of view, **"Ringa Ringa Rosie"** and **"I'll Bring You Back Something Nice,"** in which the sense of voice is also noticeably diminished. Paradoxically, despite the detachment implied in a third-person point of view, there is less of a feeling of control in these two stories than in the other seven. They are further weakened, notwithstanding the balancing force of their wry humour, by Levine's shameless indulgence in the trite, romantic theme of the struggling artist.

Unlike most fiction in a first-person autobiographical mode, Levine's seven first-person stories do not focus on the character or personality of the narrator as such, but on what he observes. Our initial impression of the narrator, consequently, is that he is merely a detached observer, coolly recording the people and places that he has witnessed—almost a feeling that the point of view is completely disembodied. Any details that we receive about the narrator, for example, serve less as a means of characterization than as straightforward exposition necessary for the narrative purposes of the story. Levine's narrators, moreover, seldom, if ever, make explicit value-judgments about, comment on the significance of, or

display overt emotional responses to the events and people that they witness. Yet, in spite of the rhetorical stance of a dispassionate observer, intensified by the consistent use of a past tense, which implies a distance from that which is being recounted, the narrator's selection of details—what he actually chooses to record—and the pattern of their arrangement suggest the meaning and values that he has perceived and that we, in turn, are invited to infer. In this pattern lies his motive for fiction, the *raison d'être* of the story. The detachment suggested in the reportorial, frequently anecdotal, tone and in the austerity of the style is thus a skillfully sustained illusion, for the very structure of the story is designed to elicit the most powerful of responses.

The rhetorical efficacy of Levine's austere or "plain" style has frequently been misjudged not only because of a failure to recognize the rhetorical functions of its detached tone, but also, it seems to me, because of prejudices about the values of complexity and simplicity that we bring to our reading. The assumption that many readers would seem to make is that the more stylistically complex a work is, the more important it is. Levine nevertheless takes rhetorical advantage of these prejudices. His narrative and sentence structures are simple; he does render descriptive and expository details precisely and economically, neither ornately nor densely textured; and he seldom indulges in conscious symbolism. Levine's spare style is in fact a cultivated simplicity—a consciously crafted and rhetorically designed understatement. And it is completely decorous or mimetically appropriate in that (although Levine is dealing with the dispossessed, alienated condition in which man finds himself) he is not exploring the complexity of man's tragic condition, the heroic dimensions of tragic man, but rather the simple day-to-day conditions of loneliness and frustration in which ordinary man lives. His stories do indeed depict man trying to come to terms with the absurd, inadequate conditions of his daily existence, but not man struggling passionately or heroically as we might expect from those in literature who have traditionally circumscribed themselves within a tragic vision of life. Levine's characters lead lives of quiet desperation, and this sort of fundamentally tragic desperation exists, Levine seems to be saying, on the simplest level of human existence. Levine's characters do not exactly accept the terms of the human condition, but they are not fiercely defiant of them either. Their survival lies somewhere in between.

Levine's low-keyed style, the apparent detachment of his narrator implied in that style, would seem to suggest an acceptance, if not an apathy, about the tragic dimensions of life. The accumulative rhetorical effect, however, is to draw attention to the pathetic meaning of the narrated events by the consciously created disparity between style and the emotional response called for by the structure of those events, although the austerity of the style also prevents pathos from descending into unwarranted sentimentality, as does the gentle ironic humour of many of the stories. In other words, the fundamental irony of Levine's habitual stylistic mode lies in the reader's expectations of an indication of feeling, of judgment, or articulated statement of meaning from the narrator. Paradoxically, the very absence of these explicit responses, the matter-of-fact style, actually generates an emotional energy in the reader. (pp. 691-92)

Barry Cameron, in a review of "Selected Stories," in Queen's Quarterly, *Vol. 83, No. 4, Winter, 1976, pp. 690-92.*

D. G. STEPHENS

Selected Stories reveals again that in Levine the Canadian short story has a master craftsman, a writer who looks back to find the meaning in his past yet without the sentimental nostalgia usually associated with the writer who looks back. (p. 94)

With care, with grace, and with elegance, he has astringently given to short fiction a new nuance in the magic of memory. He investigates, in vignette, the past, a past that his mind has, almost of its own, recollected for him. There is no doubt that Levine knows that he cannot go home again, and he seems to wonder why. What happens is that his memory can lead him into something new and valuable. He discovers a new dimension as he searches for meaning in the past; like Phyllis Webb, he wonders who can tell the apparent from the real?

The rhythm and sound patterns of the Levine prose are noticeably intrinsic to his meaning. He can, in a few deft strokes, sketch a complete scene and its mood:

> Murray Street looked drab, empty, frozen. Solemn boxes with wooden verandahs. Brown double doors and double windows. Not a soul was outside. On King Edward the snow heaped in the centre had a frozen crust. It glittered underneath the street lights. And the houses, on either side, in shadow, appeared even more boarded up, as if you would have to go through several layers before you found something living.

The scene is compacted here; the sentences are as stark as the landscape they describe. He is at once the photographer with details that are precise, sharp, clear; yet the words have connotations, yet are not diffuse within the scalpel-like effectiveness of the figurative language. Here, too, the sounds evoke the scene, the crispness of that winter night. Levine not only forces his reader to fasten on the clear-cut primary picture that he presents, but also makes the reader's mind push onto another level of meaning. He aims for a texture in his prose, and the reader must participate in recreating the experience.

This process is done by the reader filling in the gaps. Levine has said that he can "always tell a bad writer by the words he leaves in"; with him, we know he is a good writer by the words he leaves out. In **"In Quebec City,"** the narrator has just left the bed of a girl who has sneaked him into her parents' house to make love in her bedroom, and for a moment it appears as if the girl's mother will discover them; yet again, there is the suggestion that the parents of the girl know all about it, and almost encourage the girl's liaisons, of which this is the fifth. He leaves just after five in the morning:

> It was snowing. Everything was white and quiet. It felt marvellous walking, flakes slant, very fine. I didn't feel at all tired. I heard a church bell strike and somewhere further the sound of a train whistle, the two notes like the bass part of a mouth organ. The light changed to the dull grey of early morning and the darker shapes of a church, a convent, came in and out of the falling snow.

Levine suggests so much in this. And it is so Canadian, not just because of the landscape, but he captures that understatement that is so oral about the Canadian as he does describe a scene. The Canadian does not wax and wane when he reacts to his natural world; instead, he describes and lets the subtleties gauge in on their own so that the reader's response is individual and never stereotyped. It is much more than it appears to be on first glance.

The characters that Levine introduces to his readers present a similar situation. At first they appear to be stereotyped: the narrator who is often a young Canadian airman, on his way to England after or during basic training, a young man, often Jewish, on the make. There is the father, a typical Ottawa peddlar; there are the father's friends, all trying hard to make ends meet. There is poverty, there are slums. Yet something unexpected occurs with these characters, who could very well be the stereotypes so popular in stories preceding and during the war, characters emotionally stunted by the force of poverty and the desire for making it at the expense of someone else. Yet, they do not turn out that way. These people may be faced with all the temptations and acquisitiveness of a materialistic society, and for a while it appears that their capacity for happiness and love, for becoming mature and enlightened in their feelings toward others, is warped and poisoned in the bud. But they do not turn out that way; life is not joyless, hardship is not hopeless, premature old age is not a natural outcome. These people for the most part are able to reach out to the true natural world that contains their own identity. When one reads all of Levine's stories, it sometimes appears as if he were writing them from a political point of view, that the characters portray general types of social victims. Like Zola, Levine does use the technique of "realism" to dramatize a social condition. He does focus on representative faces in the crowd to bring the whole social condition into clearer perspective, but the types that Levine creates live, in the imagination, as individuals.

Nowhere does Levine strangle the characters because of some kind of social consciousness he wants to put across. Never are the characters forced and manipulated; never do I feel that the narrator's insights, or those of some of his characters, are obviously those of Levine. These are characters who are at once blameless and to be blamed, victims of society but of their own making, yet they are never lifeless automatons. We are not so much moved by what happens to them as we are exhilarated by their reaction to what happens. Levine appears to have added a greater depth in characterization than the short story form usually dictates. The characters are often memorable, as the three Mendels—Constance, Frieda, and Mr. Mendel—in **"In Quebec City."**

Levine has been accused of being closer to the English than to the Canadian idiom, and of an increasing tendency to rework the same themes. Though I feel that Levine does not need a defense against these criticisms, I also feel that it is important to disclaim them, mainly because some readers would get such impressions from some critics—and from general statements about his work, as in the Supplement to *The Oxford Companion to Canadian History and Literature.* In Western Canada we seem to be less concerned with whether a writer is too English or too American or not Canadian enough than we are with what he does as a writer. It is the universal in Levine's themes, the art with which he writes that is important. He may set his characters in Ottawa, Montreal, Quebec or in England, but their experiences are world wide, could happen to anyone anywhere. He takes the ordinary, and makes the reader see the ordinary in it, unlike so many writers who look only for the extraordinary in human experience.

There is, too, a strong poetic quality in the writing of Norman Levine. He writes the short story frequently with the resources and the intention of the lyrical poet. The stories should not be read as simple narratives in the usual sense, though there is much narrative movement in many of them. Instead, Levine conveys the feeling of a situation, the humanity of what is going on, the idea that this is happening to people; the stories have all the unity and shape, the concentrated diction and implied emotion of a well-finished lyric poem. As with the lyric, the stories yield their full meaning only upon re-reading, when the reader can link the implications of section with section, implications that are not always obvious upon first reading. For this reason, I do not feel that the criticism against Levine that he reworks old themes is valid; instead, by similar themes in these *Selected Stories,* separate stories illuminate each other. What may be a fragmentary moment in one story is lighted by another fragment in another story; even the characters may be different, but the emotion is similar, and its significance is apprehended more fully when it is implied again another way.

The diction of Levine's short stories, with its evocation of mood and scene and its poetic use of implication is the most important part of the fabric of his work. Yet, there is nothing vague about these short stories. Levine is assured in his craft, very knowledgeable in his composition; he always uses the right punctuation mark in the right place. He writes with a precision, knowing full well what he intends, and achieving it in his best stories with an accuracy and rightness that puts him with the best of short story writers. And without ceasing to belong to the country where he was born, he is a writer who has branched out into his contemporary world—he has been translated into both German and Dutch—and become a man of his time as well as of his country. (pp. 94-6)

> *D. G. Stephens, "Looking Homeward," in* Canadian Literature, *No. 70, Autumn, 1976, pp. 93-6.*

JOHN LOWNSBROUGH

Norman Levine, like Mavis Gallant, is a Canadian who lives and works abroad; short-story collections before *Thin Ice* have included *One-Way Ticket* and *Selected Stories,* and there were novels, *The Angled Road* and *From a Seaside Town.* Like Gallant, Levine charts the ripples of human circumstances from the dual perspective of the expatriate. His adopted habitat, though, is not exotic Paris but a small town on the Cornish coastline. There is a bleakness, an austerity to these surroundings, and such an ambience would appear to influence his prose style, which, in the present collection, can seem alternately evocative and too minimalist by half. There are times when understatement becomes almost too emphatic. Sometimes, instead of more, less can still mean less. . . .

Thin Ice suffers a kind of structural stasis. In essence, its stories are memory pieces linked as short fiction. Ostensibly, each has a different narrator, though, in fact, voice and perspective remain the same throughout. Invariably, the narrator is a writer who lives in England and ponders—ponders mightily—the tug and pull of his Canadian roots. There are occasional visits home. It is probably not coincidence that two of the more successful stories, **"Hello, Mrs. Newman"** and **"Grace & Faigel,"** work as well as they do simply because this omnipresent narrator had to relinquish more than his customary share of the spotlight to other characters. Since so much of Norman Levine's observation on human foible is pointed and shrewd, it is unfortunate that in the service of so

schematic a context his stories risk seeming tedious if not at times actually trite. In a couple of them the narrator resolves to return home and start fresh. If we are meant to understand the urgency behind this resolve, Levine may be asking too much. One man's crisis of identity is being played out here mainly on surfaces and in the shallows. Form and subject matter seem somehow at cross-purposes.

> *John Lownsbrough, "No Place Like Home," in* Maclean's Magazine, *Vol. 92, No. 47, November 19, 1979, p. 58.*

MICHAEL SMITH

Unlike many short-story writers, Levine wastes little energy on *staging*—the creation of clever, "memorable" characters, or a narrative persona independent from himself. Rather, the narrator and writer are identical, at least superficially: a Canadian Jew who grew up in Ottawa, served in the RCAF, graduated from McGill, and soon moved abroad. The premise behind most of his stories [in *Thin Ice*] is equally simple: the writer forays out—sometimes overseas, sometimes just for a walk—then returns to write down what he has learned. Often, when people find out he's a writer, they want to tell him things. "You wouldn't believe the things that have happened to me," says a man in **"By a Frozen River"**; it's a common refrain.

Compared to traditional notions about how a short story should be structured, this journalistic deliberation creates stories that are nearly formless, flirting with the mundane. No twist of the tale. No plot. No passion. Very little sex. As its title suggests, **"A Writer's Story"** is a blueprint for Levine's *modus operandi.* The writer and his wife move to the seaside. He goes for visits to two elderly people who reminisce about their pasts. The man has known D. H. Lawrence; the woman has many local ironies to tell. Then the man has a fall, and must go to live with his daughter. "We won't see him again," the old woman says. The writer and his wife move back to London. And that's it.

Yet Levine's stories manage to transcend banality, partly because he forces his readers to respond to them by implication, rather than telling us what to think. Even when, in **"Grace & Faigel,"** the writer appears to be on the verge of an extramarital affair, he hardly reveals what he's thinking about. There's no suggestion that the possibility of an affair is anything he has ever considered before. Nor any second thoughts, except for the remark that he's avoiding talking too much about his wife. As a result, the narrator is often in danger of seeming a cold fish, though in his spare reporting of events Levine successfully balances the cynical with the humane. When, as readers, our judgement waivers, he skewers us with irony:

> "Next time you're here," he said, "I'll take you out to see my plant. It's in the country. I built it all myself—the machinery—the conveyor belts—the whole process."
> We go back into his car.
> "The government health inspector is after me," he said mischievously. And grinned. "I'm a polluter."
> I like Harvey. I like his style.

The visitation theme is sustained most strongly in such stories as **"In Lower Town"** and **"Champagne Barn,"** in which the writer returns to the Ottawa of his youth; in **"A Visit"** and **"Class of 1949,"** in which visitors from the past turn up at his home; and in **"By a Frozen River"** and **"The Girl Next Door,"** in which the writer deliberately checks into lodgings in Canada and the lives of the inhabitants of adjoining rooms. Similarly, in [**"Thin Ice"**], he finds himself storm-stayed and broke in a small New Brunswick town, reliving the poverty-inspired artifice he had to practise as a young writer in order to survive. And in **"We All Begin in a Little Magazine"** he rediscovers, rather guiltily, the dependence many fledgling writers invest in the benevolent editors of small magazines, beyond which few will ever progress.

By the time these stories were written, Levine's writer-narrator has become quite a success. Journalists travel to the seaside to interview him, and his presence commands whole pages in the Ottawa papers when he returns for a visit. "You're *fame-us,"* says a retarded nephew in one story. "Me see you on TV." That's slightly more popular attention than Levine himself seems to enjoy in Canada, but he does deserve it. As the man says, I like his style. (pp. 8-9)

Michael Smith, "An Ice Place to Visit," in Books in Canada, Vol. 8, No. 10, December, 1979, pp. 8-9.

JONATHAN STEFFEN

For Norman Levine, the word 'writer' means not 'inventor' but 'observer', and he writes about what he knows with a deceptive simplicity of style. But there is nothing simplistic about the twelve starkly elegant stories of *Thin Ice* or about Levine's constant struggle to ascertain the truth about what he sees, and to render this in prose.

The stories in *Thin Ice,* all basically autobiographical, are written in the first person, and again and again we see the figure of Levine the Writer moving restlessly through the worlds of his experience, reworking, remaking them—the Ottawa of his childhood, the post-war London of his Bohemian days as an aspiring writer, the oppressively peaceful West Country where he now lives and works.

It is distances which obsess Levine—between places, between people, between past and present; the problem of reconciling a past which is not only lost, but which was actively rejected, with a present from which one incessantly contemplates that past. Levine escaped from the Jewish immigrant community of Lower Town, Ottawa, only to find that it is still where he belongs.

> Now that most of the fruit and rag pedlars are dead and Lower Town has changed—I find I am unable to stay away from it. It's become like a magnet. Whenever I can, I return.

This crumbling world, and its pervasive persistence in memory, is beautifully evoked, as is the London of the post-war generation. But though so much of Levine's work is an attempt to recreate the past in language, 'a sort of innocence that has gone', he tempers the sad passion of his quest with honesty, with a melancholy realism. . . . (p. 250)

There is no better illustration of his simple precision of observation and narration than the tiny vignette of a Merchant seaman whom Levine meets on a train, speaking of his wife left at home:

> 'I have her picture on my cabin wall', he said. 'For the first few days of the voyage she's nice and big.

> But as the weeks go by—she gets smaller and smaller and smaller . . .'

This is the quiet agony of Levine's world: the remorseless gulf opening between a person and the object of his love, be it place or person, the precarious writer's struggle with an inevitable sense of loss. 'I was a writer. In my world nothing is certain.' Thin Ice. (pp. 250-51)

Jonathan Steffen, "Too Late," in New Statesman, Vol. 99, No. 2552, February 15, 1980, pp. 250-51.

VICTORIA GLENDINNING

Canada Made Me is a reissue of Norman Levine's volume of travel, reminiscence and self-discovery first published in England in 1958, and only recently in Canada; *Thin Ice* is his new collection of short stories. To read the two books in conjunction is to take a lesson in how a writer—or this writer—uses his experience as material for fiction. Mr Levine is a very good but not an inventive writer. In **"A Writer's Story"** from *Thin Ice* the narrator, in his twenties, fears that he is running out of material. "But as the weeks went by I realized it wasn't that at all. I didn't know what my material was." Mr Levine's material is his own life, his background, the people and places he knows or used to know. . . .

Canada Made Me is the account of a journey through his native country and into his past, which he was driven to revisit by a "restless energy"; a "personal destructiveness". It was not that he felt he belonged there, for he felt he belonged nowhere. Revisiting the Lower Town quarter of Ottawa where he was brought up, he recalled the poverty-stricken immigrant families, Catholic or Jewish. Most of them, like his own parents, never learnt to speak English easily, and earned their livings by peddling rags or vegetables. That ghetto community had now changed and gone; and in the Canada of the mid-1950s he found little that appealed to him. . . .

Mr Levine's gift is for a peculiar, very personal kind of reportage. In every town he visited he walked the streets alone: "A good way I have found to get to know a place is to get lost in it." He haunted hotel lobbies, watching and listening. He has a talent for reacting to and transcribing the most ordinary encounters with a concentration that makes his travelogue as actual as film, and as dispassionate: "I thought of myself here, of 'being a camera', the detached observer."

Canada Made Me is a very good book indeed. Quite apart from the autobiographical excursions, some of his descriptions of things newly seen are startlingly effective: there is, for example, an extended account of a visit to a slaughterhouse in Winnipeg that is disturbing and unforgettable. It is when one turns to his new fiction that the "personal" seems a bit of a stranglehold. His experiences are recycled: scraps of dialogue, anecdotes, descriptions from *Canada Made Me* recur in the stories, transposed but not transformed. The Lower Town pedlars are here again; and the narrator in most cases is a Canadian writer living in Cornwall, revisiting Canada, being visited by Canadians. The writing is sad, spare, a thinned-out version of the autobiographical record.

Two of the stories seem to me to carry sufficient weight to justify so total a surrender to obsession. In [**"Thin Ice"**] an émigré, returning in triumph as writer in residence at a university in the Maritimes, is snowed up for two days in a small town with no money and no cheque book. No one there has heard of him; he is treated like a penniless vagrant. Back in the glow of an academic dinner party, he realizes the frozen wastes that lie not only around the islands of culture and conviviality but around his apparent success. In **"Class of 1949"** the Canadian writer in Cornwall is visited by a compatriot who lives an untrammeled, travelling life. The narrator, lapped in family routine, and local matters, feels inadequate and dull, and senses the tension between desire for freedom and the chains of habit.

Perhaps Norman Levine, having established himself as a gifted and dedicated writer, might apply his talent for detached observation and honest introspection to something new. Or maybe that is too facile a prescription to offer one who concluded his investigation into his heritage with these words:

> I wondered why I felt so bitter about Canada. After all . . . it was foolish to believe that you can take the throwouts, the rejects, the human kickabouts from Europe and tell them: Here you have a second chance. Here you can start a new life. But no one ever mentioned the price one had to pay; how much of oneself you had to betray.

> *Victoria Glendinning, "Peddling the Provinces," in* The Times Literary Supplement, *No. 4016, March 14, 1980, p. 289.*

ELWIN MOORE

Sorrow is gaudy, unconsidered, immediate as fire, a measure of loss; it passes. Sadness is reticent, reflective, pervasive as air, a measure of distance; it stays. And Norman Levine is a master of sad distances. *Why Do You Live So Far Away?* asks the title of this collection, and an earlier Levine title can be drafted as answer: *I Don't Want to Know Anyone Too Well.* Levine seems an expatriate spirit; a hard-eyed, clear-eyed tourist in his own life. Relentless as a camera, he records the distances between husband and wife, between son and mother, between the free rich man and the trapped poor man, between the rooted and the rootless, between wish and fact. Levine maintains, too, an artful, unstated space between reader and narrator. And he likes to end his stories with departures—a last look, a turning away. "One is always disappointed by change," says Gordon Rideau, the impoverished guest of honour at a reunion of McGill grads, shortly before he begins to follow his old university brothers into the washroom to ask them for loans.

This book gathers five short stories first published in the 1960s, another written in 1975, and a 1981 revision of the 1961 novella *The Playground.* Mostly early Levine, in other words—Levine in his time of long struggle, before his work began to win the attention it deserved. The dominant theme of the early short stories here is privation. A writer pawns his typewriter. A writer moves his family for the 14th time in five years. A writer stays indoors to avoid meeting creditors in the street. A writer's wife smuggles home chunks of firewood under the baby carriage's raincover. All this in a determinedly flat, bare, direct, and factual style, for Levine long ago mastered the technique of lowering his voice so as to be better heard. These stories give an uneasy enjoyment. The reader keeps wondering how autobiographical they are. The effect is of a feast where the food is fine and the chef is much in evidence, and emaciated.

The Playground is set in 1959-60 in the seaside town of St.

Ives, Cornwall, Levine's long-time home. We are given three seasons in the life of St. Ives and three seasons in the gossip and partying of an artists' colony that runs heavily to idlers, spongers, and pretenders. This story is almost as much a pastiche as a novella—Levine seems to have written many of its parts separately and then strung them together by inventing a narrator with the appropriate name of Bill Stringer. The people of *The Playground* don't amount to much. They're a matter of quick, usually undercutting sketches and a few good scenes. But Levine has appropriated the town. He knows it at all hours and from all vantage-points. He knows it from the castrated cats sunning themselves in the middle of summer streets to the outside house pipes painted to look like varicose veins to the gull caught head down between electric wires in October cold, "the neck arching with the wind like the neck of a kettle." The sense of place in this story is rich and dense and marvellous.

Levine's prose traditionally has been celebrated for its taut authority. Lately he seems to be letting a little more of the randomness of the world into his fiction. There's more ease in his telling. The change shows here in the 1975 story **"Continuity,"** and it showed too in the 1980 collection *Thin Ice.* One critic found the language of *Thin Ice* "almost chatty." But I think Levine has gained by surrendering himself just a bit to his material. His recent stories seem subtler, wiser, and more various in their effects. (pp. 16-17)

> *Elwin Moore, "From a Seaside Town," in* Books in Canada, *Vol. 13, No. 6, June-July, 1984, pp. 16-17.*

IRA BRUCE NADEL

Ever since its publication in England nearly twenty-five years ago, *Canada Made Me* by Norman Levine has been excluded from the mainstream of Canadian letters. Underrated as a literary work and misrepresented as a travel book, *Canada Made Me* has not been understood for what it is: a striking Canadian autobiography sharing similar themes, literary motifs, and structural features with several other major Canadian autobiographies. Common to all these works are the theme of exile, the motif of the journey, and the structural exploration of time. Two additional features, however, highlight *Canada Made Me* as a significant work: it is the pivotal text in the progress of Norman Levine as a writer and, at the same time, extends a pattern of twentieth-century autobiographical writing—expressed most clearly in the work of George Orwell and Henry Miller—to Canadian literature. (p. 69)

Safely but incorrectly categorized as a travel book by the *Literary History of Canada*, *Canada Made Me* is referred to as both "a nightmare" and "a memorable book." This paradox, however, may in part explain the nature of the work and its importance for Canadian autobiography. In 1956 Norman Levine, then living in St. Ives, Cornwall—he emigrated to England in 1949—had the idea of writing a book on Canada but when no money was available he began to do it imaginatively, creating itineraries, characters, and incidents. But there was, as he wrote, "a need for making the physical journey, I felt the need to make a reconciliation. I didn't want to run away from the country as I had originally. . . ." This desire is not so much for a reunion but for a re-departure. However, the reconciliation he seeks is within himself and, as the

"Author's Note" implies, the work is one of self-engagement in order to eliminate self-estrangement.

The epigraphs to the autobiography, one by Dante and the other by Camus, emphasize the sense of division within the self derived from a separation from place. The Dante reference is especially important because the passage from the "Purgatorio," Canto 5, is the source of Levine's title and suggests his longing to identify with the world of his past as does the speaker in the poem, the murdered Pia de Tolomei. The choice of "Purgatorio" is also significant in that it represents a middle existence where there is an intense realization of the doubleness of man's life, of identity and division, welcome and rejection. This is precisely the condition of Levine. And as one's knowledge and understanding increases in this state, so, too, does one's solitude, as Levine demonstrates throughout his autobiography. The full title of Dante's poem, a semi-autobiographical journey composed by an exile, also defines more fully the condition of the narrator in *Canada Made Me.* It is "The Comedy of Dante Alighieri, a Florentine by birth but not in character." Transposed, the appositional phrase applies equally well to Levine and his work.

Beginning his journey with a sense of alienation and of exile . . . provides Levine with the distance and objectivity to make accurate observations while experiencing them internally. Employing the traditional autobiographical structure of retrospection, revisiting and recreating a world he consciously left, Levine gives an account that is objectively valid and subjectively meaningful. The quest of *Canada Made Me* is to discover the meaning of Levine's departure and continued separation while understanding his perplexing attachment to the country. Levine is both the rootless Wandering Jew and the Defender of the Faith. It is not surprising, then, that his first destination when he returns is his home which is also the mythical centre of the country: Ottawa.

From his search to recapture the past . . . , Levine attempts to rediscover himself. "To be a writer I had to be an exile" he stated in 1980 but in 1970 he admitted that he went to England to run away from Canada. His 1956 return is not to find the country but himself. Only through writing *Canada Made Me* could Levine begin to accept his past and adjust it to his sense of the present. What he is able to do is unite memory, what he recreates of the past in the various fictional sections, with repetition, what he actually experiences when he revisits the country. As a consequence, his writing after *Canada Made Me* achieved a new directness and impact because he no longer interpreted his Canadian experiences as English and was able to perceive his history and origins more ethnically.

Initially, *Canada Made Me* was to be a travelogue but it quickly became a record of personal self-discovery. Instead of merely recording his responses to the people and places he sees as he travels from Halifax to Ucluelet, he confronts his past through associations forced on him by the immediacy of the surroundings. Whether it is his parents' life in Ottawa, the mining town of Ile-aux-Noix where he worked in the summer of 1948, or Montreal where he had been a student, Levine blends the realism of the immediate with the truth of the past. Flashbacks, superimpositions, and biographies of figures from the past and the present disrupt the linear narrative to create an absorbing text. But when he candidly describes the unhappiness, boredom, desolation, and materialism in the country, he presents an unflattering portrait. No photographs, he remarks, could possibly illustrate the book because the poetry of the country consists entirely "in the advertisements and statistics."

Analyzing his own dislocation and departure from the country, Levine remarks that he left for the sake of change, the lack of any patriotic feeling, the unpleasant reminders of his childhood and the absence of any distinctive culture; "ours is still a mixture of other cultures which hasn't fused into anything separate," he writes. Attracted to the poorer areas of the cities because "they represent failure, and for me failure here has a strong appeal," Levine focuses on the decay of the country and its dismalness as seen in flophouses, mining towns, and bars. Dominating the work is his feeling that he does not belong anywhere and that his natural condition is rootlessness. But the cause of this condition and that of the general decay is the failure of Canada to realize the dream of a golden future and provide a new beginning for its immigrants. For Levine the dream evaporates into a sordid reality, the romance quickly becoming irony. (pp. 71-3)

Following *Canada Made Me* Levine could accept a paradox he previously did not understand. He realized he could not go home again, yet he could never imaginatively or mythically ever leave it. His new stories of Ottawa, northern Ontario, or immigrant Canada, often fictionalizing experiences from his autobiography, show an unexpected vitality and conviction in his writing. **"A Small Piece of Blue,"** from *One Way Ticket,* his first collection of stories after *Canada Made Me,* illustrates this new ease with his past as he uses the experiences of his summer working in a northern Ontario mine to reassert his love of nature. **"A Memory of Ottawa,"** from the same collection and one of his most successful stories, reestablishes his Jewishness and identity with the immigrant past of Ottawa in a natural and convincing way. Written in 1958, the year *Canada Made Me* was published, **"A Memory of Ottawa"** is the fictional celebration of the self-discovery achieved from his autobiography. An elegiac story, it captures with humour a past Levine had been avoiding.

From a Seaside Town, his second novel, published in 1970, also demonstrates Levine's more ready acceptance of the condition of ambiguous exile. His Canadian hero, who lives in Cornwall as a travel writer, revisits Canada only to return to England to write fiction, freed to write imaginatively, no longer literally, about his past. The dilemma which *Canada Made Me* made clear and allowed Levine to accept is summarized in the novel by Joseph Grand in this comment on his early travel essays on Canada written while in England: "I wrote about the violence, the mediocrity of the people, the provincialism, the dullness. . . . And all the time I wanted to be there." Levine's more recent collection, *Thin Ice* (1979), continues the renewal with a Canadian past in stories like **"In Lower Town"** about his father and life in Ottawa or **"By A Frozen River,"** dealing with Jewish life in a tiny northern Ontario town. (pp. 79-80)

Ira Bruce Nadel, " 'Canada Made Me' and Canadian Autobiography," in Canadian Literature, *No. 101, Summer, 1984, pp. 69-81.*

SHERIE POSESORSKI

[Since] *Canada Made Me,* Levine's short stories have formed a chapter by chapter fictional autobiography. In **"A Writer's Story,"** the young narrator wanders around Cornwall, unable to write, not knowing "What my material was . . . trying to cut out [my] past, cover it up . . . and it made [me] boring." Once Levine discovered his material—once the affirmation of his past meant the annihilation of the "nothing" he was experiencing—it enabled him to create a body of critically acclaimed work.

Levine states that he writes in pictures. Many of the stories [in *Champagne Barn*] begin with the narrator's examination of an old photo, or a setting depicted as if it is a photo. Metaphorically, Levine sits before a photo album of his life, picking up snapshots and meditating on them; the story that ultimately emerges is an artistic shaping of his memories. Levine's use of his experience is not an exercise in nostalgia but rather an ethical examination of the narrator's behaviour in the recollected situation. His narrator frequently regrets the missed opportunities, his inability to respond to the people around him with emotional generosity, his guarded, voyeuristic relationships with others. In **"The Girl Next Door,"** he comes to Ottawa to write, meets a girl who shares his interests, then withdraws from her emotional demands. In **"A Visit,"** the narrator is wary about the unspoken demands his sister and mother may make on him in their visit. The poignant sorrow emanating from many of the stories comes from the narrator's realization that he has behaved like an interviewer: probing people for their stories, then refusing the emotional responsibility that comes with listening.

Levine's prose is laconic and pressurized. Even in his earliest stories, the narrator's tone and consciousness are so firmly established and credible that the scenes and characters never require a wordy build up—his memories become those of the readers, and a simple phrase is enough to evoke a wealth of shared knowledge.

Such is Levine's skill that his stories are planted in the reader's mind like depth charges: the reverberations linger long after putting down his books.

> *Sherie Posesorski, in a review of "Champagne Barn," in* Quill and Quire, *Vol. 50, No. 8, August, 1984, p. 30.*

LESLEY CHOYCE

Champagne Barn pulls together "a retrospective of Norman Levine's finest work" written between 1958 and 1978. . . . His fiction works in quiet, subtle ways, focusing on the beneath-the-skin, minor revolutions that direct our lives. His simple stories are unexpectedly readable and moving simply because he is (or convincingly appears to be) so intimate and honest with himself.

Levine almost always writes close to home, beginning **"In Lower Town,"** set in the Ottawa of his childhood, and moving on to his expatriate life on the Cornish coast and visits home to Canadian soil. The preoccupation with the subject of writing suggests in itself that Levine prefers to write more about the life lived than the life imagined.

"We All Begin in a Little Magazine" dips into the subculture of anxious poets and fiction writers finding (or failing to find)

a publisher and an audience. **"By a Frozen River"** and **"Thin Ice"** are probably already Canadian classics worthy of another read here. If you've been reading Levine all along, there will probably be few surprises, but *Champagne Barn* is a valuable distillation of work by a writer whose persistently uncomplicated style allows him to reveal so much by saying so little. (p. 24)

> *Lesley Choyce, "Three Hits and a Miss," in* Books in Canada, *Vol. 13, No. 9, November, 1984, pp. 23-4.*

ERIC THOMPSON

Champagne Barn contains twenty-three stories arranged chronologically in four parts: tales of adolescence, of young manhood, of the struggling young writer, and of the reflections of a seasoned author. Levine's "journey" to the past conveys portraits of many people and events which have influenced him, but considering his self-preoccupied stance it is perhaps truer to say that he is more of an anecdotalist than a shaper of purely imaginative fiction. Still, the early stories set the tone and themes of his work: the search for a destiny more fulfilling than that expected of a fruit-pedlar's son. A familiar technique begins to emerge, too, as Levine uses a before-and-after narrative scheme to contrast a past experience with a later one. What he seems to be saying is that life, like a palimpsest, is obscure, and one had to "go through several layers before you found something living."

Levine's wartime and postwar experiences as an airman and student at McGill are recalled next, and then come reminiscences about the young writer's rather pathetic attempts to establish himself in England. The largest group of stories and by far the most revealing, occupies that last part of the book. Memories of St. Ives, Cornwall, are about equally mixed with those emanating from return trips to various places in Canada. The sense of really being an outsider, of not "belonging" anywhere, is felt most acutely when he receives visits from relatives and friends. (In one story he even consents to be a tourist guide to a film-maker, thereby emphasizing his strangeness even in the villages along the Cornish coast.) Not surprisingly, he scarcely feels at home, either, in Canada. In several of these stories he is seen as a boarder or a traveller—a transient of no fixed address, or, perhaps, purpose. This sense of being alone is caught best in **"By a Frozen River"** and **'Thin Ice,"** stories in which his vulnerability is suitably underlined by the harshness of the Canadian winter. Yet—and what makes these works special in my view—Levine succeeds in them by escaping from his egoism as he relates the ironies of his situation with self-deprecating humour and, further, by fashioning a memorable assortment of characters who are similarly isolated but not defeated. (pp. 103-04)

> *Eric Thompson, "Let Us Compare Obsessions," in* The Fiddlehead, *No. 145, Autumn, 1985, pp. 103-05.*

Antonine Maillet

1929-

Canadian dramatist, novelist, short story writer, nonfiction writer, scriptwriter, and author of children's books.

Maillet's works are composed in French and document the history, language, and culture of the Acadians, a French-Canadian ethnic group largely concentrated in the New Brunswick region of southeastern Canada. Herself an Acadian, Maillet is recognized as the first author to utilize their distinctive dialect in her writings. Although best known in Canada for her drama *La Sagouine,* Maillet has garnered international praise for her novels, which feature multiple narrators and a spontaneous, anecdotal style reminiscent of the Acadian storytelling tradition. Her fiction and drama also reflect the influence of sixteenth-century French satirist François Rabelais in their use of scatological humor and grotesque fantasy. Maillet often focuses on the 1755 British destruction of the Acadian settlement in Nova Scotia and the subsequent dispersion of the Acadian people along the eastern coast of North America. Her works evoke a mythic dimension of the Acadian experience by portraying courageous heroines and lower-class protagonists in conflict with representatives of bourgeois respectability.

Maillet's archetypal Acadian character is poor, illiterate, and unrefined yet possessed of an essential integrity that ensures survival and honor. Her one-act play *Les crasseux* (1968), for instance, portrays ebullient Acadians who overcome unjust persecution by their bigoted neighbors. *La Sagouine* (1971), a one-woman play originally written as a series of radio scripts and later adapted for television, established Maillet's reputation as a major French-Canadian dramatist. The aged title character, La Sagouine, is the most famous of Maillet's Acadian protagonists and recurs in many of her subsequent works. Impoverished yet resilient, La Sagouine sets forth her personal history in short monologues and irreverently comments on such subjects as politics, philosophy, and Acadian life while scrubbing the floors of a wealthy neighbor. Maillet's next play, *Gapi et Sullivan* (1973; *Gapi and Sullivan*), is a dialogue between Gapi, an elderly lighthouse keeper who is La Sagouine's husband, and Sullivan, a sailor. Reflecting on their lives, the men compare the relative merits of Gapi's uneventful, secure existence to those of Sullivan's adventurous exploits. Another drama, *Evangéline Deusse* (1975), which Michèle Lacombe described as "a tragi-comic masterpiece," presents a revisionist version of *Evangeline,* Henry Wadsworth Longfellow's verse epic about Acadian history. Whereas Longfellow's poem depicts two young lovers who are separated during the exile of 1755, Maillet's version concerns a pair of Acadian octogenarians who meet and fall in love in a park in Montreal. Unlike Longfellow's passive, idealized heroine, Maillet's Evangéline is earthy, robust, and optimistic. Maillet presents her story in a humorous, unsentimental manner yet retains the romantic themes of Longfellow's original.

Although she first attracted significant critical recognition for her dramas, Maillet began her literary career as a novelist. Her first work of fiction, *Pointe-aux-coques* (1958), is a semi-autobiographical account of her childhood in an Acadian vil-

lage off the coast of New Brunswick that is written in standard French. Maillet's next novel, *Don l'Orignal* (1972; *The Tale of Don L'Orignal*), for which she received a Governor General's Award, explores Acadian life in greater detail and uses form and syntax to approximate her cultural dialect. A comic allegory of early Acadian history, this mock-epic novel recalls the works of Rabelais in its spirited depiction of the adventures of the Puçois, or Flea Islanders, an uncouth tribe led by an outlandish patriarch, Don L'Orignal. The persecution of the Puçois by their hostile neighbors parallels that of the original Acadian settlers in Nova Scotia. *Mariaagélas* (1973; *Mariaagelas: Maria, Daughter of Gelas*), based on Maillet's play of the same title, is set in a seaside village in New Brunswick during the American Prohibition era. This work features a daring young Acadian woman who relays illegal shipments of liquor to the United States while evading the local constabulary and a prudish widow. In *Les cordes-de-bois* (1977), Maillet depicts a group of prostitutes and indigents who incite the bigotry of their wealthy, repressed neighbors yet prove themselves superior to their hypocritical adversaries by performing charitable acts. Ronald Sutherland proclaimed *Les cordes-de-bois* "audacious and triumphant, both in its handling of language and in local colour."

Maillet's next novel, *Pélagie-la-charrette* (1979; *Pélagie: The*

Return to a Homeland), became the first work by a non-European to win the French Prix Goncourt. A historical epic set in the late 1700s, this book recounts the adventures of Pélagie, a courageous widow who leads a group of fellow Acadians on an arduous journey from the southern United States to their Nova Scotia homeland in the decade following the Acadian exile of 1755. *Pélagie* offers a detailed portrayal of events that took place during the American Revolution and incorporates many allusions to Acadian folklore and legend. *Cent ans dans les bois* (1981; republished as *La gribouille*), a sequel set a century after *Pélagie,* concerns a group of Pélagie's descendants who gather to search for a treasure willed to them by their Acadian ancestors. Maillet returns to the theme of Prohibition-era rumrunning in *Crache-à-pic* (1984; *The Devil Is Loose!*), in which a woman vies with a villainous competitor for control of her village's bootlegging trade. Paul Stuewe called *The Devil Is Loose!* "a marvellously imaginative, cleverly structured, and highly entertaining novel that should appeal to just about every literary taste."

Maillet has also adapted several of her novels for the theater, including *La veuve enragée* (1977), a dramatization of *Les cordes-de-bois,* and *La contrebandière* (1981), a revised version of *Mariaagélas.* Two other of Maillet's plays were inspired by the works of classical French writers: *Le bourgeois gentleman* (1978), a reworking of Molière's *Le bourgeois gentilhomme,* depicts the ludicrous efforts of a French Canadian to transform himself into an Anglo-Canadian, and *Les drôlatiques, horrifiques, et épouvantables aventures de Panurge, ami de Pantagruel, d'après Rabelais* (1983) transplants grotesque figures from Rabelais into an Acadian setting. In addition to her work as a dramatist and fiction writer, Maillet has garnered praise for her literary criticism. Donald Smith lauded her volume *Rabelais et les traditions populaires en Acadie* (1971) as "a brilliant study of the linguistic and cultural similarities between the Acadia of today and the French Middle Ages and Renaissance."

(See also *Contemporary Authors,* Vols. 115, 120 and *Dictionary of Literary Biography,* Vol. 60.)

BARBARA GODARD

[The novel *Les Cordes-de-Bois*] is located in familiar Maillet territory—the Acadian coast of New Brunswick between the forest and the sea with their different ways of life. Its concern, though, is not landscape but character. Antonine Maillet has peopled her town of Le Pont with a collection of comics who dramatize the problem of extreme poverty in the area, but who are familiar inhabitants of any town. . . .

The comic clash between pillars of society and outlaws has been the subject of Maillet's earlier writing as well. Here the focus is less on its dramatic implications than on the manner in which it is related. The events of the story, which centres in the 30s but the implications of which flow from events a century before, is filtered through the memories of many spinners of yarns. . . .

Maillet sees herself at the end of an oral tradition and the beginning of a written one. Her work is less metaphysical, less complex, more truly comic than that of her compeers—Jacques Ferron, Roch Carrier and Robert Kroetsch. Though

a more interesting novel in terms of narrative technique—certainly much more successful than *Mariaagelas—Les Cordes-de-Bois* is less suggestively resonant than the symbolic fable *Don l'Orignal* where her most powerful character, La Sagouine (The Charwoman), carried the day. Similarly, the Acadian dialect which was the innovative feature of her immensely successful monologue-drama *La Sagouine* is less evident here. Such a weakening in imaginative force is the price paid for increased technical strengths.

> Barbara Godard, in a review of "Les cordes-de-bois," in Quill and Quire, Vol. 44, No. 2, February, 1978, p. 45.

RONALD SUTHERLAND

With her latest novel, *Les Cordes-de-bois* . . . , Antonine Maillet has joined the company of Canada's two pre-eminent women novelists, Gabrielle Roy and Margaret Laurence. (p. 76)

All of Antonine Maillet's works explore one of Canada's richest regional cultures, the Acadian. All more or less exploit the distinctive dialect possibilities of *l'Acadie,* making them difficult reading for the uninitiated already operating in a second language and accounting, perhaps, for some of the fascination her works have generated in France. For the French, I imagine, she is a kind of Acadian Mark Twain.

Maillet's first attempt at a novel, *Pointe-aux-Coques,* was hesitant and derivative. It is a combination of *Evangeline* and *Maria Chapdelaine,* telling the story of a young school teacher who finds her way back from the United States to the land of her immediate forebears, where she finally chooses to marry a local lad and remain in a small fishing village. Some Acadian vocabulary is used in the book, but nothing which would impede the average reader unfamiliar with the dialect.

Compared with *Pointe-aux-Coques, Les Cordes-de-bois* is audacious and triumphant, both in its handling of language and in local colour. Despite the fact that the book contains a number of ideas and themes in common with other successful Canadian novels in English and French, it stands as a unique achievement, a celebration of the qualities of the indomitable Acadians. The heroine, *La Bessoune* (from *bessonne*—twin—although indications are that she was a single birth), is a striking example of the new type of protagonist who has emerged in Canadian fiction. She reminds one particularly of Hoda in Adele Wiseman's *Crackpot.* A *"fille des matelots"*—sailors' girl—descended from a runaway seaman, probably fathered by another, and given to accommodating a new generation of lusty, seafaring men whose ships are in port, she is proud, defiant and self-reliant. She makes no excuses and asks no pardon of God or man. The community she lives in is called *Les Cordes-de-bois,* a shanty town on a knoll above the town, housing a whole conglomeration of bootleggers, smugglers, misfits and outcasts from conventional society, the latter symbolized by *Ma-Tante-la-Veuve*—the double of W. O. Mitchell's Mrs. Abercrombie—and her nieces "*les sept filles de barbier.*"

Although *La Bessoune* fits the pattern of the new Canadian hero, *Les Cordes-de-bois* also provides an excellent example of the familiar, traditional *prêtre-manqué* character. Like Father Dowling in *Such is My Beloved,* Abbé Savoie in Gilles Marcotte's *A Poids de Dieu* and Philip Bentley in *As For Me and My House,* Maillet's "*petit prêtre*" is idealistic and earnest. And like the other fictional clergymen, he is eventually overwhelmed by the "respectable" citizens, amid innuendoes that his dealings with the seductive and majestic *Bessoune,* as well as with her "godless" cohorts, are not restricted to the saving of souls. (p. 77)

Maillet's novel presents a gallery of colourful characters, including the Scottish-born wood-merchant MacFarlane and a diminutive, yarn-spinning Irish seaman called Tom Thumb, who befriends the *"petit prêtre"* and is sheltered by *la Bessoune* when he jumps ship. In the final analysis, however, it is *la Bessoune* who remains imprinted on the reader's mind. While the seven daughters of the barber rock on their front porch and *Ma-Tante-la Veuve* busies herself guarding the public morality, the girl on the hill does the real work of the world. Tough, resourceful, indomitable, she embodies the qualities of the dispossessed Acadians who managed to endure and prevail against all odds. Antonine Maillet has written a fitting tribute to her people. (p. 78)

> Ronald Sutherland, "Acadian Tribute," in Canadi-
> an Literature, No. 80, Spring, 1979, pp. 76-8.

HANS R. RUNTE

A people which populated its land of once impenetrable forests and mysteriously shifting dunes with uncounted generations of necromancers, sorcerers, will-o'-the-wisps and ghosts, is today acclaiming its greatest literary exorcist. Antonine Maillet, herself well versed in Acadian folklore (*Rabelais et les traditions populaires en Acadie,* 1971), set out from the beginning of her comet-like career to "demythologize" the rich but stifling heritage of a nation which, after two centuries, still defined itself in terms of the Expulsion of 1755. A refreshing and encouraging whiff of tongue-in-cheek disrespect for the lamentations of, and about, the Acadian past wafted already through *L'Acadie pour quasiment rien* (1973). With *Mariaagélas* (1973) and *Les Cordes-de-Bois* (1977) Acadians rediscovered to their surprise and pride that they could chuckle, laugh and joke about themselves and their English neighbour and not be punished for it by Fate or Church. Even the often troubling humour of the famous *Sagouine* (1971) could not but reaffirm them in their new-found belief that what was must not obscure what is and what could be.

To be sure, after fifteen works published in just ten years, the most difficult book, the cornerstone of the Acadian "Comédie Humaine" and the triumph over the retrospection complex, still remained to be written. In her literary universe, Antonine Maillet had not ventured back much further than the Prohibition era (*Mariaagélas*), as if Longfellow, although already dismissed in 1975 (*Evangéline Deusse*), continued to loom too large. Four years later, Acadia was deemed to be ready for Pélagie LeBlanc. . . .

Pélagie-la-Charrette, characteristically, does not describe the Deportation of 1755 nor the exile of thousands of Acadians in southern North America, but the heroic, ten-year return trek from Georgia to the Memramcook valley. The outrage of Grand-Pré and the misery of fifteen cotton-picking years lose much of their traditional symbolic weight in the light of Pélagie-the-Matriarch's courageous march and triumphant repossession of Acadia. (p. 764)

Thanks to this programmatic, albeit literary, readjustment of the historical perspective and of the way in which Acadians perceive themselves, *Pélagie* is the most progressive, for-

ward-looking work of an author whose intellectual background and creative talents had begun to frustrate fellow writers and readers looking for more than quaint modernizations of century-old local folklore. From the ashes of the old myth a new, cautiously optimistic one is liable to rise, a myth which can now be nourished by writers of another kind. . . .

Pélagie, like most of Antonine Maillet's other works, is thus caught in the present dilemma of the young literature of Acadia: what is known of it beyond the shores of Bouctouche and La Pointe-de-l'Eglise has been hailed and crowned for reasons which make many an Acadian author cringe. Montreal welcomed La Sagouine and gawked at Evangéline II because Quebec, after two hundred years of colonization, had finally discovered a sister nation worse off than herself and eminently "colonizable" in turn. To certain Quebecers the "Vive l'Acadie libre" supposedly implied in Antonine Maillet's winning of the Prix Goncourt sounds just as undiplomatic as a certain Gaullicism once did to English Canada. Worse still, France herself, all agog with things Canadian from lumberjack fashions to Pelagian epics, is largely unable to look behind the Rabelaisian descriptions of a picturesque people living in an exotic land and speaking a nostalgically-remembered language, and see the real issues facing Acadia and the role of Acadian writing in defining and resolving them. Since Antonine Maillet accepted the prize that *Pélagie* won her on behalf of all of Acadia, its halo cannot but illuminate also the literature of real commitment of, for example, a Laval Goupil (*Le Djibou,* 1975) or a Jacques Savoie (*Raconte-moi Massabielle,* 1979). Pélagie led her people into the 1780's; Acadia must now choose who will lead it into the 1980's. (p. 765)

> Hans R. Runte, in a review of "Pélagie-la-
> Charrette," in The Dalhousie Review, Vol. 59, No.
> 4, Winter, 1979-80, pp. 764-65.

GILLIAN DAVIES

Don L'Orignal was apparently at one point entitled *Don L'Original* by its French publishers. *Orignal,* of course, means moose, an animal which might well be original in Paris, but which is rather less so here. It was an ironic slip. Numerous Maillet characters—La Sainte, La Sagouine, Noume, La Cruche, Michel-Archange, Gapi, Citrouille, as well as Don L'Orignal—reappear in different books in different situations, and grow older but remain essentially unchanged. (*Garrochés en paradis,* 1986, is a play in which Maillet portrays the demise of this fictional "family.") Whichever way one considers it—the presentation of Acadian society in microcosm and in folkloric guise, or a repetitive exploitation of the same few characters, spokesmen from and of the social margins—"original" is hardly the *mot juste*. This is perhaps partly to be explained by the fact that Antonine Maillet's output is prodigious . . . and perhaps that she seems unsure what *genre* is best suited to her talents: she tends to adapt her novels for the theatre (*Les Cordes-de-Bois* became a play entitled *La Veuve Enragée,* for example), so that each work may have two or three re-incarnations.

Don L'Orignal is one of the few male protagonists who have a prominent place in Maillet's fiction: most are older, more robust versions of an archetypal Evangéline, such as La Sagouine and Evangéline Deusse. The word "Don" is less a first name than the equivalent of the Spanish "Don." He is "like a new Don Quixote, ready to avenge the weak, redress wrongs, sow the wind, to reap the whirlwind, rob Peter to pay Paul, make omelettes without breaking eggs, do what must be done, come what may." He holds court from a tree stump overlooking the sea—a "domaine sans domaine," to quote Rita Scalabrini—and his mark of distinction is a fur hat with four fake horns. King of Flea Island, which arose one morning in the middle of the ocean, he and his Knights and Ladies function as irritants to the wealthier, status-conscious mainlanders. The latter are mainly petits-bourgeois—barbers, merchants, milliners, bankers—who react with righteous indignation to the exploits of the invading tatterdemalion nobility. Each chapter contains a mock-heroic exploit, and each has a sub-heading indicating what is to follow: "Concerning the conversation the Flea Islanders had one day around a keg of molasses"; "Concerning the famine which raged on the island and the second expedition of Flea Islanders to capture the keg of molasses"; "Concerning the great conference that took place on the mainland, and the strange illness from which the merchant's daughter suffered"; and other events of similar import. (pp. 135-36)

Although published later than *Les Crasseux* (1968), a play which employs largely the same cast of characters, *Don L'Orignal* relates the birth of these people who were *les Puçois,* or Flea Islanders, before they became, by association, *les Crasseux:* the slovens, or filthy ones. Maillet's tale of the battle of wits and wills between islanders and mainlanders might be construed as a history of the confrontations between Acadians and Anglophones, albeit a history which gives a new twist to the *Grand Dérangement* of 1755: the Flea Islanders are dispersed only to rear their heads once more in the place of their former overlords. In turn, the latter, in the course of a few generations, become authentic Flea Islanders. Thus the population of the mainland is entirely renewed: the "elite had given way to a tribe of hairy and bearded creatures, spitting thick and fast, and swearing by all the devils in hell. And in the midst of this developing nation stood the royal tent, topped by the horns of a moose, bearings of the first dynasty. . . . Slowly the world was changing, upsetting class structure, civilizing the barbarians, and barbarizing the urbane."

Maillet blends various episodes with local legends, such as that of the *bateau fantôme,* and places an emphasis on the sea that reflects the importance it has, and has had, in Acadian daily life. Flea Island is, amongst other things, a metaphor for revolt. The increasing irreverence and aggressiveness of the Flea Islanders towards the mainland is reminiscent of various Celtic fringes battling against colonial status. Certain Celtic affinities are apparent when, for example, she refers to characters by listing their forbears, the most memorable of these being Jos à Pit à Boy à Thomas Picoté Viens-que-je-t'arrache.

Maillet's writing, here as elsewhere, is immensely vigorous, with numerous pleasing and amusing turns of phrase. Her prevailing tone is objective and ironic, although perhaps less acerbic than usual. In *Don L'Orignal,* there is a great deal more narrative than one habitually associates with her fiction. Dialogue, whether in *chiac* or *le parler acadien,* or both, seems to be Maillet's preferred mode of narrative expression. Ronald Sutherland has suggested that, for the French, she is "a kind of Acadian Mark Twain" [see excerpt above]. Maillet herself has made a comparison with William Faulkner. I would suggest that, for the Anglophone, she is an exotic Francophone capable of blending a Voltairean irony with Ra-

belaisian language. It is this combination that is the most attractive aspect of *Don L'Orignal.* To corrupt an oft-quoted remark, "Le style, c'est la femme." Anyone who is familiar with her work and who has also heard her speak or lecture would probably concur. However, with rare exceptions in her prolific work to date, plot and character are subordinate to her overriding concern with the transcription of Acadian *oralité.* For all Maillet's stylistic and conversational panache, *Don L'Orignal* somehow fails to resonate: caricatures are not characters. (pp. 136-37)

Maillet's preoccupations have often been at odds with the increasingly militant stance of the younger generation of Acadian writers, particularly during the 1970s. Maillet would seem to be more at ease with the events of 1755 than those of Kouchibougouac—although that issue might well be construed as a contemporary version of the original Expulsion. While writers such as Gérald Leblanc and Guy Arsenault denounce today and look forward to tomorrow, Maillet delves deeper and deeper into the Acadian past, continually adding to her own collection of "petits carrés de couleurs" from the world that she sees as "une espèce d'immense mosaïque." Beyond the archivist and the transcriber of the oral tradition, there is the stylist, the philosopher, and, most essentially, the keeper of the light, the "gardienne de phare." (p. 138)

      Gillian Davies, in a review of "Don L'Orignal," in The Fiddlehead, *No. 124, Winter, 1980, pp. 135-38.*

MARCY KAHAN

[Maillet's novel *La Sagouine*] consists of 16 monologues delivered by La Sagouine, a 72-year-old Acadian washerwoman, "the daughter of a cod fisherman, a sailor's girl, and later the wife of a fisherman who took oysters and smelts." . . .

La Sagouine is an unsentimental document that details the annual rituals and unorthodox perspectives of Acadian culture with exuberance and humour. Maillet has skilfully introduced an entire community into this one-woman show, with its hardships, personal rivalries, and special legends. It is a community of have-nots who subsist on pancakes and beans, celebrate Christmas as a spectator sport, and patiently endure an enforced isolation from their more privileged neighbours in church and school. These people measure the worth of the passing year in terms of "a winter of mild weather, a summer of clams 'n a fall of elections."

Yet La Sagouine is not merely a stoical survivor. She is also a gifted raconteur, with the shrewd eye and profane tongue of a natural satirist. (p. 13)

This is a book that must be read aloud to be fully appreciated. At a time when economic exigencies are forcing theatres to rely on the resources of solitary actors, *La Sagouine* serves as a superb example of the imaginative scope and depth that may be encompassed in a one-woman show. (p. 14)

      Marcy Kahan, "Salt-Caked Irrepressible," in Books in Canada, *Vol. 9, No. 4, April, 1980, pp. 13-14.*

MARJORIE A. FITZPATRICK

Nearly two decades ago a gifted young author named Antonine Maillet published a small novel called *On a mange la dune* about childhood in an Acadian village. The work, obviously inspired by the author's own memories, was written in standard French and recounted in the third person by an omniscient narrator, but the psychological perspective was that of its eight-year-old heroine, Radi. This technical detail was an indication that the author was already preoccupied at that time with the search for an appropriate narrative voice. I mean by that term not merely the formal aspects of narration—language level, point of view, type of discourse—but also the broader areas of choice of subject matter and genre. From that promising early work to *Pelagie-la-Charrette* . . . , Antonine Maillet has explored a vast range of esthetic and substantive options in her mission to capture and transcribe the soul of Acadia. A closer look at three of her most successful works—*La Sagouine, Les Cordes-de-Bois,* and *Pelagie-la-Charrette*—will permit us to see some of the ways in which her search for the most effective narrative voice has evolved.

Maillet had at the outset two superior gifts: a remarkable talent for old-fashioned story telling, and the ability—shared with such immortal authors as Moliere—to create memorable figures with a few deft strokes of the pen. A remark here, a detail there, and Maillet's characters leap to life before us without any heavy-handed description. It is this skill that permitted Maillet to score her first major public triumph with *La Sagouine,* the dramatic monologue whose only character, the rough-hewn scrubwoman . . . , has already become a legendary figure in Canadian literature. The Sagouine does not narrate a single well-made story in the conventional sense, but spins out a series of discrete tales, each with its own internal cohesion, its own tone and characters, its own place in the texture of the scrubwoman's little world. We have no trouble visualizing the donnybrook she describes when the well-intentioned priest watches his parishioners' thin veneer of bourgeois respectability crack under jealousy and greed at the auction of church pews. We react with amusement at the naivete of the Sagouine and her fellow poor when they assure their neighbor, "poor Jos," a fitting burial by dressing his corpse in layers of their best socks and shirts and stripping their own shanties of curtains and paper bricks to provide him a watertight coffin. At the same time, the Sagouine's unself-conscious account of the incident raises the disturbing question of our own material notions of dignity. A similar alchemy occurs as we listen to the Sagouine fantasize about one Christmas when the Christ Child is born in a smelly, dirty, *real* stable—her own, perhaps, or one familiar to the other authentically poor of her village—instead of in the papiermache-and-lace world of the parish manger scene. This literal-minded vision, dismissed by the Sagouine herself as an idle and possibly sacrilegious reverie, is transmuted in the audience's mind into a meditation on the true meaning of the Nativity. All these tales and reminiscences are enhanced by the savor of the Sagouine's rich Acadian dialect, so in keeping with her humble station and yet so rich in its earthy, evocative imagery.

It is possible to read *La Sagouine* and fall under the scrubwoman's spell without having read any of Maillet's other works, but the generation and refinement of the character through some of her prior incarnations is instructive. One strain of Maillet's creative output has followed the fortunes of a clan first fully elaborated in the 1972 novel *Don l'Orignal,* a Rabelaisian fantasy that describes the mystical origins of the Sagouine's progenitors. Abandoning the contemporary setting and straightforward narrative style of *On a mange la dune* and another early semi-autobiographical novel called *Pointe-aux-Coques,* Maillet created in *Don*

l'Orignal an Acadian myth in which a mysterious island surges out of the sea one day off the New Brunswick coast. Under the alarmed eye of the lighthouse keeper the island begins to swarm, first with fleas (*puces*), and shortly thereafter with a race of flea-like creatures that prove, despite their appearance, to be human. These are the *Pucois,* headed by a horned-bonneted patriarch named Don l'Orignal, and from their midst emerges an entire cast of colorful characters who will, in various forms, inhabit many of Maillet's later works. Among these is the Sagouine, who eventually threatens the smug comfort of the respectable Land-people and their vigilant lighthouse keeper when she infiltrates their ranks as a hired cleaning-woman.

A year later the dichotomy established in *Don l'Orignal* between the Pucois and the Land-people reappeared in a different form in a three-act play called *Les Crasseux.* Many of the characters retained their names, but the modality was considerably changed. Now, in place of the almost medieval battle of mythical races seen in *Don l'Orignal,* the struggle pitted the Crasseux ("the grubby ones"), entrenched in the Lowland, against the Bourgeois Highlanders in a sort of contemporary class war. Stylized figures from the novel turn up as ordinary, if somewhat tribal, folks in the play. The clan patriarch, Don l'Orignal, has become a benevolent old godfather. The Don's knight-errant son Noume (from the Acadian pronunciation of "un Homme," the Man he longs to be) is now a soldier back from the war overseas. Pamphile, the tribal chronicler of the novel, has disappeared from the play, though versions of the character will appear in many later works in the form of a storyteller or genealogist. The Sagouine herself takes on more prominence in *Les Crasseux* and begins to display many of the characteristics she will have in the play that bears her name. Above all, the narrative mode has changed: the characters themselves tell their story in this partly-stylized, partly-naturalistic drama, leaving behind the formal third-person narrator of *Don l'Orignal.* While *Les Crasseux* contains many frankly funny scenes and ends with the triumph of the Lowlanders, who outwit the bureaucracy to seize some of the Highlanders' choicest land, it remains at heart a morality play. At the same time, the vaguely allegorical flavor of *Don l'Orignal* gives way in *Les Crasseux* to a much stronger sense of the here and now.

The evolution is completed in *La Sagouine,* in which the heroine gives no hint of being either the current bearer of some ancient Pucois escutcheon or a woman-at-the-barricades in a formal class war. The title character, full of earthy common sense and inherent human dignity, speaks for herself alone, spinning out her marvelous tales in the rich accents of her people and leaving it to the audience to extrapolate, if it must, to the larger implications of what she is saying. Under the circumstances the dramatic monologue is the ideal vehicle for the Sagouine's ruminations, and the author's use of it is flawed only at the infrequent moments when she places in the character's mouth moralistic speculations incompatible with what we know about the Sagouine's limited universe. Maillet will use this genre again in her 1976 play *Gapi,* in which the scrubwoman's husband often mentioned in *La Sagouine* delivers a monologue of his own that constitutes the entire first act.

The dramatic form had not, however, become Maillet's exclusive narrative voice. As the Pucois/Crasseux/Sagouine line developed, she had also been experimenting with other modes that would allow her to get inside the skin of her humble characters, transmit their colloquial speech, and share their perspectives, while retaining the detachment necessary to silhouette them against a broader background. In her 1977 novel *Les Cordes-de-Bois* the author uses what has proved to be her most successful technique for satisfying the two narrative needs concurrently: she appears as a first-person narrator, but the story is recounted to her in the voices of two secondary narrators who are more closely tied than she to the times, the events, and above all the people of the novel. Acadia thus speaks to us at a variety of levels at once. The author/narrator remains quiet most of the time, sitting spellbound with the reader at the knees of the centenarian Ozite and the cynical, occasionally fanciful Pierre a Tom as they recount their world. At appropriate moments, however, she acts as our surrogate, asking leading questions, challenging inconsistencies, and setting the secondary narrators off on their chains of reminiscence. Paradoxically, this use of narrators-once-removed seems to draw the reader most intimately into the Brueghelian world of the *Cordes-de-Bois.*

And what a world it is! The established dichotomies are all there—bourgeois vs. poor, highland vs. lowland, land vs. sea, conventional vs. marginal—but these elements are mixed into one grand broth in which Maillet's two greatest strengths, caricature and story telling, are the major ingredients. The tribal characteristics of the Pucois/Crasseux here come to life in the form of the rollicking, devil-may-care Mercenaires, whose establishment of squatters' rights on the forested butte above town causes them to be known as the Cordes-de-Bois. The word "hillbilly" never had a more scornful ring. Their bourgeois adversaries, including such familiar Maillet figures as a barber, a merchant, a parish priest, and an influential prude, are the townsfolk, known collectively as "le Pont" from the bridge that is the village's principal feature. The Forge, allied by background with "le Pont" but recognized as not fully sharing the townsfolk's bourgeois rectitude, stands somewhat removed from both groups. This slight detachment gives some credibility to the tales of Pierre a Tom, a Forgeman, though his penchant for bending the truth when the mood suits him is established at the outset.

The novel's main conflict is played out between two formidable women who stand out as the respective champions of their people and their life styles: Ma-Tante-la-Veuve for le Pont and La Piroune for the Cordes-de-Bois. Prefigurations of both women had appeared in some of the earlier works already mentioned. La Piroune, like the Sagouine, is disdained by her "betters," shows grit and common sense, and is more concerned with the practical problem of day-to-day survival than with the niceties of convention. Ma-Tante-la-Veuve inherits the superficial religiosity of la Sainte, one of the Pucois, as well as the starchy bourgeois attitudes of the Mayoress and the prudish hat-designer, all of whom appeared in *Don l'Orignal* and *Les Crasseux.*

The creative line leading to Ma-Tante-la-Veuve and la Piroune is more direct, however, from Maillet's 1973 novel *Mariaagelas,* in which the characters align themselves, as they do in *Les Cordes-de-Bois,* along an axis defined by pietistic hypocrisy at one end and defiant outlawry at the other. The title character, Maria, daughter of Gelas, sets her life's pattern as a child when she blacks the eye of the local schoolmistress and stalks out, never to return. From there she proceeds through the customary stages of maturing until at last she settles into her adult vocation, bootlegging. Her archenemy is la Veuve a Calixte (Calixte's Widow), a sanctimonious prude like her descendant Ma-Tante-la-Veuve, whose allies are the local merchants and bureaucrats. There are traces here of the epic struggle of the Land-people to keep from being contaminated by the Pucois, but the accent is on the individual battle of wits between Maria and the Veuve a Calixte and on the local color of the Prohibition era.

Maillet introduces in *Mariaagelas* the secondary narrator, the device she will use to such effect in *Les Cordes-de-Bois.* However, the character that fills that role in *Mariaagelas*— Soldat Bidoche's elderly fortuneteller mother—is so unobtrusive and appears so infrequently that we often forget her existence. The technique will be much more fully developed in later works. Of greater significance, perhaps, is the framework within which the characters are presented. Maria the bootlegger and her colorful successor la Piroune of *Les Cordes-de-Bois* share two important traits not found in the Sagouine: both are outlaws, and both appear to triumph over the establishment. The live-and-let-live resignation of the Pucois scrubwoman is superseded by a much more militant Piroune, thrusting down her outrageously unconventional behavior like a gauntlet before the scandalized but impotent Ma-Tante-la-Veuve. This theme of a kind of aggressive outlawry that endears its practitioners to the reader is a growing one in Maillet—barely suggested in the early autobiographical works, full-blown in the more recent ones. One can almost sense in it the growing assurance and even militancy of Acadia itself, reacting at last to two centuries of bureaucratic indifference and injustice.

There is nothing solemn about *Les Cordes-de-Bois,* however. On the contrary, the predominant tone is the earthy ribaldry known as *l'humour gaulois,* in which laughter is generated and the pomposities of convention punctured by scenes based on sexual horseplay, bodily functions, and the indulgence of man's corporal appetites in general. (pp. 4-8)

Many of the elements, both substantive and formal, that contributed to the success of *Les Cordes-de-Bois* are also present in *Pelagie-la-Charrette,* Maillet's latest and to date most impressive work. To these, however, she has added other dimensions which give her a new narrative voice in this novel. First of all *Pelagie,* though identified as a novel, may be more accurately described as an epic. The premise is that an Acadian woman, Pelagie, widowed in the British sacking of Grand Pre in 1755 and driven into exile during the Great Deportation of the survivors, gathers together the remnants of her brood fifteen years later in Georgia, packs them all in a rickety cart (the *charrette* of the title), and starts heading back to her home, the land of her ancestors. What follows is the tale of that great northward trek—part odyssey, part pilgrimage— enlivened by the description of numerous escapades en route and the introduction of myriad other characters, mostly fellow deportees, who join the caravan along the way.

Maillet's use of secondary narrators, honed in *Mariaagelas* and *Les Cordes-de-Bois,* undergoes further elaboration in *Pelagie-la-Charrette.* The Prologue introduces us to Louis a Belonie, identified as the cousin of the first-person primary narrator. Louis, in turn, is said to have received the tale he is about to recount in the form of an oral tradition transmitted in an unbroken line harking all the way back to Belonie-le-Vieux (Old Belonie), who accompanied Pelagie herself during the Great Return. The primary narrator's stake in the tale is that she is Pelagie's latest direct descendant. Moreover, part of Louis a Belonie's tale has been supplied by an intermediate member of her line, Pelagie-la-Gribouille, located in the late nineteenth century. Each of these narrators speaks in his/her own voice, but often as filtered through one or more of the others. (p. 9)

Here as elsewhere the language is casually popular. The subject, however, is serious. Maillet, through her narrator, impresses upon the reader that the storyteller is no mere entertainer. He can also be the one great link between a people and its past, the more so on the individual level that is as much real history as the bloodless narratives of the formal history books. Thus the tale of Pelagie-la-Charrette takes on, as did Alex Haley's *Roots,* the character of a precious but fragile treasure to be safeguarded by its current possessor in trust for future generations. The important point is not whether the events recounted ever actually occurred exactly as described—in the case of this novel they assuredly did not—any more than it matters if Roland really sounded his horn to summon Charlemagne. What counts for the author, as for the reader, is that there really exists a "matter of Acadia," as surely as the "matter of Brittany" exists, and that this *geste* of humble folk is no less important on its own scale than the exploits of King Arthur.

The narrative form Maillet has adopted in *Pelagie* has a number of advantages. By using a storyteller, who by definition is a dramatic monologist, she is able to reproduce much of the tale in the savory language of the Acadians themselves. The writing abounds in the vowel shifts, metatheses, and other phonetic and dialectal transformations that Maillet had already popularized in the language of the Sagouine. We see the influence of French archaisms, maritime vocabulary, peasant illiteracy, local color—in short, all the factors that permit us to distinguish the language of Maillet's Acadians from the standard French of the academicians, or for that matter of middle-class Quebecois. These traits appear both in the widely used dialogue and in the narrative sections, some of which are in the type of discourse that the French call *indirect libre*. At the same time, the continuous telescoping of narrators into and out of each other through several generations and voices permits gradations of personality and language level that add great variety to the narrative style. The first-person narrator in particular—much more prominent here than in *Les Cordes-de-Bois*—is able to interject comments on the larger implications of the Pelagian odyssey in the language of an educated Francophone (even when she speaks colloquially) without disturbing the colorful swirl of speech of the other narrators in surrounding passages. Thus the author is able to present the entire range of dramatic voices without being shackled by the constraints of writing in the purely dramatic genre.

With all its everyday homeliness, the story of Pelagie-la-Charrette also has a mythical dimension not mined so fully since *Don l'Orignal*. Pelagie's cart, the pilgrims' mode of transportation back to the homeland, gradually becomes as well a symbol of the unquenchable spirit of Acadia, battered but still striving toward life and a homeland. Moreover, it has a ghostly counterpart, Belonie-le-Vieux's Death Cart, a "somber wagon, without portiers or lamps, drawn by six flaming black horses, a cart that had been roving the world since the beginning of time." But Pelagie would not be intimidated by the Charrette-de-la-Mort, which only Old Belonie had ever seen, nor would she abandon her old friend to its gloomy beckoning:

> The Cart of Death could go mire itself in the swamps of Georgia; she, Pelagie, would lead her

> people in the cart of Life. . . . Pelagie wouldn't have had the heart to leave behind the doyen of the deportees, even if he had to drag his phantom cart with him all the way to Grand'Pree [*sic*].

And drag it he does, such that the race between the two carts becomes, metaphorically, a contest between Life and Death for Acadia, between hope for a rebirth and resignation to an inevitable extinction. (pp. 9-10)

In addition to the myths of Acadia, the historical allusions to the Great Deportation, and Pelagie's personal adventure, Maillet treats us in [*Pelagie-la-Charrette*] to several aspects of the *petite histoire* of late eighteenth-century America, captured in stunning vignettes at each of the pilgrims' major stops. We share the rescue of an imprisoned Black slave in Charleston, the travelers' thrill at finding a thriving Acadian colony in Catholic Maryland, their clash with hostile Loyalists in Boston. A favorite refrain of the homeward-bound Acadians, "And *merde* to the king of England," finds an unexpectedly sympathetic response in Philadelphia, where Pelagie's cart rumbles through just as the bells are ringing there to signal the country's newly proclaimed independence. Each of these incidents provides an excuse for Maillet to exercise her talent for spinning picaresque tales, at the same time linking the adventures to enough real events and places to give them texture.

Pelagie-la-Charrette also contains the kind of character sketches made familiar by Maillet in her earlier works. Pelagie herself, of course, towers above all the others. She has the gritty tenacity of the Sagouine coupled with la Piroune's defiant disregard for convention and her rough-spoken generosity. Even when Pelagie finds, at the end of her heroic odyssey, that her beloved Grand Pre is nothing now but a haunted cemetery, she has the tough-minded common sense to recognize that there can be a new Acadia on the New Brunswick coast to which she has led her people. Earthy and practical, she nevertheless rises to the role of symbol of the indomitable *l'Acadie,* a people and a concept that transcend the confines of mere geography. Where Pelagie and her cart come to rest, there is Acadia.

Belonie-le-Vieux is a venerable patriarch in the mold of Don l'Orignal; Beausoleil is a doer-of-mighty-deeds like his predecessor Noume as well as an heir of the seagoing Sullivan. La Catoune, orphaned in the Great Deportation and scooped up by the motherly Pelagie, has all the ripe but innocent sexuality of la Bessoune. The only prominent type from earlier works not strongly represented here is the pietistic hypocrite like the Veuve a Calixte or Ma-Tante-la-Veuve, perhaps because Pelagie's enemies are so much more formidable—nothing less than despair and Death.

The humor in *Pelagie-la-Charrette* is likewise muted in comparison with that of *La Sagouine* and especially *Les Cordes-de-Bois.* The verbal comedy in Maillet's use of Acadian dialect and the *gaulois* ribaldry of an occasional epithet still sparkle, but the novel's subject does not lend itself to the carefree hilarity provoked by the antics of la Piroune. The laughter in *Pelagie* is of the subtler, deeper sort that comes from our recognition of truth at the root of caricature, and from our joy at witnessing the triumph of the human spirit over the cruelties of men and nature.

It is this transcendant human element in all her works, from the simplest to the most ambitious, that allows Maillet to continue exploring the nooks and crannies of the "matter of

Acadia" without ever boring the reader. Like Balzac in *La Comedie humaine* she focuses the spotlight first on one, then on another, of a cast of recurring characters who collectively give us the flavor of an entire culture. However, her artistic vision extends even beyond that culture. It is at once more universal and more personal as she explained to Jean Royer of *Le Devoir* in an interview she gave just after receiving the Prix Goncourt:

> At root, I'm not even interested in Acadia. I'm interested in the world, in life. Acadia is an example of it. Acadia is where the world appears to me. That's where I first had my feet [planted], in Acadia. It's from that point of view that I have my eye on the world. Thus, I give it the color of that corner. But Acadia is not the end of the earth.

Is it true, asks Royer, that she has said she does not wish to be considered a spokesman for Acadia?

> Yes. I don't even want to be a spokesman (*porte-parole*). I want to be speech (*parole*). I am one word of Acadia. But there is the whole language which remains aside, which remains to other writers, Acadian and Quebecois. I haven't told everything. I've told myself. They must tell themselves.

Maillet's narrative voice, then, is literally that: she herself is the word, and the language is Acadia, but an Acadia whose story is valid only because it is part of the larger whole of the total human adventure. Although she has already articulated that adventure in an impressive number of different tongues—dramatic monologue, full-length play, epic, autobiography, fantasy, satire, short story—she does not fear that the source will run dry, because it is as eternal and as variegated as life itself.

"It's as though one has painted a maple tree," she told her interviewer; "there remains the cypress!"

Just as Maillet has published many more works even than those mentioned in this article, there are also many aspects of her search for a narrative voice that remain to be explored. The great predominance and variety of female types in her works, just to mention one example, could be the subject of a fascinating study. Meanwhile there is every reason to suppose that the author herself will continue to search for the next cypress beyond the maple tree. (pp. 11-13)

> *Marjorie A. Fitzpatrick, "Antonine Maillet: The Search for a Narrative Voice," in* Journal of Popular Culture, *Vol. 15, No. 3, Winter, 1981, pp. 4-13.*

DONALD SMITH

With one exception (*Le bourgeois gentleman,* a social satire of a Montrealer who dreams of becoming an English Canadian), all [of Maillet's] works involve Acadian themes. The most predominant theme is that of the family storyteller. Various recurrent characters have a unique gift. They are amateur genealogists or "défricheteux de parenté" ("family land-clearers"). For such "conteux" and "radoteux" [or storytellers], childhood acquires a collective meaning. Personal childhood turns into national childhood as one traces one's history back to the common ancestor from Touraine or Poitou, the birthplaces of the first Acadians.

History is yet another fascinating theme. Antonine Maillet treats history in such a way that traditional heroes are re-placed by new ones. She takes great pleasure in replacing some of the main figures of Québec history, who in fact dominated history books used in New Brunswick, by Acadian personalities such as Poutrincourt, founder of Port-Royal. History thus becomes a literary device of decolonization and demythification. Perhaps the most striking example is the attack on Evangeline as the symbolic heroine of Acadia. Longfellow's character represents passivity and austerity, while the real Evangelines of New Brunswick, such as Antonine Maillet's aunt or "Evangeline the second" in *Evangeline Deusse,* are strong, joyous, and positive-thinking women.

Antonine Maillet has done for Acadia precisely what Jacques Ferron accomplished in Québec. She has transcribed, reconstructed, and transformed history and legends. Ferron often refers to folklore from the Gaspé and the Beauce. He too is a master of demythification. In his writings, the Catholic soldier and renowned Indian fighter, Dollard des Ormeaux, is replaced by the Patriot and humanist doctor, Jean-Olivier Chénier. Antonine Maillet readily admits that Ferron is the author with whom she is the most at ease, to whom she feels the closest. (pp. 157-58)

The folklore of ancestral Acadia (fiddles, mouthorgans, Jew's harps, a unique way of humming a tune called "turlatage") comes alive in Antonine Maillet's works. The rich legends of Acadia (the cart of death—"la charrette de la mort"; Captain Beausoleil-Broussard and his ship; the devil and his numerous manifestations—the Northern Lights, werewolves, giant turtles, fireflies) are ingeniously integrated into her writings.

Acadia's most prolific author is what one might call a "literary mapmaker." She has mapped out in stunning detail, in realistic and poetic beauty, the landscapes of New Brunswick, centring her creative eyes on the immediate area surrounding the Bays of Bouctouche and Cocagne. Those who have read her works will never forget the dunes, the small natural harbours (the "barachois") and the long white beaches of Acadia. In the land of the dikes, of smelt cabins, oyster barrels ("pontchines d'huitres"), crooked rail-fences and piles of corded wood, in the primitive and ancient land that proudly hides the remains of Viking explorers, Antonine Maillet remains faithful to the oral tradition from which she evolved. The storytellers, troubadours and "chroniqueurs" descended from Rabelais and his spirited Gargantua are living in Acadia and very much alive. Antonine Maillet has given them new and unique forms, and in so doing, has risen to the highest reaches of literary achievement. The themes and symbols of her works entertain while at the same time forcing one to reflect on a common ideological concern: the struggle of the underprivileged. In this sense, the Acadians represent all subjugated groups.

The admirer of French writing in Canada cannot help but be struck by the newness of the symbolism used by Antonine Maillet. Her figurative world evolved from different influences than those of Quebec writers. The ocean is the dominant symbol, not the land nor the forest. In her very first novel, Antonine Maillet tells us that since the first crossing of the Atlantic by Poutrincourt and his settlers in 1604 (Madame Maillet likes to remind us that Acadia is older than Quebec by four years!), history has continually "put water in the veins of Acadians.". . . The Sagouine claims that her sunken blue eyes come from staring at the ocean, that watching out for fish in shallow water gave her high cheek-bones and close-set eyebrows, that sea salt is the cause of her hoarse voice. In an interview, Antonine Maillet further noted that the ocean and Acadia are both feminine symbols:

> Acadia is feminine, just like the ocean. It is feminine by its symbolic temperament, by its inherent symbolic qualities. Some nations are feminine, others masculine. A tree is a masculine symbol, and the Québécois are much more a people of the forest than a people of the sea.

The "feminity" of Antonine Maillet's work is reinforced by the fact that her major characters are women. The majority of other Acadian writers also tend to give women the major role. It is interesting to note that in contrast men often play the dominant role in the imaginative minds of Québec writers.

Pélagie-la-Charrette superbly illustrates the cohesive and representative nature of the writing of Antonine Maillet. The historian in the novelist created a plot founded on historical fact: around 1780, between 140 and 150 Acadian families scattered throughout the Eastern Seaboard states, made their way back to their homeland only to discover that "la Nouvelle-Ecosse" had quickly become "la Nova-Scotia." Approximately half of the former exiles decided to remain in Nova Scotia and the rest settled in New Brunswick, which was then a land of trading posts inhabited primarily by Indians.

The plot of *Pélagie-la-Charrette* has a double focus: the return to Acadia of Pélagie, Bélonie, and their friends in 1780; the narration of Pélagie and Bélonie the third, who tell the story of their illustrious ancestors. The two perspectives intermingle and provide an appropriate mixture of live action and commentary. (pp. 158-59)

Pélagie LeBlanc was born in the village of Grand-Pré. Her last name is one of the most common Acadian names, and it was in Grand-Pré that Lawrence organized the Deportation. Pélagie's husband was in fact killed during the battle with the English. . . . Pélagie is a new Evangeline, a courageous, joyous and committed leader. She is a realistic and believable character, but she is also a legend, a storybook character, a woman who tells us that "le conte," that imagination and storytelling, are essential for the survival of her people. For what is an Acadian tale if it is not an expression of hope and a way of living that transcends the real world? Pélagie is an active woman fighting for dignity and survival. She is also a fairy-tale character, the lover of the legendary hero *capitain* Beausoleil-Broussard. Pélagie and Beausoleil love each other tenderly, but because of their commitment to their people, they are destined to be alone.

Antonine Maillet immortalizes Pélagie and Beausoleil. In the imagination of the reader, they will continue indefinitely to pick up the dispersed Acadians, by cart and by boat. And because we are in the realm of legend, they are in fact "picking up" the Acadians of today who live a passive "Evangeline" life and who have given up hope of survival. The centennial friend and *compagnon* of Pélagie, Bélonie, makes it quite clear that *Pélagie-la-Charrette* addresses itself to all men and women, to all nations involved in the struggle for happiness and recognition. . . . The underlying theme of *Pélagie* is justice for the "petits peuples" and the "petits gens." This is why "le nègre" becomes a brother for the Acadians, and this is why Pélagie's son proudly marries the Indian princess Ka-

tarina, or why Pélagie sympathizes with the Americans fighting for their independence.

But *Pélagie-la-Charrette* is not a "livre à thèse" nor a political tract. The ideology conveyed by its characters is expressed allegorically and symbolically. Antonine Maillet plays with the imagination of her readers. One is continually intrigued for example by the numerous meanings given to "la charrette." The author uses in her own way the myth of "la charrette de la mort" (the devil's cart of death). "La charrette" would normally evoke death, but in the context of *Pélagie-la-Charrette,* it does not mean that the Acadians are moving towards extinction. There is no doubt that Antonine Maillet's cart is the symbol of the Acadians, "un peuple en charrettes." And it does represent, at the very least, the pushing about of a people. Yet somehow, the cart is a sign of hope. It is not going around in circles. Slowly, surely, "la charrette" is moving ahead. . . . (pp. 159-60)

Pélagie-la-Charrette is an epic tale of rebirth, a tale in praise of water. The name Pélagie comes from the Greek word "pelagos" that means "high sea." There will be no shipwreck for Acadia. Not if "Pélagie LeBlanc dite La Charrette" has anything to do with it! The Acadian revival is at high tide. And on the mainland, the salmon are finally going up stream. . . . (pp. 160-61)

> *Donald Smith, "Maillet and the Prix Goncourt," in* Canadian Literature, *No. 88, Spring, 1981, pp. 157-61.*

HANS R. RUNTE

Those who expected Antonine Maillet to complete her epic cycle and to lift the veil of mystery and misunderstanding from the least-known period of Acadia's history [in *Cent Ans dans les bois*], will be disappointed. The "Hundred Years in the Woods" of the title do not bridge the silent gap of oblivion which separates the Goncourt-crowned Pélagie of the 1780's from the heroines of *Mariaagélas* or *La Sagouine* of the twentieth century; instead, they have been compressed into the chronicle of little more than one year, from the spring of 1880 to the first Acadian national convention in July 1881, so that Jules Boudreau's *Cochu et le soleil* (1979) remains the only detailed literary treatment of at least one period of that dark age, the second expulsion of the Acadians under Joseph Wallett DesBarres in the 1830's.

Beyond the frequent allusions to this and other events, *Cent Ans dans les bois* celebrates above all the culmination of a century spent in unspeakable and indescribable misery: unbroken and proud, the refugee descendants of the first Pélagie are starting to "come out of their hole," as Laval Goupil had already called the Acadian awakening in *Le Djibou* (1975).

Antonine Maillet is convinced that no historian, no novelist even, could satisfactorily explain the extraordinary Acadian renaissance which began in 1881. What led to the Memramcook convention is so deeply buried in the guts, soul and imagination of the people that it can only be recreated by a storyteller, a balladeer or truly medieval jongleur such as Jérôme-le-Menteux or Antonine Maillet. Being thus led down the folklore path, we find that the momentous national conventions grew out of regional Committees-To-Recover-The-LeBlanc-Treasure (see *L'Acadie pour quasiment rien,* 1973), and that Memramcook ended once and for all the epic struggle not between an Upper and Lower Village as in *Les*

Crasseux (1968) or *Les Cordes-de-bois* (1977), but between The Land and The Sea as represented by Marie-Babée Poirier of Le Fond-de-la-Baie in New Brunswick and her fiancé Pierre Bernard from Egmont Bay, P.E.I.

The penultimate treasure hunt of 1880 and the final discovery that the ancestral inheritance has in fact developed into the entire city of Philadelphia . . . make for masterful storytelling and suspenseful reading. So do the tortuous love affairs of the couple-to-be. But does Acadia need another epic tale? Is she really generically unfit for, among others, novelistic treatments? Surely there is in the hallowed or avant-garde narratology labs of the world a structural and stylistic model or catalyst for dealing with even the most complex and obstreperous collective psyche. This must be found and applied soon, or else Acadian prose writing will begin to stagnate in repetitiveness.

Besides the numerous instances of *déjà lu* (the matriarch, here called Pélagie-la-Gribouille Poirier, née Léger; genealogimania; the shipwrecked amputee stranger resembling Germaine Comeau's hero in *Le Retour de Jérôme*), there is a fair amount of novelty in this tale. There is some quoting from historical sources, some inclusion of folklore lyrics, some attempt at including Saint Mary's Bay and Chéticamp in the epic, some insightful allusion to the problematic transition of an oral society to a literate one. Antonine Maillet's greatest achievement is, however, her recreation of the archetypal bard in the persons of old lady Lamant and Jérôme. Nowhere have the material existence, the imaginative processes, the narrative techniques and the recitative strategies of storytellers been more acutely felt, understood and brought back to life. Lovers and scholars of "oral" literature, from professional epicists to the readers of John Steinbeck . . . will be delighted and enlightened.

Cent Ans dans les bois, volume 55 in Leméac's "Collection Roman Québécois," is neither a novel nor Québécois. It is an opulent fresco of a land in search of the novel, of Acadia in search of herself. (pp. 583-84)

Hans R. Runte, in a review of "Cent ans dans les bois," in The Dalhousie Review, *Vol. 61, No. 3, Autumn, 1981, pp. 583-84.*

JOHN RIPLEY

Set in an Acadian coastal village during the Prohibition era, the action [of *La Contrebandière*] features the picaresque efforts of twenty-five-year-old Maria à Gélas to prove to her bootlegger-grandfather that, although a female and the fag end of the line, she is a worthy heir to the family's outlaw traditions. . . . Maria joins Old Gélas as an active partner in his rumrunning operation. Forever on the brink of arrest by Ferdinand, the dashing young Customs and Fisheries officer, she ferries illicit French booze ashore from a schooner anchored in international waters, ingeniously caches it, and arranges for its eventual transshipment to the United States. Indefatigably nipping at her heels is Calixte's Widow, the village scandalmonger and Ferdinand's self-appointed tipster. Whether the precious jugs are buried under the feet of a tethered bull, sunk full fathom five in lobster pots, or enshrined in a covent chapel, the Widow relentlessly noses them out and rallies the Law. Her pains are largely vitiated, however, by Maria's quick wits: Ferdinand, deftly distracted by lurid emergencies, consistently arrives either too late or at the

wrong place to exercise his function. In the course of frequent encounters on land and sea, Maria and Ferdinand, without giving up a jot of their vocational antagonism, discover a mutual respect which at play's end promises to ripen into love.

Mariaagélas is by no means the richest-textured of Maillet's novels; and the dramatic [stage] version [*La Contrebandière*] can ill afford the deletion of the darker strands in the prose source. Particularly regrettable is the metamorphosis of Ferdinand, the elderly customs official murdered for betraying his class, into a youthful romantic daredevil. Nor was it well-advised to advance Sarah Bidoche, the community fortune-teller, from her relative obscurity in the novel to an unjustified theatrical prominence. Now a participant in the action, now an omniscient chorus, she and her wicked pack of cards are virtually a stage fixture: yet, despite her ubiquity, her exertions prove all but irrelevant to the dramatic outcome. At best she is a picturesque appendage, and at worst, a clog to the play's momentum. . . . Most of the novel's other key characters retain a fair measure of integrity, if not always their pristine subtlety. Maria struts with winsome insouciance; the Widow pries and prays with her wonted vigour; and Bidoche, the village idiot, maunders on valiantly in a world where ignorance turns out to be something less than bliss.

La Contrebandière, if hardly the *tour de force* of *La Sagouine,* is nevertheless a fine nostalgic romp graced with memorable folk characters, and colourful, if somewhat episodic action. Opportunities for picturesque visual effects are legion, particularly the night sequence during a fog at sea when Ferdinand searches Maria's boat with a lantern. And Maillet's scrupulous re-creation of the Acadian idiom has one fairly chewing dulse and sniffing tar throughout. Underpinned by a tuneful down-East score, *La Contrebandière* might make an agreeable musical—just the thing, perhaps, to tickle the palates of Charlottetown Festival audiences. (pp. 138-39)

John Ripley, "In Mellow Mood," in Canadian Literature, *No. 95, Winter, 1982, pp. 137-40.*

EVA-MARIE KROLLER

[Maillet's subject in *Cent Ans dans les bois*] is the collective memory of an entire people; her style . . . draws on a rich oral tradition; her point of view, avoiding the solipsism of a single outlook, combines layers of narrative voices and imaginary dialogues in an attempt at evoking the complexity of Acadian history. . . . While *Pélagie* described the 1780 odyssey of a group of Acadians making their way back from the South of the United States to Acadia, after "le Grand Dérangement" (i.e., the Expulsion of 1755), *Cent Ans dans les bois* speaks of the emergence, about 1880, of the Acadians who had been hiding in the woods of New Brunswick for over a hundred years. This emergence climaxes in the first Acadian convention, in 1881, at Memramcook where a college had been founded earlier in the century, helping to revive and preserve the Acadian cultural heritage. In illustrating the Acadian renaissance during the nineteenth century, *Cent Ans dans les bois* joins two plots, held together by the overriding concern of keeping history alive in a people's stories. One narrative strand of the novel deals with the search for a treasure. As soon as the inhabitants of Fond-de-la-Baie have emerged from their hiding-places in the woods, they begin to look for a mysterious chest but find only a barrel of liquor on the beach. So far their search has been guided by bits of information, orally handed down from their ancestors. Their luck improves when a Frenchman arrives, a "survenant" (and a positive version of the arrogant "Français de la France" in such novels as Carrier's *Le Deux-Millième Etage*) from the sea, who teaches the Acadians to write, thus giving them the means to add, to the wealth of their imagination, the power of precisely recorded knowledge and communication. The Frenchman helps his Acadian students to find their treasure although it turns out to be something of a joke à la Don Quixote: it appears, from a document found, that the city of Philadelphia belongs to the Acadians; as a result, *they* ought to be the masters of the English.

The theme of communication through the written word also dominates the subplot of the novel, a love story, much of which centres upon a letter written by Pélagie-la-Gribouille to her daughter's suitor. Pélagie-la-Gribouille, a descendant of Pélagie-la-Charrette, tries to prevent marriage between her daughter Babée and Pierre Bernard because he is a sailor; as such he represents an element of incertitude and unreliability that Pélagie—whose name, ironically, suggests the sea—rejects instinctively: the trauma of the "Great Disruption" has taught Acadians the value of belonging to a place, of sinking roots into the ground. In previous novels, Maillet had conceived of the sea as a life-giving element; in *Cent Ans dans les bois,* her opposition of sea and earth is an important variation on the theme of exile versus attachment to the soil that pervades so much of French-Canadian writing (in her 1976 play *Evangéline Deusse,* Maillet explored the Acadians' exile in comparison to that of other Canadians, e.g., the Jews). The influence of women in establishing a tradition by providing a sense of continuance has been significant concern all through Maillet's oeuvre, the most popular one perhaps being La Sagouine, the charwoman. Acadian history, as Maillet has explained in an interview with *Books in Canada,* is that of a matriarchy, "Acadie is female, its virtues are all on the side of patience, a sense of time, some kind of interiority, more *viscérale* than *cérébrale.*"

When Pierre renounces the sea in order to be able to marry Babée, he finds the treasure, as it were, that the people of Fond-de-la-Baie had been looking for in vain: a settled home. La Gribouille's efforts to keep her family together are reflected, on a larger scale, in the Acadian convention in Memramcook. . . . In describing the gathering, Antonine Maillet practises the precision of the recorded word that her characters learn to appreciate as the novel proceeds: the descriptions are footnoted with references to authentic sources. Yet Maillet does not relinquish the humour created by the fictive characters' supposed comments on the sermons preached and speeches made at the convention. In fact, their reactions—questions, puzzlement, laughter—serve as a corrective to recorded history. . . . The dynamic development of dialogue, its need for expansion, correction, clarification, its use of persuasive strategies, determine much of Antonine Maillet's narrative style. Although her characters are illiterate peasants as the novel opens, the tales of Jérôme le Menteur are shaped by an instinctive knowledge of rhetoric and an anticipation of his audience's response whom he expects to be as active in the weaving of his stories as he is himself. . . . Controlling the many voices of *Cent Ans dans les bois,* although unobtrusively so, is that of a sophisticated implied author. . . . (pp. 173-74)

It is perhaps the irony and self-consciousness of this controlling voice, more than their universal symbolism and theme, that saves Antonine Maillet's novels (specifically *Pélagie-la-*

Charrette and *Cent Ans dans les bois*) from the reproach of parochialism. Indeed, Maillet has time and again insisted that she is *not* a regionalist writer, that her literary Acadia is the world *in nuce.* Maillet's protestations point toward a catch-22 typical of the post-colonial writer's situation, perhaps only to be overcome by official (i.e., political) recognition on a large scale such as the Prix Goncourt. (p. 174)

Eva-Marie Kroller, "In Remembrance," in Canadian Literature, *No. 95, Winter, 1982, pp. 172-74.*

JOHN LENNOX

As one of our oldest voices, the narrator of Maillet's [*Pélagie: The Return to a Homeland*] speaks to us with the accents and vocabulary of Acadia. . . .

I call the voice of the novel "ours" because it tells a story in which the reader is invited to participate as a listener caught up in the wholeness, pathos, and concluding affirmation of this saga of the exiles' journey home. This is a well-used motif in the fiction of French Canada. Anne Hébert employs it, as do Marie-Claire Blais and Roch Carrier, and for all three the motif is linked with the past. *Pélagie* is also rooted in the past, but its telling reminds us constantly of the present and future as hopeful rather than intimidating. Longfellow's Evangeline, long a symbol for Acadia (and until recently the name of Moncton's French-language newspaper), has been replaced by Pélagie who, like Dilsey or Miss Jane Pittman, is a gallant, tough, canny woman conceived from within her culture and forever an expression of it. (p. 157)

Much of the liveliness of *Pélagie* springs from its intervals of tale-telling which are deepened by legend, fantasy, exaggeration, and the palpable life of a story learned and told truly by heart. The narrative, in fact, includes two stories—past and present—which depict the Acadians of the eighteenth and twentieth centuries. Between the time of the story and the time of the telling a continuity is established which encompasses the history of Acadia and of North America, a tireless matriarchal line, a succession of story-tellers, and an authorial perspective that yokes medieval allegory, Rabelaisian comedy and contemporary fascination with the ironies of narrative voice. The telling of this story with its emphasis on the fabulous, on exaggeration, and on the quest motif that gives it shape reminds me of Robert Kroetsch's *The Studhorse Man* (1969). In addition, a story posing as history, told at first or second or third hand, is as interesting in its depiction of the narrator as in its content. But where Demeter is the animator of irony in his own story, Maillet's storyteller is the unselfconscious inheritor and celebrator of all the disparities of experience and memory through which the Acadians have won their way to their goal.

At the centre of *Pélagie* is the undeniable vitality of myth-making by which a culture comes to life as it passes through unknown territory, grows in stature, and defines place not only as a region, although that is undeniably important, but also as a sensibility which is big enough to include both region and reader. Antonine Maillet has declared her admiration for the work of William Faulkner and has said that she hopes to do for her people what Faulkner did for his. Faulkner's characters, however, are marked by a world-weariness and fatalism which spring from a region whose defeat plumbs the depths of despair. Maillet's characters, ostensibly defeated, set out to reclaim their place and are consequently the inhabitants, inheritors, and creators of a dynamic culture which is being born and reborn as it moves northward in the story and as the story is being told. (pp. 157-58)

In her treatment of the constructive force of the ancestral past, Antonine Maillet diverges sharply from the work of writers like Anne Hébert, Marie-Claire Blais, and Roch Carrier, all of whom freight the past with guilt, repression, and neuroses which darken the present. Maillet makes us aware of how her Acadian present rests on the shoulders rather than under the thumb of the past. For me, all these factors make *Pélagie* a work which combines the genius of place with an equally striking genius of technique and sympathy. (p. 159)

> John Lennox, *"Survivors from History,"* in Essays on Canadian Writing, *No. 28, Spring, 1984, pp. 156-59.*

JANE MOSS

From Manitoba to Acadia, Francophone dramatists have been looking to the past to find subjects for new plays. In the case of Antonine Maillet, the sources of inspiration are both literary and folkloric as she transports Rabelais' cast of characters to her native Acadia [in *Les Drôlatiques, horrifiques et épouvantables aventures de Panurge, ami de Pantagruel, d'aprés Rabelais*]. (p. 98)

The success of *Panurge* proves that in the hands of a masterful writer, old material can come alive. Madame Maillet, whose 1971 doctoral thesis at Université Laval was entitled *Rabelais et les traditions populaires en Acadie,* faithfully and wittily brings Rabelais' mock epic to the stage. The play begins with a brief account of the miraculous birth and prodigious education of Pantagruel followed by his victory in the Picrocholine War. After this burlesque prologue, Maillet introduces her main subject, Panurge's futile search for answers to the questions, "Should I marry or not?" and "If I marry, will I be cuckolded and beaten by my wife?" Rejecting the ludicrous advice of sibyls, astrologers and professional pedants, Panurge and company voyage to the New World (la Nouvelle France) in quest of "la Dive Bouteille" in the play's second part. The ship, captained by Jacques Cartier, takes them to Acadia, where the old French language and five centuries of folk stories have remained pure and eternally youthful, preserved by the cold salt air. It is in this earthly paradise that they encounter the woman who will be Panurge's faithful loving wife—none other than "La Sagouine"!

Panurge truly captures the spirit of *Gargantua* and *Pantagruel,* amusing us with its genealogy of giants (which includes Louis Cyr and Jos Monferrand), its pastiche of the "Chansons de geste," its satire of medieval superstitions and scholasticism. There are literary jokes and allusions to contemporary Canada, mixed in with broad farce, anticlerical caricatures, and scatalogical humour. Maillet's command of language dazzles us with imitations of Rabelaisian narrative, numerous songs, pedantic discourses, puns, comic insults, and all kinds of verbal comedy. The fast pace never lets up as Pantagruel, Panurge, and Frère Jean encounter a host of hilarious characters during their "drôlatiques, horrifiques et épouvantables aventures." Rabelais himself would have enjoyed this wonderful adaptation of his work. (pp. 98-9)

> Jane Moss, *"Old Themes,"* in Canadian Literature, *No. 102, Autumn, 1984, pp. 98-101.*

SAMUEL R. SCHULMAN

For those of us who are admirers of Madame Maillet's works, and we are legion, *Panurge* is a delightful work, filled with Maillet's deft touches. . . .

Yet for all its plays on words, drolleries and *trouvailles, Panurge* somehow falls short of the mark. Perhaps we have come to expect, and receive, so much better from Antonine Maillet. Not every work by a famous author can be a masterpiece. However, as in a previous play of Maillet, *Le Bourgeois gentleman,* . . . we are given to feelings of *déjà lu.*

By all means, one should read *Panurge,* if only to appreciate the charm, wit, grace, and scholarship of Antonine Maillet, whose love of learning and humanity, like that of Rabelais himself, radiates throughout the play.

> Samuel R. Schulman, *in a review of "Les Drôlatiques, Horrifiques et Épouvantables Aventures de Panurge, ami de Pantagruel, d'aprés Rabelais," in* The French Review, *Vol. 58, No. 6, May, 1985, p. 919.*

MICHÈLE LACOMBE

According to Maillet, as the first literary work to follow her Ph.D. dissertation on Rabelais and Acadian popular traditions, *La Sagouine* was also the first of her texts to arise from a direct involvement with life rather than literature, and she has identified the two women upon whom the character was based. More significantly, it was her first piece of writing to employ Acadian speech in a substantial fashion—earlier plays and novels had won prizes without gaining much popular or critical acclaim, and tended to avoid "irregular" French. According to Viola Léger, the 1968 production of Michel Tremblay's *Les Belles-soeurs,* by "blowing up the iceberg," made a Montreal public somewhat more ready to accept *La Sagouine.* However, this does not address the fact that acceptance in Montreal and Paris preceded acceptance in Moncton—a phenomenon for which we can blame demographics, colonialism, and the rather irrespectful radicalism and realism of Maillet's Acadian reprobates in the eyes of the local theatre-going elite.

If Acadian audiences were all too familiar with the Acadian subculture, Montreal and Paris audiences did not initially recognize the reality with which they were confronted. When I first saw the 1974 production in a suburban Montreal high school, the local audience began by laughing at la Sagouine's accent and gradually grew to laugh with her at the butt of her satire, namely their own middle-class assumptions; still, for many Québécois, the cultural and linguistic barrier is only partly broken down by repeated exposure to Acadian theatre. Although Parisian audiences are reported to have less difficulty understanding Acadian French than their Québécois counterparts, their sense of history and geography remains somewhat vague—in 1976 *Paris Match* described Montreal as an Acadian city, while *Le Monde,* usually more informed, identified Acadia as "an impoverished corner of Quebec."

The critics, on the other hand, are often equally obtuse regardless of their national origin: an overwhelming number of them reacted to *La Sagouine, Les Crasseux, La Veuve Enragée,* and other plays featuring the same family of characters with rather naive romantic accolades of Maillet's peasants as *"pittoresque,"* recognizing the affinities with Brueghel but not with Bakhtin. The structuralist critics who responded to the plays' more subversive contents, for their part, tended to discuss class at the expense of race and gender—perhaps because the Acadian context and language remained elusive, but more likely because Maillet's prominence as a French-speaking dramatist from outside Quebec left them in a rather awkward position as the articulators and defenders of Quebec's economic, cultural, and linguistic autonomy. Maillet, meanwhile, having made her message as clear as possible within the genre of theatre, has imperturbably, humorously, but not quietly, proceeded to move from the regional or particular to the universal in the genre of fiction, culminating in her acceptance of the Prix Goncourt for *Pélagie-la-Charrette* (1979), the first "Canadian" novel to win that prestigious prize. (pp. 59-61)

La Sagouine by no means represents an isolated instance of theatrical legerdemain prior to Maillet's more recent rediscovery of fiction. She has stated, however, that she writes for the theatre when she is short of breath—as respite between novels—and adds that if she derives her novelist's instinct from her philosophical, storytelling father, she inherits her theatrical impulse from her mother's side of the family, who dearly loved a get-together. . . . In fact, this subterfuge discloses a more serious and productive division within her artistry, signalled by her tendency to "transpose" her best novels for the theatre; the desire to foreground the language in two distinct modes of reading, the theatrical and the narrative. (p. 61)

Evangéline Deusse is atypical in Maillet's theatre of the mid-70s not by virtue of its excellence but due to its unusually simple form and complex tone. *Les Crasseux, Mariaagélas* and *La Veuve Enragée* are more intimately connected to each other and to *La Sagouine* by virtue of a shared setting and, to a lesser extent, shared characters and historical epochs. In this they remind us of Tremblay's plays, but with significant departures, while *Gapi et Sullivan* approaches the tone of *Evangéline* within an Acadian setting and features the techniques of la Sagouine's monologues applied to her rather Job-like husband. *Les Crasseux,* an early work which was not staged until 1974, uses a cast of thousands to dramatize the opposition implicit in *La Sagouine's* one-woman show; led by Don L'Orignal, the "gens d'en bas" [or poor people] go on the warpath against "les gens d'en haut" [or wealthy class], after the latter (the mayor's wife, the doctor, the barber, the merchant, etc.) have caught their fleas at a public festival, cast them out of the festivities, denied them the odd jobs which kept them alive, and refused them molasses on credit. This key play, like *La Sagouine* breaks the silence of centuries and gives a voice to an extended family of inner exiles, a ghetto-within-a-ghetto which is in real terms smaller than the ostensive symbols of Acadian nationhood and in mythic terms larger than life and the region within which that life has been contained. Maillet sees herself as situated at the meeting point of an oral tradition and its embodiment in writing; the theatre serves as the public vehicle for transporting that marginal moment from the periphery to the center of the culture and the medium. It is no accident that the definitive confrontation between "les Crasseux" and their enemies emerges, within the play, from the local equivalent of a carnival with its roots in the folk tradition but from which the "folk" have been excluded.

Mariaagélas, on the other hand, uses rum-running as a metaphor for the "true" Acadian's relationship to his land and his neighbours; here the enemy is "la Veuve" [or widow] who embodies the false values of religiosity, spiritual aridity, and a generally nosy tendency to play God in an attempt to surpass "les gens d'en haut" in virtue and value. She resurfaces and is exorcised four years later in *La Veuve Enragée;* this time she is defeated by three generations of female squatters who combine rum-running with prostitution and witchcraft, and who are ultimately aided by one of their better customers, an Irish sailor named Tom Thumb. While Maria begins by playing off the widow against the fisherfolk who illegally sell lobster off-season, she weathers the end of prohibition and rescues her "patrimoine" by accepting the advances of the local RCMP constable, who turns out to be "one of the folk" from another Acadian district, and who is learning fast. La Veuve Enragée fights a losing battle because no-one owns the woodlot, although she sells wood to passing schooners, and despite the fact that a clan of mercenaries now known as "les Cordes de Bois" settled there a century earlier. The "butte," trapped between beach and forest, is a kind of borderland and home where Tom Thumb can marry both the prostitute Piroune and her single twin daughter la Bessoune, and where the sisters Zélica and Patience can argue with each other but offer the wisdom of hags to the younger generations and even the widow herself. As one critic has noted, although the widow resists, she nonetheless speaks the language of the Mercenaries. (pp. 62-3)

[Maillet's] greatest contribution [in *Mariaagélas* and *La Veuve Enragée*] was to have perfected techniques for converting prose narrative to drama. With *Mariaagélas,* she expanded the character of Sara Bidoche, the fortune-teller whose cards punctuate moments of dramatic tension and shifts in action. With *La Veuve Enragée,* she employed a new tactic, reducing the cast of 40 characters to six crucial figures whose dialogue did not need much adjustment to compensate for the narrator's absence. Folk songs ("Michael Row the Boat Ashore" and "All Around the Circle," in the French version "La Fripe") introduced the extremely witty repartee of paired characters, and even the actors' difficulties with the dialect could not destroy the play's humour and exuberance. All the evidence points to this production as Maillet's most significant theatrical achievement since *La Sagouine,* and like the early monologues, it cannot be dismissed as "picturesque," the one adjective which resoundingly fails to describe Maillet's language, methods, and preoccupations as an Acadian playwright.

Antonine Maillet has stated that starting from the group of characters collectively known as les Crasseux, and I would include la Sagouine in this group, one can construct a sphere inside which several hundred people circulate. She adds that characters in *Mariaagélas* are not "les Crasseux," nor their enemies, but are situated somewhere between "les gens d'en haut" and those "d'en bas." It seems to me that the figures in *La Veuve Enragée* are the most tangible and yet the hardest to recognize of the Acadian everymen and -women who people Maillet's world, and that students of Canadian theatre at its best owe it to themselves not to dismiss her work with a passing glance at a much-acclaimed but still invisible Sagouine. (pp. 63-4)

Michèle Lacombe, "Breaking the Silence of Centuries," in Canadian Theatre Review, *No. 46, Spring, 1986, pp. 58-64.*

RENATE USMIANI

The Maillet opus, both novels and plays, has been hailed as a veritable epic of the Acadian nation, a social and historical panorama in which both past and present come vibrantly alive. . . . This assertion of a national identity is achieved in a large part through language. The author's scholarly and artistic interest in oral language has led her to the revolutionary decision to transpose the actual speech of her people into a literary and dramatic idiom which retains the full flavor of its popular origin.

With the novels, Maillet evokes the image of Acadian life on an epic scale; in the plays, she narrows the focus to life in the fishing village and to a small number of characters. Among her characters, there is a recurring figure, the author's own view of the archetypal Acadian woman, a reply to the romanticised character created by Longfellow, and traditionally associated with the Acadian people. In the dramatic opus of Antonine Maillet, the spotlight is on la Sagouine, her most successful character, who appears both by herself in *La Sagouine* and in play after play, under her own name or embodied in a similar character. With *Evangéline Deusse,* the demythification is made explicit: here, the author puts on stage her own anti-Evangeline, a corrected version of the traditional archetype. But of course this Evangeline is just another embodiment of la Sagouine, somewhat older and transplanted to Montreal, but exhibiting all the same character traits; perhaps it would be more correct to say that the various versions of la Sagouine are none other than embodiments of Evangeline. By any name, Maillet's archetype of Acadian womanhood can be followed chronologically from play to play. In *Les Crasseux* (1968), she creates the background for the character, and introduces her to the audience. She is now 45 years old. From the beginning, she appears with the insignia of her profession, mop and bucket. Her function in the play is to serve as the spy for the poor in their war against the rich within the village: a role she plays with brio. With the performance of *La Sagouine* (1972), she holds centre stage: aged 72, she reveals to the audience her character, and the character of her people, through a series of 16 monologues filled with reminiscences and meditations. *Evangéline Deusse* (1975) transposes the character from an Acadian fishing village to the city of Montreal, thus echoing the exile theme on which Longfellow's *Evangeline* is based; the author also parallels both love story and tragic ending, as her 80-year-old Evangéline's lover dies in the Acadian woman's arms. By adhering to the central features of the original story, Maillet brings out more strongly the contrast between the romantic figure of Longfellow and her own conception of an archetypal Evangeline. *Gapi* (1976) complements *La Sagouine,* as her husband, Gapi, takes center stage. In *La Veuve Enragée* (1977), Maillet returns to a wider view of the village as a whole, but again the focus is on a group of female figures who clearly continue in the tradition of la Sagouine: la Piroune, la Bessoune, Pātience, and Zélica.

When *La Sagouine* was first performed . . . , the impact of the play closely paralleled the impact of the premiere performance of Michel Tremblay's *Les Belles-soeurs,* in 1968. Public reactions to the two plays were the same: at home, the shock of recognition coupled with the pride of a newly-gained sense of identity; for outsiders, the discovery of a language and a people very different from the romanticised views created by works like *Maria Chapdelaine* or Longfellow's *Evangeline;* in both cases, the realization of a deeply human quality

and therefore universal appeal of the characters presented. It is interesting to note that in both cases, the authors chose female characters exclusively in their pioneering venture of bringing before the public a hitherto ignored group, in a hitherto forbidden idiom. The female here represents both the ultimate in oppression, and the spirit of subversion. Another noteworthy parallel is the fact that the two playwrights who first spoke up for their people, in the language of their people, should be a woman, in the case of Maillet, and a male author whose affinities and sensibilities are fully female, as in the case of Tremblay. In one respect, however, Maillet's approach differs radically from that of Tremblay and other Québécois pioneers in the theatre. While in Quebec it was felt that in order to establish an identity it was first necessary to cut off all ties with the (colonial) past, Maillet consciously related past and present, forever aware of the French heritage of her people. Starting with research for a doctoral thesis on *Rabelais and the popular traditions in Acadia,* she has gone on to incorporate into her work linguistic and other material dating to the sixteenth century and beyond. . . . The vocabulary of la Sagouine is sufficiently different from modern French to necessitate a glossary of some 250 expressions at the end of the French edition of the play. Grammar and syntax also go back to old French, the most striking feature being her habitual combination of a singular pronoun with the plural form of the verb ("je pouvons").

As the embodiment of her people, la Sagouine/Evangéline Deusse stands in marked contrast to the image of Acadian womanhood created by Longfellow. I would like to point out briefly four major areas of contrast, or counter-myth, before proceeding to a more specific examination of the character within the plays.

Longfellow looks upon the Acadian past from a distance which is historical, geographical, and personal; he is thus able to idealize and romanticise. Maillet, on the other hand, writes straight from her own personal experience and that of her people; the traumatic events of deportation and return have remained an integral part of the Acadian mindset to this day. (pp. 65-6)

[In *Evangeline*], Longfellow opted for a highly artificial form—the classical epic. In fact, he modelled his work on Goethe's epic *Hermann und Dorothea,* a metrical experiment, imposing a Greek form, the hexameter, on the German language. Like Goethe, Longfellow was successful in his adaptation of the hexameter, and produced a poem which exhibits all the beauty and harmony of a classical work. Maillet, however, rejects such an imitative approach on principle. . . . Thus the total linguistic realism of her texts, their earthiness, picturesque and vivid quality.

Longfellow's basic description of the character applies also to Maillet's Evangeline figures: "Lowly and meek in spirit, and patiently suffering all things." However, there are essential differences. The American Evangeline is a victim; Maillet's characters, long-suffering though they may be, are essentially survivors. For Longfellow's romantic image of the eternal virgin, Maillet has substituted vigorous motherhood: 12 children in the case of la Sagouine, 11 (all male) for Evangéline Deusse. Instead of quiet resignation to the inevitable, the new Evangeline exhibits an energetic, no-nonsense assertiveness. (pp. 66-7)

Although romantic love figures in both versions of the Evangeline story, it has been de-emphasized by Maillet, from the end-all and be-all of life to one of those tragedies a woman must cope with reasonably, and get on with her life. Both la Sagouine and Evangéline Deusse settle down to ordinary, no-nonsense marriages. A similar demythification process applies to the area of religious faith. Longfellow's Evangeline finds great comfort in religion. In the midst of tragedy, she "remembered the tale she had heard of the justice of Heaven. Soothed was her troubled soul, and she peacefully slumbered till morning." She also relies on her parish priest as a loyal and trusty friend. La Sagouine, on the other hand, suffers from severe religious doubts, is filled with fear of the afterlife, and finds communication with members of the clergy impossible to achieve.

The treatment of the theme of exile differs essentially in Maillet's version from Longfellow's original interpretation. Where the American poet emphasizes the loss of the homeland and the wanderings of Evangeline, the more positive Acadian writer stresses the return, a matter of enormous pride to her people. . . . Maillet also further expands the theme of exile: la Sagouine, after the return, still feels like a stranger in her own country, surrounded by an oppressive anglophone majority; the characters in *Evangéline Deusse,* all expatriates, underline the universality of this situation in the contemporary world.

Let us now look more specifically at the plays to see how Maillet creates her counter-myth. *Les Crasseux* centers around the class conflict in the village between the rich, the "gens d'en haut," and the poor, the "gens d'en bas." "La traque" serves as a clearly defined dividing line between the two halves of the village. When the conflict escalates into full-fledged war, la Sagouine takes the initiative. . . . Using her charwoman's paraphernalia to gain access to the enemy's stronghold, she serves as the official spy for the "gens d'en bas." She also actively serves the cause by a house-to-house campaign in the upper village to lure the rich into a trap prepared for them by the poor. Her personal philosophy is based on no-nonsense acceptance of the facts of life; if her daughter earns a living as a *fille de joie,* that is only normal in a society where the two main sources of survival come from the sea: fish, and sailors with money in their pockets.

With the 16 monologues of *La Sagouine,* Maillet's anti-Evangeline is fully developed. Her name already evokes most unromantic associations of ideas: a *sagouin* is a small South American monkey, known for its particular propensity towards uncleanliness. In this play, la Sagouine is a 72-year-old fisherman's wife, once a *fille de joie* herself, now reduced to plying her mop and bucket in other people's houses. Throughout the work, she gives evidence of enormous strength, wisdom, and an almost infinite capacity to endure as she philosophizes and reminisces while contemplating her own reflection in a bucket of spillwater. Divided thematically, six of the sixteen monologues deal with topics related to religion; seven present scenes of everyday life; two recount specific episodes of village life; and one deals with the problem of Acadian identity and nationality.

The character of la Sagouine comes through as that of a strong-willed woman who bears her miserable lot with dignity and resignation. In this she comes close to the romantic Evangeline as she accepts social differences as one of the absolute and unchangeable facts of life. But she differs essentially from the earlier character in her tenacious will to survive, whatever the cost—which usually means the abandoning of an ideal. . . . To make ends meet is usually problematic, and

demands any number of compromises. Even to fulfil basic religious obligation can be difficult: la Sagouine would like to attend Sunday mass, but cannot, because she does not own suitable clothes. This detail evokes Longfellow's contrasting description of Evangeline on her way to church, "Down the street she passed, with her chaplet of beads and her missal wearing her Norman cap, and her kirtle of blue, and her earrings." La Sagouine faces the pathos of poverty quite matter-of-factly, but becomes agitated whenever her thoughts turn to religion. Her exposure to the teaching of the Church, far from providing solace and comfort, has only succeeded in making her anxiety-ridden and confused. Because of her acute native intelligence, she finds herself doubting the validity of some of the teachings; the doubts in turn produce guilt, and fear of hellfire. She is unable to come to terms with the obvious inconsistencies in the moral rulings of bishops in different dioceses. Confession time poses more problems: how to explain that breaking certain rules (such as making home brew, or having sex in a room shared with your children) cannot be avoided if you are very poor.

All of the monologues dealing with religion offer an eloquent comment on the oppressive influence of the Catholic Church in the Acadian villages, a total reversal of the idyllic relationship between priest and parishioners described in the Longfellow poem. Perhaps the most interesting of all the monologues, however, is "Le Recensement." The census-taker appears in the village, asks any number of embarrassing questions, and eventually has everyone fully baffled when it comes to the entry on "citizenship and nationality." Here Maillet takes the opportunity to underline the alienation of her people, as they search for an answer to the vexing problem, and find themselves forced to reject one suggestion after another: they cannot see themselves as "Americans," or "Canadians," or "French Canadians" (this would mean "Québécois"). The term "Acadian" on the other hand, is not acceptable to the census-taker. The experience leads her to a long and moving tirade on the difficulties of being homeless within your own country.

With *Evangéline Deusse,* Maillet has made her mythopoeic intentions fully clear: the play is dedicated *"au peuple Acadien,"* a gift offering of a new and more realistic *"patronne du pays."* It is a play about exile and old age; it is also a hymn to life. At the age of 80, Evangeline has retained all of her vigour and energy. The reader is made to feel that here we indeed have a mythical figure, eternally young. Like Longfellow's poem, the play is also a love story; but what binds Maillet's octogenarian lovers in their exile are the bonds of a common linguistic background. (pp. 67-70)

Although Maillet's next play, *Gapi,* focuses on two men, Gapi the sedentary lighthouse keeper, and Sullivan, sailor and eternal wanderer, we do get some glimpses which serve to round out the character of la Sagouine. Gapi, now widowed, reminisces about life with her, which was not always easy, while his friend Sullivan confesses his lifelong love for that remarkable woman.

With *La Veuve Enragée,* Maillet returns to female archetypes; this time, three generations of women represent the tradition embodied in la Sagouine. All of the *mercenaires* have been *filles à matelot* in their day. The two older sisters, Zélica and Patience, now in their sixties, have retained the full verve of youth like Evangéline Deusse; one is a bootlegger, the other "un peu sorcière" [or magician]. Their household is completed by a niece, la Piroune, fortyish, and her daughter, la Bessoune, a mother-daughter configuration which corresponds to the Sagouine-Cruche pair of *Les Crasseux. La Veuve Enragée* returns to the village scene and the battle between two factions, as the prudish and self-righteous but rich and powerful widow tries to put a stop to the *mercenaire* women's loose living and devil-may-care attitudes. This play is written in a lighter tone than the preceding ones, with a fairy-tale quality. Even so, it once again restates Maillet's consistent image of energetic Acadian womanhood. Most recently [in *Panurge*], the author has created another link between present and past, providing for her Sagouine a final apotheosis. Adapting a selection of scenes from Rabelais for the stage, she adds her own version of Panurge's quest: instead of ending his journey at the oracle of the *Dive Bouteille* with its ambiguous message, she has him land in New France, there to find the wife of his dreams.

With her creation of a series of anti-Evangelines, Maillet has thus successfully countered the romanticised view of Acadia and Acadians based on Longfellow; she has also produced a new archetype of her people. But the impact of her work goes far beyond Acadia. . . . (pp. 70-1)

> Renate Usmiani, *"Recycling an Archetype: the Anti-Evangelines," in* Canadian Theatre Review, *No. 46, Spring, 1986, pp. 65-71.*

PAUL STUEWE

The rum-running Rabelaisians of *The Devil Is Loose!* are constantly stumbling over one another's poorly concealed caches of illegal spirits, and in much the same way reviewers don't have to scratch very hard to unearth the reasons for Antonine Maillet's popularity. Her stories of life in Acadie, those French-speaking enclaves in the Maritimes that have preserved their distinctive cultural inheritance, combine the delightful simplicity of folk tales with the intriguing complexity of advanced literary techniques. Unlike the objectively depressing human specimens who infest so much contemporary literature, the inhabitants of Maillet's world are too busy experiencing and enjoying life to devote much time to wallowing in obsessional neuroses or bemoaning the dissolution of society; and if their actions don't always turn out for the best, their "nothing ventured, nothing gained" approach ensures that boredom will never be a problem for either her characters or her readers.

The Devil Is Loose! is set in the early 1930s, a period when bootlegging had replaced fishing as the major occupation of many coastal Maritime communities. The place is the Acadian villages of southeastern New Brunswick, where two groups of locals, one headed by a well-established grafter and the other led by a feisty young woman named Crache-à-Pic, are vying with each other and various criminal and police organizations for control of this extremely lucrative racket. Tantalized by the lure of easy money, the inhabitants of the area react by concocting a variety of devilish schemes that soon loosen the bonds of traditional social mores. (pp. 16-17)

But it would be misleading to imply that *The Devil Is Loose!* is merely an Acadian version of the revenuers-vs.-bootleggers conflicts familiar to fans of Burt Reynolds films. Overlaying this basic dramatic situation is a colourful tapestry of myth, folklore, and tall-tale telling that supplies a rich cultural background for what is essentially a simple and straightforward story. Maillet uses this material to flesh out her por-

traits of individual characters as well as to explain the social conventions of the community, and much of the appeal of *The Devil Is Loose!* comes from our awareness that we are exploring unfamiliar territory with a knowledgeable and perceptive guide.

Maillet unfolds her narrative in a chatty, discursive style that reflects the oral traditions associated with folk literature. She is writing about a culture in which everything is related to everything else: there is nothing so new or extraordinary that it will fail to evoke a "That reminds me . . ." from those who remember older days and ways, and it is through this process that a simple tale of group rivalries becomes a complex web of stories recaptured and retold. Those who prefer a more linear approach to story-telling may well find *The Devil Is Loose!* excessively long-winded; but anyone who appreciates a good yarn regardless of its twists and turnings shouldn't find it difficult to accept the narrative's penchant for genial meandering.

In terms of its author's intentions and interests, *The Devil Is Loose!* is an almost completely successful novel. If Maillet's literary palette sometimes seems limited to the primary colours, with a noticeable absence of nuance in its delineation of particular characters, this reflects her desire to portray a collective brand of consciousness rather than a collection of individual psyches. Similarly, her avoidance of anything resembling social realism, initially somewhat disconcerting in a Depression-era story set in a by no means affluent fishing community, is a perfectly apt expression of her conviction that it is the subjective aspects of history and culture that constitute a people's essential heritage. . . . *The Devil Is Loose!* comes to us as a marvellously imaginative, cleverly structured, and highly entertaining novel that should appeal to just about every literary taste, while also whetting our appetites for the 20 or so as yet untranslated titles from this enviably talented author. (p. 17)

> Paul Stuewe, *"High Spirits," in* Books in Canada, *Vol. 15, No. 6, August-September, 1986, pp. 16-17.*

BARBARA GODARD

For most Canadians, the 1930s are the lost years, the Dirty '30s—the Depression. But in one corner of the country, on the Atlantic seaboard, that decade was a high point, a time for vast dreams, enormous fortunes and heroic adventure on the high seas. A visitor, striking up conversation with an old-timer from the Acadian coast or the islands of St. Pierre and Miquelon, would find him or herself transported to cloud castles as a vision of future wealth, a forecast of unbelievable riches unfolds. This fortune will come thanks to the common market; bilingual Atlantic seafarers will act as middlemen for tax-free goods ferried from their warehouses to the welcoming markets of the United States. But try to get the old-timer to talk about disintegrating fish sheds along the shore shrouded in eternal fog, or ask a pointed question about the source of some local millionaire's fortune, and you will meet with silence.

Hearsay, rumour, fragment—these are the narratives of the past, and the stuff of Antonine Maillet's fiction. Piecing together snippets of tales, Maillet's pen has pierced the fog and unveiled the rollicking adventures of the rum-running days. Acadian fishermen, disguised as nuns, or with the help of parish priests on a visit to their families *aux états,* transferred rich Burgundies and tangy Bordeaux from St. Pierre into the greedy hands of Al Capone to slake the enormous drought of Prohibition-thirsty Americans. Maillet first set down these bootleggers' tales in the 1973 collection *Mariaagélas.* Recently translated into English as *Mariaagélas: Maria, Daughter of Gélas,* it keeps company with *The Devil is Loose!,* [a] . . . translation of the 1984 *Crache-à-Pic.* (p. 36)

While lacking the literary parody and complex meditations on narrative that made the earlier translated works exemplary postmodern specular fictions, Maillet's standard fare is nonetheless rich in humour, incident, pathos and compassion. Bouctouche, N.B., with its dune, its cliff, its lighthouse (where Maillet writes), its sharp divisions between rich and poor, and its epic internecine battles between clans, has been put on the literary map by Maillet through her tales of its inhabitants. Maillet considers herself to be the last raconteur in an oral tradition and the pioneer of a written one; in short, a gossip and a liar. She draws on local oral narrative modes of rumour mongering and giant's tales—the legacy of the folk tradition that produced Rabelais' belly laugh and outrageous hyperbole—more widely known as liar's tales. Let the reader beware her ironic narrative perspectives!

Giants grow big down east, into, like the heroine of Susan Swan's novel, the "biggest modern women in the world." Maillet has given birth to more than her share of gigantic sisters to Anna Swan. Maria, the daughter of Gélas, and Crache-à-Pic, larger-than-life "sheroes" of their respective tales, are more than worthy sisters to the Sagouine, the Mayoress, and the epic Pélagie. Gélas's and Crache-à-Pic's stories are the same: rebels both, they challenge the hegemonic male bootleggers of their communities, Big Vital and his sidekick, Casse-Cou Collette, and Dieudonné and his sidekick, Black Willy. Through their greater intelligence and daring, the women, fearlessly setting to sea in fierce storms, take on government and clergy, organized crime and the rich, to liberate themselves and the poor. Robin Hoods in skirts, with heroic forebears. Maria is the niece of the intrepid Claraagélas, who revolted against working conditions in the canning factories to become a labour activist. As the tale ends, Clara leaves her home for a second exile, accompanied by Maria, "that unique and feared descendant of the first Gélases of the village, . . . who would for a year keep everyone on the run between the portage, the sea, and the King's highway." While Maria's revolt is politically motivated, Crache-à-Pic's challenge is an accident of character (her name means spit-in-the-eye), a modern marvel or black magic, depending on your perspective in this matter of a sorcerer's ghost. The leader of the Galoshes—as the ragged crew of epileptic brother, aunt, and aging twin admirers of Crache-à-Pic's mother is called, since they can't afford boots—is the descendant of a legendary sorcerer of the same name, an immigrant from France who came to a sacrilegious end buried under the apple tree in the garden. The devil is let loose again in the girl who, from under Dieudonné's nose, steals away wine that was destined for the American president in his Bay of Fundy summer home and for that other president, Al Capone, in his mid-western capital. The plot is presented in a thumbnail sketch on the first page: "Right there off the Atlantic Coast of Canada on that first day of August 1930, her arms wrapped round the mainmast of her schooner, braving the waves splashing into her face, a pretty wench named Crache-à-Pic stood laughing and shouting headlong into the wind: 'I got him!' " Crache-à-Pic got more than Dieudonné, however. She also gets the new po-

liceman, Quicksilver, who has vowed to stamp out smuggling. Their passionate love affair increases the plot complications. The line between ally and enemy continually shifts, introducing pathos when Quicksilver is killed by Dieudonné.

In both books, the fearless girls' challenges lead to complicated chases and counterchases as the liquor is moved around the villages. It is spied by the busybody widow Calixte, lost to the lobster fishermen who haul it in with their traps, hidden in the convent barn, concealed in a hearse, and protected by a ghost fabricated by the girls to play on the credulity of their neighbours and create diversions for their nocturnal displacements. The incidents in the two novels are very similar, though they are given different narrative development. For example, in *Mariaagélas,* the policeman who is killed is the inept local agent Ferdinand who was replaced by a more efficient snooper; in *Crache-à-Pic,* the intrepid replacement, Quicksilver, is downed by the bullet. With her customary gusto, Maillet piles incident on incident at a whirlwind pace. Bootleggers outsmart bootleggers, villagers and police, until the firing of a gun brings the dizzying pace to a halt. A concluding scene in the courtroom provides new comic opportunities. The characters subvert courtroom protocol to ironic ends, for the judge in *Crache-à-Pic* does not understand French. Although both tales end with a comic upswing, with new life coming forth to regenerate the community— literally, in the case of Ferdinand, whose young widow gives birth—the novels end differently. A chance remark about her ability to write implicates Maria in the death of the policeman: she leaves town. But Crache-à-Pic takes Dieudonné aside and orders him to leave town. Her control over the village is complete.

Neither book is strong on the psychological development of character, focusing instead on action and language, which befits the tradition of the tale. However, in the decade that elapsed between the publication of the two books, a change occurred. To highlight emotional responses to action, Maillet pays increased attention to the love and loss of Crache-à-Pic. The writing of *Pélagie-la-Charrette* has left its mark on Maillet's subsequent fictions.

If incredible energy is one characteristic of Maillet's prose, another is the originality of her language. Her writing has stimulated the growth of an Acadian literature. Modelling herself on the oral storytellers, Maillet has written her texts in Acadian dialect. Indeed, much of the novelty of her work derives from the reader's surprise at discovering what has hitherto been an oral language written down on the page. It was a shock to find a glossary appended to *La Sagouine* to help decipher the text. Over the years, Maillet's use of dialect has diminished. She has evolved a highly personal style that draws heavily on dialect and archaisms, unusual and colourful turns of phrase, and lengthy sentences whose breathless rhythm is reminiscent of oral modes. (pp. 36-7)

Either one of these books provides an excellent introduction to Maillet's fiction and a "good read" for those who savour Rabelaisian fare. (p. 38)

Barbara Godard, "Of Rum and Black Magic," in The Canadian Forum, *Vol. LXVI, No. 762, October, 1986, pp. 36-8.*

Steven Millhauser

1943-

American novelist and short story writer.

Millhauser's fiction is respected for its unsentimental and perceptive exploration of the problems and pleasures of youth. Critics particularly admire his keen attention to physical and psychological details and his ability to interpret the world from a child's perspective. Viewing adolescence as a time of heightened imagination, Millhauser laments the suppression of creativity and idealism that results when restrictions and demands are placed upon impressionable young people. In addition to concerns of childhood, Millhauser's works often parody specific literary genres and abound in allusions to works of fiction. Although sometimes faulted for excessive self-consciousness and emotionally hollow characters, Millhauser is lauded for stylistic virtuosity and his capacity to evoke the undercurrents of ordinary life.

Millhauser earned critical acclaim with his first novel, *Edwin Mullhouse: The Life and Death of an American Writer, 1943-1954, by Jeffrey Cartwright* (1972). In this work, which won France's Prix Medicis Etranger for best novel by a foreign author, Millhauser satirizes literary biographies that overemphasize trivialities of a writer's life. On one level a thorough study of the language and mores of middle-class childhood, *Edwin Mullhouse* also condemns the limitations that adults impose on the creativity of children. Critics have compared the tone and characterizations of this book to those of Vladimir Nabokov's novel *Pale Fire* and J. D. Salinger's short pieces about the Glass family. Millhauser's second novel, *Portrait of a Romantic* (1977), addresses the disturbing and destructive forces of adolescence. In this story, twenty-nine-year-old Arthur Grumm relates in exaggerated prose the troubles he and his friends experienced during their early teenage years. Bored with their lives, they seek diversion in decadent literature and suicidal thoughts. Torn between pragmatic and romantic tendencies, Arthur must consider the painful consequences of submitting to either temperament.

Millhauser's next novel, *From the Realm of Morpheus* (1986), details the adventures of Carl Hausman, who by chance discovers a cave that leads to an underworld presided over by Morpheus, the Greek god of sleep and dreams. Morpheus escorts Carl through his domain, regaling him with fantastical tales about loneliness, inadequacy, frustration, and failed romance. As in his previous novels, Millhauser weaves into the text numerous literary allusions, parodies, and homages to other authors. While some critics maintained that this work lacks structure and ends inconclusively, most praised its array of stylistic forms. Michael Dirda observed: "At his best [Millhauser] can write as in our dreams we'd all like to—with the preciseness of Nabokov, the richness of Thomas Browne, the music of Keats." The short story collection *In the Penny Arcade* (1986) examines themes similar to those of Millhauser's novels, including the function of the artist in society, the superiority of fantasy over reality, and the notion that children and artists possess special imaginative powers. Robert Dunn commented: "Though his art can be hampered by too rigid conceits and occasional bad choices of subject,

[Millhauser] is a true original when he draws us into his precise, luminous awareness, when he makes our world turn amazing."

(See also *CLC*, Vol. 21; *Contemporary Authors*, Vols. 110, 111; and *Dictionary of Literary Biography*, Vol. 2.)

DENNIS W. PETRIE

[*Edwin Mullhouse: The Life and Death of an American Writer, 1943-1954, by Jeffrey Cartwright*] is a beautifully-written piece of fiction, a satire of modern American literary biography which is "balanced on the fine thin line of loving parody"—and ultimately it contains a very serious critical commentary about the genre which it parodies. For, as Aldous Huxley, the master satirist, states it in *Point Counter Point*, "parodies . . . are the most penetrating of criticisms." As a perfectly articulated chronicle of the joys and pains of childhood, *Edwin Mullhouse* is splendid. As a mock biography, the novel reveals to us the problems of literary biography in action. Concomitantly, its author, in the voice of the putative biographer, provides a running series of explanations about

and apologies for his art. . . . What one of the novel's reviewers writes regarding its evocation of childhood applies
equally to its parody: *Edwin Mullhouse* "offers a substantial
amount of truth disguised as elegant artifice."

Northrop Frye, in the "Mythos of Winter" section of his
Anatomy of Criticism, says that "two things . . . are essential
to satire; one is wit or humor founded on fantasy or a sense
of the grotesque or absurd, the other is an object of attack."
The object of Steven Millhauser's clever attack, literary biography, is made absurd because of a matter of degree, first of
all. Here we have the method of the writer of the mock-heroic
parody, who treats large, traditionally important subjects and
techniques in an ironical, trivially serious manner. Millhauser's novel is ostensibly the biography of an American
writer, Edwin Mullhouse, who produced his masterpiece, a
novel entitled *Cartoons,* at the age of ten and then died mysteriously at exactly the age of eleven. The fictitious biographer,
Jeffrey Cartwright, writing at the age of twelve, was a neighbor, classmate, and close friend of Edwin—and apparently
the only person who recognized Edwin's rare genius while he
was still alive. In the manner of Swift, Millhauser offers a pedantic "Introductory Note" to "this new edition of a major
American biography." Its author, we are led to believe, is one
Walter Logan White, a scholar who is eminently qualified for
his job because he was a sixth-grade classmate of the biographer (although White never really knew him) while Jeffrey
was writing his book.

As most reviewers have noted, there is a definite resemblance
between *Edwin Mullhouse* and Nabokov's *Pale Fire* (1962);
the characters of both White and Jeffrey have affinities with
Nabokov's Charles Kinbote, and verbal wit abounds in both
books. Certainly subtle, multidirectional satire pervades all
aspects of *Edwin Mullhouse,* but it is the explicit statements
about biography and the role of the biographer from Jeffrey's
pen that are usually the most forceful. For example, in this
passage, Jeffrey is comparing the respective tasks of the novelist and the biographer:

> God pity the poor novelist. Standing on his omni-
> scient cliff, with painful ingenuity he must contrive
> to drop bits of important information into the swift
> current of his allpowerful plot, where they are
> swept along like so many popsicle sticks, turning
> and turning. He dare not delay for one second, not
> even for one-tenth of a second, for then the busy
> and impatient reader will yawn and lay aside the
> book and pick up the nearest newspaper, with all
> those slender columns that remind you of nothing
> so much as the sides of cereal boxes. The modest
> biographer, fortunately, is under no such obliga-
> tion. Calmly and methodically, in one fell swoop,
> in a way impossible for the harried novelist who is
> always trying to do a hundred things at once, he
> can simply say what he has to say, ticking off each
> item with his right hand on the successively raised
> fingers of his left.

First, "modest" is hardly the word for this particular biographer, considering what he writes in his "Preface to the First
Edition." There Jeffrey expresses his disdain for "those smug
adult prefaces" and announces, "Let me say at once that in
this instance there are none to thank besides myself." Beyond
this, the word "simply" is the key to the whole statement. It
is used in much the same way that Virginia Woolf uses
"plod"—to tip the reader off about the absurdity of the argument. The most serious thrust of Millhauser's satiric fiction
is, in fact, ridicule of modern literary biography for supposing

that it is "under no such obligation" to attend to the formal
aspects of any well-told, interesting story.

Let us look now at the particular light which *Edwin Mullhouse* sheds on the problems of design in literary biography.
(pp. 32-4)

In *Edwin Mullhouse,* Jeffrey Cartwright's attitude toward his
subject is one of clear-eyed admiration, for he is well aware
of Edwin's shortcomings. Sounding like a pint-sized version
of William Faulkner, Edwin Mullhouse says, "The only thing
that doesn't interest me is facts." Then he adds, "Jot that
down, Jeffrey," and the pint-sized modern Boswell obeys, for
he intends to miss nothing regarding his subject—nothing,
from the variegated gurgles of the newborn baby (which are
philologically analyzed, for this book also constitutes a theory of language) to the most minute details about the mysterious demise of the novelist. Indeed, Jeffrey, although he was
only a few months old himself, was present on the very day
on which Edwin was born; and he writes, "Luckily for literary history my senses were immensely alive to the importance
of that occasion, that bright August morning." Since Jeffrey
has the opportunity to observe and analyze his subject at such
close range, the biographer's responsibility for self-analysis is
most acute. Hence, the biography also becomes an autobiography of the biographer, who nevertheless makes it perfectly
clear that "it is with no desire of thrusting myself forward,
but only of presenting the pertinent details . . . , that I must
intrude my personal history into these pages."

Because the biographer attempts to be both objective observer and participant, Jeffrey's book is an attempt to make a
magnificent fusion of art and life. At one point, Jeffrey suggests that Edwin is an artist who is in need of a "watcher";
this companion-biographer fulfills that need. But, unfortunately, there is no one to watch Jeffrey—except, of course, the
reader, who learns quickly enough that he also is needed for
"watching." For besides expanding his scope to include
lengthy descriptions of his own dreams, the biographer here
displays his own neuroses in action. For example, Jeffrey is
obsessively neat; one of his purposes is to put a meticulous
order in all things with which he comes in contact. This fact
is most evident in the shape and ornamentation of his book.
Thus, when Millhauser divides the book into sections ("The
Early Years," "The Middle Years," and "The Late Years"),
he is simultaneously satirizing one of the conventions of
scholarly literary biography and also giving Jeffrey's personality a perfect means of expression. Within his narration, Jeffrey further reveals his obsessions. At one point, for instance,
in describing Edwin's room, Jeffrey writes: "To the right of
the window stood the large gray bookcase. . . . To the left
of the window, in an imbalance so unendurable that I would
have invented a second gray bookcase if I had not known one
was coming, stood a blackboard on an easel. . . ." But with
Jeffrey, obsession is, after all, a virtue; he pauses early in his
book for a special reminder to his reader:

> I wonder if I have sufficiently emphasized a major
> theme of this biography. I refer to Edwin's natural-
> ness, his distinct lack of what is usually called
> genius. . . . The important thing to remember is
> that everyone resembles Edwin; his gift was simply
> the stubbornness of his fancy, his unwillingness to
> give anything up. . . . For what is genius, I ask
> you, but the capacity to be obsessed? Every normal
> child has that capacity; we have all been geniuses,
> you and I; but sooner or later it is beaten out of us,
> the glory faded, and by the age of seven most of us

are nothing but wretched little adults. So that genius, more accurately, is the retention of the capacity to be obsessed.

Embedded in this statement about his subject, then, is not only the biographer's bold-faced bid for the reader's good graces but also his announcement that he, certainly, has retained his genius.

Nevertheless, Jeffrey is solicitous toward his subject, and he tries always to be objective in considering his materials. After Edwin has finished the awesome task of writing his novel, Jeffrey takes one hundred hours to peck out the manuscript on a typewriter so as to "read a copy free from the distracting personality of a particular handwriting." Of one of Edwin's girl friends, the inspiration for the aborted Rose Dorn sequence of poems, Jeffrey writes, "I never liked Rose Dorn; but I do not wish to temper the strict truthfulness of this biography by painting her one stroke blacker than she was." And the biographer never ceases his crucial questioning. Such scrupulousness (one of Jeffrey's favorite words) should be repaid—and thus Jeffrey is amazed when Edwin exclaims, near the end of his life, "Phew! A biographer is a devil."

Steven Millhauser plays devilish tricks on the reader—and on Jeffrey—throughout *Edwin Mullhouse.* One such trick occurs during a walk which Jeffrey takes with Edwin. Jeffrey seems to record a conception of the inexplicable human personality that resembles the 4 September 1927 entry in Virginia Woolf's diary; he is looking down on Edwin from a cliff:

> Suddenly as I watched I was filled with the sense of his remoteness, it was as if I did not know him at all and had never known him, it was as if he were as impenetrable to my knowledge as the hard tree shading me and pressing into me with its ridges of bark, it was as if, standing there with his back to me, he were as forever unseeable as a transparent negative, which when turned around does not show the other side but the same side reversed; and I wanted to run down to him and again spin him around and make sure he was there.

The irony, of course, comes when Jeffrey goes closer. He finds that he has not been looking at Edwin after all; it is actually another little boy. Likewise, the main plot device in Millhauser's novel is a trick. Besides being a mock biography, the book is also a mystery story of sorts.

Near the end, Edwin, in a playful-somber mood, plans his suicide with a pistol, at almost the exact minute of the eleventh anniversary of his birth. Edwin even composes a suicide note in which he relates, among other profundities, "P. S. Goodbye, life. I aspire to the condition of fiction" (Jeffrey obligingly contributes this sentence—i.e., the biographer believes that the creature in his biography should be presented through those narrative techniques which we most often term "fictional"). But at the last second, when Edwin hesitates with the gun, Jeffrey, who is in attendance, rushes out of control and, gripping the weapon, turns jocularly contemplated suicide into murder—or at least assisted suicide. Millhauser thus satirically extends the old biographical question, "How much should a biographer tell?" to suggest another one regarding the real "life-relationship" that is increasingly more often involved in modern literary biography: "How much should a biographer do?" (pp. 36-9)

Edwin Mullhouse's death was thus viewed as suicide—at least until Jeffrey made his book public. Walter Logan White notes that even while he writes his new preface, "the search for Jeffrey Cartwright continues. I, for one, hope they never find him." But contrary to what Jeffrey maintains, his own actions are hardly unpremeditated; rather, they are merely the carrying through of his purposes as a literary biographer.

When Jeffrey first tells Edwin that he is going to write his biography, the novelist virtually ignores him, saying, "Anyway, how can you write my biography? I'm not dead." Looking back on the remark, Jeffrey remembers: " 'You don't have to be dead,' I sneered, though as it turned out I was mistaken." Later, when Edwin finally acknowledges that his future biographer has helped him to see a pattern in his life, to see his life as a biography, "a design with a beginning, middle and end . . . I [Jeffrey] replied that strictly speaking his life could not be considered a design with beginning, middle and end until it had ended." The scene in which Jeffrey "perceived dimly that the design [of his biography] was marred somewhat by Edwin's indefinitely continued existence" has affinities, certainly, with the passage in Richard Ellmann's book of biographical essays, *Golden Codgers,* in which Joyce's biographer notes laconically that "it's always better to wait until the subject of your biography is dead, . . . since it reduces the possibility of authoritative refutation." Finally, Jeffrey writes, "At times, I confess, I found myself thinking of Edwin as recently deceased." And he ultimately goes so far as to refer to "the final month of Edwin's pre-posthumous life"! (pp. 39-40)

In *Edwin Mullhouse,* Jeffrey Cartwright relates that he has "sometimes wondered whether all the murderers and criminals in this evil world are nothing but tormented authors, writing their unwritable books in blood. I, for one, can testify that even a modest biographer may be driven to strange devices for the sake of his throbbing book." One of Jeffrey's most "throbbing" problems in his own book seems to concern how to treat *Cartoons* (and, of course, the early short stories and poems: "At least as early as the third grade [Edwin] had a distinct sense of having produced juvenilia"). The manner in which Jeffrey treats both Edwin's life and his work might best be described with Clifford's term "interwoven"; but at one point in the biography, Jeffrey does stop to examine the "major" novel in more detail.

First, he summarizes the novel ("for the sake of those unhappy readers who may not have read it . . . and in order to provide fuel, so to speak, for the fiery remarks that follow"). Next, he gives notice of his critical intentions: "Let others beat against the rich red brick of Edwin's art their heads. There are many things that I might say about his work, but I shall limit myself to a small number of major insights." Finally, he presents his critical theory of "scrupulous distortion" ("the reader . . . must under no circumstances forget one simple fact: *distortion implies that which is distorted*"). Having perpetrated this pedantic act of criticism, Jeffrey proceeds to connect its implications with the facts of Edwin's life and, more ambitiously, to "the false images that feed our American dreams."

If Jeffrey Cartwright's purpose is to fathom the "secret soul" of his subject, then he must delve deeply not only into Edwin's creative work, but also into Edwin's personality. Although Millhauser's precocious biographer intimates throughout his biography that he is more than capable of analyzing the psychology of his subject with considerable completeness, Jeffrey is very scrupulous in his avoidance of psychological jargon. For example, in his discussion of Edwin's unrequited love for Rose Dorn, Jeffrey just gives his readers the facts and explains them "simply" (as he might say). Perhaps Millhauser is satirizing the simplistic psychological assessments that literary biographers have been known to make of their subjects, but at the same time, he is permitting his biographer to practice psychological interpretation in accordance with a kind of moderation which has become respectable in the genre. (pp. 44-5)

Under the guise of satire, some notable ideas about form in biography are introduced in Steven Millhauser's novel. Jeffrey Cartwright, biographical theorist, worries out loud at various points in his biography about the problem of time. Early in the book, for example, he stops his narrative to declare that

> memory and chronology simply do not make good bedfellows. Indeed it sometimes seems to me that I should abandon the madness of chronology altogether and simply follow my whims. . . . And yet, after all, no. My task does not resemble the making of a jigsaw puzzle. . . . [L]et chronology be the meter of my biography, memory my rhythm: now matching so closely as to be barely distinguishable, now tugging against one another, now drifting so far apart that the reader begins to frown and tug at his chin, now coming together with a bang. Where was I?
>
> (pp. 51-2)

To paraphrase James Boswell, Jeffrey Cartwright in *Edwin Mullhouse* is "strongly impregnated with the Mullhousian aether." Yet the imagery which Jeffrey conjures up in trying to suggest certain aspects of his subject's psychology often creates an impression which is far from laudatory. Jeffrey writes, for example, "Like so many creative people, Edwin was not impressive as a thinker; his brain resembled a murky aquarium, occasionally illuminated by the flickers of a faulty electrical system." This simile (satirically reminiscent, perhaps, of some of Boswell's images for Dr. Johnson's vast mind) is employed by Jeffrey for some swift short-circuiting of his own. He has always found Edwin's ideas about biography quite silly; and although he feels obligated to record them "in the strict interests of biographical accuracy," he wishes to dispose of them as quickly as possible to save the reader the trouble of working his way through this "typical mixture of subtlety and inanity." But *pace* Jeffrey, Edwin's ideas may finally be worth a brief review.

Jeffrey quotes Edwin's statement exactly: "Biography is so simple. All you do is put in everything." Then, without noticing how the word "simple" gives it a certain kinship with some of his own pronouncements, the biographer continues to tell us that Edwin was one of the aforementioned "enemies" of biography—that he claimed

> that the very notion of biography was hopelessly fictional, since unlike real life, which presents us with question marks, censored passages, blank spaces, rows of asterisks, omitted paragraphs, and numberless sequences of three dots trailing into whiteness, biography provides an illusion of completeness, a vast pattern of details organized by an omniscient biographer whose occasional assertions of ignorance or uncertainty deceive us no more than the polite protestations of a hostess who, during the sixth course of an elaborate feast, assures us that really, it was no trouble at all. And since Edwin claimed that good stories always struck him

as true, he found himself in the curious position of believing absolutely in the Mock Turtle and the Mad Hatter but experiencing Lewis Carroll, about whom his father [a college English professor] used to tell affectionate anecdotes, as an implausible invention.

Edwin, of course, is correct in saying that "good stories" are always "true." Unquestionably, they are "true" in biography if they are historically accurate; but in another sense, they are also "true" if they are worthy of our belief because they are well-told, because, for example, their shapes are aesthetically pleasing. Edwin says simply "put in everything," but he (and Jeffrey—and Steven Millhauser) is also calling for more expertise from the biographer. Ironically, as reported by Jeffrey in that final sentence, what Edwin is finally suggesting, I believe, is that biography, since it is already "hopelessly fictional," should endeavor to be *more* "fictional," that is, should utilize the (so-called) techniques of fiction more effectively to tell "good stories," "true" ones.

Without appearing to know it, Jeffrey, then, is in basic agreement with Edwin. Finally, in a brilliant burst of irony, Jeffrey says:

> It is not worthwhile, therefore, to break our heads over his useless opinions concerning the fictionality of biography. But I take this opportunity to ask Edwin, wherever he is: isn't it true that the biographer performs a function nearly as great as, or precisely as great as, or actually greater by far than the function performed by the artist himself? For the artist creates the work of art, but the biographer, so to speak, creates the artist. Which is to say: without me, would you exist at all, Edwin?

Admittedly, it is stated here in absurd hyperbole, but this idea that the biographer does, in his own way, "create" his subject is a central part of the conception of literary biography. . . . Regardless of the type of biography which the literary biographer chooses to write, it is his own point of view, it is his own artistry, ultimately, which "creates" (or more properly, perhaps, "re-creates") the Public Writer, the private man or woman, or the artist who created the literature. (pp. 55-7)

Dennis W. Petrie, "The Literary Biographer's Design: 'A Few Footnotes',' in his Ultimately Fiction: Design in Modern American Literary Biography, *Purdue University Press, 1981, pp. 27-58.*

TIMOTHY DOW ADAMS

Steven Millhauser's first novel, *Edwin Mullhouse: The Life and Death of An American Writer, 1943-1954 by Jeffrey Cartwright,* is an interesting and valuable book for a consideration of the complexities of the art of biography, especially the relationship between the biographer and subject. Millhauser's novel is the biography of Edwin Mullhouse (who wrote his only novel, *Cartoons,* at the age of eleven) written by his eleven-and-a-half year old friend, Jeffrey Cartwright. Because the biographer, Jeffrey, is a fictional character who narrates the story from his point of view, the reader is given direct access into the biographer's mind at work, and the novel becomes not only Jeffrey's biography of Edwin, but also Jeffrey's autobiographical account of his childhood with Edwin, his decision to become Edwin's biographer, and his struggles to impose order on Edwin's life. (p. 205)

During his short eleven-year life-span, Edwin is constantly

watched by Jeffrey, only six months his elder. Because he is Edwin's next door neighbor (like Kinbote in *Pale Fire*), Jeffrey is in an ideal situation to satisfy his inherent urge to write Edwin's life. "Compared to Jeffrey's zealous sense of purpose, his industrious concentration on his subject's infinite variety and plenitude of sameness," writes Pearl Bell [see *CLC*, Vol. 21], "James Boswell seems inattentive, Richard Ellman's *Joyce* slipshod, Leon Edel's *James* cursory."

Because *Edwin Mullhouse* is as much an autobiography of Jeffrey as a biography of Edwin, and because it is a novel in the form of a work of non-fiction—it fits into a sub-genre that I call mock-biography. A mock-biography combines elements of fiction and non-fiction (sometimes literally, sometimes mockingly by incorporating invented nonfiction within the fictional construct), and parodies the conventions of biography. (p. 206)

Like most mock-biographies *Edwin Mullhouse* has a false air of nonfiction about it. An introductory note, written by a fictional character named Walter Logan White, includes a reference to a "definitive article in the *Journal of American Letters*, XXII (1966), 22-43, which compares Jeffrey's very American life of Edwin with Boswell's very British life of Johnson." Jeffrey Cartwright's satiric preface mocks the usual "smug adult" prefaces by stating that the youthful author is "not thankful to Dr. and Mrs. Mullhouse for moving away with the remains" or to "Aunt Gladys for mislaying eleven chapters" and that he "has never received any encouragement at all from anyone about anything." The eleven year old biographer concludes his bitter preface by remarking: "I feel that grateful thanks are due to myself . . . for my valuable assistance in a number of points; to myself, for doing all the dirty work; and above all to myself, whose patience, understanding, and usefulness as a key eye-witness can never be adequately repaid, and who in a typical burst of scrupulousness wish to point out that the 'remains' mentioned above are, of course, literary remains."

Following the fictional introduction and the mock-preface, comes a chronological table which lists such important events in Edwin's life as the first day of kindergarten, and which divides his life into the early, pre-literate period; the middle, literate period; and the late, literary period.

Jeffrey Cartwright is a classic unreliable narrator who constantly intrudes into his autobiography by calling attention to himself, his own wonderous memory, and his devotion to biography. He explains that he first met Edwin, the potential subject of his biography, at the age of six months and three days, when Edwin was only eight days old. . . .

With all the seriousness of the most scholarly biographer, the year old Jeffrey begins to collect and record the early conversation of Edwin. Jeffrey analyzes pre-baby talk as though it contained the seeds of Edwin's future literary genius. . . . (p. 208)

Raw material for Jeffrey's biography includes sketches of Edwin's hand and foot, traced from prints taken at age six-and-a-half months, and a chronology of "First Steps," "Some Things I Said And Did," and "My Baby Hair," taken from *"My Story: A Baby Record."* Edwin's early droolings gave way to phonetic imitations of Shakespeare, Chaucer, and Dickens, authors who were read aloud to the child. . . . (p. 209)

At first Jeffrey tries to tell Edwin's life-story chronologically:

> God pity the poor novelist. Standing on his omniscient cliff, with painful ingenuity he must contrive to drop bits of important information into the swift current of his all-powerful plot, where they are swept along like so many popsickle sticks. . . . The modest biographer, fortunately, is under no such obligation. Calmly and methodically . . . in a way impossible for the harried novelist who is always trying to do a hundred things at once, he can simply say what he has to say, ticking off each item with his right hand on the successively raised fingers of his left.

But soon, realizing that biography shares many characteristics with novels, he begins to use flashbacks and flashforwards, remarking that "memory and chronology simply do not make good bedfellows." He announces a plan to "abandon the madness of chronology altogether and simply follow my whims" but decides he must get his biography back under control. Using his usual images of childhood, Jeffrey declares that writing a biography "does not resemble the making of a jig-saw puzzle . . . but one of those connect-the-dot pictures that lead you in a series of invariable steps from a seeming chaos of numbers to a sudden recognition of the still incompleted pattern of the final closing of the gap, when number 63 is at last joined by number 1 and you see before you a flower, a kitten, a weeping clown."

His brief desire to break with chronological order for a moment over, Jeffrey continues his chronicle of the budding American novelist. Like most biographers he is fond of frequent catalogues which list the raw material of his subject's life. In a parody of children's book titles, Jeffrey lists such "literary influences" on young Edwin at the age of three as "The Hippopota Mister and The Hippopota Miss," "Ho Hum and Heave Ho," "Willy of Chile," "The Little Pretzel Who Had No Salt," and "Donald Dandelion and Oopsy Daisy." Jeffrey begins to give samples of Edwin's early writings, including his first grade valentine poem to Rose Dorn, about which Jeffrey writes, "If I include this poem in my biography, it is evidence not of his artistry but of his misery." (p. 210)

Edwin's early poems gave way to short stories (Edwin and Jeffrey are now in the second grade) which Jeffrey numbers and categorizes and summarizes. (p. 211)

Soon the desire to alter chronology begins to dominate Jeffrey's biographical integrity. He rationalizes the necessity for order and pattern by arguing that "biography provides an illusion of completeness, a vast pattern of details organized by an omniscient biographer whose occasional assertions of ignorance or uncertainty deceive us no more than the polite protestations of a hostess who, during the sixth course of an elaborate feast, assures us that really, it was no trouble at all." Jeffrey begins to justify his frequent lapses from accuracy by arguing that "the fatal flaw of all biography, according to its enemies, is its helpless conformity to the laws of fiction" which hold "that all the details of the hero's life are necessarily related to . . . a central image" which is probably not true at all to the life of "the hero himself, sporting in his meadow outside the future cage of his biography." Roy Pascal comments on this tendency of the autobiographer/biographer to leave incorrect facts in his work, even when he knows that they are false: "On the one side are the truths of fact, on the other the truths of the writer's feelings . . . and we often find open admissions in autobiography of the conflict between the two truths. What is interesting is . . . that so many authors felt that their false impression was as important as the truth, and that the autobiographer has to tell us as much what the writer is as what the facts are."

Jeffrey begins to abandon all pretense at objectivity and accuracy and openly admits to deviating from the facts, and even justifies his departures from truth by claiming that "the false fusion of memory may reveal truths beyond chronology, and the fearless biographer, in his tireless search for the past, must be willing to heed the kind of evidence contradicted by clocks." (pp. 211-12)

Jeffrey's increasing difficulty at keeping to the facts concerns him greatly "lest biography degenerate into fiction," until he becomes obsessed with forcing Edwin's life to fit into his preconceived pattern. As Leon Edel writes, "there must be, I take it, a strong and compelling element in a biographer's attraction to his subject which pushes him on his difficult and often obsessive task, and it is mixed up in different degrees with all sorts of drives: a boundless curiosity, not unmixed I suppose with elements of *voyeurism;* a drive to power, common I suppose to most professions; a need for omniscience." Jeffrey's drive for power and omniscience causes him to worry about the difficulty of completing a biography while his subject's life continues to run on: "Even then I suppose I perceived dimly that the design was marred somewhat by Edwin's indefinitely continued existence, but at the time I was less concerned with hazy future than with the luminous past."

But Edwin's continued existence threatens to throw Jeffrey's biography out of proportion and he reveals with grim overtones, "I, for one, can testify that even a modest biographer may be driven to strange devices for the sake of his throbbing book." Finally what once was a slight worry, keeping chronology straight, has developed into a grim desire on the part of the biographer for the death of his subject so that he can complete his biography: "The three-part division of his life had already established itself in my mind, and it was emphatically clear to me that we had passed the middle of Part Three and were mere chapters, mere pages, from the tragic end. He had written his book: now he must bow and depart; all else was in a manner superfluous."

In the story's shocking denouement, Jeffrey and Edwin plan what Edwin thinks is only a childish game of biography in which Edwin pretends to kill himself at the exact hour, and minute—eleven years later—that he was born, to give his life a perfect symmetry. Although Edwin thinks it is only a game, Jeffrey—whose biographical impulse has driven him mad—is perfectly serious:

> And calmly raising the gun to his right temple, Edwin whispered: "Bang, I'm dead," and fell backward on the bed with his eyes shut, clutching the silent gun. A moment later his eyes opened and he said: "Now what?" In a split second I was leaning over him, gripping his gun-gripping hand; and I remember thinking, quite lucidly in the midst of a dreamy numbness, that the entry under "I Am Born" in *MY STORY: A BABY RECORD* allowed a certain leeway in the matter of seconds.

When Jacques Barzun remarked that "Every biography is something like a detective story," he could hardly have imagined the grisly ending of *Edwin Mullhouse,* in which the biog-

rapher murders his own subject for artistic effect and a smooth ending. To add further to the terror of Jeffrey's act, once he finishes his biography of the late Edwin Mullhouse, he notices that a new family has moved into the old Mullhouse home and that their youngest son, little Paul Hooper, "is really an interesting little fellow and I expect to be seeing more of him in the near future." Jeffrey has picked the subject for his next biography, and poor dead Edwin is forgotten, his mock-suicide note revealing ironically his ultimate fate: "I aspire to the condition of fiction." Edwin Mullhouse has become fiction in the form of Steven Millhauser's mock-biography. The biographer has literally "taken" his subject's life. (pp. 212-13)

Timothy Dow Adams, "The Mock-Biography of Edwin Mullhouse," in Biography, *Vol. 5, No. 3, Summer, 1982, pp. 205-14.*

MICHIKO KAKUTANI

The words "wonder," "magic," "mystery" and "secret" percolate through these stories [in *In the Penny Arcade*] by Steven Millhauser, surfacing here and there, everywhere, like talismans to an enchanted world. Indeed Mr. Millhauser and his characters, however varied, all seem blessed with a child's easy access to the world of imagination and dreams—they're open to the transformations worked on nature by time and art, and they're transfixed by the beauty in, say, the tiny gears of an antique clock, in the changing silhouette of the moon, in the unexpected appearance of a silver blimp in the sky. . . .

As in a penny arcade, all manner of pretty, frightening and amazing things happen in these stories—magicians bring statues to life with a flick of the wrist, men change themselves into automatons, snowmen—along with snow maidens, snow birds and snow unicorns—suddenly materialize in a town. More often than not, the event itself is easily enough explained—a sleight of hand trick, a case of mistaken identity, the work of children playing in the snow—but the perception of the marvelous nonetheless remains. That, in fact, is in large measure what these tales are really about. Like Mr. Millhauser's two novels (*Edwin Mullhouse* and *Portrait of a Romantic*), they are about the ability of artists and children to see things anew, to remake things through the force of their own romantic yearnings, and the dangerous consequences of that gift.

In addition, several of the stories are concerned with the loss of that ability to imagine, a spiritual disillusionment that can occur as swiftly as a change of mood, as gradually as a shift in the national zeitgeist. In the novella-length **"August Eschenburg,"** a precocious young man learns, from several painful experiences, that his art—making clockwork toys so beautifully that they seem alive—is no longer appreciated, that he has become an anachronism in an increasingly vulgar age.

In the three stories contained in the second section of this volume (**"A Protest Against the Sun," "The Sledding Party"** and **"A Day in the Country"**), young women experience a sudden diminishment of expectations, a jolting turn of mind in which a sense of the magical possibilities of life abruptly sour and darken: The appearance of a stranger wearing a parka casts a shadow over a bright day at the beach; a boy's avowal of love makes a girl feel that her life has suddenly constricted, and another woman's doppelganger awakens her to her own grief. As for the title story ["**In the Penny Arcade**"] it shows how precipitously the extraordinary can slip into the mundane—an adolescent returns to the summer carnival he so adored as a boy and discovers, in his disappointment, the innocence he's managed to misplace. . . .

In this story, as in the others, Mr. Millhauser writes with assurance and skill, equally at ease with a variety of literary genres, equally adept at recording the chatty non sequiturs of teen-agers and the dense, metaphysical musings of a 19th-century con man. "**August Eschenburg**," for instance, recalls the works of Thomas Mann not only in its concern with the role of the artist as well as the dialectic between life and art, pragmatic worldliness and esthetic absolutism—but also in its use of irony, philosophical dialogue and its rhetorical, 19th-century manner. . . .

"**A Protest Against the Sun**" and "**The Sledding Party**," on the other hand, are more reminiscent of J. D. Salinger's *New Yorker* stories—both in their portrayal of young, confused adolescents, and in their casual, conversational manner. Yet if these stories attest to Mr. Millhauser's impressive range of style and his ability to conjure up widely disparate fictional worlds, the reader still finishes *In the Penny Arcade* with a certain sense of having read the same story several times. There is a sameness to Mr. Millhauser's characters—nearly all of them are moody, sensitive souls, given to solitary musings and violent changes of mood—and their emotional afflictions of nostalgia, irritation and extreme joy also begin to feel overly familiar. Such misgivings, on the part of this reader, however, should not diminish the overall achievement of this collection. Mr. Millhauser possesses a bountiful imagination, and an ability to catch his perceptions in a bright butterfly net of prose, and those gifts lend these stories a lovely afterlife, colorful and lively, in the reader's mind.

Michiko Kakutani, "Perceptions of Marvels," in
The New York Times, *January 11, 1986, p. 12.*

DENNIS DRABELLE

The dominant image in this short-story collection [*In the Penny Arcade*] is the mechanical toy. "**Cathay**," a series of fabulous vignettes set in imperial China, begins with a long paragraph about artificial birds. So sweetly do the birds sing and so naturally do they move that only their golden forms keep them from being taken for real.

The title story ["**In the Penny Arcade**"] features a narrator's taking leave of his boyhood in a shabby carnival arcade stocked with mechanical cowboys, dancers, and fortune-tellers, all animated by coins. Seeing other children mock the deteriorating figures, the narrator realizes that he, too, is on the verge of losing his sense of wonder. "I recognized that I myself had become part of the conspiracy of dullness," he muses, "and that only in a moment of lavish awareness, which had left me confused and exhausted, had I seen truly. The figures had not betrayed me: I had betrayed them. I saw that I was in danger of becoming ordinary, and I understood that from now on I would have to be vigilant."

"**August Eschenburg**," the longest story (it comprises more than a third of the book), chronicles the life and times of a toymaker so skilled he can make a mechanical figure that not only writes legible copy but corrects its own mistake. (It's always the same mistake and the same correction, but

still . . .) After scoring a series of triumphs in the medium of the department-store window, he falls out of favor by refusing to prostitute his art. Across the street a rival has been fashioning and installing lewd figures in his store window—a stratagem Eschenburg disdains. Later he loses the backing necessary to support a theater devoted to his productions because he will not traffic in the bawdy buffoonery his audience—and his backer—demands. At the end he is left alone, somewhat like Charlie Chaplin's Tramp, with his integrity.

What are we to make of all this clockwork craftsmanship? It points toward a profound loneliness, crystallizing in a fascination with facsimile humans in lieu of the real things. "You're not much of a friend," Eschenburg's disgruntled backer complains. "There's something cold about you . . ." The boy in the penny arcade notices and feels superior to the cynical children also on the premises but interacts only with the mechanical adults.

The sense of being cut off from other people recurs in the "nonmechanical" stories as well. In "**Sledding Party**" a young woman is so perturbed by a male friend's abrupt declaration of love that she spends most of the evening brooding under a fir tree while the others gambol in the snow or dance inside the house. In "**A Protest Against the Sun**," the story of a family's afternoon at the beach, another young woman finds herself hard-put to explain her exultation in the day's radiant perfection to her witty but emotionally stiff father. In "**A Day in the Country**," a woman entering early middle age rounds out her solitary stay at a country inn with a crying jag and close brush with suicide. Encounters with other people are generally brief in these stories, conversations fleeting. The effect is rather like that of walking alone through a museum in a town where you don't know a soul. (pp. 4-5)

These are quite good stories, but, churlish to say, I expected better—or at least less traditional—ones. . . .

In the Penny Arcade merely reveals a skilled writer polishing up variations of less than dazzling originality on a single theme. Nothing wrong in that—unless it be the inevitable letdown after a writer breaks a few icons (e.g., the novelist as precious prophet) and then doesn't see any more he feels up to attacking.

In the Penny Arcade may not be a burst of literary pyrotechnics, but it is a showcase of style and grace. (p. 5)

Dennis Drabelle, "Stories That Run Like Clockwork," in Book World—The Washington Post, *January 19, 1986, pp. 4-5.*

ROBERT DUNN

"If the doors of perception were cleansed everything would appear to man as it is, infinite," William Blake wrote. In *Edwin Mullhouse,* it was clear that Mr. Millhauser would settle for nothing less. So it is cheerful to report that in his first short-story collection, *In the Penny Arcade,* Mr. Millhauser continues to pursue fiction as a mysterious, magical, enlightening experience. He still chases the Blakean infinite. Always, as he writes in one story, his fiction leads us "away from the torpor of the familiar into a dark realm of strangeness and wonder."

The book is divided into three sections. In "**August Eschenburg**," the long story that forms the first part, a German boy in the late 19th century is obsessed with mechanical devices that simulate life. The world is readying itself for the motion picture, but movies have not been invented yet, and August becomes the last great maker of automatons. He raises his craft to art, his humanoid models to the threshold of breath. August first creates models for a department store's windows, then an automaton theater—a *Zaubertheater,* though not one as soul-changing as Hesse's—which quickly loses customers to a frankly pornographic automaton theater (an overly obvious depiction of artistic debasement). August's backer, the cynical Hausenstein, who surreptitiously owns the other theater, knows that "your good blue-eyed German likes plenty of beef on his plate and plenty of beef on his women." August knows only that "his ambition was to insert his dreams into the world, and if they were the wrong dreams, then he would dream them in solitude." Frustrated, August returns to his hometown, his art "outmoded."

For Mr. Millhauser, art always has an erotic component. August creates his "dark-eyed suffering automaton girl," who has "in her walk . . . a new suggestion of ripeness, of sexual wakening," with "something akin to love-anguish." Art, like eros, stirs senses to full life, demands devotion, teases, yet delivers perfection and beauty. Can they last? "Was beauty subject to fashion?" Sadly, it appears so. This is the way of the world, Mr. Millhauser tells us: art, dreams and beauty sooner or later are vitiated. Yet he never lets his musings on the suffering and ravishment of art grow stale; the breath of human passion blows through them.

Gently yet more intentionally sensual are the next two stories ["**A Protest against the Sun**" and "**The Sledding Party**"], which deal with a young girl's awakening to the vibrancy and threat of womanhood and love. As with Edwin Mullhouse and August Eschenburg, Mr. Millhauser always works best with young people. They are lighter-than-air simulacrums of adults; unformed, they let us imagine possibility, process and fulfillment. The secret is to keep the grown-ups offstage as much as possible. . . .

Adulthood is everywhere in "**A Day in the Country**," which takes Judith, a 36-year-old technical-book editor, to a resort for a weekend. Judith is feigning insouciance after a bad love affair, and it takes a young woman with "melancholy and mutely appealing eyes," who Judith believes is following her, to get her to face the truth that she's lonely and depressed. The story is Upper West Side Hawthorne, and Mr. Millhauser, whose mysteries are so illuminating, founders with conventional psychologizing. Judith's epiphany can only lead, the reader believes, not to awareness but to an analyst's couch.

In the book's final section, character is moved to the background, and poetic, allegorical effect takes over. Since Mr. Millhauser's touch with people is usually so gentle and understanding, this comes as a slight disappointment. The first story, "**Snowmen**," gives us a suburban town seized by a frenzy of snowy replication: snowmen, snow animals, snow houses and finally snow "griffins, unicorns, and sea serpents" are magically built. As a miniature of Mr. Millhauser's art—rampant imagination supplanting dull reality—the fantasy is brilliant, but as a tour de force, there is nowhere for it to go. What happens to the snowy wonderland? It melts.

["**In the Penny Arcade**"] is reminiscent of an early scene in *Edwin Mullhouse* and of James Joyce's "Araby." A boy returning to a penny arcade visited years before finds the "majesty and mystery . . . crushed down by the shrewd, oppressive eyes of countless visitors who looked at [the figures] without seeing their fertile inner nature." The final story, "**Cathay**," which describes a fabulous city, is like one of Italo Calvino's evocations of invisible cities—a charming, open-ended artifice. Though not as intellectually rich as Calvino's fantasies, "**Cathay**" is richer in fairytale magic.

Mr. Millhauser's stories stand in rare counterpoint to his contemporaries' work in a flat, ironic, affectless realism. Though his art can be hampered by too rigid conceits and occasional bad choices of subject, he is a true original when he draws us into his precise, luminous awareness, when he makes our world turn amazing. As the narrator of "**Penny Arcade**" realizes, "I recognized that I myself had become a part of the conspiracy of dullness, and that only in a moment of lavish awareness . . . had I seen truly. [The magical figures] had not betrayed me: I had betrayed them. I saw that I was in danger of becoming ordinary, and I understood that from now on I would have to be vigilant."

Mr. Millhauser is more than vigilant; he creates for us this splendid arcade. And he asks us also to be vigilant as we venture with him into the common corners of our ragged world, where the marvelous glows and true meanings breathe life.

Robert Dunn, "First Love and the Last Automatons," in The New York Times Book Review, *January 19, 1986, p. 9.*

AL J. SPERONE

On the old *Twilight Zone* series, dolls and mannequins were always coming to life, while ordinary guys found out that they were actually robots. Steven Millhauser's collection *In the Penny Arcade* brings those metaphysical flip-flops to artier realms.

In his two novels, Millhauser devoted himself to recapturing all the details of daily life, specifically that of East Coast suburban baby-boom kids. With *In the Penny Arcade,* he adds three more slice-of-life stories to his collected works, but sandwiches them between tales of recreating life through technique. Four of the book's seven stories are about manmade imitations of life—puppets, arcade robots, ultradetailed snowmen, enchanted statues. These are fascinating artifacts, in part because they reveal Millhauser's ambivalence. He arranged the collection with "**August Eschenburg**" as Part I and the other three artificial-life stories as Part III, a setup that casts a peculiar light on the realistic stories (Part II) and the novels. More emphatically than ever, Millhauser keeps wondering whether total recall equals art.

Edwin Mullhouse: The Life and Death of an American Writer 1943-1954 by Jeffrey Cartwright (1972), which was widely praised and recently reprinted, suggests Nabokov's *Pale Fire* moved to a Connecticut elementary school. It's the purported critical biography of a child novelist, written by a classmate, Cartwright, whose theories of art and biography eventually kill their subject. *Portrait of a Romantic* (1977), which never made it to paperback, is a season-by-season chronicle of a neurasthenic teenager, Arthur Grumm, who's drawn to death-obsessed companions. Both books are about how art and literature impinge on life, and vice versa; they balance sensual pleasure with intellectual decadence, and they show everyday life as sensory overload. . . .

Edwin Mullhouse imposed a maniacal system on a fairly ordinary childhood; *Portrait of a Romantic* sprawled, defying shapeliness. *In the Penny Arcade* does a little of each. First and last, Millhauser writes about craft (or is it art?) mimicking life.

"In the Penny Arcade," the collection's weakest story, sends a 12-year-old boy back to the penny arcade that had amazed him when he was younger; he sees its true seediness, but for a moment returns to wonderment. "I recognized that I myself had become part of the conspiracy of dullness, and that only in a moment of lavish awareness, which had left me confused and exhausted, had I seen truly." What a sweet sentiment; let's all believe in Tinker Bell.

Part II takes up simple (as it were) naturalism, with stories about the fragility of moods in which nothing much actually happens—perfect for *The New Yorker,* where two out of three were published. In "A Protest Against the Sun," a beach outing gets shaken up by the appearance of a wild-eyed bum. At "The Sledding Party," as bookish high-school students trade witticisms, Peter tells Catherine that he loves her; she is appalled. In "A Day in the Country," Judith Hahn visits an inn for the weekend and projects her own misery onto another lone woman, who gently hands it back to her.

By themselves, the middle stories are vivid and well made; like August's automatons, their characters have all sorts of subtle motions and emotions. Yet placed as they are, these slight stories have to take a lot of weight: They are Millhauser's art, his own clockwork marvels, presumably defying the mass taste for less subtle titillations. As such, they call attention to his limits as well as his talent.

For one thing, they replicate scenes and situations from the novels—beach visits, suicidal notions, sound effects such as the jingling of boot buckles. Not that the rest of the collection doesn't; even the machines constructed by August Eschenburg echo the toys of Arthur Grumm's peculiar girlfriend. Coming after Millhauser's novels, the stories don't tell us much that's new about adolescence or suburbia or emotional shifts; they show Millhauser's meticulousness and his "lavish awareness," but lack resonance.

Part II seems thin by comparison to "August Eschenburg," "Snowmen," and "Cathay," which are imaginative (and schematic) as well as observant. In "Snowmen," a whole town shapes a blizzard into fanatically precise snow-sculptures—at first lifelike, then minutely phantasmagorical. The story slips away from realism as quietly and irrevocably as a Borges tale. "Cathay"—told topic by topic, like a Barthelme or Calvino story—itemizes a fabled emperor's court, where he is surrounded by such exquisite artifices as mechanical songbirds and miniature paintings on ladies' eyelids. It rejoices in its distance from verisimilitude. In the final vignette, two magicians compete. The younger turns a jade statue into a flesh-and-blood beauty; the elder transforms another statue into a jade woman, still cool and green. "His Imperial Majesty said that although there were many beautiful women at his court, there was but one breathing statue; and without hesitation he awarded the prize to the old magician." Artifice beats naturalism.

Millhauser can make his statues breathe, his puppets dance; if art is the act of carefully perceiving, as he suggests in the title story, he's a certifiable artist. Yet Millhauser's eye and ear are so good that his stories should be more than sets of impressions or dialectics about art. It's not enough to make objects move—they ought to move us, too. (p. 4)

*Al J. Sperone, in a review of "In the Penny Arcade,"
in VLS, No. 42, February, 1986, pp. 3-4.*

MICHAEL PEARSON

Edwin Mullhouse harkens back to "Rip Van Winkle," but it also echoes another early Irving tale, "The Legend of Sleepy Hollow." Millhauser, like Irving, centers his story on the conflict between the fanciful and the mundane, between fiction and fact, and although he gives us no Ichabod Crane and Brom Bones, he does give us biographer and novelist, one anchored in fact and zealous memory, the other soaring into possibility and selective forgetfulness. It is in the person of Jeffrey Cartwright, narrator of the story (whose name neatly echoes Irving's Jeffrey Crayon), that we find the source of irony. His voice strikes a comic tone, similar to Irving's and what amounts to a central chord in American literature from its beginnings, a note which sounds from the clash between the ideal and the real. In *Edwin Mullhouse,* as in "The Legend of Sleepy Hollow," much of the humor consists of the literary method as it contrasts with the trivial or mundane situation being described. This tension between modes of language is what Louis Rubin sees at the heart of American humor—a contrast between "the formal, literary . . . and the informal, vernacular language of everyday life." (p. 146)

Edwin Mullhouse is a peculiarly American novel. It has the essential American comic vision, which sees the discrepancy between aspirations and actualities, made more pronounced perhaps by the yawning gap between the glowing abstractions of a democratic society and the oftentimes more somber realities faced by the average man. *Edwin Mullhouse* also has the particularly American trait of preserving the parodoxical relationship between the impulse to take action and record facts and the tendency to dream and create new worlds. Tony Tanner in *City of Words* describes just such a specifically American dichotomy:

> There is a strong desire to step out . . . into some kind of free space; at the same time, it is not certain what would happen to the individual if he did manage to break out of all these versions, roles, structures. We have found another pervasive dread of ceasing to have identity and flowing into something as shapeless as protoplasm, jelly, or mud. It has been a constant preoccupation among [American] writers . . . to see whether some third area can be found, beyond conditioning but not so far into the flux as to mean the end of the individual altogether.

Thus, there seem to be two intrinsic elements in much American fiction: a comic sensibility toward the imbalance between ideals and realities, and a groping after some middle-ground between freedom and control. These forces are central to American literature, and they are central to *Edwin Mullhouse.*

First, *Edwin Mullhouse* is a comic novel, with strong elements of satire and parody. Millhauser satirizes academics like Walter Logan White of the fictitious introduction, in the process lampooning scholars who are pompous, self-serving, superficial, and of course, have the prerequisite triangular name. Millhauser also has his fun with biographers who have a mania for details, those who insist on telling us the size of Faulkner's shoe and the number of trout Hemingway man-

aged to catch on a fishing trip, making a mountain out of minutiae. Millhauser certainly mocks our idealized view of
childhood, our romantic intuition that childhood is actually
a Rousseauian playground, all innocence and purity. However, Millhauser's children—Edwin, Jeffrey, Rose Dorn, Edward Penn, Arnold Hasselstrom—are not innocent and pure.
They are silly, bored, frenzied, obsessed, cruel, playful, but
hardly ever innocent.

Like much of the satire, the parody has a literary focus. Akin
to caricature, parody can be caustic or loving, and Millhauser's parody is both: it places the readers' eyes where the
author wants them—on the text itself, on the fiction, both
silly and serious, a bit like life itself. The parody essentially
begins with the title, at once an imitation of a literary biography and a child's notebook, and literally abounds with allusions, from Dickens' stark "dead as a doornail" simile in *A
Christmas Carol* to a twisting of the opening of *Anna
Karenina:* "Everyone sees the world differently . . . but
nightmares are pretty much the same." What this parody
serves to do is underline the true subject of the novel, the
book itself, the act of imagining. And throughout, the novel
whispers with the ghosts of great imaginations—Dickens,
Tolstoy, Chaucer, Shakespeare, Joyce, Melville, Twain.

For Millhauser, literature is a game but a deadly serious one.
The prose style is Jeffrey's—witty, perceptive (at times), and
skillful. Jeffrey may have been fathered by Steven Millhauser
but he was born of Vladimir Nabokov, it seems, and it is
worth recalling what Humbert Humbert says early in *Lolita:*
"You can always count on a murderer for a fancy prose
style." Jeffrey's fancy prose style is just one more reflexive
characteristic of the novel, forcing the fiction to bend back
on itself, reflecting not so much the world as its own image,
"a budding and blossoming of words." In *Edwin Mullhouse,*
subject and object are the same. The central metaphor of the
novel is that childhood is a time of genius, which in turn is
simply "the capacity to be obsessed and every normal child
has that capacity; we have all been geniuses, you and I; but
sooner or later it is beaten out of us, the glory fades, and by
the age of seven most of us are nothing but wretched little
adults." Undeniably, Edwin is just an ordinary boy, but that
is precisely Millhauser's point. Edwin is each of us, but the
syllogism goes even further: art is the rib of imagination
brought to life, childhood is a time when the imagination is
at its peak, and this particular novel about a child-writer is
therefore about the imagination, about art, finally about itself.

However, *Edwin Mullhouse* is no sterile exercise in the anti-
novel, bodiless voices speaking one abstraction after another.
It is a fiction which cherishes the world, that pays careful witness to childhood, all its sounds, colors, and sensations. It
brings us back into all the comedy and pathos of that time.
In one instance, Millhauser describes Edwin, a second grad-
er, attempting to give his beloved Rose Dorn (whose name
Jeffrey makes clear rhymes with *forlorn*) a present of red wax
lips:

> On this particular day everyone except Edwin and
> Rose Dorn had returned to the room; I myself hap-
> pened to be crouching on the other side of the rack,
> reaching for a lost glove. Under the row of coats
> four legs were visible. Below her right knee was a
> small white bandaid; on her left knee a double
> scratch stood out darkly against a bright red back-
> ground of mercurochrome. "I've got this stupid
> thing anyway. This is such a stupid coatroom. Oh

> where is that stupid thing. I don't know why I
> bought this stupid thing. You probably wouldn't
> want it anyway. Here. You can throw the dumb
> thing out if you don't want it. This is such a dumb
> school. I think I'll go to China.

Poor Edwin. He was not an eloquent lover.

Nor is Rose Dorn, with battered knees and bad disposition,
the ideal woman or obvious object of Edwin's chivalric love.
This passage illustrates the clash of language modes in two
ways. First, there is the vernacular of Edwin's speech colliding with the implicit courtly love ideal. Then, there is the
adult, literary language of Jeffrey's inference plowing headlong into the triviality of the situation itself. At times, Millhauser squares the literary and childish in the same sentence.
In describing Edwin's relationship with his sister, Jeffrey
says: "Sometimes, when she would not learn, he lost his temper and shook her by the shoulders, saying, 'You stupid stupid jerk, you stupid dumbbell,' until her large, beautiful, cop-
per-flecked blue eyes filled with terror, and she burst into hysterical tears." The abrasively colloquial and the finely poetic
hold delicate balance. The playfield in *Edwin Mullhouse* is a
linguistic one, the book becoming a hall of mirrors, making
it difficult (as in Nabokov's work) to distinguish clearly between world and word. However, even this bit of narrative
complexity Millhauser transforms into a child's perspective
when he describes Billy Duda's reflexive story in the fourth
grade: "Ten boy scouts were sitting around a fire and each
boy scout had to tell a story. The first boy scout said: 'Ten
boy scouts were sitting around a fire and each boy scout had
to tell a story. The first boy scout said.' " This is a story about
a story about a story—much like *Edwin Mullhouse,* which
is an autobiographical novel (Millhauser and Mullhouse can
and should be mistaken for one another) about a boy who
writes a biography about another boy who writes a novel,
which in turn is quite autobiographical—and the circle continues. The novel is both made up of and about words.

There is a comic playfulness in all this, surely, a sense of
gamesplaying—both the province of the child and the artist—but just as a child plays games with a deadly earnest, so
does Millhauser play his game for high stakes. . . . Millhauser's game is satiric and parodic, but it is profoundly serious, too, written as Jeffrey points out "in blood," about subjects as significant as the realities of childhood, the nature of
art, the power of the imagination, and the potential loss of the
capacity to wonder. Childhood is murdered, but Edwin slyly
lives on in the book, and besides there is always another book
and another "normal healthy intelligent American child" fascinated by toys and snow and dinosaurs and such. In *Edwin
Mullhouse,* we see a verbal shoving match between world of
fact and world of fiction, in the persons of Jeffrey and Edwin,
and sometimes the shoving becomes violent, but there is a
symbiosis here, also. The world and the imagination create
one another, life becoming art, art becoming life. *Edwin Mullhouse* is a patently American fiction, no matter how far it
seems to stray from the Catskills or the frontier or the Mississippi. The conflict, as it has been from our literature's beginnings, emphasizes the separation of order and freedom, of
fact and possibility, of limitation and dream, and this conflict
is rendered in *Edwin Mullhouse,* as it is in so many American
novels before it, comically—both hilariously and poignantly.
In this way, *Edwin Mullhouse*—innovative, playful, and
bursting with ironies—actually holds up a mirror to life and

to literature, reflecting on American themes as it reflects its own image, as well. (pp. 147-50)

Michael Pearson, " 'Edwin Mullhouse': Re-Flexing American Themes," in Critique: Studies in Modern Fiction, *Vol. XXVII, No. 3, Spring, 1986, pp. 145-51.*

IRVING MALIN

Although these stories [in **In the Penny Arcade**] vary in length and setting and time, they must be read as variations on a theme—the "perfection" of art. Thus they are reflections, mazes, games; they surprise us because they are less interested in plot, character, and philosophy than in magic, dream, and metaphor. They suggest that it is the miniature detail—the sudden intrusion of illusion—which creates a transcendent beauty (if only briefly).

"Cathay" consists of many little sections; the sections range from descriptions of "summer nights" to those of "ugly women." There is no story; instead, there are odd miniatures. "Blue Horses" can be quoted in its entirety: "The Emperor's blue horses in a field of white snow." The sentence is stunning because it is so matter-of-fact *and* dreamlike—there is no meaning in the usual, everyday sense because Millhauser wants to startle us and, moreover, to place us in the *field of vision*. He does not explain why the horses are blue or, for that matter, why the snow is white. It is the revelation of sudden tension which creates the beauty of description. **"Cathay"** is so concerned with magical fields that it "ends" with a section on "the contest of magicians." (pp. 146-47)

These stories are *enchantments, magical arcades, detailed wonders*. They apparently defy explication because they recognize that words are occult worlds; they exist in the **"Cathay"** of the reader's imagination. They have, as it were, a life of their own—a Byzantine, enduring one. (p. 147)

*Irving Malin, in a review of "In the Penny Arcade,"
in* The Review of Contemporary Fiction, *Vol. 6, No. 2, Summer, 1986, pp. 146-47.*

MICHIKO KAKUTANI

Steven Millhauser's third novel, **From the Realm of Morpheus,** begins precipitously one fine summer day when Carl Hausman, a disaffected young man who's been sleepily watching a baseball game, chases a foul ball into a woodland thicket and tumbles down a hole into a hidden world. Whether he's slipped into a reverie is never really clear; in any case, he soon finds himself going down a staircase to a stone chamber, where he finds a key sitting on a little table. The key opens a door, which leads—surprise, surprise—to the secret realm of Morpheus, the god of sleep and dreams.

This prologue, of course, instantly recalls the beginning of *Alice's Adventures in Wonderland,* and by the time Carl comes to the end of his travels the reader has also counted references—homages, or downright imitations—to half a dozen other classics. There are voyages to odd, new lands, not unlike those in *The Odyssey,* as well as bizarre encounters with giants, floating islands and a huge bird, reminiscent of those in *Gulliver's Travels.* As in *The Picture of Dorian Gray,* a painting takes on the soul of a man—in this case, that of the artist, rather than the subject of the portrait. As in Jorge

Luis Borges's ficciones, mirrors possess wondrous powers, and libraries contain impossible books—books written by characters like David Copperfield, Gustav von Aschenbach and Pierre Glendinning, and such "lost" books as Flaubert's completion of *Bouvard et Pécuchet,* Byron's completion of *Don Juan.* And as in the *Divine Comedy,* the hero is ferried across a mysterious river, then taken on a tour of the underworld by a cooperative guide—though this time his name's Morpheus, not Virgil.

Like Dante and Swift, Mr. Millhauser occasionally draws comparisons between the strange inhabitants of this underworld and ordinary mortals, but his parallels tend to be so broad and obvious (for instance, that both species suffer from loneliness and disappointment) that they effectively evaporate altogether. In fact, for all his manipulation of old myths, Freudian theories and literary allusions, Mr. Millhauser seems less interested in satirizing society or scoring esthetic points than in simply exercising his imagination and his facility with language.

Certainly the discursive, episodic form of this novel gives him plenty of chances to do just that. There are few transitions in this novel and almost no cumulative action. Carl and Morpheus simply go from one setting to the next, one set of adventures to another—a few confidences are exchanged, a few crises are overcome, but while Carl experiences occasional bouts of weariness he remains pretty much a cipher, a window through whom the reader may experience the marvels of Morpheus' realm. . . .

Mr. Millhauser possesses a child's easy access to the world of dreams, and he depicts many of the wonders Carl sees with a persuasive blend of imaginative playfulness and minute, naturalistic detail. We, like Carl, are introduced to mirrors that reflect only the beautiful and true . . . a "Magic Man" capable of entering and exiting paintings at will, and books that talk and argue with the reader.

The lost kingdom of Atlantis, which has somehow ended up in this netherworld, is itself a remarkable and self-contained land, depicted with fairytale charm. . . .

Unfortunately some of the people Carl encounters underground are a good bit less gifted than the Atlanteans—and less interesting as well. Ekli and Heklo, for instance, are a fairly conventional storybook sister and brother—she's sensitive and lovelorn, he's strong and protective; their one distinguishing feature is that they happen to be giants. Volumnia, Morpheus' one-time wife, is a conniving—and predictable—shrew. And Morpheus—who describes himself as "a denizen of the dark, a magnifico of murk, a malingerer, a ne'er-do-well"—is really little but a boring male chauvinist who likes to carry on at length about the physical attributes of women and the horrors of domesticity.

Aside from offering Carl occasional swigs of wine, he isn't even a particularly compelling guide—mainly he just walks Carl about, pointing at this and that, while droning on about history and philosophy. . . .

In the end, Mr. Millhauser's tale turns out to be somewhat idle: whereas his previous books possessed an imaginative vision and vitality all their own, this volume, for all its inventiveness, feels more like clever embroidery, worked on themes and ideas patented by the masters.

Michiko Kakutani, in a review of "From the Realm

of Morpheus," in The New York Times, *September 17, 1986, p. 24.*

MICHAEL DIRDA

Morpheus, the god of dreams, governs the dark realm of illusion, romance, and fairy tale. Steven Millhauser's beautifully composed, utterly entrancing book [*From the Realm of Morpheus*] records the adventures of a young man named Carl Hausman who, one sunny summer afternoon, follows a foul ball into a thicket, discovers a cave, and slowly descends—like Aeneas, like Dante—into the underworld.

From the Realm of Morpheus certainly belongs with books as magical as Angela Carter's *Nights at the Circus,* as linguistically exuberant as Russell Hoban's *Riddley Walker,* as delightfully literary as Julian Barnes' *Flaubert's Parrot.* In it, for instance, you will come to understand the timeless rivalry between shadows and reflections, visit a library of all the books that should have been written, travel to an island of giants, to Atlantis, to the moon of Cyrano de Bergerac and H. G. Wells. Not precisely a novel, this "natural history of the unnatural" consists of loosely linked stories, most about doomed love and nearly all of them worthy of the *Arabian Nights* or the *Canterbury Tales.*

Besides an Ancient Mariner-like talent for hypnotic storytelling, Millhauser's great gift lies in his style. At his best he can write as in our dreams we'd all like to—with the preciseness of Nabokov, the richness of Thomas Browne, the music of Keats. Like Morpheus himself he takes all language for his province. (p. 1)

[A] sonorous yet exact voice dominates the first section of the book as Carl passes through the various antechambers of Morpheus' many-mansioned realm, each heavy with symbolism, classical reference and literary echoes. His descent eventually brings him to a tapestried palace. Here all is *"luxe, calme et volupté"*—beautiful women slumber in states of deshabille before a huge bed upon which a plump yawning figure reclines. Millhauser's description of this chamber of opulence and languor dutifully copies Ovid's portrait of Sleep's kingdom in the *Metamorphosis.* Morpheus, for it is he in soporific splendor, resembles Falstaff, Gargantua, Orson Welles, the very spirit of Carnival.

I am, he litanizes, a denizen of the dark, a magnifico of murk, a malingerer, a ne'er do well, a fair chessplayer, a dabbler in this and that. A gentleman of dubious extraction and uncertain means. A charming rogue, a poor fellow down on his luck, a man more sinned against than sinning. A simple country lad. Just an ordinary guy. Lover of the black flame of the night, an idle dreamer of a summer's day, a loafer in the poolhalls of the soul. A dangerous companion, a trusty guide. Not the sort of fellow you'd want to introduce to your sister.

This is a fair sample of Morphean eloquence, which modulates between the rolling periods characteristic of the 17th century and the Brooklynese of the Dead End Kids. His talk is sprinkled with oaths ("S'death" is a favorite), looks a little daunting on the page, and is riddled with quotation and a playful use of cliché. Literary references abound (in the passage just cited, *King Lear,* William Morris). . . .

In a trice Morph and Carl have become inseparable, and the god invites his new friend on a tour of the realm. Straightaway, they encounter Lord Hall, a young Regency buck whose clouded features betray a secret sorrow. Hall discloses that he is in fact merely a daub of color, a sentimental portrait come to life; just as people yearn to enter certain landscapes, so painted figures yearn to enter existence—and sometimes, very rarely, succeed. What happens afterwards to Hall is a tale worthy of E.T.A. Hoffmann—Spallanzani the automaton-maker of "The Sandman" even gets a mention—told in the style of Byron's letters, accurate down to the dashes used for all punctuation.

After taking leave of Lord Hall . . . the odd couple wander into a strange library. Here Carl glimpses the conclusions to *The Faerie Queene, Edwin Drood, The Man Without Qualities,* he notes the complete works of Enoch Soames, Gustave von Aschenbach, Bergotte, Stephen Dedalus, Edwin Reardon and Edwin Mullhouse (this last the subject of Millhauser's first novel, that wonderful evocation of childhood, *Edwin Mullhouse: The Life and Death of an American Writer, 1943-1954*). Along one tier he sees people literally devouring books; a bite from a volume by Kafka "had the taste of pure, burning-cold water." Elsewhere the travelers encounter all the classics burned with the library of Alexandria, the books that Joyce wrote after *Finnegans Wake,* Keats' later poems, Milton's epic on the life of King Arthur.

If these first opening sections recall Hoffmann and Borges, the subsequent tale of Morpheus' love for the virtuous Volumnia suggests Renaissance pastoral. It takes up a series of knotty love problems in language rising to heights of Euphuistic wordplay. . . . Following this tale of virtue rewarded (with misery all around) the companions enter a hall of "remembering" mirrors who talk of everything they've seen. Carl peers dizzily into a Speculum Mundi (shades of—or rather, reflections of—Borges' Aleph!) and learns that there's more to mirrors than meets the eye. A Prufrock-like mirror protests his brother's account of the love between a maiden and her glass: Instead, he says, "Let us speak rather of the boredom of reflection, the ennui of eidola, the acedia of sight." Carl hears several other stories, climaxing with an account of the "devouring mirror" which flourished in an age "when new lassitudes had led to darker abandons." Its hapless victims, "toward the end could feel their vital substance being drawn into the glass: and it is whispered that the final moments of dissolution were of a dark, unspeakable, intolerable voluptuousness."

This is the hothouse atmosphere of Baudelaire, and there lingers through many of Millhauser's pages the scent of the *Flowers of Evil*—sensuality, decadence, mystery. Lest they become too overpowering, he counters these *fin-de-siècle* blossoms with the heartbreaking story of the giants Heklo and Ekli, a narrative set down in prose as pure as Swift's; follows that with the brief fairy tale of Morpheus' passion for a mermaid; and in his final section moves completely into the realm of the fabulous traveler's tale. When these often slapstick adventurers, after escaping from a whale's gullet, explore sunken Atlantis, the descriptions of Atlantean artifice and mores recall Yeats' Byzantium as well as Millhauser's own **"Cathay"** (from his story collection *In the Penny Arcade*). Everything in Atlantis is fabricated: there are painted rivers, artificial flowers, hand-made clouds. The main palace looms as vast as Gormenghast, as labyrinthine as a Piranesi prison. In conversations here about the function of artifice Millhauser suggests a subtle defense of his own literary practice against the purveyors of true-to-life fiction; after all Morpheus' fantastic kingdom underpins the sunshine domain of realism. . . .

[*From the Realm of Morpheus*] is a book of romance, magic, and of the humane wisdom of that anti-Aristotelian Morpheus, the "mocker of them that know." Surrender to its dream-vision and you will, like Carl Hausman, be drawn into a world of unsuspected and exquisite wonder. (p. 14)

> *Michael Dirda, in a review of "From the Realm of Morpheus," in* Book World—The Washington Post, *September 21, 1986, pp. 1, 14.*

JOHN CROWLEY

Steven Millhauser's first novel, *Edwin Mullhouse*, was a work of great originality that seemed, at the time, magically familiar. In *From the Realm of Morpheus*, he seems bent on reversing that equation, producing a strange sport of a book, wholly odd yet purposefully unoriginal.

Carl Hausman, watching a baseball game on a sunny afternoon, follows a lost foul ball into the woods and discovers the opening to an underground world. As the heroes of such stories always do, he immediately plunges in, and so embarks on a series of adventures in the sunless realm of Morpheus, god of sleep.

Morpheus's realm is, in this book, a collection of stories and narrative ideas whose germs or originals are almost entirely derived from other books and stories. Mr. Millhauser is parodying a whole body of literature one would have thought it impossible to re-create: those old-fashioned guided tours of fanciful (as opposed to science-fictional or mythical) other worlds, complete with stories told within the story by the curious inhabitants. We are not near Jorge Luis Borges's mirror worlds or Italo Calvino's postmodern invisible cities; we are closer to Samuel Butler's Erewhon or James Branch Cabell's Poictesme, somewhere between Alice's underground and Gulliver's islands. . . .

Hausman's guide is Morpheus himself, like a painting by Magritte in derby, pipe and dressing gown, but talking incessantly in a pseudo-Falstaffian Elizabethan lingo that eventually infects Carl, who is himself a Morpheus in training. The god is jolly and self-indulgent, but his realm is not in fact ease, indulgence or sloth; the stories are largely about dissatisfaction, insufficiency, thwarted desire and love gone bad. . . .

As he is led from tale to tale, Hausman struggles to take on some life of his own. He is only fitfully successful, but after all the narrator of a book of this kind needs little independent existence if the conceits he is made to record are good ones.

The danger, which Mr. Millhauser skirts throughout and does not entirely escape, is of being taken over by one's own skill at pastiche, enjoying for its own sake the re-creation of bypassed modes, and thus creating what is in effect one more book of a kind that few care to read any longer, even in the original versions.

It may be that some such apprehension struck the author, for he ends Carl Hausman's adventures underground in the middle of nowhere. The hero is not returned above ground. Every hint that has been dropped along the way to suggest that a unified allegory or single big story was being built (about the artist's need to resort to his unconscious? the tug of darkness

over light?) is left unresolved. The thought is inescapable that the author just got bored, as the reader of a rambling Munchausen fantasy of this sort so often gets bored, and, like that reader, put his book down between one outlandish adventure and the next, and did not care to pick it up again.

> *John Crowley, "Underground with Mirrors and Mermaids," in* The New York Times Book Review, *October 12, 1986, p. 9.*

IRVING MALIN

[The very first page of *From the Realm of Morpheus,* suggests Millhauser's] obsessions. We are told that "sunshine" is "paradoxical"; its "brightness creates an intensity of shadow that troubles and allures." He continues in this disturbing, powerful way to invert notions, to mix things: "It's as if the purpose of sunlight were nothing but the revelation of these shadows, which perhaps have always lain hidden there, unseen in the imperfect light of sunless afternoons. You know those insubstantial, spiritual afternoons, when objects cast no shadows, and so do not exist." If we look closely, we can see that he tends to be paradoxical, ambiguous, philosophical. Light and shadow, existence and non-existence, perfection and imperfection, the seen and the unseen—all of these opposites are fused (barely) to make us wonder about creation.

Although the narrator is watching a baseball game—a work of art?—he is drifting into the "arms of Morpheus." The narrator's eyes, we are told, are "half closed." Once we accept the premise that the narrator is a dreamer—a very alert one!—we are able to understand that his long, beautifully shaped sentences reflect his musing, slow patterns of imagery. We move down—the section is called the "descent"—with him; we feel drugged. And as we fall we begin to see transformations; we are not sure *where* we are. Are we in this world? Are we somewhere else?

These epistemological questions haunt us especially when Morpheus—the creator and observer of all dreams—remarks that art is a complex kingdom (a magical one) in which anything can occur. . . . Morpheus is apparently fascinated by the angelic and demonic qualities of romanticism; he recognizes that we as readers are also creators. We do not have, however, real freedom to choose *one* world, *one* substance.

Millhauser gives us distortions, mirrors, twins, "incestuous" tales so that after a while we recognize that, like the narrator, we are trapped *and* liberated by art. There is a marvelous—in the true sense of the word—scene which takes place in Morpheus's library. Characters from one book chat with those from another volume; letters are alive. The "impish" scene is, if you will, a key to the entire novel.

We are, in effect, reading a fiction which assumes an almost human quality; and yet this fiction—is Millhauser the creator? is Morpheus the creator?—refuses to stay still. Words and objects change places. There are odd, sudden conversions. The novel is a playful, complex text—a text about texts. (pp. 254-55)

> *Irving Malin, in a review of "From the Realm of Morpheus," in* The Review of Contemporary Fiction, *Vol. VII, No. 3, Fall, 1987, pp. 254-55.*

Susan Musgrave

1951-

Canadian poet, novelist, and author of children's books.

Well known in Canada for her flamboyant lifestyle as well as her writings, Musgrave incorporates her personal experiences and outlook into intense, individualistic poetry that is noted for bizarre representations and disjointed syntax. Often likened to such Confessional poets as Sylvia Plath and Anne Sexton, Musgrave uses disconcerting images of death and sex to vividly evoke feelings of separation, frustration, and desire. Critics have been both offended and intrigued by her biting humor, her explicit descriptions of sexuality and violence, and her creation of such unsettling yet engaging characters as vampires, lunatics, and witches. Caroline Bayard commented: "Musgrave has immense talent. Instead of distancing us from these unusual realities, she makes their ways and movements almost credible and even, to a certain extent, admirable."

A high school dropout at age fourteen, Musgrave traveled around British Columbia and experimented with drugs and alternative lifestyles before being placed in several psychiatric institutes. During one stay, she fell in love with a fellow patient who taught English at the University of Victoria and who strongly influenced her growing interest in writing. She published her first poem in the *Malahat Review* before reaching age eighteen. Musgrave has married three times; her second husband, who was convicted for drug smuggling, was defended in court by her first husband. In 1986, Musgrave married a notorious bank robber in a widely publicized prison ceremony. Critics suggest that Musgrave's unconventional marriages have helped sharpen her talent for creating comic and satirical verse.

Musgrave's first volume of poetry, *Songs of the Sea-Witch* (1970), hints at the black humor and sensuality that have become important elements of her writing. Impressed by her powerful delineation of a barren world of death and despair, numerous critics lauded Musgrave as an important new Canadian poet. Her second major collection, *Entrance of the Celebrant* (1972), reaffirms the concerns of *Songs of the Sea-Witch* but also emphasizes the psychological basis of her mystical imagery. Musgrave's work was regarded as somewhat limited thematically until the publication of *Grave-Dirt and Selected Strawberries* (1973). The highly praised poems in this collection range from surrealistic presentations of various subjects to a series of animated odes to the strawberry in which Musgrave skillfully parodies various poetic forms and styles.

In two succeeding works, *Becky Swan's Book* (1977) and *A Man to Marry, A Man to Bury* (1979), Musgrave makes strong feminist statements that protest social pressures of marriage and conformity. The narrator of *Becky Swan's Book* graphically chronicles the abuse and victimization that women have endured throughout history. The poems in *A Man to Marry, A Man to Bury* are darkly humorous expressions of an individual whose cloistered world is bleak and loveless. While some critics stated that the extreme solitude of these personas tends to restrict reader sympathy, others

were impressed with Musgrave's adroit manipulation of words to achieve a hieratic voice, which, as Patricia Monk observed, "gives her poems their distinctive flavour, their absolute originality."

Musgrave has noted that with her next work, *Tarts and Muggers* (1982), she attempted to compose verse that is more gregarious and less self-absorbed. While acknowledging some of the pieces in *Tarts and Muggers* as expressive and provocative, most critics agree that this volume fails to match the inventiveness of her early works. Diverse topics and tones are evidenced in the verse collected in *Cocktails at the Mausoleum* (1985). Many of these poems contemplate physical desire and friendship, and in one sequence, "We Come This Way but Once," Musgrave writes fondly of camaraderie among Canadian poets.

Musgrave has also challenged social ethics and values in her two novels. *The Charcoal Burners* (1980) is the story of a Canadian girl who spurns modern society and travels across the islands of British Columbia with her Indian husband in search of a lifestyle based upon a romanticized past. The harsh reality of the present, however, interferes even in the wilderness, where exiles of contemporary society have established depraved communities. While faulting this novel as disjointed, critics commended its rich psychological detail and wry humor. Douglas Hill remarked: "I respect the myths and metaphors of *The Charcoal Burners,* admire its energy of imagination and naturalness of expression. It's a striking fictional debut." *The Dancing Chicken* (1987) offers a satirical portrait of the lives, loves, passions, and guilts of an upper-class community. The tightly structured plot of this comedy of manners revolves around a caddish lawyer whose affections and indiscretions affect nearly everyone with whom he comes into contact. Musgrave was praised for her lucid, candid treatment of social class.

(See also *CLC,* Vol. 13 and *Contemporary Authors,* Vols. 69-72.)

CAROLINE BAYARD

Susan Musgrave is never afraid of the bizarre. She even makes a conscious effort to familiarize us with its various modes. *Becky Swan's Book* is a fine illustration of this stylistic approach and it will probably leave its readers with ambivalent feelings of terror and delight, for one needs a good dose of gothic humour to appreciate her meanderings into the realm of the weird.

Her poetic world is peopled by mad clergymen (who give arsenic to their mistresses), witches, poachers, idiots, skeletons, and demons. And Musgrave has immense talent. Instead of distancing us from these unusual realities, she makes their ways and movements almost credible and even, to a certain extent, admirable. We feel close to her characters at the very moment when she snatches them away from us. The young Lucy Littlecote, for instance, who was innocently playing hide-and-seek in the garden is subsequently found bricked up in the rectory "wearing 18th-century boots". It is this constant tension between the ordinary and the horrifying that makes a reading of Musgrave's poems here an enchanting experience.

> *Caroline Bayard, in a review of "Becky Swan's Book," in* Quill and Quire, *Vol. 44, No. 8, June, 1978, p. 46.*

CARRIE MacMILLAN

Becky Swan's Book is a collection of eleven short new poems, tightly unified and elegantly crafted around the persona of their narrator, Becky Swan. It is the psychological world of Becky Swan that Musgrave reveals with her characteristic emotional intensity. Musgrave has Becky reveal herself partly through her own experiences but even more so by her observations of those of others, particularly women who are deformed or victimized or defeated. The women from Becky's portrait gallery appear to be from different periods, some mediaeval, some renaissance, some eighteenth century. A consistent source of the grief they share is marriage, although it can also be general societal pressures to conform, enforced by men or women. While they desire release from bondage, frequently making unheeded cries for help, they seldom achieve it. In those rare cases where they do, they are labelled "witches," "supernatural" or "wicked." Here are some of Becky's women: Elisa and Mary, joined together at the shoulder and hip; Lucy Littlecote, bricked up in the rectory for an affair

that does not meet with approval; Lady Eleanor, who relinquishes passion for the cold conformity of the Church; Mistress Blandy, who is poisoned by the local clergyman for her "loose tongue"; Godrich's wife, who is beheaded for adultry by her husband, after bearing him fifteen children; and finally, in the last and most dramatic poem of all, Isobel, who must remain faithful to her husband, Death:

> Isobel, Isobel
> let in no lovers.
> Are you still faithful on your
> death-bed? Are you letting it happen?
>
> Isobel, death is sly.
> You should not wear white,
> You should not paint your face or
> show a leg to the male nurses.
>
> Death wants to share everything.
> He wants to get under the covers
>
> he wants to get on
>
> he's panting to get on.

Becky herself has been forced into an unwanted marriage, though she would have preferred "to / dance with the young men in town— / I wanted to dance till they hunted me down" (**"Still They Call It Marriage"**).

It is a dark, threatened, gothic world that Becky inhabits, one perfectly controlled by Musgrave through the use of extreme economy (the longest poem consists of thirteen lines, many of which have as few as two or three words), startling, even shocking images, often of witchery or pain, and powerful, haunting rhythms, achieved by repetition of sounds, words or groups of words. Even her selection of type, Cloister Old English, contributes to the unity and effect of the whole. While the poems provide a poignant and dramatic personal portrait, the accumulated images of tortured and mutilated women dramatically rendering Becky's psyche, one cannot help but see them, presented as they are as so many women in so many periods, as making a larger statement on the condition of women. Musgrave, by employing her own characteristic style to pursue these female ancestors, makes her own fresh and powerful contribution to feminist literature. (pp. 132-34)

> *Carrie MacMillan, in a review of "Becky Swan's Book," in* The Fiddlehead, *No. 119, Fall, 1978, pp. 132-34.*

ANNE COLLINS

If Susan Musgrave had run away to join the circus at 17, instead of publishing her first poem, she would have been drawn to the lion's cage. Her poetry has the solitude of the lion tamer; her slender neck rests in death's jaws, aware that truce (perhaps truth) exists only in the moment between the beast's growl and the crack of the whip.

Unrelenting is the word [for *A Man to Marry, A Man to Bury*]. Musgrave writes from a place where hope has been murdered, shot down in the cold, blue light of the moon. Thousands of voices mourn its passing. She slips in and out of the characters of mass murderers, abortionists, lovers and witch-hunters, who yell or whisper about the same things:

love, death, the cruelty of the innocent, the casualties of survival. . . .

Musgrave has said that she writes only about what keeps her awake at night. Death, the ultimate bogeyman, is in many of the poems. It seems to inhabit some backwoods village where blood is casual and idiot children are kept locked in the attic—open secrets who stare out their windows into life that is called normal but is more like a slaughterhouse. As in **"Between Friends,"** where members of a family commit suicide by garroting, dynamite and knives, all are matter-of-fact to the onlooker: Between you and me, it isn't much worth / talking about. It was common enough / in those days, anyhow. / Death and that.

Love is here and humor, too, though it sounds like the laugh of a gravedigger. Moments of grace occur mainly in transit, on a ferry cross the ocean, on a boat cross the lake, on a train from the mountains . . . . Lovers love each other only when caught in old photographs, or when waving goodbye. The book is a thousand pinpricks meant to keep you awake at night. If it doesn't, suspect that you've already been embalmed.

Anne Collins, "Like a Shotgun to the Heart," in Maclean's Magazine, *Vol. 92, No. 9,* February 26, 1979, p. 55.

KENNETH SHERMAN

There are times I think the Governor General's office ought to give an award for the most tasteful example of necrophilia since so many Canadian poets seem to be engaged in that activity. This year's award could go to Susan Musgrave for her recently published, *A Man To Marry, A Man To Bury,* a book filled with blood moons and demon dogs, and laced here and there with severed hands that get bottled, rotting corpses that are kept and told tales to, nephews who are chopped up and eaten—all of which sounds as though it should be pretty chilling. Unfortunately, it isn't.

You see ever since Plath and Sexton, the demented dame has become something of a poetic pose for certain female writers and in this volume, Musgrave's images, because they lack a convincing emotional base, appear as a witch's mask one might put on for Hallowe'en.

And there is a distaste for men, a dislike of sex. Musgrave's persona is "impaled on the penis . . .", and, as the book's title suggests, men are to be buried, ultimately so that "Only my innocence / ever remains constant." In the poem, **"Coming of Age,"** which is central to this collection, a male outlaw, Giffey, is turned on each night by nine, nubile, touch-me-not maidens:

> we teased him until he came,
> blasting off into the moonlight

The poem closes with the eventual impotence of Giffey, while the teasing vestals

> crept home finally to our
> clean beds . . .
> . . . completed and alone

A whole lot of masturbation in the mausoleum.

In the poem **"Salad Days,"** Musgrave provides us with a fine description of her poetic self:

> *This poet is in pain. She is professional in her romanticism. She bares her chest and lops off her breasts . . .*

> The audience is satisfied

> (p. 42)

Kenneth Sherman, "Tasteful Necrophilia," in The Canadian Forum, *Vol. LIX, No. 690,* June-July, 1979, pp. 42-3.

PATRICIA MONK

In *A Man to Marry, A Man to Bury,* her ninth book of poetry, Susan Musgrave presents more of her distinctive and original poems. In the six groups of poems . . . which make up the volume, Musgrave shows herself to be a mistress of the morbid imagination, of the hieratic voice, and of the craft of words. The world she presents is her own inner world, and she moves through its strangeness as someone who knows it and is not afraid of any of its manifestations.

Her command of the morbid imagination manifests itself primarily in the theme of death which, even in the first group (a group of love poems) governs every line and phrase of every poem. She confronts suicide (**"Picking Cloudberries by Moonlight"**), accidental death (**"Between Friends"**), murder (**"I Did It To Attract Women"**), and execution (**"Due Process"**). The forms of death both attract and repel her: she cannot avoid writing about it. . . . (pp. 570-71)

To frame these deaths she conjures up a sombre and strange landscape. In her poems it is nearly always winter, nearly always night, and always cold, raining, or snowing. . . . Moreover, through this monochrome world of death and winter move its living inhabitants, with barely human semblances and demonic propensities. Sometimes their strangeness is merely physical, . . . sometimes it is psychological as it is with the murderer who "came finally with their crushed heads to the / police station—calling God as his witness—/ a good family man" (**"I Did It To Attract Women"**). All bring with them the chill of the "other", which Musgrave like other poets knows to be too easily confused with simple madness.

Most chilling of all, perhaps, is the poet's solitude in her world. We see her isolated not only from the outer world of facts and events in the creation of this inner world, but also from the world she creates. At first, in the opening group of poems she is with a lover: "Now, crossing the water, / I am certain there is only us". But later, the "flag of ourselves" which gives this group its title is shown to be "the flag of loneliness", and by the end of the group the poet and her lover have separated, and "there is something about my leaving that is / beautiful, beautiful" (**"Eddy"**). In later groups the withdrawal becomes more strongly marked, the voice more imperative as she observes "I would not want to be born joined / promise me I will not be born joined to anyone" (**"Elisa and Mary"**). It is not a rejection of an individual, but of humanity, as her persona makes clear in **"The Judas Goat"**; she "wandered from the herd to / escape humiliation" and "skirting the world's edge . . . thrived on spoils", until, as she tells us finally: "I prayed I had not become human".

Musgrave observes us all in the mirror of her imagination and removes herself from even that reflection.

This progressive and menacing isolation of self within the inner world of the poems is lightened by touches of comedy. **"Salad Days"** is a splendid satiric portrait of her fellow Canadian poets . . .; the found-poem she finds in the **"British Migraine Association Poetry Competition"** entry-form is also characterized by a bizarre comedy. Consequently, in other poems ostensibly perfectly straight-faced, lines such as "I buried you too soon, / though not deep enough" (**"Dig, He Said, Dig"**) take on a faint ambiguity and provoke a tentative, nervous laughter. Her poems as a whole, consequently, are redeemed from a total absorption in the macabre and the morbid by a spice of the comic, keeping her well away from the tortured inner worlds of Sylvia Plath and Anne Sexton.

As mistress of the hieratic voice in her poems, Musgrave speaks with unmistakable authority. . . . In **"North Beach Birth"** she speaks oracularly of the coming to birth of the child from the moment of conception, and binds child, parents, and herself into a solemn, incantatory ritual which takes shape as the poem. It is above all else, perhaps, this hieratic voice which gives her poems their distinctive flavour, their absolute originality.

The voice, moreover, is conveyed to us in words chosen by a poet sensitively submissive to the demands of her poems and at the same time mistress of all the techniques required to craft such demanding poems. She chooses her words with delicacy and verve, and manipulates them dextrously and with superb economy. If she can be faulted at all in this volume, it is on the tendency to prefer to end the rhythmic unit and the line unit together; this can fragment the poem into a series of short barks; more attention to spreading the syntactical unit over a group of lines, or even over the whole poem would eliminate this. But, finally, Musgrave must be acknowledged as both technically and imaginatively a mistress of her craft. (pp. 571-72)

> *Patricia Monk, in a review of "A Man to Marry, a Man to Bury," in* The Dalhousie Review, *Vol. 59, No. 3, Autumn, 1979, pp. 570-72.*

ANNE COLLINS

Deaths, the violent and bloody kind, are not unusual in thrillers—they add a few quick intakes of breath and that little wet tingle of fear down low in the abdomen. But after doing their work the corpses of conventional thrillers are easy to bury; they comfortably fit some cause or pattern of revenge, and don't hang around to haunt the reader. No such luck with poet Susan Musgrave's first novel [**The Charcoal Burners**], a thriller indeed, but one whose ghosts don't stay in the grave. This is a thriller about death itself, a fact not hard to miss considering that it opens with its heroine reading the obituary column and manages to record the deaths of 13 assorted beasts and humans in Part 1 alone. (p. 58)

The Charcoal Burners is also funny, amazingly enough, a combination of black humor and final darkness that perhaps only a poet with Musgrave's obsessions could pull off. It centres on the travels of Matty, a white-girl-former-anthropology-student, from trailer camp to Indian village to the forests of a misty, cedar-covered group of islands off the coast of British Columbia. She falls for her future husband, Dan Seeweed, while dancing with him:

> When she looked at him she could imagine the mask, Wild Man of the Woods. . . . There would be strings of elk teeth dangling from his neck, woodpecker scalps and feathers hanging from his waist. She could even ignore his dentures, glowing as they did under the black lights.

That's where the humor lies: Matty hungers after the Indian in Dan but his dentures are more indicative of life on the islands. The old ways of oolichan grease and salal berries have largely given way to Dream Whip, GMC pickups and alcohol. Their work rendered obsolete, the Indians are drunken, clown-like tatters of their former selves, tatters Musgrave renders wonderfully in minor characters like Spaghetti Chops, a former athlete gone to fat who spends his time, *all* his time, walking back and forth to eat in town, and whose name honors a famous recipe of his concoction (p. 59)

The whites on the island, mostly drunken loggers, are equally off-kilter. When Matty runs from her husband, after the chaos of a crazy mixed-up Indian funeral and feast of hungry souls, she heads deep into the woods where she stumbles into a commune of crop-haired white women of professional background more ludicrously out of touch than the Indians. . . . Eschewing males, they worship a male god with fertility rites and dietary restrictions all mixed up in a West Coast yin-yang jumble. They want to be primitive, the Indians want not to be, yet neither can obliterate what they were long enough to achieve their desires. Musgrave is brilliant at making comedy out of these mismatched souls.

Meanwhile, the thriller runs on, obsessively, as the reader waits to see what will happen to Matty, who is more the purveyor of a death wish than a heroine. Matty connects sex to death, birth to death and pain to herself, accepting what is done to her by her husband, men in general and the commune-dwellers in an already half-dead fashion, which seems in this black comedy the only appropriate response or lack thereof. Admittedly, to laugh at this book one has to possess a well-developed taste for the horrible—and Musgrave's own fascination with the grotesque almost undermines the book. Until the last part, in the charcoal burners' camp, she plays off against each other the dying society of the Indians and the artificially resuscitated one of the commune to luminous effect. What happens among the charcoal burners and who they turn out to be comes close to making everything a final unprofitable joke. But the death net is well-woven and ultimately stands the strain. (pp. 59-60)

> *Anne Collins, "A Death Net Well-Woven," in* Maclean's Magazine, *Vol. 93, No. 39, September 29, 1980, pp. 58-60.*

CLARK BLAISE

Anyone who doubts the existence of a distinctive Canadian literature should be asked to name the following novel:

1) A lost, vaguely rebellious girl locked in a doomed relationship flees deeper into the North woods. There she finds an encampment of fiendish Americans, despoiling nature and perverting the local mythology.

2) A young woman, sick of all the sacrifices she has made out of guilt and helplessness, walks away from an unfeeling mate

into a more spiritual relationship with an old friend. The quest for purification leads to unspeakable agony, torture, and death.

3) An internationally respected Canadian poet writes a novel saturated with sex and violence, abhorrence of the modern world, deep suspicion of the flesh, and strong identification with both the degradation and the spirituality of the Canadian Indian. The heroine's drawn-out suffering is transmuted to a kind of last-stroke beatitude.

It could have been *Beautiful Losers, Surfacing,* or *The Edible Woman.* It could almost have been *Gone Indian, Bear, The Scorched-wood People, Coming Through Slaughter, Scann,* or *The Diviners.* It could have been written, in part, by Malcolm Lowry, Audrey Thomas, Peter Such, Dave Godfrey, or W. P. Kinsella. But it's Susan Musgrave's first novel, *The Charcoal Burners.*

The point is that one sturdy branch of the Canadian novel—especially its West Coast manifestation—deals not with assaults upon Loyalist rectitude (as in the provincial literatures of Ontario and English Québec), but with something deeply romantic, whose honoured totem is the painter Emily Carr.

"I guess it's in my blood to want to be like Emily Carr," Musgrave wrote in **"Skookumchuck"** in 1976, identifying in Carr's work "the unexposed skin / the masks behind loss." That's not what I find in Carr, but certainly it's supportable; so is majesty and serenity, terror and fetishism, pietism and reclusiveness, and occasional mawkishness. For Musgrave to assert her own shared intent, or to see herself as another chip off the old arbutus (and not to appear an idolater or opportunist), she needs to give her readers more of those primary colours and less of the romantic agony. *The Charcoal Burners,* . . . attempts that large-scale exposure of flesh and suffering. The attempt falls short of success. (p. 72)

I am interested in the marriage of Matty (née Martha Clarke, Vancouver girl, pubescent poet, and third-year University of British Columbia anthropology drop-out) and Dan, her Indian husband. Totemistic Indian males make frequent ritual appearances in our literature, but rarely do our lily-white heroines actually marry the guys and learn to shop-lift dripping roasts, nurse hangovers, or tolerate their whoring, thieving, illiterate in-laws.

Dan is the best character in this broken-backed narrative: if he'd stayed around longer (Matty leaves him in the first half of the book), the author might have been forced to create a character out of Matty instead of letting her remain a dust-cloud of passive observation and wooden stage directions. If Musgrave had written her poetry with the same indifference to language and feeling ("Matty surveyed the room . . ."; "Matty went into the kitchen . . ."; "Matty paddled until her arms grew sore . . .") . . ., it's safe to say she'd still be waiting for her first publication.

The first half of the book is promising—a little harsh on Indians, but funny and "earned" through Matty's shared suffering—but the second half can only be judged, charitably, a disaster. Matty and an old UBC chum, Christian, head into the woods of Christian's remembered childhood (his parents were missionaries). It's the nature of the Canadian experience, of course, that Americans have discovered all our childhood haunts; if it's not a fried-chicken outlet or a camper jungle or a theme-park, then it might be this: Jonesville North, a feminist/vegetarian commune ruled by a horned and feath-

ered dwarf, where every kind of despicable, degraded, sadistic practice is condoned by a Nazi-inspired political homeopathy.

Matty and Christian are taken prisoner, and their agonies are drawn out just long enough to permit all the principal degenerates to expound their tedious theories. By now we're in a different novel, lacking the wit, the bite, the control of scene and character. Matty becomes a disembodied sufferer, an almost perfect victim. . . . [It] makes for timid narrative and the bluntest, dullest of resolutions.

The novel seeks to confirm attitudes (meaning prejudices) that are already well-received. We *know* what to think of white guilt, of Indian failings, of Hitler-quoting bikers, of any fanaticism with a California provenance. What we don't know is why we're being exposed to it and warned about it so stridently, so exhaustively, all over again. This has taken us far from the message of Emily Carr, from whose canvases a special cold, gloomy wind has been known to blow. Perhaps Musgrave wants us to know that the totems are all gone now, the forests are vanishing and the people are next, all of them turned to charcoal. (pp. 72-3)

Clark Blaise, "Vanishing Totems," in Saturday Night, *Vol. 95, No. 9, November, 1980, pp. 72-3.*

DOUGLAS HILL

The Charcoal Burners, by Susan Musgrave, has several strong ingredients—gritty realism, dark, intense imagery, suspense, a terrifying conclusion—that mix to produce an exceptional first novel. Musgrave, whose accomplishments in poetry are well-known, has made a remarkable transition to fiction. This is no "poet's novel", attenuated and precious or whatever the phrase is supposed to mean, but a fully developed narrative of poetic depth and power.

The central character is Martha Seeweed,—Matty—a young white woman married to, then separated from Dan Seeweed, an Indian from a British Columbia coastal settlement. In the course of the book's five parts, Matty encounters the bizarre implications and extensions of some crucial phenomena of contemporary life—race and sex, religion and cultism, nature and primitivism. Matty is pulled on her journey deeper and deeper into a North American heart of darkness. She's not at first a particularly appealing heroine. Sometimes vague and scattered, she's apparently indecisive and unformed, yet her susceptibility to circumstances and her helplessness make her victimization all the more believable and appalling. . . .

The last two sections require a strong stomach for the scenes of shock, eroticism, and grotesque horror. Throughout we get Matty's dreams, hallucinations, private images and visions, infused with her growing outrage and despair. The novel will inevitably be compared to [Margaret Atwood's] *Surfacing*—usefully, I think. Musgrave lacks the austere religious/philosophical/political structure Atwood imposes; Atwood seldom in her prose strikes so deep and so powerfully into the unconscious, into primal fears and longings, into the now lovely, now feral connections between sex and death.

Musgrave takes chances with her talents here. She refuses to be "safe", choosing instead to let her sensibility spill out. Though I admit to some difficulty in making her total vision, poetic as well as moral, cohere as fully as I'd like, I respect the myths and metaphors of *The Charcoal Burners,* admire its energy of imagination and naturalness of expression. It's a striking fictional debut.

Douglas Hill, in a review of "The Charcoal Burners," in Books in Canada, *Vol. 9, No. 10, December, 1980, p. 30.*

PAUL STUEWE

The Charcoal Burners finds Susan Musgrave, a most experienced and accomplished poet, essaying a novel that has many of the strengths of her verse but lacks some of the attributes of successful fiction. The impact of Musgrave's imagery stems from her capacity to grasp and hang on to psychic material that most of us know only as subconscious glimmers, and then display it in language at home with patterns of association ranging from the conversational to the metaphorical to the surreal. Thus taken simply as a rich assortment of evocative images, *The Charcoal Burners* is an engrossing and often deeply affecting piece of writing; but when considered as prose fiction, this collection of memorable moments does not add up to a coherent novel.

What we do have are several striking vignettes, some realistic short stories and a horror fantasy all more or less relating to the experiences of Matty Seeweed, a young British Columbia woman who suffers much and learns little. The vignettes reveal Musgrave at her most poetic in both positive and negative senses, positive in terms of sheer vividness of language and negative in terms of estrangement from the mundane realities of physical setting and temporal sequence. The realistic short stories are very well done, but they haven't been well-integrated into the rest of the book; and the force of a profoundly shocking denouement is unfortunately lessened by a series of jarring transitions between realistic and fantastic narrative voices. The overriding impression is that *The Charcoal Burners* requires either a guiding editorial hand, if intended as a novel, or else presentation in a variety of shorter and more clearly defined forms.

But these criticisms must be qualified by a recognition of the devastating, if sporadic, power of a book that contains a great deal of excellent writing despite its failure as a novel. Musgrave, too, strikes us as having experienced what she writes about in a most significant and meaningful way, and . . . she possesses the literary techniques to render it with fidelity and effect. What she has not yet mastered, at least on the evidence of *The Charcoal Burners,* is the control and interrelation of different kinds of prose writing within the form of the novel, but this will certainly come to an author who never seems to be at a loss for high-grade raw material. *The Charcoal Burners* . . . succeeds in convincing us that the experiences it transmits are true, deeply felt and worth knowing about, and in the final analysis that's all that really matters.

Paul Stuewe, "New Visions from the Darkling Plain," in Quill and Quire, *Vol. 46, No. 12, December, 1980, p. 29.*

BARBARA GODARD

Infused with the knife-like language and imagery of her poetry, *The Charcoal Burners* develops a suspense-filled story in the mode of the dystopia. Never far from the graveyard, the book opens with Matty reading the obituaries (casually composed in this community, intermingled with other want ads)

expressing the fear that she might find her own name prematurely listed here, a clue to the topsy turvy, inverted world we have entered. Musgrave turns her satirical eye on the social world of Vancouver Island, through the tense marriage of Matty, white sociologist, and Dan, drunken Indian, focusing on these two groups. In Old Mystic we encounter a world as bizarre as that of Jack Hodgins where mythology has decayed to be lost not in the fogs of rumour and gossip but in the bones of the graveyard, rifled by hungry dogs.

Musgrave gives full rein to her macabre fantasy. The result is a powerful novel which, despite the tension it provokes in the reader, compels one onward through the midnight hours to the anticipated end. Musgrave's language is under sharp control: there is no doubt about the satiric aim of the clichés . . . . Ultimately, Musgrave's readers may well be sickened by the uncompromising nature of her vision. . . . Musgrave plays the role of psychic iconoclast, pulling the categories of existence apart and presenting a broken, confused reality that her readers must put back in order for themselves. (p. 94)

Feminism, as well as alternate life styles in communes, vegetarianism, neo-fascism, great mother worship are exposed in Part Four of the novel, the "Utopian world" Ephratah in The Kisgula, a hidden river valley known to old time Indian fishermen. Purportedly seeking a return to the true old ways before the present decayed state of Old Mystic, Matty and Dan, depressed by the death of Dan's father, advance up this river in a canoe on a journey reminiscent of Arthur Gordon Pym's or the protagonist's of de Mille's *Manuscript in a Copper Cylinder.* Instead of Indians, they find there exiles from contemporary society, proponents of various current versions of Utopia, life styles Musgrave reveals to be as violent as those from which they are fleeing. Specifically singled out for examination are sex roles. At Ephratah, Matty and Dan find a community apparently based on the worship of the great mother, a community of women and children devoted to astrology, vegetarianism, nonetheless subject, as we find out, to the power of a male God, who visits the women to impregnate them. As the story develops—I'll not ruin the suspense by telling it—we find out that this lifestyle is not as pacifistic as it would seem. These discoveries are ironically foreshadowed in the book Matty reads as she begins her voyage, Atwood's *The Edible Woman,* which she sets aside for a vegetarian cookbook. Matty is thus disarmed for her encounter with "paradise." Had she reversed the order of her reading, she might have been more alert to her situation, for Musgrave has provided us with a gloss on Atwood's novel, though the image developed there symbolically is taken literally in *The Charcoal Burners.*

With its involvement in contemporary issues, *The Charcoal Burners* may not be destined for a long life. While it is around, it demonstrates several elements of contemporary fiction in Canada, notably the power of novels by poets, given their tight control of language and their compelling images. (pp. 94-5)

Barbara Godard, in a review of "The Charcoal Burners," in The Fiddlehead, *No. 132, April, 1982, pp. 94-5.*

L. KING-EDWARDS

[In *Tarts and Muggers*], Musgrave strives after arcane and mysterious poems. In **"The Pact"** her persona states:

> I am *the forest;*
> my deep scent reels
> *against the dark.*
> I unfold
> *like darkness*
> and you are lost in me.

The question that must be asked when reading these poems is, "Are these truly poems of a woman possessed by darkness and loss, or are they made by an artful woman trading on a convention?" Individually many of the poems seem convincing, but read together they become less so. Although the persona of the poems takes on the character of the dark, the instinctive, the venging female fury, I am not among those who feel that "a prophetess is in our midst." (I am more concerned that there be a poet in our midst.) Incantation can become powerful in the voice of the believer, but after all Musgrave is just a young woman, a poet who enjoys indulging herself in playing now the Whore of Babylon and now the innocent victim. The poems do not convince one that they are by a woman who is either a forest or a witch. There are some good poems and some striking images, such as:

> trailing a vague
> hand, floating
> for the shark's sake.

or

> The pit at midnight
> crusty with snow
> like a day-old bread pudding.

But if closely examined, much of the writing seems confused and inconclusive . . . . (p. 22)

One is never sure whether the contradictory nature of a poem where the persona "half-loves" and then "loved too much" is an intentional attempt at surrealism or whether it is just careless writing. Even given the benefit of many doubts, clarity is often sacrificed to portentousness and sound, which may carry the casual reader, but not the discerning one.

It is impossible to read Musgrave without thinking of other poets who have called forth the inanimate and inarticulate world to be on their side. One recalls Theodore Roethke and his divine nonsense. Her hand is not sure enough to dabble in this art.

The better poems of the book tend to be those that are less elliptical and which do not rely on the dark woman persona. They may be more pedestrian in form and in content, yet they are more intense and striking in feeling. One thinks of **"The Embalmer's Art," "Coming of Age,"** and **"For Charlie Beaulieu in Yellowknife. . . ."**

In all, these poems, selected and new, are largely selected from her earlier books. There is but a handful of new ones. . . . *Tarts and Muggers* is not about either, so don't let the title tantalize. (pp. 22-3)

> *L. King-Edwards, "Lists and Incantations," in
> Books in Canada, Vol. 11, No. 10, December, 1982,
> pp. 22-3.*

ANDREW BROOKS

I feel guilty, somehow, that I do not understand more of what is going on in Susan Musgrave's poetry, and I suspect it is a similar shortcoming in the poetry-reading public which has kept her from having acquired an even more formidable reputation than the one she now enjoys. *Tarts and Muggers* is an enigmatic work, but not so enigmatic that one cannot see the unique talents of the mind behind (within) it.

The most interesting poetry in the book is founded upon a fascinating use of syntax which seems to tap sources in the reader's mind of which he or she had been unaware. Each work is a mosaic of phrases, a cathedral built of verbal fragments seemingly lifted from conversation. Often the phrases, individually, approach "natural" speech (that ideal so often abused by poets). Yet the effect accomplished by the enjambment of many such phrases undercuts any sense of the natural. These seem to be fragments lifted from *different* conversations.

Musgrave achieves an utterly eloquent poetry capable of adjustment to any contour, not syllable by syllable or word by word, but phrase by phrase—*in segments*. Her poetry is a dazzling juxtaposition of angles—the proverbial infinity of straight lines forming a curve. . . . Musgrave's ability to build flow from segments closely parallels a basic perception of reality. Infinite, discrete bits of what is familiar blend into a continuum which jolts us with sudden, surprising resonance. Energy crackles in the joints, and the poems are as valuable for what they say implicitly—for their tangential energy—as they are for what they say directly.

In addition to her penchant for the productive subversion of syntax, Musgrave possesses a highly individual sense of drama. I say "individual" because the drama we find here consists not in that accumulation of context which comprises what is commonly called drama—Musgrave's use of disjointed (or "rejointed") phrases prevents that. Here, the accumulated thrust of a poem commonly runs at right angles to that of the individual phrase which the reader is encountering at any given moment. The drama comes from somewhere beyond, or immediately around, the actual words. . . . The absence of the conventionally dramatic makes a mockery of the mere suspension of disbelief—we question the validity of disbelief itself. It does not repossess us when we turn the final page, but remains in some fundamental sense revalued.

The truths—the identities—for which the poet is reaching are reached for obliquely. There is little directly verbal confrontation here. There is more of the quest, a hunt through a landscape of attributes and relationships often at cross purposes, or, tantalizingly, only partially revealed. At the centre there is always the firm "I" giving a focus which is stable and personal at the same time. The personality at the centre is firmly enough etched—Musgrave is really speaking to us here—that the poetry is prevented from becoming aphoristic or "clustered" like poetry by, say, Roo Borson, in which all elements of the writing and all the entities it serves are in a state of flux. I don't mean to dismiss Borson—she is as good a poet as Musgrave—but Musgrave's poetry has a unique integrity. There is hardly the slightest shift in real concentration. The poems remain firmly cemented throughout and lines more "pithy" than others are not easily lifted. Each poem is a single point of consciousness, the universe within the atom, relentlessly probed and opened up. (pp. 63-4)

Andrew Brooks, "Forms, Points, Details," in Canadian Literature, No. 98, Autumn, 1983, pp. 62-5.

JUDITH FITZGERALD

[*Cocktails at the Mausoleum*] contains seven sections; unfortunately, their logic seems arbitrary and self-conscious. There are long poems and there are long sections. This collection consists of long sections, a series of disconnections.

Musgrave's natural poetic abilities are inestimable; when she wishes, she can write circles around circles. However, much of this volume displays an uncharacteristic laziness on the part of the poet (or her muse). The easy rhyme occurs again and again, almost as if the poem had asserted its own order, its own sense of control. Meanwhile, the absent author appears as an afterthought, a sort of literary joy-rider.

Paradoxically, although the writer is missing, the persona/I in these poems insistently prevails. On its own, confessional self-obsession has a place in our literature (circa 1960); combined with a "poetic journal in the form of Musgrave's own notes to the poems," such autism ultimately induces a severe case of boredom. How often do we need to be informed of the colour of the poet's dress, the make and model of some car or other, whether a given photographer was copacetic? Not only do we sit through the original, we must also suffer the instant replay. In **"I Am Not a Conspiracy, Everything Is Not Paranoid, The Drug Enforcement Administration Is Not Everywhere"**:

> Paul comes from Toronto on Sunday
> to photograph me here in my
> new image . . .
>
> camera goes on clicking, standing naked
>   in the
> high-heel shoes I bought last summer in
>   Mexico. . . .

And later, the note from this "I": "Paul Orenstein was the photographer. Obviously I felt uncomfortable in the cornfield, far away from the ocean I'm used to being photographed beside."

At bottom, *Cocktails at the Mausoleum* contains a handful of poems; the remainder displays what Charles Olson called "the lyrical interference of the individual as ego." As an exercise in self-promotion, it works; as a collection of poems, it doesn't.

Judith Fitzgerald, "Women in the Moon," in Books in Canada, Vol. 14, No. 7, October, 1985, p. 30.

VIVIENNE DENTON

[*Cocktaiils at the Mausoleum*] bears the catchy title typical of her collections, suggestive of violence and reversal. These titles, like the language and images of punk culture, seem designed to shock. There is a fair range of subject and tone within the collection, although the poetry is chiefly erotic and the dominant genre is a sort of punk gothicism. [**"Cocktails at the Mausoleum"**], for example, features a wild dream sequence of drinking, sex, and vampirism set in a mausoleum in a forest. A few of the poems could be called love poems, but for the most part these are poems about physical desire; often crazed fantasies figuring images of animals (sharks and bears are favourites), savage teeth, dismemberment, and tor-

ture. This is very disembodied poetry on the subject of the lusts of the flesh; poems are characteristically in the form of dreams where action is not enumerated in gross physical descriptions but in a sequence of images. In fact, according to Susan Musgrave's notes, many of these poems began as dreams. At least she tells us this much of the poems in the section of the collection entitled, **"My Boots Drive Off in a Cadillac,"** a title indicative of the kind of story line of many of the poems.

Not all the poems are frenetic fantasies. One section, entitled **"We Come This Way But Once,"** comprising poetic reflections from a poetry reading tour with fellow Canadian poets Bill Bissett and George Johnston, celebrates friendship and shared experiences. Another poignant group is a series of requiems for absent friends. In this section also, one finds a longer poem, **"Requiem for Talunkwun Island,"** a lament for the rape of an island in the Queen Charlottes where logging has caused such massive soil erosion that reforestation is impossible.

Musgrave weaves fantastic fictions whose meanings are often obscure. Images are telescoped, reversed, or mingled incongruously as in dreams. At the back of the book, the poet has appended what is described on the dust jacket as a "poetic journal in the form of Musgrave's notes to the poems." . . . The journal with the poet's voice providing an introduction to her poems is, in fact appropriate, for Musgrave's is theatrical poetry, and one is very conscious of the poet speaking. The final poem in the book, **"Not a Love Poem,"** deals with the topic of poetic inspiration. It begins very prosaically, albeit provocatively, "Last night as I sat in my bath. . . ." In this collection the poet flaunts a most private, naked self; in the bath, in the bed, in her erotic fantasies. It makes for always provocative and sometimes compelling poetry. (pp. 273-74)

Vivienne Denton, in a review of "Cocktails at the Mausoleum," in CM: Canadian Materials for Schools and Libraries, Vol. XIII, No. 6, November, 1985, pp. 273-74.

SUSAN MUSGRAVE [INTERVIEW WITH ED JEWINSKI]

[Jewinski]: *What motivates you to write poetry?*

[Musgrave]: I guess much of my poetry results because things shock me—human relations especially shock me. The way people treat each other shocks me—in love, in war, in prisons, in any thing, even in everyday relationships on the street. I don't know how things work; I don't know how it all stays together. Poetry is the only way I know of trying to make sense of it.

Does poetry deal only with the bleak and depressing then?

No. Not at all. The act of writing and creating is a celebration. Perhaps the content is sometimes depressing because of the process of trying to figure out what it's all about. Still my "subjects" are about obvious violations. I write about things I feel violated by.

Are poems about happiness impossible?

Not impossible, but difficult. It's very hard to write poems about happy events. I've tried, but they don't come off. Part of the problem is fashion. The fashion's against you. Happiness dominates TV commercials, not poetry. Even consolation isn't a possible alternative anymore in modern poetry. It would be hard to write in the vein of Gerard Manley Hopkins today; people are too cynical and depressed.

Is this in part why, at least since **A Man To Marry, A Man To Bury,** *your books have taken on a new social tone?*

In that book I was able to include more of the "real" world, the world that is around me rather than focussing on the very internal, private world. I still can't write about political themes. That's very difficult for me. I don't know how to do it very well. So I try to avoid those things. My poems are more outgoing than they used to be. They used to be very inward looking. Now they are commenting on things that are happening to people.

What initiated that change?

I really liked Tom Wayman's poetry, and Al Purdy's. I liked the narrative style and I wanted to write things like that. . . .

What attracted you to Purdy and Wayman's poetry?

Their directness. Although there's a lot going on in their work, they are poets that are much more obvious. You can understand their poems; you don't have any problem with them. (p. 3)

How have you changed as a writer?

I'm not as locked up as I was when I was eighteen or nineteen, writing **Selected Strawberries** or the poems I wrote in Ireland. I felt confined by words; I wasn't looking at them in the way that I would later be and am able to now. I was at their mercy almost. I think that comes across in the poems, a kind of pathos. I almost feel sorry for the person writing, as if they were possessed by something. I felt I was really possessed, by voices. I was crazier, not knowing that I could survive. When you are eighteen and you start being crazy, there are not too many alternatives. I always thought automatically of suicide and now I realize I've gone through so many things that are terrible that, when another terrible thing comes along, I think it's just another terrible thing. You just survive. That's a great knowledge; knowledge that you have as you get older. (pp. 3-4)

[Some] readers see you as a feminist, especially some reviewers.

Yes, some do. And I have read reviews of my books that were sensible and interesting. I learned a lot from them. But some others took things totally out of context. One reviewer suggested I believed all women were "impaled upon a penis", saying this line expressed my view of sex, saying I found sex disgusting, and men, you know, worse. It's so irresponsible. I mean the poem the reviewer misquoted from was a fertility charm for Dave Godfrey's cows. In another review, one in *Books in Canada,* the reviewer misquoted my poems and pointed out how terrible my lines were. Well, *his* versions of them were terrible. Such reviewing is not fair; he made them look as bad as he wanted them to be. . . .

I often section books, and there are usually four or five sections. I think in this book there are seven. Someone asked me how I decided which poem fit in what section. It's usually to do with voice.

Do you see yourself as having a variety of voices?

I don't think my voices may be as discernible to other people as they are to me, but I have several voices, I think, don't you? There's a love poem voice, a more ironic voice, a social

voice. Each voice is used in a different section. For instance, the first section of poems written in or about South America is what was happening to me while I was there. It's my psychological geography that is South America. (p. 4)

But not all your books are sectioned. Why is this so important to you now?

Part of having sections is from the experience I had with my **Tarts and Muggers: Poems New and Selected.** I didn't have sections. In my head I had a thematic arrangement, but I didn't know whether anyone else would notice that. A lot of reviewers were confused by the book because I didn't tell which poems came from what book. I guess a lot of selected poems will name the books the poems came from. But I just ran it all together. I thought that's really how my life is, so that's how my poems should be presented.

But shouldn't your book reflect your aesthetic concerns? Doesn't this new ordering make its own artistic statement?

In a way. I wanted that. But I'm not sure that the book was all that successful. It was like a graph where I saw a movement—one poem would connect with another in some sort of way. It worked that way for me. But for other people, it might not have worked. There's always so much in my head, and there's never a chance to give a direct explanation in a book.

Is that why you added notes at the end of this newest book?

I've always wanted to do that, but I found it difficult to think of a way without explaining the poems. I've really written little prose pieces or parallels that talk about where the poems came from or what happened to me the day before I wrote it. I think that's a way around it. I think it's helpful when you introduce the poem or the poetry. It gives a kind of biographical insight. And these days, with the focus on personality, that's what seems to be liked anyway. (pp. 4-5)

A number of readers I know were shocked by [**The Charcoal Burners**]. *Did you intend to shock?*

No. I didn't, though I see it as more shocking now, after having left it for a while. When I was writing, there was just the urge to get to the end of each sentence. So the impact of the images was lost on me.

Do you still like the book?

I think it's not a bad book. At least it's alive. I want things to be alive.

Yet what if the book offends? The scene with the deer for example offended some people.

I don't care whether literature offends some people, as long as the writing doesn't bore them. I also don't like people trying to be parents to books, always worrying about other people's reactions. There can't be a "no-go" area in the world of art or writing.

I admire your determination to be direct and honest in literature. I agree that there should be no arbitrary restrictions imposed upon fiction. My main problem with **The Charcoal Burners** *is its structure. It reads like two parts that don't quite fit.*

The main character, I think, is what made it cohesive and kept it together. And it's a book about tribal society actually. You have the Indian people, the Vegetarian worshippers, the

Charcoal-burning cannibals. But I wrote it over such a long period of time, and I had a lot of trouble with the ending. It was, of course my first novel. I had four different endings, for it went through four major drafts. I can see why some readers might see it as two books. (p. 5)

Ed Jewinski, "Writers' Quarterly Interview with Susan Musgrave," in Cross-Canada Writers' Quarterly, *Vol. 8, No. 2, 1986, pp. 3-5.*

RICHARD BEVIS

Susan Musgrave at 35 has already written a dozen books and made a notable contribution to Canadian poetry. (p. 186)

The poet one encounters [in *Cocktails at the Mausoleum*] is partly the resultant of previous selves (sea-witch, man-burier), partly an evolving persona, humanized by time and pain, that I think will prove more sympathetic and likeable than either. At first Musgrave practised a kind of West Coast necromancy in words, stirring a blend of dreams, moon, fantasy, and native lore. Like most styles and spells, these worked at some times and not at others. Set next to the present volume, *Songs of the Sea Witch* looks obscure and overly dependent on snake-slime, while *Grave-Dirt and Selected Strawberries* invokes a power of Haida material—at its worst a kind of easy *shtik*—without managing to transmute it into poetry. Yet *Entrance of the Celebrant* is clearly the work of a genuine talent, at least in **"Birthstone"** and **"Dog Star,"** which are made of typical under-thirty Musgrave materials: night, spirits, dreams, and death. (pp. 186-87)

In the present collection, the moonwitch of the western isles still dreams, but generally that mode is less important now; Musgrave continues to broaden her appeal. The first section, for example, **"Coming Into Town, Cold,"** documents the Canadian encounter with Latin, especially southern cultures. Here—and to some extent elsewhere in the volume—the crucial polarity is not nature/supernature but self/other, and I would argue that the most patently autobiographical poems—or even parts of poems—are the least successful. The section's title-poem and **"Supposing You Have Nowhere to Go"** are particularly limited by chit-chat about the poet's age, financial problems, and low opinion of Miami; they are lineated journal entries. (Of the eight poems that I wish she had withheld, five are lessened by this kind of self-indulgence.) On the other hand, where she submerges herself in the human condition, as in **"Hunchback on the Buga Road," "Ordinary People,"** and **"The Unconsidered Life,"** she is a poet.

> I am the bride with
> worms around her heart
> and a skull bursting with goodness
> like a church goblet.

This is not the "I" of **"I'm over twenty-nine."**

These are three of the nine poems (in this collection of five or six dozen) that I would use to convince anyone of Musgrave's talent. . . . The last three touchstones are the title-piece and two poems in the final section. **"Cocktails at the Mausoleum"** is both a typically wacky piece of Musgrave fantasy and her Ode to Melancholy; cocktails taste better at the mausoleum, but death stares from the bottom of the glass. (p. 187)

"I Do Not Know . . ." (etc.) is a remarkably successful "exorcism" of (we learn from Musgrave's notes) Howard

Nemerov's "Death and the Maiden." Nemerov himself—or Roethke or Hughes, other objects of homage—would not spurn such a phrase as "a compass of blood in the heart's / wreckage," though it is not all that good. Both this and **"You Didn't Fit,"** however, seem to me deeply humane poems about coming to terms with parents, time, madness, and self. In the first, shrinks try to "cut the / stubborn mother from my womb"; in the second, the poet's vivid dream of her father's not fitting his coffin becomes a symbol for both of their lives: "neither of us fit." Here Musgrave has outgrown the cuteness and extrahuman obscurity that marks some of her young poems. **"I Do Not Know"** is a paring down to essentials:

> I think of the choices we made
> along the way, how things
> came to pass, or happened,
> what brings us finally together.
>
> The years will make sense of it.

These are not her most "poetic" lines, but they make immediate contact, with the warmth of a sympathetic friend who has been through it.

When Musgrave is off, she is usually, I suggested, being merely personal, though once, in **"Eaglet Tricks,"** she seems too imitative. Her other weakness is too little detachment from prose—i.e., insufficient revision—which shows up as flaccid diction in, for example, **"Three Witches Go for Lunch in Elora."** Her ear is not flawless; she needs to judge, to edit, to purge, as every good poet does. Robert Graves, to whom she once made a pilgrimage, would be one healthy guru in this respect. Another she long ago chose herself—in **"Skookumchuck"** from *The Impstone:*

> I guess it's in
> my blood
> to want to be like
> Emily Carr

It takes some work to move that desire from the blood to the hand. What is clear is that in Musgrave's case the result will be worth the effort. One could do worse than be the Emily Carr of poetry. (p. 188)

Richard Bevis, "Voice of One's Own," in Canadian Literature, *No. 115, Winter, 1987, pp. 186-88.*

JANET HAMILTON

Near the end of Susan Musgrave's *The Dancing Chicken,* the novel's hero, lawyer Cod Holmes, reflects on his youth's simplicity from the vantage-ground of mid-life's complexity. The memory that sparks his musings is one of having taken his wife a spring bouquet when their first child had been born: "but Nora had been allergic to tulips and he'd had to remove them at once. He remembered driving, in a fog, out into the country, and stopping at the graveyard to put the flowers on his grandparents' graves. He'd masturbated there, into a red tulip." Now, remembering, Cod is "thinking of how good that tulip had been and wishing life could always be that uncomplicated".

Love, sex, death, and their complications among the privileged residents of fictional Rottleston, British Columbia are the subjects of Musgrave's very funny and wholly engaging second novel. In an easy-going prose style that shows the same light touch as the author's satire, Musgrave leads us through the homes of Rottleston society, takes us to its parties, introduces us to its causes—MACCT, the Mothers Against Cutting Christmas Trees, for instance—and makes us familiar with its members' beds, affairs, longings, and guilt. This is a society where, for at least some, "a hat is essential, it's not an accessory"—a society Musgrave observes and depicts with good-natured acuity. . . .

The action of **The Dancing Chicken** takes place during the Christmas holidays and focuses on Cod Holmes, his wife, children, mother, lovers, and law partners. It is a tightly structured comedy of manners, all of whose many threads the author ravels and unravels with great skill.

The novel begins with the near shooting of Cod's daughter and her biker-friend ("NEXT TO SEX I LIKE KILLING BEST" is emblazoned on the back of the biker's denim jacket) and moves on speedily to Cod's encounters with the women in his life. There is the lustful Grace, whose " 'just wanting him to be happy' meant he would have to suffer," and his mother, Miriam, at once the source of her son's peculiarly Anglican sort of guilt and fascinated with the "Sex Beasts" Cod routinely defends in court. . . .

Finally, there is Nora, Cod's wife, who is herself in search of love or sex or some—any—combination of the two, and who by her search exchanges the hell of "trying to find a deodorant that wouldn't fight with her perfume" for another, more fierce. . . .

There are many large and small triumphs in **The Dancing Chicken.** There is the high-finish dialogue, for instance, and the way the author has of grabbing hold of a cliché and shaking it: at one point Nora Holmes finds herself looking down the barrel of a gun, "pointed right between her eyes, where only yesterday she had tweezed a few stray hairs". Musgrave conveys the sheer looniness of common sense: "When I die I want to have my throat cut," the housekeeper, Mrs Bowditch, explains. "That way if I'm still alive I won't suffer."

The author's observations of everyday details, and their meaning for us, are wonderful. Nora's world of cabbage-leaf skin packs and starch blocker tablets called Cheat and Eat and the try-before-you-buy cosmetic counter is particularly rich in this regard. In one quite touching moment Nora recalls the family's recent, failed holiday in Hawaii: "The most thrilling part of the holiday for her had been the discovery of a little packet containing complimentary thread, a needle, and two buttons in the dressing-table drawer."

One of the novel's important accomplishments is its explicit treatment of social class, which neither side-steps the importance of class in real life (as much Canadian fiction does) nor pulls the reader into a conspiracy with the author against the implicitly inferior. Musgrave is really superb in this regard, able to suggest class sensibility in an incidental comment. A Rottleston matron explains about her husband's luck with bingo on their recent Mediterranean cruise: "Anyway, he got a Bingo but he didn't want to say anything. He didn't feel it was very dignified, shouting out 'Bingo!' at the top of your lungs in a crowded place.". . .

Musgrave has the ability to sustain the comic energy of the whole while shifting tone quite suddenly, typically from hilarity to pathos. One of the most moving instances of this is when the elderly Miriam reminisces about her dead husband, Dodder. Her memories introduce the matter of love, sex, and

death, but with a difference, for Miriam is a woman who now fears neither death nor eternity, who knows that old age is not something one "gets over". Miriam remembers Dodder's proposal of marriage: "Do you think it would be *too* awful for you? If we were to marry, that is."

> *Janet Hamilton, "Musgrave Makes It with Love, Sex, and Death," in* Quill and Quire *Vol. 53, No. 10, October, 1987, p. 22.*

ELEANOR WACHTEL

The story goes that Susan Musgrave is having trouble finding a publisher for her non-fiction book, *The Joy of Sexual Failure.* Apparently the chapter on masturbation, which features a distraught shepherd who splits himself open with a twig, is offputting to Canadian houses. Undaunted, Musgrave has included an off-scene character, Destiny, in **The Dancing Chicken** who masturbates with pens, knitting needles, a meat thermometer, and finally razor blades until he "splits his penis in half, from head to root." That's the thing about fiction: there are no limits. Or, as Musgrave says, "Maybe my sense of humour is different from other people's."

Destiny goes on to murder his unfaithful wife. Well, not simply murder her, but cut her in half with a power saw. After all, he's an unemployed logger. He's defended in court by the beleaguered, middle-aged hero of **The Dancing Chicken,** a criminal lawyer named Cod. . . . Near the novel's end, Cod loses the case and Destiny is given a life sentence. (Get it?) The presiding judge, who always wears a kilt, has just revealed himself to be a pregnant transvestite.

Relying on sexual kinkiness for its laughs, **The Dancing Chicken** is being promoted as a satiric, comic novel. And perhaps not surprising, given her flamboyance, its author is being promoted front and centre. In what must be a publicist's dream, **The Dancing Chicken** is described as having gone through "six drafts and three marriages. Susan was working on it when her second husband went to prison for importing 30 tons of marijuana into the country and while her third was being *released* from prison where he'd served 14 years for gold robbery." In a rare instance of restraint, the press release fails to mention that her second husband had been defended on an earlier drug charge by her first husband. . . .

[Her] writing about those marriages—especially the last one, behind bars, to Stephen Reid—has produced some of her most comic, accessible prose. Funnier and more ironic than the broad, exaggerated, fundamentally old-fashioned farce of **The Dancing Chicken,** where everyone is sex-crazed and no one is happy. In fact for a "comic novel," **The Dancing Chicken** offers a sordid and bleak vision that isn't leavened by sexual weirdness.

The story follows the harried Cod as he juggles three women, as well as his 86-year-old mother and 17-year-old daughter, over Christmas. One of the women is his wife, Nora, who is so frustrated and disgusted by Cod's infidelities that she takes up with his one-eyed law partner, Leonard Putz. (In a book of cheap shots, where do you begin?) Putz eludes Nora, settling instead on one of Cod's other women, the enormously obese nurse, Grace Trout, RN, Virgin. . . . Then there's Ursula, an unstable divorcée Cod has acted for, who is also clamouring for his attention. She's the kind of gal who leaves pubic hair in her ashtray, goes out in a fur coat with nothing on underneath, and whose ex-husband liked to dress up in women's clothes and "be taken, rectally, with the leg of a chair." In this book, even the car radio talks about copulating, cannibalistic insects. (p. 19)

[Just] go down the checklist: there's incest, rape, a birthday cake in the shape of male genitals that's carved up and devoured at a party. Musgrave writes with confidence and bravado, but this is cartoon stuff of a particularly nasty sort.

The novel's central image comes from a San Francisco peep show. A sucker feeds a quarter into the slot, a red light illuminates a small cage and slow striptease music is heard while a scrawny chicken hops around. It's rewarded with a few grains of rice when the music stops. But the chicken keeps dancing around. In case we miss it, Cod too hops blindly around trying to keep his sadsack life together. (p. 20)

Eleanor Wachtel, "Different Strokes," in Books in Canada, *Vol. 16, No. 9, December, 1987, pp. 19-20.*

Amos Oz

1939-

(Born Amos Klausner) Israeli novelist, short story writer, nonfiction writer, editor, and author of children's books.

Considered among the most original and controversial contemporary Israeli authors, Oz often centers his fiction on ordinary domestic conflicts that serve to comment upon the political and historical heritage of Israel and its relationships with surrounding cultures. As a spokesman for the first generation of sabras, or native-born Israelis, Oz departs from his nation's tradition of optimistic social realism to examine such themes as religious fanaticism, the destructive effects of anti-Semitism upon both oppressor and oppressed, the clash between community and individuality, and the irrational motivations that often characterize marital and family relations. Writing exclusively in Hebrew, Oz has been widely praised for his use of a carefully modulated literary style blending surrealistic fantasy, symbolism, and allegory.

Born into a family of right-wing Zionist supporters that included several writers and scholars, Oz left his native city of Jerusalem during the 1950s to join a kibbutz, or collective farm. Sent to study literature and philosophy at Hebrew University in Jerusalem, Oz received his bachelor's degree in 1963 and returned to his kibbutz to concentrate on farming, teaching, and writing. In stories collected in *Artsot ha-tan* (1965; *Where the Jackals Howl and Other Stories,* revised, 1976), Oz uses the jackal as a symbol of forces that threaten the stability of an isolated kibbutz, both from outside its guarded perimeter and from within its domestic sphere. Although mildly received in Israel, this collection won praise in the United States for its accurate rendering of kibbutz life. A. G. Mojtabai praised *Where the Jackals Howl and Other Stories* as "a strong, beautiful, disturbing book. It speaks piercingly . . . of a dimension of the Israeli experience not often discussed . . . ; it reminds us of polarizations everywhere that bind and diminish us, that may yet rend us." Oz's first novel, *Makom aher* (1966; *Elsewhere, Perhaps*), also garnered acclaim for its sympathetic treatment of idealistic Jewish immigrants who risk establishing a mountain kibbutz near the Syrian border. Jacob Sonntag commented: "I know of no other book that depicts life in the Kibbutz more vividly, more realistically or with greater insight."

With his next novel, *Micha'el sheli* (1968; *My Michael*), Oz achieved popular success and established an international reputation as one of Israel's foremost authors. Set in Jerusalem during the 1950s, this work alternates between stark realism and romantic lyricism to relate excerpts from a diary that describes the ambivalent sexual fantasies of an unhappily married woman. While some Jewish nationalist reviewers regarded the book as a nearly seditious allegory of their country and its relationships with Arab Israelis, western critics compared *My Michael* to Gustave Flaubert's novel *Madame Bovary* for its restrained portrayal of an individual's private struggle against adverse social circumstances. *Ad mavet* (1971; *Unto Death*), inspired by Oz's reaction to Israel's Six-Day War with Egypt in 1967, consists of the novellas *Late Love* and *Crusade*. In *Late Love,* a Russian emigrant wanders throughout contemporary Israel predicting the destruction of

the state by Soviet Bolsheviks. *Crusade,* which was initially published in English in the American journal *Commentary,* is set in the eleventh century and concerns a French count's fanatical obsession with a religious pilgrimage to Jerusalem that leads to violent acts of anti-Semitism. Ivan Sanders contended that *Crusade* "shows how loathsome and maddeningly tentative the real world appears when seen in the distorting mirrors of perverted spirituality."

In *La-ga'at ba-mayim, la-ga'at ba-ruah* (1973; *Touch the Water, Touch the Wind*), Oz blends comic fantasy, allegory, and symbolism to chronicle the experiences of a Polish-Jewish mathematician from his interment in a concentration camp in Nazi Germany during World War II through the Six-Day War. Incorporating the protagonist's rise to world prominence and his reunion with his estranged wife with fantastical events, including the transformation of humans into animals, this novel garnered angry reactions from Israeli critics for attempting to deal with atrocities in comic or surrealistic terms. Alfred Kazin, however, declared that Oz "is an immensely clever, subtle, and mischievous writer whose new book is a brilliant scenario of all Jewish experience of our day." *Har ha-'etsah ha-ra'ah* (1976; *The Hill of Evil Counsel*) consists of three loosely connected semiautobiographical novellas narrated from the romantic perspective of a young middle-class Palestinian boy before the country and its inhabitants began to succumb to the pressures of militant Jewish nationalism in 1948. *True Repose* (1983), published prior to Israel's war with Lebanon, reflects Oz's dissatisfaction with his country's often violent response to differences with its neighbors. This novel concerns the decision of a young man to flee his confining existence in a kibbutz and seek suicidal escape in the Jordanian desert.

Oz's next novel, *Menuhah nekhonah* (1983; *A Perfect Peace*), centers on domestic conflicts that result when the son of a Zionist founder rejects his family and life in a kibbutz to escape the constrictive ideologies of his ancestors. After a naive but passionate young man who idealizes kibbutz existence joins the community and supplants him, the protagonist shames his family by inviting his successor to share his wife and home before departing to seek his identity in enemy territory. Described by Grace Schulman as "Oz's most powerful work" and by Rita Kashner as his "strangest, riskiest and richest novel to date," *A Perfect Peace* affirms the futility of all human systems when faced with the inevitability of death. *Black Box* (1988), the title of which refers to the device that records conversations between an airplane pilot and the flight crew and is often used to help determine the cause of an accident, is an epistolary novel consisting of letters exchanged between Alec, a political sociologist living in the United States, Ilana, his promiscuous ex-wife, and Boaz, their rebellious son. Alec expresses his contempt for Ilana by sending money to alleviate Boaz's delinquency, unaware that Ilana's new husband, Michel, is using his wages to purchase land on Israel's West Bank as part of an obsessive religious quest. Analyzing complex character interactions as well as differences between Alec, a Jew of European descent, and Michel, a working-class Jew, many critics regarded *Black Box* as an allegory of the state of modern Israel.

Oz is also noted for his essays on political and literary topics. *Poh ya-sham be-Erets-Yisra'el bi-setay* (1983; *In the Land of Israel*) is a collection of interviews Oz conducted with Jewish and Arab Israelis from diverse social and political backgrounds. Originally published as a series of articles in the socialist newspaper *Davar,* these pieces, according to Robert Alter, "reflect a strenuous effort to go out into Israeli society and sound its depths." Oz is also coeditor of the Israeli magazine *Siach lochamium* and has contributed articles to such journals as *Encounter* and *Partisan Review.*

(See also *CLC,* Vols. 5, 8, 11, 27, 33; *Contemporary Authors,* Vols. 53-56; and *Contemporary Authors New Revision Series,* Vol. 27.)

YAEL LOTAN

This rather long novel [*A Perfect Peace*] takes us back to the years 1965-67, and it is a measure of the changes that have taken place in Israel since those days that it reads almost like an historical novel.

Set in a kibbutz in the heart of the country, the story revolves around a young man's decision to turn his back on his entire life, on all that is known and familiar, and lose himself in strange landscapes. The kibbutz, viewed through his eyes and those of two or three other persons, seems like a composite creature, an organic entity, somewhat like an ant-hill or a beehive. If certain personalities do stand out of the mass, they are no more than noticeable features in a face. (p. 84)

Amos Oz' hearing is perfect. He manages to record the sounds of conversation—not merely the words, but the exact intonations and inflexions that characterize types and generations. Even a minor scene is thus lighted up with a verisimilitude that strikes the Israeli reader between the eyes. Similarly, he is a master of atmosphere, and in this novel he excels in portraying a kibbutz in winter, when it goes into a state of semi-hibernation.

Oddly enough, the personality of the central character, Yonatan Lifshitz, is the least discernible of the cast of characters. Perhaps this is because his rather torpid nature is essentially blurry and hard to define. The result is that his desire to get away from it all ("everything is false, I tell you!") is not entirely convincing. Similarly, his wife, Rimona, remains rather sketchy, despite certain marked characteristics, eccentric to the point of mild insanity. The personalities of some secondary characters are much more vivid and convincing. . . . (pp. 84-5)

The portrait of [Yonatan's father], Yolek Lifshitz, a lion in winter, one of the Grand Old Men of the kibbutz movement, a figure dating from the truly revolutionary days of pioneering Zionism, is brilliantly drawn. The uncompromising ideology, the dogged posture, the underlying pride, all add up to a figure which one still sees on the platforms of kibbutz movement conventions. . . . Yolek's wife, Hava, is another "old timer" whose like can be found in any of the old established kibbutzim. (p. 85)

But the most successfully evoked, and perhaps the most original character in the story, is that of the outsider, Azaria. Like a fledgling cuckoo, he plants himself in the kibbutz, where he seems to be a complete misfit with his city clothes, his compulsive talkativeness, and his refugee mentality, all eagerness and sensitivity. Yet the extraordinary circumstances and his own irrepressible good will—albeit fantastic to a degree—combine to make it possible for him to fit in after all, and better than the native son, Yonatan.

In fact, as the story progresses, the focus of interest shifts away from Yonatan and settles on Azaria. Although each of them accomplishes if only in part, what he set out to do, Azaria's quest is of considerably greater interest and originality than Yonatan's, and therefore his achievement is not only more memorable, but of greater significance, both for him and for the people around him.

The rapid decline of the older folk suggests that these young people—the aimless and complaisant Yonatan, the dreamy and eccentric Rimona, the ingenious Azaria, the hypernationalistic Oudy and his easy-going wife Anat—are the people of the present and foreseeable future. There are no giants among them, and their dreams—even Azaria's, in the final analysis—are small dreams. They will not create new worlds; at best they will be able to maintain the world created for them by their predecessors.

Amos Oz is a writer of the post-revolutionary generation. There is no impassioned grand design behind it all, as there was in the literature of the preceding generation. There is better literary quality, a mellower tempo, clearer observation, fewer illusions, and a certain melancholy. The passions are private, and so are the griefs. The country itself—its sights and sounds, its raw conflicts, its running tensions—which serves as the background to this fiction, marks it and sets it apart.

There is a curious tension in most Israeli literature today, arising from the conflict between the desire to write "universally" and the need to document the specific realities of our time and place. It takes a true literary talent, such as Amos Oz', to overcome the self-consciousness caused by this tension; and even so, it occasionally mars the quality of the writing. Time will do the rest. (pp. 85-6)

Yael Lotan, "A Certain Melancholy," in Modern Hebrew Literature, *Vol. 9, Nos. 1 & 2, Fall & Winter, 1983, pp. 84-6.*

GRACE SCHULMAN

[*A Perfect Peace* is] Amos Oz's most powerful work. . . . [The novel's events] unfold between 1965 and 1967, from the news of skirmishes near the Syrian border to the Six Day War. The reverberations of these events permeate the book, lending it an atmosphere of continual unease and anticipation, but the clashes Mr. Oz evokes are more of the domestic variety—a generational conflict over the meaning of the Israeli experience itself. In *A Perfect Peace,* he examines the disjunctions of history and the ways in which a people—and finally it is more than just the Israeli people to whom he speaks—transcend such divisions. (p. 7)

Born and raised on a kibbutz, at the age of 26 the book's protagonist, Yonatan Lifshitz, means to bolt from the claustrophobic, inquisitive, tight circle of men and women among whom he continues to live and who must bear, he feels, with the older generation's beliefs. At first he longs for new urban places; later, he has a vision of harmony that he feels he can realize only in the desert, on enemy soil, in an ancient city where human skeletons have been "bleached by the sun and preserved by the dryness and heat in a state of polished perfection."

Yonatan's father, Yolek, is an early settler with a pious faith in the utopian dignity of the kibbutz. He is the outgoing kibbutz secretary and a former cabinet minister, well known for his dedication to social reform. Young Yonatan resists the abstractions of his father's ideology. He suffers from knowing that while his father was admired for his rebellion in the name of labor Zionist doctrine, he must play the conformist if he is to carry out the same principles. But he is also tormented by what he sees as the hypocrisies of his elders—"Their hearts were not true"—and seeks a purer way of being.

The tension between father and son is temporarily relieved by the mysterious arrival at the kibbutz of young Azariah Gitlin, who, Yolek observes, was "born in the wrong generation." Because he has not grown up with the Zionist ideals, their meaning is not exhausted for him, as it is for Yonatan. Though he is a "bore," . . . Azariah's utopian romanticism nevertheless has its positive side. When in the face of continuing frustration Yonatan finally departs for the ancient—and empty—city of Petra in the southwestern desert, he leaves his wife, Rimona, to Azariah; Azariah, in turn, keeps Yonatan's house in order, hoping for his return.

As if to certify the reality of the situation he portrays, Mr. Oz has interspersed the names of actual Israeli leaders among the fictional ones throughout the book, thus reinforcing the novel's documentary tone. . . . It is, however, on a level other than the documentary that this novel succeeds so well. It is concerned with inner wholeness, and with a more profound peace than respect between generations and among countries.

Apart from the compelling tale of Yonatan's redemptive journey—after facing himself in the purifying solitude of the desert, he is able to break off his head-long journey to Petra and return home—the impact of this novel lies in the writer's creation of characters who are outwardly ordinary but inwardly bizarre, and at times fantastic. Before we learn of their inner turmoil, characters are presented to us in sharp exterior outline. Yolek, Yonatan's father, seems immediately real. . . . (pp. 7, 40)

The narrative shifts from one perspective to another, all eyes trained on the central drama of Yonatan's disaffection and subsequent flight. Rimona, his dreamy, elegant wife, gives the most magical account of his turmoil, in an interior monologue reminiscent of Ophelia's mad scene (down to a series of "Good night" greetings), and of Nicole's distracted recital in *Tender Is the Night*. We also hear about Yonatan's conflict through Azariah's distorted but adoring explanations of his own actions; from a guilt-ridden letter that Yolek writes to his friend Levi Eshkol but does not send; and from the diary of Srulik, the incoming kibbutz secretary, filled with observations about the migrations of birds, time's disintegration and the struggle in all of us between cruelty and love.

Yonatan's curious, primitive odyssey might have lacked credibility in lesser hands. Mr. Oz, however, is a master at making ordinary details unfamiliar: his characters' deeds are right because of the expressionist mist in which he envelops their reality, distorting and omitting circumstances that might document, but not explain, behavior. Just as we accept the unusual union of Yonatan, Rimona and Azariah, so Yonatan's sojourn in a desert of jackals and night birds seems natural. (p. 40)

Grace Schulman, in a review of "A Perfect Peace," in The New York Times Book Review, *June 2, 1985, pp. 7, 40.*

RITA KASHNER

[In *A Perfect Peace*], Yonatan Lifshitz decides to leave his wife and his kibbutz, to leave Israel entirely. Before he leaves, he installs in his home a voluble, screwy, socially inept young man who has found his way to the kibbutz. Azariah, the newcomer, will take over Yonatan's wife, Rimona, and their dog. The kibbutz is scandalized. Yonatan's mother, Hava, is enraged. His father, the secretary of the kibbutz and a fierce old pioneer, is heartbroken. Azariah is delighted. Rimona is unmoved in her serenity. Her calm, in fact, represents the only peace to be found in this novel, and it is clearly symptomatic either of madness or retardation.

Rimona is certainly not the legendary omnipotent Israeli maiden. She is as white and delicate as a marble sylph, and as cold. She is, in fact, a heartbreaking caricature of femininity—passive, accepting, accommodating, beautiful, and frigid, wanting nothing for herself. She simply reflects back what Yonatan tells her, in an insanely soothing litany. Her only drive is to promote peace, quiet, stillness.

CONTEMPORARY LITERARY CRITICISM, Vol. 54

OZ

For his part, Yonatan wants nothing more desperately than to be alone. Encircled as he has always been, he can't find himself. And because his father is larger than life, the boy knows he cannot be anything in that country until his father dies. . . .

It's the one thing Yolek, the father, never thought of. In him, Oz writes an elegiac portrait of the aging pioneers who fought to build the dream and now find that their children simply inhabit it, like any neighborhood they might have found themselves in. He doesn't understand Yonatan and can't hear him—he becomes increasingly deaf as the book progresses—and it breaks his heart that Yonatan runs away, perhaps to his American tycoon would-be father.

[*A Perfect Peace*] is Oz's strangest, riskiest and richest novel to date. He writes in his usual clean, blunt prose, his characters' voices ring true, and he creates a world which makes perfect sense, except that at its core is a series of impenetrable mysteries. Who, for example, is Yonatan's real father? It might be Yolek, or it might be Benya Trotsky, the radical-turned-Miami-tycoon, who lived on the kibbutz briefly and fell in love with Yonatan's mother, and who now wants to leave his empire to her son. Only the mother knows which it is, and she isn't telling.

For that matter, who is the father of the child Rimona gives birth to toward the end of the book, Yonatan or Azariah? Why does Yonatan provide his wife with a lover in the first place, and why does she simply accept the arrangement? Why is she so damned *calm?* And above all, what are we to make of Yonatan's brief and bizarre rebellion and his ultimate docile return?

In a novel with this many enigmas, with so many origins and destinations undefined and with key characters reacting in ways that seem otherworldly or mad, there is clearly allegory at work. That is usually the kiss of death for a novel—and in fact, the heavy-handed allegorical twist at the end of Oz's *Elsewhere, Perhaps* . . . was disastrous to that book. But if it is the game that Oz is playing here, it's a fine and tricky one, right up to the end. If the old men's tug of war over their son is heavy with its allegorical burden, for example, the character of Yolek is not. The long letter he writes to his lifelong political enemy, Levi Eshkol, is as canny a portrait of bewildered old age and contentious pol as I know. Oz has spent craftsman's years developing a tender, ironic humor and an accuracy of voice that serve him brilliantly here.

It is only at the end of the book that the reader may begin—the risk of Oz's game—to feel that he's been led by the nose to Yonatan's epiphanic moment of terror, which makes little sense except as symbolic act, and the ensuing tableau of the young trio plus infant may be a bit contrived, but the end of this novel is almost a coda. It's the long and rainy winter of dissatisfaction, personal pain and slow growth that is its splendid core.

> Rita Kashner, "Amos Oz: Holding Up a Mirror to
> Modern Israel," in Book World—The Washington
> Post, *July 14, 1985, p. 11.*

ROBERT ALTER

Amos Oz's latest, and most satisfying, novel [*A Perfect Peace*], originally published in Hebrew in 1982, offers a suggestive instance of how a writer can reorder and transfigure

his own constant preoccupations. Oz began work on the book in 1970, set the project aside for six years, then took it up again and completed it between 1976 and 1981. The historical framework is still the one to which he addressed himself in 1970—the tense period of a year and a half leading up to the Six-Day War of June 1967. But his handling of the materials and his sense of what is embodied in the Israeli predicament are very different from what they would have been at the beginning of the 1970s.

Nearly all of Oz's fiction through his 1976 volume of novellas, *The Hill of Evil Counsel,* is informed by the same symbolic world-picture: a hemmed-in cluster of fragile human habitations (the kibbutz, the state of Israel itself) surrounded by dark, menacing mountains where jackals howl and hostile aliens lurk. In the earlier Oz, this symbolic opposition is the vehicle for a series of troubled narrative meditations on the rationalist-idealist enterprise of socialist Zionism and, beyond that, on civilization and its discontents, for the jackals out there often find an answering voice in the jackal beneath the skin of those who dwell within the perimeter of civilization. In the new novel, there are a few passages where one can detect vestiges of this imaginative flirtation with the dark powers, but even in these instances the old obsessions have been transformed.

Let me begin with the title, which in the earlier Oz would have been mordantly ironic but which in the novel as it unfolds moves beyond irony. The phrase *menuhah nekhonah* is taken from the traditional prayer for the dead ("Grant perfect peace under the wings of the Shekhinah . . ."). For a good while, this in fact looks like a novel about the enactment of a death wish as the one clear way out of the constrictive pressures of the kibbutz and of life in Israel. The 26-year-old protagonist, Yonatan Lifshitz, is the son, though questions are raised about the paternity, of the kibbutz secretary, an old-time Zionist of the generation of Ben-Gurion and Eshkol who has served in parliament and is a leading figure in the Israeli Labor movement. Yonatan would seem to have the prototypical profile of the native male kibbutznik: unpolished, no-nonsense, taciturn, self-reliant, a tough worker, a decorated war hero. He is also suffering from a condition of psychological asphyxiation as the result of the demands and expectations laid on him by the collective; and Rimona, his sweet, spacey, solicitous, sexually unresponsive wife, is not much help to him. She leafs through illustrated volumes of Africa and dreams hazily of "the magic of Chad," while her husband's fantasies carry him to Bangkok, Singapore, any place elsewhere. . . . (pp. 38-9)

And so [Yonatan] heads southward, to a place where he can be utterly by himself, utterly himself, where he can find "a perfect peace" through death in the timeless desert that is the antithesis of reborn Israel, among the ruins of an alien civilization.

This fantasy of escape is one that has figured in a good deal of Israeli fiction and poetry over the past 15 years. . . . It generally remains on the level of a fantasy, a temptation, a mesmerizing but impossible project. In *A Perfect Peace* the fantasy brings the protagonist to the brink of suicide, hysterically firing the last rounds of his automatic rifle into the parched earth of the Jordanian desert in a weird, haunting moment of dementia unpent. Then, by slow stages, he returns, to be reintegrated into Israel, the kibbutz, and an odd reconfiguration of the family as ménage à trois.

I am not in a position to say whether this last detail is credible sociologically in a contemporary kibbutz, but it does have a certain thematic rightness. Yonatan the disaffected sabra comes to share his wife with the newcomer Azariah, a child of the Holocaust, garrulous, insecure, naively idealistic, a man full of philosophical quotations and grandiose schemes, as though a combination of hard-bitten native Israeli and quixotic Diaspora intellectual were necessary for the renewal, the qualified version of perfect peace, figured in the family and in the double-fathered child born to it at the end.

This rapid sketch of the plot is bound to be somewhat misleading, for Oz's novel is a hybrid of social realism and metaphysical brooding, and it gains its peculiar power of assertion by setting social institutions and political issues in a larger metaphysical context. There is a vivid, persuasive sense of place here—the white buildings with their red roofs in the sunshine, the laundry hanging on the line, the dress and gestures and verbal tics of the particular Israeli types—but local place is quietly evoked against a cosmic backdrop. In precisely this regard, the mentally skewed state of several of the principal characters is of particular utility to Oz, who for the most part limits narratorial perspective to the consciousness of the characters. As a writer he has always been fascinated by emotional disturbance, as though the true ontological substratum of chaos were discernible chiefly by the deranged. In *A Perfect Peace* he works toward a more nuanced perception of the nature of existence, and so shifts attention from madness to strangeness, moving from the slightly daft wife and the existentially baffled husband to the misfit newcomer. . . .

The noise of political debate, the buzz of kibbutz gossip, the quarrels between father and son, husband and wife, the threatening movements of Syrian troops on the northern border are all finally heard in [*A Perfect Peace*] against that ultimate, unchanging quiet between the stars. There is, let me hasten to say, no suggestion of a political quietism that would turn its back on urgent national issues in order to contemplate eternal things. Still, the Zionist enterprise with all its painful dilemmas is seen as a brave and necessary human project against a vast background of cosmic indifference and historical transience. That explains the special force of Yonatan's vision of Petra just before the final resolution. Reading a guidebook, he imagines . . . its [ancient] "orchards, vineyards, and gardens, winepresses and threshing grounds. . . . Until all was struck down. The ancient gods perished utterly. Man turned to dry bone."

This, the novel implies, is the inevitable fate of all that man erects. But the book does not end with the vision of the valley of dry bones, or with Yonatan's suicidal bursts of gunfire into the desert ground. Everything human may be tentative and transient; the only peace we can know may be a very imperfect one. And yet, as the final movement of return and renewal suggests, the imperfection of human things, in the family, the group, the nation, is all we have, and a kind of fulfillment can be found in them, in our wholehearted determination to make something of them.

The very last note of the novel is Srulik's, the new kibbutz secretary, who, as a German Jew, a musician, an introspective loner, is different from the run-of-the-mill kibbutznik. . . . [Srulik] is preoccupied with inhuman silences: "The earth is indifferent. The sky is mysterious. The sea is a lasting menace. And the plants and the migrating birds. The stone is as silent as death which has dominion over all." He then notes the capacity for cruelty of which no one is innocent, which in the course of the novel has been sharply manifested in the domestic sphere and darkly intimated in the political sphere as well. . . . Love, Srulik admits, is permanently beyond his grasp, while pain is an undeniable reality. "But a thing or two we can do," he concludes before setting aside his diary and picking up his flute, "and since we can, we must. As for the rest, who knows? Let's wait and see." (p. 39)

Robert Alter, "The World of Oz," in The New Republic, *Vol. 193; No. 5, July 29, 1985, pp. 38-9.*

NICHOLAS SPICE

[The problem of] utopian dreams, human cravings for a place of rest, a home—whether for the body or the spirit—is one that Amos Oz returns to time and again in the two books of his most recently to be translated into English, *A Perfect Peace* and *In the Land of Israel.* In both he suggests that coming to terms with such yearning is a precondition of maturity. . . . *In the Land of Israel* [is] a collection of polemical essays, in which through a series of interviews Oz animates a wide range of opinions on the state of Israel after the Israeli invasion of Lebanon and the massacres, in September 1982, at the Arab refugee camps of Sabra and Shatilla. *In the Land of Israel* was published in English in 1983, although it was written shortly after *A Perfect Peace.* I suggest the two books be read together. Certainly, the volume of essays enormously enhanced and enlightened my reading of the novel. On the subject of modern Israel and its complex sectarian struggles it teaches with an unusual economy and vividness, helping to place the novel in a political and historical context.

Given the power of the Exodus story as a paradigm for all narratives of personal and political striving, as well as for interpreting the course of later Jewish history, it is hardly surprising that in two books preoccupied with human aspirations (whether or not specifically Jewish) it should never be far from Oz's mind. . . . In *A Perfect Peace* it is the disappointment of a promised fulfilment which unites a father and son who in other respects have little in common and little sympathy for one another. The father is Yisra'el Yolek Lifshitz, pioneer kibbutznik and veteran of the Jewish Labour Party, chill at heart from the knowledge that he and his comrades in the struggle for a just and happy Israel will die 'each . . . in his own corner without a chance to see the end'. The son is Yonatan Lifshitz, 27 years old, whose rejection of life on Kibbutz Granot is the protest of a hurt child. . . .

It is Tlallim who observes this in Yonatan, reading the lines of hurt in the young man's face as he peers at him sleeping in the midday sun 'among the shacks and tents of Ein-Husub' near the Jordanian border. Tlallim is a desert tramp, a self-styled (Russian Jewish) nomad who lives out of the back of a beat-up jeep. He immediately divines what Yonatan is up to, guessing every detail of his plan to steal across the border by night into Jordan and visit the ruined city of Petra. And he sees the plan for what it is: a reckless and self-destructive act of defiance and revenge against a father. Ignoring Tlallim's taunts that the Atallah bedouin will rape him and chop him into little pieces, Yonatan continues on his journey into the valley of death. A fearful night-time ordeal follows, bringing him a measure of enlightenment, and the next morning he is back with Tlallim. Three months later Yonatan Lifshitz returns home.

Yonatan is accepted back on Kibbutz Granot without comment. The uproar his departure had provoked has subsided. But for Yolek his son's rebellion has brought to a head long-standing tensions with Hava his wife, and raised an old ghost, the still unsettled question of whose son Yonatan really is. . . . Meanwhile Azariah (of whom more in a moment) has established himself as the de facto husband of Yonatan's wife, Rimona, and Rimona is pregnant, though by which of the two men is uncertain. Yonatan accepts this unorthodox arrangement, as he himself has been accepted. Summer passes to winter. 1966 ends and 1967 begins, bringing with it the Six-Day War and the end of *A Perfect Peace.*

The novel is in two parts, with the transition from Part One to Part Two corresponding to a broad expressive movement from tension to release, stasis to flow, blocked development to change. Yonatan's decision to leave home is announced in the first paragraph of Chapter One, but it is not until page 209 that he actually makes it through the front door. In the meantime, we experience the conditions of suppression, stagnation and control which have brought him to the state he is in on page one. In particular, we get to know Yolek, who immobilises Yonatan by expecting him to be an extension of himself, and Rimona, whose sexual and emotional passivity borders on the pathological. As day by dreary day of that long first winter passes . . . , the magnitude of the burden which Yonatan has to throw off becomes oppressively clear.

A Perfect Peace is as much about the coming of Azariah Gitlin as it is about the going of Yonatan Lifshitz. . . . [Azariah, nicknamed Zaro], is provisionally accepted on the kibbutz because of his skill as a mechanical engineer, and also because, against his better judgment, Yolek takes a fancy to him. Azariah is fated with a manner designed to repel: egregious familiarity mixed with rudeness, effrontery tempered with fawning. But he is intellectually brilliant, artistic and sensitive, and above all, unexpectedly sincere: Azariah delivers what he promises. . . . Azariah sets about ingratiating himself with an energy and commitment that leave his critics gasping. Before long he has usurped Yonatan as Yolek's son and Rimona's husband, while somehow managing to retain him as a friend. In the end, it is by showing that he knows how to care for the ones he loves (something Yonatan still has to learn) that Azariah persuades the kibbutz to accept him as a full member.

The doubling of Yonatan and Azariah is the most striking of the weights and counterbalances, the points and counterpoints of this deeply pondered novel. Without a hint of schematisation or of a matching-up too plausible for life, Oz succeeds in portraying these two characters as entirely complementary opposites. Part of the trick here is perspective, since Yonatan is portrayed from the inside and Azariah from without. The result is that Yonatan seems clarified and empty, a young man without qualities, while Zaro, coming at us with colours hoisted high, set on making us his friends, seems dense, complicated and full. . . .

The meanings of *A Perfect Peace* are nowhere openly declared, and where they come nearest to being so, they are least interesting. Yet, as in those picture puzzles for children where the game is to discover fifty monkeys in a tree or thirty rabbits in a meadow, meanings nestle everywhere in this novel, just below the level of immediate apprehension and ready to ramify exuberantly once one stops to meditate them.

With *In the Land of Israel* open in the other hand, the rate of multiplication doubles.

In the Land of Israel argues explicitly what *A Perfect Peace* embodies. The only humane way forward is through openness, pluralism and democracy. Maturity, whether political or personal, requires of us that we tame our fierce longings for a promised land and settle instead for 'what there is'. Totalities of all kinds must be treated warily and compromises embraced. Rather than be seduced by the specious glamour of decisive action, we must learn to wait patiently. 'There is no shortcut.' The upshot of *In the Land of Israel* is clear, but since dogmatic assertion is part of what the book argues against and an enquiring scepticism so much what it recommends, its conclusions reach us through a thicket of qualifications and agnostic disclaimers: 'What will become of us?' 'What can be done?' 'Maybe you know?' The question-mark is Oz's favourite point of punctuation. The underlying problem here is accentuated in the book's epilogue, where Oz gives us a sketch of the city of Ashdod, his ideal polis:

> And what is, at best, is the city of Ashdod.
>
> A pretty city and to my mind a good one, this Ashdod . . . And she is not quite the grandiose fulfilment of the vision of the Prophets and of the dream of generations; not quite a world premiere, but simply a city on a human scale. . . .

The virtues of Ashdod are not by their nature easily argued with passion, and Oz is an incomparable polemicist whose forte is passionate argument. With his novelist's instinct for entering into the minds and bodies of his opponents, he succeeds in lending their case a liveliness his own inevitably lacks. The Devil, after all, can make jokes and be ironic, while God, as Baudelaire pointed out, never laughs.

The absence of the Devil from *A Perfect Peace* (unless we are to take Tlallim as Mephistopheles in a major key) does not in any serious way undermine the force of the book as a vehicle for Oz's morality, although it could perhaps do with a few more jokes. And it may be that the novel form is in principle a better instrument than the polemical essay through which to magnify the virtues of patience and moderation. At any rate, *A Perfect Peace* succeeds in presenting Oz's own political case with a subtlety that is beyond the register of *In the Land of Israel.*

On the face of it, *A Perfect Peace* is about personal growth and private interactions. The biggest social unit it deals with is the kibbutz. But Oz disputes the separation of the private and the public . . . , and the novel shows this in several ways. Superficially, it does so by representing politics both as pervasive in Israeli consciousness and as a family affair: the truck-driver from whom Yonatan hitches his first lift immediately makes a political statement, while Levi Eshkol, the Prime Minister, turns up on Kibbutz Granot with his shirt hanging out to adopt the Lifshitz family crisis as a matter of official concern. At a deeper level, political themes (a hatred of nationalism, a belief in the necessity for peaceful coexistence) are mirrored in the structure of personal relationships—for example, in the dual instances of disputed paternity, which all four fathers are obliged to come to terms with. . . .

A Perfect Peace is a model of democratic, open, pluralistic novel-making. No single character is allowed to dominate or monopolise our attention, and the shaping of events is represented not so much as an individual human prerogative as a generalised process in which individuals simply find themselves caught up, a flow as natural and inevitable as the transition which the novel makes from winter to spring. Indeed, for Oz, the ultimate leveller is nature herself: the seasons, the weather, the strangeness and beauty of the Israeli-landscape. So often in *A Perfect Peace,* the gaze of the characters is distracted from the near by the far, to come to rest among the 'ancient Biblical charms' of the land—on a distant range of mountains or the setting sun. 'The earth is indifferent. The sky is mysterious. The sea is a lasting menace.' It is an entry from Srulik's journal that ends the book, confirming it as a landscape with figures rather than a portrait with a background. But the ultimate poignancy and openness of *A Perfect Peace* is formal, and lies in the way its own point of rest seems to be located far beyond its boundaries—in the sense it gives at the end of only just having begun. In this most radical openness, in its eschewing not only of the 'totality of the Land' but of the totality of the novel, *A Perfect Peace* leaves us with a haunting awareness of the promise which all human lives have but which none can fulfill in the space allotted.

Nicholas Spice, "An Outpost of Ashdod," in London Review of Books, *Vol. 7, No. 14, August 1, 1985, p. 27.*

MARVIN HOFFMAN

A Perfect Peace, Oz' extraordinary new novel, is an attempt to comprehend the malaise that has ironically surfaced since Israel's stunning 1967 military victory by exploring its roots in the period immediately prior to the Six Day War. The decision to set the narrative in 1965-67 allows the author and his readers to draw on their extraliterary knowledge of the future, adding further resonance to the novel's already rich overtones. . . .

The hero of *A Perfect Peace,* Yonatan (Yoni) Lifshitz, lives on the kibbutz where he was born with his wife Rimona, a porcelain doll of a woman whose simple-mindedness alternately appears to be saintly or psychotic. She has had a stillborn child, and the doctor's recommendation that she not become pregnant again is the final blow to the marriage. As the story begins, it confirms Yoni in his earlier decision to flee the confines of the collective settlement, where life is too easy, too predictable, too circumscribed by parental expectations.

Yoni's father, Yolek, was a pioneer in Palestine. . . . Yolek's wife Hava—he insists on calling her his "friend"—has never forgiven her husband for the role she thinks he played in forcing the departure from the kibbutz of a certain Benya Trotsky. Long ago that unstable young man, driven mad by his love for Hava, had unsuccessfully attempted to shoot her, Yolek and himself, then fled to Miami where he became a millionaire hotel owner. Only Hava knows Yoni's true paternity, and she is not above using this as a weapon against Yolek.

Enter Azariah Gitlin, a self-described "Diaspora born" Jew. Just discharged from the Israeli Army, he is desperate to join the kibbutz. Yolek is intrigued by this idealistic, intense spouter of questionable Russian epigrams and idiosyncratic interpretations of Spinoza's philosophy, finding in Azariah something he does not see in Yoni: the passion and commitment of his own youth. Azariah is a character of uncommon

neurotic vitality—a high-energy molecule who invades Yoni's ennui-laden existence with unpredictable results.

While preparing his departure, Yoni gradually bequeaths Azariah his apartment, his belongings and his wife. This done, he follows the path of countless searchers for truth and takes to the desert in quest of that "perfect peace" his kibbutz had not yielded and death alone may bring. (The title is a phrase in a Hebrew prayer for the dead.) At the end Rimona repeats the previous generation's pattern, bearing a child of uncertain paternity.

Oz, the chronicler of a society built on idealism, is preoccupied here with the effects of the Zionist vision upon the visionaries and their offspring. Dreams fulfilled seem to him no less corrosive and unsatisfying than dreams deferred. As Yolek says, the first settlers gave their objectives "all kinds of high-flown names so that we could take ourselves seriously. . . . Well, now the high-flown words are rooftops and treetops." Such accomplishments should be cause for rejoicing, but in fact everything has soured. . . . The fulfillment uncannily resembles the life that had been left behind.

If the pioneers were nonetheless successful, the psychic cost paid by their children has been prohibitive. "They've spent their whole lives being right, those old folks," declares Yoni to himself. "What you think makes no difference because you belong to a generation that never learned how to think." Meant to be his father's crowning achievement, Yoni is a disappointment and a puzzle to the two of them. . . .

[An] air of melancholy, weariness and indefinable longing pervades *A Perfect Peace.* Even its physical world is drawn in gray, flat tones, although it contains rich, sensuous, animating details. . . . Almost the entire story takes place inside the floodlit perimeter of a single small kibbutz. Yet much as Thoreau traveled widely in Concord, Oz encompasses his universal themes within this little sphere. We are able to pull back from a greasy-smelling kibbutz tin tractor shed until we in turn see all of Israeli society, the knotted coupling of the Jewish people at "home" and in the Diaspora, and finally all of mankind struggling to find meaning and love in a radically imperfect world.

The ultimate message is not gloomy. Oz shows that you can look with searing honesty at the pock-marked faces of people around you and love them despite their flaws. Awareness of imperfections need not lead to surrender or revulsion. (p. 20)

Marvin Hoffman, "Flight from Kibbutz," in The New Leader, *Vol. LXVIII, No. 10, August 12-26, 1985, pp. 19-20.*

D. J. ENRIGHT

The true hero of *A Perfect Peace*—something which, we shall be unsurprised to hear, doesn't exist—is a kibbutz, Kibbutz Granot, populated largely by ex-Russians and ex-Poles. . . .

The inhabitants of Kibbutz Granot—and of Amos Oz's most engaging novel to date—are such as to make the place look like an intellectually up-market madhouse: either preternaturally loquacious, even oratorical, or abnormally taciturn, racked by violent passions or gnawed at by inward anguishes. The whole land, Major Chupka comments, is swarming with freaks. This is Old Testament country, as well as a modern national home; Gilead is not exactly theirs nor is Moab their washpot, and the troops of Midian prowl around, crossing the border to sabotage their water pumps.

What makes this state of affairs understandable to the outside reader is a modest effort of the imagination. What most alleviates and invites is the occasional touch of charming and apposite humor, conflating past and present. [For example, an] Arab youth on trial in Haifa for peeping at a woman undressing in a Jewish quarter cites in fluent Hebrew the precedent of King David and Bathsheba, and is let off with an admiring caution. . . .

It is the winter of 1965, a winter between wars. Yolek's son, Yonatan, wants to leave the kibbutz where he was born and raised, to get right out of the country; he feels that his life is passing fruitlessly by in a smoke-filled room clamorous with tedious argument. . . .

Just as he wants out, so Azariah, a wandering child of the Holocaust, wants in; for him the kibbutz is a place of joy and community, where "people still relate to each other," and justice resides. He is, he confesses, useless, but "even the broken clock is right twice a day." A pedant and a bull-shitter, and yet oddly charismatic, rattling on in platitudes and rhyming proverbs (supposedly Russian), Azariah is splendid, a creature from Dickens by way of Dostoevsky. In between abusing himself as a fink and a liar, he plans to "blaze new trails and demolish old shibboleths," first taking over Kibbutz Granot and eventually running the whole country.

That Azariah should arrive just as Yonatan is about to leave must look like blatant engineering, yet—as "the late philosopher" declared—what strikes us as pure coincidence can often be destiny. During the interval while Yonatan is plucking up heart, or heartlessness, to clear out, Azariah joins him and his wife, Rimona, a childless, frigid, and apparently imbecilic young woman, to form a remedial *ménage à trois*. . . . [He] rightly claims that Yonatan didn't go away because he moved in but Yonatan moved him in because Yonatan was going away. (p. 19)

[Yonatan] crosses the Jordanian border in the direction of Petra, meeting with strange, not to say freakish, adventures on the way. In one of the book's several schmaltzy patches, overwritten (I would guess) rather than overtranslated, he discovers the pleasures of uninhibited sex. . . . Major Chupka spots him far afield and returns him briskly to the kibbutz ("Okay. I'm back"), where he finds his barren wife with child—by which of the two men is a matter of no particular concern—and smelling now not of bitter almonds but of ripe pears.

Yet the most admirable, the most touching of Oz's portraits is Srulik, the music man, sexless and self-disparaging, a stolid German living uneasily among high-strung Slavs, outstanding in being one of the few people around who are not much larger than life. Without compassion, he muses, vision and imagination turn cannibalistic. There will always be pain in the world, but we should do our best to reduce it, "even if slightly, even if for a time." When Yolek slips into senility, Srulik is elected kibbutz secretary and, despite his fear and trembling, proves an efficient one. In his gentle way he emerges as the near-saint we had suspected him of being. It is he who conveys a balanced and rhetoric-free view, a view we may take as the author's own, of the kibbutz movement and of the country of Israel. "To some extent we have truly made better people of ourselves." (pp. 19-20)

D. J. Enright, "Jews, Have Pity!" in The New York Review of Books, Vol. XXXII, No. 14, September 26, 1985, pp. 19-20, 22-3.

AMOS OZ [INTERVIEW WITH ANITA SUSAN GROSSMAN]

[Grossman]: *In an earlier conversation with me, you said that* **In the Land of Israel** *was "technically nonfiction, but in some ways another Ozian novel." Could you amplify this remark?*

[Oz]: My method of working on **In the Land of Israel** was essentially not very different from my method of working on novels or stories. I work with a polyphony of voices without necessarily taking sides with one character or another. I try to give a fair hearing, a fair understanding, a fair voice to each one of my "fictitious" characters—which is exactly what I did in **A Perfect Peace.** I was thrilled by the variety of powerful, convincing, yet contradictory opinions when I was working on that collection of interviews. (p. 432)

[*You*] *don't seem to be on the whole what one might call a "realistic" writer, either in style or subject matter. What are you attempting to do in your narratives?*

In the first place, the term "realism" is meaningless because it comprehends everything—dream, fantasy, nightmare. Everything that humans have experienced, one way or another, is part of reality. Consequently, to me everything is equally realistic or unrealistic. I'm trying to do exactly what a tribal conjurer used to do perhaps twelve thousand years ago: tell stories in order to ease some of the pains and soothe some of the fears of my fellow-tribesmen. (p. 433)

How has being [in a kibbutz] influenced your writings?

It has in every way possible. Certainly it evoked and fed my curiosity about the strange phenomenon of flawed, tormented human beings dreaming about perfection, aching for the Messiah, aspiring to change human nature. This perpetual paradox of magnanimous dream and unhappy reality is indeed one of the main threads in my writing.

You've published fiction in a variety of styles and forms. Is there a literary prose form that you'd like to attempt that you haven't already?

I'm working now on an epistolary novel, consisting entirely of an exchange of letters between a cast of characters—letters, telegrams, a couple of legal documents, no narrator whatsoever. I find it difficult and fascinating. This one is set in the second half of the 1970s; to be more precise, in 1976. (p. 434)

How do you start a novel? What comes to you first?

Characters, characters. It's a type of possession. Characters whom I don't especially like and whom I sometimes try to resist with all my might—having surrealistic dialogues with those embryonic characters in the way of telling them to go away, to look for some other writer. **My Michael** is an interesting example of that. It is told, as you know, from a woman's point of view, in the first person, an undertaking which in sound mind I'd never take upon myself. Who am I?—which is exactly what I told this lady when she kind of invaded me. I said, "Go to a female writer. I can't possibly write your story in the first person. What do I know?" And by God, she argued bitterly, saying, "If this is the case, you can't write anybody's story. You can't write about anybody who is older than you are; you can't write about anybody who is less intelligent or more intelligent than you are; you can't write about anybody but yourself." And she might have a point there. Nonetheless, I resisted her for a fairly long time, and it was only when I felt that either I write her story for her in first person or else she'd never let me go that I wrote her in order to get her out of my system. Now a character usually brings with him or her a cast of other characters. They always come first; then setting, plot, and so on. (pp. 434-35)

Would you say that **A Perfect Peace** *was a political novel?*

In the broadest sense, anything is political. It's not a novel which conveys any specific message. It is political only in the sense that life is political, that love is political. In a way, *A Perfect Peace* is also a novel about how a group of ecstatic revolutionaries and world reformers gradually fade away, giving room—perhaps the right English word is compassion.

While Azariah is trying to get into the kibbutz, Yonatan is trying to opt out of his society. In a way, the beginning of **A Perfect Peace** *reminded me somewhat of Melville's tale of Bartleby the scrivener, who "prefers not to." Did you see any kind of inspiration there for the opening of the novel?*

I certainly never thought of it before, but now that you mention it, there might have been a certain amount of inspiration. These things do not work consciously. I won't swear an oath there was; I won't swear an oath that there wasn't, either. (pp. 435-36)

Your collection of short stories known as **Where the Jackals Howl,** *which appeared here in 1981, has a curious publication history. It was your first book, published in Hebrew in 1965 and later revised in 1976. Most novelists don't bother to revise their published writings. How come you did?*

I don't usually reread what I've published. In this particular case, I did, and I didn't like what I saw. These were frightfully early stories. Some of them I wrote at the age of nineteen or twenty, and when I began to write, I had this urge to prove to the rest of the world that I knew Hebrew better than anyone else. Consequently, I put on more or less my entire linguistic wardrobe—summer frock, winter coat, pair of shoes, boots, scarf, anything I had—because I needed at that age to show off. When I rewrote the stories, I considerably lowered the linguistic level, threw away tons of adjectives and adverbs, turned it into a less poetic and more prosaic collection. I didn't change the plots, though, or the characters. The translation is based on the later version, of course. I wouldn't allow the early version to be translated into any language. Ideally I would have destroyed it altogether if I could.

One of the themes in your fiction seems to be the opposition of rational, right-minded types and those who tend to give in to the dark forces, who aren't sensible, who are the voices of nightmare. Much of fiction seems so pessimistic and bleak.

I don't buy that. You know, optimism/pessimism—it's not part of my vocabulary, the way I think. I wish to think that, yes, I deal with demons from time to time, and with death, despair, and loneliness—but part of it is the result of the fact that I also deal with magnanimous dreams, with messianic expectations, with great believers who aspire to no less than change human nature in one blow, especially the kibbutz stories, but also in *The Hill of Evil Counsel* and *Unto Death.* Now, the deeper, the greater, the more ecstatic the vision is,

the more painful the limits of human nature seem to be. This perpetual interplay between magnanimous, meta-human dreams and petty realities—like the blocked drainage in *Late Love*—that's partly what I'm all about. (pp. 437-38)

Anita Susan Grossman, "An Interview with Amos Oz," in Partisan Review, *Vol. LIII, No. 3, 1986, pp. 427-38.*

WALTER GOODMAN

The device that serves as the title of Amos Oz's new novel [*Black Box*] is used to determine the cause of airplane crashes. The crash explored in this "Black Box" is the marriage of Alec and Ilana Gideon, which we soon learn from the letters that pass between them had rough weather all the way. Their letters and others from relatives, friends and business associates also chart Israel's entrance into dangerous areas.

The time is 1976. The Labor Government is on its way out and the religious right is preparing for the "redemption" of the territories occupied during the 1967 war. Ilana is now married to Michel Sommo, a pious Algerian Jew who is in every way a contrast to Alec, the austere intellectual author of an acclaimed book on fanaticism. . . . Michel, a religious zealot who is conscious of being a member of Israel's underclass and is accustomed to being pushed around by his betters . . . , is coming into his own.

Although Mr. Oz, a distinguished Israeli writer, is known to be no friend of zealotry or the ambitions of his country's right-wingers, he plays fair with Michel, who accepts the role of faithful husband to shaky Ilana and tough but understanding father to her troubled son, Boaz. . . . [Each] of the letter writers comes through with a distinctive voice; none entirely suit any political predilections. Alec the rationalist, who mocks the "theological disease," the "obsession with redemption," may be the most fanatic of the bunch. The embittered victim of a lonely boyhood, he could not accept the love of Ilana, who turned to promiscuity in longing and revenge. Their son has grown to be an uncontrollable, uneducated, violence-prone loner. His redemption is part of the story.

The letters begin with a plea from Ilana to "monkish, ascetic, haughty" Alec, who is teaching in Chicago, for money to help get Boaz out of trouble with the law. Alec has plenty of money, inherited from his pioneering, land-grabbing father. At first he contributes grudgingly, responding to Ilana's offer to sleep with him if that is what he wants, that "I am neither the Bank of England nor a sperm bank." But soon, out of some combination of generosity, guilt, calculation, quirkiness and less identifiable impulses, he begins to advance large sums to Ilana, Boaz and even Michel. Although the novel relies a bit much on Alec's wealth to drive the plot, Mr. Oz is a knowing guide to the personal dimensions of political movements.

One character who does not fit the definition of the fanatic at all and whose I-quit-you're-fired exchanges with Alec provide the book's touches of humor as well as shrewd insights into the way business is carried on in Israel, is Manfred Zakheim. This smart lawyer has devoted himself to creating the Gideon fortune and is determined to keep Alec from dissipating it in efforts to buy back Boaz by buying off Michel. . . .

Foreseeing the move into the occupied territories and the day when "land in the West Bank and the Sinai will be released for urban development, and every clod of earth will be worth its weight in gold," Zakheim uses Alec's money to enter into a deal with well-connected Michel . . . for picking up West Bank real estate cheap.

Mr. Oz's epistolary technique can be awkward, particularly when the letters are clearly designed less as communication between his characters than as information for his readers, or when they tell too much, too explicitly. . . .

Despite such displays of elementary psychology, the letters hold our attention as the writers swing between selfishness and generosity, despair and dreams, near lunacy and a semblance of sanity, reaching out in their individual ways for peace and love. In their inconstancy and inconsistency, these people are thoroughly human. Happiness may be beyond them, but their story leaves us with the hope of reconciliation through a simple affection that is an antidote to fanaticism.

Walter Goodman, " 'Black Box' Explores the Crash of a Marriage," in The New York Times, April 22, 1988, p. C36.

MARY GORDON

We expect the writer of a realistic novel to be, by temperament, a moderate. The body heat of most novels hovers around normal; their decibels are middle range. . . . [Amos Oz] would have no reason to fulfill these comfortable expectations we have for novels. His voice is rich, passionate, committed, febrile, intellectual. In the epistolary novel *Black Box,* he extends his impressive range.

Black Box—which takes its name from the black box on an airplane that is opened after the crash to give some explanation of the disaster—consists of a series of letters between Alec Gideon, his ex-wife, Ilana, and their son, Boaz. There are occasional exchanges between Alec and Ilana's new husband, Michel Sommo, and contributions by Alec's lawyer, Manfred Zakheim. Alec is a political sociologist and a hero of the 1973 war; he has made his international reputation by his analyses of the mind of fanaticism. He divorced his flagrantly unfaithful wife, Ilana, demonstrating in court her numerous betrayals. Undaunted by her public humiliation, Michel Sommo married her. Sommo is a Sephardic Jew, in Israel now by way of Algeria and Paris; he and Ilana live together simply in a small apartment, bringing up their little girl. Their family balance is tipped by the increasing delinquency of Boaz; Ilana writes to her ex-husband for help with the troublesome boy. Or this is the ostensible reason that she does. In truth, the bond between Alec and Ilana—a combination of sadomasochism and simple lust—has never been broken. Ilana cannot do without her husband's brand of defilement; she knows that in reinstating her connection with him she is asking for abasement. Alec does not disappoint her. He responds to her request for help with Boaz by throwing money at the problem—along with insults aimed from on high at everyone's most vulnerable spots.

It would be misleading to describe *Black Box* as a domestic tale whose subject is marriage and the strained relations among members of the modern, broken family. Mr. Oz is concerned not only with the private lives of these people, but with the life of Israel, and the characters, in revealing their inner lives, reveal, as well, the condition of the state.

Alec Gideon is the son of an old settler, one of those larger-than-life types who settled Palestine, striding across the face of the land in seven-league boots. Ilana is the daughter of postwar immigrant Poles. But the North African Michel is one of Israel's *pieds noirs,* an Eastern Jew, despised by the European Ashkenazi as deficient in culture and lineage. Alec's contempt for Ilana's new husband—conveyed from the cool perspective of an American university town—focuses on Michel's lack of intellectual sophistication and his emotional religiosity. . . . Alec's lawyer, Manfred Zakheim, an engaging mix of Machiavelli and Tevye, despises Michel for his shiny suits and his aftershave. But the differences between Michel and the others go deeper than clothing or manners—or even modes of expressive thought. Michel is pious in a way that is deeply alien to Alec and Zakheim—and estranging to Ilana and to Boaz. In accepting the gifts of the defiler, Michel is in fact giving his wife over, and at the same time making real his dream of involving himself in the attempt to restore the sacred places of the Jews to their rightful hands. With Alec's money, Michel is able to become the kind of fanatic upon whom Alec's fame rests.

The paradox, or perhaps the mystery of *Black Box,* is that it is only by pushing their natural extremism to its limits that the characters are able to come together in peace. Each of them lives his or her life on one or another hysterical edge. Alec is the cool—and cruel—secular rationalist; Michel is religious; Ilana is all id; Boaz is the inarticulate giant, overmastered by his body at first, then rescued by giving in to a pastoral vision of natural rhythms, in a neo-hippie commune he has set up on his father's childhood homestead.

The achievement of *Black Box* rests in its mastery of various voices. . . . Mr. Oz brilliantly captures both the overwrought piety of Michel, who has a scriptural passage for every occasion, and the cynical hectoring of Zakheim. He has caught the semiliterate thump of Boaz's language—the words of someone who has no faith in words. But it is in the letters of the monster Alec that Mr. Oz allows himself to go full out. They are a remarkable amalgam of venom, idea and lyrical observation of nature. . . .

Unfortunately, Mr. Oz is not nearly so successful in rendering either the voice or the character of Alec's ex-wife, Ilana. While we have a real sense of what it was in the past of Alec and Michel that formed them, Ilana seems to have appeared out of a libidinous fog. What was her war like? And what made her so compulsively unfaithful to the husband who seemed to be an ace between the sheets? We never really know. It is difficult to determine whether Ilana's verbal excesses are Mr. Oz's attempts to render the inner life of a woman who spends her days lurching from swoon to swoon. . . .

Amos Oz has always been a dualist. The root of his dualism may be a profound moral unease. For him, consciousness is the snake in the garden: the good people—Michael in *My Michael,* Rimona in *A Perfect Peace,* Boaz and Michel in *Black Box*—are always slightly out of it. They are victimized and overmastered by those around them who are sharper—unless they can set up an alternate system of perception and behavior that goes against the dominant and common modes. Another kind of unease expresses itself in the writer's repeated portrayal of women who seem unable to be satisfied by one ordinary virile man. Unease may not lead to the calm wisdom of a George Eliot or a Henry James, but in the case of Amos

Oz it creates a prose whose tensions almost force the reader to a richer understanding of his complex world.

Mary Gordon, "Abasement Was Irresistible," in The New York Times Book Review, April 24, 1988, p. 7.

RICHARD EDER

[In **Black Box**], Oz uses letters and telegrams among Ilana, her former husband, Alec, and her present husband, Michel, to tell a bitter, comic and ultimately mournful story of three talented and inflamed people whose lives and passions simultaneously sustain and strangle each other. The letters are tinder; they quarrel, goad, cajole, entreat and lament; they are a series of alarms, some of them false, that refuse to be shut down.

Years after a violent and messy divorce, Ilana writes desperately to Alec, now living in the United States as a professor and author of books on the subject of fanaticism. Their son, Boaz, in his late teens, has become unmanageable and has just been expelled from his school. Ilana's letter is a cry for help; it is also the first shot in a renewed battle, half warfare, half seduction, with her former husband.

Alec, who has inherited money, sends some, along with a brutally withering letter. He also uses his high-level political connections to rescind Boaz's expulsion. Meanwhile, Michel, a North African immigrant, a teacher of French, and the leader of an extremist religious splinter group, uses his own low-level, on-the-ground connections to locate Boaz and get him a job.

It is the first pass in a joust between the two men that continues through the book. One of the prizes is Boaz, whose stormy struggle to grow up takes him in and out of jobs and run-ins with the police until, at the end, he has become the oddly assured leader of a tiny hippie commune engaged in reviving an abandoned house and property in the countryside.

Another prize is Ilana. The bitter anger between her and Alec conceals an obsessive passion that draws them together even as they tear each other apart. Her love for Michel, more settled and maternal, remains, however; and he fights Alec for her to what will become a draw that is unresolvable except, perhaps, by death.

It has to be a draw. Because Ilana, apart from being a vivid, passionate, suffering and sometimes insufferable woman, is also the soul of Israel. Boaz, renouncing the concerns and hatreds of his elders, stands for a frail and insubstantial hope for Israel's future. Alec and Michel, warring rivals and linked at a profound level neither can fathom, are struggling with each other over the soul and future of their country.

Each man represents one side of Israel's internecine moral and political struggle. Alec is a scholar-warrior, a member of the Labor Party elite that dominated the country for its first quarter-century, and that seemed to have mastered the impossible task of combining a humane tolerance and intelligence with a formidable ability to maneuver tank battalions.

Michel, a Sephardic immigrant, is part of the underclass. Often patronized or ignored by the elite, it worked hard, prospered and gradually gained strength until, supporting Menachem Begin and the Likud, it broke labor's ascendancy and began a gradual overturn of class and politics. They stood for a big, as against a little, Israel; the settlement as well as the occupation of the West Bank, and a greater intransigence, with strong religious elements, against Arab claims.

"The Black Box"—the title, referring to the instrument that analyzes plane crashes, is an image for Alec's and Ilana's dissection of their former marriage—can become prosy at times. Occasionally, the epistolary form has to carry too much narrative and descriptive weight.

But it is astonishingly successful in fusing the histories and characters of Alec and Michel with what they represent. They are utterly visible and believable as individuals, though pitched in a perpetual emotional overdrive. Yet, in the way each one drinks coffee or takes a walk, we get an entire chapter of national history.

Oz, whose background and sympathies link him with his country's liberal tradition, seems to be harder on Alec. But ultimately, he is unsparing and loving—perhaps the word is "heartbroken"—with both.

Alec's detachment and chilly arrogance is, in a way, the author's argument that those who ran the country for so long, who were so admired abroad for their civility and prowess, had become estranged from the reality of a small Middle Eastern country. . . . The weapons he uses in his struggle with Michel are his checkbook—he keeps sending him money—and his connections with generals and Cabinet ministers.

Michel, on the other hand, knows sergeants, police chiefs and the heads of government bureaus that award building permits. His portrait is the most extraordinary thing in the book.

He is a warm, loving man. He has pillow fights with Ilana and their daughter, Yifat. He cooks them hamburgers and fried potatoes. He involves himself intimately with Boaz, using a kind of tough love. (Alec writes checks). He is intensely religious; his religion is inseparable from the clandestine efforts of his group to organize settlement in the West Bank.

None of this changes throughout the book; yet everything does. At the start, Michel is poor. Using Alec's money along with contributions mysteriously raised abroad, using the help of sympathetic middle-level officials—their level rises as the book proceeds—he gets rich.

It is Calvinist riches. Michel's holy biblical mission is to take possession of the West Bank. He and his people are buying up property there and, in the nature of things, they stand to make a killing. The killing, as Alec bitterly perceives, may someday become literal. Expansionism may destroy Israel. "You will boil in oil and mutter thrice 'Holy.' " For Michel—infinitely aggressive, kind and naive—real estate is holy war.

All this suggests only a part of Oz's accomplishments. Ilana's anguish as she struggles against Alec's and Michel's struggle, a fiery and comical correspondence between Alec and his lawyer, the elusive serenity of Boaz—is he signaling some ideal third kind of resolution for Israel?—these are some of the elements that enrich the book.

And there is a vein of poetry that runs through; a love of place, of the countryside, of Jerusalem at night. The rage and agony, after all, arise from the passion of the characters, for what each thinks of as his or her differently promised land.

Richard Eder, "A Marriage Shot Down over Israel,"

in Los Angeles Times Book Review, *May 29, 1988, p. 3.*

ELIZABETH POCHODA

Critics are tediously polite about Amos Oz, almost always giving him the good boy treatment—a mincing awe sometimes tinged with disappointment at his drifting plots. Hardly anyone mentions that for a good boy, Oz is frequently found in bad company and that his novels are run by a consortium of Israeli cranks, bigots, no-goodniks, visionaries, malcontents, hysterics, empty-headed Sabras and abused souls whose words whistle past us on their way to making a good impression on God or history or each other. The good boy is sly; he writes these people into the story and gets credit for letting God sort them out. Oz's talent may be for comedy of a compassionate sort, but make no mistake, he really enjoys his characters, even the worst of them. And so do I. I like the way they don't at all resemble their Israeli *landsmen* on the 7 o'clock news and the way they don't feel made to order for novels either. They seem to me, Oz's creations, the secret agents of great fiction—by which I mean that they have sought out the author and he has frequently allowed them to be smarter and more knowledgeable than he.

I'm also drawn to the country these people inhabit. Even if it's not a very appealing place, it nevertheless seems to contain more possibilities than the Israel I come across everywhere else these days. . . .

To the spectator Oz appears to have a comrade's relation to his malcontents. His story resembles theirs. Born in Jerusalem in 1939, he had by the age of 15 changed most of the important signposts of his life: He had run away from the city for Kibbutz Hulda . . . and he had abandoned his heritage as the son of a right-wing Zionist intellectual for the healthy life of the peasant soldier on a socialist commune. . . .

The familiarity of the Oz people and their stories—questionable paternity, love triangles, desertions and so forth—may annoy readers who want a little more fictional philandering from a writer who takes them abroad. But when Oz brings you home, he leaves you there for the same reason that Tolstoy and Faulkner do: A couple of generations of people stuck in one place allows plenty of room for observations on the phases of their fate. Oz's world is certainly no bigger than Yoknapatawpha county, and his collaborations with it, like Faulkner's with his, can produce any number of interesting inflections on character and society.

Of course, the characters in Oz's stories are not pleased by the repetitions or inflections that make up their lives. . . . That's one reason they are frequently frustrated and bored, almost to the point of madness or violence. . . . Anyone who wants to read the Oz books as allegories of the state of Israel, and I'm not sure it's always possible to avoid doing that, might meditate for a moment on the amount of suffocation and boredom running through their pages. Oz's people seem to know very few Arabs, just as Faulkner's seem to know few blacks. Their most serious problems are with each other and with the puzzling country they have inherited. They talk about peace but prefer excitement—in a pinch even war will do. Beset by higher longings—a legacy from the land that was to be a light unto all nations—teased by prophets and merchants of all sorts of redemption, they understandably have

trouble putting up with daily life. Let us look at them in their most recent incarnation, *Black Box.* (p. 796)

Once again there is a love triangle. At its points are Alec Gideon, former tank commander and intellectual in exile who has recently written a book on fanaticism; his divorced wife, Ilana Brandstetter, sex bomb and prevaricator, one of Oz's flamboyantly disruptive women; and Michel Sommo, Ilana's new husband, a poor, self-pitying Moroccan Jew who plans to ride his right-wing Zionism into the occupied territories and make lucrative investments there. There is also Boaz, the son of Ilana and Alec, and Manfred Zakheim, Alec's cynical lawyer. Boaz is a giant child of 16; he is blond, almost illiterate, physically violent and the only clear-sighted person in the book. For much of the story he is on the run.

These people are brought together by the enjoyably flimsy pretext of letters. Ilana must re-establish contact with Alec, who is in Chicago, to get his financial help in controlling Boaz. Alec must reply to her, her husband and Zakheim. So back and forth with letters, telegrams, reports, reviews of Alec's book and other documents. It's a nice form for an Oz novel: Since most of his characters are monologuists of some sort anyway, he has hit upon a way of letting them dispense with dialogue and scream into the wind. It suits them fine.

Boaz's troubles with school and the law are only an excuse for Ilana to open the black box containing the clues to her disastrous marriage with Alec. The immediate analogy is to the recording device that contains the information pertinent to an aircraft's crash, but, I think, the black box of physics is also apt. With the latter you know what goes into it and what emerges, but only through deduction can you guess at what happens inside. Both metaphors, but especially the second, widen the scope of the novelist's inquiry to include the land of Israel; he knows what went into its making, the pioneer dream of Palestine as a loose federation of rural communes, and what has come out, the nightmare of domination. He's now making some deductions about what went on in between, and he finds that marriage is the right box for his investigations, especially as it allows him to go into the matter of women.

Yes, women. If you put them all together, the women in Oz's novels know pretty much what there is to know about the spirit of total disillusionment cast by Zionism's attempt to produce the best country in the world. They are also aware of the costs of all that *goyish* normality. Some of these women deliver wonderfully shocking outbursts against the grand ideas of Israel's visionary patriarchs. . . . Others, like Hannah in *My Michael* or Rimona in *A Perfect Peace,* take their revenge upon the suffocating normality that has descended upon Israel by withdrawing into powerfully nutty worlds.

"The Zionist enterprise," Oz once remarked, "was far more demanding on women." In *Black Box* you begin to see what he means. It's not so much that Ilana has little to do in either of her marriages except iron shirts and boil vegetables, or that she realizes the egalitarian ideal of Zionism did not apply to women (except for those who, like Golda Meir, were ready to go on a permanent gender vacation). There is a deeper malaise here, which comes of two addictions: one to domination and the other to the idea of perfection. At the end of *A Perfect Peace* Srulik, the secretary of the kibbutz, writes in his diary:

> How can we overcome our dark desires to dominate others, to humiliate them, to subjugate them,

to make them dependent on us, to chain and en-
slave them with the gossamer threads of guilt,
shame, and even gratitude?

Is the old man talking about women, you want to ask, or
Arabs? Both. Is he speaking of the present or the past? Both.
The farther back Oz reaches into the history of his country
the less benign its origins look. (pp. 796-97)

In **Black Box** Ilana is the improbable historian of her
country. . . . She is obscenely drawn to her former husband's crisp contempt for compassion, gentleness and love.
Most of her overheated letters to him are meant to give him
an erotic charge, to remind him of their matching deformities—her fire, his ice—and to arrange at this late date some
fusion. It would be corny if it didn't run so deep.

Meanwhile, there is Ilana's second husband, the pint-sized
zealot Michel, who means to redeem the liberated territories.
Michel is one of Oz's finest creations. He is a bigoted, merciful maniac who wrings the present dry in pursuit of future
perfection: He intends to get every last bit of Eretz Israel
under the wire before the bell rings and the Messiah comes.
Alec has his number; like most fanatics, Michel suffers from
the theological disease of "higher longings," in whose name
any sacrifice can be made. They're quite a pair, these husbands, the first a despairing, autocratic member of the old
Ashkenazi elite who inherited the sour property and power
of Israel; the second a dark immigrant, "barely a hair's
breadth from the Arab," who represents lurid designs on the
country's future. Both reckon on being in on the ground floor
of the truth. They lack all talent for life, while Ilana shuttles
between them expressing faith in something she calls "happiness," and reminding them in one of her most beautiful letters
that "there is a land, but we have not found it."

It looks like a stalemate, but that is not where Oz leaves matters, being neither a pessimist like Alec nor a prophet of perfection. There is also Boaz, the giant child everyone wants to
control. He takes up residence in the crumbling castle that
once belonged to Alec's father and establishes there a freelance kibbutz of sorts, redesigning the pioneering dream according to his own crude commandments. . . . [These are]
appealing enough to draw his mother to his commune, and
then his dying father, and then, at least in Ilana's fantasy, Michel, his stepfather. Another happy Oz triangle in which everyone relinquishes something—a sexual version of land for
peace—comic in the tininess of its solution, capacious in its
insistence that no one owns the truth, Ozite in the irony that
this little civilization without territorial boundaries is exactly
what the Jews had for almost two millennia. (pp. 797-98)

> *Elizabeth Pochoda, "The Right Box," in The Na-
> tion, New York, Vol. 246, No. 22, June 4, 1988, pp.
> 796-98.*

GABRIELE ANNAN

Black Box and *Confessions of a Good Arab,* by Israeli authors, are both state-of-the-nation novels disguised as love
stories. The state of the nation, they tell us, is bad and sad.
Oz's principal female character Ilana loves the Zionist songs
she learned when she arrived from Poland as a child. Now
it grieves her to hear them: "There is a land but we have not
found it. Some jester in disguise has crept in and seduced us

into loathing what we have found. Destroying what was precious and will not return." . . .

Black Box is an epistolary novel. It sounds awkward: over-
colloquial and synthetic at the same time. So it starts by being
harder to like than [Yoram Kaniuk's] appealing *Confessions
of a Good Arab.* In any case, it is not in the business of soliciting affection. It is a savage modern tale about divorce, jealousy, resentment, blackmail, law suits, and property deals, and
it comes on aggressive, bitter, and sardonic, with a disquieting streak of hysteria running throughout the letters. With
the exception of a little girl and an adolescent boy, all the
characters are horrid, at least to start with.

Where Kaniuk dwelt on the incompatibility of "two jus-
tices," one for the Arabs, one for the Jews, Oz digs into the
beastliness of fanaticism. He too lines up a representative
range of Israeli types: Alexander Gideon, brilliant and
arrogant . . . , is now a professor at an American university
and writing a book . . . on fanaticism.

His older friend and lawyer Manfred Zakheim is a typical
German Jew, European, clever, joky, cynical. Alexander's
Polish former wife Ilana, oversexed and undereducated, feels
a sentimental but genuine affection for Israel. Her sister
Rahel is a worthy kibbutznik. The most topical and also the
most lively and loathsome character is Ilana's second husband, Michel, a busy, born-again fundamentalist cockroach
who came to Israel from Algeria via France, and has known
the triple humiliation of being a Jew in an Arab country, an
Arab (or for some a *pied noir*) in France, and an Oriental Jew
in Israel. He is the perfect illustration of the neo-Nietzschean
thesis of Alexander Gideon's book: that fanaticism springs
from a sense of inferiority. (p. 30)

Michel's oily letters are full of pious tags, biblical quotations,
false humility, *schnorren,* blackmail, and resentment against
European Jews who are not only more powerful and better
educated but also—this comes as a surprise—taller and bet-
ter-looking than Oriental Jews. Michel is a runt; Ilana towers
above him, a blond, sexy mother figure. Alexander combines
the brain of Isaiah Berlin with the looks of Clint Eastwood.
Boaz, his sixteen-year-old son by Ilana, is "six foot three and
still growing," strong as an ox, with long blond hair and lots
of girl friends. What are all these blond beasts doing here?

Well, they are highlighting the conflict between Ashkenazi
and Sephardi, top dog and underdog. The underdogs tend to
be religious fanatics with shaky standards of personal honesty
and souk if not gangland ethics. The top dogs are conceited,
rational, cynical, humane, and softer on Arabs; they don't behave particularly well either—nobody does. However, the
underdogs are coming up. (pp. 30-1)

The story is a wrangle over the violent but amiable dropout
Boaz and his paternal inheritance. It is fought out in a cat's
cradle of letters between Boaz himself, Ilana, Michel, Alexander, plus Alexander's lawyer and a private detective employed by the lawyer to spy on Michel. The letters express—
overexpress—their writers' personalities to the point of implausibility in such a naturalistic novel. One can accept the
brilliant articulateness of Alexander and his lawyer Zakheim,
but not Ilana's, or her lyricism. Boaz's illiteracy, on the other
hand, seems grotesquely overdone.

Alexander and Ilana have been acrimoniously divorced for
seven years, but one is meant to sense their unextinguishable
passion through the venom of their correspondence, which

occasionally breaks into erotic passages. Either way, its lack of *pudeur* makes it hard to sympathize with them, even toward the end, when a mood of resignation, forgiveness, and charity begins to make itself felt.

By this time Alexander has returned to die of cancer in his father's neglected mansion. The estate is being run as a farming commune by Boaz and a band of sweet foreign hippies. An atmosphere of peace and laid-back good will prevails. Ilana leaves Michel and moves in to nurse Alexander. This is a gruesome, humiliating process, which she unfastidiously describes in a letter of explanation and apology to Michel. Michel, for all his religiosity behaves vindictively: he forces Ilana to give up their baby daughter under a rabbinical interdiction. Ilana responds by proposing a necrophiliac *ménage à trois*. Michel is to bring the little girl back to the commune and share a bed with the dying Alexander and herself. . . . (p. 31)

Black Box was written three years after *Confessions of a Good Arab,* and as far as they are *romans d'actualite,* events in Israel have overtaken them both. . . . [It] must be significant that each harks back with nostalgia to an aristocratic father figure and a lost garden: on the one hand, Franz Rosenzweig and the garden where he first saw Azouri and which has been destroyed by Zionist settlers; on the other, Alexander's autocratic father whose neglected garden is being turned over to vegetables by his grandson Boaz. But Boaz won't stay: "The commune will disperse. Not a living soul will remain. The lizard, the fox, and the viper will reinherit the house and the weeds will return." (p. 32)

Gabriele Annan, "The Promised Land," in The New York Review of Books, *Vol. XXXV, No. 13, August 18, 1988, pp. 30-2.*

Jay (Lee) Parini

1948-

American poet, critic, novelist, editor, and translator.

Respected for its poignancy and clarity, Parini's verse demonstrates his command of classical poetic forms and techniques. He often evokes a serious, contemplative tone and draws upon personal experience while exploring universal themes. Parini has stated that his poems "arise out of a strong wish to embody things: objects, emotions, ideas. I celebrate the physical world and my relationship to it." His first collection of verse to garner substantial critical attention, *Anthracite Country* (1982), contains several nostalgic poems about his childhood among the collieries of Scranton, Pennsylvania, as well as pieces on love, death, and nature. In *Town Life* (1988), Parini employs a conversational yet philosophical tone to examine various stages of personal consciousness, beginning with age twelve and ending after death.

Parini's first novel, *The Love Run* (1980), transposes to contemporary times the Apollo and Daphne myth from Ovid's *Metamorphoses*. In this work, unrefined, slow-witted Teddy Leskovitch becomes infatuated with and kidnaps privileged Dartmouth College student Maisie Danston with the intention of marrying her. Against conventional wisdom, Maisie agrees to marry Teddy, leaving her boyfriend because he lacks Teddy's ardor and resolve. Mark Abley commented: "Parini is concerned to emphasize . . . the obsessive force of love, its unreasoning possession of mind and body." *The Patch Boys* (1986) is a humorous rite-of-passage story. Set in 1925 in a Pennsylvania coal-mining town and narrated in Italian-American idiom by a fifteen-year-old boy, this novel evokes the working class milieu of works by Henry Roth and James T. Farrell. Christopher Hawtree noted: "That adolescent sense of being on the brink of discovering everything about the world has rarely been so well captured as it is [in *The Patch Boys*]." In addition to poetry and fiction, Parini has published the critical study *Theodore Roethke: An American Romantic* (1979) and has also served as coeditor of the *New England Review*.

(See also *Contemporary Authors,* Vols. 97-100.)

EDWARD HIRSCH

Jay Parini's [*Theodore Roethke: An American Romantic*] adds to our understanding of Roethke's poetry and thus represents a solid addition to the critical literature. Parini's study offers what he calls "a map of Theodore Roethke's secret planet." He tracks Roethke's poetic development from *Open House* (1941) to *The Far Field* (1964), detailing individual lyrics and sequences in order to isolate major patterns and thus discover the poet's "mythos." Parini's essential contribution is his reading of Roethke's work as an extension of the literature of American Romanticism. He considers Roethke not merely in terms of his debt to Yeats (and it seems to me that both Roethke and his commentators have overac-

knowledged his borrowings from "the last Romantic"), but also as a late descendant of Emerson and Whitman. For Roethke is finally a poet of the egotistical sublime, celebrating and moralizing the American landscape, reading nature as "a steady storm of correspondences," a symbol of the spirit. Roethke called Reason "that dreary shed, that hutch for grubby schoolboys," and Parini interprets his plunge into the unconscious as an internalized quest romance. This enables him to consider Roethke's necessary pilgrimage in traditional Romantic terms.

Parini is at his best in defining the constellation of images, ideas, and influences animating Roethke's major sequences. (His book is weakest when it tries to fit some of the poems into mechanistic, so called "mythic" terms derived from Joseph Campbell. Must our critics continue to rely on grand, supposedly universal, obsolete anthropological models?) Parini's irrefutable argument is that the fact and symbol of his family's greenhouse stands at the center of Roethke's mature work. (p. 191)

Theodore Roethke: An American Romantic does not extend or redefine current notions of Romanticism, but it does place Roethke firmly in a Romantic tradition. As such it is a sturdy contribution to the study of Roethke's poetry. The Garden Master is himself gone, but this book helps to demonstrate why his work stands not on the peripheries but at the center of our literature. (p. 192)

Edward Hirsch, in a review of "Theodore Roethke: An American Romantic," in Criticism, *Vol. XXII, No. 2, Spring, 1980, pp. 191-92.*

RICHARD BRADFORD

In *The Love Run,* Maisie Danston, a Dartmouth undergraduate, has everything: a flawless face, a splendid figure, a hearty libido, a rich daddy, a presentable boyfriend, a sense of humor. . . . (pp. 14, 34)

Maisie also has a secret admirer, Teddy Leskovitch, a soiled and dimwitted young man who lurks about the woods and lanes of Hanover, N.H., aching for a glimpse of her and weaving pathological fantasies starring himself and his dream girl.

The Love Run has some of the eerie beast-chasing-the-beauty overtones found in John Fowles's *The Collector,* but Teddy isn't a particularly interesting madman. He really isn't mad at all, just incalculably stupid. He doesn't want to add Maisie to his collection, and his mind isn't on rape. He loves this girl. He wants to take her away, marry her, live in a cottage and have beautiful children. With the help of his friend Nick—a lout even dimmer than Teddy—he kidnaps her. . . .

A sensitive, sheltered girl, Maisie seems curiously unmarked by this nightmare episode, which for most people would qualify as trauma. She returns to Dartmouth and severs all amorous ties with her lover, whose attentions, while gentlemanly, lack Teddy's passion and commitment. Mr. Parini implies that she's truly grown up now, having learned something important about love and life. (p. 34)

Richard Bradford, "Young Types," in The New York Times Book Review, *June 8, 1980, pp. 14, 34.*

JEROME MAZZARO

Jay Parini's *Theodore Roethke: An American Romantic* places Theodore Roethke in a context of Romantic ideas. Parini shows Roethke's debts to Ralph Waldo Emerson, whose "Nature" (1836) Roethke had read and heavily underscored, as well as to Wordsworth, William Blake, W. B. Yeats, Gerard Manley Hopkins, Walt Whitman, Freud, and Evelyn Underhill. (p. 502)

Parini provides excellent digests of the philosophical, critical, artistic, and psychological backgrounds which bear directly and indirectly on Roethke's work. He judiciously moderates the psychoanalytical excesses of Karl Malkoff's *Theodore Roethke: An Introduction to the Poetry* (1966) and makes good use of subsequent studies of Roethke's writing by Richard Blessing (1974), Rosemary Sullivan (1975), and Jenijoy La Belle (1976). His major debts, however, are to Kenneth Burke's pioneering essay (1950), Mills's Minnesota pamphlet (1963), Arnold Stein's anthology (1965) and Stanley Kunitz' *New Republic* appraisal (1965). Parini makes little effort to answer critics who, like Randall Jarrell, complain of an absence in the poetry of "hydrogen bombs, world war, Christianity, money, ordinary social observations, [and] everyday moral doubts," or like William Meredith, value negatively the experiments of *Praise to the End!* (1951). Parini admits that Roethke was "comically uninformed on political matters" and offers to those who are discouraged by a first read-

ing of *Praise to the End!* the prospect that "after several readings, the sequence becomes more intelligible; the symbols begin to inform each other, and the strange dream imagery coheres." Parini does little with Roethke's indebtedness to D. H. Lawrence and slights the influence of Rainer Maria Rilke, translations of whose poems Louise Bogan began sending Roethke in 1935 and who was part of a course Philip Shelley and Roethke taught in 1939. Nonetheless, *Theodore Roethke: An American Romantic* is a readable and useful introduction to Roethke's work, and Parini's application of aesthetic principles to the poems of *Open House* and *The Lost Son* ably demonstrates his own fine presence as a critic. (p. 503)

Jerome Mazzaro, in a review of "Theodore Roethke: An American Romantic," in American Literature, *Vol. 52, No. 3, November, 1980, pp. 502-04.*

MARK ABLEY

The Love Run has as its epigraph a passage from Book One of Ovid's *Metamorphoses* describing Apollo's pursuit of a frightened Daphne, and much of the novel is an American retelling of that myth. The part of Daphne, young, beautiful and long-haired, is taken by Maisie Danston, the daughter of a Boston executive, a girl who floats effortlessly through a sunny life. Her boyfriend, an ambitious plodder called Burt, has the physical grace of Apollo, but the maniacal passion of the god animates an unemployed working-class youth called Teddy Leskovitch who follows Maisie relentlessly, even to the point of kidnapping. Parini is concerned to emphasize, in the hedonistic context of a shining summer, the obsessive force of love, its unreasoning possession of mind and body. Although Teddy's passion is futile, it succeeds in shocking its target into a deeper understanding.

Such a plot could have provided the framework of a compelling tale, but Parini's weaknesses as a storyteller blend with what one assumes to be the demands and expectation of his publisher and his intended audience to create a dismal book. *The Love Run* is regularly irrigated by sex scenes, at which the author shows no great originality, whereas his evocations of the natural world (the source of much of his best poetry) are kept strictly to a minimum. The conversations are inane . . . and Parini is unable to transfer the occasional intensity of his ideas into the narrative; the need to write a "readable" novel produces pages as bland as porridge. Furthermore, the characters are desperately predictable, as if, before the author began to write, he had made a brief list of their physical characteristics and behaviour patterns from which he never looked up. Parini's examination of love rarely rises above the level established by that other retailer of Ivy League romance, Erich Segal.

Mark Abley, "Ovidian Pursuits," in The Times Literary Supplement, *No. 4084, July 10, 1981, p. 786.*

ANNE STEVENSON

The poems in Jay Parini's first collection *Anthracite Country* are recognizably American; their diction is American and their prevailing tone both nostalgic and serious. But they also reflect Parini's awareness of his non-American literary ancestors; in the first poem we are invited to compare the poets of Boston and Vermont with Horace on his Sabine farm. The poem is an epistle in a classical style, conforming to the rules of iambic pentameter:

> My friend, we follow in the Roman colter's
> wake in our own ways, not really farmers,
> but poachers on the farm Maecenas
>   granted.
>
> Now weekly gossip flows along the wires
> from Boston to Vermont; the capital's
> alive, but Caesars in their private jets
> want nothing of us now. The mailman
>   comes
> with letters to aggrieve us, forms to fill.
> I pay my debts, as you do, with a shrug
> and turn to cultivate the ground, protected
> by the barbed-wire fencing of our prose.
> Unpatronized, we groom this inward land.

Such neatness, such modesty, so fair a perspective on the not-so-very-Roman present suggest a comparison with Hecht, yes, but also with English poets such as Anthony Thwaite. . . .

In Jay Parini America has a poet whose impulses are classical, while his matter is immediate and personal. It is the personableness of these poems that makes *Anthracite Country* so readable, and yet Parini's firm control of technique is most evident in poems about his childhood, spent among the collieries of the Susquehanna and Lackawanna rivers in Pennsylvania.

Ironically (and lamentably for those critics who insist on the isolationist purity of American verse) the poet who seems to have influenced Parini most is Seamus Heaney. Here, in *Anthracite Country,* is the same deeply felt nostalgia; here are the stanzas neatly counted out on the page, diction pulling against rhythm in careful counterpoint.

Since the title poem [**"Anthracite Country"**] is perhaps the finest in the book it will stand as an example of Parini's skill:

> The culm dump burns all night
> unnaturally blue, and well below heaven.
> It smolders like moments almost forgotten,
> the time when you said what you meant
> too plainly and ruined your chance of love.
>
> Refusing to dwindle, fed from within
> like men rejected for nothing specific,
> it lingers at the edge of the town, unwatched
> by anyone living near. The smell now
> passes for nature. It would be missed.
>
> Rich earth-wound, glimmering
> rubble of an age when men
> dug marrow from the land's dark spine,
> it resists all healing.
> Its luminous hump cries comfortable pain.

If that last line, with its tonguing relish of syllable—*lum*inous *hump cries com*fortable pain—seems Heaneyish, it is worth noticing, too, that the sounds it makes are American. Parini's poems do, sometimes, steer a little too closely in the wake of his master. . . .

But for all that, as a first collection *Anthracite Country* not only compares favourably with *Death of a Naturalist:* it is a more ambitious book. It takes risks which are characteristically American, especially in the love poems which, though in imitation of Ovid, rarely give an impression of artificiality. Several poems in the last section edge towards a surrealism

of which [Donald] Hall might approve, especially those poems which dwell on the colour blue. **"Skater in Blue"**, however, inherits something from John Crowe Ransom; and the last poem, **"High Gannet"** suggests the natural eye and speech of Robert Penn Warren, to whom it is dedicated.

It will be clear by now that Parini has had to work his way through a number of influences to achieve the high standard of technique in the poems he has written to date. If he goes on to develop his own voice—a voice which begins to emerge in poems such as **"Anthracite Country"**—he may well lead a number of potentially "classical" poets out of the wilderness. There are only so many ways to be original, and, despite the perennial cry of *make it new,* making it old is usually a prerequisite for true departures. But whatever its importance to American poetry in the abstract, *Anthracite Country* will be read for its honesty, for its emotional commitment to experience and its artistic commitment to a craft.

Anne Stevenson, "Making It Old," in The Times Literary Supplement, *No. 4143, August 27, 1982, p. 916.*

JAMES FINN COTTER

In his first poetry collection [*Anthracite Country*], Jay Parini contrasts classical eros with modern industrialism, dividing his book between Ovidian *Amores* and the anthracite landscape of northeastern Pennsylvania. A prologue, **"The Sabine Farm,"** draws on the literary analogy between farming land and cultivating verse, but notes that poets no longer enjoy patronage as Horace did. This theme of language as landscape develops further with poems about excavations into the rock of boyhood memories in and around Scranton, and recollections of relatives and friends, meetings and deaths. Like Jarman a minister's son, Parini contrasts visions of Zion with the mine pits, slag heaps, coal trains, and grimy-grim Lackawanna River. Nevertheless, the poet looks back with affection more than with anger, recalling **"Spring in the New World"** when children of the block went down to the swollen Susquehanna, past the wrecked cars and junk:

> The children flowed,
> a tributary stream of blood,
> and skin encountering the air
> and icy water. Children
> washed the winter from their
> bodies, floating on their
> backs beneath the rail bridge
> arching overhead, the iron
> rainbow of a diesel world.

No paradise or promised land, and yet a place for innocence and temptation. The miracle of naked bodies in a world of rock and metal strikes Parini with amazement: how could eros evolve from such harsh beginnings? . . . In childhood, despite warnings from fathers, the boy plays in an abandoned shaft until overcome with his own "black fear." He experiences death in **"The Miner's Wake,"** a quiet elegy for an uncle killed in a mining accident, as in **"Naming the Losses"** the poet later mourns a friend killed in a plane crash. In his poetry Parini answers the summons to remember and to declaim, with honesty, humor, and grief. We share his gratitude in **"Illimitable Kingdom"** for the silence out of which poetry comes and goes:

> Alone in this wordless room,

I am grateful for the life
that will not give in, that keeps
on coming when the words are gone,
this world within world,
illimitable kingdom.

Out of the depths which human flesh is heir to, the emptiness
that we feel and the fullness that we seek, the poet offers "this
world within world" of loving opposition. (pp. 481-82)

> James Finn Cotter, "Poetry of Opposites," in The
> Hudson Review, *Vol. XXXV, No. 3, Autumn, 1982,
> pp. 471-82.*

LOUIS L. MARTZ

The first book of poems by Jay Parini shows an equal originality when he is writing about his own best-remembered
subject, **Anthracite Country,** memories of boyhood in the
coal regions of Scranton, Pennsylvania—which make up
about half of this volume. If one thinks of D. H. Lawrence
here, it is only because he opened the way toward writing
about such topics and in *Sons and Lovers* showed how mine
and field and hill could be accepted as a natural setting into
which one was born. Thus Parini comes to accept **"The Lackawanna at Dusk,"** even though his mature mind tells him that
this is "a river lost to nature," and many details show the mature vision fighting nostalgia and a sense of boyhood
harmony. . . . **"Working the Face"** creates a grim heroic
picture of a lone miner "stalking the village at 6 p.m., / having been to the end of it, / core and pith / of the world's rock
belly." Meanwhile **"Spring in the New World"** is celebrated
by the children who follow an irresistible impulse to bathe in
the swollen, dirty Susquehanna, "floating on their / backs beneath the rail bridge / arching overhead, the iron / rainbow
of a diesel world." . . . We watch the boy **"Walking the Trestle"** on a dare, and feel him jolting awake three times a night
when the coal train goes by. Best of all, perhaps, is the poem
"Playing in the Mines," which develops the memory of a
childhood fear into a rich complex of implications and ambiguities:

> Never go down there, fathers told you,
> over and over. The hexing cross
> nailed onto the door read DANGER, DANGER.

"The hexing cross" belongs to the Pennsylvania setting, since
only a few miles to the southeast one can find those barns
marked with the Dutch hexing symbols. But here they do not
ward off danger, for "playing in the mines once every summer, / you ignored the warnings. The door / swung easier
than you wished." The pause on "door" is good: it marks the
hesitation and the half-wish that entry had been impossible.
Still, "the sunlight / followed you down the shaft a decent
way." The use of "decent" is both slangy and precise: a good
distance, an easy, clear path, quite decent of the sun to shine
so far. "No one behind you, not looking back"—though one
must have felt a strong urge to do so—

> you followed the sooty smell of coal dust,
> close damp walls with a thousand facets,
> the vaulted ceiling with a crust of bats,
> till the tunnel narrowed, and you came
> to a point where the playing stopped.
> You heard old voices pleading in the rocks;
> they were all your fathers, longing to fix you
> under their gaze and to go back with you.

These are the voices of all the miners who died in those workings, all of them fathers who warned against the danger and
who now beg to save themselves and you from their fate. Perhaps the pause on "longing to fix you" contains a threat of
entrapment:

> But you said to them NEVER, NEVER,
> as a chilly bile washed round your ankles.
> You stood there wailing your own black fear.

The cry NEVER, NEVER, may be taken doubly: never will
he be caught in such a fate, and never will those fathers return
to the light.

Such firm control of his materials is a sign of Parini's appreciation of many poetical masters, both ancient and modern, as
one can see from his fine opening tribute to Horace, his occasional echoes of the techniques of Williams and Roethke
(Parini has written a good critical study of Roethke), his
command of Frost's manner in the drama of a small child
drowning under the ice (**"Skater in Blue"**). . . . And finally
we have the closing acknowledgment of his admiration for
Robert Penn Warren, in the poem **"High Gannet"**. . . . But
these masters are absorbed: Parini has achieved his own
voice. (pp. 78-80)

> Louis L. Martz, "Ammons, Warren, and the Tribe
> of Walt," in The Yale Review, *Vol. 72, No. 1, Octo-
> ber, 1982, pp. 63-84.*

ROGER POOLEY

[In **Theodore Roethke: An American Romantic,** Parini as-
serts] that Roethke's career can best be described in terms of
the ideas and poetics of Romanticism. The Wordsworthian
analysis of childhood as a privileged, visionary time is central
to his analysis of Roethke's greenhouse poems, his 'autobiographical myth'. But the American side of the Romantic tradition gets more extended treatment. Emerson, with his sense
of Nature as the symbol of the Spirit, is in the forefront of the
argument, followed by Whitman (the poet as prophet) and
Wallace Stevens (expression versus mimesis). Roethke's own
mentors, most notably Kenneth Burke, are given full credit;
and indeed Burke's early essay on Roethke provides Parini
with many of his guide-posts. In fact, all through the book
Professor Parini is modifying and building on such early
mapping-out essays, Louis L. Martz being the other principal
contributor. It is often the way with books on near-
contemporary writers, and it is not meant as a criticism. He
is rightly critical of later, over-ingenious book-length system-
atizations.

Professor Parini is no simple pro-Romantic either. He needs
to gloss his argument about Roethke's childhood repressions
with the idea that psychoanalysis is the completion of Romanticism (Norman O. Brown is quoted with approval a
number of times). And the best part of the book is where he
deals with the pitfalls of self-absorption in the Romantic process of self-discovery. That, and the determined attempt to
explicate as much of the 'Lost Son' sequence as will yield to
recuperation, makes the book a useful contribution to the
study of an important poet.

I suppose 'important' is the word; Professor Parini is good at
evaluating comparatively *within* Roethke's work, but he pulls
away from a broader estimate of its value, even within the
confines of American Romanticism. My other cavils are less

important. The quotations from Roethke's notebooks are so interesting and suggestive that it would have been good to have more, or at any rate some fuller description of what is being excerpted. The descriptions of myth and meditation read like explication for students rather than debate with established concepts. There is some inconsistency between the dismissive remarks about the stultifying formality of the early poems and the admirable formal 'plain style' of 'Four for Sir John Davies' in Roethke's later *oeuvre*. Perhaps the latent historicism of the Romantic thesis is surfacing here; one formality had to be transcended for Roethke's development to be as it was, the other is acceptable as part of a Yeatsian (and thus Romantic) trajectory in Roethke's later years. Despite these reservations, though, the book is still a useful fleshing-out of our picture of Roethke's poetry, perhaps even a first book to go to for students of his work.

Roger Pooley, in a review of "Theodore Roethke: An American Romantic," in The Modern Language Review, *Vol. 78, Part 2, April, 1983, pp. 439-42.*

WILLIAM H. PRITCHARD

Jay Parini's [*Anthracite Country*] is perfectly titled, naming with directness and economy the territory in which the first and best section of his book (consisting of sixteen poems) takes place. Maybe, since I grew up only sixty miles north of Anthracite Country, and heard about Scranton and the mines only as a place my father's family was glad to get out of, my high estimate of Mr. Parini's poems is too much a "personal" one (in Matthew Arnold's sense of that word) rather than a "real" one. But I don't think so, even though like Parini I spent my early years close by the Lackawanna tracks, just a stone's throw away down in the ravine:

> Three times a night it woke you
> in middle summer, the Erie Lackawanna,
> running to the north on thin, loud rails.
> You could feel it coming a long way off:
> at first, a tremble in your belly,
> a wire trilling in your veins, then diesel
> rising to a froth beneath your skin.

("Coal Train")

Yes, that's the way it was. . . . (p. 178)

If it sounds as if I'm saying that Parini has written poems which, in the immortal words of the student, I can Relate To, I'm afraid it's true. But even someone who had to grow up in Mobile or Walla Walla, rather than southern New York or northern Pennsylvania, would admire the simplicity and closeness of observation with which his poems are written. The illusion is often that we are placed in the presence of *things,* not mere words:

> The dirt road rose abruptly through a wood
> just west of Scranton, strewn by rusty wire,
> abandoned chassis, bottles, bits of food.

This is poetry that doesn't need to play games with us, much less with itself (no poems about writers' colonies in *Anthracite Country*) because it is interested only in having us share in the remembered materials, grittily memorable as they are: garbage, poisoned fish, the "mounds of culm" which burn softly near the Lackawanna at dusk.

Parini's voice can also take on real warmth, especially in the opulently prefatory poem to the volume, **"The Sabine Farm."**

Here he gracefully and lovingly imagines a landscape which has everything Scranton and environs lacked:

> You spoke of Horace on his Sabine farm,
> his lime-deep valley, hyacinth in bloom,
> with holm oak forests shuffling in the breeze.
>
> He loved the spring, the clover-laden grass
> his herds would feed on, drizzle-sweetened hills.

This is where, as a poet, he wants to live, and access to which is constantly made difficult by the way life insists on being composed of gossip and debts and the "barbed-wire fencing of our prose." But though he and his fellows are merely "poachers on the farm Maecenas granted," Parini shows, in this poem and others, that he cultivates his lands with a fine hand and a generous spirit. Nothing in the remainder of *Anthracite Country* quite matches the vigor and authority of its first third. But Jay Parini is clearly a poet who has arrived on the scene knowing that, above all else, the poem should illustrate what a "hell of a good time" (Frost's phrase) the poet had in writing it. So the reader is similarly pleased. (pp. 179-80)

William H. Pritchard, "Intelligence and Invention," in Salmagundi, *No. 60, Spring-Summer, 1983, pp. 176-85.*

RICHARD TILLINGHAST

Jay Parini brings to his poetry a calm self-assured tone of voice, a classical sense of balance, and a rare skill at the art of writing verse. I hope the absence of flashiness will not cause readers and reviewers to ignore this very accomplished book [*Anthracite Country*]. My mention of Mr. Parini's classical qualities is not fortuitous: he has clearly studied Latin poetry, and its presence can be felt in the opening poem of the volume, **"The Sabine Farm,"** as well as in the section entitled "Amores," in which several of the poems are indebted to Ovid.

"The Sabine Farm" is a tribute to Horace, who "loved the spring, the clover-laden grass / his herds would feed on, drizzle-sweetened hills. / He lived, well free of Rome, as if the world / were leafy and reposed." Horace's farm becomes a *paysage moralisé:* "private earth / in which to plough the furrows of our verse, / to separate the tangled roots of speech." The poem ingeniously turns to a wry account of the contemporary poet's patronless dilemma: "Now weekly gossip flows along the wires / from Boston to Vermont; the capital's / alive, but Caesars in their private jets / want nothing of us now." It is a pleasing urbane poem, moving smoothly from phrase to phrase, from line to line, in a way even Horace would have admired.

Parini's poetry evidences his sense of humor and his sensuality. The humor is compassionate, and all the more effective for being so. In **"The Missionary Visits Our Church in Scranton,"** for example, the parishioners become figures of fun for poet and reader, but they are not skewered, as they "wheezed in unison, / waiting for the slides: the savage women / dandling their breasts on tawny knees, / the men with painted buttocks / dancing in a ring." Parini is restrained, gentle: "The congregation loosened their collars, / mopped their brows, all praying / that the Lord would intervene." Spiritual uplift is achieved, with the women "in makeshift bras, the men in shirts"; and we are left with this gentle reassurance:

"They were said to be singing a song of Zion. / They were said to be wishing us well in Scranton." (p. 475)

The poems in **Anthracite Country** are written with gusto and, at the same time, with delicacy and care. (p. 476)

> *Richard Tillinghast, "Ten New Poets," in* The Sewanee Review, *Vol. XCI, No. 3, Summer, 1983, pp. 473-83.*

JAMES D. BLOOM

[**The Patch Boys**] covers the familiar working-class territory explored by Henry Roth, James T. Farrell and numerous others. Using this staple of American fiction, Mr. Parini evokes creditably an ethnic coming-of-age that takes place during the summer of 1925 in the coal mines and scarred hills of northeastern Pennsylvania. The title refers to the Exeter patch, a neighborhood shared by Italian and Polish miners' families, including Sammy di Cantini, the precociously articulate and unrealistically ambitious narrator, and his troubled family. The oldest brother, gifted with a mean fast ball and smoldering eyes, is consumed by his work organizing the miners' union. Another brother is on the verge of becoming a prominent Manhattan hoodlum, and Sammy's restless 17-year-old sister is the kind of girl who "always fell for a Buick." A nagging, nurturing immigrant mother—widowed by a mine collapse—keeps a weekend speak-easy and presides over this turbulent household. Sammy's parentless, Huck-like best friend, Will Denks, and Will's idyllic riverside lean-to harbor Sammy in his frequent flights from family stress. True to genre, Sammy's vexing love interest is the blonde daughter of his benevolent high school principal. Out of such stock ingredients, Mr. Parini has produced a subtly paced narrative.

> *James D. Bloom, in a review of "The Patch Boys," in* The New York Times Book Review, *December 28, 1986, p. 18.*

CHRISTOPHER HAWTREE

Not a great deal happens (it hardly could) in [**The Patch Boys,** an] account of a fifteen-year-old's summer in a Pennsylvanian mining town during 1925. The mines are there as a background, a threat of what might well lie ahead in an existence which, for the moment, is happily passed swimming in a river of questionable purity and, less equably, stifling erotic yearnings which focus on one Ellie Maynard. That adolescent sense of being on the brink of discovering everything about the world has rarely been so well captured as it is here. Parini allows his first-person narrator, Sammy di Cantini, neither to indulge in irony at the expense of his younger self nor to let rip with torrents of rhapsodic, "poetic" recollection.

All is held in check by a prose that is no less vigorous for being finely controlled: the farce of a swim in the buff with Ellie is duly balanced by the writing of verse of a fearful sincerity. A visit to a loan-shark brother in New York comes to an equally unfortunate, messy end and contrasts with the grim sweat of life below ground back home—all of it subject to the confession-box and Father Francis. The melodrama of the ending comes as an inevitable part of life in a town where forces are always present to quell those such as Sammy, who

have gained a glimpse of the possibilities beyond it. "Whatever the world threw at me now, I would throw back in spades."

> *Christopher Hawtree, "Boys on the Brink," in* The Times Literary Supplement, *No. 4402, August 14, 1987, p. 873.*

THOMAS D'EVELYN

At a time when poetry dithers at the margins of the arcane or the trivial, Jay Parini hits the mark. In doing so, he shatters some critical categories such as modernism and postmodernism. His poems [in **Town Life**] look traditional— American blank verse, English ode—but the inner demands of the modern spirit are being negotiated at every turn. (p. 19)

Parini is an industrious (two novels, two collections of poetry, a critical study, a textbook) and even ambitious writer whose quiet voice belies his achievement. That achievement is to have taken modern poetry back to its source, to bring the Callimachean spirit of subtlety and independence into American poetry just when it needs it most.

Specifically, Parini's style goes back to Horace, whose indebtedness to Callimachus, richly documented in scholarly editions, is beyond question. In one of Parini's Horatian odes on himself, he reveals the moral center of the modern spirit:

> . . . Do I deceive myself
> like all the others, whom I once thought dull,
>
> incapable of heights or depths of soul,
>   the vulgar mob; *odi et arceo,*
>   as Horace said,
>   that prince of language
> in whose dainty steps I've trod, do tread,
>
> will tread forever until Death or, worse,
>   Dementia absorb my impulse
>   to put words
>   to things, . . .

But, in fact, it's not the "dainty steps"—wicked epithet!—of Horace's odes that Parini most follows, but the Horace of the later epistles, the relaxed, philosophical Horace, the Horace who combined Callimachean polish and philosophical self-analysis in one of the truly great achievements in world literature. In these poems Horace added weight and substance to Callimachean subtlety and litheness without betraying them.

Parini's renewing of the Horatian balance is true innovation. Parini has not been afraid to make sense. I had fun outlining the argument of his three-page poem **"Things of This World."** I was reassured—nay, delighted—to find the old art of rhetoric being used so unobtrusively by a contemporary poet. Parini's verse is simultaneously sinewy, lyrical, philosophic, and conversational.

It all comes together in **"At the Ice Cream Parlor."** Unity is everything in the Callimachean/Horatian tradition, and here the transitions between local detail and philosophic concerns happen with lightning speed. Study the poem and it will just be there for you, like your own room when you turn the lights on.

The *mise-en-scène,* the local ice cream parlor with its chairs made of "black curlicues of iron, ice-cream parlor perfect," introduces a discussion of "that chair," and its Platonic prototypes. The subtle Callimachean touch is to draw this out from the variation on the "picture perfect" idiom. In his easy-to-listen-to Horatian style, Parini talks about the relationship between the particular and the universal. The voice never becomes thin, shrill, or ghostlike: It is always that of a nice man holding forth over ice cream. Finally, in the manner of Horace, it all comes down to ironic self-depreciation, without narcissism.

In the end, Parini shows how our search "for essences in what's been given" opens on the supremely personal, supremely universal question: *What claim do I have to being a good man?*

Along with everything else, Parini's poems manage to suggest that a truly modern poetry is up to whatever life throws our way. (pp. 19-20)

Thomas D'Evelyn, "The Poet in the Ice Cream Parlor," in The Christian Science Monitor, *February 17, 1988, pp. 19-20.*

W. C. HAMLIN

The heart of [*Town Life*] is given over to nine "portraits of the artist": a 12-year-old boy at his baptism experiencing his first rebirth; a high school pitcher losing, crying, his father in the stands; a college revolutionary chanting against the Vietnam War; a youth abroad, full of poetry and Scotland; a young professor in New Hampshire teaching Milton against the odds; a paunchy traveler at 37, in Bangkok, trying to climb out of the rut; a father with his sons, probing his own vulnerability; an old man in 2038, looking toward the end and looking back; finally, the artist at peace, after life. The last few poems, particularly **"At the Ice Cream Parlor,"** are quietly reflective, tender without sentimentality or confession. Overall, the poems offer a marvelous diversity of imagery and form and attest greatly to the illusion of artlessness and freedom born of total control.

W. C. Hamlin, in a review of "Town Life," in Choice, *Vol. 25, No. 9, May, 1988, p. 1405.*

Mervyn Peake

1911-1968

English novelist, poet, short story writer, author of children's books, illustrator, dramatist, and scriptwriter.

Peake is regarded as an important author of fantasy literature as well as one of the foremost book illustrators of his era. His most famous works are a series of Gothic novels known as the Gormenghast Trilogy, which depicts a medieval world inhabited by lonely eccentrics. Reflecting the influence of Charles Dickens in its intricately detailed plot developments and grotesque characters, this triad also recalls the works of Franz Kafka in its evocation of a bizarre and often irrational world. The flamboyant style of these novels prompted Henry Tube to call Peake "a master of the rolling period, the purple passage and the grand set-scene." Although his fiction usually revolved around strange and horrific events, Peake also exhibited a whimsical sense of humor, especially in his nonsense verse and stories for children.

Peake's first novel, *Titus Groan* (1946), introduces the gloomy world of Gormenghast, an ancient, decaying castle inhabited by a peculiar family of aristocrats and their servants. This work chronicles the birth and early infancy of Titus Groan, heir to Gormenghast and the hero of the series. Various subplots in the novel include the villainous activities of Steerpike, a servant who aspires to become ruler of Gormenghast, and the romantic adventures of Keda, Titus's nurse. *Gormenghast* (1950), the second novel in the series, depicts the childhood and adolescence of Titus, who gradually rebels against the ritualized, traditional way of life forced upon the inhabitants of Gormenghast. This novel also follows Steerpike's attempts to take over Gormenghast through murder, seduction, and deceit. At the end of *Gormenghast,* Steerpike is defeated by Titus. A work often discussed in conjunction with the Gormenghast Trilogy is the novella *Boy in Darkness* (1957), a nightmarish allegory in which the fourteen-year-old Titus confronts forces of evil embodied in a sinister white lamb that transforms human beings into grotesque beasts.

Peake intended to write several more novels documenting various stages in the life of Titus Groan. During the 1950s, however, he was stricken with Parkinson's disease, a degenerative nervous disorder that ended his career by the early 1960s. The last novel of the Gormenghast Trilogy, *Titus Alone* (1959), portrays the twenty-year-old hero's experiences in the outer world. Set in a technologically advanced city that some reviewers likened to Oceania in George Orwell's novel *Nineteen Eighty-Four,* this book details Titus's first romantic encounters and his struggles to overcome his emotional attachment to Gormenghast. Because Peake's illness affected his ability to concentrate, the original manuscript of *Titus Alone* was heavily edited to correct various textual errors and inconsistencies, resulting in a disjointed narrative style radically different from that of the first two books in the series. A more complete version of *Titus Alone,* based in part on Peake's original manuscript, was issued in 1970. Although they received positive reviews when first published, the Gormenghast novels did not acquire a large audience until the mid-1960s, when a resurgence of popular interest in fantasy

literature led to the rediscovery and critical reexamination of Peake's works. Bryn Gunnell noted: "Peake stands in a class by himself, and one of the reasons why he has generally been greeted with puzzled praise is that he is our only true representative of the *surrealist* approach to art. . . . Gormenghast is an eruption of the subconscious. It is also a protracted dream, at once familiar and frightening, full of blinding flashes of beauty and areas of threatening darkness."

During his prolific career, Peake produced works in diverse genres. The pieces contained in such early poetry collections as *Shapes and Sounds* (1941) and *The Glassblowers* (1950) reflect Peake's fondness for colorful, arcane language and striking visual imagery, while his later verse often focuses on realistic subject matter. The title poem of *The Rhyme of the Flying Bomb* (1962), for example, describes the bombing of London during World War II, and "The Consumptive, Belsen, 1945" draws upon Peake's experiences as an army illustrator at the liberation of the Nazi concentration camp in Belsen, Germany. In addition to his serious verse, Peake composed nonsense poems in the tradition of Edward Lear and Lewis Carroll. These verses are featured in *Rhymes without Reason* (1944) and *A Book of Nonsense* (1972). While such writings attracted a relatively limited readership, Peake wrote a number of works that he hoped would appeal to a more mainstream audience. These compositions include the novel *Mr. Pye* (1953), a humorous fable about an evangelist whose good deeds cause him to sprout angel's wings, and the play *The Wit to Woo* (1957), a romantic farce written in blank verse. Peake also wrote and illustrated humorous stories for children, most notably *Captain Slaughterboard Drops Anchor* (1939) and *Letters from a Lost Uncle* (1948).

In addition to writing novels and poetry, Peake also maintained a distinguished career as an artist. Closely related to his fiction in style and content, Peake's drawings accompanied the texts of several of his books. Among his most admired accomplishments are his illustrations for such literary classics as Lewis Carroll's *Alice's Adventures in Wonderland* and *Through the Looking-Glass,* Samuel Taylor Coleridge's *Rime of the Ancient Mariner,* and Robert Louis Stevenson's *Treasure Island.*

(See also *CLC,* Vol. 7; *Contemporary Authors,* Vols. 5-8, rev. ed., Vols. 25-28, rev. ed. [obituary]; *Contemporary Authors New Revision Series,* Vol. 3; *Something about the Author,* Vol. 23; and *Dictionary of Literary Biography,* Vol. 15.)

EDWIN MORGAN

[The essay from which this excerpt is taken was originally published in Chicago Review, *Autumn-Winter, 1960.]*

A writer who is also an artist, with a strongly developed visual imagination and a distinct flair for portraying the grotesque and the strange, tries his hand at the novel. He sees this literary form, this great tract so ill-defined in shape and purpose, apparently welcoming a lavish and indulgent play of imagination, a story-telling rich with fantastic incident, whose sole necessity is to enthrall. This is a freedom he will find deceptive, but only partly deceptive. He discovers that the 'necessity to enthrall' involves him willy-nilly with human feelings and experiences, and that the novel is oddly tenacious of its verisimilitudes, even when it is shading off towards fairy-tale or allegory. If he can learn this lesson, humanize his fantasy, localize his strangeness—he has the chance of proving how important the imagination is, in a form which is constantly being pushed towards documentation and naturalism. It would be wrong, certainly, to judge *Wuthering Heights* without reference to how life was lived in the north of England in the early nineteenth century; but the lack of imaginative life in the novels of, for example, C. P. Snow is a more serious fault than the lack of a minute realism in Emily Brontë, because it leads to dullness, and nothing is worse than dullness. Poetry has to be periodically brought down to earth; the novel has to be periodically lifted off.

Mervyn Peake is one writer who has made this experiment, and within fantastic narratives (I am thinking especially of *Titus Groan* and *Gormenghast*) that are superficially of great self-indulgence and escapism he has been able to show the emergence of a positive imaginative power of a peculiar and valuable kind. What I want to do is to try to define this peculiarity and this value.

Apart from his work as an artist (drawings, paintings, book-illustrations) . . . , Peake has produced two volumes of poetry, a play, four novels, and a long short story. Of these, it is only the novels and the short story that are important,

though many an interesting and idiosyncratic touch will be found in his other writings. The poems (*Shapes and Sounds,* 1941; *The Glassblowers,* 1950) are romantic and exploratory, with some striking imagery, but for the most part they fail to achieve the necessary distinction of form. Often one feels the excitement that lies behind the poem, without feeling that the excitement has been made meaningful or fully worked out in poetic terms. Strong reactions to 'shapes and sounds'—as in the title-poem **"The Glassblowers"**—stamp his poetry with the fluent sensuousness that is found in all his work. His poetic comedy, *The Wit to Woo,* was produced [in 1957]. . . . This, like the poetry, shows Peake using a medium where he cannot extend himself in the special way he requires. A fantastic love-story, set in the hall of a country house, with a good deal of verbal humour (e.g. four tipsy undertakers 'primed in our roles and rolling in our prime'), the play came too close in atmosphere and diction to the work of Christopher Fry, at a time when drama had moved away from the verbal-poetic mode, to have a full success on the stage. It has a nice lyrical feeling, but the 'reality' of the love theme is too flimsily illustrated by the dramatic action.

It is in prose that the 'literature of imagination' tends to be written—by Beckford or Bunyan, Poe or Kafka, Rabelais or Wells, Orwell or Asimov. The literature of imagination requires at least two things that prose can best command: strong pictorial visualization (for the strange has to be made credible), and dramatic action (since the author has a story to keep up). In his book-illustrations and original drawings Mervyn Peake had already shown his capabilities as a visualizer of haunting and penetrating images, both grotesque and realistic, and this power did not desert him when he turned to prose narrative: his descriptions are alive, and almost Dickensian in the way that they call out for illustration, and his often detailed accounts of physical action—a rare pleasure in an epoch of psychology!—appear as an extension of his artist's control of gesture, an animation of the tense but arrested movements of another medium.

Even his minor works of fiction succeed admirably on their own terms. *Mr. Pye* (1953) is a light and amusing novel about the sojourn of Harold Pye, a plump little 'sleuth of glory', on the island of Sark (where Peake himself has done much of his writing). Mr Pye, whose sole desire is to turn Sark into a paradise of goodness and love, finds that his missionary efforts result in his sprouting a rather troublesome pair of wings. To counteract the embarrassment he tries to do evil, but as the wings diminish on his back, horns push through on his forehead. At the end his good nature accepts the winged state, and on the last page we see Pye (rather like Wells's Pyecraft) becoming airborne and floating off from the island. As in many fantasies, a small island is chosen as a naturally isolated spot where marvellous events might be looked for; but the treatment here is gently humorous rather than seriously imaginative.

Boy in Darkness (1956) is very different: it is a *nouvelle,* a sinister epic incident, a reflection in miniature of the world of *Titus Groan* and *Gormenghast.* The story is separate from the two big novels, but has the same hero, the boy Titus. The Boy, aged fourteen, undergoes a testing allegory of adolescence, and successfully outwits the three horrible half-human figures of the Goat, the Hyena, and the Lamb, into whose country he strays. The blind, dead-white Lamb with his hyperacute hearing and soft musical voice is a more appalling Comus, transforming his human captives into a shape halfway towards the animal which their ruling passion or quality suggests. When the Boy kills him, he kills an enchantment. 'There was no blood, nor anything to be seen in the nature of a brain.' The danger had in one sense been real: he had experienced the first shock of identity, of being not a boy but a man, a free and individual soul whom others (including the most evil) would now begin to trouble, cover, touch, and attack. But the danger and the dread are presented as a dream, a nightmare which he himself will forget—or remember only as an unexplained strengthening of his courage in moments of temptation or terror in waking life.

With the long novel *Titus Groan* (1946) and its two sequels *Gormenghast* (1950) and *Titus Alone* (1959), we reach Mervyn Peake's major work. Here, the full range of his imagination rouses itself, from weird fantasy and farcical humour to horror, pathos, and moral and social allegory.

The action of the first two books of the trilogy takes place in or near the enormous ritual-ridden castle of Gormenghast, in a highly organized and ancient society. At the top of the hierarchy are the Earl and Countess of Groan, Sepulchrave and Gertrude; abstracted, solitary figures, Sepulchrave immured with his books, Gertrude with her cats and birds. The family includes the Earl's twin sisters, Cora and Clarice, single-minded in jealous hatred of the Countess; his daughter Fuchsia, awkward, passionate, hungering for the love that her remote parents have denied her; and his newly born son Titus, who is still a baby at the end of *Titus Groan* but has already given signs of an independent spirit by throwing certain sacred objects in the lake. The privileged ranks of society are headed by the eccentric but good-hearted Dr Prunesquallor and his man-hunting sister Irma. Then come the vast array of servants, from the knee-cracking head valet Flay down to the versatile but Machiavellian kitchen-boy Steerpike who becomes the focus of interest in *Titus Groan.* Lowest of all are the Outer Dwellers living in huts in the shadow of the castle walls—a different race. . . . (pp. 35-8)

The story, which is continued in *Gormenghast* to the point where Titus is a young man, and in *Titus Alone* to the hero's first experience of life and love beyond the castle walls, presents a crisis in the life of this society. Gormenghast is threatened, in the first place by the coldblooded and ambitious Steerpike, who is willing to use murder, arson, and seduction as stepping-stones to power, and hopes for eventual dictatorship, replacing the Groan dynasty with an even more rigid and frustrating régime. He overreaches himself, and is killed by Titus. But Titus himself represents a second and perhaps more serious threat. His motives for destroying Steerpike are personal rather than public, and he becomes, ironically, the deliverer of a society he is eager to reject. The laws and rituals of his forebears . . . , with which he is bound to comply whatever the heroism or indifference of his personal character, stifle his adventurous spirit. 'What do I care,' he exclaims to his mother, 'for the symbolism of it all? What do I care if the castle's heart is sound or not? I don't want to be sound anyway! Anybody can be sound if they're always doing what they're told. I want to live!' His mother assumes that this is the natural and temporary rebelliousness of youth, and does not try to stop Titus when he rides off alone from the castle on the last page of *Gormenghast* in search of a freer existence. . . . Life in Gormenghast, as in many human communities, has become morbidly stiff and encrusted with meaningless ceremonies; Titus sees it not merely as the world of his boyhood which he must outgrow, but also as a world

that has become unnaturally resistant to change. With Steerpike's death, Gormenghast has a breathing-space; but with Titus's departure—the defection of the heir—a criticism is made of the old ways which is deeper than the Countess knows. Like a spore of new life breaking off from some great colony in decay, Titus bears with him an impress of tradition and order and authority of which he is himself hardly aware, but he will not re-enter the ancient castle, and if some day he founds a castle of his own it will only be 'Gormenghast' as a man is the son of his parents, not as a king succeeds a king. At the end of the third volume, *Titus Alone,* the young hero returns to Gormenghast Mountain, after many adventures in an alien country where the people's mocking disbelief in his noble origin gave him an intense homesickness for the very things he had tried to escape from; but as soon as he hears a ritual salvo booming from the still invisible walls, his old rejection of Gormenghast is suddenly confirmed and strengthened, and he swings off in another direction, away from the castle. (pp. 38-9)

These three novels are in fact commenting—neither directly nor by strict allegory but by significant juxtaposition and mingling of the grotesque and the human—upon society, upon the relation of the individual to traditional forms, upon what Guillaume Apollinaire called

> . . . cette longue querelle de la tradition et de
> l'invention
>   De l'Ordre de l'Aventure.

They do this, admittedly, with a profusion of romantic, exciting, and sometimes lurid incident, but the point must be made that they are by no means 'Gothick' in their total effect. (The American edition of *Titus Groan* was sub-titled *A Gothic Novel,* against the wishes of the author.) . . . Far from 'having no more connection with the reality of living than *The Hunting of the Snark,*' as one reviewer asserted of *Gormenghast,* the novels give an impression of relevance to life that is all the more extraordinary because it might seem incompatible with the undoubtedly 'Gothick' material— crumbling turrets, hooting owls, guttering candles—which Peake doesn't hesitate to incorporate. This material falls into a wider imaginative scheme: it is not at the centre of the novels. It is the almost wanton richness of the author's imagination that gives his work something of the richness of life itself. Images are thrown off which would be irrelevant to the more didactic and narrow fantasy of a William Golding or a George Orwell, but which here (rather as in Kafka and Melville) reinforce credibility with sudden pleasure. When Steerpike is exploring the tremendous ramifications of the castle roofs, he sees very far off in the sunlight a tower half-filled with rainwater.

> In this circle of water whose glittering had caught his eye, for to him it appeared about the size of a coin, he could see that something white was swimming. As far as he could guess it was a horse. As he watched he noticed that there was something swimming by its side, something smaller, which must have been the foal, white like its parent.

These horses are not like Chekhov's gun; they don't have to be there. But it is such details—details here of a world within a world—that make the fantasy leap into verisimilitude.

The novels are not without faults. The recapitulation at the beginning of *Gormenghast* slows up our entry into the main action. I am not quite happy about the position and meaning of the Outer Dwellers (it is hinted that they may be concerned in some way with the rejuvenation of Gormenghast), and the primitive simplicity of their portrayal was perhaps a mistake: they remain unassimilated. *Titus Alone,* which introduces a new set of characters, has some fine scenes but shows rather less certainty of purpose than the two earlier volumes. And there are, throughout, curious solecisms and misspellings which could have been tidied up.

But what matters is the many truly remarkable passages in these three books which are unfolded with a narrative energy and descriptive brilliance not commonly found among more conventional novelists today. Let me recommend in particular four scenes which show the unusual range of Peake's effectiveness: Steerpike's reconnoitring climb over the complex of the castle roofs and battlements (*Titus Groan*); the nightmarish duel between Flay and Swelter in the Hall of Spiders (*Titus Groan*); Irma's soirée with the Professors and her dallying with the Headmaster in the moonlight arbour—surely one of the funniest scenes in modern fiction (*Gormenghast*); and the ghastly Dostoevskian throngs of the Under-River (*Titus Alone*). A man climbs over a roof. Two men fight. A woman holds a party. A man explores a sewer. This basis in recognizable experience, highly particularized and circumstantial, is what preserves Peake's grotesque from whimsy and from crude melodrama. Yet his greatest quality is the sweep of free imagination with which he fills a large and tumultuous canvas. In his finest pages he leaves the grotesque behind. At the climax of *Gormenghast* there is a deluge which almost ruins the castle physically at the moment when Steerpike is striking at its soul. The description of the storm, the evacuation of the vast crowded mass of buildings floor by floor as the floodwaters rise, the final stark encounter of hero and villain when Titus hunts Steerpike among the ivy, and the eventual receding of the water and re-emergence of the castle, and the return to everyday life—all this has an epic quality of multitudinousness and grandeur and inevitability of action. The dead Fuchsia is ferried across the water to her burial-place on Gormenghast Mountain, and Peake gives us a last look at his creation from that vantage-point.

> From this location the castle could be seen heaving across the skyline like the sheer sea-wall of a continent; a seaboard nibbled with countless coves and bitten deep with shadowy embayments. A continent, off whose shores the crowding islands lay; islands of every shape that towers can be; and archipelagos; and isthmuses and bluffs; and stark peninsulas of wandering stone—an inexhaustible panorama whose every detail was mirrored in the breathless flood below.

Artist and writer, outward and inward eye, combine to produce an image which is in its own way an image of the world. (pp. 39-42)

> Edwin Morgan, "The Walls of Gormenghast: An Introduction to the Novels of Mervyn Peake," in his Essays, Carcanet Press, 1974, pp. 35-42.

HENRY TUBE

The new edition of *Titus Groan,* first published in 1946, is an occasion for celebration. Not that Mervyn Peake's great Gormenghast trilogy has ever been undervalued by those who know it, but so comparatively few seem to be aware of its existence. Whether this is because the work is in the generally

'Gothic' style, or because its author is also a notable illustrator and people tend to be suspicious of a man with two talents, it is something which can now be remedied. . . .

At first reading, the qualities that make the most striking impression are Mr Peake's boldness of language and the powerful movement of his narrative. These are, of course, the natural bonuses which accrue to any writer daring enough to essay the Gothic novel, for whatever disadvantages may come in tow—and Mr Peake suffers from some of them—he can at least dress his thoughts in any fantastic garb he pleases, while the heightened happening is his stock-in-trade. Mr Peake seizes this opportunity with both hands. He is a master of the rolling period, the purple passage and the grand set-scene. Indeed, if the book were brand-new, a reviewer might well close his account with the mere evocation of some of its finest effects: the infernal scene in the kitchens, as the sweating chef, Abiatha Swelter, bullies his apprentices; the young villain Steerpike's harrowing journey over the castle's roofscape—. . . .

Let there be no mistake about this. I suspect that the slight air of contempt people wear at mention of 'Gothic' writing, or even 'grotesque' illustration—the other string to Mr Peake's bow—is due to their belief that it is somehow 'easier' than naturalism. But no one falls harder on his face than the Gothic writer who lacks the imagination and the stamina to weave and control his fantasy. Mr Peake succeeds in passage after passage because he has both in lavish measure.

Beyond this again, the structure of the whole book has, like Gormenghast itself, 'a certain ponderous architectural quality.' Moving slowly, as it can afford to do when there are other volumes to follow, the opening chapters introduce us one by one, or in small groups, to the characters of the drama, and it is not until we have been properly absorbed into the engrossing rituals of Mr Peake's world that the narrative is allowed to gather pace. Even then, it is never 'snatched,' the slow heavy rhythms are most wonderfully deployed against the excitement of the action.

But it is only when these larger virtues of his art have become a little familiar, that one begins to appreciate its real core. What makes him, so far as I know, unique among writers, is what also makes him a great illustrator of other writers—Stevenson, Coleridge, Dickens—his gift for seeing: 'What Fuchsia wanted from a picture was something unexpected. It was as though she enjoyed the artist telling her something quite fresh and new.' Who but Mervyn Peake would have seen one-legged Long John Silver *without* a cloak, and the peculiarly youthful and therefore much more sinister effect that would have on him? Who but Mervyn Peake would have placed the Ancient Mariner at the very bottom of the picture, hardly more than a speck, beneath enormous tattered sails? Who but he could have written this:

> Swelter is shifting the soft, dace-like areas of his feet backwards and forwards, a deliberate and stroking motion, as of something succulent wiping itself on a mat?

(p. 105)

Swept along by the narrative, buoyed up by the rhythmic prose and time and again ravished by these visual insights, one is in no mood to cavil too severely at Mr Peake's faults. Nevertheless, if only in order to set off what he is so good at, and because, as Anthony Burgess in his introduction to the new edition points out, [**Titus Groan**] is now safely a modern classic, it is worth glancing at them. He has, in the first place, never mastered dialogue. Characters who command our deepest respect, visually and in action, wither away at the touch of speech, amid uneasy echoes of Lewis Carroll.

This weakness gives rise to another. Since he is unable to throw open his characters mentally and psychologically, he is gravely hampered when it comes to spinning the moral thread of his saga. For the world of Gormenghast, though on one level providing a superbly spacious canvas for its author's special visual techniques, is also on another the arena for a straightforward conflict between good and evil. Alas, Mr Peake can do no more than present this conflict undigested in the most second-hand and tawdry terms, which at their worst become frankly sentimental, as in the episodes concerning Keda, the girl from the huts outside the castle wall, as well as many of those concerning Fuchsia, the Earl's daughter. For although when he is sketching the teenage Fuchsia's dawning sexuality he understands perfectly what he is about, her creator is lost when he has to convey her 'good'-ness.

But, abandoning these dark thoughts, let us return to Mr Peake's apotheosis. If the illustrations included in this new edition are disappointing the reason is quite simply that they are redundant. The central glory of **Titus Groan** is that it is a series of verbal illustrations of outstanding quality. The story, though a good one and well told, is not exceptional; the characters are borrowed types and, as we have seen, do not speak well; even the prose, though often exhilarating, is not wholly original. But what does any of this matter? In taking his story, in taking his characters, his prose, from wherever he took them—Dickens, Stevenson, Carroll and perhaps Kafka—Mr Peake had one purpose only, to *see* them as they had never been seen before. He has succeeded triumphantly. The outcome is that we must see him not as a man with two talents, but as a genius with two nibs. (pp. 105-06)

> *Henry Tube, "His Nibs," in* The Spectator, *Vol. 220, No. 7283, January 26, 1968, pp. 105-06.*

MICHAEL WOOD

[**Titus Groan**] first appeared in 1946, to a chorus of firm but puzzled praise. One understands the puzzlement. The book is impossible to describe and therefore hard to recommend coherently.

It presents a world which, like Kafka's, demands to be discussed in its own terms—the reverse of an allegory. It is a world of fantasy, peopled by creatures with names like Sepulchrave, Rottcodd, Prunesquallor and Sourdust, a closed, self-sufficient creation. Yet it is a world without whimsy, and it touches our own at many points. It is frightening and familiar, like an old dream, or an obsolete, forgotten wish. The conflicts, illusions and deaths of its characters are both sinister and comic, like the games of children growing up.

> *Michael Wood, "Gruesome and Good," in* The Observer, *April 14, 1968, p. 27.*

C. N. MANLOVE

Peake was probably best known to the public for his drawings. These are either representational or illustrations to a given text or both which may explain how he could turn to writing fiction: though a caricaturist he rarely drew abstracts or 'unrecognizable' shapes. Some of his drawings have been collected; and his illustrations for books include *The Hunting of the Snark* (1941), *The Ancient Mariner* (1943), *Alice's Adventures in Wonderland* (1946), the *Household Tales* of the brothers Grimm (1946) and *Treasure Island* (1949). Goya is an obvious influence on his style, and El Greco, Poussin and Claude Lorrain. His bent as a caricaturist seems to have been primarily for elongation or compression: and the most frequent vision in his art seems to be of verticality struggling against a dense and crushing medium—precisely the vision that we are to be given of Gormenghast (both the castle and the people). Consider, for instance, how Peake plays the horizontality of the sea, or the thickness of the atmosphere or darkness (or even 'downwards' verticality, in the case of the hanging rags of the ship's sails) against the tiny upright figure of the sailor in *The Ancient Mariner,* or the pressure of the sky on Jim on the island in *Treasure Island;* or the use of right-angles in the postures of the figures in *The Hunting of the Snark.* It is to Peake the artist and draughtsman that much of the manner of the 'Titus' trilogy—the descriptions, precise to the point of pedantry, the recurrent use of chiaroscuro, the sheer sense of space and the slowness of the narrative—can be attributed.

Peake also received recognition as a poet. Most of his poetry appeared in **Shapes and Sounds** (1941), **The Glassblowers** (1950), **The Rhyme of the Flying Bomb** (1962) and **A Reverie of Bone** (1967); . . . . 'Of every form of human expression,' Mrs Peake writes, 'poetry moved Mervyn more than any other.' His own, however, rarely catches fire. It is best when he is dealing with immediate experience; worst when he meditates, generalizes or analyses his feelings after the event. Any distance from an intense present, as in his own life, is false. Thus in the finer poems—for instance **The Rhyme of the Flying Bomb**, 'The Glassblowers', 'To Maeve', 'A Reverie of Bone', 'El Greco', or 'Heads Float About Me'—the experience and its significance to him are fused. Elsewhere the poetry is frequently shrill, melodramatic, or uncertain and rambling; much of it is too simply derivative, lacking in individual style.

If his poetry is often too earnest, we find the reverse in Peake's children's books—**Captain Slaughterboard Drops Anchor** (1939) and **Letters from a Lost Uncle from Polar Regions** (1948)—and in his nonsense verse—**Rhymes without Reason** (1944). Delightful inconsequentiality is of the essence. **Captain Slaughterboard** is mainly drawings of the life of a pirate captain who comes to give up his violent life and settle down on a pink island with a lonely Yellow Creature; **Letters from a Lost Uncle,** also heavily illustrated, consists of the letters to his nephew of an explorer who is hunting the White Lion of the Arctic with a sulky turtle-like creature called Jackson. The nonsense verse shows the debt of Peake's imagination to Lear and Carroll, though this is far from overwhelming. Peake has a special ability at the verse of 'pointlessness': witness the ocean and story in **'The Frivolous Cake,'** or this from a drifting mariner,

> There was no one to love me
> Nor hope of being found—
> When, on the blurred horizon,
> (So endlessly a-drip),
> I saw—all of a sudden!
> No sign. . .of any. . .ship. (**Mr. Pye**)

It is when Peake's imagination fuses its sense of point and

pointlessness, of gravity and absurdity that we have a genuine imaginative vision, as we shall see in *Titus Groan.* There the Ritual is pointless, its meaning forgotten, but as a central fact of existence in the castle it gives purpose and direction to every character; and the characters themselves are at once bizarre and tragically human.

Something of this vision is also present in *Mr. Pye* (1953). This novel, set in Sark, describes a little man who comes from nowhere to the island and by skill and personal magnetism turns it into a paradise of Christian behaviour—only to find that as a result a pair of angelic wings has started to grow out of his back. When, to make these disappear, he sets about doing as much evil as he can, a pair of horns sprouts from his forehead. To remove these, he humiliates himself before the people of Sark, at which his wings re-appear and he is able to escape the popular wrath by literally flying from the island, never to return. This book deserved much better than to have been remaindered on its first appearance: Peake's grip on the character of Mr Pye is very sure and the unsentimental love of Sark and its people out of which the story grew gives it depth, humour and economy. However it seems an unusual theme for him to have chosen. Perhaps one can relate it to the 'Titus' trilogy by seeing it as his way of saying that one takes a risk in trying to change oneself or other people: Gormenghast, too, is a place of 'no change'. (pp. 212-14)

Peake's primary literary indebtedness was to Dickens—both to his sense of the grotesque and to his preoccupation with crippling ritual and tradition, decay and smothering. In some degree [*Titus Groan* and *Gormenghast*] are a re-creation of *Bleak House* (a book for which Peake did a series of unpublished illustrations), with one major difference: for Dickens, decay and rot grind down separate identities to a kind of universal sludge, whereas Peake's Gormenghast thrives on decay and neglect, producing more and more etiolated and bizarre stalks of personality and setting.

Peake probably also took something from another imagination which owed much to Dickens—that of Kafka; the particular book is of course *The Castle* (1926). In that book the edifice itself, a cluster of little two-storey buildings with only one sprouting a modest tower, is not readily a prototype of Peake's stronghold; but the sheer gulf between the people of Kafka's castle and those of the village outside suggests that between Gormenghast and the Outer Dwellings; and perhaps Peake got some of his idea of the Ritual from the elaborate, nightmarishly indifferent bureaucracy of the castle in Kafka's book. Certainly, too, Kafka has isolated the setting of his book as Peake has: the Land Surveyor K. has come in from the outside world, but that world is, apart from one mention by Frieda of France and Spain as places she would like to escape to, wholly ignored, as if it did not exist.

Titus Alone may well have owed much to the book which was also the source of Orwell's *Nineteen Eighty-Four*—Yevgeny Zamyatin's *We*—for the ideas both of the search for identity and of an antiseptic scientific world of glass, concrete and metal outside which the unruly world of rejected nature continues to exist. Certain incidental features afford particularly striking parallels—the hovering spy-planes, the sabotaged state scientific project, the constant shadowing of the protagonists by strange police 'guardians', the notion of underground tunnels leading to contact with the more passionate side of life (or in terms of mental symbolism, the *id*). There are no animals in Zamyatin's One State: Peake may have been refining on this in putting the only beasts in his world behind

the bars of Muzzlehatch's (eventually-destroyed) zoo, and in calling human characters like Cheeta, the scientist's daughter, by animal names.

The narrative of Peake's trilogy may be briefly told. It begins with the birth of Titus and the origin of the schemes of the kitchenboy Steerpike against the society of Gormenghast. Steerpike, by Machiavellian means, gains both power and favour until he is in a position to strike against the family of Groan. He drives the old Earl Sepulchrave to madness and suicide, starves Cora and Clarice, the sisters of the Countess Gertrude, to death, and slays Barquentine, the Master of Ritual, to secure his influential office for himself. With the help of loyal retainers, Titus, now a youth, discovers Steerpike gloating over the dead sisters, but the murderer escapes. Prodigious rains flood Gormenghast until it is a Venetian archipelago, and Steerpike, driven like everyone else to the higher towers, is eventually sighted and finally slain by the young Earl. But at the same time as he slays the traitor of his ancestral home, Titus becomes an open traitor himself and leaves his realm in search of further horizons. *Titus Alone* describes the technological world—much more like ours—that he finds. Few of the people in it believe in the existence of Gormenghast, and Titus is almost driven mad by his own increasing doubt. In the end he returns homewards, and comes at last to a rock beyond which he knows he will be able to see Gormenghast. But he does not go forward: 'He had no longer any need for home, for he carried his Gormenghast within him.' He turns away, and sets out on a new path into the unexplored world. (pp. 215-17)

Gormenghast, considered both as place and society, is the most important character of the trilogy—is indeed its first and (in synonym) its last word—and defines the very nature of the first volume. Its role in the eventual urge of Titus to escape is crucial. . . . It is isolated—more isolated than any other fantastic realm—from our world and indeed from any continuum of time or space. Our reality is simply never mentioned. *Where* Gormenghast is, and how it came into being Peake does not suggest. Titus is the seventy-seventh Earl of Groan, but what those before his father, the seventy-sixth, were like, or indeed what their home was like before the first of them, remains a mystery; what, too, will happen to Gormenghast when at the end Titus flees the place leaving no heir, is blank. With the prerogative of the artist, Peake captures a life or a moment, and if we look for a before and an after we will find only the frame. Not that time, history and tradition are unimportant: they are the castle's very lifeblood. To us, however, they are presented as a result rather than a process; are seen in their effect on Titus as data rather than through analysis of their growth. (pp. 217-18)

Titus' reason for wanting to leave Gormenghast seems simple enough. For him life can never be free because he must always be imprisoned by the Ritual, the immemorial observance required constantly of the lineal Earls and, less frequently, of their relatives. The Ritual is enshrined in the ancient Tomes of Procedure, which lay down the exact activities to be performed at every minute of the day by the Earl. Most of these activities have a symbolic significance now forgotten, but the law of Gormenghast decrees that they continue, and that a hierophantic Master of Ritual is kept in office to ensure their survival. (pp. 230-31)

There is here certainly a ground-plan for a life of misery. Yet Peake strangely fails to show any convincing Ritual stranglehold on the life of Titus. In *Titus Groan* he is only one year old by the end of the book, and is only occasionally, and un-consciously, made the centre of Ritual observance. Through-out *Gormenghast* and his development from childhood to youth, his life is almost entirely occupied with pleasure or ad-ventures—the joys of schoolboy wickedness, the thrill of rid-ing beyond the confines of the castle, and later of hunting down Steerpike. Rarely is he found in the shackles of the Rit-ual. When, very occasionally, Peake mentions any duties to which Titus has to submit, they are always oddly attractive—his Tenth Birthday Party in the woods or the occasion on which he has to stand beside the castle moat wearing a plaited grass necklace and throw a golden coil in such a way that it bounces off the water, soars over the reflection of a particular turret and finally sinks in that of a gaping window at which his mother stands. Though Peake makes something of Titus' loathing for Barquentine, the repulsive Master of Ritual, it is nevertheless stressed throughout that the latter has carried his office to an extreme of inhuman zeal (which we know from comparison with his more likeable father Sourdust); and the fact that both Barquentine and his treacherous suc-cessor Steerpike are dead by the end of the book further di-vides the Ritual from its exponents. In any case Barquentine and the supposed forces of repression have little actual im-pact on the freedom of Titus or indeed of anyone else in the book. Peake thus fails to make the Ritual an adequate justifi-cation for escape from Gormenghast. (pp. 231-32)

Titus' role in the trilogy loses credibility from the start. He is supposed to be the first Earl of Groan to have rebelled, but nothing in his nature seems to make him peculiar. The sense of duty and observance has until Titus been 'immemorial' in Gormenghast. It might be possible to allegorize and say that his ancestors represent the period of feudal loyalty and obedi-ence, while he is a new Renaissance individualist: but Renais-sances must have causes—shifts of interest, new intellectual discoveries, forces from outside—and there is no change in Gormenghast, or any real influence from beyond its walls.

Peake had several problems before him with the theme of freedom. First, since the essence of Gormenghast is that it does not change, it is well-nigh impossible to give adequate explanation for the existence of a heretical earl. Second, to give a convincing reason for leaving the castle, some quality or person of equal weight of reality must be offered to us to set against the place: and because Gormenghast is the natural home of his imagination, Peake finds it difficult to do this. Thirdly, it is equally a difficulty for him to condemn the place from within—really to show us, for example, that the Ritual is a poisoning influence on Titus, or, say, that his surround-ings and his society are stunting his vision and his humanity. He cannot do this because it would mean judging Gor-menghast simply, and his involvement with the place is far too complex to allow this: he will not side with Titus so far. The result of all this is a split between Peake's ostensible and real commitments.

Throughout *Gormenghast* he shows his uneasiness in a con-tinual search for some way of accounting for Titus' quest. He offers a confused variety of motives which still beg the ques-tion as to where they come from in the first place. (p. 238)

Titus' escape from Gormenghast is unreal. At the very end, when he hastily takes leave of his mother and his home, and the Countess asks him where he is going, both he and his cre-ator are so bankrupt of motives that all that can be offered is a pretence that they are too deep, rather than too nebulous, to be explained: ' "I am leaving. . .I am leaving Gor-

menghast. I cannot explain. I do not want to talk. I came to tell you and that is all." ' As Titus makes for the door, he hears his mother's voice at his back articulating our own feel-ings: ' "There is nowhere else," it said. "You will only tread a circle, Titus Groan. There's not a road, not a track, but it will lead you home. For everything comes to Gormenghast".'

Largely as a result of Peake's difficulties with the theme of freedom, *Gormenghast* misses the complex vision of *Titus Groan.* On the one hand he is committed to supporting Titus' rebellion, and on the other, to its ostensible cause, Gor-menghast. Because Titus' heresies occupied only a small part of *Titus Groan,* Peake's attitude to the castle could there re-main complex and latent, but their centrality in the second volume polarizes and simplifies his loyalties and his sensibili-ty alike. (pp. 246-47)

At first sight *Titus Alone* might seem to deny the declaration of the Countess at the end of *Gormenghast,* for in his new world Titus becomes gradually obsessed by doubt that his home exists. What seems to start this process is his shock at the self-sufficiency of his new and strange environment. It was this very quality in the Thing, this total indifference to the castle and its life, that made her and what she stood for so fascinating to Titus originally: she made him 'Haunted by the thought of this other kind of world which was able to exist without Gormenghast.' Yet when he finds this far realm that has never heard of his home he asks, 'How was it that they were so self-sufficient, these women in their cars, or Muzzle-hatch with his zoo—having no knowledge of Gormenghast, which was of course the heart of everything?' In the previous book we were shown Titus standing against Gormenghast be-fore separating himself from it: now we find the denial of all this, the pull backwards. If only Peake had portrayed Titus' original urges in a more ironic light, admitting that he could not cut himself as cleanly from the castle as he thought, then we could feel that the drag of his home in *Titus Alone* repre-sented his feelings coming home to roost. But no: Peake in fact starts the third volume by maintaining that he is finished with the past, 'It was no more than a memory now; a slur of the tide; a reverie, or the sound of a key turning.' This sounds like fresh woods and pastures new: but in a few lines we dis-cover that the propitiatory elegy is still to come, 'He only knows that he has left behind him, on the far side of the sky-line, something inordinate; something brutal; something ten-der; something half real; something half dream; half of his heart; half of himself.' That Titus should spend all his time away fixated by Gormenghast is what we would expect, but not what we were *meant* to expect. (pp. 249-50)

The question which remains is why, if despite Peake's efforts it fails to convince, the theme of freedom has any place at all in the trilogy, why he was driven in the first place to fasten on the one issue guaranteed to fail. The explanation may lie in the very world of fantasy which he has created. He has made a world so isolated from any other that he may have been driven to make the connections he denied. The process . . . would be like a spring: the greater the distance, spiritual or physical, of the fantastic world from any other, the more the pull backwards on its creator—even though, un-molested, his world may by virtue of a self-consistent reality already stand in richly symbolic relation to our own.

To ask why Peake chose the theme of freedom is, ultimately, to ask why he portrayed Gormenghast as he did. If the castle had not been founded on changelessness, if it had not been an island universe, then the ideas of change and of other worlds would not have been so nebulous beside it. And perhaps the artist was behind this—the artist who will put only one place in his frame, and whose visions are, essentially, 'still life'. Peake wanted, however, to generate from within this world of repose and stasis a condition of flux and becoming, to show the central figure of his picture coming to independent life from inside, and then walking out of the painting, out of the frame altogether, like the man in M. R. James' 'The Mezzotint'. Why he felt this wish is, however, a question which perhaps only other artists might be able to answer.

Nevertheless, whatever Peake's reasons for choosing the theme, and whatever its disastrous effect on his trilogy, that very failure is in part a testimony to the power of *Titus Groan*, in which the castle of the Groans is so brilliantly realized. *Gormenghast* and *Titus Alone* are not the creations of a fading genius, but—and this is well enough illustrated by the way in which Peake's imagination surfaces, as hugely as Gormenghast itself, in the account of the flood before Titus leaves the castle—the products of a real, even a great literary ability strangled in its own toils. (pp. 256-57)

> C. N. Manlove, "Mervyn Peake (1911-68)—The 'Titus' Trilogy," in his Modern Fantasy: Five Studies, *Cambridge University Press, 1975, pp. 207-57.*

HILARY SPURLING

Mervyn Peake's premature decline and death coupled with his years of almost complete neglect, have lent an exhilarating—and entirely righteous—crusading indignation to the public rediscovery in the past decade of this powerful and highly peculiar talent; but even the staunchest enthusiasts may find themselves welcoming this gargantuan volume of first drafts, rough sketches and bungled or abandoned projects [*Peake's Progress: Selected Writings and Drawings of Mervyn Peake*] with something not unlike the fixed expression of the pirate Mr Grinner ('Tortured by Indians in his callow days his face now presented to the world an unalterable smile') in Peake's hitherto unpublished story, **'Mr Slaughter-board.'**

The character comes to a frightful end along with practically everyone else in this early, X certificate version of what eventually emerged as the children's classic, *Captain Slaughterboard Drops Anchor,* here set aboard a sort of rudimentary, sea-going Gormenghast. It is one of the best things in a collection that builds perhaps too much on that fatally soft ground which constitutes Peake's undeniable attraction for literary cranks and cult practitioners.

His limitations—a tendency to mawkishness and whimsy, accompanied by a certain self-indulgent prolixity or linear slackness—were well understood by Peake himself, if one may judge by his repeated injunctions to students to cultivate the habits of critical intelligence and rigorously accurate observation. 'The whole idea was to be sharp, matter-of-fact and, if you understand me, rather original and grandiose,' as he explains in **'I Bought a Palm-Tree,'** a flimsy tale which demonstrates his theory by default.

Other fragments like **'The House of Darkstones'**—a dogged, fumbling, stumbling first attempt at *Titus Groan*—make it very plain that his own richest and most prodigal effects were achieved only by hard labour. . . .

[The] book is by no means without minor pleasures: a macabre story called **'Same Time, Same Place,'** worthy of M. R. James in its masterly combination of the humdrum and the monstrous; a handful of fine poems, including the lovely **'To Maeve';** some notes for a projected autobiography which enigmatically evoke Peake's Chinese childhood, as in this memo on his parents' cook: 'TA-TZE-FU. His starling to market. The way he killed hens and peeled sticks.'

Perhaps most intriguing of all, among material not previously published elsewhere, is the text of *The Wit to Woo,* the poetic drama whose unenthusiastic reception in 1957 played such a disastrous part in precipitating Peake's last illness.

Much else will no doubt interest Peake specialists; but one can't help feeling that, if books could speak, this one would say with Percy Trellis, in a memorably ungainly image from *The Wit to Woo,* 'I am the dottle in that one-time pipe-full: I am the acrid ullage in the keg.'

> Hilary Spurling, "Dottle and Ullage," in The Observer, *January 29, 1979, p. 34.*

JONATHAN KEATES

1968, the year of the Paris *événements* and the Russian invasion of Czechoslovakia, was the year when I failed to finish *Titus Groan*. I tried very hard, manfully swallowing that awful title ('Vespasian Shriek' or 'Nero Shudder' would have done as well) and gulping down names like Flay and Lord Sepulchrave—but it was no use. Added to the fact that the 'Gormenghast' novels were so obviously the longed-for replacement for Tolkien, part of the wave of late-Sixties floral-patterned infantilism (of which *Watership Down* is an insidious vestige) there was the unwelcome sensation of reading something by an author who couldn't really write, and whose true métier clearly lay elsewhere. A decade later this feeling persists: it is not that Peake doesn't savour words and respond to certain obvious literary influences, or that he fails to exercise the same potent, haunted imagination which established his deserved success as an illustrator. The truth is that language won't do what he wants, that cliché, orotundity and vagueness keep getting in the way, and the result is curiously gawky and shambling, like one of the knobbly, stringy figures in his drawings.

This latest bulky anthology of ungathered pieces, [*Peake's Progress*], has the additional interest of being readable as an autobiography. Almost the best thing it contains is, indeed, Peake's own skeleton account of his boyhood as a missionary's son in northern China, at Tientsin Grammar School ('Its windows were mouths that shouted "I know I'm ugly and I like it" ') and Shanghai ('a frozen, icy, tinkling horror of mules and motor cars, western houses, and narrow, banner-hung hovel streets'). Rough and unforced, his description of travelling by night in a cart along a mountain road among camel and mule caravans has an intensity altogether lacking from the more self-consciously polished prose extracts.

We are also reminded that he wrote verse. Who, for Christ's sake, doesn't? None of these poems is especially good, and even the nonsense verses fail to transcend the level of the merely nonsensical to create an independent logic. Much, including the once admired **'The Cocky Walkers'**, now has the mournful interest of the yellowing newspaper cuttings which occasionally drop out of old books. The idiom in nearly every case belongs less to its author than to the period or to the mass of eagerly absorbed reading which underlies it. For a taste, read the four poems on painters written during the early Fifties, so strangely redolent, in words like 'graved', 'enswathen', 'quenchless' and 'thieven', of a Pater and Meredith world of High Art drawing rooms.

Precisely the same suggestion of a modified fin-de-siècle aestheticism, of words as things somehow precious and brittle, which might come to pieces if not reverently handled, clings to the longer poems **'A Reverie of Bone'** and **'The Rhyme of the Flying Bomb'.** The first, a versified 'Urne Buriall', relates directly to Peake's preoccupation as a draughtsman with the ridges and angles of the human physique. The second, frankly imitative in form and style of 'The Ballad of Reading Gaol', is nearly successful as a concentrated evocation of London's experience of wartime bombardment. Both, like practically everything else Peake ever wrote, are portentous, hyper-literary, magniloquent and ultimately empty of life.

Nor indeed are the plays and stories much better. The enormous verse play *The Wit to Woo* flopped at the Arts Theatre in 1957, for reasons, alas, easy to appreciate. Its satirical aims get quickly lost in thickets of arch jocularity and the pacing of the dialogue is simply amateurish throughout. Among the longer prose pieces is the potentially absorbing *Boy In Darkness,* a sub-species of *Titus Groan,* in which the characters and action are heavily allegorical, but here too intention flouts technique. A clutch of short stories conveys an identical urge to get over the hurdles of style, narrative rhythms and character-drawing, in order to make the point before it escapes absolutely.

Exactly what Peake was good at emerges at once in the illustrative material drawn from his sketches. . . . As an artist with brush and pencil, nothing comes between him and his subject: the medium is triumphantly established as his own. As a writer he can never break out of an enduring awkwardness with words, as though his hands were grasping bunches of them in a desperate effort to make them carry his ideas. His true poetry was visual: his place as a literary figure is with interesting Gothick failures like Lord de Tabley and Thomas Lovell Beddoes. More vividly than others of its kind this anthology reminds us that a *violon d'Ingres* can sometimes prove a ukulele. (pp. 222-23)

Jonathan Keates, "Quenchless," in New Statesman, *Vol. 97, No. 2500, February 16, 1979, pp. 222-23.*

RONALD BINNS

A creatively restless man, Peake's central achievement remains the [Gormenghast] trilogy; without it he would probably only be half-remembered as a minor poet of the 'forties, or as a brilliant book illustrator. Despite the popularity of his work, however, Peake's trilogy has attracted little academic recognition. It belongs to no obvious tradition, lacks an ordered structure, is occasionally careless in detail, and breaks in two after the second volume, at the point where Titus Groan abandons Gormenghast for a picaresque journey through a quite different, more futuristic world. Peake's language is narcotically rich, spilling over with adjectives, sometimes to the point of self-indulgence. The springboard of his imagination is his talent for bizarre characterisation, but the plotting which binds his strange creatures together against the vast static tableau landscapes (loosely called Gothic, but only tenuously deriving from the traditional Gothic novel)

appears largely haphazard, unmoving in any exploration of psychological or moral dilemma. Gormenghast remains truly *sui generis,* yet oddly English, both in its characterisation (which clearly owes a great deal to Dickens) and in the nature of the sluggish, unchanging aristocratic castle society it portrays (though there is no specific attempt at allegory).

An important part of Peake's productivity went into creating for children (*Captain Slaughterboard Drops Anchor, Letters From a Lost Uncle, A Book of Nonsense*), and the Gormenghast trilogy is powerfully charged for adolescent readers. Titus Groan is only twenty when the third volume ends, and in its own way the trilogy forms a *Bildungsroman,* reworking in a heightened form of pure myth the ordeals of a youth endeavouring to break free from the grip of his family. It's also significant that Peake really only achieved substantial popularity towards the end of the 'sixties, at a time much more disposed to works of fantasy, and when various cultural myths of innocence and antirationalism were predominant.

Leslie Fiedler, pointing to the division between fiction as entertainment and fiction as high art invoked by Henry James, has argued that perhaps Stevenson's 'A humble remonstrance' to James's 'The art of fiction' was right after all, 'having reached a time when *Treasure Island* seems somehow more to the point and the heart's delight than, say, *The Princess Casamassima'.* The problem with the argument that fiction should shed the weighty moral imperatives of the social novel and delight instead in fabulation and fun is that as literature becomes divorced from social experience it increasingly runs the risk of seeming merely trivial. The deterioration of the Gormenghast trilogy and of Peake's own career seems to stem from precisely this tension, with the novelist labouring painfully to make fantasy fiction true to his own disturbing experiences in war-shattered Europe. . . . By coincidence *Treasure Island* was one of Peake's favourite books, and though his trilogy has often been appropriated as a similar kind of light escapism to understand it we need to look beyond its status as an hermetic fiction, as fantasy, and instead situate its meaning in relation to the period in which Peake wrote and to the writer's own experiences.

In the poem **'Is there no love can link us?'** published in his first collection *Shapes and Sounds* (1941), Peake considered what his relationship was as a writer to the victims of the developing world war:

> Is there no thread to bind us—I and he
> Who is dying now, this instant as I write
> And may be cold before this line's complete?

The poem concludes pessimistically that there is none at all, except a connection in time:

> There is no other link. Only this sliding
> Second we share: this desperate edge of now.

But to be connected only in time is scarcely to be connected at all, and in another poem **'The two fraternities'** Peake asserts that the 'doomed' companionship of the living is more horrible than 'death's brotherhood'. The poems are slight, but that Peake in the period when these poems were written (1939-41) should have been considering his position as a writer and puzzling over ideas of human fraternity is surprising. John Watney's useful though rather brief biography [*Mervyn Peake*] gives us the picture of a writer who almost always endeavoured to retreat from the world rather than engage with it. For a novelist born in 1911 this is unusual. In the 'thirties no young or unestablished writer could afford to ignore the question of the writer's role in society or towards international politics. . . . Apart from one slightly curious incident when he travelled off to stay among unemployed miners in the Rhondda Valley, Peake's career seems to have been atypical of the period; indeed, his first book and only publication during the decade was an illustrated story for children, *Captain Slaughterboard Drops Anchor,* published by *Country Life* in 1939. It's ironic, therefore, that just at the moment when disillusion and withdrawal affected many writers upon the signing of the Hitler-Stalin pact, Peake began to turn his attention outwards.

The language of *Shapes and Sounds* makes it clear that Peake, temperamentally inclined to the Gothic and the fantastic, was influenced by the ideas and practice of the 'New Apocalypse' school. His style is indulgent and archaic, full of references to angels, centaurs, skulls, battlements, coffins, doom, hemlock, 'autumn grief', 'dagger'd roses', and so on. This is *Grand Guignol*—war imagined from a distance, not war experienced. There is, however, a counter-pull within the collection, where the writer goes outside the enclosed world of his imagination and finds inspiration in bored youths hanging around the streets, in miners, people in a dancehall, a group of people singing hymns in public, a hunchback. These encounters are, though, muffled and romanticised, hampered by Peake's inability to forge a distinctive style, and perhaps also by his inability to empathise with the psychology of others. He does seem to have found it difficult to understand other people as rounded individuals, and in his drawings and prose Peake appears happiest with caricature, with a retreat into pure imagination which permitted a delighted or obsessive exploitation of the weird and the grotesque. This grasp of detail but not of psychology is half-admitted by the writer himself: 'If I could see, not surfaces / but could express / What lies beneath the skin . . .' Though moved by human suffering Peake failed to understand its causes. His historical perspective remained apocalyptic: events piled up, horribly and meaninglessly, and he personified History as 'that witless chronicler'.

In *Enemies of Promise* (1938) Cyril Connolly forecast that writers in the future would be 'required to live within their imagination's income', which is precisely what 'New Apocalypse' writers failed to do. 'Forties poets notoriously failed to develop, and Peake, who during the rest of his life published only two more slim volumes of verse, anticipated several of his more prominent contemporaries in abandoning verse for prose. The poetry remains important, however, for the tensions and contradictions it reveals in Peake's make-up as a writer, and which were to erupt to the surface after 1945— the contrary pulls of a yearning for solidarity existing alongside a mandarin disdain for political engagement, a hazy compassion for humanity matched by a monk-like retreat from society wherever possible, and the contradiction between the enchantments of fantasy and the claims of the real world.

The first draft of *Titus Groan* seems to have been written very quickly between 1940 and 1942. It was later revised stylistically but the plot remained intact. In prose Peake had at last found the best medium for his pictorial imagination, though it seems he only began to conceive of further Titus Groan novels after completing the first volume. His imagination had piled up a fantastic world, yet after five hundred pages his hero was only fifteen months old. The titles of the first two

volumes seem in fact oddly misplaced, for it is *Titus Groan* which establishes the gigantic, decaying world of Gormenghast, and *Gormenghast* which concentrates on Titus's adolescence and initiation into manhood. Perhaps the example of *Tristram Shandy* was in his mind as Peake built up his fictional world with a provocative slowness, and with the nominal hero virtually absent. Much of the first volume is concerned with lavish description of the decaying world of the castle and its environs, together with the dramatisation of a range of weird and eccentric characters who have only a marginal relationship to the plot.

Titus Groan is prefaced by an epigraph taken from Bunyan's 'Author's apology' which precedes *The Pilgrim's Progress:* 'Dost thou love picking meat? Or would'st thou see A man in the clouds and have him speak to thee?' Whereas Bunyan is nervously apologetic about using something as potentially sinful as a fiction for his Puritan myth-making, Peake makes the distinction between sensual pleasure and the cerebral delights of the imagination almost dissolve, since his language is characterised by excess, lushness, a sensual delight in playing with language. . . . What is disturbing about *Titus Groan,* however, is not so much the density of the language, or what Anthony Burgess has described as the 'almost paranoiac' attention to detail, but the grotesque angles of the narrative viewpoint. (pp. 21-5)

Gormenghast is a world transformed from tranquillity and unchanging ritual to one of disturbance and tension. Though represented as a separate world, feudal and pre-industrial, twentieth-century phrases and concepts appear discreetly in the text: Peake talks of sociologists, Steerpike decides that Barquentine is 'to be liquidated'—an expression new to George Orwell as late as 1938. There are a range of questions we might ask about the absences in Gormenghast (producers, police, politics) but Peake never invites them. The density of the description is so lavish, the canvas so broad, that the gaps and ambiguities are all but invisible. As in a Shakespeare history play, Gormenghast is a kingdom legitimised by the forces of nature, and when Steerpike rebels he violates a mystical order that makes his doom inevitable.

The final two paragraphs of the novel capture something of this authoritative but mystifying rhetoric which Peake deploys when considering the fortunes of Gormenghast:

> Through honeycombs of stone would now be wandering the passions in their clay. There would be tears and there would be strange laughter. Fierce births and deaths beneath umbrageous ceilings. And dreams, and violence, and disenchantment. And there shall be a flame-green daybreak soon. And love itself will cry for insurrection! For tomorrow is also a day—and Titus has entered his stronghold.

As a conclusion this is not very satisfying. Peake originally planned to end *Titus Groan* with the word 'Nevertheless'—a word suggesting a continuation, but also some kind of qualification or negation of what has previously happened. His endeavour to close the narrative with a vague suggestion of panoramic, romantic destinies in the offing is overconventional. As Roger Bromley has pointed out, traditional escapist popular fiction always ends in foreclosure, in a prescriptive conclusion where fantasy is endorsed and consciousness is 'bricked in'. *Titus Groan,* however, differs from popular romance through its structural contradictions. Expectations are raised, only to be comically deflated or left in suspension.

Titus Groan rebels against his imposed role as heir to the throne and pushes the regalia of Lordship into the lake. Fuchsia's future is left in doubt, her sexual exploitation by Steerpike an unanswered possibility. Marriage and family life (the holy grail of popular romance) is rendered as grotesque and absurd. Peake's characters retreat from the meaningless rituals of the castle into solipsism, yet their private worlds are corrupt, perverse or puerile. In the fate of the seventy-sixth Earl the apparently hermetic world of Gormenghast is itself brought into question: 'His sensitive mind had ceased to function, for it had played so long in a world of abstract philosophies that this other world of practical and sudden action had deranged its structure.' *Titus Groan* ends, like the outcome of the war in Europe when Peake finished his first draft of the novel, unresolved, a tangle of sinister questions and unanswered possibilities.

Until 1945 Peake had led a very sheltered life, but suddenly, rather late in the day, he was employed as a war artist. He travelled across Germany and witnessed at first hand the sufferings of displaced nationals and the horrors of the concentration camp at Belsen. This last experience seems to have been traumatic, and one from which Peake never recovered. His brief, disturbing **'London fantasy'**, which meditates on loss and failure ('The talents that never bore fruit or even flowered; the forgotten talents; the murdered talents . . .') possibly registers some of the pain and confusion he felt in the face of such atrocities. The closing paragraph of the Fantasy, a vision of faces in a London street, returns us to the perspectives of his earlier poems:

> Beneath the electric glare; in fog; in downpour; in sunlight; in wind; at sunrise or at dusk there is no end. Each desperate moment, clutching Entirety, sinks with a smouldering fistful of raw plunder; sinks into nullity while time slides on, and the heads move by and are huge, as they nod; huge as they turn and stare: huge as the heads of mammoths.

As in **'Is there no love can bind us?'** reality is reduced to a succession of desperate, unrelated moments; the perceiver is overwhelmed. London is seen from the viewpoint of a pictorial artist, but also from that of a child. Human beings transform into objects, grotesque, threatening and huge. The notion of artistic possibility as 'plunder' seems oddly childish in conception (a word which conjures up Peake's fondness for *Treasure Island* once again). The reference to mammoths suggests that the world is in the grip of an ice age; the syntax hurries us on to a final notion of apocalypse. Peake was certainly disturbed by his inability to feel for the suffering victims of the war. His poem **'The consumptive, Belsen 1945'** expresses his anguish at being merely a detached observer. After Belsen Peake was no longer at home in the world: his poem **'Suddenly, walking along the open road'** describes a frightening sense of alienation suddenly overwhelming him in a tranquil English landscape, and pictures the world as merely a toy, 'A marble spinning through the universe'.

Gormenghast, written between 1946 and 1949, seems both to retreat from and engage with the Belsen experience. The first half of the novel, up to chapter thirty-seven, is relatively mellow, with the focus on Titus's schooldays and the headmaster's comic pursuit of Irma Prunesquallor. Initially Peake seems to have shut out his awareness of the contemporary world and indulged in a certain amount of autobiographical reverie with his nostalgic treatment of Titus's schoolboy ad-

ventures, which softens the tone of the novel. Bellgrove's courtship of Irma, climaxing in a ludicrous romantic evening involving hot-water-bottle false breasts that slip, is pure pantomime and likewise draws attention away from the darker undercurrents of the trilogy. Only in the second half of the novel does the tone darken as Steerpike's murderous quest for power reaches its end—though even here the plot retains a boys' adventure book dimension, featuring what is really a gigantic game of hide and seek.

This second volume is more conventional in its plot, but Peake gives it a perculiarly modern twist at the end. Instead of reclaiming his kingdom after defeating Steerpike in the traditional way, Titus, now seventeen, spurns it and departs for all time from the enclosed world of Gormenghast, unhoused, a perpetual refugee. This unexpected ending seems significant as an expression of the novelist's wavering attitudes to the claims of pure fantasy and the real world that lies outside the imagination.

Although many of the characters old and new remain solitaries, *Gormenghast* contains a shift in emphasis from the previous volume by dealing with three pairs of relationships: the comic farce of Irma and the headmaster, Steerpike's sinister pursuit of Fuchsia, and Titus's infatuation with 'the Thing'. Steerpike's planned seduction is frustrated at the last moment, and Fuchsia is left to her lonely day-dreams. Peake's view of her isolation seems implicitly a critique of the world of Gormenghast itself. Cut off from society Fuchsia, a child imprisoned in a woman's body, is left with her withered fantasies. The dreamed-of prince never comes except in Steerpike's deformed and malignant figure (mutilated by fire, like Charlotte Brontë's Mr Rochester), and Ophelia-like she drowns.

Titus's relationship is more complex. There are incestuous overtones in his attraction towards his foster-sister, the mysterious and ethereal 'Thing'. Her sexual identity remains indeterminate for some time, and when she is revealed as female it's in a curiously sexless way. When Titus traps her he discovers that she is dumb, and he attempts to rape her (this is the closest that Peake ever comes to actually mimicking *Titus Andronicus*). Whether or not the rape is successful is ambiguous; Peake's language at this point is contradictory, and he shies away from plain statement. Titus's escapade nevertheless involves 'the death of his imagination', which makes the opposition between adolescent romance and adult sexuality finally explicit. The 'Thing' is conveniently killed by lightning; thereafter all that is left for the guilty Titus to do is destroy Steerpike and depart into another world, a fallen man.

Peake's work in the 'fifties perpetuated the elements of uncertainty and lack of direction in his career. He quickly wrote a third novel, *Mr Pye* (1953), hoping to produce a bestseller. Peake sadly misjudged the mood of the times; *Lucky Jim* and *Hurry on Down* were the successes of that year, besides which his own novel was merely a slight, whimsical piece—fancy, rather than imagination. The characterisation is shallow and lacks the full-blooded zest of the caricature-creatures of Gormenghast. The dilemma that Mr Pye, a thumb-sucking, eccentric evangelist, constantly invoking God as 'the Great Pal', is faced with—wings sprouting from his back one day, horns from his brow the next—is grotesque and disturbing rather than comic. A greater disaster for Peake was the failure of his play *The Wit to Woo* in 1957. Though given a West End première his brand of whimsy and fantasy, written in iambic pentameters, failed miserably in a London still recovering from the shock of *Waiting for Godot* and *Look Back in Anger,* both staged in the previous year. Drama was not a form in which Peake seemed likely to distinguish himself.

Among the debris of Peake's abortive and abandoned projects from the 'fifties appear two important fictions: *Titus Alone* and the novella *Boy in Darkness,* commissioned for a science-fiction anthology. This last work remains an astonishing *tour-de-force,* and though usually overlooked properly belongs with any consideration of the trilogy. The Boy, fourteen years old, and clearly Titus, runs away from his castle home, crosses a strange river, and arrives in a waste land denuded of all life except for the nightmarish figures of a hyena, a goat and a lamb. As the Boy journeys deeper across this terrifying landscape of men transformed into animals, to encounter the source of all bestiality and evil, the atmosphere is reminiscent of a tale by the Brothers Grimm crossed with 'Childe Roland to the dark tower came' and *The Island of Dr Moreau*—though at another level perhaps it expresses Peake's version of his own stunned trip across ruined Europe which culminated in the nightmare of Belsen.

Unusually for Peake the narrative is written in short, breathless sentences. There is no humour to soften the horror of this world, and the terse, economic presentation marvellously builds up a chilling atmosphere of suspense. The impact of the piece is deepened by Peake's provocative inversion of traditional cultural associations: whiteness symbolises evil, and the lamb, emblem of Christ, is made to represent ultimate evil. Perhaps *Boy in Darkness* expresses Peake's final despair and incomprehension at the course of history, which in the past he had so easily and glibly apostrophized. The only dissatisfying feature of this dazzling novella is the perfunctory ease with which the Boy outwits the monstrously cunning lamb and destroys it; the victory over evil seems rather artifically tacked on.

'There comes a time when the brain, flashing through constellations of conjecture, is in danger of losing itself in worlds from which there is no return', Peake commented in *Boy in Darkness.* Before the progress of mental illness necessitated permanent hospitalisation Peake did manage largely to complete *Titus Alone.* The chapters are much shorter, and the world that Titus, now twenty, discovers outside Gormenghast, is radically different to anything previously experienced in his homeland. Gormenghast conjured up an ancient, feudal world, and evil contained itself in the single figure of Steerpike. By contrast, in the unidentified world of *Titus Alone* we get a vision of the future, more science fiction than Gothic romance, more urban and contemporary than the temporally and geographically remote society of Gormenghast. Titus enters a world of cars, slums, police, prostitution, prisons, courts and asylums, at the heart of which lies the sinister factory, a place of death and evil, surrounded by the stench of burning bodies. This last feature, together with the dying girl, Black Rose, reveals that Belsen still preyed on Peake's mind, though it's worth noting the ambivalence of Titus's response to the suffering girl: ' "I can't sustain her. I can't comfort her. I can't love her. Her suffering is far too clear to see. There is no veil across it: no mystery: no romance. Nothing but a factual pain, like the pain of a nagging tooth." ' This seems to be Peake speaking as much as Titus, expressing his anguish at a world which had cruelly violated the fancies of his tranquil earlier life. A realistic portrayal of Belsen was outside the scope of his imagination; instead he placed his memories of the camp inside the larger, despairing vision of a futuristic, highly technological totalitarian society.

The characterisation in *Titus Alone* is impoverished in comparison with the earlier two volumes of the trilogy. Muzzlehatch reincarnates Flay, and the beautiful, demonic Cheeta is reminiscent, more than just in name, of the cunning beasthumans of *Boy in Darkness.* It seems significant that the other main character, Juno, the first woman whom Titus has a sexual relationship with, should turn out to be a kind of mother-substitute, twice his age and at the other extreme from the wispy 'Thing'. The final scene in the novel serves as a reminder of the theme of repressed or displaced sexuality which runs through the trilogy. At the end a vast, foul explosion (perhaps Peake had the atom bomb in mind) obliterates the factory. Titus survives and flees, returning one day, by accident, to the very edge of his domain, arriving back at the cave where his attempted rape of the 'Thing' expelled him for ever from the world of imagination and romance. At the close of the trilogy the outcast Titus, unlike David Copperfield, has still not met a woman who is his equal. He seems doomed to perpetual solitude; as Fiedler puts it, for this kind of romance protagonist 'it is hard to imagine a real acceptance of adult life and sexuality, hard to conceive of anything but continuing flight or self-destruction'. From Peake's sketchy jottings for a fourth volume it seems, indeed, that he merely envisaged further picaresque adventure, further flight. But if Titus is still in some ways a child at the end of *Titus Alone* he is nevertheless a particularly twentieth-century figure: unhoused, a refugee whose responses are 'no longer clear and simple', a youth whose burden of knowledge is one of 'tragedy, violence and the sense of his own perfidy'.

In 1958 Peake wrote to his wife from hospital, 'I have almost lost my identity . . . I will never write about mad people again . . . It has done something to me. I have played too much around the edge of madness', and it's significant that the macabre climax of *Titus Alone* involves a battle for identity, more exhausting and perilous than the clean-cut boyish heroics of the final victory over Steerpike. Cheeta maliciously arranges an elaborate masque for Titus, gambling that by confronting him with the figures from his past, assembled in the form of grotesque puppets, she will succeed in toppling him into madness. For once Titus is unable to save himself, and only the fortuitous intervention of Muzzlehatch spares him. It's odd that a mere representation of the past should be sufficient to threaten Titus's sanity, and there's a sense that the materials of the trilogy were themselves feeding on their creator, who channelled his own crisis back into the novel. Whereas Titus narrowly escapes with his personality intact, Peake, tragically, didn't. The last glimpse of his hero's world which he gave us before falling silent and spending the long last years of his life in a mental hospital, is far removed from the ordered, balanced world of Gormenghast with which the trilogy began: 'All futility: disordered: with no end and no beginning.' Through the Gormenghast trilogy we can, then, trace the gradual collapse of Peake's epic vision as the tension between the exploration of fantasy for its own sake and the truth of his own experience in the real, social world became too great for him to bear. (pp. 27-32)

Ronald Binns, "Situating Gormenghast," in Critical Quarterly, *Vol. 21, No. 1, Spring, 1979, pp. 21-33.*

JOSEPH L. SANDERS

During Mervyn Peake's life, his writing received just enough critical and financial encouragement to keep him trying, never enough to give him any assurance that a substantial number of people cared about what he wrote. That has changed. Today Peake's fiction, especially the works concerned with Titus Groan, have been republished, widely distributed in paperback, and, most importantly, admired by an increasing number of serious readers. We do care, and we are now trying sympathetically to understand what about Peake impresses us. (p. 75)

At first glance the Titus stories appear to have little kinship with a fantasy novel like Tolkien's *The Lord of the Rings,* filled with monsters, wizards and magic rings. Yet the real purpose of fantastic elements in Tolkien's story is to extend human desires and fears far beyond their normal range. Magic and monsters objectify human passions that disrupt the natural order. In Tolkien's fantasy, fears take physical shape and desires become supernaturally achievable. In *The Lord of the Rings,* the Ring represents a common wish, the craving to master all knowledge and power, while the creatures and wizards show alternative ways to achieve that goal by brute force or study. Tolkien views life as a terrible struggle between desires and moral impulses, which one cannot understand let alone direct but in the midst of which he must trust in divine benevolence and hope for final victory. By accepting healthy tradition and trying to submit to the purposes that tradition offers, one can at least haltingly participate in satisfying action.

Peake's type of fantasy also moves outside normal setting and familiar devices to present his conception of the human condition. It works, however, from a quite different viewpoint in a quite different manner. Peake does not accept the orthodox religious tradition that undergirds Tolkien's fiction. Furthermore, he does not believe that true power can be trapped in a ring, diagrammed by a sage, or seized by violence. In fact the systematic study of supernatural power, in religion or magic, is impossible; Peake not only rejects any particular religion but denies that man can gain any benefit from using a religious/ethical tradition as an aid to understanding. Thus, though forces beyond human comprehension sometimes are at work in Peake's stories, they resist easy labeling. The supernatural empathy between Titus and Keda's child, in *Titus Groan* and *Gormenghast,* is one such fantastic element. The mysterious certainty that guides Keda through the last month of her life may be another. However, clairvoyance or other violations of familiar natural order are very rare in these first two books; the major fantastic element is found not in the action's foreground but in its background. The action in these first two books takes place in or near Gormenghast—an immense castle, self-sufficient and completely cut off from contact with any outside society. One character, Dr. Prunesquallor who is familiar with astronomy, observes the "evening star" in the night sky, suggesting that Gormenghast is located on this Earth. Elsewhere, however, it is revealed that Gormenghast must have been totally isolated in its wilderness for at least 368 years. Gormenghast appears to have no real counterpart in past or present, and it is difficult to imagine the castle as part of a future that would leave it so undisturbed. It exists in its own world, one similar to the real world but not part of it.

Gormenghast's unnatural existence allows Peake to examine the human condition from a fresh perspective. At the same time, the lack of overtly fantastic forces in Gormenghast reflects Peake's attitude toward the basis of responsible action. In *Titus Groan* and *Gormenghast,* there are no easy magical tools by which one can manipulate Gormenghast's power, but on the other hand the characters actually need not fear such a power's violent intervention in their lives. In a completely different setting, *Boy in Darkness* uses many more elements that are overtly fantastic: *Titus Alone,* set in still another part of Peake's special world, uses others. However, in these works, too, characters lack full control over themselves and cannot pledge allegiance to some superhuman source of control; at the same time, still, they need not be controlled by tradition or ritual. Although most characters are not aware of it, because the human passions that went into their society's creation are hidden by the aura of revered mystery, they are free. No "god" appears directly or indirectly in the Titus stories. Instead, men worship a set of physical objects and the tradition associated with them. Peake believes that man's desires and fears created the setting and the tradition that envelopes it. He pictures man as the source of all meaning and all delusion, and shows one particular young man, Titus, becoming aware of himself in those terms and rousing himself to fight free of tradition and the settings that enforce it. (pp. 75-7)

For Peake, tradition embodies the most stultifying of human impulses—the will to dominate, to see the world remade in terms of self—its failure hidden only by its own self-sanctified mysteriousness. Tradition promises a share in the delight of dominating nature. In return a man must surrender his individual self to the greater self. The worshiper feels himself a part of a power that fits his deepest urges (though he is not created in *its* image, as the tradition states), within which he can follow any desire as long as he consciously frames his actions in traditional images. But the worshiper is thus prevented from developing his individual self. Such tradition can show a man only a distorted, deadening image of himself. Yet, as in Gormenghast, most people accept a role determined by tradition in preference to developing themselves freely. They are willing to imagine no other existence. (p. 82)

Titus Groan and *Gormenghast* form a unit by themselves. . . . These two books contain a richness of detail, a convincing grasp of psychology, and a depth of human concern that mark a great work. The vividness with which Gormenghast is described, the careful presentation of characters—and in particular of Titus' passionate groping toward a true sense of himself—all work with Peake's thorough presentation of his thesis concerning individual freedom versus tradition. I believe *Titus Groan* and *Gormenghast* form a unified, successful whole.

Peake's next work dealing with Titus, the novelette *Boy in Darkness,* was commissioned by Peake's publishers for a collection of three original stories, *Sometime, Never.* Although *Boy in Darkness* could fit chronologically somewhere in the middle of *Gormenghast,* it represents a major step toward the world shown in *Titus Alone.* Apparently Peake was preparing himself to write another major novel to carry Titus forward into another stage of development.

In **Boy in Darkness,** Titus is just fourteen years old, still imprisoned within the castle's ritual. He already knows that he hates "the eternal round of deadly symbolism," and on the night of his fourteenth birthday he instinctively seizes the chance to escape. His flight takes him into a nightmarish country outside the castle. There, captured by two grossly ugly, semi-human creatures, the Goat and the Hyena, Titus is carried toward their master, the Lamb—in the person of whom Peake simultaneously attacks religion and science. (pp. 96-7)

Titus Alone was written during a very difficult period for Peake. Describing his purpose, in a letter to his wife, Peake says he wishes "to canalize my chaos. To pour it out through the gutters of Gormenghast." But chaos was gaining on him. Maeve Gilmore, Peake's widow, describes his appalling nervous deterioration and the increasing difficulty he experienced in concentrating—and even in the physical activity of writing.

In addition Peake faced a major test of his creative power in this final book, since Titus now must struggle toward greater maturity. As part of the escape from Gormenghast, Peake evidently had decided to let Titus find his way in what Gilmore calls "a world which was probably closer to this one [than Gormenghast] and yet alien." With his flight from Gormenghast, Titus has ceased to be a boy; to become a man he must find his way in a setting that adult readers can at least half-recognize, confronting a tradition that stems more directly from modern life. (p. 99)

Because Peake's illness probably affected the writing of *Titus Alone* and because the series is itself a developing and incomplete structure, it is difficult to evaluate Peake's books about Titus as a finished work. Perhaps a fairer question is whether or not the stories accurately represent man's sense of himself as an unfinished, growing being. I believe that they do. The Titus series is overwhelmingly concerned with Becoming, rather than with fallen man's unchangeable state of Being, and shows great faith in the individual's ability *to become* a stable, free individual. Peake offers no moral judgments of a young person's actions as he matures. For Peake, the weight of moral standards comes from their being part of a tradition, and any tradition lies outside the individual's potential and needs. Thus adherence to a morality impedes development of the whole self and denies real maturity. Titus' values are based on what works or fails for him, what pleases him or makes him feel shame. Man lives, Peake shows us, in a fantastic world, unfathomable by any mind; therefore, one cannot rely on outside teaching, but must throw himself headlong into life, transcending any limiting scheme. Titus lives through a series of vivid experiences, developing through them in a convincing manner. Titus grows beyond the limits of his tradition to become a freeminded, sympathetic man.

As a presentation of this idea, Peake's work is very impressive. In particular, his first novels—*Titus Groan* and *Gormenghast*—form a vivid and convincing unit. Even in their unfinished state, Peake's stories of Titus Groan deserve their popularity for their successfully humanistic conception of contemporary man. It is unfortunate that physical illness kept Peake from continuing his depiction of Titus' development. But there is joy and wonder in what he completed. (pp. 103-04)

> *Joseph L. Sanders, " 'The Passions in the Clay': Mervyn Peake's Titus Stories," in* Voices for the Future, Vol. 3, *edited by Thomas D. Clareson and*

> *Thomas L. Wymer, Bowling Green University Popular Press, 1984, pp. 75-105.*

MICHAEL MOORCOCK

With Peake's mental and physical decline there grew in the media an image of a doomed, romantic figure, tortured by madness and the prospect of imminent death. Had he remained in good health, his amiable, quick-witted and sardonic manner would easily have contradicted those who saw him as a brooding Gothic poet haunted by bizarre images of immense, gloomy castles, of human grotesques locked in perpetual, petty conflicts and bewilderments. Certainly the Titus books contain these elements, as do some of his drawings, but much of the rest of his work, either humorous or realistic (frequently both), better represents the artist as he seemed to his intimates. *Mr Pye* perfectly displays this more "ordinary," gentler, lighter-hearted Peake, and his U.S. publishers while producing an excellent edition (in line with their editions of the Titus books and the compendium *Peake's Progress*) rather mislead the reader by calling it "a novel of sin and salvation." *Mr Pye* is a humorous fable much closer to T. H. White than to Kafka. . . .

Peake's talent was unique. He was as skilled a draftsman as he was a narrator. His earliest publicists were chiefly people not usually associated with works of fantastic imagination; they included Elizabeth Bowen, John Brophy, Graham Greene, John Betjeman, Angus Wilson and Hilary Spurling. His great trilogy has not yet discovered its potential readership, I suspect, because of its association with the romances of Tolkien and C.S. Lewis, with which it has little in common. Peake's prose is as vital and accurate as his line (see his drawings of Belsen, where he was the first war artist inside the camp). His eye always held steady when regarding human evil but his concerns were never morbid or abstract; they were firmly rooted in reality, as were his characters. His work is grotesque only in the way that Dickens' is—amplified but never distorted—with a similar compassion, a hatred of cruelty, an understanding of the nature of evil (never represented by shadowy super-villains with grand designs but by self-pitying individuals motivated by malice and envy against those they think luckier than themselves).

Perhaps a wider range of Peake must be read before the American public comes to recognize his seminal importance. In the meantime *Mr. Pye* serves as a good introduction to those who have steered clear of Peake, expecting his darkness, as it were, always to be utter. For those already convinced of his complex and sophisticated talent, this fable should shed new light on the nature of Peake's particular genius.

> *Michael Moorcock, "The Magic of Mervyn Peake," in* Book World—The Washington Post, *October 28, 1984, pp. 1, 3.*

Irina Ratushinskaya

1954-

Russian poet, essayist, and memoirist.

Ratushinskaya writes lyric verse in the tradition of such early twentieth-century Russian poets as Osip Mandelstam, Boris Pasternak, and Marina Tsvetaeva. An outspoken advocate of human rights in the Soviet Union, Ratushinskaya was sentenced in 1983 to serve seven years in a labor camp for female political dissidents but was released in 1986. Although her poetry is considered subversive by the Soviet government, Ratushinskaya seldom writes directly about political concerns. Her verse written before her imprisonment examines such traditional subjects as love, Christian theology, and artistic creation. Ratushinskaya's later poems, which differ in tone and imagery from her earlier work and display proficiency in a variety of forms, recount her struggles to survive the physical and mental hardships of prison life. Tom Deveson observed: "[The] very qualities that make [Ratushinskaya] so outstanding a person also inform her poetry—generosity and adventurousness of spirit, strict adherence to truth, uneffaceable lyrical delight in the world."

Ratushinskaya's first volume of poetry, *Stikhi* (1984; *Poems*), which contains verse written before her arrest, was published in the West while she was serving her jail sentence. The collections *No, I'm Not Afraid* (1986), *Beyond the Limit* (1987), and *Pencil Letter* (1988) include poems that Ratushinskaya composed on bars of soap and memorized during her incarceration. These pieces starkly depict Ratushinskaya's daily existence as an inmate and reveal her determination to maintain an optimistic outlook while resisting promises of better treatment from her jailers had she renounced her antitotalitarian beliefs. In her review of *Beyond the Limit,* Maria Carlson stated that Ratushinskaya's poems "are proof of [her] blood tie to the lyrical tradition of Russian poetry. . . . [They] raise the powerful themes that have always tortured Russian poets: memory, history, fate, love, poetry, faith and freedom." Ratushinskaya has also written *Grey Is the Color of Hope* (1988), a memoir that further documents her prison experiences.

ALAN SHAW

> To hide a poet behind bars is like breaking a watch; it is a falsification of time, for poetic meter is nothing other than restructured time. What's referred to as the music of poetry, what's regarded as the poet's lyricism, is the fusion of time and language, the illumination of language by time.
>
> —From the Introduction [to Irina Ratushinskaya's ***Poems***] by Joseph Brodsky.

The odd thing about Brodsky's statement, to ears conditioned by the American poetical scene, is his emphasis on meter. Naturally we cannot but share his indignation at young Irina Ratushinskaya's fate (she is in a labor camp for the crime of "manufacturing and disseminating" anti-soviet poetry), and this makes it all the more puzzling to find that the martyr, in the next clause, is not the poet's "individuality" or her "self-expression" (as we might have said), but that impersonal thing "poetic meter", a notion that to many American poets bears more resemblance to the prison bars than to the soul imprisoned within them. One of the effects of a traditional meter is to make any utterance less individual, and this, to the contemporary American poet, is in itself an evil. Individuality, in our poetry, is a sort of badge worn by everyone who aspires to the profession. We do not demand, as earlier ages conventionally did, that the poet express common feelings in a timeless manner; the value of poetry to us, on the contrary, is that it allows us to assert our personal quirks of language and perception against what we take to be a threatening standardization.

Irina Ratushinskaya's poetry is not individual in this sense. Very little Russian poetry of any significance is. Even Brodsky, whose work, in English, often seems to approximate to the American ideal of quirkiness, sounds far more classical in Russian. This is not entirely an accident of differing traditions. The sort of standardization that threatens the Russian

379

poet, after all, is not only mental or metaphysical: it can be brutally physical and real.

> Where instead of air—a busload of profanity,
> Instead of a housewarming, a barrack's snoring . . .

Under these conditions individuality is hardly an adequate defense: what one needs is a traditional, rational and freely accepted law to oppose to the grotesque parody of law set up by the state. The laws of nature tell us that life is short; the totalitarian state, parodying nature, boasts that history will march over our heads, what we think and feel is of no consequence, our resistance is absurd. The laws of meter, on the other hand, admonish us reasonably: "Yes, life is short, and only if you will submit to me, cut out your inessential syllables, and give up a few of your cherished idiosyncracies, will you find time to say all that needs to be said." The keener sense of the passage of time that meter imposes is what makes language lyrical and, paradoxically, timeless, since only by this sort of reembodiment of time into itself can the language gain a foothold outside of time. Only then can it do what Auden asks of it:

> In the prison of his days
> Teach the free man how to praise.

And yet this gain involves a loss of sorts, since to expect to carry all of one's individuality into such a setting would be like expecting to wear one's latest clothes into eternity. (pp. 514-16)

In her introductory prose piece [to *Poems*] Ratushinskaya movingly describes her search for some such alternative, truer law and her discovery of it in Mandelstam, Tsvetaeva and Pasternak. The experience had the strength, it seems, of a religious conversion. The Western reader may be at a loss to understand why. What was it that she found so new in these poets of Russia's "silver age"? Their technical innovations were minor, their diction did not represent any sharp break with the classical Russian poets enshrined in the Soviet schools. The answer is that the sense of newness, for Russian poets in this century, has come less often through technical innovation than through rediscovery of the vitality of a tradition that was supposed to be obsolete. It was all very well for Pushkin, in the days of serfdom, to write in a timeless manner about things that, as socialism predicted, were fated to disappear, but to write "timelessly" *in* and *about* the Soviet era, as Mandelstam had done, was not only not desirable, it was an affront to that era, an even graver affront, in a sense, than outright protest would have been, since protest at least accords a special importance to its object, whereas from the lyrical perspective the creations of the Soviet "new man" were seen to be as ephemeral as any others; his massive crimes fade into the brutality and folly of the ages. . . . No, it was not technical innovation that she found (although she, like Brodsky and others, follows the silver age poets in the occasional use of imperfect rhymes and looser meters), nor, on the other hand, was it a mere repertoire of lost techniques. Traditional rhyme and meter remained, in fact, the preferred medium of official Soviet poetry (after the short-lived period of experimentation following the revolution), and official poets continue to make use of them much as the party makes use of the courts. But when rhyme and meter are seen, not as vehicles for a preconceived truth, but as instruments for the discovery of their own truth (which is the way any real poet uses them), then they become as subversive to official reality as the delib-

erations of a truly independent judiciary would be to the party. Moreover, they give the poet's words a ring of authority they would not otherwise have. It is as if not one individual, but the Russian language itself, were passing judgment on the new era.

Besides the lyrical tradition, Ratushinskaya has inherited, since her imprisonment, something of the more recent and homelier vein of camp literature, which at first sight seems closer to pure protest or chronicle. There is, for instance, a satirical piece in which her cutting of a tooth is seen as a plot against the state, since nothing is supposed to grow without permission. But here as elsewhere her concern is for what will enrich the language and not merely render a situation. (pp. 516-17)

Alan Shaw, in a review of "Poems," in Michigan Quarterly Review, *Vol. XXIV, No. 3, Summer, 1985, pp. 514-17.*

BARBARA HELDT

The tripartite book *Stikhi/Poems/Poèmes* [by Irina Ratushinskaya] contains original poems in Russian, followed by English and French translations. Each section consists of a two-page introduction by Joseph Brodsky, an autobiographical sketch in prose by the author, and thirty-three of her poems. . . . Some of the poems, in the tradition of Tiutchev, Blok, Bely, and others, refer to the motherland as the mother-stepmother, destroyer of her own children. A few mention God or the Mother of God. Looking out the window, the poet asks the Pasternakian question. "Whose footsteps are heard in Petrograd?"; and soon the metaphor of fear becomes reality. The innocent are roused early from their bed. The good or saintly, like the man who helps others survive in the camps, are doubly punished. Ratushinskaya writes about youth, a perennial Soviet theme, with a different twist. A youthful dreamer goes off to the war in the South to die. In a dream, in another poem, a former schoolmate visits the poet in her cell. She is about to be shot at sunrise, and he will vacation in the Crimea as a reward for his job of executioner (better him than some total stranger, he says). Like Akhmatova, the poet uses mirror images to suggest both the splitting of the self and the multiplication of the single life of the speaker.

The poetry is good. A rhetorical questioning occasionally mars the imagery and tone.

Barbara Heldt, in a review of "Stikhi/Poems/Poèmes," in World Literature Today, *Vol. 59, No. 3, Summer, 1985, p. 450.*

TOM DEVESON

Irina Ratushinskaya, aged 32 and a physics teacher, is serving a sentence of seven years hard labour in a Soviet "strict regime" camp. . . . Her crimes in the camp have been to hunger-strike on behalf of other prisoners and to demand basic human rights; her crimes in the outside world were to write and circulate these poems [*No, I'm Not Afraid*]. Clearly she's a remarkable, brave woman whose cause (backed by Amnesty) demands support; dissidence, however, needn't itself guarantee poetic gifts. But the very qualities that make her so outstanding a person also inform her poetry—

generosity and adventurousness of spirit, strict adherence to truth, uneffaceable lyrical delight in the world.

She adopted the Catholicism of her Polish forebears and in her twenties had what amounted to a second conversion when she discovered the poets of Russia's Silver Age. There are echoes of Akhmatova's *Requiem* in her insistence on both remembering and forgiving, and of Mandelstam's consolatory classical allusions. But her individual voice is stronger than these influences. Set down "on the squares of the monstrous chessboard", knowing she's deprived of "the childish, flouted right to beauty", she celebrates undefeated the moment when "a word stirs under my hand / like a starling". The courage and the gift are one.

Tom Deveson, "Lines from Irina," in The Times Educational Supplement, No. 3651, June 20, 1986, p. 28.

JOHN BAYLEY

One of Ratushinskaya's poems [in *No, I'm Not Afraid*] describes a dream in which John the Baptist appears in the Gulag, filthy and ragged, and is succoured by one of the female inmates before he gets ready to fly away. She longs for a miracle, to see her daughter, and begs him to perform it. But he is silent, weeping, and she wakes up from a dream that is no longer happy. Yet the poem says:

> Is there any place from which one can love
>   more powerfully
> Than from here?

Prophetic images, images of faith and miracles, make a natural appearance in the poems, among the circumstances of camp life. The state is pushing the poet towards the role of prophet, seer and truth-teller. Yet nowadays this role is in itself a negative one. Ratushinskaya's husband observes that her poems are 'remote from politics. In order to call for the overthrow of a regime one must have some idea of what one wishes to replace it with. For Irina herself the most suitable social structure would be democracy on the Western model—but she has always been quite clear in her mind that such a structure would not suit the overwhelming majority of people in the Soviet Union.'

That is a significant point. The spiritual élite today knows that it is no use appealing to the masses. At previous moments in Russian history, or wherever revolutions were planned or foretold, the great idea was to convert the people, to indoctrinate the masses and get them on one's side. Lenin's highly realistic revolution showed that this can only be done after power has been seized by other means. But Ratushinskaya knows quite well that nothing can be done, and that may be why the authorities particularly fear her sort. With a counter-revolutionary, or a new sort of revolutionary, you know where you are, but the KGB could only find her guilty of 'an unenthusiastic way of thinking'. A splendid phrase that tells much, but it would make Dostoevsky, even Pushkin, shake their heads as sorrowfully as the KGB shake theirs. A prophet with no message except 'human rights'? No wonder the masses pay no attention. After his years in Siberia, and his persecution at the hands of the Tsarist regime, Dostoevsky found his own kind of popular role as a prophet: not as a prophet opposed to the government, but, on the contrary, as one who saw the government's true purpose as a spiritual one—the purgation of Russia by suffering and the salvation

of Europe by Russia's example. Even Pushkin wrote: 'In hope of all the good and glory, I look ahead devoid of fear.' What kind of hope and regeneration does Ratushinskaya see for her country? Evidently none at all, and that makes the essential hopefulness of her nature and her poems all the more poignant. . . .

Joseph Brodsky says that Irina Ratushinskaya is 'a poet with a voice of her own, piercing but devoid of hysteria', who has been influenced but not taken over by the majestic voices of the Russian poets of the persecuted epoch—Mandelstam, Tsvetaeva and Akhmatova. Certainly the individual tones come across, even in English . . . , although in the absence of the Russian text it is not possible to 'give way' to them as one does to authentic sound in a poem. But the atmosphere of fresh reality—the flavour of the camps, dreams, visions, moments of liberation in them—is unmistakable. One of the most striking things is the way in which religious imagery—'the bitter face of a brown icon / And the solid murmur of a thousand swords'—enters the poems without seeming to be summoned or made use of, and almost against the conscious will of the poet. It is as if in this predicament, and with a poet's talent, she cannot help but see seraphim in 'winged Decembers', hear tolling bells. (p. 15)

John Bayley, "Censorship," in London Review of Books, Vol. 8, No. 14, August 7, 1986, pp. 15-16.

THOMAS D'EVELYN

[*Beyond the Limit*] is more than a document in the endless history of cruelty and suffering imposed on creative people by the Soviet communist regime.

The true nature of the book is suggested by the strange path it took on its way West.

While she was 300 miles southeast of Moscow in the strict-regime camp at Barashevo, Ratushinskaya's husband . . . received her poems from others who had either memorized them or had received copies from those who had. Once Gerashchenko had the completed book, he sent a typed Russian copy to the translators of this volume.

How did the poems come to be composed? Ratushinskaya was not allowed to have paper. After all, she was in prison precisely because she wrote "beyond the limit." Ratushinskaya composed her verses on bars of soap. After she had polished and memorized them, she washed her hands, destroying the incriminating evidence. . . .

Later, at night, she would recite the lines to her fellow prisoners. Eventually they too knew her poems by heart.

Recited and memorized by the prisoners, the poems became part of the inner life of the prison. (p. 21)

Beyond the Limit is quite simply a marvelous book of poetry. Far more than a miscellany, it has the unity of Keats's odes or Catullus' poems or Shakespeare's sonnets. Composed during the first 17 months of her term, 42 out of 47 are dated. As a whole, the book clearly shows the growth of the poet's understanding of what it means to go—or be pushed—beyond the limit.

The work is intimately tied to its context. Ratushinskaya addresses several prisoners by name, and the notes indicate the fate of some of them. Many poems describe the conditions of prison life, the cold of the isolation cell where prisoners were allowed only light dress—no blankets, no jacket—and slippers contaminated by previous occupants. (pp. 21-2)

Ratushinskaya's sharp vision is universal—and not unrelated to her awareness of her religious roots in the Polish Roman Catholicism of her grandparents. The poems are also varied in tone, imagery, and genre. Lullabies follow plain, confessional poems; historical scenes, visions. There is irony and apocalypse, intimacy and historical sweep.

And bad as the situation was, *Beyond the Limit* is a triumph of the human spirit. It describes a spiritual rebirth. . . .

Very occasionally a book comes along that not only makes news, but history. *Beyond the Limit* is such a book. Indeed, the time Ratushinskaya spent at Barashevo must be a special time for all who love poetry and freedom, and the isolation cell a special place. From it, Ratushinskaya addresses not only fellow *zeks,* but all mankind. (p. 22)

> *Thomas D'Evelyn, "Writing Lines Beyond the Limit," in* The Christian Science Monitor, *June 17, 1987, pp. 21-2.*

MARIA CARLSON

The Soviet Union, as Russia was before it, is a land where poet is the proudest and the most dangerous of all professions. Russian poets have always exercised the power of moral authority, and they have paid for that privilege with their freedom and even their lives. Irina Ratushinskaya wrote a poem in 1984—to honor the poets Aleksandr Pushkin, shot in a duel on the shore of the Black River in 1837, and Marina Tsvetayeva, who hanged herself in Elabuga in 1941—in which she says:

> Don't ask yourself—are you a poet or not?
> They won't waste time—they'll raise you to poet-
>   hood!
> All roads—from bullet to noose—
> open to you from birth.
> And when it begins to beat like a human's
> you'll understand, recalling the tune:
> from Elabuga to Black River—
> *Broad is my native land.*

That is one of 250 poems Miss Ratushinskaya wrote while she was a political prisoner in a Soviet labor camp. She scratched her poems onto a bar of soap with a matchstick, memorized them and then washed away all evidence of her forbidden creations. Forty-two of her prison poems, written between June 1983 and August 1984, along with several others, have now been translated and published in *Beyond the Limit.* . . .

The poems in *Beyond the Limit* are proof of Miss Ratushinskaya's blood tie to the lyrical tradition of Russian poetry. She is heir to the line that stems from Pushkin and is represented in the 20th century by Anna Akhmatova, Osip Mandelstam, Boris Pasternak and Marina Tsvetayeva. Her poems dig deep into the Russian tradition and raise the powerful themes that have always tortured Russian poets: memory, history, fate, love, poetry, faith and freedom. Using the potent imagery of cold, earth and execution, Miss Ratushinskaya finds beauty in frost on the prison window and transforms the "violence of prism-ice" into a "holiday" and a "gift." In her prison poems she intensely appreciates life and

freedom ("may we only survive!") as only a person who has risked losing both can do. She transcends the prison experience, taking her reader with her into the world of unvanquished spirit, "beyond the gates, beyond the boundary," "beyond the border / that cannot be crossed," "beyond the limit." . . .

Miss Ratushinskaya's poems were rendered by Frances Padorr Brent, a poet and co-editor of the journal Formations, and Carol J. Avins, who teaches Slavic languages and literatures at Northwestern University. Their translation strives for the compactness of Russian, but sacrifices the grammatical clarity of the original. Seeking to please the American reader trained in Pound and Eliot, they leave out much of the helpful punctuation marks of the original, making the poems more obscure and sometimes unnecessarily nebulous. Finally, there are several subtle mistranslations here and the whole translation is in one key; it does not convey the extraordinary range of this gifted poet, whose voice moves naturally from the rustic to the refined, from the conversational to the lyrical. No English rendering, alas, can capture Miss Ratushinskaya's rich Russian rhythms, cadences and sonorous assonances. . . .

Even though the Brent-Avins rendition mutes Miss Ratushinskaya's full-throated, alternately vigorous and tender voice, it succeeds in conveying her powerful imagery. Even in translation, reading her poetry is a profound emotional experience.

> *Maria Carlson, "Victims of Yesterday and Tomorrow," in* The New York Times Book Review, *June 28, 1987, p. 12.*

EDWIN MORGAN

Of the two books by Irina Ratushinskaya [*Grey is the Colour of Hope* and *Pencil Letter*], *Grey is the Colour of Hope,* the documentary prose account of her imprisonment in a camp for women political dissidents in Mordovia, gives much the stronger impression, and not merely on account of its subject-matter. The poor food, the rough or thin clothing, the intense cold, the desultory medical attention, the petty regulations, the lax or sadistic officers, the letters which might or might not be sent, the meetings with relatives which might or might not take place, the fearful general arbitrariness of events—all these are described with the minute detail which no amount of philosophizing could have replaced. What emerges most strikingly is the unremitting obstinacy with which the "politicals" (as distinct from the ordinary criminals nearby), and especially Ratushinskaya, tried to pursue what they knew to be their constitutional rights, measuring the size of a punishment cell and taking its temperature, demanding entitlements of food and medical treatment, gaining a point here, losing it there, but going on strike, or hunger-strike, at the first sign of unfairness or oppression. . . .

Pencil Letter contains new translations and also translations already published in *No, I'm Not Afraid.* Fourteen persons were involved in the translating, but even allowing for this hotch-potch approach, it would be very rash to assert that Ratushinskaya is another Tsvetayeva, as some have claimed. The Russian texts of her poems are now available for inspection, partly in her own tiny handwriting at the end of this book, partly in collections published in Frankfurt and New York. They show a modest lyrical talent, but hardly match up to the greatness which has been thrust on her. The best poems are those in which she distances herself from immediate concerns, and uses characters from history, legend, or fantasy: Lady Godiva riding through Coventry, Jacob wrestling with the angel, a man carrying a carpet roll which may yet become a flying carpet. All three suggest, of course, analogies with her own situation.

> And till dawn the master will smoke his pipe there,
> And watch the sparkling town below.
> And then in the blue he'll dwindle away. . . .

She has said that no living Soviet poet interests her—her admirations stop with Tsvetayeva and Mandelstam. Yet she grew up, in the 1960s, in an atmosphere of renaissance in Russian poetry—Voznesensky, Yevtushenko, Akhmadulina, Aigi, Sosnora, Morits and many others—and it must be clear that her quarrel with Soviet society in general forbade her to see and to use the potential which was really there, and that is a pity.

> Edwin Morgan, "From the Personal Outwards," in The Times Literary Supplement, No. 4456, August 26-September 1, 1988, p. 940.

FRANCINE DU PLESSIX GRAY

With the exception of Eugenia Ginzburg's memorable accounts of Stalin's gulags, the vast literature that has documented Soviet camp life has been a predominantly male genre. One of the many fascinations of Ms. Ratushinskaya's memoir [*Grey Is the Color of Hope*] is that it records that experience through the prism of an acutely female sensitivity. It thus offers unique insights into the different tactics of psychic survival chosen by men and women inmates.

Four principal factors contributed to Ms. Ratushinskaya's ability to tolerate the sadism of Soviet prison life, particularly the hardships of the isolation cells and hunger strikes which she endured in deliberate protest for many months of her jail term. One was the tenacious love of her husband, Igor Gerashchenko, who was allowed to see his wife only once during her imprisonment, and who spent those years relentlessly publicizing her plight to the free world. Another was the example of Aleksandr Solzhenitsyn, whose cardinal principle for all prisoners of conscience the author adopts as a credo. "Never believe them," he wrote about jailers, "never fear them, never ask them for anything." But of perhaps even greater importance in Ms. Ratushinskaya's survival are the power of her religious faith and the extraordinarily loyal, loving bonds she forged with her community of female inmates. . . .

During Ms. Ratushinskaya's stay in the Small Zone [a tiny hut reserved for female political prisoners] this community of women ranged in size from 5 to 11. And, apart from a temporary K.G.B. informer whose attempts to disrupt the prisoners' mutual loyalties were comically inept, the Small Zone's inmates acted with astounding solidarity to uphold those very principles of truth, justice, freedom and compassion that Soviet camps are designed to destroy. Experiencing a constant tension between the will to live and the will to remain absolutely pure, they structured their conduct on the "honor" or "dishonor" of particular prison rules. With serene unanimity, for instance, they labored conscientiously on their work assignments—sewing protective workmen's gloves—because such labor is honest and useful to any com-

munity. As Ms. Ratushinskaya puts it, "We turn out first-class gloves as a point of honor."

Yet with equal solidarity the women refused to wear the cloth identification tags prison authorities assigned to them, seeing them as a symbolic surrender of their autonomy. . . .

Admittedly, the work camps of the 1980's offer prisoners an immeasurably greater chance of survival than the 1930's compounds described by Ginzburg, places in which a poet of Osip Mandelstam's stature could disappear without anyone knowing to this day the precise circumstances of his death. Apart from their far less arduous conditions, contemporary Soviet "politicals," unlike the totally isolated inmates of the Stalin era, are diligently monitored by a number of human rights groups (American PEN was particularly militant on the Ratushinskaya case). As a poet who was beginning to be published in the West, this is a privilege of which Irina Ratushinskaya remains highly conscious. "What if they'd thrown me a little bit harder? Uproar! . . . just think of the unfavorable publicity: a political prisoner killed!"—so the author muses as she returns to consciousness after suffering a severe concussion. (She had engaged in a hunger strike while in SHIZO [an acronym for *shtrafnoy izolyator*, isolation cell] to protest against the mistreatment of one of her Small Zone companions and the guards threw her, head first, against a wooden trestle when she yelled to all the SHIZO inmates that she refused to be force-fed.) (p. 11)

Some of the most startling passages in Irina Ratushinskaya's memoir are those in which she describes the many female ceremonies of domesticity and civility that helped her companions to maintain their loving ties and to create, in this heart of darkness, a make-believe microcosm of a free world. In the scant leisure time of work camps, the male inmates of Aleksandr Solzhenitsyn's, Vladimir Bukovsky's, Natan Sharansky's memoirs have solved chess problems, fantasized about means of escape, ceaselessly discussed politics. In contrast, the women of the Small Zone (lawyers, physicists, poets) spent weeks secretly preparing celebrations of one another's birthdays and name days, managing to make the birthday celebrant a fancily ruffled embroidered skirt out of discarded sheets, crowning her with a wreath of laurel leaves collected from their frugal broth, making a cake out of some oil and flour surreptitiously passed on by some charitable criminal *zek* (abbreviation for *zaklyuchenny*, prisoner). And it is interesting to note that unlike most "politicals" described by male authors, throughout their years together the women of the Small Zone continued to address one another in the formal *vi*—the second person plural—however intimate their friendships became. . . . (pp. 11-12)

In the same mood of domestic, almost liturgical, formality, on warm summer nights the Small Zone sisterhood set its frugal dinner table out of doors, decorated it with a centerpiece of wild flowers, garnished the barely edible mush with finely chopped wild nettles and chives. Among this community of women who, with a single exception, were religious believers of four different Christian sects, Easter and Christmas were observed twice, according to both the Catholic and Orthodox calendars. During a particularly arduous SHIZO stay imposed on Ms. Ratushinskaya because she protested the improper medical treatment of a sick friend, she embroidered table napkins for her mother-in-law and sprayed a Christmas tree design with tooth powder on the door of her cell. In one of the most exalting passages of the memoir, her community engaged in an Epiphany ritual particular to northern Russia and to the author's native Ukraine. In 25 below zero weather, the women ran naked through the snow and doused themselves with buckets of ice water. . . .

The passage is archetypal. For it is precisely these festive, archaic female rituals that give Irina Ratushinskaya's memoir an idyllic, exultant tone unprecedented in camp literature. It also exemplifies the specific kind of religiousness—syncretic, deeply felt but lightly worn—that informs her text and makes her survival possible.

But her ironic wit is as ample as her piety. She also offers many earthy glimpses of women's camp life. She describes, with compassion and horror, the violence of the lesbian community in the criminal section of the work camp—their ardent jealousies, the frequent suicide attempts caused by lovers' infidelities. She records with an impeccable ear the feisty voice of a woman *zek* who has murdered her drunkard husband with an ax: "I don't regret it—not for a moment I don't. I spent three months in prison, and the guards only hit me once. Before, I'd get bashed around practically every day."

I have one major reservation about this splendid book. There is a disturbing incongruity between Ms. Ratushinskaya's high regard for her own poetic gifts and the poems she scatters throughout her memoir. But then, there is also a considerable difference of quality between her volumes of published verse—traditional, accomplished, but hardly memorable—and the unforgettable book she has forged out of her jail experience. (p. 12)

> *Francine du Plessix Gray, "Sisterhood in the Small Zone," in* The New York Times Book Review, *October 30, 1988, pp. 11-12.*

DAVID M. BETHEA

There are, according to Solzhenitsyn's worldview, two basic ways of surviving the prison camp experience while maintaining *inner* (spiritual or psychic) independence. The first is to believe in a higher court of justice and to give up one's will to this sense of a benign and proprietary "Other": perhaps the clearest example of this tendency is Alyoshka the Baptist in *One Day in the Life of Ivan Denisovich,* Alyoshka, like his namesake in *The Brothers Karamazov,* has a simple, spontaneous faith that allows him to persevere almost serenely in the face of repeated hardship. By renouncing his own will and refusing to judge, and by claiming that his trials in this world have some ulterior meaning hidden from view, Alyoshka is given back a redoubled will to live. . . .

The second major means of surviving with one's personal dignity intact is diametrically opposed to the first, a fact which at first glance may seem paradoxical but is upon closer scrutiny quite logical. Those individuals like Bobynin in *The First Circle* and Y-81, the old-timer in *One Day* with the ramrod-straight back and the gums hard as teeth, are the purest essence of will and self-control. From all appearances they do not believe in a higher realm, do not pray or ask for God's help, do not depend on anybody or anything. They are as defiant (within the rules of the camps) as Alyoshka is pliable and passive. And they are able to sustain their defiance because the Stalinist state has made the fatal mistake of taking everything from them and thus, in Bobynin's own words, "made them free all over again." What they have left is an inner freedom and self-worth that is theirs alone, earned through countless trials and torments. They are not even

afraid of death, the state's ultimate bargaining chip, and they have nothing to leave prison for. (p. 312)

Irina Ratushinskaya survived her trials with dignity. Her poetry constantly questions the injustice of her and her comrades' position, but it does so within the context of a Christian faith and an old nobility of values (i.e., one stemming from her *Polish* aristocratic past) that, more than any crude ideological or political import, brought down the wrath of the state on her. She seems to believe in or at least invoke the possibility of a higher court, but that belief does not mute her wrath, sarcasm, or bitterness. Her faith cannot be called simple, that is, a version of Alyoshka the Baptist's; it simultaneously hurls verbal Molotov cocktails at both courts, the higher and the lower, the one for judging man "from above" and the other for judging man "from below": "How will You dare to pass judgement, / By [the laws of] what court? / What will you answer, when I break through and come— / When I stand before you, leaning my shoulder against the glass wall— / And when I give You a look, / And ask you about nothing." But unlike Tsvetayeva, whose stylistic presence haunts this poetry, Ratushinskaya is not yet ready, in the notorious formulation of Ivan Karamazov, "to return her ticket" to God. Quite the opposite, she has just found Him, that is, found a lively Christian dialectics and culture that is a sign of psychic health in a world whose spiritual values have long since atrophied and withered.

In this regard, Ratushinskaya's early development as a "metaphysical" poet parallels that of two older contemporaries, Joseph Brodsky, her most eloquent champion in the West, and Dimitry Bobyshev, the most decidedly "Christian" of modern Russian poets. . . . [Both] Brodsky and Ratushinskaya have expressed the view that their *real* education was in some way postponed until their mid-twenties, when the combination of spiritual and cultural values (the Bible in Brodsky's case, the poetry of Mandelstam, Tsvetayeva, and Pasternak in Ratushinskaya's), which had been such a vital part of early twentieth-century Russian poetry but which their generation(s) had been denied access to, became known to them with the force of revelation. Brodsky was, of course, by far the more precocious of the two: Self-educated at a much younger age, a voracious reader of forbidden native and Western cultural fruit, someone already steeped in the literary mythology of old St. Petersburg and its "Silver Age" through his close association with Anna Akhmatova, Brodsky did not need to discover the wonders of Mandelstam or Tsvetayeva at age twenty-four. Those wonders had long since entered into that durable duffel bag of poetic sounds and images which accompanied him on his gypsy wanderings across his homeland. But his reading of the Bible was a major late discovery, and with it came the important turn away from the "purer" lyricism of his early verse and the turn toward the "metaphysical" manner—"Elegy for John Donne," for example—associated with his maturity. Ratushinskaya's development is the chronological reverse of Brodsky's: the religious heritage—the Roman Catholicism from her Polish aristocratic past—was always there through her grandparents. (See the lovely poem **"To the world beyond I'm posting,"** in *Stikhi;* her parents, on the other hand, denied this past and tried to adapt and "Russify" themselves and their daughter.) Her faith had to be ignited by the "revelation" of a modern Russian poetry that could be called genuine and a poetic language worthy of the name.

Like Brodsky, Ratushinskaya discovered her voice by discovering a past that had been cut off from her and her generation. It had none of the cant or cliché, what Brodsky would label language struck dead in its tracks, that one might associate with the fundamentalist brand of Christianity in the West. Rather it was, above all, a *linguistic* way out of "internal exile." It possessed insight into "another reality" that was transcendent and, mercifully, independent of the various prescriptive plots and immanent causalities foisted on Soviet schoolchildren as an antidote to consciousness. And its "drive axle," to use a favorite Stalinist metaphor, was poetic speech.

Poetry, as Brodsky is fond of saying, is nothing other than the *restructuring of time,* especially time as it is defined according to Marxist historiography. Because poetic language is "older" than the state, with a built-in "memory" of things whose existence predates any revolutionary calendar, it is that state's mortal enemy. Mandelstam had something like this in mind when he claimed in an essay of 1922 that the Russian language is "so highly organized, so organic" that it is "not merely a door to history, but history itself." The *sotto voce* rhythms of Brodsky's "keening muse", Akhmatova, resonate in both directions, *back* to a Silver Age culture with a memory of the world before 1917 and *forward* to an ideal future reader who has *outlived* the language of Marxism-Leninism. They are modeled—*structured from within*—on a Christian time of meaningful beginnings and ends that wrests the plot from human hands and seats it at the right hand of myth and metaphor. It is, therefore, this simple linguistic fact that underlies the ancient adversarial relationship between poet and tyrant. And having learned their lesson well and having graduated to a worldview and cultural tradition of *ars longa, vita brevis,* Brodsky and Ratushinskaya can now be said to have become "exiles" in several senses. In both time (they choose a past that is more alive than the present) and space (one is a Jewish "outcast" from his native Russia, the other a "closet Pole"), they no longer see themselves as belonging to history, but to History.

Christian metaphysics, Silver Age culture, and a profound personal and collective urge for justice—these are the forces motivating Ratushinskaya's poetry. . . . If Ratushinskaya enters into the first ranks of Russian poets, it will be because of her words and their distinct combinations, not her noble actions as a political prisoner. To be sure, part of a poet's "aesthetic" biography, that which makes his "lyrical I" multidimensional and interesting, are the facts that subsequently lend themselves to becoming legend, like Lermontov's self-forseen (*in a poem!*) fatal duel. But the knowledge that Ratushinskaya is a poet who was a political prisoner does not, by definition, make her poetry more worthy of our attention. What will remain of Ratushinskaya's legacy, now that she is free in the West, is twofold: her art, which is written for that other sense of time she shares with Brodsky, and the record of her political acts of conscience, which were played out for (or actually against) the "present," the cynical view of history imposed on her and her colleagues by her government. In order to protect the sanctity and integrity of the first (the "free speech" which is the poet's supply of oxygen), she has been forced to wage her uphill battle for the second. Nevertheless, the language of these two causes (the artistic and the political) are *not* the same, except in a dangerous blurring of metaphorical terms, and while Ratushinskaya must continue to insist on the right to write the kind of verse that first placed

her in Barashevo, she cannot lose sight of which time she is writing for and which language she is writing in.

Discussion might be made more concrete with what I take to be a negative example. **"I had a strange dream,"** a poem which focuses solely on the injustice of the poet's position, is in its own way a powerful statement, full of savage sarcasm with absolutely no Aesopian pulling of punches, but it speaks, alas, in one, ideological, language. It concerns a dream the poet has about her own execution. She is taken out to be shot by a former classmate, who is genuinely fond of her and thus tries to excuse his role through a series of self-justifications. . . . (pp. 312-17)

A narrative poem with only one story to tell, **"I had a strange dream"** assails the time-honored concept of *poshlost'*, of philistinism and self-serving vulgarity that is all too willing to trade higher values for a safe spot in this world. The litany of people and things (children, mother, pink-tiled bathroom, washing machine, pass to a sanatorium) that the state uses as leverage to force the old schoolmate to carry out the death sentence is precisely . . . what makes him unfree. He has too much to lose, and so he loses his soul instead. The poem derives its rhetorical power from its Solzhenitsyn-like sarcasm. Everything the executioner says sincerely in his own behalf is undercut by what the reader knows to be a greater truth: the state is able to manage its most cynical and notorious crimes through petty bargaining and incremental compromises. It is not our obvious enemies but our friends and acquaintances who can, and do, become our executioners. However, once the sarcasm (ultimately a crude form of irony) is decoded, the poem has no other meaning, and thus reads primarily as a political, rather than poetic, statement. (pp. 317-18)

Ratushinskaya is still at the beginning of her career. Her language is not yet heavy with the culture of Mandelstam or Brodsky, but there are sure signs that she has found her voice and that it is authentic. Her "signature" is the angel's wings that often appear near a poem's closing to alert the reader to the possibility of divine intervention, of passage out of this world and its time. (In this she is—though presumably unwittingly—a protégé of the émigré poet Khodasevich, Nabokov's favorite among contemporaries.) (p. 318)

[The] best of what Ratushinskaya has written up to now is endowed with a stereoscopic quality, a sense of seeing one reality through the other. This "second sight" almost always has a hidden religious, or revelatory, message. It surfaces suddenly in "The imprint / Of two wings" on "the burnt-out masonry" of a wall where a prisoner is about to be shot (**"The Ballad of the Wall"**); it wryly contemplates the "bedraggled angel" that has somehow managed to fall asleep in the cigarette smoke and the crackling sound of radio interference as someone's sentence is being read (**"The incoherent radio"**); it transforms the spider into a "potty genius" that ends up being "crucified" on its own coordinates, an "eccentric Pythagoras" and "half-witted prison prophet" that tries valiantly to count the days of the speaker's sentence (**"The Spider-Mathematician"**); and it makes possible "the first beauty" experienced by the poet in captivity [**"I will live and survive"**]:

> A frost-covered window! No doors, nor walls,
> Nor cell-bars, nor the long-endured pain—
> Only a blue radiance on a tiny pane of glass,
> A cast pattern—none more beautiful could be
> dreamt!

> The more clearly you looked, the more powerfully
>   dawned
> Those brigand forests, campfires and birds!
> And how many times there was bitter cold weather
> And how many windows sparkled after that one—
> And never was it repeated,
> That upheaval of rainbow ice!

Here is the freedom-within-captivity to study one's soul of which Solzhenitsyn has spoken so often. All spatial barriers—which also stand in for the ultimate temporal barrier of the sentence—fall away as the speaker catches sight of the cast pattern on the window. Doors, walls, and cell-bars no longer exist in the sprung logic and *openness* of revelation. The forests, campfires, and birds tell of a nomadic, fairytale existence *beyond* the law (the *brigand* forests), beyond the pull of gravity and history (the flight of the birds). Who has cast this pattern, upheaved the rainbow ice? It is the same Other from outside and beyond that is the addressee in many of these poems and that makes meaning possible to those still trapped within—prison bars, Soviet society, Marxist historiography, the language of Socialist Realism.

Recent history has shown that Ratushinskaya, both as citizen and artist, is someone who resists all manner of (en)closure, so I should like to complete this survey with a brief mention of two of her most powerful and open-ended poems: **"To the world beyond I'm posting"** (*Stikhi*) and **"Over Russia's wheatfields once"** (*Stikhi*). The first involves an imaginary letter which the poet sends to her now-deceased grandparents; the second tells of a young gymnasium student who enlisted in the army and was killed in battle. These poems strike me as little masterpieces—especially in the Russian—both because of what they say and what they don't. The rhetorical balancing-act between truculent irony and heart-stopping pity here reaches the point of perfection; the tragic absence created by missed possibilities (what the poet might have been in another place and time, what would have become of this bright, impressionable lad had he not joined the army) is "almost" compensated for by the presence of a remarkably vivid and full-throated lyricism. The poet gently chides her grandmother for giving her herbal baths (so evocative of childhood and another time), since now that fragrance is wasted on K.G.B. thugs. But of course it is not, since it returns to life in the authenticity of the particular image and the *bon mot*. And the courtly virtues of her grandfather that are so grotesquely out of place in the surroundings of the camp are for the creator of these lines literally *parts of speech,* building blocks in her lexicon. The "funny high school kid" of **"Over Russia's wheatfields once"** is so in love with spring that, like Pushkin's Lensky or Tolstoy's Petya Rostov, he dies before he has time to discover that immortality is a literary cliché. Yet he, too, is retrieved from a nameless passing by the marvelous catalogue of his mental wanderings—poring over Magellanic maps, warming himself under Sorrento's orange groves, escaping on high-sounding Latin phrases as though they were plane tickets abroad, imagining sultry slave girls dancing in vats of grapes. There is no answer, nor ever has there been one, to the poet's concluding question: "Why this [his death—DMB]? Why us? can you tell / Us, God? It's impossible" (*Stikhi*). What there is, however, is the quality of the questioning.

And for this we have Irina Ratushinskaya, poet first of all and ex-political prisoner second, to thank. Time will tell whether she, like Tsvetayeva, Khodasevich, and Brodsky, will be able to turn the difficult status of émigré and exile, the stigma of

"otherness" and "marginality," into poetic triumph. Now she will have to face, in Khodasevich's wry words written more than a half-century ago, not the burdens of "societal demand" (*sotsial'nyi prikaz*), but that of "societal rejection" (*sotsial'nyi otkaz*), of a readership that may have other agendas and priorities. But émigré backwaters, especially where national literatures in exile are concerned, can and do become mainstreams. We wish her well in her new surroundings and hope that she will not only "live and survive," but become the major poetic voice that her country, both "mother and stepmother," and its version of literary history would silence. (pp. 320-22)

> *David M. Bethea, " 'What Does a Six-Winged Seraphim Taste Like?',"* in *Parnassus: Poetry in Review, Vol. 14, No. 2, 1988, pp. 310-23.*

CHRISTIAN McEWEN

On March 5, 1983, the day after her 29th birthday, Irina Ratushinskaya was sentenced to seven years' hard labor, to be followed by five years of internal exile. She had written articles in defense of human rights. She had been found with "anti-Soviet literature" in her possession. She was responsible for "oral agitation and propaganda." But above all, she was guilty of writing poems.

From the versions available in English, . . . it is difficult to understand what all the fuss was about. Russian-speaking experts praise the intricacy of the poems: their rhyme, their metrical range, their mixture of "zek-talk" (prison camp slang) with the language of philosophy, fairy tale, and nursery rhyme. But the English-speaking reader has to take all this on trust. Ratushinskaya in translation is Ratushinskaya drastically reduced, a quiet, flat, anecdotal writer whose moments of luminous realism (the frost pattern in the window, "bluish light in the smallest glass") are far outweighed by her half-hearted diary poems and the fey jingles of her children's verse.

In the context of *Grey Is the Color of Hope,* however, it seems a Western luxury to haggle over such matters. Whether Ratushinskaya is the literary daughter of Tsvetayeva or simply a talented, personable, and well-publicized young writer is at this point immaterial, a fact of which she herself is well aware:

> Don't ask yourself—are you a poet or not?
> They won't waste time—they'll raise you to poet-
>   hood!
> All roads—from bullet to noose—
> Open to you from birth.

Singled out as a poet (and severely punished as such), Ratushinskaya accepts both the honor and the responsibility of that position. Her book is more than a personal memoir of life in the camps; it is political testimony, literature as argument, as lived experience, a veritable textbook of survival. "I will remember," she asserts near the beginning. "I know what must be done.

How would I cope if something truly terrible were to happen to me? How would I survive a famine, war, a prison sentence? Would I crack under pressure? Would I come through? At some time or another, all of us have asked ourselves such questions. It is part of their allure that they mostly go unanswered. We dabble in the horror for a moment, and then we back away. Someone else, some Ratushinskaya, is living through it all instead of us. We lavish praise on her, of course. We call her wonderful. But with that praise, the bargaining begins. If we honor her sufficiently, then maybe we ourselves will be excused. If we idealize her, if we call her "heroine," then a gulf will open up between ourselves and her. She will become inhuman and unreal, too perfect altogether, and we will have succeeded, not for the first time, in betraying our own strengths and possibilities. *Grey Is the Color of Hope,* in every small exacting choice, refuses us such cobbled self-diminishings. Here, Ratushinskaya tells us, is how to last the course, or, in the words of the camp motto, how to make it "back to freedom with a clear conscience." (p. 55)

[On] the whole, it is impossible not to be impressed by *Grey Is the Color of Hope.* Memoir, testimony, spiritual journey: it is a triumph of integration, both literary and moral. There, in the very text of the book, Ratushinskaya addresses the KGB man who will be asked to read her work in search of information. There too, alive as always to the power of accurate publicity, she addresses her growing Western audience. And through it all she maintains her focus, her command of those thousands of fiercely remembered details, her absolute narrative drive.

Over the last year, Gorbachev's *perestroika* has altered some of the realities Ratushinskaya describes. According to a recent article in *The Nation,* over 400 political prisoners have been freed since last January, and political arrests and trials have virtually ceased. Among the reforms openly discussed in the Soviet press are plans to dismantle the system of internal exile, to repeal some of the laws used to imprison dissidents, to give detainees access to lawyers before they stand trial, and to eliminate capital punishment. Ratushinskaya herself was officially released on October 9, 1986, and now lives in London. It is perhaps inevitable that some will use her words to minimize the recent changes, but that is hardly her fault. Her book needs neither *glasnost* nor her own identity as poet to make it well worth reading. (p. 56)

Christian McEwen, "The Courage of Her Convictions," in The Village Voice, *Vol. XXXIV, No. 3, January 17, 1989, pp. 55-6.*

Léopold Sédar Senghor

1906-

(Has also written under pseudonyms of Silmang Diamano and Patrice Maguilene Kaymor) Senegalese poet, essayist, nonfiction writer, critic, and editor.

An influential statesman who served as President of the Republic of Senegal for twenty years following its independence from France in 1960, Senghor is also considered an important poet and essayist whose work affirms the rich traditions of his African heritage. He is perhaps best known as one of the most outspoken proponents of négritude, a literary ideology that urges black people worldwide to resist the cultural manifestations of European colonialism and to reclaim and embellish their African past. Many commentators have noted elements of both European and African culture in Senghor's poetry, attributing this synthesis to his French education and his long service in the French government. Robert W. July, however, contended that Senghor's works are not exclusive to one group. He argued that "the value of Senghor's poetry rests squarely on its own merits which are not parochial but universal. . . . Thus the special pleading of négritude fades before the eloquence of the poet whose humanity represents and refreshes us all." A recipient of many honors and literary prizes, Senghor became the first black member of the Académie Française upon his election in 1983.

Senghor was born in the predominantly Islamic province of Joal, French West Africa. Raised as a Roman Catholic, he attended French missionary schools in preparation for the priesthood but abandoned his religious studies in favor of the classics and modern literature. Upon graduation from the Lycée of Dakar in 1928, Senghor earned a scholarship to study at the Sorbonne. While in Paris, he met the West Indian writers Aimé Césaire and Léon Gontran Damas, who introduced him to the works of such Harlem Renaissance authors as Claude McKay, Countee Cullen, and Langston Hughes. The affirmation of African-American culture that Senghor discovered in their books profoundly influenced his writings, as did the verse of such French poets as André Breton, Paul Claudel, and St.-John Perse. In 1933, Senghor became the first black African to graduate from the Sorbonne with the agrégé de grammaire, the highest degree granted in French education. The following year, with Césaire and Damas, he founded the literary and cultural journal *L'etudiant noir,* which helped delineate the principles of négritude and published the works of other francophone writers. During this period, Senghor also taught Latin, classical literature, and African history at several secondary schools in suburban Paris.

The poems in Senghor's first major collection, *Chants d'ombre* (1945), were written during the 1930s. Although largely traditional in structure and meter, these pieces also evoke the intricate rhythmic patterns of compositions by musicians in Senghor's native village. In such poems as "Neige sur Paris" and "Nuit de Sine," Senghor describes the loneliness and alienation that he experienced during his first years in Paris. He also reflects upon his boyhood in Joal and devotes several poems to his parents and a maternal uncle. *Hosties noires* (1948) evidences Senghor's growing interest in

Pan-Africanism and contains some of his strongest attacks on French colonialism. The majority of the poems in this collection relate his experiences as a soldier and prisoner of war while serving in the French Colonial Army during World War II. In the poem "Camp 1940," for example, Senghor recalls the fraternal bonds that he formed with black American and West Indian GIs during his incarceration. He also celebrates the humility and endurance of Senegalese soldiers in "Aux tirailleurs Sénégalais" and "Désespoir d'un volontaire libre," equating their battlefield experiences with the sufferings of their ancestors under colonialism. The angry, militant tone of Senghor's verse in this collection provoked some critics to label négritude a racist movement. With the advent of Fascism and Nazism in Europe, however, Senghor tempered his views. Jonathan Peters declared: "Senghor wishes that the threat to the free existence and expression of a national will and consciousness will be a lesson to France and the rest of Europe in dealing with colonies under their management and that the inhumanity of the encounter will give birth to a new and multi-cultural humanism."

Following World War II, Senghor became active in politics. In 1946, he began serving his first term as Senegalese député in the French National Assembly in Paris, and in 1948, he formed the socialist party Bloc Démocratique Sénégalais in his own country. Senghor also remained involved in literary pursuits, playing a significant role in the establishment of the literary journal *Présence africaine* in 1947 and a year later editing *Anthologie de la nouvelle poésie nègre et malgache de langue française,* which features the works of writers from the Caribbean, French West Africa, and Madagascar. Senghor also published his own verse during this period, most notably the volume *Chants pour Naëtt* (1949), which contains love lyrics addressed to a woman whose physical attributes and spiritual temperament serve as metaphors of the African landscape.

Éthiopiques (1956) is regarded by many commentators as Senghor's most conciliatory collection of verse. The poems in this book were composed during the early 1950s, when Senghor served as French delegate to the United Nations General Assembly and was reelected to the French National Assembly. The sequences "Epîtres à la Princesse" and "La mort de la Princesse," which depict the courtship of a European princess by an African diplomat, were interpreted by several critics as allegories of Senghor's political orientation and his marriage to a French woman. Also included in *Éthiopiques* is the long dramatic poem "Chaka," which recounts the final days of the nineteenth-century Zulu warrior king who conquered the leading South African tribal groups through mass murder and tyranny. Based in part on Lesotho writer Thomas Mofolo's 1926 historical novel *Chaka,* Senghor's poem was regarded as a highly idealized and apologetic rendition of Chaka's ruthless exploits. John Reed and Clive Wake stated: "Chaka's excuse that it was necessary to destroy, like a farmer burning the bush before a new season, is a simile which it is impossible to apply in detail."

Senghor continued to publish poetry following his election as President of Senegal. *Nocturnes* (1961) contains a series of elegies discussing the nature of poetry and the role of the poet in contemporary society. This collection also reprints in its entirety Senghor's volume *Chants pour Naëtt* as a sequence of poems entitled "Chants pour Signare." *Selected Poems* (1964) made Senghor's most significant verse accessible to American and British readers through English translation. In a review of this volume, a critic for *Newsweek* observed: "Like Walt Whitman, Senghor taps private sources deep within himself to discover in his experience the consciousness of his people and the drama of his continent. . . . Conquest over despair, acceptance, and pride drive through the poems like a strong river, unifying them by its powerful currents." During the 1970s, Senghor published *Elégie des eaux* (1971; *Elegy of the Waters*) and *Lettres d'hivernage* (1973), which expand upon his usual themes. In recent years, Senghor has revised several early volumes of verse, including *Poèmes* (1964; revised, 1984), which features a cycle of elegies dedicated to his deceased son as well as other meditations on life and death.

In addition to his poetry, Senghor has also published several nonfiction works, including *Rapport sur la doctrine et le programme du parti* (1959; *Report on the Principles and Programme of the Party*), *Liberté I: Négritude et humanisme* (1964; *Freedom I: Négritude and Humanism*), and *Ce que je crois: Négritude, francite, et la civilisation de l'universel* (1988).

(See also *Contemporary Authors,* Vols. 116, 125.)

JOHN REED AND CLIVE WAKE

Senghor's poetry is critically best examined not as the poetry of a new African poetic tradition because, though Senghor's poetry may be important for the foundation of such a tradition, speculation about it now can hardly throw light on Senghor's poetry itself. It is best examined as the work of a man in a particular situation making use of a French poetic tradition which is at hand. In fact the outstanding qualities of Senghor's work do come from the situation of the man himself. If we look at his situation at the moment, he is President of the Republic of Senegal. His life has been devoted and devoted with success to politics as well as to poetry. . . . The circumstances which enabled—almost one might say, drove—Senghor to become both poet and politician can be set out. They in turn have given a quality to his poetry—or enabled his poetry to retain qualities which are hard to find in European poetry. Perhaps the most important is the holding together without strain personal and public issues, a poetry which furnishes a myth and at the same time allows the poet to remain an acceptable hero of his own poetry. . . . We could say that the value of Senghor's poetry comes more from the combination of poet and politician than the combination of African and Frenchman but the two combinations in the end are inseparable, because the circumstance which has allowed Senghor to be both poet and politician without the one spoiling the other is precisely the circumstance that he is one of the small group of Africans with whom the French colonial policy of assimilation—half-heartedly believed in and only spasmodically applied—really took its course. It is because Senghor is an African so deep in the culture of the French language that he was for a time a teacher of French in a Parisian Lycée, that the personal nostalgia which gives rise to his earliest poetry must lead by way of a sentimental journey back to Africa, to political involvement. It is his possession of French culture which among his own people makes him one of a small group of leaders. The process of acquiring this culture takes him to Europe where he experiences not only exile but the peculiar predicament of having a black skin in a white society. It is through the culture whose acquisition has brought this predicament, that the predicament can be expressed. But this culture also gives the status of a leader, so that for Senghor the predicament is not personal, and not resolvable merely through poetic utterance but through political action. . . . The French gave to Senghor and those like him everything French culture could offer, not to enable them to carry their countries to independence but to make them Frenchmen, local dignitaries in the overseas provinces of France. The independence of Senegal was not foreseen by Senghor's teachers, nor indeed by Senghor himself until well into the 1950's. Even so, Senghor's life has been largely a working out of the inevitable if unforeseen logic of the French colonial policy of assimilation, and if it has provided the context for his whole achievement, it is also something which overtook him like his fate. He writes somewhere how his father used the white school to which he was eventually sent as a threat of punishment while his mother wept and pleaded that he was too young to go away. But if French culture was a fate that overtook Senghor, it was a fate of human devising. The negro in the New World finds his fate in his black skin. His destiny is being who he is. And although the society which despises him is of human devising and in the last resort his predicament comes from the human actions and decisions which made up the centuries of the slave trade, the literature of the New World negro expresses an existential rather than a social predicament. The only genuine poetry which emerges is defiant, and destructive. (pp. viii-x)

Senghor's white education was a preparation for leadership which led to personal problems which could only be resolved by the assumption of that leadership. But they could be solved in that way. Within this particular situation, private and public problems fall almost exactly together; a private personality and a public personality become compatible. Hence Senghor's cultivation of poetry did not render him incapable of taking the political action the situation demanded, his political offices have not meant the death of the poet; further, the poetry itself has a quality of being at the same time profoundly personal poetry and public poetry, a poetry in which the aspiration of his people, in which the generalized manifesto of new African consciousness are expressed. Poetry of this kind does not exist in Europe, and perhaps it cannot exist even in Africa outside the particular conditions which have surrounded Senghor's life. It is these conditions which give real validity to the literary concept of *négritude*. For Senghor, a scrupulous and honest, that is, poetical expression of himself, is also a political expression. Hence the criticisms which are made of this concept by some English-speaking Africans have a general validity, but fail to understand how the concept in circumstances different from their own can still be valid. Ezekiel Mphahlele, the South African critic, writes that the artist at work and the nationalist are not one and the same person. Usually they are not, but in Senghor they are.

Even in the earliest published verse, the personal is never separated from the larger situation from which the personal situation arises: a racial, political and colonial situation. The main themes in **Chants d'Ombre** (1945) are exile, the loneliness and homesickness of an African student in Paris in the 1930's. . . . [The] nostalgia for the paradise of childhood with its 'innocence of Europe' brings an awareness of a conflict between his African heritage and European culture. This conflict is felt personally, but not only as a personal problem—it is also the problem of the conflict between Africa and Europe. His own role as the spokesman for his people is already present. Poems which take their rise in the evocation of mood or in erotic experience, like **"Nuit de Sine"**, reach their conclusion in a mood of impatience, as if all this only reminded the poet of a task of speaking on behalf of others which has still to be achieved. . . . The conflict is traced most fully in **"For Koras and Balafong"**, where Soukeina and Isabella, sister and foster-sister, stand for Africa and Europe. If he had to choose one and reject the other, he says he would choose Soukeina, but the very imagery of sister and foster-sister shows that Senghor does not expect to be driven to make this choice. It is his good fortune to live in a situation where colonialism resolves into affirmatives and not negatives. He can take with both hands, and his poetry finds a fullness of expression to correspond to the fullness of his cultural position, just as his theoretic writing on *négritude* postulates an ultimate all-inclusiveness in the concept of the Culture of the Universal. At the same time, the poetry although it is autobiographical never has that sharpness which is the tone of the individual at war with the world found in some European poetry. Even at its most bitter, Senghor's poetry is poetry of fulfilment rather than of decision. Though he rejects much of Western civilization, Senghor is a poet at ease in two cultures, unlike many modern European poets and indeed some African poets, who are at ease in none. Even his task of expressing the vision of his native culture through the means and methods of an acquired culture sets him problems which are much

more immediately rewarding in their solution than the problem which faces an original artist in Europe who often has to express a new vision through the means and methods of a culture that upholds an older and incompatible vision. This is why so much modern poetry contains destructive elements—ugliness, cacophony, nonsense—which are necessary before anything new can be said. These destructive elements are absent from Senghor's poetry. Now and then we catch an echo of the idiom of surrealism, but Senghor's poetry in its use of language and in its attitude towards the civilization of its time is at the opposite pole from surrealism. (pp. x-xii)

To the period of the War belongs much of Senghor's bitterest but also most moving poetry. He joined the French Army as a private soldier, was captured by the Germans and remained in the prison camp *Front-Stalag* 230 until 1942. The War confirms Senghor's loyalty to France, and through that loyalty he finds a new solidarity with his own people and also with the common people of France. Yet military life reveals the continuing prejudice against the blackman, and one of the themes of the second collection of poems, **Hosties Noires** (1948) is the humiliation of the African soldier. In the camps Senghor celebrates the humility and endurance and creativity of his own people. Europe in its distress has needed to use them and will not be able to turn them away from their part in building the new world. A mythic battle in the future is foreseen, but it is not a war of African against European, but a great revolutionary struggle of all the oppressed peoples and the white workers who belong with them. Much of the poetry is still personal, but Senghor has taken on the impersonality of the African soldier. The heroes of this volume are the *tirailleurs* of Senegal, and Senghor in his own person finds justification in being their poet. . . . . **Chants pour Naett,** first published in 1949, and afterwards republished as part of the volume **Nocturnes** (1961), under the title **Chants pour Signare,** is a series of short love poems. The woman addressed is in a way identified with Africa, as the women in his earlier poetry are almost always seen and expressed in terms of landscape. The image usually has strongly maternal characteristics. Love is a going back to the emotional world of Africa and of childhood, a retreat from the harsh bright demands of the West. These poems seem written from inside Africa, and the nostalgia of exile and the bitterness of the despised soldier are mostly absent, and with them much of the emotional turbulence of the earlier verse. These poems are less rhetorical, less violent, less public. Although the literal meaning is often obscure, the tone is without ambiguity and the quality of imagery and melody is rich. (p. xiii)

In **Ethiopiques,** a collection published in 1956, the lyrical quality in his previously highly personal poetry has become the self-confident rhetoric of the man who represents his people, who has become their trumpet. Even in the poems of the group called **"Épîtres à la Princesse"**, which are the only ones in the volume which seem to be personal in subject matter, he takes up, perhaps half playfully, the position of a leader in an old-fashioned traditional Africa of the imagination. It is not that there is no distinction between public and private life, but the poems occur at that point when a private friendship seems to have public implications. They are about two people who, like medieval sovereigns, in their personal relations establish symbolically the relations between their realms. Senghor is once more the hero of his own poetry, but not now as a person in a predicament or a man discovering solidarity with his fellows, but as their symbol, speaking for them with an air of confidence, as personal and impersonal as an hereditary monarch.

In the **"Épîtres à la Princesse"**, Senghor presents himself, the poet-ruler, in a poetic world built up out of his own personal relationships and African history, owing something perhaps to the princes who found cities in Saint-John Perse's *Anabase*. There is, however, another image used by Senghor in which this notion of the compatibility of the poet and the ruler is deeply challenged—the image of Chaka the Zulu. Senghor's dramatic poem about Chaka is inspired by the remarkable historical novel written in Sesuto by Thomas Mofolo and published in 1926. . . . Mofolo, a Christian and writing before it was fashionable to glorify every aspect of the African past, sees Chaka as a bloodthirsty tyrant and at the end a crazy megalomaniac. Yet he is also born under a curse, led astray by supernatural soliciting, a figure not unlike Macbeth. Senghor chooses the moment at the very end of Chaka's life, and makes him a martyred figure, a man who has sacrificed himself body and soul for his people. Critics have objected to this cavalier use of history, and yet the attempt to reinterpret historical figures in a startling way is not unusual, even outside poetry, and Senghor does not in fact do violence to any of Mofolo's events. . . . [Senghor's **"Chaka"**] fails as a justification of Chaka's actions and read in this way is quite intolerable. Chaka's excuse that it was necessary to destroy, like a farmer burning the bush before a new season, is a simile which it is impossible to apply in detail. However, Senghor is not really concerned with Chaka's actions; his drama is without action and concerns Chaka's state of mind alone, and so we must see the death of Noliwe, for example, not as the death of another human being, but as the sacrifice Chaka himself makes, giving up what he loves and even his power to love.

In this poem, Senghor is less concerned with the crimes which those who have power may have to commit, than with the sacrifices of love and of their real creativity which they may have to make. . . . [He] makes Chaka a poet who has to sacrifice his poethood to undertake the liberation of his people. In reading the poem, it is difficult to avoid seeing Senghor himself as Chaka and at the same time noticing how different Senghor's own situation seems to be. We notice it is the White Voice that identifies poet and politician.

> My word, Chaka, you are a poet . . . a fine speaker,
>   a politician . . . !

Chaka himself distinguishes them. A politician is a man of action alone, he killed the poet in himself. He was dead himself before the first of his victims. Yet in the second part of the poem, set now not against the accusing White Voice but against the Chorus and its leader, Chaka is once more established in his poethood. The politics of violence becomes the politics of a new kind of creation through rhythm. Chaka is no longer the Lion, the Elephant, the Buffalo, but the athlete, the dancer, the lover. Power is against the vocation of the poet, but it is also the testing and the purgatory of the poet. Chaka, who has been called by the White Voice the poet of the Valley of Death, is declared Poet of the Kingdom of Childhood, creator of the words of life. The poet who died to make the politician, lives again and the politician dies. Chaka's own definition of the poet in his last utterance is 'the one-who-accompanies, the knee at the side of the drum, the carved drumstick'. The poet is in this sense not incompatible with the political leader, because the poet is not a creator, but the spokesman; he speaks for his people. As earlier in Seng-

hor's verse, we find the repeated image of the trumpet, the ambassador. Alternatively, though not the creator, he provides the rhythm for the creative activities of the whole people.

In his most recent poems, the **"Odes"**, Senghor seems to treat more directly the problems of the nature of poetry and the sources of poetic inspiration. The direct but antithetic imagery of the **"Elegy of Midnight"** deals with the aridity and the creativity of the poet. Poetry springs from childhood, into which the poet must be born again. But it also springs from the sleep of death. In the **"Elegy of the Circumcised"**, he tells how poetry affirms life and overcomes the fear of death, but only by surrendering to the process of life. The poem must give up structure, become only rhythm. Poetry lives only if the words are allowed to go. (pp. xiv-xvi)

A comparison between Senghor's **"Elegy of the Waters"** and Claudel's Ode "L' Esprit et l' Eau" immediately suggests itself. As we have seen, there is no point in trying to isolate Senghor's poetry from the tradition of French poetry; it is difficult to see how recognizable poetry can be written in any language without reference to the poetic traditions already existing in that language. As a poet of the French literary tradition, Senghor is not an innovator. The reasons for this have been discussed earlier in this introduction. We could say Senghor is a poetic innovator in an African poetic context, but not in the European. On the other hand, he enters the French poetic tradition at a point where it was most open, the point at which an awareness of the world outside Europe and the excitement of non-European culture was powerfully felt, in the poetic tradition of Paul Claudel and Saint-John Perse. Senghor is of course not an imitator, and he has said that the material for *Chants d'Ombre* and *Hosties Noires* was already in his drawer before he discovered Saint-John Perse. Still, he recognizes them as cognate poets: Claudel, the professional diplomat, living most of his adult life outside France, an expert on oriental civilizations; Saint-John Perse, also a career diplomat, also living almost continuously outside France, preoccupied with the theme of exile. Yet both these poets are profoundly European, in the sense that traditional European values are stressed in their work. They are poets whose sentiments are patriotic and reactionary, poets of civilization, men who were able to combine eminent careers in the public service with poetic creativity. Senghor's poetry shares with theirs the freedom from regular metrical form, a use of language which is rhetorical, drawing on rich but not eccentric sources of vocabulary and dependent on highly charged words, like 'blood', 'gold', and 'night', elaborating a few central images and symbols.

The differences are, however, important. Senghor, like them, is a poet of civilization, but his attitude is less arrogant, less insistent, more humane. His work is also more intensely personal than the French poets'. Claudel and Saint-John Perse have not written the kind of occasional verse which makes up most of Senghor's collections. At the same time Senghor's poetry is less egotistical. It is also in its sympathies both aristocratic and popular, profoundly traditional, not only in the African context, but also in the European, and at the same time revolutionary. Senghor has been called the poet of unity. It would perhaps be more correct to call him the poet of reconciliation, which is not the same thing. This conciliation is not only found in the thought and feeling of the poetry, but also in its techniques. It is not a poetry of paradox, of sharp metaphysical distinctions, or far-fetched imagery which suddenly reveals similarities in unexpected places, and at the same time, unexpected contradictions. It is poetry without wit. It is poetry in which the great commonplace symbols are used, sometimes conventionally, sometimes idiosyncratically, but never rigidly to create absolute distinctions. Night and day, black and white, become ambiguous. This is helped by the way in which European languages impose a symbolism of white and black which an African poet tends to repudiate, as Sartre points out in his essay *Orphée Noir*. Senghor's poetry, like his cultural philosophy, is inclusive, rather than exclusive. His world is ultimately without negation, which means that the relation between the word and the reality is always a direct one. Nothing can be defined by negatives. Nothing can be mentioned in a poem to be excluded. Hence poetry is a listing of things, a bringing of them together, in a relationship which is not structural or architectural, but rhythmic and living. A speaking of names is intended to establish a relation.

> And I repeated your name: Dyallo!
> And you repeated my name: Senghor!
> ("Mediterranean")

The word, as in African thought, and indeed in all the prephilosophic thought of Europe, is active and creative; the master of language is the master of things.

Poetry of this kind is hard to find in English, where the use of wit and of definition by exclusion has had a triumph much more complete than in France, and where so much of our poetry is devoted to suggesting the disquietingly unsure relationship between language and reality. The nearest equivalent in the English language to the idiom which Senghor uses is the idiom of Whitman and his followers. Indeed Whitman is an indirect source of Senghor's style, for his work was an important influence around the turn of the century on the whole school of free-verse writing in France from which Senghor derives. (pp. xvii-xix)

Some passages in Senghor sound very like Whitman. Others sound like Robinson Jeffers. But there is a certain French literary quality about his work which makes it wrong to model the style of a translation closely on existing poetry in English. Senghor's language is not archaic, although he does permit himself now and then surprising archaisms in vocabulary, but it is impossible to render him into an altogether colloquial modern English idiom. His heightened rhetorical language in English often sounds turgid. On the other hand the direct use of language means that much of his poetry can survive direct translation. Like Saint-John Perse he is attractive to the translator, though his verse in translation, like Saint-John Perse's, is not immediately attractive to the English reader. Even T. S. Eliot's version of the *Anabase* would be perplexing to read on its own as an English poem. (p. xix)

> *John Reed and Clive Wake, in an introduction to*
> Selected Poems *by Léopold Sédar Senghor, translated by John Reed and Clive Wake, Atheneum, 1964, pp. vii-xix.*

WOLE SOYINKA

The mystic may be a narcissist, but the poet insists on mysteries only at the peril of truth. Of all known areas of hibernation, none is more suited to the narcissist than the womb. . . . To reduce exploration to the endless hazing of predictable courses, to the tortuous burrows of fundamental

fluids—these are the well-known tactics of the totemic poet, blissful in self-center at the heart of the community. The audience waits hopefully for the venturing, waits for the man to desert the matrix.

Léopold Sédar Senghor proves in every line that we may believe the poet's totem, but the totem's poet is a much harder creation. Such a poet would be a psychic mouthpiece, wholly animist and possessed of mystic penetrations. Consider, then, the poet who would *be* the totem of the tribe. Thrusting up the self-totem through every word and image is a hazardous method of persuasion. Oppressed by such insistence, we think the poet exhibitionist or, at the best, narcissistic. For, confounded by the hardened skin-patch on the navel, quite impenetrable, the poetic eye becomes glazed from hopeful concentration, turns its own mirror. From then on, all venturing ceases, only reiteration of totemic features, lineage by lineage, lineament for lineament, and a substitution of this for poetic vision.

Nevertheless, it is from this totem-narcissistic phase that a different kind of poet has begun to emerge, one who goes back to real knowledge—namely, the knowledge that hot sterilizing pads sealed the cord at birth but that such discouraging facts need not condemn the poet to exile. And so exploration begins from the acceptance; the poet rejects the navel's fascination, seeks his path through experience, through liberation, through self-surrender. (p. 53)

That the African writer is full of the burden of self-consciousness is therefore not a crime. Poets feed first of the self, anyway; it is the extension of "self" into history and mythology, into society, and even into contemporary responsibility, which is a conspicuous development in the self-consciousness of most African writers, since it does not appear to correspond to the degree of creative processing. Narcissism begins when the writer fails to distinguish between self-exploration and self-manipulation. The latter, overburdened with metaphors usually of thinly disguised preconcepts, is indeed a work of love, motivated by external responsibility. But self-love is self-love and is far more superficial than the bereavement, the curiosity, or the revelation. (p. 54)

It would be intriguing to know whether the hero would still emerge as narcissist, even in the context of action, once writers became more preoccupied with the violence of the contemporary African situation. Senghor's **"Chaka"** implies a contradiction between the poet and the "politician," and this immediately arouses speculation on similar kinds of dissections, which, misdirected, become the poet's excuse for narcissistic indulgence. Whether it is true or not that most Negroes dream of playing Othello, most African writers are convinced that they *are* Hamlet. Senghor's **"Chaka"** is Hamlet after the event. Contrasting his historical escape is the fantasy of Camara Laye's *Radiance of the King,* a work in which the two opposing halves are, firstly, narcissistic inflation, then truth. . . . Truth begins and triumphantly explodes through the second half of the work only when the poet (totemist and sensualist) fuses life with imagination. It is *The Dark Child,* however, which quietly proves that animist introspection need not involve narcissistic inflation.

In any culture, the cycle of rediscovery—*négritude* or Renaissance enlightenment or pre-Raphaelite—must, before the wonder palls, breed its own body of the literature of self-worship. African writing has suffered from an additional infliction; apart from his own rediscovery, the African writer has experienced discovery by the external eye. It is doubtful if the effect of this has any parallel in European literature. Not to be confused with it is the literary narcissism of the psychoanalytic game, which operates at once an individualist assertiveness and a revolt against a long tradition of realism. The African writer is subject to its stylistic influence, but a similar indulgence of his self is extended again into his totemic urge. He proclaims its essence or bewails its loss.

Intellectualism plays an ambivalent role in the work of poets like Senghor, so that even now there is no predicting what shape writing will take when the narcissistic impulse—whose active sustenance has been drawn from the intellectual concepts of the African, consciously or subconsciously—is lost. That it may be transmuted into a new and equally intellectualized individualism is one suggestion of a work like **"Chaka,"** even of the inferior manner of William Conton's *The African,* and of much of Peter Abrahams's work. The evidence seems to be that the writer is thrown back more and more on himself, on a more individual relationship to his society, whereas formerly this could be evaded in the reversion to collective myths and the animist transference of endless self-adulation. Senghor is one poet who does not disguise his addiction:

> I could not stay deaf to the innocence of shells, of
> fountains, and mirages on the sea flats

Or, somewhat more to the point:

> Bless you, Mother
> Recognize your son by the look in his eyes, the
> authenticity of his heart his lineage

And, commanding admiration by its directness:

> I am standing up, strangely lucid
> And I am handsome as the hundred yards runner,
> as the black Mauritanian stallion in rut.
> I wash down in my blood a river of seed to make
> fertile all the Byzantine plains
> And the hills, the austere hills
> I am the Lover and the locomotive with well-oiled
> piston.

Always the objective vanishes, even the real self vanishes, for the purpose of his poetry. Its celebrative assertiveness turns into a kind of paradox, his intensification of the physical responses into objective centers from within which the poet's ecstasy rises, throws the self into a set of communal concretions, not essences, among which the self is even most clamant in its own adulation. In a hundred forms Senghor has wrung the self, and through a hundred victims of the deception; the glorification of man and poet—the black poet, sensation of the black poet—which culminates in the inspired deception of Chaka, the poet-politician. A search into the nature of poetry? Or a new ploy for the old tale of love?—self to self, the declaration of concrete sensations turning and returning into themselves? (pp. 55-7)

To be a poet is presumably to be persuaded not only of the inexhaustible poetry of the self, but to presume the even more transcendentalist view that the poetic self is in itself inexhaustible. It would appear that Senghor's poetic mission is to exhaust both possibilities in the creation of a quasi-religious kingdom of black denomination. Not for him the world beneath the matter, the realities of the mystic kingdom in which other black writers are wont to explore lineaments of body or soul. He takes it instead to its furthest conceit, the pretense to activity within the existential kingdom of black poesy—the

separation of action and sensitivity. This tendency remains a common inclination among the narcissistic writers, as if action is contradictory to poetry; but rarely is it made into such an overt declaration of faith as we find it in Senghor's **"Chaka."** There is no pretense, of course, to an exploration of the psyche. If there were, a distinct poetic motion would be clear in the entry or intermesh of one level of experience and another. And Senghor's poetry is static; vigorous, clamant, constantly celebrative, it nevertheless stays still.

Could it be the encroaching realization of a closure to the real essence of poetry which gave birth finally to **"Chaka"** and the plaint of destitution? Yet even here, the chronic ailment continues manifest in the parallel separation, the denial of the poetry, not merely of action but of violence. Forced to substitute accord for penetration, acclamation for "insight," the poet batters the mystic barrier of the very heart of his poetic concept with cumulative imagery and reverberating lyrics. But the elusive heart, the more elusive for its *certain* existence in poetic knowledge and in intellectual formulation—this essence remains beyond the possession of the poet. The solution that Senghor and similar poets have adopted to meet the problem—reducing all experience to the narrowest matrix of values, to the "intimate" capsule where the area of the chase is limited—does not, alas, guarantee that the quarry is within the quarantine. What it does ensure is the increasing "intimacy" with the self and a distorted view of it, of an exaggeration of its value: in lieu of primary penetration by the developed sensibility, a regression into the ecstatic state of innocence or its delusion; glorification of the womb because object experience seals its inner nature. But poetry is selective, it is inhibiting. The poetry of the narcissist lacks inhibition, and even the intellectual content is subordinated to the extrinsic exposition of the object of the quest. Intellectualism need not be externalized.

"Chaka" underscores poetic despair? This is too easy. For a start, the narcissistic intrusion into the character of Chaka has diffused the heroic stature of the man. Action now seems a purpose to the eventual narcissistic kingdom of man; action has been corrupted by the very process that seeks a quality for movement that has not sprung from within action and is not justified even by the thoughts of the hero for his own motivation:

> Work is holy, but work is no longer gesture
> Drum and voice no longer make rhythm for the
> gestures of the seasons.

This is merely sentimental.

In explication of the real problem of Senghor in the interpretation of **"Chaka,"** which cannot be solved by the poetic self-identification, the essence of Ogun, the Yoruba god of war and the creative principle, probably offers the best assistance. Senghor's **"Chaka"** is something even more dangerous to the poet than self-identification; it is first of all an intellectual fabrication, a composite from external pieces, yet paradoxically true. Primogenitor of the artist as the creative human, Ogun is the antithesis of cowardice and Philistinism, yet within him is contained also the complement of the creative essence, a bloodthirsty destructiveness. Mixed up with the gestative inhibition of his nature, the destructive explosion of an incalculable energy. Contradictory as they are, it is necessary to experience these aspects of the god as a singly comprehended essence, a habit of psyche impossible for the Christian-oriented mind, which, to give one example, can conceive of

God the Father, God the Son, God the Holy Ghost (Destroyer, Intercessor, Mystic) in singly felt entities. No such dissection is valid in the comprehension of Ogun. There is no separation, except in analytical exercises of this kind, of the scientist from the artist in him, of the explorer from warrior, the warrior from artist, and so on. The face and the essence are the same, and the human psyche is disrupted only when, as in **"Chaka,"** there has been an abnormal development of the one aspect at the expense of others. Thus is born the monster.

Senghor's **"Chaka"** suggests that the poet's answer to antihumanism lies solely in sublime or aesthetic conceptions. The implication is that poetry is not in itself a force for violence or an occasional instrument of terror. That it combats fear by the revelation of beauty is undoubtedly one of poetry's functions; hence, the social responsibilities of the artist—his "politics," as **"Chaka"** would have it—are not in themselves a contradiction of the poet. A true Ogun sensibility that is African, or should be, recognizes this at once and does not seek the negativity of escapism, which blasphemes against the very existence of a poet. There cannot be more than a remote suggestion that Senghor is a poet of escape; the structure lies in his poetic practice and the intellectual content of a work like **"Chaka,"** the danger it presents in distorting the poetry of action, and the narcissistic fluff it shares with much of African writing. (pp. 57-60)

To say that Senghor's **"Chaka"** is not intended to be a poem of action is to beg the question. The poem becomes a living organism, and what we constantly seek when it claims its right to be static is the movement that accompanies introspection, a movement within the image, shall we say, not merely a crescendo of passions. A pause even into the heart of image which has left the poet's lips gently or been violently wrenched from him. It is at such moments that the poetic self is suspended and the phrase, the concept, lives on its own, freed from all subordination to the poet's self-interest. Senghor permits no such comradeship, no such sympathy for the moment of imagic separation. (p. 63)

Senghor hurls experience to the center of physical reiteration, and it proves a cumulative barrier to true response. It is as if his poetic skin has never breathed, as if, in response to Okigbo's lines:

> Stretch, stretch O antennae
> to clutch at this hour

Senghor seems eternally to stretch but never truly to touch the elusive moment; his dissatisfaction is exposed in the bisected warrior Chaka. And here is another irony. The character of Senghor's protagonist, Chaka, refutes the narcissism of Senghor's poetry, refutes the implication that narcissism must be a concomitant of physical exploration or experiential. Chaka's intensification of the body's endurance has become a vehicle for Senghor's self-worship; the entire concept of poetic identification is an elaborate occasion for his own physical idealization, his self-saturation in the historical (and other externalized) richness of his Negro-poetic heritage. (pp. 63-4)

Self-sacrificial in the process, Senghor's art has coursed a lifetime calling forth the essence of a new poetic heritage, but it is not itself the essence. (p. 64)

Wole Soyinka, "And After the Narcissist?" in African Forum, Vol. 1, No. 4, Spring, 1966, pp. 53-64.

HAROLD SCHEUB

The dominant metaphor in the poetry of Léopold Sédar Senghor of Senegal is, explicitly or implicitly, that of the phoenix of Egyptian mythology, that curious and fabulous creature which lived for five hundred years, then consumed itself in flames and was thereby reborn, purified and regenerated, to live for another five hundred years. A mythic death-purification-regeneration theme and a concomitant quest for self-identity form the central focuses of Senghor's poetic work and reproduce in contemporary terms the phoenix metaphor: man's alienation from his past, and the terrifying loss of identity and sense of cosmic harmony; the attempts to regain identity and therefore dignity by means of a spiritual, poetic voyage to a historical, often mythical past, a metaphorical journey to the soul; and the hope for rebirth, a renewal of the individual human in league with the community, a quest for a "civilization of the universal," where "life is born again color of whatever is." Senghor's poetry combines these themes—alienation, renewal, universal brotherhood—into a progression, an odyssey that is reminiscent in some respects of the philosophical journey of the English poet, William Blake, moving from the pure innocence of childhood into the often repellent but unavoidable world of experience, and finally, hopefully, into a new innocence, an innocence born of experience, a "New Jerusalem."

The poetry of Léopold Senghor explores the impact made by the West on Africa, the effect his own European experience has had on him. He examines the resultant contradictions in his character: Senghor the African, the nostalgic traditionalist, remembering the golden past, cherishing the bold and humane African past; Senghor the western-style intellectual, the Parisian cosmopolite, the Roman Catholic, European educated, European centered. Soukeîna and Isabelle, Africa or Europe—which shall he choose? He learns that he has no choice, and his poetry traces this learning process, from rejection of western ideals to a conclusion that *négritude* has a broad meaning and wide applications. In his love-hate relationship with the West, Senghor does not finally wholly reject the West, although he brings western values under close and critical scrutiny. He realizes that he is not purely a traditionalist African; he concludes that if there is a solution to his dilemma, it is not just an *African* solution. He is indeed repulsed by much that a bankrupt Europe stands for, but he does not seek an insular Africa nostalgically and not very productively turned in upon itself and its past; rather, he recognizes the reality of Europe and the historical fact of Africa's cultural ties with Europe. He finally searches for a synthesis that will partake of both cultures, which will, moreover, have validity not only in Africa but in the West as well. In ministering to an agonized Africa, Senghor also doctors an ailing Europe. *Négritude* ironically becomes a solution for Europe as well as for Africa.

Senghor adopts as his frame of reference the historical and more recent plight of the black man, yet his concern consistently transcends *femme noire* and [his birthplace] Joal—these become, finally, symbolic of a more universal preoccupation. Indeed, his racial pronouncements often seem more rhetorical than genuine. This is not to diminish the major role played by the black man in his poetry. He himself is black, and his finest poetry illuminates his personal experience. The black man, furthermore, is the alienated man par excellence, condemned by the same soul-flattening reliance on technology and reason which is destroying the white man, yet simultaneously ostracized from the world of technology and reason because of his skin color. In the European, American, and colonial African milieux, the black man is a part of a bankrupt world, yet apart from it: the black man is truly alone. Senghor is, however, ultimately dealing with a universal problem which happens to find its most dramatic figure in the black man.

His argument essentially is this: the "black" man must extricate himself from the "white" man's corrupt world, reestablish his connections with his past and his rapport with nature, which is to say with both his own nature (self-awareness, self-identity, self-esteem) and the world around him. Then, as an equal, he will reenter the world community, prepared to participate in the purification of a dying world and to act as midwife to its rebirth.

Color is a major motif in **"Neige sur Paris,"** a poem in which Senghor plays almost defiantly, certainly with sarcasm, upon the word "white" and its usual western connotations of peace, goodness, and purity. The poet accepts, for the sake of argument, the white man's premise that "white is good," and he turns it against the white man by means of a catalogue of African grievances and the consequent exposure of the white man's hypocrisy. The poem is composed in the form of a prayer directed to the white man's god, and irony is the chief weapon and poetic device as Senghor assails the corrupt white world, at the same time reversing the European's ethnocentric definitions of "white" and "black."

God's vengeance and mercy are represented in **"Neige sur Paris"** through images of nature: "snow of your peace," which is also a snow of God's vengeance; "mountain of your peace," "sun of your gentleness," and "hands like dew," all of which bring God and nature into a kind of unity, the god of the poem being a kind of God-nature. Man's lack of harmony with nature is thereby equated to his lack of harmony with God. The whiteness of God's snow purifies and brings peace, and is contrasted with the powdered, spurious whiteness of the white man's hands which bring destruction.

The first seven lines of the poem constitute its opening movement, the establishment of the basic image and the immediate transformation of that image into a symbol. God sends the snow to purify Paris, to purge it "By white death." So effective is God's visitation that "even the factory chimneys," symbols of industrialized Europe, are singing in unison, "Flying white flags," and chanting "Peace to Men of goodwill." God's snow has done its work: Europe has been purified, making plain its surrender to God, and the sterile product of the industrial revolution has been brought into harmony with God—alienated man has been brought back into a rhythmic union with nature.

Things have been anything but unified prior to this time, however, and the second [and third] . . . movements of the poem expose what a debased Europe has done to Africa and to itself: it was an alienated, "a divided world . . . a divided Europe. . . ." Spain has been "torn apart" in a revolutionary war; "And the rebel" against God disrupted God's peace. Ironically, it is the Jew and the Catholic—representing the ideological and spiritual bases of western civilization—who defy God, who fire their "1,400 guns against the mountain of your Peace." The image suggests man's assault on God-nature, a Europe out of harmony with God and nature, a Europe divided against itself.

The poet himself has not been without taint. His heart, filled with hatred toward the white man, must also be purified by the "incorruptible cold / By white death." The poet is humble: "Lord, I have accepted your white cold more burning than salt." Snow is again the purifier, the cleanser, and the action causes a burning sensation as it purges the heart of its hatred. That work accomplished, the poet's "heart melts like snow beneath the sun." The effect is immediate, and "Under the sun of Your gentleness," the animosity melts away. "And I forget."

Whether or not he actually forgets is of no significance; the images that follow in the third movement are too vivid, too stringently anti-European to support an attitude of forgiveness. It is the *process* that is important, as Senghor telescopes the stages of this metaphorical journey. Forgetting implies forgiveness, on which the final stage of the odyssey is dependent. Man must first recover what he has lost, and only then can he forgive, the prelude to deliverance and regeneration. Symbolically, both Europe *and* the poet have been brought back into rapport with God-nature. (pp. 199-203)

[Civilization] (which Senghor mockingly capitalizes), the sterile whiteness, invaded Africa, and destroyed nature, disrupting man's relationship with nature. And again the irony: the white man destroyed nature to save his own civilization, but it is that civilization which is now dying. There is further irony. The poet has been speaking of God's white "snow of peace" and of the white man's "chalk-white hands," then he injects yet another color into the color-sensitive imagery: God's hands are not white, as the white man has insisted, they are "brown hands." The detail achieves significance in this instance because it is immediately contrasted with the Europeans' white hands and with the white snow, and hence cannot be ignored. The poet might have concluded that God's hands are pure white, not powdery white; this would have been consistent with the general use of color in the poem. But there is an abrupt color change. It is possible that Senghor is suggesting here that this white man's God is in fact closer to the world of the black man than he is to the world of the white. If so, then this is the crowning irony of the poem. Nature and God are very close, if not one; the black African, closer to nature, is closer to God.

The fourth and final movement of **"Neige sur Paris"** deals with the poet, now cleansed by God's gentle sun. "Lord," the poet says,

> I know I will not bring out my store of hatred
> against the diplomats who flash their long teeth
> And tomorrow will barter black flesh.

Again, these are not the words that would be chosen by a man filled with forgiveness. The poet is not yet cleansed; he is merely mapping out the way to deliverance. The final movement is concerned with the future, the world after God's peace efforts have had their effect, after God has dissolved the black man's hatred and the white man's deceitfulness and penchant for destruction, and brought them back into union with nature (and therefore with one another). God's gentleness is generous: it is also applicable "to my enemies, to my brothers with white hands without snow." Though those chalk-white hands bring anything but peace, God's "hands like dew" cleanse white and black alike.

While **"Neige sur Paris"** is more concerned with the havoc the white man spread throughout Africa, it also contains the seeds of redemption. That vague promise of deliverance requires exploration, and this is found in the poem, **"Que** m'accompagnent kôras et balafong" ("For Koras and Bala-fong"). (pp. 204-05)

"Que m'accompagnent kôras et balafong" both intensifies and ameliorates Senghor's attacks on white civilization, the poem betraying the poet's own attraction to Europe while at the same time broadening the condemnation of that society for its bankrupt ideology and its rape of Africa. The promise of hope is elaborated somewhat, but the poem is caught in the dramatic tension that exists within the poet, torn as he is between the two worlds. This conflict is resolved to some extent, but as **"Neige sur Paris"** was primarily concerned with the present plight of alienated man, so **"Que m'accompagnent kôras et balafong"** turns to the past and becomes enveloped in a somewhat romantic examination of the concept of *négritude.* (p. 206)

In Part I of **"Que m'accompagnent kôras et balafong,"** Senghor introduces a leitmotif which he will develop in various ways throughout the work: the fountain of Kam-Dyame, the image of water, of thirst satisfied and not satisfied. It is at the fountain where the poet, naked, flowers adorning his body, "drank your mystical waters out of my cupped hands." The fountain represents the mystical connection with the past, rhythm, the sap within man that rises and struts and dances.

This was his early childhood, and later there were other fountains, the fountains of Europe: his schooling, where the "Latin Muses" were "proclaimed as my guardian angels," but he rejects the shade provided by those muses as being too narrow. . . . His European education did not quench his thirst; those European fountains were insufficient. After partaking in that world of "grilled and salted pistachios," which only served to quicken his thirst, he turned to the past, to another fountain, the "Fountain-of-Elephants, where the stammering water is good," symbolizing as it does a broader wisdom and a deeper experience—that of his forefathers who, "with solemn eyes," perceived the very source of things. So he did not succumb to the muses of Europe; he was guided through that Scylla and Charybdis by Africa and Verdun. It is true that he has forgotten much of the past to which he now retreats. . . . He has retained his innocence and now recalls, if vaguely, the mystical rhythm of his past.

Part III of the poem introduces the conflict between the two worlds, and intimates that the poet's innocence has been sternly tested. The conflict is announced in the child's verse that prefaces the section: his mother suggests that he is a white man "Kissing the prettiest girl," implying that he has compromised and been won over by the white world. But it is not that simple. He dislikes the fact that he must choose, "deliciously torn" as he is "between these two friendly hands. . . ." But he must make a decision, because friendly though those hands may be, they represent "two antagonistic worlds." Shall it be Soukeîna or Isabelle? Africa or Europe? He "cannot tell now which is my sister and which is my foster-sister"; he has pleasant remembrances of each. He protests; he would like to make "those two hands" one.

Still, if he must choose, he chooses Africa, "the verset of streams and of winds and of forests / The assonance of plains and rivers"; he chooses "the rhythm of blood in my naked body." And he chooses harmony, "the harmony of strings and brass that seem to clash." But the "plains and rivers" are not assonant, the "strings and brass" do not clash when one is in rhythmic contact with nature. The poet has made that choice, he has chosen the "Swing swing yes chosen the swing

/ And the far-off muted trumpet." In another poem, **"Chants pour Signare" ("Elle me force sans jamais répit"),** he rejects the music of Europe: "I cannot sing your plain chant that has no swing to it, I cannot dance it." Dance—rhythm is the essence of *négritude,* enveloping man biologically, emotionally, spiritually, bringing him into harmony with nature and with an Africa that is as real as the beat of his pulse. Europe is out of tune; its music is plain, and the poet cannot dance it. And dance is everything: "She dances, she lives," he proclaims in **"Epîtres a la princesse" (V, "Princesse, ton épître");** his nobleness, he tells the princess, "is to live that land according to that land." It is rhythm, the rhythm of the drums, the rhythm that throbs up within him and possesses him, rhythm with nature. . . . And this drum roll, this rhythm is not only the hope of Africa, it will also resurrect a dead Europe: "the burst of the trumpet [no longer muted] over the snowy graveyards of Europe."

The poet, in almost apologetic tones, speaks in Part IV of **"Que m'accompagnent kôras et balafong"** of his intimate relations with Europe. But he has already rejected Europe and Isabelle in favor of Africa and Soukeîna, and there is more than mere rejection here. Underlying the comments about Europe is the knowledge that he has something far more desirable than pale occidental offerings: not the arid plains of European knowledge but the fountain of *négritude,* "where the stammering water is good." He "was not always a shepherd of fair heads," teaching in European schools. Not always. There was something that he had long ago, before he taught the white children, before he became a deferential official, the proper colleague, "smiling but rarely laughing." It is that primordial state of innocence of which he speaks, and the memory of his origins intensifies the aridity of "Old France old University, all the old routine." Age has nothing to do with it; his "childhood is as old as the world and I am as young as the everlasting youth of the world's dawn." He will be delivered from the acute sense of alienation, which is Europe's contribution, by a new sense of his own identity, an identity which will become known to him through *négritude,* a reestablishment of contacts with his past, with "The poetesses of the sanctuary" and the "authentic legend of my race," a new union symbolized by the rhythmic "sounds of the high *kôras.*"

The essence and lesson of that past are indicated in Part V in the description of one of the poet's forebears, Koumba Ndofène Dyouf, a vassal and a governor, important here because the past makes him a rhythmic counterpart of nature; origins, nature, and rhythm, all are accounted for as the poet describes the peregrinations of this "royal pilgrim," who, accompanied by the *dyoung-dyoungs,* gives "ear in the wood to the murmured grievance," listens to "the prattle of birds," and heeds "the conch eloquent among the prophetic tombs," that is, the ancestors. While they wept in the evening because their own fragile peace (the peace spoken of in **"Neige sur Paris"**) is threatened, there is yet no disruption of that man-nature union; he and his fellows are "Cousins in peace," continuing their traditional way of life. The ancestors are symbolic of man's roots, and are important to Senghor's poetry particularly in this symbolic sense: man's quest for identity will end with a reestablishment of ties with the past, and hence the emphasis on links with the ancestors. They are a part of the harmony, and once the break with the past is complete, the harmony too is shattered. The present blends into the past; the two cannot be separated: "I was myself the grandfather of my grandfather / I was his soul and his ascendancy."

On "the high pyre" of war (a fracture of God's peace, again referring to a disruption of man's relations with nature and a consequent slide toward a state of alienation), the "dusty riches" of the past go up in flames. The present is imprisoned ("my house, the wives who have mothered my sons"); the past is destroyed ("Furniture of the sanctuary, solemn masks, ritual garments")—all are consumed. Yet in that smoldering rubble lies hope; the flames of destruction can be transposed, through the effects of *négritude,* into the flame of regeneration, and from the devastation will rise the new phoenix: "Sleep, heroes, in this evening which brings new life to birth, in this night heavy with grandeur." All is not destroyed: "saved is the Singer," the *griot* who creates the poem, embodiment of rhythmic calm. The survival of the singer is all-important, for rhythm is life, and "my pagan sap that rises, struts and dances" will give birth to a regenerated and purified mankind.

The roles of the poet and the poem are essential in this process. "This complex notion" of *négritude,* Sartre has written, "is essentially pure poetry." There is no more appropriate symbol of the agent who will resurrect a moribund Europe and revive a dying Africa than the *griot* who will blow the trumpet "over the snowy graveyards of Europe." The trumpet is the poem. But the poetic word alone is not sufficient: "What makes the *négritude* of a poem is less its theme than its style, the emotional warmth which gives life to words, which transmutes the word into the Word." This statement has meaning only when one considers the emphasis Senghor places on rhythm and the interpretation he gives to it. Without rhythm, the word is sterile: "It is rhythm that lends it [the word] its full effectiveness, that transforms it into the verb. It was God's verb, that is to say the rhythmic word, that created the universe." When Senghor speaks of "the Word," he is not suggesting objective and rational interpretation. It is "intuitive reason" that he is referring to; not necessarily spoken or written, it is "a certain affective attitude towards the world." It is hence not a reasoned interpretative process, but rather a state of being. . . . (pp. 206-13)

The Word is *négritude,* which is rhythm, which is life. This rhythm is given form in art—in the sound of the drums, in the metrical movement of the poem. This is not to suggest that the form of the poem is the end; the rhythmic beats are illustrative and symptomatic of "the Negro's being-in-the-world." Poetry is not something to be merely read, and drums are not to be simply heard—they are felt, as a part of man's being. It is not a question of searching for the meaning of a poem; what is important is that one feels the poem. . . . The "message" or theme, if there is one, is felt, and it is more than a mere vicarious experience: it *is* experience. The poem simultaneously expresses in outward form the rhythmic rudiments of man's union with "the Other," but more important, it is an ecstatic heightening of that union. The dance is the most obvious example: the pulsating beat of the blood within man, of his throbbing rapport with nature, and of the beat of the drums—all converge, and while it is true that such an experience is a symbol of the larger experience, it is at the same time an experiential encounter during which man is most keenly aware of his identity. So with the poem: the poetic experience is not simply a microcosm of that larger symphony; it is in itself an experience, a moment when man's sense of harmony is heightened and acute, and the harmony itself is

complete, perfect. One does not explicate such poetry: "He has no need to think, but to live the Other by dancing it. . . . Now to dance is to discover and to recreate, to identify oneself with the forces of life, to lead a fuller life, and in short, to *be*. It is, at any rate, the highest form of knowledge. And thus, the knowledge of the African negro is, at the same time, discovery and creation—re-creation." Such a form of "knowledge" is alien to European experience, not because of race but because the European has, through his continual insistence on rationalism at the expense of feeling, widened the gap between himself and his origins. He studies rather than participates in the object, and he thereby misses the point: "It is a matter of *participating* in the object in the act of knowledge; of going beyond concepts and categories, appearances and preconceptions produced by education, to plunge into the primordial chaos, not yet shaped by discursive reason." (pp. 213-14)

In Part VII of **"Que m'accompagnent kôras et balafong,"** Senghor addresses the Africa of the past, present, and future. This "Africa," rather than rob the people of their identities (an accusation which the poet immediately rejects), prepares them to survive the onslaughts of those who would destroy that innocence. . . . In such difficult times, Africa (*négritude,* the primal sympathy) will rise to drive the enemy off; it is the fortress, "the chief organizing the force to forge / The arm." And as "your people are honored in you / . . . You are your people." (Man is not simply a part of Africa, he *is* Africa, "Africa" suggesting that natural rapport.) It is this lush fertility and its bold promise of creativeness, mixing the bloods of all men, these bloods mingling in the poet's veins, which make him a part of the totality of humanity. Africa is rhythm—"only the naked clapping of hands," nothing else is important. This is the promise of that symbolic Africa, it is "the song of Africa to come." In a word, it is this same "Africa" which signals an end to mankind's torment.

The poet hopes to carry this message "to the gatherings of the people," thereby preparing the way for the regenerated phoenix. But before he can carry out his mission of purification, the poet must himself be purified, and he naturally turns to nature:

> O desert shadowless desert, austere earth, pure
> earth, from all my pettiness
> Wash me clean, from all contagions of civilized
> man.

These two lines capsulize Senghor's concept of the initial stages of *négritude:* a purgation of the spirit, washing away the contamination of civilization, and a return to the earth. The poet will return to his roots, find his original identity which is full accord with nature, and reclaim the dignity, now lost, which had flowed from that accord. Using the imagery of Africa's past to illumine the present and to embody the promise of the future, the poet can now set out on his pilgrimage, "together with all the buried greatness of the past" (not a historical past but a reminder of rhythmic origins—the historical references are mere symbols of that rhythm), his voyage identical to that of his forebear, Koumba Ndofène Dyouf, bursting with the same promise and beset by the same dangers. He will march in a procession of "seven thousand new negroes," regenerated humans, "seven thousand peasants humble and proud / Who carry the authentic riches of my race on their musical shoulders." (pp. 215-16)

This reestablished rapport with the forces of the universe is thrown into stark relief by the abrupt shift, in Part IX of **["Que m'accompagnent kôras et balafong"]**, to the situation in Europe. The poet has already noted that he owes his deliverance not to the European fountains of knowledge, but rather to the fountains of wisdom and feeling which have their source in the African past. . . . The waters of Europe flow red with blood: "see how the Somme and the Seine and the Rhine and the savage Slav rivers are red under the Archangel's sword." The poet escaped the fury of that sword because, in Claude McKay's words, he "was in closer biological kinship to the swell of primitive earth life. And maybe this apparent failing under the organization of the modern world was the real strength that preserved him from becoming the thing that was the common white creature of it." A renewed feeling of attraction for this Europe nevertheless wells up within the poet, but he immediately represses it: "I have my orders, my duty is to go on." Still, there is hope, and his love for this destructive Europe leads him to "find a little comfort" in the possibility that his "double loves" may "go wandering every night." There is that dim hope that this torn Europe may, through its attachment to Africa, be saved.

The inner fountain of blood, a symbol of the poet's affinity to nature, has now become a symbol of alienation: those same rhythmic "bloods mingled in my veins" are drained in Europe because of war, the primary image of Europe's spiritual bankruptcy and consequent sense of aloneness. In the remainder of the poem, by concentrating on the ingredients of his own deliverance, the poet proposes a solution for Europe's barrenness. From that sickening sight of European bloodletting, the poet retreats to his past, the sense of union now finding its symbol in "African night." He returns to that first innocence, returns to those "distant nights" when his uncle led him "through the shadows and the signs." . . . The uncle thereby becomes the vehicle, bringing the young poet back into contact with his past and with nature. It is quiet, the calmness of man in tune with nature—the flowers, the glowworms, the stars, grass, trees, all woven into his being by "the muffled tom-tom, the far-off breathing of the night." The ancestors (representing that past) explain the mysteries of nature (the only worthy education), which means simply that the poet, in harmony with the past, is a part of those mysteries, feels them and thereby has an intuitive understanding of them—this is wisdom, not mere knowledge. All is unified: the poet, his Africa, his past, the spirits, ancestors, nature, and the pulse of the drums. "Africa" is all of this; it is self-awareness. (pp. 217-18)

The poem ends on a brief note of hope, the attempt again to bridge the gulf between the two worlds of "Africa" and "Europe." Though he has now accepted Africa, he has not completely cut his ties with Europe. He has brought back with him "only this friend" (his European wife?), who, like the poet, is yet a child whose eyes, having survived "Breton mists," are still bright, still attuned to "Africa." With this slim hope for a regenerated Europe in mind, Senghor develops the final phase of his odyssey. (p. 219)

Read on a literal level, Senghor's poems require little explanation. The African, enslaved for centuries and humiliated by the colonial powers, gradually lost his dignity as a man; in the eyes of the white conqueror, he was an inferior being. This was serious enough, but the state of the black man became disastrous when he himself began to accept the white man's premise. One of the most pathetic manifestations of this loss of identity was the concept of the *assimilado:* the black Afri-

can who tried to become a white European, forsaking his own history and identity, attempting to become what he was not. The experiment was doomed from the beginning, and the African became a double exile: psychologically and physically, he was alienated. Cut off from his origins and adrift in a world in which, because of his skin color, he would always be a stranger, the African was prevented from participating in the world of the present and from aiding in the creation of a more productive future world. The present situation of Senghor's African, then, is one of destruction,

> the tearing of self from self
> From the tongue of my mother, from the skull of
>   my Ancestor, from the drum of my soul.
>   (pp. 226-27)

But Senghor, in his poetry, goes beyond the shores of Africa. One of the probable reasons for misconceptions arising from the poetry of *négritude* is that unfortunate word itself. However it is translated—"blackness," "negrohood," "niggerness"—it leads one to assume that it is a peculiarly racial (or even racist) concept. Poets like Aimé Césaire and Léon Damas have compounded this confusion; their poetry is uncompromising in its attacks on white civilization, their artistic images and idealistic quests marred by an overwrought emotionalism. The subject of Senghor's poetry is indeed blackness; the error is to stop there, with the mere personal and historical data and imagery. It is *not* the theme of the work. "I am not really a Pan-Africanist," Senghor told a London press conference in 1961, "I am a humanist." And his poetry supports this claim; it is a humanistic vision rather than a racial justification that characterizes his work. (pp. 227-28)

> *Harold Scheub, "Soukeîna and Isabelle—Senghor and the West," in* Africa & the West: Intellectual Responses to European Culture *by James W. Fernandez and others, edited by Philip D. Curtin, The University of Wisconsin Press, 1972, pp. 189-230.*

GERMAINE BRÉE

If, for Africa, 1960 was the "year of destiny," for many Africans it was also the beginning of a long and difficult process of national construction. It opened the decade in which some forty new African nations acquired sovereignty. What "nationalism" had meant in the years of the struggle for independence could no longer apply to their postindependence situation. Among the men who most articulately and consistently voiced the feelings and the concepts that so deeply marked the emerging new values and who helped to shape their course, President Léopold Sédar Senghor of Sénégal is a figure who stands apart. From the year 1934, when he founded, with Aimé Césaire of Martinique and Leon Damas of Guyana, the review *L'étudiant noir,* to the present, when he presides over the destiny of the Republic of Sénégal, he seems single-mindedly to have followed a straight itinerary as poet, literary critic, spokesman for francophone Black Africa, and statesman. A figure of quiet dignity, less flamboyant than his more eloquent and dramatic friend Aimé Césaire, yet a man possessed by an inner vision, his work as poet and essayist so far has received little attention in this country. His literary output is considerable and varied: six collections of poems published between 1945 and 1961; a number of articles, prefaces, translations, and essays that cover a wide range of topics: studies in linguistics, literary criticism, definitions of cultural problems, political discussions of topical issues. From none of these, however brief or purely ceremonial, has Africa ever been absent, much as it has never been absent from Senghor's effort to make explicit and define those traits of the "black personality" evoked by the word "Négritude."

In his introduction to the first volume of his collected prose writings, *Liberté I: Négritude et humanisme,* alluding to that title and to the title of a further volume *The Concept of Nation and the African view of Socialism (Nation et voie africaine du socialisme),* President Senghor remarked: "Everything the author has written, for twenty-five years, constitutes only *variations* on these four particular themes," i.e., Négritude, humanism, nationalism, and socialism. "In fact, since his years in the 'Quartier latin,' the author has been preoccupied only by those four ideas, which truly became an *obsession.* They explain his life and his work, even when he speaks of French poetry in the sixteenth century." It seems to have been that obsession which first really "informed," as Gide would have said, the poet in Senghor, sending him back to the poetic forms alive in the oral literature of his people; the poet in turn then "informed" the statesman. One can, in a sense, organize the four obsessive themes in a kind of circular interdependence with the concept of Négritude at the dynamic core determining the content of the three others. Senghor's thesis concerning the particular non-Marxist form of socialism through which the new nations of Africa could best be organized rests upon his vision of the humanistic aspirations peculiar to black Africans, expressed in their art and literature as well as in their social organization. These all reveal the cultural values cherished, values which bear the stamp of and perpetuate a characteristic affectivity. Art in all its forms is the expression of that affectivity. Poetic speech or song is central then to the life of the community. (pp. 374-75)

Very early in his career, Senghor defined his role as poet in relation to his people and to their traditions. He was to be the Dyâli, the singer poet, who among the Serère tribes—to which Senghor belongs—celebrates the greatness of a high personage; but the personage, for Senghor, was to be no single human being but a people. (p. 376)

To that people in a fervent and prophetic prayer addressed to the "Elephant of Mbissel," one of the legendary mediators between men and the powers of the cosmos, he dedicated his life, words, and action:

> Grant that I may die for the quarrel of my people,
>   and if need be in the odor of powder and cannon.
> Preserve and root in my liberated heart the primor-
>   dial love of that people
> Make of me your Master of language; but now, ap-
>   point me its ambassador.

For Senghor, literature and art can only be, as he himself has indicated, "functional, collective and committed." Political action and poetry cannot be separated. Yet rare in Senghor's verse are the militant themes, the cries of revolt that we have come to associate with the rich vein of literary expression characteristic of the black "renaissance," and more particularly of the Martiniquean poet Aimé Césaire. The poet in Senghor's world is a courtly figure; he celebrates, illustrates, praises; and by naming he rekindles in the memory and imagination of his people the noble legends, myths, and achievements of the common past. In his introduction to the Seghers anthology of Senghor's poems, Armand Guibert questioned the appropriateness of one of Senghor's poems, entitled **"Chaka,"** a "Dramatic poem for several voices" dedicated to

the "Bantu martyrs of South Africa" and included in *Ethiopique.* A Zulu warrior and tyrant, sometimes known as the Black Napoleon of Africa, Chaka had conquered vast stretches of South African territory, which he had plunged into a blood bath, eventually massacring his own mother and fiancée. The Bantu epic had already been sung by an African poet, Thomas Mofolo, and translated into French in 1940. Guibert's objection to Senghor's interpretation of Chaka's revolt was that it glorified and justified unwarranted and bestial butchery. Understandably, the reproach mistakes the particular role of the poet as Senghor sees it. In the figure of Chaka, "pinned to the ground by three spears" and about to die, it is not the historic chieftain Senghor evokes, but the passion of a whole people incarnated in the proud figure of the man who sacrificed his private love for a woman to his revolt against the white invader, his vocation as poet to his role as leader. The poem, a dirge for the martyred Bantu, is the transmutation of the man, his renaissance beyond defeat as the "poet," the annunciator of a new dawn for his oppressed race. It is, Senghor believes, the poet's task "to prophesy, to awaken declining hope, to announce the final victory and the renaissance," rather than to denounce. The personal sense of poetry as a perpetual recall of man's highest dignity bestowing upon men's acts the aura of beauty, hence meaning, sets Senghor apart among his black contemporaries and links him to a French poet he admires, St. John Perse.

When "on the morning of August 20, 1960" the Senegalese nation was born and Senghor became its first president, few had been his references to that nation as such. The allusion in the poem just quoted is an exception. When in *Black Hosts (Hosties noires)* he speaks to and for the Senegalese soldiers killed or made prisoner in France—"the Senegalese prisoners obscurely lying on the soil of France"—whose destiny he shares, or when he recalls the family home, it is without a trace of exclusiveness. (pp. 376-78)

One among the anonymous soldiers designated by the French as the Senegalese *tirailleurs* ("sharpshooters"), Senghor merges into the group of all his brothers alive and dead the 500,000 men thrown by France into its battlefields; they in turn draw around them all their African brothers, and beyond them all the oppressed, the infantrymen in all the armies of the world, including those of France, to which Senghor remained loyal in her defeat. This merging of the poet's own individual situation with the great mass of humanity through ever-widening circles is characteristic of Senghor's poems, reflecting his natural inclination to reach out and gather all others into the circle of his poem. Senghor's "peuple" then people the earth; through the mediation of his own situation, seen through French eyes as a black from the colonial territory of Sénégal, the privileged boy from the royal Sérère tribe becomes brother to all exploited human beings on this earth. Black Africa is then the mediator, conferring upon the poet the gift of social innocence, the mission of liberator. It becomes the spiritual homeland of the "wretched" of the earth, and the African is thus today, whether he knows it or not, a man charged with a mission. When Senghor speaks as he sometimes does of an "African nation," he is referring to that Africa as much as to the geographical and complex continent itself. It is a "seamless" whole that wipes out all frontiers: between the self and the other; between Senghor the privileged Sérère poet and the men of his own tribe; between the Sérère and the Senegalese; between the

Senegalese and the other blacks; between the blacks and the whites. (pp. 378-79)

The word ["Négritude"] first expressed his sense of his own separate identity with regard to the French culture he had so eagerly absorbed, and his bonds with French-speaking blacks of whatever origin. Négritude also accompanied his active partisanship, among his own people as well as the French, for the creation of an independent French Black African group of nations, within a French Commonwealth, with equal rights for all its citizens. Consciously a *métis* ("half breed") culturally, he first rehabilitated and sought out the African component in his "métissage," namely, the Négritude through which, acceding to his own inner kingdom, he simultaneously transcended the mental and more especially spiritual provincialisms of what he sometimes called the "hexagone." Borrowed from the abstract political jargon of the time—when the concept of the French Commonwealth was superseding the concept of a colonial empire—the word, in Senghor's use of it, took on the quality of an ideogram, a quality he most particularly attributes to the use of images in African languages: it quietly relegated French power to its geographic limits. Used by a man who was never inclined to attack French culture indiscriminately, who rather pointed only to the vast areas of its self-deceits—it was as powerful a form of demystification as the virulent denunciations of white humanity. The distinctions between the purveyor of culture and the receiver, between the superior civilized colonizer and the inferior colonized blacks were quietly dismissed.

In his famous and influential preface to Senghor's *Anthology of the New Black and Madagascan Poetry* (*Anthologie de la nouvelle poésie nègre et malgache*) (1948), Sartre dramatically defined the common source of inspiration for black lyricism in terms of the black revolt against the white image imposed upon the blacks by colonial masters, itself the obverse of the deified mask of himself created by the white to hide his real face from himself. Desecration, denunciation, and destruction of the white image, and celebration of all things black were then the natural means of liberation from the constraining judgment of the "Other," and with them the concomitant and necessary violence. But whether prose or poetry, such forms of exorcism are rare in Senghor's writing. Rather, with regard to the European man, we find a stern accounting, more specifically for his mercantilism and his disregard for the suffering he inflicts. This is the theme of the postwar **"Prière de paix"** ["Prayer for Peace"] the last poem in *Black Hosts,* written to be spoken to the accompaniment of the great church organs. It is an indictment of the Europeans' murderous waste of human lives over the centuries, but a prayer too for their pardon, and a fervent plea for God's aid in crushing "the serpent of hatred that rears its head in my heart, the serpent I had thought was dead."

There was a time, admittedly, recorded in poems like **"Le retour de l'Enfant Prodigue"** (**"The Return of the Prodigal Son"**) when, in his Parisian "exile," he rejected all things French, the French language among them. It was, he later rather humorously remarked in a speech addressed to his Sorbonne masters, necessary "pour les besoins de ma thèse." But his Négritude was not, as Sartre would have it, a mere by-product of the white man's presence. Senghor, as we shall see, could stand his own ground. Curiously, and revealingly, Senghor does not shun the word "white" in his poems, nor does he equate it with forms of evil. It generally appears quite

naturally among the gamut of colors he uses; when on one occasion in the poem **"Chaka,"** "the white voice" is the voice of the accuser, it is not necessarily the voice of the white. The "return to the sources" for him was the rediscovery of his cultural inheritance as a son of the Sérère clan. It involved a new awareness of the forms of its oral literature, the integration of words, song, and dance. This was a time when he translated the poems of the village poetess, Marône. And it was the time when he found his own idiom as Sérère poet, writing in the French language. Senghor's poems, in the main, elaborate upon the suggestions of that oral tradition. Many of them are songs, formally designed and modulated according to diverse poetic purposes or intentions: a "taga," for the celebration of a human being or specific action; a "way" or ode; an elegy or satire. Each of these he writes for accompaniment by specific instruments, tam-tams extraordinary in their diversification: dyoung-dyoung or royal tam-tam of Sine, gorong, mbalakh, ndeundere, sabar, talmblatt and tama; balafong (xylophone); khalam (guitar); rîti (viola); flute or modern jazz orchestra. It is not by chance then that the **"Prayer for peace"** was written for organ music. The theme of the return to the sources was indeed more than a thesis; it was a necessary prelude to the poet's discovery of his own idiom.

Senghor, in fact, loves literature too deeply to renounce the pleasures and sustenance it offers. Corneille, Lautréamont, Rimbaud, Péguy, Claudel, and "le grand Hugo" are among the masters who opened up to him worlds of thought and poetry, and he once called French "the language of the Gods"; that is to say, French considered in its literary, "universalizing" usage. Of the contemporary French poets, the one to whom he is most drawn, whose conception of poetry and the poet's mission most clearly approximated his own, is St. John Perse, the West Indian Creole poet. Perse's idiom moved him more deeply than that of his friend Aimé Césaire. Politically and intellectually, the thinker who most deeply influenced Senghor—besides Marx, with whom he felt that same affinity—was the Jesuit ethnologist and philosopher, Teilhard de Chardin. St. John Perse is a "cosmic poet" who celebrates the epic of man's spiritual odyssey on this planet, apparent in the often tempestuous course of the civilizations he temporarily sets up, and in the inventions or "sea-marks" that chart his course in the uncharted stretches of space and time. The poet, according to St. John Perse, is he who records the adventure, each great poem itself a "sea-mark," at one and the same time the story of its own emergence and of the creation of the world, poetry itself being the eruption of the word that merges world and consciousness, the singer with the surge. Poetry is then the advent or incarnation of the spiritual in the material that gives all things, sweeping through space and time, a transcendental unity and human meaning. To see things whole is perhaps the gift of the poet; it is certainly the essential need of the human being in Senghor's world. (pp. 379-82)

Senghor's sense of himself as African crystallized around quite different images, the memory of a childhood "royal" in its wonder, happiness, and freedom. It produced a recurrent image in his poetry, which sometimes emigrates into his prose, what he would perhaps call rather than a symbol an "ideogram": "le Royaume d'Enfance," the Childhood Kingdom. At the heart of "le Royaume d'Enfance" is the memory of a happy childhood in a prosperous family in the Sérère village of Djilar. "Almost all the people and things they evoke," he wrote of his poems, "are from my small region, a few Sérère villages lost among the *tanns,* the woods, the *bolongs,* and the fields. I need only name them to live once again the *Royaume d'Enfance* [*The Kingdom of Childhood*]."

Senghor's personal quest for what he has called the "Grail-Négritude" always leads back to that kingdom from which both his poems and his political vision and action draw their substance. Because of it the Senegalese sharpshooter, shivering and abandoned in his prisoner-of-war camp, is kin to the legendary *quelwár* or nobleman of the great legendary kingdoms of the past. The poet will clad him again in this ancestral nobility through the nobility of language, he whom "the merchants and bankers proscribed from the Nation," as they proscribed the volunteer Senghor and "upon the honor of [his] arms, engraved 'mercenary.' " No bitterness touches the "Royaume d'Enfance" which knew nothing of colonialism, harking back to the "ancient kingdom of Sine." In an early poem **"Joal"** (**"Songs of the Shade"**) Senghor recalls the fabulous visits to his father's house of the last of Sine's kings, Koumba N'Dofène. As a small boy in his native village of Djilos, Senghor left the cultural confines of his home to listen to the tales and legends told him by his mother's brother; and along with black mythology, he absorbed a sense of participation of all things and beings in the cosmic whole, including the presence of the "blood" of the common Ancestor in his own veins that linked him to the wide community of the family.

It was during the Paris "exile" that Senghor made the passionate discovery of Frobenius and the group of ethnologists who described the present and past civilizations of Africa and reversed the European image of the primitive black barbarian, whereupon the "Royaume d'Enfance" became the very incarnation of Négritude, giving it a peculiarly Senghorian coloring. Adapting Frobenius's thesis concerning the unity of the Negro-African world, Senghor saw in it an archetype, a model of African civilization, that made it the very essence of Négritude. For him the word designates "the configuration of cultural values of the Black world as they are expressed in the life, institutions and works of the Blacks" but seen in the perspective of their "absence," the perspective of exile and memory. This too is the perspective of poetry.

In a 1963 preface, **"Black Dominion"** (**"Domaine noir"**), to a volume [edited by Michel Huet] called *African Africa* (*Afrique Africaine*) illustrating diverse aspects of Africa, Senghor, drawing upon the work of many ethnologists, fully developed his theory of black sensitivity, constantly turning to his own "pays du Sine" and to its pastoral civilization for a relevant example. The Negro he defines as "l'homme de la nature," a "thinking man" but one who thinks "forms and colors and more especially odors, sounds and rhythms" without "filtering intermediaries." To this physical and mystical sense of the earth he attributes the black esthetic of art as a synthesis of all media—dance, music, language, sculptured mask—actively involving all the sensory apparatus of the human body in the act of creation, which is in fact the symbolic act of liberation from domination by the material forces of the cosmos. The same sense of physical participation links mother and son, the mother through whom the "flame of life" is transmitted with the blood of the ancestor. The African family he notes is the "microcosm, the first cell that through extension is reproduced by all the concentric circles which form the different levels of society, village, tribe, kingdom, empire," a harmonious community which colonialism disrupted, whose central concern was the integration of each member into the spiritual whole and the concern that he bring to

the whole, as individual, the full participation which is the measure of a man's freedom and his share in the perpetual re-creation of the integral spiritual whole and its liberation from domination by the inhuman powers of the cosmos.

For Senghor, the outer social configuration then corresponds to a cosmic, spiritual, and mystical design which reproduces the natural expansive movement of his own sensitivity apparent in his poems. Quite clearly, he has incorporated into that design the mystical spiritual community of the Christian church, to which Senghor nonetheless addressed the reproach that it had "torn from [his] too loving heart the chains that linked him to the pulse of the world." For Senghor, the social pattern of the African clan thus idealized is itself an "ideogram," the inscription in a concrete social organization of the central African concern with the wholeness of the human being, suggesting, beyond it, an archetype. In spirit, it reflects the harmony of innocence and timeless order of the "Royaume d'Enfance." **"Domaine noir"** was published in 1963, the year Senghor also wrote the preface to *Négritude et humanisme,* the articles the volume contains being in a sense a record of his public pronouncements over more than a quarter of a century. The central theme running through the book is "the conquest of freedom"—his own, one feels, and his people's, a conquest whose several stages he recalls as "the recovery, affirmation and illustration of the collective personalities of the Black people, of 'Negritude.' " The "illustration" is manifest in all forms of culture, poetry, and political institutions alike. Consciously and carefully, in his *The Concept of Nation and the African View of Socialism,* Senghor defined "nation" in terms both of the archetype and of the political and social realities of Africa. The nation he distinguishes from a Barrèsian *patrie;* the *patrie* is the heritage transmitted by the ancestors, "a land, blood, a language or at least a dialect, mores, customs, folklore, art, a culture rooted in the soil and expressed in a race," precisely the concept often equated with nationalism. The nation is then the next higher circle in the African design: a "voluntary" creation or "restructuration" of the individuals formed by the *patrie* conceived on a larger scale in terms of the common virtues to which each *patrie* had attuned their emotions. The nation then, like the clan, is created anew each day in the "souls" of its members. The state is the means whereby the inner creation is in fact incarnated. Marx is then, as Senghor had noted when discussing the ideas in Teilhard de Chardin, turned upside down, and modern African socialism wedded to the "collective personality of the Black peoples, of 'Négritude.' " The "new Negro" and "new nation" is a new incarnation and conscious recreation of the African humanistic civilization in terms of the modern environment.

Over the years, Senghor tirelessly fulfilled his role as intellectual, within the design he had formulated for it: the task of the intellectual was to reiterate the black values "in their truth and excellence," engraving as it were, ever more deeply, the image of "virtues rediscovered," those virtues once obscured by the foreign conqueror. (pp. 384-87)

This is the realm of all culture, in relation to a civilization as such, and thereby, specific though it is, no culture need exclude another. As the nation transcends but does not negate the *patrie,* so culture transcends but does not negate a civilization. It is in his definition of the "virtues rediscovered" that Senghor comes full circle back to the "imaginary continent" within himself. To Négritude he attributes the African peasant's "mystical sense of the earth" which makes "the healthiest and strongest people" and the gift of emotion, "the royal domain of the Negro," which is also the key to the "realm of art and poetry," that ultimate aspiration of all culture which is to allow men "to produce works of beauty and to enjoy them." To the European he allots reason as against imagination for the African, discursive knowledge as against unitary vision, science as against art and the freedom attained by the black; a political freedom to be sure, but in part also the freedom acquired with the sense of his own creativity in the practice of his art. (p. 388)

No one more clearly than Senghor himself has diagnosed the mythical quality of a vision, poetic in essence, and created out of the very absence of the reality that engendered it: "Here he is, today's poet, grey in winter in a grey hotel room. How could he not think of the 'Royaume d'Enfance,' of the Promised Land of the future in the nothingness of the present time? How could he not sing 'Négritude arise'?" For Senghor, clearly, the black is the poet, not the political or the racial figure, and Africa the inner continent of his longing. The "continent of the imagination" bridged the present that negated it. For Senghor the political and the poetic vision were one; and he lived to see the unity of these visions in part realized through his own action. The potential contradictions and immediate practical incompatibilities within the dream have perhaps now become apparent; yet it would seem that a goal was set and a personal credo faithfully lived. "We lived," wrote the Guadeloupean poet Paul Niger, "on an unreal 'négritie' [negrity] built on the theories of sociologists and other scholars who study men behind plate-glass windows." This could not be the case with Senghor who, even if he renounced his role as spokesman for all Africa or Négritude, could still combine in the fine balance of his love of beauty, imagination, and concrete practical sense, in a time of violence, his total fidelity to his own inner universe and his dedication to a people, his, and yet linked to all humanity. (p. 390)

> *Germaine Brée, "Senghor's Africanism and the Francophone Mode," in* The Cry of Home: Cultural Nationalism and the Modern Writer, *edited by H. Ernest Lewald, The University of Tennessee Press, Knoxville, 1972, pp. 374-91.*

SYLVIA WASHINGTON BÂ

In his prefatory remarks to the appendix of **Nocturnes,** Senghor states his intention of writing first of all for his people. Yet what of these same illiterate "peasants" to whom his poetry remains inaccessible? He explains further the full import of his declaration: it is by reaching French-speaking Africans that he will best be able to reach the French and, ultimately, all men. His mission is to bear witness to what he believes to be his truth, a duty he has admirably fulfilled in many capacities. In fact, his mission is twofold. He must galvanize the forces of his own people so that they too may respond to the call of their spokesman. (p. 152)

The messianism of Senghor's poetry is the pivotal element that makes it "at the same time profoundly personal poetry and public poetry, a poetry in which the aspiration of his people, in which the generalized manifesto of new African consciousness are expressed." Not only does he foretell deliverance from political and cultural bondage, he also leaves no doubt as to the evangelistic role of his poetry, frequently using the literal translation of the word "gospel": good news. His sense of the moral excellence of his mission and his faith

in the efficacy of the poetic word in the realization of the future cause him to assume a vindicatory tone in affirming his role.

> Such my answer and my two-headed scepter:
> Lion's jaws and Sage's smile.

Force and wisdom: such are the black poet's talents and duties in regard to his own people. But Senghor's ultimate aim is the elaboration of the values of negritude and their participation in the "Civilization of the Universal," the panhuman convergence toward which mankind is tending. Before such a civilization can be realized, there remains a crucial issue to be reckoned with: the so-called crisis of western civilization. Not only must the black poet lead his own people to salvation; all poets are called upon to re-establish true humanistic values, to lead man back to himself. The poet's mission is redemption, the revival of hope by the prophecy of man's victory over brute force. The poet's tool is language. He alone can manipulate the magic of the creative power of the word, he alone can reveal the moral value of words that has been obscured by the function of utility. Chaka laments the fact that the white man arrived bringing civilization but also "the naked word." Senghor quotes Teilhard de Chardin on the subject: "The more the world becomes rationalized and mechanized, the more it needs 'poets' as the saviors and leaven of its personality."

That true human values have been stifled by the technological civilization of the west is the subject of much concern and discussion. Moralists decry the imbalance between technical perfection and moral disarray; men of religion note the despiritualization rampant in modern existence, both in the strict sense of organized religion and in the broad sense of human spiritual values. Surrounded by his Frankensteins, the contemporary western man is the victim of alienation from his humanity in much the same way that the black man has known alienation from society. By an ironic twist of history, the colonizer has brought upon himself the very fate to which he subjected the colonized and is victimized by the results of the very force in whose name he launched his undertaking: progress.

> It was the year of Discovery. From their eyes they spit yellow fire. And the waters of the rivers flowed with gold and sweat. The capitals were bursting with them. The naked men were reduced to slaves, and the parents sold their children for one guinea coin.
>
> Then it was the year of Reason. From their eyes they spit red fire. And hatred knotted men's necks in twisted ganglions, and the soldiers bathed in the mud of the blood. The executioners and the learned were decorated; they had found the way to kill a man twice.
>
> Then it will be the year of Technology. From their eyes they will spit white fire. The elements will separate and aggregate governed by mysterious attractions and repulsions. The animals' blood and the plants' sap will be but whey. The white men will be yellow, the yellow men white, all will be sterile.

Senghor's résumé-prophecy accurately depicts the devolution of the double process of alienation and the interaction of practical aims and means and their concomitant moral results. The politico-economic rationale of slavery and colonization nurtured avarice and hate, with its intellectual counterpart of racism, and the entire process culminated in the moral sterility of dehumanized technology. . . . It must be this atrophied, devitalized condition that accounts not only for the modern *taedium vitae* but also for the deplorable and shocking connection between progress, technology, and science and death and destruction, between material wealth and injustice and oppression. As Senghor has remarked, "Civilization" is not the exploits of outer space per se. If such exploits are devoid of human values and purposes, they will only contribute further to the "barbarism of civilized men." It is at this point that negritude transcends its narcissistic and combative aspects and becomes constructive. Senghor believes that the black man's culture should be recognized as real and valid as a matter of human justice, but primarily because the values of negritude can be instrumental in the reintegration of positive values into western civilization and the reorientation of contemporary man toward life and love. (pp. 153-56)

Before the west can be expected to welcome the values of negritude, it has a right to know exactly what the term embraces and the extent of its objective validity. . . . Senghor's definition of the concept as the sum of these cultural values is deceptively simple and is based on a certain assumption that is obviously valid in his own experience but that demands substantiation when applied universally and seemingly on the basis of color alone. Superficial or biased reading of Senghor's essays and poems can leave us with erroneous or contradictory impressions. Random reading of critical commentary on Senghor's writings tends to leave us in a quandary also. We may be faced with analyses based on any of several of Senghor's pronouncements on the subject, most of them quite profound and in a variety of contexts. Or, we may encounter critics who insist upon assessing literary merits by political criteria; appreciations too strongly governed by personal preferences and temperaments; or reviewers unequipped to understand the many facets of Senghor's formation, situation in history, and vocation as poet and statesman. A convenient method for evaluating negritude is the consideration of the two main elements that constitute it and under which all the themes, concepts, and connotations may be grouped. These two divisions are what may be described as (1) situational or historical negritude and (2) the more basic theory of essential negritude.

Historical negritude concerns generally the fact of being black in a white world, and specifically the twentieth century's awakening to that fact. The origins of racial prejudice are disputed, but the fact constitutes a historical reality responsible for the common heritage of all black men. If this heritage was not brought about initially because of color, it has been perpetuated on that basis and is at the heart of the contemporary black existence. Whatever sociological, cultural, or ideological expressions of black men are rooted in that heritage may be grouped under the descriptive tag of negritude. The twentieth-century black *évolué*'s awareness of his situation, which produced the contemporary search for identity and self-assertion, is the pivotal moment of negritude. The negritude movement, itself a product of history, is at the crossroads and must reckon with its heritage in terms of its future. (pp. 158-59)

Essential negritude as advanced by Senghor is a far more controversial concept, since the idea of a black African personality, a black specificity, is based on the explosive notion of race. This word is so highly charged in contemporary human relations that the slightest reference to it risks interpretation out of all proportion to reality. The Nigerian poet and playwright, Wole Soyinka, has countered with his now famous sally ridiculing the idea of a tiger's having to proclaim his tigritude. Jean Ghéhenno protests that he could no more believe in the values of negritude than in those of "whiteness": "The human spirit has no color." Their point is clear enough but is based on the sophism that avoids the affirmation of the supremacy of European values implicit in the refusal to recognize African culture. Ideally, the necessity of values' having to be specified as white or black should never exist, but in view of the division produced by history, it is rather naïve to expect the black man to vindicate his humanity without first vindicating that aspect of it that has been so discredited. . . . In a wry though not entirely unfounded remark, LeRoi Jones (Imamu A. Baraka) points out the folly of a hasty judgment on negritude: " . . . it is usually made to seem by European commentators like the crafts program of the Black Muslims." Before countering with the cry of "antiracist racism," we would do well to understand what Senghor means by race and how he links race-color with an avowed humanistic ideology. (p. 160)

The principal issue is one of definition, since connotation and usage often extend terms beyond their true meaning. In the very strictest sense, race is a matter of homogeneity: the continuity of a physical type. Race defines a physical community presenting an ensemble of common hereditary physical traits. The term that properly applies to a cultural community, which may be but most often is not biologically homogeneous, is "ethnic group." A purely historical phenomenon, this reality addresses itself to the socio-psychological aspect of a group, its psycho-cultural properties. (p. 161)

No discussion of race can overlook the fact that racial purity is a rare thing. Though history has somewhat obscured the fine details of racial components, it has left one aspect to assume the role of prime differentiating factor: pigmentation. For this reason, and especially in the case of the black man, the realities of *race, ethnic group,* and *culture* have come to designate one reality. Negritude defined as "the same reaction to the same events" among blacks throughout the world transcends the geographical factor in favor of the historical factor.

What happens to the claim of universal essential negritude in the instance of North and South American blacks centuries removed from their origins? Senghor takes this into account, recognizing that a different cultural milieu eventually exerts decisive influence, but notes that he is less struck by the permanence of physical traits among blacks of the Americas than by the permanence of characteristic psychic traits *in spite of* the new milieu. Though segregation may account for this permanence of traits to some extent, it is not the sole factor in view of the case of Latin American blacks who have known less absolute forms of segregation. The black diaspora poses the problem of the chicken and the egg: which came first? To what extent has perpetuating cultural values and attitudes served to maintain characteristic psychic traits and to what extent has the permanence of the black man's psycho-physiological make-up contributed to the perpetuation of his cultural expression?

Black American writers and intellectuals are divided in their views on the reality of race in regard to culture. Senghor had an ally in Langston Hughes whom he quotes as saying just after World War I: "We, the creators of the new generation, want to give expression to our *black personality* without shame or fear. . . ." . . . Some who object to Senghor's views on the permanence of racial traits do so on the basis of what they believe to be the implications of such views. They feel that the affirmation of such permanence is synonymous with a denial of their cultural "American-ness." There is a difference of emphasis that explains the divergence of views. Because of the separatist connotations of the idea of a black specificity and the American blacks' experience with separatist views, some are wary of such an attitude. They interpret Senghor's ideas as meaning that they should cultivate their "blackness" to the exclusion of their "American-ness." Others, among them many voices of the "new black youth" of America, champion the separatist notion, though their complete line of thinking would not be seconded by Senghor. (pp. 161-63)

[For] those who are unconvinced of the validity of essential negritude, Senghor has yet another angle, which is aesthetic or stylistic negritude. In his famous *Anthologie de la nouvelle poésie nègre et malgache de langue française,* he says: ". . . what makes the negritude of a poem is less the theme than the style, the emotional warmth that gives life to the words, that transmutes the *parole* into *verbe."* In his preface to this *Anthologie,* "Orphée noir," Sartre makes an observation which, despite his noble intentions and often brilliant insights, attests to some confusion on his part in regard to negritude. After quoting this same remark of Senghor's, Sartre says: "We could not be better advised that negritude is neither a state nor a definite ensemble of vices and virtues, of intellectual and moral qualities, but a certain affective attitude toward the world." Many, including Senghor himself, have seized upon the final phrase of this observation as the most succinct and accurate definition of essential negritude, yet no one has taken issue with Sartre on the rest of his statement in the light of Senghor's elaboration of the philosophy of negritude. (pp. 165-66)

Any consideration of essential negritude and its validity ultimately rests upon the validity of Senghor's analysis of black African culture as based on the philosophy of life forces. The unity of this culture must be established before its principles and values can be presumed to be transmitted and maintained throughout the black world. Dissenting voices among black Africans themselves, especially inhabitants of former British colonies, refute the very foundation of negritude, on the basis of the diversity of African personalities. These objections are not based solely on whatever formative influences the various colonial powers may have exerted on African ways of life; they refer to profound cultural differences that predate sustained contact with the west. They object to the notion of a "single archetypal African culture," which the Haitian writer Jacques Stéphen Alexis suggests is "an idealised portrait of Senghor's own local Serer culture." One of the most outstanding of African writers, the South African Ezekiel Mphahlele, is one of the most vociferous and derisive critics of Senghor's views, objecting to his "pretension to a mystical unified whole." Though Senghor's fervor in regard to negritude may smack of the mystical, this term would hardly be applicable to his views on the basic cultural unity of black Africa. "Despite these differences and contrasts, of which any serious student of African culture soon becomes aware, there are underlying similarities between cultures of neighboring African peoples and in the processes of culture change for sub-Saharan Africa as a whole. . . ." This situation poses no problem when we consider an obvious analogy: European civilization and its German, Spanish, French, Italian, etc.,

components. The individuality of each people sacrifices nothing to their general "European-ness"; " . . . serious inquiry does not hesitate to trace the mainstreams of the European heritage to their sources, nor to seek the common cultural ground on which Western men stand." (pp. 167-68)

One very noticeable problem which characterizes much of the adverse criticism of negritude is the unwillingness or inability of many commentators to go beyond a certain superficial approach to language and ideas. Only such a failing could account for the censure of a sort of popular folklorism when Senghor means culture as he has defined it. There is the same tendency to read traditionalism for moral tradition, retrogression for "moral rearmament," and racism for the cultivation of negritude, of which love is set forth as one of the primary virtues. This backfires when the commentators are faced with such Senghorian ideas as the opposition of European discursive reason and black African intuitive reason or the primacy of rhythm. Out of the context of his detailed analysis of black African culture according to his definition of culture, these ideas inevitably seem to be nothing more than infuriating corroborations of traditional, distorted views on black Africa. There can be no fruitful dialogue with Senghor until some commentators abandon their superficial approach to his ideas.

The most marked difference between Senghorian negritude and the ideology of younger militant poets is precisely the element and tone of militancy. Senghor is definitely of another generation, that of discovery and elaboration. This present generation finds Senghor's philosophy outmoded from various points of view. (pp. 169-70)

Senghor's love of France adds an ironic note to his campaign on behalf of black African culture. To condemn this affection is to lose sight of the fact of Senghor's and his generation's unique position in history. It was they who had to adjust to the realization that the education afforded them by assimilationist policy was at once a singular opportunity, an indispensable means of achievement, and a falsification of themselves. That Senghor was able to avail himself of the good in this situation and use it against the evil of the same situation, yielding to only a temporary bout with "antiracist racism" is no negligible achievement. The way in which negritude has been misunderstood and misinterpreted is rather forcefully demonstrated by the fact that the same ideology can be accused of racism and nonmilitancy, of reactionary views because Senghor hopes to build a future on moral force derived from the past. (p. 170)

The younger generation finds little "relevance" in Senghor's poetry. His dream of the kingdom of childhood is too divorced from the aspirations and realities of their Africa today to touch those actively involved in contemporary progress and turmoil. . . . [These] younger blacks are more for dynamic change than for continuity. They reproach Senghor for not living up to the tradition he professes to uphold: "In the African traditions which Senghor quotes incessantly, it is the bards who galvanize the warriors' energies. Toward what destinies is this writer trying to lead the African people by the grace of poetry?" Though Sartre proclaimed black poetry a revolutionary force by its very existence and Senghor deemed the First World Festival of Negro Arts "an undertaking much more revolutionary than the exploration of the cosmos," cultural revolution does not conform to the idea of revolution entertained by those who would have poetry *engagé.* There is another irony in the fact that Senghor's political commitment has interrupted his poetic vocation. It is generally true that there was more black African poetry published before independence than after and that the impetus supplied by that cultural means was instrumental in bringing about that independence. And it is true that all writing is a commitment.

In the current atmosphere of tension and showdown in places where the black struggle is at a white heat, the attitude of "action now" is understandable. . . . But such action, brought about by violence if need be, is still not the final solution. Progress cannot exist in a void and Senghor's cultural militancy seeks to provide the necessary framework for meaningful change, identity, and self-realization. (pp. 171-72)

There is some truth in the observation that Senghor's poetry has lost much of its actuality in relation to the Africa of today and the approach to her problems. What was revelation in 1945 is now history. The quarrel is not with the quality of Senghor's poetry as poetry but rather that today's world demands more than pure poetry. Senghor thinks differently: "Poetry is not prose. Poetry does not aim at efficacy; it *is,* by virtue of which it is efficacious, ripping out the soul and turning it inside out like tripes in the sun." But the idyllic world of his poetry seems to the younger poets a deformed image of the present instead of an inspirational view of the past. This aspect of Senghor's poetry and its counterpart in his political ideology pose a problem not only for younger Africans but also for some of his contemporaries who, for various reasons, cannot understand the value of a vision of the past in the elaboration of the future.

One of the most poignant examples of the inability to appreciate an idyllic past is the case of the South African Ezekiel Mphahlele, who finds that Senghor's poetry "reflects a defective poetic vision." . . . It is incontestable that Senghor's belief in the regenerative power of a "return to the sources" is possible because he had the grace of knowing a kingdom of childhood such as he describes and of fulfilling himself in the way he so ardently advocates to his fellow Africans. Negritude as a romantic myth can remain so for those who have no such past to which to relate or who can not sympathize with Senghor's brand of cultural militancy. Negritude is a myth for Senghor also, but in the etymological sense of the word: it is explanatory and fundamental, inspirational and operative. Since a golden age is part of every literary tradition, he feels that Africa is entitled to hers. (pp. 173-74)

The militant realists take issue with the idealized picture of purity and innocence that Senghor paints in his analyses and poetic images of black African society. Certainly he is far too intelligent to do so with intent to deceive the world and Africans themselves. It would seem rather that he assumes that the realities of poverty, ignorance, squalor, internecine rivalries, witchcraft, superstition, cannibalism, graft, greed, ambition, etc., are too well known to require emphasis, having already received their fair share of it. He prefers to outline the ideal in the hope—itself ideal—of judging what is best, although potential, in man and thereby realizing that potential. To the pragmatist, Senghor's way is a terribly roundabout, intellectualist way of helping Africans, Africa, and the black man in general. The conception of freedom differs greatly among men and strikingly so between Africans of former British and French colonies. The English-speaking African cannot understand the Gallic penchant for systematizing thought and actions into movements and "isms." His pragmatic view dispenses with cultural and intellectual luxuries

and attacks the problem at hand by the most direct, most efficient means. (pp. 174-75)

Prospective negritude is the final step in the long progression from narcissistic through combative and constructive negritude. Borrowing Gaston Berger's "philosophy of the distant future," which studies the future of the world in an effort to predict its evolution, Senghor situates negritude in the universal context that would be its fulfillment. The development and increasing complexity of the sciences and of communications, and the universal effects of wars and balance of power, inevitably bring continents, races, and nations into contact with one another. The exchange of ideas, goods, and techniques necessarily results from this contact, and tends to lead toward a planetary civilization whose only hope for survival will be in the symbiosis of all civilizations. According to Senghor, each civilization has cultivated only fragments of the total human reality; the ideal civilization of the twenty-first century, the "Civilization of the Universal," would welcome the positive values and virtues of each civilization in a symbiosis of "giving and receiving." "True culture is being firmly rooted and being uprooted. Firmly rooted in the native land, in one's spiritual heritage. But, being uprooted: open to the rain and the sun, to the enriching contributions of foreign civilizations."

A Wolof proverb says, "Man is the remedy of man." The black problem is a universal problem and black culture has ramifications throughout the world. Too often we choose to ignore very real parallels in underdevelopment. The Third World is certainly economically underdeveloped, but the Great Powers suffer from spiritual and moral underdevelopment no less debilitating. For these deficiencies, negritude proposes remedies in the form of humanizing virtues. "The 'Civilization of the twenty-first century' . . . will surely be *superindustrial,* that is, technological. It will be *humanism* or *barbarism,* depending on whether or not the peoples of the Third World, and among them the black peoples, will have brought to it their contributions."

During his most recent visit to the United States, Senghor challenged America to become the prototype of the civilization of the future:

> . . . you have all the necessary ingredients, it is you who can give it a truly universal dimension. Your population is composed of every major European and Asian ethnic group, but even more important, those from Africa as well. . . . Thus it is the Americas, more particularly the United States, which already anticipates the world of the twenty-first century and holds in its strong but faltering hands not only its own destiny, but the destiny of the entire world. For it is the destiny of America to summon negritude to its rightful place in the civilization of the twenty-first century.
>
> (pp. 179-80)

Sylvia Washington Bâ, in her The Concept of Negritude in the Poetry of Léopold Sédar Senghor, *Princeton University Press, 1973, 305 p.*

GERALD MOORE

[Léopold Sédar Senghor] is many things to many men. The points at which his mind or his life touch those of others are exceptionally various; as must be the case with any man who claims equal eminence as poet, scholar, and statesman. Among African presidents, Senghor shares this distinction with Agostinho Neto of Angola, a man for whom he had little political sympathy, and it must be said of both men that the policies they pursued in power are very much those we would expect from their poetry. Senghor's preoccupation with acknowledging an equal heritage from Africa and from Europe, the constant search in his poetry for the keynote of reconciliation, are the marks also of his astute but accommodating foreign policy, of his almost limitless collaboration with France. And his poetic claim to representative status, as the champion of his people, is matched by the skill with which he has dominated Senegalese political life for over twenty years. The revolutionary fire and passionate aspiration of Neto's poetry, by contrast, should also prepare us for the very different kind of struggle the Angolan people have had to undergo, and the very different political leadership they have enjoyed. . . . Both wrote like men who confidently expected to play a leading part in the affairs of their countries. It is even possible that Africa would have little time for a prominent poet who did not have such expectations.

This representative note is struck very early in Senghor's work, in these lines from **"The Return of the Prodigal Son"**:

> Tomorrow I take the way of Europe,
>   way of the ambassador
> In longing for my black country.

Exile, then, is seen neither as escapism nor as the search for a purely personal advantage, but as a duty and a sacrifice. It is no accident that Senghor is a Senegalese, for his career embodies the Senegalese dilemma. (pp. 17-18)

As both a beneficiary and a victim of the assimilationist educational system, Senghor felt its effects from the age of seven, or perhaps earlier, through the influence of an already *assimilé* father, a Catholic in a predominantly Moslem society, and a prosperous trader in a land of widespread poverty. The intention and the effect of the system was to distance the child step-by-step from his own culture and values, exposing him at the same time to the very real seductive power of French civilization, ranging from the tangible delights of red wine (a specially favoured import), good bread and *charcuterie* to the more rarefied ones of Voltaire's prose or Rousseau's libertarian sentiments. This alienation from oneself, coupled with the prolonged exile in France then necessary to any higher education, called forth the counter-assertion of negritude, but it was a counter-assertion made very much in the intellectual terms, as well as in the language of the conqueror. The ambivalence of Francophone African policies is one which lies also at the heart of negritude itself. Senghor is not only the leading theoretician of negritude, of the black personality and its unique qualities, but also one of the leading practitioners of those black policies which often tie Dakar, Abidjan and Libreville so intimately to France that they sometimes seem only a Métro ride from Paris, rather than so many thousands of miles on the map.

To recognize this ambivalence is not to belittle Senghor as a poet, but to prepare ourselves for an understanding of the conflicting materials out of which his poetry and his life have been built. It's more than fifty years since the young Senghor arrived in France; more than forty since his first poems and critical essays began to appear. His work contains within itself much of the tension, anguish, hope and striving which

characterized Senegalese and African experience during those same years.

Senghor was one of the first Africans to pursue a French academic education to a high level, and the first to complete his *agrégé*, the state qualification for teaching in senior schools. . . . In his boyhood he moved among the Serere farmers and fishermen of the district, listening to the tales of the poets and the old women about the ancient Africa which preceded the French conquest. . . . This was a period of his life which was to achieve great significance in retrospect, a period which he is constantly opposing to the velleities of 'assimilation', using it as a kind of touchstone of original virtue and sincerity; it is his 'kingdom of childhood'. Dominant in the memory of those years is the figure of his maternal uncle Tokô'Waly, who was his principal instructor in the traditional culture of the savannahs. . . . (pp. 21-2)

But from the age of seven Senghor began an intensive study of the French language. . . . In 1928 he sailed for France to continue his studies at the Lycée Louis-le-Grand and the Sorbonne in Paris. Here he was soon joined by Aimé Césaire, seven years his junior, and the two men began the long series of conversations and experiments which, as they saw it, prepared them for the task of 'giving a tongue to the black races'. Another acquaintance of this period was Léon Damas of French Guiana. None of these three men began to publish until the late 1930s; they had first to master the strange status of the 'assimilated' man living in a society to which he does not belong. We discover from Senghor, as later from Camara Laye, that the overwhelming impression of the star pupil from French Africa who won his way to Paris was one of isolation. Only in this new context did he discover the fallacy that had underlain his whole education: he was not and could never be a Frenchman. He had therefore to settle down and rediscover what it was to be an African. To this task he was able to bring all the intellectual curiosity, the mastery of language and the knowledge of literature which were the abiding and noble parts of the education he had been given. The supreme irony of 'assimilation' is that it has inadvertently contributed more than anything else to this process—the rediscovery of Africa. (pp. 22-3)

The style which Senghor made for himself actually owes little to the scornful whiplash of Césaire's poetry, or to the staccato lines and typographical tricks of Damas, inspired partly by the latter's reading of American poetry. But Césaire undoubtedly exercised a powerful and liberating influence on Senghor through his intellect and personality, an influence which Senghor has generously acknowledged in his memorable **"Letter to a Poet"**. . . . Curiously, despite the passionate warmth of this poem, Senghor casts Césaire very much in his own image; for it is the African poet who more habitually sings of 'Ancestors, Princes and Gods' and whose verse 'breathes like the night'. Césaire is far more the poet of blazing tropical noon, of volcanic menace and the dry crack of the tornado. (pp. 23-4)

With Césaire he began to develop the new literary programme of negritude, which demanded of its poets a strong verbal rhythm, a wealth of African allusions and a general exaltation of 'the African personality'. The true past of the black man must be rediscovered beneath the layers of colonial history, his culture vindicated, and his future prepared. Senghor alone, however, insisted upon the musical aspect of rhythm, even demanding that his poetry should be recited to the accompaniment of African instruments. Almost at once we find him creating, through the use of the long line, that rolling, deep-breathed sound which distinguishes all his verse. (pp. 24-5)

In *Chants d'Ombre* Senghor had already asserted not only his personal music but the major preoccupations which haunt his verse to this day. Chief among these is his insistence on communion with the dead, with the ancestors and defeated princes of his people, from whom his own education sought to isolate him. How far this is a poetic attitude, how far a deep conviction, it is impossible to say. Senghor, in any case, has expressed unforgettably the classical African view of the dead as the principal force controlling the living, benevolent but watchful. In a poem like **"In Memoriam"**, he invokes the dead from his lonely exile in Paris, seeking to draw strength from their company and example. . . . Here the dead serve as a bridge between Senghor and everything which his education has turned him away from. By mingling the names of the Seine, the river of Paris, with those of his homeland (Sine, Gambia, Saloum) he stresses the universality of their presence. Looking out from his attic window, he suddenly sees the blood of the French conquest filling the narrow streets; but he sees also the presence which can reconcile him with his strange white brothers. It is to the dead, or in other poems, to his mother, that he seeks to justify his present life, his present interests, his apparent immersion in the affairs of a Parisian savant. . . . (pp. 28-9)

This, then, is 'negritude upright'. With this key Senghor has unlocked his lips and sent forth a river of rich sombre melody. Yet as we read on into his second volume, *Hosties Noires* (*Black Wafers,* 1945), we do begin to wonder how far Senghor's negritude can be seen as embodying what Wole Soyinka has called a genuine 'self-apprehension', an untrammelled apprehension of himself as an African. Sometimes it seems to contain a suspiciously large element of apprehension in terms of the Other. It must be remembered that Senghor's early years in Paris coincided with those in which many white scholars, such as Maurice Delafosse, Georges Balandier and Marcel Griaule, were saying the same sort of things about black personality and civilization that Senghor was saying. Even Catholic racist writers like Charles Maurras were at least in agreement about the profound differences between white and black cultures, even if they went on to rationalize from this a hierarchy of values with France at the top. But the whole tendency of Senghor's mind is towards synthesis rather than separation. Having established the unique qualities of African cultures, his desire is not to hold them in isolation, but to pool them in what he calls 'The Civilization of the Universal'. This notion, derived in part from the biologist Teilhard de Chardin, regards human cultures as organic and evolutionary, with a tendency to combine themselves into new wholes.

It seems that Senghor's construct of 'La Civilization Négro-Africaine' (Black African Civilization), a construct made up essentially in exile, is built not only out of materials remembered from his childhood, but out of his reactions to such writers as those just mentioned. It is partly an argument with Europe, rather than a free, spontaneous expression; and perhaps this is inevitable, because Senghor's public life in these years was frequently one of argument. As a professor of French language and literature in the *lycées* of Tours and Paris, a position which he occupied from 1935 to 1940, the poet must have felt the continual need to assert his difference if he were not to sink entirely into the imposed role of a Black

Frenchman. Such an assertion, though humorously made, can be found in the poem, **"Que M'accompagnent Koras et Balafong" ("Let Koras and Balafong Accompany Me")**, written during those years. . . . (pp. 29-30)

But in *Hosties Noires* the poet's position has become still more ambivalent than that of the black shepherd of blond heads, for if Senghor was not obliged to remain in France after his graduation (he had not yet entered parliamentary politics), he carried his allegiance to the French part of his heritage still further by taking French citizenship and by volunteering to fight a war which many black intellectuals regarded as an irrelevance, except in so far as it might indirectly further African liberation. (pp. 30-1)

Senghor, who swiftly found himself a prisoner-of-war in German hands, could only mourn the thousands of Senegalese riflemen who fell on the battlefields of Europe, as others were later to fall in Indo-China and Algeria, fighting in what was now quite clearly the imperial interest of France. But, despite the warmth and compassion of these poems, perhaps he might have done better to tell the soldiers, as Léon Damas had already done, to 'go and invade Senegal!"

It is these anomalies which make much of the more public, less personal poetry of *Hosties Noires* difficult to read, and which culminate in the last stanzas of the closing poem, **"Prayer for Peace"**. After enumerating some of the worst colonial excesses of France and Europe, Senghor cries:

> Bless this people who have brought me Your
>   Good News, Lord, and opened my
>   heavy eyelids to the light of faith.
> They have opened my heart to knowledge of the
>   world, showing me the rainbow in the new
>   faces of my brothers.
>
> (p. 31)

Here, as elsewhere in *Hosties Noires,* Senghor's perpetual search for reconciliation has betrayed him; he appears before us with a paper dagger and an ingratiating smile. It is assimilation rather than negritude which triumphs in such writing.

His poetry is often at its best when he abandons the search for reconciliation and is content to register a single emotion without too much care for the consequences. The love poems of *Chants pour Naëtt (Songs for Naëtt)* (1949) have this quality of abandon and seem to derive a lot of their rhythmic energy from it. Senghor's verse here moves faster than usual and his imagery glows with an extraordinary warmth. . . . A different but equal satisfaction can be found in a poem like **"New York"** from *Ethiopiques* (1956). This achieves a completely acceptable stance of negritude by its sincere and illuminating opposition of downtown Manhattan and Harlem. The structure of this poem is extremely successful, with its explosive opening, its gradual mounting sense of dry sterility, its sudden transition to the refreshing warmth and smell of Harlem, and the splendid broad gesture which ends it. . . . A similar strength and wholeness are achieved when Senghor turns aside from his long love affair with France, from his obsession with being 'Ambassador of the Black Peoples', and plunges himself into communion with his childhood, with his native landscape, with the broad night of the savannah, with all that he associates with his ancestors. Here the poet has no need to justify or excuse anything. He is serene, and this serenity fills his verses with its quiet music. In such a mood Senghor's sincerity marks the page and he writes unforgettably. The following lines are taken from *Ethiopiques,* a volume in which too much space is devoted to lamentations of exile— and now it is exile *from* Europe that the poet is lamenting, exile from all that is symbolized by 'the Princess de Belfort' (a synonym for his second wife, a Norman aristocrat). But in this extract of his poem, **"Pour Khalam"**, Senghor breaks free from all that, and rediscovers his purest vein of introspection:

> I don't know when it was, I always confuse child-
>   hood with Eden
> As I mix up Death and Life—a bridge of kindness
>   joins them.
>
>   (pp. 32-4)

Notable also in **Ethiopiques** is the stronger drive of Senghor's rhythm, which now develops a shorter breath and a more regular fall. His poem **"L'Absente"** yearns for the coming of spring to the dry savannah and equates it with the long-predicted arrival of the Queen of Saba ('The Absent') from the East. Perhaps this Ethiopian figure symbolizes for him the integration of his Christian faith and his African identity, just as the rape of Ethiopia in 1935-6 symbolizes the continued spoliation of the continent. . . . (p. 34)

Here the more regular fall of the metre is countered by the forward rush of the poem. But turning from **Éthiopiques** to **Nocturnes** (1961), one is conscious of a certain slackening of energy. Nowhere is this more evident than in the poet's decision to republish the **Chants pour Naëtt,** originally issued in 1949 in honour of his black wife Ginette Eboué, and to suppress all mention of their original subject, Naëtt. The effect is to render the poems less compelling as the expression of a passionate lyrical urge.

Also, the five Elégies which follow the love-songs, and complete the volume, despite a sombre richness of sound, do occasionally collapse into unabashed nostalgia and escapism. . . . The tendency of these poems is more and more in divergence from the tendency of his actual life-style, for the Presidential Palace in Dakar represents a more drastic exile from the Kingdom of Childhood than even his Parisian exile did. The poetry has become compensation for the time and energy his public life now consumes.

The composition of the Elégies coincides with the years 1957 to 1959, when Senghor was becoming almost entirely absorbed in affairs of state, and when he was fighting vainly to arrest the deliberate balkanization of West Africa by the French government by means of the *loi cadre,* which encouraged the growth of petty 'independent' territories, relying heavily on French military and financial support. His success in dominating Senegalese political life for twenty years has been marred by his failure to achieve a wider association with his neighbours, even if one doubts whether the achievement of a greater federation would significantly have altered the conservative and pro-French bent of his foreign policy.

These twenty years of power, though rich in policy statements and refinements of his theoretical position, have been thin in poetry. But what poet has not found public life to be the enemy of the muse? The harvest of those years, at any rate, is represented by the thirty short poems published with his collected volume in 1973, as **"Lettres de l'Hivernage"**. The title can only be translated as **"Letters of the Rainy Season"**, since Senghor specifically tells us that, in his region, 'l'Hivernage' is not winter, but summer and the advent of au-

tumn. He now addresses Africa, not as a poet, but as a statesman. Hence, the quieter, more domestic tone of these poems, which no longer carry the burden of the writer's hopes, ambitions and concerns. They do not merely express escapism, as happened occasionally with the Elégies, but they are an escape by their very nature from the incessant anxiety and activity of statesmanship. . . . (pp. 34-6)

Senghor once defended himself from the charge of exoticism in a somewhat mannered essay, **"As the Manatees go to Drink at the Source"**. There he argued that he was writing primarily for an African audience, to whom such words as *kora, balafong, dyali* and *khalam* were familiar. If they were exotic to the French reader, that was not his concern. They were not in intention picturesque, but descriptive;

> For all is sign and sense at the same time for the African Negro; each being, each thing; but also the matter, the form, the colour, the smell and gesture and rhythm and tone and timbre: the colour of the lappa, the shape of the kora, the design of the bride's sandals, the steps and gestures of the dancer, the mask and so on.

Reading such passages, the suspicion grows that what Senghor is describing is the unifying faculty of the artist in man, not specifically in African man. The enemies of spontaneity and passion move amongst us all, and they do not always carry white masks. But Senghor's claim that he writes primarily for his people, although dismissed by Reed and Wake [see excerpt above], has perhaps been validated by events. When he began writing in Paris over forty years ago, it is probable that his readership, beyond the immediate circle of his friends, was largely French. But with the spread of literacy in French over those same years, with the public readings which are a feature of his life in Dakar, with the ascent of Senghor himself to a position of international fame, it seems likely that his poetry is now and will for many years remain among the best known in Africa. (pp. 36-7)

> *Gerald Moore, "Assimilation or Negritude," in his* Twelve African Writers, *Indiana University Press, 1980, pp. 17-38.*

JANICE SPLETH

The theory of Negritude had its beginnings in the 1930's when, as an attempt to define the distinctive features of the African personality, it was forged into a cultural complement to the growing nationalist movements in Africa. Léopold Sédar Senghor, who was later to serve as Senegal's first president and who has recently attracted international attention by becoming the first black member of the French Academy, was among those writers who were most directly involved in formulating the Negritude concept and in proclaiming its value both in his numerous essays and in his poetry. In the period since nationhood, however, both Senghor and the concept of Negritude have been the targets of extremely negative criticism, and some of that criticism has focused specifically on the way in which Senghor's attempts to characterize African culture and society seem to have drawn rather too overtly from the ideas of Romantic primitivism in general and the motif of the Noble Savage in particular. The principal objections here seem to be first that a racial theory based on such foundations merely confirms established stereotypes. Secondly, a literary myth constitutes a poor practical basis for solving the real problems of Africa today. Furthermore, there is some danger here that under the influence of primitivism the qualities of traditional precolonial society may be over-idealized. It would be virtually impossible to argue that Senghor's theories do not owe a great deal to Romanticism, and, indeed, we intend to show something of the extent of that debt. On the other hand, we would like to suggest that the very element that has attracted so much censure to Senghor's prose writings on race and culture can, in fact, be viewed as an especially compelling component of his poetry. (p. 112)

In a well-developed study of the history of primitivism in Romantic literature as it relates to the African people, Edna L. Steeves presents strong evidence for considering the concept of the Noble Savage as the legitimate ancestor of Negritude. Steeves does not look closely at Senghor's philosophy and interprets it rather broadly as a variation on the Afro-American theme: "Black is beautiful." An examination of the specifics of Senghor's thinking, however, only serves to confirm Steeves' findings. Although the Senegalese writer has articulated his ideas in detail on a number of occasions, the essay, **"Eléments constitutifs d'une civilisation d'inspiration négro-africaine"** . . . , provides an especially well organized and coherent point of reference for the study of his concept of the African personality and culture. He begins, in fact, with a depiction of African climatic conditions in order to give Negritude a scientific basis derived from environmental determinism. His description, however, has a number of points in common with the classical notion of the Golden Age. He reminds us, for example, that Africa is called the "cradle of civilization," and he claims that the soil and weather are extraordinarily suitable to the needs of cultivation, even under the simplest of technologies. Because the African is generally a farmer, he is closer to nature than those who live in an industrialized urban society. It is, in part, this closeness to nature that endows the African with an instinctive spirituality, a special sensitivity to cosmological forces. Senghor emphasizes the African sense of family and community and also points out that private property, which Rousseau considered the root of civilization's evils, is virtually non-existent in traditional Africa. In a section on ethics, [Senghor] implies that the pagan African may be more virtuous than the European professing Christianity inasmuch as the former practices his code of behavior while the latter merely recites his catechism. Even from this brief overview, Senghor's portrait of the African and his society can be considered a revival of the Noble Savage concept. While what he says about Africa is often accurate, his idealized vision of the continent and its people is also highly selective and certainly invites the criticism it has received. (pp. 113-14)

The affinities existing between the theory of Negritude and the exotic motifs of the Noble Savage and the Golden Age are equally visible in the poetry of Negritude, but the romantic echoes that have tended to place the validity of Senghor's social theories in question are considerably more palatable in the poems. In fact, they penetrate nearly every aspect of his verse—setting, characters, and subject matter—and, somewhat paradoxically, what has seemed so difficult to accept as the basis of a scientific premise endows the literary works with exceptional emotional power. . . . [These] time-honored exotic concepts constitute an important source of Senghor's poetic language and ideas and serve furthermore to enhance his poetry by appealing to a universal desire to escape from the here and now into a better, simpler place and time.

Crucial to Senghor's view of the universe is his image of the kingdom of childhood. It becomes not merely the object of his personal nostalgia, but also the symbol of precolonial Africa as it existed before its contamination by Western civilization. In this sense, his description of childhood becomes a form of chronological primitivism drawing liberally from the conventions related to both Eden and the Golden Age. The association between Paradise and childhood in Senghor's work is an explicit one with the poet telling us at one point that he has always confused the two. In the poem **"Que m'accompagnent kôras et balafong,"** he further cements the relationship by drawing from the Biblical description of Eden as a source for his description of his own childhood. . . . He seems to recall here the third chapter of Genesis where God stations an angel with a flashing sword at the gate of paradise. There is of course a natural association between innocence and childhood, but innocence was also an essential attribute of Eden before the fall. By extension, it even comes to characterize Senghor's depiction of traditional Africa as if, as one critic phrases it, "the black Adam and Eve had never sinned and had always lived in the black paradise in all innocence." In this same poem, we also find passages reminiscent of the myth of the Golden Age. Except for the use of African names, the pastoral setting of these verses with their flower-bedecked dancers and the distant notes of a flute might well have been inspired by some classical poet; indeed, we should not forget that Senghor was a serious student of both Latin and Greek and often employs expressions that reflect those studies. In **"Joal,"** for example, the descriptions of processions, palms, triumphal arches, and nubile dancers could have been drawn from the pages of Homer. Since our image of the Golden Age is primarily a classical image, such borrowings become significant with respect to our discussion of chronological primitivism, for it is difficult, especially with Senghor's constant reiteration of the term "paradise," not to perceive the connotations inherent in Senghor's choice of vocabulary. In this respect, he resembles the engravers who touched up the sketches made during the South Sea voyages of Captain Cook in order to make them appear more classical in character, more in keeping, that is, with their own conventions of the Golden Age with which they associated these newly discovered island paradises. Likewise, the exoticism we find in Senghor's description of Africa is not exclusively tropical but has its origins as well in man's longing for some perfect state now lost to him forever. It is perhaps this association more than realistic geographical details that renders Senghor's kingdom of childhood so inviting for the general reader, who finds in these very unfamiliar surroundings the reflection of his own dreams.

Because Senghor's memories of Africa and childhood, with their Edenic connotations, are so uniformly favorable and infused with nostalgia, the resulting depiction of the land and the people emerges as almost entirely pleasurable and appealing, a tropical setting that is truly paradise. Some of his most effective poems are those that take this setting as a backdrop for romance. The series of short poems dedicated to the poet's first wife under the title **Chants pour Naëtt** (1949) and later reissued as **Chants pour Signare** in the collection **Nocturnes** (1961) has been cited by several critics as being among his most enduring works, and much of what can be said about these verses can also be said of the little series in the same vein entitled **"D'Autres chants"** published in **Ethiopiques** (1956). Most of these poems sing the poet's love for a woman who is generally depicted against an African setting. Like the childhood kingdom, she too is an idealization. . . . The woman in the poems might easily have been patterned after the Indian maidens of the 18th- and 19th-century novels. Like her predecessors, she is equated with the purity which can only be bestowed on those who have avoided the contamination of civilization; she is variously a "pure flower," the "Virgin of black silk," and the "angel of the prodigal son." A relatively passive creature, she rarely speaks and seems to serve for the most part as just one more charming attribute of the exotic decor. Senghor has, in fact, been criticized for his failure to develop realistic portraits of African women. . . . In a sense, however, Senghor's love affair is as much with the land and the culture incarnated by the woman as with the woman herself, and, thus, the idealization is appropriate in this context, with the association between the woman and Africa defining the symbolic nature of her role. Furthermore, Senghor's depiction of his feelings for this truly exotic creature endowed with all the mystery and fascination of his beloved Africa is effective and capable of involving the reader's emotions as evidenced by the reactions of the critics.

But what of the actual "noble savage" himself? Part of the glamour of the Noble Savage concept lies in the sentiments aroused by the acts of a man who pits his strength against the forces of nature without the aid of civilization and its technologies. . . . In **"L'Homme et la Bête,"** for example, he has his protagonist engaged in fierce combat against a powerful, unknown beast. In **"Congo,"** the narrator becomes a native boatman struggling against the rapids of the mighty river. Both **"Teddungal"** and **"Messages"** tell of perilous journeys through jungle and desert as does another poem from about the same period, **"Chant de l'initié."** Each of these works serves in some way as a vehicle for the poet's ideas, but, by couching those ideas within the framework of the confrontation between man and nature, Senghor stirs emotions in the reader akin to those aroused by the works of Hemingway, whose characters, too, are often close relatives of the Noble Savage.

In addition to its influence on the setting of the poems and on the way Senghor depicts his central figures, the concept of the Noble Savage underlies the essential message of the poems, for what is afterall the objective in these works if not to confer nobility on the so-called "savage," to point out the ways in which the African, so long patronized by the colonial master, has indeed much to offer. It is, in fact, pretty clear that Senghor feels Africa's gifts may well constitute the salvation of mankind in an era that has lost the humanity it knew in a pre-technological age. Such is his message throughout the collection of war poems entitled *Hosties noires* (1948) where the black soldiers come to incarnate the principle of life in the face of the European machines of death. . . . He speaks of them explicitly as "noble warriors" and renders them so excessively virtuous that one critic has asserted rather cynically that, for Senghor, "all black soldiers are strong and loyal." Perhaps the most dramatic depiction of the soldiers' nobility occurs in the poem, **"Désespoir d'un volontaire libre."** Based on a true story, it describes the suicide of a Senegalese rifleman for whom military service emerges as merely another chapter in a long history of exploitation. Senghor transforms the act into a manifestation of that African sense of honor which he treats at length in his writing on traditional ethics.

In addition to its use in *Hosties noires,* the ideological impli-

cations of the Noble Savage motif, with its implied criticism of civilization and tacit praise for man in his "natural" state, appear elsewhere in various poems where African and European ideas are brought into confrontation. **"Messages,"** a poem from *Chants d'ombres* (1945), finds the narrator assuming the role of a warrior called, through time and space, to the seat of the Ancestors to be lectured on the ills suffered by his people under colonial domination and to be reminded of the values of his own cultural heritage. Needless to say, "civilization" does not stand up well in the comparison. Another example of the juxtaposition of African and Occidental can be seen in the series of poems entitled **"Epîtres à la Princesse,"** published in *Ethiopiques* (1956). In verses which recount the courtship of a nordic princess by an African ambassador, the poet foretells the eventual self-destruction of the West in an atomic holocaust. The envoy offers his beloved a chance to escape the cataclysm by inviting her to join him in his own land, which he characterizes as technologically simpler, but more in tune with the rhythms of nature and life. . . . This work differs from our previous example in that it does not specifically represent a charge against colonialism, but rather it joins the voice of the poet with that of others concerned that modern technology has surpassed our ability to control it. The central theme of the poem, which counters the possibility of a nuclear disaster with a flight into primitivism, is one that occurs elsewhere in contemporary literature as well as in the real-life movements of the survivalists. Throughout history, the literature of the Noble Savage has often served to attack contemporary values: Montaigne's cannibals, for example, enabled the writer to criticize the religious and political practices of the 16th century, and Voltaire's Huron in *L'Ingénu* allowed his creator to call into question the prevailing customs of the 18th century. Indeed, as the issue of nuclear war attracts increasing concern, the Noble Savage may be due for a revival in our own time.

It is easy to see why critics—and especially African critics—have found the close relationship between Negritude and Romantic primitivism objectionable when the two are wedded together and offered up as a racial theory. The literary amalgam, however, deserves a better reception. The bond Senghor so effectively establishes between his own ideal state and that of Eden or the Golden Age permits us to see in the poet's longing for his childhood kingdom a desire common to all men and engages our imagination. The notion of a tropical paradise peopled with pure maidens and heroic warriors also has a universal fascination that surges from the very depths of our subconscious. The dichotomy between nature and progress that lies at the heart of Senghor's poetry has a highly reputable literary heritage, and although it is intended to serve as a vehicle for the concept of Negritude, it manages at certain points to transcend that concept and to give these works broader philosophical implications. While the view of Africa in Senghor's poems, in spite of the undeniable cultural insights it offers, is far from realistic and is undoubtedly not intended to be, it is profoundly poetic. (pp. 115-20)

Janice Spleth, "Senghor and the Concept of the Noble Savage: A Defense," in French Literature Series, *Vol. XIII, 1986, pp. 112-21.*

Elizabeth Smart

1913-1986

Canadian novelist, poet, memoirist, and essayist.

Smart earned significant critical attention in North America following the 1975 republication of her first novel, *By Grand Central Station I Sat Down and Wept* (1945), an intense, self-analytical work that prompted comparison to the confessional writings of Sylvia Plath and Anne Sexton. Stylistically influenced by William Blake and such metaphysical poets as John Donne and George Herbert, Smart's fiction combines verse, prose, and autobiographical elements to depict the spiritual exaltation and collapse that results from a woman's sexuality and artistic expression. Of Smart's work Anne Stevenson noted: "A piercing note of sexual insult prevails throughout, together with a cry of pain, a smile of pity, a declaration of honesty and pride, and a challenge to the world to gainsay her. Miss Smart's books are more public manifestos in a private language than they are 'true confessions.' "

Born into an affluent family in Ottawa, Ontario, Smart rebelled against the restrictions that were placed upon women of her social class and pursued a bohemian lifestyle in England, the United States, and Mexico. Upon publication of *By Grand Central Station I Sat Down and Wept,* Smart's mother, scandalized by the novel's content, influenced Canadian Prime Minister William Lyon Mackenzie King to ban its sale, and the work remained largely unnoticed until its 1975 reissue. *By Grand Central Station I Sat Down and Wept* closely parallels the early years of Smart's love affair with English poet George Barker, as the unnamed female narrator achieves transcendence through her romance with a married man during the 1940s only to face reality when he abandons her and their unborn child. Although some critics found the novel pretentious and self-indulgent, others praised Smart's ability to integrate intensely lyrical prose with unsentimentalized personal experience and biblical texts to express the spiritual quality of both sexual and artistic love. Michael Brian Oliver commented: "[This] little book is a triumph of style. Miss Smart's energy, virtuosity, and vision are truly overwhelming. *By Grand Central Station* not only speaks but actually clarifies—once and for all—the language of love which nobody understands." *The Assumption of the Rogues and Rascals* (1978), a sequel to *By Grand Central Station I Sat Down and Wept,* details the difficulties that the protagonist encounters as a single parent and artist living among the "rogues and rascals" of the London literary community. Written over the previous thirty years, during which Smart raised the four children she bore by Barker, *The Assumption of the Rogues and Rascals* departs thematically from her earlier novel in its rejection of romantic love and its acceptance of painful experience as the primary vehicle for self-discovery.

In addition to her novels, Smart published works in other genres. *A Bonus* (1977) features poetry written between the mid-1940s and the mid-1970s. *In the Meantime* (1985) includes an early novella, *Dig a Grave and Let Us Bury Our Mother,* along with autobiographical essays and verse composed during the late 1970s. The posthumously published *Necessary Secrets: The Journals of Elizabeth Smart* (1986)

chronicles Smart's personal and artistic life during the years prior to the publication of *By Grand Central Station I Sat Down and Wept.* Alice Van Wart observed: "[These] journals are the private record of the heart of a woman, a woman who never overtly rejects the standards and expectations placed upon her but quietly begins to construct her own personal values. Rather than accept abstract ideologies or material ambitions, she searches for the vital connections she believes could be found only in love, art, and the natural world."

(See also *Contemporary Authors,* Vols. 81-84, Vol. 118 [obituary].)

ADELE FREEDMAN

[Sometimes] a book falls into neglect almost as soon as it is written and lies there passively like Sleeping Beauty awaiting resuscitation. One of these is a slim volume with a fat title written by Elizabeth Smart, a Canadian now resident in England: *By Grand Central Station I Sat Down and Wept.*

This book was completed in 1941, published in London in

1945, reprinted with an incandescent introduction by Brigid Brophy in 1966—and issued for the first time in North America in 1975 with the modest tag of "major fiction discovery."

Why *Grand Central Station* took 30 years in reaching our shores is not only a mystery, it is an embarrassment. No doubt its publication at this time owes much to the feminist spirit hovering over publishing houses, and rightly so. Although Brophy sets Smart in company with Genet, Baudelaire, Ovid and King Solomon, it is precisely Smart's difference from these men, namely her sex, that makes this book special.

Smart's narrator sits down to cry by Grand Central Station for the same reason that women have been weeping for centuries. Her affair with a married man has ended and she is awaiting the birth of a baby alone. But what makes her experience noteworthy is both the way she expresses it—in lush biblical cadences and a feeling for imagery that is positively Elizabethan—and what she emblazons on her tightly textured manifesto like a 20th century armed Venus: Love is as strong as death.

The affair Smart describes is set against the backdrop of the Second World War and the two events are so closely fused as to cast a welcome feminist glow on that incorrigible eternal couple, love and war. . . . [Spoken] by a woman the images of blood and water that course through centuries of literature take on a personal, biological dimension necessarily denied male writing.

Smart's book is drenched in uterine imagery. At first it prefigures disaster. . . . But once the narrator has worked through the guilt she feels on account of her lover's wife whose heart she breaks "like a robin's egg," the blood and water are transfigured by love into oceans of fulfillment and largesses. . . .

The woman's womb enlarges to include, at least potentially, the entire world within its sphere. . . .

But the embattled world she is anxious to comfort refuses to be incorporated into the perfect circle of love. Smart centers her woman's rejection by society around a visit to the narrator's (and her own) home, Ottawa. Coming back pregnant from California after being separated from her lover, she hopes to find understanding and support in a country which has not hardened into ten cent tradition, where there is "a waiting unself-conscious as the unborn's, for future history to be performed upon it." But even in Canada love is covered over with the thickest blanket of patriotism and the placid acceptance of the death of soldiers. . . .

Smart's woman is left shouting her defiance without a sympathetic hearing and you can sense in the stridency of her promise to "bring forth new worlds in underground shelters while the bombs are dropping above" and her divine determination to "put the whole untidy world into a nest" the final rally of love before it is murdered.

The war ends. The woman's lover returns to his wife. The woman herself is a war casualty who waits for a last minute reprieve "like an egg for the 21st day." In *Grand Central Station* the full horror of life without passion comes alive as fully as the narrator's magnificent vision of love's potency. If you want to see real death, she says, just look around you at the dollar worshippers, the status seekers. Mr. and Mrs. Middle America, the smug pragmatists who make the world go round. Smart reserves her wickedest satire for these slouching beasts who survived the war to create a loveless void.

Grand Central Station is a very special book. In its message, intensity, unity, structure, psychology—in everything, to cut this paean short, that makes a piece of writing memorable and meaningful—it is uncompromising. How reassuring it would have been if Smart had won the war. Under the circumstances, however, it is at least good to be able to report: Smart lives! (p. 37)

Adele Freedman, "Vibrant Sleeper," in The Canadian Forum, *Vol. LVI, No. 660, April, 1976, pp. 36-7.*

ANITA KRUMINS

"No morbid adolescent ever clutched toward melodramatic conclusion so wildly," says the nameless female "I" who wept by Grand Central Station (and in other places). This is a rare moment of insight on the part of the narrator; it is also true. Feverishly and self-indulgently, our "heroine" describes the pain of love with metaphors made of metaphors. In true adolescent fashion, she centers the entire world upon herself; she does not give all for love; her love is all. Squeezed in among the already crowded tropes is an allusive framework which is astonishing both in its scope and in its audacity, as the universal is forced to serve the trivial. Had the song "Teen Angel" existed when this "hymn to love" was composed, a more appropriate source for allusion would have been available. . . .

[*By Grand Central Station I Sat Down and Wept*] is not really about love, but about the UNEQUALLED AGONY thrust on a soul of superior sensitivity (who is the unmarried third of a love triangle) by a world which envies the "lineaments of gratified desire."

The entire work is one long writhing. Arrests are made and throats are cut, but one becomes so numbed by the excruciation of constant torment that one can only experience events intellectually and with growing suspicion. One watches the weeper, but never weeps oneself. More than that, one seeks respite in finding comedy where none exists. (p. 85)

What disturbs me most about this work is its celebration of weakness, its glorification of a succumbing to misery, its cheapening of human suffering and emotion with mawkish self-pity. . . . [The heroine's] sanity is "besieged" and the imagery of sharp-teethed animals is used to enunciate her own ferocity toward herself. "Fear," for instance, is a "terrible fox at my vitals under my tunic of behaviour." Alone in a cheap hotel room, she is frustrated:

> I am over-run, jungled in my bed, I am infested with a menagerie of desires: my heart is eaten by a dove, a cat scrambles in the cave of my sex, hounds in my head obey a whip-master who cries nothing by havoc as the hours test my endurance with an accumulation of tortures.

As a description of experience, one cannot argue that this communicates a certain stark urgency, but one can dispute the beauty of lolling in this lonely bed all day so the jungle feeling won't go away.

She justifies her self-flagellation by calling it fate. . . . Love is her only strength. . . . Her lover is her "entire goal." To her lover she says of herself: "I am not the ease, but the end" (he does not, apparently, agree). The world is going to war, and of the newspaper she says: "It is my worst antagonist for most often it won him away." "Why," she asks, "should even ten centuries of the world's woe lessen the fact that I love."

With her lover gone back to his wife (forsaking Love for Pity), she goes "whoring after oblivion." The distillation of philosophy she says is: "If you can't Take It, Get Out." Can she take it? "I can't take it," she says, "so I lie on the hotel bed dissolving into chemicals." She imagines her lover with his wife, and what she resents is that "It is *her* tears he feels trickling over his breast each night." This is obviously not a strange course for her jealousy to take. (pp. 86-7)

She has no strength within herself and for herself. She has not even a healthy acceptance of her own sex. . . . There is no meaning in her life without this man who, having left her pregnant, refers to her martyrdom as "minor."

Her struggles to free herself are indeed small:

> I will not think of the thing now. I have no time.
> When I have washed my stockings I will. When I
> have sewn on a button I will. When I have written
> a letter I will.

Obviously we are meant to think of Scarlett O'Hara's "I'll think about that tomorrow," but what a difference between the two! Scarlett builds a business; the weeper sews on a button. There is no time for a career when a-laying in bed a-weeping. Passion is everything. (p. 87)

She is intrigued by her own suffering and relishes its continuance. . . . Her lover seems superfluous except as a catalyst for her self-consideration; she exhibits very little actual feeling for him as a person. . . . She is "dying for love," going toward the "one river" that "waits" and "lusts" for her. The rest of the world is interested in war and lace doilies (not necessarily in that order); it is envious of her beautiful love; it is a world which prefers "corncobs to the genitals of the male." Better a corncob than such total and willing annihilation of body, spirit and mind. (p. 88)

Anita Krumins, "A Paean to Pain," in WAVES, *Vol. 4, No. 3, Spring-Summer, 1976, pp. 85-8.*

JEREMY TREGLOWN

This week's Corny Rhetoric And Pretentiousness awards have been decided as follows:

Most Rhetorical Question: Elizabeth Smart, for 'Thence cometh the catatonic?' jointly with 'Is it reprehensible alchemy to pleasure yourself with inevitable cataclysm?' Least Vivid Simile: Elizabeth Smart, for 'Night has fallen, comfortably patterned like pain'. Softest Cliché: Elizabeth Smart, for 'the terrible nature of the naked truth, Least Pithy Epigram: Elizabeth Smart, for 'the price of careless rapture is a twisted history chronicled by envy'.

In future, the CRAP awards will include a new category, Most Obscure Title. Meanwhile, Ms Smart also walked off with the vocabulary competition prize. Challenged to produce the shortest sentence including the words *ready, forgive, even, mistletoe, miseries, bright-eyed, underground* and *activities,* she came up with this winning formulation: 'Be ready to for-

give, even if her mistletoe miseries are bright-eyed with underground activities.'

In their citation, the judges said they yielded to anyone in their admiration for this author and regretted that they were not allowed to make a retrospective award for over-ratedness to her earlier *By Grand Central Station I Sat Down and Wept.* In *The Assumption of the Rogues and Rascals* they detected an (if anything) increased self-indulgence, noting the failure to realise any characters other than the narrator, and a proneness to embarrassing gestures of love towards unimportant objects . . . gestures which, it was felt, devalued the similar affection the narrator claims for the human rogues and rascals of her title. They were not convinced that her book justified the importance attached in it to drink and Celtic romanticism as alternatives to sober Anglo-Saxon reason, and felt that indeed an argument could be made for saying that the narrator herself embodies the worst consequences of her enthusiasms. In conclusion, recalling 'Niagra', 'annointed' and 'lanscape' in the recent reprint of *By Grand Central Station,* they observed that Ms Smart's spelling and/or proof-reading showed little improvement, citing *'Quia amore langeo'* as a memorable example of pretentious misquotation.

Jeremy Treglown, "With Nobs On," in New Statesman, *Vol. 95, No. 2451, March 10, 1978, p. 330.*

ANNE STEVENSON

[There is] a tradition of personal confession in writing which, though it has its own integrity, is not art but journalism. Confessions of this nature—whether in poetry or prose—are in some cases more popular in our own time than "art" because we want so much to break down social and cultural conventions in order to get at the "truth". This is the tradition to which Elizabeth Smart belongs.

The Assumption of the Rogues & Rascals and the earlier *By Grand Central Station I Sat Down and Wept* are not public or private forms of art at all, but urgent forms of self-analysis and therapy. More than this, they are flagrant presentations of the naked self. They are also calls to arms. A piercing note of sexual insult prevails throughout, together with a cry of pain, a smile of pity, a declaration of honesty and pride, and a challenge to the world to gainsay her. Miss Smart's books are more public manifestos in a private language than they are "true confessions". When you finish *The Assumption of the Rogues & Rascals* you think not "what a marvellous book" but "what a splendid woman"—or, if you disapprove of Miss Smart, "what a bore".

Indeed, *The Assumption of the Rogues & Rascals* leaves you with the impression that, while you know very little about the particulars of the author's experience, you know a great deal about her, and maybe about yourself too. A kind of intimacy has been willy-nilly established through her relation of a skeletal series of events. *By Grand Central Station* . . . left the author deserted by her lover, weeping on her own in the middle of New York City. *The Assumption of the Rogues & Rascals* takes place in post-war London where the author has to work in an office to support herself and her four children. The rogues and rascals are the habitués of the Chelsea streets and Soho pubs among whom Miss Smart moves, finding consolation, sympathy, and even love in the company of these emotional cripples whose conversation about drink, money and sorrow contrasts agreeably with the respectability of the successful half of the world against which Miss Smart invariably finds herself pitted.

There is more fury than humour in this story, as there is more feeling than art in its telling. Melodramatic overwriting suits the style of the book:

> Cowering before the blow of life, how can she open to accept the remedy? How can the engine of regeneration ever work? . . . That she should *need* to beg from the day! To insist on pity where there's the roar of love!

Passion, however, yields to pity (not self-pity—there is little of that) when Miss Smart tears "aside the veils that cover other people's pain". A publican's wife, a poor woman deserted by her husband, Doris who sells sweets, a dead father, a forgotten Canadian who brings back memories of childhood: these figures do not so much come to life as bestow life (or hope, or courage) on the author during her struggle upwards towards the light with her "burden" of children on her back. There is little about the children themselves, except as they represent the "load" that she "had to get through." . . . But there is a lot of unsqueamish, frank exhortation and advice in this book—to herself as a writer and to similarly situated readers. Miss Smart finishes with intimations of happiness and bursts of resolute self-knowledge. . . .

> Anne Stevenson, "Reeling and Writing," in The Times Literary Supplement, No. 3963, March 10, 1978, p. 273.

MICHAEL BRIAN OLIVER

In 1945 Elizabeth Smart, who was at that time a young Canadian exile, published a book called *By Grand Central Station I Sat Down And Wept*. . . . *By Grand Central Station* was met with a few surprised, confused, but favourable notices, and as the years went by it gradually became an underground classic in England, a rare book appreciated by a cult of readers who were able to attune themselves to the intense, personal vision presented by the obviously gifted young writer. The fact that during all this time Miss Smart published no further books naturally served to increase the literary and spiritual value of her singular masterpiece.

Sadly though, Elizabeth Smart's only opus remained almost totally unknown in Canada and the United States until 1975 when it was reissued. . . . Even then few North American journals noticed it, although it had received rave reviews in England when it was first reissued . . . in 1966. . . . No doubt the main reason the journals missed it is their inherent bias against paperback reprints. To this day there are probably some people actually professing to teach Canadian Literature who have never heard of *By Grand Central Station I Sat Down And Wept*, even though Elizabeth Smart was born and grew up in Canada and finished writing her book on the coast of British Columbia just a few miles from where Malcolm Lowry was simultaneously finishing *Under the Volcano*. . . . It is deplorable that Canadian readers have so long paid tribute to Lowry, the exile among us, yet so long been ignorant of Elizabeth Smart who chose, for reasons at least partly cultural, to exile herself to Britain and has stayed there for more than thirty years especially when we realize that her literary accomplishment is even more unusual than Lowry's. This essay is an attempt to correct that very unfortunate oversight by bringing Canadian readers up to date on Eliza-

beth Smart and by offering a reading of *By Grand Central Station,* in recognition.

During 1977 many things happened to Elizabeth Smart in the cultural mass media, and most of these things were calculated to make her a celebrity. As I write this she is becoming famous at last, a found literary treasure. . . . The dust jacket of [*By Grand Central Station*] suggests the ultimate reason for Miss Smart's sudden, burgeoning popularity. There on the cover the reader can see a cloudy black and white photograph, taken by a street photographer in New York during the war, showing Elizabeth Smart and George Barker, dressed à la 1940s, hurrying along the sidewalk into destiny. In other words, Elizabeth Smart is now being promoted by the media—women's magazines, British TV, *et cetera*—as a Romantic Lady Recluse with hints of Tragedy in her past. Unfortunately all this publicity misses the point, a fact that Miss Smart is painfully aware of personally. Instead of ignoring her, readers are now recognizing her for the wrong reason, paying too much attention to her life and not enough attention to her art.

Such a mistake is understandable, if not forgivable. . . . [Her] art is poetry—not fiction—and her subject is herself. It is no wonder both England and America want to make her a star. Still it is Miss Smart's writing that readers should recognize first and foremost.

I have carefully avoided calling *By Grand Central Station* a novel, because it isn't one, really. Similarly her new book, *Assumptions Of The Rogues And Rascals,* is written in what she calls "concentrated prose." The difference between this and the familiar term "poetic prose" is simply, but significantly, the difference between metaphor and simile: poetic prose is only *like* poetry, whereas concentrated prose *is* poetry—a new understanding of the word, an extension of the usage, but still poetry. Elizabeth Smart is an experimental and original poet, and *By Grand Central Station* is an extensive and very special poem. This is not a claim I make solely on Miss Smart's own definition of her work; the book itself exhibits every quality known to poetry. From beginning to end it is dramatically lyrical, deeply metaphoric and allusive, and far too tense thematically to be read with any normal regard to the fictional conventions of narrative, scene, and characterization. Elizabeth Smart can do in ten pages what it would have taken Tolstoy a hundred pages to approximate.

Before turning to the text though, I should briefly describe *By Grand Central Station* and indicate where it stands in relation to the main body of twentieth century literature. First, there is a narrative, but it is a mythical one: a passionate and intelligent young woman loves a complex older man who is already married to a longsuffering wife. The theme is love, and the tone is both joyous and elegiac, but there is nothing melodramatic or sentimental about the book. Nor is it romantic, even though the setting might be called American Wartime. . . . [The] characters are concerned with eternity, not America. The point of view is purely subjective, the principle of narration is surreal, and the language is powerful and brilliant page after page after page. *By Grand Central Station* is the young woman's testament, urgent as an ultimatum, and the young woman, who goes nameless throughout the book, is Elizabeth Smart herself.

I do not mean that *By Grand Central Station* is a portrait of the artist as a young woman. The dullest reader could not help thinking that the book is in some way "autobiographical," but in reality it is much more than a *kunstlerroman,* more too than a memoir or a diary. The reason is, when Miss Smart wrote the book she refused to take refuge in either distant objectivity or naïve privacy. Instead she applied vision to herself, her intimate self happening in space and time. The result is unusual, almost paradoxical: the "I" of the narrative is not separated by age and values from the author, yet neither is she limited in her understanding of herself. Just the same, the author is left open and unprotected against the misunderstanding and cynicism of the superficially educated reader. Elizabeth Smart definitely wrote about herself in this book, but, for the record, it should be noted that she wrote the first part of the book last . . . and the rest of it piece by piece as it happened. From the beginning her vision was equipped with design. Not surprisingly, this method of composition is essentially poetic. *By Grand Central Station* achieves, confidently and nonchalantly, a brave lyrical balance between lived experience and aesthetic retreat, though none of the author's emotions were recollected in tranquility and the red-hot coal of her mind faded very little in creation.

Such real subjectivity constitutes a heresy in twentieth century literature which has so long prided itself on countless displays of *ironically* emotional speakers. . . . Thus, certain uninspired readers, who can trust only invention's dark fancy, will probably persist in criticizing *By Grand Central Station* because it presents a real suffering voice instead of a fake suffering voice.

Obviously Elizabeth Smart has more in common with confessional poets like Sylvia Plath and Anne Sexton than with most modern or post-modern novelists. No one even knows if there is such a thing as "novelry" any more; that is, creative prose as a genre distinct from poetry. (pp. 106-10)

By Grand Central Station begins with a vision of nature. Part One shows us the young woman playing hostess to a man and his wife who are visiting her in California. Already she loves the man, already she pities the wife, who is pictured as innocent, "trusting as the untempted." Her pity for the wife ironically foreshadows what she will eventually learn about love, but at first her mind wants to avoid the imminent, "the Beginning." Her heart, though, will not allow her to evade physical reality: "Nature, perpetual whore, distracts with the immediate." This is one of the major images in the book, nature as the Whore of Babylon, which is, of course, common Christian theology, and, by the way, standard Blakean philosophy. Throughout the book the young woman describes herself as a whore, always with ironic intention, but always too with symbolic truth in her voice. Thus before "the Beginning" mind works against heart, conscience works against nature. Coincident with this struggle a second tension appears. The young woman's role as whore is set against the wife's role as nun, her emulation of Christ's sacrifice. . . . As for the man, he is obviously torn, his wife unconsciously perceiving him as a teaching Christ and the young woman seeing him as a loving angel. This is another major image in the book, man as angel. We should remember here that in the original Greek, *angel,* or *aggelos,* means "messenger." We should also keep in mind the biblical teaching that "Jesus was made a little lower than the angels for the suffering of death." . . . Clearly the young woman wants something "higher" from the man than the wife wants.

The idea that the man is an angel also corresponds with the young woman's realization that "he is the hermaphrodite whose love looks up through the appletree with a golden in-

determinate face." Angels are not limited by maleness or femaleness. . . . She sees him as a messenger of love, not sex, and their union transcends what Blake calls "division." All this simply points to the universal truth that the experience of God, or grace, is the experience of unity: the dialectics of time and space, good and evil, ego and ego, even male and female, disappear in the imaginative perception of "all there is."

As the summer wears on, nature and the angel proceed to tear the young woman's mind to shreds. . . . [Smart's allusions to Blake's] "Ah! Sun-Flower" and "I asked a thief" both symbolize, ironically, the inability of love to flourish under the regime of a moral world view. The fact that her problem cannot be solved mentally is sharply expressed by the ambiguity of her cry to the "angelic orders": the real angels of eternity will not listen to moral invocations, and the moral angels of this world will not recognize the reality and importance of desire.

Inevitably, and fortunately in the light of Smart's overall vision, the angel touches nature and love is consummated. . . . Creation is consummation, temptation should never be refused. This is the message the young woman receives from God. Nature is not fallen away from God, if we only recognize that it is not. In her revision of *Genesis* Smart shows us a new Eve who loves and heals the wound of sex immediately. She does not grieve for God, she finds God in man, she loves the angel down here on the real earth. Now that "the Beginning" has happened the young woman realizes the imperative of love and she boldly states her creed:

> To deny love, and deceive it meanly by pretending
> what is unconsummated remains eternal, or that
> love sublimated reaches highest to heavenly love,
> is repulsive, as the hypocrite's face is repulsive
> when placed too near the truth.

Part One ends with "a long black rainbow," a beautiful parody of God's promise to Noah after the Deluge. Though joined to the angel, the young woman is not yet free of her puritanical heritage and its dread of punishment. (pp. 112-15)

Part Two takes us into the autumn, or "fall" archetypally speaking, and it depicts the young woman tormenting herself because of her love. "Not God, but bats and a spider who is weaving my guilt keeps the rendezvous with me, and shame copulates with every September housefly." As she often does, Smart recalls John Donne here, his "spider love, which transubstantiates all," and this dark parody of holy communion is grimly appropriate for the young woman's feelings of remorse about her own communion with God. Indeed, for most of Part Two she entertains the ghastly objections of her conscience and fights the good fight against her natural desire. Eventually she appeals to two more Metaphysicals, and to two more angels as well:

> What was your price, Gabriel, Michael of the ministering wing? What pulley from headlong man pulled you up in the nick of time, till you gushed vegetable laughter, and fed only off the sun? Was it your reward for wrestling successfully with such despair as this?

How can angels ascend while humanity falls? This is one of the central problems of man's moral inquiry. The allusion to George Herbert's "The Pulley," which suggests that the more man pulls down away from God in restlessness the more he is pulled up to the restfulness God offers, implies that the young woman is wondering if the fall of her humanity might not, paradoxically, cause the elevation of her being to angel consciousness, what she here calls "vegetable laughter." This phrase in turn suggests Andrew Marvell's "vegetable love," meaning the leisurely, almost timeless, quality of love in its proper state. Thus the despair of Donne's "spider love" is tentatively replaced by the hope of a metaphysical balancing of the consequences of action, a view of existence that transcends the divisive dialectics of rational morality. The young woman's thinking suggests that the angels do not pity, nor do they sacrifice. If they did they would lose contact with God, or fall away from the sun like "headlong man." Obviously the young woman is carrying on a complicated, erudite argument with herself in a nightmarish attempt to justify her love philosophically and conquer her despair. . . . (pp. 115-16)

Still, this passage is haunted by a shadowy Blakean intimation in the phrase "vegetable laughter," and Smart is always closer to Blake than she is to the Metaphysicals. . . . Read with Blake in mind "vegetable laughter" implies nature's mockery of imagination, an idea which has the feel of foreshadowing about it. Then when we remember that in Blake's vision of the Last Judgement "the Eternal Consummation of Vegetable Life & Death with its Lusts" strips and burns "Mystery" or the Whore of Babylon, we cannot help seeing the ambiguity in the young woman's allusive phraseology: if creation demands constant consummation to maintain union with God, nature may eventually disappear, burn itself up in apocalypse. Where does this leave the body of love? Or, on the other hand, nature may devour vision. By identifying with the Whore of Babylon and following her natural desire the young woman has achieved a higher level of consciousness than is normal, but can it last? Will the metaphysical pulley always balance imagination and nature, joy and despair?

The answer the young woman finds comes to her from outside her rarefied, super-literate flow of consciousness: "the texts are meaningless," as she realizes. Instead, "My heart is its own destructive. It beats out its poisonous rhythm of truth." This is a direct statement of her adherence to nature's dictates. Nature *is* sexual, however noxious that may be to the mind. . . . [In] true Metaphysical fashion, poisoned she is purified, cleansed of self-doubt, and she ends the second phase of her love calmly, "breathing like a workman setting out on a job."

Part Three is a hymn in praise of ecstasy. "This is the state of the angels," the young woman exclaims, and no one—certainly not Milton, not even Blake—ever described perfection with more positive delight. Continuing the Biblical motif she established in the first two parts, the young woman uses the analogue of creation to portray her fulfilment:

> It has happened, the miracle has arrived, everything begins today, everything you touch is born; . . . all the world solicits me with joy, leaps at me electrically, claiming its birth at last.

This answers the question she asked herself in Part Two: "Is an infant struggling in the triangular womb?" Yes, the infant is ecstasy, angel consciousness. Birth is the third major image of the book, not just the birth of an individual from love, but the birth of the world from love. The experience of love, Smart suggests, is not only constant consummation but also constant birth, constant introduction to wonder and fresh-

ness and life, eternal genesis. The man, her angel, is "land emerging from chaos" and she is borne away in "tidals of love." Seen in this light the wife's previous loss of a child symbolizes the spiritual sterility of her pose as nun or saint, contrasted with the fertility of the Whore of Babylon. (pp. 116-18)

She realizes too that her attainment of grace is paradoxical, perhaps even miraculous. . . . The necessity of reaching your wit's end, of replacing hope with faith, is common to both Zen and Christian teaching, and this serves once again to illustrate the universal scope of the young woman's vision. Nevertheless, she relies intrinsically on Christianity for her mythology. I do not mean that she is orthodox. Her Eden is not easy: "There is no room for pity, of anything. In a bleeding heart I should find only exhilaration in the richness of the red." This is the central fact of angel consciousness: pity is precluded, all is yes.

In Part Four, after having united imagination and nature in herself, and having united herself with the man, the young woman meets the world for the first time as an angel:

> But at the Arizona border they stopped us and said Turn Back, and I sat in a little room with barred windows while they typed.
>   What relation is this man to you? (My beloved is mine and I am his: he feedeth among the lilies).
>   How long have you known him? (I am my beloved's and my beloved is mine: he feedeth among the lilies).
>   Did you sleep in the same room? (Behold thou art fair, my love, behold thou art fair: thou hast dove eyes).
>   In the same bed? (Behold thou art fair, my beloved, yea pleasant, also our bed is green).
>   Did intercourse take place? (I sat down under his shadow with great delight and his fruit was sweet to my taste).

This parody is surely one of the best examples of black humour in modern literature, a fact that readers often miss when they comment on the book's relentless seriousness. This is a very funny scene, if it is read properly, especially if it is read aloud before an audience. Still the sharp irony of the scene certainly adds to the tension of both the external narrative and the internal depiction of consciousness. Perhaps the greatest effect of this satire is its illustration of the essential difference between ordinary human thoughts and feelings and what I have been calling angel consciousness. Admittedly, the police inspector is caricatured, but basically he represents the rational, common sense attitude—in other words, the ordinary, puritanical American's attitude—towards love, especially illicit love. The difference is not simply one of deeper or shallower levels of perception, though this is part of it. What is more important is that the puritan judges experience and fearfully tries to control it, whereas the angel enjoys experience bravely for what it is, however lawless. The puritan thinks love is a matter of responsibility and free will; the angel believes love is inevitable and uncontrollable. The difference is made even more obvious when *she* interrogates *him*: "Are all Americans chaste? All, by law." . . . The ultimate irony of the confrontation is that society very easily views love as a crime, yet at the same time it professes to believe that love is sacrosanct. Indeed, if we recall the status of the *Song of Solomon* in conventional Judaeo-Christian observance, we can see that Smart was aiming at the icy heart of puritanism when she chose this holy text for her burlesque of American morals. Most worshippers prefer to forget the *Song of Solomon,* but officially this series of erotic lyrics, spoken plainly in the tones of the angels, is interpreted as a didactic allegory. . . . Such deliberate hypocrisy boggles! No wonder the young woman concludes, in bewilderment, "Who is for us if these are so fiercely against?"

The next two parts of the book make it clear that no one is for them. In Part Five the young woman describes her train trip back to Canada, to her parents' home in Ottawa. . . . It is now October, almost November, symbolically well into the fall. As she watches the gold and scarlet foliage out the window, the young woman is certainly an angel looking homeward, as she herself hints, but she is afraid that only misunderstanding awaits her. . . . She refers to herself, ironically, as "another prodigal daughter," and once again we see how Smart is constantly rewriting the *Bible* as she goes along. Realistically, the young woman doubts very much that her family will be able to forgive her. . . . Almost there, she realizes that going home promises "a plentitude not to be borne," and the pun on still birth—symbolically the loss of union with God—undercuts any hope of being understood.

Part Six contains a crucial, and surprising, turn. Action, consciousness, theme, and style all pivot in the middle of this section as everything changes for the young woman. . . . On New Year's Eve she says good-bye and set out to face the final consequences of her love. Suddenly she starts speaking directly to the man, as if he is already lost to her. This abrupt change of voice is very moving, coming as it does after many pages of rising, courageous, and positive introspection. The very fact that she has to explain, persuade, and practically cajole almost takes her breath away:

> Not that I wish to blaspheme, or to say, See what I am. I wish only to say, Remember Ottawa on New Year's Eve: On that day which so threatened and whose antagonists it was not nothing to have said Pooh to, I did choose without influence or fanfare or any signpost to point me anywhere but away from you. . . .

Much of this is in keeping with what she has already said, her strong–hearted faith in love for example, and her understanding of the paradoxical quality of grace, even the quotation from the *Song of Solomon*—this time straight: "Love is as strong as death." But there is one great difference: *I did choose*. . . . Before, nature and vision carried her up to the state of the angels, possessed her. Now love demands a cold decision, a sober choice made in the face of the fallen world. The young woman's love is perfect; she does not hesitate.

Her problem now is that she fears the man may not be as strong as she is. She realizes that he is in danger of falling headlong back into submission and sacrifice. . . . [He] may be no better than the average American puritan who both desires and fears the Whore of Babylon. She reminds him of their true identity and their proper activity:

> Who weeps for the angels though, or notices when they turn aside to stiffen their upper lips.
> Not that I claim to be an angel, too. But I know that to be even gently bright and happy raises enemies.
> Only remember: I am not the ease, but the end. I am not here to blind you but to find you. . . .

This is rhapsody, but it is very tough. Elizabeth Smart is no sentimentalist. Her urging is nothing less than anarchy: let

us be angels, all of us, she suggests, instead of scapegoats, pseudo-Christs deferring to law and order and custom in such a routine, fearful fashion that God gets lost forever. Nor is she mystical. What she describes is not only accessible, it is inevitable. Consummation happens; it is real. What distinguishes Miss Smart here is her implication that collecting the apple is an infinite act, and that this truth must be faced for love to work.

Part Seven relates a troubled dream that the young woman experiences after leaving Ottawa. Her fears about the man's inability to maintain angel status invade and dominate her unconscious mind. She has made a conscious decision, but she still seems possessed, and this is both her despair and her glory. . . . The mythical surrealism of the young woman's dream resembles her waking thoughts very closely, especially in the recurrence of biblical imagery, and her dream recalls all that has happened to her so far. But one prophetic image and one idea dominate. The image is blood, which is ambiguous (birth if love is strong, death if it is not); the idea is her realization that, more and more, the man sees her womanhood, and possibly all of nature, as monstrous and threatening (the belly of the whale). Consummation destroys him as it creates her. . . . (pp. 118-24)

In Part Eight the young woman has awakened, but what she experiences is worse than a nightmare. . . . The man has gone back to his wife. The young woman is left in a cramped, dirty hotel room in New York in the dead of winter, pregnant. Both the winter and the pregnancy are oppressively factual as well as symbolic. Part Eight of *By Grand Central Station* is one of the most devastating portraits of love's despair ever written. . . . Love is meaningless to the young woman if it does not bear fruit, if it does not fulfil its promise of eternally creating the world, eternally communing with God. Nowhere is her understanding of the falseness of sacrifice more vivid than when she tries to understand her angel's absence. . . . (p. 124)

> He did sin against love, and though he says it was in Pity's name, and that Pity was only fighting a losing battle with Love, he was useless to Pity, and in wavering, injured Love, which was, after all, what he staked all for, all he had, ungamblable.

Pity is the only force that can destroy love. This is the ultimate truth of the book, and it challenges the ideological foundation of our society which has tried desperately, and for a very long time, to equate love with pity. Such an equation assumes that the world is fallen forever and that pity is therefore essential to human dignity.

This returns us, once again, to Smart's constant reappraisal of reality. "But what is important in life, what is it for?" the young woman asks the police inspector in Part Four, and she will not let us avoid this question. Smart's answer is that life—in other words, nature—exists for imagination to love, consume, and continuously perceive God in. Life is not a consolation prize. Only those who have failed to live, those who have tried to make life something it is not, need pity, in Smart's view, and pity draws us arrogantly away from God down towards the *only* human, away from our angelic birthright. (p. 125)

The young woman's angel is only a ghost now, after his departure. Nature in the form of hard, cold facts suddenly takes over her mind and all cerebral activity becomes a mockery. . . . Still her love never dies:

> This is the grass of hope that grows indomitably over my mind, which dares not admit that perhaps tonight his mouth, like the centre of all roses, closes over a mouth not mine, burrowing with apologies and love, like a baby at the breast.

By the end of Part Eight the man has totally metamorphosed in her imagination all the way from an angel into a baby, and this means, symbolically, that he has totally failed at love, for as man he should be sharing the act of creation with her, the Whore and the Angel of Babylon, generating birth, instead of being suckled himself by a frail wife-madonna. Elizabeth Smart's image of woman suggests a positive but unique attitude in these times of women's liberation. She is positive partly because she sees woman as being strong, certainly stronger than the man in this book, but even more so—and this is how she is unique—because she sees woman as necessarily merging herself with man in order to perceive God and celebrate the world, whereas most feminists attempt to divide male and female as much as possible.

Part Nine portrays the full extent of the young woman's desolation. . . . She returns to California and wanders along the lonely cliffs. She listens as her gossipy neighbours inquire about her pregnancy in one breath and in the next brag about their own vapid attempts to make the American Dream come true. She tries to read. Most of all she tries to keep love alive. Just as the texts are meaningless, so too is her own experience. "What is love?" she mockingly asks herself, but this question comes to her, and to us, from a much deeper source than usual. In fact, she has almost ceased to exist on the conscious level:

> I reach the cherry tree and we all blossom. Or I reach the cherry tree and we die. But I reach the tree. That is my entire plan and all the goal for my remaining forty years, if as seems impossible, so many remain.

Once again Smart returns to biblical mythology to explain her own vision of earthly life, and once again the echo is ironic. The young woman's taking the forbidden fruit has brought her "the nightmare of knowledge-too-late," but not the knowledge of good and evil. Instead she now knows that even angel lovers betray. It is as if the young woman has been seduced by, or seduced, one of the cherubims guarding the tree of life, only to have this angel cast her out of paradise again when he remembers his moral duty. The obsession with the cherry tree symbolizes the young woman's great determination to return, not to innocence, but to grace, the paradoxical, peaceful union of innocence and experience. She simply will not be denied. She will settle for nothing less than love, perpetual angel consciousness.

"But relentless Spring goes on and dares to finish itself without him." This is when she understands, bitterly, that nature's purpose may not be love after all, that sensuality may not lead to Blake's apocalyptic "lineaments of gratified desire," one of her favourite texts, but simply to the propagation of the species. Common, literal pregnancy. "Nature is using me," she cries, "I am the seedbag." This is surely the most poignant realization in the book. In "the Beginning" nature prompted the young woman's imagination to love, but once satisfied, nature deserts vision and even tries to drag it down into time and space. She sees too that "No one can throw me

a pulley." None of her mentors can help any more, not the Metaphysicals, not even Blake. Her religious training fails her most of all. . . . She will not accept martyrdom, nor will she accept "natural salvation," the prospect of motherhood offered her by the "officious housewife nature." Finally her imagination decides that she must make one last attempt to recover her "lost angel."

In Part Ten the young woman returns to New York. By this time her mind has grown so wild and active it is like "Judgement Day." As she wanders around the city alone, the starkness of her loss contorts itself into a madly lucid vision of the final and total reality of love. The very first line of the ending, the title line "By Grand Central Station I sat down and wept," really says it all, if we follow the allusion to its completion. "Psalm 137" ends like this:

> O daughter of Babylon, who art to be destroyed; happy *shall he be,* that rewardeth thee as thou hast served us.
> Happy *shall he be,* that taketh and dashest thy little ones against the stones.

The Whore of Babylon, the natural woman, is more than fallen; she is about to be destroyed, and so is her offspring—yet *he* shall be happy. This is exactly what the young woman sees when she returns. The man is now a crucified Christ. . . . But he is all right, if not happy, at least alive and reasonably secure, quite content to let his wife attend him. . . . And the wife too is content. "This one was the perfect sacrifice. All civilized men will weep for her." Those who sacrifice, those who pity and accept pity, those who separate God and nature, survive. Those who regard creation as finite, and mankind as pathetic, prevail. Those who seek refuge in morality find it. "But O, they totter into it blind and unprotesting," says the young woman, "And from their sin, the sin of accepting such a pimp to death, there is no redemption. It is the sin of damnation."

By now it should be obvious that Elizabeth Smart has succeeded in rewriting the *Bible.* Her vision denies the necessity, and even hints at the impossibility, of spiritual redemption, which after all presumes finite, linear time in order for us to fall away from God or eternity. Smart's point, like Blake's, is that we do not need to return to God, we *are* God. In this book Jesus, at least the Jesus most church-goers worship, is little more than a mama's boy, an impotent, happy victim, instead of the eternally creative Word of God, his proper role in Smart's view of things. The church-goers themselves are simply lovers of death. As far as Adam is concerned, the young woman even suggests that the real original sin was his desire to separate woman from himself in the first place. . . . Here is the ultimate image of the failure of love: not only the woman but the whole universe is withered, simply not born, not created, when the man—mythically—refuses the fruit and chooses pity instead. There is a deep implication in this that the world only appears to be fallen because of most men's false need to project a female comforter who will play madonna to their Christ, and this is perhaps the most damning indictment of masculinity ever penned by a woman, for instead of blaming men for desiring women sexually, Smart blames men for not desiring women *enough* sexually.

By Grand Central Station ends with the young woman's final dream of her beloved. For pure erotic grief it is unparalleled. . . . Taken literally this passage portends suicide, but such an interpretation violates the symbolic and visionary argument of the book as a whole. True, the young woman seems to be intent on killing herself, but we must remember that the river can just as easily signify her sense of imminent childbirth. So too the frozen waterfall echoes two previous scenes: "under the waterfall" is where she first made love with the man, and the frozen Chaudiere Falls later symbolize the world's reaction to her love. In Part Three she calls her ecstasy "the water of love that floods everything over," and this indicates the ultimate meaning of this final vision, namely that she is no longer borne aloft on the tidal waves of love—now she is drowned. Thus water suggests all of its archetypal meanings here: death and birth, the underworld of the mind, and primeval femininity. Even in the dream she realizes the futility of dying for love, for it would change nothing as far as the man is concerned. "Only the fact has potency," and the fact is she is already totally, hopelessly separated from her lost angel. Suicide would be a sacrifice, a complete denial of all that love has shown her, an all-too-human act. As she says, just after the dream, "All martyrdoms are in vain." The last line of the book—"My dear, my darling, do you hear me where you sleep?"—indicates the greatest irony of all: even in love's desolation the young woman is more awake, more alive, than her lost angel, the man who turned away from love and went back to pity, back to simple human consciousness.

"All there is" is too much for most readers. *By Grand Central Station* reveals an insight into love and existence that challenges both our beliefs and our perceptions. Elizabeth Smart's world is a deeper, higher, wider world than most people ever inhabit. It is the world of unconscious sensuality, the continuously expansive point in reality where imagination and nature, spirit and body, the miraculous and the ordinary, meet forever. . . . For Smart the original myth is everything. Reality is literally mythical. Eden never stops. Every moment we are about to fall away from angel consciousness; every moment we must create the world, bountifully, by loving, by fusing imagination and nature in our actions. And here is where she differs from even Blake. The young woman is not intent on forging nature into art, nor is she afraid of the prison of the five senses. She needs both imagination and nature to live in eternity. The tragedy is not that her physical reality betrays her visionary reality, but that the man betrays her completely. Other people exist for Smart as they never really did for Blake. There are infinite Adams, infinite Eves in her world, not just one Albion. This is one important reason why her vision is unusually credible. It is extreme, but it is neither solipsistic nor mystical. *By Grand Central Station* is more vividly intense, and far more magnificent, a book than most readers are accustomed to, but everything happens in a recognizable context, and though almost everyone is liable to be dumbfounded by the young woman's faith, no one can doubt the authenticity of her love.

In fact, it is the complete nature of love that Elizabeth Smart displays in this masterpiece. As I suggested before, some readers may mock the young woman's exceptional intensity and determination. Some readers may call these qualities "romantic," and thereby imply that she is suffering from an illusion, and that sooner or later she will "come to her senses." . . . But the young woman does not change, even in desolation. This is the whole point of the book: perfect love is real, it exists. (pp. 125-31)

"Heathcliff's look bored a hole through England which generations of heather on the wild moor never erased." The young woman's empathy with Emily Brontë's dark, undeni-

able angel is perhaps the most appropriate allusion in her mind. For generations imaginative readers have been fascinated by the stormy genius of *Wuthering Heights*. Charlotte Bronte spoke for almost everybody when she wrote that she neither comprehended Heathcliff nor ever saw the like of her sister on earth. Even today critics are still puzzled about *what* Heathcliff is. The answer is accessible. Heathcliff is Emily Brontë. And, in a visionary way, Heathcliff is Elizabeth Smart. No wonder it is so difficult to recognize her. (p. 132)

Michael Brian Oliver, "Elizabeth Smart: Recognition," in Essays on Canadian Writing, No. 12, Fall, 1978, pp. 106-33.

JEAN MALLINSON

The Assumption of the Rogues & Rascals is clearly written as a sequel to *By Grand Central Station I Sat Down and Wept.* Its substance indicates that the author views it as a continuation of and a commentary on the earlier work; and its form—discontinuous vignettes as a variety of modes, lyrical, anecdotal and reflective, with an oblique relation to narrative—indicates that the earlier book established for Smart the frame within which she chooses to work. Both works are distinguished by titles . . . which contain rhetorical surprises epitomizing the fiction which the novel elaborates.

The captivating and memorable brilliance of the title of the early work compared with the brisker, less striking incongruity of the title of Smart's recent novel is a measure of the difference in accomplishment between the two books. It is, of course, significant that the element of surprise in both titles occurs in a religious context; but in the early work, the title links the book firmly to a text—the Psalms, and by extension the whole of the Old Testament—whereas the title of the new novel, though specifically religious, referring to the doctrine of the assumption of the Virgin Mary into heaven, does not link the work to a text which provides a sustaining framework for the discontinuous vignettes which make it up.

It was not for nothing that the young Elizabeth Smart had one of Blake's Proverbs of Hell printed above the doorway of her lodging in Pender Harbour. *The Assumption* is her version of *The Marriage of Heaven and Hell*. Its import is essentially the same: a declaration that goodness has nothing to do with conventional morality and that, as her title suggests, the kingdom of heaven is at hand. In form it shares some characteristics with Blake's *Marriage:* both are episodic, in mixed modes and a variety of tone, ranging from the satirical, through the conversational, to the rhapsodic; and both move toward what Frye calls the "epiphanic point of view." The doctrine that informs Smart's work is now, as it was in *By Grand Central Station,* the doctrine of Blake's "The Everlasting Gospel": the rejection of moral virtue; the forgiveness of sins; the raising up of the publican the vagrant, the harlot, the adultress.

The Assumption is also related to the prototypical modern work: Eliot's *The Waste Land.* . . . Like *The Waste Land,* Smart's novel is discontinuous, allusive, apparently fragmentary, its episodes tangential to an unstated centre. And, like the earlier poem, it is a vision of judgement, a summoning, a reckoning. It is more transparently personal, less opaquely symbolic, than Eliot's poem; and—though, like *The Waste Land,* it is to some extent a cento—the fragments which sustain her, the texts to which she alludes, are not Eliot's. It is interesting to observe that she echoes his "give, sympathize, control" in the context of a pub scene, and what she says is:

> I try to enter into the spirit. To give, sympathise, entertain. I think: their needs may be greater than mine.

Her pub scenes have a quality quite different from the one in *The Waste Land,* which I have always particularly disliked for its implicit suggestion that the lives depicted in the words Eliot puts into the mouths of his speakers are tawdry and trivial. . . . Smart is a spiritual democrat who insists on gathering everyone into heaven with her. Indeed the apotheosis in her book takes place in a pub, although the whole city of London participates in it. . . . (pp. 134-36)

> The rogues and rascals have radiant faces in the Queen's Head. They rise and welcome me. They raise their stolen hats and buy me a bitter with borrowed cash. . . . But there is still enough love. It flows back faster than they squander it, and as regular as the managing director's salary. The jackets they nabbed while their host lay sleeping shine like saint's robes.
>
> They are received into heaven.

The literary allusions which sustain this beatification of the downtrodden are, besides Blake and Eliot, references to Desdemona, Cordelia, Vaughan, Traherne, and the Ancient Mariner. In accord with the Everlasting Gospel at the centre of the text, the reference is to the moment of communion in *The Ancient Mariner:* the heading for Part Six following the apotheosis in the pub, is "Paving-stones play the part of the water snakes in the 'Ancient Mariner'." . . . At the unstated heart of the book is an affirmation of life and death. . . . (pp. 136-37)

It is the nightmare of history which lies over *The Waste Land,* but a visionary writer like Smart can always break through history into the transient but noetic certainty of epiphany. And, in addition, the time that matters in *The Assumption* is not the time of history, but the time of breeding, gestation, giving birth: natural rhythms, as imperative, necessity, sentence, and redemption. . . . (p. 137)

Since she is essentially not interested in history, but rather in those moments when it is possible to imagine,

> . . . going down into the gulf of the Underground, that you were being borne along the birth gulley, out into the new world, amazed, for the first time. Then, then tremendous things might happen. People's faces would astonish. Everything would delight, because it would have no connotations, no history, no meaning but its looks.

it follows that she has only a minimal interest in narrative. It thus makes sense that she would look to texts like Traherne's *Centuries of Meditations,* Blake's *The Marriage of Heaven and Hell* and Eliot's *The Waste Land* as models. In Part Seven, "Lament of a Maker", she shows that she is aware of the problem such a perspective imposes, in terms of both substance and form . . . . In Part Nine, "The Story of Our Life," she tries on a few stories for size, and they are little parodies of the archetypal and banal: "they were born. they were bewildered. they loved. they suffered. they were pacified. they died." She tells little stories now and then, but—as is suitable to her real genre, which is not the novel or even the romance but the visionary miscellany, which follows the

arc or toss of illumination—her tales are short and exemplary, and serve a purpose either emblematic or evocative. So, in Part Eleven, subtitled "Trying to Write, Trying to Survive," after speculating:

> I suppose we need a drama. Well, a climax, not to say an orgasm, to make an experience—a rising to a height, and a subsiding.
>
> There will have to be a few humans? Snapped in action? identifiable? They are usually called for, wanted, found necessary for a story.

she replies:

> Speak.
>
> What is it? Glimpses, flashes in the medley, sudden revelations impossible to recall, except for their absoluteness—the rock revealed by lightning.

Once again, the undersong in this passage is provided by echoes of Eliot, but it nevertheless comes across as her own *credo.* And the unit she works with is not the poetic line, but the sentence. "Only the verb works" is the message the transfigured rogues and rascals give to her, and she has devised a sentence which at its unmistakable best can be recognized as an Elizabeth Smart sentence. *By Grand Central Station* taught us this sentence, and it is still central to whatever formal strength her new work possesses. Which is not to say that the book has no larger shape: in general, it is a searching of memory, leading to an apotheosis, followed by another search—the quest for her vocation as a writer, how to set it all down.

It is not nothing to have come upon a sentence which speaks unmistakably with your own voice, and so far this seems to me to be Elizabeth Smart's achievement. It is a sentence which has to do with rapture rather than narrative, and this leaves her with formal problems which were solved by the transumptive or pervasively allusive frame of *By Grand Central Station* and which have been only partially dealt with in *The Assumption,* which too often falters, drifts off, lags. But when it works, listen:

> Child lying stiff on one elbow like a frozen prayer, don't listen to chaos below. Will vigilance avert calamity? Relax into innocence. Go and cry in a secret part of the wood, where a wild clematis will compensate for pain. Build a bush house and kiss unresisting worms. It rains and you are enveloped. The wind blows and you know what you face. The mud reminds you of the comfortable beginning of the world, before the immense edict shrugged us into isolation.
>
> Over the uncooperative landscape, inertias and despairs find their way, make nests in every likely corner, so that none can hold a hopeful surprise which might, at the last trump, have come running with a golden solution held up in a happy finger.
>
> (pp. 138-40)

The Assumption is, like *By Grand Central Station* but with a difference, a celebration of life. It is also a lament, a taking of account; it is not as big with promise and agape with defiant hope as the early book. The structure of the early work was abetted by a pattern of allusion in which the horizontals and verticals, the latitudes and longitudes, were discernable. There are many more oblique and tangential lines in *The As-*

sumption. But the new work is a sequel to and a commentary on the early one. In a sense, they are contrapuntal to one another.

The poems in *A Bonus* provide marginal commentary on both prose works. This is their main interest. Smart says, in the first poem, "Reputations, by people with nothing to do,/ Are footballs kicked down the years./ But the goals are never true." By and large, I agree, and I feel diffident about judging her poems; but her own uneasiness about them is expressed in a number of the poems. . . . The poems are partly obsessive jottings, partly essays within a narrow range of styles which rarely come off quite right. If I am correct in thinking that the sentence is her natural vehicle, then the kind of concentration appropriate to her is not the imagistic concentration of contemporary poetry but the concentration of aphorism: not the aphorism of wit, but the aphorism which is sibylline, prophetic in Blake's sense. It is interesting to observe how many of her poems start with questions in a manner reminiscent of Blake's "The Everlasting Gospel". One of these, and one of my favourites, is **"Are Flowers Whores?"** which is also very like Blake in substance; in a pert and forthright way it states the doctrine implicit in *The Marriage of Heaven and Hell* and *The Assumption of the Rogues & Rascals.* . . . (pp. 141-42)

The reader interested in Smart's prose will find the poems moving and fascinating in their anxious musing on her vocation as a writer, her brooding on the meaning of domesticity, the squalor and mystery of looking after children. Blake, that sturdy visionary, turns up by name in the last poem, *"Blake's Sunflower".* The only woman—other than herself—who provides substance for a poem is that "lovely terrible person", Marjery Kempe. Smart clearly feels akin to her, an "excessive lady", with "fourteen children, husband and sins behind her", "Nosily full of herself and her new vision". Sensuous, domestic, visionary, and committed to telling, to bearing witness, Smart shares these attributes with Margery. (pp. 142-43)

> Jean Mallinson, "Smart's Proverbs of Hell," in Essays on Canadian Writing, *No. 12, Fall, 1978, pp. 134-43.*

MICHAEL BRIAN OLIVER

The Assumption of the Rogues & Rascals begins . . . in nothingness. In [*By Grand Central Station I Sat Down and Wept*] Elizabeth Smart revealed how she once achieved and then lost doubleness, or the state of grace, where all the opposites are fused: male and female, time and space, good and evil, appearance and reality—ultimately, beauty and truth. In her new book she reveals how she has had to deal with nothingness ever since. Love is now reduced to flashes of memory . . . but she characteristically refuses the comfort of self-pity. . . . For the first half of *The Assumption of the Rogues & Rascals* truth in the form of hard, cold facts virtually torments the memory of beauty. The fact that truth is now operating separately and in opposition to beauty indicates that events are now unfolding in the fallen world, or nothingness. The ravaged city and the post-war economic crisis shared by all Londoners provide Miss Smart with a frightful metaphor for her own depression. Her love affair and the war itself merge into a guilty "passion" that must be paid for. Her own reparation takes the form of solitary child-rearing. In fact, the greatest separation in this book is the gulf between God and nature. Love once united the narrator's spiritual and physical desires, but neither her man nor God is present when she bears her children and has to cope with raising them alone. Throughout the book Miss Smart suggests that being dominated by nature and deserted by God is part of what it means to be a woman, at least in the everyday world of nothingness where she finds herself after the lovemaking is over.

These first years after the war are especially desolate. . . . Still, following the pattern of everyone who has ever despaired, she attempts for a while to find comfort in the fallen world, to adjust herself, cynically and profitably, to facts. . . . [She] realizes the identity she must assume, if she is to make the rest of her life meaningful:

> The rogues and rascals have radiant faces in the Queen's Head. They rise and welcome me. They raise their stolen hats and buy me a bitter with borrowed cash. . . . But there is still enough love. It flows back faster than they squander it, and as regular as the managing director's salary. The jackets they nabbed while their host lay sleeping shine like saint's robes.
>
> They are received into heaven.

The rogues and rascals are writers—poets such as Dylan Thomas and Patrick Kavanagh—and their assumption is a double one. First, they assume what Elizabeth Smart decides to accept: "The price of life is pain, since the price of comfort is death and damnation." Then, because they have made such a brave acceptance, they are assumed into heaven, or the state of grace. Being a writer: that is the answer Miss Smart finds to her post-war, post-love desolation, and that is what this book is all about.

Part Seven, the chapter called "Lament of a Maker," deserves to stand with such documents as Shelley's *Defence of Poetry* as a major statement of the imperatives of being a writer:

> But where, woman wailing above your station, is it you want to go, get to, accomplish, communicate? Can't you be amply satisfied with such pain, such babies, such balancing? . . .

The first sentence of this passage, with its allusion to her own first book and to Coleridge's demon—or angel—lover, sets the tone of Elizabeth Smart's writing since the war and since her love affair. Her eye is now on truth more than on beauty, and as a result there is both a decrease in sensuousness or concern for nature and an increase in irony and aesthetic distance. This would seem to suggest that Miss Smart has given up her stance as a genuine Romantic and adopted an orthodox Modernist attitude. If this is so, the change has been made against her heart's desire, and much of the pain the devoted reader of *By Grand Central Station* will find in this new book can be traced to the feeling that the author has lost her truest source of inspiration. *By Grand Central Station* is often richly and bitterly ironic, but throughout that book Miss Smart is able to maintain a belief in one of her favourite texts, taken from *The Song of Solomon:* "Love is as strong as death." But in the absence of her lover she has *only* pain to combat death. . . . The rest of *The Assumption of the Rogues & Rascals* reveals many painful moments in Elizabeth Smart's life, from the poignancy of her feelings about her father's death to the futility of many wasted nights in a Soho pub. She even gives us a new—and perhaps final—vision of love, and this is the image that appears on the dust jacket of the book:

> In the smeared glass jar are two ecstatic newts in a long immobile embrace. . . . Is it their pale glowing colour that brings primeval memories, or their frozen rapturous dance, poised above the decaying vegetable matter, the mud and stones, and the wet snake in the bottom of the jar. So private a preoccupation, so regardless, stirs up dreams of perfection, so sad from where I stand.

Watching doubleness she feels like nothing! This is excellent poetry and it recalls in a flash Miss Smart's earlier vision of love as constant consummation and creation of a perfect, elevated world. Needless to say, the terrible sadness the author now feels will most certainly be shared by ardent readers of *By Grand Central Station I Sat Down And Wept.*

The Assumption of the Rogues & Rascals ends with God—who is now "unimaginability" and "the non-me"—being found once again, this time by accepting pain instead of love as the rule of life and as the necessary creed of the writer. . . . I cannot help feeling, though, that something important is lost whenever tragedy is succeeded by comedy, which Miss Smart—following Samuel Beckett, one of her heroes—finally decides is "a better form." Certainly writing is a viable alternative to loving, but *must* pain succeed love when the lovers do not die but simply go on living apart from each other? I believe that the Elizabeth Smart who wrote *By Grand Central Station I Sat Down And Wept* could have gone on unchanged forever, if George Barker had loved her the same way she loved him. Of course, if that had happened, the world would never have received this excellent new book, and whether the words that stream from Miss Smart's furious pen tell of angel consciousness or of artist consciousness, the stream itself is fresh, lucid, strong, and beautiful. All lovers and all writers should read both of her confessions. Together they complete a life. (pp. 129-31)

> *Michael Brian Oliver, "Double or Nothing," in* The Fiddlehead, *No. 126, Summer, 1980, pp. 127-31.*

LORRAINE McMULLEN

Elizabeth Smart's *By Grand Central Station I Sat Down and Wept* is an unusual novel. Closer in many ways to a symbolist poem, an impressionist painting, or a piece of music than to the traditional novel, it is most aptly termed a lyrical novel.

When pieced together, events of the novel strike us as ordinary, perhaps even mundane. A young woman falls in love with a married man and has a brief affair with him; he returns to his wife and she finds herself alone and pregnant. Magazine racks are filled with stories of such unhappy love affairs, but the classics, too . . . , give us tales of ill-starred romances. The mode of expression, not the plot line, dictates whether a work is a world classic or pulp magazine fiction. Elizabeth Smart is aware of the paradox that what may appear sordid and disreputable in one form may appear lyrical and magnificent in another. She is aware also that the experience which is central to her novel encompasses the sordid and the marvellous, the sacred and profane; and her language is devised and structured to reflect these polarities. (p. 133)

The novel begins with the first meeting of the protagonist with her future lover and ends with her realization that the affair is ended. While the novel involves a circular journey tracing a path from west to east, north to Canada, south to New York, west again and once more east, it is also, and more importantly, a voyage of mind and heart, which traces the complex graph of the protagonist's emotions throughout the affair. The novel is created of this emotional voyage. While we have come to expect a novel to concern itself with events and character development, in this lyrical work, events and character are subordinate to effect. Using words less as a language of communication than as an expression of emotion, the novel directs itself to rendering the texture of experience. "I was trying to say that this is how it is," the author explains. "How it is"—the inner reality—is the focus of this work.

As a lyrical novel, *By Grand Central Station* is something of a hybrid, combining aspects of two genres. Time, place, character, and event still exist: events occur within the space of a year; setting shifts from west to east and back; three characters interact. At the same time, much as in lyrical poetry, incantatory rhythm, lyrical and evocative language, daring and extravagant imagery heighten emotional expression. While novels are associated with storytelling, and the reader expects to find a character with whom he can identify and a plot in which he may become involved, in this novel emotional experience rather than external experience or individual character is central. The skeleton of barely identifiable events exists so that the resulting emotional effects can be expressed. Narration is subordinate to lyricism. Because it is the voice of the unmarried woman protagonist that we hear, from her perspective that we enter into experience, and her emotions that we share, the fictional world of the novel is her internal world. Events and individuals become aspects of the poetic vision, raw material for imagery. The protagonist shapes the world she sees to the expression of feeling. Objects, scenes, characters exist as images within the protagonist's lyrical subjective point of view, while the underlying plot fuses the array of disjointed images. Intensely emotional and lyrical, hence romantic in expression, the language of feeling is never out of control. Analogies and conceits, however exaggerated and even startling, are never ill-conceived or inappropriate. Literary allusions link the love affair with expressions of love throughout the ages, and biblical allusions underline its essentially sacred and eternal nature.

Interior monologue can be used to present realistic details filtered through an individual consciousness. To some extent this is what Smart does in seeking to describe "how it is". But because the reality she seeks to present is the protagonist's sensibility, the point of view is lyrical and confessional. A design of images and motifs takes form from the loose, disjointed series of events, recollections, conversations, displacing the external world or shifting from the external to the internal world to reveal the protagonist's mind and heart. Her emotional journey becomes a quest in which she abstracts impressions from the concrete world and refashions them into the texture of lyric poetry.

Characters exist to serve the lyrical intentions of the novel. The protagonist is the lyrical "I", as in a lyric poem; others are image-figures with which she interacts. Neither the protagonist, nor her lover, nor his wife, is named: all three remain shadowy figures in the lyrical acting out an archetypal pattern. Nor is any of the three described except for a few evocative details. On first meeting, the wife is seen first by the waiting protagonist, before the husband, as indication of how she is to continue to stand between the two. As the traditionally-termed injured party, the wife is portrayed as trusting and vulnerable, appealing in her very helplessness. . . . In a technique of reversal, not uncommon in this paradox-filled novel, this married woman, compared to a madonna and a nymph, appears virginal. She is associated with the fragility and innocence of flowers and birds. Her innocence is both childlike and saintly. . . . (pp. 133-35)

When first seen, the protagonist's love ". . . fumbles with the tickets and the bags, and shuffles up to the event." . . . "Shuffle" and "fumble" are hardly the action verbs one associates with a long-awaited romantic hero. Nor does he ever prove to be particularly heroic. This man is even more imprecisely described than his wife; in fact, he never becomes more than a silhouette or a shadow. Neither his appearance nor his personality is important. What is important is his effect on the protagonist: ". . . he, when he was only a word, was able to cause me sleepless nights and shivers of intimation.". . . The word "shadow" recurs insistently. . . . From the protagonist's lyrical point of view, the lover appears as a spectral, fateful, and often threatening figure.

The protagonist herself is passive. Her own personality is even less clearly drawn than that of her lover or his wife. Like them she is a figure in a drama which she watches unfold. She, too, serves the lyrical intention of the novel. The closer to the heart of the experience, the less concretized the individual. The protagonist remains only a voice.

Setting takes on the texture of imagery. Like the characters, it is mirrored through the eyes of the protagonist as an adjunct to emotional expression. The lush California setting presides over the lover's apotheosis, imaging its eroticism, its ecstasy, and its dangers. Like the protagonist's love, the setting appears excessive, larger than life. . . . Menace is hidden within the beauty of the landscape: "But poison oak grows over the path and over all the banks, and it is impossible even to go into the damp overhung valley without being poisoned. Later in the year it flushes scarlet, both warning and recording fatality." The description underlines the sensuousness of the surroundings: "Round the doorways double-size flowers grow without encouragement.". . . As the lush and sensuous flowers grow without encouragement, so does emotion, and it is in the lush and sensuous, and at the same time menacing, valley that the love is first consummated, a love which is to contain at least as much agony as ecstasy. . . . (pp. 135-37)

In similar, though less lyrical, fashion, the Canadian winter mirrors the response of family and acquaintances, ". . . how sympathetic the frozen Chaudière falls seem under the December sky, compared with these inflexible faces.". . . Finally, the all-night café at New York's Grand Central Station, a hangout for derelicts, where the novel ends is equally appropriate. Here the protagonist sits alone, deserted: "These tables are topped in leather on which the blood has never dried."

A lyrical novel is itself a paradox in its combination of features of two genres, its use of elements of the novel for lyrical purposes. In **By Grand Central Station** the aesthetic arrangement of the traditional elements is designed to express the pleasure and pain of love in a paradoxical structure, with motifs and symbols designed to show the existence of the polarities of joy and sorrow. The protagonist sees the world and experience in terms of paradox. While joyously embracing her experience, she is always aware of its dangers and of the inevitability with which sorrow follows happiness. (p. 137)

The first words of the novel create oppositions which mirror the dialectic within the mind and heart of the protagonist. Awaiting her first meeting with her future lover, she says, ". . . all the muscles of my will are holding my terror to face the moment I most desire." By linking the two seeming contraries, "terror" and "desire", she sets the stage for the continuing paradoxical structure of the novel and her own ambivalent, sometimes contradictory, emotions. In the next sentence, with the words, "Apprehension and the summer afternoon keep drying my lips. . . .", she links emotion with physical sensation, fusing the two worlds, the emotional and the physical, as she will continue to do throughout the novel.

All elements of the novel contribute to the tension of opposites within the experience. As the effects of love and joy, of grief, ecstasy, and despair, birth and death are the opposites to which the narrator returns obsessively, so blood and water, the central symbols to which she returns insistently, are paradoxical. Blood, while associated with birth, is also linked with passion, suffering, sacrifice, and death. Water, most often linked with life and creativity, is also associated with death.

Love is viewed by the protagonist as a flood on which she is borne, by which she may be swept away, and in which she might drown. (pp. 137-38)

Blood, associated with sorrow and death, is also linked with birth. . . . "Not all of the poisonous tides of the blood I have spilt can influence the tidals of love." The association of blood with "tidals of love" fuses the two central images, blood and water as do the words, "But the sea that floods is love, and it gushes out of me like an arterial wound. I am drowning in it," an image which at the same time links love with death. The flood of love on which the protagonist is borne does become the flood in which she drowns. . . . The emotion which carried her to ecstasy carries her to despair.

Birth as a motif is linked with love from the novel's beginning. . . . The birth motif embraces several kinds of birth, linking three levels of experience: the birth of a passionate love affair, the birth of a child, the creation of a lyrical work.

The narrator turns to the classics and the Bible for analogies and symbols adequate to express her passion. She makes of herself and her love archetypal figures acting out their love in the world of myth and legend. Their experience and emotions rise above the temporal and parochial to become constituents of the eternal and the infinite. By their association with gods and heroes, the lovers are mythologized. The protagonist links herself with others loved by gods. . . . Implicit in the classical allusions is recognition of the inevitability of the protagonist's acceptance of love and of the unhappiness, even disaster which will be its inevitable result. She associates herself with other women involved in tragic love situations, such as Ophelia and Isolde. When deserted by her lover, the protagonist associates herself with Dido, the queen of Carthage who committed suicide when deserted by Aeneas. . . . With this analogy, the narrator also lends cosmic significance to her experience, a significance amplified by association of herself with the natural world and translation of her experience into hyperbolic and dramatic metaphor and symbol. . . . (pp. 138-39)

Along with the cosmic significance which such metaphors,

analogies, and classical allusions lend to the love affair, there are important religious overtones. The biblical cadence of the novel's rhythms contributes to the love's apotheosis. The most dramatic of the biblical allusions underlining the religious dimension is the use of verses from the Song of Solomon which, in the voice of the protagonist, are counterpointed with the crude questioning of the police who stop the couple at the Arizona state border. This counterpointing of voices points out the dichotomy between the two ways of looking at the experience: for the protagonist, her love is sacred and lyrical; for the police, as outsiders, it is adulterous and sinful.

The interweaving of the lyrical, cadenced biblical language with the direct and brutal words of the interrogators also recalls to the reader the inextricable link between the sensual and the spiritual; the sensual is not denied but made transcendent, the marvelous is shown to exist within the corporeal. In her use of the Song of Solomon, Smart comes full circle: the lyrically erotic language which in the Old Testament was transposed to express a divine love, to image a transcendent world which can only be expressed through the concrete, now is turned back, still carrying its sacred implications, to add to an erotic experience the resonance of the spiritual, to underline one of the main paradoxes of the novel, that to be human is to be both flesh and spirit, human and divine.

The intermeshing of the spoken words of the police with the silent discourse of the protagonist is achieved by the use of parenthesis for the silent discourse. In the conjunction of the exterior dialogue (which is actually a dramatic monologue, since only one side of the conversation is given) with the interior monologue, the impression is created of the spoken words entering the protagonist's consciousness, the dialogue entering the monologue frame. An ironic tension is created and developed between outer appearance (the words of the police) and inner reality (the protagonist's recitation from the Song of Solomon). While to some extent the effect may be compared to that of an aside in drama, the emphasis remains with the interior monologue. The opposition of the views expressed by the two voice levels underlines the impossibility of communication. . . . (pp. 139-40)

While such other voices impinge upon the consciousness of the lyrical "I" through whose sensibility the world is filtered, we never hear, directly or indirectly, the voices of the lover or his wife, the two other figures central to the lyrical experience. Distanced from the reader, they remain shadowy figures in the experience of the narrator-protagonist, acting out their parts in an elemental pattern. Other voices heard directly are those of secondary figures, largely unsympathetic, acting as a kind of chorus. These voices express an attitude and a reaction antithetical to hers. Through them, the world in general is shown to be unsympathetic, capable of viewing the affair only from the most superficial level, but capable, nevertheless, of passing judgment.

Brief comments of family and acquaintances, directly reported as scattered bits of conversation recalled by the protagonist, tend to isolate her further: " 'Love? Stuff and nonsense!' my mother would say, 'It's loyalty and decency and common standards of behaviour that count' "; ". . . the well-meaning matrons who, from their insulated living say, 'My dear, I think you would regret it afterwards if you broke up a marriage.' . . . The clichés spoken by these observers reflect the conventional and unthinking views of onlookers to any adulterous affair.

For the most part, the novel consists of the present tense discourse of the lyrical "I" which is overheard by the reader. Verbalization is synchronized with action or experience. In the course of the interior monologue, the lyrical "I" conveys to us what she is doing and what is happening to her, and what she is feeling. Present-tense discursive language lends a sense of directness and immediacy as the reader overhears the lyrical "I" in the act of responding to her situation.

There are times when the monologuist addresses her thoughts to others, human or divine. When considering her feelings of guilt at injuring her lover's wife, she addresses God: "God, come down out of the eucalyptus tree outside my window. . . ." After her recitation from the Song of Solomon, she addresses Solomon in language ironically more appropriate to her crude interrogators. . . . Travelling to rejoin her lover she addresses him as "you." Such make-believe communication further underlines her loneliness and isolation.

While most of the novel is narrated in the present, that present shifts in its mode of operation. We think of the present in its most common use, expressing immediate action, emotion, or response, but there are times when the present becomes a timeless present shifting to the expression of a generalization. . . . (pp. 141-42)

At times too, the present modulates from instant present to habitual present to indicate a repetition or a longer duration. Such uses of the present contain, at least implicitly, such adverbs as whenever, sometimes, always, never. (p. 142)

In keeping with these varied modes of present tense, are the paradigmatic scenes, which, while they are in themselves individual scenes, are representative of other similar scenes. Such a scene occurs in the home of the Wurtles, a couple with whom the lovers stay for a short time. . . . Here the present tense shifts from a brief scene in the instant present to expression of a generalization in the timeless present, and shifts back to another instant moment in another brief scene. The impression created is that of the lyrical "I" speaking to herself while involved in these scenes.

While the present tense in its various modes is used most, a recurrent feature of this monologue is the manner in which from time to time shifts are made to other tenses. For example, while the protagonist's thoughts remain in the present as she travels home, the next episode, in which she considers the unsympathetic and uncomprehending attitude of family and friends, takes place in the past tense. . . . Recollected words of others are then interjected in present tense direct discourse in a dramatization of recollected attitudes. In such a situation, present experience giving way entirely to a remembrance of incidents and attitudes, the narrator's monologue becomes a memory monologue. In similar fashion, the episode with the police, which begins with the counterpointing of interior and exterior voices, continues in past tense narrative. When the past tense is used, it is never simply to narrate what has occurred but rather to comment upon past situations. . . . (pp. 143-44)

In the final and most emotionally wrought part of the novel, the monologue shifts rapidly from present to past to future in a surreal structure. Bits of action and event are interwoven with lyrical effusions, and the protagonist shifts from speaker to listener to speaker, and from interior to exterior, in a kaleidoscopic shifting of scene and tense. . . .

In its handling of voice and language *By Grand Central Station* is a remarkable accomplishment. Even more remarkable is that it is the first novel of a very young woman, and was written in 1941. (p. 144)

Equally remarkable is the history of *By Grand Central Station.* Appearing first in England in 1945, during the last months of the war, it was an underground success, but was not widely known until 1966 when it was republished. . . . It was still almost unknown in Canada. It is said that Elizabeth Smart's family blocked its importation into Canada. The first North American publication, the Popular Library edition in 1975, finally brought the novel to attention in Canada. Now at last *By Grand Central Station* joins the list of Canadian classics. (p. 145)

Lorraine McMullen, "Elizabeth Smart's Lyrical Novel: 'By Grand Central Station I Sat Down and Wept'," in Modern Times: A Critical Anthology, Vol. III, edited by John Moss, NC Press Limited, 1982, pp. 133-45.

HEATHER HENDERSON

Elizabeth Smart was 31 when she published her first novel, the harrowing, exquisitely crafted *By Grand Central Station I Sat Down and Wept.* She was 63 when she published her second, *The Assumption of the Rogues and Rascals.* Those silent years, 1945 to 1977, haunt *In the Meantime,* a new collection of the Ottawa-born writer's poetry and prose. "Her Muse screamed," writes Smart, in rueful acknowledgement of her silence, "but children louder.". . . But in old age, still driven by the need to speak, Smart displays new bite and vigor. Her voice has become infinitely more powerful, if less beautiful, capable of cracking over the soul like lightning.

In the Meantime combines a novella and a cycle of poems from Smart's youth with diaries, poetry and autobiographical essays written in the late 1970s. The early pieces are romantic and lyrical, while her pared-down, almost brutally harsh later work bears witness to the toll that time has exacted. Despite the radical simplification of her style, *In the Meantime* displays a striking thematic continuity. For Smart, only one drama animates the human soul, a passion play that begins with a person's first terrifying separation from his or her mother. Betty, the heroine of the semiautobiographical 1939 novella *Dig a Grave and Let Us Bury Our Mother,* flees to Mexico to carve out her own identity as a woman and an artist. But she finds that she cannot escape her maternal bond. . . .

Smart's recent prose, essays and diary return to the theme of primal loss. But they are flawed by a certain formlessness: her unbridled emotionalism needs the discipline of poetry. Still, the writing is galvanized by an almost religious belief in the healing power of art. Indeed, some of her most passionate work bursts out in defiance of approaching death. . . . *In the Meantime* is by no means an even collection: the prose is inconsistent and only the poetry is uniformly well crafted. Still, beneath its dishevelled surface bubbles the magic energy of a late and lovely spring.

Heather Henderson, "Breaking the Silence," in Maclean's Magazine, Vol. 98, No. 26, July 1, 1985, p. 65.

ALICE VAN WART

[From *Necessary Secrets: The Journals of Elizabeth Smart* emerges] a remarkable personality—passionate, vibrant, extravagant, sensitive, yet subject to lethargy and self doubt. Her entries, rapidly written, usually at night while propped up in bed, were sometimes daily and sometimes sporadic accounts of events, sights, sensations, and feelings. There are glimpses of her social life, her family, her friends; there are detailed records of her trips and of her relationships; there are lists of people she has met, poems she is reading, books she has bought and read; there are lists of names of flowers, plants, and trees; there are pages of French vocabulary, philosophy notes, articles she is writing, poems she is learning, and poems by Alice Paalen and George Barker; and there are recipes, grocery lists, and accounts of money she has spent. But more important, the journals are the private record of the heart of a woman, a woman who never overtly rejects the standards and expectations placed upon her but quietly begins to construct her own personal values. Rather than accept abstract ideologies or material ambitions, she searches for the vital connections she believes could be found only in love, art, and the natural world.

Because the journals are both a private revelation of the self and an apprenticeship into writing, they vary considerably in content and style. Despite the difficulty of doing so, Smart had a profound urge to express herself and there is a cumulative sense of emotional and artistic development within the journals. They begin with an external focus and an interest in character and event, apparent in the **"Juvenilia,"** in the accounts of her early life in London and Ottawa, in the records of her trips, and in her first full-length fictional work, **"My Lover John."** However, the external focus gradually shifts to an internal one, and with the consequent movement away from incident and character, the journals reveal a growing need to articulate the voice of her soul in its search for fulfillment. The changes in voice and style correspond to the growing complexities in Smart's life. As the journals progress, her language also changes: to express emotion it relies on image and metaphor, and it begins to resonate with allusions. The style that characterizes *By Grand Central Station I Sat Down and Wept* is already apparent in the journal entries that comprise the first draft of Smart's novella, *Dig A Grave and Let Us Bury Our Mother* (published for the first time in *In The Meantime*), a seminal work that shows the burgeoning of Smart's distinctive style and voice.

Dig a Grave and Let Us Bury Our Mother is important not only as an apprentice work but also as a means of understanding the genesis and evolution of *By Grand Central Station I Sat Down and Wept.* By the time Smart had written the novella, she knew what she wanted to write and even how it should be written. In a journal entry of November 26, 1939, she states, "I want my book to be about love," and in a later entry, December 6, 1939, she says, "Poems, notes, diaries, letters, or a prose such as in *The House of Incest* or in *The Black Book,* only meet my need. . . . But I need a new form . . . each word must rip virgin ground. No past effort must ease the new birth." Not only is her novella a precursor of *By Grand Central Station I Sat Down and Wept* in style, voice, and form, but also parts of the novel were written before Smart had met the poet George Barker, and before their celebrated love affair. She had already found a voice and a style;

the relationship with Barker provided her with the subject she wanted—finally, subject and voice coincided.

Far too much has been written about the biographical implications of *By Grand Central Station I Sat Down and Wept.* Quite simply, it is the book she had been preparing for ten years to write. Art does come out of life, but in the final analysis, *By Grand Central Station I Sat Down and Wept* is not so much about the love affair between two people as it is about Smart's life-long love affair with language. Words are not life, but they are a testament to it. (pp. xi-xii)

> *Alice Van Wart, in an introduction to* Necessary Secrets: The Journals of Elizabeth Smart, *edited by Alice Van Wart, Deneau, 1986, pp. ix-xii.*

AUDREY THOMAS

I disagree with the editor's [Alice Van Wart's] premise that we see [in *Necessary Secrets*] a young writer serving her apprenticeship, searching for a voice, the voice that will sing forth in *By Grand Central Station* [see excerpt above], called by Brigid Brophy "one of the half dozen masterpieces of poetic prose in the world." (I disagree with that as well.) Certainly we discover what Elizabeth Smart was *reading* in the years before she met George Barker and wrote *Grand Central Station* (not necessarily in that order). She read the metaphysical poets, Virginia Woolf, Katherine Mansfield, D.H. Lawrence, Anaïs Nin, Henry Miller, the Song of Solomon. And all of these are there in the novel. But the journals are fascinating, to me at least, for quite other reasons.

They are the record of a young woman of wealth, beauty, and great personal charm who is obsessed with the idea of finding someone to worship, preferably a poet, and, I think, preferably a poet who would make her suffer. . . . Given those goals she picked a winner. And pick him she did: "He is the one I picked out from the world. It was cold deliberation." . . . (p. 17)

In many ways, as these journals unwittingly reveal, she was a very conventional woman. She wanted a mate—and for life. That was her first, her prime, objective. In Palestine in 1937 she turns away from the ideal of the kibbutz, although she admires the dedicated young women, saying "I seek a mate, not a way of life" and "I must satisfy nature before I invite God." She also says, in another section **"Trying to Write,"** "To be in a very unfeminine, very unloving state is the desperate need of anyone trying to write."

She wanted a man who was successful in his chosen field (and hers); she wanted to have his babies. When he turns out to be neither a prince nor charming (or only charming when he chooses to be, on his terms), in some strange way she even remains "well-bred" in her decision not to rage and moan against him but to shoulder her burden . . . and raise the children herself. Free Spirit or Patient Griselda?

I think there was a deep laziness in Elizabeth Smart and this laziness, in addition to her own conventionality (and we must remember the times and her "station" in life), kept her from being a writer of any stature. Lazy, you say, with *four babies?* I am speaking of artistic laziness. I don't think this is at all the same thing as what Tillie Olsen discusses in *Silences.*

The Assumption of the Rogues and Rascals, published more than 30 years after *Grand Central Station,* is really not much more than jottings, notes for a possible novel or group of linked stories. *A Bonus* (poems), published the year before, is a slim volume indeed. *Grand Central Station* has some lovely-sounding lines but needed more work. It's by a prose writer trying to be a poet. (pp. 17-18)

[By reading *Necessary Secrets*] one becomes more and more aware of what a spoiled, narcissistic brat the young Betty Smart was, but also of what talent she had and how she squandered it. For she had a deep knowledge of and feeling for external nature . . . and the descriptions she jots down—descriptions of landscape, flora and fauna—are superb. . . .

I put these journals down thinking, "What a waste. What a terrible waste." The best of her writing is in here.

It did not surprise me to learn from an editor's note that J.M. Barrie was one of Smart's favourite authors. (She describes her only meeting with him in the journals.) Somehow I think that although she avowed she wanted to be like Peter Pan, a free spirit, a high-flyer, who she really wanted to be was Wendy. (p. 18)

> *Audrey Thomas, "Fool for Love," in* Books in Canada, *Vol. 16, No. 3, April, 1987, pp. 17-18.*

PATRICIA MORLEY

[*Necessary Secrets* forms] a tiresome and fascinating work of considerable beauty and depth. The tiresome bits belong largely to the early pages and the very young Elizabeth, who is turning twenty at the time of the first entries. Some rapturous passages written in 1940 in the throes of love might also tire the less romantic. As for the beauty and wisdom of this prose, however, they shine from every page. The journals disclose an exceptional spirit and sensibility, a rare talent. Mercifully it need no longer be secretive, since most of the great and not-so-great named in its pages are now dead. (p. 225)

Most students of Smart's work will agree with Van Wart that too much has been written about the affair with the poet who remained married to his original wife, and that her first novel is "not so much about the love affair between two people as it is about Smart's lifelong love affair with language." The journals support this view.

They cover eight years (1933-41), a critical period for the Western world and for Smart, serving her apprenticeship as a writer. Part One (1933-35) is the weakest, not surprisingly, yet it offers intriguing insights into the budding sensuality and spirituality which co-exist at the heart of Smart's literary vision. That spirituality includes an almost mystical feeling for nature, and a concern for what Patrick White calls "lovingkindness." . . .

In Mexico in 1939 Smart stayed with Wolfgang and Alice Paalen, both writers. The relationship that developed with the beautiful Alice must have been liberating for Elizabeth, whose sexuality had been constrained by a conventional background and highly strung mother. It would be celebrated later in a tender novella entitled *Dig a Grave and Let Us Bury Our Mother,* the story of a love affair between two women which acts as a means of confronting and breaking away from the mother/womb. (p. 226)

She soon moved on to Hollywood where she lived briefly with a French painter, Jean Varda. The diaries are purposely ambiguous; from the wording it seems possible that the two were never lovers. Throughout this period Smart's thoughts were on [George] Barker. . . . Initially she did not know that he was married. Later, he told her that he would leave his wife, an intention that seems to have never been genuine.

Smart agonizes over the pain they are causing Barker's wife, but guilt had no power to quench the fires. . . . [The] two eventually had four children. Smart brought them up by herself, earning a living as a journalist in London. Small wonder that "labour" becomes the central pun in her brilliant second novel.

The journals sparkle with vitality and wit. The span of eight years allows us to see the developing style of the woman who was always a poet, one whose writing abolishes the barriers between prose and poetry. The complexity of the style matches and reflects the complexity of Smart's personality, which stands revealed as vain, selfish, selfless, kind, generous, humorous, cruel, voluptuous, and deeply loving. Smart felt herself cursed with "a New England conscience." Cursed or blessed, her life is one to confound the moralists and edify the forgiving. (pp. 226-27)

Patricia Morley, "Surprised by Joy," in Canadian Literature, *No. 116, Spring, 1988, pp. 225-27.*

Ellen Bryant Voigt

1943-

American poet.

Voigt's poems often reveal a profound love of family and nature through recollections of her childhood on a Virginia farm. Although essentially a pastoral poet, Voigt writes in the Southern Gothic tradition, paying homage to her heritage and birthplace and combining descriptions of violence with intensely sexual motifs. While sometimes faulting Voigt for laconic phrasing, critics applaud the detailed richness of her works. Edward Hirsch commented: "[Voigt's] poems often strike directly for the emotional core of their subject, but just as often they do so slowly, patiently, with a lush sense of their own verbal wanderings and enjambments, with a deep sense of the dense, discursive wealth of language."

In her first collection of verse, *Claiming Kin* (1976), Voigt divulges sentiments about relatives and the external world. While maintaining that Voigt's graceful lyrics and use of understatement seem unsuited to her references to such topics as concentration camps and murder, several critics praised her sonnets that examine themes of marriage and the intrinsic self. *The Forces of Plenty* (1983) comprises poems that explore how the mutuality of happiness and misfortune ultimately governs human existence. The tense, controlled narratives in this volume focus primarily on disappointment and loss; several pieces depict problems encountered in marriage, while others concern the death of a loved one. Penelope Mesic observed: "[*The Forces of Plenty*] is so quietly various, so intense yet decorous, so aloof from common impatience and fully fledged with wit that Voigt's voice could never be confused with another's." In *The Lotus Flowers* (1987), Voigt seeks to understand life's enigmatic blend of good and evil. In a review of this work, Reginald Gibbons noted: "Voigt's poems are utterances which themselves seem to have come from that realm of lost things that she explores. They have that kind of authority."

(See also *Contemporary Authors,* Vols. 69-72 and *Contemporary Authors New Revision Series,* Vol. 11.)

HELEN VENDLER

[Ellen Bryant Voigt] has mixed success in her first book, ***Claiming Kin.*** There are good things in almost all of the poems—and bad things, too. She . . . feels her way well into her vowels and consonants; her rhythms . . . are rigid and tense, on purpose; and she alternates between a fine clarity and a sporadic want of taste. It is hard to bring off lines like "a piece of love, our mother lode / of tradition, our nigra mammy"; and what reader of poetry can help remembering Williams's "asphodel, that greeny flower" when a young poet writes of "catalpa, that beany tree"? There is in Voigt an interest in the lurid—a man shoots his wife by mistake; a girl is buried alive. It is not clear whether these are to be seen as exceptions or rules. The better poems inhabit a small lyric

frame embracing the private self, marriage, and childlessness. There are memorable lines: "Confronting frost, / the trees assume their attitudes of pain"; a woman is "like a hawk adrift in its fine solution of clouds." The most successful single poem, again a poem of American homage to an eternal subgenre, is **"Harvest,"** which retains mystery even in its explicitness:

> The farmer circles the pasture
> checking fences. Deep
> in the broomstraw, the dove withholds
>
> her three notes. The sky
> to the southwest is uniformly
> blue. Years of plowing under
>
> have brought this red clay to its
> green conclusion.
> Down back,
>
> the herd
> clusters to the loading pen.
> Only disease or dogpack
>
> could alter such order. Is that
> what he asks for in the late
> fields, the falling afternoon?

The shapeliness of such a poem avoids both the evil of enumeration-too-long-continued and the evil of banality. When Voigt is banal, she seems to step out of poetry altogether: finding her father asleep, when she visits, she writes in flat-footed sentiment:

> Why isn't he out in the fields, our common passion?
> I want to wake him with kisses,
> I want to reach out and stroke his hand.
> But I turn away, without speech or gesture,
> having for so long withheld my body from him.

These alternations of talent and flaccidity make this a baffling collection. One would like to read more from the Voigt who sees an infant's fist, with its "palm / already mapped and pencilled in." . . . (pp. 410-12)

> *Helen Vendler, in a review of "Claiming Kin," in*
> The Yale Review, *Vol. LXVI, No. 3, Spring, 1977, pp. 410-12.*

PETER SCHJELDAHL

Ellen Bryant Voigt is a poet from Virginia who attended the Iowa Writers' Workshop. A lot about [*Claiming Kin*] is illuminated by those circumstances. First there is a sense of land and of family, of being obliged to deal with a stubborn heritage, which seems peculiarly Southern. Then there is the form of the poems, a correct free verse possessed of all the minor virtues which, being the aspects of poetry easiest to talk about, tend to be inculcated by workshops. Those things aside, what is interesting in Voigt's work—alternately impressive and appalling, actually—is evidence of a pretty ferocious sensibility: powerful sexual yearnings and repulsions, fascinations with physical rot and murderous impulses. Much of the book intimates a nature, including human nature, red in tooth and claw. However, some of Voigt's most harrowing perceptions are cast in a well-bred elegiac mode that seems inappropriate to them. A delicately phrased meditation on Auschwitz shows particularly poor judgment.

> *Peter Schjeldahl, in a review of "Claiming Kin," in*
> The New York Times Book Review, *May 1, 1977, p. 69.*

STANLEY PLUMLY

Ellen Bryant Voigt's first volume of poems [*Claiming Kin*] offers a Bishop's eye for diction and detail—

> Graceful in water, they labor now
> toward palmetto and tufted
> hillocks, the hot sun bleaching
> and drying out. Their fins dig into
> something solid, the broad flukes
> spade, then anchor in the sand.

This is a careful study. The poem is entitled **"Suicides."** It begins something like: "Ink blot, sperm on a slide, a squirm / of minnows from the helicopter's / view, the whales have beached." At a look, the first full third of Voigt's collection appears to be a bestiary of such studies, from cranes to rabbits to cats to whales to storks. Interspersed among the animals, however, are other vulnerables, other kin, including parts of her own body.

> Heavy in her hammock, she makes

ready for mating. All black,
black love in the pit of her
eye, she lolls at the center,
a soft black flower.

This rendering of the black widow, that soft black flower, is just one of a whole book-length series of strict sexual motifs, alternately recessive or dominant, opening or closing, that sustain the prevailing metaphor of Voigt's interest. . . . Even death, that "grief-perfected Rose," that "black mouth like a scar," assumes the sexual burden . . . "There the two bodies / nestle together under the common stone." What all this adds up to is uncertain. Voigt is a very skillful poet, with an ear as good as her eye. The kin being claimed are blood as well as sexual relatives, and they comprise, in their geneological sequence, perhaps the finest four poems in the book. By title, we go from grandmother, in **"Birthday Sestina,"** to mother, in **"Claiming Kin,"** to **"Sister"** to daughter, in **"The Hen."** But underpinning, and undercutting, all the kin here, whether actual, sexual, or animal, is a dimension of violence that does not sort well with the elegance at hand. It would be silly to draw on the Southern stereotype of Voigt's background, as some reviewers have, and assign various Virginia Freudian motives as the sore and source of her concern. Yet the formal surface of her poems does sublimate, even contradict, the sexual hostility beneath it. In a tonally subdued prose poem called **"Gathering,"** the entire sexual cycle, from inception to conception to birth, is treated in the fairly dark context of death ("They were bringing in the bodies from the sea each one wrapped in burlap. Long slender cigars, how easily they slid into that open mouth.") and decay ("After all she's twelve months pregnant. Everyone laughed.") and death ("But slowly the hand closed like a dried leaf, the palm was curling, the thumb moved up to pinch, and hooked at last the last end of the small, flowered, flannel nightgown."). The raw material in this piece is likely literal, but so much of its potential power is trimmed and qualified, prose poem or not, by its use of allegorical outline, its theatrics of the absurd, that its commitments seem confused. . . . Voigt invariably proposes understatement for the clear, full acknowledgment of the statement itself. She allows her imagination, sexual and/or self-destructive, to yield to the authorization of the language. It all hurts more than she is telling us. Writing well is no substitute, in Stevens' phrase, for finding what will suffice. Metaphor is not an ellipsis, some gesture directed at the silence; it is the embodiment of a discovery, an embrace.

> *Stanley Plumly, in a review of "Claiming Kin," in*
> The American Poetry Review, *Vol. 6, No. 4, July-August, 1977, p. 43.*

EDWARD HIRSCH

[In *Claiming Kin*], Ellen Bryant Voigt writes with a Southerner's devotion to family and a naturalist's devotion to the physical world. It would be difficult to think of a first book that claims a deeper or more abiding kinship with the rose-bush and the catalpa, the stork and the hen, the black widow and "the gray creative worm." . . . Her work abounds with a plenitude of adjectives, with thick dreamy descriptions of a summer spent on some imaginary island or late autumns in rural Vermont. Her poems characteristically encounter the wealth of the natural world at some final moment, on the borders of a wintry death, or at the edge of a ripe harvest, a red clay ploughed to its "green conclusion." [**"Tropics"**], for example, spends six of its ten stanzas detailing the rich life of six species of wildlife. And it concludes by yoking these inhabitants of an imaginary Garden of Eden to two lovers turning to each other in the first tropical movement out of sleep. . . .

Ellen Bryant Voigt is a poet so immersed in the material, physical world that even when writing of people she naturally compares them to plants and animals. Speaking of a farm wife, drawn into a fatal lock step of domesticity, she asks only that the woman be able to "float / like a fat gull that swoops and circles." And in the title poem, **"Claiming Kin,"** she addresses the rockbed of what she later calls "the family / the circle of fire" and in doing so, in speaking of her life as a child pulled down to her mother's kitchen, she concludes by comparing herself to a single house plant growing in the shade. . . .

Barrenness is a subject that Voigt returns to over and over again; it is her darkest compulsion. Sometimes this takes the form of "Vacant cornstalks [that] rattle in the field." More often and more affectingly, it is deeply maternal, more desperate and wounded, more womanly. Thematically the poems encapsulate different kinds of childlessness, of loss. . . . These poems—raw, deathly, and fierce—have another kind of lining, a sort of Plathean intensity, a bleak energy of mourning. At her worst Voigt descends into the melodramatic, but her best poems have a lush descriptiveness and a keen-edged knifelike clarity.

There are two linked, but somewhat different aesthetic impulses in *Claiming Kin.* Voigt's achievement is to have reconciled them. The first is for a poetry that is harsh, rapturous, wounded, regal. These poems tend to be short-lined and short-winded, carrying news of executions, suicides, drownings and burials. The second impulse strains after a poetry that is richer and more diverse, more patient and playful, more observant of sensuous detail. . . .

Ellen Bryant Voigt's high-pitched and incisive poems often strike directly for the emotional core of their subject, but just as often they do so slowly, patiently, with a lush sense of their own verbal wanderings and enjambments, with a deep sense of the dense, discursive wealth of language. When Voigt speaks of Rich November as "our season of opulence. / Festive, extravagant," she might also be speaking of her own poems. As a book *Claiming Kin* is restless, sometimes violent, always physical. Its poems stand on both sides of a barren winter. But in the end, through the magical, saving grace of language, Ellen Bryant Voigt's poems resist and transcend their seasons of hard weather. *Claiming Kin* is a stunning first collection.

Edward Hirsch, "Season of Opulence," in The Nation, *New York, Vol. 225, No. 4, August 6, 1977, p. 123.*

SARAH McGOWAN

[A] sense of yin and yang figures heavily in Voigt's poetry. The interrelatedness of light and dark which governs our lives is vividly described [in *The Forces of Plenty*]. Although the "forces of plenty" are represented, it is the forces "of loss" which predominate in the poet's mind, forcing the reader to believe that these forces do not play "equally on the human soul."

Voigt's poetry is unsentimental and realistic, presenting pictures which often deal with nature, farm or family. Although these subjects are familiar, the images Voigt uses are far from traditional or expected. . . .

In **"Sweet Everlasting"** Voigt links a second grade class' plant identification expedition with her father's death. In **"Daughter"** she describes a parent's life saving "kiss so urgent, so ruthless" it brings life back to a choking child. The poems are intense and incisive and are not so much dealing with "forces of plenty" as they are "of loss," and are, therefore, more often solemn than not.

Disagreeing with an artist's concept of beauty does not make the painting any less a work of art. So it is with poetry and with *Forces of Plenty,* a book of forceful and imaginative poems which jar the senses and provide pause for thought. But, as sobering as these poems are they must be heralded for their uniqueness and their quality.

Sarah McGowan, in a review of "The Forces of Plenty," in Best Sellers, *Vol. 43, No. 5, August, 1983, p. 187.*

BRUCE BENNETT

Ellen Bryant Voigt's poems are written from the vantage point of early middle age. Her title, *The Forces of Plenty,* comes from the poem **"The Spire,"** which describes two figures in a Bavarian steeple who emerge each hour to strike a bell:

> By legend
> they are summer and winter, youth and age,
> as though the forces of plenty and of loss
>
> played equally on the human soul.

Carefully, precisely, she tests that tentative "as though," calculating whether those forces are in fact equal. Individual poems provide partial answers, but the book offers no final resolution. The conviction grows on one that the forces of plenty are not quite holding their own.

Each poem poses the question anew, often creating an atmosphere of suspense and anxiety. This is most intense in **"Year's End"** and **"Daughter,"** harrowing accounts of small children's narrow escapes from death, and **"Quarrel,"** in which a husband and wife carry on a day-long argument at a terrific pitch. Less dramatically but with equal effect, the poet anatomizes ambivalence in herself and a man she is attracted to in **"Blue Ridge."** Throughout the book's middle section, such poems about love and marriage balance longing and desire against loneliness and the threat of loss. In **"A Marriage Poem,"** the couple is portrayed as having arrived at equilibrium:

> Spared grief, they are given dread
> as they tend the frail on either side of them.
> Even their marriage is another child.

In a sonnet, **"Liebesgedicht,"** the poet uses imagery to define her lover as something other than a pale reflection of her self, but she is compelled by that imagery to conclude that he can therefore be taken away from her.

In the final section the focus shifts to those frail ones the couple tends—children and dying parents. Mrs. Voigt accepts that she cannot protect them or alter events, yet she maintains her vigil. Her poise and control, everywhere evident, are well exhibited in **"For My Mother."** The family has gathered round the deathbed:

> My sister has put your rings
> on my finger; it seems like your hand
> stroking the white brow,
> unable to release you,
> not even after you have asked for death—
>
> And we know nothing about such pain,
> except that it has weaned you from us,
> and from the reedy, rusted
> sunflowers outside the window,
> drooping over the snow like tongueless bells.

> *Bruce Bennett, in a review of "The Forces of Plenty," in* The New York Times Book Review, *July 17, 1983, p. 22.*

PENELOPE MESIC

There are regional poets whom one feels would be forced to stop writing if they were ever cut off from their native or adopted swamps and bayous, their bays and mists, their granite ridge and mean annual snowfall. But Ellen Bryant Voigt, while explicit in her references to the Vermont landscape [in *The Forces of Plenty*], could clearly flourish as a poet anyplace. Her style is intimate and flexible, her range of approaches to a technical problem so varied that one may read a succession of poems with a sense of increasing familiarity but no nag of repetition. The drama of her narratives never seems contrived: one feels she invents only enough to allow what she has observed to show itself clearly.

The terrible, natural tension of **"Year's End,"** a poem in which the accidental death of one child is balanced against the recovery from illness of another, turns upon the significant near-rhyme of "breathe" and "grieve":

> For a long time we stayed in the room,
> listening to him breathe,
> like refugees who listen to the sea,
> unable to fully rejoice, or fully grieve.

"For My Husband," which begins with a couple hunched over a ouija board, depends for its effect on the mockingly wide range of words beginning with "l, o, . . ."—the inconclusive point at which the planchette has stalled—which appear throughout the poem and reveal the couple to be somewhere between love and loss. "[C]an't we say outloud the parent word, / *longing*, / whose sad head / looms over any choice you make?" the wife at last inquires.

In an entirely different mode of diction and lineation is the flowing **"Liebesgedicht,"** a torrent of sweetness in which one line runs quickening into the next, echoing the sense of its central metaphor:

> This is how the earth loves the river,
> and why its least fold solicits each
> impulsive stream until the gathered water

The collection of poems is so quietly various, so intense yet decorous, so aloof from common impatience and fully fledged with wit that Voigt's voice could never be confused with another's. (pp. 295-96)

> *Penelope Mesic, in a review of "The Forces of Plen-*

> *ty," in* Poetry, *Vol. CXLIII, No. 5, February, 1984, pp. 295-96.*

CAROLYNE WRIGHT

"Magic is not earned and is not fair," says Ellen Bryant Voigt in **"The Gymnast,"** one of the finest poems in her second book, *The Forces of Plenty.* This line could be taken as a comment on the volume as a whole, which, despite the early promise of *Claiming Kin* . . . , does not, unfortunately, excite or edify me as much as I had hoped. About half of the poems included are of the substance, the verbal and emotive richness I have come to look forward to in Voigt's work; too many of the remaining thirty-one poems rely on description to build up a suspense for which there is not always a dramatic payoff. (pp. 122-23)

Another characteristic I find disturbing is the (to my mind) gratuitous insertion of weighty and abstract pronouncements ("Any abstraction / names a consequence," "Music depends / on its own diminishing") or questions ("Who can distinguish knowledge / from belief?") which may sound impressive because they are obscure, but do not seem earned by their contexts. Truisms ("The long habit of living / indisposes us to dying") and editorializings ("There is one grief worse than any other") are annoying because they interrupt the poems' momentum, forcing them to start up again, as it were, after being brought to a halt. Sometimes the poem is stopped before it starts: why couldn't **"The Apology"** have begun with its current second line ("A hurt friend circles the house"), since this is the poem's situational given, instead of with the statement "Hurt dogs crawl under a bush"? The parallel seems belabored, even sentimental—a set-up for the final two lines (". . . the way one greets an animal / extending the hand.") whose finely balanced revelatory power is thus undercut from the beginning. (pp. 123-24)

I am nitpicking, but if I did not admire Voigt's work, and applaud the standards she has set for herself, I would not be so fussy. The whole manuscript wants to be as fine as its strongest poems and passages; with further editing, it easily could have been. Knowing what she is capable of, and presented with a volume that almost achieves it, is frustrating for the reviewer who can neither dismiss nor unilaterally praise the work. Certainly these poems are more "mature" in tone than those of *Claiming Kin* more reflective, more able to meditate on their subjects with simultaneous aesthetic distancing and full emotional commitment. Among them are some of Voigt's best poems—**"The Spire," "The Medium," "The Gymnast," "The Couple," "For My Mother,"** and the second section of **"A Marriage Poem"**—which, with their wealth of linguistic texture, generous imagery, and full lines, permit the exploration of complex, deeply felt insights into the "forces of plenty and of loss" against which all human love strives to maintain itself. There is a serious acceptance, even embracing, of the truths which only living can reveal to us, and which we are powerless to change. The speaker of these poems has reached the midsummer of her life, "coming [as she does / from [her] strong marriage," her children, her keen sense of the pastoral beauty of her surroundings; she nevertheless knows that the heart cannot help but yearn for the impossible continuance of such fullness, for the impossible stoppage of time. . . . (pp. 124-25)

[Ellen Bryant Voigt is concerned with the losses] of early middle age: the deaths of parents, the blurring of youthful vigor and cosmetic beauty, the realization of her own lack of immunity to aging and death. . . . "Death is the mother of beauty," Wallace Stevens said in his own meditation on the subject, "Sunday Morning," and Voigt knows from experience what he meant. Confronted with the realities of the life cycle, both in their ascendancy and the first degrees of their decline, she can only love that well which we must all leave 'ere long. She has learned some of the consolations of increasing age as well—the deepening of insight, the opening of the reflective powers, the awakening of the mind as the body's youthful imperatives subside, or at least come into perspective. In **"Blue Ridge,"** the speaker and a friend are watching a fireworks display and talking about the advantages of growing older; given the sexual tension between the two of them, however, the benefits cited become gently ironic:

> He said we were watching youth at a great distance,
> and I thought how the young
> are truly boring, unvaried as they are
> by the deep scar of doubt, the constant afterimage
> of regret—no major tension in their bodies, no tender
> hesitation, they don't yet know
> that this is so much work, scraping
> from the self its multiple desires . . .

Happily, the abstractions in this passage (doubt, regret) arise of necessity from the dramatic context; we are privy to the speaker's mingled attraction and hesitation, the companion's subtle defensiveness, and we comprehend both the truth of the declarations and their immediate function here as the speaker's attempts to come to terms with her failure to attract him.

Some of the most intriguing poems here are those in which loss (or perpetual deprivation in some form) is suggested obliquely, through the filter of a persona. The speaker of **"The Gymnast"** is a young woman athlete, but not Nadia [Comanechi], not the Olympic gold medal winner. She appears to be a less talented, or merely less charismatic, teammate—the one whose "long hours of practice" at Nadia's side do not result in stardom. She has "beaten the blank mat"; but for Nadia herself, the effort bears the fruits of the magic that cannot be earned. The poem is a patient and clear-headed evocation of genius from the perspective of the less gifted, the simultaneous stirring and relinquishment of envy as futile in the face of unchangeable differences of ability. . . . The poem is moving because we all have experienced failures of this sort—of not being the strongest, the fastest, the most attractive; of not, in short, being the winner or the star.

Ellen Bryant Voigt's strengths seem to reside in cultivation of the longer line, the denser linguistic texture, the accumulation of sensory experience played off against abstractions demanded by their imagistic occasions—prosodic devices, in short, that can mirror the fullness and subtlety of nuance she is drawn to in the world. She is not a "minimalist"; her best work is that of the cornucopia, not the stripped cornfield of November. The reductive image and lean phrase lose energy in her lines, as demonstrated by attempts in this mode in *The Forces of Plenty.* The title, moreover, could not be better chosen, reflecting as it does her concerns with family, with kinship and relation, with the loveliness and evanescence of the world in which we so briefly sojourn, with loss and reconciliation to its finality. (pp. 125-26)

> Carolyne Wright, "Pain and Plenitude: First and Second Books by Maria Flook and Ellen Bryant Voigt," in The Literary Review, *Fairleigh Dickinson University, Vol. 30, No. 1, Fall, 1986, pp. 118-26.*

EDWARD HIRSCH

The Lotus Flowers is a book of fierce regard and passionate attention. The narrator who animates its pages is unblinking, inquisitive, even—to borrow a word an old friend uses to describe her at 19—*"acquisitive."* In those days, she "wanted it all, / every exhilaration, every grief," although, almost 25 years later, she seems hungry not so much for experience as for understanding. She is determined to hold what she can of the vanishing world,

> to salvage
> something from my life, to fix
> some truth beyond all change.

Against her losses, Ms. Voigt poses a loving and fiery attentiveness to her world, balancing grief and exhilaration, mourning and joy.

The woman who speaks throughout *The Lotus Flowers* is poised at mid-life between the gravitational pull of the past and its "cruel perfected music" and the flaming world of the present. She feels the gap widening between her Virginia childhood and her New England adulthood, between the lost world of her parents and grandparents and the fresh discoveries of her children. . . .

As she feels the past receding, as she observes herself giving up mourning and grief, as she notices that "The horseshoe hung in the neck of the tree sinks / deeper into heartwood every season," Ms. Voigt's poems increasingly meditate not only on what passes away but also on what survives, how the past determines and informs the present, how it infuses and complicates our adult experience.

In the final poem of *The Lotus Flowers,* **"Dancing With Poets,"** Ms. Voigt envisions "all the poets of exile / and despair, unfit for this life, all those who cannot speak / but only sing"—Berryman, Frost, Dickinson, Keats—dancing together in a local bar, "not / lifted out of grief but dancing it." That vision is entirely characteristic. James Wright once said he wanted to write the poetry of a grown man. In her dream of community, in her passionate determination to sing her losses and dance her griefs, in her complex allegiance to the dual countries of childhood and adulthood, the past and the present, Ellen Bryant Voigt is writing the poetry of a grown woman.

> Edward Hirsch, "Heroes and Villanelles," in The New York Times Book Review, *August 23, 1987, p. 20.*

REGINALD GIBBONS

A patient searching for the revealing, conclusive sign marks Voigt's second book, *The Forces of Plenty,* and [*The Lotus Flowers*], her third collection. Sometimes, the sign may even appear in the obvious place of the first or the final image in a poem—a tangible thing like a berry, or a more symbolic item like an imagined aeriel view of a house that makes it seem the bull's eye of a target whose concentric circles are lawn and gravel and fence. But wherever it is found in a poem, the sign often seems something rescued from the past.

In many of the poems there's a brooding sense of anxiousness over the vulnerability of life to frightening or saddening developments (which might come as the result either of change, or lack of change). All this suggests that Voigt is an elegist, and the epigraph to **The Lotus Flowers** shows that she sees herself that way: it's Yeats's "Man is in love and loves what vanishes."

Something about her book—something about its accessible manner which yet conceals or gives way to more difficult states of feeling—suggests that **The Lotus Flowers** is a kind of diagnostic book of poems of this time, in this country. . . . (pp. 225-26)

Voigt's artistic life belongs to the latter half of our century, and as her contemporary I find in her poems a poignant sense of having presided unwillingly over a world-change unlike any other. . . . Having inherited a poetics of images set like ornaments in free verse, as opposed to metrical manipulation of sound and syntax, our latter-day poets look to an image as earlier poets might have looked to an idea or a poetic rhythm. Voigt's manipulation of image is happily balanced by a more-than-usually musical sense of phrase and line. In this way she is very "mainstream"—Frost, and perhaps Bishop, and Yeats himself, are faint shadows sometimes whispering along with the voice of her poems. Maybe the plain straightforwardness of Jarrell also opened her way for her. . . . Voigt doesn't seem interested in technical originality so much as technical sufficiency, with which she fashions the unassuming, but always polished, vehicle of her moral inquisitiveness.

It's not that Voigt's poems give the answers: they only pursue the questions with care and subtlety. . . . She very carefully *describes* a great deal. In a way Voigt is very old-fashioned: the manner of her art insists in every poem that the deep connections are indeed there, and that language, trained and mustered and encouraged, like a kind of smart hound, can indeed find them and bring them back. The poems are of a kind to give a reader confidence, because it's clear from the first one that Voigt isn't interested in putting her own perceptions and feelings on display, but in getting somewhere—in making a connection between her faculties and capacities as poet and the multitudinous stories and things racing past us in time, faster than we can register. She wants to guide; and she can make a reader want to be guided. That's a matter of "eye," "ear," and all other poetic gifts; but the poems' confident bearing isn't a technical matter, nor does it have anything to do with such waves of literary fashion as "new formalism." Voigt's work has more to do with what Seamus Heaney defines as "technique," to mean "a stance toward life." The success of the poems owes much to the sheer human preparation behind them. Which is as it should be with serious work—for a poem's validity as an artistic work does not finally *depend* on craft, as all the great craftsmen know. Voigt's poems are utterances which themselves seem to have come from that realm of lost things that she explores. They have that kind of authority. (pp. 226-27)

Reginald Gibbons, in a review of "The Lotus Flowers," in TriQuarterly 71, *No. 71, Winter, 1988, pp. 225-27.*

JAMES FINN COTTER

[In **The Lotus Flowers,** Ellen Bryant Voigt has] found her voice as a storyteller. Many of the tales deal with family and neighbors in the farm country of Virginia. Even a dog secretly killing sheep at night while faithfully guarding his own flock by day offers a subject for compactly staged narrative that reflects on the animal instinct to kill and the human need to tame. **"Feast Day"** recalls the Advent ritual of shooting mistletoe out of trees for Christmas, while **"Short Story"** describes a grandfather's killing a stubborn mule, a story grown fuzzy in the course of family retelling. Unlike her sister who stays at the homestead each summer (**"The Visitor"**), the author's life has moved her further away from scenes to which she can return in memory alone and art. Some poems, like **"The Riders"** and **"Good News,"** view their protagonist from such a distance that it is hard to know what, if anything, has happened. Sometimes purple patches of description distract from the purpose of a story. **"Memorial Day,"** for example, starts out as a description of spotting American redstart warblers:

> In field guides they are always in repose:
> tiny female, olive-gray, so like the local birds;
> the male, shiny black with tailstripes, wingbars,
> "shoulder coloration" such a vivid orange
> I might have recognized him in the elm.

Fair enough, although the words themselves smack of the field guide. The poet elaborates on the mythic theme of the meanings of birds, and the language swells with phrases like "the terrible dark winters of retribution." The author admits: "I am overrun with signs and omens." The impulse to go on writing has taken over, and the poem ends flatly by returning to the guide's description. . . . More often, however, she has something to say and one can feel the subject guiding the voice in the choice of incidents and detail. **"Bright Leaf"** is the best thing in poetry or prose that I have read about tobacco picking and curing, the hard lot of both the black workers and the struggling white farmer. **"At the Movie: Virginia, 1956"** effectively depicts segregation through the eyes of a child who thought the Negroes' balcony seats reflected "a special privilege" because they enjoyed a superior vantage and freedom. Trained as a classical pianist, the author reviews the rise and fall of her vocation in **"The Chosen,"** a poem that embodies music in its story and lines. (pp. 228-29)

James Finn Cotter, "The Voice of Poetry," in The Hudson Review, *Vol. XLI, No. 1, Spring, 1988, pp. 225-32.*

PETER HARRIS

Ellen Bryant Voigt's **The Lotus Flowers** keeps straying back to her upbringing on a farm in Virginia, a place which was partly idyllic and partly a vale of tears. She explores her origins from the complex perspective of someone who finds home a place that's necessary to leave and to return to. Voigt's speaker at one point describes herself as having embarked on a lifelong swim, leaving the island of her origins, heading toward, but never arriving at, a distant mainland. The poems embody stages of her passage, both in the swim and above it, in a vantage of provisional transcendence. (pp. 262-63)

Virtually every one of her poems contains clusters of images rich enough to resist the simple discursive glosses that less accomplished poems invite and sometimes supply. We're almost always left with an image or phrase that takes us somewhere inevitable, yet unexpected. In **"The Field Trip,"** for example, Voigt describes a nature walk taken by a group of 13-year-old school children. One troubled boy in particular holds the speaker's attention because he's studiously ignoring the others while courting danger out on the edge of a cliff. When he ironically becomes the first to spot a passing hawk, it strikes in the speaker a deep chord of rueful sympathy. She wants to praise the boy,

> so much does he resemble
> if not the hawk then the doomed shrub
> fanned against the rockface there beside him,
> rooted in a fissure in the rock.
> But soon the hero swings back up to earth,
> the group divides. Just like that
> they're ready for home, tired of practicing:
> sixteen children, two adults, and one
> bad boy who carved a scorpion on his arm.

This is a passage written by a poet who knows how to end a poem. Voigt prompts us to see the boy in a montage, first as a predatory hawk, next as a doomed cliff shrub. Then, to close, the montage finds summary focus in the self-incised scorpion tattoo, an image of self-predation that fuses and amplifies the implications of the hawk and the shrub.

Voigt lets much of her meaning be released through natural imagery, often in a rural landscape, where her command of detail is very strong. But she can be just as resonant in her descriptions of the city. In the sinister **"Nocturne,"** a poem about a woman being trailed home by a rapist, she dramatizes his menace by stressing how at home he is in the urban hunt:

> Trailing her from the bus, deft as a cab
> in the dense streets, as a dog on the broad common,
> he's neither hungry nor afraid, a man with a knife
> evolving coolly from the traffic of strangers.

The two similes—comparing the stalker's movements with the assuredness of a cab and then a dog—are as misleadingly benign as the observation "he's neither hungry nor afraid." But the truth emerges: he's "a man with a knife," a stark reality which she then holds in the light of an elegant abstraction, describing the man as "evolving coolly from the traffic of strangers." Because of the densely circumstantial background out of which it arises, this abstraction carries a devastating charge of inevitability, as if the rapist were not an anomaly but a natural function of the estrangement of the urban landscape.

Every reader of Voigt will be struck by how palpable her poems are, yet a phrase like "coolly evolving from the traffic of strangers" embodies an equally distinctive, though less pervasive, signature: her capacity to wield abstraction with magisterial elegance. In a poem which seems to grow from a Virginia landscape, a farmer is suddenly attacked by the bees he's been keeping for years. The poet explains the farmer survived because his system had been immunized by a lifetime of small, miscellaneous stings, "like minor disappointments, instructive poison." In its context at the end of the poem, the quietly precise "instructive poison" provides a fine

consummating epitome that lets us see the bee stings as emblematic of an entire life informed by disappointment.

Moreover, the phrase "instructive poison" indicates something essential about Voigt's whole experience of the past. In a given situation, she's acutely sensitive to its tragic dimensions, to the sting of mortality; but at the same time, she's resourcefully determined to be instructed and enlarged, not overwhelmed, by what she has faced, what she has owned. (pp. 263-65)

Peter Harris, "Four Salvers Salvaging: New Work by Voigt, Olds, Dove, and McHugh," in The Virginia Quarterly Review, *Vol. 64, No. 2, Spring, 1988, pp. 262-76.*

MICHAEL COLLIER

Like Donald Justice, Ellen Bryant Voigt is preoccupied with the past, memory, and the emblematic innocence of childhood. But where Justice finds in his childhood the genesis of a sublime sensibility, Voigt finds in hers the blood ties that link her physically and emotionally to the Virginia landscape of her parent's farm. Both poets return to the South for their childhoods, yet their methods—Justice's impressionistic and Voigt's realistic—differ immensely. Whereas Justice sounds the clear ramifying nostalgia of Jarrell's *The Lost World*, Voigt echoes the dense particularity of Roethke's greenhouse poems. To this she adds something of the Southern Gothic—a fascination with the terrible spiritual power of violence. . . .

Behind the naturalistic detail of Voigt's poems [in *The Lotus Flowers*] we feel the pressure of a moral world with its paradox of good and evil. In **"Night-shade"** she writes, "without pure evil in the world, / there was no east or west, no polestar / and no ratifying dove." The first two sections of *The Lotus Flowers* attempt to justify or resolve this paradox or at least find a place where "grieving has an end." But there is no such place, and in the final section Voigt leads us to the discomforting but inescapable knowledge that only death—through its mysterious silence—resolves the moral paradox. Occasionally the moral weight of a poem, such as **"At the Movie: Virginia, 1956,"** feels too heavy and strains the delicacy of its detail and incident.

The Lotus Flowers is a full and mature work, and it marks the culmination of themes and concerns which Ellen Bryant Voigt set out for herself in her first two books, *Claiming Kin* and *The Forces of Plenty*. This is a book that will attract many more admiring readers to Voigt's work, especially those who believe that a poem should be clear and accessible and concern itself with the rescue and transformation of a life.

Michael Collier, in a review of "The Lotus Flowers," in Partisan Review, *Vol. LV, No. 3, Summer, 1988, p. 491.*

☐ Contemporary Literary Criticism

Indexes

Literary Criticism Series
  Cumulative Author Index
Cumulative Nationality Index
Title Index, Volume 54

This Index Includes References to Entries in These Gale Series

Contemporary Literary Criticism

Presents excerpts of criticism on the works of novelists, poets, dramatists, short story writers, scriptwriters, and other creative writers who are now living or who have died since 1960. Cumulative indexes to authors and nationalities are included, as well as an index to titles discussed in the individual volume. Volumes 1-54 are in print.

Twentieth-Century Literary Criticism

Contains critical excerpts by the most significant commentators on poets, novelists, short story writers, dramatists, and philosophers who died between 1900 and 1960. Cumulative indexes to authors, nationalities, and titles discussed are included in each new volume. Volumes 1-33 are in print.

Nineteenth-Century Literature Criticism

Offers significant passages from criticism on authors who died between 1800 and 1899. Cumulative indexes to authors, nationalities, and titles discussed are included in each new volume. Volumes 1-22 are in print.

Literature Criticism from 1400 to 1800

Compiles significant passages from the most noteworthy criticism on authors of the fifteenth through eighteenth centuries. Cumulative indexes to authors, nationalities, and titles discussed are included in each new volume. Volumes 1-10 are in print.

Classical and Medieval Literature Criticism

Offers excerpts of criticism on the works of world authors from classical antiquity through the fourteenth century. Cumulative indexes to authors, titles, and critics are included in each volume. Volumes 1-3 are in print.

Short Story Criticism

Compiles excerpts of criticism on short fiction by writers of all eras and nationalities. Cumulative indexes to authors, nationalities, and titles discussed are included in each new volume. Volumes 1-2 are in print.

Children's Literature Review

Includes excerpts from reviews, criticism, and commentary on works of authors and illustrators who create books for children. Cumulative indexes to authors, nationalities, and titles discussed are included in each new volume. Volumes 1-18 are in print.

Contemporary Authors Series

Encompasses five related series. *Contemporary Authors* provides biographical and bibliographical information on more than 92,000 writers of fiction, nonfiction, poetry, journalism, drama, motion pictures, and other fields. Each new volume contains sketches on authors not previously covered in the series. Volumes 1-126 are in print. *Contemporary Authors New Revision Series* provides completely updated information on active authors covered in previously published volumes of *CA*. Only entries requiring significant change are revised for *CA New Revision Series*. Volumes 1-26 are in print. *Contemporary Authors Permanent Series* consists of updated listings for deceased and inactive authors removed from the original volumes 9-36 when these volumes were revised. Volumes 1-2 are in print. *Contemporary Authors Autobiography Series* presents specially commissioned autobiographies by leading contemporary writers. Volumes 1-8 are in print. *Contemporary Authors Bibliographical Series* contains primary and secondary bibliographies as well as analytical bibliographical essays by authorities on major modern authors. Volumes 1-2 are in print.

Dictionary of Literary Biography

Encompasses three related series. *Dictionary of Literary Biography* furnishes illustrated overviews of authors' lives and works and places them in the larger perspective of literary history. Volumes 1-78 are in print. *Dictionary of Literary Biography Documentary Series* illuminates the careers of major figures through a selection of literary documents, including letters, notebook and diary entries, interviews, book reviews, and photographs. Volumes 1-6 are in print. *Dictionary of Literary Biography Yearbook* summarizes the past year's literary activity with articles on genres, major prizes, conferences, and other timely subjects and includes updated and new entries on individual authors. Yearbooks for 1980-1988 are in print. A cumulative index to authors and articles is included in each new volume.

Concise Dictionary of American Literary Biography

A six-volume series that collects revised and updated sketches on major American authors that were originally presented in *Dictionary of Literary Biography*. Volumes 1-3 are in print.

Something about the Author Series

Encompasses two related series. *Something about the Author* contains heavily illustrated biographical sketches on juvenile and young adult authors and illustrators from all eras. Volumes 1-54 are in print. *Something about the Author Autobiography Series* presents specially commissioned autobiographies by prominent authors and illustrators of books for children and young adults. Volumes 1-7 are in print.

Yesterday's Authors of Books for Children

Contains heavily illustrated entries on children's writers who died before 1961. Complete in two volumes. Volumes 1-2 are in print.

Literary Criticism Series
Cumulative Author Index

This index lists all author entries in the Gale Literary Criticism Series and includes cross-references to other Gale sources. References in the index are identified as follows:

Author Index

Author Index

Author Index

Author Index

Author Index

Author Index

Author Index

Author Index

CLC Cumulative Nationality Index

Nationality Index

Nationality Index

Title Index